Sister Reformations III

Schwesterreformationen III

Sister Reformations III
Schwesterreformationen III

From Reformation Movements to Reformation
Churches in the Holy Roman Empire and
on the British Isles

Von der reformatorischen Bewegung zur Kirche
im Heiligen Römischen Reich und auf den
britischen Inseln

Edited by / Herausgegeben von

Dorothea Wendebourg, Euan Cameron
and/und Martin Ohst

Mohr Siebeck

Dorothea Wendebourg war zuletzt ordentliche Professorin für Mittlere und Neuere Kirchengeschichte/Reformationsgeschichte an der Humboldt-Universität zu Berlin.

Euan Cameron ist Henry Luce III Professor am Union Theological Seminary New York.

Martin Ohst ist ordentlicher Professor für Kirchengeschichte und Systematische Theologie an der Bergischen Universität Wuppertal.

ISBN 978-3-16-158932-4 / eISBN 978-3-16-158933-1
DOI 10.1628/978-3-16-158933-1

Die Deutsche Nationalbibliothek verzeichnet diese Publikation in der Deutschen Nationalbibliographie; detaillierte bibliographische Daten sind über *http://dnb.dnb.de* abrufbar.

© 2019 Mohr Siebeck Tübingen. www.mohrsiebeck.com

Das Werk einschließlich aller seiner Teile ist urheberrechtlich geschützt. Jede Verwertung außerhalb der engen Grenzen des Urheberrechtsgesetzes ist ohne Zustimmung des Verlags unzulässig und strafbar. Das gilt insbesondere für die Verbreitung, Vervielfältigung, Übersetzung und die Einspeicherung und Verarbeitung in elektronischen Systemen.

Das Buch wurde von Gulde-Druck in Tübingen auf alterungsbeständiges Werkdruckpapier gedruckt und von der Großbuchbinderei Spinner in Ottersweier gebunden.

Printed in Germany.

Vorwort

Der vorliegende Band enthält die Beiträge der dritten deutsch-angelsächsischen Tagung *Schwesterreformationen*, die in den Tagen vom 9. bis zum 11. April 2018 an der Humboldt-Universität zu Berlin stattfand. Die erste Tagung von 2009 hatte ein breites Spektrum verschiedener Themen im Zusammenhang der Reformation im Heiligen Römischen Reich und in England und namentlich ihrer Beziehungen behandelt (dokumentiert in: Sister Reformations – Schwesterreformationen. Die Reformation in Deutschland und England, hg. v. Dorothea Wendebourg, Tübingen 2010) und die zweite von 2012 sich mit der Ethik in der Reformation hier und dort befaßt (dokumentiert in: Sister Reformations II – Schwesterreformationen II. Reformation und Ethik in Deutschland und England, hg. v. Dorothea Wendebourg u. Alec Ryrie, Tübingen 2015). Die hier dokumentierte dritte Tagung nun, wegen des alle Kräfte bindenden Reformationsjubiläums von 2017 erst sechs Jahre nach der letzten veranstaltet, ging der Frage nach, wie diesseits und jenseits des Kanals aus der reformatorischen Bewegung Institutionen, evangelische Kirchen wurden; tastend wurde der Blick erstmals auch nach Schottland gerichtet.

Das Programm der Tagung gliederte sich in vier Teile. Den Anfang machten drei großflächige Überblicke, in denen skizziert werden sollte, wie reformatorische Impulse in England, in Schottland und im Heiligen Römischen Reich geschichtlich wirksam wurden. Da für das Reich ein solcher Überblick nicht zustandekam, an diesem Punkt aber keinesfalls eine Lücke bleiben durfte, haben drei Teilnehmer (DOROTHEA WENDEBOURG, ANDREAS STEGMANN, MARTIN OHST) sie nachträglich gefüllt, das aber nicht in Form einer Darstellung, sondern in einer Reihe knapper Thesen. Deren Anliegen ist es herauszustellen, wie der von Wittenberg ausgehende reformatorische Impuls in Umformungen des kirchlichen Lebens auf allen Ebenen wirksam wurde, dabei aber selbst zugleich Klärungen und Modifikationen erfuhr, die sich in einer Pluralität verschiedener evangelischer Kirchen niederschlugen.

ASHLEY NULL widmete sich der Reformation in England. Sein Beitrag identifiziert als Schlüssel für die Anziehungskraft der vom Kontinent herüberkommenden evangelischen Einflüsse wie für die Theologie der von Thomas Cranmer verfaßten Formulare der Kirche von England die affektive Frömmigkeit des spätmittelalterlichen Englands. Humanisten der Tudorzeit, die von dieser Frömmigkeit geprägt waren, fanden in Martin Luthers Konzeption der in der Heiligen Schrift mitgeteilten bedingungslosen Gnade und der dadurch ausgelösten antwortenden Liebe als Motivation christlichen Handelns die Erfüllung ihrer Anliegen. Unter Eduard VI. schrieb Cranmer diese lutherische Soteriologie in die offiziellen Formulare der Anglikanischen Kirche ein. Erst unter Elisabeth trat eine eher reformierte Konzeption in den Vordergrund, nach der Gehorsam und Furcht die Motive christlichen Handelns sind. Doch die ältere Sicht blieb in der Privatfrömmigkeit des englischen Protestantismus die ganze frühe Neuzeit hindurch lebendig.

JOHN MCCALLUM bot den Überblick über die schottische Reformation. Sein Beitrag konzentriert sich auf die Einflüsse der früh eingedrungenen reformatorischen Ideen und auf den Prozeß, in dem die ihnen anhängenden Gruppen sich zu einer protestantischen Nationalkirche entwickelten. Wie er zeigt, kam die nationale Reformation von 1559–60 zwar spät und in mancher Hinsicht unerwartet, doch als sie kam, war das ein dramatisches Geschehen. In den folgenden Jahren lag die Hauptherausforderung darin, protestantische Institutionen in einem Land zu entwickeln, das zuvor nur wenig offenen protestantischen Aktivismus erlebt hatte. Entscheidend für das Gelingen waren die Amtsträger und die *kirk sessions* in den Gemeinden.

Der zweite Teil galt *Faktoren des Kirchwerdens*, d.h. institutionellen Elementen und Orten, die, durch die Reformation transformiert, zu Mitteln und Räumen ihrer spezifischen Institutionalisierung wurden. ALBRECHT BEUTEL beschäftigte sich mit der Predigt. Sein Beitrag vergleicht zunächst die während der Reformationszeit in Deutschland und England entfaltete Theologie der Predigt, die nun, anders als zuvor, der gottesdienstlichen Verkündigung des Wortes Gottes eine exklusive heilsmittlerische Funktion zuerkannte. Er wendet sich dann den volkssprachlichen Bibelübersetzungen zu und stellt das seinerzeit unreflektiert gebliebene Konkurrenzproblem heraus, dass auch die privatreligiöse Bibellektüre als Möglichkeit einer unmittelbaren Glaubensapplikation des Wortes Gottes in Betracht kam. Im ausführlichsten dritten Teil werden am Beispiel namhafter, exemplarisch ausgewählter Kanzelredner weitgehende Analogien, aber auch signifikante Differenzen der in Deutschland und England gehaltenen Reformationspredigt herausgearbeitet.

KONRAD KLEKS Thema war das Singen. Sein Beitrag beschreibt das Singen der Gemeinde als *das* Medium der Durchsetzung der Reformation – diese werde zu Recht als Singebewegung bezeichnet. Den Sitz im Leben der am Anfang stehenden Lieder Martin Luthers sieht er im Alltag, auf Straßen, am Arbeitsplatz und in der Familie, nicht in der – evangelischen –

Messe, wo der Chorgesang vorgeherrscht habe. Liturgisch wirksam sei das Singen der Gemeinde hingegen in den übrigen Gottesdiensten gewesen. Dort, wo sich die Messe nicht hielt, sondern der Predigtgottesdienst sich als Hauptgottesdienst durchsetzte, habe es von vorneherein eine größere Rolle gespielt, so in Straßburg, Württemberg, Genf, hier in Gestalt des gesungenen Psalters. Dieser verbreitete sich auch in England, obgleich das *Book of Common Prayer* dem Gemeindegesang gegenüber zurückhaltend war. Der Beitrag schließt mit dem Fazit, der Liedgesang der Reformation lasse sich der Polarität *Luthergesangbuch* versus *Liedpsalter* zuordnen.

Bei THOMAS KAUFMANN ging es um das Buch, genauer, um einen spezifischen Ausschnitt reformatorischer Buchproduktion. Da aufgrund der insularen Lage Englands hier Repressionsmechanismen in Bezug auf Druckwaren wirkten, die im Reich nicht funktionierten, bemühten sich englische Anhänger der Reformation, im Reich drucken zu lassen. Bekannt ist das Beispiel William Tyndales. Kaufmann stellt dar, daß die englischen Glaubensexulanten im Reich um Tyndale weniger den Kontakt zu den etablierten Reformatoren der sich formierenden ›Lager‹ suchten als zu Buchproduzenten, die den Druck englischen Schrifttums förderten. Anhand der Verbindungen zu Köln und Worms werden Interaktionen zwischen klandestin operierenden deutschen und englischen Buchproduzenten sichtbar.

WOLF-FRIEDRICH SCHÄUFELE handelte von der häuslichen Gemeinschaft. Wie sein Beitrag zeigt, erfuhren Ehe, Familie und ›Haus‹ in der Reformation eine umfassende theologische Neubewertung, wobei die Reformatoren auf dem europäischen Kontinent dieses Thema schon seit den 1520er Jahren behandelten, in England sich ihm aber vor allem puritanische Autoren seit dem ausgehenden 16. Jahrhundert widmeten. Übereinstimmend kam es einerseits zu einer Entsakramentalisierung der Ehe, andererseits zu einer starken Aufwertung des Ehestandes als Gottes Stiftung und Gebot oder Schöpfungsordnung. Ehe, Familie und Haus wurden als Keimzelle der Gesellschaft und der staatlichen Ordnung gewürdigt. Zugleich waren sie als Ort religiöser Kindererziehung und häuslichen Gottesdienstes eine ›kleine Kirche‹.

SUSAN KARANT-NUNNS Beitrag vergleicht die Ansichten von der Natur der Frau und ihrer gesellschaftlichen Stellung im nachreformatorischen deutschsprachigen und englischen Protestantismus des späten 16. und frühen 17. Jahrhunderts. Er fragt nach den Medien, durch die das Volk auf beiden Seiten des Kanals über die rechte Stellung christlicher Männer und Frauen belehrt wurden, sowie nach dem Inhalt, der durch diese Medien verbreitet wurde, und vergleicht dann die Aussagen hier und dort. Wie sie zeigt, waren auf dem Kontinent viele Bände mit Traupredigten führender

Theologen verbreitet. Deren Zahl war in England deutlich geringer, weil die Traupredigt dort nur erlaubt, aber nicht geboten war. Dennoch gab es in England eine Reihe von Schriften zu jenem Thema. Die Gegenüberstellung ergibt, daß die englischen Autoren erheblich härter über angebliche sexuelle Verirrungen von Frauen schrieben und daß sie im Vergleich etwa mit Martin Luther eine deutlich negativere Einstellung zur Sexualität, selbst innerhalb der Ehe, hatten. Gewalt gegenüber ungehorsamen Ehefrauen wurde freilich hier wie dort selten bejaht. Abschließend mahnt der Beitrag, die Vorstellungen der Prediger und Autoren nicht mit dem realen Leben zu verwechseln.

AMY BURNETTS Thema war das Leben der Gemeinden. Ihr Beitrag stellt heraus, daß in vorreformatorischer Zeit Gemeinden in Deutschland und der Schweiz gegenüber England erheblich mehr Glieder umfaßten, was die angemessene geistliche Versorgung durch die Pfarrer erschwerte. Städter hatten mehr religiöse Optionen außerhalb ihrer Gemeinde, was sie empfänglicher für die Ideen der Reformation machte. Dabei spielte das Predigen in der frühen Reformation in Deutschland und der Schweiz eine viel größere Rolle als in England. Doch am Ende des 16. Jahrhunderts besaß es auch in England große Bedeutung. Glieder dörflicher Gemeinden pflegten auf beiden Seiten des Kanals weiterhin ein gemeinschaftsorientiertes Christentum, das Wert auf den Erhalt sozialer Harmonie und eine zufriedenstellende Amtsführung des Pfarrers legte.

ANDREAS STEGMANN schließlich befaßte sich mit dem neuen Typ von Pfarrer, wie er von der Reformation geformt wurde und ein entscheidendes Element der Kirchwerdung der Reformation darstellte. Wie der Beitrag zeigt, waren für den neuen Typus des Pfarrers entscheidend zum einen die Aufgabe der Verkündigung, die theologische Aus- und Weiterbildung erforderte, weshalb kirchliches Amt und Bildungswesen eng miteinander verklammert wurden (necessaria coniunctio scholarum cum ministerio evangelii), und zum anderen die Einordnung der kirchlichen Amtsträger in die bürgerliche Welt, die u.a. die neuartige Lebenswelt des Pfarrhauses hervorbrachte. Deutsche und englische Reformation unterscheiden sich in den Grundlinien des neuen Verständnisses des geistlichen Amts kaum, doch wurde der neue Typ von Pfarrer hier und dort auf unterschiedliche Weise Wirklichkeit: In Deutschland vergleichsweise schnell und konsequent, wie am Beispiel des brandenburgischen Luthertums gezeigt wird, in England dagegen über einen längeren Zeitraum und mit vielen Kompromissen.

Im dritten Teil der Tagung ging es um *alte und neue Traditionen*, d.h. um institutionelle Formen, die von der sich institutionalisierenden reformatorischen Bewegung übernommen und verändert wurden und die deren

Institutionalisierung ihrerseits prägten. DOROTHEA WENDEBOURG handelte vom Gottesdienst. Ihr Beitrag vergleicht den Weg, der im Heiligen Römischen Reich und in England von der reformatorischen Kritik an der
überlieferten Messe zur Ausbildung und Einführung neuer, evangelischer
Liturgien führte. Wie sie zeigt, gab es in verschiedenen Territorien und
Städten des Reiches längere, z.T. auch experimentelle Prozesse der Abweichung vom bisherigen Gottesdienst und liturgischen Veränderung auf
der Ebene der Gemeinden, bis die alte Liturgie offiziell, von Räten und
Fürsten, durch – mehrere – neue ersetzt wurde. In England dagegen gab es
keine Zwischenphase. Das straffe Kirchenregiment der Krone machte bis
zum Tod König Heinrichs VIII. jede liturgische Abweichung und Veränderung unmöglich, bis unter seinem Nachfolger dann ebenso zentral ge-
steuert sehr schnell eine – einzige – neue Liturgie für das ganze Land
eingeführt wurde. Einzige Ausweichmöglichkeit für Anhänger der Reformation außer dem Exil war bis dahin die Äquivokation.

ANDREW SPICERS Beitrag befaßt sich mit dem liturgischen Raum. In
Martin Luthers wie in John Knox' Augen waren bestimmte Einrichtungsgegenstände für den Gottesdienstraum erforderlich. Doch die Kirchen der
Lutheraner und der reformierten *kirks* wiesen in ihrer Ausstattung deutliche Unterschied auf. Luther betrachtete die Ausstattung von Kirchen als
adiaphoron (heilsindifferent) und machte dazu folglich keine Vorschriften.
Es ergab sich ein gewisses Maß an Kontinuität in der Gestaltung des Kir-
cheninneren, andererseits aber auch eine allmähliche Veränderung, insofern die Einrichtungsgegenstände, die erhalten blieben, den neuen liturgischen Verhältnissen angepaßt wurden. Im Gegensatz dazu drangen die
schottischen Reformatoren darauf, die Kirchen von allen ›monuments of
idolatry‹ und mit der Zelebration der Messe verbundenen Gegenständen
zu reinigen. Wie der Beitrag zeigt, spiegelt diese Veränderung nicht zuletzt
eine Differenz zwischen der deutschen lutherischen und der schottischen
reformierten Kirche hinsichtlich der Sakramentsverwaltung, genauer hinsichtlich der Häufigkeit der Abendmahlsfeier, die entscheidende Konsequenzen für die Ausstattung des Gottesdienstraumes hatte.

ALEXANDRA WALSHAM untersuchte, wie sich der Übergang des Protestantismus von einer Protestbewegung zur kirchlichen Institution in der
materialen Kultur niederschlug. Ihr Beitrag, der sich auf Objekte konzentriert, die antikatholische Vorurteile und Feindseligkeit förderten, beschreibt, wie konfessionelle Identität im häuslichen Rahmen gebildet wurde. An jenen Artefakten und ihre Bildprogrammen zeigten sich der dau-
ernde Austausch und die Wanderungsbewegungen kultureller Praktiken
und Bildmotive zwischen den Schwesterreformationen im nördlichen Europa. Damit werde zugleich das konventionelle Stereotyp in Frage gestellt,

wonach der reife Protestantismus asketisch ist, und neues Licht auf die protestantische Haltung zu Muße und Spiel geworfen.

CHRISTOPHER VOIGT-GOYS Thema war das Recht. Sein Beitrag verfolgt die Ausbildung der Reformationskirchen Wittenberger Prägung und in England unter dem Aspekt ihres je spezifischen Umgangs mit dem kanonistischen Rechtsinstitut des Kirchenguts. Im Fall der Wittenberger Reformation lässt sich nach Voigt-Goy eine Transformation feststellen, die darin besteht, daß das hergebrachte anstaltsrechtliche Verständnis des Kirchenguts, gemäß dem als Rechtsträger des Kirchenguts die geistlichen Institutionen qua juristische Personen fungieren, durch Verweis auf den Zweck des Kirchenguts, in allen Ständen den »Gottesdienst« zu fördern, modifiziert wird. In England hingegen findet eine »reformatorische Adaption« des Kanonischen Rechts in der Weise statt, dass die Kirchengerichte der Church of England die bestehende kanonische Rechtsvorstellung und -rechtsprechung grundsätzlich weiterführen, dabei aber als reformatorisch illegitim eingestufte Sachverhalte ausscheiden. In beiden Fällen wird somit der im Kanonischen Recht betonte Anstaltscharakter des Kirchenguts in seinen Grundzügen erhalten.

Bei GEOFFREY DIPPLE ging es um die ›radikalen Geister‹. Sein Beitrag setzt mit der Feststellung ein, daß die Geschichtsschreibung auf dem Kontinent die sog. radikalen Geister als Teil der frühen, ›wildwüchsigen‹ Reformation betrachte, aus der sie allmählich verdrängt worden seien, während sie auf den Britischen Inseln als ursprünglich fremde Gewächse angesehen werden, die sich weitgehend am Rande der Hauptgeschichte der Reformation befunden hätten, bis sie im 17. Jahrhundert mit Macht auf die Bühne drängten. Diese Differenz der Perspektive sei zumindest teilweise auf die unterschiedlichen Haltungen gegenüber den Erfahrungen der ›Radikalen‹ bei den Historikern hier und dort zurückzuführen. Beide Einordnungen dieser Gruppen und Individuen verdunkelten aber die Ähnlichkeiten, die zwischen den Erfahrungen der Radikalen diesseits und jenseits des Kanals bestünden – Verdunkelungen, die auch damit zusammenhingen, wie die ›radikalen‹ und ›mainstream‹-Bewegungen sich zu Kirchen entwickelten hätten.

Die an der Reformation beteiligten Menschen waren sich dessen bewußt, daß sie Geschichte machten. Sie haben ihr Tun und Erleben gedeutet und in Konzeptionen eines übergreifenden, letztlich theologisch zu verstehenden Geschichtszusammenhanges gestellt. Diesem Aspekt galt der vierte und letzte Block der Tagung, in dem die *Selbstdeutungen der Reformation* zur Sprache kamen. EUAN CAMERONS Beitrag galt dem Bild der Wittenberger und der Schweizer Reformation von sich selbst. Danach war für viele Reformatoren, insbesondere Luther, die Kirche, wie ein christli-

ches Individuum, immer zugleich ›gerecht und Sünder‹. Gleichwohl waren
fast alle überzeugt, daß die Kirche nach relativer Reinheit in der Spätantike
im Mittelalter verfallen sei, ein Zustand, aus dem die Reformation sie ge-
rettet habe. In diesem Zusammenhang wird der Gebrauch patristischer
Belege bei Philipp Melanchthon und John Jewel verglichen. Schließlich
wird anhand dreier Beispiele untersucht, wie in Wittenberg und in der
Schweiz der lange Verfall der Kirche erklärt wird: am Beispiel der Abkehr
des Mönchtums von seinen ursprünglichen Impulsen, der Selbstüberhebung des Papsttums und der Ausgestaltung der Abendmahlsliturgie.

KRISTEN WALTONS Thema war das Selbstbild der schottischen Reformation. Ihr Beitrag zeichnet zunächst die Anfänge der schottischen Reformation und deren Durchführung durch John Knox und das Reforma-
tionsparlament von 1560 nach, bevor er sich George Buchanans und anderer Deutung der schottischen Reformation zuwendet. Diese Männer
hätten die Reformation gefördert und die schottische Kultur verwandelt,
indem sie argumentierten, daß die Reformation nichts anderes sei als die
Wiederherstellung der alten schottischen Kirche, nachdem diese von Rom
pervertiert worden sei. Damit hätten sie zugleich eine neues Bild der
schottischen Geschichte entworfen.

Bei MARTIN OHST ging es um die englische Reformation. Sein Beitrag
stellt als Dokument *eines* Selbstbildes dieser Reformation die beiden *Books
of Homilies* (1547 und 1563) vor, die zu den normativen Lehrdokumenten
der Anglikanischen Kirche gehörten. Er zeigt, daß die *Books of Homilies*
für ein Verständnis der Reformation als Rückführung der Kirche zu ihrer
Normgestalt in Leben und Lehre werben, wie sie die Bibel und die Alte
Kirche miteinander bezeugten. Besonders positiv werde dabei hervorge-
hoben, dass die Reformation ein Akt der Krone war und dass sie die
Krone – wieder – als irdisches Kirchenoberhaupt etablierte – gegen das
Papsttum und seine antichristischen Herrschaftsansprüche.

In diesem Sammelband wird viel neues Material präsentiert, und wo Be-
kanntes aufgegriffen wird, steht es im Licht neuer Perspektiven. Dabei
bilden die Beiträge in der Vielfalt ihrer Inhalte und Methoden ein Ganzes,
weil in ihnen allen Veränderungen beschrieben und analysiert werden,
welche das kirchliche Leben im Heiligen Römischen Reich, in England
und in Schottland in den drei Menschenaltern zwischen 1500 und 1575 bis
hin zur Institutionalisierung der Reformation durchlaufen hat. Freilich
drängt sich beim Lesen immer wieder die Frage nach der Vergleichbarkeit
der Vorgänge und ihrer Ergebnisse auf – und es wird zugleich deutlich, mit
welchen Schwierigkeiten alle komparatistischen Unternehmungen konfrontiert sind. Wie die politisch-sozialen Strukturen überhaupt, so waren

auch die kirchlichen Strukturen im Reich, in England und in Schottland im Spätmittelalter ganz unterschiedlich ausgebildet. Sie prägten die konkreten Artikulations- und Rezeptionsgestalten allgemein kirchenreformerischer und spezifisch reformatorischer Programme. Und folglich gestalteten sie auch die Ergebnisse reformerischer und reformatorischer Anstrengungen ganz unterschiedlich. Wenn man auf einen in der gegenwärtigen deutschen Reformationshistoriographie gern benutzten Terminus zurückgreifen will, kann man konstatieren: Die Beiträge dieses Bandes bezeugen zunächst einmal eine – sicher noch vermehrbare – Reihe von *Transformationsprozessen*, die einmal parallel verlaufen, einmal divergieren, einmal konvergieren oder einander schneiden.

Nun ist das bloße Konstatieren von ›Transformationen‹ trivial und nichtssagend. Bedeutung gewinnt es erst, wenn transformierende Faktoren identifiziert und von ihren Voraussetzungen, Folgen und Sekundärursachen unterschieden werden. Und Vergleiche zwischen unterschiedlichen Transformationsprozessen werden nur dann zu diskussionswürdigen Ergebnissen führen, wenn sie eben zu der Frage nach den transformierenden Faktoren selbst vorstoßen und untersuchen, welche Interaktionen und Interdependenzen zwischen ihnen nachgewiesen werden können. Von hier aus werden sich dann stichhaltige Einschätzungen von Fremdheits- und Verwandtschaftsverhältnissen zwischen unterschiedlichen Phänomenen und Ereignissen gewinnen lassen. Diesen Punkt haben wir noch nicht erreicht.

Der Eindruck, daß noch viele Aufgaben historischer Forschungs- und Deutungsarbeit vor uns liegen, war allen deutlich, die mit ihren Vorträgen und Diskussionsbeiträgen das Berliner Symposium Schwesterreformationen III im Frühjahr 2018 gestaltet haben. Die Herausgeber geben das Buch mit der Erwartung an die Öffentlichkeit, daß es zu weiteren Arbeiten in dieser Richtung anregen möge.

Finanziert wurde die Tagung von der Deutschen Forschungsgemeinschaft (DFG) und der Evangelischen Kirche in Deutschland (EKD). Beiden Institutionen sei hiermit herzlich gedankt.

Berlin, New York, Wuppertal
Herbst 2019

Dorothea Wendebourg
Euan Cameron
Martin Ohst

Preface

This volume presents the contributions to the third German/Anglo-Saxon conference *Sister Reformations* which took place on April 9th–11th at the Humboldt-University of Berlin. The first conference in 2009 had comprised a wide scope of different topics concerning the Reformations in the Holy Roman Empire and in England, not least the relations between them (documentation in: Sister Reformations – Schwesterreformationen. The Reformation in Germany and England, ed. Dorothea Wendebourg, Tübingen 2010). The second one in 2012 had dealt with ethics in both Reformations (documentation in: Sister Reformations II – Schwesterreformationen II. Reformation and Ethics in Germany and England, ed.s Dorothea Wendebourg and Alec Ryrie, Tübingen 2015). The third conference whose contributions are published here – which because of the Reformation jubilee of 2017 that tied up all forces took place only six years after the previous one – asked how on both sides of the Channel the Reformation movements became Reformation churches. For the first time also Scotland was included, though only with a first touch.

The program of the conference was divided in four parts. The point of the first part was to present three large scale overviews which outlined how evangelical impulses took historical effect in England, Scotland, and the Holy Roman Empire. Since for the Holy Roman Empire such an overview was not realized, and must in no way be lacking, three participants (Dorothea Wendebourg, Andreas Stegmann, Martin Ohst) have subsequently filled the gap, not, however, by writing an essay but by formulating a set of theses. These theses point out how the Reformation impulse starting from Wittenberg took effect in various transformations of the ecclesial life and how in the course of these transformations the impulse itself underwent clarifications as well as modifications which were embodied in a plurality of Protestant churches.

Ashley Null's topic was the Reformation in England. His contribution finds the key to understanding both the original appeal of evangelical thought in England and the missional theology of Thomas Cranmer's formularies in late medieval English affective piety. Some Tudor humanists who were influenced by this piety found what they looked for in Martin Luther's conception of God's unconditional grace communicated through Holy Scripture and the believer's love brought about by this communication as motivation of Christian ethics. Hence, under Edward VI, Cranmer embedded this Lutheran soteriological conception into the formularies of the Church of England. Only Elizabeth's *Second Book of Homilies* began to move towards a more Reformed conception where obedience and fear replaced love as the motivation for Christian ethics. However, the former view continued to remain central to private devotions in Protestant English piety throughout the Early Modern Period.

JOHN MCCALLUM provided the overview of the Scottish Reformation. His essay focuses on the processes by which early reforming ideas and dissenting groups developed into a national Protestant Church. Although the national Reformation of 1559–60 was late in coming, and in some senses unexpected, when it did arrive it was a dramatic moment of transition. In the years that followed, the central challenge was developing Protestant institutions in a country which had only witnessed limited overt Protestant activism previously. The clergy, and the parish kirk sessions, were central to the Church's successes in meeting this challenge.

The second part was dedicated to *factors contributing to the emergence of evangelical churches*, i.e. institutional elements and places which, transformed by the Reformation, became instruments and spaces of its institutionalization. ALBRECHT BEUTEL's subject was the sermon. His contribution, firstly, compares the theologies of the sermon which now, differently from before, attributed to the proclamation of the Word in the liturgy a unique function of communicating salvation. Secondly, Beutel's contribution deals with the translations of the Bible in the vernacular and points out the problem, not discussed at the time, of a competitive relationship between the sermon and private reading of the Bible as a possible way of direct communication of the Word of God. Thirdly, in the longest section, several exemplary preachers are singled out, to show far-reaching analogies as well as significant differences between evangelical sermons preached in Germany and in England.

KONRAD KLEK dealt with singing. According to his essay singing was *the* medium which implemented the Reformation – the Reformation is often rightly described as a »movement of singing«. In Klek's view the *Sitz im Leben* of the hymns by Martin Luther which marked the beginning of this movement was everyday life on the streets, at the working place, and in the family, not the – evangelical – mass, where choir singing predominated. However, in the other church services besides the mass, congregational singing had its place within the liturgy. In regions where the mass was not preserved, but preaching service became the main liturgy on Sunday, congregational singing in church from the start played a greater role, e.g. in Straßburg, Württemberg, Geneva – here in the form of the sung

Psalter. The sung Psalter also spread in England, although the *Book of Common Prayer* was reserved as regards to congregational singing. Klek's concluding remark is that singing in the Reformation can be attributed to two poles: *Lutheran hymn book* and *sung Psalter*.

THOMAS KAUFMANN's topic was the book. In fact, his contribution looks at a specific case of book production in the Reformation. Since due to England's insular position mechanisms of repression against book printing took effect which would not have worked in the Empire, English adherents of the Reformation tried to get books printed in the Empire. The example of William Tyndale is well known. As Kaufmann demonstrates, the circle of English evangelical exiles around Tyndale in the Empire were less interested in contacts with the leading Reformers of the protestant camps on the way to institutionalization than with book-producers who would help printing English books. Tyndale's connections with Cologne and Worms show interactions between Germans and Englishmen clandestinely working on the book market.

WOLF-FRIEDRICH SCHÄUFELE's paper spoke about marriage, family, and household. As his chapter shows marriage, family, and the ›home‹ through the Reformation received a new theological appreciation. This is obvious in writings by the continental Reformers starting from the 1520s and by English protestant authors, predominantly Puritans, who wrote on marriage and family life from the late 16th century. All of them, on the one hand, refused to regard marriage as a sacrament, but, on the other hand, they raised its status as an estate instituted by God and a divine commandment, in other words, as a created order. Marriage, family, and ›house‹ were valued as the nucleus of society and political order. At the same time they, as place of religious education and private devotion, were seen as a ›little church‹.

SUSAN KARANT-NUNN's essay on clerical advice for the sexes, marriage, and the household compares teachings on women's nature and position in society during the later sixteenth and early seventeenth centuries in German and English Protestantism. It inquires into the media used in teaching the populace concerning the proper roles of Christian men and women as well as their content, and compares what was said in this respect on both sides of the Channel. As the essay shows, on the continent many volumes of wedding sermons given by leading divines were published and widely disseminated. In England their number was considerably smaller because nuptial preaching was permitted but not required. Nevertheless there, too, existed writings on the same topic. The result of a comparison of both groups is that, in general, the English writers are harsher than their continental counterparts in their description of the alleged aberrations of women. They also have a more negative attitude toward sexuality than Martin Luther, even within marriage. However, husbands' beating their disobedient wives was rarely approved. In the final section the reader is admonished not to mistake the ideas of the preachers and authors for reality.

AMY BURNETT's subject was life in the parish. As her contribution demonstrates, in comparison to England, parishes in Germany and Switzerland before the Reformation were much more densely populated making it difficult for parish priests to provide adequate pastoral care. Urban laypeople had a wider variety of religious options outside of the parish. This made them more receptive to evangelical ideas. Preaching played a much greater role in the early Reformation in Germany and Switzerland than in England, but by the end of the sixteenth century preaching had an important place also in English towns. In both Germany and England, rural parishioners continued to practice a communal Christianity that emphasized maintenance of social harmony and the pastor's satisfactory performance of his duties.

Finally ANDREAS STEGMANN dealt with the new type of pastor brought forth by the Reformation as a decisive element of the institutionalization of the Reformation. According to Stegmann two aspects were essential for this new type: Firstly preaching as the central task of the pastor's office, requiring theological studies and continued education – which is why ministry and academia were tightly connected (necessaria coniunctio scholarum cum ministerio evangelii), and secondly the integration of the minister into civil society, which among other things led to the new world of the protestant parsonage. Stegmann underlines that the basic lines of the understanding of the new type of pastor were similar in the German and English Reformation, but that its realizations differed. In Germany the process was relatively swift and thorough-going as is shown at the example of the Lutheran Church in the electorate of Brandenburg, whereas in England it took longer and involved more compromises.

The third part of the conference was dedicated to the examination of *old and new traditions*, i.e. institutional elements which were taken over as well as changed by the Reformation in the process of its institutionalization, and which in turn left their mark on this institutionalization itself. DOROTHEA WENDEBOURG's theme was worship. Her chapter compares how the Reformers' criticism of the traditional mass led to the formation and eventual introduction of new evangelical liturgies. In many territories and cities of the Empire there were lengthy and at times also experimental processes of deviation from the traditional church service as well as liturgical changes on the parish level before the old liturgies were officially replaced by several new, evangelical ones through city councils or princes.

In England, however, there was no intermediate phase. The king's firm grip on the church made any liturgical deviation and change impossible until the death of Henry VIII, when under his successor the equally centralized introduction of a single new liturgy for the whole country took place in very little time. Until then the only evasion possible besides exile was equivocation.

According to ANDREW SPICER's essay on liturgical space, both Martin Luther and John Knox recognized that certain liturgical furnishings were necessary for places of worship. Yet the appearance and arrangement of Lutheran churches and Reformed kirks were markedly different. Luther considered church furnishings as *adiaphora* (matters indifferent for salvation), so he did not prescribe what was required in this respect. There was a degree of visual continuity in the appearance of church interiors, but nonetheless over time a gradual change took place, and while former Catholic fittings may have survived, they were often altered to meet the needs of the new liturgical reality. By contrast, the Scottish reformers sought to strip their churches of all ›monuments of idolatry‹ and items associated with the celebration of the mass. As Spicer demonstrates, these changes to the setting of worship also reflected the difference between the German Lutheran and Scottish Reformed churches in the administration of the sacraments, particularly as regards the frequency of the eucharist, which had significant implications in determining the arrangement and liturgical fittings of their places of worship.

ALEXANDRA WALSHAM looked at material culture. Her essay shows how Protestantism's transition from protest movement to institutionalized church manifested itself therein. Focusing particular attention on objects that fostered anti-Catholic hostility and prejudice, it explores how confessional identities were forged in the forum of the home. These artefacts and their iconographies illustrate the continuing exchange and traffic of cultural practices and pictorial motifs between the sister Reformations of northern Europe. They also raise questions about the conventional stereotype of mature Protestantism as morally ascetic and shed fresh light on reformed attitudes to leisure and play.

CHRISTOPHER VOIGT-GOY's theme was law. His contribution looks at the institutionalization of the Wittenberg church and the Church of England with an eye on their use of the canonical institution of ›ecclesiastical property‹ (Kirchengut). In the Wittenberg Reformation the traditional, medieval understanding according to which the ecclesial institutions which own this property function as legal entities, was transformed with reference to its purpose, the promotion of church service in all estates. In England, however, the adaptation of canon law in the context of the Re-

formation took place in such a way that the Church of England's ecclesiastical courts continued the traditional canonical concepts and court ru-
lings but eliminated those matters which, according to the categories of the
Reformation, were illegitimate. Thus in both cases the institutional character of the ecclesiastical property was in principle upheld.

GEOFFREY DIPPLE's essay on ›radical spirits‹ starts with an observation
regarding Reformation scholarship on the continent and on the British
Isles: They describe the place and experiences of radical spirits in very
different terms. On the continent the radical spirits appear as an integral
part of the early Reformation *Wildwuchs*, until they are gradually tamed
over the course of the sixteenth century; while on the British Isles they
arise initially as foreign growths, largely peripheral to the main Reformation story, until they explode onto the scene in the seventeenth century.
Dipple argues that these differences in perception derive, at least in part,
from the different approaches to the experiences of the radical spirits adopted by scholars of the continental and British Reformations. He main-
tains that both the methods employed to identify the groups and individuals identified as radical spirits, obscure similarities in experiences between the continent and Britain. Finally, the essay suggests that those similarities have been hidden by processes involved in the transition of movements, both radical and mainstream, into churches.

Those who partook in the Reformation knew that they were writing
history. They interpreted what they did and experienced and integrated it
in conceptions of an overarching historical continuity which in the end is
to be understood theologically. The fourth and last part of the conference
took up this perspective. It explored how the Reformation was understood by its own adherents as a distinct phase in the history of the Christian Church. EUAN CAMERON's topic was the self-image of the Wittenberg and Swiss Reformation. As his contribution demonstrates, for many
reformers, Luther especially, the Church was always, like a Christian individual, both righteous and sinful. Nevertheless, nearly all were convinced that it had lapsed from relative purity in late antiquity into a medieval
decline, from which the Reformation rescued it. The chapter compares the
use of patristic evidence in Philipp Melanchthon and John Jewel. Then it
explores how historians from Wittenberg and the Swiss Confederation
accounted for the Church's long decline in three specific areas: the diversion of the monastic instinct from its first impulse; the self-aggrandize-
ment of the papacy; and the progressive elaboration of Eucharistic ritual.

KRISTEN WALTON dealt with the Scottish Reformation. Her essay dis-
cusses the early roots of the Reformation and addresses the work of Knox
and the other reformers to implement the Reformation in Scotland follo-

wing the 1560 Reformation Parliament, before she looks at how George Buchanan and others interpreted the Reformation. In fact, in order to change the Scottish culture and further the Reformation ideas, these men created a new history of Scotland arguing that the Reformation was actually just a restoration of an ancient Scottish church that had been perverted by Rome.

Finally MARTIN OHST's task was to look at the self-image of the English Reformation. As a document of *one* such self-image his contribution presents the two *Books of Homilies* (1547 und 1563) which were part of the official documents of the Church of England. He demonstrates how these documents advertised an image of the Reformation as return of the Church in life and doctrine to its normative form, testified to both by Holy Scriptures and the ancient Church. What is seen as a particularly positive feature is the fact that the English Reformation was brought about by the crown and that the crown was again installed as the church's – temporal – head, against the papacy and its Anti-Christ-like claims of supremacy.

Altogether this volume presents a lot of new material, and where material is presented which was not new, the aim was to look at it in the light of new perspectives. The contributions, although manifold as regards contents and methods, nevertheless must be seen as a whole because all of them aim to describe and analyze changes which Christian life and the Church have undergone during the three generations between 1500 and 1575 up to the institutionalization of the Reformation in the Holy Roman Empire and on the British Isles. More than once the question imposes itself on the reader how far the developments that took place here and there and their results are really comparable. Indeed, it is obvious what are the difficulties faced by every comparative endeavour. As the social-political structures in general, so the ecclesial structures in the Empire, in England, and in Scotland differed from each other widely. They had considerable impacts on all programs of church reform as well as on the Reformations. Thus the results in each case were equally different. Taking up a term frequently used in the present historiography on the Reformation one could say: The contributions of this volume show a string of transformation processes which at times run parallel, at times in different directions, at times on convergent lines, and at times intersecting each other. Their number could certainly be increased.

Of course simply to state »transformations« is trivial and means little. It makes sense only when the factors responsible for the transformations are identified and distinguished from their presuppositions, consequences, and secondary causes. Therefore comparisons between different processes of transformation will only yield results worth discussing when they advance as far as to the transforming factors and then show which interactions and interdependencies can be found between them. On this basis it would be possible conclusively to identify relationships of kinship and foreignness between different phenomena and events. We have not yet reached that point.

All persons present at the Berlin conference Sister Reformations III in April 2018, those who gave papers as well as those who participated in the discussions, shared the impression that there are many tasks ahead on various levels of historical research and interpretation. The editors hand this volume over to the public hoping thereby to stimulate further work on the same field.

The conference was financed by the German Research Foundation (DFG) and the Evangelical Church in Germany (EKD). Our sincere thanks to both of them.

Berlin, New York, Wuppertal
Autumn 2019

Dorothea Wendebourg
Euan Cameron
Martin Ohst

Inhalt – Contents

I.

Von der kritischen Gruppe zur evangelischen Kirche im Heiligen Römischen Reich, in England und in Schottland. Ein Überblick

From Dissenting Groups to Evangelical Churches: An Overview

II.

Faktoren des Kirchewerdens

Factors Contributing to the Emergence of Evangelical Churches

III.

Alte und neue Traditionen

Old and New Traditions

IV.

Das Bild der Reformation von sich selbst

The Reformation's Self Image

I.

Von der kritischen Gruppe zur evangelischen
Kirche im Heiligen Römischen Reich,
in England und in Schottland
Ein Überblick

From Dissenting Groups
to Evangelical Churches
An Overview

Protestant England:
From Movement to Institution

John Ashley Null

»All the world's a stage, / And all the men and women merely players.«
With these famous words Shakespeare concisely captured the Sixteenth
Century's ›self-fashioning‹ approach to life. Although human beings had
to play a role in society which was largely pre-determined, they were still
expected to perform their part with as much insight and artifice as possible. The challenge was to discern the right model to imitate, the best
script to follow. For Jaques, Shakespeare's libertine-turned-philosopher
who uttered those memorable lines in *As You Like It*, his goal in life was
to find the true way of discharging the foul infections, both corporal and
spiritual, which he had acquired on his many world travels. At the end of
the play, Jaques pinned his hopes for a return to wholeness on meeting the
former persecuting Duke Frederick who had abandoned the pomp of
court life to become a monastic penitent:

»To him will I. Out of these convertites / There is much matter to be heard and
learn'd.«[1]

Of course, in Shakespeare's England none of those in his audience who
wished to purge themselves of the world could actually avail themselves of
Jaques' solution, for English converts no longer congregated in monasteries. The reason lay in changes beginning much earlier during the reign of
Henry VIII in the 1520s and 1530s. At that time courtiers like Sebastian
Newdigate and Sir John Gage could still convert in the traditional medieval meaning of the word by turning from a life lived in this world to the
retreat of a monastic way-station in preparation for admittance to heaven
after death.[2]

   Others, however, took conversion in a completely different direction.
Concerned that the medieval emphasis on human effort obscured the suf-

---

[1] William Shakespeare, *As You Like It*, Act II, Scene 7, lines 139–40; Act V, Scene 4,
lines 184–85. For the theme of ›self-fashioning‹ in the English Renaissance, see Stephen
Greenblatt, *Renaissance Self-Fashioning: From More to Shakespeare* (Chicago, 1980).
[2] Peter Marshall, *Religious Identities in Henry VIII's England* (Cambridge, 2006),
27, n. 40.

ficiency of Christ's redeeming work on the cross, they sought to cleanse themselves of their sins by rejecting much of the church's established belief and practice. Returning to the fountainhead of the Christian faith, they found a new model to follow for forgiveness, a script based only on the plain sense of the Bible, as read through the prism of the writings of St. Paul. These dissenters from both the world and the church insisted that a true Christian should give priority to this radically new script over everything else in shaping one's life:[3] priority over culturally-hegemonic beliefs like purgatory, pardons, and penance; priority over universally cherished devotional practices like praying to saints and burning lights before their images; priority over time-honoured ›unwritten verities‹ and centuries of well-reasoned biblical interpretation that authorised such practices; priority over even the ancient institutional authority of the church itself which had notoriously endorsed them. After the sword of scriptural authority had cut away centuries of error, what remained, these reformers believed, was the simple message of salvation by faith in Christ alone. This ›fervent biblicism‹ was the coat-of-arms by which they presented themselves on the doctrinal battlefield and by which they recognized their comrades-in-arms.[4]

1. Recent Historiography of the English Reformation

A. G. Dickens famously portrayed the rise of these English gospellers as a popular movement arising as a natural response to the »rational appeal of a Christianity based upon the authentic sources of the New Testament«.[5] For in his view, Protestant conversion in England was simply a matter of intellectual insight,[6] rather than an experience of an existential inner resonance, including Luther's own *Turmerlebnis*.[7]

---

[3] Ibid., 93–105.

[4] Ibid., 7.

[5] A. G. Dickens, »The Shape of Anti-clericalism and the English Reformation«, in *Politics and Society in Reformation Europe: Essays for Sir Geoffrey Elton on his Sixty-Fifth Birthday*, eds. E. I. Kouri and Tom Scott (London, 1987), 379–410, at p. 380.

[6] »Luther declared war between bible-Christianity and churchly, scholastic Christianity. Within this intellectual context, by 1530 widely apparent, we should also locate the core of the English Reformation«, Dickens, *The English Reformation*, 2nd ed. (London, 1989), 21.

[7] »Whatever the importance of the tower-experience, it should not be regarded as a ›religious experience‹ as one applies this term either to medieval mystics or modern revivalists. [...] The tower-experience was something different; it taught [Luther] what he believed to be the true sense of the Scriptures, the understanding of something objective, of something God had long ago thrown open to the insight of men«, A. G. Dickens, *Martin Luther and the Reformation* (London, 1967), 30.

Dickens took as his baseline an essentially negative view of the medieval English church:

»English Catholicism, despite its gilded decorations, was an old, unseaworthy and ill-commanded galleon, scarcely able to continue its voyage without the new seamen and shipwrights produced (but produced too late in the day) by the Counter-Reformation.«[8]

In contrast, however, with the advent of an increasingly educated populace, Protestantism's book-based faith was inevitably more persuasive than the medieval church's affective ritualism and ignorant popular piety. This thesis is, of course, as old as John Foxe himself:

»[A]s printing of books ministered matter of reading: so reading brought learning: learning showed light, by the brightness whereof blind ignorance was suppressed, error detected, and finally God's glory, with truth of his word, advanced.«[9]

Since Dickens saw the English Reformation as essentially following an intellectual script based on the Bible alone, he naturally linked its eventual success to the surviving underground network of England's previous bible-based lay church reform movement, the Wycliffe-inspired Lollards, who were still being actively suppressed by English church officials in the early decades of the Sixteenth Century. According to Dickens, »Scholars who seek an historical understanding of the English Reformation would be wise to think a little less about Bucer, Bullinger, and even Cranmer, and somewhat more in terms of a diffused but inveterate Lollardy revivified by contact with continental Protestantism.«[10] And again, »The Lollards were the allies and in some measure the begetters of the anticlerical forces which made possible the Henrician revolution, yet they were something more, and the successes of Protestantism seem not wholly intelligible without reference to this earlier ground-swell of popular dissent.«[11]

Of course, at the heart of Dickens' reformation from below is a whiggish assumption of the inherent superiority of a ›rational‹ Protestantism over an ignorant, moribund medieval church life, an assumption which has been so successful challenged by revisionist Tudor historians of the last thirty years.[12] On the one hand, Eamon Duffy has illuminated how tra-

---

[8] Dickens, *English Reformation*, 108.

[9] John Foxe, *Ecclesiasticall history contaynyng the Actes and Monumentes of thynges passed in euery kynges tyme in this Realme* (London, 1570), 838. Spelling has been modernized in all quotations from this text. Cf. Ethan H. Shagan, *Popular Politics and the English Reformation* (Cambridge, 2003), 2–3.

[10] A. G. Dickens, *Lollards and Protestants in the Diocese of York 1509–1558* (London, 1982), 243.

[11] Dickens, *English Reformation*, 59.

[12] Shagan, *Popular Politics and the English Reformation*, 4–5. Cf. Hebert Butterfield, *The Whig Interpretation of History* (London, 1931).

ditionalist religious beliefs and practices were just as appealing to members of the educated classes as they were to rural labourers.[13] Indeed, Richard Rex has helpfully shown that English humanism, the force that Dickens posits as leading inevitably to Protestant thought, was in fact originally a flowering of late medieval Catholic learning in support of traditionalist belief which then fuelled the Counter-Reformation as much as the Reformation.[14] On the other hand, Alec Ryrie has found little evidence for Dickens' grass-roots movement of Protestant conversions. According to Ryrie, »most English people never experienced a dramatic, individual conversion; Protestant England was formed by pragmatic gospellers«.[15]

In the face of the demise of the Dickens' model, what have we learned in the last thirty years? The late medieval English catholicism remained vibrant, if not as idyllic as Eamon Duffy first seemed to present in his landmark *Stripping of the Altars*, which he made sure to clarify in his introduction to the revised edition;[16] that parish life was cohesive and remarkably well-financed;[17] that parishes could be the recalcitrant, if ultimately unsuccessful, in responding to mandated religious changes from above;[18] there were »as many Reformations as there were monarchs on the Tudor throne«, from Henry VII through Elizabeth;[19] that England might

---

[13] Eamon Duffy, *Stripping of the Altars: Traditional Religion in England c. 1400–1570* (London, 1992).

[14] Richard Rex, »The Role of English Humanists in the Reformation up to 1559«, in N. S. Amos, A. Pettegree and H. van Nierop, eds., *The Education of a Christian Society: Humanism and Reformation in Britain and the Netherlands* (Aldershot, 1999), 19–40.

[15] Alec Ryrie, »Counting sheep, counting shepherds: the problem of allegiance in the English Reformation«, in Peter Marshall and Alec Ryrie, eds., *Beginnings of English Protestantism* (Cambridge, 2002), 84–110, at p. 105.

[16] »*The Stripping of the Altars*, then, was at one level an elegy for a world we had lost, a world of great beauty and power which it seemed to me the reformers – and many historians ever since – had misunderstood. [...] In attempting to offer a corrective to conventional assessments of medieval religion, I opted for a thematic, analytic treatment of a vast and intractable mass of source material. That decision about procedure exacted a price, similarly acknowledged in the introduction, in terms of the elimination of narrative, and the consequent muting of a sense of change and development within the thematic sections of the first and longer part of the book. I had indeed gone so far as to use the phrase ›the social *homogeneity*‹ of late medieval religion. By that phrase, however, I certainly did not mean to suggest that all was well in an harmonious pre-Reformation Merry England, a consensual garden of Eden only spoiled by the arrival of the serpent of reform«, Eamon Duffy, *The Stripping of the Altars: Traditional Religion in England c. 1400–c. 1580*, 2nd ed. (New Haven, 2005), xiv, xx.

[17] See Beat A. Kümin's examination of ten church warden accounts in *The Shaping of a Community: The Rise and Reformation of the English Parish, c. 1400–1560* (Aldershot, 1996).

[18] See Eamon Duffy's examination of one conservative Devon village and its priest from the 1520s to the 1570s, Sir Christopher Trychay, in *The Voices of Morebath: Reformation and Rebellion in an English Village* (London, 2001).

have become a clearly Protestant nation in 1547, but it did not become a nation of Protestants until well into Elizabeth's reign in the 1570s.[20] Indeed, some historians would argue for longer periods of Reformation, up to the Restoration Church of 1662 or even 1800, although by then what was really being debated was what the Reformation as a past event meant for England in the following centuries, rather than being the part of its process;[21] that the eventual advent of Protestant England was the result of a process of mutual cultural accommodation between the religious policies of Tudor regimes, and the populace, who modified them along the way according to their own interests.[22]

And what of the Lollards and their influence on the English Reformers? No consensus has yet emerged.[23] On the one hand, Duffy and Rex argue that Lollardy was a spent force by the Reformation era, marginal to both late medieval English religion and the Reformers' critique of it.[24] On the other hand, Diarmaid MacCulloch has noted that the geographic areas known for a strong Lollardy presence correspond to the same parts of England where Protestantism had its first major advances among the populace, the so-called ›great crescent‹ from Norwich to East Anglia to Kent to the Thames Valley.[25] Moreover, there are a number of instances of their interaction, both Lollards distributing Tyndale Bibles and reformers pub-

---

[19] Diarmaid MacCulloch originally made this point with reference to Tudor rulers »after the break with Rome« in »The Church of England, 1533–1603«, in Stephen Platten, ed., *Anglicanism and the Western Christian Tradition* (Norwich, 2003), 18, but the insight applies equally to Henry VII and his mother's Catholic humanist renewal movement as well.

[20] Patrick Collinson, *The Birthpangs of Protestant England: Religious and Cultural Change in the Sixteenth and Seventeenth Centuries* (Basingstoke, 1988), ix.

[21] See Peter Marshall, »(Re)defining the English Reformation«, *Journal of British Studies* 48 (2009), 564–586, at p. 567; Nicholas Tyacke, ed., *England's Long Reformation, 1500–1800* (London, 1998).

[22] In embryo, see Geoffrey Elton's *Policy and Police: The Enforcement of the Reformation in the Age of Thomas Cromwell* (Cambridge, 1972) which showed the Henrician regime's necessary reliance on both power and persuasion to implement religious change; for this thesis more recently distilled, see Ethan H. Shagan's *Popular Politics and the English Reformation* and Peter Marshall's *Heretics and Believers: A History of the English Reformation* (New Haven, 2017), although Shagan sees the local responses as more pragmatic secularism, while Marshall wants to insist on the fundamentally religious nature of those choices.

[23] See Peter Marshall, »Lollards and Protestants Revisited«, in Mishtooni C. A. Bose and J. Patrick Hornbeck II, eds., *Wycliffite Controversies* (Turnhout, 2011), 295–318.

[24] See Duffy's robust rejection of the criticism that *The Stripping of the Altars* failed to appreciate the dynamic force of Lollardy in late Medieval England in the »Preface to the Second Edition«, xviii–xxviii, as well as Richard Rex's more extended argument for the marginal nature of the movement in *The Lollards* (Basingstoke, 2002).

[25] Diarmaid MacCulloch, *The Later Reformation in England, 1547–1603*, 2nd ed. (Basingstoke, 2001), 106.

lishing Lollard books, if only to show where their church was before Luther.[26] Yet, one stubborn undisputed fact remains. While Lollardy may have aided English Protestantism's advance, the leaders of the movement, the Reformers themselves, came from orthodox Catholic backgrounds.[27] We cannot find the origins or even the momentum for early English Protestantism in Lollardy itself.

For that we must re-examine not only Dickens understanding of the medieval church but also his assessment of the first gospellers. In essence, he split the human being in two, dividing head from heart, assigning emotionalism to popular medieval piety and intellectualism to Protestant believers. Therefore, much revisionist ink has been well-spilt to show that medieval Christians held head and heart together. Yet why should this not be equally true of the first English Protestants, since they were late-medieval catholics, too? Just as English piety on the eve of the Reformation did not solely focus on the affections, the script which began the process of the English Reformation did not merely appeal to the intellect.

Susan Karant-Nunn has shown this dual head-heart dynamic was true across confessions in Germany. She has investigated the emotion scripts for Roman Catholic, Lutheran and Reformed preachers during the German Reformation, highlighting the emphasis in each on the importance of a ›heartfelt‹ response to God in the light of their doctrine. For Roman Catholics, that meant contrition through identification with the physical sufferings of Christ for their sins. For Lutherans, that meant *Trost* – Comfort because of justification *sola fide*, leading to gratitude and love, and for the Reformed that meant in the face of the clear preaching of predestination, human self-abasement, divine glorification and gratitude for salvation, but amongst the elect alone.[28] Alec Ryrie has also shown in *Being Protestant in Reformation Britain* that Elizabethan and Stuart Protestants

---

[26] Marshall, *Heretics and Believers*, 137–140; Anne Hudson, »No newe thyng‹: the printing of medieval texts in the early Reformation period«, in *Middle English Studies Presented to Norman Davis in Honour of his Seventieth Birthday* (Oxford, 1983), 153–174; Susan Brigden, *London and the Reformation* (London, 2014), 336, 358. For John Bale and John Foxe's description of Wycliffe as the *stella matutina* of the Reformation, see Marget Aston, »John Wycliffe's Reformation Reputation«, *Past and Present 30* (1964), 23–51, especially at pp. 24–27.

[27] »When we can ascertain anything about the religious antecedents of the English Reformers, we find that they came from highly orthodox backgrounds [...] Reformers were no doubt happy to recruit Lollards to their ranks. But we find no Lollards among the movers and shakers of the English Reformation. [...] The key to the success of the English Reformation lies not in the conversion of Lollards, but in the conversion of Catholics«, Rex, *Lollards*, 133, 141–42.

[28] Susan C. Karant-Nunn, *The Reformation of Feeling: Shaping the Religious Emotions in Early Modern Germany* (Oxford, 2010).

were deeply committed to cultivating their feelings to strengthen their service to God. If English Protestants held head and heart together at the end of the Reformation period, what about the role of emotions at its beginning? The source for that script lay not in Lollardy, but in the medieval English affective tradition, a piety which the moralist focus of Lollard preaching rejected.[29]

2. New Insights into Tudor Evangelical Conversion

The heart of Tudor Protestantism was not right doctrine but right desire. The mystical and mixed-life writings of Richard Rolle and Walter Hilton had trained devout early Tudor Christians to embrace affective piety as the hallmark of true faith. Rolle, the most popular devotional writer for fifteenth-century England, encouraged his readers to embrace celibacy and to ruminate on the Scripture so that they would experience a sensible burning love for Christ.[30] Hilton also stressed the supernatural power of the Bible to transform human affections, but he was of a more practical mind than Rolle. Rather than seeing contemplation as a gateway to God-given physical sensations of ecstasy, Hilton encouraged his readers to channel their newly received divine love into a striving for moral perfection.[31] As a result, unlike Rolle, he encouraged devout lay people to stay in their current secular spheres of responsibility to better serve their fellow Christians, but to cultivate a rich contemplative life in private to sustain their work in the world as well.[32] Thoroughly embracing this ›mixed-life‹

---

[29] As Duffy himself pointed out: »Like the Lollard preachers, Langland had no interest in and no sympathy for the affective tradition of meditation on the Passion which was the dominant devotional mode of the late Middle Ages«, *Stripping of the Altars*, 2nd ed., xxviii. Cf. »The Lollards appealed to the same educated lay cadre as [Walter] Hilton, but their call was to action, not to contemplative thought. Lollard literature, like the works of Wyclif himself, carried no hint of a devotional disposition«, Jeremy Catto, »1349–1412: Culture and History«, in Samuel Fanous and Vincent Gillespie, eds., *The Cambridge Companion to Medieval English Mysticism* (Cambridge, 2011), 120.

[30] For a brief introduction to his life and works, see Rosamund S. Allen, ed., *Richard Rolle: The English Writings* (New York, 1988), 9–63. For the most thoroughly study, see Wolfgang Riehle, *Englische Mystik des Mittelalters* (Munich, 2011), 117–208, and, in the light of Riehle's critique, Nicholas Watson, *Richard Rolle and the Invention of Authority* (Cambridge, 1991).

[31] For a short introduction see, Walter Hilton, *The Scale of Perfection*, translated by John P. H. Clark and Rosemary Dorward (New York, 1991), 13–68. For a more thorough study, see Margarethe Hopf, *Der Weg zur christlichen Vollkommenheit. Eine Studie zu Walter Hilton auf dem Hintergrund der romanischen Mystik* (Göttingen, 2009).

[32] See »Epistle on the Mixed Life«, in Barry Windeatt, ed., *English Mystics of the Middle Ages* (Cambridge, 1994), 108–30.

tradition herself, Lady Margaret Beaufort, the mother of Henry VII, promoted its piety as part of her highly influential humanist education program for the English church,[33] since continental humanism also stressed that Scripture's power to transform the affections would lead to moral reformation. Indeed, the great humanist scholar Erasmus insisted that the Gospel was the living mind of Christ whose words had the power to reprogram the human heart and mind so that people could lead godly lives.[34]

We can see this progression from scriptural meditation to transformed affections in the conversion narratives of the early English reformers Thomas Bilney and Katherine Parr. According to Bilney, he often »felt a change« in himself »from the right hand of the Most High God« when he read Scripture. It happened for the first time while reading Erasmus' new Latin translation of the Bible.

»I chanced upon this sentence of St. Paul (Oh most sweet and comfortable sentence to my soul!) in I Tim. 1: ›It is a true saying and worthy of all men to be embraced, that Christ Jesus came into the world to save sinners, of whom I am the chief and principal.‹ This one sentence, through God's instruction [...] working inwardly in my heart, did so gladdened it – which before was wounded by the awareness of my sins almost to the point of desperation – that immediately I felt a marvelous inner peace, so much so that my bruised bones leapt for joy. After this, the Scripture began to be more pleasant to me than honey or the honey comb.«[35]

Katherine Parr, the widow of Henry VIII, used the same emotive language to describe the result of her reading of Scripture.

---

[33] For the best treatment of Lady Margaret, see Michael K. Jones and Malcolm G. Underwood, *The King's Mother: Lady Margaret Beaufort Countess of Richmond and Derby* (Cambridge, 1992); for the wider Mixed-life movement, see Hilary M. Carey, »Devout Literate Laypeople and the Pursuit of the Mixed Life in Later Medieval England«, *Journal of Religious History* 14 (1987), 361–81.

[34] For Erasmus' rhetorical theology, see Marjorie O'Rourke Boyle, *Erasmus on Language and Method in Theology* (Toronto, 1977), and Manfred Hoffmann, *Rhetoric and Theology: The Hermeneutic of Erasmus* (Toronto, 1994). For texts, see especially *Paraclesis* in the contemporary translation by the English Reformer William Roye, *An exhortation to the diligent studye of scripture* (Antwerp: J. Hoochstraten, 1529), A 2r/v, A 5v–A 6r. For the background of this translation, see the recent critical edition, Douglas H. Parker, ed., *William Roye's An exhortation to the diligent studye of scripture; and, An exposition in to the seventh chapter of the pistle to the Corinthians* (Toronto, 2000), 28–36.

[35] John Foxe, *Actes and Monuments* (London, 1570), 1141–43. Bilney's description of his conversion is contained in correspondence to Bishop Cuthbert Tunstall during Bilney's 1527 heresy trial. Foxe has given two versions, the original Latin and an English translation. The quotations here are the author's revision of Foxe's translation in the light of the original Latin.

»Cum to me al ye that labour, and ar burdened, and I shall refresshe you. What gentle, mercyfull, and comfortable wordes ar these, to all sinners? [...] What a most gracious comfortable, and gentle, saying was this, with suche pleasant and swete wordes, to allure his enemies to cum unto him? [...] [W]hen I behold the benignitie, liberalitie, mercy, and goodnes of the lord, I am encoraged, boldened, and stirred to ask [for] suche a noble gift [as living faith]. [...] By this fayth I am assured: and by thys assurance, I fele the remission of my sinnes: this is it that maketh me bolde, this is it that comforteth me, this is it that quencheth all dispayre. [...] Thus I feele my selfe to cum, as it were in a newe garment, before god, and nowe by his mercye, to be taken iuste, and rightwise.«[36]

»I felt a supernatural change within«, »gladdened my heart«, »I felt inner peace«, »leapt for joy«, »more pleasant than honey«, »pleasant and sweet words«, »I am assured«, »I feel the remission of my sins«, »I feel myself in a new garment«: To borrow a term from T. S. Eliot, the first English reformers clearly »felt their thought«.[37] But what in their affective reading of the Bible led them to leave behind the unquestioned orthodoxy of Lady Margaret's humanist renewal movement and embrace the evangelicalism of Luther and his followers?

Justification by faith was the doctrinal bridge by which the scriptural affective piety of medieval English spirituality and Renaissance humanism crossed over into early Protestantism. For traditionalists, the gift of divine love through reading Scripture was the foundation of a person's inherent righteous which justified them before God. Hence, Hilton had taught that a continual desire for God – defined as a constant loathing of all worldly bliss coupled with an intense yearning for heavenly joy – was the heart of authentic Christianity.[38] For gospellers, however, divine love was the fruit of gratitude for having been previously justified because of faith inspired by reading God's Pauline promises. Only by first experiencing the un-conditional love of God made known in salvation as a free gift could human beings ever begin to find the power of loving him in return. Bilney had implied his acceptance of the latter understanding by his meditating on Paul's soteriology. Katherine made hers unquestionably explicit.

---

[36] Katherine Parr, *The Lamentation of a Sinner* (London, 1547), B 2ᵛ–[B 4]ᵛ.

[37] T. S. Eliot, »The Metaphyscial Poets«, *Times Literary Supplement*, 20 October 1921, 669–70.

[38] »Seynt Austyn seith that the liyf of eche good Cristen man is a continuel desire to God. [...] And what is this desire? Sotheli, [no thinge] but a lothynge of al this wordlis blisse, of this fleschi likynge in thyn herte, and a wondirful longynge with a trustfull yernynge of endeles blisse and heveneli desire and joie«, Walter Hilton, »Epistle on the Mixed Life«, in Windeatt, *English Mystics of the Middle Ages*, 121.

»Then began I to dwel in god by charitie, knowing by the louyng charitie of god in the remission of my sinnes, that god is charitie as Saint John sayeth. So that of my faythe (wherby I came to knowe god, and wherby it pleased god euen because I trusted in hym, to iustifie me) sprang this excellent charitie in my harte.«[39]

She helpfully added that because she had at last experienced a life-chang-ing redirection of her affections, she knew the »new learning« was the true interpretation of Scripture:[40]

»than I knewe it was no illusion of the deuill, nor false, ne humain doctrine I had receyued: when suche successe came thereof, that I had in detestacion and horrour, that which I erste [i.e., formerly] so muche loued and estemed.«[41]

In short, Katherine's account of her conversion makes clear that she adop-ted solifidianism not as a repudiation of her late medieval emotive piety, but precisely because she found its grace and gratitude theology much more effective in moving her affections than the traditional medieval means.

Here is the context for understanding William Tyndale's individualist ›feeling faith‹.[42] Like Bilney and Katherine, Tyndale began his journey towards Protestantism as an Erasmian humanist, in his case translating the *Enchiridion* for the Walsh family who employed him as an explanation for why he disputed with the clergy who called at their home.[43] And like Bilney and Katherine, he believed that saving faith produced a clearly sensible experience. When More demanded that Tyndale explain by what authority he accepted the Scriptures, if not like Augustine on account of the church's endorsement, Tyndale argued that the Bible was self-authen-ticating because the Holy Spirit worked through its proclamation to birth a sensible faith in the elect.[44]

»And therefore, when thou asked why thou believest that thou shalt be saved through Christ, and of such like principles of our faith; answer, Thou wottest and feelest that it is true. And when he asketh, How thou knowest that it is true; answer, Because it is written in thine heart. And if he ask who wrote it; answer, The

---

[39] Parr, *Lamentation*, [B 6]$^{r/v}$.

[40] For the sixteenth-century use of the term ›new learning‹ to refer to emerging Protestant doctrine than to Renaissance humanism *per se*, see Richard Rex, »The New Learning«, *Journal of Ecclesiastical History* 44 (1993), 26–44.

[41] Parr, *Lamentation*, [B 6]^r.

[42] »I answer, ›That there are two manner faiths, an historical faith, and a feeling faith‹«, Henry Walter, ed., *An Answer to Sir Thomas More's Dialogue, The Supper of the Lord* [...] *and William Tracy's Testament Expounded by William Tyndale* (Cambridge, 1850), 50.

[43] Arne Dembek, *William Tyndale (1491–1536)* (Tübingen, 2010), 33–38. *NB* that Dembek rightly argues Tyndale's emphasis on morality more likely comes from the influence of Erasmus than Lollardy, ibid., 35, n. 129.

[44] Ibid., 309–12.

Spirit of God. And if he ask how thou camest first by it; tell him whether by reading in books, or hearing it preached, as by an outward instrument, but that inwardly thou wast taught by the Spirit of God.«[45]

Tyndale further clarified that by the term ›feeling faith‹ he meant ›experiential‹, like the difference between children being told a candle flame would burn their fingers, and then children actually touching the flame and getting burned.[46] What, then, was the experience which left the elect no doubt about their salvation? Although he left no spiritual autobiography, Tyndale's description of the conversion process suggests that his ›feeling faith‹ was nothing other than a renovation of the affections resulting in trust and love.

»[The heart] in believing is saved from the fear of everlasting death, and made sure of everlasting life; and then, being overcome with this kindness, beginneth to love again and to submit herself unto the laws of God, to learn them and to walk in them. Note now the order: first God giveth me light to see the goodness and righteousness of the law, and mine own sin and unrighteousness; out of which knowledge springeth repentance. [...] Then the same Spirit worketh in mine heart trust and confidence, to believe the mercy of God and his truth, that he will do as he hath promised; which belief saveth me. And immediately out of that trust springeth love toward the law of God again.«[47]

Thomas More may have despised Tyndale's ›felyng fayth‹ as a German import foreign to the faith and faithfulness of the English church.[48] In reality, it was but the unexpected offshoot of England's own orthodox fifteenth-century lay piety movement. As recent scholars have noted, Tyndale's ›feeling faith‹ »seems to share important features« with Hilton's own call for the reformation of the affections, for the Reformers' Scripture-induced sensible experience of inner renewal issuing forth in outward loving service was in fact also the hallmark of the medieval English affective tradition.[49]

3. Spreading the Faith

Early English Protestantism was not only a book-based faith, it was a book-disseminated faith. With the publication of Henry VIII's *Assertio*

---

[45] Walter, *An Answer to Sir Thomas More's Dialogue*, 55.

[46] Ibid., 51.

[47] Ibid., 195–96.

[48] Thomas More, *The Confutation of Tyndale's Answer*, ed.s Louis A. Schuster et al., *The Complete Works of St. Thomas More* (New Haven, 1973), Vol. 8, Part II, 663, 741, 926.

[49] Hilton, *Scale of Perfection*, 9–10.

Septem Sacramentorum in 1521, England was left in no doubt that the leadership of the government as well as the church was actively opposed to Lutheran ideas coming to England.[50] Open evangelical preaching would not be tolerated. Nor was the importation of foreign heretical books, and books printed at home now had to be licensed. Hence, 11 February 1526, saw a grand service in St. Paul's Cathedral. In front of Cardinal Wolsey with thirty-six bishops and mitred abbots, Fisher preached against Luther and then banned books which had been ferreted out were burned before the Rood at the North Door. But the display of such pomp and power, the very fact that »great basketfuls« of confiscated tomes were fed into the flames showed simultaneously both the great determination of officials to stop the heretical book trade and their on-going failure.[51] England's immensely important commercial ties to both Antwerp and the Hanseatic League gave too many legitimate foreign trade opportunities to smuggle Protestant writings and, especially Tyndale's New Testament (1526), into England. Indeed, the merchants themselves represented the ideal target audience for perspective readers, educated laymen who might find a printed English Bible helpful for their mixed-life devotions. After all, it was an orthodox humanist Catholic layman, who sponsored Tyndale to go to Hamburg but also asked him to say masses for his parents' souls. Not surprisingly, young lawyers at London's Inns of Court found the books inspiring as well.[52]

Besides smuggling at sea, the English gospellers used subterfuge at home as well, especially subterfuge shaped by late medieval devotional practice. When Bilney heard Hugh Latimer argued strenuously against Melanchthon for his BD, he converted him through asking Latimer to hear his confession. Both Bilney and Latimer were also known for visiting prisoners, helping the needy and feeding the hungry. Bilney was especially mindful to help those, like he once was, in despair over sin.[53] By being

---

[50] See Richard Rex, »The English Campaign against Luther in the 1520s«, *Transactions of the Royal Historical Society* 39 (1989), 85–106.

[51] Edward Hall, *Hall's Chronicle* (London, 1809), 708; Marshall, *Heretics and Believers*, 135; Bridgen, *London and the Reformation*, 158.

[52] Marshall, *Heretics and Believers*, 129–134; Bridgen, *London and the Reformation*, 106–18.

[53] For Latimer's own description of his conversion through Bilney's confession and their visits to prisoners, see G. E. Corrie, ed., *Sermons and Remains of Hugh Latimer*, 2 vols. (Cambridge, 1844–5), I,344–45. For a second reference by Latimer to his conversion through Bilney, see »Conferences with Latimer« in Henry Christmas, ed., *The Works of Nicholas Ridley* (Cambridge, 1843), 118: »Sir, I begin now to smell what you mean: by travailing thus with me, you use me, as Bilney did once, when he converted me. Pretending as though he would be taught of me, he sought ways and means to teach me; and so do you.« For Foxe's account of Latimer's conversion and his good works, see *Actes and Monuments* (1570), 1152, 1903, 1905.

very public in their good works, they at once conformed to the outward expectations of the church for pious Christians, while giving living testimony that the change in their affections made possible justification by faith did indeed fuel such a life. Yet, in these eyes of their traditionalist opponents, such an outward appearance of holiness was merely another devious subterfuge to win the innocent to their heretical cause, since the reformers' teaching was merely based on pleasing their corrupt affections rather than right judgment and the testimony of their consciences.[54]

Thomas Farman, President of Queens' College, Cambridge, and rector of All Hallows, London,[55] was another of those, in the words of Thomas More, »that bear two faces in one hood«, a gospeller among gospellers, but a dissembler before the public.[56] Indeed, Farman deeply frustrated his bishop Tunstall, because Farman's sermons in the pulpit always seemed absolutely conventional, but he, too, was know for using the sacrament of confession to convert those he came to him for spiritual consolation. Farman also had a second mission strategy. He was a major disseminator of banned books. And what did he see as his market? Young humanist scholars who could be persuaded. Indeed, he sent his curate, Thomas Garrett, back to Oxford in December 1527 with two very large loads of books.[57] His assignment was clear: to look for »all siche wiche wer gevyn to greke, ebrew and the polyt latyn tonge«. Under the subterfuge of seeking instruction in the biblical languages, he was to introduce his supposed teachers to »bokes of new thinges to allewer [i.e., allure] them«.[58]

We need to note Garrett's emphasis on »new thinges«. He did not present himself to his mission field as peddling the old Lollard heresies, but the fresh insights of cutting-edge scholarship. Secondly, this word »allewer« was of deep significance for the English Reformers, for they believed that the changes in the affections brought about by this new doctrine of justification *sola fide* would naturally draw others to their cause. Persuasion through conventional means was, therefore, their preferred method, as Thomas Becon later made clear:

---

[54] As former evangelical William Barlow made clear in his *Dialogue describing the original ground of these Lutheran factions* (London, 1531), [B 4]ᵛ–C 1ᵛ; Marshall, *Heretics and Believers*, 142.

[55] *NB* that Thomas Farman is also know by Robert Forman (Brigden, *London and the Reformation*) and Robert Farman (Marshall, *Heretics and Believers*). I follow Richard Rex (*Henry VIII and the English Reformation, Cambridge Companion to Thomas More*) based on records at Queens' College and Cambridge University which Rex has identified.

[56] Thomas More, *Dialogue concerning Heresies*, eds. T. M. C. Lawler *et alia*, *The Complete Works of Thomas More* (New Haven, 1981), Vol. 6, Part 1, 399.

[57] Bridgen, *London and the Reformation*, 113–16.

[58] A Report of Dr. London to the Bishop of Lincoln, 25 Feb. 1528, National Archives, State Papers 47/1, 16ᵛ.

»As I maye unfaignedly reporte vnto you the affect of my herte, verely synce that ye declared to vs the goodnes of God the father toward vs thorow Jesus christ I haue felte in my herte such an earnest fayth and burnyng loue towarde God and his worde, that me thynke a thousande fyres coulde not plucke me away from the loue of hym. I begynne nowe vtterlye to contemne, despyse, reiecte, cast awaye, and sette at nought al the pleasures of this world, wherein I haue so greatlye reioyced in tymes past. All the thretes of god, all the displeasures of God, al the fyres and paynes of hell coulde neuer before this daye so allure me to the loue of God, as you haue now done by expressynge vnto me the excedyng mercye and unspeakable kyndenes of God towarde vs wretched synners, insomuch that now from the very herte I desyre to knowe what I maye do, that by some meanes I maye shewe agayne my herte to be full fyred on the sekynge of his glory. For I nowe desyre nothyng more then the auancement of his name.«[59]

The English authorities also tried persuasion at first, convincing Bilney, Forman and Garrett to abjure.[60] Fisher even offered in print to meet confidentially with any young scholar having doubts:

»I trust in our lorde / that finally we shall so agre / that either he shal make me a Lutheran / or els I shal enduce hym to be a catholyke / and to folowe the doctryne of Christis churche«.[61]

However, as Heinrich Heine observed in the *Almansor: Eine Tragödie* (1823): »Dort wo man Bücher verbrennt, verbrennt man auch am Ende Menschen.«[62] Bilney (1531), Tyndale (1536) and eventually Garrett (1540) died in the flames of heresy.

4. The First Major Turning Point: Henry's Divorce

How then was this new evangelical emotion script institutionalized in the Church of England? The first major step was the break from Rome to enable Henry's ›Divorce‹ in 1533, and the declaration of royal supremacy the following year. From then on, the Henrician regime went from suppressing Continental influences for similar reform in England, to trying to manage them within certain not always entirely clear limits. Henry's case for his annulment depended on Scripture, as interpreted by other Scripture in good Erasmian fashion, having the authority to reject papal decisions and medieval church tradition.[63] Consequently, henceforth all doctrine

---

[59] Thomas Becon, *A Christmas Banquet Garnished with Many Pleasant and Dainty Dishes* (London, 1542), F 4ᵛ–F 5ʳ.

[60] Marshall, *Heretics and Believers*, 152–54.

[61] »Epistole vnto the reder«, in John Fisher, *A Sermon had at Paulis* [...] *concernynge certayne heretickes* (London, [1526]), [A 4]ʳ.

[62] »Where they burn books, in the end they will also burn people«, Heinrich Heine, *Almansor: A Tragedy*.

and ceremonies in the independent Henrician Church of England had to be proven by the Word of God, albeit in view of the writings of the early church by governmental authority. For convinced evangelicals like Cranmer, Henry's new archbishop of Canterbury, royal supremacy and the new emphasis on Scripture offered the best hope for bringing the truths of the Reformation to the English people. In the midst of the doctrinal uncertainty, they used their powers of patronage to send forth evangelical preachers and propagandists.[64] Thomas Cromwell, vice-gerent in spirituals since 1535, even persuaded the king to agree to the ultimate evangelical goal for forwarding their movement: the authorization for and public display of an English Bible in every parish church in 1537–38.[65] For the archbishop's traditionalist opponents, however, the king's new-found authority and loathing of Luther remained the best means of stopping the heretics' advancement. For the king was deeply suspicious of any suggestion that obedience to the crown was not necessary for salvation. As a result, Henry supported changes broadly in line with Erasmian humanism, including closing of all religious houses and deciding that confession was helpful but not required for salvation.[66] Nevertheless, the king would not accept justification by faith alone nor tolerate any deviation from the mass.

As part of the new doctrinal landscape, in 1537 Cromwell gathered together a group of both traditionalist and evangelical bishops to draw up a lengthy set of standard sermons to be read in parishes. The result was the *Institution of a Christian Man*, popularly known as the Bishops' Book. An attempt at theology by committee, the resulting work was a patchwork compromise. Steven Gardiner disparagingly compared the book to a barn where all parties were able to store up their favorite things and then point them out to the rest when needed.[67] Yet to a gospel man like Cranmer, even this hodgepodge was a decided step forward, precisely because so much Protestant theology had at last made its way into official church teaching, regardless of the theological company it was required to keep

---

[63] See Ashley Null, »Princely Marital Problems and the Reformers' Solutions«, in *Sister Reformations: England and the German Empire in the Sixteenth Century*, ed. Dorothea Wendebourg (Tübingen, 2010), 133–49.

[64] Susan Wabuda, »Setting Forth the Word of God: Archbishop Cranmer's early patronage«, in Paul Ayris and David Selwyn, eds., *Thomas Cranmer: Churchman and Scholar* (Woodbridge, 1993), 75–88; Diarmaid MacCulloch, *Thomas Cromwell: A Life* (New Haven, 2018), 236–37, 416–20, 460–61, 506.

[65] MacCulloch, *Cromwell*, 415; Marshall, *Heretics and Believers*, 256–57, 263–64.

[66] For Henry and confession in the Act of Six Articles, see Ashley Null, *Thomas Cranmer's Doctrine of Repentance: Renewing the Power to Love* (Oxford, 2000), 154–55.

[67] James Arthur Muller, ed., *The Letters of Stephen Gardiner* (Cambridge, 1933), 351.

there. In the sacrament of penance, we see the private evangelical confessional subterfuge of the 1520s now institutionalized as require preaching and practice throughout the country. Under the guise of describing sacramental contrition, the Bishops' Book actually preaches the Lutheran soteriology of Law and Gospel:

»The penitent and contrite man, muste firste knowledge the fylthines and abhomination of his owne synne (vnto whiche knowledge he is brought by herynge and consyderinge of the wyll of God declared in his lawes) and feelynge and perceyuyng in his owne conscience, that god is angry and displeased with hym for the same: he must also conceyue not onely great sorowe and inwarde shame, that he hath so greuously offended god, but also great feare of goddis displeasure towardes hym, consyderynge he hath no workes, or merytes of his owne, whiche he may worthily lay before god, as sufficient satisfaction for his synnes. Whiche done, than afterwarde with this feare, shame, and sorowe muste nedes succede and be conioyned [...] a certayn faithe, trust, and confidence of the mercy and goodnes of god, wherby the penitente muste conceyue certayne hope and faithe, that god wyll forgyue hym his synnes, and repute hym iustifyed, and of the nombre of his electe chyldren, not for the worthynes of any merite or worke done by the penitent, but for the onely merites of the blode and passion of our sauyour Jesu Christe.«[68]

By traditionalist standards, this paragraph merely described the lower standard of attrition (sorrow out of fear of punishment) rather than true, saving contrition (sorrow out of love for God).[69]

When Henry VIII criticized such Protestant sections of the Bishops' Book, Cranmer wrote back in 1538 seeking to reinforce the affective evangelical principle that love for God and king was the inevitable spiritual fruit of justification by faith:

»But, if the profession of our faith of the remission of our own sins enter within us into the deepness of our hearts, then it must needs kindle a warm fire of love in our hearts towards God, and towards all other for the love of God, – a fervent mind to seek and procure God's honour, will, and pleasure in all things, – a good will and mind to help every man and to do good unto them, so far as our might, wisdom, learning, counsel, health, strength, and all other gifts which we have received of God, will extend, – and, *in summa*, a firm intent and purpose to do all that is good, and leave all that is evil.«[70]

Doctrine, rightly taught, would birth desire, but desire would enable that doctrine to be embraced and lived out in behavior. The intellectual and emotion script worked together to produce the pursuit of godliness.

However, Henry rejected Cranmer's counsel. Starting with the Act of Six Articles in 1539[71] and Cromwell's execution for harboring heretics in

---

[68] *The Institution of a Christen Man* (London, 1537), 37[r/v].
[69] Null, *Cranmer's Doctrine of Repentance*, 37–44.
[70] J. E. Cox, ed. *Miscellaneous Writings of Thomas Cranmer* (Cambridge, 1846), 86.
[71] Glyn Redworth, »A Study in the Formulation of Policy: The Genesis and Evo-

1540,[72] Henry permitted a traditionalist resurgence which gradually eroded the earlier evangelical gains. Its culmination was the publication of the King's Book, a new set of official sermons with the king's expressed approval, which replaced the Bishops' Book in 1543.[73] Its teaching explicitly rejected all the key points of evangelical soteriology, including the previous Lutheran description of contrition[74] and any suggestion of justification without works.[75] However, true to Henry's anti-clericalism, confession to a priest was described as the church's ordinary pastoral directive, but not ultimately necessary for salvation *de divino jure*.[76] In the same year, Cranmer barely survived a plot for him to go the way of Cromwell.[77] In the end, he remained alive and in office, but he would have to wait for the next reign to renew his campaign to use his affective evangelical piety to shape the formularies of the Church of England.

5. The Edwardian Regime

Under the boy-king Edward VI (1537–1553), Cranmer was at last free to reform the teaching and practices of the English Church according to his understanding of biblical truth. During the next six-and-a-half, short years, Cranmer worked hard to produce a new, Protestant blueprint for

---

lution of the Act of Six Articles«, *Journal of Ecclesiastical History* 37 (1986), 42–67; Rory McEntegart, *Henry VIII, the League of Schmalkalden and the English Reformation* (Woodbridge, 2002), 131–166.

[72] MacCulloch, *Cromwell*, 506–531.

[73] Formally known as *A Necessary Doctrine and Erudition for any Christen Man* (London, 1543): Marshall, *Heretics and Believers*, 288–89.

[74] The King's Book now demanded true contrition: »Herevpon the said penitent, moued and stirred with the great loue and goodnes of god, shewed before towardes hym on the oone partie, and his owne ingratitude or vnkindnes towardes god on the other partie, conceiueth an earnest sorowe«, *A Necessary Doctrine*, F 1ʳ.

[75] »And thus is faith taken of saint Paule, in the other places of scripture, where it is saide, that we be iustified by faith. In whiche places men maie not thynke, that we be iustified by faith, as it is a seuerall vertue separated from hope and charitie, feare of god and repentance: but by it is ment Faith, neither onely ne alone, but with the foresaid vertues coupled togither, conteinyng as it is aforesayd, the obedience to the hole doctrine and religion of Christ«, ibid., [A 7]ᵛ–[A 8]ʳ.

[76] »It is also to be noted, that confession to the prieste, is in the churche profitably commaunded to be vsed and frequented [...] specially for this cause, that they whiche by custome be drowned in synne [...] maie [...] be stirred [...] that not onely contricion shall arise in the herte to the pleasure of god, but also satisfaction ensue [...] yet in case there lacke a minister [...] if he truly repent him of his synfull lyfe [...] he shal vndoutedly haue pardon«, ibid., F 3ʳ/ᵛ.

[77] Diarmaid MacCulloch, *Thomas Cranmer: A Life*, rev. ed. (New Haven, 2016), 297–322.

the Church of England. He oversaw the publication of an official set of sermons called the *Book of Homilies* (1547). Required reading in every parish, the Homilies taught *sola scriptura*[78] and justification by faith.[79] Next he brought out a progressively more Protestant *Book of Common Prayer* (1549 and 1552). The first Prayer Book insisted on English as the language of the liturgy, restored systematic reading of Scripture[80] and removed all references to both personal merit and the mass as a propitiatory sacrifice.[81] The *Ordinal* (1550) grounded the role of deacons, priests and bishops in New Testament practice of pastoral care based on instructing people in the Word of God.[82] The revised, second *Book of Common Prayer* (1552) went even further than the first, making clear that Christ's eu-

---

[78] According to the *Homily on Scripture*, »there is no truth, nor doctrine, necessary for our justificacion and everlastying salvacion, but that is, or may be, drawen out of that fountain and welle of truth [...] Let us diligently searche for the welle of life in the bokes of the New and Old Testament, and not ronne to the stinkyng podelles of mennes tradicions, devised by mannes imaginacion for our justificacion and salvacion«, Ronald B. Bond, *Certain Sermons or Homilies (1547) and A Homily against Disobedience and Wilful Rebellion (1570)* (Toronto, 1987), 61.

[79] The *Homily on Salvation* stressed that justifying righteousness was an alien righteousness: »Because all men be synners and offendors against God [...] every man of necessitie is constrayned to seke for another righteousnesse, or justificacion, to be received at Gods awne handes«, ibid., 79. Moreover, the righteousness given to the believer through faith was not true inherent righteousness: »And this justificacion or righteousnesse whiche we so receive by Gods mercie and Christes merites, embraced by faithe, is taken, accepted and allowed of God for our perfect and full justificacion«, *ibid.* Therefore, the only possible means of salvation was the imputation of an alien righteousness by faith: »Christe is nowe the righteousnesse of all them that truely doo beleve in hym [...] forasmuche as that whiche their infirmitie lacketh Christes justice hath supplied«, ibid., 81.

[80] A new lectionary was appointed for Morning and Evening Prayer which read through most of the Bible in one year. The Psalter was read through monthly. As the first lesson, the remainder of the Old Testament was read over ten months, »except for certain books and chapters, which be least edifying«. For the other two months readings came from the Apocrypha. As the second lesson, the New Testament was read three times a year, except for Revelation, which was used sparingly for certain proper feasts. See Joseph Ketley, ed., *The Two Liturgies, A. D. 1549, and A. D. 1552* (Cambridge, 1844), 200–212.

[81] See James A. Devereux, »Reformed Doctrine in the Collects of the First ›Book of Common Prayer‹«, *Harvard Theological Review* 58 (1965), 49–68.

[82] »And now we exhort you [...] to have in remembrance [that] ye be called [...] to be the Messengers, the Watchmen, the Pastors, and the Stewards of the Lord, to teach, to premonish, to feed, and provide for the Lord's family: to seek for Christ's Sheep, that be dispersed abroad, and for his children, which be in the midst of this naughty world, to be saved through Christ for ever. [...] Be you persuaded that the holy scriptures contain sufficiently all doctrine, required of necessity for eternal salvation, through faith in Jesu Christ? And are you determined with the said scriptures to instruct the people committed to your charge, and to teach nothing, as required of necessity to eternal salvation, but that you shall be persuaded, may be concluded, and proved by the scripture?«, Ketley, *Two Liturgies*, 175, 177.

charistic presence was spiritual in nature, a holy communion in the heart of the believer through personal faith.[83] Finally, in the last months of the boy-king's life, Cranmer drew up an official statement of theological beliefs called the *Articles of Religion* (1553). Summing up the doctrinal beliefs that had underpinned the Edwardian Church, the Forty-Two Articles applied reformed scriptural exegesis to the controversial issues of the day, including predestination.

Clearly, the Edwardian Church of England was Protestant, but was it Lutheran, Reformed, or something in between? Alec Ryrie has suggested that by the end of Henry's reign Lutheranism as the leading gospel movement in England had died. Its most important tenet, justification by faith, had ceased to be the »evangelical rallying cry«, because as »an abstract doctrine«, it was merely »a learned man's game« whose time on the front lines had passed. Open opposition to Henry now required a clearer target, grounded in everyday practice, and that target was the sacrifice of the mass. The more extreme Reformed doctrine on the lack of any bodily presence of Christ in the sacrament made the charge of idolatry against this chief traditionalist devotional practice all the easier to stick. Hence, over the course of Henry's last summer, the evangelical opposition was radicalized into the Reformed camp.[84]

It is hard to deny that the Edwardian regime did indeed embrace a Reformed, rather than a Lutheran, theology of the sacraments.[85] Yet, that in no way would require its leaders to abandon promoting a Lutheran, emotive soteriology as central to their campaign for the Protestant conversion of England. What better way to appeal to a Christian culture deeply shaped by the medieval spiritual tradition of Rolle and Hilton? Surely that was the regime's purpose in having Queen Katherine Parr publish her own solifidian-inspired, but still highly affective, conversion story less than ten months into the new reign.[86] Indeed, it can be argued that Cranmer himself came to embrace a reformed view of Holy Communion precisely because this teaching was more in keeping with his love-propelled understanding of sanctification, i.e, that the miracle of the sacrament was not a change in the elements but in the human hearts of the

---

[83] Cf. the Words of Administration: »The body of our Lord Jesus Christ which was given for thee, preserve thy body and soul unto everlasting life« (1549) versus »Take and eat this, in remembrance that Christ died for thee, and feed on him in thy heart by faith, with thanksgiving« (1552), ibid., 92, 279.

[84] Alec Ryrie, »The Strange Death of Lutheran England«, *Journal of Ecclesiastical History* 53 (2002), 64–92, at p. 90.

[85] See Diarmaid MacCulloch, *Tudor Church Militant: Edward VI and the Protestant Reformation* (London, 1999), 85–95.

[86] *A Lamentation of a Sinner*, see above 9–10.

faithful, enabling them to more »perfectly love [God], and worthily magnify [his] holy name«.[87]

Not surprisingly, then, Cranmer's formularies consciously sought to institutionalize the Lutheran emotion script into the regular rhythms of English life. Firstly, the *Book of Homilies* followed the Lutheran pattern of preaching first law, then Gospel,[88] first doctrine, then discipleship.[89] Even more importantly, its »Homily on Salvation« explicitly taught that the spiritual comfort provided by free forgiveness fueled a love for God Christians would express by loving him and their neighbors more.[90] Secondly, by instituting daily Morning and Evening Prayer in every English parish with the first *Book of Common Prayer*, Cranmer took the very final step in the two-hundred-year-long process of completely laicizing monastic affective scriptural meditation. Since his Word-based services were fitted around the average person's work day, Cranmer had made it possible for the mixed life's tradition of biblical rumination to be the rhythmic daily norm for every English person, not just a special, holier, privileged few. Here is the end point of that earlier long reformation. Thirdly, Cranmer's second *Book of Common Prayer* placed his *loci communes* of Lutheran *Trost* at the very heart of the Communion Service. The alluring power of four New Testament Comfortable Words were strategically placed immediately before the *Sursum corda* to draw the communicants'

---

[87] The Collect of Purity; Ketley, *Two Liturgies*, 77; For Cranmer's theology of the sacraments, see Ashley Null, »Thomas Cranmer«, in Justin S. Holcomb and David A. Johnson, eds., *Christian Theologies of the Sacraments: A Comparative Introduction* (New York, 2017), 209–33.

[88] It was no accident that the homilies were to be read in order. Homily 2 was »The Misery of All Mankind«. Homily 3 was »Salvation of All Mankind«. Their similar titles underline their inner connection, namely, the first corresponds to the Lutheran understanding of preaching the Law, the second to preaching the Gospel.

[89] The first six homilies proclaim doctrine: »Scripture«, »Human Misery«, »Human Salvation«, »Faith«, »Good Works«, and »Christian Love«. The next six sermons address practical discipleship issues: »Swearing«, »Declining from God«, »Fear of Death«, »Obedience«, »Adultery«, and »Strife«. Cf. Melanchthon, *De modo et arte concionandi* (1537–9) in, Paul Drews and Ferdinand Cohrs, *Supplementa Melanchtoniana* (Leipzig, 1929), V.2: 33, 35–37, 51–52; Uwe Schnell, *Die homiletische Theorie Philipp Melanchthons* (Berlin, 1968), 88–99.

[90] »For the right and true Christian faith is not onely to beleve that Holy Scripture and all the forsaied articles of our fayth are true, but also to have a sure trust and confidence in Gods mercifull promises to be saved from everlastynge dampnacion by Christe, wherof doeth folowe a lovyng harte to obey his commaundementes. [...] These greate and mercifull benefites of God, if they be well considered [...] if we be not desperate persones and oure hartes harder then stones, they move us to rendre our selfes unto God wholy, with all our wil, hartes, might and power, to serve him in all good dedes, obeyng his commaundementes during our lifes, to seke in al thinges his glory and honor [...] [and] to be ever redy to geve our selfes to our neighbours«, Bond, *Certain Sermons*, 86–87.

hearts upward towards God.[91] Lastly, even the highly contentious doctrine of predestination was presented in the Forty-Two Articles as a great source for *Trost* which would then move the affections of the elect to love God and others.[92] Clearly, the Edwardian Church combined a Lutheran script for its affective soteriology with a Reformed approach to its sacraments.

6. Towards the Elizabethan Settlement

Edward VI died on July 6th 1553, bringing Mary Tudor to the throne for what turned out to be a five-year Roman Catholic interregnum. Although the Marian regime would repudiate Cranmer's formularies, they responded to their effectiveness by emulating his method for national change. They, too, issued standard homilies for those not qualified to preach. Yet Pole was also convinced that the Word would hinder the people's restoration to the true Catholic faith, rather than help, if its proclamation were not joined to the promotion of affective rites and rituals which encouraged willing obedience to the Marian church authorities.[93] Consequently, the Legatine Synod's first decree instituted a new ritual. On St. Andrew's Day (30 November) – the anniversary of England's return to Roman obedience – everyone in every English village, town and city was required to attend a public procession preceded by a mass with a sermon or reading explaining the reason why this was such a joyous occasion.

Elizabeth's accession in 1558 brought another alteration in religion. First, there was a careful cull of secular offices filled by those whose primary qualification was their commitment to the Roman faith. Then, the 1559 Parliament declared the Elizabeth to be supreme governor and reissued both the 1547 *Book of Homilies* and a slightly amended 1552 *Book of Common Prayer*. In 1563 the bishops also approved a new, second *Book*

---

[91] See Ashley Null, »Comfortable Words: Thomas Cranmer's Gospel Falconry«, in John D. Koch, Todd H. W. Brewer, eds., *Comfortable Words: Essays in Honor of Paul F. M. Zahl* (Eugene, 2013), 218–42.

[92] *NB* the highly affective language: »As the Godlie consideration of predestination, and our election in Christe is ful of swete, pleasaunte, and vnspeakable coumfort to godlie persones, and soche as feele in themselues the woorking of the spirite of Christi, mortifying the workes of the flesh, and their earthlie membres, and drawing vp their minde to high and heauenly thinges, aswel because it doeth greatly stablish and confirme their faith of eternal saluation to bee enioied through Christe, as because it dooeth feruentlie kindle their loue towardes Godde«, Charles Hardwick, *A History of the Articles of Religion* (Cambridge, 1859), 296.

[93] Eamon Duffy and David Loades, *The Church of Mary Tudor* (Aldershot, 2006), 177–86, 197–98.

of Homilies and the revision of the Forty-Two articles into Thirty-Nine in 1571. Finally, in the same year, Alexander Nowell's catechism was required to be used in schools. In addition, along side the official formularies, as Ian Green has shown, throughout her reign there was a massive publishing program of catechisms to supplement Nowell.[94] Indeed, as Mary Hampson Patterson points out, »much of the energy for reformation was not primarily official«, and consequently she has looked at three massive bestsellers, those with over twenty-five editions, including an affective devotional for the dying by Thomas Becon.[95]

But what of Cranmer's affective program institutionalized in the Church of England's formularies? Did it continue to dominate the Sunday liturgical experience of Elizabethans? A noticeable change can be seen in the *Second Book of Homilies*. The struggle to defeat papist teachings successfully revived under Mary pushed the *Second Book of Homilies* to include two significant revisions of Cranmer's theology. Firstly, the archbishop routinely preached to the people such benefits of election as assurance of salvation, but he always refrained from describing its grounding in God's decision rather than the individual's. »On Almsdeeds«, however, appealed to an explicit explanation of God's role in predestination in order to exclude any possibility of personal merit contributing to either salvation or sanctification:

»God, of his mercy and especial favour towards them whom he hath appointed to everlasting salvation, hath so offered his grace effectually, and they have so received it fruitfully that [...] the Spirit of God mightily working in them unto obedience to God's will and commandments, they declare by their outward deeds and life [...] that they are the undoubted children of God.«[96]

Secondly, while Cranmer acknowledged the fear of punishment's preparatory role in driving sinners to God, he continually stressed that the true motivation for repentance and amendment of life was loving gratitude for the free gift of salvation. The Elizabethan homilies had several passages that trumpeted Cranmer's emotion script of *grace and gratitude*.[97] Yet the trauma of the Marian reaction had evidently stolen much of its wind. Many more passages throughout the collection emphasized repentance in

---

[94] Ian Green, *The Christian's ABC: Catechisms and Catechizing in England c. 1530–1740* (Oxford, 1996); idem, *Print and Protestantism in Early Modern England* (Oxford, 2000).

[95] Mary Hampson Patterson, *Domesticating the Reformation: Protest Best Sellers Private Devotion, and the Revolution of English Piety* (Cranbury, New Jersey, 2007), esp. 302.

[96] John Griffiths, *The Two Books of Homilies Appointed to be Read in Churches* (Oxford, 1859), 390.

[97] Ibid., 391, 408–10, 424–26, 470.

order to avoid another experience of God's wrath against the nation. In fact, the Second Book literally begins and ends with »the common peril and plague hanging over us«.[98] Nothing makes the shift in tone any clearer than »On Repentance« which offers five reasons to repent: duty to God, hope of forgiveness, shame for sin, suddenness of death and fear of divine punishments.[99] However, no mention is made of grace-inspired gratitude or love.

Thus, the *Second Book of Homilies* began to preach predestination explicitly to safeguard salvation *sola gratia*, while at the same time emphasizing the benefits of moralism as the basis for repentance. It has been suggested that such mixed signals in early Elizabethan preaching contributed to the development of Reformed Protestantism's new federal theology. To avoid confusion, the typical Tudor concern for the nation's morals was incorporated into the covenant of works, whereas the utter gratuitousness of salvation was ensured by the covenant of grace.[100] Despite the queen's reluctance to embrace new developments in Protestant theology, the seeds for a Church of England Calvinist consensus and its preaching were already present in the collection of sermons she personally reviewed in 1563.

As the continuing popularity of Becon's devotional demonstrated, the Lutheran emotion script would always have an audience in Reformation England. But, as Ryrie has shown, the advent of preaching on predestination shifted the mainstream discussion of the affections away from assumed assurance to its pursuit, from Luther's comfort and love to Puritan uncertainty and desiring desire.[101] For Jacques's Elizabethan audience, no monasteries now offered assistance. Many might still find comfort in Cranmer's liturgy, as Judith Maltby has shown.[102] Others in the oft recommended twice-daily family prayers or hearing a minister's sermon.[103] Yet the ultimate answer remained the transforming power of Scripture. The Calvinist doctrinal consensus of the Elizabethan Church still had not moved too far from its early English Reformation affective roots. According to Ryrie,

---

[98] Ibid., 153, 597–600.

[99] Ibid., 545–49.

[100] Michael McGiffert, »Grace and Works: The Rise and Division of Covenant Divinity in Elizabethan Puritanism«, *Harvard Theological Review* 75 (1982), 463–502.

[101] Ryrie, *Being Protestant in Reformation Britain*, 17–98.

[102] Judith Maltby, *Prayer Book and People in Elizabethan And Early Stuart England* (Cambridge, 1998).

[103] Ryrie, *Being Protestant in Reformation Britain*, 351–74.

»George Herbert's words on the subject – ›Oh Book! infinite sweetnesse! let my heart / Suck ev'ry letter, and a hony gain‹ – could be dismissed as versifying. However, there is more direct testimony that this was a widespread Protestant experience. [...] [Indeed] Nicholas Byfield advised his readers to make a note of the Biblical verses which they ›finde sensible comfort and rauishing of heart in‹. Most, he assumed, would be able to find between twenty and fifty such passages.«[104]

Far more than the four verses Cranmer used for his *locus communis* on *Trost* in his liturgy for Holy Communion.

---

[104] Ibid., 280.

Von der reformatorischen Bewegung zur evangelischen Kirche
Das Heilige Römische Reich

Dorothea Wendebourg, Andreas Stegmann, Martin Ohst

1.1. Die reformatorische Bewegung begann, als Gedanken Martin Luthers, in denen die Erstgestalt einer neuen, nachmittelalterlichen Art westlichen Christentums Gestalt gewann, durch die schnelle Aufnahme in der Breite der Bevölkerung geschichtswirksam wurden: Zunächst als Kritik an bestimmten kirchlichen Institutionen, Lehren und Handlungsmustern formuliert, wirkten sie überzeugend wie polarisierend und riefen Zustimmung und Ablehnung hervor. Publizistisch-medial von Anfang an meisterhaft präsentiert, aktualisierte und aktivierte der von Wittenberg ausgehende Impuls dabei weit verbreitetes – humanistisches, konziliaristisches, antiklerikales, mystikaffines u.a. – Unbehagen. In der Überzeugung durch diesen Impuls geeint, wurden heterogene Gruppen, wie es schien, zu einer einzigen großen Bewegung.

1.2. Im Zentrum von Luthers reformatorischer Theologie stand das Evangelium, das den rechtfertigenden Heilsglauben schafft. Von hier aus bestimmte er auch die Kirche: als die durch das Evangelium konstituierte, in der und für die Kommunikation des Evangeliums existierende Gemeinschaft der Glaubenden. Wenn dieses Evangelium zum Zentralgehalt und seine Verkündigung zur Zentralaufgabe alles Kommunikationsgeschehens in der Kirche werden sollte, folgte daraus eine radikale Umgestaltung der bestehenden kirchlichen Institution. Das wurde umso deutlicher, als die papstkirchliche Hierarchie, sich dieser Konsequenzen schnell bewußt, alle durch Luther aufgeworfenen Fragen von Anfang an zu Fragen der kirchlichen Autorität erklärte, wie der alsbald eingeleitete Häresieprozeß zeigt.

1.3. Die von Wittenberg ausgehende reformatorische Bewegung hielt jedoch, ebenso wie die dann von Zürich, Straßburg und Genf ausgehenden, an *einer* seit dem Frühmittelalter etablierten Konstante unbeirrbar fest: Alle Getauften sind strikt verpflichtet, ihre Kinder taufen zu lassen, und jeder getaufte Christ gehört als solcher einer Pfarrei an (»Pfarrbann«). Damit hat die Kirche den Auftrag, alle Menschen – mit Ausnahme der Glieder der jüdischen Gemeinden – zu Christen zu erziehen – eine Aufgabe, an der die Papstkirche in den Augen der Reformatoren auf breiter Front gescheitert war.

1.4. Da somit die Kirche wie schon nach mittelalterlichem, so auch nach reformatorischem Verständnis nicht ein Segment innerhalb der Gesellschaft war, sondern die Gesellschaft selbst in ihren religiösen Deutungen, Riten und Gestaltungen, betraf die sich abzeichnende Umgestaltung der kirchlichen Strukturen und Kommunikationsmuster alle Dimensionen des gesellschaftlichen und individuellen Lebens.

1.5. Als die umfassenden Dimensionen der sich abzeichnenden oder bereits eingeleiteten Neuausrichtungen sichtbar wurden, kam es zu Scheidungen. Konvergenzen von Idealen und Interessen erwiesen sich als illusionär, Sympathisanten Luthers, etwa unter den Humanisten oder in der akademischen Theologie, wurden zu unerbittlichen Kritikern und Gegnern.

1.6. Aber auch die Gruppe derer, die in der Grundintention einer umfassenden Umgestaltung der Kirche vom Evangelium her weiterhin mit ihm übereinstimmten, war alles andere als homogen. Andere Protagonisten der frühen Reformation wie Philipp Melanchthon, Andreas Karlstadt, Thomas Müntzer, Ulrich Zwingli oder Martin Bucer nahmen Luthers Impuls in eigener Weise auf. Sie verbanden diesen Impuls mit ihren eigenen Prägungen – etwa humanistischen oder monastischen; sie reagierten auf je spezifische Herausforderungen – etwa die städtischer oder territorialstaatlicher Gesellschaften; und sie zogen divergierende, z.T. gegensätzliche kirchenreformerische Konsequenzen.

1.7. Das institutionelle Wirksamwerden des reformatorischen Impulses in dauerhaften Umgestaltungen des kirchlichen Lebens, also der Übergang von der reformatorischen Bewegung zur Kirchwerdung der Reformation, vollzog sich somit konkret in einer Vielzahl von Kirchwerdungen.

1.8. Die institutionelle Vielgestaltigkeit, die das Ergebnis dieser Prozesse war, stand als solche nicht im Widerspruch zum auslösenden Impuls. Denn die von Wittenberg ausgehende Reformationsbewegung bejahte oder verneinte kirchliche Institutionen nicht als Selbstzweck, sondern nach dem Maßstab ihrer Dienlichkeit für das leitende Ziel, die Kommunikation des Evangeliums – Beispiele hierfür sind die Stellung zum Bischofsamt oder zur Liturgie. Deshalb war die Anknüpfung an unterschiedliche Traditionen und das Eingehen auf unterschiedliche gesellschaftliche Kontexte keine notgedrungen akzeptierte Last, sondern entsprach dem Verständnis der kirchenreformerischen Aufgabe.

1.9. Die entstehenden institutionellen Gestalten reformatorischen Christentums erhielten auf diesem Wege ihre eigentümlichen Charaktere. Umgekehrt empfing in den Prozessen der Kirchwerdung der reformatorische Impuls selbst Klärungen, Akzentuierungen und teils auch gegensätzliche Modifikationen durch die Vorgaben, in deren Transformation er einging und wirksam wurde. Das sollte sich an der Entwicklung der später sog. »lutherischen« Kirchen – die ihrerseits in manchen Hinsichten wie Liturgie, Ausgestaltung der Ämter oder der genaueren Bestimmung des Bekenntnisstandes voneinander abweichen – und der »reformierten« mit ihren sehr unterschiedlichen Flügeln zeigen, um nur die wichtigsten Vertreter zu nennen.

2.1. Die reformatorische Bewegung, die sich Anfang der 1520er Jahre formierte und in der Folgezeit in den frühen Zentralregionen der Reformation im Reich (Sachsen, Thüringen, Franken, Schlesien, Hessen, Südwestdeutschland) und der deutschsprachigen Schweiz ganz oder weitgehend durchsetzte, schlug sich, vor allem in den Städten, von Anfang an in Veränderungen des religiösen Lebens und kirchenreformerischen Umsetzungen nieder – in der Minderung von Ablaßkäufen, dem Auszug aus Klöstern, dem Rückgang und der Unterbrechung von Messen und Prozessionen, liturgischen Veränderungen, neuen sozialdiakonischen Maßnahmen u.a.m.

2.2. Träger waren zunächst einzelne, meist Prediger, und kleine Gruppen. Doch die hier aufbrechende Dynamik wurde meist sehr schnell von städtischen und territorialen Obrigkeiten – Fürsten und Räten – aufgegriffen, die einerseits mit der neuen Bewegung sympathisierten, sie – nötigenfalls auch gegen geltendes weltliches und geistliches Recht – schützten und für die Reform der Kirche fruchtbar zu machen suchten, andererseits aber auch ihre Energie kanalisieren wollten, womit zugleich der seit dem Spätmittelalter im Gang befindliche Prozeß der Einordnung der Kirche in das – territoriale oder städtische – Gemeinwesen befördert wurde. So war in den meisten Fällen die Kirchwerdung der Reformation – wie deren gegenreformerische Bekämpfung – ein Prozeß, an dem die weltliche Obrigkeit maßgeblichen Anteil hatte.

2.3. Diese Rolle der weltlichen Gewalt bejahend und in Anspruch nehmend – im Falle Luthers und Calvins nicht ohne grundsätzliche Grenzziehung und Vorbehalt –, gaben die zuständigen Reformatoren Maßstab und Inhalte von Verkündigung und Lehre der sich formierenden kirchlichen Institutionen vor und arbeiteten die Hilfsmittel aus, in denen und durch die sich die Institutionalisierung der Reformation vollzog (Bibelübersetzungen, Postillen, Liturgien, Katechismen, geistliche Lieder, Bekenntnisse, Ordinationsrituale, Kirchenordnungen etc.).

2.4. Freilich wurde in Teilen der reformatorischen Bewegung der reformatorische Impuls auch in Weisen aufgenommen, die die Einordnung der Christengemeinde in den städtischen oder territorialen Rahmen und eine tragende Rolle der Obrigkeit bei der Institutionalisierung der Reformation ausschlossen; an die Stelle des Pfarrbanns sollten Organisationsmodelle treten, die die Zugehörigkeit zur Kirche auf die eigene Entscheidung gründeten. Dreh- und Angelpunkt war die Säuglingstaufe, die hier abgelehnt wurde.

2.5. So kam es zu Ansätzen von Kirchbildungen, die sich von der Wittenberger und der oberdeutsch-schweizerischen Reformation absetzten und zum offenen Konflikt führten, etwa bei Thomas Müntzer in Allstedt und Mühlhausen, bei Balthasar Hubmaier in Waldshut und bei den Zürcher Täufern. Die Konflikte und der geringere Erfolg dieser Gruppen dürfen aber nicht übersehen lassen, daß es sich auch in ihren Programmen um spezifische Aufnahmen, Entwicklungen und Modifikationen des ihnen mit ihren Gegnern gemeinsamen reformatorischen Impulses handelte, die im Maße der Klärung, Präzisierung und Festigung der Wittenberger und der oberdeutsch-schweizer Reformation ausgeschieden wurden.

3.1. Im Rahmen der politisch-gesellschaftlichen Bedingungen des Heiligen Römischen Reiches wurde das – territoriale oder reichsstädtische – Landeskirchentum zur Normalgestalt der institutionalisierten Reformation. Die Konsolidierung evangelischer Landeskirchen, zunächst lutherischer, dann auch reformierter, wurde ermöglicht durch die relative Autonomie der Reichsstände und gesichert durch die immer engere religionspolitische Kooperation der mit der Reformation sympathisierenden bzw. sich ihr anschließenden Reichsstände auf Reichsebene. Wo weltliche Obrigkeiten die Reformation bekämpften oder sich weder für noch gegen die Reformation entschieden, konnte die Basis nur wenige Veränderungen durchsetzen und allenfalls die partielle Institutionalisierung eines evangelischen Kirchenwesens erreichen.

3.2. Die jeweilige – reichsterritoriale oder reichsstädtische – Landeskirche war der primäre institutionelle Bezugsrahmen evangelischen kirchlichen Lebens. In diesem Rahmen wurden etwa die Berufung und Beaufsichtigung des kirchlichen Personals, die Visitation der Kirchengemeinden, die mit der Kirche verklammerte schulische Bildungsarbeit, die Regelung finanzieller Belange, die akademische theologische

Lehre und Forschung und die – weitgehend durch der weltlichen Obrigkeit verantwortliche Instanzen geleistete – Verwaltung der Kirche wahrgenommen.

3.3. Gleichwohl entwickelte sich über die Grenzen der Landeskirchen, ja, die über die Reichsgrenzen hinweg ein Zusammengehörigkeitsbewußtsein im Rahmen der jeweiligen – lutherischen oder reformierten – Konfession, das in gemeinsamen Bekenntnissen zum Ausdruck gebracht und in Lehrkontroversen bekräftigt wurde. Ein wichtiger Differenzmarker nach innen wie nach außen war die von den Lutheranern nachdrücklich auf die eigene Konfession beschränkte Abendmahlsgemeinschaft.

3.4. Die Kirchwerdung der Reformation erfaßte nicht das gesamte Heilige Römische Reich, Deutschland wurde nur zum Teil evangelisch und nicht monokonfessionell. Die Reichsstände, die sich der reformatorischen Erneuerung nicht anschlossen, setzten ihr nach und nach eine Reformalternative entgegen, die auf die Bildung eines konfessionellen Kirchentums im Zeichen des Trienter Konzils hinauslief. Die Konkurrenzsituation, noch dadurch verstärkt, daß die protestantischen Stände ihrerseits konfessionell gespalten waren, bedeutete einerseits eine Belastung durch immer neue Konflikte. Andererseits schärfte sie auf allen Seiten die Profile und beförderte die Identitätsbildung. Ja, indem der Wettstreit der Kirchen allenthalben mit intensiver und extensiver Steigerung auf den Feldern von Bildung, Künsten und Wissenschaften einherging, trug er zum Aufblühen der Konfessionskulturen um 1600 bei.

From Reformation Movement to Evangelical Churches
The Holy Roman Empire

Dorothea Wendebourg, Andreas Stegmann, Martin Ohst

1.1. The Reformation Movement began when the ideas of Martin Luther in which the first form of a new, post-medieval kind of Christianity developed became a historical force, through its swift reception among large parts of the populace. These ideas, at first brought forward as criticism of certain ecclesial institutions, doctrines, and patterns of behaviour, convinced as well as polarized those who read and heard them: they elicited assent, but also rejection. The stimulus which came from Wittenberg, from the start presented masterfully in the media of the time, renewed and activated widespread feelings of uneasiness which had already been fostered in humanist, conciliarist, anticlerical, mystically inclined, and other circles. United in the positive response to that stimulus, heterogenous groups, as it appeared, became one large single movement.

1.2. The center of Luther's evangelical theology was the Gospel which creates the justifying, salvific faith. In this perspective, the Church was understood as the communion of the faithful which is created by the Gospel, and exists by and for the communication of the Gospel. When the Gospel thus had to be the central content, and its proclamation had to be the central task, of all communication in the Church, the consequence was radical reform of the existing ecclesial institution. This consequence became all the clearer since the hierarchy of the papal church from the start declared all critical questions Luther asked to be questions of ecclesial authority, as the heresy trial against him which was initiated almost immediately showed.

1.3. However, the Wittenberg Reformation movement, as those later ones which had Zurich, Straßburg, and Geneva as their centers, held on to one constant firmly established since the early Middle Ages: All faithful were obliged to have their children baptized, and every baptized Christian as such belonged to a parish (»Pfarrbann«). Therefore it was the duty of the Church to educate everybody – except for the members of the Jewish community – to be Christians. In this task, according to the Reformers, the papal church had failed miserably.

1.4. Since thus according to the Reformers, as before in the Middle Ages, the Church was not a segment of society but society itself in the perspective of its religious design, interpretation, and rites, the reform of the ecclesial structures and patters of communication which became apparent affected all dimensions of both social life and individual existence.

1.5. When the comprehensive dimensions of the new arrangements, whether still on the horizon or already initiated, became clear, separations happened. Convergences of ideals and interests proved to be illusory, as some of Luther's sympathizers, e.g. in academic theology or among the humanists, became fierce critics and opponents.

1.6. But the group of those who continued to agree with him in the intention to aim for a comprehensive reform of the Church on the basis of the Gospel were also far from homogenous. Other champions of the early Reformation like Philip Melanchthon, Andreas Karlstadt, Thomas Müntzer, Ulrich Zwingli, or Martin Bucer took up Luther's stimulus in their own way. They blended with it theological views derived from their personal backgrounds – e.g. humanist or monastic. They brought it to bear in response to specific challenges – e.g. territorial or municipal settings of society. And they drew different, in part contradictory consequences as regards the sought-for comprehensive reform.

1.7. Thus the institutionalization of the fundamental stimulus of the Reformation in a permanent new shape of the Christian life, in other words the transition from Reformation movement to Reformation church actually took place as the shaping of a plurality of churches.

1.8. The plurality of institutions which resulted from this process does not in itself conflict with the stimulus that set them all off. For the movement which started in Wittenberg approved of or rejected ecclesial institutions not for their own sake, but according to their usefulness for the governing aim, the communication of the Gospel – two examples are the different stances taken with regard to the office of bishop and to the liturgy. Therefore the connection to different traditions and the entering into different social contexts was not a burden taken up only by necessity; rather it corresponded to the Reformers' understanding of their task.

1.9. In this way the institutional embodiments of Reformation Christianity gained their specific characters. Conversely, in the processes of ecclesial institutionalization the Reformation stimulus itself was further clarified, emphasized, and modified – partly in ways contrary to each other – by the pre-conditions in which it took effect and which it transformed. This became apparent in the development of the so-called Lutheran churches – which differed among themselves in several respects like liturgy, the arrangement of offices, or the collection of official confessional writings – and of the Reformed churches with their very different wings, just to name the most important examples.

2.1. The Reformation movement which took shape in the beginning of the 1520s and then prevailed completely or to a large extent in the early central regions of the Reformation in the Empire (Saxony, Thuringia, Franconia, Silesia, Hesse, South-Western Germany) as well as in German-speaking Switzerland from the start, particularly in the cities, found expression in changes of religious life and implementations of ecclesial reforms – e.g. by a drop in the purchase of indulgences, a massive exit of monks and nuns from the monasteries, a decline in or interruptions of masses and processions, liturgical alterations, new measures of charity and diakonia.

2.2. The main agents of change in the beginning were individuals, mostly preachers, and small groups. But the dynamic erupting in the early Reformation very soon was seized upon by the municipal and territorial authorities – city councils and princes – who, on the one hand, sympathized with the new movement, protected it – if necessary against secular and canon law –, and tried to make it bear fruit for the reform of the Church. On the other hand, they also wanted to channel its energies, and thereby at the same time to further the integration of the Church into the body politic (territorial or municipal) which had been under way since the late Middle Ages. Thus in most cases the development of the Reformation into Reformation churches was – like the battle against it by the Counter Reformation – a process in which the secular political authorities had a significant share.

2.3. While affirming and using this role of the secular authorities – though in the case of Luther and Calvin, only with fundamental limits and reservations – the responsible Reformers prescribed the yardstick and contents of the proclamation and doctrine of the emerging ecclesial institutions, and composed the instruments in and through which the institutionalization of the Reformation took place (translations of the Bible, postils, liturgies, catechisms, hymns, confessional writings, ordination rituals, church orders etc.).

2.4. However, in parts of the Reformation movement the Reformation impulse was taken up in ways which excluded the integration of the Christian congregation into the municipal or territorial context as well as a leading role of the secular authorities for the institutionalization of the Reformation; the medieval system of *Pfarrbann* (see above) was to be replaced by models of organization which based church membership on personal decision. The key issue was infant baptism which was rejected.

2.5. Thus in the initial stages of ecclesial formation, paths were taken which differed from the Wittenberg as well as from the Swiss Reformation and led to open conflict, as in the case of Thomas Müntzer in Allstedt and Mühlhausen, of Balthasar Hubmaier in Waldshut, and of the Anabaptists of Zurich. These conflicts and the poor success of those groups must not cause one to overlook the fact that their programs, too, were specific ways of reception, development, and modification of the common Reformation impulse, which, however, were eliminated as the Wittenberg and the Swiss Reformations underwent processes of clarification and consolidation.

3.1. Within the social and political structure of the Holy Roman Empire the territorial church (»Landeskirche«) – of a territory or an Imperial city – became the normal pattern of the institutionalized Reformation. The consolidation of evangelical territorial or municipal churches – first Lutheran ones, then also Reformed – became possible through the relative autonomy of the Imperial estates and was secured through the ever tighter cooperation in matters of religious politics between those estates which sympathized with the Reformation or joined it, on the level of the Empire. Where the secular authorities fought the Reformation or decided neither for nor against it, people at the grass roots could effect only small changes, and at the most achieve only a partial institutionalization of an evangelical church.

3.2. The *Landeskirche*, whether territorial or municipal, was the primary frame of reference of evangelical ecclesial life. Within this framework the clergy were appointed and controlled, and visitations of congregations took place. The same holds true for the educational work of the schools which was connected with the church, for academic theological teaching and research, for the regulation of the churches' financial matters, and finally for the ecclesial administration, which to a large extent was done by authorities responsible to the princes or city councils.

3.3. Nevertheless within the frameworks of the respective – Lutheran or Reformed – confessional communions, a sense of belonging together in a specific way developed which went beyond the borders of the *Landeskirchen* and even the Empire. This sense was expressed in common Confessions and confirmed in doctrinal controversies. An important marker of difference inwardly as well as outwardly was communion at the Lord's table which the Lutherans confined firmly to their own confessional church.

3.4. The institutionalization of the Reformation did not extend to the whole Empire. Germany became protestant only in part, it did not become mono-confessional. The Imperial estates who did not join the Reformation gradually opposed it with an alternative ecclesial reform which led to the formation of a confessional church according to the Council of Trent. This competitive situation, which was intensified even more by the divisions within Protestantism, on the one hand meant a burden of ever new conflicts. On the other hand it sharpened the confessional profiles and furthered the formation of identities on all sides. Indeed, since their competition was accompanied by an enormous increase of efforts in education, arts, music, literature, and academia it contributed to the blossoming of confessional cultures in the 17th century.

Protestant Scotland:
From Dissenting Groups to Institution

John McCallum

This paper aims to provide an overview of the Scottish Reformation with particular emphasis on the current state of the secondary literature on the process of building and developing reforming movements into a Church. In anticipation of the specialist comparative papers elsewhere in the volume, it will set the scene in terms of what was happening in Scotland, and draw attention to some of the recent developments in the study of the Scottish Reformation. It follows a roughly chronological structure, starting with the emergence of dissenting groups in parts of Scotland, through the transition of power which was centered around the Reformation Parliament of August 1560, through to the processes of building and developing the workings and culture of an established Protestant Church.

One relatively well-known characteristic of the Scottish Reformation is that it was late in coming, especially in comparison to the other territories addressed in this collection. Although there were flashpoints and moments of opportunity, the Protestant cause did not look a particularly optimistic one until as late as the late 1550s in Scotland.[1] When official Reformation did come in 1559–60 however, it was dramatic and immediate. It has even been described as a »revolution« by Alec Ryrie.[2] The central transitional year of 1559–60 has dominated a lot of attention in the discussion of the Scottish Reformation. It was certainly pivotal, quite literally in the sense that the nation swung from a Catholic to Protestant settlement in a way which, superficially at least, appears at first more clear-cut than the chronological and geographical complexity and variety of English and German Reformations.[3] The centrality of that date has also been greatly questioned

---

[1] Key surveys and narratives of the Scottish Reformation include G. Donaldson, *The Scottish Reformation* (Cambridge: Cambridge University Press, 1960); I. B. Cowan, *The Scottish Reformation: Church and Society in Sixteenth-Century Scotland* (London: St Martin's Press, 1982); A. Ryrie, *The Origins of the Scottish Reformation* (Manchester: Manchester University Press, 2006). See also I. Hazlett (ed.), *The Brill Companion to the Scottish Reformation* (forthcoming, Leiden: Brill).

[2] Ryrie, *Origins of the Scottish Reformation*, 198.

[3] Ibid., 197–204; J. Dawson, *Scotland Re-Formed, 1488–1587* (Edinburgh: Edinburgh University Press, 2007), 212–15.

by Scottish historians in recent years, and it was in many ways just the starting-point for a more complex set of institutional and cultural reformations.[4]

1. Dissenting Groups Prior to 1560

As the Reformation was making progress in England and in the Holy Roman Empire, dissent in Scotland began in forms which were highly geographically focused, and socially selective. Sixteenth century Scotland was geographically diverse, and far less urbanised than England or the Holy Roman Empire. As in the sister reformations discussed elsewhere in this collection, there was no single or normative experience of reform. Some counties or regions have generally been considered to have been more receptive to reforming opinion in the early decades prior to the 1550s. For example, Ayrshire, in the south-west of the country, is conventionally seen as disproportionately sympathetic to evangelical ideas. It has even been suggested that there were links here to the descendants of the Lollard tradition.[5] And in Angus there were signs of reforming opinion amongst the lairds, albeit few signs of a more socially diverse dissenting group.[6] Naturally, as elsewhere in Europe urban areas were particularly associated with the early Reformation, and towns on the central east coast such as Dundee and St Andrews witnessed discussions of evangelical ideas as well as the famous martyrdoms of Patrick Hamilton and George Wishart in the university town.[7] Again, however, there were few signs of a truly popular movement or broad social appeal, and dissent was often associated with university scholars or relatively small groups of local eli-

---

[4] M. Cowan, »In the Borderlands of Periodization with ›The blythnes that hes bein‹: The medieval/early modern boundary in Scottish History«, *Journal of the Canadian Historical Association* 23 (2012): 142–75; J. McCallum, »Introduction«, in J. McCallum (ed.), *Scotland's Long Reformation: New Perspectives on Scottish Religion c. 1500–1660* (Leiden: Brill, 2016), 18–20.

[5] M. Sanderson, *Ayrshire and the Reformation: People and Change, 1490–1600* (East Linton: Tuckwell, 1997); M. Cowan, *Death, life, and religious change in Scottish towns c. 1350–1560* (Manchester: Manchester University Press, 2012), 161–63.

[6] F. Bardgett, *Scotland Reformed: The Reformation in Angus and the Mearns* (Edinburgh: John Donald, 1989), 24–37, 48–52.

[7] J. Dawson, »›The Face of Ane Perfyt Reformed Kyrk‹: St Andrews and the Early Scottish Reformation«, in J. Kirk (ed.), *Humanism and Reform: The Church in Europe, England and Scotland 1400–1643* (Oxford: Oxford University Press, 1991); I. Flett, »The conflict of the Reformation and Democracy in the Geneva of Scotland 1443–1610: an Introduction to edited texts of documents relating to the Burgh of Dundee« (unpublished MPhil Thesis, University of St Andrews, 1981); I. B. Cowan, *Regional Aspects of the Scottish Reformation* (London: Historical Association, 1978), 10–11.

tes.[8] In Perth however, there was an apparent association between the reformation cause and the craftsmen in their challenge to the authority of the more powerful merchant burgesses.[9] Other parts of the country seem to have been less promising environments: especially Aberdeen and the north-east, and the highlands.[10] As in English reformation historiography, there have also been revisionist attempts to balance early demands for reform and the antecedents of the reformers, with the ongoing vitality and strength of Catholic opinion.[11] Although there were major institutional and financial problems with the Church, Audrey-Beth Fitch and Mairi Cowan have identified an important lay spirituality and investment which echoes Eamon Duffy's *The Stripping of the Altars*.[12] Recent studies of towns as associated with the Protestant cause as Dundee and St Andrews have pointed to the health of Catholic opinion and structures alongside the emergence of some statements of reforming opinion.[13] As this brief summary suggests, drawing on the lessons of revisionist historiography elsewhere, Scottish historians are now far more cautious about the extent and scope of evangelical dissent prior to the precipitation of reformation in 1559–60.

This is not to say, however, that this dissent was insignificant. Although they proved not to be transformative in the longer term, key flashpoints such as Arran's ›godly fit‹ in 1543 or the siege of St Andrews Castle

---

[8] Cowan, *Regional Aspects of the Scottish Reformation*, 10; Ryrie, *Origins of the Scottish Reformation*, 118–21; cf. J. Kirk, »The Religion of Early Scottish Protestants«, in Kirk (ed.), *Humanism and Reform*.

[9] M. Verschuur, *Politics or Religion? The Reformation in Perth, 1540–1570* (Edinburgh: Dunedin Academic Press, 2006).

[10] A. White, »Religion, Politics and Society in Aberdeen, 1543–1593« (unpublished PhD Thesis, University of Edinburgh, 1985); Ryrie, *Origins of the Scottish Reformation*, 121; Cowan, *Regional Aspects of the Scottish Reformation*, 14.

[11] C. Haigh, »The Recent Historiography of the English Reformation«, *Historical Journal* 25 (1982): 995–1007; P. Marshall, »(Re)defining the English Reformation«, *Journal of British Studies* 48 (2009): 564–586 at p. 565.

[12] A. Fitch, *The Search for Salvation: Lay Faith in Scotland 1480–1560* (Edinburgh: John Donald, 2009); Cowan, *Death, Life and Religious Change*; E. Duffy, *The Stripping of the Altars: Traditional Religion in England c. 1400–c. 1580* (New Haven: Yale University Press, 1992).

[13] E. Rhodes, »Property and Piety: Donations to Holy Trinity Church, St Andrews«, in McCallum (ed.), *Scotland's Long Reformation*; T. Slonosky, »Civil Reformations: Religion In Dundee and Haddington c. 1520–1565« (unpublished PhD Thesis, University of Pennsylvania, 2014). Fittingly, this means that Dundee's traditional status as the ›Geneva‹ of Scotland, a title conferred long before modern research, especially by W. Naphy, had fully explored the contested and challenging road to reform in Geneva, has now been balanced by a slightly more nuanced version of Dundee's reformation. Flett, »The conflict of the Reformation and Democracy in the Geneva of Scotland«; W. Naphy, *Calvin and the Consolidation of the Genevan Reformation* (Manchester: Manchester University Press, 1994).

in 1546–7 highlighted the possibilities of reformation, and the potential
threat of active dissent.[14] And less dramatically, pockets of Protestant
opinion and activity were to prove crucial in paving the way for what
would become Protestant victory.[15] Both the extent and the nature of these
pockets has been hotly debated. Alec Ryrie's work has persuasively questioned the idea of large numbers of ›privy kirks‹, or secret congregations
of Protestants, existing in the 1550s as simple forerunners of the national
reformed church of 1560 onwards.[16] This is partly because the evidence for
their scale, numbers and importance is questionable, but also because they
were »more diverse, more disorganized and more doctrinally untidy« than
the conventional story suggests.[17] Hardly any seem to have been real privy
kirks in the sense of fully formed and orthodox (but secret) congregations:
many were irregular gatherings in noble households, or reading groups,
lacking a sense of uniform faith and discipline as in the post–1560 settlement, and lacking formal structures.[18] There was no straight line from
these pre–1560 groups to the post–1560 Church. The upheaval of 1559–60
did not simply catapult these groups, or versions of them, into power.
Instead it was a transition brought about through the actions of noble
leaders, bolstered by evangelical preaching, not least by the returning exile
John Knox, and written into a single Church by ministers in the summer
of 1560.[19]

The narrative of events by which the Protestant party took power in
1560 is not the main concern for the themes of this collection. But it is
worth drawing attention to the relative speed with which the tide turned
against the Franco-Catholic interest. It was not something that could easily have been expected (as Ryrie argues, it might have been expected that
Mary of Guise would act more decisively to quell opposition, or that the
minority of radical activist Protestants might have been more forcefully
opposed by the rest of the country).[20] The Wars of the Congregation,
between the Protestant nobles generally known as the Lords of the Con-

---

[14] Ryrie, *Origins of the Scottish Reformation*, 68, 80; see also Kristen Post Walton's
paper in this collection.

[15] James Kirk, »Religion of Early Scottish Protestants«; Dawson, *Scotland Re-Formed*, 188–89.

[16] A. Ryrie, »Congregations, Conventicles and the Nature of Early Scottish Protestantism«, *Past and Present* 191 (2006): 45–76.

[17] Ibid., 47–49.

[18] Ibid., 75–76. Edinburgh's privy kirk was the only exception, in Ryrie's view (67).

[19] Dawson, *Scotland Re-Formed*, 202–12; J. Wormald, *Court, Kirk and Community:
Scotland, 1470–1625* (Edinburgh: Edinburgh University Press, 1981), 114–17; Ryrie,
Origins of the Scottish Reformation, 201–02.

[20] Ryrie, *Origins of the Scottish Reformation*, 197.

gregation, and Mary of Guise's Franco-Catholic forces ended up going in favour of the Lords of the Congregation, for reasons including but not limited to Elizabeth I's intervention.[21] But at the start of 1559 few would have predicted Protestant victory by the following summer. And there was certainly no fully-formed Protestant church waiting in the wings. Indeed, the summer of 1560 was hugely important in the setting out of the agenda for the new Church, even if implementing that agenda would not always prove to be so straightforward.

The Reformation Parliament abolished papal jurisdiction, forbade the Mass and the Catholic sacraments, and mandated Protestant worship.[22] It established an orthodox Reformed Confession of Faith.[23] The production of a Book of Discipline was a little slower and more complicated, but by 1561 the structures and organisation of an institutional Church were set out in blueprint, even if there would continue to be disagreement about funding.[24] And of course it is hardly a minor footnote that questions of power, authority and structure in the Protestant Kirk would go on to be deeply and sometimes violently contested for the next century and a half. But a new Church, and a new situation, was brought into being in 1560 and – as Ryrie puts it – »[u]nexpectedly, almost accidentally, Scotland had stumbled into a new world«.[25]

Protestant victory was, then, driven by a relatively small and dispro-portionately powerful group of deeply committed elite evangelicals, against the backdrop of international politics.[26] Few would now argue that the numerical balance of opinion across the country as a whole had a significant impact on the course of events, and in many senses what evan-gelical reformers had going for them was not their simple numbers but their commitment, resilience, and willingness to act when the time came. However, when the task was to build national churches, to turn a refor-mation movement into a reformation church, the fact that the wider po-pulation was not necessarily »crying out for reformation« becomes more significant.[27] They had to be brought on board, and a more inclusive re-

---

[21] Dawson, *Scotland Re-Formed*, 208–11; see also A. Blakeway, »The Anglo-Scottish War of 1558 and the Scottish Reformation«, *History* 102 (2017): 201–224.

[22] Dawson, *Scotland Re-Formed*, 212–13.

[23] Ryrie, *Origins of the Scottish Reformation*, 201–02; for the text of the confession see *The Scots Confession, 1560* (Edinburgh: Saint Andrew Press, 1960).

[24] J. K. Cameron (ed.), *The First Book of Discipline* (Edinburgh: Saint Andrew Press, 1972); Donaldson, *Scottish Reformation*, 68–72.

[25] Ryrie, *Origins of the Scottish Reformation*, 204.

[26] Ibid., esp. 118.

[27] The »crying out« quotation is from O. Chadwick, *The Reformation* (London: Penguin, 1964), 11.

formed church established. A key area of emphasis in recent studies has been identifying the processes by which this could have happened.

2. The development of an evangelical Church
after 1560

Arguably the most important mechanism for the construction of reformation churches across Scotland was the preaching ministry. This institution was of course crucial elsewhere, including in German and English Reformations.[28] But particularly for a dispersed and mainly rural population, with a less established print culture than much of England and the Holy Roman Empire, the ministers were the most important and often only mouthpieces of the Reformation. It has been established that progress in training and providing ministers to parishes was gradual and geographically patchy, especially before around 1600.[29] For many, access to a minister was shared and the normative experience of worship was not a full sermon, but the reader's service, involving scriptural readings, prayers and psalm-singing. This actually suggested some continuity with pre-Reformation models of parochial worship with intermittent visits from a preaching friar, perhaps. More research on the readers is needed, but it is apparent that they were more likely to have served in the Catholic church, to be lower-paid and less likely to be university educated.[30] Certainly regular Reformed preaching was not introduced into most Scots' lives overnight. Instead, depending on where one lived, it was gradually rolled out over the post–1560 decades. I have suggested this may have actually been unintentionally helpful in allowing for a smoother and less intrusive or aggressive transition towards local Protestant settlements, although this is not a hypothesis that can be decisively proved or disproved one way or the other.

---

[28] R. O'Day, *The English clergy: the emergence and consolidation of a profession, 1558–1642* (Leicester: Leicester University Press, 1979); A. N. Burnett, *Teaching the Reformation: ministers and their message in Basel, 1529–1629* (Oxford: Oxford University Press, 2006); C. Scott Dixon and Luise Schorn-Schütte (eds), *The Protestant clergy of early modern Europe* (Basingstoke: Palgrave, 2003). See also the chapter on preaching by Albrecht Beutel later in this volume.

[29] M. Lynch, »Preaching to the Converted: Perspectives on the Scottish Reformation«, in A. A. Macdonald, M. Lynch and I. Cowan (eds), *The Renaissance in Scotland* (Leiden: Brill, 1994); J. McCallum, *Reforming the Scottish Parish: The Reformation in Fife, 1560–1640* (Farnham: Ashgate, 2010), ch. 1.

[30] McCallum, *Reforming the Scottish Parish*, ch. 3.

Where they were present, and once they were in place across the low-lands by the early seventeenth century, there is no doubting the impor-tance of the parish minister in the Protestant Church.[31] As in other coun-tries, clerical dynasties emerged, and the clerical household acted as an important feature of the godly parish (although it has been suggested that the proportion of ministers' wives who were daughters of the manse was not as high as might be expected, with many marriages within a wider circle of lower elites and middling sorts).[32] A 2017 conference and forth-coming volume on *The Clergy in Early Modern Scotland* testifies to the growing range of research on their work not just as preachers, but as religious communicators in other forms (including through poetry), and within clerical networks which linked communities and enabled a sense of Reformed identity through processes such as fundraising for international Calvinist causes as well as, more famously, presbyterian activism.[33]

The parochial kirk session – Scotland's adaptation of the consistory – is one of the distinctive and increasingly well-known institutions of Scottish Protestantism. Staffed by the minister, elders and deacons of the parish, it was responsible for reformed discipline, amongst other things.[34] It was central to the modern stereotype of Scottish Calvinist culture as strict, disciplinarian, and uncompromising. And although some recent scholar-ship has tended to stress the elements of flexibility and accommodation in kirk session discipline, and the ways in which they operated with the grain (rather than against the grain) of early modern Scottish society, the em-phasis on kirk sessions as harsh, punitive and perhaps unpopular with many Scots has persisted most recently and eloquently in the work of the late Jenny Wormald.[35] In any case, there is little question that kirk sessions were the linchpin of the new Protestant kirk across lowland Scotland. The

---

[31] Dawson, *Scotland Re-Formed*, 220–21; J. McCallum, »The Reformation of the Ministry in Fife, 1560–1640«, *History* 94 (2009): 310–327.

[32] I. Whyte and K. Whyte, »Wed to the Manse: The Wives of Scottish Ministers, c. 1560–c.1800«, in E. Ewan and M. M. Meikle (eds), *Women in Scotland, c. 1100–c. 1750* (East Linton: Tuckwell, 1999), 223.

[33] C.R. Langley, C. McMillan and R. Newton (eds), *The Clergy in Early Modern Scotland* (forthcoming, Woodbridge: Boydell and Brewer). See also the Mapping the Scottish Reformation project, which promises to provide by far the most detailed ana-lysis of the clergy to date: http://mappingthescottishreformation.org (accessed 27th July 2018).

[34] M.F. Graham, *The Uses of Reform: ›Godly Discipline‹ and Popular Behavior in Scotland and Beyond, 1560–1610* (Leiden: Brill, 1996), 28–46, 73–129.

[35] M. Todd, *The Culture of Protestantism in Early Modern Scotland* (New Haven: Yale University Press, 2002); McCallum, *Reforming the Scottish Parish*, ch. 7; J. Wor-mald, »Reformed and Godly Scotland?«, in T. Devine and J. Wormald (eds), *The Oxford Handbook of Modern Scottish History* (Oxford: Oxford University Press, 2012), 207–08.

first was operational in St Andrews prior to the Reformation Parliament of 1560, testifying to the precocious organisation of reformed institutions in certain locations.[36] But although the *First Book of Discipline* envisaged their immediate establishment across the country, the process of instituting and developing their work was one which took decades rather than years, especially in the rural lowlands, and they were far from an unvarying presence in the parish for many Scots throughout the first generation or two from the Reformation.[37] Nevertheless, there was undeniably a rigorous Calvinist discipline by c. 1600, perhaps initially focusing on sexual offences before widening its remit to encompass a range of offences especially slander, sabbath-breach, and drunkenness.[38] Crucially, its emphasis on protecting the Sabbath and the sermon (and the infrequent communion celebration) was important for ensuring attendance and conformity with Protestant worship. They were also vital in enforcing engagement with catechesis, and more generally they ensured that the Church was able to scrutinise the lives of its members to a previously unprecedented degree. And although it remains open to debate how far this scrutiny was effective in increasing either doctrinal or moral conformity, any effectiveness achieved surely came in large part from the intense localism of kirk session discipline. Kirk sessions were of course staffed by men who were often of high standing in the local community, but Scots came to be disciplined not by distant or anonymous authority figures but by their neighbours.[39]

The kirk sessions were not, however, simply enforcers of discipline. They were also, as Margo Todd's work shows, vital agents of change, and at the same time the creators of by far the richest source material for understanding the religion in the pew, and the ways in which a Scottish Protestant culture emerged. In the *Culture of Protestantism in Early Modern Scotland*, the book which defines the subject, she uncovered a process of accommodation and flexibility in bringing around that transition. Elements of ritual and symbolism, for example through the sacrament of communion, were still included. Protestantism might have been logocentric, but the choreography of worship, and the drama of the public repentance ceremony, among other things, ensured that the experience in the pew was not confined to the verbal and textual.[40] And there was flexibility

---

[36] Graham, *Uses of Reform*, 77–97.
[37] Cameron (ed.), *The First Book of Discipline*; McCallum, *Reforming the Scottish Parish*, ch. 2.
[38] Graham, *Uses of Reform*, 219–20, 257.
[39] McCallum, *Reforming the Scottish Parish*, 160–67.
[40] Todd, *Culture of Protestantism*, esp. 125–26, 168–69.

and sensitivity on ›superstitious‹ rituals as the kirk session elders gradually worked to shape more godly communities. Todd also argues that kirk sessions provided the ›carrot‹ of social services as well as the ›stick‹ of discipline – they were active in conflict resolution, intervening in family and local disputes and carved out a role as the most important parochial mediators and keepers of the peace. This applied to feuds between neighbours, and also to breakdown within families and marriages. And they oversaw arrangements for the care of orphans and the needy.[41] The kirk sessions' work in providing poor relief has been foregrounded further in my recent work on welfare. The kirk sessions held regular collections, and acquired funds from fines and other sources, to support their provision of carefully-considered and thoughtful poor relief. Indeed they were very well-suited to acting as welfare providers in Scotland's diffuse rural parishes especially, and I have argued that their practices in this area were relatively effective.[42] Their knowledge of the local community was, again, vital to these wider and more ›positive‹ aspects of their mission. And the evidence of regular and careful relief certainly suggests a greater degree of success for the Kirk in achieving some of the initial reforming and church-building aims of 1560 than has been allowed, especially where the failure to acquire ecclesiastical revenues has been foregrounded.[43]

Similarly, another of the *First Book of Discipline*'s aims for the social policy of the Kirk was education: most famously the idea (or myth) of a widespread provision of education for all. The recent posthumous work of John Durkan has provided a huge step forward in our knowledge of schooling across the lowlands, based on incredibly painstaking archival work, especially tracing schoolmasters in the registers of deeds as witnesses to documents.[44] Progress towards ›a school in every parish‹ was, like progress on the clergy, very gradual – but there was a growing range of local schoolmasters including in rural areas, especially by the seventeenth century. Some (though by no means all) of these were associated with the parish through the kirk session.[45] And given the intertwining of elemen-

---

[41] Todd, *Culture of Protestantism*, esp. 221–26, 263, 275–84, 302–11.

[42] J. McCallum, *Poor Relief and the Church in Scotland, 1560–1650* (Edinburgh: Edinburgh University Press, 2018).

[43] T. C. Smout, *A History of the Scottish People, 1560–1830* (London: Fontana, 1969), 85; I. Whyte, *Scotland Before the Industrial Revolution* (London: Longman, 1995), 99–100.

[44] J. Durkan, J., rev. and ed. J. Reid-Baxter, *Scottish Schools and Schoolmasters, 1560–1633* (Woodbridge: Boydell and Brewer, 2013).

[45] S. M. Holmes, »Education in the Century of Reformation«, in R. Anderson, M. Freeman and L. Paterson (eds), *The Edinburgh History of Education in Scotland* (Edinburgh: Edinburgh University Press, 2015), 61–67.

tary schooling and catechism, this must have expanded the extent to which Scottish youth could be exposed to core Protestant doctrine, albeit again rather gradually.[46]

Overall, studies of these subjects raise the possibility that the kirk session (and presbyterian) system made for less of a variegated and patchwork reformation than England, in the mainland lowlands at least. There were lots of subtle variations at the very local level, between nearby villages and towns.[47] But there was also a great deal of institutional uniformity, and important mechanisms for keeping order and maintaining standards, enabling the emergence of a well-integrated and connected local church. Todd's arguments currently dominate the field, and where they have been challenged is not primarily in their account of the nature of the Protestant culture which emerged, but in the practicalities and timescale of its emergence. Based primarily on later sixteenth and seventeenth century records, especially from towns, the applicability of the arguments to earlier post–1560 practice has been the most questioned: some would suggest that kirk sessions and reformed preaching of the sort she emphasises took a long time to emerge and were geographically uneven.[48] Another noticeable critical point – especially for the theme of this collection – is Christopher Haigh's critique of Todd's suggestion that the community work of the kirk session helps to explain Scotland's smoother transition, in comparative terms, to a fully reformed populace. Haigh suggests that the English churchwardens were undertaking some similar if less obviously documented work, and that the English system was not an entirely contrasting, distant, inefficient and inflexible cousin of the Scottish kirk session system.[49] How distinctive and unique the work of the kirk sessions was in a wider geographical context is beyond the scope of this chapter, but *The Culture of Protestantism in Early Modern Scotland* remains the definitive account of how Scotland's national Reformation manifested itself in what would become energetic local Reformed churches.

---

[46] Our knowledge of university education is also expanding: see especially S. J. Reid, *Humanism and Calvinism: Andrew Melville and the Universities of Scotland, c. 1560–c. 1625* (Farnham: Ashgate, 2011).

[47] H. Cornell, »Gender, Sex and Social Control: East Lothian, 1610–1640« (unpublished PhD Thesis, University of Edinburgh, 2012), 263; McCallum, *Reforming the Scottish Parish*, 192–203; Graham, *Uses of Reform*, chs 3, 6.

[48] J. Goodare, »Review of Margo Todd, *The Culture of Protestantism in Early Modern Scotland*,« *Albion* 36 (2004): 376; McCallum, *Reforming the Scottish Parish*, 4.

[49] C. Haigh, »The Clergy and Parish Discipline in England, 1570–1640«, in B. Heal and O. Grell (eds), *The Impact of the European Reformation: Princes, Clergy and People* (Aldershot: Ashgate, 2008).

Much of the preceding discussion has essentially been about the Lowlands, and the course of the Reformation in the Gaelic-speaking highlands is often told as a separate story, perhaps justifiably since there was a substantial distinction between the two halves of early modern Scotland. The highlands did not follow the lowland model, but Jane Dawson has shown how Calvinism did still manifest itself, albeit in a way which was highly distinctive to Gaelic society and culture. Although a Gaelic Bible translation was slow to come, evangelical preaching and catechism did much to compensate for this in a culture geared to oral literacy and memory. The structure of parish churches, kirk sessions and presbyteries were harder to replicate for obvious geographical reasons than in the lowlands, but highland ministers adapted by employing a more itinerant and flexible approach. They saw themselves as good Gaels and good Calvinists, and if their branch of the church sometimes appears less developed or even less reformed, it was more because of the preconceptions of lowland observers, whose judgements on the Gaelic church shaped previous understandings.[50]

Of course, at the same time that local evangelical churches and religious culture was developing, Scottish Protestantism was beginning to experience ecclesiological conflict. This was a subject which was often seen to define the aftermath of the Scottish Reformation (and certainly for a long time defined, and perhaps still defines its historiography).[51] The division into presbyterian and episcopalian tendencies, and ultimately churches, has been shown to be a far more contingent development of the early seventeenth century than a direct consequence of 1560, and there was considerable fluidity and flexibility for a long time, rather than two permanently and entirely opposed camps.[52] And work by David Mullan and others has stressed common spiritual impulses and even a common ›puritan‹ culture which was by no means the preserve of presbyterians, and the same goes for the disciplinary work of the kirk sessions.[53] Aaron Denlinger's more directly theological research has recently helped to develop this sense of a relatively broad orthodoxy within much Scottish Protestantism.[54] One of the implications of these trends is the need to avoid

[50] J. E. A. Dawson, »Calvinism and the Gaedhealtachd in Scotland«, in A. Pettegree, A. Duke and G. Lewis, *Calvinism in Europe, 1540–1620* (Cambridge: Cambridge University Press, 1994).

[51] A. R. MacDonald, *The Jacobean Kirk 1567–1625: Sovereignty, Polity and Liturgy* (Aldershot: Ashgate, 1998), 2–4; McCallum, »Introduction«, in McCallum (ed.), *Scotland's Long Reformation*, 3–5.

[52] MacDonald, *Jacobean Kirk*, 173–78; Reid, *Humanism and Calvinism*, 10.

[53] D. Mullan, *Scottish Puritanism, 1590–1638* (Oxford: Oxford University Press, 2000), 66, 87; McCallum, *Reforming the Scottish Parish*, 51.

[54] See for example A. C. Denlinger, *Reformed Orthodoxy in Scotland: Essays on Scot-*

thinking in terms of an evangelical Scottish Presbyterian Church which emerged if not at 1560, then soon after, and which was fundamentally at odds with a conservative episcopalian and royal faction. In Scotland as elsewhere, there is now a suggestion of more of a consensual and broad-based religious culture and theology.[55] This in no way lessens the significance (and increasing ferocity) of the tensions and divisions over church polity and authority, and the way that for many this solidified into distinct identities in the seventeenth century. It is certainly not a conflict which can be entirely ignored when reflecting on the emergence of reformed churches in the British Isles, even if we now understand it in more nuanced terms.

Conclusion

The processes by which the reformed Church emerged and took shape in Scotland were complex and gradual, with Protestant institutions and culture developing at a slow, or perhaps calm pace after the late and dramatic Reformation of 1559–60. But what emerged was also rich and engaging, an intensely local and communally-based set of mechanisms for overseeing a broad religious change. And this may have been particularly important given the way in which the Reformation played out – or rather failed to play out – in Scottish communities prior to 1560. This overview has also touched on some divisions and divides – between the highland and lowland experience, between presbyterian and episcopalian, and of course we should not forget the more subtle and intangible but perennial divide between the enthusiast and the conformist. But there were also unifying and common institutions, in particular the minister and the kirk session, which shaped and provided some consistency in the reformed Church. Through its record-keeping the latter also serves as a unique and important source of evidence, and offers ways in which historians can explore themes which have not been addressed here but are important in the specialist chapters, such as gender and the family, sacred space, and worship.

---

tish Theology, 1560–1775 (London: Bloomsbury, 2015), 102; A. C. Denlinger, »Swimming with the Reformed Tide: John Forbes of Corse (1593–1648) on Double Predestination and Particular Redemption«, *Journal of Ecclesiastical History* 66 (2015): 67–89 at p. 73, 84, 86–87.

[55] A. Ryrie, *Being Protestant in Reformation Britain* (Oxford: Oxford University Press, 2013), 469–72.

II.

Faktoren des Kirchewerdens

Factors Contributing to the Emergence
of Evangelical Churches

Die Predigt

Albrecht Beutel

Geschwisterliche Eintracht gedeiht allemal dort am besten, wo ihr eine distinkte Binnendifferenzierung zugrunde liegt. Diese Lebensweisheit, deren triviale Evidenz kaum zu bestreiten ist, gilt gleichermaßen für Familien und Reformationen. Wer die immanente Spezifizierung, die jede verwandtschaftliche Analogie strukturiert, zur krassen Antithese übertreibt, disqualifiziert sich damit als ein beziehungsgestörter Autist.

Indessen hat die komparatistische Reformationsgeschichtsforschung solche Depravationen seit Jahrzehnten schon überwunden. Die These, in Deutschland sei die Reformation von unten, in England hingegen von oben, hier durch eine basale Predigtbewegung, dort durch einen souveränen »act of state«[1] ausgelöst worden, ist an der Komplexität der historischen Sachverhalte längst irreparabel zerschellt. Denn bekanntlich spielten auch in Deutschland obrigkeitliche Schutz- und Fördermaßnahmen eine tragende Rolle, obgleich sie nicht von einer Zentralgewalt, sondern durch zahlreiche »acts of state«[2] realisiert wurden. Und in England stellte die evangelische Predigt nicht eine Folgeerscheinung, sondern ein konstitutives Ermöglichungs- und Begleitmoment der Entscheidung dar, den König als »Protector and Supreme Head of the English Church and Clergy« auszurufen. Insofern dürfte sich das Predigtthema für die Aufgabe, die binnendifferenzierte Analogie der englischen und deutschen Reformationsschwestern auszuloten, als ein vorzüglicher Indikator erweisen.[3]

---

[1] FREDERIC MAURICE POWICKE, The Reformation in England, Oxford 1941, 1.

[2] OTIS CARL EDWARDS, A History of Preaching, Nashville 2004, 351.

[3] Für den deutschsprachigen Bereich vgl. die mit reichen Literaturhinweisen versehenen Übersichten: ALBRECHT BEUTEL, Art. Predigt VIII. Evangelische Predigt vom 16. bis 18. Jahrhundert (in: TRE 27, 1997, 296–311); DERS., Art. Predigt II. Geschichte der Predigt (in: RGG⁴ 6, 2003, 1585–1591); DERS. u.a., Art. Predigt (in: Historisches Wörterbuch der Rhetorik 7, 2005, 45–96). – Für den englischen Bereich vgl. insbesondere: PHILIP EDGCUMBE HUGHES, Theology of the English Reformers, London 1965, 119–188; CHRISTOPHER MATTINSON DENT, Protestant Reformers in Elizabethan Oxford, Oxford 1983, 201–220 u. passim; CHRISTOPHER HAIGH, English Reformations. Religion, Politics, and Society under the Tudors, Oxford 1993, 268–283 u. passim; ERIC JOSEF CARLSON, The Boring of the Ear: Shaping the Pastoral Vision of Preaching in England, 1540–1640 (in: Preachers and People in the Reformations and Early Modern Period, hg. v. Larissa Taylor, Leiden u.a. 2001, 249–296); ANNE T. THAYER, Penitence, Preaching

Wenn wir uns im Folgenden, ohne die historischen Kontexte ausblenden zu wollen, auf die jeweilige reformatorische Gründergeneration und dabei näherhin auf die Meisterprediger Martin Luther und Hugh Latimer konzentrieren, so ist diese Beschränkung nicht etwa durch alliterative, sondern ausschließlich durch ökonomische Gründe veranlasst. Dergestalt dürfte es sachdienlich sein, zunächst die Grundzüge der reformatorischen Predigtlehre, sodann das Komplementärphänomen der volkssprachlichen Bibelübersetzung und schließlich die hier und dort geübte Praxis der reformatorischen Predigt in holzschnittartigen Umrissen kenntlich zu machen.

1. Die Relevanz des Wortes Gottes:
Zur Theologie der Predigt

Die soteriologische Zentrierung des Wortes Gottes erwies sich als das Proprium reformatorischer Theologie. Um diese programmatische Neuausrichtung zu unterstreichen, pflegte man das überkommene Predigtwesen als Negativfolie in den dunkelsten Farben zu malen. Dass die Bibel im Papsttum »unter der banck ym stawb«[4] gelegen habe, wurde für Luther seit 1520 zur stehenden Wendung.[5] Als notwendige Folge dieser Missachtung meinte er ein fast vollständiges Verstummen der Evangeliumspredigt wahrnehmen zu können. Dem entsprach der von englischen Reformatoren diagnostizierte Befund: Die meisten Kanzeln, klagte Bernard Gilpin, seien mit Staub bedeckt gewesen, und von den seltenen Kanzelreden, die man allenfalls habe hören können, verdienten es nur die wenigsten, als ›Predigt‹ bezeichnet zu werden.[6] Natürlich waren solche Pauschalurteile höchst polemisch und ungerecht: Die spätmittelalterliche Prädikantenkultur stand in hoher Blüte, in England sah sich die evangelische Verkündigung namentlich von den Lollarden kontinuierlich geübt.[7]

---

and the Coming of the Reformation, Aldershot 2002; EDWARDS, A History (s. Anm. 2), 350–387.

[4] WA 6,460,18f. (1520).

[5] Weitere Belege bei STEFAN MICHEL, Die Kanonisierung der Werke Luthers im 16. Jahrhundert, Tübingen 2016, 20, Anm. 10.

[6] »A thousand pulpits in England are covered with dust. Some have not had four sermons these fifteen or sixteen years [...] and few of those were worthy of the name of sermon« (Bernard Gilpin, 1552; zit. nach CARLSON, The Boring [s. Anm. 3], 249).

[7] Für die vorreformatorische Predigt in England vgl. etwa GERALD ROBERT OWST, Preaching in Medieval England. A Introduction to Sermon Manuscripts of the Period c. 1350–1450, Cambridge 1926; EAMON DUFFY, The Stripping of the Altars. Traditional Religion in England c. 1400–c. 1580, New Haven u. London 1992; EDWARDS, A History (s. Anm. 2), 210–282.

Diese notwendigen Relativierungen schmälern den reformatorischen Neuaufbruch nicht im geringsten. Denn nun wurde, anders als bisher, das *verbum praedicatum* programmatisch zum zentralen Konstitutionsfaktor jedes Gottesdienstes erklärt. Es sei, mahnte Luther,

>»auffs erst tzu wissen, das die Christlich gemeyne nymer soll zu samen komen, es werde denn da selbs Gottis wort gepredigt [...], es sey auch auffs kurtzist«.[8]

Das damit postulierte Grundprinzip teilten selbstverständlich auch die Reformatoren in Zürich und Genf.[9] Dergestalt mutierte die Predigt vom spätmittelalterlichen »special event«[10] zum Regelfall reformatorischer Liturgie, und die Funktionsbestimmung des geistlichen Amtes wandelte sich dementsprechend vom Priester zum Prediger, vom Treuhänder der Gnade zum Lehrer des Wortes Gottes.[11]

Für den Formierungsprozess der jungen Reformationsgemeinden war die Zentralkontinuität der Predigt von signifikanter Bedeutung: In ihrer Komplementärfunktion der nach außen gerichteten Differenzfixierung und der nach innen gerichteten Homogenisierungsleistung trug sie in entscheidendem Maße zur konfessionellen Identitätsbildung bei.

Auf den spätmittelalterlichen Kanzeln dominierte die Themapredigt, die weithin von kirchlicher Moral- und Institutionenlehre bestimmt war. Demgegenüber hat die Reformation die Gattung der Themapredigt zwar nicht verabschiedet,[12] aber doch weit hinter die textuale Auslegung der Bibel zurückgestellt. Damit sollte das göttliche *verbum scriptum* nicht etwa nur erklärend glossiert, sondern in Gestalt des göttlichen *verbum praedicatum* wieder in den ursprünglichen mündlichen Aggregatzustand des Evangeliums überführt werden. Zwingende Voraussetzung dieser sakramentalen Worthaftigkeit war allerdings, dass der Prediger das Wort

---

[8] WA 12,35,19–21 (1523).

[9] Vgl. DOROTHEA WENDEBOURG, Reformation und Gottesdienst (in: ZThK 113, 2016, 323–365, hier: 324f.).

[10] »In the years before the Reformation the sermon never lost its sense of being a special event« (ANDREW PETTEGREE, Reformation and the Culture of Persuasion, Cambridge 2005, 16).

[11] *The Bishop's Book* (1537) benannte als oberste Pflicht der Geistlichen »to preach and teach the word of God unto his people« (zit. nach CARLSON, The Boring [s. Anm. 3], 260). Entsprechend hieß es im Katechismus von Thomas Becon: »the first and principal point of a bishop's and a spiritual minister's office [is] to teach and preach the Word of God« (THOMAS BECON, The Early Works, hg. v. John Ayre, Bd. 1, Cambridge 1843, 320).

[12] Man denke nur an Luthers *Invokavit-Predigten* von 1522 (WA 10/3,1–64). – Zu Luthers Predigtverständnis und Predigtpraxis: ALBRECHT BEUTEL, In dem Anfang war das Wort. Studien zu Luthers Sprachverständnis, Tübingen 1991, 352–357, 468–472 u. passim; HELLMUT ZSCHOCH, Predigten (in: Luther Handbuch, hg. v. Albrecht Beutel, Tübingen ³2017, 358–365 [Lit.]); ROLAND M. LEHMANN, Reformation auf der Kanzel. Luthers Predigten außerhalb Wittenbergs, Habil. masch., Jena 2018.

Gottes in unvermischter Gestalt vergegenwärtigt: Was immer er sagt, schärfte John Jewel ein, müsse allein aus der Bibel bezogen sein.[13] Damit, fuhr er fort, verbinde sich dann auch die Gewähr, dass wir auf der Kanzel nichts anderes sagen als das, was vor uns die Kirchenväter, die Apostel und Christus selbst schon gesagt haben.[14] Für dieses Kontinuitätspostulat findet sich bei Luther eine wörtliche Parallele, freilich mit dem einzigen Unterschied, dass er dabei die Väter der Kirche verschwieg.[15] Und wenn Latimer davor warnte, in der Predigt das Wort Gottes mit menschlichen Träumen und Erfindungen anzureichern,[16] so gaben hierzu die berühmten blauen Enten, die Luther einem wichtigtuerischen Prediger zu erzählen unterstellte,[17] eine grelle, aber sachidentische Verbildlichung ab. Im Übrigen, hieß es in Cambridge und Wittenberg übereinstimmend, sollten Undank und Desinteresse der Leute den Prediger nicht zur Resignation, sondern im Gegenteil zu verstärkter homiletischer Anstrengung provozieren.[18] Biblische Predigt, war man sich einig, ergehe allemal ohne Ansehen der Person – weder der eigenen, die von Natur aus auf Beliebtheit und Anerkennung erpicht ist, noch der des Hörers, und sei es der eigene Landesfürst[19] oder König: Ein guter Prediger, wusste Latimer,

»verbessert und kritisiert selbst den König, er fürchtet keinen Menschen, sondern fasst allein Gott in den Blick«.[20]

Die bekannte Formel Heinrich Bullingers »praedicatio verbi dei est verbum dei«[21] fixierte einen gesamtreformatorischen Basiskonsens, der, unbeschadet jeder graduellen Nuancierung,[22] allenthalben begegnet,[23] gelegent-

---

[13] Vgl. HUGHES, Theology of the English Reformers (s. Anm. 3), 121.

[14] »Remember, we are the sons of the prophets. [...] It is not our doctrine that we bring you this day; we wrote it not, we found it not out, we are not the inventors of it; we bring you nothing but what the old fathers of the Church, what the apostles, what Christ our Saviour Himself hath brought before us« (JOHN JEWEL, The Works, hg. v. John Ayre, Bd. 2, Cambridge 1847, 1034).

[15] Vgl. etwa WA 12,521,23 f. (1523); WA 43,536,27 f. (1530/32).

[16] »These be the properties of every good preacher: to be a true man; to teach, not dreams nor inventions of men, but *viam Dei in veritate*« (The Works of Hugh Latimer, hg. v. George Elwes Corrie, Bd. 1, Cambridge 1844, 292).

[17] »Wo nicht geystlicher verstand und der geyst selbst redet durch die prediger [...], so kompts doch endlich dahyn, das ein iglicher predigen wird was er will, und an stat des Euangelii und seyner auslegunge widderumb von blaw endten gepredigt wird« (WA 19,95,9–14 [1526]).

[18] Vgl. HUGHES, Theology (s. Anm. 3), 122.

[19] Vgl. WA.Br 10,33,17–27 (1542).

[20] »The preacher [...] must correct and reprove him [sc. the King] with the spiritual sword; fearing no man; setting God only before his eyes, under whom he is a minister, to supplant and root up all vice and mischief by God's word« (The Works of Hugh Latimer [s. Anm. 16], 86).

[21] Marginalie zur Confessio Helvetica Posterior I (BSRK 171).

[22] Vgl. WENDEBOURG (s. Anm. 9), 328.

lich auch, etwa bei Bischof Edwin Sandys, in christologischer Präzisierung:

»Wenn du den Pfarrer die Wahrheit predigen hörst, dann hörst du nicht ihn, sondern den Sohn Gottes, den Lehrer aller Wahrheit, Jesus Christus«.[24]

Was hierbei dem Hörer zur Glaubensvergewisserung dient, wird für den Prediger zum homiletischen Elementarunterricht: Er soll sich den Prediger Christus zum Vorbild nehmen,[25] und dies gleichermaßen hinsichtlich der biblischen wie der rhetorischen Sachtreue. Christus, lehrte Luther einmal bei Tisch,

»hat am aller einfeltigsten geredt vnd war doch eloquentia selbst. [...] Drumb ists am besten vnd die hochste eloquentia simpliciter dicere«.[26]

Die Pluralität der katholischen Heilsangebote wurde von den Reformatoren in ein solitäres Integral überführt: Das aktuell verlautbarte Wort Gottes galt ihnen als das *medium salutis* schlechthin. Das paulinische *fides ex auditu* (Röm. 10,17) diente Luther als Angelpunkt seiner aus der Fundamentalrelation von Wort und Glaube entwickelten Rechtfertigungslehre. Latimer bezeichnete die Predigt schlicht als »God's instrument of salvation« und dementsprechend das Predigtamt als »the office of salvation«.[27] Dieser worthaften Heilsvermittlung wusste man auch die Sakramente zugeordnet, deren Proprium William Tyndale, durchaus repräsentativ, als »a preaching function«[28] erkannte.

---

[23] Vgl. etwa die bekannte Sequenz aus Luthers Schrift *Wider Hans Worst*: »Ein Prediger mus nicht das Vater unser beten, noch Vergebung der sünden süchen, wenn er gepredigt hat (wo er ein rechter Prediger ist), Sondern mus [...] mit S. Paulo, allen Aposteln und Propheten trötzlich sagen: Haec dixit Dominus, Das hat Gott selbs gesagt. [...] Denn es ist Gottes und nicht mein wort, das mir Gott nicht vergeben sol noch kan, Sondern bestetigen, loben, krönen und sagen: Du hast recht geleret, Denn ich hab durch dich geredt, und das wort ist mein. Wer sich solchs nicht rhümen kan von seiner predigt, der lasse das predigen anstehen, Denn er leugt gewislich und lestert Gott« (WA 51,517,22–34 [1541]). Für analoge Positionierungen bei Calvin und im schottischen *First Book of Discipline* vgl. WENDEBOURG (s. Anm. 9), 328, Anm. 24.

[24] »When thou hearest the minister preaching the truth, thou hearest not him, but the Son of God, the teacher of all truth, Christ Jesus« (The Sermons of Edwin Sandys, hg. v. John Ayre, Cambridge 1841, 278).

[25] »Christ is the preacher of all preachers, the pattern and the exemplar that all preachers ought to follow« (The Works of Hugh Latimer [s. Anm. 16], 155).

[26] WA.TR 4,664,22–24 (1540).

[27] The Works of Hugh Latimer (s. Anm. 16), 178, 349. – Ähnlich etwa auch Edmund Grindal: »If there be no salvation but by faith, no faith but by hearing the word of God, how should the people be saved without teachers?« (zit. nach HAIGH, English Reformations [s. Anm. 3], 269).

[28] Vgl. HUGHES, Theology (s. Anm. 3), 132. Auch John Jewel erkannte in der Zusammenschau von Predigt und Sakramenten die Wortverkündigung als den »principalist part of this office« (JOHN JEWEL, The Works, hg. v. John Ayre, Bd. 3, Cambridge 1848, 1130 f.).

In der Metaphernwahl kamen deutsche und englische Reformatoren exakt überein: Für Luther bot die Predigt nicht weniger als den Schlüssel zum Himmelreich,[29] für Richard Greenham galt sie als »the gate of heaven«.[30] Bisweilen allerdings manifestierte sich daneben eine signifikante Explanationsdifferenz. Während die deutschsprachigen Kanzelredner die Form der diskursiven Entfaltung bevorzugten, erläuterten englische Reformationstheologen die Heilsnotwendigkeit der Predigt gern durch einen syllogistischen Kettenschluss:

»No preaching, no faith; no faith, no Christ; no Christ, no eternal life«,

schlussfolgerte etwa Arthur Dent.[31] Oder auch:

»Wer den Himmel haben will, muss Christus haben. Wer Christus haben will, muss den Glauben haben. Wer den Glauben haben will, muss die Predigt haben«.[32]

Besonders markant wurde die *scala coeli* von Latimer formalisiert. In Aufnahme des in Röm. 10,13 zitierten Profetenwortes »Wer den Namen des Herrn anrufen wird, der soll errettet werden« (Joel 3,5a) machte er sich die paulinische Erläuterung (Röm. 10,14) unmittelbar zu eigen:

»How shall they call upon him, in whom they have not believed? [...] How shall they believe in him, of whom they never heard? [...] How shall they hear without a preacher?«

Als Conclusio dieser dem Apostel nachgebildeten logischen Operation präsentierte Latimer dann die bekannte Formel:

»Take away preaching, take away salvation«.[33]

Insofern war es nur konsequent, wenn Elnathan Parr festhielt, nach Christus stelle die Predigt die größte Wohltat dar, die Gott der Menschheit gegeben habe.[34] Indes widerstanden nicht alle Reformatoren der damit riskierten Gefahr, der Person des Predigers eine aktive Heilsmittlerschaft zuzuschreiben. So meinte etwa William Jones, ein Mensch könne nur dergestalt selig werden, dass ihn der Prediger auf seinen Schultern in den Himmel hineintrage.[35] Um solcher fehlgeleiteten Hypostasierung zu weh-

---

[29] »Per hoc verbum aperitur coelum, remissio peccatorum consequitur« (WA 15,720,35 f. [1524]).

[30] RICHARD GREENHAM, The Workes, London 1605, 779. Ähnlich etwa auch Richard Hooker, der die Predigten als »the keyes to the kingdom of heaven« bezeichnete (RICHARD HOOKER, Of the Laws of Ecclesiastical Polity, The Folger Library Edition of the Works of Richard Hooker, Bd. 2, hg. v. W. Speed Hill, Cambridge 1977, 87).

[31] ARTHUR DENT, The Plaine Mans Pathway to Heaven: wherein every man may clearly see whether hee shall saved or damned, London 1625, 336.

[32] A.a.O., 336 f.

[33] The Works of Hugh Latimer (s. Anm. 16), 123.

[34] »Faith and the promised good things cannot be attainded without preaching. Next to Christ, it is the greatest benefit which God hath given to men« (The Workes of [...] Elnathan Parr, London ⁴1651, 130 f.).

ren, unterstrichen Luther, Latimer und mit ihnen viele andere die bloße Instrumentalität des Predigers, der nicht zum selbstmächtigen Himmelspförtner, sondern lediglich als ein Werkzeug in der Hand Gottes berufen sei.[36] Luther stellte dies in der von ihm oft gewählten dialogischen Form dar:

»Ich hore wohl die predigt, aber wer redet? Der pfarherr? Nicht also, du horest nicht den pfarherr. Die stimme ist wohl sein, aber das wortt, das ehr fhuret oder redet, das redet mein Gott«.[37]

Analog dazu befand Latimer, den Predigern sei nicht mehr als treue Pflichterfüllung aufgetragen, während der Erfolg allein dem verborgenen Wirken Gottes anheimgestellt bleibe:

»They can do not more but call; God is he that must bring in; God must open the hearts«.[38]

Das göttliche *verbum praedicatum* erschien den Reformatoren so unabdingbar, dass sie es nicht notwendig auf den Raum einer Kirche beschränkt wissen wollten. Zwar biete dafür die Kanzel allemal die beste Gelegenheit, doch wenn eine solche nicht zur Verfügung stehe, eigne sich gleichermaßen auch jeder andere Ort. Wie Jesus umstandshalber sogar von einem Schiff aus gepredigt hatte (Mt. 13,1–9), so könne, befand Latimer, ein guter Prediger auch auf einem Pferd oder im Baum sitzend das Wort Gottes austeilen.[39] In Wittenberg sah man die Sache nicht anders: Auch auf dem Dach eines Hauses, meinte Luther, und sogar auf der Elbbrücke[40] oder »unter einer grünen Linde oder Weiden«[41] könne das Evangelium, wenn es not tut, unter die Leute gebracht werden. Moderne Liturgiker mögen sich wundern, scheint sich damit doch selbst der *Gottesdienst im Grünen* als ein Vermächtnis der Reformation zu erweisen.

---

[35] William Jones, A Commentary upon the Epistles to Philemon, and to the Hebrewes, London ²1636, 633.

[36] »Sumus instrumentum per linguam, per quam deus praedicat. Sic omnia officia in mundo ghen in gotlicher gestalt. Nos non sumus deus ut Christus, sed tantum particulam acquirimus gotlicher gstalt, da ghet die lere an, ut sua forma fiat servus« (WA 27,94,15–18 [1528]). – Entsprechend Latimer: »Preachers are Christ's vicars [...] [and] the mighty instrument of God« (The Works of Hugh Latimer [s. Anm. 16], 349).

[37] WA 47,229,30–33 (1540). – Ähnlich a.a.O., 211,9–14: »Wenn ich dich schlechts hörete predigen, so gebe ich nicht einen Strohalm fur deine Predigt. Aber Gott redet da, ehr teuffet und wircket und ist selbst gegenwerttig da. Derhalben so hat der prediger nicht für sein person gepredigt, sondern gott, der himlissche vater, und du soltest sagen: Ich hab gott selbst gesehen teuffen und das Sacrament des altars reichen und das wort hören predigen«.

[38] The Works of Hugh Latimer (s. Anm. 16), 285.

[39] A.a.O., 206.

[40] »Wu Gott redt, da wohnt ehr. Wo das wortt klingt, do ist Gott, do ist sein hauß [...]. Wen ehr auch klunge uff dem dach adder under dem dach, und gleich uff der elbbruckenn, ßo ists gewiß, das ehr do wohne« (WA 14,386,28–387,10 [1523/24]).

[41] WA 16,105,20 (1524); vgl. a.a.O., 105,15–28.

2. Die Fasslichkeit des Wortes Gottes:
Zur volkssprachlichen Bibelübersetzung

Man könnte meinen, mit einem Seitenblick auf die Bibelübersetzungen der Reformation drohe das eigentliche Thema aus dem Blickfeld zu rücken. Bedenkt man es indes näher, so kann damit die Wahrnehmung des reformatorischen Predigtverständnisses noch in erheblicher Weise geschärft werden. Volksbibel und evangelische Predigt stellten ein Komplementärphänomen dar; sie erwuchsen gleichermaßen, in Deutschland und England, aus der von den Reformatoren ins Werk gesetzten soteriologischen Zentrierung des Wortes Gottes.

Selbstverständlich gab es volkssprachliche Übersetzungen von biblischen Büchern schon längst in vorreformatorischer Zeit. Sie begannen im deutschen und englischen Sprachraum, wollte man von der gotischen Wulfila-Bibel absehen, jeweils im 8. Jahrhundert und blühten im Spätmittelalter kräftig auf, wobei hierzulande insbesondere der *Mentelin-Bibel* (1466) und dem *Zainer-Plenar* (1485), auf der Insel der *Lollard Bible* (um 1380) ausstrahlende Bedeutung zukam. In Deutschland war wenig später die *Luther-Bibel* (NT 1522, Vollbibel 1534) von epochalem Gewicht, hinter den Grenzen des Luthertums zunächst auch in der Schweiz – in Basel wurde Luthers Neues Testament 1522/23 nachgedruckt, versehen mit einem dort höchst notwendigen Glossar – sowie in verschiedenen altgläubigen Plagiaten.[42]

Eine Keimzelle der englischen Reformationstheologie lässt sich in einem Gasthaus zu Cambridge verorten, wo seit Beginn der 1520er Jahre etliche Dozenten und Priester zusammenkamen, um die Publikationen Luthers zu lesen und zu erörtern. Namhafte Teilnehmer dieses bald »Little Germany« genannten Kneipenzirkels waren etwa Miles Coverdale und Thomas Cranmer, Tyndale und Latimer. Hier wurzelten neben der liturgischen und lehrhaften Neubesinnung auch die Bemühungen um eine neue englische Übersetzung der Bibel. Während die Tyndale-Ausgabe im alttestamentlichen Teil fragmentiert blieb, konnte Coverdale 1535 eine Vollbibel vorlegen, aus der wenige Jahre später die *Bishop's Bible* (1537) sowie die *Great Bible* (1540) erwuchsen. Nun erließ Heinrich VIII. die Verfügung, in jeder Gemeindekirche sollten eine englische Bibel öffentlich ausgelegt und die Eingepfarrten zu deren Lektüre ermuntert werden.[43]

---

[42] Vgl. ALBRECHT BEUTEL, Art. Bibelübersetzungen. II. Christliche Übersetzungen in europäische Volkssprachen seit dem Mittelalter. 1. Übersetzungen in germanische Sprachen (in: RGG⁴ 1, 1998, 1498–1505).

[43] Gute Übersichten bieten etwa GÜNTHER GASSMANN, Die Lehrentwicklung im Anglikanismus. Von Heinrich VIII. bis zu William Temple (in: Handbuch der Dogmen-

Tatsächlich waren die reformatorischen Volksbibeln mit ihrem Bemühen um sprechsprachliche Verständlichkeit auf das Ziel gerichtet, jedem elementar gebildeten Menschen das Wort Gottes in seiner authentischen Gestalt unmittelbar zugänglich zu machen. Dies sollte nicht allein der privatreligiösen Erbauung zugute kommen, sondern durchaus auch der Ermöglichung einer bibeltheologischen Laienkompetenz und, damit verbunden, eines unabhängigen homiletischen Urteilsvermögens. Denn die Reformatoren wiesen, jedenfalls in der Anfangszeit, den Gemeinden die Aufgabe zu, die Lehre ihrer Pfarrer auf biblische Sachtreue zu überprüfen. Den Predigern, mahnte Latimer, sei nur so weit zu folgen, wie sie ihrerseits Christus folgten.[44] Und auch Tyndale machte es den christlichen Laien zur Pflicht, die Botschaft ihrer Geistlichen am biblischen Wort Gottes zu prüfen und diese notfalls auch zu ermahnen.[45] *Dass eine christliche Versammlung oder Gemeine Recht und Macht habe, alle Lehre zu urteilen*,[46] galt also zunächst nicht nur im Einflussbereich Wittenbergs, sondern auch auf der britischen Hauptinsel.

Damit war nun unversehens, von den Reformatoren kaum bemerkt oder bedacht, eine Konkurrenz aufgebrochen zwischen dem für die Predigt reklamierten Anspruch auf exklusive Heilsmittlerschaft und der für die Bibel postulierten suffizienten Authentizität des Wortes Gottes.[47] Luther unterlief das Problem gelegentlich mit dem Hinweis, die Predigt sei eine populartheologische Gattung und darum zwar für Hänslein und Elslein, aber nicht für Gelehrte wie Johannes Bugenhagen, Justus Jonas oder Philipp Melanchthon bestimmt.[48] Richard Hooker fasste es allgemeiner

---

und Theologiegeschichte, hg. v. Carl Andresen, Bd. 2, Göttingen 1988, 353–409, hier: 354–369); VIVIANE BARRIE-CURIEN, Die Reformation auf den Britischen Inseln (in: Die Zeit der Konfessionen [1530–1620/30], hg. v. Marc Vernard, Freiburg i. Br. u.a. 1992, 524–572, hier: 524–539).

[44] »It is a dangerous thing to follow men; and we are not bound to follow them, further than they follow Christ. [...] Therefore let us follow them as they follow Christ [...]. So that we ought to follow them that teach the truth; but when they do naught, we should not follow them« (The Works of Hugh Latimer [s. Anm. 16], 514; vgl. a.a.O., 523).

[45] The Works of the English Reformers: William Tyndale, and John Frith, hg. v. Thomas Russel, Bd. 2, London 1831, 269f.

[46] WA 11,408–416 (1523).

[47] Vgl. ALBRECHT BEUTEL, Erfahrene Bibel. Verständnis und Gebrauch des verbum dei scriptum bei Luther (in: Ders., Protestantische Konkretionen. Studien zur Kirchengeschichte, Tübingen 1998, 66–103).

[48] »Man sol auff der cantzel die zitzen herauß ziehen und daß volck mit milch trencken, den eß wechst alle tage eine newe kirch auff, quae indiget primis principiis. Drumb sal man nur den catechismum vleisig treiben und die milch außteylen; dj hohen gedancken und stucken soll man fur dj kluglinge privatim behalten. Ich wil Doctorem Pommeranum, Jonam, Philippum in meyner predigt nicht wissen, den sie wissens vorhin baß den ich. Ich predige ihnen auch nicht, sondern meinem Henslein und Elslein; illos observo« (WA.TR 3,310, 5–12 [undatiert]).

und erklärte das Bibellesen zu einem gegenüber dem Predigthören gleich-
wertigen Weg zum Heil.[49] Andere englische Theologen stimmten ihm darin bei: Die Bibel zu lesen, befand Martin Fotherby, sei eine höchst machtvolle Spielart der Predigt, zumal dort kurz, klar und einfach geschrieben
stehe, was auf den Kanzeln oft nur langatmig, dunkel und abgehoben zu
hören sei.[50] Erstaunlicherweise sah sich dafür sogar Paulus als Kronzeuge
berufen. Dessen einschlägigen *locus classicus* »Der Glaube kommt aus dem
Hören« (Röm. 10,17) erläuterte John Downe durch lebensweltliche Em-
pirie: Wer einen Brief erhält, der sage doch, er habe von jemandem *gehört*.
Und demgemäß habe der Apostel mit jenem Satz nicht, wie Luther übersetzte, die Predigt, sondern das Lesen heiliger Schriften als den Quell-
grund des Glaubens bezeichnet. Ein Lehrer der Kirche, fuhr Downe fort,
könne in dem, was er sagt, jederzeit irren, aber die Bibel, das verschrift-
lichte Wort Gottes, irre niemals.[51]

Für die Karriere der reformatorischen Predigt fiel dieses Konkurrenzproblem zwischen dem geschriebenen und gepredigten Gotteswort nicht
ins Gewicht. Gleichwohl blieb die dogmatische Erörterung und Klärung
dieser in der Soteriologie aufbrechenden Ambivalenz ein bemerkenswertes
reformationstheologisches Desiderat.

3. Die Vermittlung des Wortes Gottes: Zur Praxis der Predigt

Im lutherischen und englischen Bereich lag der Predigt des sonn- und
festtäglichen Hauptgottesdienstes zumeist die altkirchliche Perikopenordnung zugrunde. Dagegen übte Ulrich Zwingli in Zürich von Anfang an die
Praxis der *lectio continua*, also der fortlaufenden Auslegung biblischer Se-
quenzen oder Bücher, die Luther lediglich für die Nebengottesdienste be-
vorzugte, sofern er dort nicht eine predigthafte Auslegung des *Kleinen
Katechismus* vortrug. Das 1549 erstmals publizierte *Book of Common
Prayer*[52] stellte die Perikopentexte des gesamten Kirchenjahrs zur Verfügung.

In der Auslegungspraxis ergab sich bald eine wichtige, wenn auch letztlich nur graduelle Differenz. Während die deutsche Reformation jedem
Pfarrer die theologisch selbstständige Auslegung des biblischen Predigt-

---

[49] The Works of [...] Richard Hooker, hg. v. Isaak Walton, Bd. 1, Oxford 1845, 493.
[50] MARTIN FOTHERBY, Foure Sermons, lately preached, London 1608, 28f.
[51] JOHN DOWNE, Certaine Treatises, Oxford 1633, 18–29.
[52] The Book of Common Prayer. The Texts of 1549, 1559, and 1662, hg. v. Brian
Cummings, Oxford 2011.

textes zur Pflicht machte, wurde in England die Lizenz zur eigenverant-
wortlichen Predigt nur äußerst restriktiv verliehen.[53] Allerdings waren die
Pfarrer auch in Deutschland dieser Aufgabe zunächst kaum gewachsen;
eine entsprechende Ausbildungsreform und die Produktion homiletischer
Hilfsliteratur kamen nur langsam in Gang. Als interimistische Alternative
schlug Luther deshalb in seiner *Deutschen Messe* die Verlesung der unter
seinem Namen veröffentlichten Postillenpredigten[54] vor, zumal ihm damit
neben der Entlastung unzureichend gebildeter Pfarrer[55] auch die positi-
onelle Identitätswahrung der evangelischen Kanzelverkündigung garan-
tiert schien.[56] Selbst noch aus dem Abstand von Jahren bezeichnete Luther
die *Wartburgpostille* als »mein aller bestes buch, das ich yhe gemacht habe«,[57] obschon er deren Weitschweifigkeit, die der homiletischen Nach-
nutzung abträglich war, selbstkritisch eingestand.[58]

Die Postillen Luthers blieben bis ins 18. Jahrhundert stark frequentierte
Quellen der Predigtvorbereitung. Allerdings erwiesen sich die darin gebotenen Musterpredigten für den gewöhnlichen Gottesdienst als viel zu
lang. So kam es zu einem auch literaturgeschichtlich bemerkenswerten

---

[53] »England was unusual in a number of respects, not least in instituting a separate
tier of licensed preachers as an individually selected subset of the parish ministry. Elsewhere in Protestant Europe it was taken for granted that a properly called minister
would be a preaching minister« (PETTEGREE, Reformation [s. Anm. 10], 35).

[54] Von Luthers eigener Hand stammen nur der Advents- und Weihnachtsteil, die sog.
Wartburgpostille (WA 10/1/2,1–208; WA 10/1/1,8–728 [1522]), die Stefan Roth 1525
durch einen Fastenteil zur *Kirchenpostille* (WA 17/2,5–247) ergänzt hat. Von unterschiedlichem, jedoch durchweg geringerem Wert sind die von Roth kompilierte *Sommerpostille* (WA 10/1/2,213–441 [1526]), *Festpostille* (WA 17/2,252–514 [1527]) und *Winterpostille* (WA 21,5–192 [1528]) sowie Veit Dietrichs *Hauspostille* (WA 52,10–732
[1544]) und Caspar Crucigers *Sommerpostille* (WA 21,203–551; WA 22,3–423 [1544]).

[55] In den von ihm selbst verfassten Postillenpredigten (vgl. Anm. 54) hat Luther die
Perikopentexte nicht gemäß seinem *Septembertestament*, sondern jeweils in uneleganter
Wörtlichkeit übersetzt, um damit den biblischen Urtext für altsprachlich ungebildete
Prediger möglichst exakt abzubilden. Welche Unterschiede sich dabei ergaben, lässt sich
am Prolog des Johannes-Evangeliums (Joh. 1,1–14) exemplarisch studieren (vgl. BEUTEL,
In dem Anfang [s. Anm. 12], 6–29).

[56] »Es were das beste, das man verordnete, die postillen des tages gantz odder eyn
stucke aus dem buch dem volck fur zu lesen, nicht alleyne umb der prediger willen, die
es nicht besser kunden, sondern auch umb der schwermer und secten willen zuverhüeten« (WA 19,95,4–8 [1526]).

[57] WA 23,278,13f. (1527). Dieses Urteil hat Luther später allerdings revidiert, indem
er Wolfgang Capito am 9. Juli 1537 brieflich mitteilte, von seinen Schriften schätze er
allein *De servo arbitrio* und den Katechismus (WA.Br 8,99,7f.).

[58] »Occasio facit praedicatorem, nam ex contionibus meis postillaribus ne unum quidem sermonem colligo, ut eodem modo praedicarem. Ich kan mich nicht mit worten
binden lassen. [...] Si iunior essem, multa resecarem in postilla, nam immodice fui copiosus. Eam copiam nemo assequi aut imitari potest, neque omnia sunt accommoda[nda]
omnibus temporibus« (WA.TR 1,488,24–489,2 [erste Hälfte der 1530er Jahre]); vgl. etwa
auch Luther an Nikolaus Gerbel, 27.11.1535: WA.Br 7,329,14–20).

Funktionswandel, der die Postillen Luthers nicht allein zu homiletischen Meditationshilfen, sondern daneben zusehends zur Grundlage der privat-religiösen Erbauung werden ließ. Daraus erklärt sich im Übrigen auch das rasante Aufblühen einer evangelischen Postillen- und Predigtliteratur,[59] deren Fernausläufer bis ins 20. Jahrhundert zu spüren gewesen sind.

In England war die gottesdienstliche Verlesung vorgefertigter Kanzel-reden ebenfalls nur als temporärer Notbehelf auferlegt worden, erwies aber, anders als in Deutschland, eine bis in die Gegenwart reichende Be-harrungskraft. Die 1547 erstmals erschienenen *Books of Homilies* boten zwölf Musterpredigten, deren Zahl sich in der zweiten Ausgabe von 1562 nahezu verdoppelte. Während dabei die basalen Glaubenslehren kaum verändert fortgeschrieben wurden, intensivierte die Vermehrung der zwei-ten Ausgabe vor allem die konkrete moralische Unterweisung. So erwei-terten sich die Predigtthemen bis hin zu der Ermahnung, den Kirchen-raum sorgfältig zu reinigen, und der Warnung vor Trunksucht, Völlerei, Faulheit und modischem Prunk.[60] Die Kritik, die mancherorts laut wurde, entzündete sich einerseits pragmatisch an der liturgisch nicht praktikablen Länge der Musterpredigten, andererseits aber auch grundsätzlich an der Unmöglichkeit, damit auf die jeweils speziellen Bedürfnisse vor Ort ein-gehen und die Herzen derer, die im Gottesdienst versammelt sind, errei-chen zu können.[61] Manche Engländer nahmen deshalb längere Reisen auf sich, um eine Predigt, die »freshly created«[62] war, zu goutieren.[63] Doch solchen Luxus konnten sich nur wenige leisten, und so spendeten die Pragmatiker mit der Weisheit des Sprichwortes Trost, es sei einstweilen, bevor jede Gemeinde mit einem selbsttätig predigenden Pfarrer versorgt ist, allemal besser, man besitze einen halben Laib als gar kein Brot.[64]

---

[59] Symptomatisch erscheint das Beispiel des Tübinger Kontroverstheologen Tobias Wagner (1598–1680), dessen Verleger nur dann bereit war, die schwer verkäuflichen Streitschriften Wagners zu drucken, wenn er von diesem weiterhin mit offenbar sehr viel besser laufender Postillen- und Erbauungsliteratur versorgt würde (vgl. ALBRECHT BEU-TEL, Lehre und Leben in der Predigt der lutherischen Othodoxie. Dargestellt am Beispiel des Tübinger Kontroverstheologen und Universitätskanzlers Tobias Wagner, in: DERS., Protestantische Konkretionen [s. Anm. 47], 161–191, hier: 172 f.).

[60] Vgl. The two Books of Homilies appointed to be Read in the Churches, hg. v. John Griffiths, Oxford 1859.

[61] Vgl. HUGHES, Theology (s. Anm. 13), 122 f.; EDWARDS, A History (s. Anm. 2), 357–359; CARLSON, The Boring (s. Anm. 3), 278–282.

[62] EDWARDS, A History (s. Anm. 2), 359.

[63] Solche Ausbrüche aus der parochialen Zugehörigkeit und dem Verantwortungs-bereich des Ortspfarrers wurden gelegentlich sanktioniert (vgl. MATTHEW MILNER, The Senses and the English Reformation, Farnham 2011, 309).

[64] »Better half a loaf than no bread« (EDMUND GRINDAL, The Remains, hg. v. William Nicholson, Cambridge 1843, 382 f.).

Die großen Reformatoren predigten beständig, Zwingli nahezu täglich, Luther selbst bei angegriffener Gesundheit und neben aller anderen Arbeit gewöhnlich drei- bis viermal pro Woche, in Extremzeiten bis zu viermal am Tag.[65] Dementsprechend ermahnten sie alle evangelischen Pfarrer,[66] in ihrer kontinuierlichen Arbeit auch unter widrigen Umständen niemals müde zu werden. Samuel Hieron fasste diese homiletische Treuepflicht in das drastische Bild, ein gefangener Fisch zapple verzweifelt, um sich wieder aus dem Boot zu werfen, zurück in das Meer der Unwissenheit, des Elends und der Sünde.[67] Daneben gebrauchte man gern auch agrarische Bilder: Der Prediger, hieß es bei Greenham, gleiche dem Bauern, der sich nicht mit der einmaligen Aussaat begnügen kann, sondern die Felder das ganze Jahr über betreuen und pflegen muss.[68]

Berühmtheit erlangte die *Predigt vom Pflug*, die Latimer am 18. Januar 1548 in London vortrug.[69] Gleichnishaft und bibelnah erklärte er das Wort Gottes zum Saatgut, die Gemeinde zum Acker, der bestellt werden soll, und den Pfarrer zum Landmann. Als solcher, fuhr Latimer fort, habe er das ganze Jahr über zu tun, müsse nach der Aussaat beständig weiterarbeiten, gleichwie der Prediger beständig gefordert sei, hier das Gesetz und dort das Evangelium zu verkünden, hier zu ermahnen, dort zu trösten, zu lehren, die Herzen zu erwecken und vieles mehr. Deshalb sei die Predigt so notwendig wie das tägliche Brot – und nicht wie die Erdbeere, die nur einmal heranreift und rasch verdirbt.

»Therefore preach and teach, and let your plough be doing«.[70]

Daraufhin präsentierte Latimer der Gemeinde ein erstaunliches Ratespiel.

»Wer«, fragte er, »ist in ganz England der fleißigste Prediger? Wer investiert alle Kraft in sein geistliches Amt? Wer hat in seiner Verkündigung den größten Erfolg?«

Weil damals die Dialogpredigt noch nicht erfunden war, gab Latimer die Antwort selbst:

---

[65] Vgl. BEUTEL, Art. Bibelübersetzungen (s. Anm. 42), 297f.

[66] Deren Zahl lässt sich für die Anfangszeit kaum ermessen. Aus England ist bekannt, dass Latimer, als er 1535 Bischof von Worcester wurde, dort bereits eine Gruppe von evangelisch gesinnten Geistlichen vorfand (vgl. CLAIRE CROSS, Church and People 1450–1660. The Triumph of the Laity in the English Church, Fontana 1976, 76).

[67] Zit. nach CARLSON, The Boring (s. Anm. 3), 270.

[68] Vgl. KENNETH L. PARKER, ERIC J. CARLSON, »Practical Divinity«: The Works and Life of Reverend Richard Greenham, Ashgate 1998, 147.

[69] HUGH LATIMER, Sermon of the Plough (in: The Works of Hugh Latimer [s. Anm. 16], 59–78).

[70] A.a.O., 65.

»Es ist der Teufel! Er ist der beliebteste Prediger von allen, er verlässt niemals seine Gemeinde [...]; rufe nach ihm, wann immer du willst, er ist stets zu Hause, [...] er steht immer hinter seinem Pflug«.[71]

Darum, schloss Latimer, sollten sich die faulen Prediger ein Beispiel am Teufel nehmen, ihre Arbeit ebenso gewissenhaft verrichten und in beständigem Eifer das Korn der guten Lehre auswerfen.[72] Diese persuasive Verwegenheit mag ein Spezifikum der englischen Kanzelrhetorik sein; für Luther, in dessen Predigten der Teufel ebenfalls oft zu Gast war, ließe sich eine solche pastoralpädagogische Inanspruchnahme des Bösen kaum denken.

In der homiletischen Zielbestimmung, die Hörer nicht etwa nur frontal zu belehren, sondern ihnen eine aktive Rezeptivität abzuverlangen, sie also zu eigenem Verstehen anzuleiten und zur individuellen Applikation der Predigtbotschaft herauszufordern,[73] kamen die Reformatoren allesamt überein. Bei Calvin, der im Regelfall manuskriptfrei annähernd eine Stunde zu predigen pflegte, ging es anspruchsvoll zu: Neben einem gewissen Hang zur Gesetzlichkeit stellte auch die nicht immer stringente Gedankenführung eine rezeptive Erschwernis dar. Demgegenüber predigte Luther unmittelbar hörernah. Unter Verzicht auf kunstvolle Ausformung und filigrane Gliederungssystematik, wie sie später in der altprotestantischen Predigtkunst üblich wurde, benannte er meist unvermittelt den zentralen Predigtgedanken, den er dann vielfach variierend umkreiste. Seine Sprache war schlicht und plastisch, bisweilen derb, doch stets von erdhafter Lebendigkeit, die er durch fiktive Dialogisierung noch zu steigern wusste. Eine narrative Verwässerung des Evangeliums war ihm zuwider. Dagegen hat er die metaphorisch-allegorische Rede nicht nur predigtpraktisch geschätzt, sondern sie als ein unverzichtbares Kommunikationsmittel auch theoretisch gewürdigt: Die Gleichnisrede galt ihm als »ein seiden tuchlein, do ich den verstand deste bas einfasse und behalt«.[74] Bei jedem Predigttext zielte Luther darauf ab, der Gemeinde den biblischen Stoff als ihren eigenen aktuellen, christologisch fundierten Lebens- und Glaubensraum zu eröffnen. Das verlieh seiner Kanzelarbeit eine gewisse Gleichförmigkeit und bot, gepaart mit seinem unmittelbar ansprechenden rhetorischen Talent, den Hörern höchst unterhaltsame Monotonie.[75]

---

[71] A.a.O., 70.

[72] A.a.O., 77f.

[73] Die Rede von dem den Predigthörern zugemuteten »eare-labour« prägte Henry Smith (HENRY SMITH, The Sermons, London 1593, 640). Vgl. die erhellende Arbeit von ARNOLD HUNT, The Art of Hearing. English Preachers and Their Audiences, 1590–1640, Cambridge 2010.

[74] WA 36,640,8f. (1532).

Auch der englischen Reformationspredigt war, wie es das *Book of Common Prayer* (1549) programmatisch darlegte,[76] an einer aktiven Rezeptionsleistung der Gemeinde gelegen. Im Bewusstsein der eschatologischen Verantwortung, die ein Prediger trug, neigte man nicht selten zu starkem emotionalen Engagement. Von Greenham wurde berichtet, er habe sein Hemd in jeder Kanzelrede so vollständig durchgeschwitzt, als hätte man es aus dem Wasser gezogen.[77] Durch diese schonungslose affektive Hingabe wirkten seine Predigten mitunter geradezu überwältigend. Einmal, während er auf der Kanzel stand, brach eine Frau in lautes, verzweifeltes Schluchzen aus, weil sie sich als eine verdammte Seele zu erkennen meinte. Daraufhin unterbrach Greenham die Predigt, stieg von der Kanzel herab, ging zu ihr hin und beruhigte sie mit den Worten: »Sei getrost, du hast die Sünde gesehen, gleich wirst du von der Vergebung der Sünde hören«.[78] Gemäßigter temperierte Gemüter suchten sich für das »tricky business«,[79] das die Predigt darstellte, vorab zu wappnen. Elnathan Parr unterschied dabei vor allem zwei Risiken: Wenn man die Hörer zu milde anspreche, verharrten sie in der Sünde; wenn man sie aber zu hart angehe, würden sie widerspenstig oder stürzten in heillose Verzweiflung.[80] Um solcher Gefahr zu begegnen, riet John Frewen, sich als Prediger jederzeit um eine liebevolle, väter- und mütterliche Affektation zu bemühen.[81]

Dies schloss eine klare, unverblümte, konkret eindeutige Kanzelsprache keineswegs aus. So zog Zwingli in unerschrockener Direktheit gegen die in Zürich waltende Sittenverderbnis zu Felde und scheute dabei nicht einmal die namentliche Anklage einzelner Stadtbürger. Auch Luther hat sich als Prediger immer wieder zu brennenden Zeitfragen geäußert, wobei er den Konflikt mit der Obrigkeit, wo er ihm nötig schien, durchaus nicht

---

[75] Vgl. ZSCHOCH, Predigten (s. Anm. 12); ALBRECHT BEUTEL, Verdanktes Evangelium. Das Leitmotiv von Luthers Predigtwerk (in: DERS., Spurensicherung. Studien zur Identitätsgeschichte des Protestantismus, Tübingen 2013, 63–78).

[76] Vgl. GASSMANN, Die Lehrentwicklung im Anglikanismus (s. Anm. 43), 362f.

[77] Vgl. SAMUEL CLARKE, The Life of Master Richard Greenham, London ³1677, 12.

[78] PARKER, CARLSON, Practical Divinity (s. Anm. 68), 252.

[79] CARLSON, The Boring (s. Anm. 3), 266.

[80] »In this, two sorts of Ministers much faile: First, those which are so tender and studious to please, that they are loath to speake any but sweet words, though men rot in their sinnes. Secondly, those which are as farre on the other extreme, accounting all prefacing and loving speaking to be dawbing, and no sentence to be zealously delivered, unlesse Damnation and damned be at the end of it: whereby many times they drive them farther from Christ, whom they would have converted unto him« (The Workes of [...] Elnathan Parr [s. Anm. 34], 74).

[81] JOHN FREWEN, Certain Fruitfull Instructions and Necessary Doctrines meete to Edify in the Fear of God, London 1587, 294.

scheute.[82] Stärker als die sozialkritischen Themen war in seinen Kanzelreden freilich die kontroverstheologische Polemik präsent, so dass seine Hörer bisweilen den Eindruck gewinnen mochten, der römische Papst residiere heimlich in Wittenberg. Das Motiv der durch antithetische Abgrenzung gestärkten eigenen Konfessionsidentität war auch in englischen Predigten der Reformationszeit allgegenwärtig.

Gleichwohl erscheint der Eindruck nicht unbegründet, als habe dort der sozialkritische Aspekt die Predigtanliegen noch wesentlich stärker beherrscht. Dass ein Prediger die Sünde in allen Sorten und Graden benennen müsse, ohne auf den gesellschaftlichen Stand der Beklagten Rücksicht zu nehmen, war eine vielfältig wiederholte Ermahnung.[83] Überhaupt scheint bei den englischen Reformationspredigern das Sündenthema in hoher Beliebtheit gestanden zu haben. Neben diversen individuellen Verfehlungen traten dabei insbesondere drei sozialkritische Beschwerden hervor. So wurde vielfach der Missbrauch des Landes als Spekulationsobjekt angeprangert, desgleichen die wachsende strukturelle Not des arbeitenden Bauernstandes.[84] Darüber hinaus war es das frühkapitalistische Zins- und Wucherwesen, das die großen Prediger oft als eine evangeliumswidrige Störung der von Gott gesetzten Gesellschaftsordnung beklagten. Zumal in dieser Hinsicht genossen die reformatorischen Pfarrer bald hohes allgemeines Ansehen. So fand die von Thomas Wilson 1572 veröffentlichte Schrift *A Discourse Upon Usury* rasche Verbreitung. In Gestalt eines platonischen Dialogs diskutieren darin ein evangelischer Geistlicher, ein Jurist und ein Kaufmann über das Thema des Wuchers. Während sich der Jurist um kasuistische Differenzierung bemüht und der Kaufmann die gewerbliche Notwendigkeit eines überhöhten Zinssatzes unterstreicht, entlarvt der Pfarrer den Wucher im Rückgriff auf das Neue Testament und

---

[82] Vgl. beispielsweise Luthers Predigt über 1.Joh. 5,4ff. vom 13.4.1539 (WA 47,721–730), in der er die Gemeinde darüber aufklärte, die gegenwärtige Angst vor Hans Kolhase werde von den Grundherren ganz bewusst geschürt, weil sie damit die drastische Anhebung des Getreidepreises legitimieren wollten; während sie Kolhase als einen Strohmann aufbauten, plünderten sie ärger als jeder »Landstrassen Reuber« das eigene Volk, weshalb man sie nicht einmal mehr Säue und Kühe heißen könne, sondern nur noch »morder, Teuffel, landsfeind« (a.a.O., 725,6–8). Vgl. dazu ALBRECHT BEUTEL, Luther und Kolhase. Eine Fallstudie zur cura conscientiae des Reformators (in: DERS., Reflektierte Religion. Beiträge zur Geschichte des Protestantismus, Tübingen 2007, 1–20, hier: 15).

[83] »For as god, a most righteous judge, will punish all sin, so must His preachers indifferently warn and rebuke all sorts of sinners; or else God will require their blood and their hands, if they perish without their warning« (JAMES PILKINGTON, The Works, hg. v. James Scholefield, Cambridge 1842, 98f.).

[84] Vgl. PAUL MEISSNER, England im Zeitalter von Humanismus, Renaissance und Reformation, Heidelberg 1952, 402–404.

altkirchliche Autoritäten als ein Zeichen der Endzeit. Damit vermag er die Disputanten dann auch zu überzeugen, der Jurist verstummt kleinlaut, und der Kaufmann, frisch bekehrt, sieht die Zinsnahme nun auf einer Stufe mit der Straßenräuberei. Es dürfte mentalitätsgeschichtlich aufschlussreich sein, dass der Figur des evangelischen Predigers auch im literarischen, also außerkirchlichen Raum bald die höchste moralische Reputation und Überzeugungskraft zuerkannt wurde.[85]

Unter den englischen Reformationspredigern kommt Latimer gewiss besondere Bedeutung zu;[86] der Kirchenhistoriker Horton Davies attestierte ihm mit guten Gründen »a popular preaching at its best«.[87] Latimer hatte in Cambridge Erasmus persönlich kennengelernt und sich früh mit den Schriften Luthers auseinandergesetzt. Bereits 1529 trat er entschieden für das von Luther erneuerte Konzept der Glaubensgerechtigkeit ein.[88] Allerdings legte er auf die Feststellung Wert, er sei nicht durch Luther, sondern durch Thomas Bilney zu evangelischer Einsicht gelangt.[89] Dabei musste Latimer gewusst haben, dass Bilney seinerseits nicht zuletzt durch lutherisches Gedankengut zu seinen evangelischen Überzeugungen gebracht worden war.[90] In vorgerücktem Alter fand Latimer zu einer entspannten Würdigung des Reformators von Wittenberg.[91]

Als Prediger zeichnete er sich durch klare biblische Fundierung aus,[92] ferner durch die Vorliebe für lebensweltliche Exempel und Anekdoten,

---

[85] Vgl. das Kurzreferat der Schrift a.a.O., 396f.

[86] Vgl. etwa ALLAN G. CHESTER, Hugh Latimer. Apostle to the English, Oxford u.a. 1954; DAVID M. LOADES, The Oxford Martyrs, London 1970; ARTHUR F. BUTLER, Hugh Latimer. The Religious Thought of a Reformation Preacher, Ann Arbor 1980; NATALIE A. GALDI, Hugh Latimer. Humanism and The English Reformation, Ann Arbor 1980.

[87] HORTON DAVIES, Worship and Theology in England, Bd. 1: From Cranmer to Hooker, 1534–1603, Princeton 1970, 248.

[88] »Now then, if men be so foolish of themselves, that they will bestow the most part of their goods in voluntary works, which they be not bound to keep, but willingly and by their devotion; and leave the necessary works undone, which they are bound to do; they and all their voluntary works are like to go unto everlasting damnation« (The Works of Hugh Latimer [s. Anm. 16], 23).

[89] HAIGH, English Reformations (s. Anm. 3), 58f.

[90] Vgl. mitsamt den dort gebotenen Hinweisen auf die Sekundärliteratur MARIE-LUISE EHRENSCHWENDTNER, Art. Bilney, Thomas (in: RGG[4] 1, 1998, 1598f.).

[91] »I will not stand to it that all that he wrote was true; I think he would not so himself: for there is no man but he may err. He came to further and further knowledge: but surely he was a goodly instrument« (zit. nach ROBERT DEMAUS, Hugh Latimer. A Biography, London 1903, 183).

[92] Das lutherische Sola-scriptura-Prinzip (vgl. ALBRECHT BEUTEL, »Sola scriptura mus sein«. Begründung und Gebrauch des Schriftprinzips bei Martin Luther, in: Sola scriptura heute? Rekonstruktionen – Kritiken – Transformationen, hg. v. Stefan Alkier, Tübingen 2019, 29–58) teilte Latimer vollauf.

durch geschärfte sprachliche Sensibilität und feinen Humor. So erzählte er angelegentlich von einer Frau in London, die stets einen bestimmten Prediger aufsuchte, weil sie unter dessen Kanzel am leichtesten Schlaf finden konnte. Anstatt solchen Missbrauch zu tadeln, nahm Latimer die schlafgestörte Frau nicht bloß in Schutz, sondern ehrte sie sogar durch den Vergleich mit Augustin, der die Predigten des Ambrosius zunächst ebenfalls aus unwürdigen Motiven aufgesucht habe und gleichwohl von ihnen bekehrt worden sei.[93] Wenn seine frei gehaltenen Kanzelreden zu lang gerieten – und sie gerieten fast immer zu lang –, pflegte Latimer sie manchmal durch ein Gebet zu unterbrechen. Im Unterschied zu Luther hielt er meist an der Gattung der Themapredigt fest und fokussierte seine Predigtbotschaften nicht durchweg auf Christus.

Beachtung verdient überdies, dass Latimer manchmal sogar die Predigtlehre zum Predigtgegenstand machte. Seine letzte, 1550 vor Eduard VI. vorgetragene Predigt[94] kann dafür als symptomatisch gelten. Hier deutete er die Bußrede, die der Profet Jona den Menschen von Ninive hielt (Jon. 3), als einen homiletischen Musterfall: Jona war allein, er predigte nur kurz, verzichtete auf allen rhetorischen Prunk, auf kuriose Geschichten und Pfaffengehabe und sprach klar zur Sache, woraufhin sich unter dem Eindruck seiner Predigt die ganze Stadt bekehrte. Von diesem Ideal sah Latimer die meisten seiner Berufskollegen sehr weit entfernt. Deren Gemeinden verharrten in Sünde, weil die Kanzelreden, die sie hörten, viel zu ausführlich und zu selbstgefällig gerieten, auch weil sie im Überfluss offeriert würden und weil, dies zumal, die gegenwärtigen Prediger aus falsch verstandener Diskretion unangemessene Rücksicht nähmen auf die Persönlichkeit ihrer Hörer. Die Schlussfolgerung war vernichtend: Würde Jona damals so gepredigt haben, wie es im gegenwärtigen England üblich ist, er wäre in dem Auftrag, mit dem ihn Gott nach Ninive gesandt hatte, kläglich gescheitert.[95] Als Adressaten hatte Latimer in diesem Fall den König zwar nicht in Person, aber als Haupt der Kirche von England und ganz gewiss auch die späteren Leser der gedruckten Predigt vor Augen. In den Fürstenpredigten deutscher Reformatoren düften solche breiten predigtreflexiven Ausführungen schwerlich zu finden ein.

Die Erfahrung, dass der treue Kirchgang nicht selbstverständlich war und die physische Teilnahme am Gottesdienst nicht notwendig auch auf intellektuelle Partizipation schließen ließ, wurde von allen Reformatoren geteilt. Dass Luther zu Beginn des Jahres 1530 in einen drei Monate an-

---

[93] Vgl. The Works of Hugh Latimer (s. Anm. 16), 201 f.
[94] A.a.O., 239–281.
[95] A.a.O., 239–242.

dauernden Predigtstreik trat,[96] war als Ausdruck einer gemeindepädago-
gischen *ultima ratio* zu verstehen, selbst wenn man dabei seine besondere
charakterliche Disposition nicht außer Acht lassen sollte. Auch machte er
sich über den Rezeptionsbedarf seiner Hörer keinerlei Illusionen:

»Wenn man articulum iustificationis predigt«, klagte er einmal bei Tisch, »so
schlefft das volck und huset; si autem inceperis historiam aut exemplum, tum
arrectis auribus cum summo silentio attendunt«.[97]

Dass Luther die Menschen inmitten solcher Frustrationen weiterhin zu
beständigem Kirchgang anhielt, war für ihn gleichwohl selbstverständlich.

Es scheint, als sei Latimer darüber hinaus auch auf sophistische Wider-
stände gestoßen. Jedenfalls widmete er sich solchen Einwänden, die in
theologischer Bemäntelung auftraten, eingehend. So referierte er etwa das
Argument, wenn die Heiligung das Werk von Gottes verborgenem Wirken
im Herzen sei, könne er solches Werk doch auch außerhalb der Predigt
verrichten. Latimer erwiderte darauf in der ihm eigenen, den Gegner *ad
absurdum* führenden Weise: Freilich, gab er zu, kann Gott mein Leben
auch ohne Essen und Trinken erhalten, aber treten wir deshalb in einen
Hungerstreik? Und freilich kann Gott mich aus dem Feuer erretten, aber
laufe ich deshalb vorsätzlich in die Flammen hinein?[98] Die Gegenfragen
ergingen selbstverständlich rhetorisch, und deshalb, schloss Latimer, solle
man beim Leibes- und Seelenerhalt jederzeit diejenigen Wege wahren, die
Gott uns dazu verordnet hat.[99]

Einen weiteren Einwand quittierte er wiederum dialogisch.[100] Der Frage, ob unsere Vorfahren, da ihnen nicht evangelische Prediger, sondern nur
falsche Lehren verfügbar waren, wohl allesamt als verdammt gelten müssten, hielt er den Hinweis entgegen, es stünden Gott durchaus verschiedene
Möglichkeiten zu Gebote, einen Menschen zu retten. Wäre dann aber,
fasste der fiktive Gesprächspartner nach, nicht auch heute die für die Predigt reklamierte soteriologische Exklusivität zu bezweifeln? Darauf repli-
zierte Latimer mit geschichtstheologischer Gegenwartsdeutung: Durch die
Reformation habe Gott für sein den evangelischen Predigern aufgetragenes
Wort die Tore des Himmels geöffnet. Wer dieses Heilsangebot mit pseu-
dotheologischem Räsonnement zu relativieren suche, der verweigere sich

---

[96] MARTIN BRECHT, Martin Luther, Bd. 2: Ordnung und Abgrenzung der Reformation 1521–1532, Stuttgart 1986, 280f.
[97] WA.TR 2,454,17–19 (1532).
[98] The Works of Hugh Latimer (s. Anm. 16), 306.
[99] »I must keep the way that God hath ordained, and use the ordinary means that
God hath assigned, and not seek new ways. This office of preaching is the only ordinary
way that God hath appointed to save us all by. Let us maintain this, for I know no other;
neither think I God will appoint or devise any other« (ebd.).
[100] A.a.O., 525–528.

dem geoffenbarten Willen Gottes und verharre damit mutwillig in sündiger Selbstüberhebung.[101]

Andere englische Reformationstheologen, so etwa John Jewel[102] oder William Jones,[103] waren offenbar ganz ähnlichen Einwänden ausgesetzt. Auch sie verwiesen dann wie Latimer auf die exklusive Heilsmittlerschaft, die Gott dem evangelischen Predigtamt verliehen habe. Durchmustert man ihre Antworten aufmerksam, fällt allerdings auf, dass sie dieser Auskunft jedesmal das Adjektiv ›ordinary‹ noch hinzufügten. Dies indizierte keineswegs ein stilles Einlenken auf die Argumente der predigtmüden Sophistiker, sondern wollte allein die absolute Souveränität Gottes gewahrt wissen.[104] Damit war die schiere Instrumentalität, die das Selbstverständnis der reformatorischen Prediger auszeichnete, abermals eindrücklich unterstrichen.

Das mag als ein provisorischer Überblick zur deutschen und englischen Predigtkultur der Reformationszeit einstweilen genügen. Wenn dabei ausnahmslos die Vertreter der theologischen Avantgarde berücksichtigt wurden, so gründet dies nicht in der Absicht eines elitären Themenzugriffs, sondern in der Defizienz der verfügbaren Wissensbestände. Wie damals in Stackelitz und Romsey, in Kursachsen und England, im Kanton Zürich und in Schottland flächendeckend, bis in die kleinsten Dörfer hinein, tatsächlich gepredigt worden ist, davon wissen wir bis heute noch immer so gut wie nichts.

---

[101] »In our time, God hath sent light into the world; he had opened the gates of heaven unto us by his word; which word be opened unto us by his officers, by his preachers; shall we now despise the preachers? Shall we refuse to hear God's word, to learn the way to heaven, and require him to save us without his word? No, no; for when we do so, we tempt God, and shall be damned world without end« (a.a.O., 528).

[102] HUGHES, Theology (s. Anm. 13), 125.

[103] JONES, Commentary (s. Anm. 35), 633.

[104] CARLSON, The Boring (s. Anm. 3), 277f.

Preaching

Albrecht Beutel

Sibling harmony always thrives best when it is based on distinct internal differentiation. The self-evidence of this life maxim is difficult to dispute and applies equally to families and reformations. Anyone who forces the inherent particularity that structures each relational analogy into a stark antithesis is disqualified as communicatively and relationally dysfunctional.

Comparative historical research on the Reformation has already overcome such inadequate theories for decades. The thesis that the Reformation in Germany was initiated from below through a grass roots preaching movement, whereas in England it was induced from above by a sovereign »act of state«,[1] has long been irreparably shattered by the complexity of the historical facts. For it is well known that magisterial protection and support measures also played a decisive role in Germany, even though they were not implemented by a central authority but by numerous »acts of state«.[2] And in England Protestant preaching was not an after-effect, but decisively accompanied and enabled the decision to proclaim the king »Protector and Supreme Head of the English Church and Clergy«. In this respect, preaching topics should prove an excellent indicator to gauge the internal differentiations between the English and German sister Reformations.[3]

---

[1] FREDERIC MAURICE POWICKE, The Reformation in England, Oxford 1941, 1.

[2] OTIS CARL EDWARDS, A History of Preaching, Nashville 2004, 351.

[3] For the German speaking area see the overviews that provide abundant reference literature: ALBRECHT BEUTEL, art. Predigt VIII. Evangelische Predigt vom 16. bis 18. Jahrhundert (in: TRE 27, 1997, 296–311); ID., art. Predigt II. Geschichte der Predigt (in: RGG⁴ 6, 2003, 1585–1591); ID. et al., art. Predigt (in: Historisches Wörterbuch der Rhetorik 7, 2005, 45–96). For the English-speaking areas see particularly: PHILIP EDGCUMBE HUGHES, Theology of the English Reformers, London 1965, 119–188; CHRISTOPHER MATTINSON DENT, Protestant Reformers in Elizabethan Oxford, Oxford 1983, 201–220 (passim); CHRISTOPHER HAIGH, English Reformations. Religion, Politics, and Society under the Tudors, Oxford 1993, 268–283 (passim); ERIC JOSEF CARLSON, The Boring of the Ear: Shaping the Pastoral Vision of Preaching in England, 1540–1640 (in: Preachers and People in the Reformations and Early Modern Period, ed. Larissa Taylor, Leiden et al. 2001, 249–296); ANNE T. THAYER, Penitence, Preaching and the Coming of the Reformation, Aldershot 2002; EDWARDS, A History (see note 2), 350–387.

Without wanting to obscure the historical context, the following will focus on the generation of respective Reformation founders and, more precisely, on the master preachers: Martin Luther and Hugh Latimer. This limitation is not prompted by alliterative reasons but solely economic ones. Thus, it would be pertinent to first identify with broad strokes the main characteristics of the Reformation doctrine of preaching, then the complementary phenomenon of vernacular Bible translations, and finally the practice of Reformation preaching as carried out in the two respective movements.

1. The Relevance of the Word of God
for the Theology of preaching

The soteriological centrality of the Word of God proved to be the *proprium* of Reformation theology. To underline this new programmatic orientation, the traditional manner of preaching was cast in a very negative light. The fact that the Bible in the papacy was »under the bench in the dust«[4] had become a catchphrase for Luther since 1520.[5] As a necessary consequence of this contempt, Luther descried an almost complete silencing of the preaching of the Gospel. This corresponded with the findings of the English Reformers. Most of the pulpits, Bernard Gilpin lamented, were covered with dust, and – of the few sermons one could hear – exceedingly few deserved to even be called »sermons«.[6] Of course, such generalizations were highly polemical and unjust. The late medieval homiletical culture was in its heyday, and scripture-based preaching in England was practiced continuously, particularly by the Lollards.[7]

These necessary qualifications do not in the least diminish the Reformation as a new awakening. For now, unlike in the past, the *verbum praedicatum* was programmatically declared to be the central constituent factor of every service. It was, Luther urged,

---

[4] »unter der banck ym stawb«: WA 6,460,18f. (1520). Compare LW 44,204 and LW 31,76.

[5] For additional evidence: STEFAN MICHEL, Die Kanonisierung der Werke Luthers im 16. Jahrhundert, Tübingen 2016, 20, n. 10.

[6] »A thousand pulpits in England are covered with dust. Some have not had four sermons these fifteen or sixteen years [...] and few of those were worthy of the name of sermon« (Bernard Gilpin, 1552; cited in CARLSON, The Boring [see note 3], 249).

[7] For pre-Reformation preaching in England see, for example, GERALD ROBERT OWST, Preaching in Medieval England: A Introduction to Sermon Manuscripts of the Period c. 1350–1450, Cambridge 1926; EAMON DUFFY, The Stripping of the Altars. Traditional Religion in England c. 1400–c. 1580, New Haven and London 1992; EDWARDS, A History (see note 2), 210–282.

»auffs erst tzu wissen, das die Christlich gemeyne nymer soll zu samen komen, es werde denn da selbs Gottis wort gepredigt [...] es sey auch auffs kurtzist« (it is to be known first of all that a Christian congregation should never gather together without the preaching of God's Word and prayer, no matter how briefly).[8]

Of course, the Reformers in Zurich and Geneva also shared this core principle.[9] Thus, the sermon, from being a »special event« in the late Middle Ages,[10] became the norm of Reformation liturgy, and the functional definition of ecclesiastical ministry transformed accordingly – from priest to preacher, from custodian of grace to teacher of the Word of God.[11]

The central continuity of the sermon was of great significance for the formation process of the congregations of the early Reformation; its complementary function of an outward-looking fixation on differences and an inward-facing homogenization contributed decisively to the formation of denominational identity.

The late medieval pulpits were dominated by the topical sermon, which was largely determined by the church's moral and institutional doctrine. While the Reformation did not bid farewell to the genre of the topical sermon,[12] it placed this genre far beneath the textual exegesis of the Bible. Thus, the divine *verbum scriptum* should not merely be interpreted for clarification, but should – in the form of the divine *verbum praedicatum* – be conveyed afresh in the original oral state of the Gospel. However, the essential prerequisite for the word to be understood sacramentally was that the preacher should make the word of God present in an unmixed form: whatever he says, John Jewel exhorted, must be based on the Bible alone.[13] With that he connected the assurance that we should say nothing

---

[8] WA 12,35,19–21 (1523). Compare LW 53,11.

[9] DOROTHEA WENDEBOURG, Reformation und Gottesdienst (in: ZThK 113, 2016, 323–365, here: 324–5).

[10] ANDREW PETTEGREE, Reformation and the Culture of Persuasion, Cambridge 2005, 16: »In the years before the Reformation the sermon never lost its sense of being a special event.«

[11] *The Bishop's Book* (1537) named the supreme duty of the clergy »to preach and teach the word of God unto his people« (cited in Carlson, The Boring [see note 3], 260). Accordingly, the catechism of Thomas Becon said »The first and principal point of a bishop's and a spiritual minister's office [is] to teach and preach the Word of God« (THOMAS BECON, The Early Works, ed. John Ayre, vol. 1, Cambridge 1843, 320).

[12] We only need to consider Luther's *Invocavit Sermons* (WA 10/3,1–64 [1522]). For Luther's preaching insights and practices cf. ALBRECHT BEUTEL, In dem Anfang war das Wort. Studien zu Luthers Sprachverständnis, Tübingen 1991, 352–357, 468–472 (passim); HELLMUT ZSCHOCH, Predigten (in: Luther Handbuch, ed. Albrecht Beutel, Tübingen ³2017, 358–365); ROLAND M. LEHMANN, Reformation auf der Kanzel. Luthers Predigten außerhalb Wittenbergs, Habil. masch., Jena 2018.

[13] HUGHES, Theology of the English Reformers (see note 3), 121.

in the pulpit but what the church fathers, the apostles, and Christ himself have said before us.[14] In Luther, we find a literal parallel to this demand for continuity, admittedly with the sole difference that he did not mention the church fathers.[15] Latimer warned against enriching the preaching of the word of God with human dreams and inventions;[16] this is analogous to the famous blue ducks that Luther attributed to the story of a pompous preacher[17] in a glaring, yet fitting depiction. Incidentally, there was agreement in Cambridge and Wittenberg that the people's ingratitude and disinterest should not provoke the preacher to resignation, but on the contrary, to stronger homiletical efforts.[18] Biblical sermons, it was agreed, are always delivered irrespective of the person, neither with regard for the preacher – who is by nature eager for popularity and recognition – nor with regard for the listener, even if he were one's own prince[19] or king. A good preacher, Latimer knew, »corrects and criticizes even the king, he fears no man, but sets his sights on God alone.«[20]

Heinrich Bullinger's well-known phrase »praedicatio verbi dei est verbum dei«[21] set a basic consensus for the whole Reformation, which – regardless of any gradual nuances[22] – was encountered everywhere.[23] It

---

[14] »Remember, we are the sons of the prophets [...]. It is not our doctrine that we bring you this day; we wrote it not, we found it not out, we are not the inventors of it; we bring you nothing but what the old fathers of the Church, what the apostles, what Christ our Saviour Himself hath brought before us« (John Jewel, The Works, ed. John Ayre, vol. 2, Cambridge 1847, 1034).

[15] Cf. for example, WA 12,521,23–4 (1523); WA 43,536,27–8 (1530/32).

[16] »These be the properties of every good preacher: to be a true man; to teach, not dreams nor inventions of men, but *viam Dei in veritate*« (The Works of Hugh Latimer, ed. George Elwes Corrie, vol. 1, Cambridge 1844, 292).

[17] »Wo nicht geystlicher verstand und der geyst selbst redet durch die prediger [...] so kompts doch endlich dahyn, das ein iglicher predigen wird was er will, und an stat des Euangelii und seyner auslegunge widderumb von blaw endten gepredigt wird (WA 19,95,9–14 [1526]).

[18] HUGHES, Theology (see note 3), 122.

[19] Cf. WA.Br 10,33,17–27 (1542).

[20] »The preacher [...] must correct and reprove him [that is, the King] with the spiritual sword; fearing no man; setting God only before his eyes, under whom he is a minister, to supplant and root up all vice and mischief by God's word« (The Works of Hugh Latimer [see note 16], 86).

[21] Marginal note in: Confessio Helvetica Posterior I (BSRK 171).

[22] Cf. WENDEBOURG (see note 9), 328.

[23] Cf. for example the well-known sequence from Luther's writing *Wider Hans Worst*: »Ein Prediger mus nicht das Vater unser beten, noch Vergebung der sünden süchen, wenn er gepredigt hat (wo er ein rechter Prediger ist), Sondern mus [...] mit S. Paulo, allen Aposteln und Propheten trötzlich sagen: Haec dixit Dominus, Das hat Gott selbs gesagt [...]. Denn es ist Gottes und nicht mein wort, das mir Gott nicht vergeben sol noch kan, Sondern bestetigen, loben, krönen und sagen: Du hast recht geleret, Denn ich hab durch dich geredt, und das wort ist mein. Wer sich solchs nicht rhümen kan von seiner predigt, der lasse das predigen anstehen, Denn er leugt gewislich und lestert Gott«

was also found occasionally in a precise Christological sense, as for instance in Bishop Edwin Sandys' statement that:

»If you hear the pastor preaching the truth, then you do not hear him but the Son of God, the teacher of all truth, Jesus Christ.«[24]

Here, what serves the listener for reassurance of faith becomes basic homiletic education for the preacher. He should take Christ the preacher as an example[25] and both the biblical content and rhetorical form should adhere faithfully to this paradigm. Christ, Luther once taught at the table,

»taught to everyone in the simplest fashion and was the essence of eloquence. [...] Therefore the best and highest eloquence is to speak simply.«[26]

The Reformers transformed the plurality of Catholic offers of salvation into one single point: they considered the word of God that was currently being proclaimed to be the *medium salutis* par excellence. The Pauline *fides ex auditu* (Rom 10:17) served as the linchpin of Luther's doctrine of justification, which developed out of the fundamental relationship between word and faith. Latimer characterized the sermon simply as »God's instrument of salvation« and, accordingly, the ministry of preaching as »the office of salvation.«[27] The sacraments also formed a part of this word-based means of salvation: William Tyndale, representative in this respect, referred to their proper function as a »preaching function«[28]

In their choice of metaphors, German and English Reformers were of one accord. For Luther, the sermon offered nothing less than the keys to the kingdom of heaven;[29] for Richard Greenham it was considered »the gate of heaven«.[30] Sometimes, however, a significant variance in explana-

---

(WA 51,517,22–34 [1541]). For an analogous position in Calvin and the Scottish *First Book of Discipline* cf. WENDEBOURG (see note 9), 328, n. 24.

[24] The Sermons of Edwin Sandys, ed. John Ayre, Cambridge 1841, 278.

[25] »Christ is the preacher of all preachers, the pattern and the exemplar that all preachers ought to follow« (The Works of Hugh Latimer [see note 16], 155).

[26] Christus »hat am aller einfeltigsten geredt vnd war doch eloquentia selbst. [...] Drumb ists am besten vnd die hochste eloquentia simpliciter dicere«: WA.TR 4,664,22–24 (1540).

[27] The Works of Hugh Latimer (see note 16), 178. 349. Similarly, for example, Edmund Grindal: »If there be no salvation but by faith, no faith but by hearing the word of God, how should the people be saved without teachers?« (cited in HAIGH, English Reformations [see note 3], 269).

[28] HUGHES, Theology (see note 3), 132. John Jewel also recognized in the synopsis of preaching and sacraments that the proclamation of the Word of God was the »principalist part of this office« (JOHN JEWEL, The Works, ed. John Ayre, vol. 3, Cambridge 1848, 1130 seqq.).

[29] »Per hoc verbum aperitur coelum, remissio peccatorum consequitur« (WA 15,720,35–6 [1524]).

[30] Richard Greenham, The Workes, London 1605, 779. Likewise, Richard Hooker, who characterized the sermons as »the keyes to the kingdom of heaven« (RICHARD

tory styles was manifest. While the German-speaking pulpit orators preferred the style of discursive development, English Reformation theologians readily explained the need for salvation through a chain of successive syllogisms. For example, Arthur Dent concluded,

»No preaching, no faith; no faith, no Christ; no Christ, no eternall life.«[31]

Or likewise,

»Whoever wants to have heaven, must have Christ. Whoever wants to have Christ, must have faith. Whoever wants to have faith, must have preaching.«[32]

Particularly striking was the *scala coeli* formalized by Latimer. In taking up the prophetic words cited in Romans 10:13, »He who calls on the name of the Lord shall be saved« (Joel 3:5), Latimer directly adopted the Pauline interpretation (Rom 10:14),

»How shall they call upon him, in whom they have not believed? [...] How shall they believe in him, of whom they never heard? [...] How shall they hear without a preacher?«

To conclude this logical process that emulated the apostle, Latimer then presented the familiar formula:

»Take away preaching, take away salvation.«[33]

Thus, it was only natural when Elnathan Parr maintained that, after Christ, preaching represents the greatest blessing God has bestowed upon humankind.[34] However, not all Reformers resisted the danger of attributing an active mediating role to the person of the preacher. For instance, William Jones thought that a human being could only be saved by being carried to heaven on the preacher's shoulders.[35] To ward off such misguided conjecturing, Luther, Latimer, and many others underscored the mere instrumentality of the preacher; he was not appointed to be a self-empowered gatekeeper of heaven, but rather as a mere tool in the hands of God.[36] Luther depicted this in his oft-chosen dialogical form:

HOOKER, Of the Laws of Ecclesiastical Polity, The Folger Library Edition of the Works of Richard Hooker, vol. 2, ed. W. Speed Hill, Cambridge 1977, 87).

[31] ARTHUR DENT, The Plaine Mans Pathway to Heaven: wherein every man may clearly see whether hee shall saved or damned, London 1625, 336.

[32] Ibid., 336–37.

[33] The Works of Hugh Latimer (see note 16), 123.

[34] »Faith and the promised good things cannot be attained without preaching. Next to Christ, it is the greatest benefit which God hath given to men« (The Workes of [...] Elnathan Parr, London ⁴1651, 130–1).

[35] WILLIAM JONES, A Commentary upon the Epistles to Philemon, and to the Hebrews, London ²1636, 633.

[36] »Sumus instrumentum per linguam, per quam deus praedicat. Sic omnia officia in mundo ghen in gottlicher gestalt. Nos non sumus deus ut Christus, sed tantum particulam acquirimus gotlicher gstalt, da ghet die lere an, ut sua forma fiat servus« (WA

»To be sure, I do hear the sermon; however, I am wont to ask: ›Who is speaking?‹ The pastor? By no means! You do not hear the pastor. Of course, the voice is his, but the words he employs are really spoken by my God.«[37]

Analogously, Latimer contended that the preacher was instructed with no more than doing his duty faithfully – success was left to the hidden work of God alone:

»They can do not more but call; God is he that must bring in; God must open the hearts.«[38]

The divine *verbum praedicatum* seemed so indispensible to the Reformers that they did not want it to be necessarily confined within the ambit of the church. Although the pulpit always offers the best opportunity, if one is not available then any other place is equally suitable. Just as Jesus once preached even from a ship (Matt 13:1–9), so a good preacher, Latimer decided, could deliver the Word of God on a horse or sitting in a tree.[39] In Wittenberg, the matter was envisioned no differently. Even on the roof of a house, Luther opined, and even on the Elbe Bridge[40] or »under a green linden or willow tree«[41] the Gospel could, if necessary, be brought to the people. Modern liturgists may be surprised that even »worship in the open air« seems to be a legacy of the Reformation.

2. The Comprehensibility of the Word of God: Vernacular Translations of the Bible

With a cursory glance at Bible translations of the Reformation, one might think we risk moving our actual topic out of focus. However, by considering these translations more closely, our awareness of the Reformation

---

27,94,15–18 [1528]). According to Latimer »Preachers are Christ's vicars [...] [and] the mighty instrument of God« (The Works of Hugh Latimer [see note 16], 349).

[37] »Ich hore wohl die predigt, aber wer redet? Der pfarherr? Nicht also, du horest nicht den pfarherr. Die stimme ist wohl sein, aber das wortt, das ehr fhuret oder redet, das redet mein Gott« (WA 47,229,30–33 [1540]). Likewise ibid., 211,9–14: »Wenn ich dich schlechts hörete predigen, so gebe ich nicht einen Strohalm fur deine Predigt. Aber Gott redet da, ehr teuffet und wircket und ist selbst gegenwerttigk da. Derhalben so hat der prediger nicht für sein person gepredigt, sondern gott, der himlissche vater, und du soltest sagen: Ich hab gott selbst gesehen teuffen und das Sacrament des altars reichen und das wort hören predigen« (cf. LW 22, on John 4:9).

[38] The Works of Hugh Latimer (see note 16), 285.

[39] Ibid., 206.

[40] »Wu Gott redt, da wohnt ehr. Wo das wortt klingt, do ist Gott, do ist sein hauß. [...] Wen ehr auch klunge uff dem dach adder under dem dach, und gleich uff der elbbruckenn, ßo ists gewiß, das ehr do wohne« (WA 14,386,28–387,10 [1523/24]).

[41] WA 16,105,20 (1524); cf. 105,15–28.

understanding of preaching can be considerably sharpened. The *Volksbibel* and Protestant preaching represented complementary phenomena; they grew similarly in Germany and England out of the centering of salvation on the Word of God that the Reformers set in motion.

Of course, there were already vernacular translations of biblical books in the pre-Reformation period. They began in the German and English-speaking worlds (except for the Gothic Wulfila Bible) in the 8th century and flourished vigorously in the late Middle Ages. Whereas in this country the *Mentelin Bible* (1466) and the *Zainer Bible* (1485) were influential, on the British Isles it was the *Lollard Bible* (ca. 1380–1395). Shortly thereafter in Germany, the *Luther Bible* (NT 1522, full Bible 1534) was of revolutionary importance beyond the boundaries of Lutheranism – initially in Basel, Switzerland where Luther's New Testament was reprinted in 1522/23 and furnished with a glossary that was much needed there. Luther's translation also exerted influence through various plagiarized versions published by conservative Catholics.[42]

A nucleus of English Reformation theology can be traced to an inn in Cambridge where, since the beginning of the 1520s, a number of teachers and priests gathered to read and discuss Luther's publications. Renowned participants of this soon-to-be-called »Little Germany« pub circle were, for example, Miles Coverdale, Thomas Cranmer, Tyndale, and Latimer. Taking root here alongside new liturgical and doctrinal reflection were efforts to find a new English translation of the Bible. Whereas the Tyndale edition remained fragmentary in respect of the Old Testament, Coverdale was able to produce a full Bible in 1535 – from which the *Bishop's Bible* (1537) as well as the *Great Bible* (1540) arose a few years later. Now, Henry VIII issued the decree that an English Bible should be publicly displayed in every parish church and the parishioners should be encouraged to read it.[43]

In reality, the Reformation Bibles for the masses, with their efforts toward linguistic intelligibility, were aimed at making the Word of God in its authentic form directly accessible to every rudimentarily educated person. This endeavor would not only prove advantageous for private reli-

---

[42] Cf. ALBRECHT BEUTEL, art. Bibelübersetzungen. II. Christliche Übersetzungen in europäische Volkssprachen seit dem Mittelalter. 1. Übersetzungen in germanische Sprachen (in: RGG⁴ 1, 1998, 1498–1505).

[43] For example, GÜNTHER GASSMANN offers a good overview in: Die Lehrentwicklung im Anglikanismus. Von Heinrich VIII. bis zu William Temple (in: Handbuch der Dogmen- und Theologiegeschichte, ed. Carl Andresen, vol. 2, Göttingen 1988, 353–409, esp. 354–369); VIVIANE BARRIE-CURIEN, Die Reformation auf den Britischen Inseln (in: Die Zeit der Konfessionen [1530–1620/30], ed. Marc Vernard, Freiburg i.Br. et. al. 1992, 524–572, esp. 524–539).

gious edification but would also facilitate a biblical theological lay competence and, therewith, independent ability to judge the quality of sermons. The Reformers, at least in the early days, allocated to the church community the task of examining whether the doctrine of their pastors adhered to biblical standards. Preachers, warned Latimer, were only to be followed in so far as they themselves followed Christ.[44] Tyndale also made it a duty of the Christian laity to examine the message of their clergy with the biblical word of God and also, if need be, to admonish them.[45] Luther's claim »that a Christian congregation or community has the right and power to judge all teaching«[46] was not only valid within Wittenberg's sphere of influence but also on the main island of Britain.

At that time, unexpectedly and barely noticed or considered by the Reformers, a rivalry had broken out over the claim of exclusive mediation of salvation, a contention between the sermon, which claimed this for itself, and the sufficient authenticity of the word of God that the Bible postulated.[47] Luther sometimes circumvented the problem by pointing out that the sermon was a popular theological genre and, therefore, intended for Hänslein and Elslein, not for scholars like Philip Melanchthon.[48] Richard Hooker expressed it more generally and explained that reading the Bible and listening to the sermon were equivalent as paths to salvation.[49] Other English theologians agreed with him: reading the Bible, Martin Fotherby noted, is a most powerful form of the sermon, especially since it is concise, clear, and simply written; that which is often heard in the pulpits is simply long-winded, obscure, and out of touch.[50] Surprisingly, even Paul saw himself as called to be a key witness. John Downe explained

---

[44] »It is a dangerous thing to follow men; and we are not bound to follow them, further than they follow Christ. [...] Therefore let us follow them as they follow Christ [...]. So that we ought to follow them that teach the truth; but when they do naught, we should not follow them« (The Works of Hugh Latimer [see note 16], 514; cf. ibid., 523).

[45] The Works of the English Reformers: William Tyndale, and John Frith, ed. Thomas Russel, vol. 2, London 1831, 269–70.

[46] WA 11,408–416 (1523).

[47] Cf. ALBRECHT BEUTEL, Erfahrene Bibel. Verständnis und Gebrauch des verbum dei scriptum bei Luther (in: ID., Protestantische Konkretionen. Studien zur Kirchengeschichte, Tübingen 1998, 66–103).

[48] »Man sol auff der cantzel die zitzen herauß ziehen und daß volck mit milch trencken, den eß wechst alle tage eine newe kirch auff, quae indiget primis principiis. Drumb sal man nur den catechismum vleisig treiben und die milch außteylen; dj hohen gedancken und stucken soll man fur dj kluglinge privatim behalten. Ich wil Doctorem Pommeranum, Jonam, Philippum in meyner predigt nicht wissen, den sie wissens vorhin baß den ich. Ich predige ihnen auch nicht, sondern meinem Henslein und Elslein; illos observo« (WA.TR 3,310,5–12 [undated]).

[49] The Works of [...] Richard Hooker, ed. Isaak Walton, vol. 1, Oxford 1845, 493.

[50] MARTIN FOTHERBY, Foure Sermons, lately preached, London 1608, 28–29.

Paul's relevant *locus classicus* »Faith comes from hearing« (Rom 10:17) by using the empirical evidence of real life: Whoever receives a letter says that he has *heard* from someone. And, accordingly, with that phrase the apostle did not identify the sermon as the wellspring of faith (as Luther had interpreted it) but rather the reading of Holy Scriptures. A teacher of the church, Downe continued, could always be wrong in what he says, but the Bible – the written Word of God – never errs.[51]

For the future development of Reformation preaching, this problem of competition between the written and proclaimed word of God was of little consequence. Nevertheless, the dogmatic explanation and clarification of this emerging ambivalence in the theology of salvation remained a significant unfulfilled aspiration of Reformation theology.

3. The Mediation of the Word of God: On the Practice of Preaching

In Lutheran and English regions, preaching for the main Sunday service and feast days was largely based on the sequence of pericopes established in the old church. Ulrich Zwingli, in contrast, practiced from the beginning *lectio continua*, the successive reading of scripture. Luther only preferred *lectio continua* for the *Nebengottesdienste* (services without holy communion) unless he preached an interpretation of the *Small Catechism* there. The *Book of Common Prayer*,[52] first published in 1549, made the pericopes of the entire church year available.

An important, albeit only gradual, difference soon emerged in the practice of exegesis. Whereas the German Reformation charged every pastor with the duty of a theologically independent interpretation of the biblical sermon text, in England the license for independent preaching was granted very restrictively.[53] Admittedly, the pastors in Germany were hardly equal to the task at first; a corresponding educational reform and the production of ancillary homiletic literature got underway only slowly. Therefore, as a provisional alternative, Luther suggested that the postil sermons[54] publi-

---

[51] JOHN DOWNE, Certaine Treatises, Oxford 1633, 18–29.

[52] The Book of Common Prayer. The Texts of 1549, 1559, and 1662, ed. Brian Cummings, Oxford 2011.

[53] »England was unusual in a number of respects, not least in instituting a separate tier of licensed preachers as an individually selected subset of the parish ministry. Elsewhere in Protestant Europe it was taken for granted that a properly called minister would be a preaching minister« (PETTEGREE, Reformation [see note 10], 35).

[54] Only the Advent and Christmas portions (*Wartburgpostille*) stemmed from Luther's own hand (WA 10/1/2,1–208; WA 10/1/1,8–728 [1522]), which Stefan Roth supp-

shed under his name be read in his *German Mass*. In addition to relieving inadequately educated pastors,[55] this seemed to guarantee that preaching in Protestant pulpits would keep to the appropriate theological stance.[56] Looking back years later, Luther described the *Wartburg Postil* as »mein aller bestes buch, das ich yhe gemacht habe« (altogether the best book that I ever wrote)[57] although he was critical of its prolixity, which he confessed was detrimental to its continued use.[58]

Luther's postils continued to be heavily used as sources for preaching preparation until the 18th century. However, the model sermons offered therein proved too long for ordinary services. Thus, a change of function came about, significant in terms of literary history, whereby Luther's postils became not only aids for homiletical meditation but also increasingly the basis of private religious edification. Incidentally, this also explains the rapid proliferation of a Protestant collection of postils and preaching literature[59] whose distant offshoots could still be felt until the 20th century.

---

lemented in 1525 with a fasting portion *Kirchenpostille* (WA 17/2,5–247). Of varying, but consistently lesser value are the *Sommerpostille* compiled by Roth (WA 10/1/2,213–441 [1526]), the *Festpostille* (WA 17/2,252–514 [1527]), and the *Winterpostille* (WA 21,5–192 [1528]) as well as Veit Dietrich's *Hauspostille* (WA 52,10–732 [1544]) and Caspar Cruciger's *Sommerpostille* (WA 21,203–551; WA 22,3–423 [1544]).

[55] In the postil sermons he wrote (see note 54), Luther did not translate the pericope texts according to his »September Testament« but rather in more inelegant, literal terms in order to depict the original biblical text as precisely as possible for linguistically uneducated preachers. The differences that arose in this process can be illustrated in the prologue to the Gospel of John (John 1:1–14; cf. BEUTEL, In dem Anfang war das Wort [see note 12], 6–29).

[56] »Es were das beste, das man verordnete, die postillen des tages gantz odder eyn stucke aus dem buch dem volck fur zu lesen, nicht alleyne umb der prediger willen, die es nicht besser kunden, sondern auch umb der schwermer und secten willen zuverhüeten« (WA 19,95,4–8 [1526]).

[57] WA 23,278,13–4 (1527). However, Luther later revised this judgment. In a letter to Wolfgang Capito on July 9th, 1537, Luther shared that, of his writings, he only appreciated *De servo arbitrio* and the Catechism (WA.Br 8,99,7–8).

[58] »Occasio facit praedicatorem, nam ex contionibus meis postillaribus ne unum quidem sermonem colligo, ut eodem modo praedicarem. Ich kan mich nicht mit worten binden lassen […]. Si iunior essem, multa resecarem in postilla, nam immodice fui copiosus. Eam copiam nemo assequi aut imitari potest, neque omnia sunt accommoda[nda] omnibus temporibus« (WA.TR 1,488,24–489,2 [first half of the 1530s]); cf., for example, Luther to Nikolaus Gerbel, 27th nov. 1535: WA.Br 7,329,14–20).

[59] The example of Tübingen's controversial theologian Tobias Wagner (1598–1680) appears symptomatic of this. Wagner's publisher was only prepared to print Wagner's more difficult to sell pamphlets if he continued to supply him with apparently much better-selling postils and devotional literature (cf. ALBRECHT BEUTEL, Lehre und Leben in der Predigt der lutherischen Orthodoxie. Dargestellt am Beispiel des Tübinger Kontroverstheologen und Universitätskanzlers Tobias Wagner, in: ID., Protestantische Konkretionen [see note 47], 161–91, esp. 172–3).

In England the liturgical reading of ready-made sermons had likewise been imposed merely as a temporary measure, but, unlike in Germany, this proved a persistent force up until the present day. The *Books of Homilies*, first published in 1547, offered twelve sample sermons; this number almost doubled in the second edition of 1562. While the fundamental doctrines of the faith were hardly altered, the proliferation of the second edition particularly strengthened concrete moral instruction. Preaching topics were expanded to include admonitions to thoroughly purify the church as well as warnings against drunkenness, gluttony, slothfulness, and showiness in dress.[60] Criticism became vociferous in some places and was ignited, on the one hand, by pragmatic concerns over the impracticable length of the model sermons in the liturgy and, on the other hand, because it was impossible to respond to the specific local needs and to reach the hearts of those gathered in worship.[61] Some Englishmen, therefore, took longer trips to enjoy[62] a sermon that was »freshly created«.[63] But only a few could afford such luxuries, and so the pragmatists were comforted with the wisdom of the saying that it was only a matter of time before each parish would be provided with a preacher who could preach his own sermons: it is always better to have »half a loaf than no bread« at all.[64]

The great Reformers preached constantly. Zwingli preached almost every day and Luther, even in bad health and in addition to all his other activities, usually three or four times a week (in extreme periods up to four times a day).[65] Accordingly, they exhorted all Protestant pastors[66] to never grow weary of continuous homiletic work, even under adverse circumstances. Samuel Hieron captured this allegiance with the dramatic image of a snared fish, flailing desperately to throw himself out of the boat and back into the sea of ignorance, misery, and sin.[67] In addition, agricultural im-

---

[60] The Two Books of Homilies Appointed to be Read in the Churches, ed. John Griffiths, Oxford 1859.

[61] Cf. Hughes, Theology (see note 13), 122–23; Edwards, A History (see note 2), 357–359; Carlson, The Boring (see note 3), 278–282.

[62] Such examples of breaking away from parochial affiliation and from the parish priest's area of responsibility were occasionally sanctioned (cf. Matthew Milner, The Senses and the English Reformation, Farnham 2011, 309).

[63] Edwards, A History (see note 2), 359.

[64] Edmund Grindal, The Remains, ed. William Nicholson, Cambridge 1843, 382–83.

[65] Cf. Beutel, art. Bibelübersetzungen (see note 42), 297–98.

[66] Their number in the early days can hardly be estimated. In England, it is known that when Latimer was Bishop of Worcester in 1535, he already came across a group of clergy with Protestant views there (cf. Claire Cross, Church and People 1450–1660. The Triumph of the Laity in the English Church, Fontana 1976, 76).

[67] Cited in Carlson, The Boring (see note 3), 270.

agery was also utilized: Greenham said that the preacher is akin to the farmer, who cannot be satisfied with sowing one time but must oversee and tend the fields throughout the entire year.[68]

The *Sermon of the Plough*,[69] which Latimer presented on January 18th, 1548, achieved great renown. Allegorical and true to scripture, it declared that the word of God is the seed, the church is the soil to be tilled, and the pastor is the farmer. As such, Latimer continued, he has something to do all year round; after sowing he must continue working steadily, just as the preacher was constantly required to proclaim the law here and the gospel there, here to admonish and there to comfort, to teach, to awaken hearts, and much more. Therefore, preaching is as indispensable as daily bread – and not like the strawberry that ripens only once and spoils quickly.

»Therefore preach and teach, and let your plough be doing.«[70]

With that, Latimer presented the community with a guessing game.

»Who«, he asked, »is the most diligent preacher in all of England? Who invests all of his strength in his ministry? Who has the greatest success in his preaching?«

Because the dialogical sermon had not yet been invented back then, Latimer answered himself:

»It is the devil! He is the most popular preacher of all. He never leaves his church [...] call him whenever you want, he is always home [...] he is always behind his plow.«[71]

Therefore, concluded Latimer, indolent preachers should take the devil as an example, perform their work just as diligently, and scatter the grain of good doctrine with steady zeal.[72] This persuasive boldness may be a peculiarity of English pulpit rhetoric. For Luther, in whose sermons the devil was also a frequent guest, one could hardly conceive of such a pastoral, pedagogical utilization of evil.

The Reformers all agreed that the defining goal of homiletics was not merely to instruct the listener head-on but to demand an active receptivity from them, thus guiding them to their own understanding and challenging them to individually apply the message of the sermon.[73] As for Calvin,

---

[68] Cf. KENNETH L. PARKER, ERIC J. CARLSON, »Practical Divinity«: The Works and Life of Reverend Richard Greenham, Ashgate 1998, 147.

[69] HUGH LATIMER, Sermon of the Plough, 1548 (in: The Works of Hugh Latimer [see note 16], 59–78).

[70] Ibid., 65.

[71] Ibid., 70.

[72] Ibid., 77–78.

[73] Henry Smith coined the word »eare-labour« to describe the effort of hearing the sermon (HENRY SMITH, The Sermons, London 1593, 640). Cf. the enlightening work of ARNOLD HUNT, The Art of Hearing. English Preachers and Their Audiences, 1590–1640, Cambridge 2010.

who generally preached for nearly one hour without a manuscript, it could be demanding. In addition to a certain propensity for legalism, his thought processes were not always rigorous, which presented difficulties for those hearing them. Luther, in contrast, preached directly to the needs of his listeners. Without recourse to artistic forms and filigree organizational systems, as would be customary later in the *altprotestantischen* art of preaching, Luther usually named the central idea of his sermon quite suddenly and would then circle around it in many different ways. His language was simple and easy to grasp, sometimes coarse but always with an earthy liveliness that he knew how to enhance through fictional dialogues. A narrative watering down of the Gospel was repugnant to him. Instead, he not only valued metaphorical-allegorical speech as practical for preaching, but also appreciated it theoretically as an indispensable means of communication. He considered the parables as »a silken cloth, with which I wrap around and hold on to the meaning«.[74] With each sermon text, Luther aimed to open the biblical subject matter to the community as a relevant, Christologically based space for their life and faith. This gave his preaching a certain uniformity and, paired with his instantly appealing rhetorical talent, provided the listeners with the most entertaining consistency of tone.[75]

The English Reformation sermon, as the *Book of Common Prayer* (1549) programmatically set forth,[76] also depended on the active reception of the community. Because of their awareness of their eschatological responsibility, preachers quite often expressed a powerful emotional commitment. It was reported that Greenham's shirt was thoroughly soaked in sweat at every sermon as if it had been drenched in water.[77] Through his relentless, affective dedication his sermons sometimes seemed almost overwhelming. Once, while he was standing at the pulpit, a woman broke out in loud desperate sobs because she recognized that she was a damned soul. Greenham then interrupted the sermon, descended from the pulpit, went to her and comforted her with the words, »Rest assured, you have seen the sin, and now you will hear about the forgiveness of sin.«[78] Moderate, tempered minds sought to brace themselves for the »tricky business«[79] that

---

[74] WA 36,640,8–9 (1532).

[75] ZSCHOCH, Predigten (see note 12); ALBRECHT BEUTEL, Verdanktes Evangelium. Das Leitmotiv von Luthers Predigtwerk (in: ID., Spurensicherung. Studien zur Identitätsgeschichte des Protestantismus, Tübingen 2013, 63–78).

[76] GASSMANN, Die Lehrentwicklung im Anglikanismus (see note 43), 362–63.

[77] SAMUEL CLARKE, The Life of Master Richard Greenham, London ³1677, 12.

[78] PARKER, CARLSON, Practical Divinity (see note 68), 252.

[79] CARLSON, The Boring (see note 3), 266.

the sermon presented. Elnathan Parr distinguished between two risks in particular: if the listeners are addressed too mildly, they will remain in their sin, but if you approach them too harshly, they will become recalcitrant or plunge into a state of utter despair.[80] To confront such danger, John Frewen advised that preachers strive at all times for a loving motherly and fatherly affectation.[81]

This by no means precluded a sermon that was clear, direct, concrete, and unambiguous. Thus Zwingli, with unflinching candor, railed against the moral corruption prevailing in Zurich and did not shy away even from castigating individual citizens of the city by name. As a preacher, Luther also commented frequently on burning current issues, never shying away from conflict with the authorities when it seemed necessary to him.[82] Controversial theological polemics admittedly had a stronger presence in his sermons than socio-critical topics, so his listeners might have occasionally had the impression that the Roman pope was secretly residing in Wittenberg. The motif that one's own confessional identity was strengthened through antithetical distinctions was also ubiquitous in English sermons of the Reformation period.

Nevertheless, the feeling that the socio-critical aspect dominated sermon matters more powerfully does not seem unfounded. That a preacher must call out sins of all kinds and various degrees, without taking into account the social status of the defendant, was an oft-repeated exhortation.[83] In general, the topic of sin seems to have enjoyed high popularity

---

[80] »In this, two sorts of Ministers much faile: First, those which are so tender and studious to please, that they are loath to speake any but sweet words, though men rot in their sinnes. Secondly, those which are as farre on the other extreme, accounting all prefacing and loving speaking to be dawbing, and no sentence to be zealously delivered, unlesse Damnation and damned be at the end of it: whereby many times they drive them farther from Christ, whom they would have converted unto him« (The Workes of [...] Elnathan Parr [see note 34], 74).

[81] JOHN FREWEN, Certain Fruitfull Instructions and Necessary Doctrines meete to Edify in the Fear of God, London 1587, 294.

[82] See, for example, Luther's sermon on 1 John 5:4seqq., dated April 13, 1539 (WA 47,721–730), in which he explained to the community that the current fear of Hans Kohlhase was deliberately stoked by the landlords, because they wanted to legitimize a drastic increase in the grain price; meanwhile, while they set Kohlhase up as a straw man, they plundered their own people worse than any highway robber, which is why they could not even be called sows and cows anymore but only »morder, Teuffel, landsfeind« (ibid., 725,6–8). Cf. ALBRECHT BEUTEL, Luther und Kolhase. Eine Fallstudie zur cura conscientiae des Reformators (in: ID., Reflektierte Religion. Beiträge zur Geschichte des Protestantismus, Tübingen 2007, 1–20, esp. 15).

[83] »For as god, a most righteous judge, will punish all sin, so must His preachers indifferently warn and rebuke all sorts of sinners; or else God will require their blood and their hands, if they perish without their warning« (JAMES PILKINGTON, The Works, ed. James Scholefield, Cambridge 1842, 98–99).

with the English Reformation preachers. In addition to various individual transgressions, three social criticisms came particularly to the fore: the misuse of the land as an object of speculation was denounced many times, as well as the mounting structural hardships of the working peasants.[84] Moreover, the great preachers often decried the proto-capitalist interest-taking and usury as antithetical to the Gospel and as a disruption of the social order established by God. Especially in this regard, the Reformation pastors soon enjoyed a high level of public esteem. Thus Thomas Wilson's *A Discourse Upon Usury*, published in 1572, was widely disseminated. In this work, a Protestant clergyman, a lawyer, and a merchant discuss the matter of usury in the form of a platonic dialogue. Whereas the lawyer strives for casuistic differentiation, the merchant underscores the commercial necessity of an excessive interest rate. The pastor, however, exposes usury as a sign of the end times with recourse to the New Testament and early church authorities. In doing so, he is able to persuade the disputants; the lawyer falls sheepishly silent, and the merchant – who is freshly converted – now recognizes that taking interest is tantamount to highway robbery. It may be enlightening in terms of the history of mentalities that the figure of the Protestant preacher was soon awarded the highest moral reputation and possessed power of persuasion even in the context of non-religious literature.[85]

Among the preachers of the English Reformation, Latimer surely holds a special significance.[86] The church historian Horton Davies describes him for good reasons as exemplifying »popular preaching at its best«.[87] Latimer met Erasmus personally at Cambridge and had grappled with the writings of Luther early on. As early as 1529, he advocated resolutely for Luther's concept of the righteousness of faith.[88] However, he underscored that his determination had not come through Luther, but rather he arrived at his

---

[84] Cf. PAUL MEISSNER, England im Zeitalter von Humanismus, Renaissance und Reformation, Heidelberg 1952, 402–404.

[85] Cf. the Summary of this text: ibid., 396–97.

[86] Cf. for example: ALLAN G. CHESTER, Hugh Latimer. Apostle to the English, Oxford et. al. 1954; DAVID M. LOADES, The Oxford Martyrs, London 1970; ARTHUR F. BUTLER, Hugh Latimer. The Religious Thought of a Reformation Preacher, Ann Arbor 1980; NATALIE A. GALDI, Hugh Latimer. Humanism and The English Reformation, Ann Arbor 1980.

[87] HORTON DAVIES, Worship and Theology in England, vol. 1: From Cranmer to Hooker, 1534–1603, Princeton 1970, 248.

[88] »Now then, if men be so foolish of themselves, that they will bestow the most part of their goods in voluntary works, which they be not bound to keep, but willingly and by their devotion; and leave the necessary works undone, which they are bound to do; they and all their voluntary works are like to go unto everlasting damnation« (The Works of Hugh Latimer [see note 16], 23).

Protestant views through Thomas Bilney.[89] And yet, Latimer must have known that Bilney, in turn, had been brought to his Protestant beliefs not least by Lutheran ideas.[90] Late in life, Latimer discovered a comfortable appreciation for the reformer of Wittenberg.[91]

As a preacher, Latimer was characterized by a clear biblical foundation[92] as well as a preference for life-like examples and anecdotes, a heightened linguistic sensitivity, and a subtle sense of humor. Thus, he recounted a story about a woman in London who always visited a certain preacher because it was easiest for her to get some sleep under his pulpit. Instead of reprimanding such misconduct, Latimer not only came to the sleep-deprived woman's defense but even honored her through a comparison to Augustine – who also initially sought out Ambrose's sermons with ulterior motives and nevertheless was converted by them.[93] If his sermons without notes turned out to be too long – and they usually were – Latimer was wont to interrupt them now and then with a prayer. Unlike Luther, he usually adhered to the genre of the topical sermon and did not focus his sermon messages exclusively on Christ.

It is also noteworthy that Latimer sometimes even made the doctrine of preaching itself the subject matter of his sermons. His last sermon,[94] presented in 1550 before Edward VI, can be considered symptomatic of this proclivity. Here, he interpreted the call to repentance that the prophet Jonah delivered to the people of Nineveh (Jonah 3) as a model homiletical case: Jonah was alone, he preached only briefly, dispensed with all oratorical pomp, funny stories, and priestly affectations, and spoke clearly and to the point. Consequently, the whole city converted under the impact of his sermon. Latimer deemed most of his colleagues to be very far away from this ideal. Their congregations remained in sin because the sermons they heard were much too elaborate and too complacent; they also remained in sin because these sermons were offered in abundance, and, particularly, because the current preachers – out of a misconceived

---

[89] HAIGH, English Reformations (see note 3), 58–59.

[90] Cf. together with the references provided there, MARIE-LUISE EHRENSCHWENDT-NER, art. Bilney, Thomas (in: RGG⁴ 1, 1998, 1598–9).

[91] »I will not stand to it that all that he wrote was true; I think he would not so himself: for there is no man but he may err. He came to further and further knowledge: but surely he was a goodly instrument« (cited according to ROBERT DEMAUS, Hugh Latimer. A Biography, London 1903, 183).

[92] The Lutheran Sola Scriptura principle (cf. ALBRECHT BEUTEL, »Sola scriptura mus sein«. Begründung und Gebrauch des Schriftprinzips bei Martin Luther, in: Sola scriptura heute? Rekonstruktionen – Kritiken – Transformationen, ed. Stefan Alkier, Tübingen 2019, 29–58) Latimer shared completely.

[93] Cf. The Works of Hugh Latimer (see note 16), 201–02.

[94] Ibid., 239–281.

desire to be tactful – were showing improper consideration for the personality of their listeners. The implication was devastating: if Jonah had
preached back then as is customary in present-day England, he would
have failed miserably in the mission for which God sent him to Nineveh.[95]
Indeed, in this case Latimer did not address the king in person, but had his
sights on him as the head of the Church of England and certainly also as a
prospective reader of his printed sermon. In the German Reformers' sermons to the princes, such passages that reflect broadly on the sermon itself
are difficult to find.

All Reformers shared the experience that faithful church attendance
was not to be taken for granted and that physical participation in worship
did not necessarily imply intellectual participation. The fact that Luther
entered into a three-month preaching strike[96] at the beginning of 1530 was
understood as expressing a pedagogical *ultima ratio* for the community
(even though we should not lose sight of his particular character and disposition). He also had no illusions about the reception needs of his listeners:

»If one preaches the doctrine of justification, the people sleep and cough; but if you
begin a story or an example, then they pay attention with ears pricked up in total
silence.«[97]

That he must continue to encourage consistent church attendance amidst
such frustrations was nevertheless self-evident for Luther.

It seems that Latimer also encountered sophistical obstacles. In any
case, he devoted himself to such objections that emerged under a theological guise. For instance, he addressed the argument that if sanctification
was through God's hidden work in the heart, then God could also carry
out such work outside of the sermon. Latimer replied in his own unique
way, by leading the opponent ad absurdum. Of course, he admitted, God
could sustain my life even without food and drink, but does that mean we
embark on a hunger strike? And, of course, God could save me from fire,
but does that mean I run deliberately into the flames?[98] These questions
were obviously issued rhetorically; thus, Latimer concluded that we
should always observe the ways God has prescribed for us to preserve
body and soul.[99]

---

[95] Cf. ibid., 239–242.
[96] MARTIN BRECHT, Martin Luther, vol. 2: Ordnung und Abgrenzung der Reformation 1521–1532, Stuttgart 1986, 280–81.
[97] WA.TR 2,454,17–19 (1532).
[98] Cf. The Works of Hugh Latimer (see note 16), 306.
[99] »I must keep the way that God hath ordained, and use the ordinary means that
God hath assigned, and not seek new ways. This office of preaching is the only ordinary

He countered yet another objection dialogically:[100] the question of whether our ancestors must be regarded as damned since they only had false doctrines available to them and not Protestant preachers. He countered with the suggestion that God certainly had different ways at his disposal to save a person. But then, would not the fictional interlocutor follow up by questioning the soteriological exclusivity that is claimed for the sermon today? Latimer replied to this with a historical-theological interpretation of the present times. Through the Reformation, God has opened the gates of heaven for us by dispensing his word to Protestant preachers. Anyone who seeks to relativize this offer of salvation with pseudo-theological reasoning refuses to accept the revealed will of God and thus willfully persists in sinful hybris.[101]

Other theologians of the English Reformation, such as John Jewel[102] or William Jones,[103] were apparently subjected to quite similar objections. Like Latimer, they also referred to the exclusive mediating role of salvation that God had bestowed on the Protestant ministry of preaching. If we carefully examine their answers, it is certainly noticeable that they added the adjective *ordinary* to this information every time. This by no means indicated that they softened their tone towards the arguments of the sermon-weary Sophists; rather they wanted to ensure that the absolute sovereignty of God was safeguarded.[104] This, once again, impressively highlights the pure instrumentality that characterized the self-understanding of the Reformation preachers.

This may suffice, for the time being, as a more provisional overview of the German and English preaching cultures of the Reformation. If, in the process, only representatives of the theological avant-garde were considered, this was not intended as an elitist grasp on the subject matter but stems from a dearth of available knowledge. What was preaching actually like in Stackelitz and Romsey, in Saxony and England, in the canton of Zurich and in Scotland all the way down to the smallest villages? To this very day, we still know almost nothing about it.

---

way that God hath appointed to save us all by. Let us maintain this, for I know no other; neither think I God will appoint or devise any other« (ibid.).

[100] Ibid., 525–528.

[101] »In our time, God hath sent light into the world; he had opened the gates of heaven unto us by his word; which word be opened unto us by his officers, by his preachers; shall we now despise the preachers? Shall we refuse to hear God's word, to learn the way to heaven, and require him to save us without his word? No, no; for when we do so, we tempt God, and shall be damned world without end« (ibid., 528).

[102] HUGHES, Theology (see note 13), 125.

[103] JONES, Commentary (see note 35), 633.

[104] CARLSON, The Boring (see note 3), 277–78.

Singen

Konrad Klek

1. Einleitung

Im neuen katholischen Gesangbuch Gotteslob (2013) finden sich einige
Lieder reformatorischen Ursprungs, als Bußlied zur Fastenzeit Luthers
erstes Psalmlied *Aus tiefer Not schrei ich zu dir* (GL 277). Allerdings fehlt
die zweite Strophe:

»Bei dir gilt nichts denn Gnad und Gunst,
die Sünde zu vergeben.
Es ist doch unser Tun umsonst
auch in dem besten Leben.«

Dem Benehmen nach hat ein Bischof sein Veto dagegen eingelegt. Auf
allerhöchster ökumenischer Ebene gibt es ja die gemeinsame Erklärung
der Kirchen zur Rechtfertigungslehre vom 31. Oktober 1999,[1] aber: »Papier ist (offensichtlich) geduldig«. Singen dagegen ist der Ernstfall. Der
Bischof meinte wohl, seine katholischen Kirchenmauern davor schützen
zu müssen, ins Wanken zu kommen, wenn in ihnen gesungen würde *Es ist
doch unser Tun umsonst / auch in dem besten Leben.*

2. Singen und Reformation als Thema der Forschung

Das Singen war tatsächlich der Ernstfall bei der Durchsetzung der reformatorischen Bewegung im 16. Jahrhundert. Das ist europaweit zu konstatieren und wäre Thema für ein eigenes Symposion zur differenzieren-
den und vergleichenden Betrachtung. Deutsche evangelische Hymnologen
zitieren gerne die Bemerkung des Münchner Jesuiten Adam Conzen
knapp 100 Jahre später (1620), Luthers Lieder hätten mehr Seelen in die
Verdammnis geführt (occiderunt) als seine Schriften und Predigten (scripta

---

[1] www.theology.de/religionen/oekumene/evangelischerkatholischerdialog/gemein-
sameerklaerungzurrechtfertigungslehre.php, hier Absatz 15: »Allein aus Gnade im Glauben an die Heilstat Christi, nicht auf Grund unseres Verdienstes, werden wir von Gott
angenommen und empfangen den Heiligen Geist, der unsere Herzen erneuert und uns
befähigt und aufruft zu guten Werken.«

et declamationes).[2] Vielfach sind im deutschen Sprachraum Vorgänge dokumentiert, wo gesungener Protest im Medium von »martinischen Liedern« erfolgreich war. (Leider gibt es dazu bisher keine Quellensammlung.) Der Kulturwissenschaftler Patrice Veit spricht sogar vom »Liederkrieg« und von »Revolution durch Gesang«.[3] Prägnant ist ein aus dem Rathaus von Lemgo erzählter Dialog: In die Gottesdienste als Spione ausgeschickten Ratsdiener kommen zurück und melden: »Herr Bürgermeister, sie singen alle!« Dessen Reaktion: »Ei, alles verloren!«[4]

Ich vermisse bei den Darstellungen zur Reformationsgeschichte, auch in den jüngsten Publikationen zum Jubiläumsjahr 2017, die Thematisierung und Aufarbeitung des Phänomens »Reformation als Singbewegung« – eine etwas moderatere Bezeichnung als »Revolution«. Bei meinen Bemühungen, in der deutschsprachigen Literatur etwas Substantielles dazu zu finden, bin ich enttäuscht worden. Bei englischsprachigen Autoren wird man da eher fündig – auch in Forschungen zu Deutschland![5] Das Singen neuer, volkssprachlicher geistlicher Lieder damals an allen möglichen und unmöglichen Orten scheint hierzulande nicht weiter der Rede wert, obwohl es seinerzeit so subversiv wirkte, dass es explizit verboten werden musste.[6] Im Bereich der reformierten Reformationsgeschichte ist es wohl etwas mehr im Blick, da mit dem Genfer Psalter ein klares Bezugs-Korpus gegeben ist, dessen eminente Wirkkraft zu evident ist, um übergangen werden zu können.

Immerhin hat Johannes Schilling zum 2017er-Jubiläum zusammen mit dem Musikwissenschaftler Jürgen Heidrich im Reclam-Verlag eine mit Faksimiles bebilderte Edition der Lieder Luthers in ihrer zeitgenössischen Verbreitung vorgelegt, wo sich im Apparat auch manches Detail zur Wirkungsgeschichte aufspüren lässt,[7] In Halle erschien eine weitere bebilderte

---

[2] Belegt bei PATRICE VEIT, Kirchenlied und konfessionelle Identität im deutschen 16. Jahrhundert (in: Hören Sagen Lesen Lernen. Bausteine zu einer Geschichte der kommunikativen Kultur, FS Rudolf Schenda, hg. v. Ursula Brunold-Bigler u. Hermann Bausinger, Bern u.a. 1995, 741–754, hier: 741).

[3] A.a.O., 744, 745.

[4] So (ohne Quellenangabe) widergegeben bei KARL MEIER-LEMGO, Geschichte der Stadt Lemgo, Lemgo 1962, 78.

[5] CHRISTOPHER BOYD BROWN, Singing the Gospel. Lutheran Hymns and the Sucess of Reformation, Cambridge u. London 2005; ROBIN A. LEAVER, Luthers's Liturgical Music. Principles and Implications, Grand Rapids u. Cambridge (UK) 2007.

[6] Siehe die Belege dazu bei INGE MAGER, Lied und Reformation. Beobachtungen zur reformatorischen Singbewegung in norddeutschen Städten (in: Das protestantische Kirchenlied im 16. und 17. Jahrhundert. Text-, musik- und theologiegeschichtliche Probleme, hg. v. Alfred Dürr u. Walther Killy, Wiesbaden 1986, 25–38).

[7] MARTIN LUTHER, Die Lieder, hg. v. Jürgen Heidrich u. Johannes Schilling, Stuttgart 2017.

Lutherlied-Edition von Hans-Otto Korth.[8] Der Musikwissenschaftler Martin Geck veröffentlichte Essays zu sechs Lutherliedern unter dem schönen Titel *Luthers Lieder. Leuchttürme der Reformation*.[9] Der Verlag Vandenhoeck & Ruprecht hat jüngst noch nachgelegt mit 24 Luther-Lied-Porträts in eher populärwissenschaftlicher Erklärung.[10] Der Buchmarkt also ist durchaus empfänglich für das Thema Reformation, namentlich Luther und das Lied, der fachwissenschaftliche Diskurs offensichtlich kaum!

Dorothea Wendebourg allerdings thematisiert die Bedeutung des Liedersingens in ihren Ausführungen zur Gottesdienstreform.[11] Und sie hat nun dafür gesorgt, dass »Singen« ein Vortragsthema auf dieser Tagung ist. Ich kann in der Kürze der Zeit nur weniges skizzieren und erlaube mir dabei Unschärfen. Das mag Anstoß geben zu gründlicherer Forschung und Ausarbeitung.

Thema dieser Tagung sind die Institutionalisierungsprozesse bei der Reformation. Das Singen spielte dabei gewiss eine Rolle, aber dergestalt, dass es »domestiziert« werden musste, wie es Patrice Veit nennt.[12] Dem »subversiven« Agieren der Menschen im Medium der Lieder wurden Gesangbücher als Kanon des erlaubten Repertoires und Kirchenordnungen als Regelung der kirchlichen Singpraxis gegenüber gestellt. Es ist meiner Einschätzung nach aber nicht sachgemäß, schon den Ursprungsimpuls zum Singen und Liederdichten primär in kirchlichen Regelungsprozessen zu verorten, namentlich bei der Gottesdienstreform.[13] Wenn das Singen von »martinischen Liedern« nicht die Straßen und Märkte, die Handwerkerstuben und die Häuser erobert hätte, wäre das Lieder-Dichten nicht so zum Selbstläufer geworden, nachdem Luther zunächst ja Schwierigkeiten hatte, Mitstreiter zu finden. Und das Lieder-Singen hat im Protestantismus trotz der kirchlichen »Domestikation« weiterhin sein originäres Protestpotential behalten. So konnte es in den folgenden Zeiten immer wieder zu »Singbewegungen« gekommen gerade in Verbindung mit Protestströ-

---

[8] Lass uns leuchten des Lebens Wort. Die Lieder Martin Luthers. Im Auftrag der Franckeschen Stiftungen anlässlich des Reformationsjubiläums 2017 vorgelegt und erläutert von Hans-Otto Korth, mit einem Nachwort von Patrice Veit, Halle u. Beeskow 2017.

[9] MARTIN GECK, Luthers Lieder. Leuchttürme der Reformation, Hildesheim u.a. 2017.

[10] Mit Lust und Liebe singen. Lutherlieder in Porträts, hg. v. Ilsabe Alpermann u. Martin Evang, Göttingen 2018.

[11] DOROTHEA WENDEBOURG, Reformation und Gottesdienst (in: ZThK 113, 2016, 323–365).

[12] VEIT, Kirchenlied (s. Anm. 2), 742. 746–749.

[13] WENDEBOURG, Reformation und Gottesdienst (s. Anm. 11), 348f.

mungen gegen die verfasste Kirche (z.B. Pietismus). Wer das Singen als Sprachform des Glaubens frei lässt, wird immer wieder Probleme haben, es kirchlich oder theologisch zu bändigen, zu zähmen. Diese Erfahrung machte auch Martin Luther sehr schnell. So gesehen ist es aber auch besonders spannend, die kirchlichen Ordnungsstrategien gerade beim Singen genauer anzusehen.

3. Reformation und Singen – einige Skizzen

Ich reihe nun skizzenartig einige Beobachtungen aneinander, die für unser Thema wichtig sein dürften.[14]

3.1. Luthers erstes Lied

Ein neues Lied wir heben an – Luthers erstes Lied ist überhaupt kein Kirchenlied, sondern ein typisches Zeitungs-Lied, ein Erzähllied zum Märtyrertod der beiden Augustinermönche in Brüssel am 1. Juli 1523. Forum für solch ein Lied sind Marktplatz und Wirtshäuser. Es dient der publizistischen Agitation und findet Verbreitung mit dem Druckmedium Flugblatt (Einblattdruck). Offensichtlich überraschte der Absatz-›Erfolg‹ damit Luther selber und motivierte ihn zum Weiterdichten!

3.2. Luthers erstes geistliches Lied

Nun freut euch, lieben Christen gmein – Luthers wohl erstes dezidiert geistliches Lied wählt dieselbe Form des Erzählliedes und kommt auch via Einblattdruck auf die öffentlichen Plätze.[15] Es ist ebenso ein Vortragslied und mit Luthers eigener Melodie schlecht geeignet für hymnischen Gemeindegesang. Am nur begrenzten Vorkommen in den späteren Kirchenordnungen sieht man, dass es liturgisch schwer integrierbar ist. Dabei ist gerade dieses Lied eine pointierte Entfaltung der reformatorischen Erkenntnis von der Rechtfertigung des Sünders.[16]

---

[14] Weitere Literatur zu Luthers Liedern, auf die ich mich beziehe: GERHARD HAHN, Evangelium als literarische Anweisung. Zu Luthers Stellung in der Geschichte des deutschen kirchlichen Liedes, München 1981; MARTIN RÖSSLER, Liedermacher im Gesangbuch. Liedgeschichte in Lebensbildern, Stuttgart 2001, 35–81.

[15] Siehe das in Heidelberg erhaltene Exemplar Augsburger Provenienz in: SCHILLING, HEIDRICH, Luthers Lieder (s. Anm. 7), 15.

[16] HAHN, Evangelium (s. Anm. 14), 104–133.

3.3. Der Brief an Spalatin

Das Liederdichten wird als reformatorische Strategie Luthers identifizierbar in seinem nicht genau zu datierenden Brief an Spalatin von Ende 1523, in dem er diesen als Dichter gewinnen will.[17] Erwägungen zur liturgischen Verortung der Lieder spielen hier überhaupt keine Rolle. Die Intention ist sehr allgemein »quo verbum Dei vel cantu inter populos maneat«. Als Sujet für die Lieddichtung schlägt Luther bestimmte Psalmen vor, primär die sieben Bußpsalmen. Selber ist er mit dem Lied zum Bußpsalm 130 *Aus tiefer Not schrei ich zu dir* in Vorlage gegangen, das er dem Brief beigelegt hat. Die Stoßrichtung ist also eher allgemein katechetisch oder sogar volksmissionarisch. Das Wort Gottes im rechten Verständnis von Buße und Gnade soll über die Lieder im Volk verwurzelt werden. Auch das Lied Luthers zu Ps. 130 wird dann auf der Straße vorgesungen und als Einblattdruck verkauft – dokumentiert am 6. Mai 1524 in Magdeburg.[18] Und fünf Jahre später, am 24. August 1529, werden Handwerker in Göttingen mit diesem *Aus tiefer Not* in der Kehle lautstark eine Bußprozession stören, die wegen einer Seuche angeordnet worden war – ein inhaltlich profilierter Protestakt, der als Auslöser des reformatorischen Umbruchs in Göttingen gilt.[19]

3.4. Deutsche Lieder in der Formula missae

In der *Formula missae et communionis*, die am 4. Dezember 1523 vorliegt, also etwa zeitgleich zum Spalatin-Brief, äußert Luther den Wunsch nach möglichst vielen volkssprachlichen Gesängen, »quae populus sub missae cantaret«.[20] Er beklagt, dass es dafür noch an Poeten mangle und nennt daher einige ältere, inhaltlich akzeptable deutsche Lieder. Warum nur, muss man sich fragen, hat Luther im Spalatin-Brief als erwünschte Lied-Sujets nicht jene liturgischen Topoi genannt, die er in der Formula missae als Orte für ein deutsches Lied kennzeichnet, »iuxta gradualia, item iuxta Sanctus et Agnus dei«? Als Erklärung wäre für mich plausibel: Luthers Überlegungen zum Liedersingen in der Messe wurden sozusagen überholt durch den »Erfolg« der Flugblattlieder auf der Straße. Das brachte ihn auf die weiter reichende volksmissionarische Lied-Strategie ohne Fixierung auf liturgische Abläufe.

---

[17] WA.Br 3, Nr. 698. Das lateinische Schreiben ist neu übersetzt von Schilling in: Heidrich, Schilling, Luthers Lieder (s. Anm. 7), 193. Vgl. dazu Dorothea Wendebourg, Martin Luther und das Kirchenlied im lutherischen Protestantismus (in: Das Kirchenlied zwischen Sprache, Musik und Religion, in: BThZ 28, 2011, Heft 2, 230–245).

[18] Heidrich, Schilling, Luthers Lieder (s. Anm. 7), 163.

[19] Mager, Lied und Reformation (s. Anm. 6), 33.

[20] WA 12,218.

3.5. Luthers erste *Lieder und die* Formula missae

Bekanntlich war Luther bei seiner Suche nach Dichtern zunächst nicht erfolgreich und hat darum in einem Zug 1523/1524 selber über 20 Lieder geschaffen »zum gutten anfang und ursach zu geben denen die es besser vermögen«.[21] Darunter sind einige Lieder für die liturgische Position »iuxta gradualia«, nämlich die Festlieder und -hymnen. Namentlich durch die Erweiterungen der mittelalterlichen Vorlagen sind sie unabhängig von der liturgischen Position aber auch gut katechetisch als Lehrlieder zu verwenden.[22] Zur Abendmahlsliturgie liefert Luther 1524 keine passenden Gesänge, sondern präsentiert ein Lehrlied auf der Basis einer böhmischen Vorlage (*Jesus Christus, unser Heiland, der von uns den Gotteszorn wand*) und eine erweiterte Fassung des sub communione-Liedes *Gott sei gelobet und gebenedeiet*, was auch als Lied »iuxta Agnus dei« gedeutet werden kann. In der Formula missae nennt Luther die Segensformel in Ps. 67 als Schlusssegen-Variante, weshalb Paul Speratus in der deutschen Ausgabe (Januar 1524) Luthers Lied zu diesem Psalm beifügt (*Es wollt uns Gott genädig sein*). Daraus wird geschlossen, dass Luther dies als liturgisches Segenslied konzipiert habe.[23] Ps. 67 ist aber wie Ps. 12, wozu Luther das Lied *Ach Gott, vom Himmel sieh darein* vorlegt hat, einer der im Betbüchlein 1522 als Mustergebet für den Alltag präsentierten Psalmen. Er ist dort überschrieben »zu beten um Erhebung des Glaubens«. Dieser Psalm war im Stundengebet fester Bestandteil der Laudes und Luther als morgendliches Alltagsgebet vertraut.[24] Sein Lied dazu wird so primär als gesungenes Alltagsgebet intendiert sein. Im Medium Lied eröffnen sich neue Formen für individuelles wie gemeinschaftliches Beten unabhängig von kirchlichen oder klösterlichen Institutionen.[25] Luthers Lied zu Ps. 67 wurde ebenfalls am 6. Mai 1524 in Magdeburg auf der Straße im Einblattdruck feilgeboten, was die Inhaftierung des Verkäufers nach sich zog – und einen Bürgerprotest, der zu dessen umgehenden Freilassung führte.

---

[21] Vorrede zu J. Walters Chorgesangbuch 1524/25: WA 35,474.

[22] Musterbeispiel ist *Gelobet seist du, Jesu Christ*, von einer Leisen-Strophe auf ein siebenstrophiges Lied erweitert.

[23] HEIDRICH, SCHILLING, Luthers Lieder (s. Anm. 7), 163.

[24] KATHARINA WIEFEL-JENNER, [EG] 280 Es wolle Gott uns gnädig sein (in: Liederkunde zum Evangelischen Gesangbuch, hg. v. Ilsabe Alpermann u. Martin Evang, Heft 23, Göttingen 2017, 28–34, hier 29f.).

[25] Vgl. die Titelformulierung des ersten »Gesangbuchs« (Erfurter Enchiridion 1524): Eyn Enchiridion oder Handbüchlein, eynem ytzlichen Christen fast nutzlich bey sich zu haben / zur stetter vbung vnd trachtung geystlicher gesenge vnd Psalmen.

3.6. Luthers Psalmlieder

Luthers Psalmlieder, seine für das Liedersingen in den verschiedenen protestantischen Kirchen so folgenreiche Erfindung, sind nach meiner Einschätzung alle nicht liturgisch motiviert.[26] Das bereits genannte *Ach Gott,
vom Himmel sieh darein* entwickelte denn auch eine starke Stoßkraft als
›subversiver‹ Gesang, worauf zahlreiche amtliche Dokumente mit Nennung des Liedtitels verweisen.[27] Ein Forum der Auseinandersetzung um
die rechte Lehre waren allerdings Prädikanten-Gottesdienste, wo schon
immer vor und nach der Predigt Gelegenheit zum Volksgesang war. So
konnte jetzt mit spontan angestimmtem *dein Wort man lässt nicht haben
wahr* (aus Str. 1) der altgläubige Prediger kritisiert oder gar niedergesun-
gen werden.[28] Auch in späteren Jahren werden Psalmlieder als aktuelle
Zeit-Lieder gedichtet, als »Trost«-Gesänge in konkreter Bedrohungssitu-
ation und als Stoßgebete des Volks zu Gott. Auch wenn es dann schon
Gesangbücher gibt, werden sie weiterhin im Wortsinn auf den Markt gebracht in Einblattdrucken, beispielsweise *Der neun und siebentzigste
Psalm / zu diesen [ge]ferlichen zeiten / allen Christen zu trost / zu singen
und zu beten / In Reime gestalt* (Justus Jonas, 1546).[29]

3.7. Psalmlieder in Straßburg

In Straßburg sieht das mit den Psalmliedern anders aus. Von Anfang an
werden sie in die Gottesdienstordnung integriert. Das *Straszburger kirchen ampt* (1525) führt bereits im Titel die Angabe »mit lobgesengen und
goetlichen Psalmen«.[30] Straßburger Musiker entwickeln auch sofort ein
neues Melodiemodell, das funktioniert beim Singen einer Volksmenge und
zudem religiös erhebend wirkt, während Luthers Lieder weiterhin den
Vortragslied-Gestus bevorzugen und eher aufrüttelnd, appellativ sich ge-
bärden.[31] In Straßburg werden an den Werktagen viele Predigtgottesdienste abgehalten. Vor und nach der Predigt ist hier ein idealer Ort für Psalm-

---

[26] Zur selben Zeit, als diese Lieder entstanden, war Luther mit der Übersetzung des
Psalters befasst!

[27] MAGER, Reformation und Lied (s. Anm. 6), 36–38.

[28] A.a.O., 30, 34.

[29] STEPHANIE MOISI, Die Medialität des geistlichen Liedes im Zeitalter der Reformation (1517–1555) am Beispiel deutschsprachiger Psalmlieder (in: Musik in neuzeitlichen Konfessionskulturen – 16. bis 19. Jahrhundert. Räume – Medien – Funktionen, hg.
v. Michael Fischer u.a., Ostfildern 2014, 31–52, hier 48). Vgl. die analoge Funktion von
Luthers *Ein feste Burg* (zu Ps. 46).

[30] LEAVER, Luther's liturgical music (s. Anm. 5), 14–21.

[31] Siehe das Gegenüber der beiden *Aus tiefer Not*-Melodien von Luther und aus
Straßburg im Evangelischen Gesangbuch (1993), EG 299.

lieder als Volksgesang. So werden Lieder zu allen 150 Psalmen zusammen getragen und in zwei verschiedenen, nicht stringent konzipierten Editionen 1537 und 1538 veröffentlicht.[32] Bei Johannes Calvin sind es die positiven Erfahrungen mit den Psalmliedern im Straßburger Exil, die ihn motivieren zum Projekt Gesangbuch = Liedpsalter, um damit das kirchliche Singen zu reglementieren. Der Genfer Psalter entsteht in verschiedenen Editionsschritten ab 1542 und liegt 1562 komplett vor. Auch für die Entwicklung in England ist der Straßburger Psalmliedgesang essentiell, denn Miles Coverdale, der Herausgeber des ersten reformatorischen Gesangbuches (*Goostly psalmes*, 1535), lebt im Exil ab 1540 in Straßburg und im Elsaß, und neben ihm weitere für die liturgische Entwicklung in England später wichtige Personen.[33]

3.8. *Luthers* Deutsche Messe *und der Gemeindegesang*

Gemeinhin gilt, dass Luthers *Deudsche Messe*, publiziert 1526, den Gemeindegesang in liturgischer Funktion festschreibt und so zur nota ecclesiae erhebt.[34] Der Musikwissenschaftler Konrad Küster hat in seinem Buch zum Jubiläumsjahr, *Musik im Namen Luthers*, nachdrücklich in Frage gestellt, dass seit dieser Deutschen Messe der Gemeindegesang als konstitutiver Bestandteil des Gottesdienstes gilt und in lutherischen Landen auch so praktiziert wird. Küster konfrontiert Luthers Schrift mit dem Wittenberger Gottesdienstprotokoll des Wolfgang Musculus von 1536 und hinterfragt aufgrund des Musculus-Befundes die bisherigen Lesarten von Luthers Formulierungen zum Singen in der Deutschen Messe.[35] Meinen die Formulierungen »wir singen«, »singet man«, »mit dem gantzen Chor« wirklich Gemeindegesang? Ist da nicht eher Chorgesang im Blick? Anstatt nur auf Latein agieren die Knaben aus der Lateinschule jetzt eben zusätzlich mit volkssprachlichen Gesängen, einerseits in Psalmrezitation (in der *Deutschen Messe* zu Beginn beispielhaft ausnotiert), andererseits mit Liedern. Zur Unterscheidung von Chorgesang dient dann Luthers eindeutige Formulierung

---

[32] BEAT FÖLLMI, Der Genfer Psalter als Medium. Die Rolle von Straßburg und Genf bei der Ausbildung eines musikalischen Repertoires als Ausdruck reformierter Identität (in: Musik in neuzeitlichen Konfessionskulturen – 16. bis 19. Jahrhundert. Räume – Medien – Funktionen, hg. v. Michael Fischer u.a., Ostfildern 2014, 53–64, hier 60f.).

[33] ROBIN A. LEAVER, »Goostly Psalmes & Spirituall Songes«. English & Dutch Metrical Psalms from Coverdale to Utenhove 1535–1566, Groningen 1987, 21.

[34] WENDEBOURG, Reformation und Gottesdienst (s. Anm. 11), 349; DIES., Luther und das Kirchenlied (s. Anm. 17), 243–245.

[35] KONRAD KÜSTER, Musik im Namen Luthers. Kulturtraditionen seit der Reformation, Kassel u. Stuttgart 2016, 19–28.

»Nach dem Euangelio singt die gantze kirche den glauben zu deutsch / Wir glauben all an eynen Gott.«[36]

Im Bekenntnis des Glaubens soll es keine liturgische Substitution mehr geben. *Wir glauben all* ist wörtlich im Gesang der »ganzen Kirche« umzusetzen. Luther hat dazu eine einstrophige Vorlage erweitert zum trinitarisch dreistrophigen, lehrhaft entfalteten Lied (EG 183).

Allerdings notiert Musculus, dass am Sonntag Exaudi, 28. Mai 1536, nach dem Evangelium die Orgel gespielt habe, worauf der Chor mit *Wir glauben all* folgte.[37] Musculus listet dann mit unpräziser Passivformulierung – »canebatur«[38] – die Gesänge zum Abendmahl auf. Wenn da erstmalig die Gemeinde gesungen hätte, wäre das von Musculus sicher explizit benannt worden (wie im Protokoll vom Vorsonntag in Eisenach). Im Übrigen weist er darauf hin, dass »maior pars populi« nach der Predigt gegangen sei (auch Luther selbst mit Melanchthon wegen eines Schwindelanfalls) und es nur sehr wenige Kommunikanten gab.[39] Zum Singen der Gemeinde wären wohl gar nicht mehr genügend da gewesen. De facto hat an diesem Sonntag die Gemeinde in der Messe unter den Augen Luthers offensichtlich gar nicht gesungen. Das wird kein Sonderfall gewesen sein!

3.9. Gemeindelieder in lutherischen Kirchenordnungen

In Korrespondenz zu Luthers *Deutscher Messe* ist ein Blick auf die evangelischen Kirchenordnungen der nächsten Jahrzehnte geboten. Das Singen in der sonntäglicher Frühmesse und Messe, in der Sonntagsvesper und in den Werktaggottesdiensten musste geregelt werden. Eine (oberflächliche) Durchsicht der Sehling-Edition hat ergeben: In Sachen »Kirchen Gsang« operieren die Ordnungen stets mit dem Chor – »der Schulmeister mit den Knaben«[40] heißt es etwa in Weißenburg (Mittelfranken) 1528. Ordnungen greifen regulierend eben bei Institutionen, und die Schule ist eine zentrale Institution bei der Konsolidierung der Reformation. Im Vordergrund steht in den Kirchenordnungen der Ausgleich zwischen den Sprachen Latein und Deutsch, nicht die Beteiligung der Gemeinde. Die liturgische Tradition und das gängige musikalische Chor-Repertoire geben dem Lateinischen den Vorzug, was um der Lateinschüler willen auch weiter kultiviert werden soll, aber das Deutsche muss um des »Volks« willen eben auch

---

[36] WA 19,95.

[37] Evangelischer Gottesdienst. Quellen zu seiner Geschichte, hg. v. Wolfgang Herbst, Göttingen ²1992, 103–109, hier 107.

[38] A.a.O., 108.

[39] Ebd.

[40] Die evangelischen Kirchenordnungen des XVI. Jahrhunderts, begründet v. Emil Sehling, Bd. 11/1, 1961, 658.

sein. Deutsche Gesänge werden überwiegend folgendermaßen festgeschrieben:
- ein deutscher Psalm oder ein Lied am Beginn, oft nur als fakultative
  Variante zu lateinischem Gesang;
- als Regelfall ein Lied zwischen den Lesungen, also in der Gradualposition;
- »der Glauben deutsch«, also Luthers *Wir glauben all* ebenso als Regelfall;
- zwei oder drei Lieder sub communione;
- ein Schlusslied, zunächst überwiegend *Es wolle Gott uns gnädig sein*, in
  späteren Jahren *Erhalt und Herr bei deinem Wort* mit *Verleih uns Frieden.*[41]

Wie bei Luthers *Deutscher Messe* muss man auch in diesen Ordnungen
genau hinsehen, welche Akteure die Wendung »singet man« jeweils meint.
Da Volksgesang oft explizit benannt wird, wird mit »singet man« in der
Regel der Gesang des Schülerchores gemeint sein. Als Volksgesang benannt wird meistens Luthers Glaubenslied in der Credo-Position (»Patrem«) und ein Lied in der Gradualposition zwischen Epistel und Evangelium. Auch sub communione sind vielfach zwei bis drei Liedtitel als
Gemeindegesang vorgesehen, wobei die Führung des (einstimmigen) Gesangs stets Sache des Schülerchors ist, so dass für den geregelten Ablauf
letztlich unerheblich ist, ob »das Volk« sich beteiligt oder nicht.[42]

Die Ordnungen von 1533 in meinem regionalen Umfeld, Nürnberg
und die Brandenburgisch-fränkischen Territorien, thematisieren als Problem denn auch das Fehlen von Schülerchören auf den Dörfern. Da sollen
»christenliche teutsch geseng nach gelegenheit jedes orts« die sonst er-
wünschten lateinischen Chorgesänge ersetzen. »Wo aber das volk solich
geseng nicht könnte, sollens die pfarherr anrichten zu lernen.«[43] »Nach
Gelegenheit jedes Orts« heißt, man muss eben singen, was vor Ort bekannt und möglich ist. Und damit das nicht allzu kümmerlich ist, sollen
sich die Pfarrer – andernorts die Küster – drum kümmern. Ich lese in
diesen Formulierungen ein Unbehagen darüber, dass man die Sache mit
dem Volksgesang auf den Dörfern nicht so regulieren kann wie den Chorgesang der Knaben in den Städten. Als Gesamttendenz lässt sich etwas
überspitzt formulieren: Deutsche Gesänge des Chores in Maßen, und
wenn's passt, auch zusammen mit dem Volk.

---

[41] Diese beiden Luther-Lieder sind erst später publiziert worden (1543, 1529).
[42] Siehe die Praxis in Wittenberg laut Musculus 1536.
[43] Kirchenordnungen (s. Anm. 40), 188.

Dies gilt wohlgemerkt für die Lande mit Wittenberger (oder Nürnberger) Leitkultur. Im Straßburger Einflussbereich sieht das anders aus. Hier werden zur Führung und Schulung des Gemeindegesangs ausdrücklich Vorsänger bestellt. Martin Bucer geht es essentiell um den Gesang »von ganzter gemein« und ein schlechter Gemeindegesang wäre für ihn »Gotteslästerung«[44] (1525). In meiner Heimat Württemberg, nicht weit von Straßburg (Konstanz und Zürich) entfernt, wird der Predigtgottesdienst zum Normalfall erklärt. Die erste Kirchenordnung (1536) fordert demgemäß Volksgesang vor und nach der Predigt – unter Anleitung von Schulmeister und Schülerchor. Latein als Gottesdienstsprache und dem entsprechende Musikdarbietung wird hier kategorisch ausgeschlossen, Lateinschulen hin oder her.[45]

3.10 Gesangbücher

Das zweite Instrument zur Regulierung des Singens sind Gesangbücher, die einen Liedkanon definieren.[46] Im Reformationsjahrhundert gibt es zunächst keine landeskirchlichen Gesangbücher. Die ersten Gesangbücher sind Liedsammlungen von Verlegern, die da einen neuen Markt wittern.[47] Sie fassen Flugblatt-Drucke zusammen. Mein schwäbischer Hymnologie-Lehrer Martin Rößler bezeichnet das württembergische Gesangbuch von 1583 dann als erstes »bewusst gestaltetes Gesangbuch der lutherischen Orthodoxie«, ein Landesgesangbuch auf obrigkeitliche Anordnung.[48] Bis dahin hat sich die Kanon-Frage fast von selbst geregelt durch die Autorität von D. Martinus Luther. Erstmals 1529 hat er ein Gesangbuch redigiert und bei Klug in Wittenberg zum Druck gebracht,[49] das zu seinen Lebzeiten mehrere Folgeauflagen erlebte. Im Jahr 1545 erschien dann bei Babst in

---

[44] LEAVER, Goostly Psalmes (s. Anm. 33), 17.

[45] MARTIN RÖSSLER, Württembergische Gesangbuchgeschichte zwischen der Reformation und dem Dreißigjährigen Krieg. Erstes württembergisches Landesgesangbuch 1583 (in: DERS., Geistliches Lied und kirchliches Gesangbuch, München 2006, 213–275, hier 222f.).

[46] ERIC DREMEL, Sammeln und Sichten – Gesangbücher als Liedkanon (in: Davon ich singen und sagen will. Die Evangelischen und ihre Lieder, hg. v. Peter Bubmann u. Konrad Klek, Leipzig 2012, 45–61).

[47] Siehe die Konkurrenz der beiden Erfurter Enchiridien.

[48] RÖSSLER, Gesangbuchgeschichte (s. Anm. 45), 275. Vgl. a.a.O., 239, das Faksimile des Titelblatts: »auß gnädigem Befelch des Durchleuchtigen Hochgebornen Fürsten und Herrn«.

[49] Geistliche lieder auffs new gebessert zu Wittenberg. D. Mart. Luth. – Luthers Name wird also quasi im Autorenstatus bereits auf dem Titelblatt genannt. Siehe die Faksimile-Edition der zweiten Auflage: Das Klug'sche Gesangbuch 1533 nach dem einzig erhaltenen Exemplar der Lutherhalle zu Wittenberg, ergänzt und herausgegeben von Konrad Ameln, Kassel u. Basel 1954.

Leipzig eine im Umfang erweiterte, mit Bildern und Zierleisten prächtig ausgestattete Revision dieses Luther-Gesangbuchs. Es enthält eine neue Vorrede Luthers und wurde für die nächsten Jahrzehnte als autoritativ erachtet. Da es quasi zeitgleich mit Luthers Tod auf den Markt kam, galt es als sein letzter Wille in Sachen Kirchengesang. Die Liedauswahl in anderen Gesangbüchern wie in den lutherischen Kirchenordnungen orientiert sich eindeutig am Repertoire dieser beiden Gesangbücher (Klug und Babst).

Luthers Gesangbuchkonzeption von 1529 ist eigentlich kleinlich und engstirnig. Dem Vorwort nach geht es ihm primär um korrekte Fassungen seiner eigenen Lieder, die mit Namen gekennzeichnet und komplett vorangestellt werden. Das Gesangbuch fungiert also als Werkausgabe im Interesse des Copyrights. Der zeitgenössischen Lieddichtung, inzwischen zur Liederflut angeschwollen, steht Luther sehr reserviert gegenüber. Es sei »wenig Guts«[50] dabei und der »mehrer teil nicht sonderlich taugen«.[51] Lediglich 17 weitere Gesänge »der unsrigen« finden Aufnahme und fünf vorreformatorische Gesänge, in denen Christus »recht erkannt«[52] sei. Bei der letzten Auflage dieses Wittenberger Gesangbuchs (1543) erscheint auf dem Titelblatt eine mit »D. M. L.« signierte »Warnung« in Gedichtform, welche 1545 auch ins Babstsche Gesangbuch übernommen wird[53]:

»Viel falsche Meister jetzt Lieder dichten,
sieh dich vor, und lern sie recht richten.
Wo Gott hin bauet sein Kirch und sein Wort,
da will der Teufel sein mit Trug und Mord.«

Diesem Ausgrenzungs-Eifer des Doktor Martinus steht gegenüber, dass in der Folgezeit der von ihm definierte reformatorische Lied-Kanon als »Stamm« vieler Gesangbuchausgaben zwar beibehalten wird, die »Anhänge« mit zeitgenössischen Neudichtungen aber immer stärker wachsen. Die Sorge vor »falschen Meistern« wird also (zum Glück) nicht bestimmend. Und im Gegenüber zur kirchlichen ›Domestizierung‹ des Singens via Luther-Kanon und Kirchenordnungen kommt es bei den Christenmenschen zu vielfältigen Prozessen der Kommunikation des Evangeliums im Medium des Liedes. Darin geht Luthers volksmissionarische Lied-Strategie im Spalatin-Brief 1523 voll auf! Sie trägt sozusagen Frucht hundertfach. Das Evangelium zirkuliert in und mit den Liedern unter den Leuten. Nicht zuletzt wird das Lied als »Trost-Lied« (das Luther-Lehrlied weniger) zur zentralen Sprachform für die persönliche Frömmigkeit. Das von Luther

---

[50] »Ein newe Vorrede« (s. Anm. 49; vgl. WA 35,475).
[51] A.a.O., fol. 94 (in der Einleitung zu den neuen Liedern anderer im Gesangbuch).
[52] A.a.O., fol. 86 (in der Einleitung zu den »alten Liedern«).
[53] Siehe die von Konrad Ameln herausgegebene Faksimile-Edition: Das Babstsche Gesangbuch von 1545, Kassel 1929.

propagierte Priestertum aller Gläubigen realisiert sich gerade unabhängig von jeder Kirchenordnung in der je individuellen Aneignung von Gesangbuchliedern, die zu »Lieblingsliedern« werden. Seit der zweiten Hälfte des 16. Jahrhunderts profilieren Leichenpredigten die persönliche Frömmigkeit der Verstorbenen gerade mit der Nennung von solchen Liedtiteln.[54]

3.11. Der Erfolg der Psalmlieder in Europa

Das Luther-Gesangbuch ist prägend nicht nur in Deutschland, es wirkt namentlich in nordische Länder, vorrangig Dänemark. Eine größere Ausstrahlung in Europa gewinnt aber das Prinzip Liedpsalter.[55] Dies kommt auch im elisabethanischen England zum Zug, nachdem Coverdales *Goostly Psalmes* von 1535 noch stark am Luther-Gesangbuch orientiert waren, dieses fast eins zu eins ins Englische übertrug.[56] Zur Rezeption dieses Liederbuches gibt es kaum Quellen. Sicher wurde es im häuslichen Rahmen da genutzt, wo reformatorisches Gedankengut Einzug gehalten hatte.[57]

Speziell am Hofe Eduards VI. wurde dann das Singen von »Metrical Psalms« beliebt, Psalmlieder im Gegensatz zur gregorianischen Psalmodie. Es gibt eine um 1547 konzipierte, nicht vollständige Sammlung von »Certayne Psalms«, die das Straßburg/ Genfer Melodiemodell imitiert.[58] Die englische Exilgemeinde im deutschen Wesel sang dann zahlreiche Lieder daraus.[59] Nicht nur in Straßburg, auch in Genf erlebten viele englische Exulanten das Psalmlied-Singen. Es wurde sogar eine englische Version zum Genfer Psalter ediert.[60]

Der Einzug des Psalmensingens zurück in London ist dokumentarisch belegt mit Datum 21. September 1559. Henry Machyn notiert in sein Tagebuch, dass in St. Antholin's Church zu Beginn des morning prayer um 5 Uhr »after Geneva fassyon« ein Psalm gesungen wurde, und er hält fest: »men and women all do syng, and boys«.[61] Dieses Psalmliedsingen der Gemeinden greift schnell auf andere Kirchen in London über und wird zur reformatorischen Singbewegung ganz Englands. Zeitgleich mit dem

---

[54] VEIT, Kirchenlied (s. Anm. 2), 750f.

[55] Siehe die prägnante Übersicht bei JAN ROHLS, Der Genfer Liedpsalter und das Liedschaffen im reformierten Protestantismus (in: Das Kirchenlied zwischen Sprache, Musik und Religion, BThZ 28, 2011, Heft 2, 246–261, hier: 252–256).

[56] Siehe das Inhaltsverzeichnis bei LEAVER, Goostly Psalmes (s. Anm. 33), 66–69. 15 von 41 Liedern waren allerdings bereits Psalmlieder.

[57] A.a.O., 75f.

[58] A.a.O., 120–123.

[59] A.a.O., 202–218.

[60] A.a.O., 228–235.

[61] A.a.O., 252.

kompletten Genfer Psalter liegt 1562 auch *The Whole Book of Psalms* vor, das in den Folgejahren enorme Verbreitung findet.[62] Offensichtlich dient es vielfach auch als Hausgesangbuch. Bei diesen »Metrical Psalms« kommt es zu einer eigenen musikalischen Dynamik, indem die Melodien teilweise popularisiert und dann auch auf wenige Singmodelle reduziert werden. Die Engländer müssen sich ja nicht an die Genfer Melodie-Dogmatik Calvins halten und können ihre Psalmlieder als »Popsongs« mit hohem Identifizierungsgrad weiterentwickeln.

Das 1559 wieder verbindlich erklärte *Book of Common Prayer* erhält zum Singen einen neuen Absatz 49, der wenig reguliert und vieles offenlässt: Zunächst wird allerdings betont, dass alles, was in den Gottesdiensten gesungen wird, »a modest and distinct song« sein müsse, »that the same may be as plainly understanded, as if it were read without singing«. Unter dieser Vorgabe aber wird zugelassen

»that in the beginning, or in the end of Common Prayers, either at morning or evening, there may be sung an hymn, or suchlike song, to the praise of Almighty God.«[63]

Volksgesang als Rahmenprogramm stört die Liturgie nicht, ob diese »hochkirchlich« in den Kathedralen sich gebärdet als künstlerisch ambitionierten Kult mit Chor und professionellen Kräften oder eher schlichter in den Parish Churches.[64] Das Rahmenprogramm kann aber auch dem Hauptprogramm die Show stehlen, zur eigentlichen Attraktion werden:

»You may now sometimes see at Paul's Cross (London), after the service, six thousand persons, old and young, of both sexes, all singing together and praising God«

staunt am 5. März 1560 ein in der Literatur oft zitierter Briefschreiber.[65]

3.12 Luther-Gesangbuch oder (Genfer) Psalter?

Es ist deutlich geworden, dass die Entwicklung des geistlichen Singens in der Reformationszeit und seine kirchliche Regulierung sehr komplexe Vorgänge sind. Das kann nur durch präzise Einzeluntersuchungen erhellt werden, die möglichst viele Dimensionen erfassen, auch die kultur- und sozialgeschichtliche. Alles geistliche Singen, in künstlerischer Elaboration wie in der Elementarform Lied, ist Teil der gesellschaftlichen Kulturpraxis.

---

[62] Siehe die Inhaltsangabe a.a.O., 264–266. In Schottland führt John Knox 1564 den Genfer Psalter ein.

[63] A.a.O., 251.

[64] Beachte die Detail-Studie zur Polarität Kathedrale-Parish Church von JONATHAN WILLIS, Church Music and Protestantism in Post-Reformation England. Discourses, Sites and Identities, Farnham u. Burlington 2010.

[65] LEAVER, Goostly Psalmes (s. Anm. 33), 252.

Die unterschiedliche Entwicklung der künstlerisch ambitionierten Figuralmusik in den reformatorischen Kirchen habe ich gar nicht thematisiert.

Etwas plakativ lässt sich die Entwicklung des reformatorischen Singens benennen in der Polarität *Luther-Gesangbuch versus Liedpsalter*. Diese Polarität in weiteren Forschungen zu profilieren, wäre eine lohnende Aufgabe.

Nachtrag: Erst nach Abschluss dieses Beitrags erhielt ich Kenntnis von der sehr gründlichen Studie von Joseph Herl: Worship Wars in Early Lutheranism. Choir, Congregation, and Three Centuries of Conflict, New York 2004. *Die Ausführungen in Punkt 3.1. bis 3.10. werden hier durch eine Fülle von Quellenmaterial und überwiegend analoge Deutung bestätigt.*

Singing

Konrad Klek

1. Introduction

The new German Catholic hymnbook Gotteslob (2013) contains some hymns of Reformation origin, e.g. as a penitential hymn for Lent Luther's first psalm-based hymn *Aus tiefer Not schrei ich zu dir* (GL 277) – *From trouble deep I cry to thee*. But the second stanza is missing:

»Bei dir gilt nichts denn Gnad und Gunst,	With thee counts nothing but thy grace
die Sünde zu vergeben.	forgiving all our failing.
Es ist doch unser Tun umsonst	The best life cannot win the race,
auch in dem besten Leben.«	good works are unavailing.

A bishop obviously has vetoed it. At the highest ecumenical level, there is the Joint Declaration of the churches on the Doctrine of Justification of 31 October 1999,[1] but: »Paper is patient«. Singing is the real thing. The bishop probably meant that he had to protect his Catholic Church walls from shaking when singing in them *The best life cannot win the race, good works are unavailing.*

2. Singing and Reformation as a topic of research

Singing was indeed the real thing (Ernstfall) in the implementation of the Reformation movement in the 16th century. This claim holds good across Europe and would be a topic for a symposium of its own, to observe differences and make comparisons. German Protestant hymnologists like to quote the remark of the Munich Jesuit Adam Conzen almost 100 years later (1620) that Luther's hymns had brought more souls into condemnation (occiderunt) than his writings and sermons (scripta et declamationes).[2] In many cases, in German-speaking countries processes are docu-

---

[1] www.theology.de/religionen/oekumene/evangelischerkatholischerdialog/gemeinsameerklaerungzurrechtfertigungslehre.php (15).

[2] PATRICE VEIT, Kirchenlied und konfessionelle Identität im deutschen 16. Jahrhun-

mented, where sung protest in the medium of »Martinian hymns« was successful. (Unfortunately, there is no source collection to date.) The French cultural scientist Patrice Veit even speaks of the »hymn war« and of »revolution through hymn«.[3] The point can be summed up from an exchange reported from the city hall of Lemgo: council servants, sent to spy on the church services came back and reported: »Mayor, they are all singing!« His reaction: »Ah, all is lost!«[4]

I miss in the most recent publications to Reformation history for the anniversary year 2017, the exploration and processing of the singing movement »Reformation als Singbewegung« – a somewhat more moderate term (than »revolution«). I have been disappointed in my efforts to find something substantial in the German-language literature. From English-speaking authors, one will find rather more – especially in research on Germany![5] The singing of new, vernacular spiritual hymns at all possible and impossible places in this country does not seem worth mentioning to modern scholars, although it was so subversive at the time that it had to be explicitly banned.[6] In the area of the reformed history of the Reformation, it is probably somewhat more conspicuous, since with the Geneva Psalter one confronts a body of text, whose significance is too evident to be ignored.

Nevertheless, Johannes Schilling and the musicologist Jürgen Heidrich prepared an edition of Luther's hymns, published with facsimiles by Reclam-Verlag, for the 2017 anniversary that contains also details about the story of their impact.[7] In Halle, another illustrated Luther hymn collection edited by Hans-Otto Korth was published.[8] The musicologist Martin Geck published essays on six hymns of Luther under the beautiful title »Luther's hymns. Lighthouses of Reformation«.[9] Vandenhoeck & Ru-

---

dert (in: Hören Sagen Lesen Lernen. Bausteine zu einer Geschichte der kommunikativen Kultur, ed.s Ursula Brunold-Bigler and Hermann Bausinger, Bern et al. 1995, 741–754, esp. 741).

[3] Ibid., 744–45.

[4] Karl Meier-Lemgo, Geschichte der Stadt Lemgo, Lemgo 1962, 78.

[5] Christopher Boyd Brown, Singing the Gospel. Lutheran Hymns and the Sucess of Reformation, Cambridge and London 2005; Robin A. Leaver, Luther's Liturgical Music. Principles and Implications, Grand Rapids and Cambridge (UK) 2007.

[6] Inge Mager, Lied und Reformation. Beobachtungen zur reformatorischen Singbewegung in norddeutschen Städten (in: Das protestantische Kirchenlied im 16. und 17. Jahrhundert. Text-, musik- und theologiegeschichtliche Probleme, ed.s Alfred Dürr and Walther Killy, Wiesbaden 1986, 25–38).

[7] Martin Luther, Die Lieder, ed.s Jürgen Heidrich and Johannes Schilling, Stuttgart 2017.

[8] Lass uns leuchten des Lebens Wort. Die Lieder Martin Luthers. Im Auftrag der Franckeschen Stiftungen anlässlich des Reformationsjubiläums 2017 vorgelegt und erläutert von Hans-Otto Korth, Halle and Beeskow 2017.

precht recently added 24 »portraits« of Luther hymns with an explanation aimed at a more popular readership.[10] The commercial book market is therefore quite receptive to the subject of the Reformation as it relates to Luther and the hymn, the scholarly discourse apparently barely so!

However, Dorothea Wendebourg has discussed the significance of singing hymns in her remarks on worship reform.[11] And she has now ensured that »singing« is a lecture topic at this conference. In the short time, I can only sketch a few things and please allow me to be somewhat impressionistic. This may give impetus to more thorough research and development.

The subjects of this conference are the institutionalization processes during the Reformation. Singing certainly played a role, but in such a way that it had to be »domesticated«, as Patrice Veit calls it.[12] The »subversive« behaviour of the people through the medium of hymns was juxtaposed with hymn-books as a canon of the permitted repertoire, and church orders for regulation of the practices of singing in Church. In my estimation, however, it is not appropriate to locate the original impulse for singing and hymnody primarily in ecclesiastical regulations, specifically in the reform of worship.[13] If the singing of »Martinian hymns« had not conquered the streets and markets, the craftsmen's shops and the houses, hymnody would not have become self-sufficient, after Luther initially had difficulties finding those who would help him in the struggle. And singing continued to retain its original protest potential in Protestantism, despite ecclesiastical »domestication«. So, again and again in successive ages there would arise »singing movements« in connection with protest movements against the established church (such as Pietism). Anyone who liberates singing as a language of faith will always have problems taming it ecclesiastically or theologically. This discovery was also made by Martin Luther very early. In this sense, it is also particularly exciting to take a closer look at strategies in the church ordinances regarding congregational singing.

---

[9] MARTIN GECK, Luthers Lieder. Leuchttürme der Reformation, Hildesheim et al. 2017.

[10] Mit Lust und Liebe singen. Lutherlieder in Porträts, ed.s Ilsabe Alpermann and Martin Evang, Göttingen 2018.

[11] DOROTHEA WENDEBOURG, Reformation und Gottesdienst (in: ZThK 113, 2016, 323–365).

[12] VEIT (see note 2), 742, 746–49.

[13] WENDEBOURG (see note 11), 348–49.

3. Reformation and Singing – a few Sketches

I now sketch a series of observations that may be important to our topic.[14]

3.1. Luther's first song

Ein neues Lied wir heben an (A new song be by us begun) – Luther's first hymn is not a hymn at all, but a typical newspaper hymn, a narrative hymn to the martyrdom of the two Augustinian monks in Brussels on July 1, 1523. The natural environment for such a hymn was the market-place and tavern. It served to arouse popular agitation and found its distribution through the medium of the printed broadsheet. Obviously, the success of this publicity venture surprised Luther himself and motivated him to continue his work!

3.2. Luther's first »spiritual song«

Nun freut euch, lieben Christen gmein (Dear Christians, one and all, rejoice) – Luther's first decidedly spiritual hymn chose the same form of narrative hymn and also reached the public square via broadsheet.[15] It is also a lecture hymn, and with Luther's own melody seems poorly suited for congregational singing. From its limited occurrence in the later church orders it appears that it was difficult to integrate this hymn liturgically. Yet this hymn offers a focused exposition of Reformation understanding of the justification of the sinner.[16]

3.3. The letter to Spalatin

The writing of poetic hymns becomes identifiable as a reforming strategy of Luther's from his letter (not exactly dated) to Spalatin in late 1523, in which he expressed the desire to have him become a poet.[17] Reflections on the liturgical location of the hymns played no role here at all. The intention was very general: »quo verbum Dei vel cantu inter populos maneat«

---

[14] Important for my research in Luthers hymns are also: GERHARD HAHN, Evangelium als literarische Anweisung. Zu Luthers Stellung in der Geschichte des deutschen kirchlichen Liedes, München 1981; MARTIN RÖSSLER, Liedermacher im Gesangbuch. Liedgeschichte in Lebensbildern, Stuttgart 2001, 35–81.

[15] HEIDRICH, SCHILLING, Luthers Lieder (see note 7), 15, a broadsheet, printed in Augsburg, in the library of University of Heidelberg.

[16] HAHN, Evangelium (see Note 14), 104–133.

[17] WA.Br 3, no. 698. On this letter see further DOROTHEA WENDEBOURG, Martin Luther und das Kirchenlied im lutherischen Protestantismus (in: Das Kirchenlied zwischen Sprache, Musik und Religion, BThZ 28, 2011, vol. 2, 230–245).

(by which means the word of God may remain in people's minds also by means of song). As a subject for hymn lyrics Luther suggested certain psalms, primarily the seven penitential psalms. As a model Luther proposed his hymn based on the Penitential Psalm 130 *Aus tiefer Not schrei ich zu dir* (From trouble deep I cry to thee) which he attached to the letter. The thrust was thus more generally catechetical or even evangelistic. The Word of God, in respect of the right understanding of repentance and grace, should be rooted in the people through hymns. The hymn of Luther based on Psalm 130 would then be sung on the street and sold as a broadsheet – as was documented on May 6, 1524 in Magdeburg.[18] Five years later, on August 24, 1529, craftsmen in Göttingen while singing this *From trouble deep* loudly disturbed a penitential procession, which had been ordered because of a plague. This singing amounted to a substantive act of protest, which came to be considered the trigger of the reformatory upheaval in Göttingen.[19]

3.4. German hymns in the Formula missae

In the *Formula missae et communionis*, which was published on December 4, 1523, thus at about the same time as the Spalatin letter was written, Luther expressed the wish for as many vernacular hymns as possible, »which the people may sing during the Mass«.[20] He complained that there was still a shortage of poets and therefore listed some older German hymns, whose content was acceptable. Why did Luther, one may ask, in his letter to Spalatin not identify the liturgical locations which he marked in *Formula missae* as places for a German hymn, »iuxta gradualia, item iuxta Sanctus et Agnus dei«? A possible explanation might be, that Luther's reflections on hymn singing in the Mass were, so to speak, outbid by the ›success‹ of the broadsheet hymns on the street. This brought him to devise a broader evangelistic hymn strategy without fixation on liturgical processes.

3.5. Luther's first hymns and the Formula missae

As we know, Luther was not very successful at first in his search for poets and therefore created more than 20 hymns in a single exercise in 1523/1524 »to give a good beginning and cause those who can do better«.[21] Among

---

[18] HEIDRICH, SCHILLING, Luthers Lieder (see note 7), 163.
[19] MAGER, Reformation und Lied (see note 6), 33.
[20] WA 12,218.
[21] WA 35,474 (Introduction to J. Walter, Chorgesangbuch, 1524/25).

them were some hymns for the liturgical location »iuxta gradualia«, namely the festival hymns and hymns. However, through the development
from medieval models they became independent of their liturgical location
and appropriate for catechetical use as teaching hymns.[22] For the liturgy of
the Lord's Supper Luther did not deliver suitable hymns in 1524, but
instead presented a catechetical song based on a Bohemian model (*Jesus
Christus, unser Heiland, der von uns den Gotteszorn wand / Jesus Christ,
our Savior, who turned God's wrath away from us*) and an expanded
version of the *sub communione* hymn *Gott sei gelobet und gebenedeiet*
(God be praised and blessed), which could also be used as a hymn »iuxta
agnus dei«. In the *Formula missae*, Luther called the blessing formula in
Psalm 67 a final liturgical blessing, which is why Paul Speratus in the
German edition (January 1524) added Luther's hymn to this psalm (*Es
woll uns Gott genädig sein, May God bestow on us his grace*). It may thus
be concluded that Luther conceived this as a liturgical blessing.[23] Psalm 67,
however, is like Psalm 12, to which Luther has presented the hymn *Ach
Gott, vom Himmel sieh darein* (Oh God, look down from heaven), one of
the psalms presented in *Betbüchlein* (1522) as a model prayer for everyday
life. The Psalm at that point had the superscription appended »to pray for
increase of one's faith«. This psalm was an integral part of Lauds in the
liturgy of the hours and therefor familiar to Luther through the morning
prayers.[24] His hymn would therefore be intended primarily as an everyday
sung prayer. The medium of hymns opened up new forms of individual
and common prayer, independent of ecclesiastical or monastic institutions.[25] On May 6, 1524 Luther's hymn about Psalm 67 was also offered
on the street in Magdeburg as a broadsheet, which led to the imprison-
ment of the seller – and a protest from the citizens, which led to his
immediate release.

---

[22] See as best example *Gelobet seist du, Jesu Christ* (Let us praise you, Jesus Christ),
originally only one stanza, now seven stanzas.
[23] HEIDRICH, SCHILLING, Luthers Lieder (see note 7), 163.
[24] KATHARINA WIEFEL-JENNER, [EG] 280 Es wolle Gott uns gnädig sein (in: Liederkunde zum Evangelischen Gesangbuch, ed.s Ilsabe Alpermann and Martin Evang, vol.
23, Göttingen 2017, 28–34, esp. 29–30).
[25] See also the title of the first »hymnbook«, Erfurt Enchiridion, 1524: Eyn Enchiridion oder Handbüchlein, eynem ytzlichen Christen fast nutzlich bey sich zu haben /
zur stetter vbung vnd trachtung geystlicher gesenge vnd Psalmen (for permanent exercise and meditation of gostly songs and psalms.)

3.6. Luther's psalm-based hymns

All Luther's psalm-derived hymns, an invention which proved so influential for singing in various Protestant churches, are in my estimation not motivated by the needs of the liturgy.[26] The already mentioned *Ach Gott, vom Himmel sieh darein* also developed a strong impact as a »subversive« hymn, as evidenced by numerous official documents which refer to the hymn's title.[27] However, a forum for controversy about right doctrine always was worship focused on the sermon, where an opportunity for congregational singing was always offered before and after the sermon. So now, with a spontaneous singing of *Thy Word men shall not let remain* (St. 1) the conservative traditionalist preacher could be criticized or even silenced by the power of the hymn.[28] Even in later years, psalm-based hymns were written as hymns for contemporary circumstances, as a »consolation« hymn in a situation of some specific threat, and as prayers of the people to God. Even when collected volumes of hymns were available, individual hymns would continue to be released on the market as single sheets, for example *The seventy-ninth psalm, made into rhyme for all Christians to sing and to pray for consolation in these dangerous times* (Justus Jonas, 1546).[29]

3.7. Metrical psalms in Strasbourg

Strasbourg presents a quite different aspect in regard to psalm-based hymns. From the beginning they were integrated into the order of worship. The *Straszburger kirchen ampt* (1525) already mentioned the titles under the sections »lobgesenge[ ]« and »goetliche[ ] Psalmen«.[30] The Strasbourg musicians also immediately developed a new melodic model, which suited a large number of singers and was also religiously uplifting, while Luther's hymns continued to favour the style of the expository song, arousing one to conforming conduct.[31] In Strasbourg, many sermon worship services were held on weekdays. Before and after the sermon was an

---

[26] At the same time Luther was busy translating the Psalter!

[27] See MAGER, Reformation und Lied (see note 6), 36–38.

[28] Ibid., 30, 34.

[29] STEPHANIE MOISI, Die Medialität des geistlichen Liedes im Zeitalter der Reformation (1517–1555) am Beispiel deutschsprachiger Psalmlieder (in: Musik in neuzeitlichen Konfessionskulturen – 16. bis 19. Jahrhundert. Räume – Medien – Funktionen, ed.s Michael Fischer et al., Ostfildern 2014, 31–52, esp. 48). See also Luther's hymn *Ein feste Burg* (Psalm 46).

[30] LEAVER, Luther's liturgical music (see note 5), 14–21.

[31] See for comparison both melodies for *Aus tiefer Not* by Luther and from Strasbourg in the German hymnal: Evangelisches Gesangbuch (1993), EG 299.

ideal place for psalm-based hymns for congregational singing. Thus, hymns based on all 150 psalms were collected and published in two different editions, not precisely conceived, in 1537 and 1538.[32] In the case of John Calvin it was his positive experience with psalm-based hymns during his exile in Strasbourg that inspired him to the project of the book of metrical psalms, in order to regulate church singing. The Geneva Psalter was produced in various partial editions from 1542 and became available in its entirety in 1562. The Strasbourg psalm-based hymnody was also essential for developments in England, because Miles Coverdale, the publisher of the first reformation hymn book (*Goostly psalmes* 1535), lived in exile from 1540 in Strasbourg and in Alsace; following him came others, who would be important for liturgical developments in England later on.[33]

3.8. Luther's German Mass *and congregational singing*

It is generally held that Luther's *German Mass*, published in 1526, codified congregational singing as a liturgical practice and thus raised it to a *nota ecclesiae*.[34] The musicologist Konrad Küster, in his book to the anniversary year, *Musik im Namen Luthers* (2016), has brought into question whether, since this German Mass, congregational singing was considered a constitutive part of worship and was indeed so practiced in Lutheran lands. Küster confronts Luther's writing with the Wittenberg worship protocol of Wolfgang Musculus in 1536 and questions the previous readings of Luther's formulations for singing in the *German Mass* on the basis of the Musculus findings.[35] Does »wir singen«, »singet man«, »mit dem gantzen Chor« really mean congregational singing? Is it not choral singing that is envisaged? Instead of singing only in Latin, the boys from the Latin school now also sang in the vernacular, on the one hand in the recitation of Psalms (as is for example noted at the beginning of the *Deutsche Messe*), and on the other with hymns. Luther's unequivocal formulation then served to distinguish clearly from choral singing: »After the Gospel the whole church sings the Creed in German, We all believe in one God«.[36] In

---

[32] See BEAT FÖLLMI, Der Genfer Psalter als Medium. Die Rolle von Straßburg und Genf bei der Ausbildung eines musikalischen Repertoires als Ausdruck reformierter Identität (in: Musik in neuzeitlichen Konfessionskulturen – 16. bis 19. Jahrhundert. Räume – Medien – Funktionen, ed.s Michael Fischer et al., Ostfildern 2014, 53–64, esp. 60–61).

[33] See ROBIN A. LEAVER, »Goostly Psalmes & Spirituall Songes«. English & Dutch Metrical Psalms from Coverdale to Utenhove 1535–1566, Groningen 1987, 21.

[34] See WENDEBOURG, Reformation und Gottesdienst (see note 11), 349, and ID., Luther und das Kirchenlied (see note 17), 243–245.

[35] KONRAD KÜSTER, Musik im Namen Luthers. Kulturtraditionen seit der Reformation, Kassel and Stuttgart 2016, 19–28.

[36] WA 19,95.

the confession of faith there should be no liturgical substitution. *We all believe* is literally implemented in the hymn of »the whole church«. To this end, Luther extended a single-pronged model to the trinitarian, three-paragraphed, hymn of doctrinal exposition.

However, Musculus noted that on Sunday Exaudi, May 28, 1536, the organ played after the reading of the gospel, after which the choir follow-ed with *Wir glauben all* (We all believe).[37] Musculus then listed the hymns for the Lord's Supper with an imprecise passive formulation – »caneba-tur«[38]. If the whole church had sung for the first time at this point, it would certainly have been explicitly noted by Musculus (as in the protocol of the previous Sunday in Eisenach). Incidentally, he pointed out that »maior pars populi« were leaving after the sermon (even Luther himself with Melanchthon because of a dizzy spell) and that there were very few communicants.[39] There would not have been enough to sing congregati-onally. In fact, on this Sunday, the congregation did not sing at the Mass – and Luther saw this. That will not have been a special case!

3.9. Congregational hymns in Lutheran church orders

Alongside Luther's *German Mass*, a look at the church ordinances of the next decades is required. The singing in Sunday mass, high mass, Sunday vespers and weekday services had to be regulated. In the Sehling edition of the church orders one can see: In the matter of »Kirchen Gsang«, the orders always operate with the choir – »the schoolmaster with the boys« is what is said in Weißenburg (Middle Franconia) in 1528.[40] Regulations re-gulate institutions, and school is a central institution for the consolidation of the Reformation. In the foreground in the church orders stands the balance between the Latin and German languages, not the participation of the congregation. The liturgical tradition and the musical repertoire give preference to Latin, which should be further cultivated for the sake of the Latin student, but German must also be for the sake of the »people«. German hymns are predominantly written as follows:
- a German psalm or a hymn at the beginning, often only as an optional variant to Latin singing;
- as a rule, a hymn between the readings, so in the Gradual position;

---

[37] Evangelischer Gottesdienst. Quellen zu seiner Geschichte, ed. Wolfgang Herbst, Göttingen ²1992, 103–109, esp. 107.
[38] Ibid., 108.
[39] Ibid.
[40] Die evangelischen Kirchenordnungen des XVI. Jahrhunderts, ed by Emil Sehling, vol. 11/1, 1961, 658.

- »der Glauben deutsch«, thus Luther's *Wir glauben all* also as a rule;
- two or three hymns *sub communione*;
- one postlude, in the beginning primarily *Es wolle Gott uns gnädig sein*, in later years *Erhalt und Herr bei deinem Wort* mit *Verleih uns Frieden*.[41]

As in Luthers *German Mass* one must consider carefully in each of these orders, which actors the phrase »singet man« (one sings) means. Since congregational singing is often named explicitly, I suspect that »singet man« usually means the singing of the school choir. Luther's hymn of faith in the position of the Credo (»Patrem«) and a hymn in the Gradual Position between the Epistle and the Gospel are usually called congregational hymns. Also *sub communione* there are often two or three hymn titles provided as a congregational hymn; but there the leadership of the hymn (in unison) is always the responsibility of the choir, so that ultimately it is irrelevant to the regular process, whether »the people« get involved or not.[42]

The church orders of 1533 in my own region, Nuremberg and the Brandenburg-Franconian territories, also address the problem of the lack of school choirs in the villages. There, »christenliche teutsch geseng nach gelegenheit jedes orts« should replace the otherwise desirable Latin choral hymns. »Wo aber das volk solich geseng nicht könnte, sollens die pfarherr anrichten zu lernen.«[43] »Nach Gelegenheit jedes Orts« means that you must sing what is known and possible on the spot. And so this is not too puny, the pastors – elsewhere the sexton – should take care of it. I read in these formulations a discomfort that one cannot regulate congregational hymn-singing in the villages in the same way as the choral singing of the boys in the cities. The general preference can be expressed thus: German choral singing in moderation, and if it fits, also together with the people.

This applies, of course, for those regions influenced by the prevailing culture of Wittenberg (or Nuremberg). The Strasbourg area of influence looks different. Here, precentors were specifically ordained for the guidance and training of congregational singing. Martin Bucer regarded it as essential to have singing »by the whole congregation« and bad church singing would be a »blasphemy«[44] for him (1525). In my native Württemberg, not far from Strasbourg (Constance and Zurich), the preaching service was regarded as normal. The first church order (1536) accordingly

---

[41] This Luther-hymns were published later (1543, 1529).
[42] See the praxis of singing in Wittenberg 1536, as Musculus referred.
[43] Kirchenordnungen (see note 40), vol. 11/1, 188.
[44] LEAVER, Goostly Psalmes (see note 33), 17.

demanded congregational singing before and after the sermon – under the guidance of the schoolmaster and boys choir. Latin as the language of worship and its use in musical performances were categorically excluded here, Latin schools or not.[45]

3.10. Hymnals

The second kinds of instrument for the regulation of singing were hymn-books that defined a canonical list of hymns.[46] In the Reformation century, there were initially no territorial church hymnals. The first hymn-books were collections of hymns by publishers who smelt a new market there.[47] They summarized broadsheet prints. My Swabian hymnology-teacher Martin Roessler called the Württemberg hymnal of 1583 the first »purposely arranged hymnal of Lutheran Orthodoxy«, a state hymnbook ordained by the authorities.[48] Until then, the canon question had almost settled itself by the authority of D. Martinus Luther. For the first time in 1529 he edited a hymn book and brought it to Klug in Wittenberg for printing,[49] which received several reprinted editions in his lifetime. In 1545, Babst in Leipzig published a revised version of this Luther hymn book, which was enlarged in scope and beautifully decorated with pictures and borders. It contained a new preface by Luther and was considered authoritative for the next decades. It came to the market almost simultaneously with Luther's death and was considered his last will in church singing. The hymn selection in other hymnbooks as in the Lutheran church orders was clearly based on the repertoire of these two hymnals (Klug and Babst).

Luther's hymnbook concept of 1529 is actually petty and narrow-minded. According to the preface, he was primarily concerned with correct versions of his own hymns, which were labeled with his name and

---

[45] See MARTIN RÖSSLER, Württembergische Gesangbuchgeschichte zwischen der Reformation und dem Dreißigjährigen Krieg. Erstes württembergisches Landesgesangbuch 1583 (in: ID., Geistliches Lied und kirchliches Gesangbuch, Munich 2006, 213–275, esp. 222–3).

[46] ERIC DREMEL, Sammeln und Sichten – Gesangbücher als Liedkanon (in: Davon ich singen und sagen will. Die Evangelischen und ihre Lieder, ed.s Peter Bubmann and Konrad Klek, Leipzig 2012, 45–61).

[47] In Erfurt 1524 there were published two Enchiridions in competition.

[48] RÖSSLER, Württembergische Gesangbuchgeschichte (see note 45), 275. See ibid., 239, the cover of the hymnal: »auß gnädigem Befelch des Durchleuchtigen Hochgeborrnen Fürsten und Herrn«.

[49] Geistliche lieder auffs new gebessert zu Wittenberg. D. Mart. Luth. (Luther is named on the cover like an author! See the reprint of the second edition: Das Klug'sche Gesangbuch 1533 nach dem einzig erhaltenen Exemplar der Lutherhalle zu Wittenberg, ed. Konrad Ameln, Kassel and Basel 1954).

consistently placed first. So the hymnal functioned thus as a collected edition for the sake of copyright. Luther was very reserved though in terms of the contemporary hymn poetry, now swollen to a flood of hymns. There is »wenig Guts«[50] and »der mehrer teil nicht sonderlich taugen«.[51] Only 17 other hymns »der unsrigen« are included and five pre-Reformation hymns in which Christ is »recht erkannt«.[52] In the last edition of this Wittenberg hymnbook (1543) a »warning« as a poem signed »D. M. L«. appears on the title page, which is also incorporated into the Babst hymnbook in 1545[53]:

»Viel falsche Meister jetzt Lieder dichten,	Many wrongful masters versify in hymn,
sieh dich vor, und lern sie recht richten.	watch out, learn not to judge them wrong.
Wo Gott hin bauet sein Kirch und sein Wort,	Where God builds his Church and Word for us to see,
da will der Teufel sein mit Trug und Mord.«	with deception and slaying the devil wants to be.

In direct opposition to this exclusionary zeal of Doctor Martinus, in the following period, although the Reformation hymn canon which he had defined was retained as the »root« of many hymnal editions, the »appendices« with contemporary new compositions grew more and more. Worrying about »false masters« did not (fortunately) become determinative. In contrast to the ecclesiastical »domestication« (Veit) of singing via the Luther canon and church orders, there were many means of »communicating the gospel« in the medium of the hymn by and to the Christian people. Luther's folk-missionary hymn strategy in the Spalatin letter 1523 was thus fully received, and bore fruit a hundredfold, so to speak. The gospel circulated in and with the hymns among the people. Not least, the hymn as »consolation hymn« (the Lutheran catechetical hymn rather less) became the central mode of expression for personal piety. Irrespective of any church order, Luther's priesthood of all believers was realized in the individual appropriation of hymnal-songs, which become »favorite hymns«. From the second half of the 16th century onwards, funeral sermons profiled the personal piety of the deceased precisely by mentioning such hymn titles.[54]

---

[50] Ein newe Vorrede (see note 49; cf. WA 35,475).

[51] Loc. cit., fol. 94 (introduction to the new hymns of other poets).

[52] Loc. cit., fol. 86 (introduction to the »old hymns«).

[53] See the reprint-edition: Das Babstsche Gesangbuch von 1545, ed. Konrad Ameln, Kassel 1929.

[54] VEIT, Kirchenlied (see note 2), 750–51.

3.11. The success of metrical psalms in Europe

The Luther hymnbook was not only influential in Germany; it was especially influential in Nordic countries, primarily Denmark. However, the idea of the metrical psalter enjoyed a greater diffusion across Europe.[55] It was also the book of choice in Elizabethan England, after Coverdale's *Goostly Psalms* of 1535 were based on the Luther hymnbook, with an almost word by word translation.[56] »Of the reception of this hymnbook there is precious little detail recorded.« – »Coverdale's hymns were undoubtly sung and used during daily devotions in those homes where Reformation faith and commitment had entered.«[57]

Especially at the court of Edward VI the singing of *Metrical Psalms* became popular: these were psalm-based hymns quite unlike Gregorian psalmody. There was an incomplete collection of *Certayne Psalms* conceived around 1547 that imitated the Strasbourg/Geneva melodic model.[58] The English exile community in the German town Wesel then sang numerous hymns from it.[59] Not only in Strasbourg, but also in Geneva, many English exiles experienced metrical psalm singing. There was even an English version of the Geneva Psalter published.[60]

The return of Psalm-singing to London is attested in documentary evidence dated September 21, 1559. Henry Machyn noted in his diary that in St. Antholin's Church at the beginning of the morning prayer at 5 o'clock a psalm was sung »after Geneva fassyon«, and he says, »men and women all do syng, and boys«.[61] This congregational psalm-based hymn-singing quickly spread to other churches in London and became the *Reformation Singing Movement* throughout England. Contemporary with the complete Geneva Psalter 1562 there was published *The Whole Book of Psalms*, which found enormous popularity in the following years.[62] Evidently, it also often served as a house singing book. With these »Metrical Psalms« there emerged a distinctive musical dynamic, in that the melodies were partially popularized and then reduced to a few singing models. The Eng-

---

[55] JAN ROHLS, Der Genfer Liedpsalter und das Liedschaffen im reformierten Protestantismus (in: Das Kirchenlied zwischen Sprache, Musik und Religion, BThZ 28, 2011, vol. 2, 246–261, esp. 252–256) .

[56] See the content of the hymnbook in LEAVER, Goostly Psalmes (see note 33), 66–69. However 15 of 41 hymns were psalm-hymns.

[57] Ibid., 75–76.

[58] Ibid., 120–23.

[59] Ibid., 202–18.

[60] Ibid., 228–35.

[61] Ibid., 252.

[62] Ibid., 264–66. In Scotland the Genevan Psalms were introduced by John Knox 1564.

lish did not have to adhere to Calvin's Geneva melody-dogma, and could develop their psalm-based hymns as ›pop songs‹ with a high degree of identity-formation through them.

The Book of Common Prayer, which was revised and reissued in 1559, had a new paragraph 49 on singing, which regulated very little and left much open. First of all, however, it emphasized that everything that is sung in the services must be »a modest and distinct hymn«. »That the same may be as plainly understood, as if it were read without singing«. Under this provision, however, – »it may be permitted, that in the beginning, or in the end of Common Prayers, either at morning or evening, there may be sung a hymn, or suchlike hymn, to the praise of Almighty God«.[63] Congregational singing as a supporting program does not disturb the liturgy, whether this is conducted as an artistically ambitious »high church« worship with choir and professional resources in the cathedrals, or rather more simply in the Parish Churches.[64] The supporting program can also steal the show from the main program, and become the actual attraction:

»You may now see sometimes at Paul's Cross (London), after the service, six thousand persons, old and young, both singing together, all singing together and praising God«

marveled on 5 March 1560 a letter writer often quoted in the literature.[65]

3.12. Luther's hymnals or (Genevan) psalter?

It has become clear that the development of spiritual singing in the Reformation and its ecclesiastical regulation are very complex processes. This can only be elucidated by precise detailed research projects that cover as many dimensions as possible, including cultural and socio-historical aspects. All spiritual singing, in artistic elaboration as in the elementary hymn, is part of social-cultural practice. I did not even discuss the different development of artistically ambitious, figural music in the churches of Reformation. – The development of Reformation singing could be strikingly expressed in this polarity: *Lutheran hymn book versus Metrical Psalm*. To profile this polarity in further research would be a worthwhile task.

Addendum: After having completed this article I became aware of Joseph Herl's comprehensive study Worship Wars in Early Lutheranism. Choir, Congregation, and Three Centuries of Conflict, *New York 2004. Herl confirms my remarks in*

---

[63] Ibid., 263.
[64] Details to music in cathedrals and parish churches presents JONATHAN WILLIS, Church Music and Protestantism in Post-Reformation England. Discourses, Sites and Identities, Farnham and Burlington 2010.
[65] LEAVER, Goostly Psalmes (see note 33), 252.

sections 3.1. to 3.10. with a wealth of source material and an analogous interpretation.

Literarisch-publizistische Interaktionen zwischen England und dem Heiligen Römischen Reich Beobachtungen zur frühen Reformation[1]

Thomas Kaufmann

In all jenen Territorien und Städten, in denen die weltlichen Obrigkeiten die frühreformatorischen Entwicklungen maßgeblich steuerten und verantworteten – dem Heiligen Römischen Reich, Dänemark, Schweden und einigen osteuropäischen Ländern – kam der Gruppe der sogenannten »Reformatoren«[2] eine Schlüsselrolle zu. Mit dem traditionellen und notorisch starken Interesse an diesen amtlich bestallten, kirchlich, städtisch oder universitär alimentierten Akteuren, denen eine entscheidende Aufgabe bei der Etablierung, Organisation, Legitimation und Kommunikation der Kirchenreform und ihrer theologischen Grundlegung zukam, ging eine gewisse Wahrnehmungsschwäche gegenüber anderen Personen einher, die ohne amtliche Stellung, z.T. auch ohne festen Wirkungsort und -kreis, als vagierende Intellektuelle und freie Publizisten zugunsten einer Veränderung der bestehenden kirchlichen und gesellschaftlichen Verhältnisse wirkten. In Bezug auf die Trennlinie zwischen sogennanten ›radikalen‹ und ›magistralen‹ Reformatoren im Reich kommt der soziologischen Differenz ihrer Positionen eine signifikante Bedeutung zu; mit Ausnahme der ephemeren täuferischen Stadtreformatoren Balthasar Hubmaier und Bernhard Rothmann agierten ›radikale Reformatoren‹ der frühen Reformation quasi ›aus dem Untergrund‹, d.h. als Personen, deren Schritt in die Subversion mit dem Verzicht auf ein öffentliches Amt verbunden war.

In Bezug auf die Frühphase der englischen Reformation stellen sich die Verhältnisse anders dar; hier war der soziologische ›Normalfall‹ einer reformatorischen Existenz quasi der eines Exulanten. Im Falle der Interaktionsprozesse zwischen den Akteuren der frühen englischen und der Re-

---

[1] Dieser Beitrag stimmt in seiner Substanz überein mit einem Anhang in meinem Buch *Die Mitte der Reformation. Eine Studie zu Buchdruck und Publizistik im deutschen Sprachgebiet, zu ihren Akteuren und deren Strategien, Inszenierungen und Ausdrucksformen* (Tübingen 2019, hier: 701–718).

[2] Thomas Kaufmann, Reformatoren, Göttingen 1997; Das Reformatorenlexikon, hg. v. Irene Dingel u. Volker Leppin, Darmstadt ²2016.

formation im Reich gewinnt man freilich den Eindruck, dass einige Exulanten eher den direkten persönlichen Kontakt zu einigen ›Radikalen‹ suchten als zu den etablierten Reformatoren. Dass William Tyndale in Wittenberg war, gilt als eine Art Konsens der Forschung; dass er den Kontakt zu Luther oder Melanchthon gesucht hat, ist hingegen nirgends bezeugt. Dass er schließlich im Sommer 1525 die englische Übersetzung des Neuen Testaments zusammen mit seinem Landsmann William Roye zunächst in Köln und später in Worms in den Druck brachte (s.u.), ist gesichert. Dass die beiden Engländer dafür nicht die im Sommer 1525 mit ca. acht Offizinen bereits sehr stark ausgebaute typographische Infrastruktur Wittenbergs nutzten, sondern sich stattdessen auf die Gefahren der Buchproduktion in der zu diesem Zeitpunkt bereits antireformatorisch profilierten Reichsstadt Köln einließen, ist merkwürdig und – so denke ich – erklärungsbedürftig. Dem geläufigen Argument der günstigen Transportbedingungen der gedruckten Fracht über den Rhein würde ich zunächst die nicht minder attraktive Elbverbindung von Wittenberg nach Hamburg entgegenhalten – zumal Tyndale über die Hansemetropole am ›Tor zur Welt‹ ins Reich eingereist sein soll.[3]

Sollte Tyndale zwischen Frühjahr 1524 und Sommer 1525[4] in Wittenberg gelebt haben, nahm er vielleicht Folgendes wahr: den Beginn der Kontroverse zwischen Erasmus und dem Wittenberger Reformator Luther; einen ersten Höhepunkt der innerreformatorischen Verwerfungen in Gestalt von Luthers Polemik gegen Karlstadt; dessen Ausweisung aus Kursachsen; Luthers Kampf gegen Müntzer und dessen Fall; die im Frühjahr 1525[5] in Wittenberg aufgetauchte niederländische Gruppe von Sektie-

---

[3] ARNE DEMBEK, William Tyndale (1491–1536). Reformatorische Theologie als kontextuelle Schriftauslegung, Tübingen 2010, 47.

[4] Folgt man der eindrucksvollen Rekonstruktion von JAMES FREDERICK MOZLEY (William Tyndale, London 1937, 53), dann hat aufgrund des Wittenberger Matrikeleintrages »Guilelmus Daltici ex Anglia« vom 27. Mai 1524 dieses Datum als terminus ante quem von Tyndales Ankunft in der kursächsischen Universitätsstadt zu gelten. Geht man sodann davon aus, dass Tyndale Wittenberg gemeinsam mit seinem Landsmann William Roye, der sich am 10. Juni 1525 in die Wittenberger Matrikel eintrug, verließ (DEMBEK, Tyndale [s. Anm. 3], 47, 54 ff.), ergibt sich der etwaige Zeitraum von Tyndales Präsenz.

[5] »Novum genus prophetarum ex Antwerpia hic habeo asserentium, spiritum sanctum nihil aliud esse quam ingenium & rationem naturalem« (Luther an Spalatin, 27.3.1525: WA.Br 3,464,9–11). Die Forschung identifiziert diesen Hinweis mit dem Schieferdecker Eloy Pruystick, dem »Haupt der Sekte der ›Loyisten‹«, der mit einigen Anhängern im März 1525 in Wittenberg war. Dieser Besuch soll den Anlass für Luthers *Sendschreiben an die Christen in Antwerpen* (WA 18,547–550; JOSEF BENZING, HELMUT CLAUS, Lutherbibliographie. Verzeichnis der gedruckten Schriften Martin Luthers bis zu dessen Tod, zwei Bände, Baden-Baden ²1989–1994 [= BENZING, CLAUS], Nr. 2200; VD16 L 4149), gebildet haben, das in eine starke zeitliche Nähe zu diesem Besuch datiert wird

rern, die Eloyisten; die Auswirkungen des Bauernkriegs und die Anfänge des Abendmahlsstreites mit den Schweizern[6]. War Tyndale aufgrund dieser Erfahrungen mit der Wittenberger Reformation verstört? Diese Frage zu stellen, ist m.E. unumgänglich; sie offen zu lassen, leider auch. Allerdings wird man mit der Möglichkeit rechnen müssen, dass Tyndales deutliche Absage an Thomas Mores Behauptung, er stehe in einem ›Bund‹ mit Luther[7], nicht nur taktischer Natur war. Sie könnte auch einer durch die Wittenberger Erfahrungen gespeisten inneren Distanz zu dem kursächsischen Reformator entsprochen haben.

Angesichts des spezifischen Quellencharakters von Bugenhagens gedruckter *Epistola ad Anglos* und Luthers ›Privatbrief‹ an Heinrich VIII. vom 1. September 1525[8] halte ich es methodisch im Unterschied zu anderen[9] für geboten, zwischen beider Intentionen deutlich zu unterscheiden. Bugenhagens *Epistola*, die in je einem Wittenberger Erstdruck auf Latein und auf Deutsch erschienen war[10], richtete sich an »die Heiligen in

---

(»als April 1525«: WA 18,545). Luther selbst rekurriert allerdings nicht auf diesen persönlichen Besuch sondern gibt als Ursache seiner Schrift an: »Ich bin bewegt worden aus Christlicher liebe und sorge, an euch [sc. die Christen in Antwerpen] diese schrifft zu tun, Denn ich erfaren habe, wie es bey euch regen die yrrigen geyster, wilche die Christliche lere hyndern und besudeln sich unterwynden, wie denn an mehr orten auch geschicht, auff das ich, so viel an myr ist, meyne pflichtige trewe und warnunge an euch beweyse, und nicht auff mich durch meyn schweygen kome yrgents blut« (WA 18,547,5–12).

[6] Bugenhagens den Abendmahlsdissens mit Zürich erstmals öffentlich thematisierende *Epistola contra novum errorem*, der eine wichtige Bedeutung bei der Konfliktseskalation des innerreformatorischen Abendmahlsstreites zufiel (THOMAS KAUFMANN, Die Abendmahlstheologie der Straßburger Reformatoren bis 1528, Tübingen 1992, 282ff.), lag Mitte Juli 1525 gedruckt vor. Ein handschriftlicher Eintrag Luthers auf einem Exemplar des [Wittenberger] Urdrucks [Melchior Lotters] (GEORG GEISENHOF, Bibliotheca Bugenhagiana, Leipzig 1908, Nr. 171; VD16 B 9385) datiert auf den 19. Juli 1525 (Ex. UB Heidelberg, Sign. Sal 80/21; KAUFMANN [a.a.O.], 282, Anm. 65).

[7] Vgl. DEMBEK, Tyndale (s. Anm. 3), 46 mit Anm. 197.

[8] WA.Br 3,562–565 (Nr. 914).

[9] So DOROTHEA WENDEBOURG, Die deutschen Reformatoren und England (in: Sister Reformations, hg. v. ders., Tübingen 2010, 53–93, hier: 66f.).

[10] Epistola Ioannis Bugenhagii Pomerani ad Anglos, Wittenberg [N. Schirlentz] 1525 (VD16 B 9302); Ein Sendbrief an die Christen ynn Engeland, warynnen ein Christlich leben stehet, Wittenberg [J. Klug] 1525 (VD16 B 9307). Die [Augsburger] Offizin [S. Ruffs] brachte sowohl eine lateinische als auch eine deutsche Ausgabe heraus (VD16 B 9301, B 9306). Ansonsten erschien eine lateinische Ausgabe, die bisher noch nicht zugeordnet wurde (s.l., 1525; VD16 B 9300) und eine [Kantz] in [Altenburg] zuzuschreibende deutsche (VD16 B 9305) Ausgabe. Interessanterweise sind die außerhalb Wittenbergs erschienenen deutschen Ausgaben beide Neuübersetzungen. Zu Cochläus' kommentierender Ausgabe der *Epistola* [Köln, Quentel] 1526 (VD16 B 9303/9304) siehe unten Anm. 22. In der Ausgabe von Bugenhagens Briefen (Dr. Johannes Bugenhagens Briefwechsel, hg. v. Otto Vogt, mit einem Vorwort und Nachträgen von Eike Wolgast, Hildesheim 1966) ist die *Epistola* nicht erwähnt.

Christo, die in England sind«[11]. Hätte ein mit dem Wittenberger Reformatorenkreis in Kontakt stehender Engländer als Übersetzer zur Verfügung gestanden, wäre kaum verständlich, warum nicht auch eine englische Version des lediglich einen Quartbogen umfassenden Schriftchens gedruckt worden wäre.

Den Erscheinungszeitpunkt von Bugenhagens *Epistola* innerhalb des Jahres 1525 einzugrenzen, ist, soweit ich sehe, unmöglich; irgendwelche Nachrichten über eine potentielle Hinwendung des englischen Königs zur Reformation oder über die Person Heinrichs VIII. enthält Bugenhagens Schreiben – im Unterschied zu Luthers Brief vom 1. September – nicht. Die *Epistola* gibt allenfalls vage Hinweise auf die Situation der »Engländer«, die der Wittenberger Pfarrer voraussetzt: Zum einen habe das Evangelium in England Zuspruch gefunden, also die Reformation an Boden gewonnen; zum anderen aber würden »viele Schwache« durch irgendwelche Unruhen (rumores) und Gerüchte über die Wittenberger verunsichert oder zur Abkehr veranlasst.[12] Auch wenn Bugenhagen – ähnlich wie Luther[13] – gemäß Mt. 5,11 in der üblen Nachrede, die ihm bzw. den Wittenbergern widerfahre, einen Beweis für die Wahrheit ihrer Position sah und einschärfte, dass die sittliche Verfassung kein Hindernis für den Glauben sein dürfe[14], ließ er sich doch darauf ein, dass »das, was über uns Böses gesagt werde«[15], der Annahme des Evangeliums bzw. der Ausbreitung der Reformation in England entgegenstehen könne. Vor allem die zahlreichen Streitthemen, die nun aufgekommen seien, könnten den »Einfältigeren« als probater Einwand gegen die von Wittenberg ausgehende Reformation erscheinen: Willensfreiheit, Gelübde, Genugtuungsleistungen, der Umgang mit Verstorbenen etc.[16] So sei der Verdacht aufgekommen, dass sich hinter der Vielfalt der Positionen ein »geheimes Gift« verberge.[17]

---

[11] »Sanctis in Christo qui sunt in Anglia« (VD16 B 9302, A 1ᵛ).

[12] »Non potuimus non gaudere quando audivimus et in Anglia Evangelium gloriae dei apud quosdam bene audire, Caeterum et illud nobis nunciatum est, multos infirmiores adhuc averti, propter rumores nescio quos, qui isthic feruntur ab illis qui Evangelio dei adversantur de nobis« (ebd.). Das Personalpronomen »nobis« dürfte in beiden Fällen *uns*, die Wittenberger, meinen.

[13] Vgl. Luthers Reaktionen auf die ihm bekannt gewordene Kritik an seiner zweiten Bauernkriegsschrift in der Korrespondenz des Sommers 1525: WA.Br 3,515,7ff.; 517,3ff.

[14] Epistola (s. Anm. 11), A 2ʳ.

[15] »Hoc vero miramur cur sacrum Christi Evangelium quidam isthic verentur suscipere propterea quod de nobis mala dicuntur, ignorantes quod oportet filium hominis reprobari a mundo et stulticiam haberi predicationem crucis« (ebd.).

[16] »Verum aiunt rudiores, quis ista tam varia capere potuit? disputatur enim de libero arbitrio, de votis et sectis monasticis, de satisfactionibus, de abusu venerandae eucharistiae, de cultu sanctorum defunctorum etc.« (a.a.O., A 2ʳ/ᵛ).

[17] »Alij aiunt. Veremur ne sub ista varietate lateat venenum« (a.a.O., A 2ᵛ). Die Wittenberger Übersetzung interpretiert: »Die andern sagen / wir fürchten uns das nicht

Ob die aufgrund der »varietas« gewonnenen Argumente gegen die Wittenberger Reformation primär die Auseinandersetzung mit der ›römischen‹ Seite betraf oder aber auch die ›innerreformatorischen‹ Kontroversen, ist nicht leicht zu entscheiden. Indem Bugenhagen allerdings den Satz »Christus est iustitia nostra«[18] als den einen und maßgeblichen Artikel herausstellte, der »von uns« gelehrt werde[19], markierte er die Grenze gegenüber all jenen Positionen, die er nicht mehr als »christlich« anzuerkennen bereit war – gleichviel ob es sich um traditionelle ›Altgläubige‹ handelte oder im Zuge der reformatorischen Bewegung entstandene ›Sekten‹.[20] Mit dem Bild des guten Baumes, der gute Früchte bringt, trat der Wittenberger Stadtpfarrer auch dem Haupteinwand gegen die evangelische Rechtfertigungslehre, nämlich dass sie zu einem Niedergang der guten sittlichen Werke führe, entgegen.[21] Aus dem Rechtfertigungsglauben folge das rechte Gottes- und Weltverhältnis und ein Christi Einsetzung entsprechendes Verständnis der Sakramente.[22]

Die *Epistola ad Anglos* dürfte – so möchte ich folgern – vor allem darauf abgezielt haben, der Skepsis erasmianisch geprägter Kreise in England entgegenzutreten, die fürchteten oder gar verbreiteten, dass die von Wittenberg ausgehende Reformation zu Zwiespalt und Sittenverfall führe. Wäre es nicht denkbar, ja wahrscheinlich, dass Tyndale und Roye, jene beiden Engländer, deren Aufenthalt in Wittenberg wir im Jahre 1525 voraussetzen können, den Anlass für jenes patstorale Schreiben Bugenhagens geliefert hätten? Besitzt es nicht sogar eine gewisse Wahrscheinlichkeit, dass sich die *Epistola* auf verstörte Reaktionen bezog, die das ›germanische Spektakel‹ des Sommers 1525 auf die von außen kommenden, gegenüber den reformatorischen Entwicklungen im Reich verunsicherten Engländer ausgelöst hatte? Ich vermute, dass der durch Tyndale und Roye mit ent-

---

yrgent ein gyfft unter solcher mancherley handlung und Disputation begraben und verborgen sey?« (VD16 B 9307, A 2ʳ).

[18] VD16 B 9302, A 2ᵛ.

[19] »Et ne varietatem doctrine excuses breviter dico, unum tantum articulum a nobis doceri, utcunque quotidie multa praedicamus, multa scribamus, multa agamus contra adversarios et ut ipsi salvi fiant. Est autem articulus ille. Christus est iustitia nostra« (ebd.). Die letzten vier Worte ließ Bugenhagen in einer dreimal größeren Type drucken.

[20] »Quisquis hoc [sc. den Hauptartikel] non dederit nobis, non est Christianus, quisquis autem fatebitur nobiscum, apud eum statim cadet alia quaecunque iusticia humana, Nihil hic erit Pelagiana haeresis, qua licet mutatis verbis infecti sunt qui vel solos se Christianos gloriantur, nihil valebit omnis sectarum quae hodie sunt et operum fiducia, quam abnegato crucis Christi scandalo nostri iustificarii nobis invenerunt, dum opera pro Christo nobis venditarunt« (a.a.O., A 3ʳ).

[21] A.a.O., A 3ᵛ–A 4ʳ.

[22] »Sobrie itaque pie et iuste vivet [sc. der Christ], adorabit deum in spiritu et veritate non in elementis mundi, cibis et vestitu, aut alia hypocrisi, sentiet de sacramentis quod Christus docuit et instituit« (a.a.O., A 4ʳ).

sprechender Skepsis konfrontierte Wittenberger Stadtpfarrer mittels der *Epistola* und der Konzentration auf das seines Erachtens essentiell Reformatorische diesen Einwänden zu begegnen versuchte.

Im Februar 1526 gab Johannes Cochläus eine kommentierte Ausgabe der Bugenhagenschen *Epistola* in der [Kölner] Offizin [Peter Quentels] heraus[23]; darin verbreitete er die Auffassung, dass Bugenhagens Brief fiktiv sei und in Deutschland den Eindruck erzeugen sollte, dass die Insel der Reformation zuneige; Letzteres bestritt Cochläus nachdrücklich.[24] Ansonsten lieferte Cochläus' *Responsio* an Bugenhagen instruktive Anhaltspunkte dafür, dass es dem Wittenberger Stadtpfarrer vor allem um die innerreformatorischen Fraktionierungen gegangen sei.[25] Die Behauptung

---

[23] Epistola Iohannis Bugenhagii Pomenrani ad Anglos. Responsio Iohannis Cochlaei, 1526 (VD16 B 9303/9304; Datum der dem Kölner Senator Hermann Rinck gewidmeten Vorrede: »III. Idus Februarias« [11.2.]: A 2ʳ). Zu Cochläus: MONIQUE SAMUEL-SCHEYDER, Johannes Cochläus, humaniste et adversaire de Luther, Nancy 1993.

[24] »Ad quos tu [sc. Bugenhagen] scripseris nescio, scio autem hoc excusae per Chalcographos epistolae tuae exemplar, quod in manus meas pervenit, ex Ulma huc esse transmissum [sc. vermutlich der Augsburger Druck, s. Anm. 10]. Scio item in Angliam non posse hanc aut consimilem epistolam tuto perferri publice. Suspicari itaque licet, a te fraude conficutam esse, ad hoc ut Germaniae populi eo facilius vestra recipiant dogmata, quo difficilius admissuros & accepturos credunt Anglos, quorum Rex tam egregium contra Lutherum iam pridem scripsit & emisit librum. Per mathematicam [i.S. von ›fantastisch‹] vero hanc epistolam tuam decepti credant nunc. Regem illum simul cum tota gente sua in partes concecisse vestras« (VD16 B 9304, C [5]ᵛ).

[25] Das von Bugenhagen verwendete Stichwort der *libertas Christiana* (VD16 B 9302, A 1ᵛ) nahm Cochläus folgendermaßen auf: »Qua obsecro fronte aut quibus verbis defendas, quae sub praetextu Evangelij Christianaeque libertatis hoc anno [sc. 1525] a Lutheranis Rusticis in plaerisque superioris Germaniae provincijs perpetrata sunt?« (VD16 B 9304, A 3ᵛ). In Bezug auf die Auseinandersetzungen über den ›freien Willen‹ führte Cochläus neben Erasmus Bischof John Fisher und sich selbst, der gegen Melanchthon geschrieben habe (De libero arbitrio hominis adversus locos communes Philippi Melanchtonis, [Tübingen, U. Morhart d.Ä.] 1525; VD16 C 4342), an; in Bezug auf die Gelübde nannte er Johannes Dietenberger, der auch bezüglich der Frage der Genugtuungsleistungen (»de satisfactionibus«, a.a.O., B 1ᵛ) neben Fisher, Eck und Clichtoveus hervorgetreten sei. Hinsichtlich der Abendmahlsfrage aber formulierte er: »De abusu Eucharistiae quanta sit impietas vestra, horret profecto animus dicere. Ut omittam, quae Rusticorum vulgus Luthericum hoc anno [sc. 1525] perpetravit in capsulis & ciboriis horendissima, vestra vos produnt scripta. Num ignoras [sc. Bugenhagen] quam absurda & impia protulerit male uxoratus vester Archidiaconus [sc. Karlstadt], quem Lutherus ipse reprobavit? Qualia vero sunt Lutheri? Quando unquam constitit sibi ipsi? Utcunque nunc ad populum, cui Archidiaconi vestri obsurditas nimium displicet, aduletur, certe ad Vualdenses scribens [sc. WA 11,431–456], dicebat, externam Eucharistiae venerationem minime necessariam esse neque damnandos, qui eam non adorare aut venerari dignantur« (a.a.O., B 1ᵛ). Hinsichtlich der Differenzen innerhalb des reformatorischen Lagers notierte Cochläus sodann: »Quae inter paucos annos adeo varia multiplexque facta est, ut tot fere sint inter vos fidei opiniones diversae, quot capita, quot factionum duces. Aliter enim praescribit credendi formulam Lutherus, aliter Carolstadius, aliter Zuuinglius, aliter Oecolampadius, aliter alij, quisque pro beneplacito sui popelli ac pro cerebelli proprii phantasia« (a.a.O., B 2ʳ). Und noch einmal gegen den besonders verachteten

des entschiedenen Luthergegners, Bugenhagen habe sich die Anhänger der Reformation auf der Insel lediglich ausgedacht, stand allerdings in einer schwer vermittelbaren Spannung dazu, dass er den zeitweilig in engen Beziehungen zu König Heinrich und seinem Kanzler Kardinal Wolsey stehenden Kölner Ratsherrn Hermann Rinck[26], dem er seine Erwiderung auf Bugenhagen gewidmet hatte, in einem Widmungsschreiben dazu aufforderte, den englischen König vor den immensen Gefahren zu warnen, die von der soeben im Bauernkrieg explodierenden lutherischen Lehre ausgingen.[27]

Sodann spricht gegen Cochläus' Behauptung, nennenswerte Sympathisanten der Reformation gäbe es in England nicht, dass er selbst gegen die wohl aus Wittenberg nach Köln gereisten englischen Glaubensexulanten Tyndale und Roye vorging. In ihrem klandestinen Tun, nämlich der Drucklegung der ersten Ausgabe des englischen Neuen Testaments in der Offizin [Peter Quentels][28], sah der seit Frühjahr 1525 vorübergehend in der Rheinmetropole lebende Kontroverstheologe späteren Rückblicken zufolge eine immense Gefahr für den Bestand des englischen Katholizismus, dessen historisch frühe und enge Verbindung zu Rom zu erwähnen

---

Karlstadt: »Et Archidiaconus vester neminem post apostolos melius quam se scripsisse iactitat de sacramento Eucharistiae [vgl. WA 15,335,29–32]. Cum interim rerum eventus nos doceat. Nihil minus quam Evangelium dedisse Lutherum. Nec quempiam sceleratius de sacramento Eucharistiae scripsisse quam vestrum Archidiaconum« (a.a.O., B 3ᵛ–4ʳ). Ähnlich wie [Emser] in Dresden die innerreformatorische Kontroversistik dadurch anzufeuern versuchte, dass er Bugenhagens *Epistola contra novum errorum* nachdruckte (VD16 B 9388), tat dies Cochläus mit Luthers *Rhatschlag* zum Widerstandsrecht von 1530 (THOMAS KAUFMANN, Konfession und Kultur. Lutherischer Protestantismus in der zweiten Hälfte des Reformationsjahrhunderts, Tübingen 2006, 43ff.) und mit *Wider die räuberischen und mörderischen Rotten der Bauern* (BENZING, CLAUS, Nr. 2161–2163: Köln, P. Quentel, teils unfirmiert = VD16 L 7501f., L 7485; weitere gegnerische Nachdrucke: BENZING, CLAUS, Nr. 2137. 2164–2167).

[26] Einige Hinweise auf Rincks Verbindungen zum englischen Königshof sind seinem Brief an Kardinal Wolsey vom 4. Oktober 1528 zu entnehmen (in: EDWARD ARBER, The First Printed English New Testament, London 1871, Nr. 4, 32–36). Cochläus charakterisiert ihn folgendermaßen:»Herman Rinck / ein Cöllnischen Gschlechter und Ritter / so etwa der Keyserlichen Mayestat und des Königs von Engellandt Rath und Diener gewest« (COCHLÄUS, Historia Martini Lutheri, VD16 C 4280, 292).

[27] »Diabolus enim non dormit, sed tanquam Leo rugiens circuit quaerens quos devoret. Circuivit apud nos per hanc factionem tam diu, donec supra centum milia Rusticorum Lutheranorum, ipso etiam ferente sententiam Luthero, devoravit, necdum tamen tanto sanguine sic fuso satiatus est, cum nusquam satis fidam adhuc pacem esse sinat. Expedit igitur, Prudentiss[ime] domine Hermanne[,] ut primo quoque tempore Regem, cui tot annis laudabiliter A consiliis fuisti hodieque esse cognosceris, super his periculosis insidiis certiorem facias, ne Germaniae incommoda sub falso Evangelii praetextu Angliae quoque regnum, quod florentissimum est, invadant ac perturbent« (COCHLÄUS, Epistola [s. Anm. 23, VD16 B 9304], A 2ʳ).

[28] VD16 B 4569. Ein fragmentarisch erhaltenes Exemplar (31 Bl. [bis inklusive Bg. H]: STC 2823) ist über EEBO zugänglich.

er nicht müde wurde.[29] Im Jahre 1533, also acht Jahre nach den Ereignissen selbst, berichtete Cochläus erstmals nicht ohne Stolz öffentlich darüber, wie es ihm gelungen sei, die Drucklegung von »Lutheri novum testamentum in linguam Anglicanam«[30] zu verhindern; insgesamt drei Mal erzählte er die Geschichte in Druckschriften.[31] Ich folge der ausführlichsten Version aus seiner Lutherbiographie: Zwei englische Apostaten, die in Wittenberg Deutsch gelernt hätten, seien nach Köln gekommen, um dort heimlich die englische Übersetzung des Neuen Testaments in einer Auflage von 3000 Exemplaren drucken zu lassen. Ihr Ziel sei gewesen, England heimlich dem Luthertum zuzuführen. Cochläus, der in Konkurrenz zu einer bei Johann Petreius in Nürnberg erscheinenden protestantischen Ausgabe in der Kölner Offizin Peter Quentels Drucke Rupert von Deutz' betreute[32], habe zufällig ein Gespräch in der Offizin, in dem sich einige Drucker über die gelehrten Engländer und ihr Vorhaben austauschten, gehört. Daraufhin habe der entschiedene Lutherfeind »etliche Trucker«[33] in seine Herberge eingeladen; »auß wolthat des Weins«[34] konnte Cochläus dann von einem der Drucker »den gantzen Handel«[35] in Erfahrung bringen. Demnach sollten die 3000 Exemplare des englischen NT auf Kosten englischer Kaufleute hergestellt und heimlich verschifft werden. Gegenüber den Druckern verstellte sich Cochläus; am kommenden Tag aber kontaktierte er den bereits erwähnten Kölner Patrizier Herman Rinck. Dieser ließ in der Werkstatt [Quentels] umgehend Nachforschungen anstellen und fand Cochläus' Angaben bestätigt; auch die entsprechend gro-

---

[29] Zur Mission des Mönchs Augustins im Auftrag Papst Gregors I. vgl. VD16 B 9304, A 2ᵛ–A 3ʳ, A 4ʳ/ᵛ (gelegentlich in Konfrontation zu dem sich aufblasenden ›Kaff‹ Wittenberg).

[30] JOHANNES COCHLÄUS, An expediat laicis legere Novi Testamenti libros lingua vernacula, [Augsburg, Weißenhorn] 1533 (VD16 C 4235), A [6]ʳ.

[31] In der folgenden Darstellung lasse ich die drei Versionen (JOHANNES COCHLÄUS, Scopa in araneas Morysini Angli, Leipzig 1538 [VD16 C 4382], B 2ʳ; DERS., Commentaria de Actis et Scriptis Martini Lutheri, Mainz [S. Behem] 1549, ND o.J., 132–135; deutsche Ausgabe: Ingolstadt 1582 [VD16 C 4280], 292–294; COCHLÄUS, An expediat [s. vorige Anm.]) ineinander fließen; Einzelnachweise gebe ich nur im Falle direkter Zitate. Den Hinweis auf diese Ausgaben verdanke ich GERGELY M. JUHÁSZ, Translating Resurrection. The Debate between William Tyndale and George Joye in its Historical and Theological Context, Leiden u. Boston 2014, 249, Anm. 644. Vgl. zu Cochläus' Lutherbiographie: ADOLF HERTE, Das katholische Lutherbild im Bann der Lutherkommentare des Cochläus, drei Bände, Münster 1943.

[32] Vgl. VD16 R 3782–3784; R 3796. Zu den Petreiusschen Rupert-Drucken: THOMAS KAUFMANN, Die Mitte der Reformation. Eine Studie zu Buchdruck und Publizistik im deutschen Sprachgebiet, zu ihren Akteuren und deren Strategien, Inszenierungs- und Ausdrucksformen, Tübingen 2019, 243 ff.

[33] COCHLÄUS, Historia Martini Lutheri (VD16 C 4280), 292.

[34] A.a.O., 293.

[35] A.a.O., 292.

ße Papiermenge war in der Werkstatt bereits vorhanden. Rinck sprach daraufhin beim Kölner Rat vor und erreichte, dass der Druck abgebrochen werden musste. Den beiden Engländern aber gelang die Flucht, wobei sie die bereits gedruckten Quartbögen mitnahmen; ihre Flucht führte sie rheinaufwärts ins reformatorisch geprägte Worms. Man wird voraussetzen können, dass sie sich bei der Flucht abermals der Unterstützung der Kaufleute bedienten. Rinck und Cochläus aber richteten Briefe an den englischen König, Kardinal Wolsey und Bischof John Fisher, in denen sie vor den gefährlichen Druckwaren warnten und scharfe Einfuhrkontrollen nahelegten.

Gewiss – Cochläus erzählte diese Vorgänge erst lange Zeit nachdem sie sich ereignet hatten. Allerdings ist bereits für seine *Responsio* gegen Bugenhagen die Zusammenarbeit mit Herman Rinck im Kampf um das katholische Profil Englands bezeugt. M. E. ist es wahrscheinlich, dass Cochläus in Bugenhagens *Epistola* ein Zeugnis dafür sah, wie akut die drohende Gefahr eines reformatorischen Umschwungs im Inselreich war. Dies öffentlich zuzugeben aber hätte der gegnerischen Seite gedient. Aus den genannten Indizien ergibt sich deshalb folgende Hypothese: Bugenhagen war mutmaßlich in Wittenberg durch Tyndale und Roye damit konfrontiert worden, dass englische Sympathisanten »des Evangeliums«, die einen humanistischen Bildungshintergrund hatten, durch das Zerwürfnis mit Erasmus und die im Sommer 1525 offen zu Tage liegenden inneren Konflikte der reformatorischen Bewegung im Reich verstört waren. Bugenhagen versuchte die damit gegebene Herausforderung dadurch aufzufangen, dass er die Rechtfertigungslehre als integrierendes Kriterium der wahren Lehre herausstellte. Dass Tyndale selbst der gegenüber dem polemischen Positionalismus Wittenbergs skeptischen Position der englischen Reformationssympathisanten zuneigte, ist wahrscheinlich. Dass die reformatorische Entwicklung Englands – unbeschadet der Lektüre Luthers – von ihren frühesten Anfängen an einen gegenüber dem Wittenberger Reformator und den doktrinalen Fixierungen im Reich eigenständigen Charakter besaß, war – so scheint mir – auch eine Folge dessen, dass ihre frühesten Repräsentanten, die Glaubensexulanten auf dem Kontinent, die innerreformatorischen Zerwürfnisse zutiefst befremdeten. Dass die entscheidenden Unterstützer der beiden ›Apostaten‹ Tyndale und Roye englische Kaufmänner und Landsleute waren, dürfte ihre Eigenständigkeit gegenüber Wittenberg und den anderen frühen Etablierungszentren der Reformation im Reich begünstigt haben.

In seinen Rückblicken auf den durch ihn veranlassten Abbruch des Kölner Erstdrucks des Tyndaleschen Neuen Testaments nannte Cochläus folgende Gründe dafür, dass die Rheinmetropole als Druckort gewählt worden war: Köln sei quasi eine Nachbarstadt Englands, ein berühmter Handelsplatz, verfüge über geeignete Verschiffungsbedingungen und habe den Exulanten nach dem Bauernkrieg günstige Möglichkeiten des Unterschlupfs geboten.[36] Ob die Entscheidung Tyndales und Royes für Köln aus eigenem Antrieb erfolgt war, ist freilich ungewiss. Das Projekt eines Drucks des englischen Neuen Testaments in einer Auflagenhöhe von 3000 Exemplaren – was exakt dem Volumen des Lutherschen Septembertestaments entsprach[37] – erforderte einen erheblichen logistischen und vor allem finanziellen Planungsvorlauf. Allein die Papierkosten waren gewiss mit deutlich über 1000 fl. zu veranschlagen. Da Cochläus ausdrücklich erwähnte, dass die Papiermenge für den Druck der 3000 Exemplare bereits vorhanden war, war deren Finanzierung entsprechend gesichert. Dass sich Tyndale und Roye zum Druck nach Köln begeben hatten, war aller Wahrscheinlichkeit nach also eine Folge dessen gewesen sein, dass hier jenes Netzwerk an zahlungskräftigen und -willigen Sympathisanten reformatorischer Entwicklungen existierte, ohne das ein Großprojekt dieser Art undenkbar war. Offenbar war von vornherein nicht an einen Verkauf der gedruckten Exemplare auf dem Kontinent – etwa mittels eines Transports zur Frankfurter Buchmesse – gedacht; vielmehr sollte die gesamte Auflage nach England überführt und heimlich verbreitet werden.[38] Diese Strategie zur Verbreitung der evangelischen Botschaft dürfte vor allem vor dem religionskulturellen Hintergrund einer jahrhundertelangen Jagd nach den Resten lollardischer Bibeln zu interpretieren sein.[39]

---

[36] »Etenim ante annos octo, duo ex Anglia Apostatae, qui Vuittenbergae Teuthonicam edocti linguam, Lutheri novum testamentum in linguam Anglicanam verterant, Coloniam Agrippinam venerunt, tanquam ad urbem Angliae vicinorem, mercatuque celebriorem, & navigiis ad transmittendum aptiorem, ibique post rusticorum tumultum latitantes, conduxerunt sibi in occulto Chalcographos, ut mox primo agressu tria milia exemplarium imprimenent« (COCHLÄUS, An expediat laicis [s. Anm. 30, VD16 C 4245], A 6ʳ).

[37] Näheres in: KAUFMANN, Mitte der Reformation (s. Anm. 32), 377ff. Vgl. WOLFGANG SCHELLMANN, Luthers Septembertestament von 1522. Neue Erkenntnisse zu Auflagenhöhe und Ökonomie (in: Archiv für Geschichte des Buchwesens 72, 2017, 1–22).

[38] »Der Uncosten [sc. des Drucks] wurde dißfahls uberflüssig von den Engelischen Kauffleuthen dargewendt / welche das gantze getruckte Werck in Engellandt führen / und eh solchs der König / oder Cardinal [Wolsey] erführen / hin unnd wider heimlich außbreitten wurden ec.« (VD16 C 4280, 293).

[39] Zu den Lollarden: RITA COPELAND, Pedagogy, Intellectuals, and Dissent in Later Middle Ages. Lollardy and Ideas of Learning, Cambridge 2004; ANNE HUDSON, Premature Reformation. Wycliffite Texts and Lollard History, Oxford 1988; WOLF-FRIEDRICH SCHÄUFELE, Wegbereiter der Reformation? »Vorreformatorische« religiöse Bewegungen und ihre Anhänger im 16. Jahrhundert (in: Entfaltung und zeitgenössische Wirkung der Reformation im europäischen Kontext, hg. v. Irene Dingel u. Ute Lotz-Heumann, Gütersloh 2015, 137–153, hier: 142ff.).

Vieles spricht dafür, dass das Druckprojekt von längerer Hand vorbereitet war und dass die entsprechenden Kontakte bereits vor dem Sommer 1525 bestanden hatten. Die Anwesenheit der beiden englischen *exules Christi* am Druckort Köln bzw. in der Offizin [Quentels] stellte ohne Zweifel eine notwendige Voraussetzung für den Satz in der fremden Sprache und die Korrekturprozesse dar. Dass der [Quentel-] Druck nach Auskunft des Cochläus' bis zum Bogen K gelangt war[40], setzte – auch beim Einsatz von zwei oder mehr Pressen – eine Produktionszeit von mehreren Wochen voraus.[41] Dass [Quentel] während dieser Zeit darauf verzichtet hätte, auch anderes Schrifttum zu drucken, ist unwahrscheinlich, da dies eine gewiss unerwünschte Aufmerksamkeit auf das klandestine Druckprojekt des englischen NT gelenkt hätte. Wahrscheinlich hing Cochläus' Besuch in der Quentelschen Offizin damit zusammen, dass er selbst dort regelmäßig zu tun hatte, weil er dort eigene Werke drucken ließ bzw. andere herausgab oder sonstige Druckwaren erwerben wollte.[42]

---

[40] Demnach hatte Cochläus bei seinem Herbergsgespräch mit den Druckern der Quentelschen Offizin erfahren: »Es wären gleich jetzo underm truck drey tausent Exemplar des Lutherischen in die Englische Spraach gebrachten newen Testaments / und man wäre nun biß an Buchstaben K. in Ordnung des Alphabeths kommen« (COCHLÄUS, Historia Martini Lutheri, VD16 C 4280, 292f.). Das erhaltene Fragment des Drucks (s. Anm. 28) reicht nur bis Bogen H; aufgrund dieses Befundes sehe ich allerdings keine Ursache, Cochläus' Nachricht zu misstrauen.

[41] Setzt man – mit ANDREW PETTEGREE (Die Marke Luther, Berlin 2016, 120) – eine Produktionsleistung von 500 Ex. eines Quartbogens pro Tag als Durchschnittswert einer Presse an, kommt man bei 10 Bögen (A-K, in der Regel ohne J) einer Auflage von 3000 Ex. auf ein Druckvolumen von 30.000 Bogen; dies entspräche ca. 60 Arbeitstagen mit einer Presse bzw. 30 auf zwei, 20 auf drei etc.

[42] Mit dem Datum des 25.2.1525 war Cochläus' Schrift *De Petro et Roma adversus Velenum* bei Quentel in Köln erschienen (VD16 C 4353/4354; HANS-JOACHIM KÖHLER, Bibliographie der Flugschriften des 16. Jahrhunderts, Teil 1: Das frühe 16. Jahrhundert [1501–1530]. Druckbeschreibungen, Bd. 1, Tübingen 1991, Nr. 559). In seiner Vorrede hob Cochläus die Verdienste des englischen Bischofs John Fisher um die Verteidigung der römischen Petrustradition gegen die 1520 bei [Cratander] in [Basel] und bei [S. Otmar] in [Augsburg] erschienene Schrift des jungen tschechischen Humanisten Odlřich Velenský (Ulrichus Velenus) *In hoc libello gravissimis [...] rationibus [...] probatur Apostolum Petrum non venisse [...] Romam* (VD16 V 504f.) hervor, der bestritten hatte, dass der Apostelfürst jemals in Rom gewesen sei (dazu: ANTONIE JAN LAMPING, Ulrichus Velenus [Oldřich Velenský] and his Treatise against the Papacy, Leiden 1975; vgl. auch THOMAS KAUFMANN, Der Anfang der Reformation, Tübingen [2]2018, 48. 278f., sowie DERS., Das Ende der Reformation, Tübingen 2003, 349f.; zu Luthers Aufnahme seiner Gedanken: WA.Br 2,260,11f.). Wohl vorher war die gleichfalls auf 1525 datierte, mit Kolophon gedruckte Ausgabe von Predigtexzerpten Luthers mit Widerlegungen Cochläus' herausgekommen: Confutatio XCI. Articulorum: e tribus Martini Lutheri sermonibus excerptorum, Authore Iohanne Cochlaeo, Köln, Quentel 1525 (VD16 L 5500f.; Datum der Vorrede: Mainz 3.11.1524, A 1ᵛ). Eine von Cochläus kompilierte Zusammenstellung von 400 häretischen Artikeln aus 36 Predigten Luthers veröffentlichte Quentel im September 1525: Articuli CCCC Martini Lutheri. Ex sermonibus eius sex & Triginta, Köln, Quentel 1525 (VD16 L 6657; Datum der Vorrede: 3.8.1525). Auch die

In den 1520er Jahren war der Drucker Peter Quentel der produktivste unter den Kölner Druckern. Er war der Erbe eines in die 1470er Jahre zurückreichenden Traditionsbetriebs. Auch als Verleger war Peter Quentel tätig und gehörte der einflussreichen »Kaufleutegaffel Eisenmarkt«[43] an; zudem übte er einige Ratsämter aus. In dem uns interessierenden Jahr 1525 hatte er eine Art Doppelexistenz begonnen. Neben einer sehr reichhaltigen gegenreformatorischen Druckproduktion, die mit Bernhard von Luxemburg[44], Jakob von Hoogstraeten[45], Johannes Dietenberger[46], Johannes Eck[47], Johannes Cochläus oder John Fisher[48] die profiliertesten Reformationsgegner umfasste, brachte Quentel in einigen nicht – firmierten Drucken auch reformatorische Literatur in Umlauf: Neben dem englischen Neuen Testament[49] waren dies mindestens drei niederdeutsche Drucke ›erbaulichen‹ Inhalts.[50] Vielleicht war das Wissen um Peter Quentels zeit-

---

niederdeutsche (VD16 L 7506; BENZING, CLAUS Nr. 2166) und die hochdeutsche (VD16 L 7485) Sammelausgabe von Bauernkriegsschriften Luthers, u.a. *Wider die räuberischen* [...] *Rotten der Bauern*, brachte Quentel in firmierten Drucken 1525 heraus. Den Lutherschriften war Cochläus' Schrift *Ein kurtzer Begriff* (VD16 C 4338), ein Beitrag zum Bauernkrieg, der insbesondere Luthers Verantwortung für das Desaster, herausstellte, beigedruckt. Insofern war klar, dass auch diese öffentlichen Drucke Quentels ein ›gegenreformatorisches‹ Profil hatten. Auch 1526 war Cochläus für Quentel ein wichtiger Autor; aufgrund seines Engagements für die Rupert-Drucke (s. Anm. 32; vgl. VD16 C 4382, B 2ʳ) ist davon auszugehen, dass Cochläus auch 1526 eine wichtige Aufgabe für die Akquise neuer Druckaufträge für Quentel spielte.

[43] CHRISTOPH RESKE, Die Buchdrucker des 16. und 17. Jahrhunderts im deutschen Sprachgebiet. Auf der Grundlage des gleichnamigen Werkes von Josef Benzing, Wiesbaden 2007, 432. Zum zeitgenössischen Kölner Druckgewerbe in der frühen Reformationszeit: WOLFGANG SCHMITZ, Buchdruck und Reformation in Köln (in: Jahrbuch des Kölnischen Geschichtsvereins 55, 1984, 117–154); DERS., Beten und Lesen im Untergrund. Evangelischer Buchdruck in der katholischen Reichsstadt Köln bis zum Ende der kölnischen Reformation ca. 1547 (in: Reformation und Buch, hg. v. Thomas Kaufmann u. Elmar Mittler, Wiesbaden 2016, 85–104).

[44] 1525/6: VD16 B 1991, B 1995.

[45] 1525/6: VD16 H 4805, H 4817.

[46] 1525/5: VD16 D 1484, D 1480.

[47] 1525/6: VD16 E 329f., E 255, E 334f.

[48] 1525: VD16 F 1219, F 1226f., F 1238–1240. Die *Defensio Regie assertoris contra Babylonicam captivitatem* [...] *per Reverendum* [...] *Ioannem Roffensem Episcopum. In quo respondet pro illustrissimo* [...] *Anglorum Rege Henrico* (VD16 F 1226f.) erschien in erster Ausgabe im Juni 1525 bei Quentel in Köln. Von dem ›sichtbaren‹ Druckprofil der Quentelschen Druckerei her legte sich die Wahl dieser Offizin für den Druck klandestiner englischsprachiger Literatur also schwerlich nahe. Insofern besitzt es eine gewisse Wahrscheinlichkeit, dass die Finanziers, die Geschäftsbeziehungen zu Quentel besessen haben mögen, diese Entscheidung getroffen hatten.

[49] Der Druck des NT (VD16 B 4569; STC 2823; s. Anm. 28) bei [Quentel] enthielt einen von Tyndale verfassten Prolog auf das Matthäusevangelium (in: Doctrinal Treatises and Introductions to Different Portions of the Holy Scripture by William Tyndale, martyr, 1536, hg. v. Henry Walter, The Parker Society, Cambridge 1848, 1–28; zum Inhaltlichen: DEMBEK, Tyndale [s. Anm. 3], 68ff.).

weilige religionspolitische Ambiguität, die wirtschaftliche wie persönliche Gründe gehabt haben mag, auch dafür verantwortlich, ihm den gewiss lukrativen Druckauftrag des englischen Neuen Testaments anzuvertrauen.

Die Inkriminierung des Drucks des Tyndaleschen Neuen Testaments erfolgte dadurch, dass Rinck ein entsprechendes Verbot durch den Kölner Rat erreichte. Da es Tyndale und Roye gleichwohl möglich war, bei ihrem Abgang aus Köln die bereits bedruckten Bögen mitzunehmen und diese mit dem Schiff nach Worms zu bringen[51], ist wohl nicht nur von einer weitergehenden Unterstützung durch Kaufleute auszugehen, sondern auch davon, dass sie vorab gewarnt worden waren.

Warum die Wahl der englischen Glaubensexulanten oder ihrer Unterstützer auf Peter Schöffer in Worms fiel, ist unklar. Peter Schöffer war, ähnlich wie Peter Quentel, der Sohn eines sehr berühmten Druckers aus Gutenbergs erster Werkstatt; die Druckerfamilien Quentel und Schöffer werden sich gekannt und auf den Frankfurter Messen, deren Besuch auch durch Tyndale bis 1528 gesichert ist[52], regelmäßig begegnet sein. Cochläus erwähnte, dass »der gemeine Mann mit viler unsinnigkeit das Lutherische Evangelium«[53] in Worms angenommen habe[54], was gewiss ein unbehelligteres Drucken ermöglichte. Vielleicht hatte sich Schöffer auch durch ein eben gedrucktes deutsches Neues Testament empfohlen.[55]

---

[50] Und zwar eine niederdeutsche Auslegung einer Vaterunser-Auslegung Luthers (VD16 L 4066; Benzing, Claus, Nr. 279), ein Gebetbuch Luthers (VD16 L 4120; Benzing, Claus, Nr. 1308) und des Braunschweiger ›Frühreformators‹ Gottschalck Kruse (über ihn: Im Aufbruch Reformation 1517–1617, hg. v. Heike Pöppelmann u. Dieter Rammler, Dresden 2017, 428ff.; Antje Rüttgart, Klosteraustritte in der frühen Reformation. Studien zu Flugschriften der Jahre 1522 bis 1524, Gütersloh 2007, 21ff.) Schrift *Von Adams und unserm valle* (VD16 K 2473).

[51] Bei Cochläus heisst es, dass Rinck nach entsprechenden Nachforschungen an den Kölner Rat herantrat: »und brachte endtlich die Sachen dahin / daß den Truckern undersagt wurde / in dem Werck [sc. dem englischen NT] weiters fortzufahren. Hierauff flohen die zwen verloffne Englische Münch mit den getruckten Quatern dem Rein nach aufwerts nach Wormbs« (VD16 C 4280, 293 f.).

[52] Magret Popp, Eberhard Zwink, Verwirrspiel um eine Bibel. Der englische Reformator William Tyndale und sein Neues Testament: Das Stuttgarter Exemplar (in: Philobiblon 45, Heft 4, 2001, 275–324, hier: 281). Aus Rincks Brief an Wolsey vom 4. Oktober 1528 (s. Anm. 26) geht hervor, dass Juden in den Transfer englischer Bücher nach Frankfurt involviert waren (Arber, First Printed English New Testament [s. Anm. 26], 33).

[53] VD16 C 4280, 294.

[54] Zur Reformation in Worms: Stephen Buckwalter, Die Priesterehe in Flugschriften der frühen Reformation, Gütersloh 1998, 256ff.; Sabine Todt, Kleruskritik, Frömmigkeit und Kommunikation in Worms im Mittelalter und in der Reformationszeit, Stuttgart 2005.

[55] VD16 B 4364. Busso Diekamp (The Newe Testament, Worms 1526 – William Tyndale und sein Drucker Peter Schöffer d.J., in: Der Wormsgau 30, 2013, 107–158, hier: 116), weist darauf hin, dass die Titeleinfassungen des deutschen und des englischen

Für das Wahrscheinlichste aber halte ich, dass ein noch ins Jahr 1525 zu datierender Wyclif-Druck Schöffers – der erste Druck des großen englischen Ketzers überhaupt! – auf eine Verbindung des Wormser Druckers zu den englischen Exulanten und zu dem Straßburger ›Buchakteur‹ Otto Brunfels, der in den Wyclif-Druck involviert war, schließen lässt. Im Unterschied zu Melanchthon, der sich wohl im Vorjahr, 1524, gegen eine Publikation der ihm vermutlich durch Tyndale bekannt gemachten Dialoge Wyclifs ausgesprochen hatte, hatte Brunfels deren Drucklegung betrieben. Wahrscheinlich bestanden also bereits vor der Entscheidung für Quentel als Drucker des englischen NT Kontakte Tyndales zu Schöffer.[56]

Drucks des NT, die Schöffer herstellte, identisch waren. Zu Schöffer grundlegend: ALEJANDRO ZORZIN, Peter Schöffer d.J. und die Täufer (in: Buchwesen in Spätmittelalter und Früher Neuzeit, FS Helmut Claus, hg. v. Ulman Weiss, Epfendorf 2008, 179–213); KAUFMANN, Mitte der Reformation (s. Anm. 32). Aufgrund der sorgfältigen bibliographischen Analyse dieses ersten Schöfferschen Bibeldrucks und seiner Beziehungen zu dem Straßburger Drucker Knobloch ist P. Pietsch aufgrund eines unvollständigen Ex. zu der Datierung »[1524/5]« gekommen (WA.DB 2, Anhang, 705–708). Das Titelblatt, das die Datierung 1526 trägt, lässt allerdings keinen Zweifel daran, dass Schöffer wohl mit oder auch für Knobloch gedruckt hat, was die Identität einzelner der verwendeten Bilder erklärt. Möglicherweise kann man bei der Datierung innerhalb des Jahres 1526 an den Anfang gehen. Zwingende Gründe dafür, dass Schöffer ›sein‹ deutsches vor dem englischen NT gedruckt hatte, sehe ich allerdings nicht. Denkbar ist also auch, dass der lukrative Auftrag zum Druck des Tyndaleschen NT für Schöffer den Eintritt in den Bibeldruck bedeutete.
[56] IO Wiclefi Viri Undiquaque pii. Dialogorum libri quattuor [...] Excusum Anno a Christi nato MDXXV. Die VII Martii, [Worms, Peter Schöffer d.J.], VD16 W 4688 (kritisch hg. v. Gotthard Lechler: Joannis Wiclif Trialogus cum Supplemento Trialogi, Oxford 1869, zur Ausgabe von 1525: 11 f.; s. auch KAUFMANN, Mitte der Reformation [s. Anm. 32], 598 f.). Entgegen früheren Überlegungen bezgl. der Herausgeberschaft der Wyclif-Schrift (KAUFMANN, Abendmahlstheologie [s. Anm. 6], 267 f., Anm. 909), die ich in Unkenntnis des Brunfelsschen Briefes an Luther aus dem April 1525 (WA.Br 3,476–478, Nr. 858) angestellt habe, scheint mir die maßgebliche Verantwortung Brunfels' für die [Schöffersche] Wyclif-Ausgabe evident zu sein. Vielleicht wird man davon ausgehen können, dass Brunfels durch böhmische Vermittlung an das Wyclif-Manuskript gelangt war und es zu den ›anderen‹ (Geistlicher Bluthandel, VD16 G 983, A 1ʳ) gehörte, die er von dort erhalten hatte. Denkbar ist aber auch, dass er direkten Kontakt mit Engländern hatte, die sich in Straßburg aufhielten. Aus einem undatierten Brief Melanchthons (MBW.T 2,220 [Nr. 363]: 1524?) geht allerdings hervor, dass auch dieser eine Handschrift des *Trialogus* gesehen hatte, allerdings von einer Drucklegung desselben nichts hielt (MBW.T 2,220,4 f.), da die in ihm enthaltenen Dialoge teilweise bedeutungslos, teilweise vom sprachlich-logischen Kolorit ihrer Epoche geprägt seien (»partim leves disputationes partim obscurissimiae et ex mediis scholis dialecticorum illius temporis depromptae«: MBW.T 2,220,5 f.) – ein Einwand gegen den Text, den auch der Humanist [Brunfels] geltend machte (VD16 W 4688, A 2ᵛ). Sollte die Ansetzung des Melanchthon-Briefes auf ca. 1524 zutreffen, wäre natürlich denkbar, dass Tyndale ihm das Manuskript gezeigt hatte. Nach WILLIELL R. THOMSON, The Latin Writings of John Wyclyf, Toronto 1983, 79, sind heute acht z.T. fragmentarische Handschriften des *Trialogus* bekannt. Instruktive Hinweise zu den überlieferungsgeschichtlich maßgeblichen Verbindungen nach England und den Wyclif-Handschriften in Böhmen: JOHANN LOSERTH, Huss und

Vermutlich wandten sich Tyndale und Roye, nachdem sie in Köln ›aufgeflogen‹ waren, also an jenen Drucker, mit dem sie bereits zuvor in direktem oder indirektem Kontakt gestanden hatten. Durch eine Notiz Georg Spalatins, der am Rande des ersten Speyrer Reformationsreichstages von dem Humanisten Hermann von dem Busche einschlägige Informationen erhalten hatte, ist bezeugt, dass sich Tyndale in der Zeit, als Schöffer das englische Neue Testament druckte, zeitweilig mit zwei Landsleuten in Worms aufgehalten hat und dass die Auflage gegenüber dem Quentelschen Erstdruck auf 6000 Exemplare verdoppelt worden war.[57] Sollte dieser Hinweis zutreffen, dürfte der gewiss durch englische Kaufleute finanziell abgesicherte lukrative Großauftrag entscheidend dafür verantwortlich gewesen sein, dass Schöffer bald darauf imstande war, seine ambitionierte Prophetenausgabe[58] zu finanzieren. Der sich daran anschließende Einstieg Schöffers in die klandestine Druckproduktion zugunsten von Täufern und Spiritualisten war initial durch den ökonomischen Erfolg infolge der Herstellung des englischen Neuen Testaments möglich geworden.

Geht man gemäß der Cochläus-Überlieferung davon aus, dass Peter Schöffer, der schließlich erfolgreiche Erstdrucker des englischen Neuen Testaments, das nur in einem einzigen Exemplar erhalten geblieben ist[59], die Möglichkeit gehabt hatte, die Bogen A-K des abgebrochenen Quentelschen Drucks zu verwenden, fällt auf, dass das Buch, das Schöffer schuf, etwas Neues und Anderes war. Im Unterschied zu Quentel wählte er ein Oktavformat und verzichtete auf die langen und typographisch problematischen Randglossen Tyndales sowie die Vorreden; stattdessen stellte er lediglich ein an Luthers Septembertestament orientiertes Inhaltsverzeich-

---

Wiclif. Zur Genese der hussitischen Lehre, München, Berlin 1925, 193–203. Ein weiteres Indiz für eine direkte typographische Verbindung zwischen Straßburg und Schöffer ist in dessen Druck des sogenannten Hoen-Briefes (Epistola Christiana [...] ex Bathavis missa [...] tractans coenam dominicam, [Worms, Schöffer 1525], VD16 ZV 8053; zum Verhältnis dieses Drucks zum Straßburger: KAUFMANN, Abendmahlstheologie [s. Anm. 6], 292ff.; dagegen: BART JAN SPRUYT, Cornelius Henrici Hoen [Honius] and his Epistle on the Eucharist [1525]. Medieval Heresy, Erasmian Humanism, and Reform in the Early Sixteenth-Century Low Countries, Leiden u.a. 2006) gegeben.

[57] »Item Wormatiae VI. mille exemplaria Novi Testamenti Anglice excusa. Id operis versum esse ab Anglo, illic cum duobus aliis Britannis divertente, ita VII linguarum perito, Hebraicae, Graecae, Lintinae, Italiae, Hispaniae, Britannicae, Gallicae, ut quamcunque loquatur, ea natum putes« (GEORG SPALATIN, Excerpta quaedam e Diario Georgii Spalatini Msto, in: Amoenitates literariae 4, 1725, 389–432, hier: 431; vgl. POPP, ZWINK, Verwirrspiel [s. Anm. 52], 280f., Anm. 4).

[58] ULRICH OELSCHLÄGER, Die Wormser Propheten von 1527. Eine vorlutherische Teilübersetzung der Bibel (in: BPfKG 75, 2008, 331–362 [Ebernburg-Hefte 42, 2008, 19–50]).

[59] Landesbibliothek Stuttgart, Sign. T 7 N°. 202 / 8° B engl 1526 01 (VD16 B 4570). Vgl. POPP, ZWINK, Verwirrspiel (s. Anm. 52).

nis, das Hebr., Jak., Jud. und Apk. ohne Zählung aufführte, voran. Im
Falle der Vorrede zum Röm ist eine von Schöffer separat gedruckte »compendious introduction« überliefert;[60] ob – wie ich vermute – auch zu den
anderen biblischen Schriften entsprechende Vorreden gedruckt worden
waren, die, wie die gesamte nach England verschiffte Produktion Schöffers, vernichtet worden ist, muss offen bleiben. Dem Druck des *New Testament* war ein knappes Nachwort »To the Reder« beigefügt, das Tyndale
zugeschrieben wird.[61] Es bot einige elementare hermeneutische Orientie-
rungen: An das Wort der Schrift sei mit einem reinen Geist heranzutreten;
unsichere Stellen sollten von den »manyfest places«[62] her gedeutet werden;
die Unterscheidung von »lawe and gospell«[63] galt als elementar; Buße und
Glaube erschlössen den Sinn der Schrift. Der Anonymus schloss mit einem Bekenntnis zu seinen eigenen Grenzen als Übersetzer, der Hoffnung
auf eine stetige Verbesserung der englischen Übersetzung und der Bitte:
»praye for us«.[64] Nach allem, was wir wissen, war dies das erste erfolgreich
gedruckte Wort, das ein englischer Glaubensexulant an seine Landsleute
gerichtet hat. Ob man es als spezifisch ›reformatorisch‹ identifizieren sollte, ist durchaus schwer zu entscheiden.

Das weitere Schicksal dieses Buches ist bekannt; durch das Mandat des
Erzbischofs von Canterbury (3.11.1526) wurde verfügt, dass alle Exemplare des Drucks aufgespürt und vernichtet werden sollten.[65] Unter den
geopolitischen Bedingungen des englischen Königreichs funktionierte also
das traditionelle Instrument der Inquisition und der Ketzerbekämpfung,

---

[60] STC 24438 (nicht nachgewiesen in VD16). Einziges Ex.: Oxford, Bodl. Libr. (abgedruckt in: WALTER, Doctrinal Treatises [s. Anm. 49], 484–510; vgl. DEMBEK, Tyndale
[s. Anm. 3], 83 ff.).

[61] VD16 B 4570, Tt 1ᵛ–Tt 2ᵛ (abdruckt in: WALTER, Doctrinal Treatises [s. Anm. 49],
389–391; vgl. DEMBEK, Tyndale [s. Anm. 3], 81 ff.).

[62] VD16 B 4570, Tt 1ᵛ.

[63] Ebd.

[64] A.a.O., Tt 2ᵛ.

[65] POPP, ZWINK, Verwirrspiel (s. Anm. 52), 281, 288 ff. Zum Text des Mandats: Letters
and Papers foreign and domestic of the reign of Henry VIII, Bd. 4, Teil 2, 1158, Nr.
2607. Dem Mandat ist in der Edition eine Liste verbotener englischer und lateinischer
Bücher angefügt. U.a. genannt werden: »The Supplication of Beggars [s.u. Anm. 75]. The
Revelation of Antichrist of Luther [s.u. Anm. 73]. The New Testament of Tindall. Oeco-
nomia Christiana [s.u. Anm. 78]. [...] An Introduction to Paul's Epistle to the Romans.
A Dialogue betwixt the Father and the Son. [...] Captivitas Babylonica. Johannes Hus in
Oseam. Zuinglius in Catabaptistas. De Pueris Instituendis [s.u. Anm. 68]. Brentius De
Administranda Republica. Lutherus ad Galatas. De Libertate Christiana. Luther's Ex-
position upon the Pater Noster.« Wegen der z.T. späteren Erscheinungsdaten kann die
Liste allerdings nicht von 1526 stammen. Zu dem Hinweis auf den Kaufpreis von zwei
Schilling und acht Pence, dem Kaufkraftäquivalent von 5 kg Rindfleisch bzw. dem Ar-
beitslohn für fünf Tage Maurerarbeit: POPP, ZWINK, ebd.; vgl. The New Testament.
Translated by William Tyndale, XVf.

die Bücherverbrennung[66], nach wie vor leidlich; im Reich war dieses Instrument infolge der territorialen Zersplitterung sowie der Diversität und Vielfalt der typographischen Infrastrukturen faktisch zur weitgehenden Wirkungslosigkeit verdammt.

Bevor Antwerpen von den späten 1520er Jahren an für einige Jahre zum maßgeblichen Publikationsort der frühreformatorischen englischen Dissenter wurde, hatte Straßburg kurzfristig eine ähnliche Rolle gespielt. Als der Kölner Patrizier Herman Rinck den zu dieser Zeit vornehmlich für Otto Brunfels tätigen Straßburger Drucker Johann Schott auf der Frankfurter Herbstmesse des Jahres 1528 nach dem Verbleib Royes und Tyndales fragte und in Erfahrung brachte, dass englische Bücher an Frankfurter Juden verpfändet worden waren,[67] besiegelte er, wie es scheint, das Schicksal Straßburgs als Exils- und Publikationsort der Engländer. Johann Schott, dem vor allem daran gelegen war, seine Auslagen für Papier und Arbeitskosten zurückzuerhalten, war bereit, sie dem meistbietenden Käufer zu überlassen. Durch entsprechende Aufwendungen vereitelte Rinck, dass die gedruckten Bücher nach England geschmuggelt wurden.[68]

Bei diesen englischen Titeln wird es sich um eine Kardinal Wolsey als Verbrenner des Wortes Gottes scharf attackierende Versdichtung mit dem Titel *Rede me and be nott wrothe For I saye no thynge but trothe*, die Roye und Barlowe zugeschrieben wird[69], und um die von Roye angefer-

---

[66] Grundlegend ist Thomas Werner, Den Irrtum liquidieren. Bücherverbrennungen im Mittelalter, Göttingen 2007. Zu antireformatorischen Bücherverbrennung im England der 1520er Jahre, beginnend am 12. Mai 1521: John D. Fudge, Commerce and Print in the Early Reformation, Leiden u. Boston 2007, 76 ff. Eine im Februar 1526 nach dem Auftauchen auf dem Kontinent gedruckten reformatorischen Schrifttums in England durch John Fisher veranlasste Bücherverbrennung erwähnen Popp, Zwick, Verwirrspiel (s. Anm. 52), 297.

[67] »However, I [sc. Rinck], as a most humble, faithful and diligent servant, three weeks [sc. um den 1. September 1528 herum] before receiving your grace's letters, heard and perceived that those very books had been pawned to the Jews at Frankfurt for a certain sum of money [...]. The engraver, John Schott, demanded beside the interes for the Jews, the pay for his labour and the expense of the paper, and said that he should sell them to whoever would give the most money« (Arber, English New Testament [s. Anm. 26], 32 f.). Zu Schott: Reske, Buchdrucker (s. Anm. 43), 873 f.; Kaufmann, Mitte der Reformation (s. Anm. 32), 253 ff.

[68] »I [sc. H. Rinck] might scrape and heap together all those books from every place; which was done in three or four places, so that I hope that all those books yet printed are in my possession, except two which your grace's [sc. Kardinal Wolsey] commissary the above named John West asked for and received from me for the greater profit and advantage of the king's grace and yours. Two books indeed, I gave him [...]. Unless I had discovered it, and interfered, the books would have been enclosed and hidden in paper covers, packed in ten bundles covered with linen and conveyed in time by sea«. Als Akteure hätten englische Kaufleute zu gelten, die die Bücher bei den Juden auslösten und Schott bezahlten (Arber, English New Testament [s. Anm. 26], 33).

[69] [Straßburg, Johann Schott 1528], STC 1462.7, VD16 R 434. Zur Verfasserfrage und

tigte englische Übersetzung von Capitos dialogisch formuliertem Katechismus *De pueris instituendis* bzw. *Kinderbericht und Fragstuck*[70] gehandelt haben. Dass Roye die katechetische Schrift dieses Straßburger Reformators übersetzt hatte, dürfte vor allem darauf zurückzuführen sein, dass
Capito in jener Zeit das besondere Vertrauen der ›Radikalen‹ und ›Dissenter‹ besaß und öffentlich dafür eintrat, den innerreformatorischen Abendmahlsstreit zu entschärfen bzw. in seiner Bedeutung herunterzuspielen.
Capito wurde, wie es scheint, in der weiteren Geschichte der englischen
Reformation zu einer wichtigen, freilich bisher nicht identifizierten Quelle
spiritualistischer Sakraments- und Kirchenvorstellungen.[71]

---

zum Inhalt: WILLIAM A. CLEBSCH, England's Earliest Protestants 1520–1535, Yale 1964,
230ff. Im Jahr 1546 erschien eine Neuausgabe der Schrift (STC 1462.9), die eine aktuelle
Vorrede und einige kleinere Erweiterungen aufwies. Wahrscheinlich handelte es sich hier
um einen Amsterdamer Druck. In der Vorrede des Drucks von 1528 sprach Roye einen
ungenannten »Master. P.G.N[.]O.« (VD16 R 434, a 2^r), der offenbar sein Landsmann
war, an. Demnach hatte Roye das Reimgedicht vorab handschriftlich versandt und die
Aufforderung erhalten, es in den Druck zu geben. Dass er dem Publikationswunsch des
Ungenannten entsprach, begründete [Roye] folgendermaßen: »Which thynge [sc. den
Druck] (the bonde of charite / where with not alonly you and I / but we with the whole
nomre of Christis chosen flocke / remaynge amonge oure nacion of englisshe men / are
knet together / purly for the truthes sake pondered) I could do no lesse but fulfill and
accomplysshe« (ebd.). Tyndale sah in dem Wolseys Kampf gegen das englische Neue
Testament scharf attackierenden Reimgedicht allerdings einen Anlass, sich von Roye zu
distanzieren (DEMBEK, Tyndale [s. Anm. 3], 61f.; CLEBSCH, Protestants [s.o.], 230f.). In
Bezug auf die Schärfe gegen die Kirche von England gab es also offenkun-
dige ›Temperamentsunterschiede‹ zwischen den englischen *exules*.
   [70] Der zunächst auf Latein, dann auf Deutsch erschienene Katechismus Capitos war
1527 bei [Herwagen] (VD16 C 833) und [Köpfel] (VD16 834–836) in [Straßburg] erschienen. Die englische Übersetzung durch William Roye brachte Johann Schott heraus
(ADOLF WOLF, William Roye's Dialogue between a Christian Father and his Stubborn
Son, Wien 1874, 10f.; BEATE STIERLE, Capito als Humanist Gütersloh 1974, 210, Nr.
29e). Die Übersetzung wurde 1550 erneut von Gwalter Lynne unter folgendem Titel in
den Druck gegeben: The true beliefe in Christ and his sacramentes, London [S. Mierd-
man] for Gwalter Lynne 1550 (STC 24223.5). Lynne, der Herausgeber des Drucks, teilte
über die Herkunft des Textes Folgendes mit: »The author of the boke I know not. Only
this I finde that it was fyrste written in the duche long, and then translated into latine.
But whoso he were that first wrote it, or that translated it into latine: certen I am that it
is a ryght Godly, & worthy to be often times reade of al Christen men. It declareth
effectuously and very pytyly the. Xii. Articles of the Christian faith and insidently the
righte understandige of the sacraments. So that it maye rygthe well be called the summe
of Christianitie, or rather the perfect rule of Christen religion« (a.a.O., A 2^v).
   [71] CLEBSCH, Protestants (s. Anm. 69), 234, dem mit weiten Teilen der sonstigen englischen Forschung – auch DEMBEK, Tyndale (s. Anm. 3, 61, Anm. 51), spricht davon, dass
der »Verfasser« »unbekannt« sei (vgl. auch MOZLEY, Tyndale [s. Anm. 4], 122; DAVID
DANIELL, William Tyndale. A Biography, Yale 1997, 143f.; WALTER, Doctrinal Treatises
[s. Anm. 49], 39f.) – entgangen ist, dass Capito der Verfasser des von Roye übersetzten
›Dialogs‹ von Vater und Sohn war, fasst die Bedeutung der Schrift folgendermaßen
zusammen: »*A Brefe Dialoge* first stated in English the viewpoint of the Reformation
radicals. The position won few adherents before its ecclesiology was adopted by sepe-

Dass sich die publizistischen Aktivitäten der englischen Dissenter im Jahre 1529 nach Antwerpen verlagerten, dürfte vor allem damit zusammengehangen haben, dass die Transporte der Druckwaren über die englischen Kaufleute von der niederländischen Metropole aus offenbar reibungs- und gefahrloser funktionierten als dies bei der Route vom Oberrhein abwärts der Fall war.

Die Sehnsucht vieler Engländer nach einem volkssprachlichen Neuen Testament[72], die wohl auch vor dem Hintergrund der Geschichte der Lollarden und des stetigen Kampfes gegen englische Bibeln, der das späte Mittelalter begleitet hatte, zu verstehen ist, wurde von den einschlägigen Appellen des Erasmus[73] ebenso wie von der Wittenberger Praxis des deutschen Bibeldrucks bestärkt. Insofern sollten die Bemühungen um die volkssprachliche englische Bibel m.E. nicht vorschnell mit einer spezifischen theologischen ›Nähe‹ zur Reformation im Allgemeinen oder zu Luther im Besonderen identifiziert werden.

Nennenswerte Bemühungen der auf dem Kontinent publizistisch aktiven englischen Glaubensexulanten, Luthersche Texte in ihrer Muttersprache bekannt zu machen, hat es außer im Sommer 1529, als immerhin zwei seiner Schriften in z.T. gekürzter Form in der [Antwerpener] Offizin [Johannes Hoochstratens] in Übersetzung erschienen sind, nicht gegeben.[74] Bei einem dieser Drucke war ein spezifisches Interesse an Luthers

---

ratists after 1580, although sacramental spiritualism found advocates among some more radical English Protestants in the reign of Edward VI.«

[72] »Anglos enim, quamvis reluctante & invito Rege, tamen sic suspirare ad Evangelion, ut affirment, sese empturos Novum Testamentum, etiamsi centesis milibus aeris sit redimendum« (von dem Busche, in: SPALATIN, Excerpta [s. Anm. 57], 431 f.).

[73] HEINZ HOLECZEK, Humanistische Bibelphilologie als Reformproblem bei Erasmus von Rotterdam, Thomas More und William Tyndale, Leiden 1975, 138 ff.; KAUFMANN, Anfang (s. Anm. 42), 78 ff.

[74] Bis zu Luthers Tod sind nach Ausweis von BENZING, CLAUS zehn Drucke Lutherscher Schriften in der englischen Sprache erschienen. Die früheste und mit zwei Drucken erfolgreichste war die englische Übersetzung von Luthers Brief vom 1. September 1525 (zum Kontext: WENDEBOURG, Die deutschen Reformatoren [s. Anm. 9], 62 ff.; WA.Br 3, Nr. 899; WABr 3,500 f. mit Anm. 3; WABr 3, Nr. 914; WA 23,18 ff.), die natürlich durch Heinrich VIII. bzw. andere Reformationsgegner veranlasst war und seine in der Hoffnung auf eine Hinwendung des englischen Königs zur Reformation erfolgte Selbsterniedrigung öffentlich bekannt machen sollte (vgl. BENZING, CLAUS, Nr. 2402a/b). Die m.W. ersten reformationsaffinen Übersetzungen Luthers in die englische Sprache erschienen im Sommer 1529 in der [Antwerpener] Offizin [Johannes Hoochstratens]. Dabei handelte es sich um eine auf die Offenbarung des päpstlichen Antichristen fokussierte Teilübersetzung von Luthers acht Jahre zuvor erschienener *Schrift gegen Ambrosius Catharinus* (WA 7,701 ff.; zur Sache: KONRAD HAMMANN, Ecclesia Spiritualis. Luthers Kirchenverständnis in den Kontroversen mit Augustin von Alvendt und Ambrosius Catharinus, Göttingen 1989) bzw. der Antithesen des *Passionals Christi und Antichristi* (dazu: KAUFMANN, Mitte der Reformation [s. Anm. 32], 646 ff.) durch John Frith (BENZING, CLAUS, Nr. 888; STC 11394; datiert auf 12.7.1529; dazu: CLEBSCH,

Lehre vom päpstlichen Antichristen und der dieser antithetisch gegenübergestellten Kirche Christi zu erkennen. Außerdem betonte der Übersetzer John Frith in seiner Vorrede an den Leser, dass Sündenerkenntnis und Rechtfertigungsglaube engstens zusammenhingen.[75]

In der gleichzeitig in Amsterdam erschienenen Schrift Simon Fishs *A Supplicayon for the Beggars,*[76] die die Form einer an Heinrich VIII. gerichteten Rede hatte, warnte der Exulant vor der sich auf jede erdenkliche Weise bereichernden tyrannischen Klerisei, die die politische Ordnung und den ›gemeinen Nutzen‹ unterminiere und das englische Neue Testament bekämpfe. Der König solle um seiner Untertanen willen endlich den Kampf gegen die römische Geistlichkeit, den Antichristen, aufnehmen. Dieser scharfe Antiklerikalismus Fishs hatte mit dem, wofür Luther und die Seinen gegen Ende der 1520er Jahre standen, nicht mehr viel zu tun. Dass Simon Fishs *Supplicayon* im Jahr ihres Erscheinens – soweit ich sehe als einziger Text eines der englischen ›erliest protestants‹ – in einer deutschen Übersetzung Sebastian Francks erschienen ist,[77] bestärkt den Ein-

---

Protestants [s. Anm. 69], 85 ff.) unter dem Pseudonym Richard Brightwell und eine William Roye zuzuschreibende englische Version von Luthers Auslegung von 1.Kor. 7 (WA 12,90 ff.), datiert auf »Malborow in the lande of Hesse. M. D.xxix. xx. daye Iunij.« (BENZING, CLAUS, Nr. 1680; vgl. CLEBSCH, Protestants [s. Anm. 69], 230 f.; DERS., The Earliest Translations of Luther into English, in: The Harvard Theological Review 56, 1963, 75–86). Sämtliche anderen Lutherübersetzungen werden in die Zeit ab 1534 (Wider den neuen Abgott: WA 15,175 ff.; BENZING, CLAUS, Nr. 1926: [London], Wyer 1534) datiert und sind in England selbst produziert worden. Es handelt sich um BENZING, CLAUS, Nr. 647, 766, 605, 2034, 3216, 3290, 863. Sofern eine solche Aussage angesichts des bescheidenen Befundes überhaupt berechtigt sein kann, handelt es sich vornehmlich um kleinere exegetische Werke Luthers.

[75] »It is not therfore sufficient to beleve that he is a sauiour and redemer: but that he is a sauior and redmer anto the / and this canst thou not confesse / excepte thou knowleg thyself to be a sinner / for he that thinketh him silf no sinner / neadith no sauvior and redemer. [...] There fore knowledge thy silf a sinner y' thou maist be iustifyed« (A pistle to the Christen reader The Revelation of the Antichrist, [Antwerpen, Johann Hoochstraten], 12.7.1529, STC 11394, 3ʳ; BENZING, CLAUS, Nr. 888).

[76] STC 10883. Dazu: CLEBSCH, Protestants (s. Anm. 69), 240 ff.; DUSTAN ROBERTS, Simon Fish, A Supplicacyon for the Beggars, STC 10883 (in: The EEBO Introduction Series). Siehe auch: SIMON FISH, A Supplicacyon for the beggars. Now reedited by Frederick J. Forewall, Early English Text Society 13, London 1871 (ND New York 1973). Dieser Druck wird der [Antwerpener] Druckerei des Johannes Grapheus (vgl. über ihn: Contemporaries of Erasmus, hg. v. Peter Bietenholz, Bd. 1, Toronto 1986, 123) zugeschrieben.

[77] Klagbrieff oder supplication der armen dürfftigen in Engenlandt an den König daselbs gestellet, [Nürnberg, Friedrich Peypus] 1529 (VD16 F 1211/2). Vgl. auch die Druckbeschreibung in: SEBASTIAN FRANCK, Sämtliche Werke. Kritische Ausgabe mit Kommentar, Bd. 1: Frühe Schriften, Bern, Berlin u.a. 1993, 476–481 (abgedruckt a.a.O., 216–235). In seiner Vorrede hob Franck darauf ab, dass die »Feinde des Kreuzes Christi« die in Apk. 9 erwähnten Heuschrecken seien. Die Kritik am Klerus und den Gelehrten dürfte sich wohl bereits auf die Vertreter der Kirche in allen sich bildenden ›Konfessi-

druck, dass die englischen Glaubensexulanten eher den Kontakt zu Dissentern im Reich als zu den etablierten Reformatoren suchten.

Offenkundig war es einigen der englischen Exulanten wichtiger, eine Ermahnung zum Bibelstudium aus der Feder des Erasmus[78] und die aus dem Geist der Devotio moderna gespeiste, irenische *Summa der godliker Scrifturen*, die dem Niederländer Heinrich Bommelius zugeschrieben wird,[79] in ihre Muttersprache zu übersetzen als den Wittenberger, den Basler oder den Zürcher Reformator. Die entsprechende Drucke erschienen gleichfalls 1529 in Antwerpen. Soweit ich sehe hat außer Robert Barnes, dem Ordensbruder Luthers, der 1528/9 mit Hilfe englischer Kaufleute über Antwerpen nach Wittenberg floh,[80] keiner der sich im Reich auf-

---

onen‹ beziehen. Zur Interpretation der Schrift im Rahmen der frühen Theologie Francks: CHRISTOPH DEJUNG, Sebastian Franck, Sämtliche Werke, Bd. 1: Frühe Schriften, Kommentar, Stuttgart-Bad Canstatt 2005, 293ff.; VASILY ARSLANOV, »Seliger Unfried«. Modalitäten und Strategien der Popularisierung historischen Wissens bei Sebastian Franck (1499–1542), Leipzig 2017.

[78] Erasmus von Rotterdam, An exhortation to the diligent studye of the scripture, [Antwerpen, Joh. Hoogstraten] 1529 (STC 10493; vgl. CLEBSCH, Protestants [s. Anm. 69], 234f.). Es handelt sich um eine von William Roye ausgeführte Übersetzung von Erasmus' *Paraclesis*. Ein fingiertes Kolophon (weitgehend identisch mit STC 11394 [s. Anm. 74] lautet: »At Marborow in the lande of Hesse. M. D.XXIX.XX daye Juny. By my Hans Luft.« Aus welchem Grunde der Name des seit 1523 in Wittenberg tätigen Druckers Hans Lufft (vgl. RESKE, Buchdrucker [s. Anm. 43], 996) gewählt wurde, ist schwer zu entscheiden. Sollte er den Engländern 1525 den Druck des englischen NT verweigert haben? Vgl. dazu aber: K. BECKEY, Der niederländische Buchdrucker Johannes Hoochstraten zu Antwerpen, alias »Adam Anonymus te Bazel«, alias »Hans Luft te Marburg« in einer dritten, bisher unbekannten Maske als »Steffen Rodt te Marborch in Hessen« 1530 (in: Het Boek 26, 1940, 27–38); H. STEELE, Hans Luft of Marburg (in: The Library 3th. ser. 2, 1911, 113–131); M. E. KRONENBERG, De geheimsinnige druckers Adam Anonymus te Bazel en Hans Luft te Marburg ontmaskerd 1526–1528, 1528–1530 en 1535 (in: Het Boek 8, 1919, 241–280).

[79] Eine deutsche Übersetzung dieser außerhalb des deutschsprachigen Gebietes seit 1523 sehr erfolgreichen Schrift, die eine elementare katechetische Darstellung der ganz auf Glauben, Rechtfertigung und Schriftlesung zentrierten, weitgehend unpolemischen evangelischen Lehre bietet, hat Karl Benrath vorgelegt: Die Summa der Heiligen Schrift. Ein Zeugniß aus dem Zeitalter der Reformation für die Rechtfertigung aus dem Glauben, hg. v. Karl Benrath, Leipzig 1880; vgl. WA 18,542; vgl. JEAN TRAPMAN, De summa der godliker scrifturen [1523], Leiden 1978, hier zum Zweifel an der Autorschaft Bommels: 52ff. Der niederländischen scheint eine auch unter dem Namen *Oeconomica Christiana* verbreitete lateinische Version zugrunde gelegen zu haben (HERMAN J. SELDERHUIS, PETER NISSEN, The Sixteenth Century, in: Handbook of Dutch Church History, hg. v. Herman J. Selderhuis, Göttingen 2015, 157–258, hier: 186). Als Übersetzer der englischen Ausgabe von 1529 (The summe of the holye scripture, [Antwerpen, Joh. Hoochstraten] 1529; STC 3036) gilt Simon Fish (STEVEN W. HAAS, Simon Fish, William Tyndale, and Sir Thomas More's ›Lutheran Conspiracy‹, in: JEH 23, 1978, 125–136, hier: 125 Anm. 5, 135 Anm. 2). Am 27. Mai 1530 beschloss eine englische Bischofssynode eine Liste von 92 Irrtümern, die in *The summe of holye scripture* enthalten seien (DAVID WILKINS, Concilia Magnae Britanniae et Hiberniae, London 1737, Bd. 3, 730–732).

[80] KATHARINA BEIERGRÖSSLEIN, Robert Barnes, England und der Schmalkaldische Bund (1530–1540), Gütersloh 2011, 37ff.

haltenden englischen Exulanten aus der Frühzeit der Reformation engere Kontakte zu den ›etablierten‹ theologischen Repräsentanten der magistralen Reformationen aufzubauen versucht. Vermutlich wollte man vermeiden, sich für eines der ›Lager‹, die einander seit Mitte der 1520er Jahre unversöhnlich gegenüberstanden – des ›lutherischen‹ und des ›reformierten‹ der Kontrahenten im Abendmahlsstreit und der ›Erasmianer‹ – entscheiden zu müssen.

Auch nach 1534 orientierte man sich – ungeachtet einiger weniger Lutherübersetzungen, die nun erschienen – bekanntlich nicht einfach an den kontinentalen Reformatoren. Dass man die wohl Konrad Pellikan zuzuschreibende, anonyme Flugschrift *Vom alten und neuen Gott, Glauben und Ler*[81], die eine ›vorkonfessionelle‹, weitgehend unpolemische, katechetische Darstellung ›evangelischen Christentums‹ repräsentierte, im Juni 1534 »mit königlichem Privileg« in englischer Übersetzung herausbrachte,[82] verdeutlicht, an welcher Art reformatorischer Theologie man interessiert war: biblisch, mit reichen Bezügen zur historischen Tradition des Christentums in Antike und Mittelalter, antipapistisch und gegenüber dem Mönchtum zurückhaltend, doch ohne doktrinalen Positionalismus nach innen. Der theologische ›Sonderweg‹ des englischen Protestantismus begann, wenn ich recht sehe, bereits mit den sich von den innerreformatorischen Parteiungen fern haltenden humanistisch geprägten exules Christi der 1520er Jahre. Insofern sind die deutsche und die englische Reformation zwei eher fremde Schwestern.

---

[81] Zu Pellikans Verfasserschaft: KAUFMANN, Anfang (s. Anm. 42), 528 ff. Abdruck der Schrift in: Judas Nazarei, Vom alten und neuen Gott, Glauben und Lehre. (1521.), hg. v. Eduard Kück, Flugschriften aus der Reformationszeit XII, Halle a. S. 1896.

[82] STC 25127; London, John Byddell für William Marshall, 15.6.1534. Möglicherweise existierte bereits eine frühere Ausgabe, die heute bibliographisch nicht mehr nachzuweisen ist. Dies würde jedenfalls erklären, warum KÜCK, Judas Nazarei [s. Anm. 81], Xf., im Anschluss an andere von einem Erscheinen der englischen Übersetzung bald nach 1522 spricht. Der Londoner Druck von 1534 ist nämlich datiert.

Literary and Promotional Interactions in the Reformation: Observations on Anglo-German exchange in the Early Reformation

Thomas Kaufmann

The princely Reformation as manifested in the Holy Roman Empire, Denmark, Sweden and a number of territories in Eastern Europe, was subject to the controlling influence of a new breed of man: the Reformer.[1] Drawn from the ranks of the Church or administration, the Reformer was entrusted with considerable powers to drive and shape the energies unleashed by the new Theology. With these powers he established and communicated a Church settlement tailored to the interests and expectations of his political master. The rise of this novel species of political-cum-ecclesiastical actor and his often far-reaching importance has served to obscure our view of the wider Reformation terrain, making us less sensitive to the relative significance of other actors. Historians have therefore paid much less attention to the contribution of a range of intellectuals and writers not rooted in any specific location or office.

When differentiating between the so-called ›radical‹ and ›princely‹ Reformers in the Empire, we often find a sociological difference between the office-holders of the magistrate's Reformation and the radical Reformers, who acted while rejecting any official position and often from what today we would call the ›underground‹. The only exceptions to this taxonomy which spring to my mind are the (albeit ephemeral) cases of the Anabaptist preachers Balthasar Hubmaier and Bernhard Rothmann, who proclaimed a radical municipal Reformation from an official pulpit.

From this vantage point, the early English Reformation presents an entirely different case to that of the continent. Nearly all the early English Reformers came from continental exile to bring the new faith back home to their compatriots. One forms the impression that English Reformers sought out the representatives of the radical Reformation more than those of the ›magisterial‹ Reformation.

---

[1] Cf. Thomas Kaufmann, Reformatoren, Göttingen 1997.

One such influence in the early English Reformation is the celebrated Bible scholar and translator William Tyndale. Whilst it has been established that Tyndale spent a certain amount of time in the epicentre of the German Reformation, Wittenberg, no evidence has ever been found to establish that he sought to make contact with either of its leading lights, Luther and Melanchthon.

It is striking that Tyndale and his colleague William Roye chose to print Tyndale's translation of the New Testament in Cologne, the authorities of which were openly hostile to the Reformation cause, before completing their task in Worms in the summer of 1525. Why did they not simply go to Wittenberg? Not only did the town boast eight separate printing presses, furnishing the itinerant theologians with an excellent printing infrastructure, it would have provided a far more welcoming political climate. The common argument stressing the good transport links along the Rhine from Cologne to a port from which the pair could then sail to England is not convincing, when we consider the direct route from Wittenberg to Hamburg via the Elbe. Tyndale most probably landed in Hamburg in 1524. Why should he not have returned by the same route?[2]

Had Tyndale lived in Wittenberg from early 1524 to the summer of 1525 as many suppose,[3] he would have had immediate access to the debate between Luther and Erasmus and read the bitter invective which he employed against the insurrectionary peasants and a wide range of rival Reformers and Reformed groups – Karlstadt, Müntzer, the »Eloyists« (a group of sectaries who originated in the Netherlands)[4] and the Zwinglians

---

[2] Cf. ARNE DEMBEK, William Tyndale (1491–1536). Reformatorische Theologie als kontextuelle Schriftauslegung, Tübingen 2010, 47.

[3] If FREDERICK MOZLEY's impressive reconstruction is correct (William Tyndale, London 1937, 53 seqq.), the date of the entry in the matriculation records of Wittenberg university »Guilelmus Daltici ex Anglia« which is May 27th, 1524 is the terminus *ante quem* of Tyndale's arrival. If one also takes into consideration that Tyndale left Wittenberg together with his country man William Roye, whose entry in the Wittenberg matriculae dates from June 10th, 1525 (cf. DEMBEK [see note 2], 47, 54 seqq.), one can roughly conclude that the time span of Tyndale's presence in Wittenberg was the one given above.

[4] »Novum genus prophetarum ex Antwerpia hic habeo asserentium, spiritum sanctum nihil aliud esse quam ingenium & rationem naturalem« (WA.Br 3,464,9–11: Luther to Spalatin, March 27th, 1525). Recent research connected this remark with the slater Eloy Pruystick, the »head of the sect of the ›Loyists‹«, who, together with a group of followers, visited Wittenberg in March 1525. This visit supposedly occasioned Luther's *Sendschreiben an die Christen in Antwerpen* (WA 18,547–550; JOSEF BENZING, HELMUT CLAUS, Lutherbibliographie. Verzeichnis der gedruckten Schriften Martin Luthers bis zu dessen Tod, zwei Bände, Baden-Baden ²1989–1994 [= BENZING, CLAUS], no. 2200; VD16 L 4149), which bears a date very close to Pruystick's visit (»als April 1525«: WA 18,545). Luther himself, however, does not refer to this visit but rather gives the following reason for his writing: »Ich bin bewegt worden aus Christlicher liebe und sorge, an euch [sc. the

over the beginnings of the Eucharistic controversy[5] – all which threatened the unity of the Evangelical movement. Was Tyndale distressed with the Wittenberg Reformation because of these controversies? The question must be posed but will never find a satisfactory answer. Questions of personality may even have been supplanted by political considerations with an eye to his domestic audience, namely Tyndale's concern not to nourish Sir Thomas More's accusation that he was in league with Luther.[6] Whether these tactical considerations were reinforced by personal proclivities or vice versa is a matter which we cannot resolve.

Viewing the Anglo-German Reformation exchange from the German perspective, I find the distinct intention of the two texts from Luther and Johannes Bugenhagen sufficiently striking as to warrant separate treatment.[7] Bugenhagen's *Epistola ad Anglos*,[8] first published in German and Latin, addressed itself to a wide Christian audience in England (»die Heiligen in Christo, die in England sind«[9]); Luther's ›private letter‹ to Henry VIII from September 1st 1525[10] claimed to address itself to an individual

---

Christian in Antwerp] diese schrifft zu tun, Denn ich erfaren habe, wie sich bey euch regen die yrrigen geyster, wilche die Christliche lere hyndern und besudeln sich unterwynden, wie denn an mehr orten auch geschicht, auff das ich, so viel an myr ist, meyne pflichtige trewe und warnunge an euch beweyse, und nicht auff mich durch meyn schweygen kome yrgents blut« (WA 18,547,5–12).

[5] Bugenhagen's *Epistola contra novum errorem*, which for the first time publicly mentioned the dissent with the theologians of Zurich about the Lord's Supper and was to play a significant role in the escalation of the strife among the Reformers about this topic (cf. THOMAS KAUFMANN, Die Abendmahlstheologie der Straßburger Reformatoren bis 1528, Tübingen 1992, 282seqq.) was printed by the middle of July 1525. An entry from Luther's hand in a copy of the Wittenberg original print [Melchior Lotter] (Geisenhof no. 171; VD16 B 9385) stems from July 19th, 1525; copy UB Heidelberg Sign. Sal 80/21; KAUFMANN, ibid., 282, note 65.

[6] Cf. DEMBEK (see note 2), 46 with note 197.

[7] Others, such as DOROTHEA WENDEBOURG, have come to a different conclusion: see DOROTHEA WENDEBOURG, The German Reformers and England, in: Sister Reformations. The Reformation in Germany and in England, ed. Dorothea Wendebourg, Tübingen 2010, 94–132, esp. 106seqq.

[8] Epistola Ioannis Bugenhagii Pomerani ad Anglos, Wittemberg [N. Schirlentz] 1525 (VD16 B 9302); Ein Sendbrieff an die Christen ynn Engeland, warynnen ein Christlich leben stehet, Wittenberg [J. Klug] 1525 (VD16 B 9307). The Augsburg printing press of S. Ruff placed a Latin as well as a German version on the market (VD16 B 9301, B 9306). Besides, there is a Latin edition which could so far not be assigned to a place and a printer (s.l., 1525; VD16 B 9300) and another Latin one to be attributed to Kantz in Altenburg (VD16 B 9305). Interestingly the later German editions are all fresh translations. For Cochlaeus' edition and commentary [Köln, Quentel] 1526 (VD16 B 9303, B 9304, cf. below note 22). The edition of Bugenhagen's letters (Dr. Johannes Bugenhagens Briefwechsel, ed. Otto Vogt, mit einem Vorwort und Nachträgen von Eike Wolgast, Hildesheim 1966) does not mention the *Epistola*.

[9] »Sanctis in Christo qui sunt in Anglia«: *Epistola*, VD16 B 9302, A 1[v].

[10] WA.Br 3,562–565 (no. 914).

recipient. If there had been a resident Englishman in contact with the circle of Wittenberg reformers, able to supervise a translation, it would be almost incomprehensible why there would not also have been printed an English translation of Bugenhagen's short epistle (running to no more than a quarto): this further suggests that relations with Tyndale were not strong.

As far as I can see, it is not possible to date Bugenhagen's letter to 1525. Unlike Luther's missive, it makes no reference to Henry's potential interest in the Reformation. Instead, it contains only vague reflections on the »situation of the English« who he believed to have welcomed the reformed faith; other weaker brethren in England were said to have been disquieted by rumours about the Wittenberg Reformation and thus moved to abandon the true Gospel that the Wittenbergers proclaimed.[11] Bugenhagen followed Luther's argumentation[12] that (in accordance with Matthew 5:11) criticism of his message only served to underscore its truth – indeed he reminded the reader that the moral standing of the sinner was no hurdle to saving faith.[13] However, he did make some effort to defend himself against the rumours being spread about the Wittenbergers[14] in order to facilitate the spread of the Gospel in England. To this end, he addressed himself to the large number of controversial topics which could hold back the »weaker-minded« from embracing the new teachings: »free will, vows and monastic orders, satisfactions, the abuse of the Holy Eucharist, the cult of dead saints, etc.«[15] In so doing, he sought to address the charge that a »secret poison« lay at the root of the plurality of reformed positions regarding these often intractable questions.[16] It is unclear whether the charge of *varietas* which Bugenhagen sought to address was a response to Roman

---

[11] »Non potuimus non gaudere quando audivimus et in Anglia Evangelium gloriae dei apud quosdam bene audire, Caeterum et illud nobis nunciatum est, multos infirmiores adhuc averti, propter rumores nescio quos, qui isthic feruntur ab illis qui Evangelio die adversantur de nobis« (ibid.). The personal pronoun »nobis« in both cases most probably means »us«, i.e. the »Wittenbergians«.

[12] Cf. Luther's reactions to the criticism of his second writing on the Peasants' War in his letters from July 1525 (WA.Br 3,515,7 seqq., 517,3 seqq.).

[13] *Epistola* (see note 10), A 2[r].

[14] »Hoc vero miramur cur sacrum Christi Evangelium quidam isthic verentur suscipere propterea quod de nobis mala dicuntur, ignorantes quod oportet filium hominis reprobari a mundo et stulticiam haberi predicationem crucis« (ibid.).

[15] »Verum aiunt rudiores, quis ista tam varia capere potuit? disputatur enim de libero arbitrio, de votis et sectis monasticis, de satisfactionibus, de abusu venerandae eucharistiae, de cultu sanctorum defunctorum etc.« (ibid., A 2[r/v]).

[16] »Alij aiunt. Veremur ne sub ista varietate lateat venenum« (ibid., A 2[v]). The Wittenberg translation interpretes this sentence in the following way: »Die andern sagen / wir fürchten uns das nicht yrgent ein gyfft unter solcher mancherley handlung und Disputation begraben und verborgen sey?« (VD16 B 9307, A 2[r]).

Catholic criticisms or disagreements amongst the evangelical movement. Nevertheless, Bugenhagen's recourse to the tenet *Christus est iustitia nostra*[17] as the foundational article of the Wittenberg Reformed faith,[18] served to delimit the doctrinal boundaries of Christianity and cast all other positions which Bugenhagen regarded as unbiblical – whether held by the ›old believers‹ or Reformed sects – outside the pale of the Church.[19]

Using Matthew's image of the good tree which yields good fruit, Bugenhagen sought to counter the key Catholic criticism of the Reformed doctrine of justification, to the effect that it would result in general moral decay.[20] From the belief in justification would follow a proper relationship towards God and the World, and a Christologically rooted understanding of the sacraments.[21] As such, I interpret the *Epistola ad Anglos* as an attempt to defuse the Erasmian scepticism of influential English opinion-formers. In seeking to allay fears that adopting the new teachings would result in the importing of conflict and moral decline, Bugenhagen hoped to clear the way for the spreading of Lutheran doctrine in England.

Is it not conceivable or even probable that the presence in Wittenberg in 1525 of the Englishmen Tyndale and Roye even provided the occasion for Bugenhagen to put pen to paper in the cause of a Reformation in England? Could not he even have grasped the quill as the result of disagreement with the pair or in response to their negative reactions to the ›German uproar‹ of 1525 and the apparent self-inflicted chaos in the Evangelical movement? I surmise that confronted by the scepticism of Tyndale and Roye, Bugenhagen felt compelled to defend the reputation of the Lutheran Reform movement in England.

Writing in a commented edition of Bugenhagen's *Epistola* published in Cologne in February 1526,[22] Johannes Cochlaeus decried the letter as a

---

[17] VD16 B 9302, A 2ᵛ.

[18] »Et ne varietatem doctrine excuses breviter dico, unum tantum articulum a nobis doceri, utcunque quotidie multa praedicamus, multa scribamus, multa agamus contra adversarios et ut ipsi salvi fiant. Est autem articulus ille. Christus est iustitia nostra« (ibid.). Bugenhagen had the last four words printed in letters three times bigger than the rest.

[19] »Quisquis hoc [sc. the main article] non dederit nobis, non est Christianus, quisquis autem fatebitur nobiscum, apud eum statim cadet alia quaecunque iusticia humana, Nihil hic erit Pelagiana haeresis, qua licet mutatis verbis infecti sunt qui vel solos se Christianos gloriantur, nihil valebit omnis sectarum quae hodie sunt et operum fiducia, quam abnegato crucis Christi scandalo nostri iustificarii nobis invenerunt, dum opera pro Christo nobis venditarunt« (ibid., A 3ʳ).

[20] Ibid., A 3ᵛ–A 4ʳ.

[21] »Sobrie itaque pie et iuste vivet [sc. the Christian], adorabit deum in spiritu et veritate non in elementis mundi, cibis et vestitu, aut alia hypocisi, sentiet de sacramentis quod Christus docuit et instituit« (ibid., A 4ʳ).

[22] Epistola Iohannis Bugenhagii Pomerani ad Anglos. Responsio Iohannis Cochlaei,

device intended to convince German opinion that the Reformation was spreading in England, a land which he insisted, had hitherto proved largely resistant to its claims.[23] It is worth considering Cochlaeus' *Responsio* not just as a product of anti-Lutheran Catholic Humanism, but for the light which it sheds on Bugenhagen's possible concern in writing the letter.[24]

1526 (VD16 B 9303, B 9304). The date of the preface dedicated to the senator of Cologne Hermann Rinck: »III. Idus Februarias«, i.e. Febr. 11th (A 2[r]). On Cochlaeus cf. MONIQUE SAMUEL-SCHEYDER, Johannes Cochläus, humaniste et adversaire de Luther, Nancy 1993.

[23] »Ad quos tu [sc. Bugenhagen] scripseris nescio, scio autem hoc excusae per Chalcographos epistolae tuae exemplar, quod in manus meas pervenit, ex Ulma huc esse transmissum [presumably the Augsburg print, cf. note 8]. Scio item in Angliam non posse hanc aut consimilem epistolam tuto perferri publice. Suspicari itaque licet, a te fraude confictam esse, ad hoc ut Germaniae populi eo facilius vestra recipiant dogmata, quo difficilius admissuros & accepturos credunt Anglos, quorum Rex tam egregium contra Lutherum iam pridem scripsit & emisit librum. Per mathematicam [in the sense of ›in their fantasy‹] vero hanc epistolam tuam decepti credant nunc. Regem illum simul cum tota gente sua in partes concecisse vestras« (VD16 B 9304, C [5][v]).

[24] Cochlaeus took up the key word *libertas Christiana* used by Bugenhagen (VD16 B 9302, A 1[v]) in the following way: »Qua obsecro fronte aut quibus verbis defendas, quae sub praetextu Evangelij Christianaeque libertatis hoc anno [sc. 1525] a Lutheranis Rusticis in plaerisque superioris Germaniae provinciis perpetrata sunt?« (VD16 B 9304, A 3[v]). Regarding the debate on the *liberum arbitrium* Cochlaeus named, besides Erasmus, bishop John Fisher und himself who had written on this topic against Melanchthon (De libero arbitrio hominis adversus locos communes Philippi Melanchthonis, [Tübingen, U. Morhart the Elder] 1525; as for the monastic vows he referred to Johannes Dietenberger who also had written on the »satisfactions« [»de satisfactionibus«], ibid., B 1[v]), as had Fisher, Eck and Clichtoveus. However, as regards the Lord's Supper he wrote: »De abusu Eucharistiae quanta sit impietas vestra, horret profecto animus dicere. Ut omittam, quae Rusticorum vulgus Luthericum hoc anno [sc. 1525] perpetravit in capsulis & ciboriis horendissima, vestra vos produnt scripta. Num ignoras [sc. Bugenhagen] quam absurda & impia protulerit male uxoratus vester Archidiaconus [sc. Karlstadt], quem Lutherus ipse reprobavit? Qualia vero sunt Lutheri? Quando unquam constitit sibi ipsi? Utcunque nunc ad populum, cui Archidiaconi vestri obsurditas nimium displicet, aduletur, certe ad Vualdenses scribens [sc. WA 11,431–456], dicebat, externam Eucharistiae venerationem minime necessariam esse neque damnandos, qui eam non adorare aut venerari dignantur« (ibid., B 1[v]). Then he said about the difference between the Reformers: »Quae inter paucos annos adeo varia multiplexque facta est, ut tot fere sint inter vos fidei opiniones diversae, quot capita, quot factionum duces. Aliter enim praescribit credendi formulam Lutherus, aliter Carolstadius, aliter Zuuinglius, aliter Oecolampadius, aliter alij, quisque pro beneplacito sui popelli ac pro cerebelli proprii phantasia« (ibid., B 2[r]). Finally he inveighed once more against Karlstadt whom he particularly despised: »Et Archidiaconus vester neminem post apostolos melius quam se scripsisse iactitat de sacramento Eucharistiae [cf. WA 15,335,29–32]. Cum interim rerum eventus nos doceat. Nihil minus quam Evangelium dedisse Lutherum. Nec quempiam sceleratius de sacramento Eucharistiae scripsisse quam vestrum Archidiaconum« (ibid., B 3[v]–4[r]). As Emser in Dresden tried to stoke in Dresden the controversies between the Refomers by publishing anew Bugenhagen's *Epistola contra novum errorem* (VD16 B 9388), Cochlaeus used Luther's *Rhatschlag* about the right to resistance from 1530 (cf. THOMAS KAUFMANN, Konfession und Kultur Tübingen 2006, 43 seqq.) as well as his second writing on the Peasants' War (cf. BENZING, CLAUS, no. 2161–2163: Köln, P. Quentel, in part with-

The charges levelled at Bugenhagen, that the English Lutherans of his address existed only in his imagination are weakened, by Cochlaeus' own entreaties to the Cologne Councillor Hermann Rinck in the foreword[25] to warn Henry VIII and Cardinal Wolsey of the immense dangers posed by Lutheran teachings to the established order, as demonstrated by the massive insurrections which they had recently fomented.[26]

Moreover, Cochlaeus' attempt to downplay the nascent Lutheranism in England is contradicted by his energetic campaign against Tyndale and Roye after they entered Cologne. He viewed their attempt to print their English translation of the New Testament in Cologne[27] as a latent threat to English Catholicism. For Cochlaeus, the early and close links established between England and Rome made it a key battle-ground in the Counter-Reformation.[28] Eight years later in 1533, Cochlaeus was still proud of having hindered the printing of »Lutheri novum testamentum in linguam Anglicanam«,[29] an achievement which he mentions three times in his published work.[30]

---

out the printer's name = VD16 L 7501 seqq., L 7485; for more republications of evangelical writings by opponents see BENZING, CLAUS, no. 2137, no. 2164–2167).

[25] More indications of the connections of Rinck with the English Royal Court can be found in his letter to Cardinal Wolsey from October 4th, 1528, ed. in: EDWARD ARBER, The First Printed English New Testament, London 1871, no. 4, 32–36. Cochlaeus described him like this: »Herman Rinck / ein Cöllnischen Gschlechter und Ritter / so etwa der Keyserlichen Mayestat und des Königs von Engellandt Rath und Diener gewest« (VD16 C 4280, 292).

[26] »Diabolus enim non dormit, sed tanquam Leo rugiens circuit quaerens quos devoret. Circuivit apud nos per hanc factionem tam diu, donec supra centum milia Rusticorum Lutheranorum, ipso etiam ferente sententiam Luthero, devoravit, necdum tamen tanto sanguine sic fuso satiatus est, cum nusquam satis fidam adhuc pacem esse sinat. Expedit igitur, Prudentiss[ime] domine Hermanne [,] ut primo quoque tempore Regem, cui tot annis laudabiliter A consiliis fuisti hodieque esse cognosceris, super his periculosis insidiis certiorem facias, ne Germaniae incommoda sub falso Evangelii praetextu Angliae quoque regnum, quod florentissimum est, invadant ac perturbent« (ibid., A 2^r).

[27] VD16 B 4569. A copy which however has been preserved only in fragments (31 fol., going to H iv^r; STC^2 2823; accessible via EEBO).

[28] Regarding the mission of Augustine the monk to Kent on the orders of Pope Gregory I cf. VD16 B 9304, A 2^v–A 3^r, A 4$^{r/v}$ (partially in comparison with the self-promoting »hole« of Wittenberg).

[29] Johannes Cochläus, An expediat laicis legere Novi Testamenti libros lingua vernacula, [Augsburg, Weißenhorn] 1533 (VD16 C 4235, A [6]^r).

[30] In the following presentation I shall merge the three versions (JOHANNES COCHLAEUS, Scopa in araneas Morysini Angli, Leipzig 1538; VD16 C 4382, B 2^r; ID., Commentaria de Actis et Scriptis Martini Lutheri, Mainz, S. Behem 1549; later print s.a., 132–135; German edition: Ingolstadt 1582, VD16 C 482, 292–294; COCHLAEUS, An expediat [see note 29]); specific references shall be given only in cases of quotations. I owe the knowledge of these editions to GERGELY M. JUHÁSZ, Translating Resurrection. The Debate between William Tyndale and George Joye in its Historical and Theological

The most detailed account of the episode is to be found in Cochlaeus' biography of Luther, in which he recounts how two English apostates who had learnt German in Wittenberg came to Cologne to undertake a secret printing of their English-language translation of the New Testament in an edition of three thousand copies of this document. They intended to return to England and convert it to Lutheranism. Cochlaeus, who was overseeing an edition of Rupert of Deutz in Peter Quentel's office in Cologne, in competition with a Protestant edition appearing with Johann Petreius in Nuremberg,[31] happened to overhear a conversation in the office, in which some printers exchanged views on the learned Englishmen and their plans. Then the resolute enemy of Luther invited a number of printers to his quarters, where with the help of the wine, Cochlaeus was able to bring the whole business to light from one of the printers. 3,000 copies of the English New Testament were to be paid for by English merchants and then shipped to England.[32] The next day, Cochlaeus contacted Herman Rinck, whose agents found a large quantity of paper intended for the completion of the English New Testament. Rinck convened the Cologne city council and obtained a warrant ordering the abandonment of the project. Unfortunately for him, the two English itinerants had managed to flee Cologne in possession of the pages already printed. Escaping along the Rhine to Protestant Worms, we can assume that they were assisted in their progress by merchants. For their part, Rinck and Cochlaeus wrote to the English King, Cardinal Wolsey and Bishop John Fisher to warn them of the impending arrival of the two fugitives with their cargo of New Testaments.

Although this account was composed some time after the event, Cochlaeus' alliance with Herman Rinck in the struggle to maintain England's Catholic soul was documented earlier in his response to Bugenhagen. I believe it is very likely that Cochlaeus viewed Bugenhagen's *Epistola* as indicative of an acute threat posed to England's Catholicism; concession of this danger would however nourish the very cause which he sought to check. The evidence available would seem to support the following hypothesis: through meeting Tyndale and Roye in Wittenberg, Bugenhagen

---

Context, Leiden and Boston 2014, 249, note 644. For Cochlaeus' biography of Luther cf. ADOLF HERTE, Das katholische Lutherbild im Bann der Lutherkommentare des Cochläus, 3 vols., Münster 1943.

[31] Cf. VD16 R 3782–3784, R 3796. On the Petreius edition of Rupert see THOMAS KAUFMANN, Die Mitte der Reformation. Eine Studie zu Buchdruck und Publizistik im deutschen Sprachgebiet, zu ihren Akteuren und deren Strategien, Inszenierungs- und Ausdrucksformen, Tübingen 2019, 243 seqq.

[32] COCHLÄUS, Historia Martini Lutheri (VD16 C 4280), 292–93.

learnt that English sympathizers with the Reformation, shaped by Humanist ideas, were appalled at Luther's break with Erasmus and distressed not only by the way in which the Wittenberg circle dealt with their Protestant brethren, but also by the resulting divisions which Luther's pugilistic manner engendered. Worried at the effect that such appearances would have on the Reformation in England, Bugenhagen attempted to assuage any fears developing amongst the Reform-minded English by stressing the doctrine of justification as the integrating principle of true religion.

Although early English Reformers certainly engaged with Lutheran ideas, they maintained a clear independence from his doctrinal concerns. Repulsed most probably in my view, by Luther's idiosyncratic and authoritarian style, exile theologians such as Tyndale sought to avoid the error and divisions which it caused. The penniless and homeless English exiles were able to maintain their independence both financially and doctrinally from Wittenberg and other centres of the German Reformation through the support of English merchants abroad. This financial, practical and moral support enabled them to able develop their own emerging theology and approach to Church reform independently of the German Reformers.

This important consideration explains, for me, the otherwise puzzling decision by Tyndale and Roye to base their operations in the difficult context of Cologne. Looking back on his efforts to interrupt the printing of an English New Testament, Cochlaeus believed that the English itinerants had chosen Cologne as the base for their activities due to its distance from the fighting of 1525 and its excellent transport links to England.[33] Whether Tyndale and Roye actually chose Cologne or were forced to take refuge there remains a matter of speculation. Nevertheless, to print 3000 copies of the New Testament – the same print run as Luther's September Testament[34] – required considerable planning and financial outlay. The cost of the paper alone is estimated to run to 1000 fl. As Cochlaeus clearly stated that Tyndale and Roye already had the paper for the printing, we can assume that they had raised the money to pay for it. As such, financial

---

[33] »Etenim ante annos octo, duo ex Anglia Apostatae, qui Vuittenbergae Teuthonicam edocti linguam, Lutheri novum testamentum in linguam Anglicanam verterant, Colonbiam Agroppinam venerunt, tanquam ad urbem Angliae viciniorem, mercatuque celebriorem, & navigiis ad transmittendum aptiorem, ibique post rusticorum tumultum latitantes, conduxerunt sibi in occulto Chalcographos, ut mox primo agressu tria milia exemplarium imprimerent« (COCHLAEUS, An expediat laicis [see note 29], VD16 C 4245, A 6ʳ).

[34] More details in: KAUFMANN, Mitte (see note 31), chapter 2. Cf. WALTER SCHELLMANN, Luthers Septembertestament von 1522. Neue Erkenntnisse zu Auflagenhöhe und Ökonomie (in: Archiv für Geschichte des Buchwesens 72, 2017, 1–22).

constraints best explain the decision to base their operation in Cologne: their network of backers on which their project, entire continental existence and subsequent escape rested, must itself have been based in Cologne. A large international centre of trade such as Cologne would be likely to host such a nexus of wealthy Englishmen. It is most likely that the New Testaments were not intended for sale on the continent – for example at the Frankfurt book fair – but circulation in England.[35] The strategy of advancing the Evangelical cause by disseminating the Bible is probably grounded in the specific ecclesiastical history of England and the century-long search for the remaining Lollard Bibles.[36]

The weight of evidence points to the printing project having been planned long before the summer of 1525. The task of printing and correcting the New Testament in English meant that Tyndale and Roye must have been in Cologne some weeks before Cochlaeus learned of their presence. The project had advanced to at least the letter »H«[37] at the time of discovery, which meant that even with the use of two or more presses, Quentel had been at work for a number of weeks.[38] It was unlikely that he would have declined other (legal) jobs for fear of drawing attention to his clandestine activities. Indeed, Cochlaeus' visit to Quentel was most likely to supervise one of his own print projects or to make purchases.[39]

---

[35] »Der Uncosten [sc. of the printing] wurde dißfahls uberflüssig von den Engelischen Kauffleuthen dargewendt / welche das gantze getruckte Werck in Engellandt führen / und eh solchs der König / oder Cardinal [Wolsey] erführen / hin unnd wider heimlich außbreitten wurden« (VD16 C 4280, 293).

[36] On Lollardy and the Reformation cf. RITA COPELAND, Pedagogy, Intellectuals, and Dissent in Later Middle Ages. Lollardy and Ideas of Learning, Cambridge 2004; ANNE HUDSON, The Premature Reformation. Wycliffite Texts and Lollard History, Oxford 1988; WOLF-FRIEDRICH SCHÄUFELE, Wegbereiter der Reformation? »Vorreformatorische« religiöse Bewegungen und ihre Anhänger im 16. Jahrhundert (in: Entfaltung und zeitgenössische Wirkung der Reformation im europäischen Kontext, ed.s Irene Dingel and Ute Lotz-Heumann, Gütersloh 2015, 137–153, esp. 142 seqq.).

[37] According to his report Cochlaeus had gathered the following information in his conversation with the printers from the printing firm Quentel: »Es wären gleich jetzo underm truck drey tausent Exemplar des Lutherischen in die Englische Spraach gebrachten newen Testaments / und man wäre nun biß an Buchstaben K. in Ordnung des Alphabeths kommen« (Historia, 1582, VD16 C 4280, 292–3). The fragment of the print (cf. note 27) only goes to sheet H; however, I see no reason to doubt Cochlaeus' report because of this fact.

[38] If one assumes – in agreement with Pettegree (ANDREW PETTEGREE, Die Marke Luther, Berlin 2016, 120) – 500 copies of one quarto sheet as average daily output of a printing firm, 10 sheets (A–K, in general without J) of an edition of 3000 copies resulting in 30,000 correspond to roughly 60 workdays with one printing press or 30 with two, 20 with three etc.

[39] Cochlaeus' treatise *De Petro et Roma adversus Velenum* was published by Quentel in Cologne with the date February 25th, 1525 (VD16 C 4353/4354; HANS-JOACHIM KÖHLER, Bibliographie der Flugschriften des 16. Jahrhunderts, part 1: Das frühe 16.

In the 1520s, the printer and publisher Quentel was one of the most productive printers in Cologne. Having inherited his business from his father, he was well-established in Cologne and was both a member of the iron merchants' trade guild[40] and held a number of council offices. His printing business profited from the custom of leading figures in the Counter-Reformation including Bernard of Luxemburg[41], Jakob von Hoogstraeten[42], Johannes Dietenberger[43], Johannes Eck[44], Johannes Cochlaeus and John Fisher[45] whilst producing clandestine pro-Reformation copy.

Jahrhundert [1501–1530]. Druckbeschreibungen, vol. 1, Tübingen 1991, no. 559). In his preface Cochlaeus praised the service done by the English bishop John Fisher in defending the Roman Petrine tradition against the treatise of the young Czech humanist Oldrich Velenský (Ulrichus Velenus) *In hoc libello gravissimis* [...] *rationibus* [...] *probatur Apostolum Petrum non venisse* [...] *Romam* (VD16 V 504–505), published in 1520 by Cratander in Basel and by S. Otmar in Augsburg. Velenský had challenged the view that Peter had ever been in Rome (on Velenský: Antonie Jan Lamping, Ulrichus Velenus [Oldrich Velenský] and his Treatise against the Papacy, Leiden 1975; Kaufmann, Der Anfang der Reformation, Tübingen ²2018, 48, 278 seqq.; Id., Das Ende der Reformation, Tübingen 2003, 349 seqq.). As for Luther's reception of Velenský's thoughts see WA.Br 2,260,11 seqq. Cochlaeus' *Confutatio XCI. Articulorum: e tribus Martini Lutheri sermonibus excerptorum, Authore Iohanne Cochlaeo* (Köln, Quentel 1525, VD16 L 5500 seqq.; date of the preface: Mainz November 3rd, 1524, A 1ᵛ), an edition of excerpts from sermons by Luther together with refutations by the editor printed with colophon, most probably appeared earlier in the same year. In September 1525 Quentel also published a collection of 400 »heretical« articles from 36 sermons of Luther: Articuli CCCC Martini Lutheri. Ex sermonibus eius sex & Triginta, Köln, Quentel 1525 (VD16 L 6657; date of the preface: August 3rd, 1525). In 1525 the same Quentel published a Low German (VD16 L 7506; Benzing, Claus, no. 2166) and a High German (VD16 L 7485) collection of writings by Luther concerning the Peasents' War. To Luther's writings was added Cochlaeus' *Ein kurtzer Begriff* (VD16 C 4338), a writing about the same topic which particularly blames Luther for the disaster. Thus it was obvious that the public prints of Quentel also had a Counter Reformatory profile. Equally in 1526 Cochlaeus was an important author for Quentel, not least because he played an important role in the acquisition of new printing jobs for Quentel.

⁴⁰ Christoph Reske, Die Buchdrucker des 16. und 17. Jahrhunderts im deutschen Sprachgebiet. Auf der Grundlage des gleichnamigen Werkes von Josef Benzing, Wiesbaden 2007, 432. For the printing business in Cologne during the early Reformation cf. Wolfgang Schmitz, Buchdruck und Reformation in Köln (in: Jahrbuch des Kölnischen Geschichtsvereins 55, 1984, 117–154); Id., Beten und Lesen im Untergrund. Evangelischer Buchdruck in der katholischen Reichsstadt Köln bis zum Ende der kölnischen Reformation ca. 1547 (in: Reformation und Buch, eds. Thomas Kaufmann and Elmar Mittler, Wiesbaden 2016, 85–104).

⁴¹ 1525/6: VD16 B 1991, B 1995.

⁴² 1525/6: VD16 H 4805, H 4817.

⁴³ 1525/5: VD16 D 1484, D 1480.

⁴⁴ 1525/6: VD16 E 329 seqq., E 255, E 334 seqq.

⁴⁵ 1525: VD16 F 1219, F 1226 seqq., F 1238–1240. The first edition of the *Defensio Regie assertoris contra Babylonicam captivitatem* [...] *per Reverendum* [...] *Ioannem Roffensem Episcopum. In quo respondet pro illustrissimo* [...] *Anglorum Rege Henrico* (VD16 F 1226 seqq.) was published in June 1525 by Quentel in Cologne. According to its ›visible‹ profile Quentel's firm thus did not suggest itself for the printing of clandestine

Having already printed an English New Testament[46] and a handful of low German devotional texts,[47] his practice of serving both sides of the Reformation divide was doubtless well-known in certain circles; this probably explains the move on the part of either Tyndale and Roye or their backers in Cologne, to commission him with the printing of Tyndale's translation of the New Testament.

The banning of the printing of Tyndale's New Testament followed, as Rinck obtained a decree to that effect from the Cologne city council. The fact that it was possible for Tyndale and Roye to take the already printed sheets with them and bring them by boat to Worms, suggests that they not only had support from other merchants, but that they were forewarned in advance. It is unclear why the English exiles or their supporters chose Peter Schöffer in Worms.[48] Like Peter Quentel, Peter Schöffer was the son of a famous printer from Gutenberg's first workshop. As his Cologne colleague, he was a well-known figure at the Frankfurt book fair, an event which Tyndale is known to have visited by 1528.[49] Cochlaeus mentioned Worms as open to the Reformation,[50] where »the common man from the

---

English literature. There is some probability that the financiers who might have had business connections with Quentel took the decision.

[46] Quentel's printing of the NT (VD16 B 4569; STC 2823; cf. note 26) comprised a prologue to the Gospel of Matthew written by Tyndale, which is edited in: Doctrinal Treatises and Introductions to Different Portions of the Holy Scripture by William Tyndale, martyr, 1536, ed. Henry Walter, Cambridge 1848, 1–28. For the content cf. DEMBEK, Tyndale (see note 2), 68 seqq. In 1532/33 Tyndale also published an exposition on Matthew V-VII in which he took up Luther's sermons on the same texts from 1532 (cf. ID., Political Ethics in the English and German Reformation. William Tyndale and Robert Barnes as Interpreters of Luther's Doctrine of the two Regiments, in: Sister Reformations, vol. 2: Reformation and Ethics in Germany and in England, eds. Dorothea Wendebourg and Alex Ryrie, Tübingen 2014, 262–265).

[47] Namely a Low German version of an exposition of the Lord's Prayer by Martin Luther (VD16 L 4066; BENZING, CLAUS, no. 279), a prayerbook by Luther (VD16 L 4120; BENZING, CLAUS, no. 1308) and the writing *Von Adams und unserm valle* (VD16 K 2473) by the Braunschweig ›early Reformer‹ Gottschalck Kruse (about him: Im Aufbruch Reformation 1517–1617, eds. Heike Pöppelmann and Dieter Rammler, Dresden 2017, 428 seqq.; ANTJE RÜTTGART, Klosteraustritte in der frühen Reformation. Studien zu Flugschriften der Jahre 1522 bis 1524, Gütersloh 2007, 21 seqq.).

[48] According to Cochlaeus, Rinck after some enquiries approached the City Council of Cologne and succeeded in ending the project (»brachte endtlich die Sachen dahin / daß den Truckern undersagt wurde / in dem Werck [sc. the English NT] weiters fortzufahren. Hierauff flohen die zwen verloffne Englische Münch mit den getruckten Quatern dem Rein nach aufwerts nach Wormbs«: VD16 C 4280, 293–4).

[49] MAGRET POPP, EBERHARD ZWINK, Verwirrspiel um eine Bibel. Der englische Reformator William Tyndale und sein Neues Testament: Das Stuttgarter Exemplar (in: Philobiblon 45, no. 4, 2001, 275–324, esp. 281). According to Rinck's letter to Wolsey from October 4th, 1528 (see above note 25) Jews were involved in the transfer of English books to Frankfurt (ARBER, First Printed English New Testament [see note 25], 33).

[50] For the Reformation in Worms cf. STEPHEN BUCKWALTER, Die Priesterehe in Flug-

greatest lack of sense« has accepted the Lutheran Gospel«,[51] a situation which promised an easier climate for an English printing of the New Testament. Probably Schöffer recommended himself through his recently printed German New Testament.[52]

However, I believe it to be most probable that an edition of Wyclif printed by Schöffer – dated to 1525 – the first printing of the great English heretic ever! – suggests a connection between the Worms printer and the English exiles and the Strasbourg book entrepreneur Otto Brunfels, who was involved in Wyclif printing. In contrast to Melanchthon, who argued in the previous year, in 1524, against a publication of Wyclif's dialogues, probably made public by Tyndale, Brunfels had seen to their publication. Indeed, it is likely that Tyndale had contacts with Schöffer, whether direct or indirect even before he settled on Quentel as the first printer for his translation of the New Testament,[53] thus making him an easy replacement

schriften der frühen Reformation, Gütersloh 1998, 256seqq.; SABINE TODT, Kleruskritik, Frömmigkeit und Kommunikation in Worms im Mittelalter und in der Reformationszeit, Stuttgart 2005.

[51] VD16 C 4280, 294.

[52] VD16 B 4364; BUSSO DIEKAMP (The Newe Testament, Worms 1526 – William Tyndale und sein Drucker Peter Schöffer d.J., in: Der Wormsgau 30, 2013, 107–158, esp. 116) points out that the ornaments of the title pages of the German and English prints of the NT Schöffer produced were identical. For Schöffer see the fundamental article by ALEJANDRO ZORZIN, Peter Schöffer d.J. und die Täufer (in: Buchwesen in Spätmittelalter und Früher Neuzeit. FS Helmut Claus, ed. Ulman Weiss, Epfendorf 2008, 178–213); KAUFMANN, Mitte (see note 31). After a painstaking bibliographical analysis of this first edition of the NT by Schöffer and his connections with the Straßburg printer Knobloch, P. Pietsch on the basis of an incomplete copy concluded the date to be »[1524/5]« (cf. WA.DB 2, appendix, 705–708). However, the title-page which bears the date 1526 makes it probable that Schöffer printed also for or with Knobloch, which explains why some of the pictures used are identical. Possibly one can understand the date 1526 as meaning the beginning of this year. In any case I do not see cogent reasons to assume that Schöffer printed »his« German NT before the English one. Thus is could also be that the lucrative commission to print Tyndale's NT was Schöffer's entry into Bible printing.

[53] IO Wiclefi Viri Undiquaque pii. Dialogorum libri quattuor [...] Excusum Anno a Christi nato MDXXV. Die VII Martii, [Worms, Peter Schöffer d.J.] (VD16 W 4688). Critical edtion by Gotthard Lechler: Joannis Wiclif Trialogus cum Supplemento Trialogi, Oxford 1869 (referring to the edition from 1525: 11–12). Cf. also KAUFMANN, Mitte (see note 31, 598seqq.). Contrary to my own former thoughts about the editor of Wyclif's work (KAUFMANN, Abendmahlstheologie [see note 5], 267–68, note 909), which were due to the fact that I did not know the letter of Brunfels to Luther from April 1525 (WA.Br 3,476–478 [no. 858]) I now find it evident that Brunfels was primarily responsible for Schöffer's edition of Wyclif. Possibly Brunfels had received the manuscript through Bohemian intermediaries, together with the »other« material he had received from there (Geistlicher Bluthandel, VD16 G 983, A 1ᵛ). On the other hand, it could also be the case that he was in direct contact with Englishmen present in Strasbourg. However, it is clear from an undated letter of Melanchthon (MBW.T 2,220 [no. 363]: 1524?) that he had also seen a manuscript of the *Trialogus*, but thought little of having it printed (MBW.T 2,220,4–5) since the dialogues it comprised were in part insignificant and in

as printer after the flight from Cologne. Georg Spalatin recorded a conversation with the humanist Hermann von dem Busche on the margins of the first Speyer Reformation Reichstag, which suggests that Tyndale was in contact with two of his countrymen in Worms during the time at which Schöffer was printing the English New Testaments, and that the first printing was raised to 6,000 copies, twice the run planned by Quentel.[54] Were this report reliable, it is clear that this commission, financially secured by English merchants, enabled Schöffer to fund his ambitious edition of the Old Testament Prophets completed in 1527.[55] Schöffer's new career as an underground printer of Anabaptist and Spiritualist literature was probably launched on the economic success of the English New Testament.

If we follow Cochlaeus' account, by which Peter Schöffer was able to use the quires A to K (or possibly A to H) of the interrupted printing by Quentel, to complete the first-ever edition of the English New Testament, surviving in one unique copy,[56] it becomes clear that Schöffer completed something new and different. In contrast to Quentel, he printed the text in an octavo format, and did not reproduce either Tyndale's long and typographically complex marginal notes, or his foreword. Instead, he used a

---

part highly obscure and dependent on the mediocre schools of their time (»partim leves disputationes partim obscurissimae et ex mediis scholis dialecticorum illius temporis depromptae«: MBW.T 2,220,5–6) – a criticism equally voiced by the humanist Brunfels (VD16 W 4688, A 2ᵛ). If it is correct to assume about the year 1524 for Melanchthon's letter it is, of course, also possible that Tyndale had shown the manuscript to him. According to WILLIELL R. THOMSON, The Latin Writings of John Wyclyf, Toronto 1983, 79, today eight manucripts of the *Trialogus* are known, some of them only in fragments. For information regarding the relevant connections and manucripts of writings by Wyclif in Bohemia cf. Johann Loserth, Huss und Wiclif. Zur Genese der hussitischen Lehre, Munich, Berlin 1925, 193–203. Another indication for a direct typographical connection between Strasbourg and Schöffer is Schöffer's print of the so-called Hoen-letter (Epistola Christiana [...] ex Bathavis missa [...] tractans coenam dominicam [Worms, Schöffer 1525], VD16 ZV 8053). For the relationship of this printing to the Strasbourg edition cf. KAUFMANN, Abendmahlstheologie (see note 5), 292 seqq.; differently: BART JAN SPRUYT, Cornelius Henrici Hoen (Honius) and his Epistle on the Eucharist (1525). Medieval Heresy, Erasmian Humanism, and Reform in the Early Sixteenth-Century Low Countries, Leiden et al. 2006.

[54] »Item Wormatiae VI. mille exemplaria Novi Testamenti Anglice excusa. Id operis versum esse ab Anglo, illic cum duobus aliis Britannis divertente, ita VII linguarum perito, Hebraicae, Graecae, Lintinae, Italiae, Hispaniae, Britannicae, Gallicae, ut quamcunque loquatur, ea natum putes« (in: Excerpta quaedam e Diario Georgii Spalatini Msto, in: Amoenitates literariae 4, 1725, 389–432, here 431; quoted after POPP, ZWINK, Verwirrspiel [see note 49], 280–81, note 4).

[55] Cf. ULRICH OELSCHLÄGER, Die Wormser Propheten von 1527. Eine vorlutherische Teilübersetzung der Bibel (in: BPfKG 75, 2008, 331–362 [= Ebernburg-Hefte 42, 2008, 19–50]).

[56] Landesbibliothek Stuttgart, T 7 Nº. 202 / 8° B engl 1526 01 (VD16 B 4570; cf. POPP, ZWINK, Verwirrspiel [see note 49]).

contents page based on Luther's September Testament, which listed Hebrews, James, Jude and Revelation without sequential numbers. In the case of the preface to the Romans, a »compendious introduction« printed separately by Schöffer has survived. Whether, as I suspect, similar prefaces had been printed to the other biblical writings, which, like the entire production of Schöffer shipped to England, had been destroyed, must remain an open question. The New Testament only included a short postscript »To the Reder« which has been attributed to Tyndale.[57] It offered basic hermeneutic orientation: to approach Scripture with a pure spirit; uncertain passages should be interpreted in the light of the »manyfest places«[58]; the differentiation of »lawe and gospel«[59] was taken to be elementary, whilst repentance and faith unlocked the sense of Scripture. Tyndale finished his anonymous text with an avowal of his own limitations as a Biblical translator and hoped that the text would only be used as the starting point for many subsequent improvements. He finished with the injunction »praye for us«.[60] As far as we know, this is the first successful printing of a text addressed by an Englishman exiled for his faith to his compatriots. Whether it should be taken as specifically ›Reforming‹ is difficult to decide.

The subsequent fate of the book is well-known. The Archbishop of Canterbury's mandate of 3 November 1526 ordered that all copies of the printing were to be tracked down and destroyed.[61] The destruction of heretical books functioned as the traditional English anti-heresy measure,[62]

---

[57] VD16 B 4570, Tt 1ᵛ–Tt 2ᵛ (ed. in: WALTER [see note 46], 389–391; cf. DEMBEK, Tyndale [see note 2], 81 seqq.).

[58] VD16 B 4570, Tt 1ᵛ.

[59] Ibid.

[60] Ibid., Tt 2ᵛ.

[61] POPP, ZWINK, Verwirrspiel (see note 49), 281, 288 seqq. For the text of the instruction cf.: Letters and Papers foreign and domestic of the reign of Henry VIII, vol. 4, part 2, 1872, no. 2607. To the instruction is added a list of forbidden Latin and English books, among them: »The Supplication of Beggars [see below note 75]. The Revelation of Antichrist of Luther [see below note 73]. The New Testament of Tindall. Oeconomia Christiana [see below note 78]. [...] An Introduction to Paul's Epistle to the Romans. A Dialogue betwixt the Father and the Son. [...] Captivitas Babylonica. Johannes Hus in Oseam. Zuinglius in Catabaptistas. De Pueris Instituendis [see below note 66]. Brentius De Administranda Republica. Lutherus ad Galatas. De Libertate Christiana. Luther's Exposition upon the Pater Noster.« Since some of these writings were published later the list cannot be from 1526. – The price of the NT was two shilling, eight pence, which was the equivalent of 5 kilograms of beef or of the wages for five days of a mason's work (POPP, ZWINK, Verwirrspiel [see note 49], 288 seqq.; The New Testament. Translated by William Tyndale. The text of the Worms edition of 1526 in original spelling. Edited for the Tyndale Society by W[illiam] R[ichard] Cooper with a preface by David Daniell, London 2000, XV-XVI).

[62] Fundamental for this topic: THOMAS WERNER, Den Irrtum liquidieren. Bücherver-

an option rendered relatively effective by the island nature of the Kingdom. Such an approach would have been of little consequence on the
continent, where a plethora of bordering jurisdictions each with their own
printing infrastructure meant that the supply of books and pamphlets easily outstripped any attempt to destroy them.

Before Antwerp became the authoritative publication site of the early
Reformation English Dissenters for some years from the late 1520s, Strasbourg had played a similar role in the short term. When the Cologne
patrician Herman Rinck asked the Strasbourg printer Johann Schott (then
working mainly for Otto Brunfels) at the Frankfurt Autumn Fair in 1528
for the whereabouts of Roye and Tyndale, and learned that English books
had been pledged to Frankfurt Jews,[63] it seems that he sealed the fate of
Strasbourg as the place of exile and publication for the English. Johann
Schott, who was particularly anxious to recover his paper and labor costs,
was ready to hand them over to the highest bidder. With the appropriate
expenditure, Rinck prevented the printed books from being smuggled into
England.[64]

Besides these English titles, there was a piece of verse severely attacking
Cardinal Wolsey as »one who burned the Word of God«, entitled *Rede me
and be nott wrothe For I saye no thynge but trothe* attributed to Roye and
Jerome Barlowe,[65] also Roye's translation of Capito's catechism in dia-

---

brennungen im Mittelalter, Göttingen 2007. For the burning of evangelical books in the
England during the 1520s, starting on May 12th, 1521, cf. JOHN D. FUDGE, Commerce
and Print in the Early Reformation, Leiden, Boston 2007, 76 seqq. A book burning in
February 1526, instigated by John Fisher after evangelical writings printed on the continent appeared in England is mentioned by POPP, ZWICK, Verwirrspiel (see note 49),
297.

  [63] »However, I [sc. Rinck], as a most humble, faithful and diligent servant, three
weeks [sc. about Sept. 1st, 1528] before receiving your grace's letters, heard and perceived
that those very books had been pawned to the Jews at Frankfurt for a certain sum of
money [...]. The engraver, John Schott, demanded beside the interest for the Jews, the
pay for his labour and the expense of the paper, and said that he should sell them to
whoever would give the most money« (ARBER, English New Testament [see note 25],
32–33). For Schott cf. RESKE, Buchdrucker (see note 42), 873–74; KAUFMANN, Mitte (see
note 31, 253 seqq.).

  [64] »I [sc. H. Rinck] might scrape and heap together all those books from every place;
which was done in three or four places, so that I hope that all those books yet printed
are in my possession, except two which your grace's [sc. Cardinal Wolsey] commissary
the above named John West asked for and received from me for the greater profit and
advantage of the king's grace and yours. Two books indeed, I gave him [...]. Unless I had
discovered it, and interfered, the books would have been enclosed and hidden in paper
covers, packed in ten bundles covered with linen and conveyed in time by sea« (ARBER,
English New Testament [see note 25], 33).

  [65] [Strasbourg, Johann Schott 1528]; STC 1462.7; VD16 R 434; EEBO. For the question of the authorship as well as for the content: WILLIAM A. CLEBSCH, England's
Earliest Protestants 1520–1535, Yale 1964, 230 seqq. In 1546 a new edition was published

logue form De pueris instituendis (»On educating children«).[66] The fact
that Roye had translated the catechetical writing of this Strasbourg reformer, may be mainly due to the fact that Capito had at that time the special
confidence of the »Radicals« and »Dissenters«, and publicly advocated
defusing the intra-Reformation communion dispute or downplaying its
significance. Capito, it seems, became in the further history of the English
Reformation an important, though hitherto unidentified source of spiritualist concepts on the sacraments and the church.[67] The fact that the
publishing activities of the British Dissenters relocated to Antwerp in
1529, may have been mainly related to the fact that the transport of printed goods by English merchants from the Dutch metropolis was apparent-

---

(STC 1462.9; EEBO) which comprised an up-to-date preface and a few minor additions.
It had probably been printed in Amsterdam. In the preface of the 1528 print Roye
addressed an unnamed »Master. P.G.N[.]O.« (VD16 R 434, a 2ʳ) who obviously was his
countryman. According to this preface Roye had sent him the poetry before as manuscript and been asked to have it printed. He explained his fulfilment of the addressee's
wish by saying: »Which thynge [sc. the printing] (the bonde of charite / where with not
alonly you and I / but we with the whole nomre of Christis chosen flocke / remaynge
amonge oure nacion of englisshe men / are knet together / purly for the truthes sake
pondered) I could do no lesse but fulfill and accomplysshe« (ibid.). For Tyndale the
polemics in this poetry against Wolsey's fight against the English New Testament were a
reason for distancing himself from Roye (DEMBEK, Tyndale [see note 2], 61–62;
CLEBSCH, Protestants, 230–1). There were clearly differences in ›temperature‹ between
the English exiles regarding their polemics against the English church authorities.

[66] Capito's catechism was published first in 1527 in Latin, then in German by Her-
wagen (VD16 C 833) und Köpfel (VD16 834–6) in Strasbourg. The English translation
by William Roye was published by Johann Schott (ADOLF WOLF, William Roye's Dialogue between a Christian Father and his Stubborn Son, Vienna 1874, 10–11; BEATE
STIERLE, Capito als Humanist, Gütersloh 1974, 210, no. 29e). This translation was edited
again in 1550 by Gwalter Lynne with the title: The true beliefe in Christ and his sacramentes, London [S. Mierdman] for Gwalter Lynne 1550 (STC 24223.5). Lynne wrote
the following about the origins of the text: »The author of the boke I know not. Only
this I finde that it was fyrste written in the duche tong, and then translated into latine.
But whoso he were that first wrote it, or that translated it into latine: certen I am that it
is a ryght Godly, & worthy to be often times reade of al Christen men. It declareth
effectuously and very pythyly the. Xii. Articles of the Christian faith and insidently the
righte understandige of the sacramentes. So that it maye rygthe well be called the summe
of Christianitie, or rather the perfect rule of Christen religion« (The true beliefe in
Christ, A 2ᵛ).

[67] CLEBSCH, Protestants (see note 65), 234, overlooking – like most other English
historians (MOZLEY, Tyndale [see note 3], 122; DAVID DANIELL, William Tyndale. A
Biography, Yale 1997, 143–44; WALTER, Doctrinal Treatises [see note 48], 39–40) as well
as DEMBEK [see note 2, 61, note 51], according to whom the author is »unknown«) – that
Capito was the author of the »Dialogue« between Father and Son translated by Roye
summarizes the significance of the text with the following words: »A Brefe Dialoge first
stated in English the viewpoint of the Reformation radicals. The position won few
adherents before its ecclesiology was adopted by separatists after 1580, although sacramental spiritualism found advocates among some more radical English Protestants in the
reign of Edward VI.«

ly smoother and safer work than was the case on the route from the Upper Rhine.

English yearnings for a vernacular New Testament,[68] which must also be understood against the backdrop of the history of the Lollards and the constant struggle against English Bibles in late Middle Ages, were strengthened both by Erasmus' support for vernacular Bibles[69] and the publication of a German-language Bible in Wittenberg. As such, the mere fact of the appearance of an English Bible in the 1520s should not necessarily, in my view, be taken as indicative of any theological acceptance of Reformation doctrine in general or Lutheranism in particular.

Significant efforts on the part of English people in exile for their beliefs on the continent to make texts by Luther known in their native language are lacking, except in the summer of 1529, when at least two of his writings appeared in partly abbreviated form from the (Antwerp) printery of Johannes Hoochstraten.[70] One of these editions showed a specific interest in Luther's doctrine of the papal Antichrist and of the Church of Christ,

---

[68] »Anglos enim, quamvis reluctante & invito Rege, tamen sic suspirare ad Evangelion, ut affirment, sese empturos Novum Testamentum, etiamsi centensis milibus aeris sit redimendum« (von dem Busche, in: SPALATIN, Excerpta [see note 54], 431–2).

[69] HEINZ HOLECZEK, Humanistische Bibelphilologie als Reformproblem bei Erasmus von Rotterdam, Thomas More und William Tyndale, Leiden 1975, 138 seqq.; KAUFMANN, Anfang (see note 39), 78 seqq.

[70] According to BENZING, CLAUS until Martin Luther's death ten editions of writings from his hand appeared in English. The earliest which was also, with two editions, the most successful, was the translation of his letter from September 1st, 1525 (for the context cf. WENDEBOURG, The German Reformers [see note 7], 104 seqq.; WA.Br 3, no. 899; WA.Br 3,500–1 with note 3; WA.Br 3, no. 914; WA 23,18 seqq.), a public testimony of self-humiliation caused by the hope that the English king would turn towards the Reformation (cf. BENZING, CLAUS, no. 2402a/b). As far as I see the earliest English translations of writings by Luther which expressed the spirit of the Reformation were published in summer 1529 in Antwerp by the printing firm of Johannes Hoochstraten. One of them is a partial translation, concentrating on the revelation of the Antichrist, of the *Response to Ambrosius Catharinus* published eight years before (WA 7,701 seqq.; cf. KONRAD HAMMANN, Ecclesia Spiritualis. Luthers Kirchenverständnis in den Kontroversen mit Augustin von Alvendt und Ambrosius Catharinus, Göttingen 1989), the second one a translation of the antitheses of the *Passional Christi und Antichristi* (KAUFMANN, Mitte [see note 36], 646 seqq.) by John Frith (BENZING, CLAUS, no. 888; STC 11394; cf. CLEBSCH, Protestants [see note 65], 85 seqq.) under the pseudonym Richard Brightwell, and the third one an English version by William Roye of Luther's *Auslegung von 1 Kor 7* (WA 12,90 seqq.), bearing the date »Malborow in the lande of Hesse. M. D.xxix. xx. daye Iunij.« (BENZING, CLAUS, no. 1680; CLEBSCH, Protestants [see note 65], 230–31; cf. ID., The Earliest Translations of Luther into English, in: The Harvard Theological Review 56, 1973, 75–86). All other translations of writings by Luther date from the period after 1534 (Wider den neuen Abgott: WA 15,175 seqq.; BENZING, CLAUS, no. 1926: [London], Wyer 1534). They were mostly produced in England itself (BENZING, CLAUS, no.s 647, 766, 605, 2034, 3216, 3290, 863). If this small output allows such a statement at all, they are primarily minor exegetical works of Luther.

antithetically opposed to it. In addition, in his preface to the reader, the translator John Frith emphasized that awareness of sin and justifying faith were closely related.[71]

In Simon Fish's *A Supplicacyon for the Beggars*, published at the same time by Johannes Grapheus of Antwerp, which took the form of a speech addressed to Henry VIII, the exile author warned against the tyrannical clerics, who enriched themselves in every conceivable way, undermined the political order and the common good, and opposed the English New Testament. For the sake of his subjects, the king should finally take up the fight against the Roman clergy, the Antichrist. Fish's sharp anticlericalism had no longer much to do with what Luther and his followers stood for at the end of the 1520s. The fact that Simon Fish's *Supplicacyon* appeared in a German translation by Sebastian Franck in the year of its publication – as far as I can see is the only text of one of the English ›earliest Protestants‹ to do so – reinforces the impression that the English exiles preferred to be in contact with Dissenters in the Reich, rather than with the established reformers.[72]

Evidently it was more important for some of the English exiles to translate into their mother tongue an exhortation to study of the Bible from the pen of Erasmus,[73] and the irenic *Summa der godliker Scrifturen*,

---

[71] A pistle to the Christen reader The Revelation of the Antichrist [Antwerp, Johann Hoochstraten], July 12th, 1529 (BENZING, CLAUS, no. 888; STC 11394; EEBO), 3[r]: »It is not therfore sufficient to beleve that he is a sauiour and redemer: but that he is a sauiour and redemer unto the / and this canst thou not confesse / excepte thou knowleg thyself to be a sinner/ for he that thinketh him silf no sinner / neadith no sauiour and redemer. [...] There fore knowledge thy silf a sinner y[t] thou maist be iustifyed.«

[72] Klagbrieff oder supplication der armen dürfftigen in Engenlandt an den König daselbs gestellet [Nürnberg, Friedrich Peypus] 1529 (VD16 F 1211/2; cf. the description of the print in: SEBASTIAN FRANCK, Sämtliche Werke. Kritische Ausgabe mit Kommentar, ed. Peter Klaus Knauer, vol. 1: Frühe Schriften, Bern, Berlin et al. 1993, 476–81; ed. in ibid., 216–35). Franck stressed in his preface that the »enemies of the cross of Christ« are the locusts mentioned in Rev. 9. The criticism of the clergy and the scholars probably already has in mind the representatives of all denominations which were then taking shape. For an interpretation of Franck's writing in the context if his early theology (CHRISTOPH DEJUNG in: Sebastian Franck, Sämtliche Werke, vol. 1: Frühe Schriften, Kommentar, Stuttgart-Bad Canstatt 2005, 293 seqq., and the most recent study: VASILY ARSLANOV, »Seliger Unfried«. Modalitäten und Strategien der Popularisierung historischen Wissens bei Sebastian Franck [1499–1542], Leipzig 2017).

[73] ERASMUS VON ROTTERDAM, An exhortation to the diligent studye of the scripture [Antwerp, Joh. Hoogstraten] 1529; STC 10493; cf. CLEBSCH, Protestants [see note 65], 234–5). This text is a translation by William Roye of Erasmus *Paraclesis*. A fictional colophon (largely identical with STC 11394 [see note 73]) reads: »At Marborow in the lande of Hesse. M.D.XXIX.XX daye Juny. By my Hans Luft.« It is difficult to guess why it gives the name of the printer Hans Lufft who since 1523 worked in Wittenberg (cf. RESKE, Buchdrucker [see note 40], 996). Could it be that Lufft in 1525 had refused the English the printing of the English New Testament? But cf. K. BECKEY, Der nie-

inspired by the spirit of the *Devotio Moderna*, probably written by the Dutch Heinrich Bommelius,[74] than anything by the reformers of Wittenberg, Basle or Zurich. The corresponding editions appeared in the same year of 1529 at Antwerp. As far as I can see, except for Robert Barnes, a fellow-brother of Luther's order, who fled via Antwerp to Wittenberg with the help of English merchants in 1528/9,[75] none of the British exiles who remained in the Reich from the early days of the Reformation sought to build closer contacts with the ›established‹ theological representatives of the Magisterial Reformation. Presumably one did not want to have to decide for one of the ›camps‹ that had become irreconcilable with each other since the mid–1520s – the ›Lutheran‹ and ›reformed‹ antagonists in the sacramental dispute, and the ›Erasmians‹.

Even after 1534, notwithstanding a few Luther translations that now appeared, there was not a conscious straightforward orientation towards the continental reformers. That there appeared in June 1534, with royal privilege, in English translation, the anonymous pamphlet attributed to Konrad Pellikan, *Vom alten und neuen Gott, Glauben und Ler* (On the Old and New God, Faith and Teaching),[76] which represented a ›pre-con-

---

derländische Buchdrucker Johannes Hoochstraten zu Antwerpen, alias »Adam Anonymus te Bazel«, alias »Hans Luft te Marburg« in einer dritten, bisher unbekannten Maske als »Steffen Rodt te Marborch in Hessen« 1530 (in: Het Boek 26, 1940, 27–38). Cf. also H. STEELE, Hans Luft of Marburg (in: The Library 3th, ser. 2, 1911, 113–131), and M. E. KRONENBERG, De geheimsinnige druckers Adam Anonymus te Bazel en Hans Luft te Marburg ontmaskerd 1526–1528, 1528–1530 en 1535 (in: Het Boek 8, 1919, 241–280).

[74] Karl Benrath has produced a German translation of this tract, which is an elementary catechetical presentation of evangelical teaching, concentrating on faith, justification, and Bible reading and largely unpolemical, and which since 1523 was very successful outside of the German-speaking lands: Die Summa der Heiligen Schrift. Ein Zeugniß aus dem Zeitalter der Reformation für die Rechtfertigung aus dem Glauben, ed. Karl Benrath, Leipzig 1880. Cf. WA 18,542. Cf. JEAN TRAPMAN, De summa der godliker scrifturen, Leiden 1978 (esp. 52 seqq. on doubts about Bommel as author). The Dutch version seems to be based on a widespread Latin one which also carried the title *Oeconomica Christiana* (cf. HERMAN J. SELDERHUIS, PETER NISSEN, The Sixteenth Century, in: Handbook of Dutch Church History, ed. Herman J. Selderhuis, Göttingen 2015, 157–258, here: 186). The translation into English from 1529 (The summe of the holye scripture [Antwerp, Joh. Hoochstraten] 1529; STC 3036; EEBO) is attributed to Simon Fish (STEVEN W. HAAS, Simon Fish, William Tyndale, and Sir Thomas More's ›Lutheran Conspiracy‹, in: JEH 23, 1978, 125–136, here: 125, note 5, 135, note 2. On May 27th, 1530 a synod of English bishops passed a list of 92 errors which supposedly were comprised in in *The summe of holye scripture* (DAVID WILKINS, Concilia Magnae Britanniae et Hiberniae, London 1737, vol. 3, 730–732).

[75] KATHARINA BEIERGRÖSSLEIN, Robert Barnes, England und der Schmalkaldische Bund (1530–1540), Gütersloh 2011, 37 seqq.

[76] For Pellikan's authorship: KAUFMANN, Anfang (see note 39), 528 seqq. The pamphlet is edited in: Judas Nazarei, Vom alten und neuen Gott, Glauben und Lehre. (1521), Flugschriften aus der Reformationszeit XII, ed. Eduard Kück, Halle a. S. 1896.

fessional‹, largely non-polemical, catechetical representation of »Evangelical Christianity«, makes it clear what kind of Reformation theology English readers were interested in.[77] It should be biblical, rich in references to the historical tradition of Christianity in antiquity and the Middle Ages, anti-papal and with reservations regarding monasticism, but without any internal stating of doctrinal stances.

The theological *Sonderweg* of English Protestantism began, if I am right, already with the humanistic ›exiles for Christ‹ of the 1520s, who held themselves aloof from intra-Reformation partisanship. To this extent, the German and English Reformations are two rather remote sisters.

---

[77] STC 25127; London, John Byddell für William Marshall, 15.6.1534; EEBO. There might have been an earlier edition which there is no longer a bibliographic record. This would explain why Kück, Judas Nazarei (see note 76, X-XI), following other historians, writes that the English translation was published soon after 1522. For the London edition carries the date 1534.

Ehe, Familie und Haus in der Reformation im Heiligen Römischen Reich und in England

Wolf-Friedrich Schäufele

Eine klassische, theologisch orientierte Reformationsgeschichte wird bei der Beschreibung des »Kirchewerdens« der reformatorischen Bewegungen in erster Linie die theologische Lehre, den Gottesdienst und die Kirchenverfassung in den Blick nehmen. Nicht minder bedeutend waren aber die von der Reformation bewirkten Veränderungen der sozialen Formationen und Mentalitäten. In diesem Sinne stellte bereits 1892 Waldemar Kawerau fest, dass die kirchliche Reformation auch zu einer »Reformation des häuslichen Lebens« geworden sei.[1] In den vergangenen Jahrzehnten hat sich eine sozial- und kulturgeschichtlich orientierte Forschung ausgiebig mit Geschlechterbeziehungen und sozialen Praktiken im Kontext von Ehe, Familie und Haus in der Reformationszeit beschäftigt[2] und dabei bestätigt, dass diese nicht nur an der Peripherie der reformatorischen Neugestaltungen standen.[3] Ich setze im Folgenden diese Forschungen voraus, versuche selber aber, wieder stärker auf die normativen theologischen Konzepte und ihre Begründungsstrukturen zurückzukommen. Demge-

---

[1] WALDEMAR KAWERAU, Die Reformation und die Ehe. Ein Beitrag zur Kulturgeschichte des 16. Jahrhunderts, Halle 1892, 4.

[2] So z.B. STEVEN E. OZMENT, When Fathers Ruled. Family Life in Reformation Europe, Cambridge (Mass.) u. London 1983; PATRICK COLLINSON, The Birthpangs of Protestant England. Religious and Cultural Change in the Sixteenth and Seventeenth Centuries, Basingstoke u. London 1988, 60–93; LYNDAL ROPER, The Holy Household, Oxford 1989 (dt.: Das fromme Haus. Frauen und Moral in der Reformation, Frankfurt a.M. u. New York 1995); HEIDE WUNDER, »Er ist die Sonn', sie ist der Mond«. Frauen in der Frühen Neuzeit, München 1992, bes. 65–76; JACK GOODY, Geschichte der Familie, München 2002, 101–124; CHRISTINE PETERS, Patterns of Piety. Women, Gender and Religion in Late Medieval and Reformation England, Cambridge ²2005, 314–342; WOLFGANG REINHARD, Lebensformen Europas. Eine historische Kulturanthropologie, München ²2006, 199–226; DIARMAID MACCULLOCH, Die Reformation 1490–1750, München 2003, 784–856.

[3] Z.B. ROPER, Das fromme Haus (s. Anm. 2), 11: »Die Geschlechterbeziehungen [...] wurden durch die Reformation keineswegs nur am Rande berührt. Sie standen im Gegenteil im Zentrum der Reformation. Die konservative Umdeutung der Glaubenslehren der reformatorischen Bewegung kreiste um die Bestimmung der Rolle der Frau in Ehe und Haushalt. Dieses konservative Umschreiben der evangelischen Botschaft war der Schlüssel dazu, die Reformation erfolgreich einzuführen und zu verankern.«

genüber sollen die viel diskutierten und durchaus kontrovers beantworteten Fragen, inwieweit der Protestantismus über die Einführung der Priesterehe hinaus substantielle Veränderungen im täglichen Leben der Familien hervorgebracht,[4] ob er eine soziale Besserstellung der Frauen bewirkt[5] oder, zumal in Gestalt des englischen Puritanismus, zu einer emotionalen Vertiefung der familiären Beziehungen beigetragen habe,[6] hier nicht eigens erörtert werden.

Die Quellen, auf die ich mich vornehmlich stütze, sind für den Bereich der lutherischen Reformation Luthers Sermon *Vom ehelichen Leben* von 1522[7] und die *Oeconomia Christiana* des Eisenacher Superintendenten Justus Menius (1449–1558) von 1529[8]; dazu kommen weitere Schriften von Luther, von Johannes Mathesius, Erasmus Sarcerius und Andreas Fabricius. Exemplarisch für die Zürcher Reformation steht Heinrich Bullingers (1504–1575) *Der Christlich Eestand* (1540).[9] Zugleich wirkte Bullinger mit diesem Buch aber auch stark auf die frühe englische Reformation: Miles Coverdale übersetzte es unmittelbar nach seinem Erscheinen ins Englische; der Erstdruck erschien Ende 1541,[10] und bis 1575 folgten acht weitere Auflagen. Ebenfalls sozusagen auf der Grenze zwischen der deutsch-

---

[4] COLLINSON, Birthpangs (s. Anm. 2), 81–90; McCULLOCH, Die Reformation (s. Anm. 2), 793.

[5] Vgl. z.B. CLAUDIA ULBRICH, Frauen in der Reformation (in: Die Frühe Neuzeit in der Geschichtswissenschaft. Forschungstendenzen und Forschungserträge, hg. v. Nada Boškovska Leimgruber, Paderborn 1997, 163–177).

[6] Vgl. z.B. COLLINSON, Birthpangs (s. Anm. 2), 63 f.

[7] MARTIN LUTHER, Vom Eelichen Leben, Wittenberg 1522 (VD16 L 7025; USTC 700025). Hier benutzt: die Edition in WA 10/2,267–304. Ausführlich zu Luthers Ehetheologie: CHRISTIAN VOLKMAR WITT, Martin Luthers Reformation der Ehe. Sein theologisches Eheverständnis vor dessen augustinisch-mittelalterlichem Hintergrund, Tübingen 2017; THOMAS KAUFMANN, Reformation der Lebenswelt: Luthers Ehetheologie (in: DERS., Der Anfang der Reformation. Studien zur Kontextualität der Theologie, Publizistik, und Inszenierung Luthers und der reformatorischen Bewegung, Tübingen 2012, 550–564); UTE GAUSE, Art. Ehe/Familie (in: Das Luther-Lexikon, hg. v. Volker Leppin u. Gury Schneider-Ludorff, Regensburg 2014, 181f.).

[8] JUSTUS MENIUS, Oeconomia Christiana das ist von christlicher Haußhaltung, Wittenberg 1529 (VD16 M 4541; USTC 636874). Hier benutzt die Edition in: Ehe und Familie im Geist des Luthertums. Die Oeconomia Christiana (1529) des Justus Menius, hg. v. Ute Gause u. Stephanie Scholz, Leipzig 2012, 35–139.

[9] HEINRICH BULLINGER, Der Christlich Eestand. Von der heiligen Ee herkumen / wenn / wo / wie / vnnd von wäm sy ufgesetzt/ vnd was sy sye, Zürich 1540 (VD16 B 9578; USTC 632939). Moderne deutsche Übersetzung: HEINRICH BULLINGER, Schriften, Bd. 1, hg. v. Emidio Campi, Detlef Roth u. Peter Stotz, Zürich 2004, 417–575. Vgl. ALFRED WEBER, Heinrich Bullingers »Christlicher Ehestand«, seine zeitgenössischen Quellen und die Anfänge des Familienbuches in England, Leipzig 1929.

[10] HEINRICH BULLINGER, The Christen state of matrimonye: The orygenall of holy wedlok: whan, where, how, and of whom it was instituted [and] ordeyned: what it is: how it ought to proceade: what be the occasions, frute and commodities therof, Antwerpen 1541 (ESTC S108927; USTC 410898).

sprachigen und der englischen Reformation steht Martin Bucer (1491–1551) mit seinem König Eduard VI. von England gewidmeten Spätwerk *De regno Christi* (1550), das allerdings schließlich nicht in England, sondern erst sieben Jahre später in Basel gedruckt wurde und 1563 auch in deutscher Übersetzung erschien.[11]

Aus dem Umkreis der englischen Reformation wurden das elisabethanische *Book of Common Prayer* von 1559[12] und die Traupredigt aus dem 1571 fertiggestellten zweiten *Book of Homilies*[13] herangezogen. Alle anderen englischen Quellen stammen fast ausschließlich von puritanischen Autoren des späten 16. und beginnenden 17. Jahrhunderts: von dem umfangreichen Katechismus von Thomas Becon (1560)[14] über eine Hochzeitspredigt von Henry Smith aus dem Jahr 1591[15] bis hin zu den umfang-

---

[11] Martin Bucer, De Regno Christi Iesu servatoris nostri, libri II. Ad Eduardum VI Angliae Regem, annis abhinc sex scripti. Basel: Oporinus, 1557 (VD16 B 8906; USTC 631342). Hier benutzt: Martini Buceri Opera Latina, Bd. 15: De regno Christi libri duo, 1550, hg. v. Francois Wendel, Paris 1955. Deutsche Übersetzung: Vom Reich Christi, Straßburg 1563 (VD16 B 8907; USTC 701665). Vgl. Martin Greschat, Martin Bucer. Ein Reformator und seine Zeit (1491–1551), Münster ²2009, 270–276; Basil Hall, Martin Bucer in England (in: Martin Bucer: Reforming church and community, hg. v. D. F. Wright, Cambridge 1994, 144–160, hier: 154–158).

[12] The Boke of common praier, and administration of the Sacramentes, and other rites and Ceremonies in the Churche of Englande. London: Richard Grafton, 1559 (ESTC S93763; USTC 518068). ND: The Book of Common Prayer commonly called The First Book of Queen Elizabeth. Printed by Grafton 1559, London 1844. Neben dem liturgischen Formular zur Eheschließung findet sich hier auch eine Ermahnung auf der Grundlage der neutestamentlichen Haustafeln, die vom Priester anstelle einer Traupredigt verlesen werden konnte (a.a.O., 99^{r/v}).

[13] The Two Books of Homilies Appointed to be Read in Churches. Oxford 1859, hier: 500–515 (»A Homily of the State of Matrimony«). – Die von Thomas Cranmer 1547 bzw. John Jewel 1571 zusammengestellten *Books of Homilies* sind Sammlungen reformatorischer Musterpredigten: vgl. Ashley Null, Official Tudor Homilies (in: The Oxford Handbook of the Early Modern Sermon, hg. v. Hugh Adlington, Peter McCullough u. Emma Rhatigan, Oxford 2011, 348–365). Die erste Hälfte der Traupredigt ist eine kaum veränderte englische Übersetzung einer ursprünglich deutschen, bei Nikolaus Selnecker lateinisch überlieferten Traupredigt von Veit Dietrich (The Two Books of Homilies, 500, Anm. 1).

[14] Thomas Becon, A new Catechisme sette forth Dyaloge wise in familiare talke betwene the father and the son, s.l., s.a. [1560]. Wieder in: The Catechism of Thomas Becon, with other pieces written by him in the reign of King Edward the Sixth, ed. John Ayre, Cambridge 1844, 1–410. Thomas Becon (Beccon, ca. 1511–1567) war ein Vertrauter Cranmers und Kanoniker an der Kathedrale von Canterbury; ca. 1556–1559 lehrte er an der Universität Marburg: Alexander Balloch Grosart, Art. Becon, Thomas (in: DNB 4, 1885, 92–94); Derrick Sherwin Bailey, Thomas Becon and the Reformation of the Church of England, Edinburgh u.a. 1952.

[15] Henry Smith, A preparatiue to mariage The summe whereof was spoken at a contract, and inlarged after. Whereunto is annexed a treatise of the Lords Supper, and another of vsurie, London 1591 (ESTC S104139). Hier benutzt: Henry Smith, A Preparative to Marriage, in: Ders., The Sermons, gathered into one volume, London 1937, 9–47. – Henry Smith (ca. 1550/60–1591), auch bekannt als »silver-tonged Smith«, war

reichen Handbüchern von William Perkins (1609),[16] William Whately (1617)[17] und William Gouge (1622)[18]. Das dürfte kein Zufall sein, zeichnete sich der Puritanismus doch durch sein besonderes Interesse an der religiösen Heiligung des Alltags aus.[19]

Die literarischen Gattungen der betrachteten Schriften aus dem Heiligen Römischen Reich wie aus England gehen fließend ineinander über: von Traupredigten über theologische und ethische Traktate über den Ehestand und die Pflichten von Eheleuten bis hin zur Hausväter- und Ratgeberliteratur[20] und den puritanischen »conduct books«[21]. Dabei stehen als biblische Referenztexte regelmäßig die sogenannten Haustafeln aus Eph. 5,21–6,9, Kol. 3,18–4,1 und 1.Petr. 3,1–7 im Hintergrund.

Eine terminologische Vorbemerkung ist erforderlich. Der Sache nach sprechen wir im Folgenden über die Bedeutung der Familie für das Kirchewerden der Reformation. Tatsächlich begegnet dieser Begriff (»Familie«, »family«, »familia«)[22] vor allem in den englischen Quellen, deutlich seltener in denen aus dem Reich. Eine förmliche Definition gibt William Perkins in seiner *Christian Oeconomie* von 1609:

Lektor an St. Clement Danes in der City of Westminster und galt als beliebtester puritanischer Prediger des elisabethanischen London: THOMPSON COOPER, Art. Smith, Henry (in: DNB 53, 1898, 48 f.).

[16] WILLIAM PERKINS, Christian Oeconomie: or, A short survey of the right manner of erecting and ordering a familie according to the scriptures. First written in Latine by the author M. W. Perkins, and now set forth in the vulgar tongue [...] by Tho. Pickering Bachelar of Diuinitie, London 1609 (ESTC S4819). Das 1590 erschienene lateinische Original ist nicht erhalten. – William Perkins (1558–1602) war Fellow am Christ's College in Cambridge und Prediger an der Great St. Andrew's Church und einer der führenden Puritaner seiner Generation. Cf. JAMES BASS MULLINGER, Art. Perkins, William (in: DNB 45, 1896, 6–9); MARTIN SALLMANN, William Perkins. Puritaner zwischen Calvinismus und Pietismus (in: Theologen des 17. und 18. Jahrhunderts, hg. v. Peter Walter u. Martin H. Jung, Darmstadt 2003, 88–105).

[17] WILLIAM WHATELY, A bride-bush; or a wedding Sermon compendiously describing the duties of married persons, London 1617 (ESTC S101310). Hier benutzt: WILLIAM WHATELY, Directions for Married Persons, London [4]1790 (ESTC N964). – William Whately (1583–1639) war Pfarrer in Banbury bei Oxford: CHARLOTTE FELL SMITH, Art. Whately, William (in: DNB 60, 1899, 430 f.). Vgl. JACQUELINE EALES, Gender Construction in Early Modern England and the Conduct Books of William Whately, 1583–1639 (in: Gender and Christian Religion, hg. v. R. N. Swanson, Woodbridge 1998, 163–174).

[18] WILLIAM GOUGE, Of domesticall duties eight treatises, London 1622 (ESTC S103290). – William Gouge (1575–1653) war Pfarrer an St. Anne Blackfriars in London und Mitglied der Westminster Assembly: ALEXANDER GORDON, Art. Gouge, William (in: DNB 22, 1890, 271–273).

[19] Zum Puritanismus vgl. WOLF-FRIEDRICH SCHÄUFELE, Art. Puritanismus (in: EdN 10, 2009, 560–566).

[20] Vgl. JÜRGEN DONIEN, Art. Hausväterliteratur (in: EdN 5, 2007, 254–256).

[21] COLLINSON, Birthpangs (s. Anm. 2), 68–74 und passim.

[22] Vgl. ANDREAS GESTRICH, Art. Familie 2. Begriffsgeschichte (in: EdN 3, 2006, 791 f.).

»A Familie, is a naturall and simple Societie of certaine persons, hauing mutual relation one to another vnder the priuate government of one«.[23]

In den Quellen vom Kontinent ist demgegenüber häufiger von »Ehe« – auch »Ehestand« oder »ehelichem Leben« – die Rede (englisch »marriage« oder »matrimony«, lateinisch »coniugium« oder »matrimonium«). Freilich werden zur Ehe in diesem Sinn fast immer unmittelbar auch die Kinder und die Kindererziehung mit hinzugedacht, und nicht nur diese, sondern auch die unverheirateten Dienstboten, die mit im Haus lebten und wie die Kinder unter der gemeinsamen Aufsicht der Eheleute standen. In diesem umfassenden Sinne wird in den Quellen dann auch vom »Haus« oder der »Haushaltung« (house, household; selten: husbandry) oder der »Ökonomie« (economy, oeconomia) gesprochen.

1. Theologische Neubestimmung des Stellenwerts von Ehe und Familie

In der Neubestimmung des Stellenwerts von Ehe und Familie verbinden sich in einer spannungsreichen Dialektik zwei auch sonst zu beobachtende Grundtendenzen reformatorischer Theologie: die Nivellierung der Unterscheidung zwischen *heilig* und *profan* einerseits und damit einhergehend die religiöse Aufwertung bislang als *profan* geltender Lebensbereiche andererseits. Konkret bedeutete dies, dass die Reformatoren in Abgrenzung zur spätmittelalterlich-scholastischen Auffassung den Sakramentscharakter und damit eine besondere sakramental-institutionelle Heiligkeit der Ehe bestritten, die sie von anderen Lebensformen und -vollzügen unterschied. Zugleich werteten sie den Ehe- und Hausstand, der im Mittelalter als dem sogenannten ›geistlichen Stand‹ der Priester und Ordensleute gegenüber inferior galt, theologisch auf und erkannten ihm eine besondere religiöse Würde als von Gott gestiftete Ordnung, ja als bindendes göttliches Gebot zu.

In ihrer Bestreitung der sakramental-institutionellen Heiligkeit der Ehe vollzog die Reformation eine Gegenbewegung zu der erst seit dem Hochmittelalter von der römischen Kirche betriebenen Sakramentalisierung der Ehe. Als konstitutiv für die Ehe galt herkömmlich und weiterhin das in freiwilliger Übereinkunft gegebene Heiratsversprechen der Brautleute; mit dem geschlechtlichen Vollzug galt die Ehe dann darüber hinaus als unauflösbar. Doch seit dem 12. Jahrhundert war die Kirche bestrebt gewesen, die Eheschließung unter ihre Kontrolle zu bringen, indem die Ehe als

---

[23] PERKINS, Christian Oeconomie (s. Anm. 16), 1 f.

Sakrament gewertet wurde – eines freilich, das die Ehepartner selbst einander spendeten – und immer nachdrücklicher die Einsegnung durch den Priester als notwendiger Bestandteil verlangt wurde.[24] Diese neue Auffassung hatte sich in der Praxis noch keineswegs vollständig durchgesetzt, als sie von den Reformatoren wieder außer Kurs gesetzt wurde. In seiner Schrift *Von Ehesachen* (1530) brachte Luther die reformatorische Überzeugung auf die klassische Formel, »das die ehe ein eusserlich weltlich ding ist wie kleider und speise, haus und hoff, weltlicher oberkeit unterworffen«.[25] Damit war die Eheschließung eindeutig als weltliches Rechtsgeschäft, als Vertragsangelegenheit der Ehepartner und ihrer Familien qualifiziert. Die rechtliche Regelungskompetenz lag so beim weltlichen Gesetzgeber, nicht mehr das kanonische Eherecht war als bindend anzusehen, sondern weltliches Recht, und an die Stelle der kirchlichen, bischöflichen Ehegerichte traten in der Folge vielfach neuartige, mit weltlichen Richtern besetzte Gremien, in denen Theologen gewöhnlich nur noch eine beratende Stimme zukam.[26] Damit waren Ehe und Familie kein besonderer, religiös-kirchlicher Normierung und Jurisdiktion vorbehaltener Lebensbereich mehr, sondern in die Gesamtheit weltlicher Lebensvollzüge hinein nivelliert. Ähnlich wie Luther, so erklärte auch etwa Heinrich Bullinger die Ehe zu einem jener »äußerlichen Dinge«, die der weltlichen Obrigkeit unterworfen seien.[27]

Interessanterweise kam es in England nicht zu einer vergleichbaren Ablösung der kirchlichen durch eine weltliche Ehegerichtsbarkeit. Zwar hatte Martin Bucer im zweiten Band seines gegen Ende seines Lebens verfassten Hauptwerks *De regno Christi* König Eduard VI. (reg. 1547–1553) Vorschläge für 14 Gesetze zu einer »plena religionis restitutio« unterbreitet, von denen das zu Fragen der Ehe und Ehescheidung mit 33 von insgesamt 52 Kapiteln bei weitem am meisten Raum einnahm.[28] Ähnlich wie Luther charakterisierte Bucer die Ehe als eine »res politica«, für deren rechte Praxis es staatliche Gesetze und Gerichte brauche; die weltlichen Herrscher müssten das vom antichristlichen römischen Papsttum zu Un-

---

[24] Urs Baumann, Art. Ehe VI. Historisch-theologisch (in: LThK³ 3, 1993, 471–474, hier: 472f.); Ozment, When Fathers Ruled (s. Anm. 2), 26–28.

[25] WA 30/3,205,12f.

[26] Für die wettinischen Territorien: Ralf Frassek, Eherecht und Ehegerichtsbarkeit in der Reformationszeit. Der Aufbau neuer Rechtsstrukturen im sächsischen Raum unter besonderer Berücksichtigung der Wirkungsgeschichte des Wittenberger Konsistoriums, Tübingen 2005.

[27] »ob glych wol die Ee ouch die Seel vnd inneren menschen angadt / hört sy doch ouch vnder die eusserliche ding / die der oberkeit underworffen sind« (Bullinger, Der Christlich Eestand [s. Anm. 9], Kap. 4 [unpaginiert]: Schriften [s. Anm. 9], 436).

[28] Bucer, De regno Christi (s. Anm. 11), 152–234 (Kap. 15–47).

recht usurpierte Eherecht wieder in die eigene Verantwortung nehmen.[29] Doch kam es unter der Herrschaft Eduards nicht mehr zu einer entsprechenden Gesetzgebung, und auch beim Elizabethan Settlement blieb das Eherecht ausgespart. So kam es, dass in England das kanonische Eherecht in Geltung blieb und die bischöflichen Ehegerichte fortbestanden.[30]

Luthers Formel von der Ehe als »weltlich Ding« besagte, dass Ehe und Familie in reformatorischer Anschauung keinen religiös-rechtlichen Sonderbereich außerhalb der übrigen Lebenswelt bildeten. Sie sollte der Ehe aber keineswegs eine religiöse Bedeutung absprechen. Im Gegenteil, die Ehe war für Luther ein besonderes Werk Gottes und stand unter seiner besonderen Aufsicht.[31] Mit Bedacht hatte Gott den Menschen als Mann und Frau erschaffen und beide zur gegenseitigen Ergänzung bestimmt. Die Ehe galt Luther und den späteren Lutheranern daher als eine göttliche Ordnung und ein göttlicher Stand. Für Justus Menius war sie unter allen Ständen des menschlichen Lebens der größte und alle Mühen wert.[32] Mehr noch, der Eintritt in den Ehestand war nicht nur der schöpfungsmäßige Normalfall, sondern ein prinzipiell alle Menschen unmittelbar bindendes Gebot göttlichen Rechts, von dem nur wenige, im Neuen Testament ausdrücklich definierte Personengruppen (Mt. 19,12) ausgenommen waren.[33] Seinen Gegnern schrieb Luther ins Stammbuch, dass das Heiraten keineswegs freigestellt sei; sie sollten wissen,

»gleich wie hohe not vnd hart gebot ist / da Gott spricht / Du solt nicht tödten / Du solt nicht ehebrechen / eben so hoch not vnd hart gepot / ia vil hoher not vnd herter gepot ists / Du solt ehelich sein / du solt ein weib haben / du solt einen man haben.«[34]

Bullinger leitete den überragenden religiösen Rang der Ehe aus den Umständen ihrer Einsetzung her. So sei die Ehe als einzige Lebensordnung überhaupt noch im Paradies, also noch vor dem Sündenfall begründet worden, und ihr Urheber war Gott selber.[35] In enger Anlehnung an Bullingers Ausführungen, aber in den biblischen Bezugnahmen und Argumenten noch darüber ins Neue Testament hinausgehend, behandelte später auch Henry Smith »The excellency of marriage«.[36] Vor dem Hintergrund

---

[29] A.a.O., 126.

[30] Martin Ingram, Church Courts, Sex and Marriage in England, 1570–1640, Cambridge 1987.

[31] Witt, Luthers Reformation der Ehe (s. Anm. 7), 250–258.

[32] Menius, Oeconomia Christiana (ed. Gause / Scholz [s. Anm. 8], 44).

[33] Luther, Vom Eelichen Leben (s. Anm. 7), 277,1–280,6.

[34] Luthers Vorrede zu Menius, Oeconomia Christiana (ed. Gause / Scholz [s. Anm. 8], 38).

[35] Bullinger, Der Christlich Eestand (s. Anm. 9), Kap. 1 (Schriften [s. Anm. 9], 429f.).

[36] Smith, A Preparative to Marriage (s. Anm. 15), 9–11.

solcher Überzeugungen vom religiösen Wert der Ehe konnte Bullinger ganz unbefangen von der »heiligen Ehe« und Bucer vom »sacrum coniugium«[37] als einer »sanctissima societas«[38] sprechen.

Damit hatten Ehe und Familie nicht bloß an der allgemeinen Aufwertung der alltäglichen Lebensvollzüge der Gläubigen als gottgefälliger guter Werke Anteil – in diesem Sinne hatte Luther 1520 im *Sermon von den guten Werken* selbst das Aufheben eines Strohhalms, wenn es nur im Glauben geschehe, als Gott wohlgefälliges gutes Werk gewürdigt,[39] und ebenso dürfte auch noch das berühmte Zitat aus *Vom Eelichen Leben* zu verstehen sein, wonach Gott mit allen Engeln und Kreaturen wohlgefällig über den Familienvater lacht, der die Windeln seines Kindes wäscht.[40] Vielmehr kam dem »heiligen Ehestand« als dem bedeutendsten Stand auf Erden in den Augen der Reformatoren eine besondere, eigene religiöse Würde zu.

Die Aufwertung von Ehe und Familie hatte die Abwertung und Delegitimierung anderer Lebensformen als Kehrseite. In erster Linie ist hier natürlich an das männliche und weibliche Mönchtum und an das zölibatäre Leben der Priester zu denken. Die mittelalterliche Kirche hatte diese Formen sexuell abstinenten Lebens als religiös überlegen und verdienstvoll über das weltliche Leben der Verheirateten gestellt. Die Reformatoren kehrten diese Ordnung um. Insofern die zölibatäre und monastische Lebensform als solche keine Grundlage in der Heiligen Schrift hatte, ja mehr noch: gegen das Ehegebot verstieß, durfte sie nicht verpflichtend gemacht werden. Die grundsätzliche Möglichkeit, auf Grund einer von Gott geschenkten Gnadengabe unehelich zu leben, die anfangs durchaus noch bejaht wurde,[41] trat praktisch bald in den Hintergrund, Mönchtum und Zölibat verschwanden aus den evangelischen Gemeinden[42]. Die bedeutendste Konsequenz daraus war, dass nun auch der Pfarrer zum Ehemann wurde.[43] Ja, in Gestalt von Pfarrer und Pfarrfrau stand nun in der Mitte und an der Spitze der Gemeinde quasi ein exemplarisches, vorbildgeben-

---

[37] BUCER, De regno Christi (s. Anm. 11), 153, 164 und passim.

[38] A.a.O., 152.

[39] WA 6,206,9–11.

[40] WA 10/2,296,27–297,4.

[41] LUTHER, Vom Eelichen Leben (s. Anm. 7), 279,15–23.

[42] Zu Luthers Experiment mit einem »evangelischen Mönchtum« in den Jahren 1522 bis 1524: WOLF-FRIEDRICH SCHÄUFELE, »... iam sum monachus et non monachus«. Martin Luthers doppelter Abschied vom Mönchtum (in: Martin Luther – Biographie und Theologie, hg. v. Dietrich Korsch u. Volker Leppin, Tübingen ²2017, 119–140).

[43] LUISE SCHORN-SCHÜTTE, Die Drei-Stände-Lehre im reformatorischen Umbruch (in: Die frühe Reformation in Deutschland als Umbruch, hg. v. Bernd Moeller, Gütersloh 1998, 435–461, hier: 446–450).

des Ehepaar.[44] Damit wurde die theologisch mit der Formel vom allgemeinen Priestertum der Getauften begründete Nivellierung des Unterschieds zwischen Klerus und sogenannten Laien auch sozial manifest. Die Folge war eine (zumindest ansatzweise) soziale Homogenisierung der Gemeinde.

Doch auch auf unverheiratete »Laien« wuchs nun der Druck zum Eintritt in den Ehestand. Im Mittelalter waren viele Menschen vor allem aus wirtschaftlichen Gründen ledig geblieben, und noch für das 16. Jahrhundert schätzt man den Anteil der Unverheirateten an der ländlichen Bevölkerung auf ein Drittel, in den Städten auf ein Drittel bis die Hälfte.[45] Jetzt drängten die reformatorischen Prediger auf die Ehe als das für alle verbindliche Sozialmodell, nicht zuletzt auch deshalb, um so der Sexualität einen gesellschaftlich legitimierten und kontrollierten Ort zuzuweisen. Dabei neigten sie dazu, die damit verbundenen wirtschaftlichen Fragen mitunter allzu leicht zu nehmen. Für Luther war die Eheschließung trotz geringer Finanzmittel einfach eine Frage des Gottvertrauens.[46] Dementsprechend plädierte er für eine frühe Verheiratung: Die jungen Männer sollten mit spätestens 20 Jahren, die jungen Frauen mit 15 bis 18 Jahren in den Ehestand treten.[47] Und auch wenn William Gouge dringend empfahl, erst mehrere Jahre nach dem Erreichen des gesetzlichen Mindestalters von 14 bzw. 12 Jahren für Männer bzw. Frauen zu heiraten,[48] wird das praktisch auf das gleiche hinausgekommen sein. Auch die Schließung der Bordelle in den protestantischen Territorien gehört in den Zusammenhang der theologisch-sozialen Aufwertung der Ehe und Kontrolle der Sexualität. Im Ergebnis entstand eine gegenüber dem Mittelalter sozial deutlich stärker homogenisierte Gemeinde. Die evangelische Gemeinde war eine Gemeinde von Eheleuten und Familien.[49]

---

[44] LUISE SCHORN-SCHÜTTE, »Gefährtin« und »Mitregentin«. Zur Sozialgeschichte der evangelischen Pfarrfrau in der Frühen Neuzeit (in: Wandel der Geschlechterbeziehungen zu Beginn der Neuzeit, hg. v. Heide Wunder u. Christina Vanja, Frankfurt a. M. 1991, 109–153); SUSAN C. KARANT-NUNN, Reformation und Askese: Das Pfarrhaus als evangelisches Kloster (in: Kommunikation und Transfer im Christentum der Frühen Neuzeit, hg. v. Irene Dingel u. Wolf-Friedrich Schäufele, Mainz 2008, 211–228).

[45] OZMENT, When Fathers Ruled (s. Anm. 2), 41 f.

[46] LUTHER, Vom Eelichen Leben (s. Anm. 7), WA 10/2,302,16–303,28.

[47] A.a.O., 303,31 f. Vgl. MENIUS, Oeconomia Christiana (ed. Gause / Scholz [s. Anm. 8], 102). Dazu OZMENT, When Fathers Ruled (s. Anm. 2), 38.

[48] »if they forbeare some yeares longer, it will be much better for the parties themselues that marie, for the children which they bring forth, for the family whereof they are the head, and for the common wealth whereof they are members« (GOUGE, Of domesticall duties [s. Anm. 18], 180).

[49] OZMENT, When Fathers Ruled (s. Anm. 2), 55 f.

2. Normative Zentrierung

Es erscheint auf den ersten Blick überraschend, wie stark die neuen theologischen und juristischen Vorstellungen der deutschen und englischen Reformatoren von Ehe und Familie in den Grundzügen übereinstimmten. Offenbar gelang es in kurzer Zeit, an die Stelle der mittelalterlich-scholastischen Ehelehren eine relativ geschlossene eigene Anschauung zu setzen. Diese kann als das Ergebnis einer biblisch orientierten normativen Zentrierung[50] verstanden werden. Dabei wurden durchweg die gleichen biblischen Belegstellen und Vorschriften zugrunde gelegt, wenn auch mit nicht unwichtigen Akzentunterschieden im Einzelnen.

Theologisch wurde der Zweck der Ehe gewöhnlich dreifach begründet: Mit dem Schöpfungsbericht von Gen. 1 und der göttlichen Aufforderung »Seid fruchtbar und mehret euch« (Gen. 1,28) wurde der Ehe die Aufgabe der Fortpflanzung und der Kindererziehung zugewiesen. Aus dem zweiten Schöpfungsbericht in Gen. 2 leitete man ab, dass die Eheleute einander Gesellschaft leisten und trösten, einander beistehen und in Alltag und Beruf Hilfe leisten sollten (Gen. 2,18). Und mit Paulus in 1.Kor. 7,2 sah man in der Ehe das wichtigste Mittel zur Verhütung von Unzucht.[51] Die Muster-Traupredigt des zweiten *Book of Homilies* und William Perkins fügten als einen vierten Zweck zusätzlich die Vermehrung und Fortpflanzung der Kirche hinzu.[52]

Für Luther und für Justus Menius stand unter den drei klassischen Zwecken der Ehe die Fortpflanzung und Kindererziehung klar im Vordergrund,[53] auch wenn beide daneben die Verhütung von Unzucht als weiteres Ziel gelten ließen. Für William Whately war dagegen letztere der Hauptzweck.[54] Eine Besonderheit Martin Bucers war die betonte Herausstellung der Partnerschaft von Mann und Frau, ihres Zusammenlebens und ihrer gegenseitigen Unterstützung.[55] Den Endzweck der Ehe sah er dem-

---

[50] Das Konzept der »normativen Zentrierung« wurde von Berndt Hamm in die reformationsgeschichtliche Forschung eingeführt: BERNDT HAMM, Reformation als normative Zentrierung von Religion und Gesellschaft (in: Jahrbuch für Biblische Theologie 7, 1992, 241–279).

[51] Alle drei Aspekte deutlich etwa bei BULLINGER, Der Christlich Eestand (s. Anm. 9, Kap. 10; Schriften [s. Anm. 9], 467–472), im Trauformular des elisabethanischen Book of Common Prayer (s. Anm. 12, 96ʳ) und bei SMITH, A Preparative to Marriage (s. Anm. 15, 13–17).

[52] The Two Books of Homilies (s. Anm. 13), 500; PERKINS, Christian Oeconomie (s. Anm. 16), 13f.

[53] LUTHER, Vom Eelichen Leben (s. Anm. 7), 301,16–30; MENIUS, Oeconomia Christiana (ed. Gause / Scholz [s. Anm. 8], 28–30, 64). Vgl. WITT, Luthers Reformation der Ehe (s. Anm. 7), 258–264.

[54] WHATELY, Directions for Married Persons (s. Anm. 17), 20.

[55] BUCER, De regno Christi (s. Anm. 11), 205–208.

entsprechend in der »rerum omnium divinarum & humanarum summa cum benevolentia communicatio«.[56] Auch Henry Smith stellte diesen Aspekt an die Spitze. Die Ehe diente ihm zufolge vor allem dazu, »the inconvenience of solitarinesse« zu vermeiden:

»This life would be miserable and irksome and unpleasant to man, if the Lord had not given him a wife to company his troubles.« »Beasts are ordained for food, and clothes for warmth, and flowers for pleasure; but the wife is ordained for man, [...] a Citie of refuge to flie to in all troubles, and there is no peace comparable unto her, but the peace of conscience«. »[...] like a Turtle, which hath lost his Mate, like one legge, when the other is cut off, like one wing, when the other is clipt, so had the man been, if the woman had not been joyned to him«.[57]

Im Zuge der biblisch orientierten normativen Zentrierung der Ehelehre wurden drei zentrale Positionen des kanonischen Eherechts kritisiert und preisgegeben – die Anerkennung heimlicher Ehen, die scholastische Kasuistik der Ehehindernisse und das Verbot der Ehescheidung. Das gilt gleichermaßen für die Reformatoren im Heiligen Römischen Reich wie für die englischen Puritaner. Unbeschadet dessen haben Normen des kanonischen Rechts in den bischöflichen Ehegerichten Englands weiter Anwendung gefunden, und auch die weltlichen Ehegerichte im deutschsprachigen Raum griffen teilweise weiterhin auf Vorschriften des kanonischen Eherechts zurück.[58]

Was die heimlichen Ehen angeht – also Verbindungen, die allein auf dem gegenseitigen Eheversprechen der Brautleute beruhten, ohne dass es dafür Zeugen gab, die Eltern zugestimmt hatten oder eine kirchliche Zeremonie stattgefunden hatte –, so waren diese dem kanonischen Eherecht nach gültig, auch wenn die Kanonisten im Laufe der Zeit versuchten, sie durch Durchsetzung formaler Erfordernisse wie der Zeugenpflicht und der kirchlichen Trauung zurückzudrängen – eine Tendenz, die erst mit dem Tridentinum zum Ziel kam.[59] Demgegenüber war die Haltung der Reformatoren hier von Beginn an eindeutig. Zwar galt auch ihnen der Konsens der Eheleute als wichtigstes und konstitutives Element der Ehe, doch wurden die heimlichen Ehen generell abgelehnt. Vor allem Verlöbnisse ohne elterliches Einverständnis wurden von fast allen Autoren als ungültig verworfen.[60] Zunehmend galt auch die religiöse Einsegnung der Ehe in der Kirche als notwendiger Bestandteil der Eheschließung.[61]

---

[56] A.a.O., 189.
[57] Zitate: SMITH, A Preparative to Marriage (s. Anm. 15), 16, 13, 17.
[58] OZMENT, When Fathers Ruled (s. Anm. 2), 29–32.
[59] A.a.O., 26–28.
[60] BULLINGER, Der Christlich Eestand (s. Anm. 9), Kap. 5 (Schriften [s. Anm. 9], 440–445); BUCER, De regno Christi (s. Anm. 11), 157–161; The Catechism of Thomas Becon (s. Anm. 14), 355 f.; SMITH, A Preparative to Marriage (s. Anm. 15), 24; PERKINS, Christian Oeconomie (s. Anm. 16), 76; GOUGE, Of domesticall duties (s. Anm. 18), 446–453.

Die ausgefeilte Kasuistik möglicher Ehehindernisse, zu denen neben Blutsverwandtschaft bis zum vierten Grad ebenso Schwägerschaft und Taufpatenschaft bis in vergleichbare Verwandtschaftsgrade hinein sowie weitere Sonderfälle zählten, wurde von den Reformatoren im Reich als unbiblisch und in sich unlogisch verworfen.[62] Bereits 1522 stellte Luther den einschlägigen Vorschriften des Kirchenrechts die Aufzählung verbotener Verwandtschaftsgrade nach Lev. 18,6–18 als allein verbindliche Norm gegenüber. Damit ging eine deutliche Reduktion der Restriktionen einher; insbesondere waren danach nun Ehen zwischen Geschwisterkindern (Cousins und Cousinen) möglich.[63] Ebenfalls auf Lev. 18 und darauf aufbauende Analogieschlüsse stützte sich Bullingers ausführliche Behandlung der Ehehindernisse.[64] Bucer empfahl, sich bei einer künftigen englischen Ehegesetzgebung an die Gesetze Gottes und das Beispiel der Väter des Alten Testaments zu halten.[65] Bei den hier betrachteten englischen Puritanern spielte diese Frage dagegen überraschenderweise praktisch keine Rolle.

Die vom kanonischen Recht untersagte Eheschließung mit Nichtchristen wurde auch von den evangelischen Autoren im Reich wie in England fast allgemein abgelehnt.[66] Eine vorübergehende Ausnahme bildete allein der junge Luther, für den die Weltlichkeit der Ehe auch Verbindungen mit Juden oder Muslimen zuließ;[67] Perkins hielt immerhin für den Fall, dass einer der Partner erst nach der Verlobung vom Christentum abgefallen war, diese unter Berufung auf Paulus (1.Kor. 7,12–14) für grundsätzlich verbindlich.[68]

Die dritte große Infragestellung des kanonischen Eherechts im Zuge der normativen Zentrierung auf biblischer Grundlage betraf die Möglichkeit der Ehescheidung, die vom mittelalterlichen Kirchenrecht geleugnet, von den Reformatoren aber allgemein zugegeben wurde.[69] Dabei spielte einerseits die Überzeugung vom äußerlich-weltlichen Vertragscharakter

---

[61] BUCER, De regno Christi (s. Anm. 11), 163f.; PERKINS, Christian Oeconomie (s. Anm. 16), 94; GOUGE, Of domesticall duties (s. Anm. 18), 203–205.

[62] OZMENT, When Fathers Ruled (s. Anm. 2), 44–48.

[63] LUTHER, Vom Eelichen Leben (s. Anm. 7), 280,7–287,11.

[64] BULLINGER, Der Christlich Eestand (s. Anm. 9), Kap. 7 (Schriften [s. Anm. 9], 447–458).

[65] BUCER, De regno Christi (s. Anm. 11), 154–156.

[66] Z.B. SMITH, A Preparative to Marriage (s. Anm. 15), 25f.

[67] LUTHER, Vom Eelichen Leben (s. Anm. 7), 283,1–16.

[68] PERKINS, Christian Oeconomie (s. Anm. 16), 59–62.

[69] CORDULA SCHOLZ-LÖHNIG, Art. Eheauflösung (in: EdN 3, 2006, 52–57); OZMENT, When Fathers Ruled (s. Anm. 2), 80–99. Zu Luther: ERNST KINDER, Luthers Stellung zur Ehescheidung (in: Luther 24, 1953, 75–86); WITT, Luthers Reformation der Ehe (s. Anm. 7), 205–214.

der Ehe eine Rolle, andererseits das in diesem Zusammenhang immer wieder zitierte Herrenwort Mt. 19,9, das eine Scheidung bei Ehebruch gestattete. Tatsächlich löste der Ehebruch nach reformatorischer Überzeugung als solcher das Band ehelicher Gemeinschaft auf, so dass die Scheidung – und die Möglichkeit der Wiederverheiratung! – nur noch die notwendige Konsequenz war. Allerdings gab es in den reformatorischen Kirchen durchaus auch Widerstand gegen diese Auffassung. In England waren es ausgerechnet die Puritaner, die mit biblischer Begründung durchgehend für die Möglichkeit der Ehescheidung votierten, während sich konservative Kreise damit noch lange schwertaten. Noch 1619 etwa verursachte William Whately einen Eklat, als er in seinem *Bride-Bush* die Scheidung für erlaubt erklärte.[70] Tatsächlich wurde in England als einzigem protestantischen Land Europas das Scheidungsrecht nicht eingeführt, auch wenn dafür am Ende eher politische Zufälle ausschlaggebend waren.[71] Unabhängig davon blieben im praktischen Leben Ehescheidungen in allen protestantischen Territorien noch lange seltene Ausnahmen.

Unterschiedliche Auffassungen bestanden darüber, ob der betrogene Partner eines reuigen Ehebrechers an der Ehe festhalten konnte[72] oder vielleicht sogar sollte.[73] In jedem Fall war der unschuldig geschiedene Partner frei, sich wieder zu verheiraten; die Grundfunktion der Ehe als Mittel zur Verhinderung von Unzucht erforderte dies geradezu.[74] Die Wiederverheiratung des ehebrüchigen Partners war dagegen gewöhnlich kein Thema; in biblischer Zeit wäre er ohnehin mit der Todesstrafe zu belegen gewesen – eine Sanktion, die sich manche evangelischen Autoren auch für ihre Gegenwart vorstellen konnten.[75]

Während für manche evangelische Autoren, darunter die Puritaner Smith, Whately und Gouge,[76] Ehebruch der einzig legitime Scheidungsgrund war, erkannten andere weitere Gründe an. So subsumierte Bullinger unter den Tatbestand des Ehebruchs noch den Unglauben des Partners.[77]

---

[70] WHATELY, Directions for Married People (s. Anm. 17), 6. Vgl. SMITH, Art. Whately (s. Anm. 17), 431; PETERS, Patterns of Piety (s. Anm. 2), 330.

[71] MacCULLOCH, Die Reformation (s. Anm. 2), 848.

[72] So z.B. LUTHER, Vom Eelichen Leben (s. Anm. 7), 288,29–31; 289,29–290,1.

[73] WHATELY, Directions for Married People (s. Anm. 17), 6f.; GOUGE, Of domesticall duties (s. Anm. 18), 218f.

[74] BULLINGER, Der Christlich Eestand (s. Anm. 9), Kap. 25 (Schriften [s. Anm. 9], 574f.).

[75] Ebd. LUTHER, Vom Eelichen Leben (s. Anm. 7), 289,8–17; BUCER, De regno Christi (s. Anm. 11), 189–194.

[76] SMITH, A Preparative to Marriage (s. Anm. 15), 45; WHATELY, Directions for Married Persons (s. Anm. 17), 6; GOUGE, Of domesticall duties (s. Anm. 18), 217f.

[77] BULLINGER, Der Christlich Eestand (s. Anm. 9), Kap. 25 (Schriften [s. Anm. 9], 573).

Für Luther, der hinsichtlich des Unglaubens, wie erwähnt, anfangs anders
dachte, waren dagegen auch eine von Natur aus bestehende, erst nach der
Eheschließung erkennbare körperliche Unfähigkeit zum Vollzug der Ehe
oder die dauerhafte Verweigerung des Geschlechtsverkehrs durch einen
Partner Scheidungsgründe. Ja, selbst eine nicht zu behebende Unverträg-
lichkeit der Ehepartner konnte für ihn im Extremfall eine Scheidung recht-
fertigen, auf die in diesem Fall freilich keine Wiederheirat folgen durfte.[78]
Die wohl elaborierteste und liberalste Behandlung der Ehescheidung, ihrer
Voraussetzungen, ihres Vollzugs und ihrer Konsequenzen findet sich in
Bucers Vorlage für eine Reformationsgesetzgebung Königs Eduards VI.;
sie nimmt den Großteil des Abschnitts zur Ehe überhaupt ein.[79] Auszüge
daraus ließ John Milton 1644 in englischer Übersetzung drucken und legte
sie dem Parlament vor.[80] Neben Ehebruch, der dauerhaften Versagung
ehelicher Liebe und des ehelichen Geschlechtsverkehrs sowie der Unter-
drückung und Misshandlung des Partners war er bereit, auch die im anti-
ken Römischen Recht vorgesehenen Scheidungsgründe – bestimmte
schwere Verbrechen gegen Dritte, auswärtige Übernachtungen, den Besuch von Schauspielen ohne die Zustimmung des Partners und dergleichen
– anzuerkennen.[81]

3. Oeconomia *und* Politia
Ehe, Familie und Haus als Keimzelle der Gesellschaft

Die theologische Aufwertung von Ehe, Familie und Haus führte zur Nivellierung der Standesunterschiede innerhalb der Kirche und machte die
evangelischen Gemeinden im Prinzip zu homogenen Gemeinschaften von
Verheirateten. Doch auch im gesamtgesellschaftlichen Gefüge wurden Familie und Haus zum dominierenden Modell, zu Kern und Keimzelle der
Gesellschaft aufgewertet.[82] Die alte, letztlich auf antike Vorbilder zurück-
gehende Dreiteilung der Gesellschaft in Lehrstand, Wehrstand und Nähr-
stand – in mittelalterlicher Terminologie: *oratores*, *bellatores* und *laboratores* – setzte eine mehr oder weniger statische Hierarchie der drei Stände

---

[78] LUTHER, Vom Eelichen Leben (s. Anm. 7), 287,15–17; 290,5–291,14.
[79] BUCER, De regno Christi (s. Anm. 11), 165–226 (Kap. 22–44).
[80] The Ivdgement of Martin Bucer concerning divorce written to Edward the sixt, in
his second book of the Kingdom of Christ, and now English, London 1644. Vgl. DAVID
MASSON, The Life of John Milton, Bd. 3: 1643–1649, Cambridge 1873, 255–261.
[81] BUCER, De regno Christi (s. Anm. 11), 203f.
[82] COLLINSON, Birthpangs (s. Anm. 2), 60f.; ANDREAS GESTRICH, Art. Familie 5.
Familie und öffentliche Ordnung (in: EdN 3, 2006, 799–801); ANTJE ROGGENKAMP, Art.
Erziehung 4. Evangelische Erziehung (in: EdN 3, 2006, 524–528).

voraus, wobei sich freilich der Lehrstand aufgrund des Zölibats fortlaufend neu aus den beiden anderen Ständen ergänzen musste. Luthers Drei-Stände-Lehre,[83] die er freilich nirgends im Zusammenhang entfaltet hat, knüpft an das alte Dreiermodell an. Die drei ›Hauptstände‹ *oeconomia*, *politia* und *ecclesia* sind bei ihm als Ordnungen Gottes aber nicht nur alle gleichen Ranges und gleicher Würde. Sie erscheinen hier auch sehr viel weniger scharf gegeneinander abgegrenzt, sondern kennen verschiedene Übergänge und funktionale Überschneidungen: »der Fürst oder Herr kann zugleich Ehemann und Vater sein, ebenso der Träger eines Kirchenamtes. Ein jeder steht in mehreren Lebensvollzügen«.[84] Faktisch erweist sich dadurch am Ende der Ehe- und Hausstand oder die *oeconomia*, wie Luther sagt, als Mittel- und Ausgangspunkt der gesamten gesellschaftlichen Ordnung.

»Denn es ist der eltist stand unter allen der gantzen welt, ja, alle andere komen aus dem her, darein Adam und Eva, unser erste eltern, von Gott geschaffen und verordnet sein, darinn sie und alle jhre Gottfürchtige kinder und nachkomen gelebt haben«.[85]

Das ist keineswegs nur historisch zu verstehen. Tatsächlich ist die *oeconomia* noch heute die eigentliche Keimzelle der Gesellschaft, aus der sich auch die beiden anderen Stände rekrutieren müssen. In seiner Vorrede zur *Oeconomia Christiana* von Justus Menius hat Luther die daraus resultierende Verantwortung der Eltern betont:[86] Wenn sie ihre Kinder nicht zu gottesfürchtigen und tüchtigen Persönlichkeiten erziehen, müssen geistlicher und weltlicher Stand zugrunde gehen. Denn wo sonst sollte man Pfarrer und andere Kirchenbedienstete, Räte und Amtleute hernehmen? So liegt beiden von Gott in dieser Welt verordneten Regimenten, dem geistlichen wie dem weltlichen, letztlich der Ehe- und Hausstand als Keim und Basis zugrunde.

Diese essentielle Verbindung zwischen der *oeconomia* und der *politia*, aber auch der *ecclesia* ergibt sich speziell durch den Zusammenhang von Autorität und Gehorsam, der in Luthers Augen für alle Ordnungen des

---

[83] PAUL ALTHAUS, Die Ethik Martin Luthers, Gütersloh 1965, 43–48; BERNHARD LOHSE, Luthers Theologie in ihrer historischen Entwicklung und in ihrem systematischen Zusammenhang, Göttingen 1995, 342–344; OSWALD BAYER, Nature and Institution. Luther's Doctrine of the Three Orders (in: Lutheran Quarterly, 12, 1998, 125–159); REINHARD SCHWARZ, Martin Luther – Lehrer der christlichen Religion, Tübingen [2]2016, 153–162; SCHORN-SCHÜTTE, Drei-Stände-Lehre (s. Anm. 43); LUISE SCHORN-SCHÜTTE, Art. Drei-Stände-Lehre (in: Das Luther-Lexikon, hg. v. Volker Leppin u. Gury Schneider-Ludorff, Regensburg 2014, 174–176).

[84] ALTHAUS, Ethik Luthers (s. Anm. 83), 45.

[85] LUTHER, Predigt über Hebr. 13,4 vom 4.8.1545: WA 49,797,33–798,3.

[86] Luthers Vorrede zu MENIUS, Oeconomia Christiana (ed. Gause / Scholz [s. Anm. 8], 39–42).

menschlichen Zusammenlebens konstitutiv ist und der in der *oeconomia*
im Zusammenleben von Mann und Frau, Eltern und Kindern, Hausherrschaft und Dienstboten vorabgebildet ist und praktisch erlernt und eingeübt wird. »Kern dieser Vorstellung ist, dass in der Hausherrschaft, der
›oeconomia‹, alle Formen der Herrschaft zusammenfließen: in der Ehe
stehen sich Ehemann und Ehefrau als ›Regenten‹ gleichrangig gegenüber,
Eltern und Kinder als Form der gleichrangigen Herrschaft, Hausherrschaft und Diener als Form der hierarchischen Untertanenschaft«.[87] Zur
theologischen Begründung beriefen sich Luther und andere Reformatoren
gerne auf das Elterngebot des Dekalogs, das nicht nur innerhalb der Familie galt, sondern auch darüber hinaus das Verhältnis der Menschen gegenüber Autoritäten generell normierte. In diesem Sinne hat Luther, an
mittelalterliche Auslegungen u.a. von Thomas von Aquin anknüpfend,[88]
im *Großen Katechismus* in seiner Erläuterung zum Vierten Gebot die Ge-
horsamspflicht nicht nur gegenüber den leiblichen und Hausvätern, sondern auch gegenüber den Landesvätern – der weltlichen Obrigkeit – und
den geistlichen Vätern – in der Kirche – subsumiert.[89] Im selben Sinne
wird das Elterngebot im ein Jahr zuvor erstmals gedruckten *Unterricht der
Visitatoren* ausführlich ausgearbeitet.[90] Sehr klar hat 1529 auch Justus Menius den im Elterngebot begründeten Zusammenhang von *oeconomia* und
politia, von Haushaltung und Landesregierung, als den beiden Formen
von Gottes leiblichem Regiment herausgearbeitet und auf die überragende
Bedeutung der familiären Kindererziehung für das Gemeinwohl hingewiesen:

> »Darumb / wil man landen vnd leuten wol raten vnd helffen / das es vmb die
> Politia wohl stehe / so mus mans warlich am ersten ynn der Oeconomia mit der
> iugent anfahen«.[91]

Auch die englischen Puritaner betonen die grundlegende Bedeutung der
Familie als Modell und Bildungsstätte für die weltlich-politische Ordnung
wie für die Kirche. Maßgeblich dafür ist auch hier das Elterngebot des
Dekalogs, das nach Thomas Becon nicht nur für die leiblichen Eltern gilt,
sondern auch

---

[87] SCHORN-SCHÜTTE, Art. Drei-Stände-Lehre (s. Anm. 83), 175.
[88] VOLKER LEPPIN, Die Normierung der Frömmigkeit im »Unterricht der Visitatoren« (in: Der »Unterricht der Visitatoren« und die Durchsetzung der Reformation in
Kursachsen, hg. v. Joachim Bauer u. Stefan Michel, Leipzig 2017, 167–194, hier: 177f.,
Anm. 54).
[89] WA 30/1,152,19–35; 153,29–155,21.
[90] WA 26,206,10–211,26. Vgl. LEPPIN, Normierung der Frömmigkeit (s. Anm. 88),
177–181.
[91] MENIUS, Oeconomia Christiana (ed. Gause / Scholz [s. Anm. 8], 64).

»toward the temporal magistrates, and the ministers of God's word, and toward our elders and all such as be our superiors and governors«.[92]

Daneben finden sich heilsgeschichtliche Begründungen: So ist nach William Perkins die Familie die erste und älteste aller jener Gemeinschaften (»Societies & States«), aus denen sich die Menschheit zusammensetzt. Noch bis zur Sintflut gab es weder weltliche Regierung noch Kirche, die ganze bürgerliche und kirchliche Ordnung beschränkte sich auf die privaten Familien. Erst nach der Sintflut wurde die Familie Noahs zur gemeinsamen Mutter, aus der die beiden anderen Stände hervorgingen. Die heilige und rechtschaffene Leitung der Familie ist daher ein direktes Mittel für die gute Bestellung von Kirche und Gemeinwesen.[93] In ähnlicher Weise möchte William Gouge die Familien als »excellent seminaries [...] to Church and Commonwealth« in Anspruch nehmen:

»Necessary it is that good order be first set in families: for as they were before other polities, so they are somewhat the more necessary: and good members of a family are like to make good members of Church and common-wealth.«[94]

Haus und Familie sind im reformatorischen Verständnis insofern nicht ein dem sozialen Leben entzogenes privates Reservat, sondern haben eine eminent politische Funktion.[95]

4. Oeconomia *und* Ecclesia
Ehe, Familie und Haus als Kirche im Kleinen

Der Zusammenhang zwischen *oeconomia* und *ecclesia* ist nun aber nicht allein so zu verstehen, dass in der Familie der notwendige Autoritätsgehorsam eingeübt und das künftige kirchliche Personal herangebildet werden soll. Vielmehr ist die Familie von den Reformatoren fast durchweg auch als Ort religiöser Bildung und Einübung in Glauben und Frömmigkeit in Anspruch genommen worden. Als solcher kann die Familie und das christliche Haus als Kirche[96] oder Tempel[97] im Kleinen qualifiziert werden.[98]

---

[92] The Catechism of Thomas Becon (s. Anm. 14), 88.

[93] PERKINS, Christian Oeconomie (s. Anm. 16), Widmungsvorrede (unpaginiert).

[94] GOUGE, Of domesticall duties (s. Anm. 18), Widmungsvorrede (unpaginiert).

[95] »The home, then, was no introspective, private sphere, unmindful of society, but the cradle of citizenship, extending its values and example into the world around it. The habits and character developed within families became the virtues that shaped entire lands« (OZMENT, When Fathers Ruled [s. Anm. 2], 10; vgl. Collinson, Birthpangs [s. Anm. 2], 60f.).

[96] Z.B. PERKINS, Christian Oeconomie (s. Anm. 16), 8.

[97] Z.B. JOHANNES MATHESIUS, Oeconomia oder Bericht, wie sich ein Hausvater halten soll, Nürnberg 1561 (VD16 M 1419), (unpaginiert).

Bereits in seiner Schrift *Vom Eelichen Leben* hatte Luther 1522 die religiöse Erziehung der Kinder als das Beste an der Ehe gerühmt. Indem die Eltern ihre Kinder mit dem Evangelium bekannt machen, sind sie deren Apostel, Bischöfe und Pfarrer.[99] Seinen *Kleinen Katechismus* konzipierte Luther 1529 dementsprechend für die häusliche Unterweisung der ganzen Familie einschließlich der Dienstboten durch den frommen Hausvater; in der Überschrift jedes Katechismusstücks heißt es, dass »ein Hausvater seinem Gesinde« dieses so »einfältiglich fürhalten« soll.[100] Tatsächlich rechnete Luther später sogar mit der apokalyptischen Möglichkeit, dass das Predigtamt zum Erliegen kommen und das Evangelium fortan allein in den Häusern durch die Hausväter erhalten werden könnte.[101]

Wie genau die häusliche Evangeliumsverkündigung und religiöse Belehrung durch die Hausväter abgesehen von Luthers Katechismus aussehen konnte, haben verschiedene Autoren unterschiedlich ausführlich erläutert. Justus Menius forderte die Eltern kurz auf, ihren Kindern vor allem die Gebote Gottes einzuschärfen, sie einerseits anzuhalten, immer nach Gottes Geboten zu leben und Gottes Zorn und Gericht zu fürchten, und sie andererseits zu lehren, Gott zu vertrauen, für alles zu ihm beten und ihm für seine Wohltaten zu danken.[102] Daneben entstanden aber auch ausführliche Materialsammlungen für die häusliche Katechese an Kindern und Dienstboten wie jenes umfangreiche, mehrfach wieder aufgelegte Handbuch, das der Eislebener Pfarrer Andreas Fabricius 1569 unter dem programmatischen Titel *Die Hauskirche* herausbrachte und seinen eigenen Kindern widmete.[103] Der Untertitel erscheint bezeichnend:

»Wie ein Hausvater neben dem offentlichen Predigampt / auch daheime sein Heufflein zu Gottes Wort / vnd dem lieben Catechismo reitzen soll«.

Erasmus Sarcerius wollte 1553 mit seinem *Hausbuch* [...] *von den vornemesten Artickeln der Christlichen Religion* die »Einfeltigen Haus veter« sogar als Laien-Kontroverstheologen in Anspruch nehmen.[104] Eine summarische Anweisung zur häuslichen Elementarkatechese aus der Perspektive der schweizerischen Reformation gab Heinrich Bullinger 1540 im 21.

---

[98] MacCulloch, Die Reformation (s. Anm. 2), 848.

[99] Luther, Vom Eelichen Leben (s. Anm. 7), 301,23–25. Auch Thomas Becon spricht davon, dass jeder Hausvater »a bishop in his own house« sei (The Catechism of Thomas Becon [s. Anm. 14], 337).

[100] WA 30/1,282a,17f. (Anm.); 292a,1–3; 298a,11–13; 308a,14–16; 314a,12–14; 318a,17–19; 322a,23–25. – Zum Begriff des »Hausvaters«: Ursula Fuhrich-Grubert, Claudia Ulbrich, Art. Hausvater (in: EdN 5, 2007, 252–254).

[101] Luther, Daniel-Vorrede: WA.DB 11,122,1–5.

[102] Menius, Oeconomia Christiana (ed. Gause / Scholz [s. Anm. 8], 95).

[103] VD16 ZV 5704.

[104] VD16 S 1708.

Kapitel seines Buchs *Der christlich Eestand*. Dabei sollten sich die Eltern auf die gedruckten Katechismen in deutscher Sprache stützen, aber auch Sprichwörter zur moralischen Erziehung einsetzen. Morgen- und Abendgebet, häuslicher und schulischer Unterricht, Predigtbesuch mit anschließender häuslicher Examinierung und das lebendige Vorbild der Eltern sollten ineinander greifen.

In den Schriften der englischen Puritaner nimmt der Gedanke der religiösen Erziehung der Kinder und des religiösen Lebens im »Haus« sogar noch mehr Raum ein als in den Schriften der Reformatoren vom Kontinent. Neben die Katechese im engeren Sinn tritt hier zudem sehr viel deutlicher das Bemühen um Weckung, Förderung und Pflege der Frömmigkeit insgesamt, und das nicht nur im Blick auf die Kinder und das Dienstpersonal, sondern auch im Blick auf die Eheleute untereinander. Henry Smith zufolge soll der Hausvater wie der Seraph, der den Eifer des Propheten Jesaja entzündete, in seiner Ehefrau, den Dienern und den Kindern den Eifer für Gott entzünden und wie eine Säugamme jedem die Milch seines Wissen darreichen.[105] In seiner Familie stehe der Hausvater an Christi statt und habe ihr gegenüber dessen dreifaches Amt zu versehen: zu herrschen wie ein König, zu lehren wie ein Prophet und zu bekehren wie ein Priester.[106]

William Perkins behandelte in seiner *Christian Oeconomie* an herausgehobener Stelle schon im 2. Kapitel das, was er den häuslichen Gottesdienst (»the household seruice of God«) nannte.[107] Dieser sollte einerseits gemeinsame Bibelstunden der Hausgemeinschaft umfassen – »a conference vpon the word of God, for the edification of all the members thereof, to eternall life«[108] –, andererseits gemeinsame Gebetsversammlungen am Morgen und am Abend, dazu das Tischgebet vor und nach den Mahlzeiten. Familien, in denen diese Art von Gottesdienst gehalten werde, seien kleine Kirchen, ja eine Art von Paradies auf Erden.[109]

William Gouge rechnete die gegenseitige Fürbitte, den Ruf zur Bekehrung, die geistliche Erbauung, die Verhinderung von Sünde und die Ermunterung zum Wachstum in der Gnade bereits ausdrücklich zu den gegenseitigen Pflichten, die die Eheleute einander schuldeten.[110] Die Haus-

---

[105] »One compareth the master of the house to the Seraphin, which came and kindled the Prohets zeale; so he should go from wife to servants, and from servants to children, and kindle in them the zeale of God, longing to teach his knowledge, as a nurse to empty her brests« (SMITH, A Preparative to Marriage [s. Anm. 15], 38).

[106] SMITH, A Preparative to Marriage (s. Anm. 15), 38.

[107] PERKINS, Christian Oeconomie (s. Anm. 16), 2–9.

[108] A.a.O., 5.

[109] »little Churches, yea even a kind of paradise vpon earth« (a.a.O., 8).

[110] GOUGE, Of domesticall duties (s. Anm. 18), 235–242.

eltern sollten darüber hinaus mit Bibellektüre und täglicher Katechese ihre Kinder zu wahrer Frömmigkeit erziehen,[111] aber auch die Dienerschaft täglich im Glauben und zur Erlangung der ewigen Seligkeit anleiten.[112] Ganz ähnlich verlangte William Whately von den Eheleuten, einander mit gemeinsamem Beten und Singen und mit Gesprächen über das himmlische Vaterland im Glauben und in der Frömmigkeit zu fördern.[113] Ihre wichtigste Sorge sollte sein, dass in ihrem Haus Gott recht verehrt und seine Kenntnis und Furcht in die Herzen ihrer Kinder und Dienstboten gepflanzt werde, wozu gemeinsame Bibellesung und Gebet, häusliche Katechese, gemeinsamer Gottesdienstbesuch mit anschließender Examinierung und die Überwachung der Sonntagsheiligung vonnöten seien. Auf diese Weise werde eine christliche Familie eine veritable »Kirche«, ein Haus Gottes, in dem dieser wohne.[114]

Die detailliertesten Anweisungen für die religiöse Kindererziehung und für das religiöse Leben der »Hauskirche« finden sich bei Thomas Becon. Jeder Mann ist ihm zufolge Bischof in seinem eigenen Haus (»every man is a bishop in his own house«), und als solchem obliegt ihm die Aufgabe, zunächst und vor allem seine Ehefrau, dann aber auch die Kinder und die Bediensteten auf dem Weg zur Seligkeit anzuleiten.[115] Sein ganzes Haus soll so zu einer Schule der Frömmigkeit werden.[116] Dazu muss der Hausvater nicht nur allen mit gutem Beispiel vorangehen. Er soll auch dafür sorgen, dass alle Angehörigen seines Haushalts täglich zur gemeinsamen Morgenandacht mit Gebet, Rezitation von Credo und Dekalog und möglichst auch Bibellesung zusammenkommen und dass vor und nach allen Mahlzeiten gemeinsam Dankgebete gesprochen werden. An Sonn- und Feiertagen soll er mit seiner ganzen Familie und Dienerschaft die Gottesdienste besuchen und anschließend Kinder und Dienstboten über die gehörte Predigt examinieren.[117] Wie die Dienerschaft, so sollen die Eltern auch ihre Kinder im christlichen Glauben unterrichten und zu praktizierter Frömmigkeit anleiten:

---

[111] A.a.O., 536–543.

[112] A.a.O., 666f.

[113] WHATELY, Directions for Married Persons (s. Anm. 17), 24f., 32.

[114] A.a.O., 44.

[115] The Catechism of Thomas Becon (s. Anm. 14), 337.

[116] »For every householder's house ought to be a school of godliness; forasmuch as every householder ought to be a bishop in his own house, and so to oversee his family, that nothing reign in it but virtue, godliness, and honesty« (a.a.O., 360).

[117] A.a.O., 359f.

»In these and such like godly exercises the parents must daily and diligently train up their youth, that they, being thus acquainted with virtue from the beginning, may the more easily for ever after abstain from all sin and vice«.[118]

Dazu gehört nicht nur die heimische Unterweisung im Katechismus und die Ausrichtung der gesamten Erziehung in Familie und Schule auf die Frömmigkeit – selbst das Sprechenlernen wird hier als religionspädagogische Aufgabe aufgefasst: Schon die ersten Worte, die die Kinder sprechen, sollen vorzugsweise ernste, nüchterne und fromme Worte sein, wie »God, Jesus Christ, faith, love, hope, patience, goodness, peace &c.« Sobald sie ganze Sätze sprechen, soll man sie kurze Sentenzen lehren, die sie zu einem Leben in Tugend und zum Hass gegen Laster und Sünde anregen, z.B.:

»God alone saveth me. Christ by his death hath redeemed me. The Holy Ghost sanctifieth me. There is one God. Christ alone is our Mediator and Advocate«.[119]

In derartigen Ausführungen zur religiösen Erziehung der Kinder wird diese meist in die Verantwortung beider Elternteile, mitunter sogar in die besondere Verantwortung der Mutter gestellt. Sonst aber ist es in den hier betrachteten normativen Texten immer der Hausvater und Ehemann, der, von besonderen Ausnahmesituationen abgesehen, als Leiter des religiösen Lebens im Haus in Anspruch genommen wird.[120] Die Wirklichkeit dürfte vielfach anders ausgesehen haben. Aus dem England des 16. und 17. Jahrhunderts wissen wir, dass – namentlich in Familien der Aristokratie und der Mittelschicht – die häusliche Frömmigkeit nach allgemeiner Anschauung als Domäne der Frauen galt.[121] Überhaupt wird man damit rechnen müssen, dass auch und gerade im Bereich von Ehe, Familie und Haus den normativen Texten oft keine völlig entsprechende soziale Praxis korrespondierte.

---

[118] A.a.O., 349.

[119] A.a.O., 348.

[120] »Nun brachte nicht mehr die Mutter ihrem Kind das Ave-Maria und das Vaterunser bei, sondern der ideale protestantische Hausvater, von dem erwartet wurde, dass er seine Familie beim Gebet leite und dabei auch Spontanität und Sinn für die Besonderheit einer Situation zeige wie der Pastor bei seiner Predigt auf der Kanzel. Gewiss spielte dabei auch eine Rolle, dass in den protestantischen Kirchen das Vorbild für Glaubenstreue das Geschlecht gewechselt hatte: von der gebenedeiten Jungfrau Maria zum buchstäblich patriarchalischen Abraham« (MacCulloch, Die Reformation [s. Anm. 2], 835).

[121] Sara Mendelson, Patricia Crawford, Women in Early Modern England, 1550–1720, Oxford ²2003, 225–230. Vgl. auch Wunder, »Er ist die Sonn'« (s. Anm. 2), 115.

5. Ergebnis: Sieben Thesen

1. Ehe, Familie und Haus erfuhren in der Reformation eine umfassende theologische Neubewertung und Aufwertung.

2. Schon seit den 1520er Jahren wurden Ehe und Familie von Luther und im Luthertum literarisch thematisiert, auch die oberdeutschen und schweizerischen Reformatoren widmeten sich dem Thema ausgiebig. In England waren es vor allem puritanische Autoren seit dem ausgehenden 16. Jahrhundert, bei denen es größere Aufmerksamkeit fand.

3. Die Reformatoren erklärten die Ehe zum »weltlich Ding«, zur äußerlichen, bürgerlichen Angelegenheit. Dadurch wurde die religiös begründete Sonderstellung der sakramental verstandenen Ehe gegenüber anderen Lebensbereichen nivelliert. In den protestantischen Territorien auf dem Kontinent wurde das kanonische Eherecht und die kirchliche Ehegerichtsbarkeit weitgehend preisgegeben, in England blieb beides bestehen.

4. Andererseits wurde der Ehestand von den Reformatoren theologisch stark aufgewertet: als Gottes Stiftung und Gebot, als Schöpfungsordnung, als erste und älteste aller Sozialformationen.

5. Im Zuge einer biblisch orientierten normativen Zentrierung wurden die geheimen Ehen verworfen, die Liste der Ehehindernisse revidiert und die Möglichkeit der Ehescheidung eröffnet, wobei die Ansichten der betrachteten Autoren untereinander in Einzelheiten durchaus differierten.

6. Ehe, Familie und Haus (*oeconomia*) wurden als Keimzelle der Gesellschaft und der staatlichen Ordnung *(politia)* entdeckt. Hier wurde die universal, in allen Ständen geltende Struktur von Autorität und Gehorsam (Elterngebot!) eingeübt, von hier aus rekrutierte sich das Personal im Dienst des weltlichen wie des geistlichen Regimentes Gottes.

7. Ehe, Familie und Haus wurden als Ort religiöser Kindererziehung und häuslichen Gottesdienstes in ihrer Bedeutung als »kleine Kirche« und »Tempel Gottes« entdeckt.

Marriage, Family, and Household in the Reformation in the Holy Roman Empire and in England

Wolf-Friedrich Schäufele

In describing the transition from Reformation movements to Reformation churches, a classical theology-based history of the Reformation would focus above all on the development of theological teachings, liturgy and church order. No less significant, however, were the changes in social formations and mentalities. In this sense, Waldemar Kawerau noted as early as 1892 that the ecclesiastical Reformation of the church had also become a reformation of domestic life.[1] In recent decades, socio-cultural research has dealt extensively with gender relations and social practices in the context of marriage, family, and household in the Reformation,[2] confirming that they were not just on the periphery of Reformation reorganization.[3] In this paper, I take for granted the results of this kind of research, but will try to return to a greater extent to the normative theological concepts and their substantiations. On the other hand, the much debated and thoroughly controversial questions of the extent to which Protestantism (apart from the introduction of clerical marriage) produced substan-

---

[1] WALDEMAR KAWERAU, Die Reformation und die Ehe. Ein Beitrag zur Kulturgeschichte des 16. Jahrhunderts, Halle 1892, 4.

[2] E.g. STEVEN E. OZMENT, When Fathers Ruled. Family Life in Reformation Europe, Cambridge (Mass.) and London 1983; PATRICK COLLINSON, The Birthpangs of Protestant England. Religious and Cultural Change in the Sixteenth and Seventeenth Centuries, Basingstoke and London 1988, 60–93; LYNDAL ROPER, The Holy Household, Oxford 1989 (German translation: Das fromme Haus. Frauen und Moral in der Reformation, Frankfurt a. M. and New York 1995); HEIDE WUNDER, »Er ist die Sonn', sie ist der Mond«. Frauen in der Frühen Neuzeit, Munich 1992, esp. 65–76; JACK GOODY, Geschichte der Familie, Munich 2002, 101–124; CHRISTINE PETERS, Patterns of Piety. Women, Gender and Religion in Late Medieval and Reformation England, Cambridge ²2005, 314–342; WOLFGANG REINHARD, Lebensformen Europas. Eine historische Kulturanthropologie, München ²2006, 199–226; DIARMAID MacCULLOCH, Die Reformation 1490–1750, Munich 2003, 784–856.

[3] E.g. ROPER, Das fromme Haus (see note 2), 11: »Die Geschlechterbeziehungen [...] wurden durch die Reformation keineswegs nur am Rande berührt. Sie standen im Gegenteil im Zentrum der Reformation. Die konservative Umdeutung der Glaubenslehren der reformatorischen Bewegung kreiste um die Bestimmung der Rolle der Frau in Ehe und Haushalt. Dieses konservative Umschreiben der evangelischen Botschaft war der Schlüssel dazu, die Reformation erfolgreich einzuführen und zu verankern.«

tial changes in the daily lives of families at all,[4] whether it brought about a social emancipation of women[5] or, especially in the form of English Puritanism, an emotional deepening of family relationships,[6] will not be discussed here.

The sources on which I am primarily based are for the area of the Lutheran Reformation Luther's sermon *Vom ehelichen Leben* from 1522[7] and the *Oeconomia Christiana* of the Eisenach superintendent Justus Menius (1449–1558) from 1529.[8] Moreover, I have used other writings of Luther, Johannes Mathesius, Erasmus Sarcerius and Andreas Fabricius. Heinrich Bullinger's (1504–1575) *Der Christlich Eestand* (1540) can be regarded as exemplary for the Zurich Reformation.[9] At the same time, it had a strong impact on the early English Reformation: Miles Coverdale translated it into English immediately after its publication. The first English printing appeared in late 1541[10] and until 1575 there were eight more editions. Another author on the border between the German-speaking and the English Reformation was Martin Bucer (1491–1551) with his late work *De regno Christi* (1550) dedicated to King Edward VI of England which was, however, eventually printed not in England, but only seven years later in Basel and in 1563 appeared also in a German translation.[11]

---

[4] COLLINSON, Birthpangs (see note 2), 81–90; MACCULLOCH, Die Reformation (see note 2), 793.

[5] Cf. e.g. CLAUDIA ULBRICH, Frauen in der Reformation (in: Die Frühe Neuzeit in der Geschichtswissenschaft. Forschungstendenzen und Forschungserträge, ed. Nada Boškovska Leimgruber, Paderborn 1997, 163–177).

[6] Cf. COLLINSON, Birthpangs (see note 2), 63–64.

[7] MARTIN LUTHER, Vom Eelichen Leben, Wittenberg 1522 (VD16 L 7025; USTC 700025). Used here: the edition in WA 10/2,267–304. For a comprehensive account on Luther's theology of marriage cf. CHRISTIAN VOLKMAR WITT, Martin Luthers Reformation der Ehe. Sein theologisches Eheverständnis vor dessen augustinisch-mittelalterlichem Hintergrund, Tübingen 2017; THOMAS KAUFMANN, Reformation der Lebenswelt: Luthers Ehetheologie (in: ID., Der Anfang der Reformation. Studien zur Kontextualität der Theologie, Publizistik, und Inszenierung Luthers und der reformatorischen Bewegung, Tübingen 2012, 550–564); UTE GAUSE, art. Ehe (in: Das Luther-Lexikon, eds. Volker Leppin and Gury Schneider-Ludorff, Regensburg 2014, 181–2).

[8] JUSTUS MENIUS, Oeconomia Christiana das ist von christlicher Haußhaltung, Wittenberg 1529 (VD16 M 4541; USTC 636874). Used here: the edition in: Ehe und Familie im Geist des Luthertums. Die Oeconomia Christiana (1529) des Justus Menius, eds. Ute Gause and Stephanie Scholz, Leipzig 2012, 35–139.

[9] HEINRICH BULLINGER, Der Christlich Eestand. Von der heiligen Ee herkumen / wenn / wo / wie / vnnd von wäm sy ufgesetzt / vnd was sy sye, Zürich 1540 (VD16 B 9578; USTC 632939). A modern German translation in: HEINRICH BULLINGER, Schriften, vol. 1, eds. Emidio Campi, Detlef Roth and Peter Stotz, Zurich 2004, 417–575. Cf. ALFRED WEBER, Heinrich Bullingers »Christlicher Ehestand«, seine zeitgenössischen Quellen und die Anfänge des Familienbuches in England, Leipzig 1929.

[10] HEINRICH BULLINGER, The Christen state of matrimonye: The orygenall of holy wedlok: whan, where, how, and of whom it was instituted [and] ordeyned: what it is: how it ought to proceade: what be the occasions, frute and commodities therof, Antwerp 1541 (ESTC S108927; USTC 410898).

From the domain of the English Reformation the Elizabethan *Book of Common Prayer* from 1559[12] and the wedding sermon from the second *Book of Homilies*[13] finished in 1571 were consulted. All other English sources are almost exclusively from Puritan authors of the late 16th and early 17th century: starting from the voluminous *Catechism* of Thomas Becon (1560)[14] and a wedding sermon of Henry Smith from the year 1591[15] up to the detailed manuals of William Perkins (1609),[16] William

---

[11] MARTIN BUCER, De Regno Christi Iesu servatoris nostri, libri II. Ad Eduardum VI Angliae Regem, annis abhinc sex scripti. Basel: Oporinus, 1557 (VD16 B 8906; USTC 631342); used here: Martini Buceri Opera Latina, vol. 15: De regno Christi libri duo, 1550, ed. Francois Wendel, Paris 1955. German translation: Vom Reich Christi [...], Strasbourg 1563 (VD16 B 8907; USTC 701665). Cf. MARTIN GRESCHAT, Martin Bucer. Ein Reformator und seine Zeit (1491–1551), Münster [2]2009, 270–276; BASIL HALL, Martin Bucer in England (in: Martin Bucer: Reforming church and community, ed. D. F. Wright, Cambridge 1994, 144–160, esp. 154–158).

[12] The Boke of common praier, and administration of the Sacramentes, and other rites and Ceremonies in the Churche of Englande, London: Richard Grafton, 1559 (ESTC S93763; USTC 518068). Reprint: The Book of Common Prayer commonly called The First Book of Queen Elizabeth. Printed by Grafton 1559, London 1844. Within the wedding liturgy we find here an exhortation to the couple based on the NT conduct rules (Haustafeln) which could be read by the priest instead of a wedding sermon (ibid., 99[r/v]).

[13] The Two Books of Homilies Appointed to be Read in Churches. Oxford 1859, here: 500–515 (*A Homily of the State of Matrimony*). – The two *Books of Homilies* composed by Thomas Cranmer in 1547 and John Jewel in 1571 were collections of Protestant model sermons: cf. ASHLEY NULL, Official Tudor Homilies (in: The Oxford Handbook of the Early Modern Sermon, eds. Hugh Adlington, Peter McCullough and Emma Rhatigan, Oxford 2011, 348–365). The first half of the wedding sermon in Book II is an almost unchanged English translation of a German sermon of Veit Dietrich, a Latin version of which had been printed by Nikolaus Selnecker (The Two Books of Homilies, 500, note 1).

[14] Thomas Becon, A new Catechisme sette forth Dyaloge wise in familiare talke betwene the father and the son, s.l., s. a. [1560]. Again in: The Catechism of Thomas Becon, with other pieces written by him in the reign of King Edward the Sixth, ed. John Ayre, Cambridge 1844, 1–410. Thomas Becon (Beccon, ca. 1511–1567) was a confidant of Cranmer and canon at Canterbury Cathedral; c. 1556–1559 he taught at the University of Marburg: ALEXANDER BALLOCH GROSART, Art. Becon, Thomas (in: DNB 4, 1885, 92–94); DERRICK SHERWIN BAILEY, Thomas Becon and the Reformation of the Church of England, Edinburgh u.a. 1952.

[15] HENRY SMITH, A preparatiue to mariage The summe whereof was spoken at a contract, and inlarged after. Whereunto is annexed a treatise of the Lords Supper, and another of vsurie, London 1591 (ESTC S104139). Used here: HENRY SMITH, A Preparative to Marriage, in: ID., The Sermons, gathered into one volume, London 1937, 9–47. – Henry Smith (ca. 1550/60–1591), also known as »silver-tonged Smith«, was a lecturer at St. Clement Danes in the City of Westminster und was considered the most popular Puritan Preacher of Elizabethan London: THOMPSON COOPER, Art. Smith, Henry (in: DNB 53, 1898, 48–49).

[16] WILLIAM PERKINS, Christian Oeconomie: or, A short survey of the right manner of erecting and ordering a familie according to the scriptures. First written in Latine by the author M. W. Perkins, and now set forth in the vulgar tongue [...] by Tho. Pickering

Whately (1617)[17] and William Gouge (1622)[18]. This might not be a coin-cidence, as Puritanism was especially interested in the religious sanctifi-cation of everyday life.[19]

The literary genres of the writings considered here from the Holy Ro-man Empire as well as from England are not always clear-cut but some-times tend to merge: from wedding sermons to theological and ethical tracts on the marital status and the duties of spouses up to genuine house-holder manuals (»Hausväterliteratur«) and advice literature[20] and Puritan conduct books[21]. In most cases the so-called »Haustafeln« (conduct rules) from Eph 5:21–6:9, Col 3:18–4:1 und 1 Pt 3:1–7 serve as biblical reference texts.

A preliminary remark on terminology is required. In the following paper, we will discuss the meaning of the family for the establishment of the Reformation. In fact, we find this term (»family«, »familia«, »Fami-lie«)[22] pre-eminently in English sources, whereas it is much less common in those from the German-speaking Reformation. William Perkins in his *Christian Oeconomie* from 1609 gives a formal definition:

»A Familie, is a naturall and simple Societie of certaine persons, hauing mutual relation one to another vnder the priuate government of one«.[23]

Bachelar of Diuinitie, London 1609 (ESTC S4819). The Latin original from 1590 has not been preserved. – William Perkins (1558–1602) was Fellow of Christ's College at Cam-bridge und preacher at Great St. Andrew's Church und one of the leading puritans of his generation. Cf. James Bass Mullinger, Art. Perkins, William (in: DNB 45, 1896, 6–9); Martin Sallmann, William Perkins. Puritaner zwischen Calvinismus und Pietismus (in: Theologen des 17. und 18. Jahrhunderts, eds. Peter Walter and Martin H. Jung, Darmstadt 2003, 88–105).

[17] William Whately, A bride-bush; or a wedding Sermon compendiously describ-ing the duties of married persons, London 1617 (ESTC S101310). Used here: William Whately, Directions for Married Persons, London [4]1790 (ESTC N964). – William Whately (1583–1639) was rector in Banbury near Oxford: Charlotte Fell Smith, Art. Whately, William (in: DNB 60, 1899, 430–1). Cf. Jacqueline Eales, Gender Con-struction in Early Modern England and the Conduct Books of William Whately, 1583–1639 (in: Gender and Christian Religion, ed. R. N. Swanson, Woodbridge 1998, 163–174).

[18] William Gouge, Of domesticall duties eight treatises [...], London 1622 (ESTC S103290). – William Gouge (1575–1653) was rector of St. Anne Blackfriars in London and member of the Westminster Assembly: Alexander Gordon, Art. Gouge, William (in: DNB 22, 1890, 271–273).

[19] On puritanism cf. Wolf-Friedrich Schäufele, art. Puritanismus (in: EdN 10, 2009, 560–566).

[20] Cf. Jürgen Donien, art. Hausväterliteratur (in: EdN 5, 2007, 254–256).

[21] Collinson, Birthpangs (see note 2), 68–74 and passim.

[22] Cf. Andreas Gestrich, Art. Familie 2. Begriffsgeschichte (in: EdN 3, 2006, 791–2).

[23] Perkins, Christian Oeconomie (see note 16), 1–2.

In the Continental sources, on the other hand, the term »Ehe« – along with »Ehestand« and »eheliches Leben« – is predominant (»marriage« or »matrimony«, in Latin »coniugium« or »matrimonium«). Of course, in this sense marriage almost always includes the children and their education and also the unmarried servants who lived in the house and like the children were under the joint supervision of the spouses. In this broader sense, the sources also speak of »house« or »household« (»Haus«, »Haushaltung«) or »economy« (»Ökonomie«, »oeconomia«).

1. Theological revaluation of the significance of marriage and family

In the reassessment of the significance of marriage and family, two fundamental tendencies of Reformation theology are combined: the levelling of the distinction between »sacred« and »secular« on the one hand, and, consequently, the religious revaluation of areas of life formerly rated as »secular« on the other. Actually, this meant that, in contrast to the late medieval scholastic teachings, the Reformers denied the sacramental character and thus a special sacramental sanctity of marriage that distinguished it from other ways of life or social practices. At the same time, they revalued the status of marriage and household, which in the Middle Ages was considered inferior to the so-called »spiritual status« of priests and religious, and acknowledged its special religious dignity as an order instituted by God, or even as a binding divine commandment.

In contesting the sacramental sanctity of marriage the Reformation counteracted the ongoing process of sacramentalization of marriage pushed along by the Roman Church since the High Middle Ages. Originally, only the voluntary agreement and mutual promise of bride and groom was considered as constituting marriage. After the first sexual intercourse it was regarded as indissoluble. But since the 12th century, the Church had endeavoured to bring marriage under its control, by recognizing it as a sacrament – a sacrament, of course, administered by the spouses themselves to one another but nevertheless demanding priestly consecration as a necessary ingredient.[24] This new conception had not yet been fully established when it was repealed by the Reformers. In his tract *Von Ehesachen* (1530) Luther brought the new Reformation conviction to the classic phrase of marriage as a secular matter (»ein weltlich ding«) like clothes

---

[24] URS BAUMANN, art. Ehe VI. Historisch-theologisch (in: LThK³ 3, 1993, 471–474, here: 472–3); OZMENT, When Fathers Ruled (see note 2), 26–28.

and food, house and yard, subject to secular authorities.[25] Thus wedlock was clearly qualified as a secular legal transaction, as a matter of contract of the spouses and their families. Marital jurisdiction lay with the secular legislator. Secular, not canon law had to be applied and gradually the episcopal marital courts were replaced by novel bodies composed of secular judges in which theologians had only advisory votes.[26] Marriage and family were no longer a special domain subject to religious and ecclesiastical norms and jurisdiction, but were levelled into the whole of social life. Like Luther, Heinrich Bullinger, too, declared marriage to be one of those »outward things« which are subject to secular authority.[27]

Interestingly enough, in England there was no such replacement of ecclesiastical by secular marital courts. Indeed Martin Bucer in the second volume of his late work *De Regno Christi* had made detailed proposals to King Edward VI (r. 1547–1553) for 14 laws towards a »plena religionis restitutio« among which the law on marriage and divorce was by far the most extensive, with 33 out of a total of 52 chapters.[28] In a similar way to Luther, Bucer qualified marriage as a »res politica«, for which state laws and secular courts were required. The secular rulers should recapture the marital jurisdiction wrongly usurped by the Antichristian Roman papacy.[29] However, under the rule of Edward, no such legislation was implemented, and the Elizabethan Settlement again set aside the issue of a new law on marriage. Thus in England canon law on marriage remained valid and the episcopal courts continued to exist.[30]

Luther's characterization of marriage as a secular matter was meant to dispute the notion of marriage and family as a special religious and legal sphere apart from other issues of social life. It was not, however, intended to deny marriage any religious significance. On the contrary, for Luther marriage was a special work of God and under his special supervision.[31] God had intentionally created man as male and female, and determined

---

[25] »das die ehe ein eusserlich weltlich ding ist wie kleider und speise, haus und hoff, weltlicher oberkeit unterworffen« (WA 30/3,205,12–3).

[26] Regarding the Saxon territories cf. RALF FRASSEK, Eherecht und Ehegerichtsbarkeit in der Reformationszeit. Der Aufbau neuer Rechtsstrukturen im sächsischen Raum unter besonderer Berücksichtigung der Wirkungsgeschichte des Wittenberger Konsistoriums, Tübingen 2005.

[27] »ob glych wol die Ee ouch die Seel vnd inneren menschen angadt / hört sy doch ouch vnder die eusserliche ding /die der oberkeit underworffen sind« (BULLINGER, Der Christlich Eestand [see note 9], ch. 4, not paginated; Schriften [see note 9], 436).

[28] BUCER, De regno Christi (see note 11), 152–234 (ch. 15–47).

[29] Ibid., 126.

[30] MARTIN INGRAM, Church Courts, Sex and Marriage in England, 1570–1640, Cambridge 1987.

[31] WITT, Luthers Reformation der Ehe (see note 7), 250–258.

both to complement each other. Therefore, marriage was considered a godly order by Luther and the later Lutherans. For Justus Menius, it was the greatest and most worthwhile among all estates of human life.[32] Moreover, entering the marital status was not only the normal case based on creation, but a commandment of divine law directly binding for all human beings, of which only a few categories of people expressly defined in the New Testament (Mt 19:12) were exempted.[33] Luther stressed, against his opponents, that getting married was not at will. They should be aware that it was a divine commandment just as strict as or even stricter than the prohibition of murder and adultery.[34]

Bullinger derived the paramount religious rank of marriage from the circumstances of its establishment. Marriage was the only order still established in Paradise, that is, before the Fall, and its founder was God himself.[35] In close dependence on Bullinger's remarks, but in his biblical references and arguments going even beyond into the New Testament, Henry Smith dealt with »The excellency of marriage«.[36] On the background of such convictions about the religious dignity of marriage, Bullinger could speak without hesitation of »holy marriage«, and Bucer could call the »sacrum coniugium«[37] a »sanctissima societas«.[38]

Thus marriage and family did not only participate in the general appreciation of the everyday actions of believers as godly good works – in this sense Luther in his *Sermon von den guten Werken* (1520) had acknowledged even the lifting of a straw as a godly work when done in faith,[39] and in the same way we must understand his famous remark from *Vom Eelichen Leben* about God and all his angels complacently laughing about a father washing the diapers of his infant child.[40] Much more, as the most commendable order on earth, the »holy order of marriage« had its own religious dignity.

---

[32] MENIUS, Oeconomia Christiana (ed. Gause / Scholz [see note 8], 44).

[33] LUTHER, Vom Eelichen Leben (see note 7), 277,1–280,6.

[34] »gleich wie hohe not vnd hart gebot ist / da Gott spricht / Du solt nicht tödten / Du solt nicht ehebrechen / eben so hoch not vnd hart gepot / ia vil hoher not vnd herter gepot ists / Du solt ehelich sein / du solt ein weib haben / du solt einen man haben« (Luther's foreword to MENIUS, Oeconomia Christiana, ed. Gause / Scholz [see note 8], 38).

[35] BULLINGER, Der Christlich Eestand (see note 9), ch. 1 (not paginated; Schriften [see note 9], 429–30).

[36] SMITH, A Preparative to Marriage (see note 15), 9–11.

[37] BUCER, De regno Christi (see note 11), 153, 164 and passim.

[38] Ibid., 152.

[39] WA 6,206,9–11.

[40] WA 10/2,296,27–297,4.

The revaluation of marriage and family implied on the other side a devaluation and delegitimization of other modes of life. First and foremost, of course, this applied to male and female monasticism and the celibate life of priests. The medieval church had placed these forms of sexually abstinent life as religiously superior and meritorious over the secular life of the married. The reformers reversed this order. As the celibate and monastic form of life had no basis in Scripture, and as they moreover violated the commandment of marriage, they must by no means be made compulsory. The basic possibility of an unmarried life due to a special God-given charisma, which was initially still affirmed,[41] soon lost importance; monasticism and celibacy disappeared from the Protestant communities[42]. The most significant consequence of this was that now the pastor became a husband.[43] Indeed, with the pastor and his wife, there stood an exemplary married couple at the top of the parish community.[44] Thus the levelling of the distinction between the clergy and the so-called laity, theologically based on the principle of the general priesthood of the baptized, became socially manifest. The result was (at least to some extent) a social homogenization of the congregation.

The pressure now grew on all unmarried »lay people« to enter wedlock. In the Middle Ages, many people remained single, mainly for economic reasons, and even in the 16th century, the percentage of unmarried people in the rural population is estimated at one third, in the cities at one third to one half.[45] But the Reformation preachers urged marriage as the binding social model for all, not least in order to assign sexuality to a socially legitimate and controlled place. In this they frequently tended to take the economic issues too lightly. For Luther, marriage in spite of low financial resources simply was a question of trust in God.[46] Accordingly,

---

[41] LUTHER, Vom Eelichen Leben (see note 7), 279,15–23.

[42] On Luther's experiment of an »evangelical monasticism« in the years 1522–1524 cf. WOLF-FRIEDRICH SCHÄUFELE, »[...] iam sum monachus et non monachus«. Martin Luthers doppelter Abschied vom Mönchtum (in: Martin Luther – Biographie und Theologie, eds. Dietrich Korsch and Volker Leppin, Tübingen ²2017, 119–140).

[43] LUISE SCHORN-SCHÜTTE, Die Drei-Stände-Lehre im reformatorischen Umbruch (in: Die frühe Reformation in Deutschland als Umbruch, ed. Bernd Moeller, Gütersloh 1998, 435–461, esp. 446–450).

[44] LUISE SCHORN-SCHÜTTE, »Gefährtin« und »Mitregentin«. Zur Sozialgeschichte der evangelischen Pfarrfrau in der Frühen Neuzeit (in: Wandel der Geschlechterbeziehungen zu Beginn der Neuzeit, eds. Heide Wunder and Christina Vanja, Frankfurt/Main 1991, 109–153); SUSAN C. KARANT-NUNN, Reformation und Askese: Das Pfarrhaus als evangelisches Kloster (in: Kommunikation und Transfer im Christentum der Frühen Neuzeit, eds. Irene Dingel and Wolf-Friedrich Schäufele, Mainz 2008, 211–228).

[45] OZMENT, When Fathers Ruled (see note 2), 41–42.

[46] LUTHER, Vom Eelichen Leben (see note 7), 302,16–303,28.

he pleaded for an early marriage: men should get married at the age of 20 years, women at the age of 15–18 years.[47] And even though William Gouge strongly recommended that men and women should marry only several years after reaching the minimum legal age of 14 or 12 years, respectively,[48] the result will have been virtually the same. Another consequence of the theological and social revaluation of marriage and the social control of sexuality was the closure of the brothels in the Protestant territories. The result was a congregation that was much more homogenized compared to the Middle Ages. The Protestant congregation was a community of spouses and families.[49]

2. Normative Centring

At first glance, it seems surprising how far the new theological and legal ideas of the German and English reformers on marriage and family were in agreement, at least in their outlines. Apparently, in a short time they had succeeded to replace the medieval scholastic teachings on marriage with a relatively coherent set of their own views. This can be understood as the result of a biblically oriented normative centring.[50] The same biblical references and rules were used throughout, albeit with not unimportant differences in accent and detail.

Usually, the Reformers defined a triple theological purpose of marriage. With the Creation narrative of Gen 1 and the divine call, »Be fruitful and multiply« (Gen 1:28), marriage was assigned the task of procreation and parenting. From the second Creation narrative in Gen 2, it was derived that the spouses should befriend and comfort one another, support one another and provide assistance in everyday life and work (Gen 2:18). And with Paul in 1 Cor 7:2, marriage was considered the most important means of preventing fornication.[51] The model wedding sermon of the *Second*

---

[47] Ibid., 303,31–2. Cf. MENIUS, Oeconomia Christiana (ed. Gause / Scholz [see note 8], 102); OZMENT, When Fathers Ruled (see note 2), 38.

[48] »[I]f they forbeare some yeares longer, it will be much better for the parties themselues that marie, for the children which they bring forth, for the family whereof they are the head, and for the common wealth whereof they are members« (GOUGE, Of domesticall duties [see note 18], 180).

[49] OZMENT, When Fathers Ruled (see note 2), 55–56.

[50] The concept of »normative centering« (»normative Zentrierung«) has been introduced to Reformation research by Berndt Hamm: cf. BERNDT HAMM, Reformation als normative Zentrierung von Religion und Gesellschaft (in: Jahrbuch für Biblische Theologie 7, 1992, 241–279).

[51] All three aspects clearly in BULLINGER, Der Christlich Eestand (see note 9, ch. 10, not paginated; Schriften [see note 9], 467–472), in the wedding liturgy of the Elizabethan

Book of Homilies and William Perkins eventually added a fourth purpose: the multiplication and propagation of the church.[52]

For Luther and Menius, among the three classical purposes of marriage procreation and parenting were most essential,[53] even though both of them acknowledged the prevention of fornication as another important goal. For William Whately, on the other hand, the latter was the foremost and main purpose.[54] A special feature of Martin Bucer was his strong emphasis on the partnership of husband and wife, their harmonious coexistence and their mutual support.[55] According to him the final purpose of marriage was the »rerum omnium divinarum & humanarum summa cum benevolentia communicatio«.[56] Henry Smith, too, put this aspect in the first place. In his eyes marriage was first of all meant to evade »the inconvenience of solitarinesse«:

> »This life would be miserable and irksome and unpleasant to man, if the Lord had not given him a wife to company his troubles.« »Beasts are ordained for food, and clothes for warmth, and flowers for pleasure; but the wife is ordained for man, [...] a Citie of refuge to flie to in all troubles, and there is no peace comparable unto her, but the peace of conscience«. »[L]ike a Turtle, which hath lost his Mate, like one legge, when the other is cut off, like one wing, when the other is clipt, so had the man been, if the woman had not been joyned to him«.[57]

In the course of the Biblically oriented normative centring of marriage, three central positions of the canon law on marriage were rejected: the recognition of secret marriages, the scholastic casuistry of obstacles to marriage and the prohibition of divorce. This applies equally to the Reformers in the Holy Roman Empire and to the English Puritans. Notwithstanding, certain norms of canon law continued to be applied in the episcopal courts of England, and even secular courts on the continent partly continued to rely on canon law provisions.[58]

As far as secret marriages are concerned – unions based solely on the spouses' mutual marriage vows, without witnesses, parents' consent, or church ceremonies – these were valid under canon law, even though ca-

---

Book of Common Prayer (see note 12, 96ʳ) and in Smith, A Preparative to Marriage (see note 15, 13–17).

[52] The Two Books of Homilies (see note 13), 500; Perkins, Christian Oeconomie (see note 16), 13–14.

[53] Luther, Vom Eelichen Leben (see note 7), 301,16–30; Menius, Oeconomia Christiana (ed. Gause / Scholz [see note 8], 28–30, 64). Cf. Witt, Luthers Reformation der Ehe (see note 7), 258–264.

[54] Whately, Directions for Married Persons (see note 17), 20.

[55] Bucer, De regno Christi (see note 11), 205–208.

[56] Ibid., 189.

[57] Quotes: Smith, A Preparative to Marriage (see note 15), 16, 13, 17.

[58] Cf. Ozment, When Fathers Ruled (see note 2), 29–32.

nonists gradually tried to displace them by enforcing formal requirements such as obligatory witnesses and the church wedding ceremony – a process that only came to a close with the Council of Trent.[59] In contrast, the attitude of the reformers was clear from the beginning. Although the consensus of the couple was the most important and constitutive element of marriage, secret marriages were generally disapproved of. Especially betrothals without parental consent were rejected by almost all authors as invalid.[60] Increasingly, also the religious consecration of marriage in the church was considered a necessary part of the wedding.[61]

The sophisticated casuistry of possible obstacles to marriage, which included not only consanguinity up to the fourth degree, but also relationship by marriage and godparenthood up to comparable degrees as well as other special cases, was rejected by the Reformers in the Holy Roman Empire as unbiblical and illogical.[62] As early as 1522, Luther countered the relevant provisions of canon law with the enumeration of forbidden degrees of relationship according to Lev 18:6–18 as the only binding norm. This resulted in a notable reduction of restrictions; in particular, marriages between sibling children (first cousins) were now allowed.[63] Bullinger's detailed treatment of the obstacles to marriage was also based on Lev 18 and analogies drawn from there.[64] Bucer recommended that a future English marriage law should follow the laws of God and the example of the Old Testament Fathers.[65] On the other hand, surprisingly, this question played practically no role in the English Puritans considered here. The marriage with non-Christians prohibited by canon law was also rejected almost universally by the Protestant authors in the Empire as well as in England.[66] A temporary exception was the young Luther, for whom the worldliness of marriage also permitted weddings with Jews or Muslims.[67] Perkins at least held that if one of the partners had fallen away from

---

[59] Ibid., 26–28.

[60] BULLINGER, Der Christlich Eestand (see note 9), ch. 5 (not paginated; Schriften [see note 9], 440–445); BUCER, De regno Christi (see note 11), 157–161; The Catechism of Thomas Becon (see note 14), 355–56; SMITH, A Preparative to Marriage (see note 15), 24; PERKINS, Christian Oeconomie (see note 16), 76; GOUGE, Of domesticall duties (see note 18), 446–453.

[61] BUCER, De regno Christi (see note 11), 163–64; PERKINS, Christian Oeconomie (see note 16), 94; GOUGE, Of domesticall duties (see note 18), 203–205.

[62] OZMENT, When Fathers Ruled (see note 2), 44–48.

[63] LUTHER, Vom Eelichen Leben (see note 7), 280,7–287,11.

[64] BULLINGER, Der Christlich Eestand (see note 9), ch. 7 (not paginated; Schriften [see note 9], 447–458).

[65] BUCER, De regno Christi (see note 11), 154–156.

[66] E.g. SMITH, A Preparative to Marriage (see note 15), 25–26.

[67] LUTHER, Vom Eelichen Leben (see note 7), 283,1–16.

Christianity only after wedding, the marriage stayed valid according to the precept of Paul (1 Cor 7:12–14).[68]

The third major questioning of the canon law of marriage in the course of the Reformation normative centring concerned the possibility of divorce, which was denied by medieval church law, but generally admitted by the reformers.[69] Crucial for that position was the conviction of the outward, secular character of the contract of marriage as well as Jesus' saying in Matthew 19:9 repeatedly cited in this context, which permitted a divorce in case of adultery. As a matter of fact, adultery, according to Reformation principles, dissolved as such the bond of marital union so that divorce – and the possibility of remarriage! – was the inevitable consequence. However, there was resistance to this view also in the Reformation churches. In England, it was the Puritans who voted with biblical arguments for the possibility of divorce, while conservative Anglicans remained sceptical. As late as 1619, William Whately caused an uproar when he declared divorce permissible in his *Bride-Bush*.[70] In fact, England was the only Protestant country in Europe that did not acknowledge the possibility of lawful divorce, although in the end it was rather political coincidences than religious teachings that were decisive.[71] Regardless, divorce in all Protestant territories remained a rare exception in practical life.

There were differing opinions as to whether the betrayed partner of a penitent adulterer could[72] or even should[73] cling to his or her marriage. In any case, the innocently divorced partner was free to remarry, the basic function of marriage as a means of preventing fornication requiring it.[74] Remarriage of the adulterous partner, on the other hand, was usually not an issue; in biblical times he would have been punishable by death anyway – a sanction that some Protestant authors could also imagine for their own time.[75]

---

[68] PERKINS, Christian Oeconomie (see note 16), 59–62.

[69] CORDULA SCHOLZ-LÖHNIG, art. Eheauflösung (in: EdN 3, 2006, 52–57); OZMENT, When Fathers Ruled (see note 2), 80–99. On Luther: ERNST KINDER, Luthers Stellung zur Ehescheidung (in: Luther 24, 1953, 75–86); WITT, Luthers Reformation der Ehe (see note 7), 205–214.

[70] WHATELY, Directions for Married People (see note 17), 6. Cf. Smith, Art. Whately (see note 17), 431; PETERS, Patterns of Piety (see note 2), 330.

[71] MACCULLOCH, Die Reformation (see note 2), 848.

[72] Thus e.g. LUTHER, Vom Eelichen Leben (see note 7), 288,29–31; 289,29–290,1.

[73] WHATELY, Directions for Married People (see note 17), 6–7; GOUGE, Of domesticall duties (see note 18), 218–19.

[74] BULLINGER, Der Christlich Eestand (see note 9), ch. 25 (not paginated; Schriften [see note 9], 574–5).

[75] Ibid.; LUTHER, Vom Eelichen Leben (see note 7), 289,8–17; BUCER, De regno Christi (see note 11), 189–194.

While for some Protestant writers, including the Puritans Smith, Whately, and Gouge, adultery was the only legitimate reason for divorce, others acknowledged more and different reasons[76] So Bullinger subsumed the unbelief of the partner under the facts of adultery.[77] For Luther, who initially thought differently about disbelief, as mentioned above, a physical incapacity to consummate marriage discovered only after the wedding or the permanent denial of sexual intercourse were other valid reasons for divorce. Even an extreme case of irreconcilable mutual incompatibility of the spouses could in his eyes justify a divorce after which, however, no remarriage was allowed.[78]

The most elaborate and liberal treatment of divorce, its preconditions, its practice and its consequences can be found in Bucer's proposal for a Reformation legislation to King Edward VI; it constitutes the bulk of the large marriage section.[79] Excerpts from it were printed by John Milton in 1644 in English translation and submitted to Parliament.[80] Besides adultery, the permanent denial of conjugal love and marital intercourse, as well as the oppression and mistreatment of the partner, he was ready to accept the divorce grounds provided in ancient Roman law – certain serious crimes against third parties, overnight stays abroad, the visit of plays without the consent of the partner and the like.[81]

3. Oeconomia *and* Politia: *Marriage, Family, and Household as the Nucleus of Society*

The theological revaluation of marriage, family and household contributed to the levelling of the social differences between church members and tended to make Protestant congregations homogeneous communities of married people. But even in their overall vision of social life the Reformers upgraded family and household to the dominant model and nucleus of society.[82] The ancient model of the tripartite social order constituted by

---

[76] SMITH, A Preparative to Marriage (see note 15), 45; WHATELY, Directions for Married Persons (see note 17), 6; GOUGE, Of domesticall duties (see note 18), 217–18.

[77] BULLINGER, Der Christlich Eestand (see note 9), ch. 25 (not paginated; Schriften [see note 9], 573).

[78] LUTHER, Vom Eelichen Leben (see note 7), 287,15–17; 290,5–291,14.

[79] BUCER, De regno Christi (see note 11), 165–226 (ch. 22–44).

[80] The Ivdgement of Martin Bucer concerning divorce written to Edward the sixt, in his second book of the Kingdom of Christ, and now English, London 1644. Cf. DAVID MASSON, The Life of John Milton, vol. 3: 1643–1649, Cambridge 1873, 255–261.

[81] BUCER, De regno Christi (see note 11), 203–04.

[82] Compare COLLINSON, Birthpangs (see note 2), 60–61; ANDREAS GESTRICH, art.

clergy, nobles, and peasants and labourers – in medieval terminology: *oratores*, *bellatores* and *laboratores* – presupposed a more or less static hierarchy of the three estates, while, of course, due to celibacy the clergy had continually to be supplemented from the other two orders. Luther's doctrine of the Three Orders,[83] which he certainly never expounded coherently, is based on the old triple model. But here the three »principal estates« of *oeconomia* (household), *politia* (government) and *ecclesia* (church) are not only of the same rank and equal dignity. They also appear much less sharply demarcated, and show different transitions and functional overlaps. A prince or lord can be at the same time husband and father, as well as the administrator of a church office.[84] In the end, marriage and household, or, as Luther puts it, *oeconomia* prove to be the middle and the starting point of the entire social order.

»For it is the oldest estate of all in the world, and all others stem from it, into which Adam and Eve, our ancestors, were created by God, and in which they and their godly children and descendants used to live«.[85]

This is by no means just an historical account. In fact, *oeconomia* is still the actual nucleus of society, from which the members of the other two estates must be recruited. In his foreword to Menius' *Oeconomia Christiana* Luther emphasized the resulting responsibility of parents.[86] If they do not educate their children properly to godly and capable personalities, the spiritual and worldly realm both must perish. For where else should one take pastors and other church officials, councillors and civil servants? Thus, both governments ordained by God in this world, the spiritual and the secular, are ultimately based on marriage and household as their core and nucleus.

Familie 5. Familie und öffentliche Ordnung (in: EdN 3, 2006, 799–801); ANTJE ROGGEN-KAMP, art. Erziehung 4. Evangelische Erziehung (in: EdN 3, 2006, 524–528).

[83] Cf. PAUL ALTHAUS, Die Ethik Martin Luthers, Gütersloh 1965, 43–48; Bernhard Lohse, Luthers Theologie in ihrer historischen Entwicklung und in ihrem systematischen Zusammenhang, Göttingen 1995, 342–344; OSWALD BAYER, Nature and Institution. Luther's Doctrine of the Three Orders (in: Lutheran Quarterly 12, 1998, 125–159); REINHARD SCHWARZ, Martin Luther – Lehrer der christlichen Religion, Tübingen ²2016, 153–162; SCHORN-SCHÜTTE, Drei-Stände-Lehre (see note 43); LUISE SCHORN-SCHÜTTE, art. Drei-Stände-Lehre (in: Das Luther-Lexikon, eds. Volker Leppin and Gury Schneider-Ludorff, Regensburg 2014, 174–176).

[84] ALTHAUS, Ethik Luthers (see note 83), 45.

[85] »Denn es ist der eltist stand unter allen der gantzen welt, ja, alle andere komen aus dem her, darein Adam und Eva, unser erste eltern, von Gott geschaffen und verordnet sein, darinn sie und alle jhre Gottfürchtige kinder und nachkomen gelebt haben«: Luther, Sermon on Hebr 13:4, August 4ᵗʰ, 1545 (WA 49,797,33–798,3).

[86] Luther's foreword to MENIUS, Oeconomia Christiana (ed. Gause / Scholz [see note 8], 39–42).

This essential connection between *oeconomia* and *politia*, but also *ecclesia* results especially from the connection between authority and obedience, which in Luther's eyes is constitutive of all orders of human coexistence and is preformed, pre-trained, practically learned and practiced in the *oeconomia* in the cohabitation of husband and wife, parents and children, heads of the household and servants. In the *oeconomia* all forms of social relationships come together: the community of husband and wife as equal rulers, the equal dominion of parents over their children and the hierarchical dominion of the householders over their servants.[87] For a theological justification, Luther and other reformers used to refer to the Decalogue's commandment to honour one's parents, which they not only applied to the family, but also to the relationship to authorities in general. In this sense, Luther, following medieval interpretations like that of Thomas Aquinas,[88] gave in his *Greater Catechism* an explanation of the Fourth (otherwise Fifth) Commandment, that aimed at extending the obligation to obedience from the biological parents to the fathers of the land – the secular authorities – and the spiritual fathers in the church.[89] In the same sense, the parents'commandment was elaborated in detail in the *Unterricht der Visitatoren* printed for the first time in 1528.[90] In 1529, Justus Menius clearly pointed out the connection between *oeconomia* and *politia*, household and state government, as the two forms of God's earthly regiment and emphasized the paramount importance of family parenting for the common good:

»Therefore, if you want to advise country and people well and want to contribute to a good condition of the *politia*, then you really have to start in the *oeconomia* with the youth«.[91]

The English Puritans also emphasized the fundamental importance of the family as a model and educational institution for the secular, political order as well as for the church. Here, too, the basis for this conviction was the parents' commandment of the Decalogue, which, according to Thomas Becon, applied not only to the biological parents, but also

---

[87] SCHORN-SCHÜTTE, art. Drei-Stände-Lehre (see note 83), 175.

[88] VOLKER LEPPIN, Die Normierung der Frömmigkeit im »Unterricht der Visitatoren« (in: Der »Unterricht der Visitatoren« und die Durchsetzung der Reformation in Kursachsen, eds. Joachim Bauer and Stefan Michel, Leipzig 2017, 167–194, here: 177–78, note 54).

[89] WA 30/1,152,19–35; 153,29–155,21.

[90] WA 26,206,10–211,26. Cf. LEPPIN, Normierung der Frömmigkeit (see note 88), 177–181.

[91] »Darumb / wil man landen vnd leuten wol raten vnd helffen / das es vmb die Politia wohl stehe / so mus mans warlich am ersten ynn der Oeconomia mit der iugent anfahen« (MENIUS, Oeconomia Christiana, ed. Gause / Scholz [see note 8], 64).

»toward the temporal magistrates, and the ministers of God's word, and toward our elders and all such as be our superiors and governors«.[92]

In addition, there were reasons from salvation history: Thus, according to William Perkins, the family was the first and oldest of all communities (»Societies & States«) that make up mankind. Until the Flood, there was no secular government or church, and the whole civil and ecclesiastical order was confined to the families. It was only after the Flood that Noah's family became the common mother from which the other two estates emerged. The holy and righteous leadership of the family was therefore a direct means of a good ordering of church and community.[93] Similarly, William Gouge claimed the families as »excellent seminaries [...] to Church and Commonwealth«:

»Necessary it is that good order be first set in families: for as they were before other polities, so they are somewhat the more necessary: and good members of a family are like to make good members of Church and common-wealth.«[94]

As far as the Reformation is concerned, household and family were not a private preserve apart from social life, but had an important political function.[95]

4. Oeconomia *and* Ecclesia:
Marriage, Family and Household as a »Small Church«

The connection between *oeconomia* and *ecclesia* is not only, however, to be understood as meaning that in the family the necessary obedience to authority should be practiced and the future ecclesiastical staff be raised. Rather, the Reformers almost always claimed the family as a place of religious education and practice in faith and piety. As such, the family and the Christian household could be qualified as a church[96] or temple[97] on a small scale.[98]

---

[92] The Catechism of Thomas Becon (see note 14), 88.

[93] PERKINS, Christian Oeconomie (see note 16), Dedication (not paginated).

[94] GOUGE, Of domesticall duties (see note 18), Dedication (not paginated).

[95] »The home, then, was no introspective, private sphere, unmindful of society, but the cradle of citizenship, extending its values and example into the world around it. The habits and character developed within families became the virtues that shaped entire lands« (Ozment, When Fathers Ruled [see note 2], 10). Cf. COLLINSON, Birthpangs (see note 2), 60–61.

[96] E.g. PERKINS, Christian Oeconomie (see note 16), 8.

[97] E.g. JOHANNES MATHESIUS, Oeconomia oder Bericht, wie sich ein Hausvater halten soll, Nürnberg 1561 (VD16 M 1419), (not paginated).

[98] MACCULLOCH, Die Reformation (see note 2), 848.

Already in his tract *Vom Eelichen Leben* (1522) Luther had praised the religious education of children as the best part of marriage. As parents introduce their children to the gospel, they are their apostles, bishops, and pastors.[99] Accordingly, in 1529, Luther conceived his *Small Catechism* for the domestic instruction of the whole family, including the servants, by the pious house-father: The headline of each section stated that a house-holder should present it plainly to his servants.[100] In fact, Luther later even acknowledged the apocalyptic possibility that the preaching ministry might come to a standstill and henceforth the gospel only could be kept in the homes by the householders.[101]

How the propagation of the gospel and religious instruction by the fathers at home could be practiced apart from the instructions in Luther's catechism, was explained in detail by different authors. Justus Menius urged parents to teach their children first of all the commandments of God, to live according to God's will and to fear God's wrath and judgment, and on the other hand to teach them to trust God, to pray for everything to him and to thank him for his benefits.[102] Furthermore, there were extensive collections of material for the catechesis of children and servants like for example the voluminous manual edited by the Eisleben pastor Andreas Fabricius in 1569 under the programmatic title *Die Hauskirche (The Domestic Church)* and dedicated to his own children.[103] The subtitle is meaningful:

»How besides the public ministry of preaching a house-father shall incite his flock at home towards the word of God and the Catechism«.

In 1553 Erasmus Sarcerius with his *Hausbuch fur die Einfeltigen Haus veter von den vornemesten Artickeln der christlichen Religion* even tried to take advantage of the »simple house-fathers« as theological lay controversialists.[104] A summary instruction on domestic elementary catechesis from the perspective of the Swiss Reformation was given by Heinrich Bullinger in 1540 in the 21st chapter of his book *Der christlich Eestand*. The parents should utilize the printed catechisms in German, but also use proverbs for moral education. Morning and evening prayer, home and school lessons,

---

[99] LUTHER, Vom Eelichen Leben (see note 7), 301,23–25. Thomas Becon, too, calls every husband »a bishop in his own house« (The Catechism of Thomas Becon [see note 14], 337).

[100] WA 30/1,282a,17–8 (note); 292a,1–3; 298a,11–13; 308a,14–16; 314a,12–14; 318a,17–19; 322a,23–25. – On the term »Hausvater« (husband, householder) cf. URSULA FUHRICH-GRUBERT, CLAUDIA ULRICH, Art. Hausvater (in: EdN 5, 2007, 252–254).

[101] LUTHER, Preface to the Book of Daniel (WA.Br 11,122,1–5).

[102] MENIUS, Oeconomia Christiana (ed. Gause / Scholz [see note 8], 95).

[103] VD16 ZV 5704.

[104] VD16 S 1708.

church attendance followed by domestic examination about the contents of the sermon and the living role model of the parents should mesh.

In the writings of the English Puritans, the idea of religious education of children and of religious life in the »house« occupies even more space than in the writings of the reformers from the Empire. In addition to catechesis in the narrower sense, the effort to awaken, promote and nurture piety in a comprehensive way is much more evident here, and not only in regard to the children and the service staff, but also in regard to the spouses themselves. According to Henry Smith, the householder, like the Seraph who ignited the zeal of the prophet Isaiah, should kindle zeal for God in his wife, servants, and children, and like a nurse give the milk of his knowledge to each one of them.[105] In his family, the house-father stands in the place of Christ and has to exercise his threefold office: to rule like a king, to teach like a prophet, and to convert like a priest.[106]

In his *Christian Oeconomie*, William Perkins treated what he called »the household seruice of God« at a prominent place in the second chapter.[107] This kind of divine service should comprise »a conference vpon the word of God, for the edification of all the members thereof, to eternall life«[108], prayer meetings in the morning and in the evening, and prayer before and after meals. Families in which this kind of worship was held were small churches, yes, a kind of paradise on earth.[109]

William Gouge counted mutual intercession, the call to conversion, spiritual edification, the prevention of sin, and encouragement for growth in grace among the reciprocal duties that the spouses owe each other.[110] The parents should educate their children with Bible reading and daily catechesis to true piety,[111] but also incite their servants daily to grow in faith and to gain eternal bliss.[112] Similarly, William Whately required the spouses to encourage one another in faith and piety by praying and singing together, and conversing about their home in heaven.[113] Their main concern must be that in their house God should be properly worshipped,

---

[105] »One compareth the master of the house to the Seraphin, which came and kindled the Prohets zeale; so he should go from wife to servants, and from servants to children, and kindle in them the zeale of God, longing to teach his knowledge, as a nurse to empty her brests« (SMITH, A Preparative to Marriage [see note 15], 38).

[106] SMITH, A Preparative to Marriage (see note 15), 38.

[107] PERKINS, Christian Oeconomie (see note 16), 2–9.

[108] Ibid., 5.

[109] »little Churches, yea even a kind of paradise vpon earth« (ibid., 8).

[110] GOUGE, Of domesticall duties (see note 18), 235–242.

[111] Ibid., 536–543.

[112] Ibid., 666f.

[113] WHATELY, Directions for Married Persons (see note 17), 24–25, 32.

and that his knowledge and fear should be planted in the hearts of their children and servants, which would require joint reading of the Bible and prayer, domestic catechesis, regular church attendance followed by a domestic examination and careful observance of the Sabbath. In this way, a Christian family becomes a veritable »church«, a house of God in which he dwells.[114]

The most detailed instructions for religious parenting and the religious life of the »domestic church« can be found in Thomas Becon. According to him, »every man is a bishop in his own house«, and as such he is responsible to lead his wife, his children and his servants the way to bliss.[115] His whole house should become a school of piety.[116] Not only does the householder have to lead by his personal example. He also must ensure that all members of his household daily come together for prayer, for the recitation of the Creed and Decalogue and, if possible, for reading the Bible, and that thanksgiving be held before and after each meal. On Sundays and public holidays, he and his entire family and servants should visit the services and afterwards examine children and servants about the sermon which they had heard.[117] Like the servants, the parents should also teach their children in the Christian faith and guide them to practiced piety:

»In these and such like godly exercises the parents must daily and diligently train up their youth, that they, being thus acquainted with virtue from the beginning, may the more easily for ever after abstain from all sin and vice«.[118]

This includes not only the domestic instruction in the catechism and the orientation of the entire education in family and school towards piety – even the childrens' learning to speak is understood here as a challenge for religious education. Already the very first words they speak should preferably be serious, sober and pious like e.g. »God, Jesus Christ, faith, love, hope, patience, goodness, peace &c.« As soon as they speak complete sentences, they should be taught short phrases apt to encourage them to live in virtue and hatred against vice and sin, e.g.

»God alone saveth me. Christ by his death hath redeemed me. The Holy Ghost sanctifieth me. There is one God. Christ alone is our Mediator and Advocate«.[119]

---

[114] Ibid., 44.

[115] The Catechism of Thomas Becon (see note 14), 337.

[116] »For every householder's house ought to be a school of godliness; forasmuch as every householder ought to be a bishop in his own house, and so to oversee his family, that nothing reign in it but virtue, godliness, and honesty« (ibid., 360).

[117] Ibid., 359–60.

[118] Ibid., 349.

[119] Ibid., 348.

In such statements the religious education of children is usually placed in the responsibility of both parents, sometimes even in the special responsibility of the mother. Otherwise, however, in the normative texts considered here, it is always the husband and householder who, apart from exceptional circumstances, is called to direct the religious life in his house.[120] Reality might have looked differently. From the England of the 16th and 17th centuries we know that domestic piety was generally regarded as the domain of women, especially in families of the aristocracy and the middle classes.[121] In general, one must expect that especially in the area of marriage, family and household normative texts often do not correspond completely to social practice.

5. Conclusion: Seven Theses

1. Marriage, family and household underwent a comprehensive theological reassessment and revaluation in the Reformation.
2. From the 1520s, marriage and family received extensive discussion in writing from Luther and in Lutheranism; also, the Upper German and Swiss reformers devoted themselves extensively to this topic. In England it was mainly Puritan authors from the end of the 16th century onwards who paid special attention to matters of marriage and family.
3. The reformers declared marriage a »secular matter«, i.e. an outward, civil issue. This levelled the special religious status of the sacramentally conceived marriage in relation to other areas of life. Canon marriage law and ecclesiastical marital jurisdiction were largely abandoned on the continent, but both remained in England.
4. On the other hand, the Protestant theologians greatly valued the marital status: as God's foundation and commandment, as the order of creation, as the first and oldest of all social formations.
5. As part of a Bible-based normative centring secret marriages were rejected, the list of obstacles to marriage was revised and the possibility

---

[120] »Nun brachte nicht mehr die Mutter ihrem Kind das Ave-Maria und das Vaterunser bei, sondern der ideale protestantische Hausvater, von dem erwartet wurde, dass er seine Familie beim Gebet leite und dabei auch Spontanität und Sinn für die Besonderheit einer Situation zeige wie der Pastor bei seiner Predigt auf der Kanzel. Gewiss spielte dabei auch eine Rolle, dass in den protestantischen Kirchen das Vorbild für Glaubenstreue das Geschlecht gewechselt hatte: von der gebenedeiten Jungfrau Maria zum buchstäblich patriarchalischen Abraham« (MacCulloch, Die Reformation [see note 2], 835).

[121] Sara Mendelson, Patricia Crawford, Women in Early Modern England, 1550–1720, Oxford ²2003, 225–230. Cf. also Wunder, »Er ist die Sonn'« (see note 2), 115.

of divorce was established. In these points, however, the views of the authors differed in detail.

6. Marriage, family and household *(oeconomia)* were discovered as the nucleus of society and state *(politia)*. Here, the universal structure of authority and obedience constitutive for all estates was practiced, here the staff were recruited to serve both the secular and spiritual regiments of God.

7. Marriage, family and household were discovered as a place of religious parenting and domestic worship in their significance as a »small church« and »temple of God«.

English and German Sister Reformations
Similarities and Differences in Clerical Advice for the Sexes, Marriage, and the Household

Susan C. Karant-Nunn

I dedicate this paper to the memory of
Anne Jacobson Schutte

English-language scholars have now spent two full generations exploring the lives and status of women in both early modern England and the Holy Roman Empire of the German Nation. German colleagues especially began to add their findings around the early 1990s. We know a great deal more than we did in 1970. Additionally, during this time the study of women's history has evolved into *gender* history, meaning that we began to see women's and also men's roles as significantly defined by the cultures within which they are inscribed and conditioned. What has remained in short supply are comparative studies either of England and Germany, or casting a broad evaluative eye across more than one European linguistic and cultural-religious area. Our English counterparts do not gladly learn the languages essential to such comparisons, and, in any case, to do so would require the heaping up of expertise that adds years to any research project. The leading comparer of images of women in England and Germany during the period of our concentration is Joy Wiltenburg. Her book appeared in 1992 and needs followup investigations.[1]

Because our topic for today is the Reformation, I am leaving aside all the larger questions concerning women's standing in early modern Europe and confining myself to three questions. First, what media did the new churches use to convey to the lay public their definitions of the ideal nature and functions of Christian men and women? Secondly, what was the range of content of those media? Did they elevate women's position in society? Third, how do England and German compare?

---

[1] Wiltenburg, *Disorderly Women and Female Power in the Street Literature of Early Modern England and Germany* (Charlottesville, VA: University of Virginia Press, 1992).

1. Media Conveying Reformation Ideas

Through affected Europe, articulators of the new faiths used the same categories of media to win converts, or, after the fixation by governments of established churches, to enforce conformity. Apropos of redefining gender, as we all know, they encouraged the closure of most monasteries and convents, abolishing thereby a celibate gender that ideally attempted to discipline the physical body into better preparedness for heaven. This occurred in both England and the German-speaking lands. Marriage was rendered simultaneously non-sacramental and more sacred in that the site of its effectualization was now inside the church before the altar, or in Calvinist sanctuaries where altars were eliminated, under the pulpit and before the entire congregation. Solemn vows were introduced to the ceremony, whereas in the late Middle Ages (after 1215) and in the ongoing Catholic Church, public consent sufficed. The message to all who were undergoing the Reformation was that wedlock was of paramount importance to God. Abstinent celibacy and widowhood were in no way superior. All women should be wives and nearly all men husbands and patresfamilias. In every Protestant ceremony, biblical passages were recited that defined and enjoined upon the couple specific ways of behaving toward each other. Every adult heard the same messages repeatedly during his and her lifetime. Across Europe, the favored texts were: Genesis 2:18–25 (creation of Eve); Genesis 3:1–21 (the Fall); Proverbs 31:10–31 (activities of the good woman); John 2:1–10 (the wedding at Cana); Matthew 19:1–8 (against divorce except for adultery); I Corinthians 14:34–35; Ephesians 5:22–33 (women should submit to their husbands, and husbands should love their wives); Hebrews 13:4 (keep the marriage bed undefiled); and I Peter 3:1–7 (women's adornment should be interior; husbands should honor the weaker vessel). These were the stock and standard, but they were routinely comingled, especially in sermons and treatises, with other scriptural adductions. Often these included stories of the patriarchs and their interaction with their wives.

In the shaping of new gender definitions, England and the Lutheran German-speaking lands differed in a major respect. More affected by Calvinism than by Lutheran Evangelism, the Anglican Church did not introduce a new homiletic and literary genre, the wedding sermon.[2] At least

---

[2] Wedding sermons were not unheard of during the high and late Middle Ages. See, for example, David L. D'Avray and M. Tausche, »Marriage Sermons in *ad status* Collections of the Central Middle Ages,« *Archives d'histoire doctrinale et littéraire du moyen âge* 47 (1980), 71–119; and Rüdiger Schnell, »The Discourse on Marriage in the Middle Ages,« *Speculum* 73, 3 (1998), 771–86; and the book-length treatment by idem,

several tens of thousands of these by leading Lutheran divines were published beginning in the second half of the sixteenth century and continuing on through the seventeenth century. Unfortunately, the major examination of this entire corpus lies unpublished, in manuscript form, in the Herzog August Bibliothek, where it was written by Marjorie Elizabeth Plummer.[3] Even though the Lutheran churches continued to permit private weddings in churches, during their lifetimes, the laity must have heard the core lessons delineated many dozens of times. Their purpose was to instruct brides and grooms, and also all others who were present.[4]

Calvin and the Reformed churches that traced their descent from him did not approve of preaching that elevated individuals, whether at their nuptials or after their death. Except in the cases of high-ranking nobility or patricians, such rhetoric of praise and even of tailored instruction was discouraged. It is difficult, then, to be sure to what extent sermons were given at English weddings or what the content was. The Books of Common Prayer (1549, 1552, and 1559) do leave space for a sermon, but they admit that its occurrence is optional:

»Then shalbee sayed after the gospell a sermon, wherein ordinarily (so oft as there is any mariage) thoffice of man and wife shall bee declared according to holy scripture. Or if there be no sermon, the minister shall reade this [a compendium of scriptural excerpts] that foloweth.« *(1549)*

»Then shal begin the Communion, and after the Gospel shal be sayd a sermon, wherein ordinarely (so oft as there is any mariage) the office of a man and wyfe shalbe declared according to holy scripture: or yf there be no sermon, the Minister shall reade this that foloweth.« *(1552)*

Frauendiskurs, Männerdiskurs, Ehediskurs: Textsorten und Geschlechterkonzepte in Mittelalter und Früher Neuzeit (Frankfurt/M. and New York: Campus, 1998). Both sermons and other discursive media were mainly by, directed toward, and at the behest of, the privileged in society.

[3] Plummer, »Reforming the Family: Marriage, Gender, and the Lutheran Household in Early Modern Germany, 500–1620,« unpublished Ph.D. dissertation, the University of Virginia, Charlottesville, VA, 1996, 420 pages. The wedding sermon flourished at the same time as the funeral sermon, both kinds insisted upon by the ecclesiastical authorities. The number of early modern publications on domestic behavior is vast, and its bibliography could take up a volume of its own. The pioneer surveyor of this literature was Julius Hoffmann, *Die »Hausväterliteratur« und die »Predigten über den christlichen Hausstand«: Lehre vom Hause und Bildung für das häusliche Leben im 16., 17. und 18. Jahrhundert* (Weinheim a. d. B. and Berlin: Verlag Julius Beltz, 1959; this has been completely surpassed). My own lecture, »Hochzeitspredigten und Frauenwohlsein im 16. Jahrhundert,« given at the University of Koblenz in May 2006, and summarizing the teachings of Freder (Irenaeus), Rebhun, Mathesius, and C. Spangenberg, has not been published.

[4] Susan C. Karant-Nunn, »›Fragrant Wedding Roses‹: Wedding Sermons and the Formation of Gender in Early Modern Germany,« *German History*, 17, 1 (1999), 25–40.

»Then shal begyn the Communion, and after the Gospel shalbe saied a Sermon, wherin ordinarily (so oft as there is any mariage) thoffice of a man and wife shalbe declared, accordyng to holy Scripture, or if there be no sermon, the Minister shal reade this that foloweth.« *(1559)*[5]

The eucharist was not celebrated in tandem with continental weddings. In Lutheran instances, private masses were prohibited, and most marriages did not occur before the entire congregation. In Geneva, weddings were not held on those few Sundays when the Lord's Supper was distributed, which suggested a lingering sense of the inappropriateness of initiating marital sexual gratification on an occasion devoted to spiritual concentration. This echoed past Catholic confinement of nuptials to certain, less sacred parts of the calendar. This prohibition did not apply to England. Allocations and discouragement are themselves a medium of indoctrination.

Owing to the lack of practice that late-medieval and early sixteenth-century vicars had in preaching, the Elizabethan overseers disseminated books of homilies for clergymen to read aloud to their parishioners. *The Second Tome of Homilies*, largely written by Bishop John Jewel, contained one model on the subject of marriage.[6] I shall say more about this below.

Treatises on marriage, housekeeping, and parenting formed another medium of instruction. In Lutheran territories, these often took the form of collections of wedding sermons, which, in their whole, conveyed advice on the entire spectrum of domestic behavior. As I shall say again shortly, such manuals did exist in Reformed and Anglican regions, but they probably garnered much less attention from a broad lay public than did sermons from attendance at which parishioners could gain no exemption.

Elementary and grammar schools provided yet another setting within which young people were inculcated with the governing divines' ideals. Economic and spiritual motives were paramount on either side of the Channel for encouraging the acquisition of literacy. During the sixteenth century, opportunities for average people to learn to read in Germany were greater than they apparently were in England, where more affluent families engaged private tutors or sent only their boys to grammar schools.[7] In German cities, niche or petty schools, sometimes taught by wo-

---

[5] Respectively: http://justus.anglican.org/resources/bcp/1549/Marriage 1549; http://justus.anglican.org/resources/bcp/1552/Marriage 1552; http://justus.anglican.org/resources/bcp/1559/Marriage 1559. The spelling differences are in the originals as reproduced on-line.

[6] *An Homily of the State of Matrimony* is published in *The Two Books of Homilies appointed to be read in Churches*, ed. John Griffiths (Oxford: The University Press, 1859), 500–15. See the discussion of the Books of Homilies in Martin Ohst's chapter in this volume.

men, offered tutelage in the ABCs, and town councils themselves organized grammar schools even before 1524, when Luther wrote his treatise
urging all councils to establish urban classrooms for both girls and boys.
Lutheranism may have fostered this already established trend. The curricula were defined under the influence of pastors, and they included key
teachings on gendered demeanor. *Mädchenschulen* were designed entirely
to instruct their pupils in piety and proper female self-definition and de-
portment.[8] A corresponding enjoinder to educate girls did not exist in
England at this time, and parents determined whether their daughters
should learn to read.

2. Summary of Content

It warrants declaring at the outset that individual authors, in whichever
religio-geographic sphere, did differ from one another, in emphasis if not
in outright content. In addition, it is impossible to say how many people,
and of what standing, purchased or borrowed or heard read printed discourses on marriage. In England such expositions were far fewer than in
Germany. In both settings, we can note from surviving examples how
many editions appeared and from whose presses, yet this does not say a
great deal about lay reception.[9] In 1540–1541, just as he himself wed and
perhaps not unrelated to that step, Miles Coverdale (1488–1569), the biblical translator, translated into English and saw to press Heinrich Bullinger's (1504–1575), the Zurich divine's , tract on marriage, *Der Christlich
Eestand*. Its English title is *The Christen State of Matrimonye*.[10] Early

---

[7] For the late-medieval record, see Nicholas Orme, *English Schools in the Middle
Ages* (London: Methuen, 1973); and Jo Ann Hoeppner Moran, *The Growth of English
Schooling 1340–1548* (Princeton, NJ: Princeton University Press, 1985). These are pioneering studies only. For an overview of English girls' opportunities for basic education, see Katherine Usher Henderson and Barbara F. McManus, *Half Humankind: Contexts and Texts of the Controversy about Women in England 1540–1640* (Urbana, IL and
Chicago: University of Illinois Press, 1985), 81–98.

[8] Likewise, for Germany, see my essays, »The Reality of Early Lutheran Education:
The Electoral District of Saxony, 1528–1674, a Case Study,« *Luther-Jahrbuch* 57 (1990),
128–46; and »The Problem of Spiritual Discipline: The Indispensability of Apocryphal
Books among Sixteenth-Century Leaders of the Lutheran Churches,« in *The Bible and
Issues of Household, Family, and Gender Ethics c. 1500–1750*, New Cambridge History
of the Bible, vol. 3, edited by Euan Cameron (Cambridge, UK: Cambridge University
Press, 2016), 603–19.

[9] The literature on literacy in this period is great, if inconclusive. The rates of male
literacy were rising but never predominant or evenly distributed on both sides of the
English Channel. See at least R. A. Houston's survey, *Literacy in Early Modern Europe:
Culture and Education 1500–1800* (London: Longman, 1988), 116–54.

English Books Online registers 13 editions of Bullinger's work during the sixteenth century, six of them framed in his mother tongue by Coverdale.

Coverdale thus made available early on in the process of ecclesiastical reform a representative German-Swiss treatment of marriage to an English audience. Although not impelled by any duty to preach wedding sermons, he articulates views very similar to those of the Lutheran divines, Johannes Freder (alias Irenaeus), Johannes Spangenberg, Cyriakus Spangenberg, and Johannes Matthesius. Bullinger offers no surprises to the connoisseurs of these German marital advice books. In counteracting Catholic doctrine, the successor of Ulrich Zwingli reiterates that every Christian has the right to enter this holy estate, and he (or she) ought to marry in order to guard against evil desires (*böse Lust* in German) and the fornication to which they often lead. Marriage was ordained by God in the Garden of Eden, and after the Fall, it became a *remedium ad peccatum*. Every person should marry, Coverdale translates, so »that every one of us know how to keep his vessel in holyness and honour, not in the lust of concupiscence as do the heathen.«[11] The husband's attitude toward his wife should be loving, next, in fact, to his love of God. She should reciprocate with reverence. They should share

»the most excellent and unpaynfull seruyce, diligence and ernest labour [...] in the parts of a man's body, one doing for another, louyng, one defending, helpyng, and forbearing, suffering, also joye like pain one with another. Even so ought it to be between man and woman in wedlock.«[12]

Bullinger outlines the venerable triad of reasons why people should marry: first, to raise up a new generation of Christian people; second, to serve as a remedy to one another against lust; and third, to be helpers and companions to one another all their lives together.[13]

»Wherefore the virtue, operation, effect, and fruit now of marriage, is to comfort, maintaine, help, counsaill, to clense, to further unto goode manners, honestie and shamefastness, to expel uncleneness, to avaunce the honour of god and the publike weale, and to set up many other vertues moo.«[14]

Christians should marry within their faith – meaning here within the emerging Reformed tradition – and may never be separated. He warns harshly against adultery and believes that the capital punishment for transgressors that is prescribed in the 1530 Carolina law code should be carried out.[15]

---

[10] Antwerp: M. Crom, 1541. Coverdale was periodically in exile on the continent and published there. But ultimately five editions of his translation appeared in London.

[11] Ibid., A ii[r].

[12] Ibid., A v[v].

[13] Ibid., e.g. A vi[v].

[14] Ibid., D v[r].

In his section on choosing a mate, the Zurich Reformer inherently addresses male readers. His language is masculine. Prospective bride-grooms should not make a selection on a woman's outer beauty or fine dress. Instead, each one should ask

»whether the person be godly, wyse, discret, true, faithful, honest, sober, and lo-vyng. Item, whether she be whole and sound and not laden with sore diseases, deformed, sluttish, filthy, euilfauored«.

Think

»[h]ow fruitful, handsome, housewifely, labourious, and quyck she is.«[16]

The wife, once wed and brought home, must be entirely subordinate and obedient to the husband as provided in the Book of Genesis. But the husband should love her and not be a tyrant. Eve was created from Adam's side and not from his feet. Bullinger enumerates at length possible types of ill-behavior by a woman.[17] Although all decisions concerning the domestic establishment reside with the husband, the housewife may well exercise considerable authority within the house. Her place is exclusively within the walls:

»The wyues working place is withyn her house, there to oversee and to set all thyngs in good order, and to beware that nothing be lost, seldom to go forth, but when vrgent causes call her forth.«[18]

She should be made to memorize familiar sayings that underscore her duty to be orderly, submissive, and thrifty, such as »Don't put off till tomor-row what you could do today!« and »Whatsoever thou needest not is too dear of a ferthing« [sic].[19] Women should dress modestly and cover their hair completely when attending the sermon. Otherwise, their eternal con-demnation is so certain that they might as well be put in a sack with a millstone around their necks (and drowned).[20] In his critique of women's adornment, Bullinger repeats a standard medieval preacher's admonition reaching back to the Church Fathers.[21]

---

[15] Ibid., F i[r/v].

[16] Ibid., G i[r].

[17] Ibid., H iv[r] and passim.

[18] Ibid., J iii[r]. For a general discussion of women's and men's stereotypical work-spaces, see Barbara Caine and Glenda Sluga, *Gendering European History* (London and New York: Leicester University Press, 2000), 32–54.

[19] Ibid., J iii[v].

[20] Ibid., K iii[v].

[21] See, for example, materials gathered by Alcuin Blamires, ed., *Woman Defamed and Woman Defended: An Anthology of Medieval Texts* (Oxford: Clarendon Press, 1992), passim.

Coverdale's translation of Bullinger introduced no argument that was not already widely available throughout Europe, except – and this is a revolutionary break with the medieval and Catholic paradigm – that marriage was superior to celibacy. With the dissemination of this new model of Christian living, it became necessary to stress yet more emphatically what fifteenth-century preachers had enjoined upon wives and husbands when preaching on marriage the second or the third Sunday in January each year. Or, it may be that the goal of universal wedlock fostered a more attractive depiction of the benefits to be reaped from entering into the wedded estate. Perhaps in both England and Germany, marriage was made more desirable, the mutual love more comforting, than it had been drawn in an era of saintly and celibate paragons. We cannot know this with certainty. Universally, in any case, husbands were to rule absolutely and wives to obey immediately, sincerely. On this point, Protestant clerics replicated their Catholic forebears completely.

Despite their writers' different foci, the better known German guides to marital living were of one mind on these basic principles, which they conveyed to their readers at length and with full enthusiasm. Their outlook was binary. Women and men were not only different in their nature; they should be maintained in these contrasts. The handbooks'themes become a familiar litany for the specialist: Man should not be alone; God created a helpmeet for him, whom he named Eve; she was chiefly responsible for the Fall of humankind, hearkening to the devil; her subordination to her husband became absolute, unless he were to order her to disobey God; womankind is vain, curious, given to emotion, lacking the man's rational capacity; she is inclined to self-indulgence, and he is inclined to harshness when vexed; husband and wife should help one another to be better Christians; they should pray together; they should moderate their sexual desire and practice with one another; they should help one another to bear the »crosses« of presiding over a household, supporting a family (him), and bearing (her) and raising children; they should treat the family circle as a small church.

The sentiments available in Bullinger's translated compendium were also disseminated, to an extent that we cannot presently reconstruct, in books of homilies that were intended both to instruct parish clergy in accepted teaching and to provide them texts for their unpracticed selves to read aloud. As noted above, the *Second Tome of Homilies* (1563), »to be reade in euery paryshe churche agreablye«, contains one offering on matrimony.[22] Its opening emphasis on *unclenenesse* and *fylthynesse*, which is

---

[22] *The Seconde Tome of Homilies of such matters as were promised and intituled in*

to say sexual license, sets it apart from the normative German sermon, which typically begins with God's creation of and blessing upon the marital estate in the Garden of Eden. The second topic it presents is marital concord, of which the husband, the more able and rational spouse, must be the chief author.[23] Harmony will foster all the undertakings of the pair. This model sermon is immediately binary in its treatment of the sexes. Women are by their nature distinctly inferior to men, who are urged to give them leeway and regard them with tolerance. »For the woman is a weake creature, not endued with lyke strengthe and constancie of mynde; therefore they be the sooner disquieted, and they be the more prone to all weake affections and dispositions of minde, more then [sic] men be, and lyghter [then] they be, and more vayne in their fantasies and opinions.«[24] Husbands ought never to strike their wives despite provocation.[25] They will attain more »by gentle words then by stripes.«[26] Men should not worry about diminished manliness when they refrain from severity, for Saint Peter has commanded them (1 Peter 3) to love their wives and deal with them rationally.[27] Nonetheless, women should patiently bear the sharpness of their husbands, and God will compensate them.[28] Wives' utter subjection to their husbands is signified by their head covering.[29] The author to whom this work is attributed, John Jewel, is said to have had inclinations toward Elizabethan Puritanism but gradually felt alienated from it and denied a prebend to his friend Laurence Humphrey, President of Magdalen College, Oxford, who refused to wear a surplice.[30] The tone of his homily on marriage is moderate.

Another Elizabethan divine, Henry Smith (1550?–1591), the »silver-tongued« preacher at St. Clement Danes in London, attracted thousands to his sermons until illness forced him to withdraw from the pulpit and to take up his pen in his bedchamber. In his enforced retirement, he wrote a brief treatise on preparing to enter wedlock, *A Preparatiue to Marriage* [...] *Whereunto is Annexed a Treatise of the Lords Supper*.[31] This treatment,

---

the former part of Homylyes, set out by the aucthoritie of the Queenes Maiestie. And to be read in euery paryshe churche agreablye (London: Richarde Jugge, 1563; STC, 2nd ed., 13666.4), 253–65. See also STC (2nd edn.) Nos. 13663–65.

[23] Ibid., 255r.

[24] Ibid.

[25] Ibid., esp. 259v–260r.

[26] Ibid., 255v.

[27] Also ibid., 261r.

[28] Ibid., 258v.

[29] Ibid., 257v.

[30] *The Works of John Jewel, edited for the Parker Society by John Ayre*, 4 vols. (Cambridge: University Press, 1845–1850), iv: 1265. Letter of Jewel to Archbishop Parker, 22 December 1565.

222   *Susan C. Karant-Nunn*

the author says, originated in a sermon held at a betrothal; he enlarged it thereafter. Smith's tone is mild throughout. He deals extensively with a young man's selection of a wife and what attributes he ought to look for. She should behave always in a godly manner. The would-be groom can only know this through extensive acquaintance and observation.

»He which will know all his wiues qualities before he be married to them, must see her eating and walking, working and playing, and talking and laughing, and childing, or else he shall haue lesse with her then [*sic*] he looked for, and more then he wished for.«[32]

She should prefer silence and must be content to »keepe home.«[33] She must not be a street-wife like Tamar or a field-wife like Dinah.[34] His first duty to her as his wife is »hartie affection,« and hers to him is to obey him »because he is her better.«[35] He must be soft and gentle toward her, for she is the weaker vessel. On physical discipline, he writes,

»If he cannot reforme his wife without beating, he is worthie to be beaten for chusing no better. [...] Her cheeks are made for thy lippes and not for thy fistes.«[36]

Men who strike their own flesh should be sent to [the madhouse] Bedlam.[37] Turning to the husband as heads of households, he says, men must control their wrath.

»Instructing, correcting, and praying, make good children and happy parents.«[38]

In England, largely owing, as said, to the absence of published wedding sermons, full-scale treatises on marriage were far less numerous than in the Germanophone world, yet these too derived from the (optional) preaching at weddings. After Coverdale's introduction of Bullinger's thought, and as the consequences of English exposure to Reformed strains deepened, English Protestantism became more distinctly Calvinist in its theological orientation, in many parishes' practice, and in its mood. Calvin (not to mention John Knox![39]) took a less cheerful view of womankind in her

---

[31] Henry Smith, *A preparatiue to mariage The summe whereof was spoken at a contract, and inlarged after. Whereunto is annexed A Treatise of the Lords supper: and another of vsurie* (London: R. Field for Thomas Man, 1591; STC, 2nd ed., 22686). The part on marriage is 88 pages in length.
[32] Ibid., 33.
[33] Ibid., 43.
[34] Ibid., 62–63.
[35] Ibid., 48–49.
[36] Ibid., 54.
[37] Ibid., 57.
[38] Ibid., 81.
[39] John Knox, *The First Blast of the Trumpet against the Monstruous Regiment of Women* ([Geneva: By J. Poullain and A. Rebul], 1558), STC (2nd ed.) 15070, 9v: »For who can denie but it repugneth to nature, that the blind shal be appointed to leade and

earthly life than Luther did.[40] Emblematic of his overall position is his assertion that Christ revealed his resurrection to women first, in order to show the »humbleness of our faith« and to humiliate the disciples, who had abandoned their Lord during his Passion.[41] It is important to note here that late sixteenth-century Anglican divines's staunchly negative views reflect in part the model, Calvin, whom they took from the Continent, rather than either Luther or Bullinger. Interest in Bullinger's tract generally expired after mid-century, with one final edition, a Coverdale translation at that, appearing in 1575.[42] Scholars who study the German Reformations have not yet drawn an adequate distinction between Lutheran and Reformed teaching on marriage and sexuality.

Three English pastors in particular left a legacy of lengthy treatments of marriage that originated in sermons they had given over many years in their respective parishes. All three reached maturity during the reign of Elizabeth, when the Anglican churches were still in flux, and all became Puritans. All were highly educated. All convey a more emphatic vision of women's inferiority to men than contemporary Lutherans generally did (we could differ on degrees of denigration!), all the while purporting to esteem the feminine sex in compliance with biblical admonitions to do so. William Perkins (1558–1602) was openly Calvinist and introduced Theodore Beza's thought into England. He acknowledged, additionally, the influence of Zacharias Ursinus, the Heidelberg divine. He preached at St. Andrew the Great Church in Cambridge from 1585 until his death. While at Cambridge University in the 1580s, he espoused the doctrine of double predestination. He wrote about 40 major works. The one that is pertinent

---

conduct such as do see? That the weake, the sicke, and impotent persones shall norishe and kepe the hole and strong, and finallie, that the foolishe, madde and phrenetike shal gouerne the discrete, and giue counsel to such as be sober of mind? And such be al women, compared vnto man in bearing of authoritie. For their sight in ciuile regiment, is but blindnes: their strength, weaknes: their counsel, foolishenes: and judgement, phrenesie, if it be rightlie considered.« Knox's views in fact pertain to womankind in general and were as applicable to the small governmental unit of the household. Consulted 18 March 2018.

[40] I am persuaded by the evidence amassed by John L. Thompson, *John Calvin and the Daughters of Sarah: Women in Regular and Exceptional Roles in the Exegesis of Calvin, His Predecessors, and His Contemporaries* (Geneva: Droz, 1992); he refutes the arguments of Jane Dempsey Douglass in *Women, Freedom, and Calvin* (Philadelphia: Westminster Press, 1985). A place to begin in the primary sources would be Jean Calvin, *Sermons sur la Genèse Chapitres 1,1–11,4*, edited by Max Engammare (Neukirchen-Vluyn: Neukirchener Verlag, 2000), LXVIII + 553 pp. This is vol. XI/1 in the series, *Supplementa Calviniana: Sermons inédits.*

[41] John Calvin, *Plusiers sermons de Iehan Calvin* (n.p.: Conrad Badius, 1558), ser. 9, 269, 275, 277, 278.

[42] London: John Audeley, 1575.

to the concept of gender formation is *Christian Oeconomie, or a Short Survey of the Right Manner of Erecting and Ordering a Family According to the Scriptures.*[43] It was published twice in the same year, and the title page refers to its having been written first in Latin. If this version was printed, no copy has survived. Much of Perkins' excursus is traditional: the honorability of marriage, its divine creation and condonation in the Garden of Eden. Like many of his fellows, Perkins regards the household as a small church, a foundation stone of the larger congregation and Christianity as a faith, as well as of the English commonwealth. The man is distinctly superior to the woman.

»The male is man, of a superiour sex, fit for procreation. The female is woman of an inferior sex, fit to conceiue and bear children.«[44]

He regards betrothals themselves as a legally binding contract that can hardly ever be broken, as for example if one of the engaged parties is discovered to have leprosy.[45] A feature of the tracts of all three of the Puritan fathers presented here is that they urge all possible restraint in marital sexual relations. Perkins says,

»[f]or euen in wedlock excess in lusts is no better than plain adultery before God.«

He continues,

»[i]mmoderate desire even betweene man and wife is fornication.«[46]

Spouses should abstain from sex during menstrual periods and in times of mutually agreed-upon religious fasting. The body must be maintained in a pure state as a fit vessel of the Holy Ghost.[47] The husband must provide the entire material basis of the family through his calling. The paterfamilias rules the entire domestic enterprise, although the wife may be given charge of such functions as allocating food supplies. The wife is to be helpful as he directs her, but she may not interact regularly with the public. Her duties are two: to be subject and to obey. He states,

»The woman is not to take the libertie of wandring and straying abroad from her own house without the mans knowledge and consent.«[48]

---

[43] London: Felix Kyngston, 1609.

[44] Perkins, *Christian Oeconomie*, 24.

[45] Ibid., 78–79.

[46] Ibid., 110–11.

[47] Ibid., 111. See Alan Macfarlane, »The Regulation of Marital and Sexual Relationships in Seventeenth Century England,« M. Phil. Thesis, University of London, 1968. As far as I can tell, this was not published. A propos of Ralph Josselin, see Macfarlane, *The Family Life of Ralph Josselin: A Seventeenth-Century Clergyman* (New York and London: Norton, 1970), 83–84.

[48] Ibid., 132.

In his discussion of child-rearing, he provides a chapter on »The Sonne« but none on the daughter. This omission is significant. His sole remark on daughters (in the chapter on sons) is:

»They must yeeld [sic] obedience to their parents in all domesticall labours, that they may be skilfull in household affairs.«[49]

William Gouge (1578–1653) took a B. A. and an M. A. at Cambridge University, lectured there (controversially) on Ramist logic, and served as pastor at St. Ann Blackfriars Church for 45 years. His major work on our subject is *Domesticall Duties: Eight Treatises*, first appeared in 1622 and was republished in 1627 and 1634.[50] For Gouge, too, the family in its dwelling is the small church. Its daily functioning must make that manifest. Reflecting Christ's bond with his bride the Church, Gouge declares the basic principle,

»Loue is the chief duty of a husband; fear is the chief duty of a wife.«[51]

Like other Puritan writers, he expresses concern that spouses may feel too much libidinous desire for each other. He laments,

»Excess is either in the measure or in the time. In the measure, when either the husband or the wife is insatiable, provoking rather than asswaging lust, and weakening their natural vigor rather than suppressing their vnnaturall humor. Many husbands and wives are much oppressed by their bedfellows vnsatiableness in this kind.«[52]

Husbands may not seek satisfaction while their wives are menstruating, after they have given birth, or while they are nursing an infant – as all mothers are urged to do. Gouge and his wife Elizabeth had 13 offspring, and she died after bringing forth the last one. In the third segment of his book, he treats the place and duties of wives. They are not, unlike their husbands, created in the image of God. Even if a bride is of higher socio-economic rank than her groom, the moment she is joined to him in wedlock, she must subject herself utterly to him. She is her husband's inferior, and in marrying her, he has raised her to a place of honor. She has no authority but is exclusively his helper, carrying out his instructions. Even if her husband is »coarse, swaggering, rude, swearing, a blasphemer,« she must obey him except insofar as God forbids.[53] Her head covering and veil symbolize her complete subjection. Her whole carriage and outward manner should indicate her reverence and subordination. She should be reluc-

---

[49] Ibid., 147.
[50] London: John Haviland, 1622. The subsequent printings were at other London publishing houses.
[51] Gouge, *Domesticall Duties*, 128.
[52] Ibid., 223.
[53] Ibid., 273.

tant to speak and then only reverently.[54] Gouge even seems to withdraw from women the right to dispose of possessions that are solely theirs. They may do so only with their husbands' consent, and husbands may do so without their wives' consent.[55]

Nevertheless, husbands should take delight in their wives.[56] They should commend and reward things well done.[57] They should instruct and reprove their spouses for their faults with mildness, not when they are angry, and in private.[58] In an age in which many men beat their wives with impunity, Gouge takes the position that they should not. His arguments are three: First, he finds no warrant for it in Scripture; no patriarch struck his wife. Second, the »small disparity« between husband and wife in the household would not allow for this extreme behavior of the one against the other; children and servants could not respect a person who lived under the same disciplinary conditions as they. Third, the pastor cites the Bible:

>The wife is as a mans selfe; >They two are one flesh.< No man but a frantike, furious, desperate wretch will beat himselfe.«[59]

He concludes on this subject,

»If a case so stand that a wife must needs be beaten, it is fitter for an husband to refer the matter to a publike Magistrate [...] and not to do it with his own hands. [...] There is no hope of any good to proceede from an husbands beating of his wife.«[60]

In this matter, we today regard Gouge as enlightened.

William Whately (1583–1639) was likewise educated at Cambridge (B.A.) and then at Oxford (M.A.). He was presented to a vicarage in Banbury and attracted people from out of town to his sermons. He calls his treatise on marriage and housekeeping, *A Bride-Bush, or A VVedding Sermon Compendiously Describing the Duties of Married Persons*, a sermon, as you can see.[61] Three editions appeared between 1617 and 1623. He admits to being inspired by a wedding sermon that he had given. Whately's insistence in this work that adultery and/or desertion automatically dissolved a marriage contract and freed the innocent party to remarry without resort to law, got him in trouble. Whately was forced to recant his views on divorce by the Court of High Commission in 1621.[62]

---

[54] On speech and gesture: ibid., 281–85.
[55] Ibid., 299–300.
[56] Ibid., 360.
[57] Ibid., 368–69.
[58] Ibid., 384–86.
[59] Ibid., 389–90.
[60] Ibid., 392.
[61] London: William Iaggard, 1617.

Whately devotes several pages to recommending means of suppressing lustful urges, both when one is single and for married couples.

»The married must not prouoke desires for pleasures sake, but allay desires [...]. They must not strive by words and gestures to enflame their passions [...]. In a word, marriage must be used as seldome and sparingly as may stande with the neede of the persons married; for excess this way doth weaken the body and shorten life. [...]. Excessiueness enflameth lust and disposeth the persons so offending to adultery. Moderation kills lust and is a great furtherance to purity.«[63]

Despite the seeming dangers of the husband's and wife's physical proximity, Whately advocates at length for the emotional love of wedded partners for each other. The wife should occupy that chamber of her husband's heart, and he in hers, that is just beneath that in which resides their love for God.[64]

»Their person should be to each other the most precious of all persons.«[65]

They will increase their reciprocal affection by praying, singing Psalms, and reading the Bible together.[66] They should make it their main business to please each other.[67] Still, they are never equals.

»The man must be taken for God's immediate officer in the house, and, as it were, the King in the family. The woman must account herself his deputy, an officer substituted to him, not his equall but as a subordinate.«[68]

He is her head and her savior. She must carry herself as an inferior person.[69]

»Nature hath framed the lineaments of his body to superioritie, and set the print of government in his very face, which is more stern and less delicate than the womans; he must not suffer this order of nature to be inverted. [...] That house is a misshapen house, or a crump-shouldered or hutch-backed house, where the husband has made himself an underling to his wife, and giuen away his power and regiment to his inferiour. Without question, it is a sinne for man to come lower than God hath set him. It is not humilitie, but baseness, to be ruled by her whom he should rule.«[70]

He is the »domesticall King.« Her eye, her brow, her nostrils, her hands, her feet, her shoulders – all parts of her body, every gesture, must bear out her reverence for her husband and subordination to him.[71]

---

[62] Jacqueline Eales, »Whately, William (1583–1639), Church of England clergyman and puritan preacher«, *Oxford Dictionary of National Biography*. January 03, 2008. Oxford University Press. Date of access 23 May 2019.

[63] Ibid., 19.

[64] Ibid., 37.

[65] Ibid., 39.

[66] Ibid., 52–53.

[67] Ibid., 59.

[68] Ibid., 89.

[69] Ibid., 193.

[70] Ibid., 98.

[71] Ibid., 204.

Whately is set apart from his two comparators, and from nearly all German preachers on the wedded life in that he would permit a husband to strike a badly offending and unrepentant wife, a woman demonstrating »palpable wickedness.«

»But for blows, strokes with hand or fist, nothing should drive an husband to them, except the utmost extremities of vnwifelike carriage, unless she be peremptory and wilfull in cursing, swearing, drunkenness, etc., unless she raile upon him with most violent and intolerable termes, unless she outface him with bolde maintaining that she doeth as she doth in despite of him, unless she begin the quarrell and strike or offer to strike [...]. [...] But if such extreme putrefaction shall fall out in any mans case, I see no cause of forbidding to cut or seere ones most tenderly beloued flesh.«[72]

Not clear is whether the cutting and searing are only figurative or meant as literal possibilities. A husband should show grief on his face when he must resort to physical punishment, and even have tears in his eyes.[73] He sums up:

»Doubtless many a mans case is so desperate, that there is no other remedy, and to forbid one vse, that God allows in such a case, I confess I dare not.«[74]

He employs the metaphor of the surgeon (chirogion) who must cut away rotted flesh in order to effect healing in the good tissue that is left.[75]

In the German *Hausväter* literature, this extreme position is represented by Paul Rebhun in his *Hausfried* of 1540.[76] This Lutheran pastor in Oelsnitz (Saxony) mocks housewives who run to the neighbors when their husbands have struck them »with a baby cudgel« (*Kinderrütlin*) and caused a black-and-blue spot (*fleck*), never admitting that they provided good cause for physical discipline.[77] Sometimes wives have to be beaten in the service of domestic peace. Some women are »devilishly evil« (*teuflisch böse*).[78] Husbands should never kick their wives, however.[79]

Whately does strongly advocate mildness and rationality in the husband's treatment of his wife. He should be reluctant to perceive her flaws, and he »[h]e should reproue her with great louingness of phrase.«[80]

---

[72] Ibid., 123–24.
[73] Ibid., 172.
[74] Ibid., 170.
[75] See Frances E. Dolan, *Marriage and Violence: The Early Modern Legacy* (Philadelphia: University of Pennsylvania Press, 2008), which chronologically comes up to the twentieth century. Thanks to Merry E. Wiesner-Hanks for making me aware of this book.
[76] Wittenberg: Veit Creutzer, 1546. In his preface, Rebhun informs the reader that he has preached all the sermons that are included.
[77] Rebhun, *Hausfried*, R i[r/v].
[78] Ibid., R ii[r].
[79] Ibid., S i[v]–T i[r].
[80] Whately, *A Bride-Bush*, 167.

3. Comparison of Efforts at Gender Formation

It is virtually impossible to derive reliable information on the success of housekeeping manuals to attain their desired ends. In both England and the Protestant parts of the Holy Roman Empire, clerical leaders sought to orient their followers toward a norm – now a »sacred« norm – of marriage and childrearing. In large part – though not in every part – they followed their Catholic forebears in regarding Eve as chiefly responsible for the Fall of humankind and as, from her creation, fundamentally inferior to Adam and in need of the masculine bit and bridle. With their emphasis on persuading and disciplining the populace, the clergies of both England and Germany took on the task of inculcating gender definitions with new energy.

Both English and German preachers accepted the principle of *sola scriptura* and exploited the same biblical texts as the authorities for their program. Especially the Lutheran churches, however, resorted to a greater range of media in this endeavor, which they would have defined as reforming the family. For these clergymen, as indeed for much of society, the concept of gender did not exist, but the respective assignments of the sexes were self-evident. German Lutherans should be differentiated from both Reformed and Anglicans thinkers in their methodologies. They also show different, more permissive tendencies in their perspectives on marital sexuality. Lutheran preachers generally allowed couples to regulate their own intercourse and did not explicitly ban it during menstruation, pregnancy, and nursing. They did encourage moderation as opposed to the expression of unbridled lust. Evangelical Protestant leaders exploited art, liturgy (churching of women; wedding sermons), and elementary school curricula to imprint on the minds of young and also older attendees the indelible differences in nature and vocation between females and males. Again, they saw the universe in binary terms, and these binary terms were to their minds correct. Women were *called* to be in the place they described, as men were *called* to be in theirs. The caller, of course, was God himself. Reformed and Anglican clerics agreed on this, but they relied almost exclusively on wedding liturgy and societal norms to disseminate this view and hold it in place.

Nikolaus Hermann (c. 1500–1561), the cantor and musician of Joachimsthal and close colleague of Johannes Mathesius, put in verse Mathesius's principles of raising daughters:

»Dein Tochter halte daheim im Haus,
   Laß sie nicht viel spatzieren aus.
Gwehn sie zur arbeit vnd zum Rocken,

> Das sie nicht stetz spiel mit der Tocken.
> Der müssiggang manche verfürt,
>   Das sie thut was sich nicht gebürt.
> Zu rechter zeit gib jhr ein Man,
>   Doch das sie vor Haushalten kann.
> Auffs freundlichste gebar mit jhr,
>   Das sie ohn zwang gehorche dir.[81]

Rhymes were intended to facilitate memorization. In the end, however, it is crucial to observe that actual behavior varied immensely. It surely did not conform to the ideals of the gentlemen who held forth in the pulpit and who committed some of their convictions to writing. William Gouge observed in the dedication of *Domesticall Duties* to his parishioners that they had objected especially to two points in his sermons on marriage and family life: first, they thought that wives should be able to dispose of goods that belonged entirely to them; and second, they disagreed on the extreme degree of the wife's subjection to the husband.[82] We would like to know more, but the information is lacking. We may be sure that life as lived in England and in Germany, and the extent to which teachings on gender definition may have affected it, is a wholly other subject.[83] Alexandra Walsham has demonstrated in a forthcoming paper, for example, that mothers laid down their legacy to their progeny in writing, hoping to confirm their children's piety after the parent's death. This category of literature alone suggests a maternal exertion in the household that not only established mothers' prominence in that sphere but also, by the way, conformed to the Christian role that our theologians envisioned for housewives.[84]

---

[81] Sächsische Landesbibliothek Dresden (when I used it; now it is the Sächsische Landesbibliothek – Staats- und Universitäts-Bibliothek Dresden), Sig. G. 144, a heart-shaped book bearing a title written in during the nineteenth century: »Herzbuch der Kurfürstin von Sachsen, gebunden von Caspar Meuser,« and recorded at the back: Gedruckt zu Erffurdt: Georg Bawman, 1577), no pagination.

[82] *Domesticall Duties*, preface, n. p.

[83] For one example, see Alan Macfarlane, *Ralph Josselin*, 106–10 (see note 27). For problems in enforcing gender norms, see, for instance, Heide Wunder, »Gender Norms and Their Enforcement in Early Modern Germany,« in Lynn Abrams and Elizabeth Harvey, eds., *Gender Relations in German History: Power, Agency, and Experience from the Sixteenth to the Twentieth Century* (Durham, NC: Duke University Press, 1997), 39–56.

[84] Walsham, »The Mother's Legacy: Women, Religion, and Generational Transmission in Post-Reformation England,« forthcoming in Susan C. Karant-Nunn and Ute Lotz-Heumann, eds., *The Cultural History of the Reformation: Theories and Applications* (Wolfenbüttel: Wolfenbütteler Forschungen, probably 2019).

The Parish and Lay Religious Life

Amy Nelson Burnett

Every parish has its own history. Historians looking for the causes and consequences of the Reformation at the parish level can find anecdotal evidence to argue both for and against the deficiencies of late medieval pastoral care as an explanation for popular response to evangelical teachings. On the one hand there is the German parish of Kirchen, whose pastoral post was incorporated into the collegiate foundation of St. Peter in Basel. At the end of the fifteenth century, Kirchen's parishioners complained that over the past forty years they had been served by 29 priests, some of whom stole property from the church to support their concubines and children and most of whom performed their duties only negligently if at all. On the other hand, there is the tiny Devonshire parish of Morebath described by Eamon Duffy, which was served for many years before and after the Reformation by its conscientious parish priest Sir Christopher Trychay. Through Trychay's meticulously kept records, we see his parishioners actively involved in the religious, social, and economic life of the parish. Although Trychay and his parishioners conformed to the religious injunctions of the Tudor monarchs, they showed little enthusiasm for the Reformation.[1]

These contrasting examples illustrate why it is important to look at the larger picture as well as at individual case studies when evaluating the impact of the Reformation at the parish level. Over the last few decades the late medieval and early modern parish has received intensive scrutiny from both Anglophone and German-speaking scholars. Enno Bünz, whose massive *Die mittelalterliche Pfarrei* brings together the results of his own meticulous research, has stressed that in studying the parish one must combine the approaches of institutional, social, and cultural history in order to consider the legal and economic aspects of parish life, the role of the *Niederklerus* or lower clergy (by which he means not just parish

---

[1] Guy P. Marchal, »Eine Quelle zum spätmittelalterlichen Klerikerproletariat. Zur Interpretation der Klageartikel der Bauern von Kirchen (LK. Lörrach) gegen das Kapitel von St. Peter zu Basel,« *Freiburger Diözesan-Archiv* 91 (3. F. 23) (1971): 65–80; Eamon Duffy, *The Voices of Morebath: Reformation and Rebellion in an English Village* (New Haven: Yale University Press, 2001).

pastors but also preachers, vicars, chaplains, and *Messpriester* or chantry priests), and the religious activities of the laity. Bünz's impressive overview of research illustrates just how difficult it is to make universal generalizations about the parish system and the praxis of Christianity at the parish level at the end of the Middle Ages.[2]

It is also difficult to make comparisons of lay religious culture in England and Germany (by which I mean the Holy Roman Empire and Switzerland) because scholars of both areas have relied on quite different types of sources. Historians of England have made abundant use of wills and church wardens' accounts to describe individual and collective expressions of piety, but there are no comparable studies of such documents for Germany. Conversely, scholars of Germany have used visitation reports especially from the century after the Reformation to study popular reception of reformatory teaching. The closest equivalent to these reports in England are church court records, but these served a different purpose and so are not directly comparable.

In conscious awareness of this variety, I will attempt here to highlight those aspects of parish life and popular religion most relevant to a comparison between England and Germany. In order to illustrate the change over time, I will look at three different points in that process. I will first describe structural differences between the two areas on the eve of the Reformation, then I will contrast the introduction of reforms in each area as it impacted parishes. Finally, I will discuss the consequences of reform at the parish level in the later sixteenth century. There were significant differences in both parish structure and the reformatory process. One feature common to both England and Germany, however, was the divide between urban and rural religious praxis. This divide predated the Reformation and persisted in the century after it, and it would influence the development of lay religious life in subtle ways.

1. Structural Differences between England and Germany

By around 1200, the parish was established throughout most of Europe as the site for the provision of the *cura animarum*. This term not only means »pastoral care« as it is understood today but also had legal implications concerning the relationship between the parish pastor and his parishioners. Those parishioners were the pastor's *Untertanen* or subjects, passive re-

---

[2] Enno Bünz, *Die mittelalterliche Pfarrei*, Spätmittelalter, Humanismus, Reformation 96 (Tübingen: Mohr Siebeck, 2018); see especially his survey of research, 3–76.

cipients of the pastor's actions who owed substantial financial obligations to him in return for his services, especially in administering the sacraments.[3] The early fossilization of the parish structure meant that by the late Middle Ages there was no necessary correlation between parish boundaries and settlement patterns, a fact with important consequences for pastoral care.[4]

Significantly, at the same time that the parish pastor's rights were being undergirded by canon law, the growth of the mendicant orders undermined the pastor's actual influence over his parishioners, especially in cities. The resulting conflict between secular and mendicant clergy is well known and does not need to be described here. That conflict, however, does highlight the growing divergence between the popular practice of Christianity in the cities and in the countryside through the later Middle Ages. By the early sixteenth century, urban religion was both more varied and more individualized than that of peasants in the countryside. Without ignoring the considerable commonalities between urban and rural religious practices, city dwellers had far more options for religious expression, ranging from the competing pastoral services of mendicants and greater recourse to sermons as a result of endowed preacherships, to more elaborate forms of and more frequent opportunities for worship, and a wider range of collective religious practices both within and across parish boundaries.[5] There was a significantly higher literacy rate in the cities than in the countryside, and those who could not read themselves had greater opportunity to hear books being read aloud. This gave the urban laity access to vernacular devotional works and forms of individualized piety that their largely illiterate rural counterparts did not have. A prominent concern of this literature was instructing the laity how to live a Christian life.[6]

---

[3] Karl S. Bader, »Universitas subditorum parochiae – des pfarrers untertanen. Zu Auffassung und Bezeichnung der spätmittelalterlichen Pfarrgemeinde,« in *Festschrift für Hans Liermann zum 70. Geburtstag*, ed. Klaus Obermeyer and Hans-Rudolph Hagemann, Erlanger Forschungen A 16 (Erlangen: Universitätsbund Erlangen, 1964), 11–25.

[4] David M. Palliser, »Introduction: The Parish in Perspective,« in *Parish, Church and People: Local Studies in Lay Religion 1350–1750*, ed. S. J. Wright (London: Hutchinson, 1988), 5–28.

[5] Beat Kümin, »Reformation und Pfarreileben. Englische Landgemeinden im Spiegel ihrer Rechnungsbücher 1530–1560,« in *Landgemeinde und Kirche im Zeitalter der Konfessionen*, ed. Beat Kümin (Zurich: Chronos, 2004), 21–57, downplays these differences, but even he admits that urban parishes had significantly more resources than rural ones, and their function as social and cultural centers faced competition from other groups.

[6] On the growth of religious literature in the fifteenth century, Werner Williams-Krapp, »The erosion of a monopoly: German religious literature in the fifteenth century,« in *The Vernacular Spirit: Essays on Medieval Religious Literature*, ed. Renate

The diversity of urban Christianity would have important implications for the spread of the reformation, which appealed especially to literate city dwellers. Luther's reformation may have begun in the small town of Wittenberg, but his message was most enthusiastically adopted in the many cities of south Germany and Switzerland that had populations ranging from 5,000 to 50,000. The urban structure of England differed from that of Germany, for with the exception of London it had no large cities. This difference would prove momentous, in light of the role played by the literate urban population in the spread of the German Reformation.

A second difference between England and Germany concerns the size and density of the parish network in each area. England had roughly 9,000 parishes for an estimated population of 2.1 million, which amounts to much less than 300 people per parish.[7] In comparison, there were roughly 50,000 parishes in the Empire for a population of around 16 million, or one parish for every 3,200 people – well over ten times the average population of an English parish. While averages have to be taken with a grain of salt (one thinks of the average family size of 2.4 children), these numbers do reflect a major difference between the two areas that can be illustrated by a few comparisons. London had 106 parishes for its roughly 50,000 inhabitants, and York, a town of 10,000, had fifty parish churches.[8] In contrast, Cologne, a city of about the same size as London, had only eighteen parishes, and Basel, about the same size as York, had only six parishes. Because these German cities were episcopal seats, the number of parishes in them was relatively high in comparison to other large German cities. Nuremberg, with 25,000 inhabitants, had only two parishes, while Ulm's 18,000 inhabitants all worshiped in its single parish church.[9]

Parish density in England's towns and in the smaller cities of Germany was more comparable. Beverly's 5,000 inhabitants were divided among three parishes, while Doncaster's 2,000 communicants belonged to a single parish.[10] These numbers are not so different from Zurich, with three par-

---

Blumenfeld-Kosinski, et al. (New York: Palgrave, 2002), 239–59; cf. Geneviève Hasenohr, »Religious Reading Amongst the Laity in France in the Fifteenth Century,« in *Heresy and Literacy, 1000–1530*, ed. Peter Biller and Anne Hudson, Cambridge Studies in Medieval Literature 23 (Cambridge: Cambridge University Press, 1994), 205–21.

[7] Beat Kümin, »The English Parish in a European Perspective,« in *The Parish in English Life, 1400–1600*, ed. Katherine L. French, et al. (New York: Manchester University Press, 1997), 15–32.

[8] Susan Brigden, *London and the Reformation* (Oxford: Clarendon Press, 1989), 6, 133; York's parishes in Patrick Collinson, *The Birthpangs of Protestant England: Religious and Cultural Change in the Sixteenth and Seventeenth Centuries* (Basingstoke: Macmillan, 1988), 49.

[9] Bünz, *Mittelalterliche Pfarrei* (see note 1), 110–11.

[10] Population and number of parishes for these cities derived from Patrick Collinson

ishes for its population of 5,000, or Wittenberg's single parish for its 2,000 inhabitants. In the north of both England and Germany there were parishes that were geographically quite large, that were sparsely populated, or both.[11] My impression, though, is that rural parishes in Germany, especially in the south, were much more densely populated than those in England, and rural parishes usually included multiple settlements. Upper Hesse had between 300 and 350 locales that were divided among 85 parishes, with the typical parish containing three and some as many as a dozen settlements.[12] Most of the parishes in Basel's rural territories were comprised of three or four villages as well. There could be competition among these villages for the parish priest's time and attention, and distance from the parish church imposed significant hardships on parishioners. Studies of the diocese of Speyer and of Graubünden have documented efforts by village inhabitants to endow churches and chapels and to elevate these endowments to the level of a parish in order to increase the availability of pastoral care at the village level. These efforts focused on the regular celebration of masses in filial churches and chapels and the administration of the sacraments that marked the beginning and the end of life: baptism and the complex of confession, reception of the viaticum and extreme unction.[13]

These differences in parish size and urbanization had important ramifications for the reformation of the parish. One obvious consequence of the populous urban parishes in the major cities of south Germany is that the provision of pastoral care at the parish level was wholly inadequate

---

and Patrick Craig, ed., *The Reformation in English Towns, 1500–1640* (New York: St. Martin's Press, 1998).

[11] One could, for instance, compare Bünz's description of the development of the parish of Hof an der Saale, *Mittelalteriche Pfarrei* (see note 2), 101–04, with the parish of Halifax, William Sheils and Sarah Sheils, »Textiles and Reform: Halifax and its Hinterland,« in Collinson, *The Reformation in English Towns* (see note 10), 130–43, or with the parishes of Cumbria described in Margaret Clark, »Northern Light? Parochial Life in a ›Dark Corner‹ of Tudor England,« in French, *The Parish in English Life* (see note 7), 56–73.

[12] David Mayes, *Communal Christianity: The Life and Loss of a Peasant Vision in Early Modern Germany*, Studies in Central European Histories (Boston: Brill, 2004), 56–57.

[13] Rosi Fuhrmann, »Dorfgemeinde und Pfründstiftung vor der Reformation. Kommunale Selbstbestimmungschancen zwischen Religion und Recht,« in *Kommunalisierung und Christianisierung in Mitteleuropa. Voraussetzungen und Folgen der Reformation, 1400–1600*, ed. Peter Blickle and Peter Kunisch, Beiheft der Zeitschrift für historische Forschung 9 (Berlin: Duncker & Humblot, 1989), 77–112; Immacolata Saulle Hippenmeyer, *Nachbarschaft, Pfarrei und Gemeinde in Graubünden 1400–1600*, Quellen und Forschungen zur Bündner Geschichte 7–8 (Desertina: Kommissionsverlag Bündner Monatsblatt, 1997).

and parish discipline correspondingly weak. It is not surprising that urban laypeople found channels for religious expression outside of or in addition to the parish.[14] Where the inhabitants of a town or village belonged to a single parish, the distinction between parish and civic identity easily became blurred, a fact that would aid the secularization of the parish after the Reformation. The incorporation of a parish benefice into another ecclesiastical institution could lead to numerous abuses and high turnover among poorly-paid vicars, as the case of Kirchen demonstrates. In England, the large number of parishes with small populations provided greater opportunities for contact between pastor and parishioner and may have resulted in general lay satisfaction with the priest's performance, but many of them were also very poor, a situation that encouraged pluralism.[15] In geographically large or populous parishes the authority of the parish priest was diluted, for he could not carry out all of his responsibilities himself, especially in administering the sacraments, and some of those duties were delegated to priests attached to chapels. The level of pastoral care in these parishes would be the most directly impacted by the abolition of chaplaincies and chantries whose priests had served as assistants to the parish priest.

2. The Introduction of the Reformation

The initial process of Reformation in Germany and in England would also be quite different, reflecting not only the rural/urban divide but also the reception of Luther's teachings and foreshadowing the later division between Lutheran and Reformed. In central and northern Germany, the Wittenberg reformation spread through an area dominated by princely territories that were largely rural, and it came to the cities of the north later than to those in the south. Although Wittenberg itself was a city and Luther's reformation spread to other cities in Saxony and Thuringia, the Wittenberg reformation was associated especially with rural areas where literacy was extremely low and the chief agent of religious change was the parish pastor. As a theology professor and Augustinian friar, Luther prioritized the reformation of doctrine, and he was not as immediately concerned with the reform of worship or of institutional structures. As is well

---

[14] Eduard Hegel, »Städtische Pfarrseelsorge im deutschen Spätmittelalter«, *Trierer Theologische Zeitschrift* 57 (1948), 207–220.

[15] Patrick Collinson, »Economic Problems of Provincial Urban Clergy during the Reformation«, in Collinson, *The Reformation in English Towns* (see note 10), 147–58.

known, at his return to Wittenberg from the Wartburg he rolled back the changes to liturgy and poor relief introduced during his absence. Luther's conflict with Andreas Karlstadt over images and the reform of the mass reflects his conviction that right praxis was not a goal of reform in and of itself but would instead eventually follow from the preaching of right doctrine.

This attitude had significant consequences for the introduction of practical religious reforms in rural parishes. In Saxony, major changes to church structure, administration, and worship came piecemeal and at a much slower pace than in the cities in the south, and their introduction extended over a much longer period of time. Even after the introduction of the German mass in the fall of 1525, much worship in Wittenberg continued to be in Latin, reflecting the needs of students.[16] In 1522, Luther opposed the requirement of communion in both kinds on the grounds that people needed first to be taught why they should receive communion in both kinds; only in 1525 did he judge that the new type of communion had been explained sufficiently so that it could be introduced, and in the instructions for the Saxon visitation of 1528 he was willing to allow communion in one kind for those whose consciences were still weak.[17] The visitation instructions were the first systematic attempt to reform the many parishes within Electoral Saxony, a full decade after the 95 theses, and they focused chiefly on doctrine, not worship, conduct, or institutional structures.[18] These visitation articles would be imitated by other territories, but the imposition of structural religious reform on rural parishes was a slow and long-drawn out process that did not really begin until the 1530s and 1540s.[19]

---

[16] Joseph Herl, *Worship Wars in Early Lutheranism: Choir, Congregation, and Three Centuries of Conflict* (Oxford: Oxford University Press, 2004), 9–11.

[17] WA 26: 214–15.

[18] Ernst Sehling, et al., eds., *Die evangelischen Kirchenordnungen des XVI. Jahrhunderts* (Leipzig/Tübingen: Reisland/Mohr, 1902–2016), 1: 149–74.

[19] Of the nineteen major secular territories that adopted the Reformation between 1525–1568, only six did so before 1530: Electoral Saxony, Brandenburg-Ansbach, East Frisia, Anhalt-Köthen, Hesse, and Braunschweig-Lüneburg; Eike Wolgast, »Die Einführung der Reformation in den deutschen Territorien zwischen 1525/26 und 1568,« in *Der Unterricht der Visitatoren und die Durchsetzung der Reformation in Kursachsen*, ed. Joachim Bauer and Stefan Michel, Leucorea-Studien zur Geschichte der Reformation und der Lutherischen Orthodoxie 29 (Leipzig: Evangelische Verlagsanstalt, 2017), 12–33, esp. 22; an analysis of the early Saxon visitation records focusing on the clergy in Susan C. Karant-Nunn, *Luther's Pastors: The Reformation in the Ernestine Countryside*, Transactions of the American Philosophical Society 69/8 (Philadelphia: American Philosophical Society, 1980).

In the more densely populated area of south Germany and Switzerland, a radicalized Erasmian reformation (a more accurate term than »Zwinglian« reformation) spread outward from the cities in the first half of the 1520s. Erasmian reform focused on religious praxis, including criticism of both popular superstition and of clerical ignorance and immorality, cultivation of a warm inner affective piety, and emphasis on living an active Christian life in the world. These priorities prepared the ground for and shaped the reception of Luther's more radical reformation of doctrine. Justification by faith alone was only one part of the broader reformatory preaching that emphasized the notions of Christian freedom and the distinction between God's Word and manmade laws.[20] The Swiss and South German reformers went much further than Luther in advocating a reform of Christian praxis, and in this respect they were closer to Karlstadt than to Luther. Only a minority of these reformers were parish priests; they were instead preachers, chaplains, chantry priests, or members of religious orders. Correspondingly, their vision of reform encompassed all of society and was not as directly concerned with religious life at the parish level.[21]

One consequence of the radicalized Erasmianism in the cities of the south was a greater emphasis on the need to eliminate popular abuses and to introduce forms of worship that encouraged personal piety. Evangelical preachers mobilized the laity in the cities in the 1520s to demand a more rapid introduction of practical reforms than occurred in Saxony. Rather than assuming that the understanding of correct doctrine would gradually cause superstitious or erroneous practices to disappear, Swiss and south German reformers actively preached against those practices and advocated the Christian magistrate's intervention in church affairs. The removal of images from churches and the abolition of the mass, to be replaced by a vernacular preaching service, were central components of the official introduction of the reformation in the cities of the south already in the 1520s.

Reformation preaching was largely an urban phenomenon, but because people came to the towns to hear reformers preach, the evangelical message spread to villages in close proximity to the cities. It could also spread to more distant rural parishes through a preacher or pastor who had been exposed to the new ideas.[22] Evangelical teachings reached more rural par-

[20] Berndt Hamm, *Bürgertum und Glaube: Konturen der städtischen Reformation* (Göttingen: Vandenhoeck & Ruprecht, 1996).

[21] Robert W. Scribner, »Practice and Principle in the German Towns: Preachers and People,« in *Reformation Principle and Practice. Essays in Honour of A. G. Dickens*, ed. Philip N. Brooks (London: Scolar Press, 1980), 95–117; only 28% of the reformers he examined were parish priests, while 32% belonged to a religious order.

ishes in the densely settled areas of the south than in the relatively sparsely populated north, and in contrast to the north, one can speak of a »peasant reformation« in the south that reflected the priorities of the rural communes.[23] The reformatory message underwent further transformation as it was received at the village level. Although the peasants called for the preaching of God's Word, their understanding of the evangelical message was much closer to the radicalized Erasmian emphasis on Christian ethics than to Luther's teaching of justification by faith.[24] Peasant communes demanded the right to call their own pastors who would preach »the pure word of God,« which was understood as establishing norms of conduct leading to salvation. They also claimed the right to judge doctrine and to depose priests who did not carry out their pastoral responsibilities or who lived in an inappropriate way. Rather than the parish pastor's subjects, they wanted to be his employers, using their economic resources to ensure he performed his duties to their satisfaction.[25]

One feature of the German reformation in both its Lutheran and radicalized Erasmian forms is the importance of preaching as preparation for the introduction of practical reform. That preaching began and was sustained for several years before actual reforms were introduced. A second major commonality was the emphasis on remedial education for existing clergy and the need to train a new generation of evangelical pastors. The reformers fully supported the government's assumption of control over

---

[22] Franziska Conrad, *Reformation in der bäuerlichen Gesellschaft: Zur Rezeption reformatorischer Theologie in Elsass*, Veröffentlichungen des Instituts für Europäische Geschichte 116 (Stuttgart: Steiner, 1984), 49–56, 76–85; Peter Bierbrauer, »Die Prediger-Reformation im Dorf,« in *Bäuerliche Frömmigkeit und kommunale Reformation*, ed. Hans von Rütte, Itinera 8 (Basel: Schwabe, 1988), 63–84.

[23] Peter Blickle, »Communal Reformation and Peasant Piety: The Peasant Reformation and its Late Medieval Origins,« *Central European History* 20 (1987): 216–228, and in greater detail, Peter Blickle, *Communal Reformation: The Quest for Salvation in Sixteenth-Century Germany*, Studies in German History (Atlantic Highlands NJ: Humanities Press, 1992); Hans von Rütte, »Von der spätmittelalterlichen Frömmigkeit zum reformierten Glauben. Kontinuität und Bruch in der Religionspraxis der Bauern,« in von Rütte, *Bäuerliche Frömmigkeit* (see note 22), 33–44.

[24] Franziska Conrad, »Die ›bäuerliche‹ Reformation. Die Reformationstheologie auf dem Land am Beispiel des Unterelsaß«, in *Zwingli und Europa: Referate und Protokoll des Internationalen Kongresses aus Anlass des 500. Geburtstages von Huldrych Zwingli, vom 26. bis 30. März 1984*, ed. Peter Blickle, et al. (Zurich: Vandenhoeck & Ruprecht, 1985), 137–50; Conrad, *Reformation* (see note 22), 92–102, describes the peasants' position as influenced by Bucer – who was strongly influenced by Erasmus as well as by Luther.

[25] Peter Blickle, »Warum blieb die Innerschweiz katholisch?«, *Mittheilungen des Historischen Vereins des Kantons Schwyz* 86 (1994): 29–38. Blickle argues that the Reformation had little appeal in central Switzerland because many of its parishes and political communes had already established significant control over their parish priests.

church institutions, personnel and property, but they insisted that the church's wealth should be used to support the clergy, schools, and the poor.[26] Although some of the secularized church property was siphoned off for political purposes, a striking amount remained available to fund new schools and universities and to support boys who were being prepared for the ministry. The Reformation itself did not bring a wholesale turnover among parish clergy, but as the first generation of Protestant parish pastors began to die at mid-century, they were replaced by young men who had been trained to preach and teach at the schools founded within the city or territory.

In England, the process of reform at the parish level followed a pattern that contrasts strikingly with that in the Empire and Switzerland. This difference reflects the fact that the priority of the Henrician reforms was not correct doctrine or religious praxis but instead the end of papal jurisdiction and confiscation of the church's wealth. One of the most striking features of the early English reformation in comparison to developments in Germany is the lack of preaching.[27] The Henrician reforms were imposed on parishes where evangelical teachings were largely unfamiliar. In the 1530s, sympathy for Erasmian reform and receptivity to Wittenberg teachings existed chiefly within the court, at the universities, and among urban merchant communities with connections to the continent.[28] They had not yet infiltrated the parishes, especially outside of London and the more populous southeast, and the Henrician reforms did little to aid the spread of evangelical teachings. The measures introduced under Edward VI may have put greater emphasis on doctrine and the reform of religious praxis, especially as prescribed by the Book of Common Prayer, but studies highlighting the reluctant compliance with the Edwardian injunctions at the parish level suggest they were not much more effective at instilling evangelical beliefs.[29]

---

[26] Christopher Ocker, *Church Robbers and Reformers in Germany, 1525–1547*, Studies in Medieval and Reformation Traditions 114 (Leiden: Brill, 2006).

[27] Without differentiating between city-republics and rural territorial states, Eike Wolgast describes the introduction of the Reformation as going through three stages: preaching, communal reformation, and introduction territory-wide of official administrative measures; »Die Einführung der Reformation« (see note 19), 16. One could view the introduction of the Reformation in England as the inverse of this pattern, beginning with official measures imposed throughout the land and eventually resulting in the spread of Protestant preaching.

[28] Brigden, *London* (see note 8), 70–81, 106–28; Felicity Heal, *Reformation in Britain and Ireland* (Oxford: Oxford University Press, 2003), 226–36.

[29] See especially the work of Eamon Duffy, *The Stripping of the Altars: Traditional Religion in England 1400–1580* (New Haven: Yale University Press, 1992), and *The Voices of Morebath* (see note 1).

In some respects, the early Tudor reformation may even have hampered the spread of evangelical teachings at the parish level. The closure of monasteries and the dissolution of chantries dismantled the economic basis of medieval religion and made the reestablishment of Catholicism under Mary more difficult, but many former monks and chantry priests became parish priests, and those with conservative religious views could hinder the adoption of more clearly Protestant beliefs and practices. Just as importantly, the state confiscated ecclesiastical wealth for its own purposes rather than using it to support the education of a new generation of pastors. In striking contrast to German princes and magistrates, the early Tudors placed little priority on training ministers. This neglect was all the more significant because the English church faced the double handicap of a much greater number of parish positions to be filled in proportion to the population, and the existence of only two universities to train pastors. As a consequence, there was an acute shortage of preaching clergy even among the second generation of post-Reformation pastors, and the church had to rely on licensed preachers and readers.[30]

At least in theory the introduction of the Reformation in both Germany and England strengthened the centrality of the parish to religious life. Institutions and organizations that competed for lay religious expression were abolished. Parish discipline was enforced through mandates requiring attendance at worship on Sundays and reception of the sacraments within the parish, while the introduction of parish registers encouraged closer pastoral oversight over the laity.[31] The Tudor government increasingly relied on parishes to carry out more secular responsibilities, especially the provision of poor relief.[32] In Switzerland as well the parish became the basic unit of administration of the rural territories.

Despite these official efforts to shore up parish discipline, the Protestant emphasis on preaching undermined the religious significance of the urban parish. In Germany, church ordinances regularly prescribed daily sermons held in rotation among the city's parish churches and open to all

---

[30] Christopher Haigh, »The Church of England, the Catholics and the People,« in *The Impact of the English Reformation, 1500–1640*, ed. Peter Marshall (New York: St. Martin's Press, 1997), 235–56.

[31] Church wardens' records predated the Reformation and have been used extensively for studies of the medieval parish, but baptismal records were a sixteenth-century innovation in both Germany and England; on the latter, Will Coster, »Popular Religion and the Parish Register 1538–1603,« in French, *The Parish in English Life* (see note 7), 94–111.

[32] Palliser, »Introduction« (see note 4); on how the provision of poor relief worked at the parish level, see Nick Alldridge, »Loyalty and Identity in Chester Parishes 1540–1640,« also in Wright, *Parish, Church and People* (see note 4), 85–124.

inhabitants, which contributed to a further erosion of parish identity.[33] In England, too, those who attended worship in their parish church on Sunday morning could hear sermons preached elsewhere on Sunday afternoons and throughout the week, and by the end of the sixteenth century, more zealous Christians were criticized for their »sermon-gadding«.[34] The parish remained fundamental for the sacramental and liturgical aspects of Christianity, but Reformed theology undermined the salvific value of such external actions.

3. The Long-Term Impact at the Parish Level

Studies of the Reformation in both Germany and England focus on popular acceptance of reformatory teachings in the early years of the movement. For the development of a Protestant religious culture, though, generational change was arguably more important than the decision of individuals to adopt Protestant beliefs and practices.[35] The abolition of Catholic rituals marked a caesura, ending or transforming traditional religious practices and introducing new ones in both Germany and England. By 1560, those who had grown up within a unified medieval church were reaching the end of their lives. Their children grew up in a different ritual world, and their understanding of Christianity was shaped by liturgies and religious practices that had been reformed – however widely those practices varied or how »reformed« might be defined. This was especially true in England, where Catholic worship was suppressed. The creation of the Protestant parish and of Protestant lay religiosity was thus a process of generational change, and it developed most rapidly where the interests of the parish community and its pastor coincided.

As with the medieval parish, there has been a tremendous amount of research on popular religion in the wake of the Reformation over the last four decades. Unfortunately, much of the early work was placed within an interpretative framework of success or failure or it involved the use of anachronistic confessional standards (whether »Lutheran,« »Reformed,«

---

[33] See, for instance, the example of Basel, Amy Nelson Burnett, *Teaching the Reformation: Ministers and Their Message in Basel, 1529–1629*, Oxford Studies in Historical Theology (New York: Oxford University Press, 2006), 55–56.

[34] On this, and on the audience for preaching more generally, Arnold Hunt, *The Art of Hearing: English Preachers and their Audiences, 1590–1640* (Cambridge: Cambridge University Press, 2010), 187–228.

[35] For the example of Basel, Burnett, *Teaching the Reformation* (see note 33); for England, Norman Jones, *The English Reformation: Religion and Cultural Adaptation* (Oxford: Blackwell, 2002).

or simply »Protestant«) to evaluate religious changes.[36] It is important to remember that people in the sixteenth century thought of themselves not primarily as Lutherans, Reformed, Anglicans, or Protestants, but rather as Christians in a church that had been reformed, and so we need to consider their understanding of this reformmed Christianity, rather than use the confessional definitions of later historians to measure purported success or failure.[37]

The use of specific doctrines or confessional identity to evaluate the impact of the Reformation also obscures the continued differences between urban and rural religion. Differences in rituals and church decoration turned into visible markers of confessional identity, and by the 1570s they were the focus of conflict between Lutherans and Reformed, especially in the cities.[38] In rural parishes, however, confessional distinctions made relatively little headway through the sixteenth century.

The urban reformation introduced in south Germany and Switzerland would develop in two directions over the second half of the sixteenth century as differences in sacramental theology were codified in confessions and represented through ritual practice. In the city-republics of the Swiss Confederation, the radicalized Erasmian reformation evolved into state Reformed Churches united theologically by the Consensus Tigurinus and the Second Helvetic Confession. The Erasmian concern with piety and the reform of conduct led directly to the greater emphasis on church discipline that would characterize the Reformed churches. Over the course of the later sixteenth century a Reformed religious culture gradually took root in Switzerland. Because they were relatively small and had invested in pastoral training from the beginning of the Reformation, by the third quarter of the century the Swiss city-republics had a trained pastoral corps working to implant the new religious standards at the parish level. For the most part, these pastors did their jobs well, and by the early seventeenth century they could note that their parishioners had a basic knowledge of

---

[36] The »success or failure« question for the German reformation was introduced by Gerald Strauss, »Success and Failure in the German Reformation«, *Past and Present* 67 (1975): 30–63; for England it was a theme of the revisionist school most closely associated with Christopher Haigh, Eamon Duffy, and J. J. Scarisbrick; cf. Christopher W. Marsh, *Popular Religion in Sixteenth-Century England: Holding their Peace* (New York: St. Martin's Press, 1998), 12–17.

[37] David Mayes, »Triplets: The Holy Roman Empire's Birthing of Catholics, Lutherans, and Reformed in 1648,« in *Names and Naming in Early Modern Germany*, ed. Joel Harrington and Marjorie E. Plummer (New York: Berghahn, forthcoming).

[38] Bodo Nischan, »Ritual and Protestant Identity in Late Reformation Germany,« in *Protestant History and Identity in Sixteenth-Century Europe*, ed. Bruce Gordon (Aldershot: Ashgate, 1996), 142–58.

the catechism, a Reformed understanding of the sacraments, and could »console themselves« on their deathbeds.[39] Characteristic of this Reformed confessionalization was the establishment of disciplinary structures to oversee morals. Whether regarded as ecclesiastical or secular institutions, the morals courts and consistories of Reformed Switzerland helped preserve social harmony and enforce communal morality.[40]

The cities within the Empire moved in a different direction. Under the protection of the Peace of Augsburg, they identified themselves as »churches of the Augsburg Confession.« As successive generations of their pastors were trained in Wittenberg and Tübingen, a Lutheran confessional culture was established in those cities that had formerly been associated with the Swiss. This was not necessarily a smooth transition, and it could

[39] André Holenstein, »Reformierte Konfessionalisierung und bernischer Terrritorialstaat,« in *Territorialstaat und Calvinismus*, ed. Meinrad Schaab, Veröffentlichungen der Kommission für geschichtliche Landeskunde in Baden Württemberg B/127 (Stuttgart: Kohlhammer, 1993), 5–33; Emidio Campi, »Zurich,« in *Companion to the Swiss Reformation*, ed. Amy Nelson Burnett and Emidio Campi, Brill's Companions to the Christian Tradition 72 (Leiden: Brill, 2016), 59–125. The case of Basel would be complicated by its efforts to mediate between the developing confessions; Amy Nelson Burnett, »Basel's Long Reformation: Church Ordinances and the Shaping of Religious Culture in the Sixteenth Century,« *Zwingliana* 35 (2008): 145–59. A similar development led to a Lutheran religious culture in the rural parishes of Strasbourg; James M. Kittelson, »Successes and Failures in the German Reformation: The Report from Strasbourg,« *Archiv für Reformationsgeschichte* 73 (1982): 153–174; James M. Kittelson, »Visitations and Popular Religious Culture: Further Reports from Strasbourg,« in *Pietas et Societas: New Trends in Reformation Social History. Essays in Memory of Harold J. Grimm*, ed. Kyle C. Sessions and Phillip N. Bebb, Sixteenth Century Essays and Studies 4 (Kirksville, Mo.: Sixteenth Century Journal Publishers, 1985), 89–102. The positive reports Kittelson finds in visitation records from the end of the century are in striking contrast to those from Strasbourg's rural parishes examined by Franziska Conrad from the 1530s and 1540s; *Reformation* (see note 22), 168–75. Scott Dixon also finds complaints of poor sermon attendance and lack of knowledge of the catechism in Brandenburg-Ansbach, C. Scott Dixon, *The Reformation and Rural Society: The Parishes of Brandenburg-Ansbach-Kulmbach, 1528–1603*, Cambridge Studies in Early Modern History (Cambridge: Cambridge University Press, 1996), 143–202; his discussion of the sacraments suffers from failure to recognize the Lutheran understanding of the relationship between spiritual and material things, including the sacraments.

[40] See especially the work of Heinrich R. Schmidt, »Die Christianisierung des Sozialverhaltens als permanente Reformation. Aus der Praxis reformierter Sittengerichte in der Schweiz während der frühen Neuzeit,« in *Kommunalisierung und Christianisierung in Mitteleuropa. Voraussetzungen und Folgen der Reformation, 1400–1600*, ed. Peter Blickle and Johannes Kunisch, Beiheft der Zeitschrift für historische Forschung 9 (Berlin: Duncker & Humblot, 1989), 113–163; Heinrich Richard Schmidt, »Pazifizierung des Dorfes – Struktur und Wandel von Nachbarschaftskonflikten vor Berner Sittengerichten 1570–1800,« in *Kirchenzucht und Sozialdisziplinierung im frühneuzeitlichen Europe (mit einer Auswahlbibliographie)*, ed. Heinz Schilling, Zeitschrift für historische Forschung Beiheft 16 (Berlin: Duncker & Humblot, 1994), 91–128; Heinrich R. Schmidt, *Dorf und Religion: Reformierte Sittenzucht in Berner Landgemeinden der frühen Neuzeit* (Stuttgart: Fischer, 1995).

stretch out over two or three generations, as the case of Strasbourg illustrates.[41] But the doctrinal conflicts between and within confessions that occurred in these cities through the third quarter of the sixteenth century fostered greater awareness of confessional difference and so ultimately could be seen as aiding the development of confessional identity.[42]

The success of this cultural transformation can be measured by popular response to the so-called »Second Reformation,« where a prince imposed the Reformed faith on his previously Lutheran territory. This process involved the removal of images from churches, changes to the liturgies for baptism and the Lord's Supper, and strengthened organs for the exercise of church discipline. The strongest opposition to these measures occurred in cities, which suggests that their inhabitants had come to see themselves as Lutheran.[43] Reaction in rural areas tended to be more muted, however, reflecting weaker loyalty to specifically Lutheran doctrines and rituals.

In fact, the religious culture of many rural parishes differed from the more confessionalized Christianity of the cities. In his study of the rural parishes of Upper Hesse through the later sixteenth and into the seventeenth century, David Mayes has described an understanding of Christianity characterized by an emphasis on the collective welfare of the community, the maintenance of social harmony and the social order, and communal control over the pastor intended to ensure that he fulfilled his religious duties and lived in an appropriate manner.[44] This description of rural communal Christianity bears an obvious resemblance to the communalized religion of the late Middle Ages and the goals of the »peasant reformation« of the early 1520s.

---

[41] Lorna Jane Abray, *The People's Reformation: Magistrates, Clergy, and Commons in Strasbourg, 1500–1598* (Ithaca: Cornell University Press, 1985); James M. Kittelson, *Toward an Established Church: Strasbourg from 1500 to the Dawn of the Seventeenth Century*, Veröffentlichungen des Instituts für Europäische Geschichte Mainz 182 (Mainz: von Zabern, 2000).

[42] On the frequency of conflict (which was not necessarily confessional) among city pastors, Ernst Riegg, *Konfliktbereitschaft und Mobilität. Die protestantischen Geistlichen zwölf süddeutscher Reichsstädte zwischen Passauer Vertrag und Restitutionsedikt*, Schriften zur südwestdeutschen Landeskunde 43 (Leinfelden: DRW Verlag, 2002), 299–315. On the importance of inner-confessional conflict for developing confessional identity among the laity, Robert J. Christman, »>I can indeed respond‹: Lay Confessions of Faith in Late Sixteenth-Century Central Germany,« *Sixteenth Century Journal* 39 (2008): 1003–1019.

[43] See especially Bodo Nischan, *Prince, People and Confession: The Second Reformation in Brandenburg* (Philadelphia: University of Pennsylvania Press, 1994), 185–203; Mayes, *Communal Reformation* (see note 12), 94–104, and the literature cited there.

[44] For this characterization of rural Christianity, Mayes, *Communal Christianity* (see note 12), 30–42.

Mayes refers to this communal Christianity in Upper Hesse as aconfessional, but it departed in significant ways from Roman Catholicism in its understanding of the sacraments and of the link between the living and dead, whether the saints in heaven or family and friends in purgatory. Where late medieval peasants emphasized the parish priest's responsibility to administer the sacraments to them, the parishioners in Upper Hesse emphasized the ability of the pastor to preach and teach God's Word.[45] This communal Christianity did not emphasize doctrinal technicalities, but it fit more easily with Reformed than with Lutheran emphases. Following both late medieval and Reformed practice, parishioners understood participation in communion as an outward testimony of belonging to the community and attestation of social peace, rather than as assurance to individual sinners of their forgiveness.[46] The Reformed emphasis on church discipline could also be brought into harmony with the desire to uphold communal standards of behavior. This meant that the imposition of the Reformed faith in Hesse in 1605 went much more smoothly in rural parishes than in the city of Marburg.[47]

The situation in England was somewhat different because there was no division into rival confessions. Instead controversy concerned the rejection of practices seen as »popish« and the depth of commitment to specifically Reformed doctrines such as predestination. On this basis, people were divided between the more zealous minority of the »godly« and the majority comprised of those labeled »parish Anglicans« or »prayer book Christians« by modern historians.[48] More recently Christopher Haigh has distinguished between »godly zealots« and the lazy, indifferent, or skeptical and provided examples drawn from court records to illustrate each category.[49] Alec Ryrie has questioned this distinction and stressed instead the existence of a more broad-based religious culture that fostered

---

[45] Mayes, *Communal Christianity* (see note 12), 42.

[46] John Bossy, »The Mass as a Social Institution, 1200–1700,« *Past and Present* 100 (1983): 29–61; Amy Nelson Burnett, »The Social History of Communion and the Reformation of the Eucharist,« *Past and Present* 211 (2011): 77–119; cf. Heinrich Richard Schmidt, »Das Abendmahl als soziales Sakrament,« in *Soziale Beziehungen im Spätmittelalter und in der frühen Neuzeit*, ed. Hans-Jörg Gilomen, et al., Traverse. Zeitschrift für Geschichte 9/2 (Zurich: Chronos, 2002), 79–93.

[47] Mayes, *Communal Reformation* (see note 12), 104–160, comparing the reaction in Marburg and in the rural parishes of Upper Hesse to Duke Moritz's *Verbesserungspunkte*.

[48] Cf the overview of the debate in Judith D. Maltby, *Prayer Book and People in Elizabethan and early Stuart England* (New York: Cambridge University Press, 1998), 1–19.

[49] Christopher Haigh, *The Plain Man's Pathways to Heaven: Kinds of Christianity in Post-Reformation England, 1570–1640* (New York: Oxford University Press, 2007).

a specific mindset deepened by reading and private prayer that shaped one's view of life and the world.[50] His approach prioritizes the experiences of the literate individual, and in that sense it applies most fully to city dwellers. Moreover, Ryrie says virtually nothing about the sacraments and so downplays what was still one of the chief aspects of parish religion.

There is evidence, however, for the survival of a more communal understanding of Christianity in England, especially in rural parishes. Particularly important was the fact that parishioners were no longer the priest's subjects; instead, he was their minister, and they now had some recourse if he did not fulfill his pastoral duties. Studies of church court records suggest that parishioners had specific expectations concerning their pastor's responsibilities, whether that meant reading the prayer book service as he was required to do or using his preaching to aid social harmony rather than to undermine it. Like their German counterparts, English parishioners also saw participation in the Lord's Supper as testifying to being at peace with each another, and laypeople were particularly aware of the need to reconcile with their neighbors during Lent, in preparation for Easter communion.[51]

These examples suggest that we cannot assess the impact of the Reformation by looking at how well people in a society that was still largely illiterate understood doctrinal fine points. Over the course of the later sixteenth century, rural parishioners in both Germany and England were able to take impulses coming from the Reformation and adapt them to their own priorities and understanding of Christianity. Central to this process was the role of the parish pastor, especially in rural parishes where parishioners had more limited access to alternative forms of belief and practice. As the sacraments lost their central role in the process of salvation, especially within the Reformed tradition, the pastor's role as preacher and teacher became more important. He could have a significant long-term impact on parish religion, if he fitted his language and preaching style to the expectations of his hearers.[52] He also had some leeway to introduce new ideas and values, as long as he remained within the constraints imposed by his parishioners' expectations and did not cause undue strife

---

[50] Alec Ryrie, *Being Protestant in Reformation Britain* (Oxford: Oxford University Press, 2013).

[51] Christopher Haigh, »The Clergy and Parish Discipline in England, 1570–1640,« in *The impact of the European Reformation: Princes, Clergy and People*, ed. Bridget Heal and Ole Peter Grell, St. Andrews Studies in Reformation History (Aldershot: Ashgate, 2008), 125–41; Maltby, *Prayer Book* (see note 48), 31–82; Arnold Hunt, »The Lord's Supper in Early Modern England,« *Past and Present* 161 (1998), 39–83.

[52] Hunt, *The Art of Hearing* (see note 34), 229–91.

within the community.[53] The pastor's catechization of children was intended to help them understand sermons and public worship services, and it may ultimately have been more effective for the shaping of religious culture at the parish level than were the many sermons he delivered to adults.[54]

It is tempting to conclude that the high population density of Germany's late medieval parishes, with all of the negative implications this had for the provision of pastoral care, was an important precondition for the eager reception of the Reformation. England's denser network of parishes proved more successful at providing pastoral care in the late Middle Ages. The parishioners of Morebath were satisfied with their parish priest, but those of Kirchen suffered from both high turnover and neglect from the priests responsible for providing pastoral care. In the long run, though, the differences between Germany and England in parish population density were less significant, because Protestantism shifted the emphasis of pastoral care away from the sacraments and towards preaching. More important for the shaping of Protestant religious culture in both areas was the general divide between urban and rural Christianity that also went back to the later Middle Ages. City dwellers were more open to the preaching of the reformatory message, although it took much longer for sermons to become an important component of English Protestantism. The collective aspects of early modern Christianity remained stronger in rural parishes, and rural Christians adapted Protestant emphases to fit their own priorities, especially in enforcing social discipline and in supervising the parish pastor. This more communal understanding of Christianity persisted through the sixteenth century as a central element of lay religious life in rural areas in both Germany and England.

---

[53] Perhaps the most important of the new ideas and values was the appearance of anti-papal rhetoric at those times and places where the Roman church was perceived to be a threat, whether in England at the time of the Spanish Armada or in those Protestant German and Swiss territories that had Catholic neighbors.

[54] Ian Green, *The Christian's ABC: Catechism and Catechizing in England c. 1530–1740* (New York: Oxford University Press, 1996), 29–32, 563; Lee Palmer Wandel, *Reading Catechisms, Teaching Religion*, Brill's Studies in Intellectual History (Leiden: Brill, 2016).

Der neue Typ von Pfarrer

Andreas Stegmann

Karl-Heinrich Lütcke, von 1990 bis 2005
Propst der Evangelischen Kirche in
Berlin-Brandenburg, zum achtzigsten
Geburtstag am 20. Februar 2020

Die Veränderungen, die die Reformation für die Geistlichkeit mit sich brachte, werden anschaulich in einer Episode aus der Stadt Frankfurt an der Oder.[1] Hier arbeitete Mitte der 1530er Jahre die Tochter eines Binnenfischers in einem Bürgerhaushalt als Magd. Diese Getrud Matzke fiel auf, weil sie scheinbar aus dem Nichts Geldstücke in die Hände bekam und diese anschließend zerkaute und verschluckte. Nachts wurde sie von Alpträumen geplagt und tagsüber redete sie manchmal in dem ihr unbekannten Hochdeutsch. Für die Frankfurter war klar: Die Frau war vom Teufel besessen und musste von diesem bösen Geist befreit werden. Man holte einen Priester, der es mit den üblichen exorzistischen Handlungen und Formeln versuchte, aber keinen Erfolg hatte. In der Stadt wirkte aber auch schon der evangelische Prediger Andreas Ebert (1497–1557)[2], der den Fall Martin Luther vorlegte und die von diesem vorgeschlagenen Gegenmittel versuchte: nämlich für die Frau zu beten und mit ihr den Gottesdienst zu besuchen, um dort die Predigt zu hören – und damit Erfolg hatte. Der Frankfurter Geldteufel, der sich von geweihten Kräutern, Wasser und Rettich und den wortgewaltigen Beschwörungen des papstkirch-

---

[1] Die folgende Darstellung folgt einer 1538 in Wittenberg gedruckten Flugschrift: Wunderliche Zeitung von einem GeldTeuffel / ein selzame / vngleubliche / doch warhafftige geschicht. Zu Franckfurt an der Oder geschehen / vnd vrkundlich ausgangen, o.O. o.J. (VD16 E 173). Vgl. den Briefwechsel zwischen Luther und Ebert (WA.Br 7,482–487, 489f., Nr. 3055f.) sowie zwei spätere Darstellungen, die weitere Quellen verarbeiten: Christoph Stummel, Kurtzer Vnterricht von Wunderwercken / so in Göttlicher Schrifft vnd andern Historien beschrieben sind, Frankfurt (Oder) 1567 (VD16 S 9835), X 1ʳ–Y 1ᵛ; Andreas Engel, WiderNatur vnd Wunderbuch. Darin so wol in gemein von Wunderwercken deß Himmels / Luffts / Wassers vnd Erden / als insonderheit von allen widernatürlichen wunderlichen Geschichten grössern theils Europae, fürnemlich der Churfürstlichen Brandenburgischen Marck / vom Jahr 490. biß auff 1597. ablauffendes Jahr beschehen / gehandelt wird, Frankfurt a. M. 1597 (VD16 E 1193), 213–229.
[2] Höhle, Universität und Reformation (s. Anm. 28), 422–429.

lichen Exorzisten nicht hatte beeindrucken lassen, wich dem Gebet und
der Verkündigung des reformatorischen Predigers:

>>Als sie aber jnn die predigt gefürt / hat der Teuffel durch sie / mich [sc. Ebert]
vnter der predigt / offtmals lügen gestrafft. Vnd wenn ich dem Teufel gebot er solt
schwiegen / da hat sie geschwiegen / vnd ist also [...] durch das gemein gebet / jr
geholffen / nemlich das sie der Teuffel verlassen hat.<<[3]

Andreas Ebert, der sich selbst als >>Ecclesiastes Francofordianus<< bezeichnete[4], war einer der ersten, die im Kurfürstentum Brandenburg den neuen
Typ des Pfarrers repräsentierten: Noch vor der offiziellen Einführung der
Reformation war er von Bürgern damit betraut worden, das Evangelium
zu predigen und die Gemeindeglieder geistlich zu unterstützen – als Verkündiger des befreienden Gottesworts. Die Amtsträger der Papstkirche
dagegen standen auf verlorenem Posten: Als Vertreter der papstkirchlichen
Hierarchie hatten sie die Kirchengemeinde zu leiten und die Sakramente
zu feiern – allerdings ohne von den Menschen noch als Hilfe zur Bewäl-
tigung des Lebens in der Welt und vor Gott wahrgenommen zu werden.

Wenn es im Folgenden darum geht, die Ausbildung des neuen Typs von
Pfarrer im 16. Jahrhundert nachzuzeichnen, dann ist das angesichts der
Überfülle dazu vorliegender Forschungsliteratur nur vertretbar, wenn wenigstens teilweise Neues geboten wird. Das Neue der folgenden Ausführungen betrifft zweierlei: zum einen wird als Beispiel für die deutsche
Reformation das Kurfürstentum Brandenburg gewählt, dessen Reformationsgeschichte allzu wenig Beachtung in der Forschung findet, obwohl
während der Regierungszeit Joachims II. (1535–1571) in der Mark die für
das Luthertum charakteristischen Verhältnisse in geradezu idealtypischer
Weise geschaffen wurden,[5] zum anderen erlaubt es der Vergleich zwischen
deutscher und englischer Reformation, die jeweiligen Eigenarten bei der
Transformation der Geistlichkeit klarer zu konturieren, als das bisher geschehen ist.[6] Der Aufsatz gliedert sich in zwei Hauptteile, deren erster die

---

[3] Wunderliche Zeitung (s. Anm. 1), A 3ʳ. Vgl. zu Eberts Frankfurter Predigttätigkeit:
GOTTHARD KEMMETHER, Ein Predigtkonzept von 1539 – Autograph von Andreas
Ebert, dem ersten evangelischen Prediger in Frankfurt an der Oder? (in: JBBKG 71,
2017, 200–214).

[4] WA.Br 7,486.

[5] Zur Geschichte der brandenburgischen Reformation: ANDREAS STEGMANN, Die
Reformation in der Mark Brandenburg, Leipzig 2017; DERS., Deutung und Bedeutung
der brandenburgischen Reformation (in: Reformation in Brandenburg. Verlauf, Akteure,
Deutungen, hg. v. Frank Göse, Berlin 2017, 63–92); DERS., Die Kirchenpolitik des brandenburgischen Kurfürsten Joachim II. (in: JBBKG 71, 2017, 42–148).

[6] Indem für das deutsche Luthertum Brandenburg als Beispiel gewählt wird, fällt
auch Licht auf die Gemeinsamkeiten und Unterschiede zwischen brandenburgischer
und englischer Reformation. Die Behauptung der älteren Forschung, dass sich beide
Reformationen als Mittelweg zwischen den entstehenden Konfessionen verstehen lassen

grundlegenden Gemeinsamkeiten zwischen deutscher und englischer Reformation herausarbeitet und dabei vor allem auf das deutsche Luthertum blickt, während der zweite die Unterschiede erörtert und dabei den Schwerpunkt auf die Entwicklung in England legt.[7] Das Thema ist dabei der neue *Typ* von Pfarrer, also das Ideal des kirchlichen Amts, wie es in den frühen Programmtexten der Reformation formuliert wurde und nach und nach in der kirchlichen Wirklichkeit Gestalt gewann. Dabei ist zu beachten, dass die Wirklichkeit dem Ideal erst allmählich zu entsprechen begann und beides niemals vollständig zur Deckung kam, zumal sich die Ansprüche stets weiterentwickelten, so dass die Wirklichkeit ihnen notwendigerweise hinterherhinkte.

1. Die grundlegenden Gemeinsamkeiten am Beispiel des deutschen Luthertums

Die Entstehung und Entwicklung des neuen Typs von Pfarrer im Wirkungsbereich der Wittenberger Reformation ist ein in der Forschung vielbehandeltes Thema.[8] Auch für das Kurfürstentum Brandenburg liegt eine

---

und sie darum einander innerlich verwandt sind (JOHANN GUSTAV DROYSEN, Geschichte der Preußischen Politik, Teil 2, Abt. 2, Leipzig [2]1870, 188; EMIL SEHLING, Einleitung, in: EKO 3, 1909, 3–27, hier: 18), lässt sich angesichts des *paradigm shift* der neueren Forschung nicht halten (DEWEY D. WALLACE, Via media? A paradigm shift, in: AEH 72, 2003, 2–21; ANDREAS STEGMANN, Die »christliche Reformation« im Kurfürstentum Brandenburg. Mittelweg zwischen Rom und Wittenberg oder lutherische Reformation?, in: Theologische Literaturzeitung 141, 2016, 578–591) und wird auch durch diesen Aufsatz widerlegt.

[7] Die Entwicklungen im oberdeutsch-schweizerischen Raum sowie im Wirkungsbereich der Genfer Reformation, die grundsätzlich denen im Folgenden dargestellten ähneln, werden dabei nur punktuell verglichen, und auch die Entwicklung in Schottland und Irland, wo der neue Typus von Pfarrer in Anlehnung entweder an den kontinentalen Calvinismus oder die englische Staatskirche erst allmählich Gestalt gewann, bleibt außen vor.

[8] Wichtige Überblicksdarstellungen sind: PAUL DREWS, Der evangelische Geistliche in der deutschen Vergangenheit, Jena [2]1924, 7–72; LUISE SCHORN-SCHÜTTE, The Christian clergy in the Early Modern Holy Roman Empire: A comparative study (SCJ 29, 1998, 717–731); DIES., Priest, preacher, pastor: Research on clerical office in early modern Europe (Central European History 33, 2000, 1–39); DIES., The ›New Clergies‹ in Europe: Protestant pastors and catholic reform clergy after the Reformation (in: The Impact of the European Reformation: Princes, clergy and people, hg. v. Bridget Heal u. Ole Peter Grell, Aldershot u. Burlington 2008, 103–124); WOLFGANG E. J. WEBER, Luthers bleiche Erben. Kulturgeschichte der evangelischen Geistlichkeit des 17. Jahrhunderts, Berlin u. Boston 2017 (Weber berücksichtigt auch breit das 16. Jahrhundert; die Stärke – und zugleich Schwäche – seiner Darstellung ist die Fokussierung auf die im Druck erschienene pastoraltheologische Literatur der frühen Neuzeit, die die Wirklichkeit des pastoralen Diensts nur indirekt erschließen hilft). – Wichtige regionale Studien

Studie vor, die eine nützliche Auswertung der vorhandenen gedruckten Quellen bietet, allerdings durch weitere handschriftliche oder gedruckte Materialien ergänzt werden muss.[9] Die vorliegende Forschung ist sich durchweg einig, dass der neue Typ von Pfarrer vor allem durch zweierlei charakterisiert ist: der evangelische Pfarrer ist *Prediger* und er ist *Bürger*. Was das heißt, soll im Folgenden am Beispiel der Mark Brandenburg entfaltet werden.

---

sind: BERNHARD VOGLER, Le clergé protestant rhénan au siècle de la réforme (1555–1619), Paris 1976 (vgl. von DEMS., Recrutement et carrière des pasteurs strasbourgeois au XVIe siècle, in: Revue d'histoire et de philosophie religieuses 48, 1968, 151–174); SUSAN C. KARANT-NUNN, Luther's Pastors. The Reformation in the Ernestine Countryside, Philadelphia 1979; LUISE SCHORN-SCHÜTTE, Evangelische Geistlichkeit in der Frühneuzeit. Deren Anteil an der Entfaltung frühmoderner Staatlichkeit und Gesellschaft. Dargestellt am Beispiel des Fürstentums Braunschweig-Wolfenbüttel, der Landgrafschaft Hessen-Kassel und der Stadt Braunschweig, Heidelberg 1996; C. SCOTT DIXON, The Reformation and rural society. The parishes of Brandenburg-Ansbach-Kulmbach, 1528–1603, Cambridge 1996 (vgl. von DEMS., Rural resistance, the Lutheran pastor, and the territorial church in Brandenburg Ansbach-Kulmbach, 1529–1603, in: The reformation of the parishes. The ministry and the Reformation in town and country, hg. v. Andrew Pettegree, Manchester u. New York 1993, 85–112); ERNST RIEGG, Konfliktbereitschaft und Mobilität. Die protestantischen Geistlichen zwölf süddeutscher Reichsstädte zwischen Passauer Vertrag und Restitutionsedikt, Leinfelden-Echterdingen 2002; LOTHAR BERNDORFF, Die Prediger der Grafschaft Mansfeld. Eine Untersuchung zum geistlichen Sonderbewusstsein in der zweiten Hälfte des 16. Jahrhunderts, Potsdam 2010; MACIEJ PTASZYŃSKI, »Beruf und Berufung«. Die evangelische Geistlichkeit und die Konfessionsbildung in den Herzogtümern Pommern, 1560–1618, Göttingen u. Bristol 2017. – Einen instruktiven Überblick zur lutherischen Amtstheologie des 16. und 17. Jahrhunderts gibt JÖRG BAUR, Das kirchliche Amt im Protestantismus. Skizzen und Reflexionen (Das Amt im ökumenischen Kontext, hg. v. Jörg Baur, Stuttgart 1980, 103–138).

[9] BEATE FRÖHNER, Der evangelische Pfarrstand in der Mark Brandenburg 1540–1600 (Wichmann-Jahrbuch 19/20, 1965/66, 5–46). Fröhner wertet die gedruckten Kirchenordnungen und die im Druck verfügbaren Visitationsabschiede des 16. Jahrhunderts aus und verarbeitet das Material zu einer systematisch geordneten Darstellung, die alle wichtigen Aspekte des Pfarramts behandelt. Eine andere Quellengrundlage – nämlich die von Burkhard v. Bonin herausgegebenen *Entscheidungen des Cöllnischen Konsistoriums 1541–1704. Nach der Sammlung des Konsistorialrats und Propstes D. Franz Julius Lütkens* (Weimar 1926), die vor allem für das 17. und 18. Jahrhundert überliefert sind und aufgrund dessen einen anderen zeitlichen Fokus hat die gleichwohl auch für das Reformationsjahrhundert relevante Darstellung von HERMANN WERDERMANN, Pfarrerstand und Pfarramt im Zeitalter der Orthodoxie in der Mark Brandenburg (JBrKG 23, 1928, 53–133; Separatveröffentlichung unter demselben Titel: Berlin 1929; die Fassung im JBrKG ist partiell ausführlicher). Die Zahl von Gemeinden und Pfarrstellen in der Mark des 16. Jahrhunderts lässt sich nur schätzen. Wenn in der zweiten Hälfte des 18. Jahrhunderts 80 Städte und 1971 Dörfer sowie 858 lutherische Pfarrer gezählt werden (ANTON FRIEDRICH BÜSCHING, Lutherisch-geistliche Inspectionen in der Churmark, in: Magazin für die neue Historie und Geographie 13, 1779, 365–372), dann dürfte das den Verhältnissen im 16. Jahrhundert entsprechen, wobei die landeshistorische Forschung für das Reformationsjahrhundert die Zahl der Städte etwas höher und die Zahl der Dörfer etwas niedriger ansetzt und die Zahl der Geistlichen etwas höher gelegen haben dürfte.

1.1. Der Pfarrer als Prediger

Dass das Pfarramt für die Wittenberger Reformation vor allem als Verkündigungsamt definiert und dementsprechend auszufüllen war, ergibt sich aus Luthers rechtfertigungstheologischer Grundeinsicht, dass der Glaube aus der Predigt kommt (Röm. 10,17).[10] Das den Glauben schaffende Christuszeugnis konnte für den Wittenberger Reformator auf unterschiedliche Weisen vermittelt werden, und die frühe reformatorische Bewegung zeigt eine erstaunliche mediale Vielfalt.[11] Zentral war dabei von Anfang an die Predigt, die im späten Mittelalter stark an Bedeutung gewonnen hatte[12] und von der Reformation zum virtuos gehandhabten Propagandainstrument gemacht und ins Zentrum kirchlichen Handelns und christlicher Frömmigkeit gerückt wurde.[13] Das belegt eindrücklich die älteste erhaltene reformatorische Predigt aus dem Kurfürstentum Brandenburg: Nachdem der sächsische Kurfürst 1522 die Mendikanten der Stadt Wittenberg verwiesen hatte, begab sich der gerade zum Doktor der Theologie promovierte Lutherschüler Johannes Briesmann (1488–1549), der *als Franziskaner* für die Reformation wirken und darum sein Ordensgewand nicht ablegen wollte, in seinen Heimatkonvent Cottbus.[14] In der nieder-

---

[10] Programmatisch formuliert hat Luther den Zusammenhang von Wort und Glaube etwa in seiner 1520 erschienenen Freiheitsschrift (WA 7,12–73). Zu Luthers aus diesem Grundgedanken entwickelten Vorstellungen vom Verkündigungsamt und seiner Organisationsform: REINHARD SCHWARZ, Martin Luther. Lehrer der christlichen Religion, Tübingen 2015, Kap. 9.3–4. Einen handbuchartigen Überblick mit Hinweis auf die Literatur bis Mitte der 1990er Jahre bietet: BERNHARD LOHSE, Luthers Theologie in ihrer historischen Entwicklung und ihrem systematischen Zusammenhang, Göttingen 1995, 304–316. Die wichtigste neuere Studie zum Thema ist: CHRISTOPHER VOIGT-GOY, Potestas und ministerium publicum. Eine Studie zur Amtstheologie im Mittelalter und bei Martin Luther, Tübingen 2014.

[11] THOMAS KAUFMANN, Geschichte der Reformation, Frankfurt a. M. u. Leipzig 2009, Teil II, passim.

[12] ISNARD W. FRANK, Art. Predigt VI. Mittelalter (in: TRE 27, 1997, 248–262).

[13] ALBRECHT BEUTEL, Art. Predigt VIII. Evangelische Predigt vom 16. bis 18. Jahrhundert (a.a.O., 296–311); DERS., Kommunikation des Evangeliums. Die Predigt als zentrales theologisches Vermittlungsmedium in der Frühen Neuzeit (in: Kommunikation und Transfer im Christentum der frühen Neuzeit, hg. v. Irene Dingel u. Wolf-Friedrich Schäufele, Mainz 2007, 3–15).

[14] Zu Briesmanns Person und Wirken: PAUL TSCHACKERT, Einleitung (in: Urkundenbuch zur Reformationsgeschichte des Herzogthums Preußen, hg. v. Paul Tschackert, Bd. 1, Leipzig 1890, hier: 41–48); ROBERT STUPPERICH, Johann Briesmanns reformatorische Anfänge (JBrKG 34, 1939, 3–21); BERND MOELLER, Karl Stackmann, Städtische Predigt in der Frühzeit der Reformation. Eine Untersuchung deutscher Flugschriften der Jahre 1522 bis 1529, Göttingen 1996, 31–36. Mit Vorsicht zu benutzen ist die neueste Darstellung: HEINZ-DIETER HEIMANN, Dr. Johannes Briesmann (1488–1549): Barfüsser und gewesener Mönch. Hybride Konfessionskultur im Selbstzeugnis eines franziskanischen Gelehrten und Anhängers Martin Luthers (in: Hybride Identitäten in den preußisch-polnischen Stadtkulturen der Aufklärung. Studien zur Aufklärungsdiffusion zwischen

lausitzischen Metropole, die seit dem 15. Jahrhundert unter der Herrschaft der brandenburgischen Hohenzollern stand, predigte er im Sinne der Reformation und musste nach Konflikten mit der geistlichen und weltlichen Obrigkeit die Stadt verlassen. Was Briesmann in Cottbus predigte, fasste er nach seiner Vertreibung in einer Flugschrift zusammen, die seinen zurückgebliebenen Anhängern seine Predigten in Erinnerung halten sollte.[15] Er beschwört sie, »dem barmhertzigen gott / der seyn thewr werdes wort / ynn dießen letzten ferlichen tagen vnd grewlichen tzeytten / auch vnter euch hatt lassen predigen«, dankbar zu sein und sich nicht »von dem rechten wege des Euangelions« abwenden zu lassen.[16] Dieses Evangelium, das Briesmann in Cottbus verkündet hat, beinhaltet vor allem den Glauben an Christus und die Liebe zum Nächsten, was Briesmann beides in enger Anlehnung an Luthers Freiheitsschrift entfaltet, etwa wenn er Joh. 10 auslegt:

»Der eyngang in Christum / ist der glawb / der dyr schenckt die gerechtickeytt Christi / durch wilche du gott gnugthunde / gerecht bist / vnnd darffest furt keyner werck / durch wilche du dyr die gerechtickeyt bereytest.

Der außgang aber / ist die lieb / die dich (syntemal du mit der gerechtickeyt Christi bekleydet bist) widderumb außteylet ynn die dienste des nehsten / vnnd ynn die vbung deynes eygenen leybes / tzu hülff tzukommen der frembden dürfftickeytt vnnd armutt / auff das auch sie durch dich getzogen / mit dyr eyngehen ynn Christum.

Denn gleycherweyß als Christus ist außgangen von gott / vnnd hatt vns an sich getzogen / vnd ynn all seynem leben nicht gesuchet / das seyne / ßondern das vnßere. Alßo auch widerumb / ßo wyr seyn eyngangen durch den glawben / müsse wyr außgehen an vns tzunehmen die andern / vnd nichts anders suchen / denn alleyn das wyr allen dienende / vill mit vns seligen«.[17]

Mit dieser Predigt fand Briesmann in Cottbus Gehör und provozierte die Gegenwehr der Papstkirche. Kam seine Tätigkeit dort auch bald zu einem unfreiwilligen Ende, so wirkte sie durch die Flugschrift weiter und fand in seinem weiteren Wirken ihre konsequente Umsetzung: Über Wittenberg

---

Stadt und Land, zur Identitätsbildung und zum Kulturaustausch in regionalen und internationalen Kommunikationsnetzwerken, hg. v. Joanna Kodzik u. Włodzimierz Zientara, Bremen 2016, 173–187).

[15] Unterricht vnd ermanung Doct. Johannis Briesmans / Barfusser Ordens / an die Christlich gemeyn zu Cottbus, Anno. M.D.XXiij., o.O. [Wittenberg] 1523 (VD16 B 8307).

[16] A.a.O., A 3ᵛ.

[17] A.a.O., B 2ᵛ. Dass Briesmanns frühe Veröffentlichungen Zeugnisse der Rezeption von Luthers Freiheitsschrift sind, zeigen die ebenfalls 1523 entstandenen *Flosculi*, die die christologische begründete Zweiheit von Rechtfertigungsglaube und Nächstenliebe ausdrücklich mit der *christlichen Freiheit* in Verbindung bringen (Flosculi de homine interiore et exteriore, fide et operibus, die erste grundlegende Reformationsschrift aus dem Ordenslande Preußen vom Jahre 1523, hg. v. Paul Tschackert, Gotha 1887, 9–15).

ging Briesmann den Weg ins Baltikum, wo er zum Reformator Preußens wurde. Was Briesmann hier unter den erschwerten Bedingungen der abendländischen Peripherie aufbaute, hatte sein Vorbild in den seit den 1520er Jahren in den Kernlanden der deutschen Reformation geschaffenen Strukturen: Die für die Reformation zentrale Predigt bedurfte eines institutionellen Rahmens, inhaltlicher Normierung und kompetenter Prediger. So sehr das allgemeine Priestertum geschätzt und dem einzelnen Christen Recht und Pflicht zur Verkündigung im persönlichen Nahbereich zugesprochen wurde, so wenig konnte und wollte man auf ein geordnetes kirchliches Amt verzichten.

Entscheidend für die Ausformung dieses kirchlichen Amts in der Wittenberger Reformation wurde die *necessaria coniunctio scholarum cum ministerio evangelii*. Die von Melanchthon stammende Formel der »necessaria coniunctio«[18] ist typisch für die Wittenberger Reformation und die mit ihr bezeichnete Sache findet sich auch in der oberdeutsch-schweizerischen und der Genfer Reformation: Bildungswesen und Kirche mussten miteinander verklammert sein, um die kirchlichen Amtsträger für ihre Verkündigungsaufgabe zu qualifizieren und die Verkündigung zu kontrollieren. Den Wittenberger Theologen erschien das keineswegs als die Neuerung, die es tatsächlich war, sondern für sie gab es schon seit der alttestamentlichen Zeit Bildungseinrichtungen, die die Sprachen (litterae) und die Bibel (sermo divinus) lehrten.[19] Solche Schulen hätten die Funktion, die Lehre zu bewahren, sie auszulegen sowie in Lehrauseinandersetzung Entscheidungen zu treffen: Sie seien »doctrinae custodes, atque interpretes, & gravißimarum controuersiarum iudices«.[20] Diese für die Evangeliumsverkündigung wichtige Lehrvermittlung geschieht nach Melanchthon im Rahmen der bestehenden schulischen und akademischen Strukturen: Es brauche ein intensives Studium, bei dem die zukünftigen Prediger sich durch Vorlesungen, Disputationen und eigene Lektüre die artes liberales, die biblischen Sprachen und Texte, die Kirchenlehre und kontroverstheologisches Wissen aneigneten.[21] Wo solche Schulen nicht vor-

---

[18] PHILIPP MELANCHTHON, Oratio de necessaria coniunctione Scholarum cum ministerio Euangelij: a D. Bernhardo Zieglero recitata, 1543 (in: Selectarum Declamationum Philippi Melanthonis, quas conscripsit, & partim ipse in Schola Vitebergensi recitauit, partim alijs recitandas exhibuit. Tomus Quartus, Straßburg 1558, VD16 M 3566, 424–445; Abdruck: CR 11,606–618 [Nr. 73]). Die Rede verfasste Melanchthon den im Herbst 1543 in Leipzig promovierten Bernhard Ziegler (vgl. MBW T 12,338 f. [Nr. 3322] und 363–365 [Nr. 3338]).

[19] Selectarum Declamationum (s. Anm. 18), 429–434 (CR 11,609–612).

[20] A.a.O., 430 (609).

[21] »Valde [...] errant illi, qui pastores ex quolibet ligno sculpi, & sine literis, sine longa institutione religionis doctrinam subito percipi posse somniant. Primum genus sermonis

handen seien oder ihre Aufgabe nicht erfüllten, werde das Licht des Evangeliums ausgelöscht (amißis literis lucem Euangelii extinguj).[22] Dabei hat für Melanchthon allerdings nicht die Universität selbst das *ministerium Evangelii* inne, wohl aber sei ihre Theologische Fakultät »ministerii evangelici membrum«.[23] Das bedeutete ein neue Bestimmung der Funktion der akademischen Theologie und eine daraus folgende Aufwertung der Theologischen Fakultät für die Kirche. War in vorreformatorischer Zeit die kirchliche Hierarchie der *custos doctrinae*, der für die Tradierung und Auslegung der Lehre auf die im hohen Mittelalter entstandenen Universitäten zurückgriff und diese im späten Mittelalter anfangsweise für die Ausbildung und Kontrolle des Klerus in Dienst nahm, so wurde diese lockere und partielle Kooperation von Kirche und Universität durch die Reformation zu einer *necessaria coniunctio* verfestigt. Dass sich dieses System durchsetzen konnte, hängt nicht nur mit der amtstheologischen Notwendigkeit einer für die Verkündigungsaufgabe qualifizierten Geistlichkeit zusammen, sondern auch mit den durch die Reformation geschaffenen Möglichkeiten und Freiheiten: Die Reformverweigerung der Papstkirche und die Unterstützung der Reformation durch viele weltliche Obrigkeiten führten dazu, dass überkommene Strukturen von Grund auf verändert, Neues eingeführt und dabei das theologisch Notwendige und kirchlich Wünschenswerte in einem historisch einmaligen Ausmaß tatsächlich umgesetzt wurde. Im lutherischen Bereich wurde diese Verklammerung von humanistisch-reformatorischem Bildungswesen und evangelischer Landeskirche nicht nur in Kursachsen, sondern auch in Württemberg oder Braunschweig-Wolfenbüttel vorbildhaft verwirklicht;[24] im oberdeutsch-

---

prophetici & Apostolici cognoscendum est. Discendae sunt igitur linguae ueteres, & tota ratio formandae orationis cognoscenda est: quam ad rem bonis doctoribus ueterum monumentorum lectione, literariis exercitjs, denique etiam tempore opus est. Postea maior labor succedit. [...] Opus est autem ad explicationem controuersiarum maximarum, non solum ingenij dexteritate, & mediocri cognition sacrorum librorum: sed etiam disputandi arte, copia orationis, noticia historiae, antiquitatis, & ueterum iudiciorum« (a.a.O., 435 f. [612]).

[22] A.a.O., 434 (612).

[23] So die Formulierung in der von Melanchthon verfassten Satzung der Theologischen Fakultät Wittenberg von 1545 (in: Urkundenbuch der Universität Wittenberg, hg. v. Walter Friedensburg, Teil 1, Magdeburg 1926, 262).

[24] MARTIN BRECHT, Herkunft und Ausbildung der protestantischen Geistlichen des Herzogtums Württemberg im 16. Jahrhundert (ZKG 80, 1969, 163–175); CHARLOTTE METHUEN, Securing the Reformation through education: The duke's scholarship system of sixteenth-century Württemberg (SCJ 25, 1994, 841–851); SCHORN-SCHÜTTE, Evangelische Geistlichkeit in der Frühneuzeit (s. Anm. 8), 159–226; MARTIN KRARUP, Ordination in Wittenberg. Die Einsetzung in das kirchliche Amt in Kursachsen zur Zeit der Reformation, Tübingen 2007. Für den fränkischen Bereich, der zwar keine evangelische Universität aufwies, aber ein hochentwickeltes schulisches Bildungswesen, siehe

schweizerischen Bereich ist vor allem auf Basel zu verweisen, wo man sich während der zweiten Hälfte des 16. Jahrhunderts dem »ideal type« des aus der Verbindung von reformatorischer Theologie und Humanismus hervorgehenden »coordinated system of religious and theological education« annäherte;[25] und auch in Genf begann noch zu Calvins Lebzeiten diese Verklammerung, die zu einer raschen und umfassenden Akademisierung und Professionalisierung der Geistlichkeit führte.[26] Ebenso kam es in anderen Städten und Territorien zu der von den Wittenberger Reformatoren inaugurierten folgenreichen Verklammerung von *Bildung und Konfession*.[27]

Obwohl das Schulwesen im Kurfürstentum Brandenburg kaum entwickelt und die 1506 in der Handelsmetropole Frankfurt (Oder) neu gegründete Universität anfangs wenig anziehungskräftig war, wurde mit der Einführung der Reformation auch in der Mark die *necessaria conjunctio* geschaffen.[28] Das märkische Schulwesen erhielt durch die Reformation ei-

---

BERNHARD KLAUS, Soziale Herkunft und theologische Bildung lutherischer Pfarrer der reformatorischen Frühzeit (ZKG 80, 1960, 22–49).

[25] AMY NELSON BURNETT, Preparing the pastors: Theological education and pastoral training in Basel (in: History has many voices, hg. v. Lee Palmer Wandel, Kirksville 2003, 131–151, hier: 150). Auch die Landpfarrer hatten Teil an der Akademisierung und Homogenisierung der Basler Geistlichkeit und wurden dadurch zu wichtigen Vermittlern der reformierten Konfessionalisierung (AMY NELSON BURNETT, Basel's rural pastors as mediators of confessional and social discipline, in: Central European History 33, 2000, 67–85). Dass die Landpfarrer durchaus ähnlich gut ausgebildet sein konnten wie die Stadtpfarrer, lässt sich auch im Nürnberger Landgebiet (RIEGG, Konfliktbereitschaft und Mobilität [s. Anm. 8], 183–194) oder in Pommern beobachten (PTASZYŃSKI, »Beruf und Berufung« [s. Anm. 8], 273). Es gibt allerdings auch Indizien für einen bleibenden »unterschiedlichen Bildungsstand zwischen Stadt- und Landgeistlichkeit« (SCHORN-SCHÜTTE, Evangelische Geistlichkeit in der Frühneuzeit [s. Anm. 8], 221), die auf regionale Unterschiede hinweisen.

[26] WILLIAM G. NAPHY, The renovation of the ministry in Calvin's Geneva (in: The reformation of the parishes. The ministry and the Reformation in town and country, hg. v. Andrew Pettegree, Manchester u. New York 1993, 113–132); KARIN MAAG, Education and training for the Calvinist ministry: the academy of Geneva, 1559–1620 (a.a.O., 133–152).

[27] Weitere Beispiele aus dem deutschen und schweizerischen Raum (Heidelberg, Bremen, Hamburg, Danzig, die Grafschaften Mark und Ravensberg, die fränkischen Reichsgrafschaften sowie Zürich) werden behandelt in: Bildung und Konfession. Theologenausbildung im Zeitalter der Konfessionalisierung, hg. v. Herman J. Selderhuis u. Markus Wriedt, Tübingen 2006. Zur Pfarrerausbildung in der Deutschschweiz siehe auch BRUCE GORDON, Preaching and the reform of the clergy in the Swiss Reformation (in: The reformation of the parishes. The ministry and the Reformation in town and country, hg. v. Andrew Pettegree, Manchester u. New York 1993, 63–84).

[28] Zur Geschichte der Gründung der Viadrina und ihrer Transformation bis Mitte des Reformationsjahrhunderts: MICHAEL HÖHLE, Universität und Reformation. Die Universität Frankfurt (Oder) von 1506 bis 1550, Köln u.a. 2002. Für die zweite Hälfte des 16. Jahrhunderts ist man nach wie vor auf die älteren Aktenveröffentlichungen (Acten und Urkunden der Universität Frankfurt a. O., fünf Hefte, Breslau 1897–1903) und

nen starken Impuls, auch wenn seine Entwicklung den benachbarten Regionen nachhinkte; auf jeden Fall wurde seit der Mitte des 16. Jahrhunderts an den städtischen Lateinschulen das humanistisch-reformatorischen Grundwissen vermittelt und so die von den Reformatoren geforderte, für die Heranbildung einer geistlich-weltlichen Funktionselite grundlegende Bildungsvermittlung geleistet.[29] Während der 1540er Jahre ordnete Kurfürst Joachim II. die Finanzen der Viadrina neu, revidierte die Lehrpläne im Sinne von Humanismus und Reformation, berief neues Lehrpersonal und nahm die Landesuniversität für die Landeskirche in Dienst.[30] Anschaulich wurde die Verklammerung von Landesuniversität und Landeskirche etwa in der Person des kurmärkischen Generalsuperintendenten Andreas Musculus (1514–1581), der zugleich Frankfurter Stadtpfarrer, Theologieprofessor an der Universität Frankfurt, Mitglied des Konsistoriums und Berater des Kurfürsten war – und zahlreiche theologische und erbauliche Werke verfasste und zu den führenden lutherischen Theologen des Reichs gehörte.[31] Dass die Viadrina eine Landesuniversität war, die im Dienste der Landeskirche stand, zeigt sich daran, dass der Kurfürst immer wieder einschärfte,

---

Überblicksdarstellungen (vgl. GERD HEINRICH, Art. Frankfurt an der Oder, Universität, in: TRE 11, 1983, 335–342) angewiesen.

[29] Die Grundzüge des reformatorischen Bildungsprogramms formulierte Luther in seinen Schriften *An die Ratherren aller Städte deutschen Landes, daß sie christliche Schulen aufrichten und halten sollen* (1524: WA 15,9–53) und *Eine Predigt, daß man Kinder zur Schulen halten solle* (1530: WA 30^{II},508–588), und Melanchthon füllte es durch seine Schriften und vor allem durch seine Mitarbeit an der Reform des Bildungswesens (HEINZ SCHEIBLE, Melanchthons Bildungsprogramm, in: Lebenslehren und Weltentwürfe im Übergang vom Mittelalter zur Neuzeit, hg. v. Hartmut Boockmann u.a., Göttingen 1989, 233–248). – Das märkische Schulwesen des 16. Jahrhunderts ist wissenschaftlich unzureichend erforscht. Grundzüge der frühneuzeitlichen Bildungsgeschichte sind dargestellt in dem vorrangig an den quellenmäßig besser greifbaren 17. und 18. Jahrhundert interessierten Werk von WOLFGANG NEUGEBAUER, Absolutistischer Staat und Schulwirklichkeit in Brandenburg-Preußen, Berlin u. New York 1985. Für das 16. Jahrhundert gibt es Darstellungen zum Schulwesen in manchen größeren Städten, beispielsweise AGNES WINTER, Das Gelehrtenschulwesen der Residenzstadt Berlin in der Zeit von Konfessionalisierung, Pietismus und Frühaufklärung (1574–1740), Berlin 2008.

[30] STEGMANN, Die Kirchenpolitik des brandenburgischen Kurfürsten Joachim II. (s. Anm. 5), 129–142.

[31] ERNST KOCH, Andreas Musculus und die Konfessionalisierung im Luthertum (in: Die lutherische Konfessionalisierung in Deutschland, hg. v. Hans-Christoph Rublack, Gütersloh 1992, 250–270); JÜRGEN SPLETT, Musculus (Meusel), Andreas (in: LOTHAR NOACK, JÜRGEN SPLETT, Bio-Bibliographien. Brandenburgische Gelehrte der Frühen Neuzeit. Mark Brandenburg mit Berlin-Cölln 1506–1640, Berlin 2009, 391–423). Immer noch unverzichtbar ist die quellengesättigte Biographie von CHRISTIAN WILHELM SPIEKER, Lebensgeschichte des Andreas Musculus, Frankfurt (Oder) 1858.

»das nun hinfur die Pfarrer / Predicanten / Capellene / Physici / Schulmeister vnd Stadschreiber / aus keiner andern / dann aus berürter vnser Vniuersitet vocirt / vnd niemands derselben / durch vnsere Superintendenten Instituirt oder Inuestirt werden solle / Er bringe dann von vnser Vniuersitet ein schrifftlichen schein / das er alda studirt / vnd zu solchem Ampte geschickt gnug sey«.[32]

Hintergrund dieser Forderung war, dass angehende Geistliche in erheblicher Zahl andernorts studierten – aus der Mittelmark und der Niederlausitz wandte sich man sich vielfach nach Wittenberg, die altmärkischen Hansestädten waren traditionell auf die ›Hanseuniversität‹ Rostock hin orientiert, wo David Chyträus lehrte[33] – oder zum Teil gar kein Universitätsstudium vorweisen konnte. Leider lassen die überlieferten Nachrichten über die evangelische Geistlichkeit des 16. Jahrhunderts in der Mark Brandenburg keine statistischen Auswertungen hinsichtlich der Ausbildung zu.[34] Der Trend war aber derselbe wie andernorts: Ein Lateinschulbesuch war durchweg selbstverständlich und immer mehr angehende Pfarrer studierten an der Artes-Fakultät und nutzen auch die Möglichkeiten theologischer und pastoraler Bildung, die die Viadrina und das geistliche Leben in Frankfurt boten.

---

[32] Mandat Joachims II. vom 6. Januar 1567 (Geheimes Staatsarchiv Preußischer Kulturbesitz, Berlin-Dahlem [= GStAPK], I. HA, Rep. 47, Nr. 5 a 1, Paket 2, Nr. 2).

[33] ANDREAS STEGMANN, Die Rostocker Theologie des 16. und 17. Jahrhunderts und ihre Bedeutung für das Luthertum im Ostseeraum (in: Reformatio Baltica. Kulturwirkungen der Reformation in den Metropolen des Ostseeraums, hg. v. Heinrich Assel, Johann Anselm Steiger u. Axel E. Walter, Berlin u. Boston 2018, 375–384).

[34] Das Pfarrerbuch (Evangelisches Pfarrerbuch für die Mark Brandenburg seit der Reformation, bearb. v. Otto Fischer, zwei Bände, Berlin 1941) enthält für die Pfarrer des 16. und 17. Jahrhunderts nur wenige Angabe und ist weder vollständig noch zuverlässig. Für die Altmark wurde das Datenmaterial erneut aufgearbeitet, ohne dass sich daraus aber die Möglichkeit für statistische Auswertungen ergibt: Evangelisches Pfarrerbuch für die Altmark. Biographische Daten und Quellennachweise als Hilfsmittel zur kirchlichen Ortsgeschichte der Mark Brandenburg und der Provinz Sachsen, bearb. v. Uwe Czubatynski, Rühstädt ²2006. Die gedruckten und in den Archiven erhaltenen Visitationsakten enthalten zwar vereinzelt Hinweise auf den Ausbildungsgang von Pfarrern und ihre theologische Kompetenz, lassen aber keine Verallgemeinerungen zu. Der Versuch, ausgehend von der Unterschriftenliste des Konkordienbuchs, in der ein Großteil der 1580 amtierenden brandenburgischen Geistlichen aufgeführt ist (Concordia. Christliche Widerhole, einmütige Bekentnus nachbenanter Churfürsten, Fürste und Stende Augspurgischer Confession, Frankfurt [Oder] 1581, VD16 K 2001, B 5ᵛ–C 3ʳ), einen Überblick über den Akademisierungsstand der Geistlichkeit zu gewinnen und die in der Forschungsliteratur vorgenommene Unterscheidung einer Konstituierungs- und einer Konsolidierungsphase, die um 1580 ineinander übergehen (SCHORN-SCHÜTTE, Evangelische Geistlichkeit in der Frühneuzeit [s. Anm. 8], 191) am brandenburgischen Beispiel nachzuvollziehen, scheitert an den Mängeln der Liste und am Fehlen von Informationen über die damals amtierenden Pfarrer. Die Liste zeigt allerdings, dass die leitenden Geistlichen durchweg studiert haben und akademisch graduiert sind und ein Abgleich der Namen mit Universitätsmatrikeln und dem Wittenberger Ordiniertenbuch (hg. v. Georg Buchwald, zwei Bände, Leipzig 1894–1895) belegt, dass unter den Pfarrern einige eine Universität besucht haben.

Was umfasste nun aber das in diese *necessaria conjunctio* einbezogene *ministerium evangelii* im Einzelnen? Die Einleitung zum Lehrteil der Brandenburgischen Kirchenordnung von 1540[35] weist mit Rückgriff auf Tit. 1,9 den ›Bischöfen‹, d.h. Pfarrern, Predigern und Kirchendienern, drei Aufgaben zu: Lehren, Ermahnen und Strafen. Sie sollen 1. das grundlegende Wissen über die Bibel vermitteln und zum Verstehen der Bibel anleiten, 2. durch Gesetzes- und Evangeliumspredigt den Menschen die Lehre persönlich nahebringen und sie in ihrem christlichen Leben unterstützen und 3. diejenigen, die der Lehre widersprechen und sich der Ermahnung entziehen, konfrontativ angehen.[36] Nicht ohne Grund stehen diese Ausführungen am Beginn der Kirchenordnung und verweisen auf die wichtigste Aufgabe der Kirche, »ob der gewissen lere [zu] halten / vnd mechtig zu sein zuuermanen / vnd die wiedersacher zustraffen«.[37]

Im Mittelpunkt allen kirchlichen Handelns steht die Vermittlung des Gottesworts:

»Denn wollen wir in das Himelreich komen / so müssen wir aus wasser und geist new geborn werden / Solche geburt aber geschicht nicht aus vergenglichen / sondern vnvergenglichen samen / Nemlich / aus dem lebendigen wort Gottes / das da ewiglich bleibt«.[38]

---

[35] Kirchen Ordnung im Churfurstenthum der Marcken zu Brandemburg / wie man sich beide mit der Leer und Ceremonien halten sol, Berlin 1540 (VD16 B 6909). Abgedruckt ist der Text der Ordnung teils in Bd. 3, teils in Bd. 11 von Sehlings Ausgabe der Kirchenordnungen (EKO 3, 1909, 39–90; EKO 11, 1961, 140–279). Zu Entstehungsgeschichte, Inhalt und Bedeutung dieser Ordnung: ANDREAS STEGMANN, Die brandenburgische Kirchenordnung von 1540 (in: Reformationen vor Ort. Christlicher Glaube und konfessionelle Kultur in Brandenburg und Sachsen im 16. Jahrhundert, hg. v. Enno Bünz, Heinz-Dieter Heimann u. Klaus Neitmann, Berlin 2017, 235–288).

[36] Kirchen Ordnung im Churfurstenthum der Marcken zu Brandemburg (s. Anm. 35), 1. Hauptteil, C 1ʳ–D 1ᵛ. Neben Tit. 1,9 (1. fidelis sermo secundum doctrinam, 2. exhortari in doctrina, 3. arguere qui contradicunt) steht möglicherweise auch 2.Tim. 3,16 (1. docere, 2. arguere, 3. corrigere, 4. erudire in iustitia) im Hintergrund; beide Texte sind im frühneuzeitlichen Luthertum verbreitete Schemata der Beschreibung pastoraler Tätigkeit. – Auf das alttestamentliche Bild von Hirten und seinen Schafen, das im Neuen Testament aufgegriffen wird, verweist die Einleitung zum 2. Hauptteil der Kirchenordnung: »Ein Bisschoff Pfarherr oder Prediger / sol fleissig in der Kirchen wachen / predigen vnd auff sehen / das er nichts verseume an den Schefflein / die jm befolhen sein / vnd allen möglichen fleis ankeren / das die Schefflein mit der heilsamen lere des Göttlichen worts trewlich geweidet / geleitet vnd versorget werden« (Kirchen Ordnung im Churfurstenthum der Marcken zu Brandemburg [s. Anm. 35], 2. Hauptteil, a 3ʳ). Die im 2. Hauptteil enthaltene Predigt über das Schlüsselamt enthält eine auf Röm. 10,13–15 basierende Darstellung des kirchlichen Amts (a.a.O., ee 2ʳ–ff 4ʳ), die einleitend darauf verweist, dass »das Predigampt [...] Christus vnser Herr selbs angefangen / eingesetzt / vnd verordnet hat« (a.a.O., ee 3ᵛ–ee 4ʳ) und die in der Folge von Christi Einsetzung ordentlich berufenen kirchlichen Amtsträger der Gemeinde mit einer besonderen Verantwortung und einer besonderen Autorität gegenübertreten.

[37] Kirchen Ordnung im Churfurstenthum der Marcken zu Brandemburg (s. Anm. 35), 1. Hauptteil, C 4ᵛ.

[38] Ebd.

Darum müssen die Prediger fortwährend mit dem Gotteswort umgehen und der in der Kirchenordnung enthaltenen, auf diesem Wort basierenden Lehrdarstellung folgen. Diese Lehrdarstellung, die vorgibt, was die »Diener des worts«[39] dem »volck [...] fleissig leren«[40] sollen, findet sich in mehreren Summarien komprimiert[41] und in neun um die Rechtfertigung aus dem Glauben kreisenden Kapiteln entfaltet[42]. Seinen Sitz im Leben hatte dieses Lehren, Ermahnen und Strafen in Gottesdienst und Seelsorge, aber auch im Katechismus- und Schulunterricht und in der Kirchenzucht, was alles als Teil des *ministerium evangelii* verstanden und darum selbstverständlich zu den Aufgaben des Pfarrers gezählt wurde. Wie die Brandenburgische Kirchenordnung von 1540 vorgibt und die Ordnungen von 1543, 1551, 1558 und 1561[43] sowie die Abschiede der Generalkirchenvisi-

---

[39] A.a.O., O 3[v].

[40] A.a.O., O 1[r].

[41] A.a.O., B 1[v]–B 4[r] u. D 2[r].

[42] A.a.O., G 3[r]–R 3[v].

[43] 1543 richtete Kurfürst Joachim II. nach Wittenberger Vorbild ein Konsistorium als Kirchenverwaltungsbehörde ein, für die eine Konsistorialordnung erlassen wurde, die 1551 erste Ergänzungen erfuhr (GStAPK, I. HA, Rep. 20, Lit. A, Bd. 3, 120[r]–126[r], 126[v]–138[r]). Nach dem Augsburger Religionsfrieden ging der Kurfürst daran, die kirchlichen Ordnungen in seinem Territorium zu überarbeiten. Als erstes erschien 1558 eine Visitationsordnung für die Dörfer (Ordnung vnd satzung / so [...] vnsers gnedigsten Herrn vorordnete Visitatores / den Patronen / Pfarrern / Gotshaußleuten / vnnd Gemeinden / der Dörffer inn S. Churf: G. Landen vnnd Churfürstenthumb der Marcke zu Brandenburg / sich darnach inn Geistlichen sachen zurichten, Frankfurt [Oder] 1558, VD16 B 6919; diese Ordnung basiert auf Mandaten der Visitatoren, wie etwa dem im Archiv des Stadtgeschichtlichen Museums Spandau überlieferten Mandat an die Pfarrer der Inspektion Spandau von 1553: IV B2/17, fol. 45[r]–46[v], Abdruck im Anhang zu diesem Aufsatz). 1561 lag druckfertig die überarbeitete und stark erweiterte *Geystliche Policey: Visitation: vnd Consistorial Ordnungk* vor (GStAPK, I. HA, Rep. 47, Nr. 13, Fasz. »Consistorial-Ordnung 1561«). Eine Überarbeitung der 1540 erschienenen und 1542 nachgedruckten Kirchenordnung war geplant und mit ersten Vorarbeiten schon begonnen worden, die Neufassung erschien aber erst im Jahr nach dem Tod Joachims II. (1572: VD16 C 4778). Für die Frage nach der Amtstätigkeit und des Lebenswandels des Pfarrers ist vor allem die *Geistliche Polizei-, Visitations- und Konsistorialordnung* von 1561 relevant (s.o.), die breite Ausführungen dazu enthält (vor allem das Kapitel »Von den pfarrern, irhem ampte, lehre, sitten vnd leben«: a.a.O., 16[r]–23[r]; abgedruckt im Anhang zu diesem Aufsatz). Hier finden sich auch Regelungen zu Vokation und Präsentation (a.a.O., 10[r/v]), zur Ordination (a.a.O., 10[v]–12[v]), zur Investitur (a.a.O., 12[v]–13[v]), zur Anstellung von Kaplänen und Predigern (a.a.O., 23[r]–24[r]), zum Einkommen der Geistlichen (a.a.O., 33[v]–35[v]), zum Umgang mit den Pfarrgütern (a.a.O., 35[v]–36[r]), zu den Beitragspflichten der Geistlichen zu den dörflichen Gemeinschaftsaufgaben (a.a.O., 36[r/v]), zum Pfarrinventar (a.a.O., 36[v]–37[r]), zur Rechtsstellung der Ehefrau und Kinder des Pfarrers (a.a.O., 37[r]), zur Abgrenzung des Privatvermögens des Pfarrers vom Pfarrinventar und zur Vererbung dieses Vermögens (a.a.O., 37[r]–38[v], 38[v]–39[r]), zum Pfarrhaus (a.a.O., 39[r]–40[r]) und zur Altersversorgung von Pfarrern (a.a.O., 40[v]–41[r]). Der Text der Ordnung von 1561 – darunter alle soeben aufgezählten die Pfarrer betreffenden Regelungen – wurde in leicht veränderter Form mit einigen Kürzungen und Ergänzungen 1573 als *Visitation vnd Consistorial Ordenunge* (VD16 B 6924) gedruckt, die also die

tationen der 1540er und 1550er Jahre[44] bestätigen, rückte mit der Reformation die Verkündigung und Unterweisung in den Mittelpunkt des kirchlichen Lebens: Im sonn- und feiertäglichen Gottesdienst wurde über das Evangelium gepredigt, Teil der Liturgie für die Kasualien waren stets die entsprechenden Bibellesungen und zugehörigen Unterweisungen, in den Werktagsgottesdiensten wurde aus der Bibel vorgelesen und der Katechismus ausgelegt, im Beichtgespräch und am Krankenbett wurden Mahnung und Trost der Bibel in seelsorgerlicher Form vermittelt, in den Schulen war der religiöse Grundlagenunterricht – nunmehr anhand von Bibel und Katechismus – selbstverständlich. Die Aufwertung der Verkündigung und Unterweisung spiegelte sich in der häuslichen Frömmigkeit wieder, deren wichtigste Medien Bibel, Katechismus und Gesangbuch waren und für die zahlreiche Erbauungsbücher Anleitung gaben. Wie die Pfarrer waren auch die »Hausveter« aufgefordert,

>»an jren Kindern vnd Hausgesinde oder Dienstboten / das jre fleissig aus[zu]richten / vnd embsiglich jres Ampts [zu] warten / vnd an jren beruff zu dencken / mit predigen / vermanen / vnterweisen / bitten vnd straffen«.[45]

Auch für die Pfarrer gab es Hilfsliteratur: Die Kirchenordnung von 1540 druckte Andreas Osianders Nürnberger »Kinderpredigten« ab, die als Vorbild und Vorlage für die Katechismusunterweisung dienen konnten, daneben sollten die Pfarrer eine deutsche und eine lateinische Bibel, Luthers Haus- und Kirchenpostille und andere für ihren Dienst hilfreiche Bücher wie die Werke Luthers oder der Kirchenväter besitzen.[46]

Normvorstellungen aus der Zeit um 1560 enthält und damit die während der 1540er und 1550er Jahre erreichte kirchliche Wirklichkeit widerspiegelt.

[44] Im Druck liegen die Visitationsakten der Altmark (Die Abschiede der in den Jahren 1540–1542 in der Altmark gehaltenen ersten General-Kirchen-Visitation mit Berücksichtigung der in den Jahren 1551, 1578–79 und 1600 gehaltenen Visitationen, hg. v. Julius Müller u. Adolf Parisius, zwei Bände, Magdeburg bzw. Salzwedel 1889–1929), der Prignitz (Die brandenburgischen Kirchenvisitations-Abschiede und -Register des XVI. und XVII. Jahrhunderts [= BKVAR], Bd. 1, hg. v. Victor Herold, Berlin 1931), des Landes Ruppin (BKVAR, Bd. 2, bearb. v. Gerd Heinrich, Berlin 1963) und der Mittelmark (BKVAR, Bd. 4/1: Mittlere Mittelmark, bearb. v. Christiane Schuchard, Berlin u. Boston 2019) vor. Visitationsabschiede für weitere Regionen finden sich in Sehlings Edition der Kirchenordnungen (EKO 3, 1909, 151–384). Ansonsten ist man auf die handschriftliche Überlieferung in lokalen oder zentralen Archiven sowie auf die von Victor Herold angefertigen Abschriften (GStAPK, X. HA, Rep. 16, Nr. 161–163) angewiesen, deren Edition vor einiger Zeit wieder in Angriff genommen wurde. Da die Akten des Kurmärkischen Konsistoriums seit 1945 verschollen sind, ist ein Teil der Überlieferung wohl unwiederbringlich verloren. Für die Neumark sind wegen der Ungunst der Zeitläufte kaum Visitationsakten überliefert.

[45] Kirchen Ordnung im Churfurstenthum der Marcken zu Brandemburg (s. Anm. 35), 2. Hauptteil, a 2ᵛ.

[46] Den Ergänzungen zur Visitations- und Konsistorialordnung von 1551 zufolge soll jeder Pfarrer »an buchern eine bibel deutsch vnd lateinisch, eine hauspostilla Lutheri,

Mittelbar zur Verkündigung gehörte der vorbildliche Lebenswandel des Pfarrers. Die Brandenburgische Kirchenordnung von 1540 schreibt vor:

»Widerumb begeren wir / Ermanen gnediglich / vnd wollen mit ernst / Das die Pfarherrn vnd Priester / jres Ampts getrewlich warten / Sich tag vnd nacht / mit dem Göttlichen Gesetze / vnd der Schrifft bekümern / Auch eines Christlichen guten Wandels sich fleissigen / vnd Erbarliche Priesterliche tracht brauchen sollen / damit sie niemands ergerlich sein / Das sie auch die Leut jres gebrechens / da sichs gebüret / In der Gemein auff der Cantzel vnd sonst in sonderheit / freundlich straffen / vnd bey den halstarrigen gebürlichen ernst brauchen / Doch das sie vnnötige getzencke / vnd feindseligkeit vnter den Pfarleuten nicht erwecken / Auch der Wirtsheuser vnd vordechtiger vnzüchtiger personen sich enthalten / vnd eussern«.[47]

In der Folgezeit wurden die Verhaltensvorgaben immer detaillierter, um zu gewährleisten, dass die Pfarrer »iren wandell dahinn richten, das irhe leben mit der lehre vberein stimme«.[48] Mittelbar zur Verkündigung gehörte auch die Teilhabe des Pfarrers an der Verwaltung der Kirchengemeinde. Von der Armenfürsorge bis zur Gebäudeunterhaltung gab es viel, was ebenfalls der Predigtaufgabe zugerechnet werden kann, diente es doch der Ermöglichung der Verkündigung und zeigte deren praktische Konsequenzen. Sucht man in den Quellen aus Brandenburg nach Spuren dieser Tätigkeiten, dann wird man allerdings kaum fündig. Vielmehr machen die kirchlichen Ordnungen durchweg deutlich, dass die Verwaltung der Kirchengemeinde vorrangig in den Händen der Gemeindevorsteher lag und die Finanzen von den Kastenvorstehern überwacht wurden.[49] Für die praktischen Tätigkeiten gab es den Küster, an größeren Kirchen waren es mehrere.[50] Wie hoch der Anteil der Pfarrer an der Gemeindeverwaltung zu

---

cathecismum Lutheri groß vnnd klein, die Churfurstliche Brandenburgische kirchenordnunge« besitzen (GStAPK, I. HA, Rep. 20, Lit. A, Bd. 3, 132ᵛ). In deren erweiterter Fassung von 1561 wird – wohl mit Blick auf die Stadtpfarrer – hinzugefügt: »auch do sie des vormuegens, die gantze opera Luteri, Augustini, Hieronimi vnnd anderer christlichen vnnd vnuorfelschten theologen bucher mehr, aber sich vor aller falschen lehrer schrifte vnd bucher, das sie dodurch nicht in vorfurische irrthumb geleitet werden mogen, mit allem fleisse huetten« (s. Anm. 43, 17ʳ). – Die Versorgung der Mark mit religiöser Literatur übernahmen neben den Frankfurter Druckern (Hans-Erich Teitge, Der Buchdruck des 16. Jahrhunderts in Frankfurt an der Oder. Verzeichnis der Drucke, Berlin 2000) vor allem Drucker aus den westlich und südlich benachbarten Regionen, wo auch viele märkische Autoren ihre Werke drucken ließen. So wie Leipziger, Nürnberger, Magdeburger oder Wittenberger Drucker den brandenburgischen Markt belieferten, arbeiteten auch Frankfurter Drucker für den schlesischen Markt.

[47] Kirchen Ordnung im Churfurstenthum der Marcken zu Brandemburg (s. Anm. 35), 3. Hauptteil, Y 2ᵛ.

[48] Geistliche Polizei-, Visitations- und Konsistorialordnung (s. Anm. 43), 20ʳ.

[49] A.a.O., 28ʳ–32ᵛ u.ö. Zudem trugen die »weldtliche obrigkeitten, heupt- vnnd amptleute, auch andere gerichts vorwalttere vnd beuelhaber ihn stetten vnd dorffern« Verantwortung für »religion sachen« (a.a.O., 50ᵛ–55ʳ).

[50] A.a.O., 41ʳ–43ʳ.

veranschlagen ist und welchen Einfluss sie auf die Gestaltung der kirchlichen Verhältnisse vor Ort hatten, ist angesichts der Unterschiedlichkeit der Verhältnisse und des Fehlens von Einzelstudien zu diesem Thema kaum zu klären.

Für ihren Verkündigungsdienst mussten die Pfarrer qualifiziert sein, wobei die Vertrautheit mit Bibel und Kirchenlehre und die Befähigung zu deren Vermittlung an die Gemeinde die wichtigsten Punkte waren. Von Anfang an galt ein universitäres Theologiestudium als wünschenswert, das an den reformatorischen Universitäten ganz im Sinne der Unterstützung des *ministerium evangelii* zu einer berufsqualifizierenden Ausbildung umgestaltet wurde.[51] Die Auslegung der biblischen Zentralschriften und die dogmatisch-kontroverstheologische Entfaltung der kirchlichen Lehre standen im Mittelpunkt des theologischen Unterrichts. Auch praxisorientierte Berufsvorbereitung, etwa in Form von Predigtübungen, wurde angeboten, eine Reflexion der Berufspraxis, die wiederum auf das Lehrangebot zurückgewirkt hätte, gab es dagegen nicht. Auch das Studium an der Artes-Fakultät galt als wichtig, bedurfte es doch des hier vermittelten philologisch-philosophischen Rüstzeugs, um Theologie zu studieren, und wurde im Rhetorikunterricht einiges an Handwerkszeug für die angehenden Prediger vermittelt. Nicht selten begnügten sich allerdings angehende Pfarrer mit der Absolvierung dieses Grundlagenstudium und nutzten das theologische Lehrangebot nicht. Statistische Auswertungen der überlieferten Quellen lassen erkennen, dass in der zweiten Hälfte des 16. Jahrhunderts der Universitätsbesuch für angehende Pfarrer üblich wurde, dass

---

[51] Zur Umgestaltung und Praxis des Theologiestudiums in der Frühen Neuzeit: Rudolf Mau, Programme und Praxis des Theologiestudiums im 17. und 18. Jahrhundert (in: Theologische Versuche 11, 1979, 71–91); Marcel Nieden, Die Erfindung des Theologen. Wittenberger Anweisungen zum Theologiestudium im Zeitalter von Reformation und Konfessionalisierung, Tübingen 2006; Andreas Stegmann, Johann Friedrich König. Seine ›Theologia positiva acroamatica‹ (1664) im Rahmen des frühneuzeitlichen Theologiestudiums, Tübingen 2006. – Zur Bedeutung des akademischen Studiums für die frühneuzeitliche Geistlichkeit: Vogler, Le clergé protestant rhénan au siècle de la réforme (s. Anm. 8), Kap. 1; Schorn-Schütte, Evangelische Geistlichkeit in der Frühneuzeit (s. Anm. 8), 159–225; Thomas Kaufmann, Universität und lutherische Konfessionalisierung. Die Rostocker Theologieprofessoren und ihr Beitrag zur theologischen Bildung und kirchlichen Gestaltung im Herzogtum Mecklenburg zwischen 1550 und 1675, Gütersloh 1997, 336–349; Ders., Berufskulturelle Rahmenbedingungen des Pastorenstandes in der Frühen Neuzeit (in: Ders., Konfession und Kultur. Lutherischer Protestantismus in der zweiten Hälfte des Reformationsjahrhunderts, Tübingen 2006, 303–322); Ders., Théologie, université, société. Quelques remarques sur le premier protestantisme du point de vue de l'histoire de l'église (in: Religion ou confession. Un bilan franco-allemand sur l'époque moderne, hg. v. Philippe Büttgen u. Christophe Duhamelle, Paris 2010, 461–484, hier: 475–480); Ptaszyński, »Beruf und Berufung« (s. Anm. 8), 195–274.

aber nur eine kleine Gruppe ausführlicher Theologie studierte. Eine akademische Graduierung strebten angehende Pfarrer im 16. und 17. Jahrhundert in der Regel nicht an, es genügte der Nachweis des Universitätsbesuchs. Nur wer auf eine kirchliche Leitungsfunktion aus war, tat gut daran, einen Magistergrad zu erwerben. Den Doktorgrad erwarben nur wenige Geistliche, und zwar zumeist dann, wenn sie in ein landeskirchliches Spitzenamt aufstiegen. Auch wenn sich die Akademisierung der evangelischen Geistlichkeit während des 16. Jahrhunderts allmählich durchsetzte, ist zu beachten, dass sie für einen zwar kleiner werdenden, aber immer noch erheblichen Teil der angehenden Pfarrer nicht zwingend mit einem Universitätsstudium einherging. Die theologischen Kompetenzen, die für das *ministerium evangelii* gefordert waren, ließen sich auch an den Lateinschulen und im Selbststudium erwerben, zumal wenn man nicht ein städtisches Pfarramt anstrebte und die Berufstätigkeit vor dem Antritt der Pfarrstelle – etwa als Haus- oder Schullehrer – zur Weiterbildung nutzte. Es bedurfte keines Universitätsstudiums, um an der akademischen Professionalisierung des geistlichen Amts teilzuhaben und von der *necessaria coniunctio* zu profitieren.

Um einen Mindeststandard theologischer Kompetenz zu sichern, wurde die Ordination mit einer Prüfung verbunden und den amtierenden Pfarrern die Pflicht zur Weiterbildung auferlegt. Vielerorts trafen sich die Pfarrer eines Bezirks regelmäßig, um voreinander zu predigen und miteinander zu disputieren und so den Leitungsverantwortlichen ihr Bemühen zu bezeugen.[52] In den Städten wurden in der zweiten Hälfte des 16. Jahr-

---

[52] So schrieb etwa die Kurbrandenburgische Visitationsordnung von 1558 vor, dass die Dorfpfarrer von dem Pfarrer der benachbarten Stadt »zum Examen, oder allda zu predigen gefordert« werden sollen (s. Anm. 43, A 4ʳ). Der Visitationsabschied für die altmärkische Stadt Werben von 1551 zeigt, dass diese Vorladung vierteljährlich geschehen sollte und der Inspektor auch aufgefordert war, die Pfarrer zu unterweisen; wer dabei für das Pfarramt ungeschickt befunden wurde, musste dem Stendaler Konsistorium gemeldet werden (Müller, Parisius, Abschiede [s. Anm. 44], Bd. 2, Heft 4, 1929, 402). Dass diese Überprüfungs- und Weiterbildungsmaßnahmen nur beschränkte Wirkung entfalteten, zeigt die Visitation von 1602, als es etwa im Visitationsabschied für die Stadt Neuruppin über die zur Inspektion gehörenden Dorfpfarrer hieß, dass diese sich zwar zum Augsburgischen Bekenntnis und zur Konkordienformel bekennen würden, dass sie aber »quo ad eruditionem dermaßen ungeschicket befunden«, dass die Visitatoren nur wegen des hohen Alters oder der vielen Kinder und anderen gewichtigen Entschuldigungsgründen von einer Amtsenthebung abgesehen hätten; die Bildungsmängel seien auch Folge dessen, dass die vorgeschriebenen »conventus« nicht regelmäßig gehalten würden, weshalb die Visitatoren detaillierte Vorgaben für diese mindestens einmal jährlich abzuhaltenden Treffen machen (BKVAR 2 [s. Anm. 44], 95 f.). Andernorts scheinen diese *conventus* dagegen gut funktioniert zu haben, wie die beiden altmärkischen Pfarrerbruderschaften von Gardelegen und Tangermünde belegen, die in der zweiten Hälfte des 16. Jahrhunderts die gegenseitige Unterstützung und die theologische Weiterbildung der Geistlichen korporativ wahrnahmen (Fröhner, Der evangelische Pfarrstand in der Mark Brandenburg [s. Anm. 9], 40–42).

hunderts zudem vielerorts Kirchenbibliotheken begründet, die die Geistlichen mit theologischer Literatur versorgten.[53] Bei den Visitationen wurde der Bildungsstand der Pfarrer überprüft, wodurch die Anforderungen immer neu eingeschärft und die Bildungsbemühungen gelenkt wurden. Auch wenn es immer noch Geistliche gab, deren theologische Kompetenz hinter den Anforderung zurückblieb, so wurde doch in der zweiten Hälfte des 16. Jahrhunderts das Ideal des frommen und gebildeten Pfarrers (pietas et eruditio) etabliert, das über Jahrhunderte hinweg den Protestantismus bestimmte.

Sowohl für den schulisch-akademischen Unterricht als auch für die Diensteingangsprüfung und die Weiterbildung im Amt entstand im 16. Jahrhundert eine Fülle unterstützender Literatur. Schon während der 1520er Jahre wurden die ersten Hilfsbücher für den pfarramtlichen Dienst veröffentlicht, um nichts anderes handelt es sich nämlich bei Luthers Weihnachts- und Adventspostille, beim *Unterricht der Visitatorn* und Luthers Katechismen.[54] In der Folgezeit differenzierte sich diese Hilfsliteratur aus: Neben die Katechismen, die sich zu einer reichen und vielfältigen Literaturgattung entwickelten[55], traten theologische Lehrbücher, die oftmals gar nicht vorrangig für den akademischen Unterricht bestimmt waren, man denke etwa an Melanchthons *Examen ordinandorum*.[56] Luthers Postillenwerk bekam weiteren Zuwachs und wurde durch unzählige weitere Predigtsammlungen ergänzt. Um angehenden Pfarrern den Erwerb der für ihren Beruf nötigen Kenntnisse zu erleichtern, entstanden immer mehr Studienanleitungen, die zum Teil auch das erfolgreiche Absolvieren eines akademischen Studiums thematisierten. Speziell auf Fragen des pfarramtlichen Alltags gingen die pastoraltheologischen Handbücher ein,

---

[53] Einen Einblick in die Motivation zur Begründung solcher Bibliotheken und ihre Sammelschwerpunkt gibt der Kanzelaufruf zur Gründung der Nikolaibibliothek in Berlin von 1588 (Evangelisches Landeskirchliches Archiv Berlin, Marien- und Nikolaibibliothek, Hs. 1/1, 5ᵛ–8ᵛ). Weitere brandenburgische Beispiele werden behandelt in: Uwe Czubatynski, Armaria Ecclesiae. Studien zur Geschichte des kirchlichen Bibliothekswesens, Neustadt a. d. Aisch 1998 (hier findet sich auch ein Abdruck der eben genannten Quelle).

[54] WA 10^{I/1–2}; WA 26, 175–240; WA 30^{I}.

[55] Quellen zur Geschichte des kirchlichen Unterrichts in der evangelischen Kirche Deutschlands zwischen 1530 und 1600, hg. v. Johann Michael Reu, Gütersloh 1904–1935.

[56] CR 23,XX-CXXVIII.1–102. – Ein interessantes Beispiel eines solchen nichtakademischen Lehrbuchs aus der Übergangsphase zwischen dem Beginn der Umstrukturierung der Gemeinden und der Stabilisierung des reformatorischen Landeskirchentums, das sich ausdrücklich an unzureichend gebildete Pfarrer am Anfang ihrer Laufbahn richtet ist Urbanus Rhegius, Wie man fursichtiglich vnd on ergernis reden sol / von den furnemsten Artickeln Christlicher lere. Fur die jungen einfeltigen Prediger, Wittenberg 1537 (VD16 R 1806).

die Überblicke über Amtstheologie und Kirchenlehre mit homiletischen, poimenischen, liturgischen und kirchenrechtlichen Informationen verbanden.[57] Dass dem Buchangebot eine Nachfrage gegenüberstand und den obrigkeitlichen Vorgaben zu Buchbesitz und Studium durchaus Folge geleistet wurde, zeigen neben den Kirchenbibliotheken auch die verstreuten Informationen zum Buchbesitz von Pfarrern.[58]

Mit der Akademisierung verbunden war die Professionalisierung der Geistlichkeit. Das *ministerium evangelii* war nicht nur das in CA 5 beschriebene Predigtamt im allgemeinen, sondern das in CA 14 beschriebene

---

[57] Sechs dieser zum Teil weit ins 17. Jahrhundert hinein benutzten Handbücher von Gerhard Lorich, Johannes Rivius, Niels Hemmingsen, Erasmus Sarcerius, Konrad Porta und Felix Bidembach werden vorgestellt in AMY NELSON BURNETT, The evolution of the Lutheran pastor's manual in the sixteenth century (ChH 73, 2004, 536–565). Man könnte auch noch weitere ähnliche Werke nennen, aus dem oberdeutschen Raum etwa MARTIN BUCER, Von der waren Seelsorge / vnd dem rechten Hirten dienst (Straßburg 1538, VD16 B 8941), und aus dem mitteldeutschen Raum TILEMANN HESHUSEN, Vom Ampt vnd gewalt der Pfarrherr. Auch Wer macht / fug vnd recht hab Pfarrherrn zuberuffen (Erfurt 1561, VD16 H 3163), sowie JOACHIM MÖRLIN, Von dem Beruff der Prediger. Vnd wie fern weltliche Oberkeit macht hat / dieselbigen jres Ampts zuentsetzen / Nötiger Christlicher bericht aus Gottes wort (Eisleben 1565, VD16 M 5889). Letztere beide informieren vor dem Hintergrund der innerlutherischen Lehrstreitigkeiten über Amt und Tätigkeit des lutherischen Gemeindepfarrers und berücksichtigen dabei besonders seine Beziehungen zur weltlichen Obrigkeit. Wie das 1549 erstmals erschienene Werk von Johannes Rivius (BURNETT, The evolution of the Lutheran pastor's manual [s.o.], 543–545) zeigt, war früh schon die besondere Herausforderung des Landpfarramts im Blick. Rivius dürften dabei die sächsischen Verhältnisse vor Augen gestanden haben (HANS TRÜMPY, Eine Anleitung für protestantische Landpfarrer von 1549, in: Festschrift Matthias Zender. Studien zu Volkskultur, Sprache und Landesgeschichte, hg. v. Edith Ennen u. Günter Wiegelmann, Bonn 1972, 470–478). Bemerkenswerterweise wurde Rivius' Buch 1574 in Rostock neu aufgelegt (De officio pastorali ministrorum ecclesiae in pagis libellus, iis etiam, qui in urbibus euangelion docent, non inutilis, VD16 R 2626), versehen mit einer Vorrede des Cöllner Dompropsts Georg Coelestin, wahrscheinlich motiviert durch den Bedarf an solcher Literatur in den ländlichen Regionen des Nordostens. Allerdings geht dieses lateinische Werk kaum auf die besondere Situation auf dem Lande ein: Religiöses Desinteresse und mangelnde Disziplin dürften auch in städtischen Gemeinden ein Problem gewesen sein, und die Hinweise auf die pastoralen Pflichten (Gottesdienst, Unterweisung, Seelsorge, Ermahnung etc.) sind nicht in besonderer Weise auf ländliche Gemeinden zugeschnitten. Für den ländlichen Raum spezifische Hinweise wie die Anpassung der Predigt an das bäuerliche Fassungsvermögen (a.a.O., 32) oder die Konflikte mit dem örtlichen Patron (a.a.O., 58) sind selten.

[58] GERALD STRAUSS, The mental world of a Saxon pastor (in: Reformation principle and practice, FS Arthur Geoffrey Dickens, hg. v. Peter Newman Brooks, London 1980, 157–170); SCHORN-SCHÜTTE, Evangelische Geistlichkeit in der Frühneuzeit (s. Anm. 8), 213–225. Dass die Frage nach dem Besitz und der Lektüre von Büchern während der ganzen frühen Neuzeit den Pfarrern von den Visitatoren immer neu gestellt wurde (ERNST KOCH, Dorfpfarrer als Leser. Beobachtungen an Visitationsakten des 18. Jahrhunderts im Herzogtum Sachsen-Gotha, in: DERS., Studien zur Theologie- und Frömmigkeitsgeschichte des Luthertums im 16. bis 18. Jahrhundert, Waltrop 2005, 329–361) zeigt, dass man die Anfänge pastoraler Handbibliotheken im 16. Jahrhundert nicht überschätzen sollte.

ordinationsgebundene kirchliche Amt im besonderen,[59] das durch ein ganz
bestimmtes Tätigkeitsprofil gekennzeichnet war und bestimmte berufs-
qualifizierende Kompetenzen verlangte. Die angehenden Pfarrer absol-
vierten darum eine bestimmte Ausbildung, sie entwickelten ein berufs-
spezifisches Selbstverständnis und sie verbanden sich zu Netzwerken. Im
Amt angekommen wurden sie im Laufe der Frühen Neuzeit zu einer in
sozialer, ökonomischer und kultureller Hinsicht vergleichsweise homogenen Gruppe, für die Selbstrekrutierung und standesinterne Endogamie –
beides allerdings in geringerem Ausmaß, als von der älteren Forschung
behauptet – typisch waren. Die Forschung hat diese Entwicklung in Anlehnung an die moderne Berufswelt als *Professionalisierung* gekennzeichnet,[60] was trotz des Problems anachronistischer Verzeichnung frühneuzeitlicher Phänomene nicht unberechtigt ist, weil mit dem neuen Typ von
Pfarrer tatsächlich ein Berufsstand Gestalt gewann, der mit den Professi-
onen der modernen arbeitsteiligen Gesellschaft vergleichbar ist. Aber eben
ein Berufsstand, der in besonderer Weise durch sein ›geistliches Sonder-
bewußtsein‹[61] bestimmt war, das ihn aus der Gesellschaft heraushob – *der
Pfarrer ist anders*,[62] das galt auch schon im 16. Jahrhundert.

Damit die Pfarrer das *ministerium evangelii* leisten konnten, wurde im
Laufe des 16. Jahrhunderts ein immer detaillierter ausgestaltetes System
rechtlicher Regelung und materieller Versorgung entwickelt. Der Rechtsrahmen war durch das landesherrliche Kirchenregiment bestimmt, wobei
sich die landesherrliche Regelungskompetenz im pfarramtlichen Alltag
vermittelt durch Kirchenordnungen, Konsistorium, Generalsuperintendenten, Superintendenten, Visitatoren, lokale Obrigkeiten, Patrone und
Vertreter der Gemeinde realisierte. Die grundlegenden Vorgaben für die
Geistlichkeit finden sich in der Brandenburgischen Kirchenordnung von

---

[59] Bei CA 5 und CA 14 ist zu beachten, dass jeweils etwas anderes gemeint ist:
Während CA 14 vom *ordo ecclesiasticus*, d.h. den ordnungsgemäß berufenen Geistlichen,
deren Aufgabe die öffentliche Kanzelrede ist, spricht, ist das Predigtamt und das *ministerium docendi Evangelii* in CA 5 in funktionalem Sinne als »Mittel zur Entstehung des
Glaubens« zu verstehen und auf den der ganzen Kirche aufgetragenen »Dienst der Verkündigung und nicht spezifisch auf das institutionalisierte Amt zu beziehen« (Dorothea Wendebourg, Das bischöfliche Amt, in: ZevKR 51, 2006, 534–555, hier: 535f.,
Anm. 6). Entsprechend darf auch die die Kirche konstituierende Evangeliumspredigt
und Sakramentsverwaltung in CA 7 nicht vorschnell auf das institutionalisierte Amt
eingeschränkt werden.

[60] Hier ist vor allem auf die Arbeiten von Rosemary O'Day zur englischen Geistlichkeit zu verweisen (siehe unten Anm. 86 u. 87).

[61] Schorn-Schütte, Evangelische Geistlichkeit in der Frühneuzeit (s. Anm. 8), 393–
410; Berndorff, Die Prediger der Grafschaft Mansfeld (s. Anm. 8); Tarald Rasmussen, The Early Modern pastor between ideal and reality (in: LuJ 80, 2013, 197–219).

[62] Manfred Josuttis, Der Pfarrer ist anders. Aspekte einer zeitgenössischen Pastoraltheologie, München 1982.

1540 im Kapitel über Berufung und Ordination der Kirchendiener:[63] Ein jeder Pfarrer braucht eine Vokation von Seiten des Patrons und eine Überprüfung von Seiten des landesherrlichen Kirchenregiments. Voraussetzung für die Bekleidung einer kirchlichen Amts ist die »geschickligkeit der personen«, die vom kurfürstlichen Generalsuperintendenten und anderen vom Kurfürsten Beauftragten überprüft wird, nämlich »[o]b sie in der Leer rein / vnd sonst eins Christlichen ehrlichen wandels sein«.[64] Ist der Berufene und Überprüfte noch nicht ordiniert, empfängt er die Ordination durch einen der Landesbischöfe, die weiterhin amtieren, allerdings vom Kurfürsten in ihrer geistlichen Funktion nur anerkannt werden, wenn sie sich der Kirchenordnung unterwerfen, was nur beim Brandenburger Bischof Matthias von Jagow der Fall war.[65] Tatsächlich ging die Ordination aber bald an die im Rahmen des landesherrlichen Kirchenregiments agierenden Leitungsverantwortlichen über,[66] die zugleich auch die Auf-

---

[63] Kirchen Ordnung im Churfurstenthum der Marcken zu Brandemburg (s. Anm. 35), 3. Hauptteil, X 4ʳ–Y 3ʳ.

[64] A.a.O., X 4ᵛ.

[65] Die formelle Beibehaltung der diözesanbischöflichen Struktur neben dem landesherrlichen Kirchenregiment mit seinen Alternativstrukturen war ein politisch motivierter Zwischenschritt. Faktisch wurde die geistliche Jurisdiktion der Bischöfe, die sich laut der Brandenburgischen Kirchenordnung von 1540 auch auf die Geistlichen erstreckt (Kirchen Ordnung im Churfurstenthum der Marcken zu Brandemburg [s. Anm. 35], 3. Hauptteil, Y 2ʳ), ignoriert. – Zu den Ordinationen durch Matthias von Jagow: GUSTAV KAWERAU, Bischof Matthias von Jagow und die Ordination evangelischer Geistlicher (JBrKG 13, 1915, 56–62). – 1545 verfügte Joachim II., dass die Patrone nur noch Ordinierte als Pfarrer anstellen dürfen (JOHANNES H. GEBAUER, Die Einführung der Reformation in den Städten Alt- und Neustadt Brandenburg, in: Forschungen zur brandenburgischen und preußischen Geschichte 13, 1900, 433–477, hier: 462, nach heute nicht mehr erhaltenen Akten des Ratsarchivs Brandenburg an der Havel).

[66] Wie die Ordination gestaltet wurde, zeigt eine aus Frankfurt (Oder) überlieferte und auf die 1560er Jahre zu datierende Ordinationsliturgie (JOACHIM GOLTZ, Agenda Das ist Außerlesene Kirchen-Ceremonien Welche in den Kirchen Augspurgischer Confeßion in vblichem Brauche sein / vnnd hin vnd wieder gleich vnd vngleich Bey dem Sacrament der H. Tauffe / Administration des HERRN CHRisti Nachtmahl / Copulation Breutigams vnnd Braut / Einsegenung der Sechswöchnerinnen / vnnd Christlichen Begrebnussen gehalten werden, Frankfurt [Oder] 1614, VD17 1:083005K, N 1ʳ–N 4ᵛ). Schon 1543 soll es eine Ordnung für die Prüfung und Ordination von Pfarrern durch den kurmärkischen Superintendenten (Inhaltswiedergabe ohne Angabe des Fundorts: CHRISTIAN WILHELM SPIEKER, Geschichte der Einführung der Reformation in die Mark Brandenburg, Berlin 1839, 251–253), deren Bestimmungen 1569 von Andreas Musculus verschärft werden (GStAPK, I. HA, Rep. 47, Lit. F, Nr. 2). Auf eine weitere heute nicht mehr nachweisbare Ordinationsordnung von 1574 weist hin: GEORG GOTTFRIED KÜSTER, Bibliotheca historica Brandenburgica scriptores rerum Brandenburgicarum maxime Marchicarum exhibens, Breslau 1743, 195. Ordinationszeugnisse sowie Selbstverpflichtungen von Ordinanden sind verstreut in den Akten und der Literatur überliefert: Eintragungen in den Wittenberger Ordiniertenbüchern mit Bezug auf die Provinz Brandenburg aus den Jahren 1538 bis 1637 (JBrKG 31, 1936, 98–113, 32, 1937, 3–50); Ordinationszeugnis für Georg Bolle, 1549 (MBW, Nr. 5346); Ordinationszeugnis für Va-

sicht über der Pfarrer an sich zogen und die diözesanbischöfliche Kirchenleitung vollständig ersetzten. Die späteren Kirchenordnungen und die Visitationsabschiede fügen weitere rechtliche Rahmenregelungen hinzu, und die Fülle der personenbezogenen Einzelfallentscheidungen, die in den kirchlichen und staatlichen Archiven überliefert sind, zeigen, wie dieses Recht zur Anwendung kam. Die evangelische Geistlichkeit der frühen Neuzeit war eine Personengruppe, die in einem rechtlich stark regulierten und obrigkeitlich engmaschig kontrollierten Rahmen lebte und arbeitete.

Ein wichtiger Teil der rechtlichen Rahmenregelungen betraf die Finanzierung der Pfarrer, ja am Anfang der Umsetzung der Reformation in den Gemeinden stand die Neuordnung der Gemeindefinanzen.[67] Diese beruhte weiterhin auf dem überkommenen System der Kirchenfinanzen, das mit der Begründung des Gemeinen Kastens und der Umwidmung von Einnahmen nach und nach instand gesetzt wurde, die wachsenden finanziellen Ansprüche des akademisch gebildeten und ein bürgerliches Leben führenden Geistlichkeit zu befriedigen.[68] So machte die Brandenburgische Kir-

---

lentin Henner, 1549 (GStAPK, I. HA, Rep. 43, Nr. 27 a-c, Paket 14323); Ordinationszeugnis für Martin Strahl (SBBPK, Ms. Boruss. fol., Nr. 201, 175ʳ–176ʳ); Ordinationszeugnis für Martin Dibbus, 1558 (Fortgesetzte Sammlung Von Alten und Neuen Theologischen Sachen 1731, 539f.); Vordrucke aus der der Regierungszeit Johann Georgs und Joachim Friedrichs (Stadtarchiv Frankfurt [Oder], Bestandsabteilung I, Heinsius-Annalen, Bd. 2, 201, 417, 427f., Brandenburgisches Landeshauptarchiv Potsdam, Rep. 86, Universität Frankfurt [Oder], Nr. 37); Verpflichtungserklärung von Jakob Reineck, 1600 (GEORG GOTTFRIED KÜSTER, Memorabilia Coloniensia, Berlin 1727, 91f.).

[67] ANDREAS STEGMANN, Reformation und Geld (Praktische Theologie 52, 2017, 69–74). Bezeichnenderweise ist die erste und einzige umfangreichere kirchliche Ordnung, die für die Neumark, den selbständigen Herrschaftsbereich von Markgraf Johann von Küstrin erging, die Kastenordnung von Anfang 1540. Von dieser Ordnung ist eine Abschrift des 16. Jahrhunderts (SBBPK, Ms. boruss. fol., Nr. 83, 76ʳ–99ʳ) sowie ein Abdruck des 18. Jahrhunderts (Corpus Constitutionum Marchicarum, hg. v. Christian Otto Mylius, Teil 1, Berlin u. Halle 1737, 249–264) erhalten, die auf unterschiedlichen Vorlagen beruhen und beide Fehler und Auslassungen aufweisen, einander aber in einer Weise ergänzen, dass die Rekonstruktion der nur in handschriftlicher Form verbreiteten Ordnung möglich ist. Die Ordnung zeigt, dass die Kirchenfinanzen ein vordringliches Ordnungsproblem waren und dass man sich in einem kleinen Territorium mit einer Kastenordnung begnügen und für alles Übrige auf andere Ordnungen rekurrieren konnte.

[68] Zur ökonomischen Situation der Geistlichen in der Frühphase der sächsisch-thüringischen Reformationsgeschichte hat Susan Karant-Nunn wichtige Studien vorgelegt: SUSAN K. BOLES, The Economic Position of Lutheran Pastors in Ernestine Thuringia 1521–1555 (ARG 63, 1972, 94–125); KARANT-NUNN, Luther's Pastors (s. Anm. 8). Ein durch die Reformation neu gestelltes Problem war die Versorgung der Pfarrwitwen, die anfangs nur zeitlich und materiell eng begrenzte Versorgungsansprüche geltend machen konnten (BERND WUNDER, Pfarrwitwenkassen und Beamtenwitwen-Anstalten vom 16.–19. Jahrhundert, in: ZHF 12, 1985, 429–498; WOLFGANG PETKE, Pfarrwitwen und Pfarradjunkten. Zur Alterssicherung mecklenburgischer Pfarrer und ihrer Witwen bis zum frühen 18. Jahrhundert, in: Menschen in der Kirche. 450 Jahre seit Einführung der Re-

chenordnung den Visitatoren 1540 zur Aufgabe, die Einnahmen und Ausgaben der Kirchengemeinden genau zu prüfen und alles, was »an pechten / geltzinsen / Acker oder wiesen zu jrem enthalt / vnd den Pfarren angehörig entwand ist / oder vorenthalten wird«, einzutreiben, »[d]amit die Pfarrer / Kirchendiener / Schulen vnd Hospitalia nottürfftiglich versorgt sein vnd bleiben«.[69] Tatsächlich war die Hauptbeschäftigung der Visitatoren während des 16. Jahrhunderts, die Finanzverhältnisse der Gemeinden zu ordnen, damit die für Besoldung und Bauunterhaltung nötigen Geldmittel und Naturalien zusammenkamen. Mit seinem hohen Anteil an ländlichen Pfarreien zeigt Brandenburg das typische Bild des lutherischen Territorialstaats, wo die Naturalabgaben einen großen Einkommensanteil ausmachten und nicht wenige Dorfpfarrer selbst auf den Pfarrhufen Landwirtschaft betrieben.

Obwohl sich Kirche und Obrigkeit während des 16. Jahrhunderts bemühten die Vorgaben hinsichtlich der Geistlichkeit umzusetzen und diese sich wiederum bemühte, den – ständig steigenden – Erwartungen an sie gerechtzuwerden, blieb die Wirklichkeit hinter dem Ideal zurück. Entscheidend für die Bewertung der Errungenschaften der Reformation bei der Etablierung des neuen Typs von Pfarrer sind aber nicht die Defizite und Kompromisse, sondern die mit der *necessaria coniunctio* anhebende Veränderungsdynamik, weshalb man die Etablierung des neuen Typs von Pfarrer hinsichtlich des einen Charakteristikums – der Pfarrer als *Prediger* – als Erfolg betrachten muss.

1.2. Der Pfarrer als Bürger

Das zweite Charakteristikum des neuen Typs von Pfarrer neben der Funktion als *Prediger* war sein Status als *Bürger*.[70] Dieser Status hängt nicht

---

formation in Mecklenburg, hg. v. Helge Bei der Wieden, Rostock 2000, 165–218), durch ihre Versorgungsbedürftigkeit aber auch Einfluss auf die Stellenbesetzung nehmen konnte (Maciej Ptaszyński, »... was für große sorge und mühe ein heiliger ehestandt wehre« [1599]. Zur Lebenssituation der Pfarrwitwen am Ende des 16. und Anfang des 17. Jahrhunderts in Pommern, in: Frühneuzeitliche Konfessionskulturen, hg. v. Thomas Kaufmann u.a., Gütersloh 2008, 319–345). Einen Einblick in die Komplexität der Pfarrfinanzierung und den Regelungsbedarf gibt die *Geistliche Polizei-, Visitation- und Konsistorialordnung* von 1561 (siehe oben Anm. 43 die Auflistung der Kapitel des ersten Teils dieser Ordnung).

[69] Kirchen Ordnung im Churfurstenthum der Marcken zu Brandemburg (s. Anm. 35), 3. Hauptteil, Y 2ʳ. Detaillierte Regelungen enthält die *Geistliche Polizei-, Visitation- und Konsistorialordnung* von 1561 im Abschnitt *Vonn den pfarren vn irehn einkommenn* (s. Anm. 43, 33ᵛ–35ᵛ).

[70] Zur Frage des Bürgerrechts für Kleriker im oberdeutschen Raum im Vergleich von spätem Mittelalter und Reformationszeit: Bernd Moeller, Kleriker als Bürger (in: Ders., Die Reformation und das Mittelalter. Kirchenhistorische Aufsätze, Göttingen

unmittelbar mit der Funktion zusammen, weshalb er nicht einfach wie die
bislang genannten Punkte unter der Überschrift *Der Pfarrer als Prediger*
stehen kann. Wohl galt, dass der Pfarrer in seinem Lebenswandel für das
von ihm gepredigte Evangelium einstehen musste, aber das implizierte
nicht notwendigerweise die Preisgabe eines besonderen klerikalen Status
und der mit diesem verbundenen Lebensformen. Tatsächlich entstand der
neue Status des Pfarrers nicht aus einer theologisch begründbaren Zu-
schreibung, sondern er verdankt sich der Delegitimation von Status und
Lebensformen des papstkirchlichen Klerus, der den evangelischen Pfarrern
keine andere Möglichkeit ließ, sich als Teil der nichtklerikalen Welt zu
verstehen und wie diese zu leben. So war für Luther schon in der Adels-
schrift 1520 klar, dass der »pfarr stand, den got eingesetzt hat, der ein
gemeyn mit predigen und sacramenten regierenn muß«, abgesehen von
diesem Gegenüber zu seinen Mitchristen »bey yhnen wonen und zeytlich
hauß halten« muß.[71] Die reformatorische »Bekehrung zur Welt«, die von
allen Glaubenden eine religiös motivierte innerweltliche Existenz einforderte,[72] unterstützte diese Verbürgerlichung der Geistlichkeit: Die Pfarrer
waren aufgefordert, die allen Christen geltende Forderung, den Glauben
in der Liebe hier und heute wirksam werden zu lassen, vorbildhaft umzusetzen, gewissermaßen als Bürger des himmlischen πολίτευμα auf Erden
(Phil. 3,20; vgl. Hebr. 13,14). »Bürger« ist dabei in einem doppelten Sinn
zu verstehen: Der Pfarrer war *Glied des weltlichen Gemeinwesens*, und
zwar als *Teil einer bestimmten Gruppe*, nämlich der nichtadligen und
nichtbäuerlichen Mittelgruppe, aus der sich ein Großteil der Funktions-
träger frühneuzeitlicher Staatlichkeit rekrutierte.[73] Die Zugehörigkeit zu

---

1991, 35–52). Einige Hinweise zur im Reformationsjahrhundert beginnenden Integration der lutherischen Geistlichkeit in im Verlaufe der Frühen Neuzeit entstehende »neue
soziale Schicht der Honoratioren oder der Ehrbarkeit, oberhalb des Kleinbürgertums
und Handwerkerstands, unterhalb des Adels« gibt BERND MOELLER, Pfarrer als Bürger,
Göttingen 1972, 14–23 (Zitat: 18). Der Prozess der Verbürgerlichung der Geistlichkeit ist
vor allem von der sozialgeschichtlich orientierten Forschung herausgestellt worden (vgl.
SCHORN-SCHÜTTE, Priest, preacher, pastor [s. Anm. 8]).

[71] WA 6,441,24–26. Zur »durch lebensweltliche Teilhabe charakterisierten Struktur«
des von Luther nunmehr »funktional verstandene[n] Gemeindepfarramt[s]«: THOMAS
KAUFMANN, An den christlichen Adel deutscher Nation von des christlichen Standes
Besserung, Tübingen 2014, 308f. Hintergründig dürfte auch die Einsicht in das allgemeine Priestertum aller Glaubenden eine Rolle gespielt haben, auch wenn der Zusammenhang von allgemeinem Priestertum und lebensweltlicher Teilhabe der kirchlichen
Amtsträger in der Frühzeit der Reformation nicht ausdrücklich hergestellt wurde.

[72] Zu Formel »Bekehrung zur Welt« (Oswald Bayer) und deren Bedeutung für das
reformatorische Ethos: ANDREAS STEGMANN, Die Genese und Struktur von Luthers
Ethik – ein Überblick (in: Der christliche Neubau der Sittlichkeit. Ethik in der Kirchengeschichte, hg. v. Andreas Müller, Leipzig 2018, 55–68).

[73] Was die Zugehörigkeit zum frühneuzeitlichen Bürgertum als einer bestimmten so-

dieser bestimmten sozialen Gruppe implizierte, dass die Pfarrerschaft an der in der Frühen Neuzeit zu beobachtenden sozialen Abschließung des Bürgertums gegenüber den unterbürgerlichen Schichten einerseits und dem Adel andererseits teilhatte und in den Habitus des Bürgers hineinwuchs, der zu einem zwar kontingenten, gleichwohl aber bestimmenden Merkmal des neuzeitlichen Pfarrerstands wurde.

Das wichtigste Kennzeichen der Zugehörigkeit Pfarrer zum Bürgertum war ihre Verheiratung und die Begründung eines Hausstands, und das nicht nur, weil sich darin der Bruch mit dem alten Klerikerstand am deutlichsten manifestierte,[74] sondern weil die neue Rolle als Ehemann, Vater und Hausvorstand das Selbstverständnis und die Amtsführung der Pfarrer und die Wirtschaftstätigkeit und Heiratsverbindungen seinen sozialen Status tiefgreifend veränderten. Es entstand das Pfarrhaus[75] als eine Institution, die nicht nur den engeren Lebenskreis der Pfarrfamilie umfasste, sondern auch ein wichtiges Element des Gemeinwesens bildete. Die aufsehenerregenden Eheschließungen von Klerikern und die wegweisenden Begründungen für diesen Schritt gehören in die 1520er Jahre, so dass bei der Einführung der Reformation in Brandenburg die Verheiratung der Pfarrer von Anfang als selbstverständlich vorausgesetzt werden konnte. Die Kirchenordnung von 1540 stellt den Pfarrern die Eheschließung frei,[76] und die folgenden Ordnungen gehen davon aus, dass der Pfarrer verhei-

---

zialen Gruppen innerhalb des weltlichen Gemeinwesens bedeutet, zeigt die neuere Forschung: BERND ROECK, Lebenswelt und Kultur des Bürgertums in der Frühen Neuzeit, München ²2011.

[74] STEPHEN E. BUCKWALTER, Die Priesterehe in Flugschriften der frühen Reformation, Gütersloh 1998; MARJORIE ELIZABETH PLUMMER, From priest's whore to pastor's wife. Clerical marriage and the process of reform in the early German Reformation, Farnham u. Burlington 2012.

[75] Der Begriff »Pfarrhaus« begegnet auch in der pastoraltheologischen Literatur des 16. Jahrhunderts, und zwar im weiteren Sinn. So spricht etwa Niels Hemmingsen in seinem Handbuch von der »domus pastoritiae« (Pastor sive pastoris optimus vivendi agendique modus, Leipzig 1565, VD16 H 1869, 1) und hat dabei den Pfarrer mit seiner Familie und seinen Sozialbeziehungen im Auge. – Die Forschungsliteratur zum Pfarrhaus – das gilt gerade auch für die einschlägigen Sammelbände (Das evangelische Pfarrhaus. eine Kultur- und Sozialgeschichte, hg. v. Martin Greiffenhagen, Stuttgart 1984; Das evangelische Pfarrhaus. Mythos und Wirklichkeit, hg. v. Thomas A. Seidel u. Christopher Spehr, Leipzig 2013; Das evangelische Pfarrhaus im deutschsprachigen Südwesten, hg. v. Jürgen Krüger u.a., Ostfildern 2014) – ist hinsichtlich des Reformationsjahrhunderts wenig ergiebig. Es mangelt an sozial- und kulturhistorischen Studien, die die Frühzeit der Etablierung dieses neuen Elements des lokalen Gemeinschaftslebens in den Blick nehmen. Neben den genannten Sammelbänden ist der beste Zugang zum Thema, wenn auch mit einem Schwerpunkt in der späteren Zeit: SCHORN-SCHÜTTE, Evangelische Geistlichkeit in der Frühneuzeit (s. Anm. 8), 287–330.

[76] Kirchen Ordnung im Churfurstenthum der Marcken zu Brandemburg (s. Anm. 35), 3. Hauptteil, Y 1ᵛ.

ratet ist, also ein familiären Wohn- und Wirtschaftsbedürfnissen entsprechendes Pfarrhaus hat,[77] die für den Unterhalt einer Familie notwendigen Einkünfte bezieht und im Erbrecht nicht mehr wie ein Kleriker, sondern wie ein Bürger zu behandeln ist. Zu den Privilegien gehörte auch die Befreiung von lokalen Abgaben und Leistungspflichten und das Recht, abgabenfrei für den Eigenbedarf Bier zu brauen und zu lagern.[78] Den Rechten des nunmehr verheirateten Pfarrers stand allerdings auch eine Pflicht gegenüber, dass sich nämlich sein Verkündigungsauftrag nicht nur in seinem persönlichen Lebensvollzug, sondern im Leben des Pfarrhauses als Ganzem widerzuspiegeln hatte:

»so gebueret auch den pfarrern, ihre weiber, kinder vnnd gesinde in aller gotts furcht vnd erbaren sitten dermassen aufzuziehen, das sie in deme andern darnach zuuolgen christliche anleittunge geben, vnnd do sie es nicht thun vnnd hierinne seumig oder lessigk sein wurden, sollen sie ihres ampts dodurch priuirt sein, in erwegung, das die jenigen, so die irhen vbel ziehen, die andern nicht wol vnderweisen oder lehren konnen.«[79]

Die *oeconomia christiana* wurde exemplarisch vom Pfarrer und seiner Familie vorgelebt. Wie Eheleute sich einander gegenüber verhalten, wie sie ihre Kinder erziehen und ihr Gesinde behandeln und vor allem wie sie den christlichen Glauben weitergeben und praktizieren, sollte hier anschaulich werden. Dabei wuchs der Pfarrfrau eine eigene Verantwortung zu, für die sie eines gewissen Maßes an Bildung und Eigenständigkeit bedurfte.[80] Allerdings sind die Quellen für das Familienleben und die Rolle der Pfarrfrau für die Reformationszeit zu spärlich, als dass man beides klarer konturieren kann; vor einer Verallgemeinerung von Einzelbeispielen – wie denen Martin Luthers und Katharina von Boras oder des Straßburger Ehepaars Zell[81] – muss man absehen, und aus späteren Verhältnissen auf frühere zurückzuschließen, verbietet sich.

---

[77] Geistliche Polizei-, Visitations- und Konsistorialordnung (s. Anm. 43), Abschnitt *Von besserung vnnd bawung der pfarren* (39ʳ–40ʳ).

[78] A.a.O., 36ʳ/ᵛ u. 35ʳ/ᵛ. Die traditionellen kirchlichen Abgaben der Geistlichen und Gemeinden (synodaticum, cathedraticum, procuratio) blieben vorerst erhalten und wurden umgewidmet, wurden aber in den 1570er Jahren weitgehend abgeschafft (FRÖHNER, Der evangelische Pfarrstand in der Mark Brandenburg [s. Anm. 9], 35–37).

[79] Geistliche Polizei-, Visitations- und Konsistorialordnung (s. Anm. 43), 22ᵛ. Vgl. zu den Anforderungen an die Persönlichkeit und den Lebensvollzug des Pfarrers das Beispiel Pommerns: PTASZYŃSKI, »Beruf und Berufung« (s. Anm. 8), 140–157.

[80] HERMANN WERDERMANN, Die deutsche evangelische Pfarrfrau. Ihre Geschichte in vier Jahrhunderten, Witten ²1936; LUISE SCHORN-SCHÜTTE, »Gefährtin« und »Mitregentin«. Zur Sozialgeschichte der evangelischen Pfarrfrau in der Frühen Neuzeit (in: Wandel der Geschlechterbeziehungen zu Beginn der Neuzeit, hg. v. Heide Wunder u. Christina Vanja, Frankfurt a. M. 1991, 109–153).

[81] THOMAS KAUFMANN, Pfarrfrau und Publizistin – Das reformatorische »Amt« der Katharina Zell (ZHF 23, 1996, 169–218).

Verbunden mit der Verbürgerlichung des Pfarrers und der Entstehung des Pfarrhauses waren wachsenden finanzielle Ansprüche. Die überkommene Ausstattung der Pfarrpfründen bildete zwar weiterhin die Grundlage der Pfarrbesoldung, sie musste aber rasch aufgestockt werden, um den wachsenden Bedarf der Pfarrfamilien zu decken. Die Visitationsakten des 16. Jahrhunderts zeigen eine starke Steigerung der Einkünfte, die weit über einen Inflationsausgleich hinausgeht. Obwohl die Klagen über zu geringe Besoldung und ausstehende Zahlungen bis weit ins 17. Jahrhundert notorisch sind, war das Pfarramt doch eine attraktive Karrieremöglichkeit und bot normalerweise ein gutes Auskommen. Auf dem Lande gehörte dazu allerdings auch die Bereitschaft des Pfarrers und seiner Familie, die Pfarrhufen zu bewirtschaften und mit eigener Hände Arbeit Subsistenzsicherung zu betreiben. Einen interessanten Einblick in diese Seite des Alltags von Dorfpfarrern gibt die sechsbändige *Oeconomia* des in Schlesien und Brandenburg aufgewachsenen und später in Mecklenburg tätigen Pfarrers Johannes Köhler, die zwischen 1595 und 1601 erschien und im 17. und 18. Jahrhundert immer wieder nachgedruckt und erweitert wurde und nicht nur praktische Hinweise zu Ackerbau, Viehzucht oder Heilkunde enthielt, sondern auch zeigte, wie man als lutherischer Christ sein Leben vor Gott und der Welt zu führen hatte.[82] Häuslicher Alltag und christlicher Glaube waren zwei Seiten derselben Medaille.

Die Verbürgerlichung des Pfarrers veränderte sein Verhältnis zur Gemeinde. Einerseits war er nun Teil der weltlichen Gemeinschaft und lebte ein ganz ähnliches Leben wie seine Mitbürger, andererseits stand er aufgrund seiner Funktion und seines geistlichen Sonderbewusstseins den Menschen, mit denen er im Alltag zusammenlebte, gegenüber. Diese schwer zu bewältigende Doppelrolle als Prediger des Gottesworts und christliches Vorbild im Gegenüber zu Gemeinde sowie als Bürger und Schicksalsgenosse in Gemeinschaft mit der Gemeinde war eine stete Quelle von Problemen. Als besonders konfliktträchtig erwies sich die dem Pfarrer auferlegte Pflicht, für die Beachtung religiöser Normen zu sorgen und sich darüber hinaus für die von der weltlichen Obrigkeit forcierte Sozialdisziplinierung in Dienst nehmen zu lassen, was nicht selten als un-

---

[82] Die sechs Teile erschienen in Wittenberg (VD16 ZV 25076, 25064, 25105, 25106, 3786; VD17 12:629586R). Johannes Köhler war der Sohn des unter anderem als Professor an der Viadrina lehrenden und als Propst an St. Nikolai in Berlin amtierenden Jakob Köhler, der bereits mit einer Materialsammlung zum Thema von Haus und Wirtschaft begonnen hatte (zu ihm: Noack / Splett, Bio-Bibliographien [s. Anm. 31], 58–72; zu seinem Sohn und dessen *Oeconomia*: Philip Hahn, Das Haus im Buch. Konzeption, Publikationsgeschichte und Leserschaft der »Oeconomia« Johann Colers, Epfendorf 2013). – Zur Steigerung der Einkünfte von Pfarrern: Fröhner, Der evangelische Pfarrstand in der Mark Brandenburg (s. Anm. 9), 32 f.

zulässige Bevormundung wahrgenommen und von der Gemeinde mit Verweigerung und Widerstand beantwortet wurde.[83]

1.3. Ein vergleichender Blick auf England

Was oben aufgrund der Brandenburgischen Kirchenordnung von 1540 über die Funktion des Pfarrers ausgeführt wurde, galt für die ganze Reformation – auch für England. Vorlage für die Brandenburgische Kirchenordnung von 1540 war die Brandenburgisch-Nürnbergische Kirchenordnung von 1533 gewesen, in der unter Führung von Andreas Osiander die im fränkischen Luthertum entwickelten Idealvorstellungen kirchlicher Erneuerung kodifiziert worden waren.[84] Diese Idealvorstellungen hatte zuvor ein englischer Gast Osianders in sich aufgesogen – und sollte sie nach seiner Rückkehr nach England an führender Stelle in die unter Heinrich VIII. beginnenden und von Eduard VI. entscheidend vorangetriebenen Reformbemühungen einbringen: Thomas Cranmer, Erzbischof von Canterbury von 1532 bis 1553.[85]

Auch was England betrifft, sind die Auswirkungen der Reformation auf die Geistlichkeit ein vielfach behandeltes Thema. Neben dem Standardwerk zum Thema von Rosemary O'Day[86] und einigen empfehlens-

---

[83] HELGA SCHNABEL-SCHÜLE, Distanz und Nähe. Zum Verhältnis von Pfarrern und Gemeinden im Herzogtum Württemberg vor und nach der Reformation (Rottenburger Jahrbuch für Kirchengeschichte 5, 1986, 339–348); SUSAN C. KARANT-NUNN, Neoclericalism and anticlericalism in Saxony, 1555–1675 (Journal of Interdisciplinary History 24, 1994, 615–637); BRUCE TOLLEY, Pastors & parishioners in Württemberg during the late Reformation 1581–1621, Stanford 1995; JAY GOODALE, Pfarrer als Außenseiter. Landpfarrer und religiöses Leben in Sachsen zur Reformationszeit (in: Historische Anthropologie 7, 1999, 191–211); DERS., The clergyman between the cultures of state and parish: Contestation and compromise in Reformation Saxony (in: The Protestant clergy of Early Modern Europe, hg. v. Scott C. Dixon u. Luise Schorn-Schütte, Basingstoke u. New York 2003, 100–119, 221–226); PTASZYŃSKI, »Beruf und Berufung« (s. Anm. 8), 397–429. Dass sich die im Reformationsjahrhundert grundgelegte Konfliktkonstellation während des 17. und 18. Jahrhunderts durchhielt, zeigt HANS-CHRISTOPH RUBLACK, Der wohlgeplagte Priester. Vom Selbstverständnis lutherischer Geistlichkeit im Zeitalter der Orthodoxie (ZHF 16, 1989, 1–30).

[84] ANDREAS OSIANDER, Gesamtausgabe, Bd. 5, Gütersloh 1983, 37–177. Zu diesem Text: GUNTER ZIMMERMANN, Prediger der Freiheit. Andreas Osiander und der Nürnberger Rat 1522–1548, Mannheim 1999, 268–308.

[85] Zu Cranmers Beziehungen zu Osiander: DIARMAID MACCULLOCH, Thomas Cranmer. A life, New Haven u. London 1996, 70–72.

[86] ROSEMARY O'DAY, The English clergy. The emergence and consolidation of a profession 1558–1642, Leicester 1979. O'Day stellt in ihrer magistralen Geschichte der Erforschung der englischen Reformation nach eigener jahrzehntelanger Beschäftigung mit dem Thema fest: »The manner in which the English clergy discovered a new role makes a fascinating story« (ROSEMARY O'DAY, The debate on the English Reformation, Manchester u. New York ²2014, 211).

werten Überblicksartikeln[87] sind die zahlreichen kundigen Zusammenfassungen dieses Aspekts der Reformationsgeschichte im Rahmen von Gesamtdarstellungen[88] sowie eine Fülle an Einzelstudien[89] zu nennen. Auch

---

[87] Einen knappen Überblick über die neuere Forschungsdiskussion gibt O'DAY, The debate on the English Reformation (s. Anm. 86), 210–216. Wichtige Überblicksartikel sind: ROSEMARY O'DAY, The Reformation of the ministry, 1558–1642 (in: Continuity and change. Personnel and administration of the Church in England 1500–1642, hg. v. ders. u. Felicity Heal, Leicester 1976, 55–75); VIVIANE BARRIE-CURIEN, The English clergy, 1560–1620: Recruitment and social status (History of European Ideas 9, 1988, 451–463); PATRICK COLLINSON, Shepherds, sheepdogs, and hirelings: The pastoral ministry in post-Reformation England (in: The ministry: clerical and lay, hg. v. W. J. Sheils u. Diana Wood, Studies in Church History 26, Oxford [UK] u. Cambridge [MA] 1989, 185–220); ANDREW PETTEGREE, The clergy and the Reformation: from ›devilish priesthood‹ to new professional elite (in: The reformation of the parishes. The ministry and the Reformation in town and country, hg. v. Andrew Pettegree, Manchester u. New York 1993, 1–21); CHRISTOPHER HAIGH, Anticlericalism and clericalism, 1580–1640 (in: Anticlericalism in Britain, c. 1500–1914, hg. v. Nigel Aston u. Matthew Cragoe, Stroud 2000, 18–41); ERIC JOSEF CARLSON, Good pastors or careless shepherds? Parish ministers and the English Reformation (History 88, 2003, 423–436; Carlson reagiert mit berechtigter Kritik auf die Darstellung von CHRISTOPHER HAIGH, The taming of the Reformation. Preachers, pastors and parishioners in Elizabethan and early Stuart England, in: History 85, 2000, 572–588).

[88] ROLAND G. USHER, The reconstruction of the English church, Bd. 1, London u. New York 1910, 205–243; RICHARD L. GREAVES, Society and Religion in Elizabethan England, Minneapolis 1981, 71–111; SUSAN BRIDGEN, London and the Reformation, Oxford 1989, 43–68, 392–404 u.ö.; FELICITY HEAL, Reformation in Britain and Ireland, Oxford 2003, 179–216, 286–302, 394–402, 429–435, 457–463 u.ö.

[89] Hier eine nach Erscheinungsjahr geordnete Auswahl, wobei auch Studien zur Geschichte der Kirchengemeinde berücksichtigt wurden: ARTHUR G. DICKENS, Aspects of intellectual transition among the English parish clergy of the Reformation period: A regional example (ARG 43, 1952, 51–70) [Yorkshire]; H. GARETH OWEN, The London parish clergy in the reign of Elizabeth I, Ph.D. thesis, University of London 1957; MICHAEL L. ZELL, The personnel of the clergy in Kent, in the Reformation period (EHR 89, 1974, 513–533); FELICITY HEAL, The parish clergy and the Reformation in the diocese of Ely (Proceedings of the Cambridge Antiquarian Society 66, 1975/76, 141–163); CLAIRE CROSS, Priests into ministers: The Establishment of Protestant practice in the city of York 1530–1630 (in: Reformation principle and practice, FS Arthur Geoffrey Dickens, hg. v. Peter Newman Brooks, London 1980, 203–225); TIMOTHY J. MCCANN, The clergy and the Elizabethan settlement in the diocese of Chichester (in: Studies in Sussex Church History, hg. v. M. J. Kitch, London 1981, 99–123); R. M. FISHER, The Reformation of clergy at the Inns of Court 1530–1580 (SCJ 12, 1981, Nr. 1, 69–91); JEREMY GORING, The reformation of the ministry in Elizabethan Sussex (JEH 34, 1983, 345–366); ROSEMARY O'DAY, The anatomy of a profession: the clergy of the Church of England (in: The professions in Early Modern England, hg. v. Wilfrid Prest, London u.a. 1987, 25–63); NICK ALLDRIDGE, Loyalty and identity in Chester parishes 1540–1640 (in: Parish, church and people. Local studies in lay religion 1350–1750, hg. v. S. J. Wright, London u.a. 1988, 85–124); BEAT KÜMIN, Parish finance and the early Tudor clergy (in: The reformation of the parishes. The ministry and the Reformation in town and country, hg. v. Andrew Pettegree, Manchester u. New York 1993, 43–62); MARTHA C. SKEETERS, Community and clergy. Bristol and the Reformation, c. 1530–c. 1570, Oxford 1993; PETER MARSHALL, The face of the pastoral ministry in the East Riding, 1525–1595, York 1995; CLAIRE CROSS, Ordinations in the diocese of York 1500–1630 (in: Patronage

die Forschungsbeiträge zu der durch die Reformation aufblühenden englische Predigtkultur sind in diesem Zusammenhang zu berücksichtigen,[90] ebenso wie die reichhaltige Literatur zum spätmittelalterlichen Klerus,[91] die es erlaubt, Kontinuitäten und Diskontinuitäten der Entwicklung vom 15. zum 16. Jahrhundert näher zu bestimmen. Anders als in der deutschsprachigen reformationsgeschichtlichen Forschung wird das Thema in der

---

and recruitment in the Tudor and early Stuart church, hg. v. Claire Cross, York 1996, 1–19; inhaltlich ähnlich: CLAIRE CROSS, Realising an utopian dream: the transformation of the clergy in the diocese of York, 1500–1630, in: Pragmatic utopias: Ideals and communities, 1200–1630, hg. v. Rosemary Horrox u. Sarah Rees Jones, Cambridge 2001, 259–275); BEAT KÜMIN, The shaping of community. The rise and reformation of the English parish, c. 1400–1560, Aldershot 1996; ROSEMARY O'DAY, The professions in early modern England, 1450–1800: Servants of the commonweal, Harlow 2000, 45–110; CLAIRE CROSS, From Catholic priests to Protestant ministers: Pastoral education in the diocese of York, 1520–1620 (in: The pastor bonus. Papers read at the British-Dutch colloquium at Utrecht, 18–21 September 2002, hg. v. Theo Clemens u. Wim Janse, Leiden u. Boston 2004, 157–165).

[90] Während die ältere Forschung (ALAN FAGER HERR, The Elizabethan sermon. A Survey and a bibliography, Philadelphia 1940; J. W. BLENCH, Preaching in England in the Fifteenth and Sixteenth Centuries, Oxford 1964) vor allem literaturwissenschaftlich orientiert ist, hat die neuere Predigtforschung den kirchen-, frömmigkeits- und theologiegeschichtlichen Reichtum dieser Rede- und Textgattung aufgewiesen: PETER E. MCCULLOUGH, Sermons at court. Politics and religion in Elizabethan and Jacobean preaching, Cambridge 1998; ERIC JOSEF CARLSON, The boring of the ear: Shaping the pastoral vision of preaching in England, 1540–1640 (in: Preachers and people in the Reformations and Early Modern Period, hg. v. Larissa Taylor, Leiden u.a. 2001, 249–296); SUSAN WABUDA, Preaching during the English Reformation, Cambridge 2002; IAN GREEN, Orality, script and print: the case of the English sermon c. 1530–1700 (in: Cultural exchange in early modern Europe, Bd. 1: Religion and cultural exchange in Europe, 1400–1700, hg. v. Heinz Schilling u. István György Tóth, Cambridge u.a. 2006, 236–255); IAN GREEN, Continuity and change in Protestant preaching in early modern England, London 2009; ARNOLD HUNT, The art of hearing. English preachers and their audiences, 1590–1640, Cambridge 2010; The Oxford handbook of the Early Modern sermon, hg. v. Peter McCullough u.a., Oxford 2011 (hier vor allem die Beiträge von GREG KNEIDEL, Ars praedicandi: Theories and practice [a.a.O., 3–20], IAN GREEN, Preaching in the parishes [a.a.O., 137–154], JOHN CRAIG, Sermon reception [a.a.O., 178–197], LUCY WOODING, From Tudor humanism to Reformation preaching [a.a.O., 329–347], und ARNOLD HUNT, Preaching the Elizabethan Settlement [a.a.O., 366–386]).

[91] MARGARET BOWKER, The secular clergy in the diocese of Lincoln, 1495–1520, Cambridge 1968; PETER HEATH, The English parish clergy on the eve of the Reformation, London u. Toronto 1969; ROBERT N. SWANSON, Problems of the priesthood in pre-Reformation England (EHR 105, 1990, 845–869); PETER MARSHALL, The Catholic priesthood and the English Reformation, Oxford 1994; TIM COOPER, The last generation of English Catholic clergy: Parish priests in the diocese of Coventry and Lichfield in the early sixteenth century, Woodbridge 1999; HEAL, Reformation in Britain and Ireland (s. Anm. 88), 43–80; ROBERT N. SWANSON, Pastoralia in practice. Clergy and ministry in pre-Reformation England (in: The pastor bonus. Papers read at the British-Dutch colloquium at Utrecht, 18–21 September 2002, hg. v. Theo Clemens u. Wim Janse, Leiden u. Boston 2004, 104–127); G. W. BERNARD, The late medieval English church. Vitality and vulnerability before the break with Rome, New Haven u. London 2012, 68–86.

Regel nicht von Kirchen- sondern von Profanhistorikern behandelt, die besonderes Interesse an den sozial- und kulturgeschichtlichen Zusammenhängen zeigen.

Unter Heinrich VIII. veränderten sich Status und Funktion des Klerus kaum, vielmehr bemühte sich der König trotz aller humanistisch und machtpolitisch motivierten Beförderung von Bibel und Predigt am Überkommenen festzuhalten. Dass an der kirchlichen Basis reformatorische Ideen verbreitet wurden und es mancherorts zu ersten Veränderungen kam, änderte bis Mitte der 1540er Jahre das Gesamtbild kaum. Mit der Thronbesteigung Eduards VI. aber und vor allem mit der Machübernahme durch den Kreis seiner engsten Berater kamen weitreichende Veränderungen in Gang, bei denen es direkt und indirekt auch um Status und Funktion der Geistlichen ging. Die Programmtexte und Ausführungsbestimmungen der eduardianischen Reformation stellen dem kontinentalen Protestantismus vergleichbar einen neuen Typ von Pfarrer vor Augen, der vor allem durch seine Funktion als *Prediger* bestimmt ist. Zu diesen Programmtexten gehören das *Book of Homilies* (1547)[92], das Mustertexte für die nunmehr ins Zentrum kirchlichen Lebens rückende Predigt bereitstellte, das *Ordinal* (1549/52)[93], eine dem *Book of Common Prayer* angehängten Sammlung der Ordinationsformulare für Diakone, Priester und Bischöfe, die *42 Artikel* (1552)[94], die die ekklesiologischen und amtstheologischen Grundsätze kodifizierten, die nicht mehr in Kraft getretenen *Canons* (1551/52)[95], die das überkommene Kirchenrecht den neuen Erfor-

---

[92] The Two Books of Homilies Appointed to be Read in Churches, hg. v. John Griffiths, Oxford 1859. Zum ersten *Book of Homilies*: ASHLEY NULL, Official Tudor homilies (in: The Oxford handbook of the early modern sermon, hg. v. Peter McCullough u.a., Oxford 2011, 348–365, hier: 350–357).

[93] The forme and maner of makyng and consecratyng of archebishoppes bishoppes priestes and deacons. M. D. XLIX. (STC 16462); The first and second prayer books of Edward VI, London 1910, 291–317 (Fassung von 1549), 437–463 (Fassung von 1552 mit einigen nicht das Amtsverständnis betreffenden Veränderungen gegenüber der Erstfassung); The English rite, hg. v. F. E. Brightman, Bd. 2, London ²1921, 928–1017 (Paralleldruck der Ordnungen von 1550, 1552 und 1661). Die Ausgabe von 1559 ist ediert in: Liturgical services. Liturgies and occasional forms of prayer set forth in the reign of queen Elizabeth, hg. v. William Keating Clay, Cambridge 1847, 272–298. Zur eduardianischen Ordinationsliturgie: PAUL F. BRADSHAW, The Anglican Ordinal, its history and development from the Reformation to the present day, London 1971, 18–36.

[94] Synodalia (s. Anm. 135), 1–17; Die Bekenntnisschriften der reformierten Kirche, hg. v. E. F. Karl Müller, Leipzig 1903, 505–522 (Nr. 24).

[95] Tudor church reform. The Henrician canons of 1535 and the Reformatio Legum Ecclesiasticarum, hg. v. Gerald Bray, Woodbridge u. Rochester 2000, 145–743. Diese von Cranmer als dritte, kirchenrechtliche Säule neben den doktrinalen und liturgischen Normentexten konzipierte Ordnung ist in vielerlei Hinsicht »descriptive of conditions as they actually were« und nicht bloß »a blueprint for ›the church that never was‹« (a.a.O., CXV).

dernissen anpassten, die Predigten und Schriften der Protagonisten der eduardianischen – und frühen elisabethanischen – Kirche[96] sowie die zahlreichen *Injunctions* und *Acts*, mit denen etwa die Aufhebung des Pflichtzölibats verordnet wurde.[97]

Die ekklesiologisch-amtstheologischen Grundideen der »Reformation by the word«[98], die folgenrichtig die Predigt zum zentralen Medium der

---

[96] Hier ließe eine Fülle von Predigten, Katechismen oder Traktaten anführen. Exemplarisch sei Hugh Latimer genannt, der für seine Predigten vor dem König 1548/49 zweimal Röm. 15,4 als Predigttext wählte und über die Heilsbedeutsamkeit der Predigt und die religiös zentrale Aufgabe des Predigers sprach (HUGH LATIMER, Sermons, Cambridge 1844, 59–78, 194–215). John Jewel verteidigte in seiner offiziösen Apologie der englischen Kirche 1562 auch die ekklesiologischen und amtstheologischen Grundsätze des *Elizebethan Settlement* (Apologia Ecclesiae Anglicanae, London 1562, STC 14581, B 1ᵛ–B 3ᵛ), die diese Predigt sichern sollten. – Ausgewertet wird die Fülle der Quellen zur Ekklesiologie und Amtstheologie der führenden Kirchenmänner unter Eduard VI. und Elisabeth I. in: H. F. WOODHOUSE, The doctrine of the church in Anglican theology, 1547–1603, London 1954 (hier zum kirchlichen Amt und vor allem zu der die elisabethanischen Theologen besonders umtreibenden Debatte um das Bischofsamt: 75–92); PETER NEWMAN BROOKS, The principle and practice of primitive Protestantism in Tudor England: Cranmer, Parker and Grindal as chief pastors 1535–1577 (in: Reformation principle and practice, FS Arthur Geoffrey Dickens, hg. v. Peter Newman Brooks, London 1980, 119–133); GLEN BOWMAN, »To the perfection of God's service«: John Ponet's Reformation vision for the clergy (AEH 72, 2003, 79–101); MALCOLM B. YARNELL, Royal priesthood in the English Reformation, Oxford 2013 (auch zu Thomas Cromwell, insbesondere aber zu Thomas Cranmer). – In der Streitschriftenliteratur der zweiten Hälfte des 16. Jahrhunderts waren ekklesiologische und amtstheologische Fragen durchweg präsent – vor allem in der Abgrenzung vom römischen Katholizismus und in den Debatten um den Puritanismus –, sie bildeten aber kein Schwerpunktthema (vgl. PETER MILWARD, Religious controversies of the Elizabethan Age. A survey of printed sources, London 1977). – Martin Bucers Theorie des vierfachen Amts und seine Vorschläge zur Reorganisation der theologischen Ausbildung übten vermittelt über einzelne Protagonisten zwar einen gewissen Einfluss auf die Entwicklung aus, fanden aber keine Umsetzung (O'DAY, The English clergy [s. Anm. 86], 27).

[97] Erste, ganz auf der Linie der Kirchenpolitik seines Vaters liegende Vorgaben machten Eduards *Injunctions* von 1547 (Visitation articles and injunctions [s. Anm. 135], Bd. 2, 114–130). Erst 1549 wird der *Act to take away all positive laws against marriage of priests* verabschiedet (Documents Illustrative of English Church History, hg. v. Henry Gee u. William John Hardy, London 1910, 366–368), der 1552 noch durch den *Acte made for the Declaration of a Statute made for the Mariage of Priestes and legittimacion of their children* ergänzt wird. Die theologische Begründung für diesen Schritt entfaltete John Ponet (ca. 1514–1556) in seiner 1549 erschienenen Schrift *A defence for mariage of priestes, by Scripture and anciente wryters* (hierzu: BOWMAN, John Ponet's Reformation vision for the clergy [s. Anm. 96], 82–88). – Zur Diskussion über die Eheschließung von Geistlichen und deren rechtliche Ermöglichung: JOHN K. YOST, The Reformation defense of clerical marriage in the reigns of Henry VIII and Edward VI (ChH 50, 1981, 152–165); RICHARD M. SPIELMANN, The beginnings of clerical marriage in the English Reformation: The reigns of Edward and Mary (AEH 56, 1987, 251–263); ERIC JOSEF CARLSON, Clerical marriage and the English Reformation (Journal of British Studies 31, 1992, 1–31); HELEN PARISH, Clerical marriage and the English Reformation. Precedent policy and practice, Aldershot u.a. 2000.

[98] CATHARINE DAVIES, A religion of the Word. The defence of the Reformation in the reign of Edward VI, Manchester 2002, 87.

Erneuerung machte, werden in den *42 Artikeln* in enger Anlehnung an CA 7 bestimmt: Die Kirche ist definiert durch die reinen Predigt des Gottesworts und die rechte Sakramentsverwaltung (Art. 20). Das »munus publice praedicandi, aut administrandi Sacramenta in Ecclesia« darf nur ausüben, wer »legitime vocatus et missus« ist (Art. 24). Die zu öffentlicher Predigt und Sakramentsverwaltung berufenen Amtsträger unterliegen keinem Pflichtzölibat (Art. 31), sondern – so darf man ergänzen – verbinden mit ihrem geistlichen Amt ein Leben in der Welt. Was das *munus praedicandi* ausmacht, zeigt die Ordinationsliturgie: Die drei Ämter (Diakon, Presbyter, Bischof) sind im Kern alle als Verkündigungsämter bestimmt, weshalb der Grundbestand an amtstheologischen Aussagen bei allen derselbe ist. So heißt es im Gebet bei der Ordination des Diakons:

»illuminate al Bisshops, Pastours and Ministers of the Churche, wyth true knowledge, and understandig of thy worde, and that both by theyr preachynge and lyuing, they may sette it forth and shewe it accordingly«.[99]

Der Ordinand muß bekennen, dass das kirchliche Amt in Christi Befehl gründet und dass er sich an der Bibel orientiert und die Bibel verkündigt.[100] Die bei der Ordination des Presbyters hinzukommenden Texte schärfen die Verkündigungsaufgabe weiter ein, sind die Pfarrer doch

»the messengers, the watchemen, the Pastours, and the stewardes of the LORDE to teache to premonisshe, to feede, and prouyde for the Lordes famylye«.[101]

Das Amt der Priester ist

»of so weightie a woorke perteining to the saluation of man, but with doctryne and exhortacion, taken out of holy scripture and with a life agreable unto the same«.[102]

Es besteht

»in readyng and learnyng the holy scriptures, and in framyng the maners, both of yourselues, and of them that specially partein unto you, accordyng to the rule of the same scriptures«.[103]

Die entscheidende Frage des Bischofs an den Ordinanden ist darum:

»Be you perswaded that the holy Scriptures contein sufficiently al doctrine required of necessitie for eternal saluacion, throughe faith in Jesu Christe? And are you determined with the saied scriptures, to enstructe the people committed to your

---

[99] The first and second prayer books of Edward VI (s. Anm. 93), 295.
[100] A.a.O., 300f.
[101] A.a.O., 308.
[102] A.a.O., 309.
[103] Ebd. Vgl. die Forderung und Verheißung an die Ordinanden: »And that you wyll continually praye for the heauenly assistaunce of the holy goste, from God the father, by the mediacion of our only mediatour and sauiour Jesus Chryste, that by dayly readyng and weighing of the scriptures, ye may waxe riper and stronger in your ministerie« (ebd.).

charge, and to teache nothyng, as required of necessitie, to eternal saluacion, but that you shalbe perswaded may be concluded, and proued by the scripture?«[104]

Der Pfarrer ist also der Verkündiger der biblischen Heilsbotschaft, das heißt, er muss die Bibel kennen, Irrlehre bekämpfen und ein der Bibel entsprechendes Leben selbst führen und anderen nahebringen. Die notwendige Qualifikation dafür ist theologische Bildung: Der Ordinand ist »learned in the Latyne tongue and sufficientlye instructed in holye Scripture«.[105]

Auch die *Reformatio legum ecclesiasticarum* von 1552/53 betont in ihren Ausführungen über das Predigtamt[106] dessen besondere Bedeutung:

»Quoniam contionandi munus populo Dei maxime necessarium est, ecclesia nunquam illo destitui debet.«[107]

Ein Prediger muß *pietas* und *doctrina* aufweisen, er bedarf der Überprüfung und Beauftragung durch die kirchlichen Autoritäten, er muss rhetorisch geschult sein und hohen moralischen Standards genügen.[108] Im Normalfall ist ein Pfarrer ein Prediger, nur im begründeten Ausnahmefall soll er keine Predigterlaubnis erhalten.[109] Die Verbreitung der *sana doctrina* ist auch die vornehmliche Pflicht des Bischofs, die er selbst zu erfüllen und für die er andere heranzuziehen hat.[110] Gepredigt werden soll in Pfarrkirchen im sonntäglichen Hauptgottesdienst.[111] Zu den Amtspflichten gehört auch Seelsorge an den Schwachen, Angefochtenen und Kran-

---

[104] Ebd.

[105] A.a.O., 292.

[106] The Henrician canons of 1535 and the Reformatio Legum Ecclesiasticarum (s. Anm. 95), 238–244 (Kap. 7). Das kirchliche Amt ist zudem in Kap. 11–13 sowie in Kap. 19–20 Thema. Große Teile von Kap. 7 (De concionatoribus) wurden 1571/76 in die *Canons* übernommen, wurden also geltendes Kirchenrecht.

[107] A.a.O., 238.

[108] An einer anderen Stelle wird vorgeschrieben, dass Presbyter eine englische und lateinische Bibel besitzen, diese studieren und sich um die Predigt bemühen sollen (a.a.O., 350).

[109] »Nec hi [sc. archiepiscopi] solum in hac occupatione sanctissima debent esse, sed pastoribus etiam et parochis eadem potestas in suis gregibus concedi debet« (a.a.O., 240). In Kathedralkirchen wird an jedem Sonntag und Heiligentag für das Volk gepredigt (a.a.O., 240), auch in den Universitätsstädten wird an Sonntagen und Heiligentagen gepredigt (a.a.O., 240–242). Wenn in Stadt- und Dorfkirche an Sonntagen und Heiligentagen keine Predigt gehalten wird (vier solcher Predigten sind das jährliche Minimum), soll aus den *Homilies* vorgelesen werden (a.a.O., 242); die Bevölkerung ist zur Teilnahme an den Predigten verpflichtet (a.a.O., 242–244).

[110] A.a.O., 358.

[111] A.a.O., 334–344. Alternativ kann auch eine *homily* verlesen werden. Predigten in Kathedralkirchen finden am Sonntagnachmittag statt, um den Besuch der vormittäglichen Predigt in der Pfarrkirche zu ermöglichen. In Pfarrkirchen kann auch am Sonntagnachmittag gepredigt werden, auf jeden Fall soll dann der Katechismusunterricht stattfinden.

ken.[112] Um die Qualifikation nachzuweisen, muss vor der Vergabe eines beneficium eine Prüfung absolviert werden, bei der das Glaubensbekenntnis, die Bibel, die neueren Kontroversen und der Katechismus abgefragt werden, wobei die Formulierung erkennen lässt, dass wohl eher mit Überblicks- als mit Vertiefungswissen gerechnet wird.[113] Die *Reformatio* macht auch deutlich, dass der Pfarrer in das hergebrachte hierarchische System und die überkommenen Patronatsstrukturen eingebunden bleibt. Obwohl sein Dienst neu verstanden wird, bleibt doch der im Laufe des Mittelalters geschaffene institutionelle Rahmen erhalten.

In diesen drei kurz vorgestellten Programmtexten wie in der Fülle der übrigen Quellen zeigt sich, dass die englische Reformation in ihrer Amtstheologie und deren praktischer Umsetzung dem kontinentalen Vorbild folgte, auch wenn sie an manchen Punkten konservativer mit den überkommenen Strukturen verfuhr und den Umbau der Kirche langsamer und vorsichtiger anging. Das betraf etwa die Freigabe der Priesterehe und der Predigt, was beides zwar von Anfang an intendiert war, aber aufgrund grundsätzlicher Bedenken und praktischer Hemmungen erst mit Verzögerung – so die Verheiratung von Geistlichen – oder gar nicht – so die Freigabe der Predigt – erfolgte. Das *Elizabethan Settlement* führte die unter Eduard VI. begonnenen Reformen weiter und während der mehr als vier Jahrzehnte von Elisabeths Herrschaft wurde das Ende der 1540er, Anfang der 1550er Jahre konzipierte Reformprogramm weitgehend umgesetzt: Während der Regierungszeit Elisabeths gelang es, den Bildungsstand der Geistlichkeit entscheidend zu heben, die finanzielle Ausstattung der Stellen zu verbessern und immer mehr Stellen im ländlichen Raum mit kompetenten Pfarrern zu besetzen. In einem wichtigen Teil des kirchlichen Spektrums wurde die kirchliche Erneuerung sogar noch über die durch das *Elizabethan Settlement* gezogenen Grenzen hinaus getrieben: Theorie und Praxis des Pfarramts waren im Puritanismus entsprachen dem Genfer Vorbild und hoben sich damit deutlich von der Staatskirche ab.

Der vergleichende Blick auf England zeigt, dass in den Reformationskirchen ganz Europas das kirchliche Amt in einer Weise neu verstanden und anders praktiziert wurde, die einen deutlichen Bruch mit dem mittelalterlichen Herkommen zeigt. Unzweifelhaft gab es Kontinuitäten über den Epochenbruch hinweg, im Ganzen überwog aber die fundamentale Diskontinuität, die sich aus dem Rückgriff auf die neutestamentliche Norm ergab.

---

[112] A.a.O., 230.
[113] A.a.O., 284.

2. Die Unterschiede zwischen deutscher und englischer Reformation

2.1. Die Eigenarten der Entwicklung in Deutschland

Der neue Typ des Pfarrers bildete sich im Einflussbereich der Wittenberger Reformation und in vergleichbarer Weise auch im oberdeutsch-schweizerischen Raum bereits in den Anfängen der kirchlichen Erneuerung heraus und wurde rasch und umfassend verwirklicht. Diese Einschätzung gilt auch dann, wenn man die regional unterschiedliche Entwicklung berücksichtigt und der zahlreichen Hemmungen und praktischen Probleme eingedenk ist: Auf dem Lande verlief die Etablierung des neuen Typus langsamer als in den Städten, mancherorts behinderten der Papstkirche treue Bischöfe, Obrigkeiten und Patrone kirchliche Reformen in den Gemeinden und immer wieder scheiterte die Verwirklichung des pastoralen Ideals am Fehlen geeigneter Kandidaten, am Mangel finanzieller Mittel, an Kompetenzstreitigkeiten zwischen kirchlichen und weltlichen Instanzen, an persönlichen Verfehlungen von Pfarrern oder an der Resistenz von Gemeinden. Auch die Akademisierung der evangelischen Pfarrerschaft erwies sich als nicht durchweg erfolgreich, blieb doch das Bildungsniveau lange Zeit hinter den Ansprüchen an die angehenden Pfarrer zurück und entwickelten sich diese Ansprüche zugleich in einer Weise, dass es während der ganzen frühen Neuzeit Klagen über den mangelnden Bildungsstand der Geistlichen und Hinweise auf unqualifizierte und ihrer Aufgabe nicht gewachsene Geistliche gab.[114] Aber trotz aller Relativierun-

---

[114] Quellenzeugnisse für die Schwierigkeiten bei der Etablierung des neuen Typus von Pfarrer gibt es so viele und sie lassen sich bis weit ins 17. Jahrhundert hinein finden, dass der Eindruck entstehen könnte, dass man eher von einem Misserfolg als von einem Erfolg sprechen sollte. Dabei geht es vielfach um die mangelnde Bildung der Pfarrer, so etwa, wenn die Kurbrandenburgische Visitationsordnung von 1558 beklagt, dass manche Patrone »vngeschickte vnd vngelarte Esel / die [...] jr Ampt / wie sich gebuert / nicht zubestellen wissen«, anstellen, um einen Teil der Erträge vereinnahmen zu können (s. Anm. 43, B 4$^{r/v}$), oder wenn die *Geistliche Polizei-, Visitations- und Konsistorialordnung* von 1561 erwähnt, dass »schneider, schuster oder andere vordorbene handtwercker vnnd lediggenger, die ihre grammatica nicht studirt, vielweyniger recht lesen konnen«, Pfarrer geworden seien, und die Patrone auffordert, diesen Mißbrauch des geistlichen Amts abzustellen und nach Möglichkeit »tuchtige personnen [...], nemlich godtfurchtige menner, die nicht in offentlichen lastern leben vnnd nicht falsche, sondern die reine lehre des euangelii bekennen«, zu berufen (s. Anm. 43, 10^r; dieser Passus ist auch in die Visitations- und Konsistorialordnung von 1573 übergangen [s. Anm. 43, 10]). Gerade die brandenburgische Visitation im Jahr 1600, die erstmals ausführlicher auch den Bildungsstand der Geistlichen dokumentierte, machte Mängel erkennbar (z.B. Müller, Parisius, Abschiede [s. Anm. 44], Bd. 1, Heft 3, 1893, 183, 206, 217, 229, 243; schon die *Gravamina* der kurmärkischen Stände aus dem Vorjahr weisen auf Mängel hin: GStAPK, I. HA, Rep. 20, Lit. B, Nr. 1, 180^v–182^v, 183$^{r/v}$). Dass diese Bildungsmängel verbreitet waren

gen kann mit Blick auf Deutschland von einem Entwicklungsvorsprung
sprechen, der sich gerade im Bereich der für den neuen Typ von Pfarrer so
bedeutsamen berufsbezogenen schulisch-akademischen Ausbildung zeigt:
Es gab eine Vielzahl von Lateinschulen und Universitäten, die nach dem
Einschnitt der frühen Reformation rasch wieder aufzublühen begannen
oder neu gegründet wurden und humanistische Didaktik mit der intellek-
tuell wie existentiell herausfordernden reformatorischen Theologie verbanden; die Bereitstellung von Stipendien und die Eröffnung von Studi-
enhäusern trug dazu bei, eine territoriale Funktionselite heranzubilden;
und eine Fülle pastoraltheologischer Hilfsliteratur gab zusätzliche Hilfe-
stellungen und verdeutlichte das allmählich steigende Anspruchsniveau.

Dass sich die Neuerungen im evangelischen Deutschland vergleichsweise schnell und umfassend durchsetzten, hängt mit der besonderen politischen Struktur des spätmittelalterlich-frühneuzeitlichen Reichs zusammen: Die Territorien und Reichsstädte, wo sich die Reformation etablieren
konnte, waren weitgehend souverän, so dass sie das von Luther und seinen
Mitreformatoren so eindrücklich propagierte kirchliche Erneuerungspro-
gramm aus eigener Vollmacht umsetzen konnten, wobei die Reformverweigerung der Papstkirche es unumgänglich machte, die überkommenen
Strukturen umzubauen. Aus der doppelten Voraussetzung von Notwendigkeit der Veränderung und Möglichkeit der Neugestaltung ergab sich
eine Erneuerungsdynamik, die binnen weniger Jahrzehnte den neuen Typ
von Pfarrer als Norm und Wirklichkeit etablierte. Die weltlichen Obrigkeiten waren wichtige Triebkräfte und tatkräftige Mitgestalter dieser Entwicklung. Die große Mehrheit der im 16. Jahrhundert mit der Reformation sympathisierenden Herrscher und Magistrate engagierte sich mit Ver-
antwortungsbewusstsein und Kompetenz für die kirchliche Erneuerung

---

und von den kirchlichen Leitungsverantwortlichen in Kauf genommen wurden, zeigen
auch württembergische Prüfungsprotokolle aus dem 17. Jahrhundert: KARL MÜLLER,
Kirchliches Prüfungs- und Anstellungswesen in Württemberg im Zeitalter der Orthodoxie. Aus den Zeugnisbüchern des herzoglichen Konsistoriums (Württembergische
Vierteljahreshefte für Landesgeschichte 25, 1916, 431–488; vgl. die Darstellung von
CHRISTOPH KOLB, Zur Geschichte des Pfarrstandes in Altwürttemberg, in: BWKG
57/58, 1957/58, 74–190). Zum Patronatsrecht als hemmenden Faktor der Durchsetzung
des »Typus des akademisch studierten Pfarrers«: VOLKER LEPPIN, Die Professionalisierung des Pfarrers in der Reformation (in: DERS., Reformatorische Gestaltungen. Theologie und Kirchenpolitik in Spätmittelalter und Früher Neuzeit, Leipzig 2016, 275–292,
Zitat: 291). Leppins Darstellung krankt allerdings an der Vermischung von Ideal und
Wirklichkeit und an der Ineinssetzung von Akademisierung und Universitätsstudium:
Der neue Typus des theologisch gebildeten Predigers war durchaus ein Bruch mit dem
spätmittelalterlichen Priesterideal und etablierte sich in einer frühen Phase der Reformation; seine Umsetzung in der Wirklichkeit und vor allem die Verknüpfung von Bil-
dungsanforderungen und akademischem Studium ließen aber auf sich warten.

und schuf, dabei bewusst mit führenden Theologen kooperierend, neue, über Jahrhunderte hinweg stabile Strukturen. Ein günstiger Faktor war auch die Überschaubarkeit der Herrschaftsbereiche und die Kompaktheit der Herrschaftsstrukturen, die den chronisch schwächelnden Zentralgewalten eine Durchsetzung ihrer Ordnungsvorstellungen und die Kontrolle von deren Umsetzung ermöglichte. Damit einher ging die erfolgreiche Homogenisierung des im Zuge der Reformation diversifizierten religiösen Spektrums: In einem Territorium oder einer Reichsstadt gab es in der Regel nur eine Konfession, die zwar in sich eine gewisse Pluralität aufwies, aber religiöse Konkurrenz ausschloss. Die Lehr- und Disziplinierungskonflikte, die die Kehrseite dieser Homogenisierung waren, hatten zwar durchaus destabilisierende Folgen, diese betrafen aber in der Regel nur eine kleine Minderheit und bewirkten durchaus die intendierte Stärkung der konfessionellen Identität für die große Mehrheit. Die reformatorische Geistlichkeit wirkte also in einem von verantwortlich handelnden weltlichen Obrigkeiten grundlegend neu organisierten und auf konfessionskulturelle Homogenität angelegten Institutionengefüge, was die umfassende Verwirklichung des neuen Typs von Pfarrer ermöglichte.

2.2. Die Eigenarten der Entwicklung in England

Auch wenn es in den protestantischen Territorien und Städten Deutschland immer wieder religionspolitische Kurswechsel gab, so ging die Etablierung des Typs von Pfarrer hier doch zielgerichtet vor sich. In England dagegen gab es während der Schlüsseljahre der Reformation keine längere Zeit kontinuierlicher Entwicklung. Das Schwanken Heinrichs VIII.[115] zwischen dem Festhalten an der kirchlichen Tradition einerseits und der humanistisch motivierten, sich mit der kontinentalen Reformation teilweise überschneidenden Erneuerung andererseits hieß für den englischen Klerus, dass dessen überkommener Status und hergebrachte Funktion erhalten blieben,[116] dass er allerdings für die Abgrenzung von der römischen

---

[115] Zur Religionspolitik Heinrichs VIII.: Peter Marshall, Reformation England, 1480–1642, London 2003, Kap. 3; G. W. Bernard, The King's Reformation. Henry VIII and the Remaking of the English Church, New Haven u. London 2005.

[116] Das zeigt sich auch darin, dass das mittelalterliche pastoraltheologische Handbuch *Cura clericalis* während der Regierungszeit Heinrichs VIII. dreimal aufgelegt wurde, in dem als die vier Hauptfunktionen des Gemeindepfarrers die Feier der Messe, die Verwaltung der Sakramente, die Beichte und die Unterweisung der Gemeinde aufgezählt wurden. Wenn es zur vierten Funktion heißt »Quarto sacerdotes sunt plebis doctores ideo dicitur sacerdos quasi sacra docens hoc modo opus est eos scire adminus articulos fidei & alijs preceptis dei informari« (London 1532, STC 6126, A 1ᵛ), dann zeigt das, dass sowohl die humanistische Reform Heinrichs VIII. wie die an kontinentalen Vorbildern orientierte Reformation Eduards VI. an mittelalterliche Vorgaben anknüpften.

Papstkirche und eine partielle Erneuerung der Kirche in Dienst genommen wurde.[117] Was diese Erneuerung ausmachte und welche Grenzen sie haben sollte, wurde im Laufe der Regierungszeit Heinrichs unterschiedlich bestimmt: Auf die Phase der gegenüber der kontinentalen Reformation vergleichsweise offenen Positionierung während der Kanzlerschaft Thomas Cromwells, die sich etwa in der Beförderung der Bibelverbreitung, dem Bemühen um eine Aufwertung der Predigt, der Auflösung der Klöster und der Beschneidung traditioneller Vorstellungen und Praktiken der Frömmigkeit zeigte, folgte die Phase der Distanzierung von der Reformation, die in die Bahnen einer vom erasmianischen Humanismus inspirierten vorsichtigeren Kirchenerneuerung lenkte. Auch wenn die königliche Kirchenpolitik wechselhaft und an eine grundsätzliche Veränderung von Status und Funktion der Kleriker nicht gedacht war,[118] gab es doch einen kleinen Freiraum, der von den Reformationssympathisanten genutzt wurde. So traten in den 1530er Jahren immer wieder Geistliche auf, die ihr Amt im Sinne der Reformation als *Predigt*amt verstanden und ihre Botschaft an kontinentalen Vorbildern ausrichteten. So musste sich etwa Hugh Latimer (1485–1555), der als von der Universität Cambridge lizenzierter Prediger im ganzen Land auf die Kanzeln steigen durfte, gegen Vorwürfe des Londoner Bischofs John Stokesley verteidigen, dass er ohne Befugnis in dessen Diözese gepredigt habe.[119] Interessant an dieser Verteidigung ist in unserem Zusammenhang nicht die Frage nach der Predigt-

---

[117] Margaret Bowker, The Heinrician Reformation and the parish clergy (in: The English Reformation revised, hg. v. Christopher Haigh, Cambridge 1987, 75–93).

[118] Das zeigt etwa der Entwurf eines neuen Kirchenrechts, der »Henrician canons« (The Henrician canons of 1535 and the Reformatio Legum Ecclesiasticarum [s. Anm. 95], 1–143), der den Klerus noch ganz im traditionellen Sinn versteht, allerdings dem spätmittelalterlichen Reformbemühen folgend stärker reguliert und kontrolliert. Die *Wittenberger Artikel* von 1536 (Artickel der Cristlichen Lahr, von welchen die Legatten aus Engelland mit dem Herrn Doctor Martino gehandelt Anno 1536, hg. v. Georg Mentz, Leipzig 1905), die in Art. 9 und 14 die Amtstheologie der kontinentalen Reformation vertreten, spielten für die Kirchenpolitik Heinrichs VIII. keine Rolle und dürften ihn eher im Festhalten an der Tradition bestärkt haben, wie es in unterschiedlicher Weise und unterschiedlichem Ausmaß 1536 die *Zehn Artikel* (Die Kirche von England. Ihr Gebetbuch, Bekenntnis und kanonisches Recht, hg. v. Cajus Fabricius, Berlin u. Leipzig 1937, 585–606) sowie die königlichen *Injunctions* (Documents Illustrative of English Church History [s. Anm. 97], 269–274) und 1537 das *Bishops' Book* (Formularies of faith put forth by authority during the reign of Henry VIII., hg. v. Charles Lloyd, Oxford 1856, 21–211) belegen. Der von Heinrichs konservativen Beratern entworfene *Act of Six Articles* schärfte 1539 eigens den Pflichtzölibat als göttliche Forderung ein (Documents Illustrative of English Church History [s. Anm. 97], 303–319, hier: Art. 3) und das *King's Book* von 1543 (Lloyd, Formularies of faith [s.o.], 213–377) bestätigte das Festhalten des Königs am traditionellen Verständnis des kirchlichen Amts.

[119] Brief Latimers an Edward Baynton, Dezember 1531 (?) (in: Hugh Latimer, Sermons and remains, Cambridge 1845, 322–334).

befugnis, um die es dem Bischof ging, sondern dass Latimer einen Einblick in die Praxis evangelischer Predigt in den frühen 1530er Jahren gibt. Er sei von Leuten im Ort Abb-Church gebeten worden zu predigen, die »very desirous to hear me« gewesen seien, »pretending great hunger and thirst of the word of God and ghostly doctrine«.[120] Diesem Ansinnen habe Latimer sich nicht versagen wollen,

»for I have preached and teached but according to holy scripture, holy fathers, and ancient interpreters of the same [...]: for I have done nothing else in my preaching, but with all diligence moved my auditors to faith and charity, to do their duty, and that that is necessary to be done. As for things of private devotion, mean things, and voluntary things, I have reproved the abuse, the superstition of them, without condemnation of the things themselves, as it becometh preachers to do«.[121]

In diesen Aussagen zeigt sich die Grundsituation des evangelischen Pfarrers, dessen Hauptaufgabe es war, als Prediger den geistlichen Hunger und Durst der Gemeinde zu stillen, indem er Glaube und Liebe verkündigte und vor den Gefahren veräußerlichter Frömmigkeit warnte. Dass bei einem Teil des Episkopats tatsächlich das reformatorische Verständnis des geistlichen Amts im Hintergrund stand, zeigen Cranmers unveröffentlicht gebliebene *Dreizehn Artikel* von 1538, deren 10. in enger Anlehnung an das Augsburgische Bekenntnis feststellt:

»De Ministris Ecclesiae docemus, quod nemo debeat publice docere, aut Sacramenta ministrare, nisi rite vocatus, et quidem ab his, penes quos in Ecclesia, juxta verbum Dei, et leges ac consuetudines uniuscujusque regionis, jus est vocandi et admittendi. Et quod nullus ad Ecclesiae ministerium vocatus, etiamsi episcopus sit sive Romanus, sive quicunque alius, hoc sibi jure divino vindicare possit, ut publice docere, Sacramenta ministrare, vel ullam aliam ecclesiasticam functionem, in aliena diocesi aut parochia exercere valeat; hoc est nec episcopus in alterius episcopi diocesi, nec parochus in alterius parochia. Et demum quod malitia ministri efficaciae Sacramentorum nihil detrahat, ut jam supra docuimus in Articulo de ecclesia.«[122]

Der Titelholzschnitt der 1539 erschienenen *Great Bible*[123] ließ sich durchaus in diesem Sinne verstehen: Hier gibt der König die Bibel an die Bischöfe weiter, die sie dem Klerus weiterreichen, der sie dann auf der Kanzel der Predigt zugrundelegt. Die Reformen Heinrichs VIII. zielten allerdings nicht auf den von Cranmer und Latimer anvisierten neuen Typ von Pfarrer ab, ermöglichten aber doch Veränderungen in diese Richtung, die

---

[120] A.a.O., 323.

[121] A.a.O., 331. Auf das inhaltliche Profil der Predigt und die Erwartungen der Predigtzuhörer geht Latimer in den Brief nicht näher ein. Einige Ausführungen lassen sich im Sinne augustinisch-reformatorischer Bibelorientierung und Rechtfertigungslehre verstehen.

[122] FABRICIUS, Die Kirche von England. Ihr Gebetbuch, Bekenntnis und kanonisches Recht (s. Anm. 118), 607–628, hier: 620.

[123] The Bybble in Englyshe, London 1539 (STC 2068).

es vereinzelt während der 1530er und 1540er Jahre gegeben zu haben scheint.[124] Ob und inwieweit antiklerikale Motive diesen Prozess begleiteten und vielleicht sogar bestimmten, ist in der Forschung nach wie vor umstritten, wobei sich nach der ebenso entschiedenen Behauptung wie Relativierung der Bedeutung des Antiklerikalismus mittlerweile eine differenzierte Sicht durchgesetzt hat, die um die spätmittelalterlich-frühneuzeitliche Kontinuität dieses aus der Inkongruenz von geistlichem Anspruch und kirchlicher Wirklichkeit entstehenden Phänomens weiß, die Vorstellung von einer breiten zusammenhängenden Bewegung von entscheidender Bedeutung für die Durchsetzung der Reformation allerdings verabschiedet hat.[125]

Der Thronwechsel 1547 bedeutete einen neuerlichen religionspolitischen Kurswechsel. Eduard VI. und seine engsten Ratgeber – vor allem Somerset und Cranmer – formulierten ein ambitioniertes Reformprogramm im Sinne der kontinentalen Reformation und gingen sogleich an dessen Umsetzung.[126] Die bereits weiter oben besprochenen Leittexte dieser Reform verstanden Status und Funktion der kirchlichen Amtsträger

---

[124] So bemühte sich etwa Cranmer darum, Pfarrstellen mit akademisch gebildeten und für kirchliche Reformen aufgeschlossenen Geistlichen zu besetzen und diese durch die Erteilung von Predigtlizenzen zu Multiplikatoren zu machen (SUSAN WABUDA, Setting forth the word of God: Archbishop Cranmer's early patronage of preachers, in: Thomas Cranmer. Churchman and scholar, hg. v. Paul Ayris u. David Selwyn, Woodbridge 1993, 75–88). Cranmer setzte damit das Bemühen von John Fisher fort, der bis 1535 mit anderen Zielen als Cranmer ganz ähnliche Maßnahmen ergriffen hatte (MARIA DOWLING, John Fisher and the preaching ministry, in: ARG 82, 1991, 287–309). Andere Bischöfe engagierten sich in ähnlicher Weise für die Förderung der Predigt (SUSAN WABUDA, Bishops and the provision of homilies, 1520 to 1547, in: SCJ 25, 1994, 551–566; DIES., »Fruitful preaching« in the diocese of Worcester. Bishop Hugh Latimer and his influence, 1535–1539, in: Religion and the English People, 1500–1650. New voices, new perspectives, hg. v. Eric Josef Carlson, Kirksville 1998, 49–74). Zu den Maßnahmen gehörten etwa, wie Latimers *Injunctions* für die Diözese Worcester von 1537 (Visitation articles and injunctions [s. Anm. 135], Bd. 2, 15–18) zeigen, die Verpflichtung der Pfarrer zum Studium einer englischen und lateinischen Vollbibel, zumindest aber des englischen und lateinischen NT (Art. 3) und zur Beförderung der Predigt (Art. 9). Ähnliche Aussagen, teilweise um weitere Bestimmungen ergänzt, finden sich auch in anderen bischöflichen *Injunctions* der 1530er und 1540er Jahre, z.B. in denen Cranmers für die Diözese Hereford 1538 (a.a.O., 65) oder Bonners für die Diözese London 1542 (a.a.O., 83).
[125] DAVID LOADES, Anticlericalism in the Church of England before 1558: an ›Eating Canker‹? (in: Anticlericalism in Britain, c. 1500–1914, hg. v. Nigel Aston u. Matthew Cragoe, Stroud 2000, 1–17); PETER MARSHALL, Anticlericalism revested? Expressions of discontent in early Tudor England (in: The parish in late medieval England, hg. v. Clive Burgess u. Eamon Duffy, Donington 2006, 365–380).
[126] DIARMAID MACCULLOCH, Tudor Church Militant. Edward VI and the Protestant Reformation, London 1999; DAVIES, A religion of the Word (s. Anm. 98), hier zur Umsetzung der Reformen und der dabei wegen der zentralen Bedeutung der Predigt für die »Reformation by the word« besonders wichtigen Geistlichkeit: 87–139.

auf neue Weise und intendierten nichts weniger als die Schaffung des neu-
en Typs von Pfarrer, der durch Ausbildung und Heirat *Bürger* und durch
die Konzentration auf die Verkündigungsaufgabe *Prediger* sein sollte. Die
ambitionierten Reformen wurden während der Regierungszeit des *boy
king* allerdings nur zögerlich und in vielerlei Hinsicht wenig erfolgreich
umgesetzt. Gerade für den Klerus änderte sich vorerst nur wenig. Zwar
heiratete ein Teil der Pfarrer – je nach Region zwischen einem Drittel und
einem Zwanzigstel der Geistlichen, insgesamt ca. 1500 – und feierte den
Gottesdienst nach den neuen Vorgaben des *Book of Common Prayer*[127],
wobei wohl auch die Predigten aus dem *Book of Homilies* zur Verlesung
kamen, aber zumeist scheint doch eine abwartende, zum Teil widerstän-
dige Haltung vorgeherrscht zu haben, die wohl im Zuge einer längerdau-
ernden Herrschaft nach und nach hätte überwunden werden können.
Mehr als ein Anfang wurde während der Regierungszeit Eduards VI. mit
der Erneuerung der Geistlichkeit nicht gemacht.

Der Regierungswechsel 1553 brach mit der ganzen begonnenen Kirchenreform auch die Etablierung des neuen Typs von Pfarrer ab.[128] Königin Maria und ihre Ratgeber – vor allem Kardinal Reginald Pole – setzten sowohl hinsichtlich des Status als auch hinsichtlich der Funktion der
Geistlichen auf eine Rückkehr zum vorreformatorischen zölibatären
Priestertum.[129] Das hieß vor allem, dass verheiratete Pfarrer amtsenthoben
wurden und die römische Messe mit dem Messopfer restituiert wurde.
Mochte das von ihrem Vater herkommende Interesse an humanistischer
Predigt auch von der neuen Königin weiter gepflegt werden, so bedeutete
das doch nur eine Angleichung an die in der Papstkirche anlaufende Er-

---

[127] Tatsächlich setzte sich in der zweiten Hälfte des 16. Jahrhunderts eine verkürzte
Liturgie durch, die sogar den im *Book of Common Prayer* vorgeschriebenen Predigtgottesdienst um einige Elemente reduzierte (JOHN HARPER, The forms and orders of
Western liturgy from the tenth to the eighteenth century, Oxford 1991, 166–187). Selbst
am königlichen Hof wurden die Vorgaben des BCP, dass im Sonntagsgottesdienst auf
das Glaubensbekenntnis ein *sermon, homily, or exhortation* folgen solle, nicht konsequent eingehalten, vielmehr war ein verkürzter Gottesdienst ohne Predigt üblich. Elisabeth I. hielt aufgrund ihrer »liturgical and prayer-centred piety« Predigten nicht für
einen konstitutiven Bestandteil des Gottesdiensts, so sehr sie auch die traditionellen
Predigtenreihen – etwa zur Fastenzeit – schätzte (MCCULLOUGH, Sermons at court [s.
Anm. 90], 71 f., 76–78).

[128] ARTHUR G. DICKENS, The Marian Reaction in the diocese of York [1957] (in:
DERS., Reformation studies, London 1982, 93–157, hier zum Klerus: 93–111); EAMON
DUFFY, Fires of the Faith. Catholic England under Mary Tudor, New Haven u. London
2009, 22–28.

[129] Diese Rückgängigmachung begann mit den *Injunctions on religion* (Documents
Illustrative of English Church History [s. Anm. 97], 380–383), die die Priesterehe un-
tersagten, verheiratete Kleriker ihres Amts entbanden und von verheirateten Ordensleu-
ten die Scheidung verlangten.

neuerung, in deren Zuge die Predigt geradezu zur antireformatorischen Waffe umgeschmiedet wurde, die pastoral orientierte Bischöfe und in Priesterseminaren ausgebildete Kleriker zum Nutzen der Papstkirche führten.[130] Die Pfarrerschaft lernte aus den kirchenpolitischen Kurswechseln der zurückliegenden zwei Jahrzehnte, dass es besser war abzuwarten. Die Absetzung ihrer verheirateten und damit zumeist ihre Sympathien für die Reformation kundtuenden Kollegen hatte ihnen deutlich gezeigt, dass vorschnelle Festlegungen die eigene Stellung und vor allem den Lebensunterhalt gefährden konnten. Die rabiaten Reformen unter Eduard VI. und deren nicht weniger rabiate Rückgängigmachung unter Maria dürften im Klerus für eine noch jahrzehntelang nachwirkende Vorsicht gesorgt haben, die es vielen erschwerte, den bevorstehenden nächsten religionspolitischen Kurswechsel mitzuvollziehen und sich auf die durch diesen geschaffenen neuen Verhältnisse – von denen man ja nicht wusste, ob und wie lange sie andauern würden – einzulassen.

Das nach dem erneuten Thronwechsel etablierte *Elizabethan Settlement* bedeutete eine Rückkehr zur Reformagenda Eduards VI. Die Königin nahm auch die 1553 rückgängig gemachte Transformation des geistlichen Amts wieder auf.[131] Während der mehr als vier Jahrzehnte der Regierungszeit der letzten Tudor-Herrscherin gewann der von der kontinentalen Reformation konzipierte, von Thomas Cranmer und seinen Mitstreitern adaptierte und von den an führender Stelle wirkenden Marian exiles und ihren Sympathisanten[132] bejahte neue Typ von Pfarrer – anfangs allerdings konfrontiert mit Widerständen[133] und sich nur allmählich

---

[130] In England geschah das etwa in Gestalt des Nachfolgers des *Book of Homilies*: Der neue Londoner Bischof Edmund Bonner veröffentlichte eine Lehrdarlegung, an die dreizehn von John Harpsfield und Henry Pendleton bearbeitete Lesepredigten angehängt waren: A profitable and necessary doctryne, with certayne homelies adioyned thereunto, London 1555 (STC 3282, hierzu: EAMON DUFFY, The stripping of the altars. Traditional religion in England, c. 1400–c. 1580, New Haven u. London 1992, 536f.).

[131] Grundlegend waren die königlichen *Injunctions* von 1559 (Documents Illustrative of English Church History [s. Anm. 97], 417–442), die die Verkündigung wieder in den Mittelpunkt des pfarramtlichen Diensts rückten (a.a.O., 419–422, 430, 434).

[132] Die Schaffung einer evangelischen Geistlichkeit als eine der Hauptaufgaben des sich an der kontinentalen Reformation orientierenden Teils des elisabethanischen Episkopats behandeln O'DAY, The English clergy (s. Anm. 86), 33–48, und SCOTT A. WENIG, Straightening the altars. The ecclesiastical vision and pastoral achievements of the progressive bishops under Elizabeth I, 1559–1579, New York u.a. 2000. O'Day stellt Thomas Bentham als Beispiel für das »Reformed episcopate« (a.a.O., 33) vor und Wenig bietet einen Überblick (a.a.O., 44–48) sowie Fallstudien zu John Jewel, Edwin Sandys, James Pilkington, Richard Cox und anderen (a.a.O., 146–151, 159–161, 172–176, sowie in verstreuten Ausführungen a.a.O., 209–236).

[133] HENRY GEE, The Elizabethan clergy and the settlement of religion, 1558–1564, Oxford 1898.

durchsetzend[134] – nun wirklich Gestalt.[135] Allerdings unterschied sich diese Ausprägung des neuen Typs in mancherlei Hinsicht vom kontinentalen Vorbild. Vier Punkte sind hier vor allem zu benennen:

1. Die kirchliche Erneuerung unter Eduard VI. war als weitreichende Umgestaltung konzipiert und wurde durchaus »militant« (D. MacCulloch) begonnen, sie tastete anfangs aber die überkommenen Organisationsstrukturen der Kirche kaum an. Die Veränderung dieser Strukturen war zwar geplant, aber schon die versuchte Neufassung des Kirchenrechts war so umstritten, dass tief eingreifende Organisationsreformen aufgeschoben wurden. Auch das *Elizabethan Settlement* ging nicht über den am Ende der Regierungszeit Eduards VI. erreichten Reformstand hinaus, ja nicht einmal die zurückhaltende Neufassung des Kirchenrechts in Form der *Reformatio Legum Ecclesiasticarum*, die unter Elisabeth noch zweimal ins Parlament eingebracht wurde, konnte in Kraft treten.[136] Für die Pfarrer hieß das, dass sie einem institutionellen und rechtlichen Rahmen agierten, der in viel stärkerem Maße als bei kontinentalen Protestantismus traditionell verfasst war und die Tätigkeit der Pfarrer nicht ebenso förderte, wie es dort geschah. Zu diesen überkommenen Strukturelementen gehörten etwa das Festhalten am dreifachen Amt (Bischof, Presbyter, Diakon) und

---

[134] Zurecht weist CHRISTOPHER HAIGH (The English Reformations. Religion, politics, and society under the Tudors, Oxford 1993) darauf hin, dass die Umsetzung des *Elizabethan Settlement* sich bis in die 1570er Jahren hinein als schwieriges und nur teilweise erfolgreiches Unterfangen erwies (vgl. auch seine oben Anm. 87 genannten Aufsätze).

[135] Aus der Fülle der Quellen, in denen sich diese Entwicklung widerspiegelt, seien exemplarisch Matthew Parkers *Advertisements for due order* von 1566 (The Anglican canons 1529–1947, hg. v. Gerald Bray, Woodbridge u. Rochester 1998, 163–171), die 1571 sowie 1575/76 von der *Convocation* erlassenen bzw. von Grindal zusammengestellten *Canons* (a.a.O., 172–209, hier: 196–198; 211–215) sowie die 1585 von John Whitgift zusammengestellten *Orders for the increase of learning in the unlearned sort of ministers* (Cardwell, Documentary annals of the reformed Church of England [s.u.], Bd. 2, 21f.) genannt. Die einschlägigen Dokumentensammlungen bieten zahlreiche weitere Quellen, deren Aussagen zu Ausbildung, Weiterbildung und Dienst der Geistlichkeit sich allerdings durchweg ähneln: Synodalia. A Collection of Articles of Religion, Canons, and Proceedings of Convocations in the Province of Canterbury, from the Year 1547 to the Year 1717, hg. v. Edward Cardwell, zwei Bände, Oxford 1842; Documentary annals of the reformed Church of England; being a collection of injunctions, declarations, orders, articles of inquiry, &c. from the year 1546 to the year 1716, hg. v. Edward Cardwell, zwei Bände, Oxford 1844; Visitation articles and injunctions, hg. v. W. H. Frere u. W. P. M. Kennedy, drei Bände, London 1910. Einen Endpunkt markieren die 1604 von Jakob I. erlassenen *Constitutions and Canons Ecclesiastical*, die den unter Elisabeth I. erreichten Stand der Transformation der Geistlichkeit dokumentieren (The Anglican canons 1529–1947 [s.o.], 258–453, hier: 308–370, Nr. 31–76).

[136] GERALD BRAY, Introduction (in: The Henrician canons of 1535 and the Reformatio Legum Ecclesiasticarum [s. Anm. 95], XV-CLX, hier: XLI-CLVI). Allerdings wurden Teile der *Reformatio* auf anderen Wegen in Kraft gesetzt.

die Konservierung der diözesanbischöflichen Kirchenverfassung. Die Bischöfe waren trotz der Betonung ihres Verkündigungsamts weiterhin vor allem Diener der Monarchen, die ihren geistlichen Dienst allenfalls im Nebenamt versahen. Das Festhalten an den weiträumigen Diözesen und an deren überkommenen Verwaltungsstrukturen erschwerte die bischöfliche Aufsicht über die Geistlichkeit und die Durchsetzung der kirchlichen Erneuerung an der Basis. Verbunden mit dem Festhalten am überkommenen Bischofsamt war der fortbestehende Dualismus von Kathedral- und Pfarrklerus, deren Sphären sich kaum überschnitten.[137] Die Beibehaltung des Diakonats, das üblicherweise als Verkündigungsamt verstanden wurde,[138] sowie die Zulassung von bischöflicher Aufsicht entzogener Prediger, wie sie etwa bei vielen Adelsfamilien amtierten,[139] sorgten für eine weitere Ausdifferenzierung der Geistlichkeit. Wichtig war auch das Festhalten an der vergleichsweise selbständigen und machtvollen Kirchengerichtsbarkeit, die die Kompetenzen der Pfarrer in Sachen Kirchenzucht und Sozialdisziplinierung einschränkte und Gemeinden und Pfarrer beaufsichtigte.[140] Auf der Ebene der Gemeinden erschwerten die sich an den Verhältnissen des frühen 16. Jahrhunderts orientierende, oftmals zu schmal bemessene Finanzausstattung der Stellen[141] und die starke Stellung der Patrone, deren Anforderungen durchaus andere als die der Kirche sein konnten und die nicht selten ganz andere Interessen mit der Stellenbesetzung verfolgten[142], die Tätigkeit der Pfarrer. Die unzureichende Stellenfinanzie-

---

[137] Zur »clerical élite«: O'Day, The English clergy (s. Anm. 86), 144–158.

[138] Francis Young, Inferior office? A history of deacons in the Church of England, Cambridge 2015, 1–33.

[139] William Gibson, A social history of the domestic chaplain, 1530–1840, London u. Washington 1997.

[140] Ralph Houlbrooke, The decline of ecclesiastical jurisdiction under the Tudors (in: Continuity and change. Personnel and administration of the Church in England 1500–1642, hg. v. Rosemary O'Day u. Felicity Heal, Leicester 1976, 239–257); Ders., Church courts and the people during the English Reformation 1520–1570, Oxford 1979; Martin Ingram, Church courts, sex and marriage in England, 1570–1640, Cambridge 1987; Ders., Puritans, and the church courts, 1560–1640 (in: The culture of English Puritanism, 1560–1700, hg. v. Christopher Durston u. Jacqueline Eales, Basingstoke u. London 1996, 58–91); Beat Kümin, Parishioners in court: litigation and the local community (in: Belief and practice in Reformation England, FS Patrick Collinson, hg. v. Susan Wabuda u. Caroline Litzenberger, Aldershot u.a. 1998, 20–39); Christopher Haigh, The clergy and parish discipline in England, 1570–1640 (in: The Impact of the European Reformation: Princes, Clergy and People, hg. v. Bridget Heal u. Ole Peter Grell, Aldershot u. Burlington 2008, 125–141); O'Day, The debate on the English Reformation (s. Anm. 86), 216–224.

[141] Michael L. Zell, Economic problems of the parochial clergy in the sixteenth century (in: Princes & paupers in the English Church 1500–1800, hg. v. Rosemary O'Day u. Felicity Heal, Leicester 1981, 19–43).

[142] O'Day, The English clergy (s. Anm. 86), Kap. 6–9; D. J. Lamburn, The influence

rung führte dazu, dass es eine Zeitlang weiterhin Pfründenkumulationen und die damit einhergehende Abwesenheit von einer der Pfarrstellen gab, wobei sich besonders Kathedralkleriker und akademisch Gebildete solche Möglichkeiten zur Einkommenssteigerung zunutze machten.[143]

2. Ein weiteres Hemmnis für die Etablierung des neuen Typs von Pfarrer in England war die nur ansatzweise verwirklichte *coniunctio scholarum cum ministerio evangelii.* Während im kontinentalen Protestantismus Kirchenleitung, Bildungswesen und Pfarrerschaft eng miteinander kooperierten und sich personell an entscheidenden Punkten überschnitten – etwa in der Person des kurmärkischen Generalsuperintendenten Andreas Musculus – blieben in England Kirchenleitung, Bildungswesen und Pfarrerschaft getrennte Sphären, die nur an einzelnen Punkten miteinander in Kontakt kamen und nur in beschränktem Ausmaß Personen aus anderen Sphären offenstanden. Das soll nicht heißen, dass in England kein Interesse an der Bildung, ja Akademisierung der Geistlichkeit bestand und dass es nicht zahlreiche Einzelinitiativen gab.[144] Das Bemühen um die Klerikerbildung einte alle Strömungen innerhalb der elisabethanischen Kirche: Im Wissen um die theologische Notwendigkeit einer für ihre Aufgabe qualifizierten Geistlichkeit wurden die Standards für Ordinationen nach und nach erhöht, Universitätsabsolventen bevorzugt angestellt, biblische Unterweisung und *Divinity lectures* an Kathedralkirchen angeboten, Lateinschulen und Colleges unterstützt, Begabtenstipendien gestiftet, Pfarrer zum Bibelstudium und zur Rechenschaftsablegung vor dem Vorgesetzten und den Visitatoren verpflichtet sowie die Repetition und Vertiefung des religiösen Grundwissens verpflichtend gemacht. Aber selbst die Summierung dieser Einzelpunkte ergibt nicht die machtvolle *coniunctio,* die zum Entwicklungsmotor des kontinentalen Protestantismus wurde. Dass mit Cambridge und Oxford nur zwei – wenn auch große – Universitäten vorhanden waren und das Netz von Lateinschulen nicht allzu dicht war[145], hemmte die Entwicklung, zudem erschien die geistliche Laufbahn angesichts der vielerorts unzureichenden Ausstattung vielen nicht besonders

---

of the laity in appointments of clergy in the late sixteenth and early seventeenth century (in: Patronage and recruitment in the Tudor and early Stuart church, hg. v. Claire Cross, York 1996, 95–119).

[143] Dass das Problem sich gerade auch in Diözesen ergab, wo die Bischöfe die Reformation focierten, zeigt J. I. DAELEY, Pluralism in the diocese of Canterbury during the administration of Matthew Parker, 1559–1575 (JEH 18, 1967, 33–49).

[144] Viele englische Bischöfe bemühten schon in der Regierungszeit Heinrichs VIII. um die Förderung von Bildung, Predigt und Klerikernachwuchs, was in der Folgezeit noch intensiviert wurde: O'DAY, The English clergy (s. Anm. 86), Kap. 3–5 u.ö.; KENNETH CARLETON, Bishops and reform in the English Church, 1520–1559, Woodbridge 2001.

[145] O'DAY, The English clergy (s. Anm. 86), 140f.

attraktiv, was das Angebot an qualifizierten Bewerbern für längere Zeit beschränkt sein ließ. Zwar erlebte das schulische Bildungswesen ist im 16. Jahrhundert einen merklicher Aufschwung und die Universitäten bemühten sich durch die Umgestaltung der Studiengänge[146] und die Neuausrichtung bestehender oder durch die Gründung neuer Colleges[147] dem zuneh-

---

[146] Wie und was angehende Geistliche während der Regierungszeit Elisabeths I. in Oxford und Cambridge studierten, ist von der Forschung bislang kaum näher untersucht worden, was auch mit dem Mangel an aussagekräftigen Quellen zu tun zu hat. So sind etwa die Universitätsstatuten hinsichtlich des Curriculums und des Studienverlaufs wenig aussagekräftig (The privileges of the university of Cambrigde, hg. v. George Dyer, Bd. 1, London 1824, 157–211). An Literatur zum Thema ist zu nennen: WILLIAM T. COSTELLO, The scholastic curriculum at early seventeenth-century Cambridge, Cambridge (MA) 1958; MARK H. CURTIS, Oxford and Cambridge in transition, 1558–1642. An essay on changing relations between the English universities and English society, Oxford 1959, 161–164; S. L. GREENSLADE, The Faculty of Theology (in: The history of the university of Oxford, Bd. 3: The collegiate university, hg. v. James McConica, Oxford 1986, 295–334); JENNIFER LOACH, Reformation controversies (a.a.O., 363–396); CHRISTOPHER BROOKE, Learning and doctrine 1550–1660 (in: VICTOR MORGAN, CHRISTOPHER BROOKE, A history of the university of Cambridge, Bd. 2: 1546–1750, Cambridge 2004, 437–463); IAN GREEN, Humanism and Protestantism in Early Modern English Education, Farnham 2009, 294–299. Zum puritanischen Programm einer »mixture of scriptural study and extended instruction in purified humane learning« für das Studium angehender Pfarrer: JOHN MORGAN, Godly learning. Puritan attitudes towards reason, learning and education, 1560–1640, Cambridge 1986, 220–244 (Zitat: 241).

[147] Wichtige Zentren des Puritanismus wurden etwa Christ's und Emmanuel College in Cambridge, wo Laurence Chaderton ein zweijähriges Studienprogramm für angehende Kleriker entwickelte (»for the training up and exercising of students in divinity, whereby they may be made fit and meet to discharge the duties belonging to that profession«), das sich vor allem in gemeinschaftlichen Predigtübungen (einschließliche der vorbereitenden philologisch-theologischen Auslegung des Bibeltexts) und Disputationen vollzog (PATRICK COLLINSON, The Elizabethan puritan movement, London u. New York 1967, 126 f.; PETER LAKE, Moderate puritans and the Elizabethan church, Cambrigde 1982, 36 f.). Zum von Walter Mildmay als Pflanzstätte einer puritanischen Geistlichkeit begründeten Emmanuel College: MORGAN, Godly learning (s. Anm. 146), 245–271; PATRICK COLLINSON, The foundations and beginnings (in: SARAH BENDALL, CHRISTOPHER BROOKE, PATRICK COLLINSON, A history of Emmanuel College, Cambridge, Woodbridge 1999, 13–55); DERS., Puritan Emmanuel (a.a.O., 177–226). Die 1585 erlassenen Statuten des Emmanuel College (The statutes of Sir Walter Mildmay Kt Chancellor of the Exchequer and one of Her Majesty's Privy Councillors; authorised by him for the government of Emmanuel College founded by him, hg. v. Frank Stubbings, Cambridge 1983, 113–152) zeigen, wie durch ein sorgfältig geplantes Lebensumfeld und Unterrichtsprogramm das Ziel angestrebt wurde, »ut ex hoc seminario haberet Anglicana ecclesia, quos ad erudiendum populum pastorumque munus subeundum (rem ex omnibus maxime necessariam) evocare possit« (a.a.O., 132). Zu diesem Zweck wurde auch ein durchaus anspruchsvoller religiöser Unterricht angeboten. Das Emmanuel College sah sich – ähnlich wie Melanchthon die *scholae* in der oben besprochenen Rede von 1543 – in der Tradition der Bildungsinstitutionen seit alt- und neutestamentlicher Zeit, deren Aufgabe es gewesen sei, die Jugend »in omni pietate et bonis literis, praecipue vero in sacris et theologicis« zu unterrichten, damit die so ausgebildete Jugend »alios postea veram et puram doctrinam doceat, haereses, et errores omnes refutet, atque praeclarissimis vitae integerrimae exemplis ad virtutem omnes excitet« (a.a.O., 113).

menden Studieninteresse entgegenzukommen, aber diese Bemühungen ge-
nügten lange Zeit nicht, um den Vorsprung des Bildungswesens auf dem
Kontinent aufzuholen. Zwar wurden auch in England entsprechend dem
humanistisch-reformatorischen Programm an der Universität Griechisch
und Hebräisch gelehrt, die Bibel ausgelegt sowie patristische Studien und
Kontroverstheologie betrieben, aber eine Verklammerung von Theologie
und Kirche, wie sie Melanchthon in seiner Rede über die *necessaria coniunctio* einforderte, wurde in England nicht gezielt angestrebt und stellte
sich nur ansatzweise ein. Der angehende Pfarrer wurde in einem der besonders für zukünftige Geistliche gestifteten Colleges von den dortigen
Dozenten ausgebildet und besuchte die eine oder andere Vorlesung oder
Disputation an der Artes- und vielleicht auch der Theologischen Fakultät,
ohne dass er damit rechnen konnte, bei seinen akademischen Lehrern
kirchlichen Praktikern oder gar Leitungsverantwortlichen zu begegnen,
die Theologie bewusst als kirchliche Wissenschaft betrieben und dabei
besonderen Wert auf die für den kirchlichen Dienst nutzbar zu machende
exegetische Begründung und dogmatisch-kontroverstheologische Entfaltung der Kirchenlehre legten. Man muss allerdings damit rechnen, dass das
intensive geistliche Leben und die religiöse Unterweisung in den Colleges
– etwa in Form kursorischer Bibelvorlesungen oder im Rahmen der Katechese –, wenn es sich auch nicht um »formal pastoral instruction«
zwecks Ausbildung von »professional theologians« handelte, die Studenten zu Anwärtern auf das geistliche Amt machte, die »at very least [...]
were far better qualified academically than their predecessors in the earlier
part of the century«.[148] Viele angehende Pfarrer mussten sich mit dem
mehr oder minder gründlichen Lateinschulunterricht begnügen, der allerdings ein solides religiöses Grundwissen vermittelte und dabei auch theologisch anspruchsvoll sein konnte.[149] Die Studienquote steigerte sich allmählich, so dass um 1600 mehr als die Hälfte der Ordinanden – die Zahlen

---

[148] CROSS, Ordinations in the diocese of York (s. Anm. 89), 16. An anderer Stelle
bezeichnet Cross diese informelle Qualifizierung als »process of osmosis« (CROSS, From
Catholic priests to Protestant ministers [s. Anm. 89], 164), was die Errungenschaften der
theologischen Ausbildung eher unterbewertet. Man verdeutliche sich etwa, dass 1579 für
die Katechese in den Oxforder Colleges an Büchern die Verwendung der Katechismen
von Nowell, Calvin, Hyperius oder des Heidelberger Katechismus für die Anfänger und
von Calvins *Institutio*, Jewels *Apologia* oder der *39 Artikel* mit Erläuterungen für die
Fortgeschrittenen vorgeschrieben wurde (GREENSLADE, The Faculty of Theology [s.
Anm. 146], 327).
[149] IAN GREEN, The Christian's ABC. Catechism and Catechizing in England c. 1530–
1740, Oxford 1996, 170–229; DERS., Humanism and Protestantism (s. Anm. 146), 274–
294. Griechisch- und Hebräischunterricht wurde an Schulen nur selten angeboten und
das *NT graece* gehörte nicht zur Schullektüre (GREEN, Humanism and Protestantism [s.
Anm. 146], 254–261).

schwanken regional – einen Universitätsbesuch, der in Regel kein Theologiestudium umfasst hatte, nachweisen konnte.[150] Auch wenn bei einzelnen Gruppen der Geistlichkeit wie dem Kathedralklerus oder den lizenzierten Predigern die die Studienquote noch höher lag, so gilt doch für die meisten Pfarrer: »The first point to note about early modern English preachers is how little training most of them received.«[151] Die Diensteingangsprüfung legte der angehende Geistliche dann vor einem Vertreter der Kirche – in der Regel dem Archidiakon – ab, wobei die im Rahmen einer akademischen Beschäftigung mit Bibel und Kirchenlehre zu erwerbenden Kenntnisse und Fähigkeiten zwar – wenn vorhanden – mit Lob vermerkt wurden, aber nicht ausschlaggebend für die Zulassung zur Ordination waren.[152] Die geringere Akademisierung und Theologisierung der Pfarrer in England spiegelt sich auch in dem fast völligen Fehlen autochthoner Hilfsliteratur für die Amtsführung wider. Abgesehen von den Predigtsammlungen und verstreuten erbaulichen Reflexionen über das geistliche Amt fehlte es an allem, was im kontinentalen Protestantismus zur Unterstützung der Pfarrer diente wie etwa Studienanleitungen, pastoraltheologische Handbücher oder Homiletiken.[153] Nach und nach wurden einige

---

[150] O'DAY, The English clergy (s. Anm. 86), 3f., 6, 13, 132, 135f., 233.

[151] GREEN, Continuity and change in Protestant preaching in early modern England (s. Anm. 90), 11. Green führt das weiter aus: »The standards demanded by William Perkins, John Wilkins, and other English authors were sought to describe the ideal Protestant sermon, were not easy to attain. Compared to Melanchthon's textbooks offering advice to Lutheran pastors on how to write effective sermons, or to the carefully graded tuition in Greek and Hebrew and the confessional theology taught through advanced catechisms in the academies of Strassburg and Geneva and the universities of the Low Countries and Germany, and indeed in many Jesuit colleges on the Catholic side too, there was little by way of structured training or official advice in Elizabethan and Stuart England. Greek was taught in relatively few Tudor schools (rather more in Stuart ones, but from a literary perspective), and Hebrew was taught even less, while advanced catechisms were used haphazardly. This meant that mastery of the biblical languages and official doctrine was achieved piecemeal: in a zealous household (parental or clerical), or at university (though not every ordinand could afford to stay there for long), or from the late seventeenth century in a dissenting academy [...]. Moreover, most ordinands must have experienced problems in gaining access to the many concordances, harmonies, chronologies, and scholarly commentaries on each book of the Bible which purists like Wilkins insisted were essential aids in the preparation of a proper Protestant sermon« (a.a.O., 11f.).

[152] O'DAY, The English clergy (s. Anm. 86), 48–65.

[153] Handbücher für den pfarramtlichen Dienst gab es zwischen 1570 und 1630 – anders als im späten Mittelalter (DAVID B. FOSS, John Mirk's Instruction for Parish Priests, in: The ministry: clerical and lay, hg. v. W. J. Sheils u. Diana Wood, Studies in Church History 26, Oxford [UK] u. Cambridge [MA] 1989, 131–140) – keine (COLLINSON, Shepherds, sheepdogs, and hirelings [s. Anm. 87], 193–198; überhaupt gab es im Calvinismus an diesem Punkt einen bemerkenswerten Mangel: BURNETT, The evolution of the Lutheran pastor's manual [s. Anm. 57], 540). Was in steigendem Maße Verbreitung fand, waren Bibelausgaben und exegetische Hilfsmittel (IAN GREEN, Print and Protestantism

wenige solcher Hilfsmittel ins Englische übersetzt und gedruckt,[154] und erst um die Jahrhundertwende herum scheint es eine größere Nachfrage nach solchen Werken gegeben zu haben, auf die dann auch englische Autoren reagierten, allerdings in einer Form, die der gerade auch im 17. Jahrhundert in Deutschland in großer Vielfalt und hoher Qualität verbreiteten Hilfsliteratur nicht annähernd entspricht.[155] Das kritische Urteil Rosemary

---

in early modern England, Oxford 2000, 42–100, 101–167) sowie Homiletiken (MORGAN, Godly learning [s. Anm. 146], 132–141). Mittelbar zu den Homiletiken kann man auch die Rhetoriklehrbücher zählen, die bereits früher Verbreitung fanden (z.B. THOMAS WILSON, The Arte of Rhetorique, for the vse of all suche as are studious of Eloquence, 1553, STC 25799, hier wird beiläufig auch die Predigt erwähnt, z.B. 75[r/v]). Die überlieferten Hinweise zur Gestaltung des Studiums, die vor allem von puritanischen Autoren stammen, sind nicht besonders tiefgehend, entsprechen aber dem, was auch im kontinentalen Protestantismus erwartet wurde: Angehende Pfarrer widmen sich vor allem dem Sprach- und Bibelstudium (letzteres konzentriert auf die biblischen Hauptschriften), vertiefen sich in Bibelkommentare sowie in die Schriften der Kirchenväter und Reformatoren (von Luther bis Beza) und ordnen das so erworbene Wissen mit Hilfe von Dogmatiken wie Calvins *Institutio*, puritanischen Autoren und kontroverstheologischen Schriften, wobei vielfach die Anlegung einer Materialsammlung (Loci-Buch) empfohlen wird (MORGAN, Godly learning [s. Anm. 146], 112–117). Vgl. die ursprünglich nicht für den Druck bestimmten Hinweise zum Studium aus dem puritanischen Universitätsmilieu, wie sie sich in dem wohl aus den 1570er Jahren stammenden *Order to be used for the trayning upp and exercising of Students in Divinitye, whereby they maye be made fitt and meete to dyscharge the dewtyes belongig to that profession* von William oder Laurence Chaderton für Cambridger Studenten (The seconde parte of a register. Being a calender of manuscripts under that title intended for publication by the Puritans about 1593, hg. v. Albert Peel, Bd. 1, Cambridge 1915, 133f.), in *Mr. Cartwrights letter for direction in the study of divinity* (Cartwrightiana, hg. v. Albert Peel u. Leland H. Carlson, London 1951, 108–115) und im 1577 entstandenen *Letter of Dr. Reinolds to his friend, concerning his aduice for the studie of Diuinitie* (1613 im Druck erschienen: STC 20611) finden.

[154] NIELS HEMMINGSEN, The preacher, or methode of preaching, wrytten in latine bey Niels Hemminge, and translated into englishe by i. H. Very, necessarie for al those that by the true preaching of the word of God, labour to pull down the singoge of sathan, and to buylde vp the temple of God, London 1574 (STC 13065); ANDREAS HYPERIUS, The practice of preaching, übersetzt v. John Ludham, London 1577 (STC 11758).

[155] Das zeigt etwa die in Dialogform gestaltete ausführliche Darstellung des Predigtamts und der damit verbundenen Anforderungen von SAMUEL HIERON (The Preachers Plea: Or, A Treatise in forme of a plain Dialogue, making known the worth and necessary vse of Preaching: shewing also how a man may profit by it, both for the informing of his iudgement, and the reforming of his life, London 1604, STC 13419) oder RICHARD BERNARDS besonders die Predigtgestaltung thematisierende Hinführung zum pastoralen Dienst (The Faithfvll Shepheard: Or the Shepheards Faithfulnesse: Wherein is for the matter largely, but for the maner, in few words, set forth the excellencie and neceßitie of the Ministerie; A Ministers properties and dutie; His entrance into this function and charge; How to begin fitly to instruct his people; Catechising and Preaching; And a good plaine order and method therein: Not so as yet published. Very profitable both for yoong Students, who intend the studie of Theologie (heerein being also declared what Arts and tongues first to be learned, what kind of Authours to be read and books necessarie in the beginning, and which in the first place) as also for such Ministers as yet haue not atteined to a distinct order to study studie, write, meditate, and to preach

O'Days über Bildungsstand und pastorale Kompetenzen der englischen Geistlichkeit in der zweiten Hälfte von Elisabeths Herrschaftszeit kann darum nicht überraschen: »Despite all these efforts, in the 1580s and 1590s, however, both the educational qualifications and the vocational aptitude of the beneficed clergy almost everywhere were still deplorable«.[156]

3. Zusätzlich erschwert wurde die Durchsetzung des neuen Typs von Pfarrer durch die obersten weltlichen Herrscher. Sowohl Eduard VI. als auch Elisabeth I. verstanden sich als göttlich legitimiert und mit religiöser Letztverantwortung für ihr Königreich beauftragt.[157] Sie standen damit in der Tradition ihres Vaters, Heinrichs VIII., der mit der Suprematsakte[158] den König über die ihm seit jeher eignende geistliche Dignität[159] hinaus mit der Letztentscheidungskompetenz in allen kirchlichen Fragen versehen hatte. Das dem Herrscher zukommende im wortwörtlichen Sinne *königliche* Priestertum[160] relativierte alle Vollmacht anderer kirchlicher

---

methodically, both for their better course in deliuering the Word, and the peoples vnderstanding in hearing, and memorie in reteining the same, London 1607, STC 1939). Man vergleiche damit die Sammlung von Studienanleitungen in: Joh. Hulsemanni [...] Methodus Concionandi, auctior edita. Cui accesserunt Ejusdem Autoris Methodus Studii Theologici, in privatum quorundam usum conscripta; nec non [...] Johannis Forsteri, Methodus ac formulae concionandi, Ejusdemque & [...] Leonharti Hutteri, ac Balthasaris Meisneri [...] Consilia De studio Theologico, & lectione Biblica recte instituendis, Ob argumenti similitudinem in unum volumen collecta; & impressa, Wittenberg ³1648 (VD17 23:669097R).

[156] O'DAY, The English clergy (s. Anm. 86), 132. O'Day kann aber auch zeigen, dass sich in der Endphase von Elisabeths Herrschaft die Bemühungen um die Ausbildung der angehenden Geistlichen auszuzahlen begannen, was sich etwa an den rasch ansteigenden Zahlen von studierten und graduierten Ordinanden zeigt (a.a.O., 135f. u.ö.).

[157] Anregend, wenn auch nicht durchweg überzeugend ist die besonders auf dieses Selbstverständnis rekurrierende Deutung der englischen Reformation als historisch kontingenter Gestaltwerdung einer *religio monarchica*: JOSEF JOHANNES SCHMID, ›No bishops, no King‹ – die »religio monarchica« als unbeachtetes Element der Konfessionalisierungsdebatte (in: Das Konfessionalisierungsparadigma – Leistungen, Probleme, Grenzen, hg. v. Thomas Brockmann u. Dieter J. Weiß, Münster 2013, 165–181).

[158] Documents Illustrative of English Church History (s. Anm. 97), 243f. Vgl. Die Neufassung, die zu Beginn von Elisabeths Herrschaft erlassen und um den *Act of uniformity* ergänzt wurde: a.a.O., 442–458, 458–467.

[159] Durch den Salbungsritus bei der Krönungszeremonie wurde der englische König zu einer »persona mixta« »in whom the characters of clerk and lay are combined« (LEOPOLD G. WICKHAM LEGG, The sacring of the English kings, London 1894, 3). Die vom mittelalterlichen Rechtsgelehrten William Lyndwode stammende Sentenz »Quod Rex unctus non sit mere persona laica, sed mixta« war auch im 16. Jahrhundert noch bekannt und wurde bei Rechtskommentatoren der elisabethanischen Zeit aufgenommen und im Sinne der durch die Suprematsakte neugeschaffenen Situation ausgelegt: »Reges sancto oleo uncti sunt spiritualis jurisdictionis capaces« (a.a.O., 3, Anm. 2, hier in korrigierter Fassung zitiert). Dementsprechend zeigt das Krönungszeremoniell, »that the king is an ecclesiastical as well as a civil governor« (a.a.O., 4; das auch für die Krönung Elisabeths I. zugrundegelegte mittelalterliche Krönungsritual ist abgedruckt in: English coronation records, hg. v. Leopold G. Wickham Legg, Westminster 1901, 81–112).

Amtsträger[161], verwischte die Unterscheidung zwischen den beiden Regimenten und Reichen Gottes und führte zu einer gesteigerten administrativ-fiskalischen Indienstnahme der Geistlichkeit[162]. Besonders bei Elisabeth zeigten sich die Folgen dieses nicht nur pro forma erhobenen priesterlichen Anspruchs, etwa wenn sie die Eheschließung von Pfarrern kritisch sah und deshalb die Rücknahme der Zölibatspflicht nicht konsequent verfolgte[163] oder wenn sie von Beginn ihrer Herrschaft die Predigt beschränkt sehen wollte[164] und im Konflikt mit Erzbischof Grindal um die prophesyings[165] dieses wichtige Instrument der Weiterbildung im Amt und vor allem der Förderung der Predigtkompetenz ohne zureichenden Grund verbot. Wichtig war für die Tudor-Herrscher auch die Indienstnahme der Geistlichkeit für die Legitimation ihres Herrschaftsanspruchs, für die Einschärfung des Untertanengehorsams und für die Durchsetzung der über die religiösen Verhaltensregeln hinausreichenden *public virtue*[166] – die ge-

---

[160] YARNELL, Royal priesthood in the English Reformation (s. Anm. 96), 123–149 (Heinrich VIII., Eduard VI.), 245–256 (Elisabeth I.).

[161] Zu welchen Konkurrenzen und Konflikten das spannungsreiche Verhältnis von Weltlichem und Geistlichem führte, zeigt das Verhältnis Elisabeths zu ihren Hofpredigern, das zusätzlich durch den Umstand verkompliziert wurde, dass die Königin als Frau den Hofpredigern als inferior galt, was dieser sehr wohl bewusst war (MARGARET CHRISTIAN, Elizabeth's preachers and the government of women: Defining and correcting a queen, in: SCJ 24, 1993, 561–576).

[162] FELICITY HEAL, Clerical tax collection under the Tudors: the influence of the Reformation (in: Continuity and change. Personnel and administration of the Church in England 1500–1642, hg. v. Rosemary O'Day u. Felicity Heal, Leicester 1976, 97–122); PATRICK CARTER, ›Certain, continual, and seldom abated‹: royal taxation of the Elizabethan church (in: Belief and practice in Reformation England, FS Patrick Collinson, hg. v. Susan Wabuda u. Caroline Litzenberger, Aldershot u.a. 1998, 94–112).

[163] Ihre *Injunctions* von 1559 (Documents Illustrative of English Church History [s. Anm. 97], 417–442) setzten zwar nicht die Aufhebung des Pflichtzölibats durch ihren Halbbruder wieder in Kraft, gaben in Abschnitt 29 aber der Eheschließung von Pfarrer einen Rechtsrahmen.

[164] Es ist durchaus paradox, dass die Wiederaufnahme der Reformation durch Königin Elisabeth mit dem Generalverbot der Predigt vom 27. Dezember 1558 einherging (CARDWELL, Documentary annals [s. Anm. 135], Bd. 1, 208–210; allerdings wird die Bibellesung ohne Kommentierung ausdrücklich zugelassen). Bei der Parlamentseröffnung am 25. Januar 1559 wurde dann die erste offizielle evangelische Predigt gehalten (McCULLOUGH, Sermons at court [s. Anm. 90], 59).

[165] PATRICK COLLINSON, The Elizabethan Puritan movement, London u. New York 1967, 168–176; DERS., Archbishop Grindal, 1519–1583. The struggle for a reformed church, London 1979, 233–252. Die pastorale Weiterbildung in Form von Predigerkonferenzen, die Grindal in seinem berühmten Brief vom Dezember 1576 mit Verweis auf den Nutzen der Predigt verteidigte (COLLINSON, Archbishop Grindal [s.o.], 239–246), fand bald eine Fortsetzung in Form der *lectures by combination* (DERS., Lectures by combination: Structures and characteristics of church life in 17th-century England, in: Bulletin of the Institute of Historical Research 48, 1975, 182–213).

[166] NORMAN JONES, The English Reformation. Religion and cultural adaptation, Oxford 2002.

sellschaftliche Harmonie war ein Grundwert der Tudorzeit, zu dessen Verwirklichung vor Ort auch die Pfarrer beizutragen hatten.

4. Obwohl die Geistlichkeit in England sich während der Regierungszeit Elisabeths zu einer dank der durch Status und Funktion bewirkten
Professionalisierung sozial homogenen Gruppe entwickelte, bildete er
doch ein breites positionelles Spektrum von der konservativen Amtskirche
bis zum progressiven Puritanismus aus.[167] Die Vielfalt, die sich auf dem
Kontinent auf unterschiedliche Regionen und Konfessionen verteilte, fand
sich in England innerhalb der Staatskirche.[168] Was das heißt, kann man sich
durch eine Nebeneinanderstellung der beiden paradigmatischen Amts-
theologien aus der Spätzeit Elisabeths verdeutlichen: Für die eine Strö-
mung stehen Richard Hookers *Laws of ecclesiastical polity*[169], für die andere steht William Perkins' *Art of prophesying*[170]. Beide teilen dasselbe
protestantische Grundverständnis des kirchlichen Amts, sie entfalten dieses aber auf unterschiedliche Weise und kommen an wichtigen Punkten –
etwa was das Verhältnis von Bibel und Predigt angeht[171] – zu einander

---

[167] Außer Betracht bleibt im Folgenden der radikale Puritanismus des 16. Jahrhunderts (DAVID R. COMO, Radical Puritanism, c. 1558–1660, in: The Cambridge Companion to Puritanism, hg. v. John Coffey u. Paul C. H. Lim, Cambridge 2008, 241–258),
der sich mit dem moderaten, innerhalb der Staatskirche verbleibenden Puritanismus
überlappte, aber aufgrund seiner Haltung gegenüber der Staatskirche (PATRICK COLLIN-
SON, Night schools, conventicles and churches: continuities and discontinuities in early
Protestant ecclesiology, in: The beginnings of English Protestantism, hg. v. Peter Marshall u. Alec Ryrie, Cambridge 2002, 209–235) das geistliche Amt etwas anders verstand
und praktizierte.
[168] Außer Betracht bleibt hier, dass es des Weiteren noch die Gruppe der äußerlich
angepassten, innerlich aber der Reformation gegenüber distanzierten Geistlichen gab, die
unter Heinrich VIII. oder Maria ins Amt gekommen waren und noch für Jahrzehnte
sich der Anpassung an das neue pastorale Ideal verweigerten, ohne damit aber die Entwicklung aufhalten zu können (zu dieser Gruppe am Beispiel von Christopher Trychay,
EAMON DUFFY, The voices of Morebath. Reformation and rebellion in an English village, New Haven u. London 2001; Duffy verweist auch auf die von der Forschung
bereits behandelten Beispiele Robert Parkyn und William Shepherd: a.a.O., 176 f.).
[169] RICHARD HOOKER, Of the laws of ecclesiastical polity, Bd. 2: Book V, hg. v. W.
Speed Hill, Cambridge (MA) u. London 1977, hier vor allem die Abschnitte 76–81
(413–498). Zu Hookers Amtstheologie: WILLIAM P. HAUGAARD, Towards an Anglican
doctrine of ministry: Richard Hooker and the Elizabethan Church (AEH 56, 1987,
265–284).
[170] WILLIAM PERKINS, Prophetica, sive de sacra et unica ratione Concionandi Tractatus. Editio secunda auctior & correctior ab Authore facta, Cambridge 1592 (STC 19735;
englische Übersetzung: The Arte of Prophecying: Or A Treatise Concerning the sacred
and onely true manner and methode of Preaching. First written in Latine by Master
William Perkins: and now faithfully translated into English [...] by Thomas Tuke, London 1607, STC 19735.4).
[171] HOOKER, Laws (s. Anm. 169), Abschnitt 22 (87–110). Hooker kritisiert die puritanische Predigtauffassung (zu dieser und der daraus folgenden Predigtpraxis: HORTON
DAVIES, The worship of the English Puritans, Westminster 1948, 182–203), die das in der

entgegengesetzten Aussagen, in denen sich ein Fundamentaldissens andeutet. Die amtstheologische Theorie war durchaus ein Reflex der kirchlichen Wirklichkeit: Puritanische Geistliche[172] waren oftmals besser ausgebildet, qualifizierten sich auf Predigerkonferenzen weiter, betrachteten die Predigt als ihre Hauptaufgabe, warben auf diese Weise mit Erfolg um das Stadtbürgertum und nahmen sich dabei Freiheiten in der Befolgung der kirchlichen Vorgaben, während der Teil der Geistlichkeit, für den Hooker schrieb, durchschnittlich weniger gebildet und weniger eng in eine professionelles Kontaktnetz eingebunden war, auch andere Wege der Verkündigung – etwa durch Liturgie und Bibellesung – einschlug, häufiger in ländlichen Parochien zu finden war und die geltenden Ordnungen und bestehenden Strukturen immer höher zu achten lernte. Die sich anbahnende Auseinanderentwicklung wurde in den Kontroversen seit den 1570er Jahren auch selbst zum Thema gemacht. So kontrastiert die erste, von den Londoner Predigern Thomas Wilcox und John Field verfasste puritanische Programmschrift, die *Admonition to the Parliament* von 1572[173], die Wirklichkeit der elisabethanischen Staatskirche mit dem neutestamentlichen Ideal: Angesichts der »abuses [...] in the ministerie remainyng«[174] sei darauf zu verweisen, dass wahre Kirche definiert sei durch

»preaching of the worde purely, ministring the sacraments sincerely, and ecclesiastical discipline which consisteth in admonition and correction of faults severlie«.[175]

Was den ersten Punkt des »ministerie of the worde« angeht, so werde zwar korrekt gepredigt, in vielerlei Hinsicht aber entspreche das geistliche Amt

---

Predigt verkündigte Gotteswort besonders hochschätzt und dabei die Bedeutung des gelesenen oder gehörten Gottesworts, in dem Hooker zufolge der Heilige Geist wirksam ist und das Heil schafft, zu relativieren droht.

[172] Zur Ausbildung, Weiterbildung und praktischen Tätigkeit puritanischer Geistlicher, die ihren Ort zum Teil in neu geschaffenen, an die staatskirchlichen Strukturen angebundenen Sonderstrukturen (in puritanischen Colleges, informellen Pfarrseminaren, gestifteten Prädikaturen etc.) hatten: COLLINSON, The Elizabethan Puritan movement (s. Anm. 165), 333–345; PAUL S. SEAVER, The Puritan lectureships. The politics of religious dissent, 1560–1662, Stanford 1970; O'DAY, The English clergy (s. Anm. 86), 86–104; LAKE, Moderate Puritans and the Elizabethan church (s. Anm. 147), 35–46, 116–168; MORGAN, Godly learning (s. Anm. 146), 95–120, 121–141, 220–244, 245–271, 272–300.

[173] Puritan manifestoes. A study of the origin of the Puritan revolt with a reprint of the Admonition to the Parliament and kindred documents, 1572, hg. v. W. H. Frere u. C. E. Douglas, London 1907, 1–55. Die *Second Admonition* (a.a.O., 79–133) thematisiert die puritanische Auffassung vom geistlichen Amt noch breiter. Beide Polemiken führten zu einem Streitschriftenkrieg, in dem der benannte Dissens immer wieder diskutiert wurde (einen Überblick über die Beiträge dazu gibt: MILWARD, Religious controversies of the Elizabethan Age [s. Anm. 96], 29–32).

[174] Puritan manifestoes (s. Anm. 173), 12.

[175] A.a.O., 9.

nicht den Vorgaben des Neuen Testaments hinsichtlich Ausbildung, Berufung, Tätigkeit oder Finanzierung, was vor allem für die zentrale Verkündigungsaufgabe gelte:

»Then the ministers wer preachers: now bare readers. [...] Then, as God gave utterance they preached the worde onely: now they read homilies, articles, injunctions, etc.«[176]

Die Annäherung an das biblische Ideal bedürfe einer Reform der Strukturen, deren wichtigster Punkt sei:

»Appoint to every congregation a learned & diligent preacher«.[177]

Die Alternative ist aus puritanischer Sicht klar:

»Either must we have right ministerie of God, & a right government of his church, according to the scriptures sette up (bothe whiche we lacke) or else there can be no right religion, nor yet for contempt thereof can Gods plagues be from us any while differed.«[178]

Der Dissens zwischen den sich auseinanderentwickelnden amtstheologischen und berufspraktischen Eigenarten der unterschiedlichen Strömungen verdichtete sich in den großen Konfliktthemen, die die systemischen Alternativen auf symbolische Einzelpunkte reduzierten: die liturgische Kleidung, die kirchlichen Ämter, die Ordination oder die Kirchenzucht.[179] Diese Kontroversen und die verstreuten Informationen über die kirchliche Wirklichkeit der zweiten Hälfte des 16. Jahrhunderts und das Wirken »puritanischer« und »anglikanischer« Idealgeistlicher[180] in ihr zeigen eine Spannbreite, angesichts der die generalisierende Rede vom neuen Typ des Pfarrers, der sich während der Regierungszeit Elisabeths durchsetzte, fragwürdig erscheinen könnte.

Solche Zweifel über Generalisierungen hatten die Zeitgenossen scheinbar nicht, ja sie scheuten sich nicht zu generalisieren und zu idealisieren. So hieß es in einer Predigt, die Joseph Hall anlässlich einer Synode der Kirchenprovinz Canterbury am 20. Februar 1623 in St. Paul's in London hielt:

---

[176] A.a.O., 12.
[177] Ebd.
[178] A.a.O., 6.
[179] Zur puritanischen Kritik am *Ordinal*: BRADSHAW, The Anglican Ordinal (s. Anm. 93), 37–54.
[180] Zu solchen Idealgeistlichen stilisiert wurden von Seiten der Anglikaner Bernard Gilpin (CHARLES COLLINGWOOD, Memoirs of Bernard Gilpin, parson of Houghton-le-Spring and apostle of the north, London 1884) und von Seiten der Puritaner Richard Greenham (ERIC JOSEF CARLSON, »Practical divinity«. Richard Greenham's ministry in Elizabethan England, in: Religion and the English People, 1500–1650. New voices, new perspectives, hg. v. Eric Josef Carlson, Kirksville 1998, 147–198). Der ideale Geistliche ist auch eine Figur der zeitgenössischen Literatur: NEAL ENSSLE, Patterns of godly life: The ideal parish minister in sixteenth- and seventeenth-century English thought (SCJ 28, 1997, 3–28).

»[M]unificentissimum illud τὸ πνεῦμα [...] plerosque vestrum, Patres, Fratresque, donis instruxit cumulatissime; Quibus dotibus animi, quam singulari eruditione, quam potenti eloquentia, quanta sapientia, quanta grauitate, quanta dignitatum amplitudine? Magnum est, quod dicturus sum, dicam tamen, procul omni fastu, & assentatione; ringatur, rumpantur inuidi; Stupor mundi Clerus Britannicus. Tot doctos Theologos, tot disertos concionatores frustra vspiam alibi hodie sub coelo quaesieris«.[181]

Unter den großen Predigern Englands werden von Hall nebeneinander auch »Perkinsios« und »Hookeros« aufgezählt, zusammen mit einer illustren Reihe führender Kirchenmänner aus der Zeit Eduards VI. und Elisabeths I. Mag das Urteil »Stupor mundi Clerus Britannicus« nicht für alle ca. 9000 Pfarrer des Königreichs – bezieht man Schottland und Irland noch ein, dann liegt die Zahl noch höher – gelten und den auch in den Anfängen der Stuart-Herrschaft noch merklichen Entwicklungsrückstand gegenüber der gerade vor dem Dreißigjährigen Krieg einen ersten Höhepunkt erreichenden konfessionskulturellen Ausformung der kontinentalen Kirchentümer verschweigen, so weist es doch zurecht darauf hin, dass sich auch in England ein fundamentaler Wandel vollzogen hatte und dass der neue Typ des Pfarrers auch hier Wirklichkeit geworden war. Für die Kirchwerdung der Reformation in England spielten all diese *gelehrten Theologen* und *kundigen Prediger*, von denen Hall spricht, und all die anderen Geistlichen, die der kirchlichen Erneuerung mit mehr oder weniger Enthusiasmus dienten, eine zentrale Rolle, ja die Etablierung des neuen Typs von Pfarrer war ein wichtiger Teil dieser Kirchwerdung, weil der Glaube der Verkündigung bedurfte und diese Verkündigung durch die Umgestaltung der Kirche sichergestellt werden musste. Das gilt mutatis mutandis auch für Deutschland. Was den neuen Typ des Pfarrers angeht, war man sich diesseits und jenseits des Kanals im Grundsätzlichen einig, so sehr es Eigenheiten im einzelnen gab. Die Beschäftigung mit diesem Thema bestätigt, dass Reformation hier wie dort miteinander verwandt sind und zurecht als *Schwesterreformationen* bezeichnet werden können.

---

[181] JOSEPH HALL, Columba Noae olivam adferens iactatissimae Christi arcae. Concio Synodica, ad Clerum Anglicanum (Prouinciae praesertim Cantuariensis) habita, in Aede Paulina Londinensi. Feb. 20. 1623, London 1624 (STC 12648c), 14f. Zu diesem Text und seinen Kontexten: PATRICK COLLINSON, The religion of Protestants. The church in English society 1559–1625, Oxford 1982, 92–140. Zurecht stellt Collinson fest: »applied to the generality of the parish clergy his [sc. Hall's] slogan may sound like a joke in poor taste« (a.a.O., 93), und entwickelt aus der Spannung zwischen *excellence* und *dereliction* der englischen Geistlichkeit Anfang des 17. Jahrhunderts seine lesenswerte Darstellung, die nur wegen ihrer schwerpunktmäßigen Behandlung des 17. Jahrhunderts nicht bei der oben in Anm. 87 genannten grundlegenden Literatur zum Thema aufgeführt wurde.

Anhang

Zwei bislang von der Forschung nicht rezipierte Quellen aus der Geschichte der Etablierung der evangelischen Landeskirche in der Mark Brandenburg sollen die voranstehenden Ausführungen ergänzen. Die unregelmäßige und nicht immer eindeutig zu bestimmende Groß- und Kleinschreibung der Wörter wurde – mit Ausnahme von Satzanfängen und Eigennamen – zu Kleinschreibung vereinheitlicht und die Zeichensetzung wurde normalisiert. Im Text ist mit Hilfe senkrechter Striche die Blattzählung der Vorlage angegeben. In eckige Klammern eingeschlossen sind Ergänzungen und Zusätze des Bearbeiters.

1. Das Mandat der kurbrandenburgischen Visitatoren an die Geistlichen der Inspektion Spandau 3. Mai 1553

Vorlage: Archiv des Stadtgeschichtlichen Museums Spandau, IV B 2/17, fol. 45ʳ–46ᵛ (von den Visitatoren gesiegelte Ausfertigung). Einige Formulierungen dieses Mandats sind in die 1558 gedruckte Visitationsordnung für die Landgemeinden (VD16 B 6919; Abdruck: EKO 3,90–94) übergegangen.

45ʳ ‖ Vnd sol sich der pfarrer vnd kuster alhie vnsers gne[digsten] hern christlichen kirchenordenung allendthalb[en] in predigen, sacramendtreichung, kirchen cerem[o]nien, kirchen kleidungen, an meßgewandern, chorrocken vorhalten, vnnd wan er messe held[t], [sol er] daß hochwirdige sacramendt wie vor alters eleuiren. 5

Zum andern sol der pfarrer alhie an buchern sonderlich haben vnnd fleissig daraus lesen vnd predigen: eine biebel deutzsch vnd lateinisch, eine hauspostilla doctoris Martini, cathechismum Lutheri groß vnd klein vnd die churfurstliche brandenburgische kirchenordnung vnd sich auch sonst der visitatorn vorigen vorordnung vorhaltenn. 10

Zum dritten sollen die pauren alhie dem pfarrer auch der kirchen alhie den viertzeitten pfenningk vnd andere einkommen der pfarre vnd kirche wie vor alters geben vnd vngehindertt volgenn lassenn.

Zum vierden sol der pfarrer alhie den pfarkindern alle sontage vnd feiertage des morgendes das euangelium predigen vnd zur vesper zeit ein 15 stuck oder artickel aus dem cathechismo aus der kirchenordnung in der kirchen furlesen vnd erkleren. Auch sol der pfarrer sein weib, kinder vnd gesinde aller dorffburden vnd pauerschafften aldo ledigk vnnd frey sein.

Zum funfften, wo dem pfarrer wurden clagen oder mangel furfallenn,
20 die nicht fur dem dorffhern gehorttenn oder aldo bose, streffliche laster
geschehen, soll ers dem geistlichen gerichte zu Coln an der Sprew schreiben oder berichten, daher wirdett weitter einsehen geschehenn.

Zum sechsten sollen die fursteher der kirchen alhie jerlich dem ‖ dorff-　*45ᵛ*
hern, pfarrern, schulties vnd zweien von der gemeine von der kirchen
25 einnhame vnnd ausgabe rechnung thun.

Zum siebenden sol der pfarrer aldo keine leichtfertigkeidt treiben noch
in krugk zu biere gehenn. Dan geschehe es vnd wurde daruber von den
pauren geschlagen, sol ers nicht clagen, sondern sol daheim bleibenn vnd
studiren. So soll der pfarrer auch aldo keinen bartt noch kurtze kleider,
30 sondern lange erliche kleider, wie ire standt furdert, tragen.

Zum achten soll der pfarrer alhie die fest, die im augst gefallen, nem-
blich Marie Magdalene, Jacobi vnd Laurenti, auffm sontagk legen, domit
die leute die gantze woche durch mogen irer arbeidt gewartten. Aber die
feste visitationis Marie, Petri, Pauli vnnd assumptionis Marie sol er an den
35 tagen, daran sie gefallen, haltenn.

Zum neunden sol der pfarrer alhie seine pfarhuefen wider dem junckern noch den pauren anders vormieten, dan das er vnd seine volgende
pfarrer allewege macht behaltenn, die jedes jars wider an sich zu nhemen
oder auch einem andern austzuthun. Vnnd wan das vormieten den jung-
40 kern geschicht, das sie sollen dem pfarrer reuers geben, ime die hueffen
berurter massen wider zutzustellen. Werden aber die hueffen den pauren
vormiedt, das der pfarrer neben den pauren weren fur das consistorium zu
Coln an der Sprew kommen vnd hetten solchs wie obgesatzt auch ver-
tzeichnen lassen.

45 Zum zehenden sol der pfarrer auch alhie, was er seinem ordinarien oder
bischoff zuuor fur die procuration gegebenn, wo er es ime itzo nicht gibt,
itzo ‖ jerlich zu vnderhaltung des consistorii zue Coln an der Sprew, weil　*46ʳ*
er des zu sein vnd seiner pfarren sachen zu schutz gebrauchen mag, so
geben. Gibt ers aber dem bischoff, soll es dabey bleiben.

50 Zum eilfften, wo der pfarrer alhie wirdet von einem pfarrer der nehist
anliegenden stadt zum examen oder alda zu predigen gefordert, das er
dahin sol kommen, damit seine geschicklickeit gehort vnd er bewerdt bleibe.

Zum zwolfften sol der pfarrer vf vorurlauben der patronen nicht ab-
55 tziehen, sondern sich vff das consistorium zu Coln an der Sprew berueffen
vnnd die sachen aldo, ob er das vorurlauben vorwirckt, erkennen lasse.

Zum dreitzehenden sol der pfarrer aldo keinen pfardinst thun noch
dauon eintzukommen haben, er habe dan des patronen der pfarren presentation vnnd seins ordinarien oder aber itzo des gemeinen superinten-
60 denten institution.

Zum viertzehenden, wo der pfargebeude halben wurde clagen oder mangel furfallen vnnd der pfarrer kondte sich mit dem dorffhernn oder pauren nicht darumb vortragen, das er alsdan den assessorn des geistlichen consistorii zu Coln an der Sprew soll angeben vnnd irenn bericht vnd beuelich bitten. 65

Zum funfftzehenden, wan ein festagk gefallen vff den wochennmargk thagk in der nehisten stadt, dahin die leute alhie pflegen zum wochen-markgte zufaren, das sie des tages fur dem ampte nicht, sondern erst vff 46ᵛ den mittagk sollen ausfaren. ‖

Zum sechtzehenden soll der pfarrer alhie kein par ehevolcks vortrauen, 70 sie seindt dan zuuor in seiner pfarkirchen dreymhal vffgebotten, oder frembde leute dahin khemen vnnd woltenn sich vortrauen lassenn, sie weren bekandt oder vnbekandt, so soll er derselbigenn keins vortrauen, sie brechtenn ime dann zuuor schrifftliche kundschafft, das sie ann dem ortte, daher sie kommen, zuuor werenn dreymhall vffgebotten vnnd daß keine 75 einrede geschehenn were, warumb sie sich nicht solten nhemen, oder ob solche einrede geschen were.

Zum letzsten sol der pfarrer auch beschaffen, das in seinem abtziehen oder absterben auch das vorordente inuentarium in der pfarre gelassen werde vnnd dan der schulties vnnd fursteher darauff, das solch inuentari- 80 um also dem zukunfftigen pfarrer aldo pleibe, guthe achtung gebenn.

Actum vnter der visitatorn petschafften zu Spandow, mitwochs nach cantate, anno p. liiiᵗᵉⁿ.

2. Der Abschnitt über die Amtsausübung
und Lebensführung der Pfarrer aus der
Geistlichen Visitations-, Polizei- und Konsistorialordnung
von 1561

Als Vorlage dient die einzige überlieferte Handschrift der Ordnung, die auf Geheiß des brandenburgischen Kurfürsten Joachims II. 1561 angefertigt wurde (GStAPK, I. HA, Rep. 47, Nr. 13, Fasz. »Consistorial-Ordnung 1561«, fol. 1ʳ–92ʳ, hier: fol. 16ʳ– 23ʳ). Bei dieser Handschrift handelt es um eine Reinschrift, die als Grundlage für den nicht ausgeführten Druck der Ordnung dienen sollte. Der Text der Ordnung von 1561 ist größtenteils in die 1573 im Druck erschienene Visitations- und Konsistorialordnung von Kurfürst Johann Georg von Brandenburg eingegangen, wobei er im ganzen wie im einzelnen stark bearbeitet wurde. Der folgende Abschnitt ist in bearbeiteter Form abgedruckt in: Unser von Gotts gnaden Johansen Georgens Marggraffen zu Brandenburgk / des heiligen Römischen Reichs Ertzkammerers vnd Churfürsten / In Preussen / zu Stettin / Pommern / der Cassuben / Wenden / vnd in Schlesien zu Crossen Hertzogen / Burggraffen zu Nürnbergk vnd Fürsten zu Rügen. Visitation vnd Consistorial Ordenunge, Neudamm 1573 (VD16 B 6924), 27–43.

Von den pfarrern, irem ampte,
lehre, sitten vnd lebenn

Vnnd weil oben vormeldet, das die pfarrer vnnd ministri verbi zu predigen vnd die kirche zuregirn ordentlich vocirt vnd beruffen sein mussen, so
5 wollen wir auch, das keyne pfarrer, sie sein so gelerdt oder geschickt sie immer wollenn, in stedten oder dorffern vnsers churfurstenthumbs der marcke zu Brandenburgk in der kirchen zulehren geduldet oder zu einichem pfarampt gestadtet werden, viel weyniger ‖ inhen die einkommen 16ᵛ
oder besoldungen der pfarren volgen sollen, sie sein dan zuuorn vorhort
10 vnnd haben auf gebuerliche presentation vnsers gemeynen superintendenten gewonliche institution erhaltten vnnd erlangt vnd sein in solchen irem ampte, wie obstehet, inuestirt vnd eingewiesen.

Wen nun also die pfarrer ordentlich in ihr ampt kommen vnnd getredten, sollen sie vor irhe person gott fleissig dancken, auch das volck in iren
15 predigten zu jeder zeit zu herztlicher dancksagung trewlich vnnd fleissigk vormahnen, das der almechtige gott sein teures heilsam wordt von vnserer erlosung offenbahret hat, vnnd sie ferrer zum gebet von der cantzel anhalten, das seine gotliche maiestat, seine heylige christliche kirche fur falsche lehrer vnd vorfolger des euangelii behuetten vnnd vortheidigen, auch
20 alle christliche obrigkeitten vnnd die zuhorer in rechter, brunstiger liebe der reynen erkandten gotlichen lehre fruchtbarlich im glauben vnnd warhafftiger anruffung leitten, bestendig erhalten vnnd bestettigen, deßglei-

chen erbare gutte zucht vnd christliche disciplin in diesen landen aller
gnedigst mehren vnnd vorleihen wolle.

Vnnd auf das auch solche christliche lahr in den kirchen vnserer lande 25
wie bißhero reinn vnd vnuorfelschet geleret werden, auch ferrer zunhemen
17ʳ vnnd gedeyen moge, wollen wir, das alle pfarrer vnnd kirchendiener ||
nicht anders, dan biblische, prophetische, apostolische vnnd denselbigen
gleichformige bucher vnnd schriffte lesen vnnd predigen sollen.

Derhalben sollen die pfarrer furnemlich ahn buchern haben die bibel 30
deutzsch vnd latinisch, postillam doctoris Martini Lutheri, desselbigen cathechismum vnnd vnsere christliche kirchenordnung, auch do sie des vormuegens, die gantze opera Luteri, Augustini, Hieronimi vnnd anderer
christlichen vnnd vnuorfelschten theologen bucher mehr, aber sich vor
aller falschen lehrer schriffte vnd bucher, das sie dadurch nicht in vorfu- 35
rische irthumb geleitet werden mogen, mit allem fleisse huetten.

Weitter sollen die pfarrer das volck vnd sonderlich die jugendt zu fleis-
sigem anhoren gotlichs wordts vnnd zu offter entpfahung des heyligen
hochwirdigen sacraments vnsers einigen erlosers vnd seligmachers Jhesu
Christi leibs vnd bluts trewlich vnnd fleissig vormahnen, auch nicht an- 40
ders, dan in beider gestalt, wie es der sohn gotts selbst eingesetzt, reichen.
Deßgleichen sich sonst neben den caplenen, schulmeistern, kustern vnd
andern kirchendienern in predigen, tauffen, kirchen emptern mit dem cir-
cuitu vnnd ceremonien, auch mißgewande vnd andern kirchengetzierden
vnserer christlichen kirchenordnung gentzlich vorhaltten.   45

Es sollen auch die pfarrer beide in stedten vnd dorffern die messe nicht
17ᵛ anders, dan in allermaß vnser || christliche kirchenordnung vormagk, halt-
ten vnnd die euangelia vnd episteln des sontags oder festage fleissig predigen, auch das volck vor vnd nach den predigten christliche deutzsche
psalmen de tempore vnnd sonst nach gelegenheit der zeit singen lassen, 50
vnnd dan das ampt, wehn communicanten sein, durch auß ordentlich haltten, do aber keyne vorhanden, sol es nach der predigt inhalts vnser kirchenordnung vnnd keyne priuat oder affter meß gehaltten werden.

Also auch sollen sich die woche einmahl neben andern predigten den
catechismum den jungen vnnd vnuorstendigen volcke aufs trewlichste 55
vnnd einfelttigste furtragen, auch sie zutzeiten darinne examiniren, vnd
wo sie es je so balde nicht begreiffen kondten, nicht vbel anfahren oder
von solcher vorhor abschrecken, sondern sie fein gelinde vnd freundtlich
sich zubessern weitter vntterweisen mit ertzellung, das sie dadurch got
recht lernen erkennen, der sie auch auf solch erkandtnus endtlich selig 60
machen werde etc.

Kondten aber die jugendt vnnd gesinde wegen irher arbeith vnnd dienstes ahn den werckeltagen in die kirche nicht kommen, sollen die pfarrer,

sonderlich auf den dorffern vnd in kleynen flecken den cathechismum des
65 sontags nach mittage predigen, vnnd sie ‖ vnderweylen, was sie dauon *18ᵛ*
behaltten, recitirn vnnd aufsagen lassen, auf das sie also in den furnemb-
sten stucken christlicher lehre zunhemen mogen. Bei denen ehr aber keyne
besserung findet, soll ehr auftzeichenen vnnd solchs sampt andern gebrechen seinem superintendenten, daruntter ehr vorordent, vberschicken.

70 So sollen auch die pfarrer die haußvetter trewlich vormahnen, das sie
irhe sohne vnd tochter fleissig zur schulen haltten, darinne sie den ca-
the[ch]ismum, auch die christliche psalmen lernen vnnd dem gesinde im
hause widder furlesen vnnd singen konnen.

Es erfordert auch in alwege der pfarrer beruf vnnd ampt, das sie in den
75 hospitaln vnnd sichenheusern offtmals predigen, aldo vnnd sonst in heusern die krancken, betrubten vnd bekommerten christen in stedten vnd
dorffern, sonderlich aber in pestilentz vnd sterblichen zeitten, besuchen,
sie in der beicht vnnd sonst mit gots wordt trosten, vntterrichten, stercken
vnnd zu christlicher gedult vnnd hofnung gnediger erlosung vormahnen,
80 auch mit dem hochwirdigen sacrament vorsehen. Vnnd hietzu solen die
pfarrer nicht alleyne auff der geengsten oder betrubten leutte begern, sondern vor sich selbst willig vnd vnuordrossen ‖ auch den ahrmen so wol als *18ᵛ*
den reichen disfals bereith sein, dan sonst wurde gott der almechtige wegen irer lessigheit das bluth von iren handen als den wechtern fordern.

85 Vnnd daneben sollen sie mit fleisse achtung geben, wie die ahrmen
leutte beide in heusern vnnd hospitaln mit speiß, tranck, balbierern vnnd
anderer wardtung vorsorget werden, vnd do sie bey inhen in deme mangel
spueren wurden, sollen sie solchs dem rathe, auch den vorstehern der
hospitale vnnd gemeinen kasten, auf den dorffern aber den junckern,
90 schultzen, kirchvettern vnnd gemeynen paurn vormelden, inhen gebuerliche hulffe vnnd rath zuschaffen.

Zudeme findet man viel redtlicher leutte vnnd haußarmen, die irhe notturfft in solchen kranckheitten vnnd gebrechen niemandt clagen dorffen,
vnnd doch ahn allen orttern mangelt, sollen derwegen die pfarrer die rei-
95 chen vnnd wolhabende leutte ansprechen vnnd christlich vormahnen, das
sie solchen ahrmen ahn gelde, speyse vnnd sonst behulflich vnnd trostlich
sein, furnemlich, do es eben das werck, dabei man die christen am meisten
erkendt, ist.

Auch das volck auf der cantzel erinnern, das sie den ahrmen leutten in
100 kranckheitten vnd sonst gerne hulffe thun, auch dozu williglich in den
gemeynen casten einlegen, dorauf ‖ die pfarrer dan mit fleisse sehen sollen, *19ʳ*
das solchs vntter die armen nicht nach gunst, sondern nach eins jeden
notturfft außgetheilt, das auch sonst mit der kirchen vnnd des kastens
einkommen nicht eigener nutz gesucht, sondern zu befoderung vnnd
105 vntterhalttung der kirchen diener vnnd gebeudte gewandt werde.

Sonderlich aber sollen die pfarrer vnnd prediger mit sonderm vleisse warnhemen, das das hochwirdige sacrament der heyligen tauffe mit hochster reuerentz vnnd ehrerbiettung celebrirt vnd dobei keine vnchristliche mißbreuche oder leichtferttigheitten eingefurth oder getrieben werden. Dan obwol die hurerey von gott zum hochsten vorbotten, dannoch tregt 110 sich offte zu, das etliche kinder in der vnehe getzeugt werden vnnd die muetter eine grosse antzal gefattern vmb irhes geitzes vnnd der geschencke willen bitten lassen, also auch das sie alle zur tauffe nicht kommen konnen vnnd derwegen allerley geleche vnd gespotte darauß treiben, deßgleichen geschicht auch wol von etlichen stadtlichen leutten, die des prachts vnnd 115 hofarths halben mit grosser mennige der gebettenen gefattern die heylige tauffe in ergerlichen mißbrauch ziehen. Darumb sollen hinfuro nicht vber 19ᵛ funff ‖ gefattern gebetten, noch durch die pfarrer zur tauffe gestadtet, vnnd die gefattern sich fein zuchtig in aller andacht bei der tauffe vorhalttenn, damit die heylige dreifalttigheit, so gewißlich aldo kegenwerttig ist, 120 nicht vorletzt, vnnd gotts zorne widder vns nicht erregt werden moge.

Den pfarrern vnnd predigern gebueret auch, die gotlose, faule, trege, vnachtsame leutte, so gots wordt vnnd die predigt vorseumen oder sonst in des irer arbeidt vnd handtierunge gewardten, auch von dem gebrauch des hochwirdigen sacraments des altars sich etliche jahr eussern, deßglei- 125 chen die in vntzucht, ehebruch, hurerey, zeuberey, fulsauffen, spielen, wucher vnd andern offentlichen gots lesterungen leben, damit beruchtigt oder vordechtig sein etc., trewlich zuuormahnen, sich zu bessern vnnd von sunden abtzustehen, mit angehaffter vorwarnung vnd bedrawung, do jemandts also in vorachtung gotlichs wordts vnd rohen leben vorfarn vnnd 130 nicht bei zeitte zur buesse schreitten wurde, das deme oder den jenigen gefatter zustehen noch zu anderm christlichen vorsamlungen vnnd hendeln nicht geztogen oder gelassen, vielweyniger, do sie vorsturben, auf die kirchhoeffe alß christen begraben, sondern ohne einiche christliche vorordentte gesenge alß die vnuornunfftigen tiehre anders wohin gestubbet [?] 135 werden sollen, vnnd do sie durch solch schrecken oder gutlich vormahnen, 20ʳ sich auch nicht woltten ‖ auß dem vnbußferttigen leben begeben, soll ehr solchs zum vberfluß ahn vnser consistorium gelangen, dan in solchen vnnd dergleichen sachen ein fiscal vorordent, welcher widder solche vorbrecher, sie sein edell oder vnedell, mit processen gebuerlichen zuuorfahren be- 140 uelich hatt.

Darnach sollen auch die pfarrer, prediger vnnd andere diener gotlichs wordts, sie sein hohers oder nidders standes, sich selbst befleissigen vnd iren wandell dahin reichten, das irhe leben mit der lehre vberein stimme, auch mit keynen vbeltadten, von deßwegen sie in die weldtliche gerichte 145 getzogen werden kondten, befleckt sein, vnnd endtlich also leuchten, das

die zuhorer dodurch aller christlichen tugenden anleittungen haben, auch
gots heyliger nahme vnnd das ministerium euangelii nicht geunehret werden moge.

150 Sie sollen auch gots wordt mit grosser, brunstiger liebe also lieben vnnd
mit allen crefften vnd fleisse festiglich darahn haltten, das sie sich nicht
durch herliche wolluste, gifft, gaben vnd reichthumbe, auch nicht durch
furcht oder trewung der gefengnus vnd leibs gefahr dauon abtziehen oder
dergestalt abschrecken lassen, ethwas zureden, zuthun oder furtzunhemen,
155 so widder die gotliche wahrheit oder gerechtigheit wehre. Dan der teuffel
wirdt inhen warlich durch mannicherley anfechtungen mit ernste zusetzen,
auff ‖ das ehr von vorthsetzung des godtlichen wordts abspenstig vnnd   *20ᵛ*
abtrennig mache. Darumb mussen sie gott vmb den heyligen geist bitten
vnnd nicht allein in der religion, sondern auch artibus geschickt sein, da-
160 mit sie die lehre des euangelii vorthedigen, auch dem teuffel vnd andern
widdersachern durch zeugnussen der heyligen schrifft widderstandt thun
konnen, dan es wirdt kempffens geldten, wie die alten lehrer primatiuae
ecclesie gethan, die lieber alle gefahr leibs vnnd lebens gewerttig gewesen,
ehe sie von der heylsamen lehre gewichen sein.

165 Vnnd weil von der weldtlichen obrigkeit obseruirt wirdt, das sie keyne
vnuorehelichte personen im rathe oder zum burgermeister ampte wehlen,
wieuiel mehr ist es pillich, das es in elegendis doctoribus ecclesie auch also
gehalten werde. Derhalben sollen die pfarrer, wo sie die gabe der keuscheit
nicht hettenn, ergernus zuuormeyden, im ehestande erfunden werden, auf
170 das sie wegen der vnkeuschen gedancken ahn iren gebette vnnd studiis
vnuorhindert pleyben mogen, auch solch ampt mit mehrer furcht bestellen
vnnd vorwaldten konnen.

Vnnd sollen mit den betrubten vnd angefochtenen guttig vnnd freundtlich vmbgehen vnnd die jenigen, so des euangelii vnd erkandten ‖ wahr-   *21ʳ*
175 heit halben anders wo vorjagt sein vnnd des gutten glaubhafften schein
haben, gerne beherbergen.

Auch sollen sie sonst in wordten vnnd wercken feine, sittige, glimpff-
liche vnnd sampfftmuttige menner sein, mit denen jederman gerne zuschaffen hatt. Doch sollen sie leichtferttigheit in reden, spielen, kleydern
180 vnnd geberden meidenn, vnnd keynen auß furcht oder nutzes halben seine
sunde vnd feyle zuuormelden heuchlen, sondern gleichen schein halten,
die reichen sowoll alß die ahrmen angreiffen vnnd die offentliche gotsle-
sterungeen straffen vnnd disfals widder obrigkeit noch vndterthanen sche-
wen, doch sol es sine affectibus in gemein durch gots wordt et cum pro-
185 cessu iuxta capitulum Matthei 18. Si peccauerit frater tuus in te etc., et
Pauli ad Thimoteum contra Bresbiterum etc. beschehen. Wurden sich aber
die vorbrecher nicht bessern vnnd vber alle gotliche beuelich vnd vorbot

der rechte, auch widder ir eigen gebuer, ehr vnnd erbargheit sich nicht
weysen lassen, sollen sie irhen gots vrteill vber sie vorkundigen vnnd
solchs wie obstehet dem consistorio vormelden. 190

    Vnnd sollen die pfarrer in deme noch sonst irem gemessenen beuelich
21ᵛ nicht vberschreitten, viel weiniger sich in frembde hendell mengen, ‖ vnnd
einen fueß aufm predigstuel vnnd den andern aufm rathause haben, id est,
non simul ecclesiastica et politica negotia administrare debendt.

    Vielweiniger sollen sie jachzornige menschen sein, noch sich selbst mit 195
der faust vorthedingen, sondern wehn sie gehasset, beschedigt oder mit
wordten beleidigt werden, gerne vorgeben vnnd die vorbrecher mit dem
wordte gotts straffen vnnd schrecken. Aber vber die vnbueßferttigen mogen sie wol zornen vnnd irhe vbeltadten obberurtter massen mit ernste
angreiffen, dan solchs ist ein heiliger gotlicher zorne, damit man die sun- 200
der zu rechte bringet.

    Nachdeme auch das volsauffen ein wurtzel alles boesen ist, stehet den
pfarrern wol ahn, das sie fein nuchtern vnnd messig leben, so konnen sie
zu allen dingen geschickt sein vnd alles mit bessern fleiß vnd gluckseliger
außrichten, dan die trunckenboltze tuegen widder mit den gedancken 205
noch mit dem leibe vnnd thun zutzeitten das jenige, welchs sie nimmer-
mehr außleschen konnen.

    Also sollen sie auch nicht eigensinnige, vorwirtte, sondern richtige
kopffe haben vnd in regierung der kirchen vnd zweifelhafftigen sachen irer
22ʳ superintendenten ‖ oder benachbarten pfarrer vnnd prediger rath leben, 210
dan die zusamen vorgleichung bringet der kirchen grossen nutz vnnd gotts
segen.

    Vnnd wan sie mit iren mitgehulffen oder andern pfarrern von geistli-
chen sachen reden oder radtschlagen, sollen sie nicht alleyne auf irhe kopffe vnd sinne bestehen, sondern der andern meynung vnd gedancken auch 215
horen vnnd denen volgen, die am besten gerathen, welchs etliche kluglinge
vnd nouitii schwerlich thun konnen, dan sie sein in vorthedigung irhes
gutdunckens vnnd wahns so halstarrig, als wehre es eittel heyligthumb, do
sie doch weith feilen, noch konnen sie nicht leiden, das man inhen einre-
dett, aber dieselbigen haben kein glucke ihn irem stande vnnd furnhemen. 220

    Darumb sollen die pfarrer auf der superintendenten erfordern zum sin-
odum oder sonst gehorsamlich erscheynen, aldo der superintendenten vnd
anderer gelerdten benachbartten pfarrer meynung vnnd firma argumenta
in rebus dubiis et perplexis auch horen vnnd volgen.

    Die pfarrer sollen auch nicht wucherer, geitzigk, noch keyne kremer 225
oder hendler, bier- oder weinschencken sein, deßgleichen keyne vnehrli-
che handtierung wie die weldtlichen leutte treiben, dan ein geitziger oder
hendler kahn nicht recht, lautter vnnd clar lehren, weil ehr die gedancken

auffs guth zumehren hat, sondern sollen mitt ‖ irhen stipendiis zufrieden 22ᵛ
230 vnd, do die gleich etwas geringe sein, von gott hulffe vnnd das tegliche
brodt bitten, der wirdt inhen deßgleichen iren weib vnnd kindern sonder
zweiffel, wie ehr andern gotfurchtigen fromen kirchendienern vnd trewen
predigern, die sein wordt lautter vnd rein gepredigt vnnd irhes beruffs
mit fleiß gewardtet, alwege gethan, mit allerlei dieses lebens notturfft gne-
235 digst vorsehen.

Doch wirt gleichwoll hiedurch den pfarrern nicht vorbotten, das sie
bey irhen leben irhe weiber vnnd kinder mit wohnungen vnnd guttern, so
es mit gott vnnd ehren geschehen kan, vorsorgen, auf das sie auf ir absterben vntterhalttunge haben mogen.

240 So gebueret auch den pfarrern, irhe weiber, kinder vnnd gesinde in aller
gotts furcht vnd erbarn sitten dermassen aufzutziehen, das sie in deme
andern darnach zuuolgen christliche anleittungen geben, vnnd do sie es
nicht thun vnnd hierinne seumig oder lessigk sein wurden, sollen sie irhes
ampts dodurch priuirt sein, in erwegung, das die jenigen, so die irhen vbel
245 ziehen, die andern nicht wol vnderweisen oder lehren konnen.

Sie sollen auch irem superintendenten als iren obern gehorsam sein
vnnd in allen ehren halten, auch sie nicht bei den gewalttigen oder gemeinen ‖ volcke verkleynern, vielweyniger widder sie practiciren oder 23ʳ
rottten vnd parteyen anrichten noch jemandts widder sie vorbittern oder
250 vorhetzen, in hofnung, sie dodurch außzustechen oder von irem ampte
zudringen.

Wurden aber die dorfpfarrer selbst durch die collatores oder patronen
vorurlaubet, sollen sie ohne vnser oder vnsers consistorii erkandtnus keins
wegs abziehen oder die pfarren reumen, dan wir wollen, das keiner ex
255 affectu, sondern auß redtlichen, bestendigen vrsachen seins ampts entsatzt
werden solle.

Was den pfarrern ferrer zuthun aufferlegt vnnd zu irem ampte gehorig,
werden sie hernach weitter hin vnnd widder in den volgenden articuln
finden, darumb es alles alhie ordentlich nacheinander zusetzen von vnnot-
ten geachtet.

A new type of clergy

Andreas Stegmann

Dedicated to Karl-Heinrich Lütcke,
provost of the Evangelische Kirche
in Berlin-Brandenburg, 1990–2005,
in occasion of his eightieth birthday,
February 20th, 2020

An episode that took place in the city of Frankfurt an der Oder exemplifies the changes that the Reformation brought about for the clergy.[1] In the mid–1530s, the daughter of a freshwater fisherman, a Gertrud Matzke, working as a maidservant in the household of one of the burghers there, was seen to produce coins, apparently out of nothing, which she then put in her mouth, chewed and swallowed. In her sleep she suffered nightmares, and when awake she sometimes spoke in high German, which was unknown to her. There was no doubt: The woman must be in the clutches of the devil and had to be exorcised. A priest was called, who tried all the known actions and formulas, but without any success. In the city, however, there was at the time already a Protestant preacher, Andreas Ebert (1497–1557),[2] who submitted the case to Martin Luther and then applied the remedy proposed from Wittenberg. The remedy was to pray for the woman and to take her to church and make her listen to the sermon preached there – which proved successful. The Frankfurt money devil, who had not yielded to holy herbs, water and radishes, nor to the powerful language of the papist exorcist, took flight before the prayer and sermon of the Reformation preacher:

---

[1] From a pamphlet, printed in Wittenberg in 1538: Wunderliche Zeitung von einem GeldTeuffel / ein selzame / ungleubliche / doch warhafftige geschicht. Zu Franckfurt an der Oder geschehen / vnd vrkundlich ausgangen (VD16 E 173). Cf. the correspondence between Luther and Ebert (WA.Br 7,482–90, no. 3055–56) and two later reports that present additional information: CHRISTOPH STUMMEL, Kurtzer Vnterricht von Wunderwercken / so in Göttlicher Schrift vnd andern Historien beschrieben sind, Frankfurt (Oder) 1567 (VD16 S 9835), X 1ʳ–Y 1ᵛ; ANDREAS ENGEL, WiderNatur vnd Wunderbuch, Frankfurt a. M. 1597 (VD16 E 1193), 213–29.

[2] HÖHLE, Universität und Reformation (note 28), 422–29.

»When she was led to the sermon the devil through her, time and again called me [i.e. Ebert] a liar, while I was preaching. And when I commanded the devil to be silent, then she became silent and thus [...] through common prayer she was helped, namely that the devil left her.«[3]

Andreas Ebert, who called himself »Ecclesiastes Francofordianus«,[4] was one of the first in the electorate of Brandenburg who exemplified a new type of clergyman. Even before the official introduction of the Reformation, he had been asked by citizens to preach the gospel and offer spiritual support to parishioners, proclaiming the liberating word of God. The officials of the papal church, on the other hand, were fighting a losing battle: As representatives of the papal hierarchy it was their task to lead the parishes and to celebrate the sacraments – without, however, being considered by the people as helping them to cope with their lives in this world or before God.

Taking a new look at the development of a new type of clergyman in the 16th century can, in the light of the wealth of already existing studies, be justified only if there are, at least partially, new insights to be gained. There are in fact two new aspects in what follows. One aspect is that the example chosen here is in the electorate of Brandenburg, which has found surprisingly little consideration in Reformation historiography, although the developments of Lutheranism in the Mark during the time of Joachim II (1535–1571) can serve as a kind of model for the transformation process.[5] Secondly, the characteristic features in this process, as far as the clergy are concerned, will become more distinct than they have been so far, when the German and the English Reformations are compared.[6] This

---

[3] Wunderliche Zeitung (note 1, A 3ʳ). In regard to Ebert's preaching in Frankfurt cf. Gotthard Kemmether, Ein Predigtkonzept von 1539 – Autograph von Andreas Ebert, dem ersten evangelischen Prediger in Frankfurt an der Oder? (in: JBBKG 71, 2017, 200–14).

[4] WA.Br 7,486.

[5] On the history of the Reformation in Brandenburg: Andreas Stegmann, Die Reformation in der Mark Brandenburg, Leipzig 2017; Id., Deutung und Bedeutung der brandenburgischen Reformation (in: Reformation in Brandenburg. Verlauf, Akteure, Deutungen, ed. Frank Göse, Berlin 2017, 63–92); Id., Die Kirchenpolitik des brandenburgischen Kurfürsten Joachim II. (in: JBBKG 71, 2017, 42–148).

[6] By choosing Brandenburg as example for German Lutheranism, it can be seen what the Brandenburg and the English Reformation have in common and where they differ. The claim made in older research that both Reformations should be seen as a middle course between the emerging confessions (A. F. Pollard, The conflict of creeds and parties in Germany, in: The Cambridge Modern History, ed.s A. W. Ward et. al., vol. 2: The Reformation, Cambridge 1903, 206–45, esp. 237; Emil Sehling, Einleitung, in: Die evangelischen Kirchenordnungen des XVI. Jahrhunderts, vol. 3, Leipzig 1909, 3–27, esp. 18), is no longer tenable in sight of the *paradigm shift* of newer research (Dewey D. Wallace, Via media? A paradigm shift, in: AEH 72, 2003, 2–21; Andreas Stegmann, Die »christliche Reformation« im Kurfürstentum Brandenburg. Mittelweg

article has two main parts, with the first one focusing on the fundamental agreement shared by the German and the English Reformation and primarily taking into consideration German Lutheranism, while the second part will take a look at the differences, with special attention to the developments in England.[7] The main topic will be the new *type* of clergy, meaning the ideal of the ecclesiastical office described in the early programmatic texts of the Reformation, which took shape, by and by, in the reality of the new church. One should note that the reality of the ministry only gradually began to correspond to the ideals< expressed in the theological texts. Moreover, reality never came to be identical with the ideals: expectations kept changing at their own pace, thus reality lagged behind by necessity.

1. Fundamental agreements, with particular reference to German Lutheranism

The beginnings and the development of a new type of clergy in the sphere of the Wittenberg Reformation have been studied extensively.[8] Also for

---

zwischen Rom und Wittenberg oder lutherische Reformation?, in: Theologische Literaturzeitung 141, 2016, 578–91) and is being refuted by this article once more.

[7] A comparison to what happened in south-west Germany and Switzerland and in the influence sphere of the Geneva Reformation, basically similar to what is being described here, will be taken up only selectively, and the developments in Scotland and Ireland, where we find the new type of clergy following the example of continental Calvinism or of the English state church, will not be considered here.

[8] Important overviews are: PAUL DREWS, Der evangelische Geistliche in der deutschen Vergangenheit, Jena ²1924, 7–72; LUISE SCHORN-SCHÜTTE, The Christian clergy in the Early Modern Holy Roman Empire: A comparative study (SCJ 29, 1998, 717–31); ID., Priest, preacher, pastor: Research on clerical office in early modern Europe (Central European History 33, 2000, 1–39); ID., The ›New Clergies‹ in Europe: Protestant pastors and catholic reform clergy after the Reformation (in: The Impact of the European Reformation: Princes, clergy and people, ed.s Bridget Heal and Ole Peter Grell, Aldershot u. Burlington 2008, 103–24); WOLFGANG E. J. WEBER, Luthers bleiche Erben. Kulturgeschichte der evangelischen Geistlichkeit des 17. Jahrhunderts, Berlin and Boston 2017 (Weber deals also with the 16th century; the strength – and at the same time the weakness – of his book is his focus on the printed pastoral literature of early modern times, from which the reality of the pastoral service can only be indirectly deduced). – Important regional studies are: BERNHARD VOGLER, Le clergé protestant rhénan au siècle de la réforme (1555–1619), Paris 1976 (cf. ID., Recrutement et carrière des pasteurs strasbourgeois au XVIᵉ siècle, in: Revue d'histoire et de philosophie religieuses 48, 1968, 151–74); SUSAN C. KARANT-NUNN, Luther's Pastors. The Reformation in the Ernestine Countryside, Philadelphia 1979; LUISE SCHORN-SCHÜTTE, Evangelische Geistlichkeit in der Frühneuzeit. Deren Anteil an der Entfaltung frühmoderner Staatlichkeit und Gesellschaft. Dargestellt am Beispiel des Fürstentums Braunschweig-Wolfenbüttel, der Landgrafschaft Hessen-Kassel und der Stadt Braunschweig, Heidelberg 1996; C. SCOTT DI-

the electorate of Brandenburg some research has been done, with useful analyses of the printed source material,[9] but there is additional manuscript and printed material which needs to be considered. There is agreement among researchers that the new type of minister has two main characteristics: he is a *preacher* and he is a *citizen*. What this means shall be looked at in detail with special regard to the Mark Brandenburg.

1.1. The pastor as preacher

The definition of preaching as the first and foremost duty and activity of the clergy goes back to Luther's fundamental theological insight concerning the doctrine of justification: justifying faith comes through the preaching of the Gospel (Rom 10:17).[10] There were, for the Wittenberg

---

XON, The Reformation and rural society. The parishes of Brandenburg-Ansbach-Kulmbach, 1528–1603, Cambridge 1996 (cf. ID., Rural resistance, the Lutheran pastor, and the territorial church in Brandenburg Ansbach-Kulmbach, 1529–1603, in: The reformation of the parishes. The ministry and the Reformation in town and country, ed. Andrew Pettegree, Manchester, New York 1993, 85–112); ERNST RIEGG, Konfliktbereitschaft und Mobilität. Die protestantischen Geistlichen zwölf süddeutscher Reichsstädte zwischen Passauer Vertrag und Restitutionsedikt, Leinfelden-Echterdingen 2002; LOTHAR BERNDORFF, Die Prediger der Grafschaft Mansfeld. Eine Untersuchung zum geistlichen Sonderbewusstsein in der zweiten Hälfte des 16. Jahrhunderts, Potsdam 2010; MACIEJ PTASZYŃSKI, »Beruf und Berufung«. Die evangelische Geistlichkeit und die Konfessionsbildung in den Herzogtümern Pommern, 1560–1618, Göttingen, Bristol 2017. – For an instructive survey concerning the Lutheran theology of the Protestant ministry in the 16th and 17th centuries see JÖRG BAUR, Das kirchliche Amt im Protestantismus. Skizzen und Reflexionen (in: Das Amt im ökumenischen Kontext, ed. Jörg Baur, Stuttgart 1980, 103–38).

[9] BEATE FRÖHNER, Der evangelische Pfarrstand in der Mark Brandenburg 1540–1600 (Wichmann-Jahrbuch 19/20, 1965/66, 5–46). Fröhner evaluates church orders and visitation reports from the 16th century that have appeared in print, and orders the material systematically, considering all important aspects of the ministry. Other sources are edited by BURKHARD V. BONIN, Entscheidungen des Cöllnischen Konsistoriums 1541–1704. Nach der Sammlung des Konsistorialrats und Propstes D. Franz Julius Lütkens, Weimar 1926. These sources date mainly from the 17th and 18th centuries and are analyzed by HERMANN WERDERMANN, Pfarrerstand und Pfarramt im Zeitalter der Orthodoxie in der Mark Brandenburg (JBrKG 23, 1928, 53–133; this essay is relevant also for the 16th century; slightly shortened and with the same title it has been separately published in 1929). – The number of parishes and clerical posts in the Mark during the 16th century can only be guessed. Counting 80 cities, 1971 villages and 858 Lutheran clergy in the 2nd half of the 18th century (ANTON FRIEDRICH BÜSCHING, Lutherisch-geistliche Inspectionen in der Churmark, in: Magazin für die neue Historie und Geographie 13, 1779, 365–72), this may correspond to the situation in the 16th century. Territorial historical research puts the number of cities somewhat higher and that of the villages lower for the Reformation century; the number of the clergy will probably have been somewhat higher.

[10] For the connection between word and faith see his treatise on Christian freedom, published 1520 (WA 7,12–73). Starting from these basic ideas, Luther developed his thought about the office of the proclamation of the gospel and its organizational form:

reformer, different ways and means for preaching Christ and bringing about faith and the early Reformation movement displays a surprising diversity of means of communication.[11] From the very beginning, the sermon was at the core of the Reformation agenda: While already in the late Middle Ages it had been growing in importance,[12] the Reformation turned preaching into a effective propaganda tool and placed it in the very center of church activity and Christian piety.[13]

Evidence for this can be found in the oldest extant evangelical sermon from the electorate of Brandenburg. After the Saxon elector had, in 1522, expelled the mendicants from Wittenberg, Johannes Briesmann (1488–1549), a student of Luther, who had just earned a doctor's degree and who as a Franciscan friar wanted to help spread the Reformation and therefore did not want to quit the order, returned to his original monastery in Cottbus.[14] In this city in Lower Lusatia, under the rule of the Brandenburg Hohenzollerns since the 15th century, he preached following the teachings of the Reformation, and after conflicts with both the spiritual and the secular authorities, he had to leave. What Briesmann had preached in Cottbus, he published after his expulsion in the form of a pamphlet for his followers who remained behind, so that they should not forget his

---

REINHARD SCHWARZ, Martin Luther. Lehrer der christlichen Religion, Tübingen 2015, chap. 9.3–4. A survey including literature up to the middle of the 1990s: BERNHARD LOHSE, Luthers Theologie in ihrer historischen Entwicklung und ihrem systematischen Zusammenhang, Göttingen 1995, 304–16. Most important of the newer studies on this topic: CHRISTOPHER VOIGT-GOY, Potestas und ministerium publicum. Eine Studie zur Amtstheologie im Mittelalter und bei Martin Luther, Tübingen 2014.

[11] THOMAS KAUFMANN, Geschichte der Reformation, Frankfurt a. M. and Leipzig 2009, part 2.

[12] ISNARD W. FRANK, art. Predigt VI. Mittelalter (in: TRE 27, 1997, 248–62).

[13] ALBRECHT BEUTEL, art. Predigt VIII. Evangelische Predigt vom 16.–18. Jahrhundert (ibid., 296–311); ID., Kommunikation des Evangeliums. Die Predigt als zentrales theologisches Vermittlungsmedium in der Frühen Neuzeit (in: Kommunkation und Transfer im Christentum der frühen Neuzeit, ed.s Irene Dingel and Wolf-Friedrich Schäufele, Mainz 2007, 3–15).

[14] Concerning Briesmann's person and work: PAUL TSCHACKERT, Einleitung (in: Urkundenbuch zur Reformationsgeschichte des Herzogthums Preußen, ed. Paul Tschackert, vol. 1, Leipzig 1890, 41–48); ROBERT STUPPERICH, Johann Briesmanns reformatorische Anfänge (JBrKG 34, 1939, 3–21); BERND MOELLER, Karl Stackmann, Städtische Predigt in der Frühzeit der Reformation. Eine Untersuchung deutscher Flugschriften der Jahre 1522 bis 1529, Göttingen 1996, 31–36. Cautious reading is advised for the newest study: HEINZ-DIETER HEIMANN, Dr. Johannes Briesmann (1488–1549): Barfüsser und gewesener Mönch. Hybride Konfessionskultur im Selbstzeugnis eines franziskanischen Gelehrten und Anhängers Martin Luthers (in: Hybride Identitäten in den preußisch-polnischen Stadtkulturen der Aufklärung. Studien zur Aufklärungsdiffusion zwischen Stadt und Land, zur Identitätsbildung und zum Kulturaustausch in regionalen und internationalen Kommunikationsnetzwerken, ed.s Joanna Kodzik and Włodzimierz Zientara, Bremen 2016, 173–87).

sermons.[15] He implored them to thank »the merciful God who has let his most dear and good word be preached even among them, in these last and dangerous days and fearful times« and not to be led astray »from the right way of the Gospel«.[16] This gospel, which Briesmann had been preaching in Cottbus, was first and foremost about faith in Christ and love of neighbor, both of which Briesmann elaborated, closely following Luther's treatise on the freedom of a Christian, as when he interpreted John 10:

>The entering into Christ is faith, which gives you the justice of Christ, through which you are satisfyingly just before God and need no other works to make your own justice. Yet the going out [from Christ] is love, which again is divided (since you are clothed with the justice of Christ) between the service of your neighbor and the exercise of your own body, to help others' want and poverty, in order that they, too, will be drawn through you to enter Christ with you. For similarly Christ has come from God and has drawn us to him and has, in all his life, not sought his own, but what is ours. Therefore again, since we have entered through faith, we must go out to receive others, and to seek no other thing than that we become as servants to all, to become blessed with us.«[17]

With this sermon, Briesmann found listeners in Cottbus and provoked resistance from the papal church. While his activity there soon came to an involuntary end, it was carried on through his pamphlet and found continuation in his career. Passing through Wittenberg, Briesmann found his way to the Baltic littoral, where he was to become the reformer of Prussia. Following the Wittenberg Reformation, he helped to establish the structures developed in the 1520s in the core countries of the Reformation under the difficult conditions of the periphery of the occidental world.

What the sermon needed, being as it was of central importance for the Reformation, was an institutional framework, a standardization in regard to its content, and competent preachers. As much as the common priesthood of all believers was valued and the individual Christian was given the right and the duty to proclaim the gospel to those around him, one could not nor would one abandon the well-ordered ecclesiastical office. Of critical importance for the form which this ecclesiastical office would take in the Wittenberg Reformation was the *necessaria coniunctio scholarum cum ministerio evangelii*: the necessary relationship between study and the

---

[15] Unterricht vnd ermanung Doct. Johannis Briesmans / Barfusser Ordens / an die Christlich gemeyen zu Cottbus, Anno M.D.XXiij, [Wittenberg 1523] (VD16 B 8307).

[16] Ibid., A 3ᵛ.

[17] Ibid., B 2ᵛ. That Briesmann's early publications can serve as witness to the reception of Luther's treatise on Christian freedom is demonstrated by the *Flosculi* of 1523 that also interpret the duality of justifying faith and love of neighbor by referring to the *Christian freedom* (Flosculi de homine interiore et exteriore, fide et operibus, die erste grundlegende Reformationsschrift aus dem Ordenslande Preußen vom Jahre 1523, ed. Paul Tschackert, Gotha 1887, 9–15).

ministry of the Gospel. While the formula »necessaria coniunctio«, which goes back to Melanchthon,[18] is characteristic of the Wittenberg Reformation, its subject matter appears likewise in the Southern German, in the Swiss and in the Genevan Reformation. Education and church must be interlocking, in order to qualify the holder of the ecclesiastical office for his task of proclaiming the gospel and to have control over it. The Wittenberg theologians did not see this as such an innovation as it actually was, for according to their view there had always been educational institutions, where both languages (litterae) and the Bible (sermo divinus) had been taught, since Old Testament times.[19] Such schools functioned as protectors and interpreters of doctrine, where decisions were made in case of doctrinal disagreement: They were »doctrinae custodes, atque interpretes, & gravißimarum controuersiarum iudices«.[20] This transmitting of doctrine, which was of utmost importance for the proclamation of the gospel, had to take place, according to Melanchthon, within the existing scholastic and academic structures. What was needed was an intensified study course, where the future preacher, through lectures, disputations and his own reading, would learn the liberal arts, the biblical languages and texts, the doctrine of the church and acquire knowledge in doctrinal controversies.[21] Where this kind of school was not available or not up to the task, the light of the gospel could be extinguished (amissis literis lucem Euangelii extinguj).[22]

According to Melanchthon, the *ministerium Evangelii*, was not held by the university, rather its theological faculty was »ministerii evangelici membrum«.[23] This gave a new meaning and function to academic theology

---

[18] PHILIP MELANCHTHON, Oratio de necessaria coniunctione Scholarum cum ministerio Euangelij: a D. Bernhardo Zieglero recitata, 1543 (in: Selectarum Declamationum Philippi Melanthonis, quas conscripsit, & partim ipse in Schola Vitebergensi recitauit, partim alijs recitandas exhibuit. Tomus Quartus, Strasbourg 1558, VD16 M 3566, 424–45; reprint: CR 11,606–18 [no. 73]). Melanchthon wrote this speech for Bernhard Ziegler, who received his doctor's degree in the fall of 1543 in Leipzig (cf. MBW.T 12,338–39 [no. 3322] and 363–65 [no. 3338]).

[19] Selectarum Declamationum (note 18), 429–34 (CR 11,609–12).

[20] Ibid., 430 (609).

[21] »Valde [...] errant illi, qui pastores ex quolibet ligno sculpi, & sine literis, sine longa institutione religionis doctrinam subito percipi posse somniant. Primum genus sermonis prophetici & Apostolici cognoscendum est. Discendae sunt igitur linguae ueteres, & tota ratio formandae orationis cognoscenda est: quam ad rem bonis doctoribus ueterum monumentorum lectione, literariis exercitjs, denique etiam tempore opus est. Postea maior labor succedit. [...] Opus est autem ad explicationem controuersiarum maximarum, non solum ingenij dexteritate, & mediocri cognition sacrorum librorum: sed etiam disputandi arte, copia orationis, noticia historiae, antiquitatis, & ueterum iudiciorum« (ibid., 435–36 [612]).

[22] Ibid., 434 (612).

and consequently upgraded the theological faculty for the church. Before the Reformation the hierarchy of the church had been the *custos doctrinae*: it depended for transmission and interpretation of church doctrine on the universities, which had been founded in the high Middle Ages, and trusted them, in the late Middle Ages, with the education and control over the clergy. This loose and partial cooperation of church and university was consolidated through the Reformation as a *necessaria coniunctio*. To meet the task of the theological office of propagation of the gospel, a qualified clergy was needed, while the Reformation at the same time created new possibilities and freedoms, all of which contributed to this system. The rejection of the Reformation by the papal church, together with the support of the Reformation by many secular authorities led to a fundamental change of the traditional structures, to the introduction of new ways and to a new turn of what was theologically needed and desirable for the church.

Of the Lutheran regions, not only Electoral Saxony but also Württemberg and Braunschweig-Wolfenbüttel stand out as examples for an interaction between a humanist-Reformation educational system and evangelical territorial churches.[24] During the second half of the 16th century, in the south-west it was mostly Basel, where this »ideal type« of a »coordinated system of religious and theological education«, based on the close relationship between Reformation theology and humanism, could be found.[25] Similarly in Geneva, already during Calvin's lifetime, such an

---

[23] Quoted from the statutes of the Theological Faculty Wittenberg of 1545, drawn up by Melanchthon (in: Urkundenbuch der Universität Wittenberg, ed. Walter Friedensburg, part 1, Magdeburg 1926, 262).

[24] MARTIN BRECHT, Herkunft und Ausbildung der protestantischen Geistlichen des Herzogtums Württemberg im 16. Jahrhundert (ZKG 80, 1969, 163–75); CHARLOTTE METHUEN, Securing the Reformation through education: The duke's scholarship system of sixteenth-century Württemberg (SCJ 25, 1994, 841–51); SCHORN-SCHÜTTE, Evangelische Geistlichkeit in der Frühneuzeit (note 8), 159–226; MARTIN KRARUP, Ordination in Wittenberg. Die Einsetzung in das kirchliche Amt in Kursachsen zur Zeit der Reformation, Tübingen 2007. For the Frankish region, having no protestant university, but a highly developed school system, see BERNHARD KLAUS, Soziale Herkunft und theologische Bildung lutherischer Pfarrer der reformatorischen Frühzeit (ZKG 80, 1960, 22–49).

[25] AMY NELSON BURNETT, Preparing the pastors: Theological education and pastoral training in Basel (in: History has many voices, ed. Lee Palmer Wandel, Kirksville 2003, 131–51, esp. 150). The country parsons, too, participated in the growing academic standards and homogeneity of the Basel clergy and therefore got to be important mediators of confessionalization (AMY NELSON BURNETT, Basel's rural pastors as mediators of confessional and social discipline, in: Central European History 33, 2000, 67–85). That country ministers could be as well educated as their colleagues in the cities, can be observed in the Nuremberg region (RIEGG, Konfliktbereitschaft und Mobilität [note 8], 183–94) and in Pomerania (PTASZYŃSKI, »Beruf und Berufung« [note 8], 273). But there

interaction took place, which led to a quick and full introduction of an academically qualified and professional clergy.[26] In other cities and territories, similar developments could be observed, with a close interaction of *education* and *confession*, inaugurated by the Wittenberg reformers.[27] Although there was not much of a school system to speak of in the electorate of Brandenburg, and although the newly established university in the trading city of Frankfurt (Oder) did not have much attraction, the *necessaria conjunctio* was established in the Mark after the introduction of the Reformation, there also.[28] Through the Reformation, the school system in the Mark received a fresh impulse, although its development was still slow in comparison to the neighboring regions; in any case, from the middle of the 16th century onwards, humanist-Reformation basics were taught in the urban Latin school, which meant that the education for the spiritual-secular elite demanded by the reformers was ensured.[29] After a

---

are also regional differences that have to be taken in account (cf. the remarks about the »different educational level between city and country clergy«: SCHORN-SCHÜTTE, Evangelische Geistlichkeit in der Frühneuzeit [note 8], 221).

[26] WILLIAM G. NAPHY, The renovation of the ministry in Calvin's Geneva (in: The reformation of the parishes. The ministry and the Reformation in town and country, ed. Andrew Pettegree, Manchester and New York 1993, 113–32); KARIN MAAG, Education and training for the Calvinist ministry: the Academy of Geneva, 1559–1620 (ibid., 133–52).

[27] For more examples from German and Swiss regions (Heidelberg, Bremen, Hamburg, Danzig, the counties Mark and Ravensberg, Franconia and Zurich) see: Bildung und Konfession. Theologenausbildung im Zeitalter der Konfessionalisierung, ed.s Herman J. Selderhuis and Markus Wriedt, Tübingen 2006. Concerning the education of the clergy in German language Switzerland see also BRUCE GORDON, Preaching and the reform of the clergy in the Swiss Reformation (in: The reformation of the parishes. The ministry and the Reformation in town and country, ed. Andrew Pettegree, Manchester and New York 1993, 63–84).

[28] About the history of the founding of the Viadrina and its transformation up to the middle of the century of the Reformation see MICHAEL HÖHLE, Universität und Reformation. Die Universität Frankfurt (Oder) von 1506 bis 1550, Köln et al. 2002. For the 2nd half of the 16th century see the older publications (Acten und Urkunden der Universität Frankfurt a. O., vol. 1–5, Breslau 1897–1903), and surveys (GERD HEINRICH, art. Frankfurt an der Oder, Universität, in: TRE 11, 1983, 335–42).

[29] Luther elaborated the basic ideas for a Reformation educational program in his treatises *An die Ratherren aller Städte deutschen Landes, daß sie christliche Schulen aufrichten und halten sollen* (1524: WA 15,9–53) and *Eine Predigt, daß man Kinder zur Schulen halten solle* (1530: WA 30[II],508–88), and Melanchthon complemented this by writings of his own, and most of all through his cooperation in the reform of the educational system (HEINZ SCHEIBLE, Melanchthons Bildungsprogramm, in: Lebenslehren und Weltentwürfe im Übergang vom Mittelalter zur Neuzeit, ed.s Hartmut Boockmann et al., Göttingen 1989, 233–48). – There is insufficient research on the schools in the Mark Brandenburg in the 16th century. Basic trends of the early modern history of education may be deduced from the work by W. Neugebauer, focused on the 17th and 18th centuries: WOLFGANG NEUGEBAUER, Absolutistischer Staat und Schulwirklichkeit in Brandenburg-Preußen, Berlin, New York 1985. Studies concerning the school system in

new ordering of the finances of the university in the 1540s, elector Joachim II revised the curriculum on the basis of humanism and Reformation, installed a new teaching staff and made the territorial university answerable to the territorial church.[30] An illustration for the interaction of territorial university and church can be seen in the person of the general superintendent of the Electoral Mark, Andreas Musculus (1514–1581), who was city pastor in Frankfurt, theology professor at the university of Frankfurt, member of the consistory and counsel to the elector, all in one – in addition to writing numerous theological and devotional works, being one of the leading Lutheran theologians of his time.[31] That the Viadrina was a territorial university under the auspices of the territorial church can be seen by the repeated exhortations of the elector,

»that the pastors, preachers, chaplains, physicians, teachers and town scribes shall be called from no other than our university and that none of those shall be instituted or invested by our superintendents, unless he bring a written certificate from our university showing that he has completed his studies there and is able enough for such an office.«[32]

To understand this requirement, one has to know that a considerable number of prospective clergy had completed their studies elsewhere – from the central Mark and Lower Lusatia, many went to Wittenberg; also, a traditional connection existed between the Hanse-cities in the Altmark and the ›Hanse university‹ in Rostock, where David Chyträus was professor[33]. Some of them had no university education at all. Unfortunately the data that we have about the Protestant clergy in the 16th century Mark Brandenburg, do not lend themselves to statistical evaluation in regard to their education.[34] The trend, however, was the same as elsewhere: One usually

---

the 16th century exist for some of the larger cities, e.g. AGNES WINTER, Das Gelehrtenschulwesen der Residenzstadt Berlin in der Zeit von Konfessionalisierung, Pietismus und Frühaufklärung (1574–1740), Berlin 2008.

[30] STEGMANN, Die Kirchenpolitik des brandenburgischen Kurfürsten Joachim II. (note 5), 129–42.

[31] ERNST KOCH, Andreas Musculus und die Konfessionalisierung im Luthertum (in: Die lutherische Konfessionalisierung in Deutschland, ed. Hans-Christoph Rublack, Gütersloh 1992, 250–70); JÜRGEN SPLETT, Musculus (Meusel), Andreas (in: LOTHAR NOACK, JÜRGEN SPLETT, Bio-Bibliographien. Brandenburgische Gelehrte der Frühen Neuzeit. Mark Brandenburg mit Berlin-Cölln 1506–1640, Berlin 2009, 391–423). Indispensable is the biography, with a wealth of source material, by CHRISTIAN WILHELM SPIEKER, Lebensgeschichte des Andreas Musculus, Frankfurt (Oder) 1858.

[32] Mandate by Joachim II, January 6th, 1567 (Geheimes Staatsarchiv Preußischer Kulturbesitz, Berlin-Dahlem [= GStAPK], I. HA, Rep. 47, no. 5 a 1, package 2, no. 2).

[33] ANDREAS STEGMANN, Die Rostocker Theologie des 16. und 17. Jahrhunderts und ihre Bedeutung für das Luthertum im Ostseeraum (in: Reformatio Baltica. Kulturwirkungen der Reformation in den Metropolen des Ostseeraums, ed.s Heinrich Assel, Johann Anselm Steiger and Axel E. Walter, Berlin and Boston 2018, 375–84).

went to a Latin school, and more and more prospective pastors then went on to a liberal arts faculty and took advantage of the theological and pastoral training, that university and church in Frankfurt offered.

What exactly was this *ministerium evangelii* about, being part of the *necessaria conjunctio*? In the introduction to the doctrinal part of the Brandenburg church order of 1540[35], ›bishops‹, that is to say pastors, preachers and ministers are given a threefold office, in reference to Titus 1: to teach, to admonish and to punish. It is their task 1) to impart the fundamental knowledge concerning the Bible and to lead to a proper understanding of the Bible, 2) to acquaint the people, through their preaching of law and gospel, with the doctrine for their personal lives and to support them in leading a Christian life and 3) to confront those who contradict church doctrine and are unwilling to be admonished.[36] For

---

[34] The *Pfarrerbuch* (Evangelisches Pfarrerbuch für die Mark Brandenburg seit der Reformation, revised by Otto Fischer, 2 vols., Berlin 1941) has only limited information about the ministers of the 16th and 17th centuries and is neither complete nor reliable. The dates for the Altmark have been reviewed but without making a statistical evaluation possible: Evangelisches Pfarrerbuch für die Altmark. Biographische Daten und Quellennachweise als Hilfsmittel zur kirchlichen Ortsgeschichte der Mark Brandenburg und der Provinz Sachsen, revised by Uwe Czubatynski, Rühstädt ²2006. The visitation records make some references to the education of the ministers and their theological competence, but do not allow for generalizations. The attempt on the basis of the list of signatures under the Book of Concord (Concordia. Christliche Widerholete, einmütige Bekentnus nachbenanter Churfürsten, Fürste und Stende Augspurgischer Confession, Frankfurt [Oder] 1581, VD16 K 2001, B 5ᵛ–C 3ʳ) to attain an overview over the academic standing of the clergy and to find some evidence for the transition from a constituting phase to a phase of consolidation that (according to research literature) took place around 1580 (SCHORN-SCHÜTTE, Evangelische Geistlichkeit in der Frühneuzeit [note 8], 191), and to check this in view of Brandenburg, fails because of deficiencies in the list and lack of information about the clergy in office at the time. But the list shows that the leading clergy generally had an academic education and degree. Comparing the names in the university register with those in the Wittenberg book of ordained clergy (ed. Georg Buchwald, 2 vols., Leipzig 1894–95) proves that a certain number of the clergy in Brandenburg had been to university.

[35] Kirchen Ordnung im Churfurstenthum der Marcken zu Brandemburg / wie man sich beide mit der Leer und Ceremonien halten sol, Berlin 1540 (VD16 B 6909, text published partly in vol. 3, partly in vol. 11 of the Sehling edition of church orders: Die evangelischen Kirchenordnungen des XVI. Jahrhunderts, vol. 3, Leipzig 1909, 39–90, vol. 11, Tübingen 1961, 140–279). About this church order: ANDREAS STEGMANN, Die brandenburgische Kirchenordnung von 1540 (in: Reformationen vor Ort. Christlicher Glaube und konfessionelle Kultur in Brandenburg und Sachsen im 16. Jahrhundert, ed.s Enno Bünz, Heinz-Dieter Heimann und Klaus Neitmann, Berlin 2017, 235–288).

[36] Kirchen Ordnung im Churfurstenthum der Marcken zu Brandemburg (note 35), part 1, C 1ʳ–D 1ᵛ. Beside Tit 1:9 (1. fidelis sermo secundum doctrinam, 2. exhortari in doctrina, 3. arguere qui contradicunt) there was possibly also 2Tim 3:16 (1. docere, 2. arguere, 3. corrigere, 4. erudire in iustitia) in the background. In early modern Lutheranism, both texts were frequently used to describe pastoral duties and activities. – The introduction of part 2 of the church order refers to the Old Testament image of the

good reason, these remarks are found at the beginning of the church order, pointing out the most important task of the church, »to assess the true doctrine and to mightily admonish and to punish the adversaries.«[37] At the center of all church activity is the propagation of the word of God:

>»For if we want to enter the kingdom of heaven we must be born again from water and the spirit. Such birth, however, does not come from corruptible seed, but from incorruptible, by the word of God, which lives and abides forever.«[38]

The preachers, therefore, must always engage with the Word of God and follow the doctrines, as they are contained in this church order, based on this Word. These doctrinal expositions which laid down what the »servants of the Word«[39] must »diligently teach [...] the people«[40] are comprised in several summaries[41] and developed in nine chapters regarding justification through faith.[42] This teaching, admonishing and punishing had its ›Sitz im Leben‹ in divine worship and in pastoral care, and also in catechetical instruction, in school and in church discipline, all of which was seen as belonging to the *ministerium evangelii* and therefore being part of the duties of the pastor. The Brandenburg church order of 1540 demonstrates, and the church orders of 1543, 1551, 1558, and 1561[43] and

---

shepherd and his sheep, recurring in the New Testament: »Ein Bisschoff Pfarherr oder Prediger / sol fleissig in der Kirchen wachen / predigen vnd auff sehen / das er nichts verseume an den Schefflein / die jm befolhen sein / vnd allen möglichen fleis ankeren / das die Schefflein mit der heilsamen lere des Göttlichen worts trewlich geweidet / geleitet vnd versorget werden« (Kirchen Ordnung im Churfurstenthum der Marcken zu Brandemburg [note 35], part 2, a 3ʳ). The sermon in part 2 about the office of the keys contains a description of the clerical office based on Rom 10:13–5 (ibid., ee 2ʳ–ff 4ʳ), pointing out that »das Predigampt [...] Christus vnser Herr selbs angefangen / eingesetzt / vnd verordnet hat« (ibid., ee 3ᵛ–ee 4ʳ) and that the rightly called clerical office holders, following their being instituted by Christ, are invested with a special responsibility and a special authority in the face of the parish.

[37] Kirchen Ordnung im Churfürstenthum der Marcken zu Brandemburg (note 35), part 1, C 4ᵛ.

[38] Ibid.

[39] Ibid., O 3ᵛ.

[40] Ibid., O 1ʳ.

[41] Ibid., B 1ᵛ–B 4ʳ, D 2ʳ.

[42] Ibid., G 3ʳ–R 3ᵛ.

[43] Following the Wittenberg model, the elector Joachim II established in 1543 a consistory as an church administration, with a order for the consistory, which was first supplemented in 1551 (GStAPK, I. HA, Rep. 20, lit. A, vol. 3, 120ʳ–126ʳ, 126ᵛ–138ʳ). After the Peace of Augsburg, the elector began to revise the church orders in his territory. First was the visitation order for the villages (Ordnung vnd satzung / so [...] vnsers gnedigsten Herrn vorordente Visitatores / den Patronen / Pfarrern / Gotshaußleuten / vnnd Gemeinden / der Dörffer inn S. Churf: G. Landen vnnd Churfürstenthumb der Marcke zu Brandenburg / sich darnach inn Geistlichen sachen zurichten, Frankfurt [Oder] 1558, VD16 B 6919; this order is based on earlier mandates of the visitation commission as for example the mandate from 1553 addressed to the pastors of the

the records of the general church visitations of the 1540s and 1550s[44] all confirm, that with the Reformation, preaching and instruction moved into the very center of church life: In Sunday and holiday church services there was a sermon based on the gospel; part of the liturgy for weddings and burials were Bible readings with instructions for the listeners; weekday church services had Bible readings and instructions from the catechism; in confession and at the sickbed pastoral care was given through exhortation and comfort from the Bible; and of course the fundamental instruction in the schools rested on Bible and catechism. The value assigned to preaching and instruction is reflected in the devotion practiced in the home, where the most important media were the Bible, the catechism and the hymnal, with instructions being given in devotional literature. Similar to the pastor, the »house father« was expected,

---

Spandau district: Archiv des Stadtgeschichtlichen Museums Spandau, IV B2/17, fol. 45[r]–46[v], printed in the appendix to German version of this contribution). In 1561 the revised and enlarged *Geystliche Policey: Visitation: vnd Consistorial Ordnungk* was prepared for printing (GStAPK, I. HA, Rep. 47, no. 13, fascicle »Consistorial-Ordnung 1561«). A revision of the church order of 1540 (reprinted in 1542) had been planned and preliminary work had been done, but the revised version was not published until after the death of Joachim II (1572: VD16 C 4778). For the office and the life of the clergy see the *Geistliche Polizei-, Visitations- und Konsistorialordnung* of 1561, with extensive regulations (especially the chapter »Von den pfarrern, irhem ampte, lehre, sitten vnd leben«: ibid., 16[r]–23[r]; printed in the appendix to German version of this contribution). Here one can also find regulations concerning vocation and presentation (ibid., 10[r/v]), ordination (ibid., 10[v]–12[v]), investiture (ibid., 12[v]–13[v]), employment of chaplains and preachers (ibid., 23[r]–24[r]), remuneration of the clergy (ibid., 33[v]–35[v]), clerical property (ibid., 35[v]–36[r]), contributions by the clergy to communal duties in the village (ibid., 36[r/v]), clerical assets (ibid., 36[v]–37[r]), the legal status of the minister's wife and children (ibid., 37[r]), separation of the private property of the minister from the clerical property and the passing on of his private property (ibid., 37[r]–38[v], 38[v]–39[r]), the parsonage (ibid., 39[r]–40[r]) and old age provisions for the minister (ibid., 40[v]–41[r]). The text of this order of 1561, including all these regulations concerning the ministry, was revised and printed in 1573 as *Visitation vnd Consistorial Ordenunge* (VD16 B 6924), containing therefore the norms and values of the time around 1560 and reflecting the church reality, as it had developed during the 1540s and 1550s.

[44] Available in print are the visitation records of the Altmark (Die Abschiede der in den Jahren 1540–1542 in der Altmark gehaltenen ersten General-Kirchen-Visitation mit Berücksichtigung der in den Jahren 1551, 1578–79 und 1600 gehaltenen Visitationen, ed.s Julius Müller and Adolf Parisius, two vols., Magdeburg, Salzwedel 1889–1929), of the Prignitz (Die brandenburgischen Kirchenvisitations-Abschiede und -Register des XVI. und XVII. Jahrhunderts [= BKVAR], vol. 1, ed. Victor Herold, Berlin 1931), of Ruppin (BKVAR, vol. 2, ed. Gerd Heinrich, Berlin 1963) and of the Mittelmark (BKVAR, Bd. 4/1: Mittlere Mittelmark, ed. Christiane Schuchard, Berlin and Boston 2019). Visitation records for other regions can be found in Sehling's edition of church orders (EKO 3, 1909, 151–384). Besides that, there are manuscripts in local or central archives and copies made by Victor Herold (GStAPK, X. HA, Rep. 16, no. 161–63; work on an edition of these is in progress). Since the files of the electoral consistory are missing since 1945, a part of this tradition is probably irretrievably lost. For the Neumark, due to inauspicious times, no sizable holdings are existing.

»to diligently accomplish their duty in regard to their children and servants and busily take upon them their duty remembering their calling with preaching, admonishing, teaching, demanding and punishing.«[45]

To support the pastors the church order of 1540 contained a reprinting of Andreas Osiander's *Sermons for children* from Nuremberg, which could serve as a model for catechism instruction; and pastors should possess a German and a Latin Bible, Luther's *Haus- und Kirchenpostille* and other books helpful for their work such as Luther's writings or those of the church fathers.[46]

The life of the pastor was to be part of the proclaiming the gospel, too. The church order of Brandenburg stipulates:

»In addition we desire, we graciously exhort, and wish most earnestly that ministers and priests tend to their office truly, consider day and night the divine laws and scripture, also that they observe a good Christian walk and an honorable priestly way of life causing scandal to none, that they speak about peoples' transgressions as is due to the congregation in the pulpit and elsewhere, kindly punish and with the stubborn use due seriousness. Yet they should not raise unnecessary bickering and hostility among pastors. Also they should abstain from pubs and suspicious lewd persons and stay away from them.«[47]

As time went on, the behavioral guidelines became more detailed to make sure that ministers »direct their conduct in such a way, that their life correspond to what they teach.«[48] Also an aspect of the proclamation of the gospel, if indirectly, was the minister's share of the administration of the parish. There was much, from caring for the poor all the way to the conservation of the buildings, that could be counted as being part of the office of the preacher, since it made possible the preaching and showed its

---

[45] Kirchen Ordnung im Churfürstenthum der Marcken zu Brandemburg (note 35), part 2, a 2^v.

[46] According to the *Visitations- und Konsistorialordnung* of 1551 every minister ought to own »an buchern eine bibel deutsch vnd lateinisch, eine hauspostilla Lutheri, cathecismum Lutheri groß vnnd klein, die Churfurstliche Brandenburgische kirchenordnunge« (GStAPK I. HA, Rep. 20, lit. A, vol. 3, 132^v). In the enlarged version of 1561, it is added, probably in view of the city ministers: »auch do sie des vormuegens, die gantze opera Luteri, Augustini, Hieronimi vnnd anderer christlichen vnnd vnuorfelschten theologen bucher mehr, aber sich vor aller falschen lehrer schriffte vnd bucher, das sie dodurch nicht in vorfurische irrthumb geleitet werden mogen, mit allem fleisse huetten« (note 43, 17^r). – Frankfurt printers provided the Mark with religious literature (HANS-ERICH TEITGE, Der Buchdruck des 16. Jahrhunderts in Frankfurt an der Oder. Verzeichnis der Drucke, Berlin 2000) including printers in the neighbor regions to the South and West, where authors of the Mark had their works printed, too. As printers in Leipzig, Nuremberg, Magdeburg or Wittenberg supplied the Brandenburg market, Frankfurt printers also supplied Silesia.

[47] Kirchen Ordnung im Churfurstenthum der Marcken zu Brandemburg (note 35), part 3, Y 2^v.

[48] Geistliche Polizei-, Visitations- und Konsistorialordnung (note 43), 20^r.

practical consequences. Searching, however, in the sources from Brandenburg for traces of these activities, one will not find much. The church orders make it quite clear throughout, that the administration of the parish was to be mainly in the hands of the churchwarden and the finances under the supervision by the treasurer.[49] For all practical work, there was a sexton, while in a larger church there would be more than one.[50] It is difficult to estimate how much a pastor had to contribute in the administration of the parish and how much influence he could bring to bear on local church conditions, because of the great differences locally; in addition, not much research has been done about this particular topic.

Ministers had to be qualified for the service of proclaiming the gospel: especially important for this task were an acquaintance with the Bible and church doctrine, and the ability to transmit this knowledge to the people of the parish. From the very beginning, an academic education for the pastors was deemed desirable, which at the Reformation universities became a training qualifying for the pastoral profession in the understanding of a *ministerium evangelii*.[51] At the center of the theological curriculum were the exegesis of the essential biblical writings and theological explanations of church doctrine. Practically oriented vocational preparation and practical training in preaching was also offered at the university, but reflection on that practice was missing altogether from the curriculum. Studies at the faculty of the *Artes liberales* were deemed important, because philological

---

[49] Ibid., 28^r–32^v. In addition, »weldtliche obrigkeitten, heupt- vnnd amptleutte, auch andere gerichts vorwalttere vnd beuelhaber ihn stetten vnd dorffern« were responsible for »religion sachen« (ibid., 50^v–55^r).

[50] Ibid., 41^r–43^r.

[51] Concerning the reshaping and practice of the theological education in early modern time: RUDOLF MAU, Programme und Praxis des Theologiestudiums im 17. und 18. Jahrhundert (in: Theologische Versuche 11, 1979, 71–91); MARCEL NIEDEN, Die Erfindung des Theologen. Wittenberger Anweisungen zum Theologiestudium im Zeitalter von Reformation und Konfessionalisierung, Tübingen 2006; ANDREAS STEGMANN, Johann Friedrich König. Seine ›Theologia positiva acroamatica‹ (1664) im Rahmen des frühneuzeitlichen Theologiestudiums, Tübingen 2006. – Concerning The importance of academic education for early modern clergy: VOGLER, Le clergé protestant rhénan au siècle de la réforme (note 8), Kap. 1; SCHORN-SCHÜTTE, Evangelische Geistlichkeit in der Frühneuzeit (note 8), 159–225; THOMAS KAUFMANN, Universität und lutherische Konfessionalisierung. Die Rostocker Theologieprofessoren und ihr Beitrag zur theologischen Bildung und kirchlichen Gestaltung im Herzogtum Mecklenburg zwischen 1550 und 1675, Gütersloh 1997, 336–49; ID., Berufskulturelle Rahmenbedingungen des Pastorenstandes in der Frühen Neuzeit (in: ID., Konfession und Kultur. Lutherischer Protestantismus in der zweiten Hälfte des Reformationsjahrhunderts, Tübingen 2006, 303–22); ID., Théologie, université, société. Quelques remarques sur le premier protestantisme du point de vue de l'histoire de l'église (in: Religion ou confession. Un bilan franco-allemand sur l'époque moderne, ed.s Philippe Büttgen and Christophe Duhamelle, Paris 2010, 461–84, esp. 475–80); PTASZYŃSKI, »Beruf und Berufung« (note 8), 195–274.

and philosophical basic knowledge was seen as necessary for studying theology, and the instruction in rhetoric supplied the tools for the future preachers. Quite often, however, ministers were content with those basic Liberal Arts courses and did not take advantage of the theological courses that were offered. Statistical data derived from sources of the time indicate, that during the second half of the 16th century it became customary for prospective ministers, to attend university. They also show, however, that only a small group went on to study theology more in depth. In the 16th and 17th centuries, future ministers did not generally seek academic qualifications: proof of having attended university was sufficient. Only those who were aspiring for a leading position in the church felt the need to acquire a master's degree. Only few clergy acquired a doctor's degree, mostly those who then rose to the top of the territorial church. Although it can be said that in the course of the 16th century the Protestant clergy slowly came to be more academic, one should note that a certain group of future ministers – shrinking in size, but still quite considerable – did not receive an university education. The theological competence needed for the *ministerium evangelii* could be acquired at a Latin school or through private studies, especially if a person did not seek an urban parish, or if before entering the ministry further education was pursued, for instance while working as a house- or schoolteacher. For the future Protestant minister, to profit by the academic professionalization and being part of the *necessaria coniunctio* university training was not obligatory.

To guarantee a minimum standard of theological competence, ordination for the ministry was combined with an examination, and the clergy in office had the duty of ongoing and further studies. In many places, the clergy of a region came together on a regular basis, to listen to each other's sermons and to hold disputations, thus demonstrating before their church leaders the efforts they were undertaking.[52] Additionally in many cities

---

[52] In the electoral visitation order of 1558 it says, that the village minister should be »zum Examen, oder allda zu predigen gefordert« by the minister of the neighboring city (note 43, A 4ʳ). The visitation record for the town of Werben in the Altmark from 1551 shows that there was supposed to be a summons every three months and that the inspector had to give instructions to the ministers; if someone was found to be inept, the consistory in Stendal had to be informed (MÜLLER, PARISIUS, Abschiede [note 44], vol. 2/4, 1929, 402). That these checks and the contuinuing education had, however, only a limited effectivity, is seen in connection with the visitation of 1602 where in the final report for the city of Neuruppin it is stated that some ministers there, although they adhere to the Augsburg Confession and the Formula of Concord, they are »quo ad eruditionem dermaßen ungeschicket«, that the visiting officials refrained from their dismissal only because of their old age or the great number of their children or other important excuses. This lack of education was also seen in connection with the fact that the stipulated number of »conventus« was not regularly held. Therefore detailed regu-

libraries were founded in the second half of the 16th century, giving the clergy access to theological literature.[53] In the context of the visitation, the level of education of the minister was examined, focusing awareness of the necessity of bettering one's education. Even if there still were some members of the clergy, whose theological competence was less than it should have been, the ideal of the both pious and well-educated minister (*pietas et eruditio*) was established in the course of the 16th century, and this ideal became definitive for Protestantism for centuries to come.

In the 16th century, there was a wealth of literature regarding school and academic instruction, for the examination on entering a church profession and for the ongoing education for office holders. Already in the 1520s, books with advice and support for the pastoral profession were being published, for example Luther's *Christmas* and *Advent Postil*, his *Catechisms* and the *Instruction for the Visitors*.[54] Later this aid literature became more differentiated: Beside the catechisms, which developed into a rich and varied literary genre,[55] there were theological textbooks, often not actually designed for academic instruction, as for instance Melanchthon's *Examen ordinandorum*.[56] Luther's work of collected postils grew, and was complemented by innumerable sermon collections. To help future ministers in the acquisition of knowledge needed for their work, there appeared an increasing number of study guides, some of which focused on how to successfully go through an academic course of study. Pastoral handbooks dealt with questions arising in the daily life of the parish minister, providing summaries regarding the theology of the ministry and church doctrine, in connection with homiletical, pastoral, liturgical information in-

---

lations were made for such meetings to be held at least once a year (BKVAR 2 [note 44], 95–6). Elsewhere these *conventus* seem to have worked, as the two minister associations of the Altmark in Gardelegen and Tangermünde show, where in the 2nd half of the 16th century mutual support and theological continuing education were being practiced (FRÖHNER, Der evangelische Pfarrstand in der Mark Brandenburg [note 9], 40–2).

[53] For the motivation of such libraries and for the emphasis given their collections, cf. the appeal for the foundation of the library of St. Nicholas in Berlin in 1588 (Evangelisches Landeskirchliches Archiv Berlin, Marien- und Nikolaibibliothek Berlin, Hs. 1/1, 5[v]–8[v]). Other examples are mentioned in: UWE CZUBATYNSKI, Armaria Ecclesiae. Studien zur Geschichte des kirchlichen Bibliothekswesens, Neustadt a. d. Aisch 1998.

[54] WA 10[I/1–2]; WA 26,175–240; WA 30[I].

[55] Quellen zur Geschichte des kirchlichen Unterrichts in der evangelischen Kirche Deutschlands zwischen 1530 und 1600, ed. Johann Michael Reu, Gütersloh 1904–35.

[56] CR 23,XX-CXXVIII, 1–102. – For an interesting example of such a non-academic textbook from the transition period between the restructuring of the parishes and the stabilization of the Reformation territorial churches, explicitly for ministers not sufficiently trained at the beginning of their career: URBANUS RHEGIUS, Wie man fursichtiglich vnd on ergernis reden sol / von den furnemsten Artickeln Christlicher lere. Fur die jungen einfeltigen Prediger, Wittenberg 1537 (VD16 R 1806).

cluding that about church law.[57] This supply in books corresponded to a demand, while the guidelines set by the authorities concerning the possession of books and an academic education were being met. Evidence of the foregoing can be seen not only by the church libraries, but also through scattered information about the presence of books in the parsonages.[58]

With the better academic education of the clergy came its professionalization. The *ministerium evangelii* of art. 5 of the Augsburg Confession concerned not only the office of preaching in general, but also the ecclesiastical office of the ordained clergy, as defined in art. 14, in particular,[59]

---

[57] Six of these handbooks, partly used far into the 17th century, written by Gerhard Lorich, Johannes Rivius, Niels Hemmingsen, Erasmus Sarcerius, Konrad Porta and Felix Bidembach are presented by AMY NELSON BURNETT, The evolution of the Lutheran pastor's manual in the sixteenth century (ChH 73, 2004, 536–65). There are more similar works, in the Upper-German region e.g. MARTIN BUCER, Von der waren Seelsorge / vnd dem rechten Hirten dienst (Strasbourg 1538, VD16 B 8941), and from the central German region e.g. TILEMANN HESHUSEN, Vom Ampt vnd gewalt der Pfarrherr. Auch Wer macht / fug vnd recht hab Pfarrherrn zuberuffen (Erfurt 1561, VD16 H 3163), and JOACHIM MÖRLIN, Von dem Beruff der Prediger. Vnd wie fern weltliche Oberkeit macht hat / dieselbigen jres Ampts zuentsetzen / Nötiger Christlicher bericht aus Gottes wort (Eisleben 1565, VD16 M 5889). The last two have to be read in the context of the inner-Lutheran doctrinal disputes concerning office and activity of the Lutheran parish minister, in particular in his relationship with the secular authority. As the work by Johannes Rivius, first published 1549 (BURNETT, The evolution of the Lutheran pastor's manual [see above], 543–5) demonstrates, the country pastor was early on seen as a challenge. Rivius probably had the situation in Saxony in mind (HANS TRÜMPY, Eine Anleitung für protestantische Landpfarrer von 1549, in: Festschrift Matthias Zender. Studien zu Volkskultur, Sprache und Landesgeschichte, ed.s Edith Ennen and Günter Wiegelmann, Bonn 1972, 470–8). It should be noted that there was a reprint of Rivius' book in Rostock in 1574 (De officio pastorali ministrorum ecclesiae in pagis libellus, iis etiam, qui in urbibus euangelion docent, non inutilis, VD16 R 2626), with an introduction by the provost of the Berlin cathedral church, probably, because this type of literature was needed in the rural regions of the North-East. It should be noted, however, that the particular situation in the countryside is barely mentioned in this Latin work: Lack of religious interest and of discipline were probably found in city parishes as well, and the reminder of pastoral duties (worship service, instruction, pastoral care, admonishing etc.) does not apply to rural parishes in any special way. References in regard to the rural context such as consideration of the peasants' understanding (ibid., 32) or conflicts with the local patron (ibid., 58) are rare.

[58] GERALD STRAUSS, The mental world of a Saxon pastor (in: Reformation principle and practice, ed. Peter Newman Brooks, London 1980, 157–70); SCHORN-SCHÜTTE, Evangelische Geistlichkeit in der Frühneuzeit (note 8), 213–25. That ministers were called to account for their possession and use of books throughout the course of early modern time (ERNST KOCH, Dorfpfarrer als Leser. Beobachtungen an Visitationsakten des 18. Jahrhunderts im Herzogtum Sachsen-Gotha, in: ID., Studien zur Theologie- und Frömmigkeitsgeschichte des Luthertums im 16. bis 18. Jahrhundert, Waltrop 2005, 329–61) shows, that the beginning of pastoral libraries in the 16th century should not be overestimated.

[59] Concerning art. 5 and art. 14 of the Augsburg Confession one should note that

as it acquired a characteristic work profile and demanded a specific qualifying competence. Prospective ministers therefore went through a specific training, they developed their own, particular pastoral self-awareness and joined professional networks. In the course of the early modern period, the ministers began to form a relatively homogenous group in social, economic and cultural respects, typically characterized by recruitment from within the group and intermarriage among clergy families – both of these, however, to a lesser degree than has been stated in older research. This development has been characterized by researchers as *professionalization*, taking up with this definition the description of our modern professional world;[60] while one should avoid anachronistic distortions of early modern phenomena, it is worth noting that with this new type of clergy there emerged a professional group, which is quite comparable to the professions in modern-day society – yet a professional group, in quite particular ways defined by its ›special spiritual self-awareness‹[61], by which it was standing out in society – *the pastor is different*,[62] – and that was true already in the 16th century.

In order to enable the clergy for the *ministerium evangelii*, a more and more detailed system of legal regulations and material provisions was developed in the course of the 16th century. The legal frame was given by the territorial church administration; its legal competence in pastoral daily life was expressed in the form of church orders, consistories, general superintendents and superintendents, church visitations, local authorities, church patrons and representatives of the parish. The basic guidelines for the clergy were set down in the Brandenburg church order of 1540, in the chapter about vocation and ordination of the clergy:[63] Every minister needed a calling, i.e. to be called on the part of the patron, and he needed to be

---

something different is being referred to: In art. 14 it is a question of the *ordo ecclesiasticus*, meaning the rightly called clergy, whose duty is the public speech from the pulpit, while in art. 5 the office of preaching and the *ministerium docendi Evangelii* are understood in a functional sense as »Mittel zur Entstehung des Glaubens«, for what is assigned to the church in its entirety: the »Dienst der Verkündigung« is »nicht spezifisch auf das institutionalisierte Amt zu beziehen« (DOROTHEA WENDEBOURG, Das bischöfliche Amt, in: ZevKR 51, 2006, 534–55, esp. 535–6, note 6). Accordingly, the preaching of the gospel and the administration of the sacraments in art. 7, which are constitutive for the church, cannot be limited to the institutionalized office.

[60] See the writings by Rosemary O'Day concerning the English clergy (notes 86–7).

[61] SCHORN-SCHÜTTE, Evangelische Geistlichkeit in der Frühneuzeit (note 8), 393–410; BERNDORFF, Die Prediger der Grafschaft Mansfeld (note 8); TARALD RASMUSSEN, The Early Modern pastor between ideal and reality (in: LuJ 80, 2013, 197–219).

[62] MANFRED JOSUTTIS, Der Pfarrer ist anders. Aspekte einer zeitgenössischen Pastoraltheologie, München 1982.

[63] Kirchen Ordnung im Churfurstenthum der Marcken zu Brandemburg (note 35), part 3, X 4[r]–Y 3[r].

examined on the part of the territorial church government. Precondition for tenure of a church office was the »qualification of the persons«, and being examined and reviewed by the general superintendent of the elector or others authorized for this, namely »whether they are pure in regard to doctrine and additionally display a truly Christian way of life«.[64] After being called and examined, the person received ordination by the hand of one of the territorial bishops, who had kept their office and had been recognized as such by the elector only if they submitted to the church order; in Brandenburg this was true only for bishop Matthias von Jagow in the city of Brandenburg an der Havel.[65] In fact, soon the ordination of ministers fell to the leadership of the territorial church government,[66] who took over the supervision of the clergy and of the church administration from the bishops. Additional regulations were collected in later church orders and visitation reports; the great number of decisions concerning individual cases, kept and transmitted in church and state archives, show the application of these church laws. The Protestant clergy of early modern time was a group which lived and worked in a strongly regulated legal framework, narrowly controlled by the authorities.

---

[64] Ibid., X 4^v.

[65] The formally keeping of the diocesan episcopal structure side by side with the territorial church government with its alternative structure was a politically motivated intermediate step. The spiritual jurisdiction of the bishops, which according to the Brandenburg church order of 1540 included the clergy as well (Kirchen Ordnung im Churfurstenthum der Marcken zu Brandemburg [note 35], part 3, Y 2^r) was in fact ignored. – About the ordinations by Matthias von Jagow: Gustav Kawerau, Bischof Matthias von Jagow und die Ordination evangelischer Geistlicher (in: JBrKG 13, 1915, 56–62).

[66] The form of the ordination appears in an ordination liturgy from Frankfurt (Oder) from the 1560s (Joachim Goltz, Agenda Das ist Außerlesene Kirchen-Ceremonien Welche in den Kirchen Augspurgischer Confeßion in vblichem Brauche sein / vnnd hin vnd wieder gleich vnd vngleich Bey dem Sacrament der H. Tauffe / Administration des HERRN CHRisti Nachtmahl / Copulation Breutigams vnnd Braut / Einsegenung der Sechswöchnerinnen / vnnd Christlichen Begrebnussen gehalten werden, Frankfurt [Oder] 1614, VD17 1:083005K, N 1^r–N 4^v). Supposedly already in 1543 there existed an order for the examination and ordination of ministers by the superintendent of the Kurmark (cf. the summary given without indication of the source by Christian Wilhelm Spieker, Geschichte der Einführung der Reformation in die Mark Brandenburg, Berlin 1839, 251–3), whose regulations were tightened by Andreas Musculus in 1569 (GStAPK, I. HA, Rep. 47, lit. F, no. 2) and developed further in the 1570s (Georg Gottfried Küster, Bibliotheca historica Brandenburgica scriptores rerum Brandenburgicarum maxime Marchicarum exhibens, Breslau 1743, 195). Ordination references and self-commitments by the ordinands can be found in the files and are transmitted in literature: JBrKG 31, 1936, 98–113, 32, 1937, 3–50; MBW no. 5346; SBBPK, Ms. Boruss. fol., no. 201, 175^r–176^r; GStAPK I. HA, Rep. 43, no. 27 a-c; Fortgesetzte Sammlung Von Alten und Neuen Theologischen Sachen 1731, 539–40; Stadtarchiv Frankfurt (Oder), Bestandsabteilung I, Heinsius-Annalen, vol. 2,201, 417, 427–28; Brandenburgisches Landeshauptarchiv Potsdam, Rep. 86, Universität Frankfurt (Oder), no. 37; Georg Gottfried Küster, Memorabilia Coloniensia, Berlin 1727, 91–2.

An important part of the legal regulations concerned the financing of the ministers; in fact, the reorganization of the parish finances stood at the very beginning of the introduction of the Reformation in the parishes.[67] The traditional system of church finances was more or less kept in use, and was, with the introduction of the common chest and with the re-designation of other sources of income, enabled to meet the increasing financial demands of the academically educated and married clergy, who belonged to the better citizenry.[68] In 1540, the Brandenburg church order specified for the visitation, that parishes should be audited thoroughly in regard to their income and expenditure and that everything which »of rent, money interest, farmland and meadows for their support, as the ministers due or not given to them« had to be collected, »so that the ministers, sextons, schools and hospitals be and remain provided for, as far as there is need.«[69] And indeed, the main task of the visitations during the 16th century con-

---

[67] ANDREAS STEGMANN, Reformation und Geld (Praktische Theologie 52, 2017, 69–74). Significantly the first and only church order of sizable proportion, which was issued for Neumark, the independent region under the rule of marggrave Johann von Küstrin, is a ›Kastenordnung‹ from early 1540. A copy of this order from the 16th century (SBBPK, Ms. boruss. fol., no. 83, 76ʳ–99ʳ) is still extant as well as a reprint from the 18th century (Corpus Constitutionum Marchicarum, ed. Christian Otto Mylius, part 1, Berlin and Halle 1737, 249–64), both based on different copies and both with mistakes and omissions, but supplementing each other in such a way, that it is possible to reconstruct the order, which existed only in manuscript form. From this order it becomes clear, that church finances were a problem with high priority and that in a small territory one had to content oneself with a ›Kastenordnung‹ and for everything else had to fall back on other orders.

[68] For the economic situation of the clergy in the early phase of Reformation history in Saxony and Thuringia see the important studies of Susan Karant-Nunn: SUSAN K. BOLES, The Economic Position of Lutheran Pastors in Ernestine Thuringia 1521–1555 (ARG 63, 1972, 94–125); KARANT-NUNN, Luther's Pastors (note 8). A problem newly arising from the Reformation was the care of the ministers' widows, who in the beginning could make only very limited claims, both in regard to time as well as financially (BERND WUNDER, Pfarrwitwenkassen und Beamtenwitwen-Anstalten vom 16.–19. Jahrhundert, in: ZHF 12, 1985, 429–98; WOLFGANG PETKE, Pfarrwitwen und Pfarradjunkten. Zur Alterssicherung mecklenburgischer Pfarrer und ihrer Witwen bis zum frühen 18. Jahrhundert, in: Menschen in der Kirche. 450 Jahre seit Einführung der Reformation in Mecklenburg, ed. Helge Bei der Wieden, Rostock 2000, 165–218), but had some influence on the appointment of the new pastor (MACIEJ PTASZYŃSKI, »…was für große sorge und mühe ein heiliger ehestandt wehre« [1599]. Zur Lebenssituation der Pfarrwitwen am Ende des 16. und Anfang des 17. Jahrhunderts in Pommern, in: Frühneuzeitliche Konfessionskulturen, ed. Thomas Kaufmann, Gütersloh 2008, 319–45). For the complexity of financing the ministry and the need for regulations see *Geistliche Polizei-, Visitation- und Konsistorialordnung* of 1561 (see above note 43 the list of chapters in the first part of this order).

[69] Kirchen Ordnung im Churfurstenthum der Marcken zu Brandemburg (note 35), part 3, Y 2ʳ. Fore more detailed regulations see *Geistliche Polizei-, Visitation- und Konsistorialordnung* (1561), section: *Vonn den pfarren vn irehn einkommenn* (note 43, 33ᵛ–35ᵛ).

sisted in settling the finances of the parishes, collecting both money and contributions in kind needed for the remuneration of the church personnel and for the upkeep of the buildings. Brandenburg with its high number of country parsonages is typical for the Lutheran territorial state, where the contributions in kind made up a large part of the income and where quite a few of the country pastors were engaged in farming on their parsonage.

In the 16th century, both the church and the secular authority endeavored to fulfill the demands made concerning the clergy, and the clergy on its part strove to meet the – constantly rising – expectations, yet reality was lagging behind the ideal. Evaluating the achievement of the Reformation in regard to the establishment of a new type of clergy, it is not the deficits and compromises that are of crucial significance, but the dynamic that was setting in to transform the *necessaria coniunctio*: the establishment of a new type of clergy – new in regard to its characteristic feature as *preacher* – has to be called a success.

1.2. The Clergy as citizens

Beside the minister as preacher, the other characteristic feature of the new type of clergy is the pastor's status as *citizen*.[70] This status was not directly connected to the preaching function, and can therefore not be subsumed under the heading of »Clergy as preacher«. While the clergyman had with his way of life to vouch for the gospel he preached, that did not necessarily imply that he would have to give up a special clerical status with its specific way of life. The new social status of the clergy was not founded on theological arguments, rather it was the consequence of the delegitimization of status and form of life of the medieval clergy, for the Protestant clergy had no other choice than to see themselves as belonging to the nonclerical world and to live as laypeople did. Already in his treatise to the German nobility of 1520, Luther had written that »the clergy, instituted by God, to govern the people and the congregation with sermons and the administration of the sacraments«, being in this way opposite to the con-

---

[70] Concerning the legal status as citizen for clergy in the region of Upper-Germany in comparison between late Middle Ages and Reformation: BERND MOELLER, Kleriker als Bürger (in: ID., Die Reformation und das Mittelalter. Kirchenhistorische Aufsätze, Göttingen 1991, 35–52). For references regarding the integration of the Lutheran clergy beginning in the century of the Reformation into the »neue soziale Schicht der Honoratioren oder der Ehrbarkeit, oberhalb des Kleinbürgertums und Handwerkerstands, unterhalb des Adels«, beginning to emerge in the course of early modern time, see ID., Pfarrer als Bürger, Göttingen 1972, 14–23 (quotation: 18). The process of the clergy becoming citizenry has been treated in the first place in social-historical research (cf. SCHORN-SCHÜTTE, Priest, preacher, pastor [note 8]).

gregation, must »live with them and be a secular householder«.[71] This new reality was also supported by the *conversion to the world* that implied for every believer a religiously motivated existence in this world.[72] The clergyman was called upon to put into action the demand valid for all Christians: to let faith take effect in love here and now; and in doing so, the clergy had to assume the role of a model, as citizen of the heavenly πολίτευμα on earth (Phil 3:20; cf. Hebr 13:14). »Citizen« is here to be understood in a double sense: The minister was a *member of the secular community*, and that as *belonging to a particular group*, the middle group between nobility and peasantry which supplied the majority of the office-holders of the early modern state.[73] To belong to this particular social group implied for the clergy, that it participated in the social dissociation which developed during early modern times, separating itself from the lower levels of society on the one hand and from the gentry on the other. The clergyman began to assume the social status of a citizen, which came to be the contingent, yet defining feature of the modern understanding and self-understanding of the clergy.

That the clergy now had the social standing of citizens, showed in their being able to marry and to found a household. This change visibly marked the break with the old clergy,[74] but even more this new role of husband, father and householder changed the self-understanding and the clerical office of the Protestant minister in a profound way. So did his social status, established through his economic activities and the connections made through marriage. Thus, the parsonage[75] emerged as an institution,

---

[71] WA 6,441,24–26. For the »durch lebensweltliche Teilhabe charakterisierten Struktur« of the »funktional verstandene Gemeindepfarramt« see Thomas Kaufmann, An den christlichen Adel deutscher Nation von des christlichen Standes Besserung, Tübingen 2014, 308–9.

[72] Concerning the »conversion to the world« (Oswald Bayer) and what that means for the Reformation ethos: Andreas Stegmann, The development and structure of Luther's ethics (in: Lutheran Quarterly 33, 2019, 137–52).

[73] Recent research about what it means to belong to early modern citizenry as to a particular group within the secular community is presented by Bernd Roeck, Lebenswelt und Kultur des Bürgertums in der Frühen Neuzeit, München ²2011.

[74] Stephen E. Buckwalter, Die Priesterehe in Flugschriften der frühen Reformation, Gütersloh 1998; Marjorie Elizabeth Plummer, From priest's whore to pastor's wife. Clerical marriage and the process of reform in the early German Reformation, Farnham, Burlington 2012.

[75] The expression »Pfarrhaus« appears already in the pastoral literature of the 16th century. Niels Hemmingsen in his handbook speaks of the »domus pastoritiae« (Pastor sive pastoris optimus vivendi agendique modus, Leipzig 1565, VD16 H 1869, 1) meaning the minister with his family and his social relationships. – Research literature about the parsonage – particularly in regard to the topical collections (Das evangelische Pfarrhaus. Eine Kultur- und Sozialgeschichte, ed. Martin Greiffenhagen, Stuttgart 1984; Das evangelische Pfarrhaus. Mythos und Wirklichkeit, ed.s Thomas A. Seidel and Christopher

which not only designated the house inhabited by the minister's family, but also constituted an important part of the community. It was only in the 1520s that the weddings of clergymen and the landmark justification given for them caused a sensation. Thus, when the Reformation was introduced in Brandenburg, the married status of the clergy was taken for granted from the very beginning. In the church order of 1540, the minister was declared free to marry or not,[76] and later church orders assumed that the clergy were married and lived in a parsonage sufficient to house their families and to satisfy their economic needs.[77] It was also assumed that the pastor needed an income, and should be treated in hereditary law not as a cleric but as a citizen. Among his privileges were being freed from local contributions and duties and the right to brew and keep his own beer, tax-free.[78] To the rights, however, of the now married pastor were added the duty, that the proclamation of the gospel should be reflected and become visible not only in his own personal life, but also in that of the parsonage as a whole:

»It befits the ministers to bring up their wives, children and servants in all fear of God and honorable behavior, as they in such things give Christian instructions for others to follow, and if they were slack or tardy in this, they should forfeit their office, because that, if their own lead an bad life, others cannot be instructed and taught by them.«[79]

The *oeconomia christiana* must be lived in an exemplary way by the minister and his family. Their lives should illustrate, how a married couple behaves toward each other, how they bring up their children and how they treat their servants and, most of all, how they practice and pass on

---

Spehr, Leipzig 2013; Das evangelische Pfarrhaus im deutschsprachigen Südwesten, ed.s Jürgen Krüger et al., Ostfildern 2014) – is not very rewarding, as far as the Reformation century is concerned. There are not enough studies in social or cultural history about the early time, when this new element in the life of the local community was established. The best approach to this topic, beside the collections mentioned above, although with emphasis on the following centuries, is Schorn-Schütte, Evangelische Geistlichkeit in der Frühneuzeit (note 8), 287–330.

[76] Kirchen Ordnung im Churfurstenthum der Marcken zu Brandemburg (note 35), part 3, Y 1ᵛ.

[77] Geistliche Polizei-, Visitations- und Konsistorialordnung (note 43), section *Von besserung vnnd bawung der pfarren* (39ʳ–40ʳ).

[78] Ibid., 36ʳ/ᵛ and 35ʳ/ᵛ. The traditional church contributions of clergy and parishes (synodaticum, cathedraticum, procuratio) were for the time being kept unchanged (except that they were not any longer payed to the representatives of the papal church), but were mostly abolished during the 1570s (Fröhner, Der evangelische Pfarrstand in der Mark Brandenburg [note 9], 35–7).

[79] Geistliche Polizei-, Visitations- und Konsistorialordnung (note 43), 22ᵛ. Cf. the ideal of a Protestant minister in Pomerania: Ptaszyński, »Beruf und Berufung« (note 8), 140–57.

their Christian faith. From all of this, there arose a new responsibility belonging to the minister's wife, for which she in turn had to have some education and an independence of her own.[80] However, the literary sources for family life and the role of the minister's wife are too scarce for the time of the Reformation for us to be able to draw a clear picture; one should avoid drawing general conclusions from individual examples – such as that of Martin Luther and Katharina von Bora in Wittenberg or Matthias and Katharina Zell in Strasbourg[81] – or attributing what we know from later times back into the earlier state of affairs.

The processes by which the minister became a citizen, and the parsonage developed into an institution in society, did not come about without growing financial demands. The benefice, traditionally providing the livelihood for the clergy, still remained as the basis for the income of the minister, yet it soon had to be increased, more and more, to cover the growing needs of the ministers' families. The visitation records in the 16th century show a marked rise in income, far more than would be expected to compensate for inflation. Although complaints about a too low salary or outstanding payments have a certain notoriety, far into the 17th century, the minister's profession was attractive as a career, generally offering a good livelihood. In the countryside, however, it was also important that the minister and his family should be prepared to work the land belonging to the benefice and thus to contribute, with the work of their hands, to their security and well-being. This side of every day of rural pastors is described in the six volumes of Johannes Köhler's Oeconomia published between 1595 and 1601 and reprinted several times during the 17th and 18th centuries that reflect the situation of Lutheran clergy in the German north-east.[82] Köhler dealt not only with agriculture, cattle breeding or art

---

[80] HERMANN WERDERMANN, Die deutsche evangelische Pfarrfrau. Ihre Geschichte in vier Jahrhunderten, Witten [2]1936; LUISE SCHORN-SCHÜTTE, »Gefährtin« und »Mitregentin«. Zur Sozialgeschichte der evangelischen Pfarrfrau in der Frühen Neuzeit (in: Wandel der Geschlechterbeziehungen zu Beginn der Neuzeit, ed.s Heide Wunder and Christina Vanja, Frankfurt a. M. 1991, 109–53).

[81] THOMAS KAUFMANN, Pfarrfrau und Publizistin – Das reformatorische »Amt« der Katharina Zell (in: ZHF 23, 1996, 169–218).

[82] The six volumes were published in Wittenberg (VD16 ZV 25076, 25064, 25105, 25106, 3786; VD17 12:629586R). Johannes Köhler was the son of Jakob Köhler who served as professor at the Viadrina and as provost of St. Nicholas in Berlin and who had begun to collect material for a handbook about the domestic life (about him: NOACK / SPLETT, Bio-Bibliographien [note 31], 58–72; about his son and his Oeconomia: Philip Hahn, Das Haus im Buch. Konzeption, Publikationsgeschichte und Leserschaft der »Oeconomia« Johann Colers, Epfendorf 2013). – Concerning the rising income of pastors in Brandenburg: FRÖHNER, Der evangelische Pfarrstand in der Mark Brandenburg (note 9), 32–3.

of healing but also with the daily living of a Lutheran Christian in rural northern Germany, showing that ›economy‹ and faith were two sides of the same coin.

When the minister turned into a citizen, this also changed his relationship to his parish. On the one hand he was part of the secular community and lived a life quite similar to that of the other members of the community, on the other hand he stood apart, and because of his function and his spiritual self-awareness he stood in a distinctive relationship towards all of those, with whom he lived together every day. This double role, difficult to cope with, as preacher of the word of God and Christian model facing the parish, and as citizen, sharing the common destiny together with the parish, was a constant source of problems. A particular source of conflict was the duty of the minister to make sure that the religious norms were observed, while he was also expected by the secular authority to have a hand in the social disciplining. This activity could be seen as undue patronizing, and the parish might react with refusal and resistance.[83]

1.3. England in comparison

What has been set out on the basis of the Brandenburg church order of 1540 concerning the clergy, is true for the Reformation as a whole, including England. This church order of 1540 had been built on an earlier pattern, the Brandenburg-Nuremberg church order of 1533, where, for the Lutheran church in Franconia, ideal views of a renewed church were codified under the leadership of Andreas Osiander.[84] Already before their codification these ideals had been taken up by an English guest of Osi-

---

[83] HELGA SCHNABEL-SCHÜLE, Distanz und Nähe. Zum Verhältnis von Pfarrern und Gemeinden im Herzogtum Württemberg vor und nach der Reformation (Rottenburger Jahrbuch für Kirchengeschichte 5, 1986, 339–48); SUSAN C. KARANT-NUNN, Neoclericalism and anticlericalism in Saxony, 1555–1675 (Journal of Interdisciplinary History 24, 1994, 615–37); BRUCE TOLLEY, Pastors & parishioners in Württemberg during the late Reformation 1581–1621, Stanford 1995; JAY GOODALE, Pfarrer als Außenseiter. Landpfarrer und religiöses Leben in Sachsen zur Reformationszeit (in: Historische Anthropologie 7, 1999, 191–211); ID., The clergyman between the cultures of state and parish: Contestation and compromise in Reformation Saxony (in: The Protestant clergy of Early Modern Europe, ed. Scott C. Dixon and Luise Schorn-Schütte, Basingstoke u. New York 2003, 100–19, 221–6); PTASZYŃSKI, »Beruf und Berufung« (note 8), 397–429. That the constellation of conflicts reaching back to the Reformation century was existing still in the 17th and 18th centuries, is shown by HANS-CHRISTOPH RUBLACK, Der wohlgeplagte Priester. Vom Selbstverständnis lutherischer Geistlichkeit im Zeitalter der Orthodoxie (ZHF 16, 1989, 1–30).

[84] ANDREAS OSIANDER, Gesamtausgabe, vol. 5, Gütersloh 1983, 37–177. Concerning this text: GUNTER ZIMMERMANN, Prediger der Freiheit. Andreas Osiander und der Nürnberger Rat 1522–1548, Mannheim 1999, 268–308.

ander's who, on his return to England found himself in a leading position to introduce these ideas into the Reform endeavors begun there under Henry VIII and then decisively promoted by Edward VI: Thomas Cranmer, archbishop of Canterbury from 1532 to 1553.[85]

Much research has already been conducted on the implications of the Reformation for the clergy in England. Beside the standard work by Rosemary O'Day[86] and a number of survey articles,[87] there are quite a few expert summaries of this aspect of Reformation history in historical works in general[88] as well as a great number specialized studies.[89] In addition,

---

[85] On Cranmer's connection to Osiander: DIARMAID MacCULLOCH, Thomas Cranmer. A life, New Haven and London 1996, 70–2.

[86] ROSEMARY O'DAY, The English clergy. The emergence and consolidation of a profession 1558–1642, Leicester 1979. After working on this topic for decades O'Day, in her history of the research of the English Reformation, sums up: »The manner in which the English clergy discovered a new role makes a fascinating story« (ID., The debate on the English Reformation, Manchester and New York ²2014, 211).

[87] A short survey of recent research discussions given by O'Day: The debate on the English Reformation (note 86), 210–16. Important overview articles are: ROSEMARY O'DAY, The Reformation of the ministry, 1558–1642 (in: Continuity and change. Personnel and administration of the Church in England 1500–1642, ed.s id. and Felicity Heal, Leicester 1976, 55–75); VIVIANE BARRIE-CURIEN, The English clergy, 1560–1620: Recruitment and social status (History of European Ideas 9, 1988, 451–63); PATRICK COLLINSON, Shepherds, sheepdogs, and hirelings: The pastoral ministry in post-Reformation England (in: The ministry: clerical and lay, ed.s W.J. Sheils and Diana Wood, Studies in Church History 26, Oxford [UK] and Cambridge [MA] 1989, 185–220); ANDREW PETTEGREE, The clergy and the Reformation: from ›devilish priesthood‹ to new professional elite (in: The reformation of the parishes. The ministry and the Reformation in town and country, ed. Andrew Pettegree, Manchester and New York 1993, 1–21); CHRISTOPHER HAIGH, Anticlericalism and clericalism, 1580–1640 (in: Anticlericalism in Britain, c. 1500–1914, ed.s Nigel Aston and Matthew Cragoe, Stroud 2000, 18–41); ERIC JOSEF CARLSON, Good pastors or careless shepherds? Parish ministers and the English Reformation (History 88, 2003, 423–36; Carlson reacts with justifiable criticism to the work of CHRISTOPHER HAIGH, The taming of the Reformation. Preachers, pastors and parishioners in Elizabethan and early Stuart England, in: History 85, 2000, 572–88).

[88] ROLAND G. USHER, The reconstruction of the English church, vol. 1, London, New York 1910, 205–43; RICHARD L. GREAVES, Society and Religion in Elizabethan England, Minneapolis 1981, 71–111; SUSAN BRIDGEN, London and the Reformation, Oxford 1989, 43–68, 392–404; FELICITY HEAL, Reformation in Britain and Ireland, Oxford 2003, 179–216, 286–302, 394–402, 429–35, 457–63.

[89] Here a selection sorted by year of publication, with a number of studies about the history of the parish included: ARTHUR G. DICKENS, Aspects of intellectual transition among the English parish clergy of the Reformation period: A regional example (ARG 43, 1952, 51–70) [Yorkshire]; H. GARETH OWEN, The London parish clergy in the reign of Elizabeth I, Ph.D. thesis, University of London 1957; MICHAEL L. ZELL, The personnel of the clergy in Kent, in the Reformation period (EHR 89, 1974, 513–33); FELICITY HEAL, The parish clergy and the Reformation in the diocese of Ely (Proceedings of the Cambridge Antiquarian Society 66, 1975/76, 141–63); CLAIRE CROSS, Priests into ministers: The Establishment of Protestant practice in the city of York 1530–1630 (in: Reformation principle and practice, ed. Peter Newman Brooks, London 1980, 203–25); TIMOTHY J. McCANN, The clergy and the Elizabethan settlement in the diocese of

research about the new culture of preaching, flourishing because of the Reformation, needs to be considered here,[90] as well as the extensive literature about late medieval clergy,[91] which makes it possible to define more

Chichester (in: Studies in Sussex Church History, ed. M. J. Kitch, London 1981, 99–123); R. M. FISHER, The Reformation of clergy at the Inns of Court 1530–1580 (SCJ 12, 1981, no. 1, 69–91); JEREMY GORING, The reformation of the ministry in Elizabethan Sussex (JEH 34, 1983, 345–66); ROSEMARY O'DAY, The anatomy of a profession: the clergy of the Church of England (in: The professions in Early Modern England, ed. Wilfrid Prest, London 1987, 25–63); NICK ALLDRIDGE, Loyalty and identity in Chester parishes 1540–1640 (in: Parish, church and people. Local studies in lay religion 1350–1750, ed. S. J. Wright, London et al. 1988, 85–124); BEAT KÜMIN, Parish finance and the early Tudor clergy (in: The reformation of the parishes. The ministry and the Reformation in town and country, ed. Andrew Pettegree, Manchester, New York 1993, 43–62); MARTHA C. SKEETERS, Community and clergy. Bristol and the Reformation, c. 1530–c. 1570, Oxford 1993; PETER MARSHALL, The face of the pastoral ministry in the East Riding, 1525–1595, York 1995; CLAIRE CROSS, Ordinations in the diocese of York 1500–1630 (in: Patronage and recruitment in the Tudor and early Stuart church, ed. Claire Cross, York 1996, 1–19; likewise in content: ID., Realising an utopian dream: the transformation of the clergy in the diocese of York, 1500–1630, in: Pragmatic utopias: Ideals and communities, 1200–1630, ed.s Rosemary Horrox and Sarah Rees Jones, Cambridge 2001, 259–75); BEAT KÜMIN, The shaping of community. The rise and reformation of the English parish, c. 1400–1560, Aldershot 1996; ROSEMARY O'DAY, The professions in early modern England, 1450–1800: Servants of the commonweal, Harlow 2000, 45–110; CLAIRE CROSS, From Catholic priests to Protestant ministers: Pastoral education in the diocese of York, 1520–1620 (in: The pastor bonus. Papers read at the British-Dutch colloquium at Utrecht, 18–21 September 2002, ed.s Theo Clemens and Wim Janse, Leiden and Boston 2004, 157–65).

[90] While older research (ALAN FAGER HERR, The Elizabethan sermon. A Survey and a bibliography, Philadelphia 1940; J. W. BLENCH, Preaching in England in the Fifteenth and Sixteenth Centuries, Oxford 1964) was focused on literary studies, more recent research in preaching has shown interest in the wealth of this genre in regard to the history of the church, devotion and theology: PETER E. MCCULLOUGH, Sermons at court. Politics and religion in Elizabethan and Jacobean preaching, Cambridge 1998; ERIC JOSEF CARLSON, The boring of the ear: Shaping the pastoral vision of preaching in England, 1540–1640 (in: Preachers and people in the Reformations and Early Modern Period, ed. Larissa Taylor, Leiden et al. 2001, 249–96); SUSAN WABUDA, Preaching during the English Reformation, Cambridge 2002; Ian Green, Orality, script and print: the case of the English sermon c. 1530–1700 (in: Cultural exchange in early modern Europe, vol. 1: Religion and cultural exchange in Europe, 1400–1700, ed.s Heinz Schilling and István György Tóth, Cambridge et al. 2006, 236–55); IAN GREEN, Continuity and change in Protestant preaching in early modern England, London 2009; ARNOLD HUNT, The art of hearing. English preachers and their audiences, 1590–1640, Cambridge 2010; The Oxford Handbook of the Early Modern Sermon, ed.s Peter McCullough et al., Oxford 2011 (see the contributions by GREG KNEIDEL, Ars praedicandi: Theories and practice [3–20], IAN GREEN, Preaching in the parishes [137–54], JOHN CRAIG, Sermon reception [178–97], LUCY WOODING, From Tudor humanism to Reformation preaching [329–47], and ARNOLD HUNT, Preaching the Elizabethan Settlement [366–86]).

[91] MARGARET BOWKER, The secular clergy in the diocese of Lincoln, 1495–1520, Cambridge 1968; PETER HEATH, The English parish clergy on the eve of the Reformation, London, Toronto 1969; ROBERT N. SWANSON, Problems of the priesthood in pre-Reformation England (EHR 105, 1990, 845–69); PETER MARSHALL, The Catholic priesthood and the English Reformation, Oxford 1994; TIM COOPER, The last generation of

clearly the continuities and discontinuities of this development from the 15th to the 16th century. In contrast to the German language research concerning Reformation history, in England these topics do not belong to the research field of a church historian, but rather to that of the secular historian, focusing more on social or cultural aspects of history.

Under Henry VIII, there was not much change in status or function of the clergy, rather, in spite of all his support of Bible and preaching, motivated as it was by sympathies for humanism and power politics, the king sought to hold on to tradition. Until the middle of the 1540s the overall picture did not change much, although Reformation ideas were widespread at the church basis, in some places already bringing about changes. But with Edward's succession to the throne and most of all with the assumption of power by his closest advisers, far-reaching changes came to be introduced, directly or indirectly concerning the status and function of the clergy. In programmatic texts and in statutes which gave them implementation, the Edwardian Reformation projected a new type of minister, comparable to that of continental Protestantism, defined mainly by his function as *preacher*. The programmatic texts include the *Book of Homilies* (1547) with its exemplary texts for the *sermon*, which now began to occupy a central place in the life of the church,[92] the *Ordinal* (1549/52), a collection of ordination forms for deacons, priests and bishops, attached to the *Book of Common Prayer*,[93] the *42 Articles* (1552), a codification of the ecclesiological and ministerial principles of the English Reformation,[94] the

---

English Catholic clergy: Parish priests in the diocese of Coventry and Lichfield in the early sixteenth century, Woodbridge 1999; HEAL, Reformation in Britain and Ireland (note 88), 43–80; ROBERT N. SWANSON, Pastoralia in practice. Clergy and ministry in pre-Reformation England (in: The pastor bonus. Papers read at the British-Dutch colloquium at Utrecht, 18–21 September 2002, ed.s Theo Clemens and Wim Janse, Leiden, Boston 2004, 104–27); G. W. BERNARD, The late medieval English church. Vitality and vulnerability before the break with Rome, New Haven u. London 2012, 68–86.

[92] The Two Books of Homilies Appointed to be Read in Churches, ed. John Griffiths, Oxford 1859. Concerning the first *Book of Homilies* see ASHLEY NULL, Official Tudor homilies (in: The Oxford handbook of the early modern sermon, ed.s Peter McCullough et al., Oxford 2011, 348–65, esp. 350–57).

[93] The forme and maner of makyng and consecratyng of archebishoppes bishoppes priestes and deacons. M. D. XLIX. (STC 16462); The first and second prayer books of Edward VI, London 1910, 291–317 (version of 1549), 437–63 (version of 1552, with a number of changes in regard to the first edition that do not concern the clergy); The English rite, ed. F. E. Brightman, vol. 2, London ²1921, 928–1017 (parallel printing of the orders of 1550, 1552 und 1661). The version of 1559 is edited in: Liturgical services. Liturgies and occasional forms of prayer set forth in the reign of queen Elizabeth, ed. William Keating Clay, Cambridge 1847, 272–98. Concerning the Edwardian ordination liturgy: PAUL F. BRADSHAW, The Anglican Ordinal, its history and development from the Reformation to the present day, London 1971, 18–36.

[94] Synodalia (note 135), 1–17; Die Bekenntnisschriften der reformierten Kirche, ed. E. F. Karl Müller, Leipzig 1903, 505–22 (no. 24).

Canons (1551/52), which were designed to adapt the traditional church law to the new demands, but did not take effect in practice,[95] sermons and writings of the protagonists of the Edwardian – and early Elizabethan – church[96], and the numerous *Injunctions* and *Acts*, in which for instance the clergy were released from compulsory celibacy.[97]

[95] Tudor church reform. The Henrician canons of 1535 and the Reformatio Legum Ecclesiasticarum, ed. Gerald Bray, Woodbridge and Rochester 2000, 145–743. This order of church law, conceived according to Cranmer as third mainstay beside the doctrinal and liturgical normative texts is in many aspects »descriptive of conditions as they actually were« and not merely »a blueprint for ›the church that never was‹« (ibid., CXV).

[96] A great number of sermons, catechisms and tractates could be cited here. As an example may serve Hugh Latimer, who for his sermons before the king 1548/49 twice chose Rom 15:4 as text, preaching about the significance of the sermon for salvation and of the preacher's religious duty as his central task (HUGH LATIMER, Sermons, Cambridge 1844, 59–78, 194–215). In his semi-official apology of the English Church from 1562 JOHN JEWEL defended the ecclesiological principles of the *Elizabethan Sett-lement* and its understandig of the ministry (Apologia Ecclesiae Anglicanae, London 1562, STC 14581, B 1ᵛ–B 3ᵛ). – The numerous texts dealing with ecclesiology and theo-logy of the ministry written by leading churchmen under Edward VI and Elizabeth I are evaluated in: H. F. WOODHOUSE, The doctrine of the church in Anglican theology, 1547–1603, London 1954 (esp. 75–92, concerning the church office and above all the debate about the office of the bishop, which haunted the Elizabethan theologians); PE-TER NEWMAN BROOKS, The principle and practice of primitive Protestantism in Tudor England: Cranmer, Parker and Grindal as chief pastors 1535–1577 (in: Reformation principle and practice, ed. Peter Newman Brooks, London 1980, 119–33); GLEN BOW-MAN, »To the perfection of God's service«: John Ponet's Reformation vision for the clergy (AEH 72, 2003, 79–101); MALCOLM B. YARNELL, Royal priesthood in the English Reformation, Oxford 2013. – In the controversial literature of the 2ⁿᵈ half of the 16ᵗʰ century, questions concerning the theology of the church and the office were present throughout – especially in demarcation from Roman Catholicism and the debates with Puritanism –, but they were no main topic of discussion (cf. PETER MILWARD, Religious controversies of the Elizabethan Age. A survey of printed sources, London 1977). – Martin Bucer's theory of the fourfold office and his proposals for a reorganization of theological training, being supported by a number of protagonists, had a certain influ-ence, but did in the end find no realization (O'DAY, The English clergy [note 86], 27).

[97] Edward's first *Injunctions* of 1547 (Visitation articles and injunctions [note 135], vol. 2, 114–130) were following closely the church politics of his father. Only later, in 1549, the *Act to take away all positive laws against marriage of priests* took effect (Docu-ments Illustrative of English Church History, ed.s Henry Gee and William John Hardy, London 1910, 366–368), supplemented in 1552 by the *Acte made for the Declaration of a Statute made for the Mariage of Priestes and legittimacon of their children*. The theo-logical justification was given by John Ponet (ca. 1514–1556) in his treatise of 1549 *A defence for mariage of priestes, by Scripture and anciente wryters* (see BOWMAN, John Ponet's Reformation vision for the clergy [note 96], 82–8). – Concerning the discussion about the marriage of clergy and their possible legal justification: JOHN K. YOST, The Reformation defense of clerical marriage in the reigns of Henry VIII and Edward VI (ChH 50, 1981, 152–65); RICHARD M. SPIELMANN, The beginnings of clerical marriage in the English Reformation: The reigns of Edward and Mary (AEH 56, 1987, 251–63); ERIC JOSEF CARLSON, Clerical marriage and the English Reformation (Journal of British Studies 31, 1992, 1–31); HELEN PARISH, Clerical marriage and the English Reformation. Precedent policy and practice, Aldershot et al. 2000.

The theological principles of the »Reformation by the word«,[98] making the sermon the central medium of renewal, are defined in the *42 Articles*, closely following art. 7 of the Augsburg Confession: The church is defined by the pure preaching of the word of God and the right administration of the sacraments (art. 20). Only he who is »legitime vocatus et missus« is allowed the »munus publice praedicandi, aut administrandi Sacramenta in Ecclesia« (art. 24). The clerical officeholders, who are called and installed to publicly preach and administer the sacraments, are exempt from mandatory celibacy (art. 31), and – it could be added – combine their office of clergy with leading a life in the world. Concerning the *munus praedicandi* the ordination liturgy explains: The three offices (deacon, presbyter, bishop) are all in essence defined as propagating the gospel, therefore they rest on the same theological foundation. In the prayer at the ordination of a deacon it is asked:

»[I]lluminate al Bisshops, Pastours and Ministers of the Churche, with true knowledge, and understanding of thy worde, and that both by theyr preachynge and lyuing, they may sette it forth and shewe it accordingly.«[99]

The ordinand has to state by way of a confession, that the church office is founded upon the order of Christ, and that he will be oriented by the Bible and will proclaim the Bible.[100] The ordination of the presbyter has additional texts, emphasizing the duty of the proclamation of the gospel, since the ministers are

»the messengers, the watchemen, the Pasteurs, and the stewardes of the LORDE to teache, to premonisshe, to feede, and prouyde for the Lordes family.«[101]

The priest's office is

»of so weightie a worke pertaining to the salutation of man, but with doctrine and exhortacion, taken out of holy scripture and with a life agreeable onto the same.«[102]

It consists of

»readyng and learning the holy scriptures, and in framyng the maners, both of yourselues, and of them that specially partein unto you, according to the rule of the same scriptures.«[103]

---

[98] CATHARINE DAVIES, A religion of the Word. The defence of the Reformation in the reign of Edward VI, Manchester 2002, 87.

[99] The first and second prayer books of Edward VI (note 93), 295.

[100] Ibid., 300–01.

[101] Ibid., 308.

[102] Ibid., 309.

[103] Ibid. Cf. the demand and promise given the ordinand: »And that you wyll continually praye for the heauenly assistaunce of the holy goste, from God the father, by the mediacion of our only mediatour and sauiour Jesus Chryste, that by dayly readyng and weighing of the scriptures, ye may waxe riper and stronger in your ministerie« (ibid.).

Therefore the crucial question, which the bishop asks of the ordinand, is:

»Be you perswaded that the holy Scriptures contein sufficiently al doctrine requir-ed of necessitie for eternal saluation, through faith in Jesu Christe? And are you determined with the saied scriptures, to enstructe the people committed to your charge, and to teache nothing, as required of necessitie, to eternal saluation, but that you shalbe perswaded may be concluded, and proued by the scripture?«[104]

The minister is the proclaimer of the biblical word of salvation, which means, he must know the Bible, fight heresy and lead a life according to the Bible and make others understand this. The qualification necessary for this is a theological education: The ordinand is »learned in the Latyne tongue and sufficiently instructed in holye Scripture.«[105]

Likewise, in the *Reformatio legum ecclesiasticarum* of 1552/53, the spe-cial importance of preaching[106] is emphasized:

»Since the gift of preaching us especially necessary to the people of God, the church should never be deprived of it«.[107]

A preacher must have *pietas* and *doctrina*, he must be supervised and instructed by the church authority, he must be schooled in rhetoric and must fulfill high moral standards.[108] As a rule, the minister should be a preacher, only in a well justified exception could there be a minister with-out the licence to preach.[109] The propagation of the *sana doctrina* was the bishop's foremost duty, which he had to fulfill himself and for which he had to engage others.[110] In the parish churches, there was to be a sermon preached every Sunday in the main worship service.[111] Other duties of the

---

[104] Ibid.

[105] Ibid., 292.

[106] The Henrician canons of 1535 and the Reformatio Legum Ecclesiasticarum (note 95), 238–44 (chap. 7). The ecclesiastical office is the topic of chap.s 11–3 and chap.s 19–20. Major parts of chap. 7 (De concionatoribus) were in 1571/76 taken over into the *Canons*, therefore effectively became church law.

[107] »Quoniam contionandi munus populo Dei maxime necessarium est, ecclesia num-quam illo destitui debet« (ibid., 238).

[108] It is also stipulated that the presbyter should own an English and a Latin Bible, study it and diligently work on preaching (ibid., 350).

[109] »Nec hi [sc. archiepiscopi] solum in hac occupatione sanctissima debent esse, sed pastoribus etiam et parochis eadem potestas in suis gregibus concedi debet« (ibid., 240). In the cathedrals, sermons are preached for the people every Sunday and holy day (ibid.), similarly sermons are preached on Sundays and holy days in university cities (ibid., 240–42). If in a city or village church there is no sermon on a Sunday or holy day (four are the absolute minimum per year), there ought to be a reading from the *Homilies* (ibid., 242). There parishioners are obliged to attend the sermons (ibid., 242–44).

[110] Ibid., 358.

[111] Ibid., 334–44. As an alternative, a *homily* could be read. In cathedrals, sermons were preached in the afternoon, so that people could listen to the sermon in their parish church in the morning. It was possible to have a sermon in the parish church on Sunday afternoon, too, but in any case, this was the time for catechetical instruction.

minister were pastoral care of the weak, the sick and those plagued by temptation.[112] To prove one's qualifications, the candidate had to pass an examination with questions about the creed, the Bible, the newest controversies and the catechism. From the way the questions were formulated, it can be assumed, that what was expected here, was a general rather than in-depth knowledge.[113] It is also clearly to be seen from the *Reformatio* that the minister's position remained much as it had been in the older hierarchical system and the traditional church patronage structures. While there emerged a new understanding of his service, the institutional framework as it had been created in the course of the Middle Ages remained the same.

These three short programmatic texts show, as do numerous other sources, that the English Reformation followed the continental pattern concerning the understanding of the ministry and its realization in practical life, even though it was in some points more conservative in dealing with the traditional structures and went about the restructuring of the church more slowly and more cautiously. This concerned, for instance, the release of the clergy from celibacy or the permission to preach, both of which had been intended from the beginning, but were realized only with delay – as with the marriage of the clergy – or not at all – as with the permission to preach, because of basic misgivings and practical scruples.

With the *Elizabethan Settlement* the reforms begun under Edward VI were continued, and during the more than four decades of Elizabeth's reign the reform program, conceived towards the end of the 1540s and the beginning of the 1550s, was implemented to a far degree: During the time of Elizabeth's reign, the standard of the clergymen's education was decisively raised, the financial provision for the clerical posts was improved and more and more positions in the countryside were being given to competent ministers. Within the scope of the church, the renewal went in some parts even beyond the limits drawn by the *Elizabethan Settlement*: In the context of Puritanism, theory and practice of the minister's office were almost identical with their models on the continent, in this case the Genevan model, in marked difference to the state church.

The comparison with England shows, that in the churches of the Reformation all over Europe the clerical office was understood and practiced in a new way, displaying a clear break with the tradition handed down from the Middle Ages. Doubtless, there were continuities beyond the beginning of a new epoch, yet on the whole there were fundamental discontinuities, resulting from the return to the New Testament norm.

---

[112] Ibid., 230.
[113] Ibid., 284.

2. Differences between the German and the
English Reformation

2.1. Distinctive developments in Germany

With the beginning of church renewal, in the areas under the influence of
the Wittenberg Reformation and likewise in the region of the Upper German and Swiss Reformation the new type of clergy began to emerge, and
soon came to be realized in many places. This assessment holds good, even
though one has to admit that the development was different in different
regions, with numerous obstacles and practical problems. In the countryside, the establishment of the new type of clergy was slower than in the
cities. In some places church reforms in the parishes were being prevented
by bishops, secular authorities or patrons adhering to the Roman church.
Time and again the realization of the pastoral ideal came to nothing because there were not enough qualified candidates, or because there were
not sufficient financial resources, or because of conflicts between the
church and the secular authorities, or because of personal transgressions of
clergymen or the resistance of parishes. The academic demands in regard
to the Protestant ministry were not always successfully met, for the level
of education of the incumbents did not come up to expectations for a long
time; at the same time, these expectations rose during early modern time in
such a way that there were never ending complaints about the low standard of education of the clergy and allusions to a lack of qualifications,
and to clergymen that were not up to their task.[114] These complaint have

---

[114] There are so many sources testifying to the difficulties of establishing a new type
of clergy, far into the 17th century, that it might seem, this was more a failure than a
success. Often it is a question of a lack of education of the clergy, as for instance, when
the 1558 visitation order in the electorate of Brandenburg laments about some patrons
who have been engaging »vngeschickte vnd vngelarte Esel / die [...] jr Ampt / wie sich
gebuert / nicht zubestellen wissen«, keeping part of the allowances (note 43, B 4[r/v]), or
when it is mentioned in the *Geistliche Polizei-, Visitations- und Konsistorialordnung* of
1561, that »schneider, schuster oder andere vordorbene handtwercker vnnd lediggenger,
die ihre grammatica nicht studirt, vielweyniger recht lesen konnen«, have become ministers, and demands of the patrons to stop this abuse of the spiritual office and to call as
ministers »tuchtige personnen [...], nemlich godtfurchtige menner, die nicht in offentlichen lastern leben vnnd nicht falsche, sondern die reine lehre des euangelii bekennen«
(note 43, 10[r]; this passage became part of the visitation and consistory order of 1573
[note 43, 10]). Particularly, the Brandenburg visitation in the year 1600, which for the
first time explicitly documents the educational standard of the clergy points out shortcomings (e.g. MÜLLER, PARISIUS, Abschiede [note 44], vol. 1/3, 1893, 183, 206, 217, 229,
243; cf. the petition of the estates, filed in 1599: GStAPK, I. HA, Rep. 20, lit. B, no. 1,
180[v]–182[v], 183[r/v]). That these shortcomings were widespread and that they were tolerated by those in leading positions in the church, can be seen when looking at examination records in Württemberg from the 17th century: KARL MÜLLER, Kirchliches Prü-

to be put into perspective and one must admit that Germany was definitely leading in regard to this development of a professionally oriented education in the scholastic and academic fields for the new type of clergy: There was a great number of Latin schools and universities, which after the interruption of the early Reformation began to prosper again or were newly founded, where humanist educational techniques were combined with the existentially challenging Reformation theology; stipends and the founding of colleges helped to build a territorial elite; a wealth of pastoral-theological literature offered additional help, demonstrating the rise in the level of expectations.

The distinctive political structure of the late medieval to early modern Empire helped the innovations in Protestant Germany to take hold relatively quickly and completely: The territories and imperial cities, where the Reformation was introduced, were to a fair degree sovereign, which meant that they had the power and freedom to put into practice the reform program which had so convincingly been propagated by Luther and the other reformers, and the rejection of Reformation by the Roman church made the new ordering of the old structures unavoidable. This dual precondition of a necessity for change and a possibility for renewal led to a reform dynamic, establishing a new type of clergy as norm and reality within a few decades. Important driving forces and active partners in this development were the secular authorities. The great majority of those 16th century rulers or magistrates sympathizing with the Reformation took responsibility and competently supported church renewal and, in deliberate cooperation with leading theologians, created new structures, which lasted for centuries. Another favorable condition was the relatively small size of the territories and the compactness of the structures, enabling the chronically weak central powers to realize their idea of order and to have control over their being instituted. This was accompanied by a successfully emerging homogenization of the religious diversity brought about in

---

fungs- und Anstellungswesen in Württemberg im Zeitalter der Orthodoxie. Aus den Zeugnisbüchern des herzoglichen Konsistoriums (in: Württembergische Vierteljahreshefte für Landesgeschichte 25, 1916, 431–88; cf. CHRISTOPH KOLB, Zur Geschichte des Pfarrstandes in Altwürttemberg, in: BWKG 57/58, 1957/58, 74–190). That the patronage system could be an obstacle for the recruitment of academically trained pastors is shown by VOLKER LEPPIN, Die Professionalisierung des Pfarrers in der Reformation (in: ID., Reformatorische Gestaltungen. Theologie und Kirchenpolitik in Spätmittelalter und Früher Neuzeit, Leipzig 2016, 275–92). Leppin's reconstruction is not fully convincing: The new type of a theologically trained ministry was a break with the late medieval ideal of priesthood and was established in an early stage of the Reformation even if its full realization and especially the connection of professional requirements and academic training took its time.

the course of the Reformation: As a rule, there was only one confession within a given territory or imperial city, which in itself showed a certain plurality, but precluded religious rivalry. Doctrinal and disciplinary conflicts, being the other side of this homogeneity, did have a destabilizing effect, but as a rule they affected only a small minority and had the intended effect of strengthening the confessional identity of the great majority. The clergy of the Reformation lived in an institutional framework, which was in a fundamental way newly organized by the secular authority taking upon itself the responsibility for what it was doing and which was set up for confessional homogeneity, thus enabling the full realization of this new type of clergy.

2.2. Characteristic developments in England

In the Protestant territories and cities in Germany there were only few course changes in regard to religious politics, so the establishment of the new type of clergy went ahead mostly undisturbed. In England, on the other hand, there was no extended period of continuous development during the key years of the Reformation. Henry VIII's[115] swaying back and forth between holding on to the tradition of the church on the one hand and a renewal, motivated by humanism and partly intersecting with the continental Reformation, on the other, meant for the English clergy, that its traditional status and function remained unchanged,[116] but also that it was at the king's disposal as far as the separation from the Roman papal church and a partial renewal of the church was concerned.[117] How such a renewal was to look and where it was to have its limits, was variously defined during Henry's reign: A phase of relative openness under the chancellorship of Thomas Cromwell – with the spreading of the Bible, the upgrading of preaching, dissolving of the monasteries and cutting back

---

[115] Concerning the religious policy of Henry VIII: PETER MARSHALL, Reformation England, 1480–1642, London 2003, chap. 3; G. W. BERNARD, The King's Reformation. Henry VIII and the Remaking of the English Church, New Haven, London 2005.

[116] That the pastoral handbook of the late Middle Ages, the *Cura clericalis*, was reprinted three times during the reign of Henry VIII indicates the basic continuity of the Heinrician ideal of the clergy. As the four main functions of the parish clergy are mentioned: celebrating mass, administering the sacraments, hearing confession and instructing the parishioners. When we read about the fourth function »Quarto sacerdotes sunt plebis doctores ideo dicitur sacerdos quasi sacra docens hoc modo opus est eos scire adminus articulos fidei & alijs preceptis dei informari« (London 1532, STC 6126, A 1ᵛ), then it becomes clear that both the humanist reform of Henry VIII and the Reformation of Edward VI, which followed the continental pattern, were also continuing medieval standards.

[117] MARGARET BOWKER, The Heinrician Reformation and the parish clergy (in: The English Reformation revised, ed. Christopher Haigh, Cambridge 1987, 75–93).

traditional thinking and devotional practices – was followed by a phase of a distancing from the Reformation, leading in the direction of a more cautious church renewal inspired by an Erasmian humanism. Although the church politics of the king were unstable and a basic change in status and function of the clergy was not intended,[118] there was room for small opportunities, which sympathizers of the Reformation could exploit. During the 1530s, one finds clergymen, who understood their office in the sense of the Reformation as an office to preach, and with their preaching followed continental models. For instance Hugh Latimer (1485–1555), coming from Cambridge University with a license to preach from any pulpit throughout the country, had to defend himself against reproaches from the bishop of London, John Stokesley, against having preached in his diocese without being authorized.[119] What is interesting in his defense, in our context here, is not the authorization that the bishop had questioned, but that we get to have a look at the practice of evangelical preaching in the early 1530s. Latimer states that he had been asked by people in the place of Abb-Church« to preach, people who had been »very desirous to hear me« and »pretending great hunger and thirst of the word of God and ghostly doctrine«.[120] He, Latimer, did not want to refuse them this demand,

»for I have preached and teached but according to holy scripture, holy fathers, and ancient interpreters of the same [...]: for I have done nothing else in my preaching, but with all diligence moved my auditors to faith and charity, to do their duty, and that that is necessary to be done. As for things of private devotion, mean things,

---

[118] This shows the plan for a new church law, the »Henrician canons« (The Henrician canons of 1535 and the Reformatio Legum Ecclesiasticarum [note 95], 1–143), where the clergy is still being seen more traditionally, but also is – according the late medieval reform effort – more regulated and more controlled. The *Wittenberg articles* of 1536 (Artickel der Cristlichen Lahr, von welchen die Legatten aus Engelland mit dem Herrn Doctor Martino gehandelt Anno 1536, ed. Georg Mentz, Leipzig 1905), with their understanding of the ecclesiastical office according to the continental Reformation in art. 9 and art. 14, did not play any kind of role for the church politics of Henry VIII and might have confirmed him in holding on to tradition, as testify in different ways and to different degrees, in 1536 the *Ten Articles* (Die Kirche von England. Ihr Gebetbuch, Bekenntnis und kanonisches Recht, ed. Cajus Fabricius, Berlin and Leipzig 1937, 585–606) as well as the king's *Injunctions* (Documents Illustrative of English Church History [note 97], 269–274) and in 1537 the *Bishops' Book* (Formularies of faith put forth by authority during the reign of Henry VIII., ed. Charles Lloyd, Oxford 1856, 21–211). In the *Act of Six Articles* of 1539, by Henry's conservative advisers, compulsory celibacy of the clergy was explicitly described as divine demand (Documents Illustrative of English Church History [note 97], 303–19, Art. 3) and the *King's Book* of 1543 (LLOYD, Formularies of faith [see above], 213–377) affirmed the king's holding on to the traditional understanding of the ecclesiastical office.

[119] Letter of Latimer to Edward Baynton, December 1531 (?) (in: HUGH LATIMER, Sermons and remains, Cambridge 1845, 322–34).

[120] Ibid., 323.

and voluntary things, I have reproved the abuse, the superstition of them, without condemnation of things themselves, as it becometh preachers to do.«[121]

In these statements is expressed the basic situation of the Protestant minister, whose main office was to preach in order to satisfy the spiritual hunger and thirst of the parish, which is done by preaching about faith and love and by warning against the danger of outwardly devotion. For part of the episcopate the understanding of the spiritual office rested indeed on a Reformation background, as Cranmer's unpublished *Thirteen Articles* of 1538 show. The 10th article states, close to the Augsburg Confession:

»Concerning the ministers of the Church we teach that no-one ought to teach publicly or administer the sacraments unless lawfully called by those in the Church's ministry. According to the word of God and the laws and customs of every region, they have the right to call and ordain. No-one called to the ministry, including the Roman or any other bishop, can claim for himself as by divine right, the power to teach publicly, to administer the sacraments, or exercise any ecclesiastical function in another diocese or parish. This applies to a bishop in another diocese and to a parish priest in another parish. And furthermore, the conduct of the minister in no way detracts from the efficacy of a sacrament, as we taught above in the Article on the Church.«[122]

The title woodcut of the *Great Bible* published in 1539[123] could be understood in this way: The king hands over the Bible to the bishops, who in turn give it to the clergy, who then on the pulpit preach their sermons on the foundation of the Bible. The reforms of Henry VIII did, however, not aim at the new type of clergy, Cranmer and Latimer had in mind, yet they made possible changes in that direction, which seem to have taken place here and there in the 1530s and 1540s.[124] Whether and to what degree this

---

[121] Ibid., 331. In his letter, Latimer does not expose the content of his sermon or render more precisely the expectations of the listeners. He seems to read the Bible in an Augustinian way that is open for the Reformation doctrine of justification.

[122] English translation: GERALD BRAY, The Thirteen Articles (in: The Churchman 106/3, 1992, 244–262, here 251; Latin original: FABRICIUS, Die Kirche von England. Ihr Gebetbuch, Bekenntnis und kanonisches Recht [note 118], 620).

[123] The Bible in Englyshe, London 1539 (STC 2068).

[124] Cranmer made an effort to fill clerical positions with academically educated clergy, who were open for church reforms, and to provide them with preaching licenses for the dissemination of God's word (SUSAN WABUDA, Setting forth the word of God: Archbishop Cranmer's early patronage of preachers, in: Thomas Cranmer. Churchman and scholar, ed.s Paul Ayris and David Selwyn, Woodbridge 1993, 75–88). Cranmer thus continued the efforts of John Fisher, who up to 1535 had taken similar measures, if for different ends than Cranmer (MARIA DOWLING, John Fisher and the preaching ministry, in: ARG 82, 1991, 287–309). Other bishops likewise supported preaching in different ways (SUSAN WABUDA, Bishops and the provision of homilies, 1520 to 1547, in: SCJ 25, 1994, 551–66; ID., »Fruitful preaching« in the diocese of Worcester. Bishop Hugh Latimer and his influence, 1535–1539, in: Religion and the English People, 1500–1650. New voices, new perspectives, ed. Eric Josef Carlson, Kirksville 1998, 49–74). Some of

process was accompanied or maybe even determined by anticlerical motives, has been and still is debated in research; both the definite assertion
and the more relativizing view of the importance of anticlericalism have
given way to a more differentiated view, where it is admitted that there
was a late medieval to early modern continuity of this phenomenon, emerging from the incongruence of spiritual demand and the reality of the
church. The idea that a broad and coherent anticlerical movement was
decisive for the success of the Reformation has, however, been abandoned.[125]

With the succession to throne of Edward in 1547 came another change
of course in religious politics. Edward VI and his closest advisors – most
of all Somerset and Cranmer – formulated an ambitious reform program,
following the Reformation on the continent, and did not hesitate to act
upon it.[126] In the main texts of this reform, as quoted above, status and
function of office holders in the church were given a new meaning, inten-
ding nothing less than the creation of a new type of clergyman, who, by
way of his education and marriage, was to be a citizen and, through the
focusing on the propagation of the gospel, was to be a preacher. The
ambitious reforms were, however, only reluctantly and in many ways
rather unsuccessfully realized during the reign of the *boy king*. Especially
as far as the clergy was concerned, not much changed. Some of the clergy
married – between 5 % and 30 % of the clergymen, differing in different
regions, altogether about 1,500 – and celebrated the worship service according to the *Book of Common Prayer*,[127] making use of the sermons

---

the measures were, as we can see from Latimer's *Injunctions* for the diocese of Worcester
of 1537 (Visitation articles and injunctions [note 135], vol. 2, 15–18), the obligation of
the ministers to read the whole Bible in English and in Latin, or at least the English and
Latin New Testament (art. 3) and for a betterment of the sermon (art. 9). Similar statements, partly supplemented by further regulations, can be found in other episcopal
Injunctions from the 1530s and 1540s, e.g. by Cranmer for the diocese of Hereford in
1538 (ibid., 65) or by Bonner for the diocese of London in 1542 (ibid., 83).

[125] David Loades, Anticlericalism in the Church of England before 1558: an ›Eating
Canker‹? (in: Anticlericalism in Britain, c. 1500–1914, ed.s Nigel Aston and Matthew
Cragoe, Stroud 2000, 1–17); Peter Marshall, Anticlericalism revested? Expressions of
discontent in early Tudor England (in: The parish in late medieval England, ed.s Clive
Burgess and Eamon Duffy, Donington 2006, 365–80).

[126] Diarmaid MacCulloch, Tudor Church Militant. Edward VI and the Protestant
Reformation, London 1999; Davies, A religion of the Word (note 98), concerning the
realization of the reforms and the clergy, of special significance here because of the
importance of the sermon for this »Reformation by the word«: 87–139.

[127] In the 2nd half of the 16th century a shorter liturgy comes to be used, where in the
service with a sermon, as regulated in the *Book of Common Prayer*, a number of elements are reduced (John Harper, The forms and orders of Western liturgy from the
tenth to the eighteenth century, Oxford 1991, 166–87). Even at court, the regulations of
BCP stipulating that in the Sunday service the creed should be followed by a *sermon*,

from the *Book of Homilies*, which were read out; mostly there seems to have been a position of wait-and-see, even of resistance, which might have been overcome, if the reign had been of longer duration. For a renewal of the clergy, there was not more than a beginning during the time of Edward's reign.

Due to the change in government in 1553, to the Catholic Mary, the whole church reform process, which had just begun, came to a halt, including the institution of a new type of clergy.[128] Queen Mary and her councilors – especially cardinal Reginald Pole – were set on returning to the pre-Reformation celibate priesthood, both in regard to the status as well as the function of the clergy.[129] This meant above all that married clergy were dismissed and that the Roman mass with the holy Sacrifice was reinstituted. But the new queen was also interested in renewing the church. Sharing with her father the interest for humanist preaching she joined the beginning renewal movement in the Roman church recasting the sermon as an anti-Reformation weapon, which was used by bishops with pastoral orientation and clergy newly educated in Catholic seminaries to better serve the church of the Pope.[130] What the clergy had learned from the changes and reversals in church policy during the last two centuries was that it was best to be patient and wait. The dismissal of their married colleagues, in most cases sympathizers of the Reformation, had taught them that rash decisions could endanger one's position and above all one's livelihood. The radical reforms under Edward VI and their no less radical rescinding under Mary made sure that for decades to come the clergy showed a caution, which made it difficult for many to go along with

---

homily, or exhortation, were not strictly kept, rather a service in shortened form without sermon came to be customary. Elizabeth I, because of her »liturgical and prayer-centered piety« did not hold sermons to be a constitutive part of the worship service, as much as she valued traditional sermon sequences, such as for Lent (McCULLOUGH, Sermons at court [note 90], 71–2, 76–8).

[128] ARTHUR G. DICKENS, The Marian Reaction in the diocese of York (in: ID., Reformation studies, London 1982, 93–157, concerning the clergy: 93–111); EAMON DUFFY, Fires of the Faith. Catholic England under Mary Tudor, New Haven, London 2009, 22–28.

[129] This repeal started with the *Injunctions on religion* (Documents Illustrative of English Church History [note 97], 380–83), prohibiting the marriage of priests, dismissing married clergy from office and demanding of married members of religious orders that they divorce.

[130] In England this happened in the form of the *Book of Homilies*: The new bishop of London, Edmund Bonner, published a doctrinal exposé, with thirteen reading sermons revised by John Harpsfield and Henry Pendleton attached: A profitable and necessary doctryne, with certayne homelies adioyned thereunto, London 1555 (STC 3282, cf. EAMON DUFFY, The stripping of the altars. Traditional religion in England, c. 1400–c. 1580, New Haven and London 1992, 536–37).

the next reversals in religious policy and to get involved in the new conditions – not trusting whether or how long they would last.

After the next succession to the throne, the *Elizabethan Settlement* brought the return to the reform agenda of Edward VI. The queen resumed the transformation of the clerical office, which had been rescinded in 1553, taking up again the Reformation understanding of the ministry.[131] During the more than four decades of the last Tudor reign the new type of clergy finally took shape,[132] conceived as it was by the Reformation on the continent, adapted by Thomas Cranmer and his comrades-in-arms and affirmed by Marian exiles now returned to leading positions.[133] In the beginning it often met with resistance[134], but by and by asserted itself.[135] The English form of this new type differed, however, in a few aspects from the continental model. There are four points to be considered:

---

[131] Fundamental were now the queen's *Injunctions* of 1559 (Documents Illustrative of English Church History [note 97], 417–42), which put the proclamation of the gospel back into the center of the clerical service (ibid., 419–22, 430, 434).

[132] Out of the great number of sources reflecting this development see e.g. Matthew Parker's *Advertisements for due order* of 1566 (The Anglican canons 1529–1947, ed. Gerald Bray, Woodbridge and Rochester 1998, 163–71), the *Canons* of 1571 and 1575/76, decreed by the *Convocation* and compiled by Grindal (ibid., 172–209, esp. 196–98, 211–15) and the *Orders for the increase of learning in the unlearned sort of ministers* (CARDWELL, Documentary annals of the reformed Church of England [see below], vol. 2, 21–22), compiled by John Whitgift in 1585. There are many more sources in the relevant document collections, but what they say about training, continuing education and service of the clergy is more or less the same all over: Synodalia. A Collection of Articles of Religion, Canons, and Proceedings of Convocations in the Province of Canterbury, from the Year 1547 to the Year 1717, ed. Edward Cardwell, two vol.s, Oxford 1842; Documentary annals of the reformed Church of England; being a collection of injunctions, declarations, orders, articles of inquiry, &c. from the year 1546 to the year 1716, ed. Edward Cardwell, two vol.s, Oxford 1844; Visitation articles and injunctions, ed. W. H. Frere and W. P. M. Kennedy, three vol.s, London 1910. The final conclusion of the renewal of the clergy are the *Constitutions and Canons Ecclesiastical*, decreed in 1604 by James I, documenting the transformation reached under Elizabeth I (The Anglican canons 1529–1947 [see above], 258–453, esp. 308–70, no. 31–76).

[133] The creation of a Protestant clergy as one of the main tasks of that part of the Elizabethan episcopate, which was looking at the Reformation on the continent for orientation, is being discussed by: O'DAY, The English clergy (note 86), 33–48, and SCOTT A. WENIG, Straightening the altars. The ecclesiastical vision and pastoral achievements of the progressive bishops under Elizabeth I, 1559–1579, New York et al. 2000. O'Day presents Thomas Bentham as an example for the »Reformed episcopate« (ibid., 33) and Wenig offers a survey (ibid., 44–8) as well as case studies about John Jewel, Edwin Sandys, James Pilkington, Richard Cox and others (ibid., 146–51, 159–61, 172–6, and scattered comments ibid., 209–36).

[134] HENRY GEE, The Elizabethan clergy and the settlement of religion, 1558–1564, Oxford 1898.

[135] CHRISTOPHER HAIGH (The English Reformations. Religion, politics, and society under the Tudors, Oxford 1993) rightly points out, that into the 1570s the realization of the *Elizabethan Settlement* proved to be a difficult and only partly successful undertaking (cf. also his other articles: note 87).

1. The church renewal under Edward VI had been conceived as a far-reaching re-shaping and was initiated quite »militantly« (D. MacCulloch), but barely touched the traditional church structures. A change of these structures had been planned, but the mere attempt at a renewal of church law was so controversial, that in-depth organizational reforms were postponed. The *Elizabethan Settlement* itself did not go beyond the status the reform had reached at the end of Edward's reign, and even the very cautious new form of church law in the shape of the *Reformatio Legum Ecclesiasticarum*, twice introduced in Parliament under Elizabeth, did not take effect.[136] For the clergy this meant that the institutional and legal framework, in which they acted, was much more traditional than it was for continental Protestantism, and that it was not as encouraging for clerical activity, as it was on the continent. These traditional structural elements included for instance the preservation of the threefold office (bishop, presbyter, deacon) and the keeping of the episcopal church constitution. The bishops were, in spite of the emphasis on proclaiming the gospel, first of all servants of the monarch, with their spiritual service at best being part-time. The continuation of widespread dioceses and their traditional administrative structures made the episcopal supervision of the clergy and church renewal at the grass roots difficult. Connected with this keeping of the episcopal office was the continuing dualism of cathedral and parish clergy with their own distinctive spheres, which barely ever overlapped.[137] The clergy was further differentiated by the considerable number of deacons, who understood their office as an office for the propagation of the gospel[138], and by the domestic chaplains in the great houses, who were not subject to episcopal supervision[139].

Another important feature that was kept, were the relatively independent and powerful church courts, which limited the competence of the clergy in regard to law and order in the church and social disciplining, and supervised both clergy and parish.[140] In the parishes, difficulties arose for

---

[136] GERALD BRAY, Introduction (in: The Henrician canons of 1535 and the Reformatio Legum Ecclesiasticarum [note 95], XV-CLX, esp. XLI-CLVI). Parts of the *Reformatio* were enacted in a different context, though.

[137] Concerning the »clerical élite«: O'Day, The English clergy (note 86), 144–58.

[138] FRANCIS YOUNG, Inferior office? A history of deacons in the Church of England, Cambridge 2015, 1–33.

[139] WILLIAM GIBSON, A social history of the domestic chaplain, 1530–1840, London and Washington 1997.

[140] RALPH HOULBROOKE, The decline of ecclesiastical jurisdiction under the Tudors (in: Continuity and change. Personnel and administration of the Church in England 1500–1642, ed.s Rosemary O'Day and Felicity Heal, Leicester 1976, 239–57); ID., Church courts and the people during the English Reformation 1520–1570, Oxford 1979; MARTIN INGRAM, Church courts, sex and marriage in England, 1570–1640, Cambridge

the clergy from the oftentimes meager financial provisions, going back to the situation of the early 16th century,[141] and the strong position of the patrons, whose demands could be quite different from those of the church and who in many instances were following their own interest when filling a clerical post.[142] A consequence of the insufficient financial provision was, at least for a time, a continued holding of benefices in plurality, meaning absenteeism from clerical posts. It should be remarked that especially cathedral clergy and academically educated theologians took advantage of this possibility to better their income.[143]

2. Another impediment in regard to the establishment of the new type of clergy in England was the scarcely realized *coniunctio scholarum cum ministerio evangelii*. While in continental Protestantism there was a close cooperation between church government, educational system and clergy, intersecting in a number of decisive points – embodied in the person of Andreas Musculus, general superintendent of the Kurmark – in England church government, educational system and the clergy remained separate spheres: they came into contact only in regard to particular points, and were accessible only to a limited degree to persons from one of the other spheres. This is not to say that in England interest in education, especially academic education of the clergy, was lacking, nor that there were numerous individual initiatives.[144] All groups within the Elizabethan church agreed in their efforts for an educated clergy: Given the general awareness of the theological necessity of a qualified clergy, ordination standards were

---

1987; ID., Puritans, and the church courts, 1560–1640 (in: The culture of English Puritanism, 1560–1700, ed.s Christopher Durston and Jacqueline Eales, Basingstoke, London 1996, 58–91); BEAT KÜMIN, Parishioners in court: litigation and the local community (in: Belief and practice in Reformation England, ed.s Susan Wabuda and Caroline Litzenberger, Aldershot et al. 1998, 20–39); CHRISTOPHER HAIGH, The clergy and parish discipline in England, 1570–1640 (in: The Impact of the European Reformation: Princes, Clergy and People, ed.s Bridget Heal and Ole Peter Grell, Aldershot and Burlington 2008, 125–41); O'DAY, The debate on the English Reformation (note 86), 216–24.

[141] MICHAEL L. ZELL, Economic problems of the parochial clergy in the sixteenth century (in: Princes & paupers in the English Church 1500–1800, ed.s Rosemary O'Day and Felicity Heal, Leicester 1981, 19–43).

[142] O'DAY, The English clergy (note 86), chap.s 6–9; D. J. LAMBURN, The influence of the laity in appointments of clergy in the late sixteenth and early seventeenth century (in: Patronage and recruitment in the Tudor and early Stuart church, ed. Claire Cross, York 1996, 95–119).

[143] That this problem existed particularly in dioceses under bishops who were pushing the Reformation, is shown by J. I. DAELEY, Pluralism in the diocese of Canterbury during the administration of Matthew Parker, 1559–1575 (JEH 18, 1967, 33–49).

[144] Already during the reign of Henry VIII, many English bishops made an effort in regard to education, preaching and younger clergy, which later was intensified: O'DAY, The English clergy (note 86), chap.s 3–5; KENNETH CARLETON, Bishops and reform in the English Church, 1520–1559, Woodbridge 2001.

raised by and by; candidates with a university degree were given preference; at cathedrals biblical instruction and *Divinity lectures* were established; Latin schools and colleges were supported and special scholarships for gifted students installed. The clergy were obliged to engage in bible study and to account for their activities before their superior or the visitation committee, including the bettering and increasing of their religious basic knowledge.

But even all those individual points put together do not add up to the powerful *coniunctio*, which became the driving force of continental Protestantism. With Cambridge and Oxford, there were only two – if large – universities, and of Latin schools there were not all that many.[145] This slowed down the development, especially since this career was not very attractive, because many clerical positions were poorly provided for, which meant that for a longer period of time there were not enough qualified candidates. There was a marked upturn in the education in the schools in the 16th century, and the universities tried to meet the growing interest in a better education by introducing new curricula[146] and by giving a new direction to existing colleges or founding new colleges,[147] but for a

---

[145] O'DAY, The English clergy (note 86), 140–1.

[146] So far not much research has been done about what was taught and how clerical studies were organized at Oxford and Cambridge during the time of Elizabeth's reign, which may have to do with a lack of source material. The university statutes provide little information in regard to curriculum or course of studies (The privileges of the university of Cambridge, ed. George Dyer, vol. 1, London 1824, 157–211). Relevant literature on this topic: WILLIAM T. COSTELLO, The scholastic curriculum at early seventeenth-century Cambridge, Cambridge (MA) 1958; MARK H. CURTIS, Oxford and Cambridge in transition, 1558–1642. An essay on changing relations between the English universities and English society, Oxford 1959, 161–4; S. L. GREENSLADE, The Faculty of Theology (in: The history of the university of Oxford, vol. 3: The collegiate university, ed. James McConica, Oxford 1986, 295–334); JENNIFER LOACH, Reformation controversies (in: ibid., 363–96); CHRISTOPHER BROOKE, Learning and doctrine 1550–1660 (in: Victor Morgan and Christopher Brooke: A history of the university of Cambridge, vol. 2: 1546–1750, Cambridge 2004, 437–63); IAN GREEN, Humanism and Protestantism in Early Modern English Education, Farnham 2009, 294–9. Concerning the puritan program of a »mixture of scriptural study and extended instruction in purified humane learning« for the training of future pastors, see JOHN MORGAN, Godly learning. Puritan attitudes towards reason, learning and education, 1560–1640, Cambridge 1986, 220–44 (quote: 241).

[147] Christ's and Emmanuel Colleges in Cambridge became important puritan centers, where Laurence Chaderton developed a two year study program for future clergy (»for the training up and exercising of students in divinity, whereby they may be made fit and meet to discharge the duties belonging to that profession«), which mainly consisted of joint preaching studies (including the necessary preparation through philological and theological exegeses of the Bible text) and disputations (PATRICK COLLINSON, The Elizabethan puritan movement, London, New York 1967, 126–7; PETER LAKE, Moderate puritans and the Elizabethan church, Cambridge 1982, 36–7). Emmanuel College was founded by Walter Mildmay as plantation for puritan clergy: MORGAN, Godly learning

long time these efforts were not enough to catch up with the head start of the educational system on the continent. In England, too, Greek and Hebrew were taught at the university according to the humanist-Reformation program, the Bible was studied as well as patristic writings and dogmatic theological texts, but there were no concerted efforts of bringing together theology and church, as Melanchthon had demanded in his speech about the *necessaria coniunctio*. In England, there were only first beginnings. Future clergy were being educated in colleges founded especially for that purpose, they maybe went to some lectures or disputations at the arts or theological faculty, but it was unlikely that during their study time they should encounter among their academic teachers practitioners of the church or even persons from church government, who engaged in theology as a church connected field and taught biblical exegesis and Christian doctrine focusing on the preparation for the pastoral service. Even if the colleges did not provide a »formal pastoral instruction« for the education of »professional theologians«, it can, however, be assumed, that through the intensive spiritual life and the religious instruction there – for example in the form of cursory Bible lectures or catechetical instruction – students grew into being candidates for the clerical office, who »at very least [...] were far better qualified academically than their predecessors in the earlier part of the century«.[148] Many of the future clergymen had to content

---

(note 146), 245–71; PATRICK COLLINSON, The foundations and beginnings (in: SARAH BENDALL, CHRISTOPHER BROOKE, PATRICK COLLINSON, A history of Emmanuel College, Cambridge, Woodbridge 1999, 13–55); ID., Puritan Emmanuel (ibid., 177–226). Looking at the Statutes of Emmanuel College of 1585 (The statutes of Sir Walter Mildmay Kt Chancellor of the Exchequer and one of Her Majesty's Privy Councillors; authorised by him for the government of Emmanuel College founded by him, ed. Frank Stubbings, Cambridge 1983, 113–52), one can see to what end a thoroughly planned way of life together with the study program should lead: »ut ex hoc seminario haberet Anglicana ecclesia, quos ad erudiendum populum pastorumque munus subeundum (rem ex omnibus maxime necessariam) evocare possit« (ibid., 132). Also, for this end, there was a quite demanding religious instruction. The Emmanuel College viewed itself – comparable to Melanchthon's regard of the *scholae* in his already mentioned speech of 1543 – in the tradition of educational institutions since the times of OT and NT, with the intent to instruct youth »in omni pietate et bonis literis, praecipue vero in sacris et theologicis« in order that it »alios postea veram et puram doctrinam doceat, haereses, et errores omnes refutet, atque praeclarissimis vitae integerrimae exemplis ad virtutem omnes excitet« (ibid., 113).

[148] CROSS, Ordinations in the diocese of York (note 89), 16. Some place else, Cross describes this way of qualifying as a »process of osmosis« (CROSS, From Catholic priests to Protestant ministers [note 89], 164), quite undervaluing the achievement of theological training. One should take notice that in 1579 for the catechesis at the Oxford Colleges there were mandatory the use of catechisms by Nowell, Calvin, Hyperius or the Heidelberger Katechismus for beginners, and Calvin's *Institutio*, Jewel's *Apologia* or the *39 Articles* with explications for the advanced students (GREENSLADE, The Faculty of Theology [note 146], 327).

themselves with a more or less exhaustive Latin school instruction – which provided a solid basic knowledge und could be theologically quite demanding[149] – , but the ratio was rising over time, and by 1600 more than half of the ordinands – numbers differ regionally – had gone to university, although as a rule not studying theology.[150] While with certain groups of the clergy such as the cathedral clergy or licensed preachers the ratio was higher yet, for most clergy it is true: »The first point to note about early modern English preachers is how little training most of them received.«[151] The prospective clergyman had to appear for an entrance examination before a representative of the church – usually the archdeacon – where knowledge and competence, acquired through studying the Bible and church doctrine, were noted with approval, but were no necessary precondition for the admission to be ordained.[152]

That the clergy in England was much less academically or theologically trained, can also be seen in the fact that there is no guide or advice literature for how to lead a clerical office. Apart from collections of sermons and a few edifying reflections about the spiritual office there is a complete lack of what existed on the continent for the support of the Protestant clergy such as instructions for studying or handbooks in pastoral theology or homiletics.[153] By and by, a small number of that advice literature was

---

[149] IAN GREEN, The Christian's ABC. Catechism and Catechizing in England c. 1530–1740, Oxford 1996, 170–229; ID., Humanism and Protestantism (note 146), 274–94. Schools rarely taught Greek or Hebrew, nor was the *Novum Testamentum graece* part of what was read in school (GREEN, Humanism and Protestantism [note 146], 254–61).

[150] O'DAY, The English clergy (note 86), 3–4, 6, 13, 132, 135–6, 233.

[151] GREEN, Continuity and change in Protestant preaching in early modern England (note 90), 11.

[152] O'DAY, The English clergy (note 86), 48–65.

[153] There are no handbooks for the ministers between 1570 and 1630 (COLLINSON, Shepherds, sheepdogs, and hirelings [note 87], 193–8; for Calvinism, there is generally a remarkable deficiency: BURNETT, The evolution of the Lutheran pastor's manual [note 57], 540), in difference to the Middle Ages (DAVID B. FOSS, John Mirk's Instruction for Parish Priests, in: The ministry: clerical and lay, ed.s W. J. Sheils and Diana Wood, Studies in Church History 26, Oxford [UK] and Cambridge [MA] 1989, 131–40). Increasing was the dissemination of Bibles and exegetical aids (IAN GREEN, Print and Protestantism in early modern England, Oxford 2000, 42–100, 101–67) and homiletical books (MORGAN, Godly learning [note 146], 132–41). Indirectly, textbooks on rhetoric belong here, too, which could be found earlier already (e.g. THOMAS WILSON, The Arte of Rhetorique, for the vse of all suche as are studious of Eloquence, 1553, STC 25799, where the sermon is mentioned in passing, e.g. 75[r/v]). The advice for organizing one's course of studies, mostly from puritan authors, is rather low-level, but corresponds to what was expected on the continent: Prospective ministers should pursue first of all languages and Bible studies (concentrating on the main biblical books), read Bible commentaries and the writings of church fathers and church reformers (from Luther to Beza), and organize their acquired learning with the help of dogmatic works such as Calvin's *Institutio*, puritan authors and writings of controversial theology, with the

translated into English and printed,[154] but it took until the turn of the century that there was a sizeable demand for such literature, for English authors to begin to supply it, if only in a form which cannot be counted as equivalent in variety and quality to what existed in 17th century Germany.[155] The critical judgment of Rosemary O'Day concerning the educational status and the pastoral competence of the English clergy during the second half of Elizabeth's reign is therefore not surprising: »Despite all these efforts, in the 1580s and 1590s, however, both the educational qualifications and the vocational aptitude of the beneficed clergy almost everywhere were still deplorable.«[156]

---

advice of making a collection of ›loci‹ of this material (MORGAN, Godly learning [note 146], 112–7). Cf. the advice given in the *Order to be used for the trayning upp and exercising of Students in Divinitye, whereby they maye be made fitt and meete to dyscharge the dewtyes belongig to that profession* (originally not meant to be printed, and originating in a puritan university environment, probably going back to the 1570s, by William or Laurence Chaderton for Cambridge students: The seconde parte of a register. Being a calender of manuscripts under that title intended for publication by the Puritans about 1593, ed. Albert Peel, vol. 1, Cambridge 1915, 133–4), in *Mr. Cartwrights letter for direction in the study of divinity* (Cartwrightiana, ed. Albert Peel and Leland H. Carlson, London 1951, 108–15) and in the *Letter of Dr. Reinolds to his friend, concerning his aduice for the studie of Diuinitie* from 1577 (printed in 1613: STC 20611).

[154] NIELS HEMMINGSEN, The preacher, or methode of preaching, wrytten in latine bey Niels Hemminge, and translated into englishe by i. H. Very, necessarie for al those that by the true preaching of the word of God, labour to pull down the singoge of sathan, and to buylde vp the temple of God, London 1574 (STC 13065); ANDREAS HYPERIUS, The practice of preaching, translated by John Ludham, London 1577 (STC 11758).

[155] See the detailed description of the office of the preacher in dialogue form and the demands by SAMUEL HIERON (The Preachers Plea: Or, A Treatise in forme of a plain Dialogue, making known the worth and necessary vse of Preaching: shewing also how a man may profit by it, both for the informing of his iudgement, and the reforming of his life, London 1604, STC 13419) or RICHARD BERNARD (The Faithfvll Shepheard: Or the Shepheards Faithfulnesse: Wherein is [...] set forth the excellencie and neceßitie of the Ministerie; A Ministers properties and dutie; His entrance into this function and charge; How to begin fitly to instruct his people; Catechising and Preaching; And a good plaine order and method therein: Not so as yet published. Very profitable both for yoong Students, who intend the studie of Theologie (heerein being also declared what Arts and tongues first to be learned, what kind of Authours to be read and books necessarie in the beginning, and which in the first place) as also for such Ministers as yet haue not atteined to a distinct order to study studie, write, meditate, and to preach methodically, both for their better course in deliuering the Word, and the peoples vnderstanding in hearing, and memorie in reteining the same, London 1607, STC 1939), where some basics about preaching and an introduction the pastoral service are provided, and compare these works with the collections of continental study guides, e.g.: Joh. Hulsemanni [...] Methodus Concionandi, auctior edita. Cui accesserunt Ejusdem Autoris Methodus Studii Theologici, in privatum quorundam usum conscripta; nec non [...] Johannis Forsteri, Methodus ac formulae concionandi, Ejusdemque & [...] Leonharti Hutteri, ac Balthasaris Meisneri [...] Consilia De studio Theologico, & lectione Biblica recte instituendis, Ob argumenti similitudinem in unum volumen collecta; & impressa, Wittenberg ³1648 (VD17 23:669097R).

3. The establishment of a new type of clergy was made even more difficult by the highest secular rulers. Both king Edward VI and queen Elizabeth I saw themselves as divinely legitimized rulers charged with religious responsibility for their kingdom.[157] With this, they stood in the tradition of their father, Henry VIII, who in the *Act of Supremacy*[158] had given the sovereign, beyond the spiritual dignity, which had always belonged to the king,[159] the power to decide about all ecclesiastical causes. That the ruler was quite literally vested with the *royal* priesthood,[160] meant for ecclesiastical office holders a reduction of their powers,[161] it blurred the differentiation between the two realms and kingdoms of God and led to a situation where the clergy was more and more taken into service for administrative and fiscal tasks.[162] For Elizabeth this priesthood was no mere

---

[156] O'DAY, The English clergy (note 86), 132. O'Day, however, can show, that during the final years of Elizabeth's reign the efforts for a better education of prospective clergy began to bear fruit, with increasing numbers of ordinands, who had gone to university and had graduated (ibid., 135–6).

[157] This religious self-understanding is the starting-point for the interesting, even if not always convincing interpretation of the English Reformation as a form of *religio monarchica* by JOSEF JOHANNES SCHMID, ›No bishops, no King‹ – die »religio monarchica« als unbeachtetes Element der Konfessionalisierungsdebatte (in: Das Konfessionalisierungsparadigma – Leistungen, Probleme, Grenzen, ed.s Thomas Brockmann and Dieter J. Weiß, Münster 2013, 165–81).

[158] Documents Illustrative of English Church History (note 97), 243–4. Cf. the new Act of Supremacy, enacted at the beginning of Elizabeth's reign and supplemented with the *Act of uniformity*: ibid., 442–58, 458–67.

[159] Through the rite of anointing in the coronation liturgy the English king became a »persona mixta« »in whom the characters of clerk and lay are combined« (LEOPOLD G. WICKHAM LEGG, The sacring of the English kings, London 1894, 3). The sentence by the medieval legal scholar William Lyndwode »Quod Rex unctus non sit mere persona laica, sed mixta« was still known in the 16th century, being referred to in law commentaries of the Elizabethan time and interpreted in light of the new situation, after the Act of Supremacy was enacted: »Reges sancto oleo uncti sunt spiritualis jurisdictionis capaces« (ibid., 3, note 2, quoted in corrected form). Correspondingly it says in the coronation ceremony, »that the king is an ecclesiastical as well as a civil governor« (ibid., 4; the medieval coronation ritual used at Elizabeth's coronation is printed in: English coronation records, ed. Leopold G. Wickham Legg, Westminster 1901, 81–112).

[160] YARNELL, Royal priesthood in the English Reformation (note 96), 123–49 (Henry VIII, Edward VI), 245–56 (Elizabeth I).

[161] The tense relationship between the secular and the spiritual led to competition and conflicts, as seen in the difficult relationship of Elizabeth with her court preachers, which was made even more complex by the fact that in the eyes of the court clergy the queen as a woman was judged to be inferior – a fact of which she was quite aware (MARGARET CHRISTIAN, Elizabeth's preachers and the government of women: Defining and correcting a queen: in: SCJ 24, 1993, 561–76).

[162] FELICITY HEAL, Clerical tax collection under the Tudors: the influence of the Reformation (in: Continuity and change. Personnel and administration of the Church in England 1500–1642, ed.s Rosemary O'Day and Felicity Heal, Leicester 1976, 97–122); PATRICK CARTER, ›Certain, continual, and seldom abated‹: royal taxation of the Elizabethan church (in: Belief and practice in Reformation England, ed.s Susan Wabuda and Caroline Litzenberger, Aldershot et al. 1998, 94–112).

formal claim. For example, since she had a critical view of the marriage of clergy, she did not follow up on the revocation of the celibacy in any consistent way.[163] Likewise, at the beginning of her reign she wished to have preaching limited.[164] And in the conflict with archbishop Grindal concerning the »prophesyings« she had this important tool of clerical training in office, which served mainly to enhance the preaching competence, banned without any adequate justification.[165] For the Tudor rulers, to use the clergy for their political purposes was as important as to let them fulfill their primary duty of preaching the Gospel. The clergy had to show its loyalty by helping to legitimize the Tudor claim to the throne, and to impress on the king's and queen's subjects the importance of obedience, and generally to enforce *public virtue*[166] beyond the religious rules of behavior – the harmony of society was a fundamental value in the Tudor era, and the clergy had to contribute its share to its realization.

4. During the reign of Elizabeth, the English clergy became, through the professionalization founded on status and function, a socially homogenous group, yet at the same time it stood for a broad range of positions from the quite conservative official church all the way to a progressive puritanism.[167] This great diversity, which on the continent was shared out between different regions and confessions, all found room in England

---

[163] Her *Injunctions* of 1559 (Documents Illustrative of English Church History [note 97], 417–442) did not restore the abolition of compulsory celibacy by her half-brother. Only section 29 provided legal grounds for the marriage of clergy.

[164] Paradoxically, the resumption of the Reformation by queen Elizabeth went together with a general interdict of preaching, on December 27th, 1558 (CARDWELL, Documentary annals [note 135], vol. 1, 208–10; Bible reading without commentary was authorized). The first official Protestant sermon was preached at the opening of Parliament on January 25th, 1559 (McCULLOUGH, Sermons at court [note 90], 59).

[165] COLLINSON, The Elizabethan Puritan movement, London, New York 1967, 168–76; ID., Archbishop Grindal, 1519–1583. The struggle for a reformed church, London 1979, 233–52. Pastoral training in the form of preachers' conferences, advocated by Grindal in his famous letter of December 1576, pointing out the benefit of preaching (ID., Archbishop Grindal [see above], 239–46), was soon followed up in the form of *lectures by combination* (ID., Lectures by combination: Structures and characteristics of church life in 17th-century England, in: Bulletin of the Institute of Historical Research 48, 1975, 182–213).

[166] NORMAN JONES, The English Reformation. Religion and cultural adaptation, Oxford 2002.

[167] Not considered here is the radical puritanism of the 16th century (DAVID R. COMO, Radical Puritanism, c. 1558–1660, in: The Cambridge Companion to Puritanism, ed.s John Coffey and Paul C. H. Lim, Cambridge 2008, 241–58), overlapping with the moderate puritanism that remained inside the state church, but which because of its position in regard to the state church (PATRICK COLLINSON, Night schools, conventicles and churches: continuities and discontinuities in early Protestant ecclesiology, in: The beginnings of English Protestantism, ed.s Peter Marshall and Alec Ryrie, Cambridge 2002, 209–35) had a different understanding of the clerical office and how it was practiced.

within the state church.[168] What that means can be seen, when one sets the two paradigmatic theologies of the ministry from late Elizabethan time side by side: One of them is represented by Richard Hooker's *Laws of ecclesiastical polity*[169], the other by William Perkins' *Art of prophesying*[170]. Both share the same Protestant idea of the ecclesiastical office. They develop it, however, in different ways, which then leads them in important points – for instance concerning the relationship between Bible and preaching[171] – to opposite positions, revealing their fundamental dissent from one another. The differing understanding of the function of the clergy is reflected in the daily practice of the ministry: Puritan clergy[172] often were better educated; they attended preachers' conferences to improve their sermons; they saw preaching as their main duty. In this way they successfully set out to gain the attention of the citizenry and took freedoms in following ecclesiastical demands. On the other hand, the segment of the clergy, for whom Hooker was writing, was in comparison less well

---

[168] In addition, not considered here is the group of the outwardly adapted clergy, who had taken up office under Henry VIII or Mary and had kept their distance to the Reformation and for decades had refused to adapt to the new pastoral ideal, not, however, being able to stay the course of history (an example belonging to this group is Christopher Trychay: EAMON DUFFY, The voices of Morebath. Reformation and rebellion in an English village, New Haven, London 2001; Duffy also refers to Robert Parkyn und William Shepherd: ibid., 176–7).

[169] RICHARD HOOKER, Of the laws of ecclesiastical polity, vol. 2: Book V, ed. W. Speed Hill, Cambridge (MA) and London 1977, especially sections 76–81 (413–98). Regarding Hooker's theology of the clerical office: WILLIAM P. HAUGAARD, Towards an Anglican doctrine of ministry: Richard Hooker and the Elizabethan Church (AEH 56, 1987, 265–84).

[170] WILLIAM PERKINS, Prophetica, sive de sacra et unica ratione Concionandi Tractatus. Editio secunda auctior & correctior ab Authore facta, Cambridge 1592 (STC 19735; English translation: The Arte of Prophecying: Or A Treatise Concerning the sacred and onely true manner and methode of Preaching. First written in Latine by Master William Perkins: and now faithfully translated into English [...] by Thomas Tuke, London 1607, STC 19735.4).

[171] HOOKER, Laws (note 169), section 22 (87–110). Hooker criticizes the puritan understanding of the sermon (see HORTON DAVIES, The worship of the English Puritans, Westminster 1948, 182–203), where the word of God being proclaimed in the sermon is highly valued, while he sees the danger, that the importance of the reading and listening to the word of God, in which the Holy Spirit is effective and brings salvation, is being relativized.

[172] Concerning education, ongoing training and ministry of puritan clergy, who partly found their station in newly created special structures, loosely connected to the structures of the state church (puritan colleges, informal preachers' seminaries, preaching chantries etc.): COLLINSON, The Elizabethan Puritan movement (note 165), 333–45; PAUL S. SEAVER, The Puritan lectureships. The politics of religious dissent, 1560–1662, Stanford 1970; O'DAY, The English clergy (note 86), 86–104; LAKE, Moderate Puritans and the Elizabethan church (note 147), 35–46, 116–68; MORGAN, Godly learning (note 146), 95–120, 121–41, 220–44, 245–71, 272–300.

educated, and often less well integrated in professional networks. Thus they sought other ways of reaching their parishioners, for instance through liturgy and reading of the Bible. They were found more often in country parishes and were more likely to value the prevailing orders and existing structures. The emerging divide was revealed in the controversies from the 1570s on. In the first puritan manifesto, the *Admonition to the Parliament* of 1572,[173] by the London preachers Thomas Wilcox and John Field, the reality of the Elizabethan state church was set in contrast with the New Testament ideal: In the face of »abuses [...] in the ministerie remaining«[174] the *Admonition* pointed out, that the true church was defined through »preaching of the worde purely, ministering the sacraments sincerely, and ecclesiastical discipline which consisteth in admonition and correction of faults severlie«.[175] Concerning the first of these points, the »ministerie of the worde«, the sermons were correct, but the clerical office did in many ways not meet the demands of the New Testament in regard to training, ordination, activities or financing, especially in regard to the central task of proclaiming the gospel:

»Then the ministers wer preachers: now bare readers. [...] Then, as God gave utterance they preached the worde onely; now they read homilies, articles, injunctions, etc.«[176]

To come closer to the biblical ideal, the church needed a reform of the structures, with most importantly:

»Appoint to every congregation a learned & diligent preacher.«[177]

The alternative was quite clear, in the puritan view:

»Either must we have right ministerie of God, & a right government of his church, according to the scriptures sette up (bothe whiche we lacke) or else there can be no right religion, not yet for contempt thereof can Gods plagues be from us any while differed.«[178]

The dissent between the different, more and more diverging characteristics in regard to the understanding of the ministry and its practical perfor-

---

[173] Puritan manifestoes. A study of the origin of the Puritan revolt with a reprint of the Admonition to the Parliament and kindred documents, 1572, ed.s W. H. Frere and C. E. Douglas, London 1907, 1–55. In the *Second Admonition* (ibid., 79–133) the Puritan understanding of the spiritual office is spelled out more explicitly. The two writings led to a pamphlet war, that also took in consideration the dissent concerning the understanding of the ministry (an overview is given by MILWARD, Religious controversies of the Elizabethan Age [note 96], 29–32).
[174] Puritan manifestoes (note 173), 12.
[175] Ibid., 9.
[176] Ibid., 12.
[177] Ibid.
[178] Ibid., 6.

mance gained momentum in the great issues of debate, where the systemic alternatives were reduced to single symbolic features: liturgical vestments, offices of the church, ordination or church discipline.[179] These controversies and the scattered information about church reality in the second half of the 16th century and the activities of »Puritan« and »Anglican« ideal clergy[180] reveal a spectrum of diversity, which makes generalizing remarks about the successful establishment of a new type of clergy in the reign of Elizabeth questionable.

Such doubts in regard to generalizing remarks do not seem to have been held by the contemporaries, they were not afraid of generalizations or idealizations. In a sermon preached by Joseph Hall on the occasion of a synod of the church province of Canterbury on February 20th, 1623, he said:

»That most generous Spirit [...] has endowed many of you, Fathers and Brothers, most abundantly with gifts. With what gifts of the mind, with what exceptional learning, what powerful eloquence, with what wisdom, what gravity, what graciousness of dignity? It is a great thing that I am about to say, yet I shall say it, without any grandiose flattery – let the envious groan and be broken – the British clergy is the wonder of the world [Stupor mundi Clerus Britannicus]. You will seek in vain to find so many learned theologians, so many eloquent preachers anywhere else under heaven.«[181]

Hall counts among the great preachers of England side by side also Perkins and Hooker, together with an illustrious number of leading churchmen from the time of Edward VI and Elizabeth I. The statement »Stupor mundi Clerus Britannicus« is certainly not true for all of the ca. 9,000 Clergy in the kingdom – and more, if one counts Scotland and Ireland –

---

[179] Concerning the Puritan criticism of the *Ordinal*: BRADSHAW, The Anglican Ordinal (note 93), 37–54.

[180] On the Anglican side, Bernard Gilpin was made into such an ideal clergyman (CHARLES COLLINGWOOD, Memoirs of Bernard Gilpin, parson of Houghton-le-Spring and apostle of the north, London 1884) and on the Puritan side Richard Greenham (ERIC JOSEF CARLSON, »Practical divinity«. Richard Greenham's ministry in Elizabethan England, in: Religion and the English People, 1500–1650. New voices, new perspectives, ed. Eric Josef Carlson, Kirksville 1998, 147–98). The ideal clergyman also was a figure in contemporary literature: NEAL ENSSLE, Patterns of godly life: The ideal parish minister in sixteenth- and seventeenth-century English thought (SCJ 28, 1997, 3–28).

[181] JOSEPH HALL, Columba Noae olivam adferens iactatissimae Christi arcae, London 1624, STC 12648c, 14–5 (translation by Euan Cameron). About this text and its context: PATRICK COLLINSON, The religion of Protestants. The church in English society 1559–1625, Oxford 1982, 92–140. Rightly Collinson remarks: »applied to the generality of the parish clergy his [sc. Hall's] slogan may sound like a joke in poor taste« (ibid., 93), and starting from the tension between *excellence* and *dereliction* in the English clergy at the beginning of the 17th century he gives an account worth reading, which only because of its emphasis lying in the 17th century, has not been listed among the basic literature for this topic in note 87.

nor does it take in account the backwardness, still noticeable at the beginning of the Stuart rule, which existed in contrast to the continental churches reaching a first climax in their confessional culture before the Thirty Years' War, yet it points to the fact that the new type of clergy has become a reality, even here. The *learned theologians* and *eloquent preachers*, of whom Hall speaks, played a central role in England for the Reformation becoming a church, as did all the other clergy who gave their services to the spiritual renewal with more or less enthusiasm. Indeed, the establishment of a new type of clergy was an important step in this becoming a church, because faith needed proclamation of the gospel and this proclamation was ensured by a reforming of the church. The same is true, mutatis mutandis, for Germany. Concerning the new type of clergy, there was basic consensus on both sides of the Channel, even if there were differences in particular points. This topic thus confirms, that Reformation on both sides of the Channel is related and therefore they are rightly described as *Sister Reformations*.[182]

---

[182] English translation of this contribution by Marianne Mühlenberg, Göttingen.

III.

Alte und neue Traditionen

Old and New Traditions

Der Gottesdienst
Von Vision und Kritik zur neuen Gestalt

Dorothea Wendebourg

Von der reformatorischen Bewegung zur Kirche – was bedeutet das Generalthema unserer Tagung für das Gebiet des Gottesdienstes? Es bedeutet, den Weg nachzuverfolgen, der von der Kritik am überlieferten Gottesdienst, wie sie seit der Frühzeit der Reformation laut wurde, bis zur Etablierung neuer liturgischer Ordnungen führte. War doch überall, in allen reformatorischen Strömungen, der Umbau des Gottesdienstes ein zentrales Anliegen der Reformation und eine entscheidende, wenn nicht die entscheidende Maßnahme bei ihrer Institutionalisierung. Denn ungeachtet der mannigfachen Unterschiede, die es auch an diesem Punkt unter ihnen gab, kamen sämtliche Reformatoren und reformatorischen Gruppen in dem Urteil überein, daß das Herzstück des kirchlichen Lebens, der überlieferte Gottesdienst, mit dem sie groß geworden waren und den viele unter ihnen selbst als Amtsträger gefeiert hatten, theologisch und praktisch in wesentlichen Punkten falsch sei. Und so gehörte die Umbildung der Liturgie überall zu den unverzichtbaren Schritten der Reformation. Eine Umbildung, an deren Anfang Visionen, aus dem Neuen Testament gespeiste Visionen, vom richtigen Gottesdienst standen und dessen Endpunkt die Einführung neuer liturgischer Ordnungen war. Das galt diesseits ebenso wie jenseits des Ärmelkanals.

Bevor wir uns diesem Vorgang hier und dort zuwenden, muß allerdings gefragt werden: Ist der Ausgangspunkt jeweils derselbe? Hatte man im Heiligen Römischen Reich und in England dieselbe Liturgie vor Augen, kritisierte und reformierte man denselben Gottesdienst?[1]

---

[1] Ich beschränke mich hier auf die Messe und die aus ihr herausgewachsenen Formen, d.h., es werden weder Stundengebete noch Kasualien behandelt.

1. Der spätmittelalterliche Ausgangspunkt

Die vorreformatorische lateinische Kirche besaß keine einheitliche Liturgie. Der offizielle Geltungsradius einer liturgischen Ordnung war, sieht man von den Orden ab, das Bistum. Das schloß allerdings nicht aus, daß eine Diözese die Ordnung einer anderen übernahm. Eben dies geschah in großem Stil in England. Weite Teile des Landes, ja auch von Irland und Wales übernahmen im Laufe des 15. und frühen 16. Jahrhunderts das liturgische Regelwerk von Salisbury, den sog. *Sarum Usus* mit seinen Formularen für die Messe und die Stundengebete, seiner Leseordnung, seinem Kalender u.a.m.[2] Das heißt, in England gab es schon vor der Reformation ein höheres Maß an liturgischer Einheitlichkeit als im Heiligen Römischen Reich.

Freilich ist diese Differenz nicht überzubewerten. Denn die liturgische Ordnung von Sarum war alles in allem eine – besonders prächtige – Spielart der römischen Tradition.[3] Und das galt nicht nur ebenso für die übrigen Riten des spätmittelalterlichen Englands, sondern auch für die liturgischen Ordnungen der Diözesen im Reich. D.h., wenngleich das Spätmittelalter keine Einheitsliturgie kannte, waren doch die grundlegenden Elemente diesseits und jenseits des Kanals dieselben: die Messe als der zentrale Gottesdienst, der von allen Gliedern der Kirche mindestens einmal wöchentlich zu besuchen war, das Stundengebet als mehrmals täglich zu leistender verpflichtender Dienst religiöser Gemeinschaften und Amtsträger und, wo gegeben, als fakultative Gelegenheit für die übrigen Christen; beides eingepaßt in einen zeitlichen Rhythmus, der einerseits vom die Geschichte Jesu Christi bis zur Aussendung des Heiligen Geistes nachzeichnenden Kirchenjahr und andererseits vom Heiligenkalender bestimmt war. Konkret begegneten jene Grundelemente in verschiedenen Varianten, insbesondere die unaufhörlich zelebrierte Messe: völlig still, mit hörbar gesprochenen Anteilen, mit Gesang; ohne und mit Gemeindepräsenz, ohne und mit Kommunion, ohne und mit Predigt. Das alles gab es im Reich wie in England, wobei wir über das gottesdienstliche Programm von Kathedralen, Stiften und Klöstern besser im Bilde sind als über das,

---

[2] Dabei gab es im Einzelnen durchaus Variationen. Vgl. zu Entwicklung und Verbreitung wie auch zu den Variationen des *Sarum Usus*: RICHARD W. PFAFF, The Liturgy in Medieval England, Cambridge 2009, Kap. 10–13. Freilich erlaubte – wie auch in den deutschen Diözesen – erst der Buchdruck kontrollierte Einheitlichkeit (DERS., New Liturgical Feasts in Later Medieval England, Oxford 1970, 8).

[3] »[I]n essence the Sarum Rite was a ›local medieval modification of the Roman rite in use at the cathedral church of Salisbury‹« (D. M. HOPE, The Medieval Western Rite, in: The Study of Liturgy, hg. v. Cheslyn Jones, Geoffrey Wainwright u. Edward Yarnold, London ⁵1980, 220–248, 236; vgl. 237 zur Pracht dieser Liturgie).

was sich in kleinen Städten und Dörfern abspielte, wo die große Masse der Bevölkerung lebte[4] – für die Zeit vom 15. Jahrhundert an läßt uns der Quellenbestand aber auch hier nicht einfach im Dunkeln tappen.[5]

Zwei Elemente des spätmittelalterlichen gottesdienstlichen Tableaus müssen wegen ihrer Bedeutung für die liturgischen Entwicklungen in der Reformation noch eigens angesprochen werden. Es handelt sich um gottesdienstliche Veranstaltungen, die aus der Messe herausgewachsen waren, die Kommunionfeier und den Predigtgottesdienst – auch dies beides gab es in England wie im Reich. Die Kommunionfeier, daraus entstanden, daß innerhalb der Messe die Gemeinde kaum kommunizierte, aber wenigstens einmal im Jahr zu kommunizieren hatte,[6] umfaßte die drei Bestandteile Offene Schuld, Distribution in einer Messe konsekrierter Hostien[7] und privates Dankgebet.[8] In manchen Gemeinden gingen Abendmahlsansprachen voraus, hier und dort gab es begleitende lateinische Kommuniongesänge eines Chores.[9]

Was die Predigt betraf, so lief zwar die weit überwiegende Zahl der Messen ohne sie ab und predigten die meisten Priester nicht.[10] Gleichwohl wurde viel gepredigt,[11] und das in unterschiedlichen liturgischen Zusam-

---

[4] ANDREAS ODENTHAL, Pfarrlicher Gottesdienst vom Mittelalter zur Frühen Neuzeit. Eine Problemskizze aus liturgiewissenschaftlicher Perspektive (in: DERS., Liturgie vom Frühen Mittelalter zum Zeitalter der Konfessionalisierung. Studien zur Geschichte des Gottesdienstes, Tübingen 2011, 159–206, hier: 161).

[5] ODENTHAL, Pfarrlicher Gottesdienst (s. Anm. 4), weist für den deutschen Sprachraum unter anderem auf Pfarrbücher und Mesnerbücher hin. Zu ersteren vgl. auch MARCO BERNINI, Die Feier des Osterfestkreises im Ingolstädter Pfarrbuch des Johannes Eck, Münster 2016, Kap. A 4 (Pfarrbücher als liturgiehistorische Quellen). Für England sind u.a. die Berichte der Kirchenpfleger (churchwardens' accounts) zu nennen (dazu KATHERINE L. FRENCH, The People of the Parish. Community Life in a Late Medieval English Diocese, Philadelphia 2001, Kap. 2).

[6] S. dazu PETER BROWE, Die Pflichtkommunion im Mittelalter, Münster 1940, 43–45.

[7] Daneben wurde oft auch Spülwein, der zur Reinigung des Kelches nach der beide Gestalten umfassenden Kommunion des Priesters und zur Säuberung des Mundes nach der Brotkommunion der Gemeinde dienende Wein, gereicht, hier und da auch der Wein oder das Wasser, mit dem der Priester nach dem Opfer die Ablution seiner Finger vorgenommen hatte (MATTHIAS FIGEL, Der reformatorische Predigtgottesdienst, Epfendorf 2013, 47 mit Anm. 159; vgl. JOSEPH ANDREAS JUNGMANN, Missarum Sollemnia. Eine genetische Erklärung der römischen Messe, Bd. 2, Wien ²1949, 499–508).

[8] FIGEL (s. Anm. 7), 44–48. Ausführlich: PETER BROWE, Mittelalterliche Kommunionriten (Jahrbuch für Liturgiewissenschaft 15, 1935, 23–66).

[9] A.a.O., 57–61. Muttersprachliche geistliche Gesänge wurden, anders als im Zusammenhang der Predigt (s.u.), in der Kommunionandacht nicht gesungen (JOHANNES JANOTA, Studien zu Funktion und Typus des deutschen geistlichen Liedes im Mittelalter, München 1968, 61).

[10] Vgl. RUDOLF CRUEL, Geschichte der deutschen Predigt im Mittelalter, Detmold 1879, 639: Bei »der Menge der damaligen Geistlichen und Gottesdienste [...] ist nun freilich zu constatiren, daß die Predigt nur einen Bruchteil des Klerus beschäftigte und einen untergeordneten Platz im Cultus einnahm.«

menhängen. Zum einen gehörte die Predigt offiziell zu den Aufgaben des Pfarrers und war Teil der sonntäglichen Pfarrmesse – im Reich ein vorgeschriebener, allerdings keineswegs immer realisierter Teil,[12] in England rechtlich nicht verpflichtend, aber erwünscht.[13] Vorgeschrieben war hier hingegen, der zweite Zusammenhang, der *quarter sermon*, d.h. eine Predigt pro Vierteljahr, deren Gegenstand Stücke des Katechismus, die guten Werke und die Sakramente waren,[14] nachdrücklich empfohlen wurden darüber hinaus wöchentlich mehrere auf den Ton der Buße gestimmte Fastenpredigten während der Advents- und Passionszeit;[15] beide, *quarter sermons* wie Fastenpredigten, lagen überwiegend in der Hand von Mendikanten. Die Fastenpredigten waren Praxis auch im Reich.[16] Schließlich gab es noch eine dritte Art, die Predigt aus besonderen Anlässen. Im Reich waren die wichtigsten dieser Anlässe der Auftritt durchreisender großer Bußprediger, meist aus den Mendikantenorden, der Ablaß und die Wallfahrt, vielfach erklangen die Predigten vor großen Massen im Freien, womöglich von einer Kanzel außen an einer Kirchenwand.[17] Solche Freiluftpredigten hielt man auch in England, ja, hier wurden sie zu regelmäßigen Veranstaltungen, für die man in vielen Städten freistehende bühnenähnliche Kanzeln mit einem Kreuz als Bekrönung mauerte;[18] am bekanntesten sind die Auftritte gefeierter Prediger auf der Freiluftkanzel bei St. Paul's in London, St. Paul's Cross, um die sich oft Tausende von Hörern einschließlich des politischen Establishments bis hin zum Hof versammelten.[19] Etwas Vergleichbares zu diesen Predigten von St. Paul's Cross, die

---

[11] Obwohl die Predigt »einen untergeordneten Platz im Cultus einnahm« (s. vorige Anm.), muß doch »*die Annahme, daß während der beiden letzten Jahrhunderte vor der Reformation, im Ganzen genommen, weniger gepredigt worden sei als heutzutage,* [...] *als ein unhaltbares Vorurtheil aufgegeben werden.* Etwas andres freilich ist es, was und in welcher Weise gepredigt wurde« (a.a.O., 652, Kursive im Original gesperrt). Dieser Befund gilt allerdings nur für die Städte, wo »beinahe zuviel gepredigt wurde, [...] während es auf dem Lande [...] an Predigern fehlte« (MICHAEL MENZEL, Predigt und Predigtorganisation im Mittelalter, in: HJ 111, 1991, 337–384, hier: 377).

[12] FIGEL (s. Anm. 7), 59, 67f.

[13] SUSAN WABUDA, Preaching During the English Reformation, Cambridge 2002, 33. Im Sarum Pontificale hieß es: »Fiat sermo, si placuerit« (G. R. OWST, Preaching in Medieval England, Cambridge 1926, 145, Anm. 5).

[14] A.a.O., 145f.; WABUDA (s. Anm. 13), 34–37.

[15] OWST (s. Anm. 13), 146f. Sie sollten täglich oder wenigstens dreimal in der Woche gehalten werden.

[16] CRUEL (s. Anm. 10), § 45; FIGEL (s. Anm. 7), 97. Predigttage waren Montag, Mittwoch und Freitag.

[17] ELLEN-SENTA ALTENLOH, Sakrale Außenkanzeln in Europa von der Romanik bis zur Gegenwart, Bonn 1985, 11f., 16.

[18] OWST (s. Anm. 13), 148, 195–199, 209–214; WABUDA, Preaching (s. Anm. 13), 40–48.

[19] A.a.O., 41–47. Speziell zu St. Paul's Cross: St. Paul's Cross and the Culture of

eine wichtige Rolle für Reformation und Gegenreformation in England spielen sollten,[20] gab es im Reich nicht.[21]

Was die Predigt zu einem besonderen liturgischen Element und zum Ausgangspunkt einer eigenen liturgischen Entwicklung machte, war ihre Sprache. Sie erklang in der Volkssprache[22] und fiel so, wenn sie Teil der Messe war, als Fremdkörper aus ihrem liturgischen Rahmen heraus.[23] Weitere volkssprachliche Elemente wie Katechismusstücke, Abkündigungen und Fürbitten[24] an sich ziehend, wurde die Predigt zum Nucleus eines eigenen vernikularen Blocks, des Pronaos oder Prone.[25] Dieser Block gehörte zur Pfarrmesse immer dazu, freilich ging die Predigt selbst darin oft verloren.[26] Galt das alles *mutatis mutandis* auf beiden Seiten des Kanals, so

---

Persuasion in England, 1520–1640, hg. v. Torrance Kirby u. P. G. Stanwood, Leiden u. Boston 2014.

[20] Hier fanden, begleitet eben von Predigten, auch spektakuläre Verbrennungen von Büchern und Ketzern oder Widerrufe coram publico statt.

[21] Kirby sieht in der hier geübten öffentlichen »culture of persuasion« eine Wurzel der modernen politischen Tradition Englands, die eine Tradition der Debatten im *public space* sei (TORRANCE KIRBY, The Public Sermon: Pauls's Cross and the culture of persuasion in England, 1534–1570, in: Renaissance and Reformation Rev. 31, 2008, 3–19).

[22] JANOTA (s. Anm. 9), 70: »Als nichtliturgisch geregelter Gottesdienst unterlag die Predigt nicht dem Gebot der lateinischen Liturgiesprache.«

[23] In den spätmittelalterlichen Meßbüchern wird die Predigt nicht genannt, so wie dort überhaupt »[v]om Wortgottesdienst [...] kaum etwas« vorkommt (so DOMINIK DASCHNER, Die gedruckten Meßbücher Süddeutschlands bis zur Übernahme des Missale Romanum Pius' V. [1570], Frankfurt a. M. 1995, 86, im Blick auf die süddeutschen gedruckten Meßbücher bis 1570, aber über Süddeutschland hinaus verallgemeinerbar). Bezeichnenderweise konnte sie an unterschiedlichen Orten der Messe untergebracht werden, in England wohl »between creed and offertory, or else after the latter« (OWST [s. Anm. 13], 144f.), im Reich nach Evangelium, Glaubensbekenntnis, Offertorium oder Sanctus (JANOTA [s. Anm. 9], 68f.; FIGEL [s. Anm. 7], 98) oder sogar so, daß die Messe, von einem anderen als dem Prediger zelebriert, während der Predigt still weiterlief (JANOTA [s. Anm. 9], 68). Sie konnte auch aus der Messe heraus auf die Zeit nach dem »Sunday dinner« (OWST, 145), *post prandium*, »nach Imbis« gelegt werden, im Reich allerdings nur an Festtagen, damit sie die Feiern des Vormittags nicht störte (a.a.O., 99f.). Gemeint ist hier die eigentlich in die Pfarrmesse gehörige, in der Verantwortung des Pfarrers liegende Pfarrpredigt, nicht die ohnehin außerhalb der Messe stattfindende Predigt von Mendikanten und Prädikanten (dazu s.u.).

[24] Die in England sog. *Bidding of the Beeds* (hierzu: FRANK EDWARD BRIGHTMAN, The English Rite: being a Synopsis of the Sources and Revisions of the Book of Common Prayer, Bd. 1, London ²1921, 1020–1037; WABUDA, Preaching [s. Anm. 13], 51–53).

[25] Zum Pronaos mit seinen »Predigtannexen« im Reich vgl. CRUEL (s. Anm. 10), 220–232 (ohne den Begriff); FIGEL (s. Anm. 7), 105, 112–142; zur Herausbildung dieses Blocks, und das auch außerhalb des Reiches, siehe JOSEPH ANDREAS JUNGMANN, Missarum Sollemnia. Eine genetische Erklärung der römischen Messe, Bd. 1, Wien ²1949, 605–610. Zum Prone in England: BRIGHTMAN, The English Rite, Bd. 1 (s. Anm. 18), 1038f.; WABUDA, Preaching (s. Anm. 13), 51–55.

[26] FIGEL (s. Anm. 7), 143. So ergab sich eine von den Abkündigungen angeführte »Predigtliturgie ohne [...] Predigt« (zu dieser 143–149). D.h., die Predigt war »zur Variablen degradiert« (a.a.O., 149), und tatsächlich »wurde *intra missam* nur noch äußerst

gab es doch im Reich eine Entwicklung, die in England nicht zu verzeichnen ist: Die Gemeinde, von den liturgischen Gesängen der Messe ausgeschlossen, ergriff im Pronaos – illegalerweise – die Gelegenheit, einleitende oder antwortende Liedverse[27] in ihrer Sprache, also auf Deutsch, zu singen.[28]

War die Predigt in der Messe ein Fremdkörper, stand sie als Fastenpredigt, vielleicht auch als *quarter sermon* und auf jeden Fall als Freiluftpredigt auf eigenen liturgischen Füßen. D.h. nicht, sie hätte sich auf die Rede des predigenden Priesters beschränkt; vielmehr kamen zur Predigt Gebete hinzu, vielleicht auch ein Segen, so daß sich ein regelrechter Predigtgottesdienst ergab. In seinem Rahmen konnten im Reich auch die Gemeinden sehr viel freier auf Deutsch singen als im Predigtblock innerhalb der Messe. Der genaue Ablauf der Predigtgottesdienste, die wohl[29] bereits vom 13. Jahrhundert an von Mendikanten gehalten wurden, scheint in England und im größten Teil des Reiches variabel gewesen zu sein. Im *größten* Teil des Reiches – in einem Teil nämlich sah es anders aus, in den Städten Südwestdeutschlands, ebenso in denen der Schweiz. Hier wurde die Predigt zusammen mit weiteren Elementen, vor allem dem Allgemeinen Kirchengebet, zu einem eigenen volkssprachlichen Gottesdienst mit fester Struktur, dem sog. Prädikantengottesdienst,[30] welcher sich der im

---

selten [gepredigt]« (a.a.O., 170). Wenn in zeitgenössischen Quellen von »Predigt« gesprochen wird, ist oft die gesamte Predigtliturgie gemeint, ohne daß die Predigt im eigentlichen Sinne eingeschlossen sein muß (so z.B. im Pfarrbuch des Hilpoltsteiner Pfarrers Stephan May: JOHANN GÖTZ, Das Pfarrbuch des Stephan May in Hilpoltstein vom Jahre 1511. Ein Beitrag zum Verständnis der kirchlichen Verhältnisse am Vorabende der Reformation, Münster 1926).

[27] Freilich »bestand solcher Kirchengesang jedesmal nur aus einer kurzen Strophe, beschränkte sich auf wenige Lieder und war nicht überall Sitte« (CRUEL [s. Anm. 10], 232).

[28] JANOTA (s. Anm. 9), 44, 70–76; FIGEL (s. Anm. 7), 173–179. Solcher Gemeindegesang wurde im 15. und 16. Jahrhundert immer wieder, z.B. vom Konstanzer und Basler Konzil, verboten (vgl. DOROTHEA WENDEBOURG, Reformation und Gottesdienst, in: ZThK 113, 2016, 323–365, Anm. 141; JANOTA [s. Anm. 9], 46). Darin spiegelt sich, daß er zumindest in bestimmten Gegenden zeitweise sehr beliebt gewesen sein muß, doch scheint der Brauch im Laufe des 15. Jahrhunderts zurückgegangen zu sein (CRUEL [s. Anm. 10], 232).

[29] Ganz sicher ist das nicht, denn »[e]s läßt sich nicht exakt datieren, seit wann es den mittelalterlichen Predigtgottesdienst außerhalb der Messe gibt« (EBERHARD WINKLER, Der Predigtgottesdienst, in: Handbuch der Liturgik, hg. v. Hans-Christoph Schmidt-Lauber u. Karl-Heinrich Bieritz, Leipzig u. Göttingen ²1995, 248–270, hier: 254). Jedenfalls geht er auf die Predigttätigkeit der Bettelorden zurück.

[30] Zu ihm vgl. FIGEL (s. Anm. 7), 156–170. Zur Verbreitung der städtischen Prädikaturen, die, beginnend mit Nürnberg, in der Zeit vom späten 14. bis zum Beginn des 16. Jahrhunderts »in nahezu jeder südwestdeutschen Stadt« gestiftet wurden, a.a.O., 189. Speziell zu Nürnberg vgl. KARL SCHLEMMER, Gottesdienst und Frömmigkeit in der Reichsstadt Nürnberg am Vorabend der Reformation, Würzburg 1980, 255–260.

späten Mittelalter neben das Predigtwesen der Bettelorden tretenden Stiftung[31] von Predigtpfründen oder Prädikaturen an Kathedralen und vor allem an Pfarrkirchen verdankte.[32] Predigtpfründen gab es auch im übrigen Reich sowie in England (preaching chantries).[33] Hier wie dort führten sie dazu, daß mehr gepredigt wurde, auch über die *quarter sermons* und die Fastenpredigten hinaus, im Reich am Sonntag früh zwischen den Messen oder nachmittags.[34] Aber nirgendwo gab es so viele Predigtstiftungen wie eben in Südwestdeutschland und der Schweiz, und vor allem gewannen – worauf es hier ankommt – nirgendwo die Predigtgottesdienste eine solche

---

[31] Die Stifter waren im Südwesten meist Bürger. Es gab aber auch Prädikaturstiftungen durch Bischöfe und durch Pfarrer (vgl. u. Anm. 35). Die große Zahl dieser Stiftungen, bei denen sich der Wunsch nach seelenheilfördernder Leistung eines guten Werkes mit dem Interesse an regelmäßiger anspruchsvoller Predigt verband, änderte freilich an den Prioritäten bezüglich des kirchlichen Personals und der gottesdienstlichen Formen nichts Grundsätzliches, wenn man die Zahlenverhältnisse betrachtet: In Nürnberg mit seiner frühen und großen Prädikantentradition waren an der Lorenzkirche neben dem Pfarrer noch 22 für die Messe zuständige Priester, aber nur ein Prädikant tätig (ALBERT GÜMBEL, Das Mesnerpflichtbuch von St. Lorenz in Nürnberg vom Jahre 1483, München 1928, 11), in Heilbronn ein Pfarrer und 28 messelesende Kapläne, in Ulm ein Pfarrer und 57 messelesende Kapläne jeweils neben einem Prädikanten, wobei die Masse der pfründelosen Altaristen noch gar nicht mitgezählt ist (Lesebuch zur Geschichte der evangelischen Landeskirche in Württemberg, Bd. 1: Neue Gestalt für das bleibende Wort im 16. Jahrhundert, bearb. v. Gerhard Schäfer, Stuttgart 1992, 43). So lagen die Stiftungen von Messen denn auch weit vor denen von Prädikaturen. Das galt gleichermaßen im spätmittelalterlichen England (WABUDA, Preaching [s. Anm. 13], 166).

[32] Mit der Errichtung bepfründeter Predigerstellen für Weltgeistliche war nach der in der Karolingerzeit durchgesetzten episkopalen Predigt, in den Parochien durch Pfarrer als Vertreter des Bischofs wahrzunehmen, als Normgestalt und nach der im 13. Jahrhundert hinzugekommenen und schnell in den Vordergrund getretenen diözesen- und parochieunabhängigen Predigt der Mendikanten die dritte Stufe in der Entwicklung der Predigtorganisation der mittelalterlichen Kirche erreicht, wobei idealerweise jede Stufe als Ergänzung der anderen fungieren sollte. Vgl. zu dieser Entwicklung Menzel (s. Anm. 11).

[33] Einen Überblick über Prädikaturen im Reich gibt FIGEL (s. Anm. 7), 189–199. Freilich ließen sich noch mehr Prädikaturen außerhalb des oberdeutschen Raumes aufzählen, als Figel zusammengetragen hat (a.a.O., 198), z.B. zwei von Pfarrern gestiftete im sächsischen Zwickau, deren eine zeitweise Thomas Müntzer wahrnahm (SIEGFRIED BRÄUER u. GÜNTER VOGLER, Thomas Müntzer. Neu Ordnung machen in der Welt. Eine Biographie, Gütersloh 2016, 94f.). Zu den *preaching chantries* in England: WABUDA, Preaching (s. Anm. 13), 21–23, 166–168. Hier sollten später die Puritaner mit der Stiftung von *lectureships* in anderem, innerprotestantischem Kontext den städtischen Prädikaturstiftungen Südwestdeutschlands vergleichbare bürgerliche Aktivitäten entfalten, nämlich im Kampf gegen die elisabethanische und Stuartsche Staatskirche (PAUL S. SEAVER, The Puritan Lectureships: The Politics of Religious Dissent 1560–1662, Stanford 1970).

[34] Das waren die Predigtzeiten der Mendikanten, die auch den Prädikanten zugewiesen wurden (BERNHARD NEIDIGER, Wortgottesdienst vor der Reformation. Die Stiftung eigener Predigtpfründen für Weltprediger im späten Mittelalter, in: Rhein. Vierteljahrsblätter 66, 2002, 142–189, hier: 148).

institutionelle Festigkeit wie in den auf Stiftungen zurückgehenden Prädikantengottesdiensten.[35]

2. Die Reformation

2.1. Heiliges Römischen Reich

Am Anfang standen in Deutschland die Bilder von der wahren, evangeliumsgemäßen Messe, wie sie Martin Luther in seinen Abendmahlssermonen von 1519 und 1520, dem *Sermon von dem hochwürdigen Sakrament des heiligen wahren Leichnams Christi und von den Bruderschaften* sowie *Sermon von dem neuen Testament, das heißt von der heiligen Messe*, entwarf, und die große systematisch-theologische Attacke in seinem sakramententheologischen Traktat *De Captivitate babylonica praeludium*.[36] Diese Schriften hatten weitreichende liturgische Implikationen: Die Orientierung an der Einsetzung des Abendmahls widersprach der Kommunion *sub una specie*, sein Gemeinschaftscharakter verbot die Feier ohne Gemeinde, das Verständnis der Sakramente als zeichenhafter Heilsverkündigung forderte die Hörbarkeit und Verstehbarkeit der Einsetzungsworte, die Bestimmung des Abendmahls als Selbstmitteilung Jesu Christ an die Gemeinde schloß alle Worte und Gesten aus, die vom Meßopfergedanken bestimmt waren. Daß die Predigt ein zentrales Element der Liturgie, ja, wie im Unterschied zum Spätmittelalter mit seinem großen Predigteifer unterstrichen wurde, im Gottesdienst unverzichtbar sei, betonte Luther ohnehin – sie sei, neben dem Gebet, das wichtigste Element des Gottes-

---

[35] Dieser Sachverhalt hängt möglicherweise mit einer Differenz unter den Prädikaturenlandschaften im Reich zusammen, die NEIDIGER, Wortgottesdienst vor der Reformation (s. Anm. 34), herausgearbeitet. Danach unterschieden sich diese Landschaften u.a. dadurch, daß in Südwestdeutschland vor allem Bürger Prädikaturen stifteten und über die Besetzung wachten, während in anderen Gegenden wie Sachsen, Schlesien und Böhmen, ausgehend von amtskirchlicher Initiative (152), vor allem Pfarrer Prediger anstellten (164f.). Das emanzipative Moment, daß in der Stiftung und Besetzung durch Bürger lag, mag dazu beigetragen haben, daß sich die Prädikantengottesdienste des Südwestens zu einer dauerhaften von der Messe emanzipierten liturgischen Einheit entwickelten, während die Predigtgottesdienste in anderen Gegenden stärker im Dunstkreis der Messe blieben, die in der Hand der Pfarrer lag. Mit dieser Differenz steht wohl auch in Zusammenhang, daß, wie es scheint, die Meßverpflichtungen der Prädikanten (vgl. u. 382) in Südwestdeutschland geringer waren als in jenen Gegenden des mittel-östlichen Reiches. Nur nebenbei sei darauf hingewiesen, daß es in manchen Gebieten, etwa in Westdeutschland, gar nicht zu Prädikaturstiftungen an Pfarrkirchen kam, und das vor allem deshalb, weil hier die älteren Predigtaktivitäten der Bettelorden hinreichten (172–177).

[36] Die beiden Abendmahlssermone in WA 2,742–758 und WA 6,353–378, *De captivitate* in WA 6,497–573.

dienstes. Und sie hatte, ebenfalls im Unterschied zum Spätmittelalter, Predigt über biblische Texte zu sein.[37]

Vorstellungen davon, wie der Gottesdienst sein sollte, und Kritik an dem Gottesdienst, der nicht so ist, wie er sein sollte, sind noch keine neue liturgische Ordnung. Luther selbst ging hier bekanntlich langsam voran, legte erst 1523 und 1525/26 konkrete Vorschläge für Stundengebet, Kirchenjahr und Messe vor, die schließlich zu territoriumsweiter Etablierung einer neuen Ordnung führten. Auch andernorts war es von der Kritik zur kirchenamtlichen Reform ein jahrelanger Weg. Und währenddessen stellt sich für die Beteiligten die – ihr Gewissen belastende – Frage, wie sie mit der Realität in ihren Augen evangeliumswidriger Gottesdienste umgehen sollten. Mußten die sog. Laien sich den liturgischen *status quo* gefallen lassen? Hatten sie nicht ein Recht auf regelmäßige und evangeliumsgemäße Predigten? Auf Gottesdienste, die sie verstanden, auf Abendmahlsfeiern, die auf ihre Speisung hinausliefen und in denen sie ebenso wie und dasselbe wie die Priester zu essen und zu trinken bekamen? Störungen von Predigten und Messen, die vielerorts stattfanden,[38] waren handgreiflicher Ausdruck der Ungeduld,[39] von Bürgern eingereichte Petitionen zeigen konkrete Forderungen nach gottesdienstlicher Reform, die an der »Basis« erhoben wurden.[40]

Dem Wunsch nach evangelischen Predigten standen in weiten Teilen des Reiches die geringsten institutionellen Hindernisse entgegen. Die Predigt war ein liturgisch so flexibles, andererseits hinreichend institutionalisiertes Element des Gottesdienstes, daß evangelische Predigten ohne Schwierigkeiten einen liturgischen Ort fanden, vorausgesetzt, solche Predigten wurden nicht von der kirchlichen oder politischen Obrigkeit effizient unterbunden und man konnte einen evangelischen Prediger gewin-

---

[37] Z.B. WA 6,373,11. Zwei Jahre später nachdrücklich WA 12,35,19–21. Neben der Bibel konnte der Katechismus, der selbst als Zusammenfassung der biblischen Botschaft galt, Grundlage der Predigt sein.

[38] Beispiele bei THOMAS KAUFMANN, Geschichte der Reformation. Frankfurt u. Leipzig 2009, 327–329; NATALIE KRENTZ, Ritualwandel und Deutungshoheit. Die frühe Reformation in der Residenzstadt Wittenberg (1500–1533), Tübingen 2014, 144–151; BERND MOELLER, Die Reformation in Göttingen (in: DERS., Die Reformation und das Mittelalter. Kirchenhistorische Aufsätze. Göttingen 1991, 196–211, 328–331, hier: 196f.).

[39] Womit nicht gesagt sein soll, daß die von der Reformation angestoßene Erwartung eines anderen Gottesdienstes und die darin implizierte Kritik am tatsächlichen der einzige Grund für solche Störungen war. Es entluden sich darin auch ältere Spannungen zwischen Bürgern und Kirchenvertretern. Das zeigt z.B. KRENTZ (s. Anm. 38), Kap. 1.

[40] Exemplarisch die Petition der Wittenberger Bürger vom 10. Dezember 1525, in der sie die freie Predigt, die Kommunion unter beiden Gestalten auch für die Gemeinde, die Abschaffung der gemeindelosen Messen und dazu die Schließung von Kneipen und Bordellen forderten (HEINZ SCHEIBLE, Melanchthon. Vermittler der Reformation, München 2016, 82).

nen. Anders stand es mit dem Ritus der Messe, der jedenfalls in seinem
Kernbereich, der Opferfeier, sakrosankt und strafbewehrt feststand und
dessen Reform nicht leicht und ohne Widerstand zu bewerkstelligen war.
Was sollten evangelisch gesonnene Gemeinden und Priester tun, solange
hier die Reformen ausblieben?

Zunächst zu den Gemeinden. Ein Ausweg war, den evangeliumswidrigen Ausschluß von der Kommunion als vorläufige Geduldsprobe zu er-
tragen: Weil die gegenwärtige Messe in vieler Hinsicht, nicht zuletzt wegen
der Feier meist ohne Gemeindekommunion und des Kelchentzugs,[41]

»widerwertig der natur / und eigenschafft des sacraments / erkannt wirt [...], müssen die fromen Christen / als die armen gefangen / untter den unmilten tyrannen /
sich gedulden / und des teglichen hymelischen brots / also hungerig geraten [ent-
raten]«,

heißt es zum Beispiel bei dem Jenaer Pfarrer Martin Reinhart.[42] Doch gab
es einen geistlichen Ausgleich, von dem bereits Augustin gesprochen hatte
und der nun nachdrücklich herausgestellt wurde: die Maxime *crede et
manducasti*.[43] So rät Urbanus Rhegius evangelischen Teilnehmern an der
unhörbaren und kommunionlosen Messe:

»es ist unrecht das man sie [sc. die Abendmahlsworte Christi] verbirgt / und haim-
lich [leise] spricht / Wilt du recht meß hören / gedenck das hie ain speyß und
tranck ist / darumb müst du essen und trincken / oder dein meßhören ist nichts.
[...] Wann man dir das Sacrament nit gibt / du hörest allain meß / So nimm die wort
des testaments zů hertzen / und gedenck allda, was dein got und herr Jesus Christus für dich gethon hat [...]. Gelaub den worten und dem zaichen / so erlangst du
das verhaissen erbgůt / und geest zu gottes tisch gaistlich.«[44]

Es gab allerdings noch einen radikaleren Rat, den vollständigen Meßbe-
suchsverzicht: Da nicht nur die Kommunion, sondern »die Meß ganz von
der ordnung Christi gewendt« sei, wäre es »weger [besser] ain yeder from-
mer Christ kem nymmer zů der meß«.[45] Doch hätten die meisten ange-

---

[41] Dadurch, daß »das gemein christenvolck / gar ereussert [ist] / vom tisch gottis / das
man nit mehr / dann ain mal im iar / unter einer gstalt / den christen menschen zů lest«
(REINHART [s. folgende Anm.], A iijʳ).

[42] Unterrichte wie sich ein fromer Christ / bey den papistischen Messen / so ytzt
noch viel gehalten werden (wenn er sich nit mit gůtm fug absondern kan) halten sol das
er sich nit vorsunde / und die zeyt unütz vorlier. Item ein Christliche betrachtung so du
zů dem heyligen Sacrament wilt gehn, Jena 1524 (Vorwort unterzeichnet von Martin
Reinhart, der hier weitgehend die unten zu Anm. 48 genannte Schrift von Jakob Strauß
ausschreibt), A iijʳ.

[43] Z.B. bei LUTHER, De captivitate Babylonica: WA 6,518,19–23.

[44] URBANUS RHEGIUS, Ain kurtze erklärung etlicher leüffiger puncten / aim yeden
Christen nutz und nöt / zů rechten verstand der hailigen geschrifft / zů dienst, Augsburg
1523, C 4ᵛ–C 5ʳ. Gebete, mit denen der Teilnehmer an der Messe solches geistliche Essen
erreichen kann, bietet Rhegius in seinem unten Anm. 48 genannten Andachtsbüchlein.

[45] Jakob Strauß in dem zu Anm. 48 genannten *Underricht*, C 4ʳ.

sichts des bestehenen Meßzwangs dazu nicht den Mut.[46] Immerhin gab es auch für die Notlage unumgänglicher Präsenz bei dem evangeliumswidrigen Ritual eine Lösung, und auch sie besaß schon ältere Wurzeln: die persönliche geistliche Parallelhandlung. Hatten bereits im Mittelalter Gemeindeglieder, während am Altar die weitgehend unhörbare und ihnen meist ohnehin nicht verständliche Meßliturgie zelebriert wurde, für sich geistliche Betrachtungen angestellt und Gebete gesprochen,[47] so konnte diese Praxis jetzt reformatorisch gefüllt werden: Eigene Andachtsbücher brachten den Gläubigen vor Augen, wovon hier anstelle des falschen Ritus eigentlich gehandelt werden müßte, so daß sie darüber meditieren, entsprechend beten und so zum geistlichen Essen kommen konnten:

»Wenn du [...] zu der Meß kommst / so ist dir not / das du auff den manigfaltigen mißbrauch [...] kain auffmercken habest. Aber nym dir ain übung im glauben für / das du von deinem got und herren Christo gaistlich erreichen mögest / das dir von menschlicher unmitigkait sacramentlichen entzogen ist«,

heißt es in dem *Underricht, wie sich der fröm Christ bey den Messen / so yetz gehalten werden (wenn er sich nit mit gůtem fug darvon absündern kan) halten soll / das er sich nit versündige / und die zeit nit unnützlich verlier,* den Jakob Strauß 1522 für seine bedrängte Heimatgemeinde Hall in Tirol verfaßte und in dem er ihr mehrere meditative Abendmahlsgebete bot.[48] Und in einer Predigt empfahl Luthers ehemaliger Ordensbruder Wenzeslaus Linck, mittlerweile Pfarrer in Altenburg, 1523 evangelisch gesinnten Christen, die den Besuch der Messe nicht vermeiden konnten:[49]

---

[46] »So wir aber laider die sach nit bessern mügen / und der gebrauch am Sontag Meß zůhören [sc. der Meßzwang] / das Christen volck ängstiget. Ist von nöten den armen gefangen gewissen etwas lufft und trost zů raichen / ordnung geben« (ebd.).

[47] Einige Beispiele bei JANOTA (s. Anm. 9), 35, 55–57, und bei JULIUS SMEND, Die evangelischen deutschen Messen bis zu Luthers Deutscher Messe, Göttingen 1896, 13–15.

[48] Ursprünglich Anhang zu: Ain trostliche verstendige leer über das wort sancti Pauli. Der mensch soll sich selbs probieren / und also von dem brot essen / und von dem kelch trincken. Gepredigt zů Hall im Intal durch Doctor Jacob Strauss, 1522 (dort ab C 4ᵛ), Zitat: C 5ᵛ–C 6ʳ (weitere, separate Ausgabe bei SMEND [s. Anm. 47], 29, Anm. 3; ausgeschrieben von MARTIN REINHART [s. Anm. 42]). In ähnlicher Weise bietet evangelische meditative Gebete zur Meditation während der Messe Urbanus Rhegius in einem Andachtsbüchlein mit dem Titel *Underricht wie sich ain Christen mensch halten soll das er frucht der Mesz erlang und Christlich zů gotz tisch gangg,* s.l. et a. [1522] (vgl. a.a.O., 35–37). Die ganze Meßliturgie geht in dieser Weise entlang Oekolampads kleine Schrift *Das Testament Jesu Christi* von 1523 (verschiedene Ausgaben: a.a.O., 49). Der Text dieses möglicherweise von Jakob Strauß beinflußten (a.a.O., 68–70) Schriftchens ist abgedruckt bei SMEND (a.a.O., 51–57). Dort findet sich auch ein weiterer, von dem Straßburger Matthäus Zell stammender Versuch in dieser Richtung, und zwar in Form eines während des Meßopfers für Tote zu haltenden evangelischen Gebetes (a.a.O., 25f.).

[49] »wiewol es nit böse were, die messen / so man als opffer und gutte werck thut gar zu meyden« (WENZESLAUS LINCK, Eyn Sermon [...] Von anrueffunge der heyligen. Dar-

»Wenn du messe wilt hören so gedenck das du auffs wenigeste geystlich gespeiset
werdest / dencke nit das der meßhalter für dich opffere Christum. [...] Gedenck
auch nit das er mit der meß ein gut wercke für dich thete [...] / sunder gedenck
allaine was dein got und herre Jesus christus für dich gethan hat / und dasselbig
alles miteinander dir bescheyden und zu aygen gegeben hat unter disem Sigill /
wartzaychen / und Sacrament.«[50]

Schwieriger war die Lage für Priester, die die reformatorische Kritik an
der Messe teilten. Sollten sie, solange es keine neue liturgische Ordnung
gab, erst einmal weiterhin ein Ritual vollziehen, das in ihren Augen evan-
geliumswidrig war, sollten sie fortfahren, in dem Volk unverständlicher
Sprache, ja unhörbar zu zelebrieren, die Kommunion nur unter einer Gestalt auszuteilen und, vor allem, das als Abgötterei erkannte Meßopfer
darzubringen, die allein dazu dienenden »Winkelmessen« abzuhalten? Am
ehesten fanden einen Ausweg die als Prediger angestellten Priester – sei es,
daß sie das hauptamtlich waren wie die oberdeutschen Prädikanten oder
auch ein Thomas Müntzer in Zwickau, sei es, daß sie diese Aufgabe ne-
benamtlich versahen wie Martin Luther in Wittenberg. Sie konnten
schlicht das liturgische Element, das ihre Aufgabe war, die Predigt, in den
Dienst der Reformation stellen. Da sie das meist im Rahmen allein der
Predigt gewidmeter Gottesdienste taten, brauchten sie dabei nicht in Be-
rührung mit der Messe zu kommen.[51] Vielfach sahen die Anstellungsver-
träge der Prediger zwar auch einige Meßpflichten vor, etwa mit der Predigtpfründe verbundene Privatmessen zugunsten der Stifter, doch waren

---

neben auch vom gebet / meß hoeren und fürpit. Geprediget am Suntag der Creuetz
wochen / auff das Ewangelion Johannis am. xvj. cap. Aldenburg in Meyssen MDXXIII,
Nürnberg 1523, B 2ᵛ).

[50] Ebd.

[51] Das galt nicht nur für die spezifische Form des oberdeutschen Prädikantengottes-
dienstes, sondern auch andernorts, wo es eigens angestellte Prediger gab. Allerdings
haben wir von der liturgischen Form, in die deren Predigten eingebettet waren, keine
genaueren Kenntnisse. Vgl. etwa die Situation in Nürnberg mit seiner alten Prädikantentradition: Das Meßnerpflichtbuch der Nürnberger Lorenzkirche von 1483 macht zu
den Predigten, die Sache des dortigen Prädikanten waren, nur Angaben darüber, daß
diese nach der Mette (GÜMBEL, Mesnerpflichtbuch St. Lorenz [s. Anm. 31], 20, 48) oder
nach der Frühmesse (a.a.O., 26), nach der Vesper (a.a.O., 30) oder nach dem Ave Maria
(a.a.O., 45), wenn nicht einfach *post prandium*, also am frühen Nachmittag (a.a.O., 33)
gehalten wird – Angaben, die einerseits die Häufigkeit, andererseits den sekundären
Charakter der Predigt im Gefüge des von anderen liturgischen Vollzügen geprägten
kirchlichen Betriebs zeigen (vgl. o. Anm. 31) – aber über die liturgische Gestalt dieser
Predigtauftritte erfahren wir nichts. Vgl. auch das parallele Buch mit entsprechenden
Angaben zu St. Sebald: ALBERT GÜMBEL, Das Mesnerpflichtbuch von St. Sebald in
Nürnberg vom Jahre 1482, München 1929. Reine Predigtgottesdienste waren auch die
Aufgabe Thomas Müntzers in Zwickau, ohne daß wir über deren liturgische Gestalt
Genaueres wüßten. Erst in Allstedt war er als Pfarrer hauptamtlich für die Messe zu-
ständig – und bemühte sich umgehend um deren Reform (BRÄUER, VOGLER, Müntzer [s.
Anm. 32], 186–198).

das deutlich zweitrangige Verrichtungen,[52] und u.U. konnte man ihnen ganz ausweichen.[53] Jedenfalls löste sich das liturgische Dilemma hier durch das Nebeneinander evangeliumsgemäßer Predigtgottesdienste und evangeliumswidriger Messen in derselben Kirche, die einen deutsch gehalten, die anderen lateinisch, die einen mit Gemeindeliedern, die anderen mit Chorgesängen oder still. So waren evangelisch gesinnte Amtsträger, die erstere vertraten, von Gewissensbelastungen befreit, und evangelische Gemeindeglieder hatten eine entsprechende Alternative. In den Reichsstädten Südwestdeutschlands und in der deutschsprachigen Schweiz ging man sogar noch einen Schritt weiter und kombinierte den Predigtgottesdienst mit dem anderen ausgegliederten und ebenfalls volkssprachlichen Rumpfelement der Messe, der Kommunionfeier. Damit konnten die Evangelischen der Messe entgehen, ohne auf den Empfang des Abendmahls zu verzichten.[54] Diese Lösung sollte sich schließlich als die liturgische Norm der evangelischen Gottesdienste jener Gegenden durchsetzen. Doch erst einmal war sie, meist für Jahre, eine Maßnahme des Übergangs, denn die Messen liefen gleichzeitig weiter – in Straßburg etwa bis zum Jahr 1529, als die Messe offiziell abgeschafft wurde, in Ulm gar bis 1531. Daß jene Form – Predigtgottesdienst mit Kommunion – aber überhaupt entstand und sich schließlich sogar als Norm für die oberdeutschen und deutschschweizer evangelischen Liturgien anstelle der Messe durchsetzte, war nur im Rahmen der zu liturgisch fester Form geronnenen Prädikantengottesdiensttradition jener Gegenden möglich.

Den Ausweg reformatorisch gesinnter Prädikanten, bis zur Revision des Gottesdienstes kein Abendmahl zu feiern, wählten auch andere. Andreas Karlstadt, als Archidiaconus der Wittenberger Stiftskirche zum regelmäßigen Meßopfer verpflichtet, wich schon vor seiner spektakulären

---

[52] Für die Inhaber der neuen Predigtpfründen im 15. Jahrhundert galt meist, daß ihre »Aufgabe fast ausschließlich die Predigt war« (MENZEL [s. Anm. 11], 369); ein reduziertes Meßprogramm hatte beispielsweise Matthäus Alber mit vier Messen pro Woche zu erfüllen (FIGEL [s. Anm. 7], 86, Anm. 342).

[53] Menzel spricht von der Möglichkeit »beträchtliche[r] Freistellungen« schon im Spätmittelalter (s. Anm. 11, 381) bis hin zu der Möglichkeit, zur Predigtpfründe gehörende Meßverpflichtungen ganz »abzuwenden« (a.a.O., 382). Insofern fiel es nicht aus dem Rahmen, wenn ein reformatorisch gesinnter Prädikant wie der Heilbronner Johann Lachmann, dessen Pfründenverpflichtung auch Messen umfaßte, ab 1525 keine mehr las, obwohl die Messe in seiner Stadt bis 1531 fortbestand (FIGEL [s. Anm. 7], 326).

[54] Das heißt, das zeitweilige Nebeneinander eines nach evangelischem Urteil rechten und falschen Gottesdienstes wurde in diesen Fällen auch zum Nebeneinander rechten, in reiner Kommunionfeier bestehenden und falschen, der Meßform folgenden Abendmahls, und auch das gegebenenfalls, etwa in Straßburg, in ein und demselben Kirchenraum. Ja, im Straßburger Münster, wo das evangelische Abendmahl zunächst als reformierte Messe gefeiert wurde, gab es für kurze Zeit sogar ein Nebeneinander rechter und falscher Messe (FIGEL [s. Anm. 7], 273).

deutschsprachigen Abendmahlsfeier an Weihnachten 1521, von der noch die Rede sein wird, für längere Zeit dem Zelebrieren der »gottlosen« Messe aus.[55] Die Augustinermönche im Wittenberger Konvent stellten, als ihnen nach einem ersten Versuch evangeliumsgemäßer Meßfeier die Fortführung dieser Praxis verboten wurde, kurzerhand die Messe ein und beschränkten sich auf die Predigt.[56] Und ein Wittenberger Student schrieb im selben Herbst 1521 stolz, damit wohl übertreibend, doch eine allgemeine Stimmung wiedergebend: »Nos Wittenbergenses non audimus missas«.[57]

In einer ungleich komplizierteren liturgischen Lage als reformationsgeneigte Priester auf Predigerstellen fanden sich jene, die Pfarrstellen innehatten. War doch bei ihnen das regelmäßige Abhalten von Messen Teil des Hauptgeschäfts.[58] Sie nutzten die Predigt, die ebenfalls zu ihren Aufgaben gehörte und für die ihnen die sonntägliche Hauptmesse zustand, wie die Prädikanten für die evangeliumsgemäße Verkündigung. Aber dann hatte hier das Meßopfer zu folgen, das in Widerspruch zu dieser Verkündigung stand, von den Messen während der Woche, ohne Predigt und still, ganz abgesehen. Der Zelebration konnte sich kein Pfarrer entziehen.[59] Wie es scheint, hielten die Betroffenen die Spannung notgedrungen aus. Es gab

---

[55] SCHEIBLE (s. Anm. 40), 82. Ein entsprechender Vorsatz ist zu derselben Zeit wohl auch bei Luther zu erschließen, der auf der Wartburg angesichts des täglich einsam in der Burgkapelle zelebrierenden »Meßopferpriesterleins« (sacrificulus) schrieb, man sollte dergleichen am besten sofort abstellen oder wenigstens verringern, da diese Praxis ein »Unrecht« (iniuria) sei, das dem Wesen des Abendmahls als Gemeinschaftsgeschehen und Verkündigungshandlung in jeder Hinsicht widerspreche – ein Befund, der in den Ausruf »O Antichriste!« mündet (Brief an Spalatin vom 1.10.1521: WA.Br 2,14–19 [Nr. 434]).

[56] MARTIN BRECHT, Martin Luther, Bd. 2: Ordnung und Abgrenzung der Reformation 1521–1532, Stuttgart 1986, 35.

[57] Sebastian Helmann an Johann Heß, 8. Oktober 1521 (in: Die Wittenberger Bewegung 1521 und 1522, hg. v. Nikolaus Müller, Leipzig ²1911, 15–19, hier: 17).

[58] Gar keine Zwischenlösung gab es für die vielen Meßpriester, für die das – an den Stiftungszweck ihrer Pfründen gebundene – Lesen von Messen die einzige Aufgabe und im Allgemeinen auch ihre einzige Fertigkeit war. Sie konnten nur auf ihrer Praxis beharren oder ihre Stellen aufgeben. Nicht umsonst kam nach Einführung der Reformation aus ihren Reihen vielfach Widerspruch gegen den Einsatz im neuen, auch die Predigt einschließenden liturgischen Rahmen (FIGEL [s. Anm. 7], 58).

[59] Am ehesten entziehen konnten sie sich wohl den Messen in der Woche ohne Gemeinde, wie der Fall des Wittenberger Stadtpfarrers Simon Heins zeigt, der zwei Meßbenefizien besaß, die ihn zu einer gewissen Anzahl stiller Messen verpflichteten: Es gibt Nachrichten, daß er dies seit Ende 1521 unterließ. Andere Indizien scheinen für eine kurzfristige Wiederaufnahme zu sprechen (KRENTZ [s. Anm. 38], 246; Krentz überschätzt allerdings die Eindeutigkeit dieser Indizien, wenn er im Gewißheit suggerierenden Indikativ schreibt, es »ist davon auszugehen«; das von ihr angeführte Indiz liegt darin, daß, während im Januar 1522 bereits berichtet wurde, Heyn habe seine Pfründenverpflichtungen »verlassen«, er doch im Laufe des Jahres noch sein Geld erhalten habe; aber da wir nicht wissen, ob die Bezahlung unmittelbar an den Vollzug geknüpft war und ob dieser kontrolliert wurde, ist die Folgerung nicht zwingend.).

einen Kunstgriff, sie zu mildern, von dem mehrfach, doch der Natur der Sache gemäß eher andeutungsweise die Rede ist: im *Canon Missae*, der ja unhörbar rezitiert wurde, besonders anstößige Passagen auszulassen.[60] Angesichts der speziellen liturgischen Zwangslage, in der sich reformatorisch gesinnte Pfarrer befanden, erstaunt es nicht, daß entscheidende Anstöße zur Ausarbeitung der beiden Meßformulare, die Luther schließlich vorlegte, von einem Pfarrer, Nikolaus Hausmann in Zwickau, kamen.

---

[60] So bei Oekolampad in einer brieflichen Auskunft von der Ebernburg an Kaspar Hedio vom Juni 1522: »Nihil [...] vel ex pristinis ritibus vel ex verbis canonis omitto. [...] Ego non adeo temerarius, ut immutem, quae bona conscientia servare possum, et mihi nequaquam periculosus est canon. [...] Ut nihil a me mutatum, ita si quid precum aut verborum pia mente dedicatque opera omitterem, non peccasse me crederem in Christum« (Briefe und Akten zum Leben Oekolampads, hg. v. Ernst Staehelin, Bd. 1: 1499–1526, Leipzig 1927, Nr. 128, 188, 190; davor Nr. 127 die die Auskunft auslösende Nachfrage Hedios vom 1. Juni: »quidnam mutaris, quid omiseris« [in der Liturgie]; beide Briefe einschließlich einer von Oekolampad beigelegten Predigt erschienen auch gedruckt: Quod expediat epistolae et evangelii lectionem in Missa, vernacula sermone plebi promulgari, Oecolampadii ad Hedionem Epistola, s.l., s.a. [Augsburg, 1522]). Oekolampads Verfahren war bemerkt worden, vor allem, weil der von ihm rezitierte Kanon durch das Auslassen eines Teils der Gebete kürzer war als gewohnt. Doch fiel dergleichen in einer Burgkapelle wohl leichter auf als Zelebrationen in einer Pfarrkirche, die sich hinter dem Lettner oder an Nebenaltären abspielten. Auch der Nürnberger Priester Döber fiel auf und wurde kritisiert, daß er den Kanon sowie die Gebete für die Toten und die Anrufung der Heiligen weglasse (1524). Daß das auffiel, wird, wenn es sich auf eine lateinische Zelebration bezog, damit zusammengehangen haben mag, daß er an der kleinen Spitalkirche amtierte; möglicherweise bezog sich die Kritik aber bereits auf die von ihm ab Herbst 1524 gehaltene deutsche und laut gesprochene Messe, bei der der Wegfall jener Stücke unüberhörbar war (JOHANN BARTHOLOMÄUS RIEDERER, Abhandlung von Einführung des teutschen Gesangs in die evangelischlutherische [!] Kirche überhaupts und in die nürnbergische besonders, Nürnberg 1759, 181f.). Johann Schwebel, der Reformator Zweibrückens, der schon 1522 und damit als einer der ersten Messen in deutscher Sprache hielt und dabei auch die Kommunion unter beiden Gestalten austeilte, spricht davon, daß er den Kanon, der ohnehin nur unhörbar habe rezitiert werden dürfen, »so verberge, daß niemand sich leicht beklagen könne, er habe ihn preisgegeben« (»Canonem quem vocant Missae hactenus nefas fuit aliis audientibus legere: proinde sic eum occulto, ne facile quisquam possit conqueri me illum prodidisse«). Im übrigen – so Schwebel ähnlich wie Oekolampad – habe er keine Absicht, etwas von dem Kanon wegzunehmen oder ihm etwas hinzuzusetzen, der von Christus übergeben worden sei, von dem wolle er sich keinesfalls entfernen (»ubi vel minuam, vel augeam a Christo traditum Canonem benigne moneri cupio; nam illic derivare non cupio«). Diese Sätze werden sich nicht auf Schwebels deutsche Feiern beziehen, in denen er vermutlich ohnehin nur die Einsetzungsworte – laut – sprach, sondern auf daneben von ihm auch noch auf Lateinisch zelebrierte Messen. Sie laufen dann offenbar darauf hinaus, daß Schwebel von den – unhörbaren und damit im Vollzug schwer kontrollierbaren – Kanon nur das übrig ließ, was von Christus selbst stamme, also die Einsetzungsworte (JOHANN SCHWEBEL, Scripta Theologica, atque Tractatus absolutissimi, De praecipuis ac difficilioribus S. Scripturae Locis, atque tunc in Religionis dissidio atque negotio agitatis Controversiis, Zweibrücken 1605, 337f., ohne Jahresangabe, aber von SMEND [s. Anm. 47] plausibel auf 1522 datiert). Zur Empfehlung desselben Verfahrens in anderem Kontext durch Martin Luther siehe unten S. 388 zu Anm. 80.

Denn all die genannten Maßnahmen standen unter der Erwartung, daß sie nur für eine Übergangszeit nötig seien, daß in absehbarer Frist der Gottesdienst evangeliumsgemäß reformiert und Zwischenlösungen überflüssig sein würden. Freilich verwundert es kaum, daß nicht jeder warten wollte, ja, daß Warten manchem als Mangel an Gehorsam gegen Gottes Wort erschien. Am bekanntesten ist das Vorpreschen von Anhängern Luthers in Wittenberg, die während seiner Abwesenheit auf der Wartburg liturgische Konsequenzen aus seinen abendmahlstheologischen Einsichten zogen: Melanchthon – anders als später besonders forsch –, der mit einigen Studenten am 29. September 1521 in der Stadtkirche die Kommunion unter beiderlei Gestalt empfing,[61] was sich einige Wochen später wiederholte[62] – wie der Ritus ansonsten aussah, wissen wir nicht –, Augustinerbrüder Luthers, die in Luthers Kloster dasselbe taten;[63] die gewaltsame Behinderung der predigt- und gemeindelosen, nur dem Opfer dienenden Frühmessen in der Stadtkirche durch Studenten und Bürger Anfang Dezember;[64] an Weihnachten dann das positive Gegenstück, die schon erwähnte spektakuläre Meßfeier, die Andreas Karlstadt in der Schloßkirche unter massenhafter Beteiligung der Bürger einschließlich führender Vertreter von Stadt und Universität leitete und kurz darauf mehrfach in Schloß- und Stadtkirche wiederholte: ohne Kanon, nur mit den Einsetzungsworten, diese laut rezitiert in deutscher Sprache, gefolgt von der Austeilung beider Elemente;[65] die Parallelaktion Gabriel Zwillings, der schon im Augustinerkloster die treibende Kraft gewesen war, im nahen Eilenburg;[66] in anderen Städten Kursachsens hier und da Ähnliches.[67] Die reformierten Messen sollten keine Ausnahmeaktionen sein, sondern den

---

[61] Bericht des beteiligten Studenten Helmann (s. Anm. 57), 17.

[62] SCHEIBLE (s. Anm. 40), 77, 83.

[63] Vgl. BRECHT, Luther, Bd. 2 (s. Anm. 56), 35; KRENTZ (s. Anm. 38), 180.

[64] SCHEIBLE (s. Anm. 40), 81. In der Kirche des Franziskanerklosters zwangen Studenten am Barbaratag (4. Dezember) die Mönche, sich auf eine Messe am Hauptaltar zu beschränken (a.a.O., 82).

[65] HERMANN BARGE, Andreas Bodenstein von Karlstadt, Bd. 1: Karlstadt und die Anfänge der Reformation, Nieuwkoop ²1968, 358–361; ULRICH BUBENHEIMER, Luthers Stellung zum Aufruhr in Wittenberg 1520–1522 und die frühreformatorischen Wurzeln des landesherrlichen Kirchenregiments (in: ZSRG.K 102, 1985, 149–151, 187–189); KRENTZ (s. Anm. 23), 154–159; THOMAS KAUFMANN, Abendmahl und Gruppenidentität in der frühen Reformation (in: Herrenmahl und Gruppenidentität, hg. v. Martin Ebner, Freiburg u.a. 2007, 194–210, hier: 200).

[66] SIEGFRIED BRÄUER, »ich begere lauttern und reinen wein / So vormischt er mirn mith wasser«. Der Flugschriftenstreit zwischen dem Eilenburger Schumacher Georg Schönichen und dem Leipziger Theologen Hieronymus Dungersheim (in: Reformation und Katholizismus, FS Gottfried Maron, hg. v. Jörg Haustein u. Harry Oelke, Hannover 2003, 97–140, hier: 100).

[67] SCHEIBLE (s. Anm. 40), 83.

Ausgangspunkt dauerhafter neuer Praxis bilden, wie die Wittenberger Bürger in einer Petition an den Rat forderten.[68] Tatsächlich verfügte die im Januar 1522 erlassene *Wittenberger Stadtordnung*[69] eine liturgische Reform, die entscheidende reformatorische Anliegen umsetzte: abgesehen von der selbstverständlichen Predigt die Kommunion in beiderlei Gestalt, die Streichung des Kanons mit Ausnahme der Einsetzungsworte, die Rezitation dieser Worte, die durch den Wegfall der umgebenden Opfergebete ihren Opfercharakter verloren hatten,[70] als Evangeliumsverkündigung mit lauter Stimme und auf Deutsch, während der Rest der Liturgie, der sich an den überlieferten Meßordo hielt, noch lateinisch blieb.

Als von der Stadt verantwortetes Regelwerk konnte sich die Wittenberger Ordnung nicht durchsetzen, mußte sie dem kurfürstlichen Kirchenregiment weichen, das von reichrechtlichen Zwängen[71] ebenso wie von der persönlichen religiösen Vorsicht des Landesherrn bestimmt war. Wenn ihren liturgischen Forderungen und noch aufgeschobenen, weitergehenden Anliegen gleichwohl die Zukunft gehörte, dann wegen des Kurses, den der von der Wartburg zurückgekehrte Luther einschlug, indem er einerseits den Anspruch des kurfürstlichen Kirchenregiments bestätigte, andererseits aber die Reform bei scharfer Kritik an der Durchführung in der Sache verteidigte und für die Zukunft sicherte.[72] Dabei waren die Verhaltensratschläge für die Übergangszeit (»eyn tzeytlang«)[73], die er den Wittenbergern mündlich in den *Invokavitpredigten*[74] und schriftlich in der Flugschrift *Von beider Gestalt des Sakraments zu nehmen*[75] gab, dieselben,

---

[68] BRECHT, Luther, Bd. 2 (s. Anm. 56), 39; SCHEIBLE (s. Anm. 40), 82. Gefordert wurden u.a. freie Predigt, das Ende der Privatmessen und die Kommunion unter beiderlei Gestalt.

[69] Abgedruckt in LStA 2,525–529.

[70] Gleichwohl wurde die gemeindelose Stillmesse noch zugestanden (LStA 2,528,1 f. [Druckfassung]; zur dieses Zugeständnis nicht enthaltenden handschriftlichen Fassung: WOLFGANG SIMON, Die Meßopfertheologie Martin Luthers, Tübingen 2003, 504–507; zur offenen Frage nach der Deutung der Differenz zwischen beiden Fassungen: KRENTZ [s. Anm. 38], 193).

[71] Nämlich dem Mandat des Reichsregiments vom 20. Januar 1522, das die Herrscher der beiden Sachsen und die für ihre Territorien kirchlich zuständigen Bischöfe zur Beseitigung der reformatorischen Neuerungen aufforderte (dazu ARMIN KOHNLE, Reichstag und Reformation, Gütersloh 2001, 105–112).

[72] Zur Politik des Hofes, der wegen des genannten Reichsregimentsmandats unter Druck stand, und dem Verhalten Luthers, der einerseits die gegenüber der Stadt höhere Zuständigkeit des Hofes anerkannte, tatsächlich aber sowohl durch seine dem Willen des Kurfürsten zuwiderlaufende Rückkehr nach Wittenberg als auch durch die Verteidigung der liturgischen Neuerungen und die nur vorläufige und auch nicht vollständige Rücknahme der liturgischen Veränderungen gerade nicht der Linie des Hofes folgte, vgl. KAUFMANN, Geschichte (s. Anm. 38), 388–392, sowie unten Anm. 88.

[73] WA 10/2,31,7.

[74] WA 10/3,1–64 (LStA 2,520–558).

[75] WA 10/2,11–41.

die auch sonst zu lesen und zu hören waren: für die Gemeinde der vorläufige Verzicht auf den Kelch oder auf die Kommunion überhaupt,[76] ja, auf den Meßbesuch selbst[77] und die persönliche Deutung des Ritus vom Evangelium her,[78] für die evangelisch gesinnten Priester, die nun einmal »müssen messe halten«, die vorläufig aufrechterhaltene, doch immer seltener vollzogene Zelebration »zu dienst auß liebe« für die »armen yrrigen gewissen«, welche noch meinten, die bisherige Messe zu brauchen,[79] und die stillschweigende[80] Streichung aller auf das Meßopfer bezogenen Worte.[81] Waren das dieselben Empfehlungen wie andernorts, so standen sie in Wittenberg doch in einem eigenen Kontext und wurden in spezifischer Perspektive vorgebracht: Während Männer wie Jakob Strauß oder Urbanus Rhegius für eine Lage schrieben, in der Evangelische unterdrückt waren und auf liturgische Reformen noch warteten, hatten die Wittenberger, zu denen Luther sprach, wesentliche Reformen bereits erlebt und eingeführt und mußten mit deren zeitweiliger Rücknahme zurechtkommen.[82] Auch hier war der Auslöser politischer Druck.[83] Aber Luther, der jene

---

[76] A.a.O., 30,15–31,3. Wer nicht verzichten, sondern die eigentlich richtige Kommunion *sub utraque* empfangen will, soll das nicht ostentativ tun und die »Schwachen«, die noch nicht so weit sind, dadurch in Zugzwang und anschließende Gewissensnöte bringen, sondern zu anderer Zeit und an anderem Altar als diese (a.a.O., 30,28–31). Tatsächlich wurde dann die Kelchkommunion als Regelform vorläufig zurückgenommen, doch auf individuelles Begehren hin fand sie statt (WA.Br 2,483,21–23).

[77] WA 10/2,31,28: Die, die noch zur herkömmlichen Messe gehen, sind nur die »armen yrrigen gewissen«, die das zu brauchen meinen.

[78] A.a.O., 30,4–9.

[79] A.a.O., 31,27–32,2.

[80] Da der Opferkanon still rezitiert und von der Gemeinde nie gehört wurde, geht auch Luther davon aus, daß sie die gestrichenen Opfergebete nicht vermissen und keinen Anstoß nehmen werde: »Es kann aber der priester solchs wol meyden, das der gemeyn man nymer erferet unnd on ergerniß außrichten« (a.a.O., 29,14–16).

[81] Das sei allerdings eine Veränderung, die dem Zelebranten nicht freistehe (»das frey sey zu thun ader [oder] lassen«), sondern die geschehen müsse (a.a.O., 29,11–16). Luther fügt hinzu, wer aber »verstockt« diese Worte nicht meiden, sondern weiter rezitieren wolle, der werde sich dafür selbst – vor Gott – verantworten müssen (a.a.O., 29,16f.) – eine Bemerkung, die insbesondere auf das Allerheiligenstift zielte, mit dem es noch jahrelange Auseinandersetzungen wegen es Meßopfers geben sollte. Vor allem an diese Adresse ist auch der Abschnitt gerichtet, in dem Luther seine oft geäußerte Forderung wiederholt, die Winkelmessen, »als opffer oder gute werck gethan«, abzuschaffen, aber hinzufügt, Priester, die sie halten wollten, »nicht vom altar [zu] reyssen«, da man niemanden zum Glauben zwingen könne. Wenn lange genug dagegen gepredigt worden sei, würden diese Messen von selber fallen (a.a.O., 32,11–17).

[82] Vgl. die kritischen Einwände gegen seinen Kurs, die Luther aufnimmt (a.a.O., 24,2–4): »Ist denn nu dem gewißlich alßo und keyn tzweyffell drob tzuhaben [daß die in Wittenberg durchgeführten Reformen der Einsetzung des Abendmahls entsprechen], warum thut manß denn nicht? Ja warumb lessistu [Luther] es selbs nicht gehen tzu Wittemberg, da es angefangen ist, und anders wo mehr?«

[83] Luther spielt darauf an, sieht darin aber eine kontingente Angelegenheit (»eine

Reformen selbst mit Nachdruck propagiert hatte, drang als Prediger und
Theologe auf vorübergehende Rücknahme: Sie sei nötig aus Achtung vor
der persönlichen, nur vom Evangelium selbst hervorzurufenden Glaubensüberzeugung,[84] der die schnelle Durchführung unter Zeit- und Grup-
pendruck nicht weniger widerspreche als das papistische Gesetz.[85] Aus
dieser Diagnose folgte zum einen die nachdrückliche Betonung der theologischen Rechtmäßigkeit aller in Wittenberg um die Jahreswende 1521/22
durchgeführten und geplanten liturgischen Veränderungen.[86] Daraus folgte
zum anderen die vorläufige Rückkehr zum früheren, dem Willen Christi
nicht entsprechenden Stand der Liturgie,[87] dies aber nicht, wie im Fall der
Gemeinden, für die Strauß und Rhegius schrieben, notgedrungen wegen
des Drucks politischer Gewalt, sondern frei bejaht als zeitweiliger Re-
formverzicht aus Liebe zu den im Glauben noch »schwachen« und im
Alten verfangenen Mitchristen.[88] Was auf keinen Fall eingeschränkt werden konnte, war nach diesem Programm die evangelische Verkündigung.
Durch sie aber werde die Glaubensüberzeugung wachsen, die dann der
Gemeinde als ganzer die Reformen angemessen und erwünscht erscheinen
lassen und so den Verzicht überflüssig machen werde.[89]

ßonderliche tzufellige ursach«), auf die er nicht eingehen müsse; das Sachproblem, das er
dann erörtert, wäre auch ohne die politische Lage gegeben (a.a.O., 25,1–5).

[84] »Man soll und kann niemant tzum glawben dringen, ßondern das Euangelion frey
selbs holen lassen, wen es holet« (a.a.O., 28,7–9).

[85] Z.B. a.a.O., 26,4–14; 29,3–10; 31,7–18.

[86] Keiner der Beteiligten, der etwa das Sakrament unter beiden Gestalten empfangen
habe, dürfe deshalb ein schlechtes Gewissen haben und sich zu dem Eingeständnis bringen lassen, das sei unrecht gewesen: »Alßo auch die, ßo beyder gestallt empfangen
haben, bitten wyr und, ßo es helffen will, gepieten wir ynn dem namen unßers herrn
Jhesu Christi, das sie ia keyn gewissen drob machen, als sey es unrecht odder ubell than,
ßondern sollen das leben ehe lassen, ehe sie das wider ruffen oder verleucken unangesehen, was da widder setzt, thutt oder will Bapst, Keyser, furst und teuffell datzu. Denn
da ist der text des Euangeli ßo klar.« Das zu leugnen, hieße nichts weniger, »als wenn du
sprechist, Christus selb hett unrecht daran than und were eyn ketzer, die weyl er anders
denn der Bapst und die tzornige Papisten [...] handelt« (a.a.O., 20,23–21,5). Ebenso dürfe
auf keinen Fall für unrecht erklärt werden, daß man das Sakrament mit der Hand genommen habe (a.a.O., 17,13–23).

[87] »wyr mussens noch eyn tzeyttlang ym alten mißbrauch gehen lassen, bis [...] das
Euangelion wol unter die leutt komme« (a.a.O., 27,29f.).

[88] A.a.O., 30,9–27. Nicht in diesen Rahmen fiel für Luther allerdings das Meßopfer,
es war in seinen Augen eine Gotteslästerung und stand in solchem Widerspruch zum
Evangelium, daß es auch nicht vorläufig und vorläufig nicht hingenommen werden konnte,
weshalb er unermüdlich und mit größter Schärfe dagegen kämpfte (vgl. BRECHT, Luther,
Bd. 2 [s. Anm. 56], 129–132). Wenn er, wie oben Anm. 80 angeführt, nach Von beider
Gestalt Priester, die am Meßopfer festhielten, auf eigene Verantwortung vorerst gewäh-
ren lassen wollte, dann, weil diese, konkret einige Stiftsherren am kurfürstlichen Allerheiligenstift, noch unter dem Schutz des Hofes standen.

[89] Z.B. WA 10/2,27,16–19; 32,2.14–17.

Der Verzicht auf eine umfassende liturgische Umsetzung der gottes-
diensttheologischen Einsichten gilt auch noch für die Liturgie, die Luther
im folgenden Jahr 1523 vorlegte, die *Formula missae et Communionis*.[90]
Auch wenn er der Meinung war, daß nun die Zeit gekommen sei, von der
Einwirkung auf die Herzen durch das Wort zur reformerischen Tat über-
zugehen,[91] blieb er mit der *Formula* bewußt immer noch hinter seinem
eigenem Programm zurück.[92] Und er blieb damit auch hinter den weitergehenden Erwartungen zurück, die mittlerweile allenthalben geweckt, hier
und da auch schon zu reformerischen Schritten gediehen waren, bis hin zu
volkssprachlichen Feiern.[93] Erst mit der im Oktober 1525 erstmals gefeierten *Deutschen Messe*[94] kamen theologische Einsichten und liturgische
Ordnung umfassend zur Deckung.[95] Die Einführung der *Deutschen Messe*

---

[90] WA 12,205–220.

[91] WA 12,206,3–12.

[92] So läßt die *Formula* übergangsweise noch die stille Rezitation zu (a.a.O., 212,25 f.),
schließt die als Verkündigung zu verstehenden Einsetzungsworte grammatikalisch noch
an das Präfationsgebet an, auch wenn sie sprachlich nicht mehr als Gebet gestaltet und
durch eine Pause wie durch die Veränderung des Tones von der Präfation abgesetzt sind
(a.a.O., 212,17–24), fordert die Hinwendung des Liturgen zur Gemeinde erst beim Segen
(a.a.O., 213,12), sieht noch keinen Gesang der Gemeinde vor u.a.m. (vgl. hierzu Dorothea Wendebourg, Essen zum Gedächtnis, Tübingen 2009, 58 f., Anm. 129 f.).
Grund waren Luthers Zurückhaltung gegenüber gesetzlich erscheinenden Vorschriften,
die den Eindruck erwecken würden, die Wittenberger Liturgie sei die allgemeinverbind-
liche evangelische Ordnung (a.a.O., 206,12–14; 214,14–33; 218,36–219,7), und die Erwartung, daß man im Umgang mit dem »einstweilen« (pro tempore, nach der von Luther in Auftrag gegebenen Übersetzung von Paul Speratus, Ein weyse Christlich Mess
zuhalten, Wittenberg 1524, D 4ᵛ: »auff eyn zeit«) vorgelegten Formular weiterlernen
werde (a.a.O., 218,33 f.). Hinzu kam der Umstand, daß man noch nicht über alles verfügte, was für eine weitergehende Reform nötig war; so gab es noch nicht die für den
Gemeindegesang notwendigen deutschen Lieder (a.a.O., 218,15–23) und ließ sich die
Abstimmung von Sprache und Rezitationston, die in Luthers Augen für eine als nächstes
fällige volkssprachliche Messe notwendig war, nicht so schnell bewerkstelligen (s. die
entsprechend notierten Stücke in der *Deutschen Messe* und vgl. dazu die einige Monate
eher geschriebenen programmatischen Sätze WA 18,123,19–24).

[93] Nicht nur erinnerten sich die Zeitgenossen an Karlstadts deutsche Feier, sondern
vereinzelt wurde andernorts bereits Messe in deutscher Sprache gehalten (vgl. Smend [s.
Anm. 41], 4–6), und mit der Ordnung des Nördlingers Caspar Kantz lag seit 1522 eine
deutschsprachige Liturgie gedruckt vor (Coena Domini, Bd. 1: Die Abendmahlsliturgie
der Reformationskirchen im 16./17. Jahrhundert, hg. v. Irmgard Pahl, Fribourg 1983,
8.14–17). Das Jahr 1524 brachte dann einen regelrechten Boom deutschsprachiger Meß-
feiern, so in Nürnberg (a.a.O., 176), Wertheim (WA.Br 3,330,33–42 [Nr. 769]), Allstedt
(Bräuer, Vogler, Müntzer [s. Anm. 32], 195–197), Reutlingen (Figel [s. Anm. 7],
220 f.), Straßburg (a.a.O., 272). Bezeichnenderweise wurde die *Formula missae* selbst
kaum in ihrer Originalsprache, aber schnell und viel in ihrer umgehend gefertigten deutscher Übersetzung (vgl. Anm. 92) nachgedruckt – die deutschsprachige Meßfeier, die zu
Ostern 1525 im sächsischen Lochau »im Beisein des kurfürstlichen Hofes« gefeiert wurde (WA 19,48), dürfte der übersetzten *Formula* gefolgt sein.

[94] WA 19,72–113.

[95] Das galt nicht nur für den Schritt, neben – nicht anstelle (s.u. Anm. 96) – einer

durch kurfürstliches Mandat im Februar 1526 als Liturgie für das ganze Territorium[96] nach vollständigem Ende der mittelalterlichen Messe[97] brachte die Institutionalisierung des evangelischen Gottesdienstes ans Ziel[98] – und damit das Herzstück der Institutionalisierung der evangeli-

---

lateinischen nun auch eine muttersprachliche Liturgie vorzulegen, sondern auch für die Integration von der Gemeinde selbst gesungener Lieder und die konsequente Neugestaltung des Abendmahlsteils als Worte und Gesten zusammenbindendes Gabegeschehen (vgl. WENDEBOURG, Essen [s. Anm. 92], 59). Freilich deutet Luther auch hier an, daß das letzte Wort noch nicht gesprochen sei, und konkretisiert das für zwei Punkte. Der eine ist der Gesang der Gemeinde: Man habe – die evangelische Kirchenliedproduktion hatte ja erst begonnen – noch nicht so viele deutsche Gemeindelieder, wie man sie für die deutschen Messen, zumal an Festtagen, brauche (WA 19,112,14–16). Der andere Punkt sind die der herkömmlichen Perikopenordnung folgenden sonntäglichen Epistel- und Evangeliumslesungen, über die er sich schon in der *Formula missae* nicht glücklich gezeigt hatte (WA 12,209,16–210,4), deren Auswahl aber auch in der *Deutschen Messe* nicht verändert wurde: Das solle in Wittenberg »einstweilen« (»auff eyn zeit«, vgl. oben Anm. 92) so bleiben, was im Blick auf die vielen Theologiestudenten in der Stadt nützlich sei, die das Predigen lernen sollten und sich in ihren zukünftigen Gemeinden meist nach derselben Ordnung würden richten müssen. Doch sei nichts gegen die an anderen Orten eingeführte *lectio continua*, die in Wittenberg für den Sonntagnachmittags- und bestimmte Wochengottesdienste vorgesehen war, auch am Sonntagmorgen einzuwenden – und das »einstweilen« deutet an, daß Luther sich eine solche Weiterentwicklung auch in Wittenberg vorstellen konnte (WA 19,79,7–14). Kurz, auch für die *Deutsche Messe* gilt in manchen Punkten noch:»dis werck ist ym anheben« (a.a.O., 112,16).

[96] Bericht Georg Spalatins in seinem *Chronicon sive Annales*, in: Scriptores Rerum Germanicarum, Praecipue Saxonicarum, hg. v. Johann Burkard Mencke, Leipzig 1728, Bd. 2, 654. Daß die *Deutsche Messe* für das gesamte Kurfürstentum gelten solle, schrieb Luther schon, während er an der Ausarbeitung saß (nämlich am 27.9.1525 an Nikolaus Hausmann: WA.Br 3,585,5f. [Nr. 926]), und sagt auch die Einleitung der *Deutschen Messe* selbst (WA 19,73,6–8). Dazu steht nicht in Widerspruch, daß Luther, wenn bestimmte »Ursachen« gegeben seien – nämlich die Präsenz einer internationalen, des Deutschen nicht mächtigen Gemeinde oder die lateinische Sprache lernender Schüler –, die weitere Verwendung der *Formula Missae* vorsah (WA 19,73,32–74,21). Die Einheitlichkeit des Gottesdienstes im gesamten Territorium, von der das kurfürstliche Mandat sprach, gab es nie. Auch wenn die *Deutsche Messe* im Gebrauch weit überwog, wurde sie nicht unverändert übernommen (PAHL, Coena domini [s. Anm. 93], 30). Zum Teil setzten sich auch Formulare durch, die lateinische oder ins Deutsche übersetzte Anteile der *Formula Missae* und Anteile der *Deutschen Messe* verbanden (a.a.O., 30–32), wobei die Übernahmen aus dem älteren Formular allerdings gegenüber der Fassung von 1523 weiterentwickelt waren. Das galt auch in Wittenberg, doch mit flexibler liturgischer Praxis bei unterschiedlichen Gelegenheiten (JOHANNES BERGSMA, Die Reform der Meßliturgie durch Joh. Bugenhagen, Hildesheim 1966, 92–97).

[97] Nämlich Ende 1524, als sie auch in der letzten Bastion, dem Wittenberger Allerheiligenstift, gefallen war (KRENTZ [s. Anm. 38], 369–371).

[98] Ihr waren die Neuregelung des Kirchenjahres und aller anderen Gottesdienste, nämlich der für die Messe ergänzenden sonntäglichen Predigtgottesdienste frühmorgens und nachmittags und der die Wochenmessen ersetzenden allmorgendlichen Predigtgottesdienste sowie von Mette und Vesper, vorausgegangen. Hierfür waren bereits 1523 in der kleinen für die Gemeinde von Leisnig verfaßten Schrift *Von Ordnung Gottesdiensts in der Gemeinde* (WA 12,35–37, aufgenommen in der *Formulae missae*: a.a.O., 219,8–29) Reformen angeregt und in Wittenberg sowie andernorts entsprechende Veränderungen

schen Kirche Kursachsens. Im Jahr zuvor schon war dieser Prozeß weit
südwestlich in Zürich[99] und nordöstlich in Preußen[100] sowie in der Reichsstadt Nürnberg[101] zum Abschluß gekommen, während man in anderen
Gegenden des Reiches noch mehr oder weniger lange auf dem Wege war.

2.2. England

In England sollte man noch sehr lange auf dem Wege sein – und es fragt
sich, ob man überhaupt schon auf dem Wege war. Ein Vorzeichen vor
diesen Weg setzte die Schrift, mit der sich das Königreich England in der
Frühzeit der Reformation offiziell gegenüber dem religiösen Aufbruch im
Reich positionierte: Heinrichs VIII. *Assertio septem sacramentorum adversus Martinum Lutherum* von 1521.[102] War doch diese hochpolemische
Schrift gegen Luthers »Vorspiel« *De captivitate Babylonica* von unmittelbarer Bedeutung für das Thema Gottesdienst. Denn wie in Luthers Traktat, so stand auch in Heinrichs Replik im Mittelpunkt die Messe. Und
jedem Leser wurde klar, daß an diesem Punkt mit dem König nicht zu
spaßen sein würde. Das sollte sich das gesamte Vierteljahrhundert hindurch, das Heinrich noch regieren würde, bewahrheiten. Zwar lehnte der
König auch andere reformatorische Anliegen wie die Rechtfertigung *sola
fide* ab, doch ließ er hier abweichende Ansichten eher durchgehen. In
Fragen wie denen der muttersprachlichen Bibel, der Beichte oder der
kirchlichen Bilder bewegte er sich sogar selbst. Doch mit Kritik an der

---

in Angriff genommen worden. In der *Deutschen Messe* wird dann das ganze Tableau der
Wochengottesdienste geboten (WA 19,79,17–80,24).

[99] In der Karwoche 1525 (12. April) wurde vom Zürcher Rat die Messe verboten und
beschlossen, Zwinglis Liturgie *Aktion und Brauch* als neue Gottesdienstordnung einzuführen, was am Gründonnerstag geschah (JOHANNES VOIGTLÄNDER, Ein Fest der Befreiung. Huldrych Zwinglis Abendmahlslehre, Neukirchen-Vluyn 2013, 67).

[100] Am 10. Dezember 1525 wurde vom preußischen Landtag in Königsberg eine evangelische Gottesdienstordnung für das ganze Territorium beschlossen, die die evangelischen Bischöfe des Herzogtums auf Anweisung Herzog Albrechts ausgearbeitet hatten
und die sich an Luthers *Formula Missae* anschloß, aber auch eigene Züge trug (D.
ERDMANN, Art. Albrecht von Preußen, in: RE³ 1, 310–323, hier: 318). Siehe auch: Die
evangelischen Kirchenordnungen des XVI. Jahrhunderts, hg. v. Emil Sehling, Bd. 4,
Erlangen 1911, 30–38 (vgl. Die evangelischen Kirchenordnungen des 16. Jahrhunderts,
hg. v. Aemilius Richter, Bd. 1, Weimar 1846, 23–33).

[101] ANDREAS OSIANDER d. Ä., Gesamtausgabe, hg. v. Gerhard Müller, Bd. 1, Gütersloh 1975, 143–150; Quellen zur Nürnberger Reformationsgeschichte. Von der Duldung
liturgischer Änderungen bis zur Ausübung des Kirchenregiments durch den Rat (Juni
1524–Juni 1525), hg. v. Gerhard Pfeiffer, Nürnberg 1968, 400f., 440–447; MATTHIAS
SIMON, Wann fand die erste evangelische Abendmahlsfeier in den Pfarrkirchen zu Nürnberg statt? (in: Mitteilungen des Vereins für Geschichte der Stadt Nürnberg 45, 1954,
361–371, hier: 367).

[102] Hg. v. Pierre Fraenkel, Münster 1992.

Messe war eine rote Linie überschritten, die in keiner Hinsicht zur Debatte stand. Das machte der König immer wieder deutlich, und nicht umsonst sind noch drei der *Sechs Artikel*, die im Gefolge der fehlgeschlagenen
Verhandlungen mit Wittenberg 1539 die Abgrenzung von der dortigen
Reformation festschrieben, diesem Thema gewidmet.[103] Daß Bürger und
Bürgerinnen, die Kritik an der Messe übten, sich auf dem Scheiterhaufen
wiederfanden, stand bis zum Ende von Heinrichs Regierung fest.[104] Re-
alpolitische Voraussetzung war die für das ganze Königreich geltende
Durchsetzungskraft der Krone. Ihr zu entgehen, blieb nur das Exil jenseits
des Meeres. Damit befanden sich evangelisch gesinnte Engländer in einer
bedrängenderen Lage als die Bürger des Reiches, die, wenn sie Anhänger
der Reformation unter einem reformationsfeindlichen Fürsten waren,
leichter in ein anderes Reichsterritorium oder eine Reichsstadt ziehen
konnten. Nicht nur die vielen Verbrennungen und Emigrationen,[105] sondern auch die große Zahl von Widerrufen und Widerrufen der Widerrufe,[106] der im Reich nichts Vergleichbares gegenübersteht, spricht hier eine
deutliche Sprache – wir werden darauf zurückkommen.

Es gab aber noch einen weiteren Unterschied: Das Thema Messe hatte
für die englischen Evangelicals in der Zeit Heinrichs lange nicht dasselbe
Gewicht wie für die Evangelischen auf dem Kontinent. Von Luthers Ansichten wußte man aus der Kritik des Königs, aber auch eines John Fisher
oder Thomas Morus – Kritik macht nun einmal ihren Gegenstand bekannt. Als lateinische Fachliteratur reichten die kritischen Schriften aber
nicht über den engen Kreis des gelehrten Publikums hinaus. Das galt auch
für die Werke Luthers, die schon in den früheren 1520er Jahren und trotz
scharfer Zensur weiterhin ins Land kamen[107] und mehrfach verbrannt
wurden – ebenfalls lateinische Schriften. Unter den ohnehin wenigen Lu-
thertexten, die zu Heinrichs Zeiten ins Englische übersetzt wurden, gab es

---

[103] Statutes of the Realm, printed by command of His Majesty King George III. 1817,
739–740 (31° Henry VIII c. 14).
[104] Vgl. für die 1540er Jahre die Tabellen mit den Ursachen für antihäretische Todes-
urteile bei ALEC RYRIE, The Gospel and Henry VIII. Evangelicals in the Early English
Reformation, Cambridge 2003, 224f.
[105] Für die Jahre vom Erscheinen der *Six Articles* (1539) bis zu Heinrichs Tod 1547 vgl.
die Liste der Hingerichteten und der ins Exil Gegangenen a.a.O., Appendix I.
[106] Eine Auswahl bei SUSAN WABUDA, Equivocation and Recantation During the English Reformation: The ›Subtle Shadows‹ of Dr Edward Crome (in: JEH 44, 1993, 224–
242).
[107] Vgl. die Angaben zu den Verfassern evangelischer Bücher, die von 1535 bis 1547 in
dem besonders stark von reformatorischen Ideen ergriffenen Cambridge vorhanden waren, bei RYRIE, The Gospel (s. Anm. 104), 172. Ryrie nennt die seinen Angaben zu-
grundeliegenden Testamentsinventare »thick with the works of evangelical authors«.
Unter diesen Autoren lag Luther mit weitem Abstand vorne.

keinen zum Thema Messe oder Abendmahl; die in Deutschland so weit
verbreiteten Sakramentssermone Luthers etwa gehörten nicht dazu.[108] Erst
unter Edward erschien ein übersetzter Luthertext zum Thema, bezeichnenderweise die Abrechnung mit dem »papistischen Greuel« des Meßopfers in der Wittenberger Schloßkirche von 1524[109] – ihre Veröffentlichung
war Teil einer Schriftenoffensive gegen die überlieferte Messe, die unter
dem neuen König losbrach und dessen Gottesdienstreform, das *Book of
Common Prayer*, vorbereitete.[110]

   Kein vordringliches Thema waren der Gottesdienst im Allgemeinen
und das Abendmahl im Besonderen während der ersten Phase der Rezeption und Verarbeitung reformatorischer Gedanken auch in den Schriften,
die englische Reformatoren selber verfaßten.[111] Gegenüber dem Themen-
feld *Rechtfertigung und Ethik* standen sie weit zurück. Erst 1533 erschienen die ersten abendmahlstheologischen Traktate, Abhandlungen von
John Frith[112] und George Joye.[113] Beide stehen unter dem abendmahls-

---

[108] Vgl. zu diesen Übersetzungen Carrie Euler, Does Faith Translate? Tudor Translations of Martin Luther and the Doctrine of Justification by Faith (in: ARG 101, 2010,
80–113). Übergreifend Bernd Moeller, Luther in Europe: His works in Translation
1517–1546 (in: Politics and Society in Reformation Europe, FS Geoffrey Elton, hg. v.
E. I. Kouri u. Tom Scott, Basingstoke 1987, 235–251).

[109] Ein Sermon von der höchsten Gotteslästerung: WA 15, 765–774. Auf Englisch
enthalten in der Schrift: The Dysclosyng of the Canon [th]e popysh Masse, with a
sermon annexed unto it of [th]e famous Clerke of worthy memorye. D. Marten Luther,
London s.a. [1548?] (vgl. WA 15,761).

[110] Euler (s. Anm. 108), 91, spricht von einem »rash of polemical treatises against the
Mass« in jener Zeit. Siehe zu diesem »rash« auch John N. King, John Day, Master
printer of the English Reformation (in: The Beginnings of English Protestantism, hg. v.
Peter Marshall u Alec Ryrie, Cambridge 2002, 180–208, hier: 190–192).

[111] Vgl. den Überblick von Anthea Hume, English Protestant Books Printed Abroad,
1525–1535: An Annotated Bibliography (in: The Complete Works of St. Thomas More,
Bd. VIII/2, hg. v. Louis A. Schuster u.a., New Haven u.a. 1973, Appendix B, 1063–1091).

[112] A Book Made by John Frith [...] Answering unto M. More's Letter, Monster 1533.
Vorher geschrieben worden war ein anderer kurzer Text zu demselben Thema: A Christian Sentence, s.l. s.a. (wohl 1532, erschienen erst um 1545; The Work of John Frith, hg.
v. N. T. Wright, Oxford 1978, The Courtenay Library of Reformation Classics 7, 319–
449, 478–484).

[113] The Souper of the Lorde, s.l. 1533. Der Text wurde fälschlich William Tyndale
zugeschrieben und deshalb von der Parker Society unter dessen Namen herausgegeben:
An Answer to Sir Thomas More's Dialogue, the Supper of the lord after the true meaning of John VI. and 1. Cor. XI. [...] Expounded by William Tyndale, martyr, 1536, hg. v.
Henry Walter, Cambridge 1850, The Parker Society 3, 216–268. Tyndale verfaßte hingegen zur selben Zeit einen auch das Abendmahl behandelnden Traktat (A Brief Declaration upon the Sacraments), der allerdings erst zwölf Jahre nach seiner Hinrichtung
in Villevoorde erschien (London 1548; in: Doctrinal Treatises and Introductions to Different Portions of the Holy Scripture by William Tyndale, martyr, 1536, hg. v. Henry
Walter, Cambridge 1848, The Parker Society 1, 345–385). Dazu: Arne Dembek, William
Tyndale (1491–1536). Reformatorische Theologie als kontextuelle Schriftauslegung, Tübingen 2010, 435–451.

theologischen Einfluß der Schweiz,[114] von der aus, insbesondere seitens Bullingers, damals gerade offensiv Kontakte nach England aufgenommen wurden.[115] D.h., daß die abendmahlstheologische Reflexion sozusagen im Sprung in der – vom Kontinent aus gesehen – zweiten abendmahltheologischen Phase der Reformation einsetzte, jener Phase, die vom Streit über die Realpräsenz bestimmt war. Und Frith wie Joye sprachen sich hier für die Schweizer Sicht aus[116] – eine Option, die von der starken humanistischen Prägung der englischen Reformatoren her nahelag, in der sich aber möglicherweise auch unterschwellige lollardische Einflüsse auswirkten.[117] Kehrseite des Sprungs auf diesen Stand der abendmahlstheologischen Debatte war, daß die Anliegen, die zu Beginn der Reformation auf dem Kontinent im Mittelpunkt gestanden hatten, bei den englischen Reformatoren bloß eine marginale Rolle spielten: Zum einen die Kommunion *sub utraque specie* – für dieses im Reich schwer erkämpfte Recht erhob sich kaum[118] eine englische Stimme.[119] Zum anderen die Ablehnung der Opfer-

---

[114] Diesen Einfluß zeigt auch der gleichzeitig entstandene Traktat Tyndales (s. vorige Anm.), der dabei allerdings stärker an der abendmahlstheologischen Position des frühreformatorischen Luther festhält, welche den späteren Trennungen noch vorausliegt (DEMBEK [s. Anm. 113], 438f., s.a. 151f.).

[115] CARRIE EULER, Couriers of the Gospel: England and Zurich, 1531–1558, Zürich 2006.

[116] Die im Abendmahlsstreit ausgearbeitete Wittenberger Position vertrat von den bekannten englischen Reformatoren nur Robert Barnes, Luthers und anderer Wittenberger langjähriger Tischgenosse (CARL R. TRUEMAN, Early English Evangelicals: Three Examples, in: Sister Reformations – Schwesterreformationen. The Reformation in Deutschland und England, hg. v. Dorothea Wendebourg, Tübingen 2010, 15–28, hier: 23–27). Das heißt nicht, es habe unter den evangelisch Gesinnten in England unter König Heinrich keine Verfechter der Realpräsenz gegeben. Wie ALEC RYRIE (The Strange Death of Lutheran England, in: JEH 53, 2002, 64–92, hier: 69–74) zeigt, hielt die in den 1530er Jahren aufsteigende evangelische Partei, deren Hautrepräsentanten Thomas Cromwell und Königin Anne waren, überwiegend an der Realpräsenz fest und tat es auch in den 1540er Jahren durchaus noch mancher; eine bestimmte theologische Theorie über die Ablehnung der philosophischen Explikation hinaus, die in der Transsubstantiationslehre geboten wird, war damit nicht verbunden. Wie weit das allein schon reicht, eine Position als »lutherisch« einzuschätzen, ist fraglich (vgl. u. Anm. 120). Im übrigen ist die Rede von der Gegenwart oder vom Essen des Leibes Christi als solche noch kein Indiz für das Festhalten an der Realpräsenz – so konnten auch reformierte Theologen sprechen. Zudem machten nicht wenige Evangelische auf diesem gefährlichen Feld bewußt von Äquivokationen Gebrauch, an vorderster Front der von Ryrie (a.a.O., 90f.) umstandslos als »lutherischer« Realpräsenzverfechter angeführte Edward Crome (s. WABUDA, Equivocation [s. Anm. 106]) – den er an anderer Stelle selbst »England's master of ambiguity« nennt (The Gospel [s. Anm. 104], 34; ähnlich schon SUSAN BRIDGEN, London and the Reformation, Oxford 1991, 332).

[117] Zur radikal realpräsenzkritischen Haltung Wyclifs und der Lollarden vgl. RICHARD REX, The Lollards, Basingstoke 2002, 42–45, 60, 77.

[118] Eine Ausnahme war Robert Barnes, der sich von Wittenberg aus im achten *commonplace* seiner *Supplication unto Henry the Eighth* gegen die *communio sub una* wendet, ja sogar, im Unterschied zu Luther, die Kommunion *sub utraque* für verpflichtend

messe – auch dieses bis ins zweite Drittel der 1520er Jahre die abendmahlstheologischen Debatten auf dem Kontinent bestimmende Thema nahmen
englischen Reformationsanhänger selten auf;[120] wenn es zur Sprache kam,
geschah es meist im Zusammenhang des Fegfeuers.[121]

Alles in allem kann man sagen: Sieht man von jener zunächst kleinen
Gruppe von Theologen ab, die unter Schweizer und oberdeutschem Ein-

---

und die Abweichung für Todsünde erklärt (James P. Lusardi, The Career of Robert
Barnes, in: The Complete Works of St. Thomas More, Bd. VIII/3, hg. v. Louis A.
Schuster u.a., New Haven u.a. 1973, 1365–1415, hier: 1387–1389).

[119] Das mag auch damit zusammenhängen, daß die Lollarden, im Gegensatz zu den
Hussiten, kein Interesse daran gehabt hatten (Rex [s. Anm. 117], 73).

[120] Eine Ausnahme ist wiederum Robert Barnes, der sich in Artikel 19 seiner *Sententiae ex doctoribus collectae, quas papistae valde impugnant hodie. Per Anto. Anglum.*,
Wittenberg 1530 (deutsch in Bugenhagens Übersetzung: Fürnemlich Artikel der Christenlichen kirchen, wie die bey den alten im brauch gewesen unnd gehalten sind worden,
aber yetzt unbillich von den papisten, wider die heilige geschrifft, ihr eigen Decret,
Concilia und schrifften der Lerer verdampt werden. Erstlich in latein durch D. Anthonium auss Engelandt zusamen gebracht, neulich mit einer vorred Ioan. Pomerani
pfarherr zu Wittenberg verdeutscht, Nürnberg 1531) nachdrücklich gegen das Meßopfer
wendet. So ist die Entwicklung der Messe auch in seiner Verfallsgeschichte des Papsttums (Vitae Romanorum pontificum, Wittenberg 1536) ein ausführlich behandelter Kri-
tikpunkt (vgl. Korey D. Maas, The Reformation and Robert Barnes: History, Theology, and Polemic in Early Modern England, Woodbridge 2010, 116–119). Im übrigen
bringen die wenigen anderen englischen Theologen, die denn doch gegen das Meßopfer
schreiben oder sprechen, dazu ganz überwiegend das Argument vor, das sich vor allem
bei Zwingli und anderen Schweizern findet, nämlich daß das Abendmahl dankbares
Gedächtnis des einmaligen Opfers Christi auf Golgatha und darum nicht selbst Opfer
sei (z.B. Tyndale: Dembek [s. Anm. 112], 211, oder Crome: Brigden [s. Anm. 116], 363).
Keine Rolle spielt hingegen das Argument, das bei Luther im Mittelpunkt der Meßop-
ferkritik steht, nämlich daß das Abendmahl Gottes Gabe an die Gemeinde und nicht
deren Handeln Gott gegenüber sei. Diese Differenz wird eingeebnet, wenn Ryrie von
einer gemeinsamen »Abneigung« (dislike) gegen das Meßopfer bei Lutheranern und
Reformierten schreibt, die er darin begründet sieht, daß das Meßopfer der protestantischen Rechtfertigungslehre widerspreche (Strange Death [s. Anm. 116], 72; The Gospel
[s. Anm. 104], 141). Überhaupt ist das, was er als das spezifisch Lutherische an der
Abendmahlsauffassung des »Lutheran England« der Henricianischen Zeit wahrnimmt,
nämlich das Festhalten an der Realpräsenz bei einer ganzen Reihe englischer Evangelischer (s.o. Anm. 116), ein wenig dünn. Steht doch die Realpräsenz bei Luther nicht für
sich, sondern ist eingebettet in seine Auffassung vom Abendmahl als leiblicher Selbst-
gabe Christi im Mahl. Davon findet sich bei den von Ryrie als Anhänger der lutherischen Abendmahlslehre vorgestellten englischen Evangelischen kaum etwas. Wenn er
schreibt, am Ende, nämlich in den mittleren 1540er Jahren, »[t]he theological issue of the
sacrifice of the mass was swept away as the battle polarised over the Real Presence«
(a.a.O., 91), so ist dazu zweierlei zu sagen: Das Meßopfer war, anders als in der Reformation im Reich, eben nie ein vorrangiges Thema gewesen. Und das in England, wenn
das Thema doch aufkam, vorherrschende Gegenargument, daß die Messe ein Akt des
dankbaren Gedächtnisses von Christi Opfer und deshalb nicht selbst Opfer sei, läuft auf
jenes »sweeping away« hinaus, weil für ein als Gedächtnisakt der Kirche definiertes
Abendmahl die Realpräsenz nicht nötig, ja, darin ein Fremdkörper ist.

[121] Siehe unten S. 402.

fluß standen und die Realpräsenzfrage immer schärfer erörterten, war das Thema Messe überhaupt für die englischen Evangelischen von minderem theologischem Interesse. Wenn nur das, woran ihnen vor allem lag, die Lehre von der Rechtfertigung allein im Glauben, festgehalten wurde, dann waren sie, falls nötig, willens, »to swallow their objections to the mass«.[122] Bestätigt wird dieser Befund von den überlieferten Predigten. Auch hier gilt – mit einer Ausnahme, von der noch die Rede sein wird – der Messe kein besonderes Interesse. In den großen, englandweit bedeutenden Londoner Freiluftpredigten an St. Paul's Cross, soweit sie erhalten sind, kam sie in der Zeit Heinrichs fast nicht vor.[123] Und auch auf anderen Kanzeln war sie kein wichtiges Thema evangelischer Prediger.[124]

Was heißt das alles, wenn wir nach Schritten von der theologischen Einsicht zur institutionellen Veränderung des Gottesdienstes fragen? Ist diese für das Reich ergiebige Frage für England möglicherweise gegenstandslos – gegenstandslos, weil wir keine Quellen haben, die uns solche Schritte zeigen, oder weil es wegen der besonderen Bedingungen, unter denen sich die englische Reformation entwickelte, solche Schritte gar nicht gab? In der Tat wissen wir wenig, denn was für die Evangelischen zu Heinrichs Zeit allgemein gilt, gilt erst recht für ihr Verhalten an diesem Punkt: »They bought their survival at the [...] price of historical anonymity.«[125] Und was ihr Verhalten selbst betrifft, so ließ die eiserne Hand der königlichen Kirchenpolitik, die das ganze Land im Griff hatte, zweifellos

---

[122] RYRIE, Strange Death (s. Anm. 116), 74. Ryrie nennt diese überwiegend im Land sitzenden Evangelicals im Gegensatz zu den unter Schweizer und oberdeutschem Einfluß stehenden, vielfach im Exil schreibenden »Lutheraner«, deren Gegenwart in England bis weit in die 1540er Jahre hinein zeige, daß von einem »Tod« des »Lutheran England« jener Zeit noch keineswegs die Rede sein könne. Zu den Grenzen dieses Etiketts s.o. Anm. 120.

[123] In einer Predigt von 1536 wurde das Meßopfer als eines der vielen fälschlich als Verdienste betrachteten Werke zurückgewiesen (WABUDA, Preaching [s. Anm. 13], 85f.). Mit antievangelischer Zielrichtung sprach Simon Matthew, der den königlichen Supremat und die abendmahlstheologische Linie Henrichs verfocht, in seiner vermutlich an Karfreitag 1537 gehaltenen Paul's-Cross-Predigt Transsubstantiationslehre und Meßopfer an, indem er sie verteidigte (SIMON MATTHEW, ›Christus passus est pro nobis‹: A Good Friday Sermon [ca. 1537], hg. v. Richard Rex, in: Sermons at Paul's Cross, 1521–1642, hg. v. Torrance Kirby, Oxford 2017, 57–84, hier 62f.). Zu den Themen, die in den 1530er Jahren das Feld beherrschten, nämlich abgesehen von der Frage der königlichen Suprematie die Rechtfertigung und die Rolle der Ethik, zeitweilig auch die von Heinrich angeordnete Zerstörung kirchlicher Bildwerke und Reliquien, vgl. den Überblick von RICHARD REX, Pauls's Cross and the Crisis of the 1530s (in: St. Pauls's Cross and the Culture of Persuasion in England, 1520–1640, hg. v. Torrance Kirby u. P. G. Stanwood, Leiden 2014, 107–128).

[124] Das zeigen die Angaben zu den vielen Predigten, die WABUDA, Preaching (s. Anm. 13) auswertet.

[125] RYRIE, The Gospel (s. Anm. 104), 223.

wenig Raum für Manöver. Wenn sich hier und dort freiere Räume ergaben, dann wegen der Wendungen, die diese Politik selber nahm. Aber
Heinrichs Kehren betrafen kaum den Gottesdienst und schon gar nicht die
Messe. So scheint es auffälliges abweichendes Verhalten kaum gegeben zu
haben. Unter den Häresieanklagen gegen Laien aus London und Kent aus
den frühen 1540er Jahren findet sich der Vorwurf der Gottesdienststörung,[126] doch die Zahlen sind klein.[127] Häufiger war offenbar, jedenfalls in
London, die Gottesdienstabstinenz.[128] Daß Laien lautstark und in größeren Mengen den Gottesdienst in der eigenen Sprache, die Kommunion in
beiden Gestalten oder gar die Abschaffung der Messe gefordert, daß sie
Predigten und die Messe unterbrochen hätten, wie wir es aus dem Reich
hören, gab es in England offenbar nicht.

Doch wie im Reich bot einen gewissen Ausweg für Gemeindeglieder,
die der Messe kritisch gegenüberstanden, die geistliche Parallelhandlung:
Evangelisch geprägte *Primer*, eine Mischung von Stunden- und Andachts-
büchern für Laien, boten evangelische Auslegungen traditioneller liturgischer Stücke, über die man während des Gottesdienstes meditieren konnte, und vor allem boten sie dazu die für die Messe strikt verbotenen muttersprachlichen Versionen der gottesdienstlichen Bibellesungen und des
Vaterunsers.[129] Eine andere Parallelhandlung wurde geboren, nachdem

---

[126] Damit werden Vorkommnisse gemeint gewesen sein, wie sie aus London berichtet
wurden: Einige Gemeindeglieder seien während der Wandlung in der Kirche herumge-
laufen und hätten dabei die Mütze auf dem Kopf gelassen, auch hätten sie demonstrativ
von der elevierten Hostie weggeblickt (BRIDGEN [s. Anm. 116], 406). Wenn dort
Schmählieder gegen das Abendmahl und überhaupt gegen die Sakramente gesungen
wurden, dann handelte es sich wohl um Auftritte außerhalb der Messe (ebd.).

[127] RYRIE, The Gospel (s. Anm. 104), 225, s.a. 227. Etwas größer sind die Zahlen aus
Kent, und zwar bei Laien wie beim Klerus, die den sog. Ikonoklasmus betreffen (a.a.O.,
224f., vgl. auch 227). Doch hier konnte man immerhin daran anknüpfen, daß Heinrich
selbst sich bilderkritisch geäußert und die Entfernung und Zerstörung von Bildern und
Reliquien verfügt hatte (a.a.O., 231: »Henry VIII's regime was more unequivocally
evangelical in its attitude towards images than in almost any other area, and most even of
the Kentish iconoclasts were doing no more than pushing at the limits of royal policy«).
Freilich wäre die Formulierung »unequivocally reformed« angemessener als »unequivocally evangelical«, da die Lutheraner keine Bilderfeinde waren.

[128] A.a.O., 225.

[129] Einen Überblick über die außerordentlich populären, in vielen Ausgaben heraus-
gekommenen, auch verbotenes ausländisches Material wie anonym abgedruckte Texte
Martin Luthers enthaltenden englischsprachigen Andachtsbücher, die 1545 in den *Authorized Primer of Henry VIII* mündeten, einen »direct forerunner of the Book of
Common Prayer« gibt CHARLES C. BUTTERWORTH, The English Primers 1529–1545,
Philadelphia 1953. Eine Liste der biblischen Texte: a.a.O., 288–290 (Zitat S. VII). Das
einzige gottesdienstliche Element, für das Heinrich das Englische zuließ, ja, für das er
1544 eine offizielle muttersprachliche Fassung veröffentlichen ließ, war die Litanei – und
diese machte starke Anleihen bei Luther (BRYAN D. SPINKS, German Influences on
Edwardian Liturgies, in: Sister Reformations – Schwesterreformationen. Die Reforma-

Heinrich 1537 das Verbot zwar nicht des gottesdienstlichen Gebrauchs, doch das – im Heiligen Römischen Reich undenkbare[130] – Verbot der Lektüre der Bibel auf Englisch aufgehoben hatte. Von 1538 an lagen Exemplare des lange ersehnten Buches – angekettet – in allen Kirchen aus, und während der Messen, die ja überwiegend unhörbar und unsichtbar vor sich gingen, lasen lesekundige Gemeindeglieder sich und anderen laut daraus vor.[131] Diese Lesungen wurden zumindest in Londoner Kirchen eine regelrechte Attraktion, ein guter Vorleser wie der Schneider John Porter hatte, wie es hieß, »a greater audience« als die Messe oder die Matutin, und eine Mrs. Castle machte sich einen Namen als »a reader of the scripture in the church«. Dem Klerus gefiel das wenig, und nach wenigen Jahren wurde solches »brabbeling of the New Testament« als Gottesdienststörung verboten, ja schließlich auch wieder die Bibellektüre von Laien und insbesondere Frauen überhaupt. Mr. Porter und Mrs. Castle, die sich nicht beugten, wurden verhaftet, der Schneider starb im Gefängnis.[132] Doch so spektakulär diese Fälle erschienen, waren es doch aufs Ganze gesehen Randphänomene. Die weit überwiegende Zahl der Evangelischen verhielt sich liturgisch konform. Man nahm an den für alle Bürger des Landes verpflichtenden Gottesdiensten teil, wie immer man zu ihnen stand. Daneben gab es private Konventikeltreffen in Privathäusern – in wie großer Dichte, ist nicht bekannt.[133] Doch zu gottesdienstlichen Feiern scheinen

---

tion in Deutschland und in England, hg. v. Dorothea Wendebourg, Tübingen 2010, 175–189, hier: 180).

[130] Im Reich gab es bekanntlich schon vor der Reformation volkssprachliche Bibelübersetzungen. Die Phobie der englischen Kirche und des Königs vor englischen Bibeln, die sogar das weitgehende Verschwinden englischsprachiger Andachtsbücher (primer) zur Folge hatte, rührte davon her, daß Wicliff und die Lollarden die Forderung nach volkssprachlichen Bibelübersetzungen auf ihre Fahnen geschrieben und zum Angelpunkt ihres Programms selbständiger religiöser Beteiligung der Laien gemacht hatten. So waren in den Augen der kirchlichen Obrigkeit vernikulare religiöse Texte mit »sectarian danger« verbunden (REMIE TARGOFF, Common Prayer. The Language of Public Devotion in Early Modern England, Chicago 2001, 19). Was im Reich der Laienkelch als Symbol der hussitischen Bedrohung war, war in England die muttersprachliche Bibel als Inbegriff der lollardischen Gefahr. Etwas davon scheint noch nachzuklingen, wenn Eamon Duffy – 1992 bzw. 2005! – die Volkssprache das in die überlieferte gottesdienstliche Praxis eingeführte »Trojanische Pferd« nennt (The Stripping of the Altars. Traditional Religion in England c. 1400–c. 1580, New Haven [2]2005, 222).

[131] Das Folgende bei WABUDA, Preaching (s. Anm. 13), 101–103. Eine andere, glücklicher endende Geschichte über öffentliche Lektüre der endlich zugänglichen Bibel durch Laien in der Kirche s. bei ARTHUR G. DICKENS, The English Reformation, London [2]1989, 213.

[132] Nach BRIDGEN (s. Anm. 116), 332, wurde ihm vorgeworfen, daß er das Vorlesen aus der Bibel mit der Verbreitung häretischer Ansichten über die Natur des Brotes im Abendmahl verbunden habe.

[133] Die höchste Dichte wies London auf, wo sie 1540 in großer Zahl verhaftet wurden (RYRIE, Gospel [s. Anm. 104], 238). London war von Anfang an die Stadt mit der

diese Treffen nicht gedient zu haben, man las im Geheimen »häretische« Bücher und hörte »häretische« Predigten und fiel ansonsten nicht auf – ein Verhaltensmuster, das schon die Lollarden gepflegt hatten.[134] Kritiker im evangelischen Lager, insbesondere jene, die im Exil lebten, lehnten solchen »Nikodemismus« ab.[135]

Und wie verhielten sich die Amtsträger? Gab es evangelisch gesinnte Priester, die liturgische Konsequenzen aus ihren reformatorischen Einsichten zogen? Hielten manche vielleicht keine Messen mehr, sondern beschränkten sich auf die Predigt, um Gewissenskonflikten zu entgehen?[136] Was den letztgenannten Ausweg betrifft, so ist es fraglich, ob abgesehen von außergewöhnlichen Predigten wie jenen von Paul's Cross überhaupt eine liturgische Möglichkeit für Predigten ohne Verbindung mit einer Messe bestand, vergleichbar den Predigtgottesdiensten im Reich. So sehen wir denn auch nirgends, daß Priester von der Predigt her eine neue, evangelische Gottesdienstform entwickelt hätten. Und wie stand es mit liturgischen Veränderungen innerhalb der Messe selbst? Gab es Versuche, die Liturgie oder jedenfalls die Bibellesungen in englischer Sprache vorzutragen, die Einsetzungsworte laut und muttersprachlich zu rezitieren, die Kommunion unter beiden Gestalten auszuteilen? Wir lesen von drei Unternehmungen dieser Art: In den Gemeinden von Hadleigh und Stratford in Suffolk sei 1538 »divers tymes« die Messe auf Englisch gelesen worden,[137] und der Pfarrer der Londoner Kirche St. Mary Colechurch habe an

---

größten Zahl von »Häretikern«, sieht man von Cambridge mit seinen besonderen Umständen ab (vgl. BRIDGEN [s. Anm. 116], 187–198).

[134] RYRIE, The Gospel [s. Anm. 104], 237–239.

[135] A.a.O., 132f. Dieses auf dem Kontinent, nicht zuletzt von Bullinger und Calvin, gebrauchte Wort findet sich allerdings in England nicht (a.a.O., 84).

[136] Vielleicht war das bei Nicholas Ridley der Fall. In dem Rückblick, den Ridley in seinem Abschiedsbrief vor der Verbrennung schrieb, heißt es, als *vicar* in Kent habe er bereits »not after the popish trade but after the Christs gospel« gepredigt, aber ihm sei von Gott noch nicht »the true doctryne of the Lords supper« offenbart worden (Abschiedsbrief, abgedruckt in: Certain most godly, fruitful, and comfortable letters of such true Saintes and holy Martyrs of God, hg. v. Miles Coverdale, London 1564, 92f.; vgl. WABUDA, Preaching [s. Anm. 13], 71). Aus diesen Sätzen könnte man schließen, daß er danach, als ihm die rechte Abendmahlslehre offenbar gewesen sei, nicht mehr nach der falschen zelebriert habe. Ob er in der Position, die er anschließend bekleidete, der eines Hofkaplans, um die Meßverpflichtung herumkam, ist allerdings sehr fraglich.

[137] »[A]t Hadleigh in Suffolk and at Stratforde [...], the mass and consecration of the sacrament of the aulter was sayd in Englishe by the curats there divers tymes« (Zitat aus Wriothesley's *Chronicle*: JOHN CRAIG, Reformation, Politics and Polemics. The Growth of Protestantism in East Anglian Market Towns, 1500–1610, Aldershot 2001, 171; ein Hinweis, den ich meinem Mitarbeiter Dr. Ashley Null verdanke). Darauf bezieht sich vermutlich die Bemerkung, 1538 hätten einige »evangelische Enthusiasten« englische Gottesdienste gefeiert, bei DIARMAID MacCULLOCH, Thomas Cranmer. A Life, New Haven 1996, 223.

Ostern 1542 die Sakramente in englischer Sprache gereicht.[138] Im Fall Hadleighs hing dieser eklatante liturgische Verstoß gegen kirchliches und königliches Recht vermutlich damit zusammen, daß es sich um eine unmittelbar dem Erzbischof von Canterbury unterstehende Gemeinde (peculiar) handelte, zu jener Zeit also Thomas Cranmer, unter dessen schützender Hand man schon einmal wagen konnte, was sonst zu gefährlich gewesen wäre.[139] Jedenfalls liegen hier ganz vereinzelte Ausnahmen vor, von weiteren Orten neben den drei genannten ist nichts dergleichen bekannt.[140]

Ob der eine oder andere Priester zu der weniger auffälligen Maßnahme griff, anstößige Opfergebete wegzulassen, ist angesichts der Unhörbarkeit der Kanonrezitation nicht nachzuweisen; Nachrichten darüber wie im Fall des Reiches haben wir nicht, es wäre in England auch noch erheblich riskanter gewesen. Und im übrigen spielte die Meßopferfrage, wie schon gesagt, keine Rolle, die mit der in den kontinentalen Debatten vergleichbar war. In größeren Nöten befanden sich jene – bis weit in die 1540er Jahre die Minderheit ausmachenden – Evangelischen, die die Realpräsenz bestritten; wurde doch die leibliche Gegenwart Christi im Sakrament in einer Weise rituell zur Geltung gebracht, die für jedermann offensichtlich war: in der Elevation der konsekrierten Hostie mit der anschließenden Anbetung.[141] Nicht umsonst sollte bei der im Ganzen sehr konservativen liturgischen Reform, die das erste *Book of Common Prayer* von 1549 bot, die Abschaffung der Elevation die entscheidende, von Freund und Feind verstandene Neuerung sein.[142] Das war unter dem reformierten Regime Kö-

---

[138] BRIDGEN (s. Anm. 116), 402.
[139] CRAIG (s. Anm. 137), 152. So brachte Cranmer hier auch gefährdete Reformationsanhänger unter (a.a.O., 153; SUSAN WABUDA, Setting forth the Word of God: Archbishop Cranmer's Early Patronage of Preachers, in: Thomas Cranmer. Churchman and Scholar, hg. v. Paul Ayris u. David Selwyn, Woodbridge 1993, 75–88, hier: 84).
[140] Wenn WABUDA, Cranmer (s. Anm. 139), 88, schreibt, »it may have been evident that [Cramner's] licencees advanced changes in ceremonies and rites«, dann bleibt sie die Angabe von Quellen schuldig, auf die sich dieser Satz stützt.
[141] Meßkritische Äußerungen, die diesem Punkt gelten, gab es kaum; Ausnahmen sind wohl die Proteste gegen einen *worship* Christi im Abendmahl, die sich auf Elevation und Adoration beziehen müssen (BRIDGEN [s. Anm. 116], 351, 406). Vgl. auch Anm. 126.
[142] So lautet die einschlägige Rubrik im *Book of Common Prayer* von 1549: »These wordes before rehersed [sc. die Einsetzungsworte] are to be saied, turning still to the Altar, without any elevacion, or shewing the Sacrament to the people« (The Book of Common Prayer. The Texts of 1549, 1559, and 1662, hg. v. Brian Cummings, Oxford 2011, 31; vgl. G. J. CUMING, A History of Anglican Liturgy, London 1969, 82). Gleichermaßen war die erste liturgiebezogene Maßnahme, die die gerade an die Regierung gekommene Königin Elisabeth nach dem kirchlichen *role back* und der Wiedereinführung der Messe unter König Mary traf, das Verbot von Elevation und Adoration in der Weihnachtsmesse 1558 bei Hof (JOHN SCHOFIELD, Philip Melanchthon and the English Reformation, Aldershot 2006, 186).

nig Edwards. Wer diesen Schritt zu Lebzeiten des Vaters gewagt hätte, wäre ebenso sicher verbrannt worden wie jene Männer und Frauen, die die Realpräsenz nur mit Worten in Frage stellten. Und so tat es wohl niemand. Wer sich unter diesen Umständen außerstande sah zu amtieren, verließ das Land.

An einem Punkt, der die Messe, genauer das Meßopfer, betraf, kam es aber doch zum Zusammenstoß – die angedeutete Ausnahme. Es war die Messe für Verstorbene, die seit 1540 Gegenstand aufsehenerregender Predigtattacken und so schließlich ein Jahr vor König Heinrichs Tod zum Auslöser der letzten großen Verfolgung seiner Regierungszeit wurde. Die Kritik nahm ihren Ausgang von der schon langjährigen Bestreitung des Fegfeuers, das es nicht gebe und aus dem Menschen folglich auch nicht, wodurch auch immer, zu befreien wären.[143] Also sei auch das wichtigste Mittel, das zu solcher Befreiung aufgeboten wurde, gegenstandslos, eben die Messe für Verstorbene.[144] Verbunden ist die immer heftigere und schließlich blutige Auseinandersetzung vor allem mit dem Namen Edward Cromes (um 1580–1562), eines in Cambridge graduierten Londoner Pfarrers und gefeierten Predigers, der Latimer nahestand und zu den »legendären Evangelisten der frühen Reformation«[145] in England gehörte. Mit seinen Ansichten, die er nicht allein,[146] aber am wirkungsvollsten vertrat, war Crome schon in den 1530er Jahren aufgefallen, doch seit 1539, seit Erscheinen der *Six Articles*, standen seine Predigten gegen ein Gesetz des Königreiches. War doch dort neben Transsubstantiation und Rechtmäßigkeit der Kommunion *sub una* die Privatmesse festgeschrieben, deren Hauptsinn und -zweck im Meßopfer für Verstorbene lag. Das hielt Crome nicht davon ab, im Jahr darauf in einer Predigt die Messe für Tote als »Aberglauben« (superstition) zu bezeichnen.[147] Noch 1546 wiederholte er

---

[143] Siehe den einschlägigen kritischen Traktat aus dem Jahr 1531 von JOHN FRITH, A Disputation on Purgatory (in: The Work of John Frith [s. Anm. 112], 81–203). Friths hier geäußerte Haltung zum Fegfeuer sollte neben seiner Auffassung vom Abendmahl der Grund für seine Verbrennung sein. Zur selben Zeit begann Edward Crome, das Fegfeuer in Frage zu stellen (s. Anm. 149). Zu den Anfängen der Bestreitung des Fegfeuers in den späten 1520er und frühen 1530er Jahren (Simon Fish, Frith) vgl. BRIDGEN (s. Anm. 116), 188; zur ablehnenden Haltung Erzbischof Cranmers MACCULLOCH, Cranmer (s. Anm. 137), 152f., 162, 309.

[144] Ebenso umstritten wie die Messe für Tote war das Gebet für sie, wodurch auch das wegen der darin enthaltenen Fürbitten für Verstorbene mit reichen Stiftungsaktivitäten verbundene Interzessionsgebet *Bidding of the Beads* (s.o. Anm. 24) in Frage stand (dazu: WABUDA, Preaching [s. Anm. 13], 51–63).

[145] BRIDGEN (s. Anm. 116), 187, nennt Hugh Latimer, Crome, John Lambert und Thomas Bilney »the early Reformation's legendary evangelists«.

[146] Vgl. WABUDA, Preaching (s. Anm. 13), 57. Zu nennen ist hier vor allem Hugh Latimer, der auch mit dem König darüber stritt (MACCULLOCH [s. Anm. 137], 160, 190).

[147] BRIDGEN (s. Anm. 116), 330f. Crome war vorsichtig genug, nicht die Privatmesse

seine Kritik, ja, stellte er das Meßopfer, ob für Lebende oder Tote, überhaupt in Frage und bestritt auch die Transsubstantiation.[148]

Ob Crome und seine Gesinnungsgenossen aus der Kritik an der Messe für Verstorbene die Konsequenz zogen, keine mehr zu halten, ist unklar.[149] Schritte zur Veränderung der Messe unternahmen sie auf keinen Fall. Der spezifische Beitrag, den sie, an der Spitze der gefeierte Londoner Prediger, für die erstrebte Reform des Gottesdienstes leisteten, war etwas anderes, auf den ersten Blick Gegenläufiges: die uneindeutige theologische Rede. In einer politischen Lage, in der für liturgische Veränderungen keinerlei Spielraum bestand, sondern darauf unweigerlich Verurteilung und Tod gestanden hätten, hielt Crome vor der Öffentlichkeit den Kompaß in dieser Richtung fest, indem er immer wieder entsprechend predigte und die offizielle liturgische Praxis theologisch unterminierte. Deshalb mehrfach der Häresie angeklagt und, auf höchste, königliche Weisung, vor die Alternative von Widerruf und Scheiterhaufen gestellt, kam er immer wieder davon, während Gesinnungsgenossen verbrannt wurden, außer Landes flohen oder widerriefen. Das gelang ihm mittels der Äquivokation, der uneindeutigen Rede.[150] Er deutete die inkriminierten Predigtpassagen vor seinen Richtern so um, daß sie unanfechtbar erschienen. Und er präsentierte dogmatisch wasserdichte Texte der Ketzerrichter, die er zu unterschreiben, öffentlich zu verlesen und in einer Widerrufspredigt mit eigenen Worten zu verteidigen hatte, in einer Weise, daß sie ihm nicht zu widersprechen, ja, ihn zu bestätigen schienen.[151] So wurden bei ihm, aber auch bei anderen, aus dem verlangten öffentlichen Widerruf geradezu Auftritte evangelischer Verkündigung.[152] Am Ende war diese Strategie nicht durchzu-

---

als solche zu attackieren. Doch da deren Hauptzweck die Befreiung der Toten aus dem Fegfeuer war, lief, wie sich bei ihm selber andeutet (a.a.O., 331), das eine auf das andere hinaus.

[148] WABUDA, Equivocation (s. Anm. 106), 234. Unklar ist, ob er damit zugleich die Realpräsenz in Frage stellte.

[149] Crome ließ möglicherweise 1531, als er gegen das Fegfeuer zu predigen begann, im Rahmen für Verstorbene gestifteter und deshalb eigentlich mit Gebeten zu deren Gunsten verbundener Predigten (preaching chantries) diese Gebete weg (WABUDA, Preaching [s. Anm. 13], 56).

[150] Siehe dazu den schon genannten (Anm. 106) höchst instruktiven Aufsatz von SUSAN WABUDA, Equivocation and Recantation During the English Reformation: The ›Subtle Shadows‹ of Dr Edward Crome.

[151] Besonders dreist war sein Widerrufsauftritt an St. Paul's Cross 1541, zu dem er nach Verhör vor dem König selbst gezwungen wurde. Statt eine Predigt zu halten, die die Botschaft des von ihm unterzeichneten und öffentlich zu verlesenden Widerrufs enthielt, predigte er seiner eigenen theologischen Linie gemäß und verlas anschließend das Widerrufsdokument mit den Worten, es handele sich um einen Text seiner Majestät, den er vortragen solle, was er hiermit tue. Er rezitierte das Papier, hielt ein kurzes Gebet und ging davon (a.a.O., 233 f.).

halten, 1546, im Jahr vor Heinrichs Tod, sah Crome sich ohne jede Möglichkeit der Ausflucht vor die Alternative von Widerruf und Tod gestellt und schwor ab.[153] In der Sache keineswegs wankend geworden, sollte er wenige Monate später nichts mehr zu befürchten haben.

Cromes »canting, recanting, decanting, or rather double canting«, wie ein Zeitgenosse schrieb,[154] war noch umstrittener als der Nikodemismus der evangelischen Untergrundzirkel. In einer Lage, in der andere, nicht zuletzt einfache Gläubige ohne die dialektisch-rhetorische Rafinesse eines graduierten Theologen, für ihre Überzeugung Folter und Verbrennung auf sich nahmen,[155] wanden Crome – und andere – sich mit geschickter Rede heraus und schworen notfalls sogar ab. Insbesondere evangelische Theologen, die ins Exil gegangen waren, überwiegend der Schweizer Reformation zuneigend,[156] lehnten Äquivokationen und natürlich erst recht Widerrufe ab, wo es um das Evangelium ging,[157] und forderten ein eindeutiges Bekenntnis, auch wenn es zum Martyrium führe[158] – oder eben ins Exil.[159] Dabei ist die theologisch-geistliche Zwielichtigkeit das Eine. Auf der anderen Seite hielten Crome und seine Gesinnungsgenossen, indem sie in ihren Predigten immer wieder an die Grenze und über die Grenze des Erlaubten hinausgingen, indem sie mit ihren Äquivokationen Interpretationsspielräume ausloteten, denen die Gegner nicht leicht etwas entgegensetzen konnten, und indem sie zwar widerriefen, aber in nicht geringer Zahl anschließend das Widerrufene erneut vertraten, reformatorische Einsichten im Land präsent, die sonst vielleicht mit ihnen untergangen wären. Und sie schufen die Voraussetzung dafür, daß nach Heinrichs Tod, als sich die politischen Rahmenbedingungen umfassend veränderten, gottesdienstliche Praxis wurde, was sie nur mit Worten hatten vertreten oder halb vertreten können. Nun sollte die Stunde der Eindeutigen

---

[152] WABUDA, Equivocation (s. Anm. 106), 233, schreibt über den Widerruf dreier Gesinnungsgenossen Cromes, darunter Barnes': »Their supporters recognized their attempts to use the occasion to spread their own opinions.« Das gilt ebenso für die Auftritte Cromes, nur daß er, der »master of the ambiguous recantation« (BRIDGEN [s. Anm. 116], 332; vgl. oben Anm. 116) damit erfolgreicher war als alle anderen.

[153] Zu diesen ganz London aufwühlenden Vorgängen vgl. BRIDGEN (s. Anm. 116), 363–370.

[154] Zitiert bei WABUDA, Equivocation (s. Anm. 106), 237.

[155] So besonders aufsehenerregend die 25jährige Adlige Anne Askew (zu ihrem Martyrium: BRIDGEN [s. Anm. 116], 370–376).

[156] Zu dieser Exulantengruppe und ihrer erheblichen, doch in England wenig wirkungsvollen und erst in den letzten Regierungsjahren Heinrichs auf stärkeres Echo stoßenden literarischen Furchtbarkeit: RYRIE, Gospel (s. Anm. 104), 93–112.

[157] A.a.O., 97.

[158] So etwa John Bale, der Cromes Verhalten das in Treue zum Evangelium erlittene Martyrium Anne Askews entgegenstellte (WABUDA, Equivocation [s. Anm. 106], 237).

[159] RYRIE, The Strange Death (s. Anm. 116), 75f.

schlagen, die aus dem Exil zurückkehrten oder, wie Martin Bucer oder Petrus Vermigli, in umgekehrter Richtung als Exulanten vom Kontinent kamen und sich in den Dienst der englischen Kirche stellten. Nun wurden auch hier aus reformatorischen Einsichten verbindliche Gottesdienstformulare, liturgische Institution.

Mit den *Books of Common Prayer* von 1549 und 1552, wie in Wittenberg und andernorts mit einem konservativeren und konsequenteren Doppelschritt, geschah das in wenigen Jahren und für das ganze Königreich.[160] Eine längere Phase experimenteller und partieller liturgischer Reformen »von unten« vor dem offiziellen Schritt wie in vielen Gegenden des Reiches gab es nicht, und was an Zwischenmaßnahmen erfolgte, war von oben gelenkt: Ende 1547 wurde vom Parlament die Kommunion *sub utraque* angeordnet,[161] 1548 dafür unter dem Titel *The Order of Communion* ein liturgischer Rahmen erlassen[162] und als kleines muttersprachliches Einsprengsel in die noch herkömmliche lateinische Messe eingefügt[163] – das erste Stück der geplanten neuen Liturgie, in die es praktisch unverändert weiterwanderte. Eine Reihe von Gemeinden ging, von der geistlich-politischen Spitze ermutigt, zum Gebrauch des Englischen im Gottesdienst über,[164] und manche setzten bereits Teile des neuen Meßformulars in die Praxis um, die als Entwürfe zirkulierten,[165] bevor im Januar 1549 das Parlament die neue Liturgie verabschiedete, mit Pfingsten 1549 Terminus ad quem für die Einführung in allen Gemeinden.[166] Daß das Formular vorläufigen Charakter hatte, stand den Trägern der Reform fest,[167] das verbesserte, welches das Parlament 1552 erließ, sollte demgegenüber wirklich protestantisch sein.[168]

Wie in den evangelischen Territorien und Städten des Reiches hatte man nun auch in England eine verbindliche liturgische Regelung, die die sonn-

---

[160] SPINKS (s. Anm. 129), 184f., 186–188.

[161] CUMING (s. Anm. 142), 61.

[162] S. The Two Liturgies, A. D. 1549, and A. D. 1552: with other Documents set forth by Authority in the Reign of King Edward VI., hg. v. Joseph Ketley, Cambridge 1844, 3–8.

[163] MacCULLOCH, Cranmer (s. Anm. 137), 384–386.

[164] CUMING (s. Anm. 142), 60f.; MacCULLOCH, Cranmer (s. Anm. 137), 395f. Ermutigender Vorläufer war die Messe zur Parlamentseröffnung im November 1547, in der Cranmer bereits einzelne Stücke der Liturgie in dieser Sprache rezitiert hatte (a.a.O., 377).

[165] DIARMAID MacCULLOCH, Tudor Church Militant. Edward VI and the Protestant Reformation, London 2001, 82. Vorbild und Maßstab war die mit dem König wandernde Chapel Royal (a.a.O., 81f.).

[166] CUMING (s. Anm. 142), 68.

[167] MacCULLOCH, Cranmer (s. Anm. 137), 410f.

[168] Als Terminus ad quem für seine Einführung in den Gemeinden wurde Allerheiligen 1552 festgesetzt (CUMING [s. Anm. 142], 114f.).

tägliche Predigt, die reformierte Abendmahlsfeier und andere Gottesdienste festlegte. Und das mit ungleich größerer Einheitlichkeit. Die neue Ordnung galt für das ganze Land; ein Nebeneinander mehrerer evangelischer
Liturgien wie im Heiligen Römischen Reich, ja sogar innerhalb eines einzigen Reichsterritoriums wie Kursachsen, hatte niemand im Sinn. Mehr
noch, auch jenes Element des Gottesdienstes, das im evangelischen Reich
die größte Variable darstellte, die Predigt, war in England einheitlich festgelegt.[169] Denn anders als auf dem Kontinent hatte der größte Teil der
englischen Pfarrerschaft keine Predigt zu halten, die auf eigener Auslegung
eines Bibeltextes beruhte;[170] vielmehr waren die meisten Pfarrer verpflichtet, einen Abschnitt aus dem regierungsamtlich vorgeschriebenen *Book of
Homilies*[171] vorzulesen, allsonntäglich im ganzen Land.[172] Das Regime König Edwards war nicht weniger zentralistisch, als es das des Vaters gewesen
war. Und das hieß für den Gottesdienst: Die Institutionalisierung des neu-
en evangelischen Gottesdienstes war die Institutionalisierung umfassender
evangelisch-liturgischer »Uniformität« im englischen Königreich.[173]

---

[169] Zum Thema Predigt siehe den Beitrag von Albrecht Beutel in diesem Band.

[170] Zum eigenständigen Predigen, das anders als in den reformatorischen Kirchen auf
dem Kontinent nicht Teil der mit der Ordination übertragenen Aufgaben war, sondern
eine spezielle Lizenz neben der Ordination erforderte, war nur etwa ein Fünftel berechtigt. In der zweiten Hälfte des Jahrhunderts und erst recht im 17. Jahrhundert stieg die
Zahl beträchtlich an (IAN GREEN, Preaching in the Parishes, in: The Oxford Handbook
of the Early Modern Sermon, hg. v. Peter MacCulloch, Hugh Adlington u. Emma
Rhatigan, Oxford 2011, 137–154, hier: 138 f.).

[171] Unter Elisabeth sollte dann zu dem edwardianischen (*First*) *Book* ein *Second Book
of Homilies* hinzukommen. Siehe zu den beiden *Books of Homilies* ASHLEY NULL, Official Tudor Homilies (in: Oxford Handbook of the Early Modern Sermon [s. Anm.
170], 348–365).

[172] Zu dieser wichtigen Differenz zwischen der englischen und den kontinentalen
Reformationskirchen: WENDEBOURG, Reformation und Gottesdienst [s. Anm. 28], 331–
333. A.a.O., 333 zu der scharfen Kritik des puritanischen Flügels an solchem »playing on
a stage«.

[173] »Liturgical uniformity« war nicht nur das selbstverständliche Programm der kir-
chenleitenden Könige, sondern von Anfang an auch die Leitvorstellung Cranmers bei
seinen Gottesdienstreformen (MACCULLOCH, Cranmer [s. Anm. 137], 222).

Church Service:
From Vision and Criticism to a New Liturgy

Dorothea Wendebourg

»From Reformation Movements to Reformation Churches« – how is our general theme to be applied to the specific topic of the service of the church, i.e., the liturgy? By examining how the criticism of the existing church service which was voiced during the early Reformation led to the establishment of new liturgical systems. For in all the streams of the Reformation re-envisioning the church service was, sooner or later, high on the agenda and a decisive, if not the decisive step in the institutionalization of the Reformation. For notwithstanding the differences between them, not least regarding this subject, all Reformers and all Reformation groups agreed that the heart of the church's life, the traditional service with which they had grown up and which quite a few of them had themselves celebrated as priests, was wrong in essential theological and practical aspects. Thus everywhere the reform of the liturgy was one of the indispensable measures of the Reformation. It started with visions, New Testament led visions of the right church service, and resulted in the introduction of new liturgies. This was so in the Holy Roman Empire as well as in England.

Before we start looking at this process in both countries, however, we need to ask another question: Was the starting point the same in each case? Did the evangelicals in the Empire and in England have the same liturgy before their eyes? Were they criticizing and reforming the same church service?[1]

1. The late medieval starting point

The Latin church before the Reformation did not have a uniform liturgy. Officially each diocese had its own liturgical praxis, apart from the religious orders who had theirs, of course. However, this did not exclude the possibility of one diocese taking over the liturgy of another. In fact, in

---

[1] I shall restrict my exposition to the mass and those church services which grew out of it and discuss neither the daily nor pastoral offices including baptism.

England that was very often the case. Large parts of the country, even of Ireland and Wales, in the course of the 15th and the early 16th century took over the liturgical system of Salisbury, the *Sarum usus* with its formularies for the mass and the hours, its lectionary, and its liturgical calendar,[2] albeit with certain variations. In other words, already before the Reformation England was liturgically more uniform than the Holy Roman Empire.

Yet this difference should not be overrated. For all in all the liturgical order of Sarum was basically a variant of the Roman tradition.[3] The same holds true for the other liturgical orders in England as well as for those of the dioceses of the Empire. In other words, although the Late Middle Ages did not have a uniform liturgy, the basic liturgical elements were the same on both sides of the channel: the mass as the central church service which had to be frequented by everyone at least once a week, the hours as a daily duty of religious communities and priests and as an option for other Christians; both fitted into the rhythm of time that was shaped by the church year following the story of Jesus Christ down to the outpouring of the Holy Spirit as well as by the calendar of the saints' days. The mass itself had different shapes. It was celebrated in complete silence, with parts spoken aloud, or also with parts sung by a choir; with or without a congregation present, with or without a sermon – to name only the most important variants. All this existed in England as well as in the Empire, and in both cases we are better informed about the liturgical orders of cathedrals and monasteries than about the liturgical lives of small towns and villages where the majority of people lived[4] – although we are not completely in the dark here, either.[5]

---

[2] For the development and the diffusion of the *Sarum Use*, see RICHARD W. PFAFF, The Liturgy in Medieval England. Cambridge 2009, ch.s 10–13. In fact, it was only after the introduction of print that enforcing uniformity became possible, as was the case in the dioceses of Germany (ID., New Liturgical Feasts in Later Medieval England, Oxford 1970, 8).

[3] »[I]n essence the Sarum Rite was a ›local medieval modification of the Roman rite in use at the cathedral church of Salisbury‹« (D. M. HOPE, The Medieval Western Rite, in: The Study of Liturgy, ed. Cheslyn Jones, Geoffrey Wainwright and Edward Yarnold, London ⁵1980, 220–248, here 236; 237 about the splendour of this liturgy).

[4] ANDREAS ODENTHAL, Pfarrlicher Gottesdienst vom Mittelalter zur Frühen Neuzeit. Eine Problemskizze aus liturgiewissenschaftlicher Perspektive (in: ID., Liturgie vom Frühen Mittelalter zum Zeitalter der Konfessionalisierung. Studien zur Geschichte des Gottesdienstes, Tübingen 2011, 159–206, here: 161).

[5] For the German-speaking lands ODENTHAL, Pfarrlicher Gottesdienst (see note 4) points at the »Pfarrbücher« (pastors' accounts) and »Mesnerbücher« (vergers' accounts). Regarding the former also cf. MARCO BERNINI, Die Feier des Osterfestkreises im Ingolstädter Pfarrbuch des Johannes Eck, Münster 2016, ch. A 4 (*Pfarrbücher als liturgiehistorische Quellen*). For the English scene there are the churchwardens' accounts (cf. KATHERINE L. FRENCH, The People of the Parish. Community Life in a Late Medieval English Diocese, Philadelphia 2001, ch. 2).

Two elements of the late medieval liturgical tableau still need to be addressed in particular because of their importance for the liturgical developments in the Reformation. Both had grown out of the mass and become liturgical units on their own, in England as well as in the Empire: the communion service and the preaching service. The former which had come into being because the congregation in general did not commune within the mass but had to commune at least once a year[6] comprised the three parts: i) confession, ii) distribution of hosts that had been consecrated in a mass,[7] and iii) private prayer of thanksgiving.[8] In some cases there was also a eucharistic address or Latin communion hymns sung by a choir.[9]

As regards the sermon, by far the majority of the masses were celebrated without one, and most priests did not preach.[10] Nevertheless preaching was copious,[11] in different liturgical settings. Firstly, the sermon belonged to the official duties of a pastor and was part of the parochial Sunday morning mass – in the Empire it was stipulated as such albeit often not realized,[12] in England it was not legally compulsory but desired.[13] What was compulsory here was, secondly, the *quarter sermon*, one ser-

---

[6] PETER BROWE, Die Pflichtkommunion im Mittelalter, Münster 1940, 43–45.

[7] In addition communicants often received ablution wine, i.e. the wine that had been used for washing the chalice after the communion *sub utraque* of the priest and for cleaning the mouths of the communicants after eating the hosts. Sometimes this also included the wine or the water with which the priest had performed the ablution of his fingers after the sacrifice (MATTHIAS FIGEL, Der reformatorische Predigtgottesdienst. Epfendorf 2013, 47 with note 159; cf. JOSEPH ANDREAS JUNGMANN, Missarum Sollemnia. Eine genetische Erklärung der römischen Messe, vol. 2, Vienna ²1949, 499–508).

[8] FIGEL (note 7), 44–48. For a detailed analysis see PETER BROWE, Mittelalterliche Kommunionriten (in: Jahrbuch für Liturgiewissenschaft 15, 1935, 23–66).

[9] Ibid., 57–61. Vernacular hymns were not sung in the communion service, unlike in the context of sermons at least in the empire (see below) (JOHANNES JANOTA, Studien zu Funktion und Typus des deutschen geistlichen Liedes im Mittelalter, Munich 1968, 61).

[10] Cf. RUDOLF CRUEL, Geschichte der deutschen Predigt im Mittelalter, Detmold 1879, 639: »[Bei] der Menge der damaligen Geistlichen und Gottesdienste [...] ist nun freilich zu constatiren, daß die Predigt nur einen Bruchteil des Klerus beschäftigte und einen untergeordneten Platz im Cultus einnahm.«

[11] Although the sermon held »einen untergeordneten Platz im Cultus« (cf. n. 10), muß »die Annahme, daß während der beiden letzten Jahrhunderte vor der Reformation, im Ganzen genommen, weniger gepredigt worden sei als heutzutage, [...] als ein unhaltbares Vorurtheil aufgegeben werden. Etwas andres freilich ist es, was und in welcher Weise gepredigt wurde« (ibid., 652, italics spaced in the original text). However, this holds true only for the towns, »[wo] beinahe zuviel gepredigt wurde, [...] während es auf dem Lande [...] an Predigern fehlte« (MICHAEL MENZEL, Predigt und Predigtorganisation im Mittelalter, in: HJ 111, 1991, 337–384, here: 377).

[12] FIGEL (see note 7), 59, 67–68.

[13] SUSAN WABUDA, Preaching During the English Reformation, Cambridge 2002, 33. The Sarum Pontificale says: »Fiat sermo, si placuerit« (G. R. OWST, Preaching in Medieval England, Cambridge 1926, 145, note 5).

mon every quarter of a year whose content were parts of the catechism, good works, and the sacraments,[14] and beyond that it was at least recommended to have, during Advent and Lent, several penitential sermons per week;[15] both quarter sermons and penitential sermons lay predominantly in the hands of mendicants. Seasonal penitential sermons of this kind (Fastenpredigten) were common practice also in the Empire.[16] Finally, there was a third type of sermon, the sermon at particular occasions. In the Empire the most important occasions were the visits of famous wandering penitential preachers, mostly from the mendicant orders, as well as pilgrimages and the promotion of indulgences; often these sermons were delivered outdoors in front of large crowds, if possible from pulpits on the outer wall of churches.[17] Such open-air sermons also took place in England, but here they became regular events for which churches often built stage-like stone pulpits with crosses as crowns.[18] The most famous of these sermons from open-air pulpits came from Paul's Cross by St. Paul's cathedral, which often was frequented by thousands of listeners including members of the political establishment, even of the royal court.[19] The sermons at Pauls's Cross which were to play an important role in the English Reformation and Counterreformation[20] had no equivalent in the Empire.[21]

What made the sermon a special liturgical element and the starting point for a liturgical development of its own was its language. The sermon was in the vernacular[22] and thus, if part of the mass, an alien element within the liturgy.[23] Combined with other vernacular elements like pieces

---

[14] Ibid., 145–46; Wabuda (see note 13), 34–37.

[15] Owst (see note 13), 146–47. They should be held daily or at least three times a week.

[16] Cruel (see note 10), § 45; Figel (see note 7), 97. Preaching days were Monday, Wednesday, and Friday.

[17] Ellen-Senta Altenloh, Sakrale Außenkanzeln in Europa von der Romanik bis zur Gegenwart, Bonn 1985, 11–12, 16.

[18] Owst (see note 13), 148, 195–99, 209–14; Wabuda, Preaching (see note 13), 40–48.

[19] Ibid., 41–47. Particularly regarding Paul's Cross cf.: St. Paul's Cross and the Culture of Persuasion in England, 1520–1640, ed.s Torrance Kirby and P. G. Stanwood, Leiden, Boston 2014.

[20] Pauls's Cross was also the place of spectacular burnings of books and so-called heretics or their recantations which where accompagnied by preaching.

[21] According to Kirby, the public »culture of persuasion« exercised here is one of the roots of England's modern political practice which is a tradition of debate in public space (Torrance Kirby, The Public Sermon: Paul's Cross and the culture of persuasion in England, 1534–1570, in: Renaissance and Reformation Rev. 31, 2008, 3–19).

[22] Janota (see note 9), 70: »Als nichtliturgisch geregelter Gottesdienst unterlag die Predigt nicht dem Gebot der lateinischen Liturgiesprache.«

[23] The late Medieval missalia do not refer to the sermon, just as the liturgy of the Word is hardly mentioned there at all (Dominik Daschner, Die gedruckten Meßbücher

from the catechism and intercessions (»bidding of the beeds«)[24] the sermon, both in England and in the Empire, became the nucleus of a whole vernacular block, the *pronaos* or *prone*.[25] This block was always part of the parochial Sunday mass. Often, however, within this block, the sermon itself got lost.[26] Whereas all this *mutatis mutandis* holds true on both sides of the Channel, one development which occurred in the Empire did not have a parallel in England. The congregations which were excluded from the liturgical singing in the mass used the pronaos illegally to sing vernacular, i.e. German, verses[27] as an introduction or an answer to the sermon.[28]

Süddeutschlands bis zur Übernahme des Missale Romanum Pius' V. [1570], Frankfurt a. M. 1995, 86, with reference to the printed missalia before 1570 in Southern Germany, but this statement can be generalized beyond that region). Typically the sermon could find its place at different points in the mass, in England most probably »between creed and offertory, or else after the latter« (OWST [see note 13], 144–5), in the Empire after the Gospel, the Creed, the offertory or the Sanctus (JANOTA [see note 9], 68–69; FIGEL [see note 7], 98), or it was even delivered while the mass which was being celebrated by another priest continued silently (JANOTA [see note 9], 68). The sermon could also be taken out of the mass and be relocated after Sunday lunch (OWST [see note 13], 145); in the Empire this was allowed only on feast days so that the solemnities of the morning could proceed undisturbed (ibid., 99–100). All this refers to the parochial sermon which was really part of the parochial mass and lay in the responsability of the parish priest, not to the sermons of mendicants and preachers which took place outside of the mass anyway (cf. below).

[24] For the *Bidding of the Beeds* cf. FRANK EDWARD BRIGHTMAN, The English Rite: being a Synopsis of the Sources and Revisions of the Book of Common Prayer, vol. 1, London ²1921, 1020–1037; WABUDA, Preaching (see note 13), 51–53.

[25] Regarding the pronaos with its »annexes« in the Empire cf. CRUEL (see note 10), 220–32; FIGEL (see note 7), 105, 112–42; for the development of this block within and outside of the Empire cf. JOSEPH ANDREAS JUNGMANN, Missarum Sollemnia. Eine genetische Erklärung der römischen Messe, vol. 1, Vienna ²1949, 605–10; for the prone in England cf. BRIGHTMAN, The English Rite, vol. 1 (see note 18), 1038–9; WABUDA, Preaching (see note 13), 51–55.

[26] FIGEL (see note 7), 143. In this way what came about was »a sermon-liturgy without sermon« with announcements at its beginning (cf. ibid., 143–9). In other words, preaching became a variable (ibid., 149), and in fact, *intra missam* preaching was very rare (ibid., 170). Contemporary sources, when speaking of a »sermon« often refer to the whole block of the pronaos without necessarily including the sermon itself (e.g. the *Pfarrbuch* of the parish priest of Hilpoltstein Stephan May, see JOHANN GÖTZ, Das Pfarrbuch des Stephan May in Hilpoltstein vom Jahre 1511. Ein Beitrag zum Verständnis der kirchlichen Verhältnisse am Vorabende der Reformation, Münster 1926).

[27] Actually, what was sung was only one short verse at a time with a limited repertoire of few hymns, and such singing was not customary everywhere (CRUEL [see note 10], 232).

[28] JANOTA (see note 9), 44, 70–76; FIGEL (see note 7), 173–79. Such vernacular singing by the parishoners in the course of the 15th and 16th centuries was repeatedly banned, e.g. by the Councils of Constance and Basel (cf. DOROTHEA WENDEBOURG, Reformation und Gottesdienst, in: ZThK 113, 2016, 323–65, note 141; JANOTA [see note 9], 46). Those bans show that at least in certain regions during certain periods vernacular singing

Whereas the sermon was an alien element in the mass, as *Fastenpredigt*, if I am right also as *quarter sermon* and in any case as an open-air event, it stood on its own feet liturgically. This is not to say there was nothing but the speech of the preaching priest. Rather it was combined with other elements, namely prayers, possibly also a benediction, which together with the sermon made up a proper preaching service. In this context congregations in the Empire were also able to sing much more freely in their own language than in the prone within the mass. As it appears, the precise order of the preaching services, which were probably[29] held already in the 13th century by mendicants, was quite flexible in England and in most parts of the Empire. In *most* parts – for in one region it was otherwise, namely, in the cities of the Southwest as well as in those of German-speaking Switzerland. Here the sermon, together with other elements, first of all the intercessions, developed into a proper vernacular service with a fixed structure, the so-called *Prädikantengottesdienst*[30] which owed its existence to the creation of endowments for preaching in addition to the older preaching system of the mendicants,[31] established through donations given mostly by laypeople and mostly at parish churches.[32] Endowments

---

before or after the sermon must have been very popular, but this custom seems to have diminished during the 15th century (CRUEL [see note 10], 232).

[29] This is not completely certain, since »we cannot date at which point there was a preaching service on its own outside of mass« (EBERHARD WINKLER, Der Predigtgottesdienst, in: Handbuch der Liturgik, ed. Hans-Christoph Schmidt-Lauber and Karl-Heinrich Bieritz, Leipzig and Göttingen ²1995, 248–270, here: 254). What is certain in any case is that this service goes back to the preaching of the mendicants.

[30] For the *Prädikantengottesdienst* cf. FIGEL (see note 7), 156–70. Starting with Nuremberg between the late 14th to the beginning of the 16th century urban endowments dedicated to preaching spread to »nearly every Southwestern city« of the Empire (ibid., 189). For Nuremberg cf. KARL SCHLEMMER, Gottesdienst und Frömmigkeit in der Reichsstadt Nürnberg am Vorabend der Reformation, Würzburg 1980, 255–60.

[31] The establishment of preaching prebends for secular clergy was the third step in the development of the organisation of preaching in the medieval church. The first was the Carolingian requirement for episcopal sermons which in parishes was performed by the local priest on behalf of the bishop. The second step was the mendicant sermon starting in the 13th century which was independent of the parish system and soon played the leading role. For this development cf. MENZEL (see note 11).

[32] The donors for these endowments in the Southwest were mostly burghers. However, there were also preaching endowments at cathedrals funded by bishops and priests (cf. note 35). Despite the high number of these foundations, where the wish of doing good works for furthering the salvation of one's soul was connected with the interest in regular high-quality preaching, they did not bring about a principal change of priorities regarding the ecclesiastical personnel and the liturgical events, as figures show: E.g. in Nuremberg which had an early and strong tradition of *praedicantes*, the parish church St. Lorenz had, besides the parish priest, 22 priests responsible only for masses and just one *Prädikant* (ALBERT GÜMBEL, Das Mesnerpflichtbuch von St. Lorenz in Nürnberg vom Jahre 1483, München 1928, 11), in Heilbronn there were the parish priest and 28 chaplains for masses and in Ulm the parish priest and 57 chaplains, not to mention the

for preaching existed also in other regions of the Empire as well as in England (preaching chantries).[33] In each case the effect was an increase of sermons beyond the number of *quarter sermons* and the *Fastenpredigten*. Many towns of the Empire had preaching services every Sunday in the morning between masses or in the afternoon.[34] But nowhere were there so many preaching endowments as in the Southwest and in Switzerland, and – what is of interest here – nowhere did they reach such institutional stability as in the Southwestern *Prädikantengottesdienste* rooted in the enormous number of endowments for preaching in this region.[35]

---

host of altarists, i.e. priests for unendowed masses, but in each place only one *Prädikant* (Lesebuch zur Geschichte der evangelischen Landeskirche in Württemberg, vol. 1: Neue Gestalt für das bleibende Wort im 16. Jahrhundert, ed. Gerhard Schäfer, Stuttgart 1992, 43). Thus the funding of masses by far outweighed the provision for endowed preaching. This is equally true for Late medieval England (WABUDA, Preaching [see note 13], 166).

[33] An overview of the endowments for preaching in the Empire in FIGEL (see note 7), 189–199. One could, however, list more endowments for preaching beyond the Southwestern Empire, e.g. two that were founded by parish priests in Saxon Zwickau, one of which for a time was held by Thomas Müntzer (cf. SIEGFRIED BRÄUER and GÜNTER VOGLER, Thomas Müntzer. Neu Ordnung machen in der Welt. Eine Biographie, Gütersloh 2016, 94–95). For the English preaching chantries cf. WABUDA, Preaching (see note 13), 21–23, 166–68. In England the establishment of so-called lectureships would later be the fruit of puritan bourgeois activities similar to those of the late-medieval burgers in the Southwestern Empire, except these occurred within Elizabethan and Stuart Protestantism (PAUL S. SEAVER, The Puritan Lectureships: The Politics of Religious Dissent 1560–1662, Stanford 1970).

[34] These were the authorized hours for mendicant preaching which were also allotted to the *praedicantes* (BERNHARD NEIDIGER, Wortgottesdienst vor der Reformation. Die Stiftung eigener Predigtpfründen für Weltprediger im späten Mittelalter, in: Rheinische Vierteljahrsblätter 66, 2002, 142–89, esp. 148).

[35] Possibly this has to do with a difference between the »landscapes« of preacherships in the Empire which NEIDINGER (Wortgottesdienst vor der Reformation [see note 34]) has pointed out: According to him in the Southwest prebends for preaching were mainly established by burgers who also supervised the respective appointments, whereas in other regions of the empire like Saxony, Silesia, and Bohemia parish priests, following the initiative of the hierarchy, employed preachers (ibid., 164–5). The aspect of emancipation implied in the establishment of preacherships and the appointment of preachers by burgers may have contributed to the development of the preaching service as fixed liturgical unit independent from the mass in the South-West, whereas in other regions preaching services instead remained in the orbit of the mass which was in the hands of the parish priest. As a probable consequence of this difference the obligation of the preachers to hold mass (see below p. 418) seems to have been altogether lower in the Southwest than in those Middle and Eastern regions of the Empire. Incidentally it is worth noticing that in some regions, e.g. in the Western empire, there were no endowments for preaching at parish churches, mainly because the old tradition of mendicant sermons sufficed there (ibid., 172–7).

2. Reformation

2.1. The Reformation in the Empire

At the beginning of the criticism and call for reform of the liturgy stood Martin Luther's vision of the true mass in consonance with the Gospel which he had outlined during 1519 and 1520 in his edifying *Sermones* on the Lord's Supper and in the extensive attack on the mass in his systematic treatise *De Captivitate Babylonica Ecclesiae Praeludium*.[36] These writings had far-reaching liturgical implications: Firstly, the principal of orientating the liturgy towards the Lord's institution of the Supper contradicted distribution *sub una specie*. Secondly, the communal character of the Supper ruled out celebrations without a congregation. Thirdly, its character as a symbolic proclamation of the gospel, like that of all sacraments, required that the recitation of the Words of Institution be in a loud voice and in a language which the congregation understood. Fourthly, its essential meaning as Christ's self-giving (catabic) to the congregation excluded all words and gestures which conveyed a sacrificial (anabatic) meaning of the sacrament. Fifthly, the role of the sermon, way beyond the late medieval enthusiasm for preaching, was now considered indispensable within the liturgy, i.e. as the most important element of the church service along with prayer. Moreover, once again in contrast to the Late Middle Ages, preaching had to consist of explicating and applying biblical texts.[37]

Visions of how the church service should be and criticism of the existing service is not yet a new liturgical order. As is well known, Luther himself was slow in this respect. It was only in 1523 and 1525 that he presented concrete proposals for the hours, the liturgical year, and the mass, and these finally led to the official introduction of a new liturgical order for the whole electorate. In other places, too, the path from criticism to official reform was long. In the meantime the people involved found themselves facing a difficult question, indeed, a heavy burden on their conscience: How were they to deal with the reality of a mass which in their eyes contradicted the Gospel? Did the so-called laity simply have to tolerate the liturgical *status quo*? Did they not have a right to regular evangelical preaching of the Gospel? Did they not have a right to liturgies which they understood, to celebrations which culminated in their receiving communion, and to receiving it in both kinds like the priests? Dis-

---

[36] The two *Sermones*: WA 2,742–58 and WA 6,353–78; De captivitate: WA 6,497–573.

[37] E.g. WA 6,373,11. Two years later with particular emphasis: WA 12,35,19–21. Besides the bible, the catechism could also be the basis of sermons, since it was considered to be a summary of the bible.

ruptions of sermons and masses which took place in various towns[38] were visible manifestations of impatience.[39] Petitions which citizens handed into the authorities voiced demands from the grassroots for concrete liturgical reforms.[40]

In most parts of the Empire evangelical preaching faced the least institutional impediments. Liturgically speaking, one could easily integrate it into traditional practice, since the sermon was such a flexible and at the same time sufficiently stable element of the church service. Hence, if there were hindrances to its implementation they were not liturgical but came in the form of opposition by local ecclesial or political authorities or the failure to find an adequate preacher. The situation was entirely different with the mass which, at least in its central portion, the canon, was sacrosanct. Adherence was enforced by severe punishment for any deviation. Thus its reform could not be carried out easily and without resistance. What should evangelical congregations and priests do as long as reforms in this area failed to appear?

As for the congregations, one option was a temporary renunciation of communion. In the light of many reasons, not the least of which was that the congregation did not commune and the chalice was denied to them, Martin Reinhart, pastor in Jena, judged the present mass so terribly flawed as to be »contrary to the nature and quality of the Sacrament.«[41] Consequently,

»pious Christians, as the poor captives under the cruel tyrants, have to be patient and must hungrily renounce the heavenly bread.«[42]

---

[38] Examples given by THOMAS KAUFMANN, Geschichte der Reformation, Frankfurt and Leipzig 2009, 327–29; NATALIE KRENTZ, Ritualwandel und Deutungshoheit. Die frühe Reformation in der Residenzstadt Wittenberg (1500–1533), Tübingen 2014, 144–51; BERND MOELLER, Die Reformation in Göttingen (in: ID., Die Reformation und das Mittelalter. Kirchenhistorische Aufsätze, Göttingen 1991, 196–211, 328–31, esp. 196–7).

[39] This is not to say that the expectations of a new church service and the implied criticism of the actual service engendered by the Reformation were the only reasons for these disruptions. They were also a way to express older tensions between burgers and church representatives. Cf. e.g. KRENTZ (see note 38), ch. 1.

[40] Cf., as a particularly exemplary case, the petition of the burgers of Wittenberg of 10 Dec., 1525, in which they demanded unrestricted evangelical preaching, communion in both kinds for the congregation like the priests, the abolition of masses without the participation of the congregation, as well as the closure of pubs and brothels (HEINZ SCHEIBLE, Melanchthon. Vermittler der Reformation, München 2016, 82).

[41] »[Dadurch, dass] das gemein christenvolck / gar ereussert [ist] / vom tisch gottis / das man nit mehr / dann ain mal im iar / unter einer gestalt / den christen menschen zů lest« (REINHART [see the following note], A iijʳ).

[42] Unterrichte wie sich ein fromer Christ / bey den papistischen Messen / so ytzt noch viel gehalten werden (wenn er sich nit mit gůtm fug absondern kan) halten sol das

However, there was a spiritual alternative which Augustine had already mentioned and which was now firmly emphasized:[43] *crede et manducasti.* Thus Urbanus Rhegius advised evangelical parishioners present at a mass celebrated inaudibly and without communion:

»It is wrong that they [Christ's Words of Institution] are hidden and spoken silently. If you really want to hear mass remember that here is food and drink, causing you to eat and to drink, otherwise your hearing mass is nothing. [...] If they do not give you the sacrament and you can only hear mass, take the words of Christ's testament to heart and remember what Jesus Christ, your God and Lord, has done for you [...]. Believe the words and the sign, then you shall receive the inheritance promised to you [sc. in the testament] and eat at God's table spiritually.«[44]

There was yet a more radical option, the complete renunciation of participation in the mass. Since not only communion, but »the whole mass has departed from the order of Christ,« it would be »better if every pious Christian did not come to mass ever again«.[45] Unfortunately, in view of the canonical obligation to hear mass most people did not have the courage to do so.[46] However, even for the situation of a person's inevitable presence at a »sacrilegious« ritual, there was a solution, one that also had older roots, namely, the spiritual parallel action. Already during the Middle Ages, while the liturgy at the altar went on mostly inaudibly and unintelligibly Christians focused on their private spiritual meditations and prayers.[47] The Reformation simply adapted this practice for its own purposes. Evangelical devotional books put before the eyes of the faithful what should really be going on instead of the wrong rite, so that they were able to meditate on it, pray accordingly, and attain spiritual eating:

»When you come to the mass, it is necessary for you, that you do not pay attention to the manifold abuses [...]. But occupy yourself with an exercise in faith, in order to attain from Christ your God and Lord spiritually what human cruelty withdrew from you sacramentally.«

---

er sich nit vorsunde / und die zeyt unütz vorlier. Item ein Christliche betrachtung so du zů dem heyligen Sacrament wilt gehn, Jena 1524 (the name Martin Reinhart is printed under the foreword of the booklet, which to a large extent is a copy of the writing by Jakob Strauß mentioned in note 48), A iijʳ.

[43] Cf. e.g. MARTIN LUTHER, De captivitate Babylonica (WA 6,518,19–23).

[44] URBANUS RHEGIUS, Ain kurtze erklärung etlicher leüffiger puncten / aim yeden Christen nutz und nöt / zů rechten verstand der hailigen geschrifft / zů dienst, Augsburg 1523, C iiijᵛ seqq. Prayers through which a person present at mass can attain such spiritual eating are presented by Rhegius in his devotional booklet referred to in note 48.

[45] STRAUSS, Underricht (see note 48), C iiiijʳ.

[46] »So wir aber laider die sach nit bessern mügen / und der gebrauch am Sontag Meß zůhören [sc. the obligation to hear mass] / das Christen volck ängstiget. Ist von nöten den armen gefangen gewissen etwas lufft und trost zůraichen / ordnung geben« (ibid.).

[47] Examples in JANOTA (see note 9), 35, 55–57, and in JULIUS SMEND, Die evangelischen deutschen Messen bis zu Luthers Deutsche Messe, Göttingen 1896, 13–15.

This advice comes from a booklet with a title which is in itself telling: *Underricht, wie sich der fromme Christ bey der Messen, so yetz gehalten werde (wenn er sich nicht mit fug absündern kann), halten soll, das er sich nit versündige und die zeit nicht unnützlich verlier* (Lessons on how the pious Christian during masses as they are celebrated today – if he cannot easily stay away – should behave in such a way that he will not sin nor waste his time). The booklet was written in 1522 by Jakob Strauß for his hard-pressed home parish Hall in Tyrol, containing several evangelical meditative prayers to use during mass.[48] In a similar vein Wenzeslaus Linck, Luther's former co-friar and now parish pastor in Altenburg, advised evangelically minded Christians who could not avoid frequenting mass:[49]

»When you want to hear mass remind yourself at least to be fed spiritually; do not think that the celebrant sacrifices Christ for you. [...] Do not think either, that he does a good work for you with the mass [...], but remind yourself only of what Christ, your God and Lord, has done for you and what he has bequeathed to you and given to you as your own under this seal, symbol, and sacrament.«[50]

Priests who shared the Reformers' criticism of the mass were in a more difficult situation. Should they for the time being, as long as there was no new liturgical order, continue to perform a ritual which in their eyes was contrary to the Gospel? Should they keep on celebrating in a language people did not understand, not to mention in a quiet voice that people could not even hear, distributing *sub una specie*, and, the worst of all, offering the sacrilegious sacrifice, including private masses which had no other purpose than such sacrifice?

---

[48] Originally appendix of: Ain trostliche verstendige leer über das wort sancti Pauli. Der mensch soll sich selbs probieren / und also von dem brot essen / und von dem kelch trincken. Geprediget zů Hall im Intal / durch Doctor Jacob Strauss. 1522 (there from C iiij[v], quotation: C[v]seqq.; another, separate edition mentioned by Smend [see note 47], 29, note 3; largely copied by Martin Reinhart [see note 42]). A similar collection of evangelical meditative prayers for mass is presented by Urbanus Rhegius in his devotional booklet: Underricht wie sich ain Christen mensch halten soll das er frucht der Mesz erlang und Christlich zů gotz tisch gangg (s.l. et a. [1522]; cf. Smend [see note 47], 35–37). Johannes Oecolampadius presents evangelical meditative prayers which run alongside the whole mass in his short composition *Das Testament Jesu Christi* von 1523 (various editions ibid., 49). The text of the *Testament*, which was possibly influenced by Jakob Strauß (ibid., 68–70), is printed in Smend (ibid., 51–57). Smend (ibid., 25–26) presents yet another endeavour of this kind, namely a meditative prayer by the Strasbourg Reformer Matthäus Zell to be used during a sacrificial mass for the dead.

[49] »wiewol es nit böse were, die messen / so man als opffer und gutte werck thut gar zu meyden« (Linck [see note 50], B ij[v]).

[50] Eyn Sermon [...] Von anrueffunge der heyligen. Darneben auch vom gebet / meß hoeren und fürpit. Gepredigt am Suntag der Creuetz wochen / auff das Ewangelion Johannis am. xvj. cap. Aldenburg in Meyssen MDXXIII, Nuremberg 1523, B ij[v].

The priests who could find a way out of this predicament with the least difficulty were those who were employed as preachers – whether full-time as in the case of the Southwest-German *praedicantes* and Thomas Müntzer in Saxon Zwickau or part-time like Martin Luther in Wittenberg. They could simply put the liturgical element which was their task, the sermon, to the service of the Reformation. Since they normally delivered their sermons in services which were devoted to preaching alone there was no need for them to become involved with the mass.[51] The employment contract of the preachers often included obligations to say some masses, e.g., private masses for the deceased donor to whom they owed their preaching chantry; but these were clearly secondary duties,[52] and one could possibly evade them.[53] In such cases the liturgical dilemma was solved by the juxtaposition in the same church of masses contrary to the Gospel and preaching services in line with the Gospel, the former in Latin, the latter in the vernacular, the former with a Latin choir singing or silent, the latter –

---

[51] This was the case not only in the specific liturgical framework of the *Prädikantengottesdienst* in the Southwestern Empire but also in other regions where there were priests employed as preachers; however, we know nothing about the liturgical setting in which their sermons took place. Cf. e.g. the situation in Nuremberg with its old tradition of *praedicantes*. The information about sermons held by the preachers which are given in the *Mesnerpflichtbuch* (account of the vergers' duties) of the church St. Lorenz from 1483 only states that those sermons took place on Sundays and holy days after matins (GÜMBEL, Mesnerpflichtbuch St. Lorenz [see note 32], 20, 48) or after early mass (ibid., 26), after vespers (ibid., 30) or after the Hail Mary (ibid., 45), if not simply *post prandium*, i.e. in the early afternoon (ibid., 33) – information which on the one hand shows the frequency, on the other hand the subordinate status of the sermon in the overall system of ecclesiastical life which was primarily determined by other liturgical activities (cf. note 31), but which tells us nothing about the liturgical shape of the preaching events. The same holds true of the other important parish church of Nuremberg, St. Sebald (ALBERT GÜMBEL, Das Mesnerpflichtbuch von St. Sebald in Nürnberg vom Jahre 1482, Munich 1929). Equally services devoted exclusively to preaching were the responsibility of Thomas Müntzer as preacher in Saxon Zwickau, although we know nothing about their liturgical shape. It was only when he held the position of parish priest in Allstedt that celebrating the mass belonged to his essential professional duties – and not by chance he then immediately undertook its reform (BRÄUER, VOGLER, Müntzer [see note 32], 186–198).

[52] The incumbents of the new preaching chantries in the 15th century had as their task »nearly exclusively preaching« (MENZEL [see note 11], 369). An example of a preacher with a reduced program of masses was Matthäus Alber in Reutlingen who had only four masses per week (FIGEL [see note 7], 86, note 342).

[53] MENZEL (see note 11) writes that already in the late middle ages there was the possibility of »considerable exemptions« from the obligation to hold mass (ibid., 381), to the point that these obligations could be »averted« altogether (ibid., 382). Consequently it was nothing out of the ordinary when the preacher of Heilbronn Johann Lachmann whose preaching chantry comprised several masses, stopped saying them in 1525, although the mass itself continued to be celebrated in his town until 1531 (FIGEL [see note 7], 326).

in the Empire – with vernacular hymns sung by the people. Thus evangelical priests who held preaching positions were liberated from any burden of conscience and the evangelical faithful had an alternative in line with their convictions. Even so, the Imperial cities of Southwestern Germany and in German-speaking Switzerland took a further step. The preaching service was combined with the other liturgical unit which had split off from the mass and which was also held in the vernacular, namely, the communion service. So evangelicals could escape the mass without renouncing communion.[54] Eventually this solution would become the normative liturgical structure in the protestant churches of those regions. Yet originally, in most cases for a prolonged time, it was a measure of transition, for the traditional celebrations of the mass went on at the same time – e.g. in Strasbourg until 1529 and in Ulm even until 1531. However, the fact that this new liturgical structure came into existence and would in the end even assert itself against the mass as the liturgical norm was possible only because of the tradition of *Prädikantengottesdienst* which in those parts of the empire and of Switzerland had already become fixed liturgies in their own right.

The solution chosen by preachers, namely to stop celebrating mass until it was reformed, was also taken by other priests. Andreas Karlstadt, whose duties as archdeacon of the Wittenberg Collegiate Church of All Saints included sacrifices of the mass, avoided performing this »sacrilegious« rite already prior to his famous communion service in German at Christmas 1521, to which we shall return.[55] The Augustinian friars of the same city did likewise. When after their first celebration of a mass according to the gospel they were prohibited from repeating it, they decided not to have mass any more and limited themselves to preaching instead.[56]

---

[54] Thus the temporal juxtaposition of a wrong and a right church-service in these cases also became the juxtaposition of a wrong celebration of the Lord's Supper, namely the traditional mass, and a right one, consisting of the service of communion – sometimes in the same building, e.g. in Strasbourg. Since evangelicals in the cathedral of this city initially used a revised form of the mass for the Lord's Supper, for a short while even the right and the wrong mass were celebrated side by side here (FIGEL [see note 7], 273).

[55] SCHEIBLE (see note 40), 82. In the light of what Luther wrote from the Wartburg it would seem that he around that time had the same resolve. Looking at the »little sacrificer« (sacrificulus), the lone priest who celebrated mass every day by himself in the chapel of the castle, he wrote this would best be stopped right away or at least be reduced, since this activity was a wrong (iniuria) which contradicted the essence of the Lord's Supper as an act of communion and of proclamation in every respect – a diagnosis which led into the exclamation: »O Antichriste!« (letter to Spalatin from 1 Oct., 1521: WA.Br 2,14–19 [no. 434]).

[56] MARTIN BRECHT, Martin Luther, vol. 2: Ordnung und Abgrenzung der Reformation 1521–1532, Stuttgart 1986, 35.

A student at Wittenberg University aptly captured the general mood, if still probably exaggerating, when he proudly wrote: »Nos Wittenbergenses non audimus missas«.[57]

The situation was far more complicated for evangelically minded clergy who served as parochial priests than it was for mere preachers. For regular celebration of the mass was one of their main responsibilities.[58] Since preaching was also one of their duties, giving them the right to do so during the Sunday morning parochial mass, they, too, used their sermons to proclaim the evangelical message. But then the sacrifice of the mass had to follow which was contrary to this proclamation, not to mention the masses during the week which were performed silently and without a sermon. No parish priest could escape from celebrating.[59] It would seem that most priests in this situation simply hoped for better times and endured the tension. There was, however, still one device they could use to ease the strain. It is mentioned only a couple of times, and then in accordance with its nature only allusively: to leave out particularly offensive passages from the *Canon Missae* which was, after all, recited silently.[60] In

---

[57] Sebastian Helmann to Johann Heß, 8 October, 1521 (in: Die Wittenberger Bewegung 1521 und 1522, ed. Nikolaus Müller, Leipzig ²1911, 15–19, here: 17).

[58] No intermediary solution was possible for those priests whose only task was to say mass as the donors of their endowments had specified and who had no other skill. They could only insist on continuing as before or give up their position. Little wonder than that resistance against working in the new liturgical setting which included preaching frequently came from their ranks (FIGEL [see note 7], 58).

[59] Obviously what created the least difficulties for them was to stop celebrating private masses during the week. Cf. the case of Simon Hein, the parish priest of Wittenberg, who held two mass endowments which obligated him to say a certain number of silent masses. Some sources state that he stopped doing this at the end of 1521. Other indications seem to imply that he resumed celebrating for a short while (KRENTZ [see note 38], 246, however, overestimates the clarity of the material by using the indicative »ist davon auszugehen« which suggests certainty. Her circumstantial evidence is that while it was reported in January 1522 that Hein had »left« the duties connected with his endowments, in the course of the year he still received endowment payments. But since we do not know whether the payments were connected directly to these celebrations and whether he was being monitored for compliance, Krentz' conclusion is not compelling.).

[60] E.g. Johannes Oecolampadius writing from the Ebernburg to Kaspar Hedio in June, 1522: »Nihil [...] vel ex pristinis ritibus vel ex verbis canonis omitto. [...] Ego non adeo temerarius, ut immutem, quae bona conscientia servare possum, et mihi nequaquam periculosus est canon. [...] Ut nihil a me mutatum, ita si quid precum aut verborum pia mente deditaque opera omitterem, non peccasse me crederem in Christum« (Briefe und Akten zum Leben Oekolampads, ed. Ernst Staehelin, vol. 1: 1499–1526, Leipzig 1927, 188, 190 [no. 128]; in the preceding no. 127 Hedio's question from 1 June which had caused Oecolampadius' answer: »quidnam mutaris, quid omiseris« [in the liturgy]; both letters, together with a sermon Oecolampadius had appended to his, appeared in print: Quod expediat epistolae et evangelii lectionem in Missa, vernacula sermone plebi promulgari, Oecolampadii ad Hedionem Epistola, s.l. [Augsburg] s.a.

the light of the specific liturgical quandary in which parish priests with evangelical convictions found themselves, it is not surprising that the decisive impulse for Martin Luther to draw up his two reformed orders of the mass came from a parish priest, Nikolaus Hausmann from Zwickau.

All the measures described above were taken in the expectation that they would be necessary only for a transition period, since in the near future the church service would be reformed according to the Gospel, making intermediary solutions superfluous. However, understandably not everybody wanted to wait. Indeed, waiting to some seemed to be a lack of obedience towards the Word of God. Particularly well known is the pressing ahead of Luther's followers at Wittenberg during autumn and winter 1521/22, while he was absent on the Wartburg: i) Melanchthon (then still quite bold), together with several students on 29 september 1521 received communion in both kinds in the parish church[61] which soon after they did so again,[62] although we know nothing else about the rite which was used;

[1522]). Oekolampad's procedure had been noticed, the main reason being the unusual shortness of the canon he recited because he left out certain prayers. However, it was certainly easier to make this observation in the chapel of a castle than in a parish church where masses took place behind a screen or at a side altar. The Nuremberg priest Andreas Döber also attracted attention and was criticized for having left out the prayers for the dead and the invocation of the saints (1524). If this criticism was aimed at celebrations in Latin his liturgical alterations would have drawn notice because he was saying mass in a small hospital church; yet it is possible that the criticism was aimed at the mass which he from autumn 1524 celebrated aloud in German, thus making the omissions obvious (JOHANN BARTHOLOMÄUS RIEDERER, Abhandlung von Einführung des teutschen Gesangs in die evangelischlutherische [!] Kirche überhaupts und in die nürnbergische besonders, Nuremberg 1759, 181–82). Consider also Johann Schwebel, the Reformer of Zweibrücken, who, already in 1522, was one of the first to say mass in German and distribute communion in both kinds. He wrote he »hid« the canon, which in any case was only to be recited silently, in such a way, that nobody could easily complain he had abandoned it (»Canonem quem vocant Missae hactenus nefas fuit aliis audientibus legere: proinde sic eum occulto, ne facile quisquam possit conqueri me illum prodidisse«). Moreover, like Oecolampadius, Schwebel added that he had no intention to take anything away from or add anything to the canon which Christ had handed down and from which he had no desire to depart (»ubi vel minuam, vel augeam a Christo traditum Canonem benigne moneri cupio; nam illic derivare non cupio«). This statement most likely does not refer to Schwebel's German masses in which he presumably only recited – aloud – the Words of Institution, but to the Latin masses which he still also celebrated. Obviously, then, Schwebel's comment indicates that the only thing he kept from the canon – which could not be heard and therefore not easily checked – was what came from Christ himself, i.e. the Words of Institution (JOHANN SCHWEBEL, Scripta Theologica, atque tunc in Religionis dissidio atque negotio agitatis Controversiis, Zweibrücken 1605, 337–38; no year is given for the passage quoted, but SMEND [see note 47] convincingly argues for 1522). Cf. the recommendation of the same procedure given by Luther in a different context below p. 424 (text at note 80).

[61] Report of the student Helmann who had been present (see note 57, 17).
[62] SCHEIBLE (see note 40), 77, 83.

ii) Augustinian friars received communion in both kinds in Luther's convent;[63] iii) students and local citizen obstructed the saying of private masses in the parish church in the beginning of December;[64] and iv) at Christmas the positive counter-event already mentioned took place, i.e., the
spectacular reformed mass in the collegiate or castle church at which Andreas Karlstadt preached and presided with citizens participating in dro-
ves, amongst them leading representatives of the university and the town,
an act he soon repeated in both the city and the collegiate church. Gabriel
Zwilling who had already been the driving force behind the events in the
Augustinian convent followed Karlstadt's example in near-by Eilenburg,[65]
and similar events took place in other Saxon towns.[66] Karlstadt's rite was a
mass without the Canon, save the Words of Institution which were recited
aloud as proclamation to and in the language of the people, which then led
to the communion *sub utraque* for all.[67] It was not meant to be an exceptional event, but the starting point of a lasting new liturgy, as the citizens
of Wittenberg demanded in a petition to the city council.[68] Indeed, the
Wittenberger Stadtordnung (Order for the town of Wittenberg)[69] issued
by the council in January 1522 enacted a liturgical reform which realized
decisive requests of the Reformers, including, besides the sermon which
was a matter of course, communion in both kinds, elimination of the
canon save for the Words of Institution (which through the omission of
the surrounding prayers lost its sacrificial nature), and the recitation of
these words as proclamation of the Gospel with a loud voice and in the
vernacular.[70] The rest of the liturgy, however, followed the traditional
ordo missae and remained in Latin for the time being.

---

[63] Cf. BRECHT, Luther, vol. 2 (see note 56), 35; KRENTZ (see note 38), 180.

[64] SCHEIBLE (see note 40), 81. On St. Barbara's day (4 December) students forced the
friars of the church of the Franciscans to say only one mass at the main altar (ibid., 82).

[65] SIEGFRIED BRÄUER, »ich begere lauttern und reinen wein / So vormischt er mirn
mith wasser«. Der Flugschriftenstreit zwischen dem Eilenburger Schumacher Georg
Schönichen und dem Leipziger Theologen Hieronymus Dungersheim (in: Reformation
und Katholizismus. Festschrift Gottfried Maron, ed. Jörg Haustein and Harry Oelke,
Hannover 2003, 97–140, here: 100).

[66] SCHEIBLE (see note 40), 83.

[67] HERMANN BARGE, Andreas Bodenstein von Karlstadt, vol. 1: Karlstadt und die
Anfänge der Reformation, Nieuwkoop ²1968, 358–361; ULRICH BUBENHEIMER, Luthers
Stellung zum Aufruhr in Wittenberg 1520–1522 und die frühreformatorischen Wurzeln
des landesherrlichen Kirchenregiments (in: ZSRG.K 102, 1985, 149–51, 187–9); KRENTZ
(see note 38), 154–59; THOMAS KAUFMANN, Abendmahl und Gruppenidentität in der
frühen Reformation (in: Herrenmahl und Gruppenidentität, ed. Martin Ebner, Freiburg
2007, 194–210, esp. 200).

[68] BRECHT, Luther, vol. 2 (see note 56), 39; SCHEIBLE (see note 40), 82. They demanded, amongst other things, freedom to preach the Gospel, the abolition of private masses, and communion in both kinds.

[69] LStA 2,525–29.

[70] Silent masses without congregation were, for the time being, still allowed (printed

As an *Order* issued by the urban authorities, the *Wittenberger Stadt-ordnung* was a failure. It had to give way to the Elector's authority over the church which at that time was determined both by the necessities of imperial law[71] and by the cautious attitude in religious matters of Frederick the Wise. Nevertheless, the future would see the fulfilment of the liturgical demands of the *Order* as well as of further requests which had then still been postponed. Their eventual success was due to Martin Luther upon his return from the Wartburg, who, on the one hand, confirmed the rights of the Elector in religious matters, on the other hand, although severely critizing the way the reforms had been carried out, defended the reforms themselves and secured them for the future.[72] For an interim period (»eyn tzeytlang«)[73] he gave the citizens of Wittenberg the same advice as evangelicals heard and read in other places: In his famous *Invokavitpredigten* preached during the first week of Lent[74] as well as in the broadsheet *Von beider Gestalt des Sakraments zu nehmen* (On taking both kinds of the Sacrament)[75] he recommended to the congregation the temporal renunciation of the chalice or of communion altogether,[76] indeed, even of frequenting the mass itself,[77] and the personal reinterpretation of the liturgy in the light of the Gospel.[78] His advice to the evangelical priests

---

version: LStA 2,528,1–2; for the manuscript version which did not include this concession cf. WOLFGANG SIMON, Die Meßopfertheologie Martin Luthers, Tübingen 2003, 504–07; as to the open question of how to interprete this difference cf. KRENTZ [see note 38], 193).

[71] Namely the mandate of the imperial government from 20 January, 1522, which requested that the princes of the two Saxonies and the bishops with ecclesiastical oversight of their territories should dispense of the reformatory innovations (cf. ARMIN KOHNLE, Reichstag und Reformation, Gütersloh 2001, 105–12).

[72] For more on the politics of the court which was under pressure because of the mandate mentioned in note 71 and the conduct of Martin Luther cf. Kaufmann, Geschichte (see note 38), 388–392. Although Luther recognized the superior authority of the Elector to that of the town council, he did not in fact follow. He returned to Wittenberg against Frederick's will and defended the theological basis for the reforms, while withdrawing their practice only temporarily and even then not completely. Cf. also note 88.

[73] WA 10/2,31,7.

[74] WA 10/3,1–64 (LStA 2,520–558).

[75] WA 10/2,11–41.

[76] Ibid., 30,15–31,3. Those who did not want to do without communion in both kinds which in fact corresponded to the New Testament, should not do so ostentatiously, but rather at other times and at another altar than their »weaker« fellow-Christians who had not yet reached this stage. For otherwise these would be put under pressure to do likewise and, if they did, they would have a guilty conscience afterwards (ibid. 30,28–31). In fact the communion of the chalice was withdrawn as the normal liturgical form for the time being, but individuals could still request it (WA.Br 2,483,21–3).

[77] Those who still frequented the traditional mass were only the »poor erring consciences« who thought they needed this (WA 10/2,31,28).

[78] Ibid., 30,4–9.

who »had to say mass« was to continue for the time being, but less and less, »out of love« for those with »poor erring consciences« who still thought they needed the traditional mass,[79] as well as tacitly[80] to delete all words in the canon which referred to the mass as sacrifice.[81] These were the same proposals as we have found in Jakob Strauß, Urbanus Rhegius, and others. However, these proposals now had a different context and a different perspective. Whereas Strauß and Rhegius had written for a situation in which the evangelicals were suppressed and still waited for liturgical reforms, the burgers of Wittenberg Luther addressed had already experienced essential reforms and now had to come to terms with their temporal withdrawal.[82] In this case there was political pressure behind it as well.[83] Yet Luther who had himself firmly advocated those reforms insisted on their temporary withdrawal as a preacher and a theologian. It was necessary, he argued, out of respect for the personal conviction of faith which only the Gospel itself could evoke[84] and which peer pressure for a rapid realization of reform failed to respect just as much as the laws of the pope.[85] Two consequences followed from his analysis: i) all the liturgical reforms undertaken and planned in Wittenberg around the turn of the

---

[79] Ibid., 31,27–32,2.

[80] Since the canon was recited silently and never heard by the congregation, Luther also assumed that the parishioners would not miss the sacrificial prayers when they were left out and hence not take offence: »Es kann aber der priester solchs wol meyden, das der gemeyn man nymer erferet unnd on ergerniß außrichten« (ibid., 29,14–6).

[81] Because of the enormity of the sacrilege involved (cf. note 88) Luther did not think that this change should be left to the discretion of the celebrant, but had to be done (ibid., 29,11–16). Since for political reasons (cf. note 88) this could not be universally enforced Luther added, that whoever refused »obdurately« to avoid these words, but insisted on continuing to recite them, would have to answer for this directly to God (ibid., 29,16–17). This remark was particularly aimed at specific members of the College of All Saints with whom he would have to struggle on this topic for years. He had the same group in mind when he added a concession to his frequent request that the private masses, performed »as sacrifices and good works«, must be abolished, namely that priests who wanted to say them should not be »torn from the altar« since faith could not be forced upon anybody. With sufficient preaching against this sacrilege private masses would die out on their own (ibid., 32,11–17).

[82] Cf. the remarks voiced by his critics Luther takes up ibid., 24,2–4: »Ist denn nu dem gewißlich alßo und keyn tzweyffell drob tzuhaben [sc. the legitimacy of the reforms], warum thut manß denn nicht? Ja warumb lessistu [Luther] es selbs nicht gehen tzu Wittemberg, da es angefangen ist, und anders wo mehr?«.

[83] Luther alluded to this pressure, but he called it »a rather contingent matter« (»eine ßonderliche tzufellige ursach«) which he did not need to discuss at this point, for the real issue which he addressed instead, would still be there regardless of the present political situation (ibid., 25,1–5).

[84] »Man soll und kann niemant tzum glawben dringen, ßondern das Euangelion frey selbs holen lassen, wen es holet« (ibid., 28,7–9).

[85] E.g. ibid., 26,4–14; 29,3–10; 31,7–18.

year 1521/22 had been theologically right;[86] ii) nevertheless, it was still necessary to make a temporary return to the former state of the liturgy, even though in many respects the old rite was an »abuse« which did not correspond to the will of Christ.[87] Yet, the previous order was not to be endured because of political pressure, as in the case of Strauß and Rhegius, but accepted as a temporary sacrifice out of love for those fellow-Christians who were still »weak« in faith, entangled in the web of old things and views.[88] What could not be restricted under any circumstances according to this program was evangelical preaching. But through such preaching the faith would grow which would then make evangelical reforms seem appropriate and desirable in the eyes of the whole congregation, while rendering the renunciation of reforms superfluous.[89]

Even the new liturgical order which Luther himself presented one year later, the Latin *Formula Missae et Communionis*,[90] was still a document which postponed the full liturgical realization of the theological insights of the Reformation. Although he had come to the conclusion that it was time to move beyond just letting the Word work upon hearts and begin to make actual reforms,[91] Luther still consciously refrained from implementing his full program.[92] As a result, he also failed to live up to the extensive

---

[86] A participant who had received communion in both kinds must therefore never wound his conscience by thinking he had done something wrong: »Alßo auch die, ßo beyder gestallt empfangen haben, bitten wyr und, ßo es helffen will, gepieten wir ynn dem namen unßers herrn Jhesu Christi, das sie ia keyn gewissen drob machen, als sey es unrecht odder ubell than, ßondern sollen das leben ehe lassen, ehe sie das wider ruffen oder verleucken unangesehen, was da widder setzt, thutt oder will Bapst, Keyser, furst und teuffell datzu. Denn da ist der text des Euangeli ßo klar.« Denying this truth would mean nothing less than saying that Christ himself had been a heretic (»als wenn du sprechist, Christus selb hett unrecht daran than und were eyn ketzer, die weyl er anders denn der Bapst und die tzornige Papisten [...] handelt« (ibid., 20,23–21,5). Likewise people should absolutely not think it a sin to have received the sacrament in their hand (ibid., 17,13–23).

[87] »wyr mussens noch eyn tzeyttlang ym alten mißbrauch gehen lassen, bis [...] das Euangelion wol unter die leutt komme« (ibid., 27,29–30).

[88] Ibid., 30,9–27. One thing, however, could not be treated in this way, the sacrifice of the mass. For Luther this blasphemy so contradicted the gospel that it could not be endured even out of love or even only temporarily. Therefore he fought it unceasingly with utter fierceness (cf. BRECHT, Luther, vol. 2 [see note 56], 129–132). When he remarked in *Von beider Gestalt* that priests who continued sacrificing for the time being did so at their own risk (see note 81) – meaning certain members of the college of All Saints –, he did so because the college was still under the protection of the electoral court and noting could be done.

[89] E.g. WA 10/2,27,16–19; 32,2.14–17.

[90] WA 12,205–220.

[91] WA 12,206,3–12.

[92] E.g., the *Formula* provisionally still allowed the silent recitation of the Words of Institution (ibid., 212,25–6) and still connected them grammatically to the *praefatio*

expectations which meanwhile had been awakened everywhere and had in some places already led to greater reform, including the celebration of vernacular masses.[93] It was only with his *Deutsche Messe* (German Mass),[94] celebrated for the first time in October 1525, that his theological insights and liturgical order fully coincided.[95] This liturgy was – after the complete

prayer, although they were to be understood as proclamation and therefore were no longer in the form of a prayer as in the *canon missae* and were separated from the *praefatio* through a pause and a change of tone (ibid., 212,17–24). In addition the *Formula* still required the pastor to turn to the congregation only for the final benediction (ibid., 213,12) and did not yet require hymns sung by the congregation (cf. DOROTHEA WENDEBOURG, Essen zum Gedächtnis, Tübingen 2009, 58–59, notes 129–30). Luther had two reasons for this cautious approach. On the one hand, he was wary of lawlike prescriptions that might give the impression that the liturgical order of Wittenberg was meant to be the general order of an evangelical church service (ibid., 206,12–14; 214,14–33; 218,36–219,7). On the other hand, he expected to continue to learn by doing, namely by using the *Formula* which after all was presented »for the time being« (pro tempore; in the German translation done by Paul Speratus at Luther's request: Ein weyse Christlich Mess zuhalten, Wittenberg 1524, D jjjjᵛ: »auff eyn zeit«; ibid., 218,33–4). Moreover, not everything was yet available that was needed for a more far-reaching reform: The German hymns needed for congregational singing did not yet exist in sufficient number and quality (ibid., 218,15–23) and the coordination of language and recital tone which in Luther's eyes was essential for the next step, the vernacular mass, could not be realized quickly (cf. the annotated liturgical pieces in the *Deutsche Messe* [see note 94] and Luther's programmatical sentences on this topic written a few months earlier: WA 18,123,19–24).

[93] People not only remembered Karlstadt's vernacular mass, but masses in German were already occasionally being celebrated in other places as well (cf. SMEND [see note 41], 4–6), not to mention that since 1522 there was even a German evangelical mass in print, written by Kaspar Kantz of Nördlingen (Coena Domini, vol. 1: Die Abendmahlsliturgie der Reformationskirchen im 16./17. Jahrhundert, ed. Irmgard Pahl, Fribourg 1983, 8, 14–17). The year 1524 saw a downright explosion of celebrations in German, namely in Nuremberg (SMEND [see note 41], 176), Wertheim (WA.Br 3,330,33–42 [no. 769]), Allstedt (BRÄUER, VOGLER, Müntzer [see note 32], 195–197), Reutlingen (FIGEL [see note 7], 220–1), Strasbourg (ibid., 272). Indeed, it was no accident that the *Formula missae* was printed rarely in the original Latin, but speedily and often in the German translation that had followed immediately (see note 92) – e.g. the German mass that was celebrated at Easter 1525 in Saxon Lochau »in the presence of the electoral court« (WA 19,48) was most likely based on the translation of the *Formula*.

[94] WA 19,72–113.

[95] One can see this congruity particularly in three areas: i) language – alongside, not instead of (cf. note 97), his evangelical Latin liturgy he presented a vernacular one; ii) singing – he made vernacular hymn singing by the congregation an integral part of the liturgy; iii) the Lord's Supper – he designed its rite to be a single movement in words and gestures of giving aimed at the communicants (cf. WENDEBOURG, Essen [see note 92], 59). However, even here Luther indicated that the last word on liturgical reform had not been spoken. He made this clear on two points: One, congregational singing – since vernacular evangelical hymns were just beginning to be written, there were not yet as many as were needed for German masses, especially on feast days (WA 19,112,14–16); two, the selection of gospel and epistle reading on Sundays – although in the *Formula Missae* Luther had already shown dissatisfaction with the traditional order of pericopes (WA 12,209,16–210,4), they remained unchanged in the *Deutsche Messe*: »For the time

cessation of the medieval mass[96] – introduced in February 1526 by electoral mandate as the obligatory liturgy for the whole territory.[97] The institutionalization of evangelical worship was finally realized[98] – and thus the core element of the institutionalization of the evangelical church of Electoral Saxony. In the previous year this process had already come to its conclusion in the far Southwest in Zurich[99] and in the far Northeast in Prussia[100] as well as in the imperial city of Nuremberg,[101] whereas the rest of the empire was still – for a longer or shorter while – on its way.

---

being« the traditional lectionary should be kept in Wittenberg, for it would be useful for the many students of theology in town who were learning how to preach, since most of them would have to follow the traditional order of periscopes in their future parishes. Yet Luther added, that he had no objection to the *lectio continua* system in the mass which evangelical congregations had introduced in other places to replace the pericopes whereas in Wittenberg it was the order for the readings in church services only on Sunday afternoons and on certain workdays. Indeed, Luthers's qualification »for the time being« implies that he could envisage such a development for Wittenberg as well (WA 19,79,7–14). In other words, the *Deutsche Messe* in some respects was also still a »work in its beginning« (ibid., 112,16).

[96] At the end of 1524 its last bastion fell, the traditional celebration at Wittenberg's College of All Saints where a minority of the members had maintained it until then (KRENTZ [see note 38], 369–371).

[97] Report of Georg Spalatin in his »Chronicon sive Annales« (in: Scriptores Rerum Germanicarum, Praecipue Saxonicarum, ed. Johann Burkard Mencke, Leipzig 1728, vol. 2, 654). Already when Luther was working on the *Deutsche Messe* he wrote that this liturgy should be the normative order for the whole electorate (letter of 27 September, 1525 to Nikolaus Hausmann: WA.Br 3,585,5–6 [no. 926]). He said the same in the introduction to the *Deutsche Messe* itself (WA 19,73,6–8). This statement was no contradiction to his opinion that, given certain »causes« – i.e. the presence of an international congregation who did not understand German or of students who were studying Latin – the *Formula Missae* should remain in use (WA 19,73,32–74,21). The liturgical uniformity of the whole territory which the electoral mandate stipulated never happened. And although the *Deutsche Messe* clearly predominated it was not adopted unaltered (PAHL [see note 93], 30). Often liturgies were used which combined elements of the *Formula Missae*, in Latin or in German translation, with elements of the *Deutsche Messe* (ibid., 30–32). This was also the case in Wittenberg, besides the city showing liturgical flexibility on different occasions (cf. JOHANNES BERGSMA, Die Reform der Meßliturgie durch Joh. Bugenhagen, Hildesheim 1966, 92–97).

[98] Reform had already come earlier to the liturgical calender and all other church services, i.e., those on early Sunday morning and afternoon which complemented the mass and the daily morning preaching services which replaced the weekday masses as well as matins and vespers. These changes were first recommended in 1523 in the small writing for the parish of Leisnig *Von Ordnung Gottesdiensts in der Gemeinde* (WA 12,35–37, incorporated in the *Formulae missae*: ibid., 219,8–29) and successively put into practice in Wittenberg. Other places introduced similar alterations. The *Deutsche Messe* finally presented the whole set of weekly services (WA 19,79,17–80,24).

[99] In Holy Week 1525 (12 April) the city council of Zurich banned the mass and decreed Ulrich Zwingli's liturgy *Aktion und Brauch* as mandatory order of the church service which was first introduced that Maundy Thursday (JOHANNES VOIGTLÄNDER, Ein Fest der Befreiung. Huldrych Zwinglis Abendmahlslehre, Neukirchen-Vluyn 2013, 67).

[100] On 10 December, 1525 the Prussian parliament in Königsberg decided to intro-

2.2. The Reformation in England

England would still be on the way for a long time – if it was in fact on the way at all. For in the 1520s there was a deep shadow casting darkness over the whole prospect of reform in England, namely, the treatise in which Henry VIII in the early years of the continental Reformation took his stance on this religious awakening: the *Assertio septem sacramentorum adversus Martinum Lutherum* (1521).[102] Directed against Luther's attack on the medieval sacramental system, his »prelude« *De captivitate Babylonica*, the *Assertio* had immediate implications for divine worship. Like Luther's treatise itself, the main part of Henry's highly polemical reply was dedicated to the mass around which he drew a red line. It was clear to every reader that on this topic the king would not tolerate any departure from tradition – a position which he would hold for the next quarter of a century he was to rule. Although he rejected other insights of the Reformation, too, on some issues he would more easily overlook deviations. He even changed his own position on matters like the vernacular Bible, confession, and religious images. But criticism of the mass was never tolerated. Henry made this clear over and over again. Not coincidentally three of the *Six Articles* (1539) which Henry used to show his final repudiation of the Wittenberg Reformation dealt with the mass.[103] Right to the close of his reign no one was in any doubt that citizens who spoke out against the mass would end up at the stake.[104] This was made possible by the effective power of the Tudor crown over both church and state throughout the whole kingdom. There was only one way to escape it, exile beyond the sea. Thus evangelical Englishmen were in a much more difficult position

---

duce an evangelical liturgy for the whole territory which the evangelical bishops of Prussia had composed. It was very close to Luther's *Formula Missae*, but it also had distinctive characteristics of its own (D. ERDMANN, Art. Albrecht von Preußen, in: RE³ 1,310–323, esp. 318). Cf.: Die evangelischen Kirchenordnungen des XVI. Jahrhunderts, ed. Emil Sehling, vol. 4, Erlangen 1911, 30–38; Die evangelischen Kirchenordnungen des 16. Jahrhunderts, ed. Aemilius Richter, vol. 1, Weimar 1846, 23–33.

[101] ANDREAS OSIANDER, Gesamtausgabe, ed. Gerhard Müller, vol. 1, Gütersloh 1975, 143–150; Quellen zur Nürnberger Reformationsgeschichte. Von der Duldung liturgischer Änderungen bis zur Ausübung des Kirchenregiments durch den Rat (Juni 1524–Juni 1525), ed. Gerhard Pfeiffer, Nuremberg 1968, 400–01, 440–47; MATTHIAS SIMON, Wann fand die erste evangelische Abendmahlsfeier in den Pfarrkirchen zu Nürnberg statt? (in: Mitteilungen des Vereins für Geschichte der Stadt Nürnberg 45, 1954, 361–71, esp. 367).

[102] Ed. Pierre Fraenkel, Münster 1992.

[103] Statutes of the Realm, printed by command of His Majesty King George III. 1817, 739–740 (31° Henry VIII c. 14).

[104] For the 1540s cf. the tables of causes for antiheretical death judgements in ALEC RYRIE, The Gospel and Henry VIII. Evangelicals in the Early English Reformation, Cambridge 2003, 224–25.

than evangelical citizens of the Empire who, when they lived under a local ruler opposed to the Reformation, could more easily migrate to another imperial city or territory. The many cases of burning and exile[105] as well as the high number of recantations and recantations of recantations[106] which have no parallel in the Empire speak for themselves – we shall come back to this point.

There is yet another difference. During many years for English evangelicals under Henry the mass did not have the same weight as it had for those in the Empire. One could know about Luther's views on the mass through the criticism voiced by the king, John Fisher, and Thomas More. But that was all in Latin and only reached the small circle of the learned. The same held true for those works of Luther – all Latin writings as well – which from the early 1520s in spite of severe censorship found their way into the country[107] and were repeatedly burned. Amongst the few texts by Luther translated into English during Henry's reign, there was none on the mass or the Lord's Supper, e.g., none of his *Sermones* on the sacraments.[108] It was only under Edward VI that a treatise by Luther on the mass appeared in English, not surprisingly a reckoning with the papal »sacrilege« of the mass still celebrated in the collegiate church from 1524.[109] Its publication in England was part of a campaign against the mass which broke out under the new king to prepare for his liturgical reform, the *Book of Common Prayer*.[110]

---

[105] For the years between the publication of the *Six Articles* (1539) and Henry's death (1547) cf. the table of the evangelicals who were executed or went into exile: ibid., appendix I.

[106] A selection in SUSAN WABUDA, Equivocation and Recantation During the English Reformation: The ›Subtle Shadows‹ of Dr Edward Crome (JEH 44, 1993, 224–242).

[107] Cf. the information on the authors of evangelical books which could be found between 1535 and 1547 in Cambridge in RYRIE, The Gospel (see note 104), 172. Ryrie calls the probate inventories on which he based his figures »thick with the works of evangelical authors«. Amongst these authors Luther was by far the most popular.

[108] For the English translations of works by Luther at the time of Henry cf. CARRIE EULER, Does Faith Translate? Tudor Translations of Martin Luther and the Doctrine of Justification by Faith (in: ARG 101, 2010, 80–113). For a general overview see BERND MOELLER, Luther in Europe: His works in Translation 1517–1546 (in: Politics and Society in Reformation Europe. Essays for Sir Geoffrey Elton on his Sixty-Fifth Birthday, ed. E. I. Kouri and Tom Scott, Basingstoke 1987, 235–251).

[109] Ein Sermon von der höchsten Gotteslästerung (WA 15,765–774). The English version was printed together with: The Dysclosyng of the Canon [th]e popysh Masse, with a sermon annexed unto it of [th]e famous Clerke of worthy memorye. D. Marten Luther, London s.a. [1548?] (cf. WA 15,761).

[110] EULER, Does Faith (see note 108), 91, speaks of »a rash of polemical treatises against the Mass« in those years. For this »rash« cf. also JOHN N. KING, JOHN DAY, Master printer of the English Reformation (in: The Beginnings of English Protestantism, eds. Peter Marshall and Alec Ryrie, Cambridge 2002, 180–208, esp. 190–192).

The liturgy in general or the mass in particular was also not of special interest in the writings English reformers themselves wrote during that phase of the Henrician era.[111] Questions concerning justifiction and ethics were of much greater importance. The first treatises on the Lord's Supper appeared only in 1533, writings by John Frith[112] and George Joye.[113] Both of them were heavily influenced by Swiss theologians[114] who at that time busily tried to get in contact with English evangelicals, especially Heinrich Bullinger.[115] Hence, the English reformers' reflection on the Lord's Supper jumped directly to the second phase of the continental discussion on that topic, i.e., the debate about the nature of Christ's presence. And Frith as well as Joye opted for the Swiss position[116] – an option which was obvious

---

[111] Cf. the overview of ANTHEA HUME, English Protestant Books Printed Abroad, 1525–1535: An Annotated Bibliography (in: The Complete Works of St. Thomas More, vol. 8/2, ed. Louis A. Schuster et al., New Haven et al. 1973, Appendix B [1063–1091]).

[112] A Book Made by John Frith [...] Answering unto M. More's Letter, Monster 1533; preceded by the short text: A Christian Sentence, s.l. s.a. (probably from 1532, first published around 1545) on the same topic (The Work of John Frith, ed. N. T. Wright, Oxford 1978, The Courtenay Library of Reformation Classics 7, 319–449, 478–484).

[113] The Souper of the Lorde, s.l. 1533. Since this tratise was often – wrongly – attributed to William Tyndale it was published by the Parker Society under Tyndale's name (An Answer to Sir Thomas More's Dialogue, the Supper of the lord after the true meaning of John VI. and 1. Cor. XI. [...] Expounded by William Tyndale, martyr, 1536, ed. Henry Walter, Cambridge 1850, The Parker Society 3, 216–268). About the same time Tyndale wrote the treatise A Brief Declaration upon the Sacraments which deals also with the Lord's Supper, but it was published only twelve years after his execution in Villevoorde (London 1548; in: Doctrinal Treatises and Introductions to Different Portions of the Holy Scripture by William Tyndale, martyr, 1536, ed. Henry Walter, Cambridge 1848, The Parker Society 1, 345–385). Cf. ARNE DEMBEK, William Tyndale (1491–1536). Reformatorische Theologie als kontextuelle Schriftauslegung, Tübingen 2010, 435–451.

[114] This influence can be seen also in Tyndale's treatise on the sacraments which was written about the same time (cf. the preceding note), although Tyndale adhered more strongly to Luther's position during the early years of the Reformation which predated the later protestant divisions (DEMBEK [see the preceding note], 438–39, cf. also 151–2).

[115] CARRIE EULER, Couriers of the Gospel: England and Zurich, 1531–1558, Zürich 2006.

[116] As is well known the position which Luther had developed in the course of the debate on the Lord's Supper with Andreas Karlstadt, Zwingli, and others was held only by one of the English Reformers, Robert Barnes, for many years Luther's and other Wittenbergers' table companion (CARL R. TRUEMAN, Early English Evangelicals: Three Examples, in: Sister Reformations – Schwesterreformationen. The Reformation in Deutschland und England, ed. Dorothea Wendebourg, Tübingen 2010, 15–28, esp. 23–27). This is not to say there were no supporters of the doctrine of real presence in England during Henry's reign. As ALEC RYRIE's article The Strange Death of Lutheran England (JEH 53, 2002, 64–92, esp. 69–74) has shown, the evangelical party which rose in the 1530s and whose main figures were Thomas Cromwell und Queen Anne in its majority adhered to this doctrine, and still in the 1540s there were enough adherents of it, without thereby upholding a specific theological conception beyond the rejection of the philosophical explication in the sense of the dogma of transubstantiation. Whether

in view of the strongly humanistic background of the English Reformers, but which might also reflect subliminal Lollard influence.[117] As a consequence of this jump to the second phase, the concerns in the Empire which had been in the forefront during the first phase of the debate on the Lord's Supper played only a marginal role in the writings of the English reformers under Henry: On the one hand, concerning communion *sub utraque specie* – hardly anybody[118] raised his voice in England for this right which had been obtained with such effort by the evangelicals in the Empire.[119] On the other hand, the rejection of the mass as a sacrifice – only rarely this concern was raised by English adherents of the Reformation,[120] whereas it

---

this is a strong enough reason to consider a position as ›Lutheran‹ (as Ryrie, Strange Death [see note 116], does) is questionable. Of course realist language such as speaking of the presence or the eating of the body of Christ is not in and of itself proof that someone held the a real presence positions – reformed theologians could use the same expressions. Moreover, in the light of Henry's strong sanctions, not a few English evangelicals used equivocal language on this very dangerous topic, including equivocator-in-chief, Edward Crome whom Ryrie readily presents as a »Lutheran« defender of the real presence (loc. cit., 90–91), yet at another point calls him »England's master of ambiguity« (The Gospel [see note 104], 34, similarly already Susan Brigden, London and the Reformation, Oxford 1991, 332). Cf. note 120.

[117] For the strictly critical stance of Wyclif and the Lollards regarding the doctrine of the real presence cf. Richard Rex, The Lollards, Basingstoke 2002, 42–45, 60, 77.

[118] There is one exception: Robert Barnes, who while in Wittenberg criticized the *communio sub una* in the eighth commonplace of his *Supplication unto Henry the Eighth*. Indeed, he even went beyond Luther, declaring the communion *sub utraque* as mandatory and any deviation from this rule a mortal sin (James P. Lusardi, The Career of Robert Barnes, in: The Complete Works of St. Thomas More, vol. 8/3, ed. Louis A. Schuster et al., New Haven et al. 1973, 1365–1415, esp. 1387–9).

[119] This might again have had to do with the Lollards who, in sharp contrast to the Hussites, were not interested in the *communio sub utraque* (Rex [see note 117], 73).

[120] An exception is again Robert Barnes who in article 19 of his *Sententiae ex doctoribus collectae, quas papistae valde impugnant hodie. Per Anto. Anglum* (Wittenberg 1530, German in Bugenhagen's translation: Fürnemlich Artikel der Christenlichen kirchen, wie die beyden alten im brauch gewesen unnd gehalten sind worden, aber yetzt unbillich von den papisten, wider die heilige geschrifft, ihr eigen Decret, Concilia und schrifften der Lerer verdampt werden. Erstlich in latein durch D. Anthonium auss Engelandt zusamen gebracht, neulich mit einer vorred Ioan. Pomerani pfarherr zu Wittenberg verdeutscht, Nuremberg 1531) strongly argued against the sacrifice of the mass. Accordingly the development of the mass is an important point of criticism in his *Vitae Romanorum pontificum* (Wittenberg 1536), a history of the papacy where he charted the history of the church as a history of decline. Cf. Korey D. Maas, The Reformation and Robert Barnes: History, Theology, and Polemic in Early Modern England, Woodbridge 2010, 116–19. – Besides, the few other English theologians who did write or speak against the sacrifice of the mass most often presented the central argument of Zwingli and other Swiss Reformers, namely, that the Lord's Supper was a grateful remembrance of Christ's unique sacrifice on Golgatha and could therefore not be itself a sacrifice (e.g. Tyndale [Dembek, see note 112, 211] or Crome [Brigden, see note 116, 363]); whereas, the central argument for Luther's criticism of the sacrifice of the mass played no role at all, i.e., that the Lord's Supper was God's gift for the communion of the faithful and not

had dominated the continental debates on the mass right into the second third of the 1520s – and if it was, the debate occurred most often in the context of purgatory.[121]

All in all one can conclude that for evangelicals in England, apart from the small group of theologians who were under the influence of Swiss or Southwest German theology and fought against the concept of the real presence with growing fierceness, the »mass« as a matter for theological debate was altogether of secondary interest. If the doctrine of justification by faith alone was upheld, the issue they were most concerned about, they were, if necessary, prepared »to swallow their objections to the mass.«[122] The same picture is presented by the sermons of the time. With one exception which we will examine later, they, too, did not take a special interest in the mass. The famous and influential sermons at St. Paul's Cross rarely touched the subject during Henry's reign,[123] and other pulpits did not make it a main theme either.[124]

---

their action directed to him. This difference is levelled when RYRIE speaks of a »dislike« of the Sacrifice of the mass common to Lutherans and Reformed which for him is rooted in the common diagnosis of a contradiction between the sacrifice of the mass and the protestant doctrine of justification (Strange Death [see note 116], 72; The Gospel [see note 104], 141). All in all the »Lutheran« view of the Lord's Supper which Ryrie finds in the »Lutheran England« of the Henrician period can only be called such in a very broad sense. After all, the real presence in Luther is not a stand-alone concept but is integrated into his teaching of the Lord's Supper as Christ's bodily self-giving in the meal. This aspect is of no particular concern for the English evangelicals whom Ryrie presents as adherents of the real presence. Therefore one must qualify Ryrie's conclusion that by the 1540s »[t]he theological issue of the sacrifice of the mass was swept away as the battle polarized over the Real Presence« (ibid., 91). Firstly, as stated before, the debate on the sacrifice of the mass was never an »issue« in the English Reformation to the degree to which it had been on the continent. Secondly, when the sacrifice of the mass was criticized in England, the dominant argument inevitably lead to such a »sweeping away«, since the real presence was unnecessary for, and even alien to, their description of the Supper as an act of the church's remembrance of Christ's sacrifice and not a sacrifice itself.

[121] See below p. 437.
[122] RYRIE, Strange Death (see note 116), 74.
[123] A sermon from 1536 rejected the sacrifice of the mass as one of the many works which were wrongly considered as meritorious (WABUDA, Preaching [see note 13], 85–86). In a sermon most probably preached on Good Friday 1537 Simon Matthew, a defender of the royal supremacy and Henry's line regarding the mass, spoke – with anti-evangelical thrust – on transsubstantiation and sacrifice (SIMON MATTHEW, ›Christus passus est pro nobis‹: A Good Friday Sermon [1537?], in: Sermons at Paul's Cross, 1521–1642, ed. Torrance Kirby, Oxford 2017, 57–84, here: 62–63). For more on the topics which dominated the field in the 1530s, namely the royal supremacy, justification by faith, and the role of ethics, as well as for a time the destruction of images and shrines ordered by Henry, cf. the overview by Richard Rex, Pauls's Cross and the Crisis of the 1530s (in: St. Pauls's Cross and the Culture of Persuasion in England, 1520–1640, ed. Torrance Kirby and P. G. Stanwood, Leiden 2014, 107–128).
[124] This becomes clear from the analysis of WABUDA, Preaching (see note 13).

What does all this mean for our question concerning the steps on the way from theological insights to institutional changes in the field of liturgy? Could it be that this question which is productive for the analysis of the developments in the Empire is meaningless for England, not only because of a lack of sources, but most of all because the special conditions under which the English Reformation took place excluded any such steps? There is indeed little source material which would allow an answer. For what is true for the evangelicals under Henry VIII in general, is particularly valid for their conduct in the field of liturgy: »They bought their survival at the [...] price of historical anonymity.«[125] And as far as this conduct itself is concerned, the iron fist of the king's church politics which kept the whole country under its control, undoubtedly left evangelicals little room to manoeuvre. If there was an opportunity here and there, it was largely because of the twists and turns of Henry's own policies. Yet, these rarely had to do with the liturgy and never with the mass. Thus there seems to have been little conspicuous deviation from official church practice. The lists of accusations of heresy against laypeople in London and Kent during the 1540s included the offence of »disrupting services«,[126] but the number of cases was very small.[127] What seems to have been more frequent is non-participation in masses, at least in London.[128] Laypeople loudly demanding church services in their own language, communion in both kinds, or the downright abolition of the traditional mass never arose in Henrician England as they did in the Empire.

Yet, just as in the Empire, those in England who were critical of the mass could find some relieve from their dilemma in spiritual parallel actions. Evangelical English primers presented evangelical interpretations of traditional liturgical pieces which could be meditated upon during mass,

---

[125] RYRIE, The Gospel (see note 104), 223.

[126] What most probably lies behind these accusations are events like those reported from London: Parishioners had during mass walked around in the church with their caps on their heads; they had also demonstratively looked away from the elevated host (Brigden [see note 116], 406). Other reports that people had sung insulting songs against the Lord's Supper as well as against the sacraments in general most probably referred to occurences outside of the mass (ibid.).

[127] RYRIE, The Gospel (see note 104), 225, cf. also ibid., 227. The figures from Kent are somewhat higher, both for laypeople and for clergy, where iconoclasm was the issue (ibid., 224–25, cf. 227). But in this respect one could feel justified by the king's own actions, for »Henry VIII's regime was more unequivocally evangelical in its attitude towards images than in almost any other area, and most even of the Kentish iconoclasts were doing no more than pushing at the limits of royal policy« (ibid., 231). However, »unequivocally reformed« rather than »unequivocally evangelical« would be more accurate since the Lutherans were not iconoclastic.

[128] Ibid., 225.

and more importantly, they presented vernacular versions of the biblical readings and the Lord's Prayer which were strictly forbidden for the liturgy.[129] Another parallel action came into being when in 1537 the King lifted the ban on vernacular Bibles – not on their reading in the mass, but on private reading, a ban that would have been unthinkable in the Empire.[130] From 1538 all churches held copies of the long desired book – securely fastened by chains. Since most parts of the mass went on silently and invisibly, people who were able to do so read aloud from the chained books to themselves and to others.[131] This practice became a real attraction at least in London, where a good reader like the tailor John Porter had »a greater audience« than the mass or matins, and a Mrs. Castle made a name for herself as »a reader of the scripture in the church«. The clergy did not like that, and after a few years such »brabbeling of the New Testament« was forbidden as a disturbance of the mass. In the end, reading the Bible by laypeople, particularly by women, was banned altogether. Mr. Porter and Mrs. Castle did not bend and went to prison as a result, where the tailor eventually died.[132] However, as spectacular as such cases were, on

---

[129] Cf. Charles C. Butterworth's overview of these edifying vernacular booklets which were highly popular, published in many editions, and also contained banned foreign material like – anonymously printed – texts by Martin Luther. They led in 1545 led to the *Authorized Primer of Henry VIII*, »a direct forerunner of the Book of Common Prayer« (BUTTERWORTH, The English Primers 1529–1545, Philadelphia 1953, quotation on p. VII, a list of the biblical lessons: 288–90). The only traditional Latin liturgical element which Henry permitted to be translated into English was the litany which was heavily dependent on Luther. In 1544 Henry had an official vernacular version published (BRYAN D. SPINKS, German Influences on Edwardian Liturgies, in: Sister Reformations – Schwesterreformationen [see note 116], 180).

[130] The vernacular Bibles which were published before the Reformation in the Empire were never outlawed although, of course, they were not used in the liturgy. The phobia the English church and the English king had about vernacular Bibles – which even led to a large extent to the disappearance of English primers – was rooted in Wiclyff's and the Lollards'demand for English translations of the Bible, since they taught that the Scriptures gave laypeople direct access to God and his truth; hence the authorities associated vernacular religious texts with »sectarian danger« (REMIE TARGOFF, Common Prayer. The Language of Public Devotion in Early Modern England, Chicago 2001, 19). As the chalice for the laity was the symbol of Hussite threat in the Empire, so in England the vernacular Bible was the embodiment of Lollard danger. There seems to be a faint echo of this suspicion in the wording of EAMON DUFFY who – in 1992 and 2005! – called the vernacular the »Trojan horse« that was introduced into the traditional liturgical life (The Stripping of the Altars. Traditional Religion in England c. 1400–c. 1580, New Haven ²2005, 222).

[131] For what follows cf. WABUDA, Preaching (see note 13), 101–103. For another story with a happier ending about laypeople reading the – finally available – Bible in churches see in ARTHUR G. DICKENS, The English Reformation. London ²1989, 213.

[132] According to BRIGDEN (see note 116), 332, he was accused of using the public reading of the Bible to disseminate heretical views about the nature of the bred in the Lord's Supper.

the whole they were marginal occurrences. The majority of evangelicals conformed liturgically and participated in the obligatory church services, whatever they may have thought about them. Some did participate in underground conventicles held in private houses – although we have no idea how many.[133] Yet, as far as we can ascertain, these meetings were not occasions to hold services, but secretly to read »heretical« books and listen to »heretical« sermons – a pattern of behaviour which the Lollards had already practiced.[134] In general, they passed unnoticed by the public at large, but amongst the more ardent evangelicals, particularly those in exile, such outward conformity and private dissent was dismissed as mere Nicodemism.[135]

And what about those who held ecclesiastical offices? Were there evangelical priests who drew liturgical consequences from their Reformation insights? For example, did some cease to celebrate masses and confine themselves to preaching in order to avoid conflicts of conscience?[136] As regards the last question, it is doubtful whether except for the open-air sermons, and possibly also the – relatively few – *quarter sermons*, there was any regular liturgical setting for preaching without connection to the mass which would have been comparable with the preaching services in the Empire. Consequently, we can find no evidence anywhere that English reformers attempted to develop a new, evangelical liturgical form built around the sermon. And what about changes to the mass itself? Were there attempts to read the mass in English, or at least the biblical pericopes, or recite the Words of institution aloud and in the vernacular, or to distribute communion in both kinds? We do read about three incidents of this kind. In 1538 mass in the parishes of Hadleigh and Stratford in Suffolk was said

---

[133] London had the highest concentration, participants in great numbers were arrested here in 1540 (RYRIE, Gospel [see note 104], 238). In fact, from the start London was the city with the highest number of »heretics«, apart from Cambridge with its special situation (cf. BRIGDEN [see note 116], 187–198).

[134] RYRIE, The Gospel [see note 104], 237–39.

[135] Ibid., 132–33. However, this term itself, which was common on the continent, not least with Bullinger and Calvin, was not used in England (ibid., 84).

[136] Perhaps such was the case with Nicholas Ridley. In his farewell letter before he was burned he looked back to his time as a vicar in Kent and wrote, that then he had already preached »not after the popish trade but after the Christs gospel«, but that »the true doctryne of the Lords supper« had not yet been revealed to him by God (Fairwell Letter, published in: Certain most godly, fruitful, and comfortable letters of such true Saintes and holy Martyrs of God, ed. Miles Coverdale, London 1564, 92–93, cf. Wabuda, Preaching [see note 13], 71). From this statement one might conclude that later, when he had come to the right doctrine about the Lord's Supper, he did not celebrate according to the wrong doctrine any more. However, it is highly questionable whether in the position he held afterwards, namely that of royal chaplain, he could have avoided saying mass.

at »divers tymes« in English,[137] and the curate of St. Mary Colechurch in London »ministered the sacraments« in this language.[138] At least in the case of Hadleigh, that such a blatant liturgical violation of ecclesial and royal law took place without incident most probably is connected to the parish's special canonical status. Since it was a peculiar of the archbishop of Canterbury, Thomas Cranmer could have extended his protection for liturgical experimentation which in other places would have been too dangerous.[139] At any rate, these three cases were extremely rare exceptions. No other examples are mentioned in the sources.[140]

Since the recitation of the canon was silent, whether this or that priest adopted the less obvious device of leaving out offensive sacrificial prayers is difficult to prove. In contrast to the Empire, we have no indication that this solution was ever either promoted or practiced, and in any case it would have been much more risky than on the other side of the channel. Besides, as has been said before, debate about the mass and sacrifice did not play a role in England comparable to that in the continental Reformation. For those evangelicals who denied the real presence – a clear minority amongst English reformers until far into the 1540s – the situation was more difficult. After all, the elevation of the consecrated host and its adoration gave a liturgical expression to the doctrine of the bodily presence of Christ in the mass which was obvious to everyone.[141] It was no mere accident that in the 1549 *Book of Common Prayer*, despite the otherwise generally conservative nature of that liturgical reform, the deletion of the elevation was the decisive innovation, recognized as such by both, friend and foe.[142] That was, however, under the reformed regime of king

---

[137] »[A]t Hadleigh in Suffolk and at Stratforde [...], the mass and consecration of the sacrament of the aulter was sayd in Englishe by the curats there divers tymes«, quotation from Wriothesley's *Chronicle* (JOHN CRAIG, Reformation, Politics and Polemics. The Growth of Protestantism in East Anglian Market Towns, 1500–1610, Aldershot 2001, 171; for this information I thank Dr Ashley Null). DIARMAID MacCULLOCH's remark that in 1538 »several evangelical enthusiasts »had celebrated wholly English services« seems to refer to these cases (Thomas Cranmer. A Life, New Haven 1996, 223).

[138] BRIGDEN (see note 116), 402.

[139] CRAIG (see note 137), 152. Thus Cranmer accommodated adherents of the Reformation in this parish (ibid., 153; SUSAN WABUDA, Setting forth the Word of God: Archbishop Cranmer's Early Patronage of Preachers, in: Thomas Cranmer. Churchman and Scholar, eds. Paul Ayris and David Selwyn, Woodbridge 1993, 75–88, esp. 84).

[140] SUSAN WABUDA, Cranmer (see note 139), 88, claims: »it may have been evident that [Cranmer's] licencees advanced changes in ceremonies and rites«, but she names no source upon which this assumption is based.

[141] Critical statements on the mass which referred to this point, were very rare, exceptions were occasional protests against the »idolatrous« worship of Christ in the mass which must refer to elevation and adoration (BRIGDEN [see note 116], 351, 406). Cf. also note 126.

Edward VI. Whoever would have dared such a step in the lifetime of his father would as surely have been burnt as those men and women who questioned the real presence in words alone. Thus probably nobody did. Those who could not bring themselves to celebrate under these circumstances left the country.

However, at one point concerning the mass, or more precisely concerning the sacrifice of the mass, things came to a head – the exception to which I have previously alluded. The contentious issue was the mass for the dead which from 1540 became the object of fierce preaching attacks and, one year before Henry's death, set off the last major persecution of his reign. The starting point was again not a controversy on the mass itself. The trigger was the long-standing debate about purgatory. For quite some time English evangelicals had denied its existence and, consequently, also the need for liberation from it.[143] Thus the most important means for exiting purgatory, the mass for the dead, was pointless.[144] This dispute which grew constantly fiercer and finally became bloody was linked primarily with the name of Edward Crome (ca. 1480–1562), a Cambridge educated pastor and famed preacher from London who was a close ally of Latimer and one of »the early Reformation's legendary evangelists«.[145] Although Crome was not alone in attacking purgatory,[146] he was its most

---

[142] Cf. the rubric concerning this point in the *Book of Common Prayer* of 1549: »These wordes before rehersed [sc. the Words of institution] are to be saied, turning still to the Altar, without any elevacion, or shewing the Sacrament to the people« (The Book of Common Prayer. The Texts of 1549, 1559, and 1662, ed. Brian Cummings, Oxford 2011, 31). Cf G. J. CUMING, A History of Anglican Liturgy, London 1969, 82. Likewise the first measure concerning liturgy taken by Queen Elizabeth immediately after her accession to the throne was the ban on elevation and adoration, reinstituted under Queen Mary, during the court's 1558 Christmas mass (JOHN SCHOFIELD, Philip Melanchthon and the English Reformation, Aldershot 2006, 186).

[143] Cf. the critical tract on this topic by JOHN FRITH from 1531: A Disputation on Purgatory (in: The Work of John Frith [see note 112], 81–203) – the opinion on purgatory he expressed here was, along with his statements on the Lord's Supper, the grounds for his going to the stake. At the same time as Frith's tract appeared Edward Crome started to question purgatory (see note 149). For the beginnings of the denial of purgatory in the late 1520s and early 1530s (Simon Fish, Frith) cf. BRIGDEN (see note 116), 188; for the critical attitude of Archbishop Cranmer cf. MACCULLOCH, Cranmer (see note 137), 152–53, 162, 309.

[144] Just as controversial as the mass for the dead was to pray for them. Questioning it meant questioning the intercessionary prayer *Bidding of the Beads* (cf. note 24) whose petitions for the dead were often connected to rich endowments (WABUDA, Preaching [see note 13], 51–63).

[145] BRIGDEN (see note 116), 187, about Hugh Latimer, Crome, John Lambert, and Thomas Bilney.

[146] WABUDA, Preaching (see note 13), 57. Equally outspoken was Hugh Latimer, who even had an exchange with the king about purgatory (MACCULLOCH, Cranmer [see note 137], 160, 190).

effective critic. He had attracted attention already in the 1530s, but after
the enactment of the *Six Articles* in 1539, he contradicted state law. For the
Articles confirmed not only the doctrine of transubstantiation and the
communion *sub una* but also the legitimacy of private masses whose main
purpose was for the dead. Despite the *Articles*, Crome remained undeter-
red, and in a sermon one year later he called the mass for the dead an act of
»superstition«.[147] In 1546 he repeated his initial criticism, also challenged
the sacrificial character of the mass, whether for the living or the dead, and
even questioned transsubstantiation.[148]

It is not clear whether such views held by Crome and other likeminded
priests led them to stop celebrating masses for the dead anymore.[149] However, they certainly did not undertake steps to change the liturgy. Their
specific contribution to the reform of the church service was something
else which appears at first sight to point in the opposite direction, namely,
equivocal speech. In a political situation which left no room for even the
slightest liturgical change under pain of death, Crome, as the needle of the
compass never wavers from true North, never ceased to keep this issue
before the public, over and over again he preached why and how the mass
had to be reformed, thereby undermining the liturgical practice theologically. Several times accused of heresy and confronted with the alternative
of recantation or the stake – even on royal demand – , Crome escaped
both, whereas like-minded companions were burnt, emigrated, or recanted. He managed to avoid either consequence through equivocation.[150] Before his judges he reinterpreted passages of his sermons that were under
accusation in such a way that they seemed incontestable. Similarly, when
presented with written recantations prepared by his judges which he had
to sign, read out in public, and then defend in a sermon with his own
words, he handled the required material in such a way that the
recantations did not seem to contradict his previous preaching. Indeed,
they seemed even to prove him right.[151] In this way his – and others' –

---

[147] BRIGDEN (see note 116), 330–31. Crome war careful not to attack private masses as
such. But since their main purpose was the liberation of the dead from purgatory, the
criticism of the one amounted to the criticism of the other, as his own statements
indicate (ibid., 331).

[148] WABUDA, Equivocation (see note 106), 234. It is not clear whether he also thereby
also questioned the real presence.

[149] When Crome began preaching against purgatory in 1531, it is possible that he
omitted the prayers for the dead. The context would have been preaching chantries
which had been donated in favour of certain deceased and were therefore connected with
prayers for them (WABUDA, Preaching [see note 13], 56).

[150] For Crome cf. the most instructive article by SUSAN WABUDA mentioned above (see
note 106): Equivocation and Recantation During the English Reformation: The ›Subtle
Shadows‹ of Dr Edward Crome.

public recantations became performances of evangelical proclamation.[152] In the end, however, he could not sustain this strategy. In 1546, faced with a choice between a clear repudiation of his preaching or death, Crome recanted.[153] Yet, as far as the matter itself was concerned, he was unwavering, and a few months later he would have nothing to fear any more because the old king was dead.

Crome's »canting, recanting, decanting, or rather double canting«, as a contemporary observer wrote,[154] was even more controversial than the Nicodemism of the evangelical underground conventicles. Others, including the simple evangelical faithful who did not have the dialectical refinement of a trained theologian, suffered torture and the stake for their convictions.[155] Crome and his peers, however, wriggled out of such consequences with skillful rhetoric and, if necessary, even outright recantation. The more ardent evangelicals, particularly those in exile, the majority of whose numbers tended towards the Swiss reformation,[156] rejected equivocation and even more strenuously recantation where the Gospel was at stake.[157] Instead they demanded a clear-cut confession of evangelical faith, even if it led to death[158] – or to exile.[159] Of course, the equivocators' theological and spiritual ambiguity does raise legitimate ethical questions. Nevertheless, by over and over again in their sermons going to the limits of what was allowed and beyond, by fathoming the range of possible

---

[151] He was particularly brazen in his 1541 recantation at Paul's Cross which he was compelled to give after the king himself had interrogated him. Instead of preaching a sermon expounding the text of the recantation which he had signed and was supposed to read publicly, Crome preached according to his own theological convictions. Afterwards he did read the recantation but first noted that the words were written by his Majesty for him to read, which he would now do. He then read the text, said a short prayer, and left (ibid., 233–4).

[152] WABUDA, Equivocation (see note 106), 233, writes about a recantation of three likeminded men, amongst them Barnes: »Their supporters recognized their attempts to use the occasion to spread their own opinions.« The same holds true of Crome's recantations, apart from the fact that he, the »master of the ambiguous recantation« (BRIGDEN [see note 120], 332, cf. above note 116), was the most successful amongst them all.

[153] For these events which stirred up the whole of London cf. BRIGDEN (see note 116), 363–70.

[154] Quoted by WABUDA, Equivocation (see note 106), 237.

[155] Particulary sensationally the twenty-five-year-old noblewoman Anne Askew (for her martyrdom cf. BRIGDEN [see note 116], 370–6).

[156] For this group of exiles and their literary fecundity which, however, had little effect in England and only gained some momentum during the last years of Henry's reign cf. RYRIE, Gospel (see note 104), 93–112.

[157] Ibid., 97.

[158] E.g. John Bale, who contrasted Crome's evasive conduct with the martyrdom Anne Askew suffered for her faithfulness to the gospel (WABUDA, Equivocation [see note 106], 237).

[159] RYRIE, Strange Death (see note 116), 75–76.

interpretation through their equivocations which could not easily be dis-
proven, and even by recanting and afterwards repeating the same truths as
before, Crome and his peers kept Reformation insights before the public
in their country which otherwise might have died with them. As a result,
they created the necessary conditions for change after Henry's death. With
the emergence of a new political framework, what they previously could
only advocate with words or half-way measures had at last a chance to
become liturgical reality. Now came the hour of the unambiguous, those
native sons who returned from exile and those foreigners, like Peter Martyr Vermigli and Martin Bucer, who travelled in the opposite direction as
exiles from the continent and devoted themselves to the service of the
English Reformation. Now there would be opportunities also in England
for Reformation insights to become clearly embedded in official liturgical
texts and institutions.

    As in Wittenberg and other places, this happened in two steps, an initial
more conservative and a subsequent more radical one, embodied in the
Books of Common Prayer of 1549 and 1552. The liturgical changes happened speedily and for the whole country.[160] There was no phase of experimental and partial liturgical reforms carried out from below before the
official steps, as was the case in many regions of the Empire. Intermediary
measures, if they occurred, were directed from above. Towards the end of
1547 the parliament ordered communion *sub utraque*,[161] in the following
year a liturgical framework for such communion was issued, the *Order of
Communion*,[162] a short vernacular element which was appended to the end
of the still Latin mass[163] and the first piece of the planned new liturgy into
which it was transferred practically unchanged. A number of parishes,
encouraged by the ecclesial-political leadership, went on to the use of
English for the church service[164] and several already put into practice parts
of the new order of the mass which circulated as drafts[165] before parliament authorized the new liturgy in January 1549 to begin from Pentecost

---

[160] SPINKS (see note 129), 184–85, 186–88.

[161] CUMING (see note 142), 61.

[162] Cf. The Two Liturgies, A. D. 1549, and A. D. 1552: with other Documents set
forth by Authority in the Reign of King Edward VI, ed. Joseph Ketley, Cambridge
1844, 3–8.

[163] MACCULLOCH, Cranmer (see note 137), 384–86.

[164] CUMING (see note 142), 60–61; MACCULLOCH, Cranmer (see note 137), 395–96.
The encouraging precedence was the mass for the opening of the parliamentary session in
November 1547, in which Cranmer had already recited some liturgical elements in
English (ibid., 377).

[165] DIARMAID MACCULLOCH, Tudor Church Militant. Edward VI and the Protestant
Reformation, London 2001, 82. The model was the Chapel Royal which travelled with
the sovereign (ibid., 81–82).

1549.[166] In the eyes of the Reformers it was clear that this liturgy was provisional.[167] The second one, the *Book of Common Prayer* of 1552, was meant to be fully protestant.[168]

Thus, like the evangelical territories and cities of the Holy Roman Empire, England at last also had its binding liturgical order which established the obligatory Sunday sermon, the reformed liturgy of the Lord's Supper, and that of other church services. And it did so with much greater homogeneity than in the Empire. The new order was required for the whole country – no one even considered the possibility of a plurality of evangelical liturgies like in the Holy Roman Empire and even within a single territory as in Electoral Saxony. And what is more, the very element of the church service which in the evangelical churches on the continent was the strongest variable, the sermon, was uniformly determined in England.[169] For in contrast to the continent the ordinary English ministers were not supposed to preach sermons which were based on their own explication of a biblical text.[170] Rather, they were obliged to read before the congregation a section from the officially prescribed *Book of Homilies*[171], one every Sunday throughout the whole country.[172] The Edwardian regime was not less committed to the Tudor centralization of power than Henry's had been. For the church service that meant: The institutionalization of the new evangelical liturgy was the institutionalization of a comprehensive evangelical-liturgical uniformity throughout the English kingdom.[173]

---

[166] CUMING (see note 142), 68.

[167] MacCULLOCH, Cranmer (see note 137), 410–11.

[168] *Terminus ad quem* for its introduction in the parishes was All Saints' Day 1552 (CUMING [see note 142], 114–5).

[169] For the discussion of the sermon cf. the contribution by Albrecht Beutel in this volume.

[170] Only one fifth of them was entitled to such preaching which in contrast to the Reformation churches on the continent was not part of the tasks bestowed in the ordination but required a special license. In the second half of the 16th and in the 17th century the percentage increased considerably (IAN GREEN, Preaching in the Parishes, in: The Oxford Handbook of the Early Modern Sermon, ed.s Peter MacCulloch, Hugh Adlington and Emma Rhatigan, Oxford 2011, 137–154, esp. 138–39).

[171] Under Elizabeth a *Second Book of Homilies* would be added to the Edwardian *(First) Book*. For the two *Books of Homilies* cf. ASHLEY NULL, Official Tudor Homilies (in: Oxford Handbook of the early Modern Sermon, eds. Peter McCullough, Hugh Adlington and Emma Rhatigan, Oxford 2011, 348–365).

[172] For this vital difference between the English and the Continental Reformation churches cf. WENDEBOURG, Reformation und Gottesdienst (see note 28), 331–333, esp. 333 for the fierce criticism of the puritan faction at such »playing on a stage«.

[173] Liturgical uniformity was not only the aim of the kings who governed the church but also the guiding principle of Archbishop Cranmer from his beginning as a liturgical reformer (MacCULLOCH, Cranmer [see note 137], 222).

Liturgical Space in the German and Scottish Reformations

Andrew Spicer

The late medieval landscape included many sites that had sacred associations, such as holy wells or shrines, which became places of pilgrimage and the focus of popular devotion. Alongside these religious sites, the Roman Catholic Church carefully delineated and defined what constituted liturgical space. Rites of consecration set particular buildings apart from the secular world and dedicated them for religious use, in particular for the celebration of the mass and parochial worship. These churches often stood in graveyards which had also been consecrated for the interment of the dead, separated from the rest of the community by a wall or ditch. There was a gradation of holiness from the churchyard to the church, with the most sacred site being the high altar, which was also consecrated for liturgical use.[1] Here the mass was celebrated and, through transubstantiation, Christ became manifest. The chancel was therefore divided from the remainder of the church by a rood screen and was largely the preserve of the clergy.[2] The sanctity of the church was therefore delineated by the rites of consecration and reconciliation – which restored the sanctity of a profaned site – as well as by the liturgical use of the interior. Although there was criticism of consecration, particularly because of the fees paid to the bishop for performing the rite and the cost of the celebratory banquet, it was not until the Reformation that this understanding of places of worship was fundamentally challenged.[3]

---

[1] *The Rationale divinorum officiorum of William Durand of Mende*, edited by Timothy M. Thibodeau (New York, 2007), 54–88; Eric Palazzo, *Liturgie et société au Moyen Age* (Paris, 2000), 71–77; Dominique Iogna-Prat, »L'église ‹Maison de consécration› et bâtiment d'exception dans le paysage social«, in Didier Méhu (ed.), *Mises en scène et mémoires de la consécration de l'église dans l'Occident médiéval* (Turnhout, 2007), 347–63; Derek A. Rivard, *Blessing the World. Ritual and Lay Piety in Medieval Religion* (Washington, 2009), 89–131; Will Coster and Andrew Spicer, »Introduction. The Dimensions of Sacred Space in Reformation Europe«, in Will Coster and Andrew Spicer (eds), *Sacred Space in Early Modern Europe* (Cambridge, 2005), 9–11.

[2] Miri Rubin, »The Space of the Altar«, in Lawrence Besserman (ed.), *Sacred and Secular in Medieval and Early Modern Cultures. New Essays* (Basingstoke, 2006), 167–68, 173.

The ability of Catholic rites to confer sanctity was derided by the Reformers. Martin Luther dismissed the consecration of churches as being part of »the papal bag of tricks«, which should not to be tolerated.[4] At the inauguration of the new castle chapel at Torgau in 1544, he argued that it would be »rightly and Christianly consecrated and blessed, not like the papists'church with their bishop's chrism and censing, but by God's command and will«, through preaching. Furthermore, he rejected the notion that

»we are making a special church of it, as if it were better than other houses where the Word of God is preached. If the occasion should arise that the people did not want to or could not assemble, one could just as well preach outside by the fountain [in the castle courtyard] or somewhere else«.[5]

The Genevan Reformer, John Calvin, similarly attacked the notion that any one place was more suitable than another for worship. In his *Institutes of the Christian Religion*, Calvin argued that places of worship did not

»by any secret sanctity of their own make prayers more holy, or cause them to be heard by God. But they [temples] are intended to receive the congregation of believers more conveniently when they gather to pray, to hear the preaching of the Word, and at the same time to partake of the sacraments [...] but those who suppose that God's ear has been brought closer to them in a temple, or consider their prayer more consecrated in the holiness of the place, are acting according to the stupidity of the Jews and Gentiles. In physically worshipping God, they go against what has been commanded, that, without any consideration of place, we worship God in spirit and truth.«[6]

These Reformed sentiments regarding the perceived sanctity and efficacious character of places of worship were later shared by the Scottish reformers.

Nonetheless, it was the existing parish churches that were taken over by the Lutherans in the Holy Roman Empire and the Reformed Kirk in Scotland as their places of worship. This article will consider the rearrangement of existing church interiors and liturgical space to meet the

---

[3] Andrew Spicer, »›God will have a house‹: Defining Sacred Space and Rites of Consecration in Early Seventeenth-Century England«, in Andrew Spicer and Sarah Hamilton (eds), *Defining the Holy. Sacred Space in Medieval and Early Modern Europe* (Aldershot, 2005), 210.

[4] »The Smalcald Articles«, in Robert Kolb and Timothy J. Wengert (ed.), *The Book of Concord. The Confessions of the Evangelical Lutheran Church* (Minneapolis, 2000), 326.

[5] *D. Martin Luthers Werke kritische Gesamtausgabe* (Weimar, 1883 seqq.) [hereafter *WA*], XLIX: 588, 592; Jaroslav Pelikan et al (eds), *Luther's Works*, 56 vols (St Louis, 1955–86) [hereafter *LW*], LI: 333–34, 337.

[6] John Calvin, *Institutes of the Christian Religion: 1536 Edition*, translated by F. L. Battles (Grand Rapids, 1986), 73; John Calvin, *Institutes of the Christian Religion*, edited by J. T. McNeill, 2 vols (Philadelphia, 1960), II, 893.

particular requirements of these two confessions. Although there were significant differences, the Lutherans and the Reformed both emphasised the importance of the administration of the sacraments and the preaching of the word of God. These principles underscored the adaptation of buildings initially designed for the celebration of mystery of the Catholic mass. Furthermore, by the early seventeenth century, the high regard for preaching and the sacraments led the ecclesiastical authorities to ensure that the places where this took place were appropriate, seemly and dedicated for their religious use.

1. The Holy Roman Empire

Although Luther considered that it was legitimate »to preach on the street, outside a building, without a pulpit«, he did acknowledge that it would be better to have a designated place of worship:

»for the sake of children and simple folk, it is a fine thing and conducive to good order to have a definite time, place, and hour to which people can adapt themselves and where they may assemble«.[7]

Therefore, for practical reasons, the Lutherans took over the existing churches as their places of worship. Even though Luther had derided the Catholic mass, he was reluctant to specify how these liturgical spaces should be reconfigured for worship. This was a reaction against the legalistic and prescriptive character of late medieval Catholicism.

In 1516, Luther had attacked the Church's requirement

»to build this and that church or that we ornament them in such and such a way, or that singing be of a certain kind or the organ or the altar decorations, the chalices, the statues and all of the other paraphernalia which are contained in our temples. [...] For all of these things are shadows and signs of the real thing and thus are childish«.[8]

This stance was combined with the reformers'opposition to aspects of Catholic worship that did not have biblical sanction. Luther drew a distinction between those matters »either commanded or forbidden by God and thus have been instituted by the supreme Majesty« and those »things which are not necessary, but are left to our free choice by God and which we may keep or not«.[9] Those aspects of worship that had not been ordained by God were regarded as *adiaphora* or matters of indifference; it

---

[7] *WA*, L: 649; *LW*, XLI: 173.
[8] *WA*, LVI: 493–94; *LW*, XXV: 487.
[9] *WA*, X.3: 21; *LW*, LI: 79.

was an issue of Christian freedom as to whether or not they were implemented.[10] Luther's unwillingness to be legalistic and to assume a prescriptive approach to worship is evident in the opening lines of his preface to the German mass. He argued that those who desired to use the service should

»not make it a rigid law or entangle anyone's conscience, but use it in Christian liberty as long, when, where, and how you find it to be practical and useful«.[11]

Luther's initial liturgical reforms to the mass sought

»to purify the one that is now in use from the wretched accretions which corrupt it and to point out an evangelical use«.

However, his rejection of Catholic legalism and assertion of Christian freedom meant that elements regarded as *adiaphora* – such as candles, vestments, and vessels – remained. In his German mass, he commented that

»we retain the vestments, altar, and candles until they are used up or we are pleased to make a change. But we do not oppose anyone who would do otherwise«.[12]

Luther's intention was not to alienate those who had not fully embraced the Reformation by making radical changes to the externals of worship but, nonetheless, with the expectation that in due course these could be removed.

One of the consequences of this ideological stance was that there was no major reorientation of liturgical space, although some changes were necessary in order to balance the administration of the sacraments and preaching. Initially, Luther did envisage the altar being relocated; he commented in his German Mass that

»in the true mass, however, of real Christians, the altar should not remain where it is, and the priest should always face the people as Christ doubtlessly did at the Last Supper. But let that await its own time«.[13]

In 1523, Luther gave an account of how the mass was conducted in Wittenberg:

---

[10] *WA*, VIII: 511, L: 649–51; *LW*, XXXVI: 168, XLI: 173–75. See also Caroline Bynum, »Are Things ›Indifferent‹? How Objects Change Our Understanding of Religious History«, *German History* 34 (2016), 88–112; Andrew Spicer, »*Adiaphora*, Luther and the Material Culture of Worship«, in Rosamond McKitterick, Charlotte Methuen and Andrew Spicer (eds), *The Church and Law*, Studies in Church History 56 (2020), forthcoming.

[11] *WA* XIX: 72; *LW*, LIII: 61.

[12] *WA* XIX: 80; *LW*, LIII: 69.

[13] Ibid.

»when the mass is being celebrated, those to receive communion should gather together by themselves in one place, and in one group. The altar and the chancel were invented for this purpose. God does not care where we stand and it adds nothing to our faith«.[14]

The *German Mass* of 1526 was less specific about the location for receiving communion merely instructing the faithful that

»there be a decent and orderly approach, not men and women together, but the women after the men, wherefore they should also stand apart from each other in separate places«.[15]

Although Luther sought to reject the notion that a particular part of the church was more appropriate than another for receiving communion, the liturgical importance of the east end, nonetheless, continued. Furthermore, in a number of churches, the pre-Reformation high altar remained not only in situ but also in use for the celebration of the Lutheran mass.

In his commentary on Psalm 111, published in 1530, Luther noted that

»the chancel, which since ancient times is especially built and set aside for the purpose of celebrating the Sacrament and keeping the remembrance of Christ, as is still done in the public Mass«.[16]

As the numbers who actually received communion each week were limited, the choir was large enough to accommodate the participants. A similar arrangement can be seen in other parts of northern and central Germany, particularly in areas where Johannes Bugenhagen was influential in defining and establishing Lutheran rituals.[17] In his church order for Braunschweig (1528), Bugenhagen asserted:

»The choirs were surely made for communicants for this purpose since ancient times, before the extensive singing was initiated«.[18]

The liturgical significance of the chancel was no doubt further emphasised by the removal of the side altars from the main body of the building. These had been rendered superfluous with the abolition of private and requiem masses; official orders were given for their removal in East Frisia, Mecklenburg and Weimar but elsewhere it was left to the discretion of the individual parishes.[19] The focus on the east end of the church was height-

---

[14] *WA*, XII: 216; *LW*, LIII: 33; Amy Nelson Burnett, »The Social History of Communion and the Reformation of the Eucharist«, *Past & Present* 211 (2011), 98.

[15] *WA*, XIX: 99; *LW*, LIII: 82.

[16] *WA*, XXXI.1: 406; *LW*, XIII: 365.

[17] Susan C. Karant-Nunn, *The Reformation of Ritual. An Interpretation of Early Modern Germany* (London, 1997), 119–20.

[18] Johannes Bugenhagen, *Selected Writings*, edited by Kurt K. Hendel, 2 vols (Minneapolis, 2015), II, 1359.

[19] Nigel Yates, *Liturgical Space. Christian Worship and Church Buildings in Western Europe, 1500–2000* (Aldershot, 2008), 12; Bodo Nischan, »Becoming Protestants. Lu-

ened in some German states, from the mid-sixteenth century, by the erection of small subsidiary altars at the junction between the chancel and the nave. This made the rite more visible and allowed the pastor to face the congregation, as Luther had suggested, which was not feasible at the monumental high altar. These subsidiary altars were used for weekday and Sunday services with the high altar reserved for feast days.[20]

While there was a degree of spatial continuity within the church for the German mass, this needed to be balanced with the arrangements for preaching. Although there had been preaching in German churches, principally in urban areas, before the Reformation, Luther claimed that God's word had effectively been silenced in public worship. He argued that

»a Christian congregation should never gather together without the preaching of God's Word and prayer, no matter how briefly«.[21]

Existing medieval pulpits were used for preaching,[22] although sometimes these were moved to a more convenient location in the nave which was better suited for preaching to the congregation. In some cases, this required the removal of other liturgical furnishings. At Nuremberg in 1542, for example, the city council ordered the dismantling of three side altars in the Sebalduskirche because

»they get in the way of the people hearing the Word of God and in front of them the preacher cannot be seen or heard well«.[23]

The pulpit therefore became an important liturgical focal point within the post-Reformation church interior. This was further emphasised by the iconography of the newly erected pulpits, such as in the Marienkirche and the Dom at Lübeck and the castle chapel at Torgau.[24] With their biblical

theran Altars or Reformed Communion Tables?«, in Karin Maag and John Witvliet (eds), *Worship in Medieval and Early Modern Europe* (Notre Dame, 2004), 96; Bridget Heal, *A Magnificent Faith. Art and Identity in Lutheran Germany* (Oxford, 2017), 47–48.

[20] Karant-Nunn, *The Reformation of Ritual* (see note 17), 120–21; Maria Deiters, »Epitaphs in Dialogue with Sacred Space: Post-Reformation Furnishings in the Parish Churches of St Nikolai and St Marien in Berlin«, in Andrew Spicer (ed.), *Lutheran Churches in Early Modern Europe* (Farnham, 2012), 64–67; Per Gustaf Hamberg, *Temples for Protestants. Studies in the Architectural Milieu of the Early Reformed Church and Lutheran Church* (Gothenburg, 2002), 75; Jeffrey Chipps Smith, »The Architecture of Faith. Lutheran and Jesuit Churches in Germany in the Early Seventeenth Century«, in Jan Harasimowicz (ed.), *Protestantischer Kirchenbau der Frühen Neuzeit in Europa. Grundlagen und neue Forschungskonzepte* (Berlin, 2015), 170.

[21] *WA*, XII: 35; *LW*, LIII: 11.

[22] Heal, *A Magnificent Faith* (see note 19), 49; Emily Fisher Gray, »Lutheran Churches and Confessional Competition in Augsburg«, in Spicer (ed.), *Lutheran Churches* (see note 20), 46.

[23] Quoted in Heal, »Sacred Image and Sacred Space«, in Coster and Spicer (eds), *Sacred Space in Early Modern Europe* (see note 1), 48.

references, they were in marked contrast to the 1518 pulpit at Eisenach – from which Luther preached his last sermon – with its visual references to the Virgin Mary and the cult of saints.[25] Furthermore, the role of the pulpit as the vehicle for preaching the Word of God imbued it with such significance that the authorities sought to ensure that this part of the church was treated with respect and due decorum. It symbolised the clerical office, which went one step further at Ratzberg cathedral where the portrait of the first Lutheran minister on the back wall of the pulpit gave the impression that the word of God was being constantly preached.[26]

Besides locating the pulpit in the most appropriate place for preaching to the entire congregation, the need for an attentive and receptive audience led to the rapid expansion in the construction of pews during the 1520s and 1530s. Although prominent figures – ecclesiastics, patrons, officials – often had benches or pews in their parish church before the Reformation, the new seating accommodated ordinary members of the congregation. The removal of side altars provided more space as the authorities sought to maximise the church's capacity for Lutheran rites, which was not always straightforward as the building had been designed for a different liturgical use.[27] However, the construction of pews could sometimes hamper Lutheran worship. The Church Ordinance of Electoral Saxony in 1580 addressed a »common complaint« that

»now and then seats are built in churches that prevent people from being able to see the preacher in the pulpit, or at the altar when the holy sacrament is distributed; likewise such seats are also erected in the public aisles, so that, because of these, people cannot easily come and go«.[28]

There were also difficulties for those who sat in the area between the pulpit and the altar as they needed to face in opposite directions during the course of the service. In churches, such as St Anna's in Augsburg where

---

[24] Bonnie B. Lee, »Communal Transformations of Church Space in Lutheran Lübeck«, *German History* 26 (2008), 160–62; Jeffrey Chipps Smith, *German Sculpture of the Later Renaissance, c. 1520–1580. Art in an Age of Uncertainty* (Princeton, NJ, 1994), 87–90; Joseph Leo Koerner, *The Reformation of the Image* (London, 2004), 408–10.

[25] Gotha Stiftung Schloss Friedenstein, *Martin Luther. Treasures of the Reformation* (Dresden, 2016), 360–61.

[26] Margit Thøfner, »Framing the Sacred: Lutheran Church Furnishings in the Holy Roman Empire«, in Spicer (ed.), *Lutheran Churches* (see note 20), 119–22; Heal, *A Magnificent Faith* (see note 19), 178; Chipps Smith, *German Sculpture* (see note 24), 107–08.

[27] Koerner, *The Reformation of the Image* (see note 24), 411–12; Tanya Kevorkian, *Baroque Piety: Religion, Society, and Music in Leipzig, 1650–1750* (Aldershot, 2007), 55–56; Bonnie Lee, »Communal Transformations of Church Space«, 153–54 (see note 24).

[28] Quoted in Koerner, *The Reformation of the Image* (see note 24), 415.

the pulpit was located on the north side of the building and the altar at the east end, modifications to the seats made it possible for the congregation to face both liturgical focal points during the service. The seats fitted with back rests – *drehgestühl* – which could be flipped over, meaning that the fixed seating could face in alternate directions during a service.[29]

Although the sites for communion and preaching were the most prominent liturgical spaces within the church, the location of the baptismal font was also important. Luther made only limited changes to the baptismal rite; his first liturgy including an epilogue listing various aspects of the service which survived but were regarded as *adiaphora*.[30] Medieval fonts continued to be used and survive in significant numbers across Germany, including the late fifteenth-century bronze font at Wittenberg.[31] Traditionally, fonts were located at the west end of the nave, often between the north and south doors to the building. Although Luther did not consider that there should be a prescribed position, commenting that it was just as appropriate for fonts to be found beside the Elbe, in a number of Lutheran states they remained in their original location after the Reformation.[32] Luther did emphasise the connection between preaching and the sacrament, arguing that baptism only occurred when »water and the Word of God are conjoined«.[33] The association of preaching with baptism made by Luther led some communities from the early seventeenth century to move the font to the front of the church, so that it was in closer proximity to both the altar and the pulpit.[34] Furthermore, the liturgical significance of the place of baptism resulted in elaborate screens being erected in some churches to establish a ritual enclosure for the font.[35]

---

[29] Emily Fisher Gray, »The Body of the Faithful: Joseph Furttenbach's 1649 Lutheran Church Plans«, in Andrew Spicer (ed.), *Parish Churches in the Early Modern World* (Farnham, 2016), 113; Fisher Gray, »Lutheran Churches« (see note 22), 58; A. L. Drummond, *The Church Architecture of Protestantism. An Historical and Constructive Study* (Edinburgh, 1934), 20.

[30] *WA*, XII: 46–48; *LW*, LIII: 101–03; Bryan D. Spinks, *Reformation and Modern Rituals and Theologies of Baptism* (Aldershot, 2006), 9–14.

[31] Thøfner, »Framing the Sacred« (see note 26), 113–15.

[32] *WA*, XII: 695. Silvia Schlegel, »Festive Vessels or Everyday Fonts? New Considerations on the Liturgical Functions of Medieval Baptismal Fonts in Germany«, in Harriet M. Sonne de Torrens and Miguel A. Torrens (eds), *The Visual Culture of Baptism in the Middle Ages. Essays on Medieval Fonts, Settings and Beliefs* (Farnham, 2013) 129–47, esp. 131; J. G. Davies, *Architectural Setting of Baptism* (London, 1962), 61–63, 93, 104; Sergiusz Michalski, *Reformation and the Visual Arts: The Protestant Image Question in Western and Eastern Europe* (London, 1993), 41.

[33] *WA*, XXX.1: 112; *LW*, LI: 185.

[34] Davies, *Architectural Setting* (see note 32), 104–05; Thøfner, »Framing the Sacred« (see note 26), 116–17.

[35] Thøfner, »Framing the Sacred«, 104–05, 117–18 (see note 26).

While existing churches were adapted to meet the needs of Lutheran worship as conveniently as possible, the construction of new buildings attempted to resolve some of the issues relating to the arrangement of liturgical space. The new castle chapel at Torgau might appear initially to have continued the problematic layout of the pre-existing churches. The altar was located at one end of the building while the pulpit was placed in the centre of the gallery along the side of the chapel. This did create two focal points for the congregation but for the Saxon electors seated in the first floor gallery at the west end of the chapel, the altar and pulpit were on the same alignment.[36]

Joseph Koerner has described Lutheran church building from the mid-sixteenth century as representing »a game of alignment« that sought to co-ordinate the liturgical arrangement of the building so that the administration of the sacraments and preaching could be witnessed by all of the congregation from their seats.[37] One of the earliest attempts to resolve this issue can be seen in the castle chapel erected at Schmalkalden between 1585 and 1590, which had some parallels with Torgau. However, the communion table incorporated a baptismal basin and it was overlooked by the pulpit at first floor level. The key liturgical furnishings of the chapel were therefore placed on a single vertical axis at the east end.[38] Half a century later, a similar arrangement was proposed by Joseph Furttenbach the Younger in his treatise *KirchenGebäw* (1649) which outlined the optimum design for a Lutheran place of worship in Augsburg. This included a *Kanzelaltar* or pulpit-altar at the east end, together with the small altar and font, but the design was not implemented and this *Principalstück* arrangement was not adopted by many churches before the eighteenth and nineteenth centuries.[39]

Rather than a vertical arrangement, some new churches grouped the liturgical furnishings in one part of the building. The church erected at Wolfenbüttel between 1608 and 1623 (although parts of the building were

---

[36] Koerner, *The Reformation of the Image* (see note 24), 414, 421.

[37] Ibid., 421.

[38] Hugo Johannsen, »The Protestant Palace Chapel. Monument to Evangelical Religion and Sacred Rulership«, in Hugo Johannsen, *Masters, meanings & Models. Studies in the Art and Architecture of the Renaissance in Denmark*, edited by Michael Andersen, Ebbe Nyborg and Mogens Vedsø (Copenhagen, 2010), 39–41; Dieter Großmann, »L'église à tribunes et les tribunes des églises en Allemagne au XVIᵉ siècle«, in Jean Guillaume (ed.), *L'église dans l'architecture de la Renaissance* (Paris, 1995), 259, 265; Ernst Badstübner, »Die Rezeption von Schloßkapellen der Renaissance im protestantischen Landkirchenbau, Schmalkalden und die hessische Herrschaft«, in Harasimowicz (ed.), *Protestantischer Kirchenbau* (see note 20), 260–63.

[39] Fisher Gray, »The Body of the Faithful« (see note 29), 113–17; Koerner, *The Reformation of the Image* (see note 24), 427–28.

completed later due to the disruption of the Thirty Years War) maintained the traditional pre-Reformation ground plan of a rectangular nave and chancel. The liturgical space was arranged so that preaching and the administration of the sacraments all took place around the chancel. The pulpit was sited at the junction of the nave and choir, the high altar with a monumental altarpiece at the east end, a baptismal enclosure in front it and in the foreground a second smaller altar for more regular use. The pews in the nave all face towards the liturgical focal point of the building.[40]

Heinrich Schickhardt adopted an experimental design – an L-shaped ground plan – for the church erected for the new town at Freudenstadt in c. 1608. The altar, font and pulpit were all placed at the intersection of the two arms of the church to create a single liturgical focus, which could be seen by the congregation in both wings of the building. This arrangement satisfied the requirements for Lutheran worship but also allowed for the segregation of the congregation; the men and women were both physically and visually separated.[41] This was an unusual arrangement of liturgical space that was not adopted by other communities, even the contemporary church built by Schickhardt at Montbéliard had a more traditional ground plan.[42] It was not until the eighteenth century that more imaginative and polygonal liturgical spaces were erected for Lutheran worship.[43]

These new buildings were marked out as dedicated for liturgical use through services of consecration. In spite of Luther's rejection of the practice, churches or parts of the building together with other liturgical furnishings, such as pulpits, and vessels continued to be consecrated after the Reformation.[44] This did not represent a continuation of the Catholic rite with the asperging and chrism that Luther had rejected at Torgau in 1544 but dedication through preaching. Buildings were inaugurated with sermons that drew comparisons with the Temple of Solomon and focused on function of a church and its liturgical space. They emphasised the sanctity of these places of worship as liturgical spaces, which were distinct from other buildings because of the rites performed within them. This was

---

[40] Chipps Smith, »Architecture of Faith« (see note 20), 169–70.

[41] Hamberg, *Temples for Protestants* (see note 20), 52–58; Chipps Smith, »Architecture of Faith« (see note 20), 170–73.

[42] A. Bouvard, »L'architecte Heinrich Schickhardt à Montbéliard. La construction du Temple Saint-Martin«, *Bulletin et mémoires de la Société d'émulation de Montbéliard* 109 (1986), 303–90.

[43] Koerner, *The Reformation of the Image* (see note 24), 421–24; Bridget Heal, »Better Papist than Calvinist«: Art and Identity in Late Lutheran Germany«, German History 29 (2011), 585–86.

[44] Ernst Walter Zeeden, *Faith and Act. The Survival of Medieval Ceremonies at the Lutheran Reformation* (St Louis, 2012), 51.

underscored by the increasing efforts to ensure appropriate behaviour and decorum within both the church and churchyard as well as the banning of inappropriate activities.[45]

2. Scotland

In the wake of the Scottish Reformation in 1560, the First Book of Discipline set out the parameters for establishing Reformed worship across the northern kingdom. The parish church became the focal point for worship, as other ecclesiastical buildings had been rendered redundant by the religious changes:

»Abbeyes, Monkeries, Freiries, Nonries, Chappels, Chanteries, Cathedrall Churches, Chanonries, Colledges, others then presently are parish churches or schooles [were] to be utterly suppressed in all bounds and places of the Realme«.[46]

The former Catholic parish churches were adapted by the Reformed for preaching the word of God and the administration of the sacraments. The importance of this liturgical space over private meeting places was emphasised by the First Book of Discipline, which condemned

»some idiots [...] [that] dare counterfeit in their house, that which the true Ministers doe in open congregations«.[47]

Twenty years later in 1581, the General Assembly of the Kirk also condemned the administration of the sacraments in private places.[48]

The parish churches were built for the celebration of the mass rather than for Reformed preaching, and so had to be reconfigured spatially to meet these new liturgical requirements. The First Book of Discipline ordered the abolition of idolatry which it defined as

»the Mass, invocation of Saints, adoration of images, and the keeping and retaining of the same. And finally all honouring of God, not contained in his holy word«.[49]

Following this admonition, parish churches were purged of statues and altars were cast down. In Edinburgh, it took ten workmen nine days to remove all traces of the altars and the rood screen from the principal parish church of St Giles.[50] Although these reforms were undertaken re-

---

[45] Vera Isaiasz, »Early Modern Lutheran Churches: Redefining the Boundaries of the Holy and Profane«, in Spicer (ed.), *Lutheran Churches* (see note 17), 17–37; Heal, »»Better Papist than Calvinist‹« (see note 43), 600–03.

[46] *First Book of Discipline*, edited by J. K. Cameron (Edinburgh, 1972), 94.

[47] Ibid., 205.

[48] *Acts and Proceedings of the General Assemblies of the Kirk of Scotland*, ed. T. Thomson (Bannatyne Club/Maitland Club 81, Edinburgh, 1839–45), 524–25.

[49] *First Book of Discipline* (see note 46), 95.

latively swiftly in Edinburgh, the pace of change varied across the country. In 1574, the authorities in Aberdeen, for example, were ordered by the Privy Council, to remove the »priests' stalls and backs of altars« in order to improve the space available for people to hear the sermon.[51] The pre-Reformation church interior had been compartmentalised with the liturgical space around the principal and side altars being divided by screens and curtains, which were also removed during these reforms.[52]

The church interiors were reconfigured to form a single liturgical space for the preaching of the word of God and the administration of the sacraments. The simple rectangular structure of many parish churches, particularly in rural areas, meant it was relatively straightforward to adapt many of these buildings; the rood screen was removed and the sanctuary area was integrated into the main body of the church.[53] In other places where there was a small chancel, it was sometimes demolished or, more often, sealed off from the remainder of the building. This former liturgical space was reutilised as either a mausoleum or lairds' aisle, providing a local landowning family with a private room or loft from which to follow the service with a burial space below.[54] This represented the privatisation and, to a degree, secularisation of what had previously been liturgically the most important part of the church.

The different requirements of the Reformed Kirk meant that some of the large urban parish churches had more space than was required for worship. As a result, some buildings were subdivided to accommodate

---

[50] Andrew Spicer, *Calvinist Churches in Early Modern Europe* (Manchester, 2007), 46.

[51] *The Register of the Privy Council of Scotland*, ed. J. Hillburton *et al.* 14 vols (Edinburgh, 1877–98), II, 391; M. G. H. Pittock, »The Faith of the People«, in E. P. Dennison, D. Ditchburn and M. Lynch (eds), *Aberdeen before 1800. A New History* (East Linton), 292–93.

[52] Spicer, *Calvinist Churches* (see note 50), 46. Again this could be a protracted process, the church of Foulis Easter was found to still have its rood screen when the church was visited in 1612, ibid., 48.

[53] Spicer, *Calvinist Churches* (see note 50), 48; Deborah Howard, *Scottish Architecture from the Reformation to the Revolution, 1560–1660* (Edinburgh, 1995), 177; Miles Kerr-Patterson, »Post-Reformation Church Architecture in the Marischal Earldom, 1560–1625«, in Jane Geddes (ed.), *Medieval Art and Archaeology in the Dioceses of Aberdeen and Moray* (Oxford, 2016), 102.

[54] Andrew Spicer, »Defyle not Christ's kirk with your carrion«: Burial and the Development of Burial Aisles in Post-Reformation Scotland«, in Bruce Gordon and Peter Marshall (eds.), *The Place of the Dead. Death and Remembrance in Late Medieval and Early Modern Europe* (Cambridge, 2000), 160–61; Howard Colvin, *Architecture and the After-Life* (New Haven, 1991), 295–300; Richard Fawcett, Richard Oram and Julian Luxford, »Scottish Medieval Parish Churches: The Evidence from the Dioceses of Dunblane and Dunkeld«, *The Antiquaries Journal* 90 (2010), 265, 274–75. See also Kerr-Patterson, »Post-Reformation Church Architecture« (see note 53), 104–08.

more than one congregation within the existing structure; the superfluous remaining space could also be allocated to secular use. The town council in Edinburgh resolved in 1560 to reduce the liturgical space at St Giles' Kirk. Walls were erected within the structure to provide space for a school, tolbooth (the Scots term for a town hall), prison and clerks' chamber as well as »sufficient rowme for the preiching and ministracioun of the sacramentis«.[55] The liturgical space was altered again in 1578, when a wall was built across the former choir to separate the »East Kirk« from the congregation occupying the »Middle Kirk«; a third congregation also worshipped in the building.[56] There were similar divisions of liturgical space elsewhere in Scotland; a wall erected at the crossing of the parish church of St Nicholas, Aberdeen, in 1596, created two liturgical spaces for »preaching the word of God, and ministracioun of the sacramentis«.[57]

Although the administration of the sacraments, particularly the Lord's Supper, were highly regarded in the Reformed tradition, it was preaching that became the focus of weekly worship and determined the internal arrangement of parish churches. Scottish churches were sparsely furnished before the Reformation with few having a pulpit, although most of them would have possessed a lectern, and only limited seating for the clergy and local elite.[58] The purged church interiors were rearranged to form a centralised space with the pulpit as its focal point. Usually erected at the centre of the south wall of the building, this represented a dramatic reorientation of liturgical space from the pre-Reformation east-west to a north-south axis. Furthermore, the pulpit was usually placed between two large windows ensuring that this was the lightest part of the building for preaching.[59]

The positioning of the pulpit was intended to ensure that the minister could be seen and heard by the entire congregation, but it also meant that they in turn could be seen and heard by the minister. Calvin had argued

---

[55] *Extracts from the Records of the Burgh of Edinburgh*, ed. J. D. Marwick and M. Wood, 4 vols (Scottish Burgh Records Society, 1869–82), III, 66, 99.

[56] Ibid., I, 87.

[57] *Extracts from the Council Register of Aberdeen, 1570–1625*, ed. J. Stuart (Spalding Club, 19, 1848), 135.

[58] George Hay, »Scottish Post-Reformation Church Furniture«, *Proceedings of the Society of Antiquaries of Scotland* 88 (1953–55), 53; Stephen Jackson, »Kirk Furnishings: The Liturgical Material Culture of the Scottish Reformation«, *Regional Furniture* 21 (2007), 1, 3–4; Andrew Spicer, »›Accommodating of Thame Selfis to Heir the Word.‹ Preaching, Pews and Reformed Worship in Scotland, 1560–1638«, *History* 88 (2003), 411–12, 421.

[59] George Hay, *The Architecture of Scottish Post-Reformation Churches, 1560–1843* (Oxford, 1957), 26. See also Howard, *Scottish Architecture from the Reformation to the Revolution* (see note 50), 177; Spicer, *Calvinist Churches* (see note 50), 53–54.

that the pulpit was the means by which God communicated to His people, who were to be active recipients of the word of God.[60] John Knox, himself, expressed similar sentiments regarding preaching stating that in the pulpit »I am not the master of myself but mist obey Him who commands me to speak plain«.[61]

The provision of seating was important to ensure that the parishioners remained attentive and receptive during services. There was a marked expansion in pew-building in the post-Reformation period. In 1586, the visitation of the diocese of Dunblane had enquired as to whether churches were provided a pulpit, seats and communion tables.[62] Initially, there appears to have been a combination of fixed seating installed for the more prominent members of the congregation while the majority sat on stools and benches for the service. The expectation that the entire parish would attend the sermon put pressure on the available church space. The introduction of fixed seating and allocated places made it easier to accommodate more people but also to monitor attendance. The capacity of many churches had to be increased further by the erection of galleries.[63]

The significance of the pulpit as the liturgical focal point of the church interior was further emphasised by the changes that took place regarding baptism. The pre-Reformation font had stood near the entrance to the church creating another ritual centre but the Catholic practices surrounding the sacrament were condemned in the First Book of Discipline. This sought to ensure that the rite »was voyd of all such inventions devised by man« and that there should be »the element of water onely«.[64] The requirement for churches to have »a basyn for baptisme«, implicitly meant the rejection of the font.[65] The liturgy of the Book of Common Order linked preaching with baptism by requiring that the rite took place during the Sunday service after the sermon.[66] It was an association that was further emphasised by the use of a bracket to attach the basin to the pulpit.[67]

---

[60] T.H.L. Parker, *Calvin's Preaching* (Edinburgh, 1992), 35–53.

[61] Quoted in J. Kirk, »John Knox and the Historians«, in R. A. Mason (ed.), *John Knox and the British Reformations* (Aldershot, 1998), 21.

[62] *Visitation of the Diocese of Dunblane*, ed. J. Kirk (Scottish Record Society, new series, 11, 1984), xliii, 23, 33–34, 36, 44, 54, 84.

[63] Spicer, »»Accommodating of Thame Selfis to Heir the Word‹« (see note 58), 413–15; Margo Todd, *The Culture of Protestantism in Early Modern Scotland* (New Haven, CT, 2002), 318–25.

[64] *First Book of Discipline* (see note 46), 91. See Spinks, *Reformation and Modern Rituals* (see note 30), 44–46.

[65] *First Book of Discipline* (see note 46), 203.

[66] *The Book of common order of the Church of Scotland*, edited by G. W. Sprott and T. Leishman (Edinburgh, 1901), 134; *John Knox's Genevan service book, 1556: the liturgical portions of the Genevan service book used by John Knox while a minister of the English Congregation of Marian exiles at Geneva, 1556–1559*, ed. William D. Maxwell (Leighton Buzzard, 1965), 105.

The administration of the Lord's Supper required more liturgical space than had been occupied by a pre-Reformation altar. The First Book of Discipline emphasised that the sacrament was »most rightly administered« when it came closest to Christ's own actions at the Last Supper. On that occasion

»Christ Jesus sate with his Disciples; and therefore doe we judge that sitting at a table is the most convenient to that holy action«.[68]

Congregations were required to have »tables for the ministration of the Lordis Suppar«.[69] Unlike the parish mass, this sacrament was not held every Sunday and was administered infrequently, so in most churches there was a temporary rearrangement of the liturgical space. A long table was erected for the congregation to sit around and participate in breaking the bread, drinking from the cup and passing the elements to their neighbours. The tables were usually placed in the body of the church before the pulpit and subsequently dismantled.[70] A few larger churches had sufficient space for a dedicated communion aisle, the former choir being used for this purpose at Crail, Fife and Perth; the south transept of Holy Trinity, St Andrews was similarly assigned. These more permanent liturgical spaces were railed off from the remainder of the church and reserved for the administration of the sacrament, the division also serving as a barrier for those not admitted to the Lord's table.[71]

The existing parish churches generally fulfilled the requirements for Reformed worship but in some instances, it was necessary to increase their capacity through the erection of »aisles«. Constructed at right angles to the original rectangular ground plan, these »aisles« resulted in a T-shape, which became a characteristic of many Scottish post-Reformation places of worship. The pulpit was placed at the intersection of the three parts of the T shape, to ensure that the minister could be seen and heard by the entire congregation. Some new churches were built to this T-shaped design and occasionally a fourth aisle was added to form a cross, such as at Fenwick, Ayrshire, and Lauder, Lothian, to provide accommodation for the laird.[72]

---

[67] Hay, »Scottish Post-Reformation Church Furniture« (see note 58), 48–49; Jackson, »Kirk Furnishings« (see note 58), 4–5; Todd, *The Culture of Protestantism* (see note 63), 27, 121, plate 5; Spicer, *Calvinist Churches* (see note 50), 48.

[68] *First Book of Discipline* (see note 46), 91.

[69] Ibid., 203.

[70] Todd, *The Culture of Protestantism* (see note 63), 102–03; G. B. Burnet, *The Holy Communion in the Reformed Church of Scotland, 1560–1960* (Edinburgh, 1960), 26–27; W. McMillan, *The Worship of the Scottish Reformed Church, 1550–1638* (London, 1931), 163.

[71] Hay, *The Architecture of Scottish Post-Reformation Churches* (see note 59), 26, 178–80.

The T-shape churches represented an evolution of liturgical space from more traditional Catholic designs to one that more readily accorded with the demands of preaching. The most innovative solution to the requirements of Reformed worship was the church erected at Burntisland, Fife, in the 1590s. This was very much a civic project that was intended to reflect the port's recent elevation to the status of a burgh. The church was built to a centralised, square-shaped ground plan; four central columns supported the roof. In 1602 the authorities decided to furnish the church with raked seating along three sides, presumably focused on the pulpit which was erected against one of the pillars. In the subsequent decades, the kirk session gave permission for galleries to be erected so that the occupants might more commodiously »heir & sie the minister at preaching & prayeris«. The interior resembled an auditorium, which prompted William Laud's dismissive jibe following his visit to the church in 1633 that it resembled »a square theatre« rather than a church. This experimental form of liturgical space, however, was not adopted by other Scottish church builders before the eighteenth century.[73]

Besides re-ordering the liturgical space of existing places of worship, the Reformed Kirk sought to redraw the parochial landscape. To better facilitate the preaching of the word of God and the true administration of the sacraments, it was prepared to abandon some ancient places of worship in remote or inaccessible places for new buildings that were more centrally and conveniently located for the congregation.[74] Although this was not undertaken systematically, local communities sought to resolve the difficulties they regularly faced in attending their parish church, especially in winter, which might be further away than the place of worship in a neighbouring parish. With the dispersed settlements in some rural parishes, calculations were made about the size of the farmsteads and communities as well as their distance from the parish church as part of the process of church relocation.[75]

In spite of the efforts undertaken by the Kirk to reconfigure and rationalise liturgical space, there remained a popular attachment not only to sacred sites and holy wells but also to places of worship that had been

---

[72] Spicer, *Calvinist Churches* (see note 50), 94–5, 103.

[73] Ibid., 57–60.

[74] Kerr-Patterson, »Post-Reformation Church Architecture« (see note 53), 108–12; Andrew Spicer, »Redrawing the Parochial Landscape of Post-Reformation Scotland«, (forthcoming).

[75] See Andrew Spicer, »Disjoynet, Dismemberit and Disuneited: Church-building and Re-drawing Parish Boundaries in Post-Reformation Scotland: A Case Study of Bassendean, Berwickshire« in *The Archaeology of Post-Medieval Religion* (Woodbridge, 2011), 19–3.

suppressed. In November 1581, the Scottish Parliament legislated against the

»observing of [...] superstitious and popish rights to the dishonour of God, contempt of the true religion and fostering of great error amongst the people«.

This included

»pilgrimage to any kirks, chapels, wells, crosses or such other monuments of idolatry«.[76]

The kirk session at Elgin had repeated difficulties with people who frequented the cathedral, which had been abandoned at the Reformation, rather than the parish church. In 1615, it ordered

»that nane within this congregatioun ha[u]nt the Chanonrie kirk to ther prayeris seing the prayeris ar daylie red in this kirk wher the trew word is preitched and the sacramentis celebrat, and therfor that ilk ane keip the publict meittings the tyme of preitching and nocht to go to ther avin privat prayeris in the Chanonrie kirk«.

Although the kirk session imposed fines on those who continued to visit the cathedral ruins to say their prayers, they were forced to reiterate their prohibition in 1641.[77] Beyond the town, the kirk session also condemned those who went »to the idolatrous places of the chappell at Speyside«, which was associated with a holy well.[78] The sites of former religious houses also continued to be used by some noble families for interments, where in the past their ancestors had been buried and had benefited from the prayers of the religious community. The east end or former location of the high altar were particularly favoured illustrating the continued perception of the holiness of this former liturgical space.[79]

Besides the on-going use of these sites for burial, the desire for interment within the parish church persisted in spite of the objections of the Kirk. In some instances, this became a useful source of income for the parish or the local authorities.[80] A detailed attack upon the practice was made by the minister William Birnie in his tract *The Blame of Kirk-Buriall*

---

[76] *The Acts of the Parliaments of Scotland, 1124–1707*, ed. T. Thomson and C. Innes, 12 vols (London, 1814–75), III, 212–13; *The Records of the Parliaments of Scotland to 1707*, K. M. Brown et al eds (St Andrews, 2007–2018), 1581/10/25: www.rps.ac.uk/trans/1581/10/25 (Date accessed: 3 June 2018).

[77] *The Records of Elgin, 1234–1800*, ed. W. Cramond, 2 vols (New Spalding Society, 27 (1903), 35 (1908), II, 71, 137, 144, 169, 193, 238.

[78] Ibid., II, 97, 202.

[79] Spicer, »»Defyle not Christ's kirk with your carrion‹« (see note 54), 153–55, 157–58.

[80] See Alison S. Cameron and Judith A. Stones, »Excavations within the East Kirk of St Nicholas, Aberdeen«, in Geddes (ed.), *Medieval Art and Archaeology* (see note 53), 82–98; Gordon D. Raeburn, »The Changing Face of Scottish Burial Practices, 1560–1645«, *Renaissance & Reformation Review* 11 (2009), 181–201.

published in 1606, which reflected on the appropriate use and perception of liturgical space. Birnie defined churches as being »an oratory or house of prayer« where the congregation gathered for worship; his approach accorded with other Scottish churchmen who described the building variously as »God's house«, a »temple«, a »house of prayer and spiritual exercise«.[81] Through preaching, God communicated with his people and according to the First Book of Discipline, the ministers were His mouthpiece, the »servants and ambassadors of the Lord Jesus«. The Kirk sought to ensure that parish churches were repaired and furnished for »the quiet and commodious receiving of the people« being concerned lest »the unseemliness of the place« would bring »the word of God and ministration of the Sacraments« into contempt. It was therefore not considered seemly for the place »appointed to preaching and the ministration of the Sacraments shall be made a place of buryall«.[82] While the authorities rejected the belief that churches had any inherent sanctity, they nonetheless sought to prohibit intra-mural burial and other inappropriate behaviour within places of worship.[83]

Attitudes towards liturgical space became polarised in the early seventeenth century as a result of the religious policies pursued by the crown, in particular the Five Articles of Perth – which were reluctantly accepted by the General Assembly in 1618 – and in the introduction of liturgical reforms during early 1630s, specifically the Book of Canons and the new Scottish Prayer Book. One of the most contested issues, introduced as one of the Five Articles, was the requirement that members of the congregation should receive the Lord Supper while kneeling. Half a century earlier, John Knox had vehemently opposed the practice in the context of the English Reformation.[84] The widespread opposition to kneeling rather than being seated for communion led many to absent themselves from services or attend churches where the measure was not enforced.[85] In Edinburgh,

---

[81] William Birnie, *The blame of kirk-buriall, tending to persvvade cemiteriall ciuilitie* (Edinburgh, 1606); Spicer, »»Defyle not Christ's kirk with your carrion«« (see note 54), 150–51.

[82] *First Book of Discipline* (see note 46), 102, 201–02.

[83] Andrew Spicer, »»What kinde of house a kirk is«: Conventicles, Consecrations, and the Concept of Sacred Space in post-Reformation Scotland«, in Will Coster and Andrew Spicer (eds), *Sacred Space in Early Modern Europe* (Cambridge, 2005), 90–94.

[84] Iain R. Torrance, »A Particular Reformed Piety: John Knox and the Posture at Communion«, *Scottish Journal of Theology* 67 (2014), 400–13.

[85] Burnet, *Holy Communion in the Reformed Church of Scotland* (see note 70), 77–85; McMillan, *The Worship of the Scottish Reformed Church* (see note 70), 178–82; P. H. R. MacKay, »The Reception given to the Five Articles of Perth«, *Records of the Scottish Church History Society* 19 (1975–77), 185–201. See also Laura A. M. Stewart, »The Political Repercussions of the Five Articles of Perth: A Reassessment of James VI and I's Religious Policies in Scotland«, *Sixteenth Century Journal* 38 (2007), 1013–36.

some dissidents attended conventicles held in private houses at the same time as the usual church service. Private prayer meetings spread through the southwest of Scotland during the 1620s and 1630s.[86] Mass gatherings also met to hear evangelical sermons outdoors as well as sometimes to receive the Lord's Supper.[87] These religious tensions therefore challenged the role of the parish church as the sole place for religious activities.[88]

While some were alienated by the religious policies of the 1620s and 1630s, there was a heightened view of the significance of liturgical space for those churchmen influenced by ›Laudian‹ principles. Their belief in the »beauty of holiness« meant that they sought an appropriate setting for the communion rite. The private chapel erected at Dairsie, Fife, by Archbishop Spottiswoode in 1621 reflected these changes with the floor of the east end being raised up and with a screen which separated it from the remainder of the building. In Edinburgh, Charles I ordered that St Giles's church should once again become a single place of worship and elevated it to being the seat of a new bishopric.[89] Some new places of worship were even consecrated during this period.[90] The ›Laudian‹ reordering of churches and their liturgical space was very limited and proved to be short lived in the face of widespread opposition to the crown's religious policies, which led to the signing of the National Covenant and the Glasgow Assembly in 1638.

Conclusion

There were significant differences between Lutheranism and the Reformed faith, but both confessions rejected the Catholic mass and advocated the true administration of the sacraments together with the preaching of the word of God. How these faiths translated these broad principles into actual religious practice differed markedly. The circumstances and nature

---

[86] D. Stevenson, »Conventicles in the Kirk, 1619–37. The Emergence of a Radical Party«, *Records of the Scottish Church History Society* 18 (1972), 101–08.

[87] L.E. Schmidt, *Holy Fairs. Scottish Communions and American Revivals in the Early Modern Period* (Princeton, NJ, 1989), 21–22, 28–29.

[88] D. Stevenson, »The Radical Party in the Kirk, 1637–45«, *Journal of Ecclesiastical History* 25 (1974), 136–37.

[89] Peter Lake, »The Laudian Style: Order, Uniformity and the Pursuit of Holiness in the 1630s«, in Kenneth Fincham (ed.), *The Early Stuart Church, 1603–1642* (Basingstoke, 1993), 164–74; Spicer, *Calvinist Churches* (see note 50), 71–72; Andrew Spicer, »Laudianism‹ in Scotland? St Giles'Cathedral, Edinburgh, 1633–39 – A Reappraisal«, *Architectural History* 46 (2003), 95–108. See also Leonie James, *'This Great Firebrand«. William Laud and Scotland, 1617–1645* (Woodbridge, 2017).

[90] Spicer, »›What kinde of house a kirk is‹« (see note 83), 98–102.

of regular worship came to determine the spatial arrangement and liturgical use of Lutheran churches and Reformed kirks.

Although the Reformed valued the administration of the Lord's Supper
highly, they were only willing to allow the worthy members of the congregation to participate, who had been subject to the exercise of ecclesiastical discipline. Even in the city state of Geneva, this precluded the
monthly administration that Calvin desired and it came to be held quarterly.[91] These difficulties were more acute across the 1100 parishes of the
Scottish kingdom and made more problematic by the shortage of ministers
to administer the sacrament. As a result, the Lord's Supper was held infrequently with the ritual not being administered in some churches for
several years.[92] While the Lutherans did examine the faithful on the principles of their faith, relatively few members of the congregation actually
regularly received the sacrament, even though the German mass was celebrated on a weekly basis. Furthermore, Luther's reluctance to regulate
the appropriate setting for worship or to alienate those who were less
committed in their faith by undertaking radical change, meant that there
was a degree of continuity in the use of liturgical space in the transition
from Catholicism to Lutheranism.

For Luther preaching the word of God was a fundamental part of
regular worship but it was not the only component of weekly services.
The situation was different in Scotland, where due to the infrequent administration of the Lord's Supper, the sermon became the focus of regular
worship. Liturgical space was therefore configured for preaching, in a way
that best accommodated the congregation so that they could hear and see
the minister. Only periodically was this space rearranged to allow for the
administration of the Lord's Supper. In the Lutheran churches of the empire, however, there was more than one liturgical focal point – the altar
and the pulpit as well as the baptismal font. While there were some attempts to bring together the church furnishings required for preaching and
the sacraments, this was a spatial arrangement that was only really adopted
in the eighteenth and nineteenth centuries.

Almost half a century after the German Reformer's protest against indulgences in 1517, the Scottish Kirk was not tentative in its rejection of the
setting of the mass with the abolition of idolatry and the requirement that
every church should have »a pulpit, a basin for baptism, and tables for the

---

[91] »Ordonnances ecclésiastiques«, in *Registres de la Compagnie des Pasteurs de Ge-
nève*, ed. J. F. Bergier et al. (Geneva, 1964–), I, 9; Harro Höpfl, *The Christian Polity of
John Calvin* (Cambridge, 1982), 61–63.
[92] Burnet, *Holy Communion in the Reformed Church of Scotland* (see note 70),
13–14, 16–17, 120–25.

ministration of the Lord's Supper«.[93] Luther had similarly recognised the importance of »baptismal fonts, altars and pulpits« for worship.[94] However, the circumstances surrounding the implementation of religious reform and divergent theological perceptions regarding the preaching of the word of God and the administration of the sacraments meant that there were marked differences in the configuration of liturgical space in the Lutheran churches in the Holy Roman Empire and the Scottish kirks.

---

[93] *First Book of Discipline* (see note 46), 203.
[94] *WA*, XXXVII, 670; *LW*, LVII, 187.

Mockery and Memory in the Protestant Home:
The Material Culture of Anti-Catholicism
in Reformation Europe

Alexandra Walsham

This essay explores the transformation of the Protestant Reformation from a provocative protest movement to an institutionalised church and an enduring confessional culture by investigating religious artefacts that were the victims, catalysts and conduits of anti-Catholicism in the sixteenth, seventeenth and eighteenth centuries. It focuses upon two and three dimensional objects that provoked and cemented contempt and hatred of popery and channelled cultural memory of Protestant history, exploring how they were deployed in one particular space and setting: the home. In the process, it probes the role of laughter and humour, playing and games, in undermining attachment to the Church of Rome and in creating new religious identities inflected by intolerance and prejudice. It also illuminates the shifting contours of anti-Catholicism over the course of the long Reformation and engages critically with persisting assumptions about the tensions between Protestant asceticism and leisure, piety and pleasure. As well as illustrating the distinctive dynamic that the English Reformation developed as it was domesticated, this essay underlines its participation in a pan-European Protestant movement. It investigates the ongoing traffic in ideas, texts, images and practices that continued to bind the sister Reformations of Germany, the Netherlands, and the British Isles together. The pictorial and material migrations to which I draw attention are emblematic of their mutual influences and reciprocal links.

1. Defusing the Power of Popery in the
Protestant Reformation

The early Reformation in Germany, as the pioneering work of Bob Scribner showed, was accompanied by a carnivalesque turning of the world upside down. Luther's ideas sparked both spontaneous and orchestrated protests that took ritual forms and that entailed modes of symbolic inversion rooted in traditional festive culture. Youth and students played a key part in these incidents, which frequently occurred at calendrical moments when unbridled behaviour and reversals of the social and age hierarchy were temporarily sanctioned. Catholic doctrines and practices were rudely lampooned in parodic processions that drew on an established repertoire of masking and travesty and hallowed statues and relics were taunted and desacralized in rites of violence that often had a ludic quality.[1] The same techniques were utilised to brilliant effect in the visual propaganda that poured from the presses in the early years of the movement. These were forms of graphic satire that literally inverted the established order and exposed the clergy and papacy to corrosive laughter and ridicule, turning figures that had once command respect and been the subject of reverence into jesters, fools and monsters and degrading them through the deployment of the conventional tropes of crude scatological humour in which Luther revelled.[2] One famous broadsheet took the form of a harlequinade. It used the device of a moveable flap to reveal the notorious Borgia Pope Alexander VI as the devil in disguise.[3]

Early evangelicalism in England displayed similar characteristics. Here too the culture of pastime fused with anti-Catholic zeal to inspire mock processions, as in Dover in Kent, when merchants, tradesmen and town councillors joined forces to traipse through the streets in derision of the popish liturgy and rite in 1539 in a manner that conservative critics branded as ›lewd‹.[4] As Susan Brigden demonstrated long ago, young people were prominent actors in the early decades of the English Reformation: disorderly youths composed ballads and jests in contempt of priests, dressed up dead cats in mass vestments, and engaged in other high-spirited juvenile pranks that undermined the dignity of bishops and monks, including throwing a pudding at the head of a prominent prelate.[5] Taking advantage of an ancient tradition of licensed misrule in schools, in 1554, in the wake of the Wyatt rebellion, three hundred boys gathered in Finsbury Fields in London to enact a war of religion in the guise of a mock battle. In 1548, a year before the Prayer Book Rebellion, pupils from Bodmin Grammar School had divided themselves into »two factions; the one whe-

---

[1] Bob Scribner, »Reformation, Carnival and the World Turned Upside-Down,« *Social History* 3 (1978): 303–29.

[2] R. W. Scribner, *For the Sake of Simple Folk: Popular Propaganda for the German Reformation* (Oxford, 1994 edn; first publ. 1981), esp. ch. 5.

[3] Ibid., 134–35.

[4] Benjamin Carier, *A Copy of a Letter, Written by M. Doctor Carier beyond Seas, to some Particular Friends in England* ([English secret press], 1615), 41–42.

[5] Susan Brigden, »Youth and the English Reformation,« *Past and Present* 95 (1982): 37–67.

reof, they called the olde religion; the other the new« and engaged in rumbustious games in the course of which a calf was killed by a candlestick they had turned into a makeshift gun.[6] For some iconoclasm became a sport, providing an opportunity to smash statues that were symbols of religious and political authority. Others were encouraged in the task of image-breaking by adults. When the miraculous moving crucifix or Rood of Boxley was publicly exposed as a fraud by Hugh Latimer in 1538, it was left to »rude people and boyes« to smash it into pieces.[7] In Derbyshire, local adolescents appear to have been actively encouraged to engage in irreverent tippling, piping, dancing, hoping and singing in in the disused chapel of St Anne's holy well at Buxton in the 1550s, in an episode of engineered play and profanation.[8]

A particularly telling piece of evidence is a passage in a sermon by the Catholic clergyman Roger Edgeworth, which describes how holy objects removed from churches were frequently given to children »to playe wyth all«. In it, a little girl dances with a redundant image in a »childyshe manner«, and her father joins in the laughter and makes »a gaye game« with her »idoll«.[9] In early Elizabethan Lincolnshire, in the context of a further purge of church interiors, two medieval pyxes were similarly turned over to children as playthings, while various pieces of ecclesiastical linen were recycled as dressing-up costumes.[10] This is reminiscent of incidents in Germany: in 1536 a man in Cologne reportedly pulled the arms from a crucifix and gave it to his children to use as a toy. In Biberach, many things (»viel der Ding«) were taken from monasteries and handed to toddlers and infants, who broke them.[11] It is tempting to speculate that the

---

[6] A. G. Dickens, »The Battle of Finsbury Field and its Wider Context,« in *Humanism and Reform: The Church in Europe, England, and Scotland, 1400–1643*, ed. James Kirk, Studies in Church History Subsidia 8 (Oxford, 1991), 271–87. For the Bodmin incident, see Richard Carew, *The Survey of Cornwall* (London, 1602), 124–25. See also Keith Thomas, *Rule and Misrule in the Schools of Early Modern England*, The Stenton Lecture (Reading, 1976).

[7] Charles Wriothesley, *A Chronicle of England during the Reigns of the Tudors, from AD 1485 to 1559*, 2 vols., ed. William Douglas Hamilton, Camden Society (London, 1877), i. 74–76.

[8] The National Archives, C 1/1322, 57^r. See also Ethan H. Shagan, *Popular Politics and the English Reformation* (Cambridge, 2003), 267.

[9] Roger Edgeworth, *Sermons very Fruitfull, Godly and Learned*, ed. Janet Wilson (Cambridge, 1993), 143.

[10] *English Church Furniture, Ornaments and Decorations, at the Period of the Reformation: as Exhibited in a List of the Goods Destroyed in Certain Lincolnshire Churches, A. D. 1566*, ed. Edward Peacock (London, 1866), 55, 108.

[11] Robert W. Scribner, »Ritual and Reformation,« in his *Popular Culture and Popular Movements in Reformation Germany* (London, 1987), 103–22, at p. 114. The Biberach incident is cited by Joe Moshenska in his essay, »Dolls and Idols in the English Refor-

small battered and mutilated crucifix excavated from Fiddleford in Dorset now in the British Museum may be one such object.[12] Removed out of consecrated spaces into private homes, their translation was a deliberate act of demystification, akin to and imitative of adult iconoclasm.[13] The games that were played with them defused the power of these popish images. Replicating one of the most pervasive rhetorical strategies for denouncing medieval Christianity, such practices quite literally turned them into puppets and trinkets. They trivialised them as part of the culture of children even as they made them into instruments of their re-education and socialisation.[14] Such objects helped to instruct the young in the values of a society in which Protestantism was becoming the official religion.

Such episodes were part of a climate in which it was commonplace to castigate Catholicism as a false religion that involved a mockery of apostolic Christianity and which was rooted in foolish attachment to »superstitious toys«.[15] Drawing on St Paul's invocation to put aside »childish things« in 1 Corinthians 13, this implied that popery was an infantile faith. It served as a convenient shorthand by which to dismiss its reliance upon external props and paraphernalia and its elevation of invented traditions over the canon of Scripture. This finds visual expression in an illustration of a set of scales overseen by the blindfolded figure of Justice deciding the truth of the competing Catholic and Protestant religions. The verses beneath celebrate the bible outweighing this worthless »chaff«.[16] The Eliza-

---

mation,« in *Memory and English Reformation*, eds. Brian Cummings, Ceri Law, Bronwyn Wallace, and Alexandra Walsham (forthcoming). This topic is treated more fully in his *Iconoclasm as Child's Play* (Stanford, CA, forthcoming 2019).

[12] British Museum: 1998, 0408.1.

[13] See Keith Thomas, »Children in Early Modern England,« in *Children and their Books: A Celebration of the Work of Iona and Peter Opie*, eds. Gillian Avery and Julia Briggs (Oxford, 1989), 45–77, at p. 59. Thomas cites Sir Thomas Elyot's comment in *The Boke named the Governour* (London, 1531) regarding children before the Reformation »knelynge in theyr game before images, and holding up theyr lytell whyte hands [...] as they were prayeing; other goynge and syngynge as hit were in procession«.

[14] On the ambivalence of childish play and its role in socialisation, see Nicholas Orme, »The Culture of Children in Medieval England,« *Past and Present* 148 (1995): 48–88; Lucy Trusler, »›In Play is all my Mynde‹: Children and their Toys in Renaissance England,« *Things* 13 (2000–1): 9–27.

[15] For the contemporary resonances of ›toy‹, see Oxford English Dictionary, »toy«, n. For some examples of its use as an anti-Catholic tag, see William Tuner, *A New Dialogue Wherin is Contyened the Examination of the Messe of that Kynde of Priesthood, whych is Ordained to Saye Messe* ([London, 1548]), B 8ʳ; Francis Bunny, *An Answere to a Popish Libel intituled a Petition to the Bishops, Preachers, and Gospellers, Lately Spread Abroad in the North Partes* (London, 1607), 104.

[16] *A Lively Picture Describyng the Authoritie and Substaunce of Gods most Blessed Word, Weyghing agaynst Popish Traditions*, in *The Whole Workes of W. Tyndall, Iohn Frith, and Doct. Barnes, Three Worthy Martyrs, and Principall Teachers of this Churche*

bethan homily on idolatry said that as »little Girls play with little Puppets, so be these decked Images, great Puppets for Old Fools to play with«. John Walsall's sermon preached at Paul's Cross in 1578 similarly referred to the »childishe bable« and »folly of our Popish babes«, whose devotion to crosses, altars, banners, holy water, and copes distracted them from worshipping God in spirit and truth. John Northbrooke insisted that »holy dayes [...] were invented in old time for pastimes [...] to traine up the people in ignorance and idleness«.[17] Protestant polemicists also recurrently used the vocabulary of playing and games to denigrate the miracle stories and saints' fables by which their Catholic adversaries allegedly pulled the wool over the eyes of the credulous laity. Henri Estienne's *The stage of popish toyes*, translated from French into English in 1581, scurrilously recounted a selection of these as »pleasant pastimes« to provoke Protestant laughter. The same technique was used to good effect by a range of writers, including the Irish soldier and pamphleteer Barnaby Rich, in pamphlets whose frivolous tone conceals their deadly serious intent.[18] The characterisation of the Catholic material culture brought into England by missionaries as a form of useless commodity and as lightweight ephemera – as mere trumpery and trash – continued into the seventeenth century. The woodcut of a »pack of popish trinkets« which adorned one broadside also appeared on the title-page of Jean de Chassanion's *The Merchandises of Popish Priests* in 1629.[19] Such images are closely linked with a further popular trope: that comparing priests and the pope with contemporary pedlars of inexpensive wares. One print deploying this theme first appeared in 1624 and was reissued at a further moment of anti-Catholic

---

of England (London: John Day, 1572). The print may also have appeared as a single sheet.

[17] *Certain Sermons or Homilies Appointed to be Read in Churches* (London, 1687 edn), 273; John Walsall, *A Sermon Preached at Paul's Crosse* (London, 1578), D 8[v]; John Northbrooke, *A Treatise whereing Dicing, Dau[n]cing, Vaine Plaies or Enterludes with other Idle Pastimes, &c Commonly Used on the Sabbath Day, are Reprooved, by the Authoritie of the Word of God and Auncient Writers* (London, 1579), 12[r]. See also Phebe Jensen, »Singing Psalms to Horn-pipes: Festivity, Iconoclasm and Catholicism in *The Winter's Tale*,« *Shakespeare Quarterly* 55 (2004): 279–306.

[18] Henri Estienne, *The Stage of Popish Toyes: Conteining both Tragicall and Comicall Partes* (London, 1581); Barnabe Rich, *A New Irish Prognostication, or, Popish Callender with a Calculation of all the Popish Trinkets Brought for the Pope, by his Embassadors, Doctor Sanders and Allen* (London, 1624). See also Anthony Gilby, *A Dialogue between a Souldier of Barwick, and an English Chaplain [...] and also Another Table of the Bringing in of Divers of the Popish and Superstitious Toyes, yet Remaining* (London, 1642).

[19] *A Discovery of the Jesuits Trumpery, Newly Packed out of England* (London, 1641; first publ. c. 1625); Jean de Chassanion, *The Merchandises of Popish Priests. Or, a Discovery of the Jesuites Trumpery Newly Packed in England* (London, 1629).

furore in 1641; adapted from a French precursor, the title page of a late Stuart polemical pamphlet »unveiling« the intrigues, subtle practices and »lewd and scandalous lives« of friars and other »pretended votaries« shows a monk disguised as an itinerant salesman.[20] Alongside those engaged in the haberdasher trade, pedlars were regular purveyors of amusing and titillating trifles of little value. Another place where such trinkets and toys were purchased were fairs and contemporary dramatists such as William Shakespeare and Ben Jonson keenly exploited the evolving elision between popish trumpery and children's toys in early modern minds. In *Bartholomew Fair* (1614), the puritan Zeal-of-the-Land Busy fulminates wildly against the »apocryphal wares« sold by a stallholder, comparing such bells, dragons, dolls and hobby horses with the »rancke idolls« that had drawn down divine wrath upon the Israelites of old.[21] An anti-Catholic tract produced at the height of the fictitious Popish Plot scare in the reign of Charles II – a panic provoked by the extravagant rumours fabricated by Titus Oates – likewise drew a direct analogy between the »Toys and Baubles, gaudy shews and Tricks of Legerdemain [...] Babies and Hobby Horses« available for purchase at Bartholomew Fair and the »fancies and follies« of the Church of Rome.[22]

The early modern English printmaking industry was underdeveloped by contrast with its counterparts in Germany and the Netherlands, but it did grow and develop a momentum of its own. Satirical images had circulated widely in the first phase of the Protestant movement, many of them imported and adapted from the Continent. The woodcut on a ballad surviving in the Pepys Library at Magdalene College, Cambridge, published around 1550 portrays a scene of knockabout comedy which pokes fun at the pope and shows him being outwitted by Doctor Martin Luther and a godly peasant.[23] As Adam Morton has argued persuasively, such anti-

---

[20] *The Monk Unvail'd: or, a Facetious Dialogue*, trans. C. V. (London, 1678).

[21] Ben Jonson, *Bartholomew Fair* (1614) in *The Works of Benjamin Jonson* (London, 1641), 48. The prologue addressed to the king alluded to »the zealous noyse / Of your lands *Faction*, scandaliz'd at toyes, / As Babies, Hobby-horses, Puppet-playes, / And such like rage« (sig. A 3ʳ). See also *Lambeth Faire, Wherein you have all the Bishops Trinkets Set to Sale* (London, 1641). On the sale of inexpensive toys and trifles in London shops and fairs, see Hazel Forsyth with Geoff Egan, *Toys, Trifles and Trinkets: Base-Metal Miniatures from London 1200 to 1800* (London, 2005), esp. 32–39.

[22] »The Pope's harbinger: by way of diversion«, in *The Weekly Pacquet of Advice from Rome*, 3ʳᵈ ser., no. 8 (1680), quoted in Forsyth with Egan, *Toys, Trifles, and Trinkets* (see note 21), 39.

[23] *The Husbandman. Doctor Martin Luther. The Pope. The Cardinall* ([London: s.n., 1550?]). Magdalene College, Cambridge: Pepys Library Ballads I: 16–17. See https://exhibitions.lib.cam.ac.uk/reformation/artifacts/remembering-luther–2-the-pen-and-the-sword/.

papal images must be seen not merely as an extension of rites of humiliation and shame but also as a kind of iconoclasm carried out within the forum of the printed page. They function in ways akin to forms of folk justice such as rough music and charivari and as a surrogate for the physical destruction of their subjects.[24] Although Patrick Collinson influentially argued that Protestant willingness to deploy popular media sharply declined after 1580, more recent work has traced the evolution of a rich, indigenous tradition of anti-Catholic iconography.[25] This took off in the early years of the seventeenth century when Thomas Jenner developed a lucrative trade in prints of the Protestant martyrs burnt at the stake under Mary I and the European reformers seated around a table with the Candle of the Gospel placed at the centre, which the pope and his minions try in vain to blow out.[26] Samuel Ward's *Double Deliverance* (1621) was not only a memorial to the defeat of the Spanish Armada in 1588 and the discovery of the Gunpowder Plot in 1605 but also a political cartoon directed against the unpopular proposed match between Prince Charles, heir to the throne, and the Spanish Habsburg Infanta Maria. Her father is shown conspiring with the Pope and Devil in a cabal at the centre. Ward ended up in prison for creating this impolitic picture.[27] The 1640s saw a new outpouring of anti-Catholic pictorial satire and a spirited revival of traditional polemical tropes, including a scatological print of a seven-headed »barrel-bellied beast« on stilts defecating skulls and bones into containers held out by priests and monks, with a series of belligerent verses by John Vicars beneath.[28]

---

[24] Adam Morton, »Glaring at Anti-Christ: Anti-Papal Images in Early Modern England, c. 1530–1680,« (Ph.D. Diss., University of York, 2010), esp. ch. 2.

[25] Patrick Collinson, *From Iconoclasm to Iconophobia: The Cultural Impact of the Second English Reformation*, The Stenton Lecture 1985 (Reading, 1986); idem, *The Birthpangs of Protestant England: Religious and Cultural Change in the Sixteenth and Seventeenth Centuries* (New York, 1998), ch. 4. See Alexandra Walsham, *Providence in Early Modern England* (Oxford, 1999), 250–66; Helen Pierce, *Unseemly Pictures: Graphic Satire and Politics in Early Modern England* (New Haven and London, 2008), ch. 2.

[26] *The Candle is Lighted, We Cannot Blow Out*: British Museum, 1907, 0326.31; *Faiths Victorie in Romes Crueltie*, British Museum, Satires Series 11. For discussions of these prints, see Sheila O'Connell, *The Popular Print in England, 1550–1850* (London, 1999), 129–31; Malcolm Jones, *The Print in Early Modern England: An Historical Overview* (New Haven, 2010), 59–60, 160, 162–63.

[27] *Deo Trin-uniBritanniae bis Ultori In Memoriam Classis Invincibilis Subversae Submersae* [...] *To God, in Memorye of his Double Deliveraunce from the Invincible Navie and the Unmatcheable Powder Treason* (Amsterdam, 1621), British Museum, Satires 41. See Walsham, *Providence*, 255–58, and »Impolitic Pictures: Providence, History and the Iconography of Protestant Nationhood in Early Stuart England,« in *The Church Retrospective*, ed. Robert Swanson, Studies in Church History 33 (Woodbridge, 1997), 403–24. See also Pierce, *Unseemly Pictures* (see note 25), ch. 2.

[28] John Vicars, *Behold Romes Monster on his Monstrous Beast!* (London, [1643]).

Jenner and other printmakers proved expert at harnessing imported images and recasting them for English readers. One of these was a late sixteenth-century Dutch print was an attempt to shape public opinion in the context of the Revolt of the Netherlands: it shows three Protestant gentlemen playing backgammon, cards and dice against three monks, while on the left the pope and a cardinal attempt to seize the winnings, which include church plate. The verses beneath mock the cheating papists and celebrate the demise of the mass and monasticism, even as they reflect fear that the »crowned beast« and his accomplices might still overwhelm the Calvinist cause.[29] This provided the model for a topical print engraved by Thomas Cockson in 1609, entitled *The Revells of Christendome*, which depicts James I of England, Henry IV of France, Prince Maurice of Nassau and Christian IV of Denmark playing a game of chance against the Catholic Church (fig. 1). Alluding to the Twelve Years' Truce that marked the point from which the independence of the United Provinces received formal recognition by outside powers, which was a humiliating blow for Spain, it playfully exploits the culture of gambling to score renewed points against Rome and the papacy. It adds by way of a gratuitous insult, a dog urinating on the foot of the cowled monk seated at the centre.[30] Thomas Middleton's satirical play *A Game at Chesse*, first staged in 1624, used another board game as a device for dramatising the negotiations for the Spanish match and offering a provocative critical commentary upon royal dynastic and foreign policy. Viciously caricaturing the Spanish ambassador, Count Gondomar, as the Machiavellian Black Knight, it provoked much merriment and hilarity among theatregoers, but it also created a diplomatic incident that led to the cessation of performances by order of the authorities.[31]

Laughter and satire were thus critical mechanisms in an evolving culture of anti-Catholicism which was closely linked with the unstable discourses of politics and patriotism. Their fundamental ambiguity made them multivalent. Vehicles for celebrating superiority and for reforming error, hypocrisy and vice, they served both to build solidarities and create

---

[29] British Museum, 1871, 1209.970. I am grateful to Liesbeth Corens for translating the accompanying verses.

[30] British Museum, 1849, 0315.10. On this print, see Pierce, *Unseemly Pictures* (see note 25), 35; Jones, *Print* (see note 26), 72–75.

[31] Thomas Middleton, *A Game at Chesse as it hath bine Sundrey Times Acted at the Globe on the Banck Side* ([London, 1625]).

Fig. 1
Thomas Cockson, The Revells of Christendom
London, 1609 (British Museum, 1849, 0315.10)

communities and to divide and fracture them from within.[32] They helped
to forge a prejudice whose potency and virulence should not be under-
estimated. Humour was one of the most powerful tools that Protestants
had at their disposal to combat the threat posed by the Church of Rome.
Their aim in ridiculing Catholicism as a toy and game was to reduce it to
one: to denude it of its self-importance and claims to truth and to demonstrate that it was a confection of mere stuff and nonsense. Paradoxically, they brought about its metamorphosis into a mere pastime by engaging in forms of play itself.

And they did so in a context in which leisure activities were themselves
surrounded by an aura of ambivalence and condemned by many lay and
clerical reformers as invitations to idleness and sin, if not as vestiges of

---

[32] See Mark Knights and Adam Morton (eds), *The Power of Laughter and Satire in
Early Modern Britain: Political and Religious Culture, 1500–1820* (Woodbridge, 2017),
esp. the introduction, »Laughter and Satire in Early Modern Britain 1500–1800,« and
Adam Morton, »Laughter as a Polemical Act in Late Seventeenth-Century England,«
1–26, 107–32 respectively.

pagan and popish idolatry. Such denunciations gathered pace in the context of the campaigns to reform manners and regulate unseemly behaviour that were a feature of the later Reformations in England and northern Europe. Traditional pastimes were swept up in initiatives that targeted the frivolous recreations in which people wasted their time and disorderly games that were perceived to subvert accepted hierarchies of age and rank. The mocking rhymes and carnivalesque rituals of misrule by which ordinary people gave expression to consensual moral values were themselves repressed and marginalised. These trends have long been interpreted as an assault upon the culture of »merry England« and linked with zealous puritanism and the advance of repressive social discipline.[33] In the guise of the controversial book of sports, which legitimised such activities on Sunday afternoons, they certainly became a flashpoint for conflict between Calvinist sabbatarians and those who defended these customary diversions as forms of innocent play and allowable liberty.[34] Our impulse to situate these developments in opposition to the evangelical culture of ludic inversion and transgressive laughter, however, must be firmly resisted. Instead, following the lead of Lyndal Roper and Kat Hill's work on Lutheran Germany, it is necessary to recognise how far »the dissection of sin became« an art of entertaining« itself and to acknowledge the continuing nexus between fun and loathing.[35] Anti-puritan stereotypes of godly aversion to leisure such as Shakespeare's Malvolio and Jonson's Zeal-of-the-Land Busy aside, humour remained a constituent part of Protestant discourse and piety.

---

[33] Keith Wrightson and David Levine, *Poverty and Piety in an English Village: Terling, 1525–1700* (Oxford, 1995; first publ. 1979), chs. 5–7; Ronald Hutton, *The Rise and Fall of Merry England: The Ritual Year 1400–1700* (Oxford, 1994); Martin Ingram, »Reformation of Manners in Early Modern England,« in *The Experience of Authority in Early Modern England*, eds. Paul Griffiths, Adam Fox, and Steve Hindle (Basingstoke, 1996); 47–88. On these developments in their European context, see R. Po-Chia Hsia, *Social Discipline in the Reformation* (London, 1989); Philip Benedict, *Christ's Churches Purely Reformed: A Social History of Calvinism* (New Haven and London, 2002), ch. 14. For mocking rhymes and rituals, see Martin Ingram, »Ridings, Rough Music and the »Reform of Popular Culture« in Early Modern England,« *Past and Present* 105 (1984): 79–113, and »Ridings, Rough Music, and Mocking Rhymes in Early Modern England,« in *Popular Culture in Seventeenth-Century England*, ed. Barry Reay (London, 1985), 166–97.

[34] See Alastair Dougall, *The Devil's Book: Charles I, The Book of Sports and Puritanism in Tudor and early Stuart England* (Exeter, 2011).

[35] See Lyndal Roper, »Drinking, Whoring and Gorging: British Indiscipline and the Formation of Protestant Identity,« in her *Oedipus and the Devil: Witchcraft, Sexuality and Religion in Early Modern Europe* (London and New York, 1994), 145–67, at p. 156; Kat Hill, »Fun and Loathing in Later Lutheran Culture«, in eadem (ed.), *Cultures of Lutheranism: Reformation Repertoires in Early Modern Germany*, Past and Present Supplement 12 (Oxford, 2017), 67–89.

2. The Material Culture of Anti-Catholicism in the Protestant Home

The second part of this essay develops these themes further by examining objects and images manufactured for use in the private home. In doing so it offers fresh insight into how anti-popery permeated everyday life. It begins by emphasizing the importance of the family in Protestant culture. Paralleling the literature that laid out the ideal of Lutheran »holy household« for German readers,[36] works such as William Gouge's bestselling *Domesticall duties* and Matthew Griffith's *Bethel* outlined the solemn responsibilities of English parents, and especially patriarchs, in nurturing the piety of their wives, children and servants through regimes of daily prayer, devotional reading, psalm-singing, sermon repetition, and catechising. The home was regarded as the seminary and seedbed of godly religion and good citizenship, a spiritualised space supplementary to and sometimes even a surrogate for the established church in which husbands and wives, children and servants were to be indoctrinated in the central tenets of the reformed faith and taught how to be fervent Protestants.[37] In turn, the texts and practices that became a distinctive feature of puritanism in post-Reformation England helped to sow the seeds of the pietist movement in Europe. The Dutch pastor Willem Teellinck's *Huysboek* (1639) was inspired by a nine-month stay in Banbury in Oxfordshire in 1604, where he came within the orbit of John Dod, vicar of Hanwell, and co-author of *A Godly Forme of Houshold Government*, which provided a template for his own popular manual.[38]

Instruments for training the young to become devout and virtuous adults, such conduct books laid particular stress on the duty of regularly recalling and tangibly memorialising the icon events of recent Reformation history and the triumphs of the true faith over papistical falsehood. They

---

[36] Stephen Ozment, *When Fathers Ruled: Family Life in Reformation Europe* (Cambridge, MA, 1983), esp. ch. 4; Lyndal Roper, *The Holy Household: Women and Morals in Reformation Augsburg* (Oxford, 1989).

[37] See Alexandra Walsham, »Holy Families: The Spiritualisation of the Early Modern Household Revisited,« in *Religion and the Household*, eds. John Doran, Charlotte Methuen and Alexandra Walsham, Studies in Church History 50 (Boydell and Brewer, 2014), 122–60. The classic treatment is Christopher Hill, »The Spiritualization of the Household,« in *Society and Puritanism in Pre-Revolutionary England* (London, 1964), 443–81.

[38] Willem Teellinck, *Huys-boeck, ofte Eenvoudighe, verclaringhe ende toe-eygheninghe, van de voornaemste vraegh-stucken des Nederlandtschen Christelijcken Catechismi* (Middelburg, 1639). John Dod and Robert Cleaver, *A Godly Forme of Houshold Government* (London, 1612 and later editions). See Tara Hamling and Catherine Richardson, *A Day at Home in Early Modern England: Material Culture and Domestic Life, 1500–1700* (New Haven and London, 2017), 129–30.

saw the home as an environment in which a robust hatred of Catholicism was to be cultivated, through texts, objects and images as well as oral retelling.[39] Some authors and publishers produced pocket-sized primers to help mothers and fathers in this task. Benjamin Harris's *The Protestant Tutor* (1679) was a textbook for children, teaching them how to spell, grounding them in the true religion, and revealing the »errors and deceits« of its Catholic enemies. Presented as an antidote to the tracts, catechisms, »trash and trumpery« that the papists had »dispersed like a General Infection among the youth of this Nation«, its stated objective was to »confirm this young Generation in Protestant Principles, by the [same] methods whereby they intend to Debauch them«, to arm it against the tyranny of their bloody religion, and »to Create in them an Abhorrence of Romish Idolatry«.[40] Designed for use by private tutors and filled with accounts of the persecutions and massacres perpetrated by the papists all over Europe, Edward Clark's *The Protestant Schoolmaster* (1680) was another publication in the same bellicose vein.[41]

Recent research by Tara Hamling has done much to reconstruct the didactic decorative schemes installed in sixteenth- and seventeenth-century upper and middle class houses and their constituent rooms. Illustrated bibles and emblematic prints, many of them Dutch, Flemish and German in origin, provided the patterns for tapestries, wall-paintings, overmantels and firebacks that edified spectators as well as functioned as a constant reminder of God's all-seeing eye and omnipresence as their maker and judge and of the depths of human depravity following the Fall.[42] As in Lutheran Germany, furniture and crockery were likewise deployed as what Andrew Morrall has called »a tool for provoking active rumination«: the improving moralistic inscriptions painted on mugs, cups, chargers and jugs served to encourage pious meditation and to reprove and

[39] William Gouge, Of *Domesticall Duties: Eight Treatises* (London, 1622), 541. See also Edward Topsell, *Times Lamentation: or An Exposition on the Prophet Joel, in Sundry Sermons or Meditations* (London, 1599), 51–65.

[40] Benjamin Harris, *The Protestant Tutor. Instructing Children to Spel and Read English, and Grounding them in the True Protestant Religio[n] and Discovering the Errors and Deceits of the Papists* (London, 1679), A 3ʳ–A 7ʳ.

[41] Edward Clark, *The Protestant School-master Containing, Plain and Easie Directions for Spelling and Reading English, with all Necessary Rules for the True Reading of the English Tongue* (London, 1680).

[42] Tara Hamling, *Decorating the »Godly« Household: Religious Art in Post-Reformation Britain* (New Haven and London, 2010). See also Hamling and Richardson, *A Day at Home* (see note 38). For the extent to which English decorative schemes were indebted to prints from the Low Countries and Germany, see Anthony Wells-Cole, *Art and Decoration in Elizabethan and Jacobean England: The Influence of Continental Prints, 1558–1625* (New Haven and London, 1997).

restrain gluttony, drunkenness, and other forms of improper behaviour. They were media that played »a dynamic role in shaping and conditioning social habits«.[43] Ceramic stove tiles were another set of surfaces onto which religious priorities and confessional messages were projected and etched in the German lands: in the winter months families assembled around these sources of warmth.[44] In England too, the hearth of the open fire was the heart of the home and chimney surrounds bore similar forms of decoration. The less affluent could purchase woodcuts and engravings with which to adorn their walls, including »paper monuments« to the memory of England's providential deliverances from popish malice and conspiracy.[45]

We need to balance awareness of the role that domestic iconography played in blurring the lines »between practical routine and devotional ritual« and in heightening spiritual consciousness with a sensitivity to its capacity to stimulate antipathies and hostilities that spilled out beyond the private but permeable space of the household into the streets and public sphere.[46] The pious portraits of families saying grace that became common in northern Europe, and especially among Dutch artists in the seventeenth century,[47] paint a picture of decorum and dignity that arguably eclipses other, more raucous elements of reformed culture. If Martin Luther's house in Wittenberg was the prototype of divine discourse at the dinner table, the frequently jovial and often venemous tone of his famous *Tischreden* or *Table Talk* reminds us that mealtimes were a locus for the articulation of prejudice as well as a platform for scriptural instruction and moral edification.[48] The gap between Protestant ideal and daily reality is

---

[43] Andrew Morrall, »Inscriptional Wisdom and the Domestic Arts in Early Modern Northern Europe,« in *Konstruktion, Manifestation und Dynamic der Formalhaftigkeit in Text und Bild*, eds. Natalia Filatkina, Birgit Ulrike Münch, Ane Kleine (Trier, 2012), 121–38, at pp. 128, 133; idem, »Protestant Pots: Morality and Social Ritual in the Early Modern Home,« *Journal of Design History* 15 (2002): 263–73, at . p263.

[44] See Robin Hildyard, *European Ceramics* (London, 1999), 44; David Gaimster, »Pots, Prints and Propaganda: Changing Mentalities in the Domestic Sphere,« in *The Archaeology of the Reformation 1480–1580*, eds. David Gaimster and Roberta Gilchrist (Leeds, 2003), 122–44; Ulinka Rublack, *Reformation Europe* (Cambridge, 2005), 178–79.

[45] See above.

[46] Cf. the emphasis on spiritualisation in Hamling and Richardson, *A Day at Home* (see note 38), quotation at 25.

[47] See Wayne Franits, »The Family Saying Grace: A Theme in Dutch Art of the Seventeenth Century,« *Simiolus: Netherlands Quarterly for the History of Art* 16 (1986): 36–49. On the material culture of dining, see Hamling and Richardson, *A Day at Home* (see note 38), ch. 3.

[48] For the English edition of Tidschreden, see *Dris Martini Lutheri Colloquia Mensalia: or, Dr Martin Luther's Divine Discourses at his Table, &c.*, translated by Henry Bell (London, 1652).

hinted at in the verses by Hans Sachs that accompany a 1534 German broadside by Georg Pencz entitled *Ein Tischzucht* (Table Discipline), which urge children to »proceed in a disciplined manner« and be »a model of gracefulness«, reproving their bad eating habits and warning them to guard themselves against »all shameful Words, gossip, ridicule and laughter«.[49] The godly household may have envisaged itself as a little church, but conversation in it was sometimes akin to that encountered in a tavern or alehouse.

The very pots and plates from which some Protestants ate and drank and which adorned their tables and dressers could be carriers of anti-Catholic feeling. In Germany, the motifs of polemical prints readily migrated to other media: satirical double-headed portraits of the Pope and the Devil were applied as roundels on jugs and beakers. Although this was at first an initiative of potters who supported the new faith, it also responded to a growing market for such crockery.[50] Mimicking woodcuts illustrating Revelation 17, a French enamel dish dated c. 1570, for instance, is decorated with the image of the woman of the Apocalypse seated on a seven headed beast, next to which a pope, bishop, monk and cardinal kneel in adoration.[51] Conspicuous here are the German Rhineland stoneware jugs and bottles that were imported into England and the Low Countries in large quantities in the sixteenth and seventeenth centuries (fig. 2). The origins of the Bartmann motif are obscure and some have speculated that they draw on traditions on the Wild Man. But they seem to have acquired new significance in the course of their commercial travels. In both countries they became known as Bellarmine jugs, a reference to the formidable Jesuit cardinal who was Rome's leading theologian and most redoubtable controversialist.[52] Seventeenth-century plays attest to the process by which these bearded vessels, commonly used for serving beer, became synonymous with this rotund churchman. In William Cartwright's comedy *The Ordinary* (1634) a drunken curate wittily compares an opponent with »a larger jug, which some men call a Bellarmin, but we a con-

---

[49] Reproduced and translated in Ozment, *When Fathers Ruled* (see note 36), 142–43.

[50] David Gaimster, *German Stoneware 1200–1900: Archaeology and Cultural History* (London, 1997), 148–53.

[51] British Museum, WB.31.

[52] See M. R. Holmes, »The So-Called »Bellarmine« Mask on Imported Rhenish Stoneware,« *The Antiquaries Journal* 31 (1951): 173–79; Gaimster, *German Stoneware*, 24–25, 209; Juliet Fleming, *Graffiti and the Writing Arts of Early Modern England* (Philadelphia, 2001), 146–51. The term was well established in English by the eighteenth century: see Oxford English Dictionary, »bellarmine«. For some surviving examples, see Victoria and Albert Museum, c. 31–2000; British Museum 1972, 1001.2; 1856, 0701.1619; Fitzwilliam Museum, C.4–1988.

Fig. 2
Bartmann (Bellarmine) jug,
unidentified Frechen pottery, Rhineland, Germany, 1599
(British Museum, 1856, 0701.1619)

science«.[53] Here the joke turns on the moral flexibility for which the Society of Jesus had become notorious, via its casuistry and advocacy of equivocation. The propensity of contemporaries to see a burlesque likeness of Bellarmine on the bottles in which liquor was kept is itself an index of the pervasive spread of anti-popery as a cultural habit and of the process by which it became entangled with conventional rituals of sociability and conviviality.

Other notorious Catholic figures were similarly targeted: Robert Plot and John Evelyn both reflect the widespread tendency to call such vessels after the Duke of Alva, whose role in repressing Calvinist dissent in the Netherlands using the inquisitorial Council of Blood was part of an evolving black legend. Evelyn said that his visage, »showing a malicious, stern, and merciless Aspect, fringed with a prolix and squalid Beard« and »show-

---

[53] William Cartwright, *The Ordinary a Comedy* (London, 1634), 52.

ing his meager and hollow Cheeks, Emblems of his Disposition«, could be found on thousands of jugs, pots, and tobacco boxes.[54] Protestant merry-making lubricated by drink flowed naturally into merciless mockery of the most celebrated and feared papists of the age.[55] The rituals of commensality that revolved around these objects forged bonds and fostered a sense of solidarity rooted in contempt and hatred of a convenient other.

Other household objects also served to foster prejudice by provoking laughter. A remarkable Dutch delftware plate dated 1692 and decorated with a simplified version of the Candle is Lighted print remembers Wyclif, Luther, Calvin, and Beza, but it also operates as a piece of slapstick comedy and farce at the expense of a quartet of hapless papists.[56] The base of an elaborate clock owned by James I bears an image based on another provocative anti-Catholic print, showing the Pope's nose being held to a grindstone by the king and his sons Henry and Charles. Concealed underneath, only those in the know were permitted to take pleasure in this indiscreet jest against the successor of St Peter.[57] Once again the picture itself mimics and vicariously enacts upon its victims a form of ritual punishment and humiliation. The tin-glazed earthenware tiles with which it became fashionable to decorate chimney breasts, fireplace surrounds and hearths in the later seventeenth-century were themselves sometimes decorated with anti-Catholic cartoons. A fair number narrating the unsavoury story of the Popish Plot survive in museums and private collections, including one showing the hatching of the conspiracy in Rome and the execution of the Jesuits in its aftermath.[58] Families and households gathered around the fireplace were constantly reminded of the hostility that it behoved upright Protestants to display to the pope and his besotted adherents.

---

[54] Robert Plot, *Natural History of Oxford-shire, being an Essay toward the Natural History of England* (London, 1676), 250; John Evelyn, *Numismata, a Discourse of Medals Ancient and Modern* (London, 1697), 340. See the surviving design for a tazza with a portrait of the Duke of Alva as Commander of Folly, together with the upside down head of a jester, dating from c. 1588 in the British Museum: E, 7.320. Other designs included the Whore of Babylon. Another version is 1870, 0625.38.

[55] See Angela McShane's illuminating discussion of the symbiotic relationship between intoxication and politics in »Material Culture and »Political Drinking« in Seventeenth-Century England,« in *Cultures of Intoxication*, eds. Phil Withington and Angela McShane, Past and Present Supplement 9 (Oxford, 2014), 247–76.

[56] British Museum: 1891, 0224.3. See https://exhibitions.lib.cam.ac.uk/reformation/artifacts/commemorative-tableware-a-dutch-delftware-charger/. On this item, see Walsham, »Domesticating the Reformation: Material Culture, Memory and Confessional Identity in Early Modern England,« *Renaissance Quarterly* 69 (2016): 566–616.

[57] Victoria and Albert Museum: M.7–1931. See https://exhibitions.lib.cam.ac.uk/reformation/artifacts/holding-the-popes-nose-to-a-grindstone-an-anti-catholic-clock/.

[58] See Anthony Ray, *English Delftware Tiles* (London, 1973), 35, 56–64, 114–15; Aileen Dawson, *English and Irish Delftware 1570–1840* (London, 2011), 45–47.

The template upon which these tiles were based was a pack of 52 playing cards (Fig. 3) designed by Francis Barlow, who cashed in on the success of this series with various others recalling the Rump, Rye House, Meal Tub, and other plots, as well as the reign of the overtly Catholic King James II, whose ejection in 1688 led to the accession of William and Mary and the so-called Glorious Revolution.[59] Often sold as sheets »fit to adorn studies and houses« for as little as eight pence, their iconography imitated that of earlier anti-popish prints and they were an ingenious means of spreading political propaganda for the Whig cause at low cost. Newspaper advertisements in the 1670s explicitly recommend them as a way of acquainting children with »a chronicle for above 100 years past of all the bloody purposes and devilish designs of the Papists against the Protestant Religion and the true Professors of it.«[60]

Significantly, such playing cards quite literally turned anti-popery into an amusing domestic game. They too were ludic devices for defusing the threat presented by Catholicism, sometimes by arousing unseemly laughter at grotesque bodily processes. Barlow's surviving pen and ink sketch depicts the manner in which the devil supplied the pope with plotters, by voiding them out of his arse.[61] Once again there is a curious inversionary logic at work here. The boxes in which cards were kept were also embellished with images that cemented long-standing prejudices that can be traced back to the early Reformation, including a shallow rectangular box made in the mid eighteenth century, the lid of which shows a lecherous monk stroking the chin of a well-dressed lady, a scene that has recognisable German Lutheran precedents.[62] It is surely not irrelevant that by the mid seventeenth century the word had become associated with prostitu-

---

[59] For surviving packs, see British Museum, 1896, 0501.915.1–52; British Museum, 1841, 0403.138–189; Victoria and Albert Museum, 2–366: 1–52. See also *Orange-cards, Representing the Late King's Reign, and Expedition of the Prince of Orange, (viz.) the Earl of Essex's murther. Dr Ote's Whipping [...] to which is Added, the Effigies of our Gracious K. William and Q. Mary Curiously Illustrated and Engraven in Lively Figures* ([London, 1689?]). A Dutch example of »Papacy« playing cards is British Museum, 1896, 0501.773. See William Hughes Willshire, *A Descriptive Catalogue of Playing and Other Cards in the British Museum. Accompanied by a Concise General History of the Subject and Remarks on Cards of Divination and of a Politico-Historical Character* (London, 1876) and J. R. S. Whiting, *A Handful of History* (Totowa, NJ, 1978).

[60] Quoted in Willshire, *Descriptive Catalogue* (see note 59), 244.

[61] Francis Barlow, *The Devil Supplying the Pope with Plotters* (c. 1680). British Museum 1954,0710.4.20.

[62] Victoria and Albert Museum, 860–1882. For German precedents, see, for example, Leonhard Beck's *The Monk and his Maid* (1523), in Scribner, *For the Sake of Simple Folk* (see note 2), 38.

Fig. 3
Francis Barlow (or after Francis Barlow)
Popish Plot playing cards,
London, 1679 (British Museum, 1841, 0403.138–189)

tion: »a lady of the game« was a euphemism for a woman who sold herself for sex.[63]

Card-playing had reached England in the fifteenth century and by 1628 the trade in manufacturing cards was so profitable that a livery company was formed. As a leisure activity card-playing was not uncontroversial, particularly because it was often closely connected with gambling, which some godly Protestants saw as a flagrant misuse of the solemn biblical device of the lot. Elizabethan and Stuart puritan moralists such as Thomas Wilcox and Philip Stubbes declared that carding was intolerable on the sabbath and described it, along with dice and tables, as a species of deceit and theft that robbed those who played it of their bodies and souls.[64] Such arguments were reiterated in James Balmford's *Short and plaine dialogue concerning the unlawfulness of playing at cards* (1594), dedicated to the mayor, aldermen and burgesses of Newcastle-upon-Tyne, which declared that it was sinful to make God an umpire in a game of chance.[65] Such sentiments may have contributed to the condemnation of a curious playing card found in the archives of Hatfield House, which was converted into a miniature triptych. Regarded as evidence of the »lewdness« of the Catholic religion, it was confiscated from the comb case of one of the Duke of Norfolk's men by the Lieutenant of the Tower of London in 1571. This an intriguing piece of religious dissimulation can only have reinforced the tendency to conflate popery with superstitious »toys« and idle play.[66]

However, the exaggerated outrage of the literature of complaint should not be allowed to eclipse the fact that even puritans saw a legitimate place for this form of recreation in private. The Cambridge divine William Perkins declared that the use of such things indifferent for »lawful delight and pleasure is permitted unto us« and Stubbes acknowledged that they could be efficacious in driving away melancholy passions, dispelling worries and cares, and alleviating the oppression of study.[67] Balmford's attack on card

---

[63] See Oxford English Dictionary, »game«, n., sense 4b.

[64] Thomas Wilcox, *A Glasse for Gamesters and Namelie for such as Delight in Cards & Dise: wherein thei Maie Se not onely the Vanitie, but also the Vilenesse of those Plaies Plainly Discovered and Overthrowen by the Word of God* (London, 1581); Philip Stubbes, *The Anatomie of Abuses* (London, 1583), O 6ʳ–P 1ᵛ.

[65] James Balmford, *A Short and Plaine Dialogue concerning the Unlawfulness of Playing at Cards or Tables, or any other Game consisting in Chance* (London, [1593]), A 6ᵛ. See also a broadsheet version addressed *To the Maior, Aldermen, and Inhabitants of N[ewcastle-upon-Tyne]* (London, [1600?]).

[66] Richard L. Williams, »Contesting the Everyday: The Cultural Biography of a Subversive Playing Card,« in *Everyday Objects: Medieval and Early Modern Material Culture and its meanings*, eds. Tara Hamling and Catherine Richardson (Farnham, 2010), 241–56.

playing evoked a response from the London divine Thomas Gataker, who defended the casting of lots in some instances as compatible with the rules on Christian liberty.[68] The late seventeenth-century Bedfordshire rector James Kirkwood's *New Family Book* was bound with a *Discourse about the right way of improving our time* (1693), in which he warned against the »unspeakable hurt and prejudice« that came from »being carried away by the fancy and humour« of this sport. But he also acknowledged that there were moments when it was fitting to »indulge« oneself a little in it, provided that limits and boundaries on how long one played and the quantity of money wagered were set, and any winnings were devoted to some charitable purpose:

»This would afford a great pleasure and joy to those who reap some fruit and benefit by your Recreation and Pastime«.

»Divertissements« used with due care and moderation could thus redound to the good of society at large.[69]

If some denounced cards as the »devil's picture book«,[70] then, others acknowledged that they could serve useful purposes in the building up of a godly household and commonwealth. Indeed, cards were widely deployed as educational devices in this period. Packs were devised to teach mathematics, geography, and astronomy to children; charged with biting social satire, others urged those who played with them to cleave to conventional moral dictates and to avoid idleness.[71] They were didactic devices, equip-

---

[67] William Perkins, *The Whole Treatise of Cases of Conscience* (London, 1608), 116; Stubbes, *Anatomie of Abuses*, O 7ʳ. See also Alexandra Walsham, »Godly Recreation: The Problem of Leisure in Late Elizabethan and Early Stuart Society,« in *Grounds of Controversy: Three Studies in Late Sixteenth and Early Seventeenth-Century English Polemics*, eds. D. E. Kennedy, Diana Robertson and Alexandra Walsham (Melbourne, 1989), 9–48; Alessandro Arcangeli, *Recreation in the Renaissance: Attitudes towards Leisure and Pastimes in European Culture, c. 1425–1675* (Basingstoke, 2003), ch. 4.

[68] Thomas Gataker, *Of the Nature and Use of Lots a Treatise Historicall and Theologicall* (London, 1619). Balmford replied in *A Modest Reply to Certaine Answeres, which Mr Gataker B. D. in his Treatise of the Nature, & Use of Lotts, Giveth to Arguments in a Dialogue Concerning the Unlawfulness of Games Consisting in Chance* ([London], 1623).

[69] James Kirkwood, *A Discourse about the Right Way of Improving our Time* (London, 1693), bound with *A New Family Book* (London, 2ⁿᵈ edn, 1693), 93–96.

[70] Cited in David Parlett, *A History of Card Games* (Oxford, 1991), 11.

[71] See, for example, Joseph Moxon, *The Use of Astronomical Playing-Cards Teaching any Ordinary Capacity by them to be Acquainted with all the Stars in Heaven* (London, 1692); *Tour through England and Wales, A New Geographical Pastime* (London, 1794): Victoria and Albert Museum, E.1750–1954; *The New Game of Human Life: Being the most Agreeable and Rational Recreation ever Invented for Youth of both Sexes* (London, 1790): Victoria and Albert Museum, E. 156–1933. An early deck depicting maps of the counties of England and Wales is described by A. M. Hind, »An Elizabethan Pack of Playing-Cards,« *British Museum Quarterly* 13/1 (1939): 2–4. See also Serina Patterson,

ment for a type of what Patricia Rocco has called »virtuous vices«.[72] Falling into the category of adiaphora which Christians could lawfully utilise provided they did so to the edification of their neighbours and without scandalising the weaker brethren, such games could be harmless and acceptable pastimes that served the laudable purpose of rejuvenating both the body and mind.[73] They were compatible with the cultivation and internalisation of Protestant assumptions and values, not least the visceral aversion to popery that was one of its most striking hallmarks. Revealingly, an anti-Catholic ballad entitled *Londons drollery: or, the love and kindness between the pope and the devil* published between 1678 and 81 was intended to be sung to the tune »All you that do desire to play at cards to pass the time away«.[74]

3. The Game of Pope Joan

The final set of objects requiring discussion are ceramic and wooden boards or trays designed for holding stakes in the popular eighteenth-century game known as Pope Joan. The British Museum's example from the 1770s is a rare survival; most others date from the nineteenth century (fig. 4).[75] A game for three or more players, Pope Joan used a pack of cards without the eight of diamonds. The nine of diamonds was Pope Joan; the knave or jack represented intrigue and the Queen of hearts matrimony. Pope Joan had two continental cousins: the German game of Poch, first recorded at Strasbourg in 1441, and the French one known as Nain Jaune (Yellow Dwarf). The origins of the name of the English version are unclear, and may reflect a corruption or mistranslation of the French to Nun Joan, and from thence to the better known figure of the female pope, sup-

---

»Imaginary Cartographies and Commercial Commodities: Geography and Playing Cards in Early Modern England,« in *Playthings in Early Modernity: Party Games, Word Games, Mind Games*, ed. Allison Levy (Kalamazoo, MI, 2017), 219–37.

[72] Patricia Rocco, »Virtuous Vices: Giuseppe Maria Mitelli's Gambling Prints and the Social Mapping of Leisure and Gender in Post-Tridentine Bologna,« in *Playthings* (see note 71), ed. Levy, 167–90.

[73] See Elaine McKay, »›For Refreshment and Preserving Health‹: The Definition and Function of Recreation in Early Modern England,« *Historical Research* 81 (2008): 52–74.

[74] Elkanah Settle, *Londons Drollery: or, the Love and Kindness between the Pope and the Devil. Manifested by some True Protestants, who Utterly Defie the Pope and his Romish Faction; as it was to be Seen in London, November the 17th.1680* ([London, 1678–81]).

[75] British Museum, 1887, 0210.132. For a brief discussion, see Dawson, *English and Irish Delftware* (see note 58), 124–25. For later examples, see Victoria and Albert Museum, CIRC.508–1967 (1830); W.64–1929 and E.184–1947 (19th century).

Fig. 4
Pope Joan board,
tin glazed earthenware,
English, 1750–1770
(British Museum, 1887, 0210.132)

posed to have reigned under the title of John VIII from 855 to 858.[76] The migration of this board game across the Channel was accompanied by a remaking of its meaning in keeping with the preoccupations of the culture that received it.

Although not documented until several centuries after her alleged death, by the late middle ages, the story of Pope Joan had embedded itself in countless respected texts, including the Nuremberg Chronicle and Giovanni Boccacio's *De mulieribus claris* (on illustrious women) (1353). Variously said to have been the daughter of a citizen of Mainz or of English Christian missionaries on the Continent, Joan was a cross-dresser who had acquired a doctorate and risen in the ranks of the Catholic Church to become a scholar and a cardinal by donning male disguise. Elected as the

---

[76] See Parlett, *History of Card Games* (see note 70), 86–87, 119–21, and idem, *Oxford Dictionary of Card Games* (Oxford, 1992), 206–07, 221–22. For a surviving eighteenth-century gameboard for *Le Jeu de Nain Jaune*, see British Museum, 1856, 0501.12909.1.

supreme pontiff, her exposure came when she went into labour and was delivered of an infant, conceived in a scandalous liaison with a Vatican servant, while riding in a procession near St John Lateran in Rome. Her ritual humiliation by being tied to the horse's hooves and dragged for half a league was another key part of the drama. Some accounts blamed her deception upon diabolical agency. In the fifteenth century, this fable and its associated images were in wide circulation, and like other ancient traditions it was given a fillip by the advent of print. The reformers readily alighted upon it as ammunition against the doctrines of papal infallibility and unbroken succession. Its racy elements of clerical sexual immorality lent themselves well to propaganda against the popish priesthood and its resonances with the wicked whore of Babylon foretold in Revelation 17 fostered a steady conflation of the popess with the figure of Antichrist, which itself was systematically equated with the Church of Rome.[77] This process is neatly reflected in Martin Schrott's picture book based on the Apocalypse, *Von der Erschröcklichen Zurstörung und Niderlag dess gantzen Bapstums* (On the terrrible destruction and fall of the papacy) published around 1550, which contains an illustration of a woman astride a seven-headed beast inscribed »Agnes, a woman from England, called John VII in the year 851«. In this text the national identity of the notorious female pontiff became part of the developing myth.[78] Post-Reformation woodcuts increasingly dwelt upon the ignominious downfall and degradation of this »harlot«, and the infant that emanates from between her splayed legs may be seen in the same light as scatalogical images of the pope and devil squirting out excrement.[79]

In England, the legend of Pope Joan was likewise utilised by early evangelicals as compelling evidence of the depravity of the papacy. It fitted too well into the story of the world turned upside down and of a corrupt anti-religion to be discarded by Protestants such as John Bale, for whom it simultaneously illustrated the evils of female domination and the insidious

---

[77] See Alain Boureau, *The Myth of Pope Joan*, transl. Lydia G. Cochrane (Chicago and London, 1993; first publ. in French 1988), esp. ch. 6, which covers the fifteenth to seventeenth centuries. For England, see Thomas S. Freeman, »Joan of Contention: The Myth of the All Female Pope in Early Modern England,« in *Religious Politics in Post-Reformation England: Essays in Honour of Nicholas Tyacke*, eds. Kenneth Fincham and Peter Lake (Woodbridge, 2006), 60–79; Craig M. Rustici, *The Afterlife of Pope Joan: Deploying the Popess Legend in Early Modern England* (Ann Arbor, MI, 2006); Thomas F. X. Noble, »Why Pope Joan?,« *Catholic Historical Review* 99 (2013): 219–38.

[78] See Boreau, *Myth of Pope Joan* (see note 77), 229–31, and plate 5, 106, for a reproduction of the illustration; Scribner, *For the Sake of Simple Folk* (see note 2), 171–73.

[79] See British Museum, 1880, 0710.297 (woodcut illustration from an unidentified publication dated 1539).

link between popery and prostitution. The myth became something of a hot potato in Elizabeth's reign, when the parallels with the Virgin Queen, around whom swirled similar rumours of sexual scandal, were too close for comfort and discussion of it was subdued.[80] With the accession of a male ruler in the guise of James VI of Scotland, it could safely be brought out of mothballs once more. The vicar of Leeds, Alexander Cooke's *Dialogue* on this topic dated 1610 was a vigorous attempt to prove the veracity of the legend, largely by accumulating citations from Catholic sources. He blamed her absence from other medieval works on a campaign of deliberate textual »gelding« or castration and declared that these dishonest practices reflected the tendency to feign, forge, cog, befool and lie that was intrinsic to popery.[81] Ironically, in this instance it was Protestants who bent over backwards to defend a dubious tradition, while learned Catholics from the Jesuits Georg Scherer, chaplain to the archduke of Austria and Robert Bellarmine to the leading ecclesiastical historian Caesar Baronius lined up to dismiss it as inane and fabulous.[82] Cooke's book was translated into various European vernaculars and into Latin. The title page of the two editions published in Oppenheim in 1616 and 1619 elide the child-bearing pope with the Madonna, a stratagem that is also evident in a German engraving of c. 1650.[83] In a measure of the malleability, dynamism and adaptability of English anti-Catholicism, the Pope Joan legend underwent a further revival during the Restoration. H. J.'s *History* of her life and death of 1663 is a scurrilous retelling of the tale that concludes by insisting that nothing can wash away the stain and pollution that this abomination has left upon pontifical sanctity and supremacy (fig. 5).[84] Cooke's text reappeared under the title *A present for a papist* in 1675, along with a translation of Bartholomeo Platina's sceptical biography of the popess. Its preface compared the book with a »bauble« that would please »little children and fools« but hoped that »the more rational sort of

---

[80] See esp. Craig Rustici, »»Ceste Nouvelle Papesse«: Elizabeth I and the Specter of Pope Joan,« in *Elizabeth I: Always her Own Free Woman*, eds. Carole Levin, Jo Eldridge Carney and Debra Barrett-Graves (Aldershot, 2003), 131–48.

[81] Alexander Cooke, *A Dialogue betweene a Protestant and a Papist. Manifestly Proving that a Woman Called Joane was Pope of Rome* (London, 1610). On this, see Rustici, *Afterlife of Pope Joan* (see note 77), ch. 1.

[82] See Boreau, *Myth* (see note 77), ch. 6; Rustici, *Afterlife of Pope Joan* (see note 77), ch. 1.

[83] »Johannae Papisae Bildniss aus Georg Altens Welt-Chronick«: British Museum, Bb, 8.279.

[84] H. J., *The History of the Life and Death of Pope Joane: who was Elected to the Papacy, c. 855. Under the Name of Johannes Anglus of Mentz in Germany. Published as an Advertisement to all Papists* (London, 1663).

A WomanPope (as History doth tell)
In HighProcession Shee in Labour fell,
And was Deliuer'd of a Bastard Son ;
ThenceRome some call The Whore of Babylon.

A Present for a Papist:
OR THE
LIFE and DEATH
OF
POPE JOAN,
Plainly Proving
Out of the Printed Copies, and
Manuscripts of Popish Writers and
others, that a Woman called
JOAN, was really
POPE of *ROME*;
And was there Deliver'd of a Bastard
Son in the open Street, as She went
in Solemn Procession.

By a *LOVER* of *TRUTH*,
Denying Human Infallibility.

LONDON,
Printed for *T.D.* and are to be sold at
the Ship in St. *Mary Axe*, and by
most Booksellers, 1675.

Fig. 5
Alexander Cooke, A Present for a Papist, London, 1675
(used by permission of the Folger Shakespeare Library,
shelf mark 189–219q)

men« would not be taken in by it.[85] Elkanah Settle made it the subject of a stage play called *The female prelate* in 1689.[86] Others used it to cement the link between popery and whoredom.[87] Far too useful to be discarded, its resilience was a product of the atmosphere of fetid anxiety and speculation that created and fuelled the Popish Plot and the mock processions and symbolic pope burnings that gave expression to anti-Catholic sentiment in the years immediately following.[88] The same period saw the publication of prints such as Stephen College's *Catholic Gamesters* (1680), which utilised the motif of a »dubble match of bowleing« to satirise the king's own

---

[85] *A Present for a Papist: or the Life and Death of Pope Joan* (London, 1675), A 3^v.

[86] Elkanah Settle, *The Female Prelate: Being the History of the Life & Death of Pope Joan* (London, 1689). On Pope Joan on the stage, see Rustici, *Afterlife of Pope Joan* (see note 77), ch. 5.

[87] *The History of Pope Joan and the Whores of Rome* (London, 1687; 2nd edition). See also *Pope Joan. Or, an Account Collected out of the Romish Authors* (London, 1689).

[88] See Tim Harris, *London Crowds in the Reign of Charles II: Propaganda and Politics from the Restoration until the Exclusion Crisis* (Cambridge, 1987), ch. 5.

impotent response to the plot as evidence of his own religious unortho-doxy.[89] In an uncut Dutch print of c. 1715 satirising the papacy and al-luding to the Jansenist controversy, she appears as the three of hearts.[90]

Passionate defence of Pope Joan's existence only gradually gave way to repudiation of it as an acknowledged fantasy. This was a process that did not denude her of polemical utility; it simply replaced moral outrage with corrosive laughter at popish credulity. It transformed her into a subject of comedy, into another of the superstitious »toys« and silly »pastimes« by which medieval Catholics had deluded their ignorant followers. And it did so at a time when the »toy« was becoming a discursive trope to deride the contemporary thirst for luxury and novelty, and to articulate the concerns and ambiguities surrounding a burgeoning culture of consumption.[91] The status of the legendary popess as a joke may have changed, but her ca-pacity to »reveal important cracks in established patterns of thought and activity« remained.[92] At the same time, it must be noted that she had long been associated with light-hearted conviviality: »as merry as Pope Joan« was an English proverb in common use in the mid sixteenth century.[93] Interestingly, she had also featured on European tarot cards from at least the fifteenth century.[94]

All of this is a critical backdrop to understanding the popularity of the card game that bore her name. So familiar a feature was it of the domestic scene that James Gillray depicted it in a satirical print attacking female vanity and fashion in 1796 and Charles Dickens made it the subject of a chapter of *The Pickwick Papers* in 1837.[95] Playing Pope Joan was a family

---

[89] Stephen College, *The Catholick Gamesters or a Dubble Match of Bowleing* (Lon-don, 1680), British Museum Satires 1077. On this print and its context, see Morton, »Laughter as a Polemical Act« (see note 32), 130–32.

[90] British Museum, 1859, 0709.3249.

[91] Se Ariane Fennetaux, »Toying with Novelty: Toys, Consumption and Novelty in Eighteenth-Century Britain,« in *Fashioning Old and New: Changing Consumer Prefe-rences in Europe*, eds. Brune Blondé, Natacha Coquery, Jon Stobart, and Ilja van Dam-me, Studies in European Urban History (1100–1800) 18 (Turnhout, 2009), 17–28.

[92] See Allison P. Coudert, »Laughing at Credulity and Superstition in the Long Eighteenth Century,« in *Laughter in the Middle Ages and Early Modern Times: Epis-temology of a Fundamental Human Behavior, its meaning, and Consequences*, ed. Al-brecht Clasen (Berlin, 2010), 803–29, at pp. 804–05.

[93] See Oxford English Dictionary, »Pope Joan«, n., sense 1. This is now obsolete.

[94] See the Italian example from the Italian Visconti-Sforza deck of cards of c. 1450, reproduced as the frontispiece to Boreau, *The Myth of Pope Joan* (see note 77). See also Willshire, *Descriptive Catalogue* (see note 59), 36 and 51.

[95] James Gillray, »Lady Godiva's Rout – or – Peeping Tom spying out Pope Joan,« 1796: Victoria and Albert Museum, 1232:93–1882; Charles Dickens, *The Posthumous Papers of the Pickwick Club*, ed. Robert L, Patten (Harmondsworth, 1972; first publ. 1836–7), 142.

activity that took place in the Victorian home. It must be seen in the context of a vogue for educational games, including moral race games such as one that traced the journey through human life, from cradle to grave.[96] Heirs of a humanist tradition that saw recreation as a device for teaching knowledge and virtue,[97] it served to inculcate in children the ingrained intolerance of popery that was part and parcel of being a Protestant in eighteenth-century England. Its quotient of anti-Catholic venom was sometimes diluted by other objectives, as indicated by a 1822 pack of Pope Joan cards designed to teach the names of British kings and queens.[98] Even as an undercurrent it contributed to shaping the outlook of those who played it subtly and insidiously: in Allison Levy's words, it was a »vector of sociability destined to connect but also to discriminate«.[99] Further evidence of its infiltration of the domain of the home and of its continued association with carnivalesque inversion and comic subversion is provided by a surviving toy theatre entitled »Pope Joan, or Harlequin on Card Island« created and sold in 1819.[100]

Like all toys and games, Pope Joan served as both a mirror of social values and a device for their transmission to the next generation, reinforcing and perpetuating confessional myths and stereotypes that stretched back into the sixteenth century and that tied the reformed societies of northern Europe together in diverse and dialectical ways. An agent of childrearing that inculated Protestant ideals and values, it offers insight into play's role in reproducing the more troubling features of historic societies, in this case the dark underside of that powerful component of English Protestant identity, anti-popery.[101] It opens a window onto some underexplored aspects of »the mundane friction between Protestants and

---

[96] *The New Game of Human Life*, Victoria and Albert Museum, E.156–1933. See also Iona and Robert Opie and Brian Alderson, *The Treasures of Childhood: Books, Toys and Games from the Opie Collection* (London, 1989), 160–61.

[97] See Timothy B. Husband, *The World in Play: Luxury Cards 1430–1540* (New York, 2015); Nicholas Orme, »Games and Education in Medieval England,« in *Games and Gaming in Medieval Literature*, ed. Serina Patterson (Basingstoke, 2015), 45–60.

[98] British Museum, 1896, 0501.1011.

[99] Allison Levy, »Playing the Field,« in *Playthings in Early Modernity* (see note 71), ed. Levy.

[100] British Museum, 1886, 0513.638–639. For evidence of the persisting influence of the legend, see Herbert Thurston's efforts to dispel this »fable«, which even in the early twentieth century, was »so tenaciously clung to by no-Popery lecturers«, in a pamphlet for the Catholic Truth Society: *Pope Joan* (London, 1916), 1.

[101] On anti-popery, see Colin Haydon, *Anti-Catholicism in Eighteenth-Century England, c. 1714–80* (Manchester, 1993), quotation at 13–14; Peter Lake, »Anti-Popery: The Structure of a Prejudice,« in *Conflict in Early Stuart England: Studies in Religion and Politics 1603–1642*, eds. Richard Cust and Ann Hughes (Harlow, 1989), 72–106; Linda Colley, *Britons: Forging the Nation 1707–1837* (London, 1992), ch. 1.

Papists« and extends our understanding of the »everyday, prolonged social pressures [that] were probably more distressing to most Catholics than intermittent mob or governmental action«.[102] The vicious verbal and physical conflicts that had marked the first phase of the Reformation may have waned, but antagonism remained an ever-present element in the enduring confessional culture that it engendered. Their sublimation into a light-hearted family game should not be allowed to occlude the hostility and aggression that lay beneath the surface of seventeenth- and eighteenth-century sociability, or the role that, counterintuitively, it played in social exclusion as well as inclusion and cohesion. As we have seen, anti-Catholicism had always had a ludic quality. Laughter and mockery remained intrinsic to it long after the alleged rise of the assumption that religion was a sphere in which gravity and sobriety should prevail.[103] As Protestantism progressed into maturity and adulthood and as public discourse gravitated towards politeness, the principal site in which these sentiments were expressed and inculcated became the private home.[104] Activities such as these arguably helped to ease the tensions that coexisting with those who adhered to rival faiths created in the pluralistic societies that the Reformation brought into being, even as they entrenched the very anxieties, fears, and insecurities that provoked ongoing spasms of ill-feeling.[105] They suggest that the »morose suspicion« of frivolity that has long been regarded as a lasting cultural legacy of Reformed Protestantism and puritanism may have been overstated.[106]

In conclusion, this essay has investigated the role of two and three dimensional objects as agents and conduits of early modern anti-Catholicism. It has explored how they served as vehicles of confessional identity

---

[102] For some stimulating work on other periods, see Doris Yvonne Wilkinson, »Racial Socialization through Children's Toys: A Sociohistorical Examination,« *Journal of Black Studies* 5 (1974): 96–109; Joel Best, »Too much Fun: Toys as Social Problems and the Interpretation of Culture,« *Symbolic Interaction* 21 (1998): 197–212; David Hamlin, »The Structures of Toy Consumption: Bourgeois Domesticity and Demand for Toys in Nineteenth-Century Germany,« *Journal of Social History* 36 (2003): 857–69.

[103] Cf. the argument developed in Keith Thomas, »The Place of Laughter in Tudor and Stuart England,« *Times Literary Supplement*, 3906 (21 January 1977): 77–81, at p. 79.

[104] On politeness and sociability as modes of exclusion, see Carys Brown, »Politeness, Hypocrisy, and Protestant Dissent in England after the Toleration Act, c. 1689–c. 1750,« *Journal for Eighteenth-Century Studies* 41 (2018): 61–80.

[105] See the sensitive discussion in Anthony Milton, »A Qualified Intolerance: The Limits and Ambiguities of Early Stuart Anti-Catholicism,« in *Catholicism and Anti-Catholicism in Early Modern English Texts*, ed. Arthur F. Marotti (Basingstoke, 1999), 85–115.

[106] Thomas, »Place of Laughter,« (see note 103), 81.

formation and cultural memory and examined how they infiltrated and operated within the forum of the Protestant family and household. It has situated the ritual strategies of iconoclasm, carnivalesque inversion and shaming on a continuum with rhetorical ones designed to undermine the integrity of the Church of Rome and shown how reformers in England and its neighbours in northern Europe turned Catholic artefacts, both literally and metaphorically, into playthings. It has traced how Protestantism helped to forge a denigrating discourse of trinkets and toys and to create an enduring satirical connection between popery and »childish« pastimes that reinforced its sense of its own spiritual superiority as it made the transition from a protest movement into a settled church. Paradoxically, poking fun at popery and making it into a game became a form of godly recreation and an instrument for educating the young in the art of religious intolerance. Hatred and humour, pleasure and prejudice, were connected in ways that belie lingering presuppositions about the moral austerity of Europe's sister Reformations in their second and subsequent generations.

Tradition und Innovation.
Recht

Christopher Voigt-Goy

Neben ihrer beeindruckenden Gelehrsamkeit gehörte es zum Standardrepertoire der nationalprotestantischen Kirchenrechtshistoriographie des ausgehenden 19. Jahrhunderts, die institutionelle Ausbildung der lutherischen Kirchen im Zeitalter der Reformation als unvollkommenen Ausdruck ihres »Gemeindeprinzips« zu bezeichnen. Nachgerade als Querkopf musste damals der Erlanger Jurist, Verwaltungs- und Kirchenrechtshistoriker Karl Rieker erscheinen, der schon die Annahme bestritt, dass das »Gemeindeprinzip« für die Reformatoren und ihre kirchenbildenden Anliegen von allein maßgeblichem Interesse war.[1] Vielmehr hätte, so Rieker, die Entwicklung des deutschen evangelischen Landeskirchentums auf vielfältige und oft hauptsächliche Arten und Weisen die anstaltsmäßigen Vorstellungen der vorfindlichen Kirchenorganisation fortgeführt. Diese These sicherte Rieker das kritische Interesse von Ernst Troeltsch (und einlinige Ablehnung durch Karl Holl), und machte ihn zu einem Gewährsmann für Troeltschs Analyse der Kontinuität des »Altprotestantismus« zum Mittelalter auf dem Gebiet der Kirchenverfassung.[2]

Auch abgesehen von ihrer wissenschaftshistorischen Bedeutung sind Riekers Überlegungen nach wie vor von Interesse, wenn die rechtliche Verfestigung der Reformationsbewegungen zu Kirchen im Spannungsgefüge von Tradition und Innovation betrachtet wird. Denn sie machen darauf aufmerksam, dass die Aufnahme bestehender Rechtsregelungen in den Reformationskirchen keine sachfremde Erhaltung katholischer »Restbestände« darstellt, sondern vielmehr die institutionelle Stabilisierung der Reformationskirchen in ihren je historisch eigenen Gestalten mit ermöglichte und vorantrieb. Ein Gebiet, auf dem sich diese Dynamik gut erfas-

---

[1] KARL RIEKER, Die rechtliche Stellung der evangelischen Kirche Deutschlands in ihrer geschichtlichen Entwickelung bis zur Gegenwart, Tübingen 1907, 71–74.

[2] Vgl. nur ERNST TROELTSCH, Protestantisches Christentum und Kirche in der Neuzeit (1906/1909/1922) (in: ERNST TROELTSCH, Kritische Gesamtausgabe, Bd. 7, hg. v. Volker Drehsen in Zusammenarbeit mit Christian Albrecht, Berlin u. New York 2004, 507); KARL HOLL, Luther und das landesherrliche Kirchenregiment, 1911 (in: DERS., Gesammelte Aufsätze zur Kirchengeschichte, Bd. 1: Luther, Tübingen 1923, 326–380).

sen lässt, ist die rechtliche Behandlung des Kirchenguts in den werdenden
Reformationskirchen. Dies ist natürlich ein weites Gebiet, da der Begriff
›beneficium‹, mit dessen Hilfe die mittelalterliche Kanonistik das kirchliche Vermögensrecht rechtssystematisch zu vereinheitlichen suchte, mit
vielen einzelnen Rechtsinstituten verbunden war; etwa mit Stiftungen, Inkorporationen und Patronaten, Kirchenfabriken sowie natürlich den Parochien.[3]

Wichtig für das Folgende ist es, mit Rieker festzuhalten, dass nach
kanonistischer und auch das *ius commune* prägender Rechtsauffassung der
»Eigentümer des Kirchenguts *die verschiedenen einzelnen mit juristischer
Persönlichkeit begabten kirchlichen Institute selbst*« sind, wie eben die Stiftungen, Inkorporationen, Patronate, Kirchenfabriken und Parochien.[4] Begründet ist deren juristische Persönlichkeit in ihrem ursprünglichen Er-
richtungszweck bzw. dem originären Stifterwillen, welcher in den entsprechenden Vermögensmassen bzw. Sachmitteln unveräußerlich eingeschrieben wird. Dieser institutionell-sächliche Umstand ist es, der nach
Rieker (und nicht nur ihm) den anstaltlichen Charakter der mittelalterlichen Kirchenorganisation ausmacht. Als Rechtsträger fungieren also
kirchlich zweckgebundene Komplexe, die aus Sachen bzw. Vermögensmassen und ihnen anhängenden Einzelrechten bestehen. Das Recht der
Nutzung des Kirchenguts zur Versorgung von Amtsträgern oder das
Zehntrecht verpflichten dabei zugleich, die Zweckbindung des Kirchenguts zu realisieren. Entsprechend gilt es nach kanonistischer Vorstellung
als Vergehen, wenn das Kirchengut seinem kirchlichen Zweck entweder
ganz entfremdet oder einfach einem anderen kirchlichen Zweck zugeführt
wird. Denn in beiden Fällen wird der eigentliche Rechtsträger usurpiert
(Alienationsverbot).[5]

In zwei kurzen Überlegungsgängen soll im Weiteren gezeigt werden,
wie die reformatorischen Kirchen in Adaption dieses traditionellen Verständnisses des Kirchenguts und in Konfrontation mit ihm sich institu-
tionell ausprägten. Zu Anfang steht ein Blick auf die Entwicklungen im
Alten Reich im Umkreis der Wittenberger Reformation, darauf folgen
einige Beobachtungen zur Entwicklung in England.

---

[3] Peter Landau, Art. Beneficium (in: TRE 5, 1980, 577–583).
[4] Rieker, Die rechtliche Stellung (s. Anm. 1), 189 (Hervorhebung im Original).
[5] Vgl. Peter Landau, Art. Kirchengut (in: TRE 18, 1989, 560–575, hier: 568).

I.

Inwiefern die von der Wittenberger Reformation ausgehende Kirchenbildung eine fundamentale Konfrontation mit der traditionellen Vorstellung des Kirchenguts darstellte, ist nicht eindeutig zu sagen. Denn schon in den ersten Konflikten um die Pfarrstellenbesetzungen in Altenburg und Leisnig 1522 bzw. 1523 wird zwar die zunehmende Abneigung des ehemaligen Distrikvikars der Augustinereremiten Martin Luther gegen das Rechtsinstitut der Inkorporation deutlich.[6] Jedoch bedeutete das keine prinzipielle Ablehnung des gesamten hergebrachten Kirchengutsverständnisses auf Seiten des Reformators. Nichtsdestoweniger entwarf er in diesen Kontexten eine entscheidende Grundlinie der späteren Kirchenbildung.

In beiden genannten Konfliktfällen drangen die Gemeinden der Pfarreien der kursächsischen Landstädte Altenburg und Leisnig, welche jeweils in nahegelegene Klöster inkorporiert waren, darauf, evangelisch gesinnte Prediger zu bestellen. Diesem Drängen widersetzten sich der Propst des Bergerklosters bzw. der Abt des Klosters Buch als Inhaber der Inkorporationen. Als angefragter Gutachter in beiden Fällen entwickelte Luther nun zunächst im Altenburger Fall einen Vorschlag, der explizit auf die rechtlichen Fragen nach dem Umgang mit dem bestehenden Kirchengut und Rechtsinstitut der Inkorporation nicht einging.[7] Dabei riet er Gemeinde, den neu einzustellenden evangelisch gesinnten Pfarrer eigens dadurch zu entlohnen, dass der Rat der Stadt die Pfarrpfründe verwende. Darauf habe sie – so Luther – Anspruch, weil die Gemeinde der Stadt die Predigerkirche errichtet habe.[8] Mit der schlussendlich gefundenen Lösung des Konflikts hatte Luther aber nichts mehr zu tun, weil sie durch einen kurfürstlichen Schiedsspruch zwischen dem Rat der Stadt und dem Abt zustande kam. Dieser Schiedsspruch folgte aber grundsätzlich der Richtung, die Luther schon vor Augen stand: Der Propst verzichtete auf die eigenmächtige Besetzung der Stelle sowie die Pfründe der Pfarrei[9], schnitt letztere also aus der Inkorporation heraus. Dies war in den eng gesteckten Grenzen des Alienationsverbots durchaus zulässig, da das Pfarrbenefizium ein selbstständiger Teil der Inkorporation war.[10] Der Propst musste indes

---

[6] KARL MÜLLER, Kirche, Gemeinde und Obrigkeit nach Luther, Tübingen 1910, 107–109.

[7] A.a.O., 103–110. Dazu treffend: ULRICH STUTZ, Miszelle (in: ZSRG.K 1, 1911, 309–313).

[8] KARL TRÜDINGER, Luthers Briefe und Gutachten an weltliche Obrigkeiten zur Durchführung der Reformation, Münster 1975, 58 f.

[9] WA.Br 2,538,4–5, Nr. 496 (Der Rat der Altenburger an Luther vom 22. Mai 1522).

[10] PETER LANDAU, Art. Inkorporation (in: TRE 16, 1987, 163–166, hier: 165).

nicht auf die anderen Abgaben aus der Inkorporation verzichten, die mit den restlichen Abgaben und Sachleistungen verbunden waren. Grundsätzlich waren damit die bestehenden Rechts- und Besitzverhältnisse respektiert worden.

Die Möglichkeit, eine ähnlich im Rahmen des bestehenden Rechts formulierte Lösung zu finden, zerstörte Luther in Leisniger Fall dann gründlich. Für unseren Zusammenhang aufschlussreich zeigt sich das in Luthers *Ordenung eyns gemeynen Kastens* von 1523, die aus den erwähnten gutachterlichen Zusammenhängen im Leisniger Fall entstand und als Druck schnell Furore machte.[11] In dieser Schrift schlug Luther dreierlei vor: *Erstens* solle der bisherige Inhaber der inkorporierten Pfarrei in Leisnig entsetzt werden. *Zweitens* sollten alle pfarreibezogenen Vermögen und Einkünfte kumuliert und in einem »Kasten« zusammengeführt werden. Und *drittens* solle aus dieser Vermögensmasse durch gewählte Vertreter derjenigen, die zu diesem Kasten beitragen, die Versorgung des Pfarramts, der Küsterei und der Armenfürsorge gewährleistet, sowie daraus Rücklagen für gemeindliche Notlagen gebildet und Darlehen vergeben werden. Mit diesen Vorschlägen empfahl Luther natürlich umfassende Brüche mit dem Rechtsinstitut der klösterlichen Inkorporation und Verstöße gegen das Alienationsverbot. Ganz nebenbei kassierte er auch noch die Selbstständigkeit des Pfarrbenefiziums. Allerdings brach Luther nicht mit dem, was eingangs als anstaltlicher Charakater des Kirchenguts bezeichnet worden ist. Denn die juristische Persönlichkeit, sprich: die rechtstragende und -verbürgende Instanz bleibt in Luthers Konstruktion eben der »Gemeine Kasten« selbst.[12] Daran ändert auch die genossenschaftliche Verwaltung des Kastens und Wahrnehmung der daraus sich ergebenden Rechte und Pflichten nichts, da weder die im Kasten zusammengefasste Vermögensmasse noch die Prinzipien ihrer weiteren Kumulation und Verwendung genossenschaftsrechtlichen Vorstellungen unterworfen werden. Dies lässt sich auch folgendermaßen wenden: Luthers Idee des »Gemeinen Kasten« ist nichts weniger als der Vorschlag zur Ausbildung eines neuen vermögensrechtlichen Instituts anstaltskirchlichen Charakters, das ein eigenes Alienationsverbot mit umfasst.

---

[11] WA 12,11–30. Vgl. zu den frühen Kastenordnungen CHRISTIAN PETERS, Der Armut und dem Bettel wehren. Städtische Beutel- und Kastenordnungen von 1521 bis 1531 (in: Gute Ordnung. Ordnungsmodelle und Ordnungsvorstellungen in der Reformationszeit, hg. v. Irene Dingel u. Armin Kohnle, Leipzig 2014, 239–255). Zum Leisniger Fall vgl. auch EIKE WOLGAST, Die Einführung der Reformation und das Schicksal der Klöster im Reich und in Europa, Gütersloh 2014, 29f.

[12] Treffend RIEKER, Die rechtliche Stellung (s. Anm. 1), 201.

Die rechtsbrüchigen Momente der Kastenordnung waren dennoch so augenscheinlich, dass ihr die kurfürstliche Zustimmung verweigert wurde, obwohl die Leisniger Gemeinde sie in Kraft treten lassen wollte. Ihrem Modellcharakter besonders für die Vermögensverwaltung in den zur Reformation übertretenden Städten hat dies indes keinen Abbruch getan.[13] Gerade in den Reichsstädten konnten die Kastenordnungen an die schon im Mittelalter etablierte Beteiligung der Bürger bzw. des Rats an der Kirchenverwaltung anknüpfen, so dass sie in der Praxis nicht automatisch zu einem reformatorischen Systembruch auf dem Gebiet des Kirchenguts führen mussten.[14] Dieser Systembruch wurde dann aber mit den einsetzenden Klosteraufhebungen bzw. sogenannten »Sequestrationen« ab den späteren 1520er Jahren umso deutlicher.[15] Für die Fortbildung der Kirchengutsbehandlung in den aus der Wittenberger Bewegung entstammenden Reformationskirchen waren dann reichs- und territorialpolitische Überlegungen ebenso leitend, wie auch das Reichsrecht auf die Entwicklung entscheidenden Einfluss nahm.

Die ohnehin fragile Legitimationsgrundlage, die der Speyrer Reichsabschied von 1526 für die Durchführung reformatorischer Maßnahmen darstellte[16], war mit dem Augsburger Reichstag im Jahr 1530 endgültig zerbrochen. Eine Klagewelle vor dem Reichskammergericht wegen illegitimer Enteignung und Entfremdung von Kirchen- und Klostergut drohte[17], da nicht zuletzt Philipp von Hessen das Klostervermögen seines Territoriums seinem eigenen Fiskus zugeführt hatte[18]. Zwar gelang es den protestierenden Ständen, die sich im *Schmalkaldischen Bund*[19] zusammenfanden, diese Prozesse zu verzögern. Doch eine Lösung der Kirchengutsfrage wurde aus zwei Gründen dringlich. Denn während der Nürnberger Anstand von 1532, *erstens*, in Aussicht stellte, dass der Kaiser die laufenden Prozesse vor dem Reichskammergericht suspendiere[20], fing das neue Bündnismit-

---

[13] Vgl. PETERS, Armut (s. Anm. 11), 246–252.

[14] HANS ERICH FEINE, Kirchliche Rechtsgeschichte, Bd. 1: Die Katholische Kirche, Weimar 1950, 343–352.

[15] Zur Sequestration: HANS LEHNERT, Kirchengut und Reformation. Eine kirchenrechtsgeschichtliche Studie, Erlangen 1935, 54–57.

[16] Zu den Folgen des Speyrer Reichstags von 1526: ARMIN KOHNLE, Reichstag und Reformation. Kaiserliche und ständische Religionspolitik von den Anfängen der Causa Lutheri bis zum Nürnberger Religionsfrieden, Gütersloh 2001, 277–362.

[17] DIETRICH KRATSCH, Justiz – Religion – Politik. Das Reichskammergericht und die Klosterprozesse im ausgehenden sechzehnten Jahrhundert, Tübingen 1990, 26–29.

[18] WOLGAST, Die Einführung der Reformation (s. Anm. 11), 39–51.

[19] Dazu umfassend GABRIELE HAUG-MORITZ, Der Schmalkaldische Bund 1530–1541/42. Eine Studie zu den genossenschaftlichen Strukturelementen der politischen Ordnung des Heiligen Römischen Reiches Deutscher Nation, Leinfelden-Echterdingen 2002.

[20] KOHNLE, Reichstag (s. Anm. 16), 405.

glied Herzog Ulrich von Württemberg 1534 an, seine beträchtlichen kirchlichen Pfründe seinem eigenem Haushalt einzuverleiben[21]. *Zweitens* hatten
nun auch innerhalb der reformatorischen Territorien die anderen, vornehmlich adligen Inhaber von Kirchengütern, allen voran von Patronaten,
ihrerseits angefangen, das Kirchengut ihrem Nutzen zuzuordnen.[22] In diesem spannungsreichen Kontext des Schmalkadischen Bundes wurde in der
Kirchengutsfrage eine folgenreiche Position entwickelt.[23]

Deren Leitlinien gehen wiederum auf Martin Luther zurück, der Ende
1531 im Kontext der kursächsischen Sequestrationen nach einem Gutachten gefragt worden war.[24] Grundlegend ist dabei Luthers Bestreitung, dass
mit der Einstellung des Klosterlebens in einem Kloster die Inhaberschaft
an den Gütern des Klosters dem Orden oder Klosterverband zukomme.
Vielmehr falle, so Luther, das Kloster- und Kirchengut aufgrund fehlender
Erben analog eines herrenlosen Guts (*bonum vacans*) dem Landesherren
zu. Dieser habe jedoch nicht wie bei einem *bonum vacans* die freie Verfügungsgewalt über die Güter:

»Denn das man acht habe auff der stiffter willen und meynung, Welche je nicht
anders gewest ist, Denn das sie zu Gottes dienst und ehre solche guter haben
wollen geben«.

Der eigentliche Missbrauch des Kirchenguts ist in Luthers Optik dann
auch entsprechend der falsche Gottesdienst, der das Kirchengut an Seelen-
messen u.ä. bindet. Hingegen findet für Luther der richtige Gottesdienst
in »allen guten stenden und emptern« statt, wenn auch in unterschiedlicher Gewichtung. Daher soll nach Luther das Kirchengut zuallererst und
zum größten Teil für »pfarher, prediger, Schulen und was mehr zum Gotteswort und Sacrament und seel sorgen gehoret«, aufgewendet werden.
Wenn das geschehen ist, kann das Übriggebliebene auch dem »welltlichen
regiment (welchs auch Gottes dienst, wie wol der geringer gegen ihenem)«
zukommen.[25]

---

[21] Wolgast, Die Einführung der Reformation (s. Anm. 11), 103–112.

[22] Vgl. dazu nur die landständischen Sequestrationen in Kursachsen: Uwe Schirmer,
Landstände und Reformation. Das Beispiel Kursachsen (1523–1543), in: Reformationen
vor Ort. Christlicher Glaube und konfessionelle Kultur in Brandenburg und Sachsen im
16. Jahrhundert, hg. v. Enno Bünz u.a., Berlin 2017, 55–77.

[23] Eine ausführliche Schilderung der Debatten bei Kurt Körber, Kirchengüterfrage
und Schmalkaldischer Bund. Ein Beitrag zur deutschen Reformationsgeschichte, Leipzig
1913, 83–188. Vgl. weiterhin materialreich: Klaus Bessey, Das Kirchengut nach der
Lehre der evangelischen Juristen Deutschlands im ersten Jahrhundert nach der Reformation, Diss. Masch., Tübingen 1968.

[24] Luther an Kurfürst Johann (Anfang 1531): WA.Br 6,3–10, Nr. 1766. Vgl. Trüdinger, Luthers Briefe (s. Anm. 8), 64 f., 85 f.

[25] WA.Br 6,6.

An Luthers Anschauung anknüpfend führte ein Kollektivgutachten – federführend waren wohl Justus Jonas, Johannes Bugenhagen und Philipp Melanchthon – im Kontext des Schmalkaldischen Bunds dann aus: Die Obrigkeit sei

»schuldig, dieselbigen Güter nicht den Kirchen zuentfrembden, sondern sie treulich zu erhalten [...]. Ist nun etwas übrig, so mögen auch die Obrigkeiten selbst, als Patroni, dasselbige mit genießen, dieweil sie solche Güter schützten und ordnen müßen«.[26]

Im Verlauf der weiteren Debatten waren es dann Philipp Melanchthon und Martin Bucer, die mit Bezug auf den weiteren Gebrauch des Kirchenguts durch die Obrigkeiten präzisierend und einschränkend eingriffen. Melanchthon betonte, dass der nach der Versorgung des Predigtamts übrigbleibende Rest nicht frei dem weltlichen Regiment zur Verfügung stehe, sondern zu »gemeinem Nutz« verwendet werden müsse.[27] Und Martin Bucer konkretisierte zeitgleich in seinem umfassenden Gutachten über die Kirchengüter:

»von dem veberigen erstlich die größere nodt der gar durfftigen vnnd dann aber auch verordnen zur notürfft gmeiner regierung, zu beschützung land vnnd leüt wider den Türcken, zuerhalten erliche geschlecht, zuuor die jenigen, von deren elteren den kirchenn etwas zukhommen ist«.[28]

Ein Beschluss des Bundes legte dann 1540 die Reihenfolge des Gebrauchs des eingezogenen Kirchenguts fest: Unterhaltung der Pfarrer, Prediger und Kirchendiener, Bestellung und Versehung der Schulen, Unterstützung der Armen, Unterhaltung und Aufrichtung von Spitälern und gemeinen Kästen.[29]

In der hier knapp skizzierten Debatte hat sich nun sichtlich die konkrete sächliche Zweckbindung des Kirchenguts aufgelöst. Die anstaltsförmige Vorstellung des Kirchenguts hat sich allerdings nicht gänzlich verflüchtigt. Die später noch juristisch heftig umstrittene evangelische Deutung der »eigentlichen« mit den kirchlichen Vermögensmassen und Sachmitteln verknüpften Intentionen der Kirchengutsstifter setzte nach wie vor der obrigkeitlichen Verfügungsgewalt über das Kirchengut Schranken. Diese durch und durch reformatorische Position konnte 1555 auch bean-

---

[26] Justus Jonas u.a., Iudicium Theologorum 24. Februar 1537 (in: CR 4,1040–1046 [Nr. 1532], hier: 1043).

[27] Philipp Melanchthon, Gutachten an den Rat Straßburgs vom 20. November 1538 (in: CR 3,608f. [Nr. 1752], hier: 609).

[28] MARTIN BUCER, Gutachten für den Schmalkaldischen Bund: Das Bedencken vonn Kirchengüterenn, zu Braunschweig den Stenden furgegeben 13. Juli 1538 (in: Schriften zu Kirchengütern und zum Basler Universitätsstreit [1538–1543], bearb. v. Stephen Buckwalter, Gütersloh 2007, Martin Bucers Deutsche Schriften 12, 25–78, hier: 57).

[29] KÖRBER, Kirchengüterfrage (s. Anm. 23), 181f.

502   *Christopher Voigt-Goy*

spruchen, reichsrechtlich gedeckt zu sein. Im Augsburger Reichsabschied desselben Jahres wurde in Artikel 19 ARF die bis 1552 geschehene Einziehung und Umwidmung des Kloster- und Kirchenguts zum Zweck der Kirchen-, Schul- und Armenversorgung sowie »andern sachen« anerkannt.[30] Zudem wurde in Artikel 21 ARF auch dem zukünftigen Gebrauch dieser Klöster- und Kirchengüter Grenzen gezogen:

»Und sollen dannocht von solchen obgenanten guettern die notturfftige ministeria der khirchen, pfarren und schuelen, auch die almuesen und hospitalia, die sy vormals bestellt und zu bestellen schuldig, von solchen obgemelten guettern, wie solche ministeria der khirchen und schuelen vormalen bestellt, auch nochmalen bestellt und versehen werden, ungeacht, wes religion die sein«.[31]

In der Forschung wird dieser Artikel 21 ARF vor allem als eine Beschränkung des sich ausbildenden *ius reformandi* des Landesherrn angeführt.[32] Das ist sicher richtig, und doch scheint das nur eine Seite der Bestimmung zu erfassen. Denn nicht minder folgenreich sicherte der Paragraph auch dem Kirchengut in reformatorischen Kontexten seinen verbliebenen anstaltskirchlichen Charakter. Das war durchaus ein Anliegen der Wittenberger Reformatoren. Damit war auch der Weg gewiesen, den die Kirchenordnungen des späteren 16. Jahrhunderts nahmen, als sie die im Einzelnen natürlich sehr unterschiedlichen Regelungen für den Umgang mit dem Kirchenvermögen und -gut ausgestalteten.

II.

»Mark well how many parsonages or vicarages are there in the realm, which at the least have a plow-land a-piece. Then note the lands of bishops, abbots, priors, nuns, knights of St John's, cathedral churches, colleges, chauntries, and free-chapels. For though the house fall in decay, and the ordinance of the founder be lost, yet will not they lose the lands. What cometh once in, may never more out«.[33]

Diese Klage über das unglaubliche Ausmaß und den ebenso unglaublich verrotteten Zustand des Kirchenguts in England führte William Tyndale in seiner Antwerpener Schrift *The Obedience of a Christen man, and how Christen rulers ought to govern* von 1528. Wahrscheinlich waren es Stellen wie diese, die Heinrich VIII. Anfang der 1530er Jahre angeblich über das

---

[30] Augsburger Reichsabschied vom 25. September 1555 (DRTA.JR, Bd. 20: Der Reichstag zu Augsburg 1555, Teilbd. 4, München 2009, 3103–3158 [Nr. 390], hier: 3110).
[31] A.a.O., 3111.
[32] Vgl. exemplarisch KRATSCH, Justiz (s. Anm. 17), 32 f.
[33] WILLIAM TYNDALE, The Obedience of a Christian Man, 1528 (in: DERS., Doctrinal treatises and introductions to different portions of the Holy Scriptures. Edited for the Parker Society by the Rev. Henry Walter, Cambridge 1848, 168–344, hier: 236).

Buch urteilen ließen: »This is a book for me and all kings to read«[34] – was freilich nichts daran änderte, dass Tyndale bald darauf auf Heinrichs Betreiben hin ermordet werden sollte. Obwohl Heinrich das Buch Tyndales gelesen hatte, bevor er beherzt auf das Kirchengut in seinem Land zugriff, ist ein Sachzusammenhang zwischen Lektüre und der eigentümlichen Einführung der Reformation durch Heinrich VIII. nicht herzustellen. Höchst wahrscheinlich hätte Tyndale auch gar kein Gefallen daran gefunden, wie Heinrich VIII. gegen das Klostergut vorging. Die wichtigsten legislativen Eckdaten sind hier nur kurz in Erinnerung zu rufen:[35]

Eine wichtige Vorbereitung der späteren Maßnahmen bildete schon der *Pluralities Act* von 1529. Mit ihm wurde nicht nur versucht, die Residenzpflicht der Bischöfe und Pfarrer einzuschärfen und das ausgreifende parochiale Vertretungswesen einzudämmen. Darüber hinaus verbot er – legitimatorisch auf den *Statute of Praemunire* von 1392 rekurrierend – jedem auf dem Gebiet der englischen Krone aus Rom »licenses, union, tolleracyon [or] dyspensacyon« zu erlangen und »benefices with cure« zu erhalten.[36] Damit waren zwei der wichtigsten Instrumente der Kurie, überhaupt so etwas wie eine zentralisierte Kirchenregierung auszuüben, ausgesetzt. Es folgten 1534 der berühmte *Act of Supremacy* und dann 1536 und 1539 die *Acts of Suppression* zuerst der kleineren und dann der größeren Klöster (*religious houses*). Dabei ist es bemerkenswert, wie in diesen *Acts* nicht nur der Besitz, sondern zugleich alle Rechtinstitute durch die Krone absorbiert werden, wie es der *Act* von 1536 zeigt:

»that his majesty shall have and enjoy to him and to his heirs for ever, all and singular such monasteries, priories, and other religious houses of monks, canons, and nuns, of what kinds or diversities of habits, rules, or orders soever they be called [...] manors, lands, tenements, rents, services, reversions, tithes, pensions, portions, churches, chapels, advowsons, patronages, rights, entries, conditions, and all other interests and hereditaments to the same monasteries, abbeys, and priories, or to any of them appertaining or belonging; to have and to hold all and singular the premises, with all their rights, profits, jurisdictions, and commodities«.[37]

Diese Absorption hatte in der auf die Auflösung folgende Phase der Neuverteilung des Besitzes in den folgenden Jahren, die den *Court of Augmentations* beschäftigte, zwei Folgen. Auf der einen Seite wurde die geistliche Jurisdiktion in den Diözesen im Bischofsamt gebündelt. Dies gewann

[34] DAVID DANIELL, William Tyndale. A Biography, New Haven 1994, 242.
[35] Vgl. mit weiterer Literatur: ETHAN H. SHAGAN, The Emergence of the Church of England, c. 1520–1553 (in: The Oxford History of Anglicanism, Bd. 1: Reformation and Identity, c. 1520–1662, hg. v. Anthony Milton, Oxford 2017, 28–44).
[36] 21 Hen VIII, c. 13, 1529 (in: [Great Britain], The statutes of the realm, 11 vols., n.p. 1810–1828, Bd. 3, 292–296, hier: 293).
[37] 27 Henry VIII, c. 28, 1536, (a.a.O., 575–578, hier: 575).

auch vorher den königlichen Maßnahmen und jedwedem reformatorischen Gedankengut feindselige Bischöfe, wie etwa John Longland of Lincoln für die *Church of England*.[38] Auf der anderen Seite jedoch fielen nun auch die vormals im Patronat oder der Inkorporation den Klöstern zugehörigen Pfarreien und Kirchen den meist niederadligen Neugroßgrundbesitzern zu.[39] Dies hieß freilich auch, dass die neuen Besitzer der Kirchen und Pfarreien deren Vermögensrechte wahrnahmen. Darunter bildete der Zehnteinzug die wichtigste Vermögensquelle.[40]

In seinem Kern blieb dabei das Zehntrecht in seiner kanonistischen Form unangetastet. Es war im 16. Jahrhundert nämlich schon längst Bestandteil der weltlichen Rechtsprechung geworden. Denn in England war es nach kanonistischem Rechtsverständnis gewohnheitsrechtlich zulässig, Zehntstreitigkeiten auch vor weltlichen Gerichten auszutragen. Festgehalten hat dieses Verständnis William Lyndwood[41] in seinem englisches und kanonisches Recht zusammenführenden Dekretalenkommentar *Provinciale*, der zuerst 1496 erschienen war und bis in das 18. Jahrhundert immer wieder gedruckt wurde. In der Glosse zu »Jure Patronatus« heißt es:

»licet causa Juris Patronatus sit annexa spiritualibus, et sic pertineat ad forum ecclesiasticum [...] Sed Consuetudo dat cognitionem Foro Temporali«.[42]

Unter Heinrich VIII. und dann Edward VI. wurde das Zehntrecht zwischen 1535 und 1549 allerdings durch ergänzende Gesetze novelliert. Drei Bestimmungen sind für den hiesigen Zusammenhang von besonderem Interesse: *Erstens* wurde nun Laien erlaubt, in ihrem eigenen Namen und aufgrund eigener Rechte in Zehntfällen zu prozessieren. *Zweitens* konnten wegen Zahlungsverzug bzw. -verweigerung Angeklagte nicht mehr auf ihren »leiblichen Eid« zur Wahrheitsbekräftigung zurückgreifen. Das bedeutete, dass ein Zehntvergehen einer gerichtlichen Untersuchung unterworfen wurde. *Drittens* konnte im Fall der Feststellung, dass Zehnte unrechtmäßig zurückgehalten wurden, der zweifache, unter bestimmten Bedingungen sogar dreifache Betrag zur Rückerstattung eingeklagt werden.[43]

---

[38] SHAGAN, The Emergence (s. Anm. 35), 38.

[39] LEO F. SOLT, Church and State in Early Modern England 1509–1640, Oxford u. New York 1990, 34.

[40] RICHARD H. HELMHOLZ, The Oxford History of the Laws of England, Bd. 1: The Canon Law and Ecclesiastical Jurisdiction from 597 to the 1640s, Oxford u. New York 2004, 443.

[41] Zu ihm: JOHN J. BAKER, Monuments of Endlesse Labour: English Canonists and Their Work, 1300–1900, London u. Rio Grande 1998, 43–56.

[42] Hier nach der Ausgabe WILLIAM LYNDWOOD, Provinciale, seu Constitvtiones Angliae, Oxford 1679, 316.

[43] RICHARD H. HELMHOLZ, Roman Canon Law in Reformation England, Cambridge 1990, 91 f.

Auf der Grundlage dieser Maßnahmen schwoll bis in das frühe 17. Jahrhundert hinein die Zahl der Zehntprozesse in England massiv an. Dadurch wurde der Konflikt um den »Zehnten« zu einem charakteristischen Thema der englischen Reformation des Kirchenguts.[44]

Nun läge die Annahme nahe, dass die von Heinrich VIII. initiierte Prozessdynamik den weltlichen Gerichten langfristig in die Hände spielen würde. Immerhin besaßen sie umfangreichere und unmittelbarer anwendbare Sanktionsinstrumente, was die Chancen erhöhte, die Rechtsansprüche durchzusetzen. Doch die Kirchengerichte verloren in dieser zentralen Kirchengutsfrage ihre Bedeutung gerade nicht, und Richard Helmholz hat überzeugend dargestellt, warum dies der Fall war: Grundsätzlich günstig waren nämlich die Kirchengerichte für Kläger, sowohl für Laien wie für Geistliche.[45] Das betraf vor allem die Fälle, in denen es um Klagen wegen Zehntverweigerung bzw. nicht ausreichend gezahltem Zehnten ging. Denn die Kirchengerichte hielten daran fest, dass der Zehnte *iure divino* gesetzt und daher »ein voller Zehnter der Art nach« abzuführen sei.[46] Jedwede Form der Ermäßigung dieses Zehnten musste gerichtsfest nachgewiesen werden und selbst Rechtscharakter haben. Dies machte Verteidigungen außerordentlich schwierig, die sich darauf beriefen, ihre Zehntpflicht gewohnheitsmäßig erledigt zu haben. Eine »Gewohnheit« nämlich in ihrem rechtsverpflichtenden und -bindenden Charakter nachzuweisen, war im kanonischen Prozessrecht schwierig, weil es dafür sachlich völlig einstimmiger Zeugenaussagen von mindestens zwei Zeugen bedurfte. Exemplarisch lässt sich das an einem Fall aus dem Jahr 1582 ablesen, in dem ein Pfarrer ein Gemeindeglied zur vollen Zehntpflicht verklagte. Das Gemeindeglied verteidigte sich zwar mit dem Hinweis darauf, dass seine geringeren Abgaben auf eine Abmachung mit dem Pfarrer von vor acht Jahren zurückgingen. Doch diese Abmachung war nicht schriftlich fixiert worden, und der vom Angeklagten beigebrachte Zeuge war sich in einigen Punkten unsicher. Daher wurde er zur dreifachen Rückerstattung des Zehnten verurteilt – plus Gerichtskosten.[47]

Auch in einer anderen ökonomischen Hinsicht war der gewohnheitsfeindliche Zug der Rechtsprechung der Kirchengerichte für Kläger attraktiv. Denn die strikte Handhabung des *Zehnten der Art nach* ermöglichte es ihnen, ihre Zehnteinkünfte dynamisch an die wirtschaftliche Entwicklung anzugleichen. So konnten etwa Erweiterungen eines Gartens – wie in ei-

---

[44] Zum Thema des Zehnten in England vgl. auch den Beitrag von Albrecht Beutel in diesem Band.

[45] HELMHOLZ, Roman Canon Law (s. Anm. 43), 91f.

[46] A.a.O., 95.

[47] A.a.O., 98.

nem Fall aus dem frühen 17. Jahrhundert – schnell zu einer Klage führen, die eine Erhöhung des Zehnten zum Ziel hatte. Das Gericht gab dem Kläger – in diesem Fall einem Pfarrer – Recht, da die bislang geltende Gewohnheit der Abführung eines Penny für den Garten durch den Ausbau des Garten verwirkt worden sei.[48] Neben solchen Anpassungen ermöglichte die Rechtsprechung der Kirchengerichte schließlich auch, die Abgaben in einem Zehntbezirk zu vereinheitlichen.

Für den hiesigen Zusammenhang ist an dieser Fortführung des kanonistischen Zehntrechts und seine stete strikte Restituierung durch die Kirchengerichte nun besonders bedeutsam, dass sich dadurch auch der anstaltskirchliche Charakter der *Church of England* postreformatorisch erhielt. Es dürfte nicht übertrieben sein zu urteilen, dass angesichts einer offiziell in der Frühen Neuzeit nie in Kraft gesetzten Kirchenordnung bzw. Kirchenverfassung der auf dem Kanonischen Recht aufbauenden Rechtspraxis in Fragen des Kirchenguts eine zentrale Stabilisierungsfunktion dieses Kirchentums in dieser Hinsicht zukam. Freilich: Ein eigenes reformatorisches Verständnis des Kirchenguts bedeutete das alles nicht. Daran sollte dann die *hotter sort of protestants* folgenschwer arbeiten.[49]

III.

Mit der *hotter sort of protestants* ist schon das Stichwort gefallen, das den Blick nach Schottland eröffnet. Hier ist aber eine ähnliche Dynamik, wie sie im Alten Reich und in England zu beobachten ist, nicht augenfällig.[50] Natürlich tritt die aus der reformatorischen Revolution hervorgehende *Kirk*, wie das *First Book of Discipline* (1560) zeigt, mit vehementen Forderungen für die Auflösung des bestehenden Kirchenguts ins Leben.[51] Doch diese Forderungen bleiben rechtlich erst einmal ebenso folgenlos, wie die im *Second Book of Discipline* (1578) gemäßigtere Forderung, dass die bestehenden Kirchengüter jedweder weltlicher Vereinnahmung entwunden und ihrem kirchlichen Zweck voll und ganz zugeführt werden sollen.[52] Insofern entsteht mit dem Nebeneinandertreten der presbyteri-

---

[48] A.a.O., 96f.

[49] Wegweisend: JOHN SELDEN, Historie of tithes, London 1618. Vgl. dazu GERALD J. TOMMER, Selden's »Historie of Tithes«: Genesis, Publication, Aftermath (in: Huntington Library Quarterly 65, 2002, 345–378).

[50] Vgl. die glänzende Studie von ALEC RYRIE, The origins of the Scottish Reformation, Manchester u. New York 2006.

[51] Vor allem im sechsten Artikel: The first and second booke of discipline. Together with some acts of the Generall Assemblies, clearing and confirming the same: and an Act of Parliament, [Amsterdam] 1621, 47–50.

[52] A.a.O., 83f.

alen und der bestehenden bischöflichen Kirchenorganisation in Schottland eine anhaltende Spannung, die zunächst keiner Auflösung zugeführt wurde. Hierfür könnte man womöglich den Begriff der »latenten Konfrontation« der schottischen Reformationsbewegung mit dem traditionellen Kirchengutsverständnis verwenden.

In den beiden anderen betrachteten Fällen war die Konfrontation nicht latent und hatte unterschiedliche Folgen. Im Kontext der Wittenberger Reformation und ihrer Kirchenbildung bildete sich dabei das Kirchengutsverständnis sowohl theologisch wie auch rechtlich um. Beides griff ineinander: Die evangelische Uminterpretation des ›eigentlichen‹ Zwecks des Kirchenguts, nämlich den ›Gottesdienst‹ zu fördern, ermöglichte rechtlich eine erweiterte Verwertung des überschüssigen Kirchenguts. Neben diesem Typ der ›reformatorischen Transformation‹ weist der englische Fall auf den Typ der ›reformatorischen Adaption‹ des traditionellen Kirchengutsverständnisses hin. Auffällig ist in der Rechtsprechung der englischen Kirchengerichte die maximale und durchaus rigide Weiterführung des tradierten kanonischen Rechts und seiner Normen. Dass dies ohne weiteres möglich war, zeigt *einerseits* die schon früher bestehende Eigenständigkeit und Dezentralität des kirchlichen Vermögensrechts auf. *Andererseits* deutet sich darin an, dass zumindest aus Sicht der Richter, aber auch der Kläger, das tradierte Recht in Fragen des Kirchenguts keiner Umbildung bedurfte. Es reichte das stillschweigende Ausscheiden derjenigen Materien, die als evangelisch unpassend empfunden wurden.

Beide Fälle machen zudem noch einmal darauf aufmerksam, dass die rechtlichen Faktoren in der reformatorischen Kirchenbildung in hohem Maß von den politischen Herrschaftssystemen geprägt waren, in denen diese Kirchenbildungen sich vollzogen. Allerdings ist das eben auch ein bilaterales Verhältnis, da die werdenden Reformationskirchen und ihre Vorstellungen nicht minder zu einem Teil der jeweiligen Rechtskulturen wurden, ob sie nun Eingang in das Reichsrecht fanden oder in Form der Konkurrenz die weitere Rechtsentwicklung voranbrachten. In beiden Fällen von, modern gesprochen, Deutschland und England ist ja auch gar nicht zu übersehen, dass der in der Reformationszeit erhaltene anstaltskirchliche Charakter des Kirchenguts weitreichende – und vielleicht auch gar nicht nur negative – Auswirkungen auf die späteren Entwicklungen hatte.

Tradition and Innovation:
Law

Christopher Voigt-Goy

Expressed with impressive erudition, the standard repertoire of the national Protestant ecclesiastical historiography of the late 19th century included describing the institutional formation of the Lutheran churches in the Reformation era as an imperfect expression of the »congregational principle«. Karl Rieker, a lawyer from Erlangen, historian of administrative and ecclesiastical law, was made to appear almost eccentric at that time, insofar as he had already denied the assumption that the »congregational principle« was the only consideration of decisive interest for the reformers and their church-building concerns.[1] Rather, according to Rieker, the development of the German Lutheran regional church continued the institutional ideas of the existing church organization in manifold and often fundamental ways and means. This thesis secured for Rieker the critical interest of Ernst Troeltsch (and a single-line rejection by Karl Holl), and made him a guarantor for Troeltsch's analysis of the continuity between »Altprotestantismus« (old Protestantism) and the Middle Ages in the field of church polity.[2]

Even apart from their significance for learned history, Rieker's considerations are still of interest if one reflects on the legal consolidation of the Reformation movements into churches in regard to the tension between tradition and innovation. For they draw attention to the fact that the incorporation of existing legal regulations in the Reformation churches did not represent an extraneous preservation of Catholic »survivals«, but rather enabled and promoted the institutional stabilization of the Reformation churches in their historically unique forms. One area in which this dynamic can be well grasped is the legal treatment of the church property

---

[1] KARL RIEKER, Die rechtliche Stellung der evangelischen Kirche Deutschlands in ihrer geschichtlichen Entwickelung bis zur Gegenwart, Tübingen 1907, 71–74.

[2] Cf. ERNST TROELTSCH, Protestantisches Christentum und Kirche in der Neuzeit (1906/1909/1922) (in: ERNST TROELTSCH, Kritische Gesamtausgabe, vol. 7, ed. Volker Drehsen in collaboration with Christian Albrecht, Berlin and New York 2004, 507; KARL HOLL, Luther und das landesherrliche Kirchenregiment (1911) (in: ID., Gesammelte Aufsätze zur Kirchengeschichte, vol. 1: Luther, Tübingen 1923, 326–380).

in the nascent Reformation churches. This is, of course, a broad area, since the term »beneficium«, with the help of which the medieval canonists sought to unify the legal system of church property law, was associated with many individual legal institutions, such as foundations, corporations and patronages, endowments for church maintenance and, of course, parishes.[3]

It is important for the following to note with Rieker that according to legal opinions based on both canon and common law, the »owners of the church property are *the various individual church institutions themselves gifted with legal personality*«, such as the foundations, incorporations, patronages, endowments for church maintenance and parochial churches.[4] Their legal personality is founded in their original purpose of establishment or in the original will of the founder, which is inalienably imprinted in the corresponding assets or goods. According to Rieker (and not only him), it is this primal and material circumstance that constituted the institutional character of medieval church organization. The legal entities were thus ecclesiastically purpose-bound complexes consisting of property or assets and particular rights attached to them. The right to use the church property for the supply of officials or the right to tithe at the same time obliged such institutions to ensure the earmarking of the church property. Correspondingly, according to canon law principles, it is an offence if the church property is either completely alienated from its ecclesiastical purpose or simply used for another ecclesiastical purpose. For in both cases the actual legal entity is usurped (infringing the principle that alienation is forbidden).[5]

In two short reflections it will be further shown how the Reformation churches expressed their institutional identities, both in adaptation of this traditional understanding of church property and in confrontation with it. First, there is a look at the developments in the German Empire in the Wittenberg Reformation's area of influence, followed by some observations on developments in England.

---

[3] Peter Landau, art. Beneficium (in: TRE 5, 1980, 577–583).

[4] Rieker, Die rechtliche Stellung (see note 1), 189 (original emphasis). My translation.

[5] Cf. Landau, art. Kirchengut (in: TRE 18, 1989, 560–575, esp. 568).

I.

It is not easy to determine the extent to which the church formation that began with the Wittenberg Reformation represented a fundamental confrontation with the traditional conception of church property. For already in the first conflicts over the parish appointments in Altenburg and Leisnig, in 1522 and 1523 respectively, one observes the increasingly negative stance of the former district vicar of the Augustinian Eremites, Martin Luther, towards the legal institution of incorporation.[6] However, this did not mean a fundamental rejection of the entire traditional understanding of church property by the reformer. In this context he nonetheless sketched a decisive basic line for the later church formation.

In both cases of conflict mentioned above, the communities of the parishes of the rural towns of Altenburg and Leisnig in Electoral Saxony, which were incorporated into nearby monasteries, campaigned to appoint evangelical preachers. The provost of the Bergerkloster and the abbot of the monastery of Buch, as holders of the incorporations of the parishes, resisted this pressure. As the invited expert in both cases, Luther first developed a proposal in the Altenburg case which did not explicitly address the legal questions of dealing with the existing church property and the legal institution of incorporation.[7] He advised the parish to remunerate the newly hired Protestant-minded parish priest via the city council using the parish funds. According to Luther, the council was entitled to this because the parish of the city had built the parish church.[8] In the end, however, Luther had nothing more to do with the solution of the conflict, because it came about through an electoral arbitration between the city council and the abbot. But this arbitration basically followed the direction that Luther already had in mind: the provost renounced the arbitrary filling of the position as well as the benefices of the parish[9], thus cutting the latter out of incorporation. This was quite permissible within the narrow limits of the alienation prohibition, since the parish benefice was an independent part of the incorporation.[10] On the other hand, the provost did not have to forego the other taxes from incorporation, which were

---

[6] Cf. KARL MÜLLER, Kirche, Gemeinde und Obrigkeit nach Luther, Tübingen 1910, 107–109.

[7] Cf. ibid., 103–110. In reference to this: ULRICH STUTZ, Miszelle (in: ZSRG.K 1, 1911, 309–313).

[8] KARL TRÜDINGER, Luthers Briefe und Gutachten an weltliche Obrigkeiten zur Durchführung der Reformation, Münster 1975, 58–59.

[9] WA.Br 2,538,4–5 (no. 496, city council of Altenburger to Luther, 22 May 1522).

[10] Cf. PETER LANDAU, Art. Inkorporation (in: TRE 16, 1987, 163–166, esp. 165).

connected with the remaining taxes and contributions in kind. In principle, the existing rights and ownership had been respected.

In the case of Leisnig, Luther then thoroughly destroyed the possibility
of finding a similar solution formulated within the framework of existing
law. The order of the common chest from 1523, Luther's *Ordenung eyns
gemeynen Kastens*, is instructive for the present context. It developed from
the aforementioned advisory opinions in the Leisnig case and quickly caused a furore when it was printed.[11] In this order, Luther suggested that
three things should be done: First, the previous owner of the incorporated
parish in Leisnig should be displaced. Secondly, all assets and income
related to the parish should be accumulated and brought together in a
»chest«. And thirdly, from this pool of assets the care for the office of the
parish pastor, the sacristy and the welfare of the poor should be guaran-
teed by elected representatives of those who contribute to this chest; also,
reserves should be set up for community emergencies and loans. With
these proposals Luther obviously recommended wide-ranging breaks with
the legal institution of monastic incorporation and violations of the prohibition of alienation. In addition, he also annulled the autonomy of the
parish benefice. However, Luther did not break with what was initially
described as the institutional character of church property. For the legal
personality, i.e. the instance carrying and guaranteeing the rights, remains
the same in Luther's construction of the »common chest«.[12] The cooperative administration of the chest and observance of the resulting rights
and obligations do not change this either, since neither the assets aggre-
gated in the chest nor the principles of their further accumulation and use
are subject to the ideas of cooperative law. This can also be looked at in
the following way: Luther's idea of the »common chest« is nothing less
than the proposal for the formation of a new concept of property law with
a specifically church-related character, which includes a prohibition of
alienation.

The elements of the chest order that broke the law were nevertheless so
obvious that it was refused electoral approval, although the Leisnig congregation wished to let it come into force. However, this did not diminish
its model character, especially for the administration of church property in

---

[11] WA 12,11–30. Cf. for the early orders CHRISTIAN PETERS, Der Armut und dem
Bettel wehren. Städtische Beutel- und Kastenordnungen von 1521 bis 1531 (in: Gute
Ordnung. Ordnungsmodelle und Ordnungsvorstellungen in der Reformationszeit, eds.
Irene Dingel and Armin Kohnle, Leipzig 2014, 239–255). Concerning the Leisnig case cf.
EIKE WOLGAST, Die Einführung der Reformation und das Schicksal der Klöster im
Reich und in Europa, Gütersloh 2014, 29–30.
[12] Cf. RIEKER, Die rechtliche Stellung (see note 1), 201.

the cities that transitioned to the Reformation.[13] Especially in the imperial cities, the chest orders were able to relate to the participation of the citizens or the council in the church administration, a custom already established in the Middle Ages, so that in practice they did not automatically have to lead to a Reformation-style break in the system of church property.[14] This systemic break, however, became all the clearer with the incipient abolition of monasteries or so-called »sequestrations« from the later 1520s onwards.[15] For the further development of the treatment of church property in the Reformation churches originating from the Wittenberg movement, considerations of imperial and territorial policy were equally determinative as the imperial law, which also had a decisive influence on the course of affairs.

The basis of legitimation, which the Imperial Recess of Speyer of 1526 represented for the implementation of reformatory measures[16], fragile in any case, was finally dissolved with the Augsburg Reichstag in 1530. There was a threat of a wave of legal actions before the Imperial Chamber Court for the illegitimate expropriation and alienation of church and monastic property[17], since not least Philip of Hesse had transferred the assets of the monasteries in his territory to his own treasury[18]. Though the Estates who had subscribed the *Protestation*, which had come together in the *Schmalkaldic League*[19], succeeded in delaying these processes, a solution to the question of church property became urgent for two reasons. First, while the Nuremberg »Standstill« agreement of 1532 held out the prospect that the Emperor would suspend the ongoing trials before the Imperial Chamber Court (Reichskammergericht)[20], the new League member Duke Ulrich of Württemberg began in 1534 to incorporate his considerable ecclesiastical benefices into his own household[21]. Secondly, within the Reformation

---

[13] Cf. PETERS, Der Armut (see note 11), 246–252.

[14] Cf. HANS ERICH FEINE, Kirchliche Rechtsgeschichte, vol. 1: Die Katholische Kirche, Weimar 1950, 343–352.

[15] Cf. HANS LEHNERT, Kirchengut und Reformation. Eine kirchenrechtsgeschichtliche Studie, Erlangen 1935, 54–57.

[16] Cf. for the consequences of the imperial diet of Speyer: ARMIN KOHNLE, Reichstag und Reformation. Kaiserliche und ständische Religionspolitik von den Anfängen der Causa Lutheri bis zum Nürnberger Religionsfrieden, Gütersloh 2001, 277–362.

[17] Cf. DIETRICH KRATSCH, Justiz – Religion – Politik. Das Reichskammergericht und die Klosterprozesse im ausgehenden sechzehnten Jahrhundert, Tübingen 1990, 26–29.

[18] Cf. WOLGAST, Die Einführung der Reformation (see note 11), 39–51.

[19] Cf. GABRIELE HAUG-MORITZ, Der Schmalkaldische Bund 1530–1541/42. Eine Studie zu den genossenschaftlichen Strukturelementen der politischen Ordnung des Heiligen Römischen Reiches Deutscher Nation, Leinfelden-Echterdingen 2002.

[20] KOHNLE, Reichstag (see note 16), 405.

[21] Cf. WOLGAST, Die Einführung der Reformation (see note 11), 103–112.

territories, the other, primarily noble owners of church property, above all patrons, had now also begun to assign the church property to their own uses.[22] In this tension-filled context of the Schmalkaldic League, a position on the question of church property came to be developed, which had important consequences.[23]

Its guidelines, in turn, go back to Martin Luther, who had been asked for an expert opinion at the end of 1531 in the context of the sequestrations in Electoral Saxony.[24] Fundamental to Luther's position was his denial that with the cessation of monastic life in a monastery, the ownership of the monastery's goods would fall to the Order or association of monasteries. Rather, according to Luther, the monastery and church property fell to the territorial lord due to a lack of heirs, analogous to a masterless estate (*bonum vacans*). However, the territorial lord did not have the free power of disposal over the property, as in the case of a *bonum vacans*: Luther argued »that one should be mindful of the founders' wills and opinions, which have always been, that such goods were given for the service and glory of God«. In Luther's view, the real abuse of the church property was thus the false worship, which linked church property to masses for the dead and suchlike. For Luther, on the other hand, the right worship takes place in »all good estates and jurisdictions«, albeit to a varying degree. Therefore, according to Luther, church property should first and foremost be used for »parish priests, preachers, schools and what belongs especially to God's word and sacrament and pastoral care«. When this has happened, the remainder could also go to the »worldly regiment (which also is worship, though the lesser compared to the former [spiritual activities])«.[25]

Following on from Luther's view, a collective statement of opinion – presumably drafted by Justus Jonas, Johannes Bugenhagen and Philip Melanchthon – was presented in the context of the Schmalkaldic League. It stated that: the authorities were

---

[22] Cf. for the »landständischen« sequestration in the Electorate of Saxony: UWE SCHIRMER, Landstände und Reformation. Das Beispiel Kursachsen (1523–1543) (in: Reformationen vor Ort. Christlicher Glaube und konfessionelle Kultur in Brandenburg und Sachsen im 16. Jahrhundert, eds. Enno Bünz et al., Berlin 2017, 55–77).

[23] A detailed account of the debates is KURT KÖRBER, Kirchengüterfrage und Schmalkaldischer Bund. Ein Beitrag zur deutschen Reformationsgeschichte, Leipzig 1913, 83–188. Cf. further KLAUS BESSEY, Das Kirchengut nach der Lehre der evangelischen Juristen Deutschlands im ersten Jahrhundert nach der Reformation, Diss. Masch. Tübingen 1968.

[24] Luther to Elector Johann (Anfang 1531): WA.Br 6,3–10 (no. 1766). Cf. TRÜDINGER, Luthers Briefe (see note 8), 64–65, 85–86.

[25] WA.Br 6,6. My translations.

»responsible for not alienating such goods from the churches, but of faithfully preserving them [...]. If something is left over, then the authorities themselves, as patrons, may also benefit from that surplus, while they have to protect and order such property«.[26]

In the course of the further debates it was Philip Melanchthon and Martin Bucer who intervened with regard to the subsequent use of the church property by the authorities in a precise and restrictive manner. Melanchthon stressed that the remainder remaining after the provision of the preaching office was not freely available to the secular regiment, but had to be used for »common good«.[27] And Martin Bucer at the same time specified in his comprehensive opinion on church property:

»of the rest, [it should be used] first of all for the greater need of those in poverty and then also for the order of the needs of the common government, to protect land and people against the Turks, to preserve honest families, above all those whose parents have given something to the churches«.[28]

In 1540, a decision of the League determined the order in which the confiscated church property was to be used: the priests, preachers and church servants were to be supplied, the schools were to be ordered and provided, the poor were to be supported, hospitals and common chests were to be maintained and erected.[29]

In the debate briefly sketched here the concrete material earmarking of the church property has now visibly broken down. However, the institutional conception of the church property has not completely evaporated. The Protestant interpretation of the »actual« intentions of the donors of church property tied to the church's assets and material means, which was later heavily disputed in legal proceedings, still imposed limits on the authorities' power to dispose the church property. In 1555, this thoroughly Reformation-oriented position could also claim to be covered by imperial law. In the *Augsburger Reichsabschied* of the same year, Article 19 of the Religious Peace of Augsburg acknowledged the confiscation and rededication of the monastery and church property that had taken place until 1552 for the purpose of providing for the church, school and poor as well

---

[26] Justus Jonas et al., Iudicium Theologorum 24. Februar 1537 (in: CR 4,1040–46 [no. 1532], here: 1043, my translation).

[27] Philip Melanchthon to the Strasbourg council, 20 November 1538 (in: CR 3,608–9 [no. 1752], here: 609).

[28] MARTIN BUCER, Gutachten für den Schmalkaldischen Bund: Das Bedencken vonn Kirchengüterenn, zu Braunschweig den Stenden furgegeben 13. Juli 1538 (in: Schriften zu Kirchengütern und zum Basler Universitätsstreit [1538–1543], ed. Stephen Buckwalter, Gütersloh 2007, Martin Bucers Deutsche Schriften 12, 25–78, here: 57). My translation.

[29] KÖRBER, Kirchengüterfrage (see note 23), 181–82.

as »other things«.[30] In addition, article 21 of the Religious Peace of Augsburg also limited the future use of these monastic and ecclesiastical properties:

»And so from the aforesaid resources [there shall be supported] the necessary ministries of the churches, parishes and schools, also the almshouses and hospitals, as they previously have been and should be supported, from such assigned resources, just as such ministries of churches and schools were formerly supported and should be supported and overseen in the future, regardless of which religion they may be.«[31]

In historical research this Article 21 has been interpreted as above all a limitation of the developing *ius reformandi* of the sovereign.[32] That is certainly true, and yet it seems to capture only one side of the issue. For no less momentously, the article also secured for the church property in the context of churches of the Reformation its remaining institutional character. That was definitely a concern of the Wittenberg reformers. This also pointed the way for the church ordinances of the later 16th century, when they developed the naturally very different detailed regulations for the handling of church assets and property.

II.

»Mark well how many parsonages or vicarages are there in the realm, which at the least have a plow-land a-piece. Then note the lands of bishops, abbots, priors, nuns, knights of St John's , cathedral churches, colleges, chauntries, and free-chapels. For though the house fall in decay, and the ordinance of the founder be lost, yet will not they lose the lands. What cometh once in, may never more out«.[33]

This complaint about the tremendous extent and the equally unbelievably rotten state of the church property in England was made by William Tyndale in his Antwerp writing *The Obedience of a Christen man, and how Christen rulers ought to govern* of 1528. It was probably passages like

---

[30] Augsburger Reichsabschied, 25 september 1555 (in: DRTA.JR, vol. 20: Der Reichstag zu Augsburg 1555, ed. Rosemarie Aulinger et al., vol. 4, Munich 2009, 3102–3158 [no. 390], here: 3110).

[31] Ibid., 3111: »Und sollen dannocht von solchen obgenanten guettern die notturfftige ministeria der khirchen, pfarren und schuelen, auch die almuesen und hospitalia, die sy vormals bestellt und zu bestellen schuldig, von solchen obgemelten guettern, wie solche ministeria der khirchen und schuelen vormalen bestellt, auch nochmalen bestellt und versehen werden, ungeacht, wes religion die sein«. Translation by Euan Cameron.

[32] See e.g. KRATSCH, Justiz (see note 17), 32–33.

[33] WILLIAM TYNDALE, The Obedience of a Christian Man (1528) (in: ID., Doctrinal treatises and introductions to different portions of the Holy Scriptures. Edited for the Parker Society by the Rev. Henry Walter, Cambridge 1848, 168–344, here: 236).

these that made Henry VIII in the early 1530s allegedly judge: »This is a book for me and all kings to read«[34] – which of course didn't change the fact that Tyndale was soon to be killed at Henry's instigation. Although Henry had read Tyndale's book before he boldly seized the church property in his country, there is no factual connection between reading it and Henry VIII's peculiar introduction of the Reformation. Most probably Tyndale would not have liked the way Henry VIII took action against the monastic property. The most important legislative data may be briefly recalled here:[35]

The *Pluralities Act* of 1529 already formed an important preparation for the later measures. It was not only an attempt to enforce the obligation of the bishops and priests to reside and to limit the extensive parochial substitutions. In addition, it – resorting to the *Statute of Praemunire* of 1392 for legitimation – forbade everyone on the territory of the English Crown to obtain from Rome »licenses, union, tolleracyon [or] dyspensacyon« and to receive »benefices with cure«.[36] Thus two of the curia's most important instruments to practice anything like a centralized church government were removed. This was followed in 1534 by the famous *Act of Supremacy* and then in 1536 and 1539 by the *Acts of Suppression* of the smaller and then the larger monasteries (»religious houses«). It is noteworthy how in these *Acts* not only the possession but also all legal institutions were absorbed by the Crown, as the *Act* of 1536 states:

»that his majesty shall have and enjoy to him and to his heirs for ever, all and singular such monasteries, priories, and other religious houses of monks, canons, and nuns, of what kinds or diversities of habits, rules, or orders soever they be called [...] manors, lands, tenements, rents, services, reversions, tithes, pensions, portions, churches, chapels, advowsons, patronages, rights, entries, conditions, and all other interests and hereditaments to the same monasteries, abbeys, and priories, or to any of them appertaining or belonging; to have and to hold all and singular the premises, with all their rights, profits, jurisdictions, and commodities«.[37]

This absorption had two consequences in the phase following the dissolution, the redistribution of the property in the following years, which occupied the Court of Augmentations. On the one hand, spiritual jurisdiction in the dioceses was concentrated in the episcopate through the abolition of institutions which had been exempt from episcopal oversight.

---

[34] Cf. DAVID DANIELL, William Tyndale. A Biography, New Haven 1994, 242.

[35] Cf. ETHAN H. SHAGAN, The Emergence of the Church of England, c. 1520–1553 (in: The Oxford History of Anglicanism, vol. 1: Reformation and Identity, c. 1520–1662, ed. Anthony Milton, Oxford 2017, 28–44).

[36] 21 Henry VIII, c. 13 (1529) (in: [Great Britain], The statutes of the realm, 11 vols., n.p. 1810–1828, vol. 3, 292–296, here: 293).

[37] 27 Henry VIII, c. 28 (1536) (ibid., 575–578, here: 575).

This also won over bishops who were formerly hostile to the royal measures and to the ideas of the Reformation, such as John Longland of Lincoln, for the Church of England.[38] On the other hand, however, the parishes and churches formerly belonging to the monasteries under the patronage or incorporation of the monasteries now fell to the new landowners, most of whom were of the lower nobility.[39] This also meant, of course, that the new owners of the churches and parishes exercised their property rights. Among them, the right to tithe was the most important source of wealth.[40]

At its core, the tithe in its canonical form remained untouched. In the 16th century it had long since become part of secular jurisprudence. For in England, according to the understanding of canon law, it was permissible under customary law also to settle tithe disputes before secular courts. William Lyndwood[41] enshrined this understanding in his collection of English provincial canons, *Provinciale*, which was first published in 1496 and was printed frequently into the 18th century. In the gloss to »Jure Patronatus« it states:

»licet causa Juris Patronatus sit annexa spiritualibus, et sic pertineat ad forum ecclesiasticum [...] Sed Consuetudo dat cognitionem Foro Temporali«.[42]

Under Henry VIII and then Edward VI, however, the law of tithe was amended between 1535 and 1549 by supplementary legislation. Three provisions are of particular interest for the present context: Firstly, laymen were now allowed to litigate in their own name and on the basis of their own rights in tithe cases. Secondly, defendants could no longer rely on their »corporal oath« to confirm the truth because of late payment or refusal to pay. This meant that a tithe offence was subject to a judicial investigation. Thirdly, in the case of a finding that tithes had been withheld unlawfully, a claim for reimbursement could be made for twice the amount, and under certain conditions even for three times the amount.[43]

---

[38] Cf. SHAGAN, The Emergence (see note 35), 38.

[39] Cf. LEO F. SOLT, Church and State in Early Modern England 1509–1640, Oxford and New York 1990, 34.

[40] RICHARD H. HELMHOLZ, The Oxford History of the Laws of England, vol. 1: The Canon Law and Ecclesiastical Jurisdiction from 597 to the 1640s, Oxford and New York 2004, 443.

[41] To him: JOHN J. BAKER, Monuments of Endlesse Labour: English Canonists and Their Work, 1300–1900, London and Rio Grande 1998, 43–56.

[42] »Although the case in law may be linked to spiritual [revenues] and thus belongs to the ecclesiastical court [...] custom assigns the secular court the cognizance of it.« I cite the edition: William Lyndwood, Provinciale, seu Constitvtiones Angliae, Oxoniae 1679, 316.

[43] RICHARD H. HELMHOLZ, Roman Canon Law in Reformation England, Cambridge 1990, 91–92.

On the basis of these measures, the number of tithing trials in England increased massively until the early 17th century. Thus the conflict over the tithe became a characteristic theme of the English Reformation of the church property.[44]

Now it would be reasonable to assume that the dynamics of litigation initiated by Henry VIII would play into the hands of the secular courts in the long run. After all, they possessed more extensive and directly applicable instruments of sanction, which improved the chances of winning legal claims. But the church courts did not lose their significance in this central question of church property, and Richard Helmholz convincingly explained why this was the case: In principle the church courts were favorable for plaintiffs, both for laymen and for clergymen.[45] This was particularly the case in cases of tithing refusals or insufficient tithing. For the church courts adhered to the fact that the tithe was set iure divino and therefore »a full tithe of the kind« was to be paid.[46] Any form of reduction of this tithe had to be supported by evidence in the courts and had to have legal character itself. This made it extraordinarily difficult to defend those who claimed to have done their tithe duty according to custom. To prove a »custom« in its legally obligatory and binding character was difficult in canon law procedure, because it required the factual unanimous testimony of at least two witnesses. An example of this can be seen in a case from the year 1582, in which a pastor sued a member of a parish to the full obligation of tithing. The parishioner defended himself by pointing out that his lower contributions were due to an agreement with the priest eight years ago. But this agreement had not been documented in writing, and the witness brought by the accused was uncertain on some points. The parishioner was therefore sentenced to three times the tithing fee – plus the costs of the trial.[47]

In another economic respect, too, the hostile attitude of the church courts' jurisdiction was attractive to plaintiffs. For the strict handling of the »tithe of the kind« enabled them to adjust their tithes dynamically to economic development. For example, extensions of a garden – as in a case from the early 17th century – could quickly lead to an appeal aimed at increasing the tithe. The court ruled in favour of the plaintiff – in this case a priest – because the custom of paying a penny for the garden had been forfeited by the extension of the garden.[48] In addition to such adjustments,

---

[44] For the theme of tithes and the consequences for Reformation theology in England cf. the essay of Albrecht Beutel.

[45] Helmholz, Roman Canon Law (see note 43), 91–92.

[46] Ibid., 95.

[47] Ibid., 98.

[48] Ibid., 96–97.

the jurisdiction of the church courts finally also made it possible to standardize taxes in a tithe district.

For the local context, this continuation of the canon law of tithe and its constant strict restitution by the church courts is now particularly significant in that it also preserved the institutional character of the post-reformation Church of England. It may not be exaggerated to judge that in view of the lack of an official church order or constitution in early modern times, the legal practice based on canon law in matters of ecclesiastical property had in this respect a central stabilizing effect on church polity. Admittedly, it did not mean a specifically reformed understanding of church property. The *hotter sort of Protestants* would then try to introduce such an understanding, with far-reaching consequences.[49]

III.

With the *hotter sort of Protestants*, one has the key word which introduces consideration of Scotland. Here, however, no such dynamic is visible as can be observed in the German Empire and England.[50] Of course, the Kirk which emerged from the revolution of the Reformation, as the *First Book of Discipline* (1560) shows, came into being with vehement demands for the dissolution of the existing church property.[51] But these demands remained for the time being just as unfulfilled in law as the more moderate demand in the *Second Book of Discipline* (1578) that the existing church property should be taken away from any secular occupation and fully used for its ecclesiastical purpose.[52] In this respect, the juxtaposition of the presbyterial and the existing episcopal church organization in Scotland created a lasting tension that was not immediately resolved. For this circumstance one could possibly use the term »latent confrontation« of the Scottish Reformation movement with the traditional understanding of church property.

In the other two cases considered, the confrontation was not latent and had different consequences. In the context of the Wittenberg Reformation

---

[49] Central is: JOHN SELDEN, Historie of tithes, London 1618. Cf. GERALD J. TOMMER, Selden's »Historie of Tithes«: Genesis, Publication, Aftermath, in: Huntington Library Quarterly 65 (2002), 345–378.

[50] Cf. the outstanding book of ALEC RYRIE, The origins of the Scottish Reformation, Manchester and New York 2006.

[51] Above all in the Sixth Article: The first and second booke of discipline. Together with some acts of the Generall Assemblies, clearing and confirming the same: and an Act of Parliament, [Amsterdam] 1621, 47–50.

[52] Ibid., 83–84.

and its church formation the understanding of church property changed in both theological and legal senses. Both intertwined: The Protestant reinterpretation of the »actual« purpose of the church property, namely to promote »divine worship« (Gottesdienst), made legally possible an extended utilization of church property's surplus. Compared with this type of »reforming transformation«, the English case points to the type of »reforming adaptation« of the traditional understanding of church property. In the jurisprudence of the English church courts one observes a maximal and decidedly rigid continuation of traditional canon law and its norms. That this was possible without further ado is shown on the one hand by the already pre-existing autonomy and decentralisation of church property law. On the other hand it indicates that at least from the point of view of the judges, but also of the plaintiffs, the traditional law in questions of church property did not need any transformation. It was sufficient to tacitly withdraw those matters that were felt to be inappropriate for Protestantism.

Both cases also draw attention once again to the fact that the legal factors in Reformation church formation were to a large extent influenced by the political systems of government in which these church formations took place. However, this is also a bilateral relationship, since the nascent Reformation Churches and their ideas no less became part of the respective legal cultures, whether they found their way into imperial law or advanced further legal development in the form of competition. When seen from a modern perspective, in both the cases of Germany and England it cannot be overlooked that the institutional character of the church property preserved in the Reformation period had far-reaching – and perhaps also not only negative – effects on later developments.

Radical Spirits and Their Experiences

Geoffrey Dipple

The title of my chapter begs the question: who were the radical spirits? This designation is, at the same time, strangely familiar yet oddly unfamiliar. It serves as a viable translation for a number of epithets Luther employed regularly against opponents (*Schwärmer*, *Schwarmgeister*, *Geistler*). However, Luther was unreserved in his use of these terms, levelling them against everyone from Thomas Müntzer and Andreas Karlstadt, to the Swiss Reformers, to the »papists«.[1] I have found no parallel use of this term among Luther's English contemporaries, and when it does appear in works on early modern English history, it does so as a generic term referring to no specific group.[2] This disparity is itself instructive and, as we will see, opens a window into assumptions that lie behind how we characterize the »radicals« of the Reformation era. In what follows, I will look at changing definitions of the terms »radical« and »spirit« and their significance for our understanding of the experiences of dissenters, particularly as Reformation movements became, or did not become, churches. My focus will be on the experiences of dissenters on the continent, although I will suggest some implications of those experiences for our understanding of events in the English context as well and look at their possible implications for how we understand radical spirits and their experiences in general.

1. Who Were the Radical Spirits?

Radicalism in the sixteenth century is not what it used to be. At one time, echoing George H. Williams, we could speak of a distinct Radical Refor-

---

[1] Volker Leppin, »Schwärmer«, *Theologische Realenzyklopädie* 23 (1994), 628; Amy Nelson Burnett, »Luther and the *Schwärmer*«, in *The Oxford Handbook of Martin Luther's Theology*, Robert Kolb, Irene Dingel, and L'ubomir Batka, eds. (Oxford: Oxford University Press, 2014), 511–24.

[2] Eg. Alex Cromartie, »The Persistence of Royalism«, in *The Oxford Handbook of the English Revolution* Michael J. Braddick, ed. (Oxford: Oxford University Press, 2015), 405.

mation, a European-wide counterpart to the »magisterial« Reformation, to which it was equal in scope and significance. Williams defined the criteria for inclusion in the Radical Reformation in primarily theological terms. Among the ideals shared by its adherents were: the restitution of the apostolic church, the separation of church and state, a commitment to missions, an emphasis on sanctification rather than strict espousal of the doctrine of salvation by faith alone, an emphasis on the freedom of the will, a strong eschatology, and a belief in the sleep of the soul until the Resurrection.[3] While Williams asserted that the Radical Reformation spanned the continent, he devoted little attention to radicals in the English context during the sixteenth century. Nonetheless, he followed the earlier work of Roland Bainton in describing the religious explosions of the mid-seventeenth century as a reprise of the continental Radical Reformation, which in turn laid the groundwork for the religious pluralism of the Anglo-American world.[4]

At the same time, historical writing on the English Reformation has traditionally left as a mystery how the radicalism of the early Reformation on the continent was transmitted to England in the following century. In contrast to its continental counterpart, the English Reformation has often been characterized as decidedly »unradical«.[5] Insofar as radicalism has appeared in discussions of the English Reformation, it has often been treated as synonymous with Anabaptism.[6] The most thorough treatment of this phenomenon remains I.B. Horst's study of »anabaptism« in the early years of the English Reformation – his use of the lower case for the initial vowel of the term was intentional to distinguish the English variety from its continental counterpart. Horst took seriously claims by contemporary

---

[3] George H. Williams, *The Radical Reformation*, 3rd ed. (Kirksville, MO: Sixteenth Century Journal Publishers, 1992).

[4] George H. Williams and Angel M. Mergal, eds., *Spiritual and Anabaptist Writers: Documents Illustrative of the Radical Reformation* (Philadelphia: Westminster Press, 1957), 24; Williams, *Radical Reformation* (see note 3), xxxvi; idem, »Radical Reformation«, in *The Oxford Encyclopedia of the Reformation*, Hans J. Hillerbrand, ed. (Oxford: Oxford University Press, 2005) DOI: 10.1093/acref/9780195064933.001.0001; Roland Bainton, »The Left Wing of the Reformation«, *The Journal of Religion* 21 (1941), 134. More recently, Brad Gregory has maintained this connection, »The Radical Reformation«, in *The Oxford Illustrated History of the Reformation*, Peter Marshall, ed. (Oxford: Oxford University Press, 2015), 146–51.

[5] See, for example, Roland Bainton, *The Reformation of the Sixteenth Century* (Boston: The Beacon Press, 1952), 183; A. G. Dickens, *The English Reformation*, 2nd ed. (University Park, PA: Penn State University Press, 1989), 204–05.

[6] Susan Royal, »Religious Radicalism in ›Magisterial‹ England«, in *Radicalism and Dissent in the World of Protestant Reform*, Bridget Heal and Anorthe Kremers, eds. (Göttingen: Vandenhoeck & Ruprecht, 2017), 85–87; Alec Ryrie, »Scritpure, the Spirit, and the meaning of Radicalism in the English Reformation«, in ibid., 100.

English authorities and polemicists that anabaptists lurked around every corner and behind every hedgerow and argued that anabaptism was the dominant form of religious dissent in England between the end of Lollardy and the beginning of Puritanism. Like Lollardy and Puritanism, anabaptism was initially a pejorative term applied to the anabaptists by their opponents, but, nonetheless, it was more than just the application of a new name to an old heresy. Some of its key teachings were imported from the continent, especially from the Melchiorite Anabaptism of the Netherlands, but were integrated with native traditions and practices of dissent. The result was an anabaptism that did not necessarily involve separation from the dominant church or ungodly society and anabaptists who did not necessarily practice adult baptism.[7] Horst's book met with mixed reviews when it was published and has since been largely dismissed. A consistent criticism of it has been its identifying as anabaptists dissenters who did not act like continental Anabaptists – in particular, they were not sectarians, as Anabaptists should be according to most accounts.[8]

Since then, however, new understandings of radicalism on the continent have challenged Williams' definition of, and approach to, radicals and radicalism in the Reformation from several perspectives, with potentially significant implications for comparing their experiences on the continent and in England. Scholars have questioned the extent to which all »radicals« shared the ideas he identified as radical theology and used as criteria for inclusion in the Radical Reformation. In the place of Williams' theological criteria, Adolf Laube proposed more social and political markers and Hans-Jürgen Goertz historical-cultural criteria. By these criteria, radicals were defined by their desire and attempts to change significantly contemporary ecclesiastical, political, and social institutions and practices. Initially these revisions may have reinforced the distinctiveness of the English experience, as with Laube's insistence that the social and political context of the Reformation in its birthplace, the Holy Roman Empire, distinguished it from »reformations« elsewhere.[9] However, other challenges to

---

[7] Irvin B. Horst, *The Radical Brethren: Anabaptism and the English Reformation to 1558* (Nieuwkoop: B. De Graaf, 1972).

[8] Horst's critics are legion among historians of the English Reformation, see, for example, David Loades, »Anabaptism and English Sectarianism in the Mid-Sixteenth Century«, in *Reform and Reformation: England and the Continent c. 1500–1750*, Derek Baker, ed. (Oxford: Basil Blackwell, 1979), 59–70; John Coffey, »‹The Last and Greatest Triumph of the European Radical Reformation›? Anabaptism, Spiritualism, and Anti-Trinitarianism in the English Revolution«, in Heal and Kremers, eds., *Radicalism and Dissent* (see note 6), 201–24.

[9] Adolf Laube, »Radicalism as a Research Problem in the Early History of the Reformation«, in *Radical Tendencies in the Reformation: Divergent Perspectives*, Hans

some of the basic assumptions about how we approach radicalism have reestablished the broader applicability of the label »radical« to the Reformation in different lands. For example, scholars have challenged the contention that there is a clear connection between social, political, and cultural radicalism and specific theological positions.[10] In addition, and this is largely a consequence of the preceding, there has been recognition that radicalism was situational. An individual, action, or idea could be radical at one time or in one place but not in another. Thomas Kaufmann has observed that definitions of radicalism were created in debates of the early 1520s by a process of social and theological distinction and differentiation.[11] One might add that the process did not end in the early 1520s but continued throughout the years of the Reformation. Alec Ryrie has taken this thinking to its logical conclusion, observing that »the supposedly sharp magisterial/radical division tends to dissolve into ambiguity when examined closely, in England as everywhere else«.[12]

However, the most recent, and possibly most devastating, challenge to traditional notions of the Radical Reformation and Reformation radicalism has been the awareness that radicals did not choose to be »radical«. In almost all cases, others, most often their opponents, defined and identified the radicals of the Reformation era. This procedure goes all the way back to Luther's early polemics and was fundamentally self-serving: it was usually part of a campaign to establish and defend the orthodoxy of those making the charges. The boundaries between radical and magisterial Reformers were, as a result, often porous and arbitrary. The failure to recognize this fact has led to what Michael Driedger has dubbed »caged thinking« in which early modern polemics against »radicals« have defined the categories for how they are treated in modern scholarship.[13]

Hillerbrand, ed. (Kirksville, MO: Sixteenth Century Journal Publishers, 1988): 9–23; Hans-Jürgen Goertz, ed. *Profiles of Radical Reformers: Biographical Sketches from Thomas Müntzer to Paracelsus* (Kitchener, Ont. and Scottdale, PA: Herald Press, 1982), 9–25; idem, *Pfaffenhass und groß Geschrei. Die reformatorischen Bewegungen in Deutschland (1517–1529)* (Munich: C. H. Beck, 1987); idem, »Die Radikalität reformatorischer Bewegungen: Plädoyer für ein kulturgeschichtliches Konzept«, in *Radikalität und Dissent im 16. Jahrhundert/Radicalism and Dissent in the Sixteenth Century*, Hans-Jürgen Goertz and James M. Stayer, eds. (Berlin: Duncker & Humblot, 2002): 29–41.

[10] Brad Gregory, »Reforming the Reformation: God's Truth and the Exercise of Power«, in *Reforming Reformation*, Thomas Mayer, ed. (Farnham: Ashgate, 2012), 34.

[11] Thomas Kaufmann, »Radical Political Thought in the Reformation Era«, in Heal and Kremers, eds. *Radicalism and Dissent* (see note 6), 27.

[12] Alec Ryrie, »Scripture, the Spirit and the meaning of Radicalism in the English Revolution«, in Heal and Kremers, eds. *Radicalism and Dissent* (see note 6), 101.

[13] Ibid., 100; idem, »›Protestantism‹ as a Historical Category«, *Transactions of the Royal Historical Society* 26 (2016), 68–70; Michael Driedger, »Against ›the Radical Reformation‹: On the Continuity between Early Modern Heresy-Making and Modern Historiography«, in Heal and Kremers, eds. *Radicalism and Dissent* (see note 6), 159–61.

The term ›spirits‹ is no less problematic. As my opening comments suggest, it, too, goes back to Luther's early polemics. However, in the scholarship of the continental Reformation reference to radical spirits likely calls to mind Spiritualists like Sebastian Franck and Caspar Schwenckfeld. Initially identified by Alfred Hegler, the Spiritualist typology was more clearly defined by Ernst Troeltsch and others. In Williams' conception, the Spiritualists joined Anabaptists and Evangelical Rationalists as the chief branches of the Radical Reformation, and in most accounts of these phenomena, mystically-inspired and highly individualistic Spiritualists were usually thought to have resided at the opposite end of the Radical Reformation spectrum from the sectarian, Biblicist Anabaptists.[14] Despite the attempts especially of Williams to delineate detailed and distinct Spiritualist types, the term has remained slippery and difficult to nail down. Particularly challenging has been Walter Klaassen's rejection of the division of Reformation radicals into distinct Spiritualist and Anabaptist types, describing spiritualization instead as a tendency that pervaded the entire non-Lutheran Reformation and influenced even Luther himself in the early years of the revolt against Rome. One can speak, then, of degrees of spiritualization across the Reformation.[15] Klaassen's critique has born fruit most notably in subsequent research into Anabaptism which has highlighted the extent to which Spiritualist elements permeated different Anabaptist traditions.[16]

Recently matters have become more complicated and possibly more confusing. Emmet McLaughlin has taken Klaassen's critique of the typologies of the Radical Reformation one step further, not only fundamentally redefining the criteria for judging degrees of Spiritualism, but also including all Reformers among those who spiritualized Christianity as a continuation of a general trend in the later Middle Ages. Those labelled Spiritualists by his predecessors, McLaughlin prefers to call »Radical Spiritualists«, hence bringing us closer to our own term radical spirits.[17] But

---

[14] Alfred Hegler, *Geist und Schrift bei Sebastian Franck: eine Studie zur Geschichte des Spiritualismus in der Reformationszeit* (Freiburg i Br: J. C. B. Mohr, 1892); Ernst Troeltsch, *The Social Teachings of the Christian Churches*, 2 vols. Olive Wyon, trans. (London: George Allen and Unwin, 1931), 1: 328–82, 2: 691–807; Williams and Mergal, eds. *Spiritual and Anabaptist Writers* (see note 4), 19–23; Williams, *Radical Reformation* (see note 3), xxviii–xxxvi; Heinold Fast, *Der linke Flügel der Reformation* (Bremen: Karl Schünemann Verlag, 1962).

[15] Walter Klaassen, »Spiritualization in the Reformation«, *Mennonite Quarterly Review* 37 (1963): 67–77.

[16] For a summary of this literature, see Geoffrey Dipple, »The Spiritualist Anabaptists«, in John D. Roth and James M. Stayer, eds., *A Companion to Anabaptism and Spiritualism, 1521–1700* (Leiden: Brill, 2006), 257–97.

[17] R. Emmet McLaughlin, »Reformation Spiritualism: Typology, Sources, and Si-

here, too, the situational nature of radicalism applies. For example, on the question of the relationship between the Holy Spirit and Scripture as sources of religious truth, which lay at the heart of Alfred Hegler's original definition of the term »Spiritualist«, recent studies into radical hermeneutics in the seventeenth century have identified at most subtle differences between radical and magisterial approaches.[18] When speaking of »radical spirits«, then, we are characterizing people on two related but distinct sliding scales, where the criteria are contextual and identification is determined largely by others.

Such changes in the understandings of radicalism and Spiritualism on the continent have made some inroads into historical writing on the English Reformation. Scholars have begun to clarify the social and political roots encouraging its distinct characteristics.[19] Furthermore, calls to treat radicalism as a situational rather than an essential category have led to greater recognition of its place in the English Reformation. The results, interestingly, have tended to highlight even more the distinctiveness of the English experience, in which, more than on the continent, the radical critique of the Reformation remained a part of emerging Protestantism rather than being pushed into open opposition to it.[20] However, other aspects of newer scholarship on Reformation radicalism on the continent have not made their way into the scholarship on its English variation. First, in some cases at least, the old, sharp lines between sectarian Anabaptism and individualist Spiritualism persist.[21] As well, the focus on radical thoughts and

---

gnificance«, in Goertz and Stayer, eds. *Radikalität und Dissent* (see note 9), 127–40; idem, »Luther, Spiritualism, and the Spirit«, in *Piety and Family in Early Modern Europe. Essays in Honour of Steven Ozment*, Marc R. Forster and Benjamin J. Kaplan, eds. (Aldershot: Ashgate, 2005), 28–49; idem, »Spiritualism: Schwenckfeld and Franck and Their Early Modern Resonances«, in Roth and Stayer, eds., *Companion to Anabaptism and Spiritualism* (see note 16), 119–61.

[18] Mirjam G. K. van Veen, »Spiritualism in the Netherlands: From David Joris to Dirck Volckertz Coornhert«, *Sixteenth Century Journal* 33 (2002), 129–50; Gary Waite, »The Drama of the Two-Word Debate among Liberal Dutch Mennonites, c. 1620–1660: Preparing the Way for Baruch Spinoza?« in Heal and Kremers, eds., *Radicalism and Dissent* (see note 6), 118–35; Ryrie, »Scripture, the Spirit, and the meaning of Radicalism« (see note 6), 100–17.

[19] See, for example, Ethan Shagan, »Clement Armstrong and the Godly Commonwealth: Radical Religion in Early Tudor England«, in *The Beginnings of English Protestantism*, Peter Marshall and Alec Ryrie, eds. (Cambridge: Cambridge University Press, 2002), 80–81; idem, »Radical Charity in the English Reformation«, in Heal and Kremers, eds. *Radicalism and Dissent* (see note 6), 71.

[20] Karl Gunther, *Reformation Unbound: Radical Visions of Reform in England, 1525–1590* (Cambridge: Cambridge University Press, 2014), 5, provides a valuable overview of this revision in the understanding of Anglicanism.

[21] Eg. John Coffey, »›The Last and Greatest Triumph of the European Radical Reformation‹?« (see note 8), 201–24.

practices among those who remained within the Protestant fold tends to circumvent the extent to which radicals were identified as such by their opponents. But probably most importantly, scholarship on radicalism in the English Reformation continues to focus its attention on the practices and beliefs of individuals with sufficient prominence to leave a significant paper trail and to be accounted influential within their respective movements, and it ignores exciting new attempts to capture details about the lives of rank and file dissenters from sources that may provide a more descriptive and less prescriptive account than has been the case in the past.[22] The application of such an approach to the English experience is, I believe, especially valuable as we witness the transition from reforming movements to reforming churches within both the »magisterial« and »radical« traditions.

2. Radical Spirits and the Formation of Churches

I agree with Professor Kaufmann that radicalism (and I would add Spiritualism or Spiritism) are categories created in the debates of the early 1520s. According to accepted accounts of the early years of the continental Reformation, radicalism began as loosely defined traditions of dissent which interacted with each other in a variety of ways and places. Gradually, especially in the late 1520s and early 1530s, they began to develop into distinct, more clearly defined movements. In this discussion I want to look at how those categories were recreated and redefined as the Reformation progressed into the confessional age. As recent research suggests, this redefinition was in many ways the work of people other than the radicals. However, as Kat Hill has argued, we need also to pay attention to how radicals sought to name themselves, whether they accepted the names they were given, and how they defined themselves in relation to other groups.[23] This involves investigation, then, not only of the interaction be-

---

[22] Eg. Caroline Gritschke, »*Via Media*«: *Spiritualistische Lebenswelten und Konfessionalisierung. Das süddeutsche Schwenkfeldertum im 16. und 17. Jahrhundert* (Berlin: Akademie Verlag, 2006); Anselm Schubert, Astrid von Schlachta, and Michael Driedger, eds. *Grenzen des Täufertums – Boundaries of Anabaptism: Neue Forschungen* (Gütersloh: Gütersloher Verlagshaus, 2009); Päivi Räisänen, *Ketzer im Dorf: Visitationsverfahren, Täuferbekämpfung und lokale Handlungsmuster im frühneuzeitlichen Württemberg* (Constance: UVK Verlagsgesellschaft, 2011); Kat Hill, *Baptism, Brotherhood, and Belief in Reformation Germany: Anabaptism and Lutheranism, 1525–1585* (Oxford: Oxford University Press, 2015).

[23] Kat Hill, »The Power of Names: Radical Identities in the Reformation Era«, in Heal and Kremers, eds. *Radicalism and Dissent* (see note 6), 57.

tween authorities and magisterial reformers on one side and radicals on the
other, but also of how the radicals interacted with each other in response
to external pressures.

The transition of radical movements into churches has frequently been
cast as the end of the Radical Reformation. George Williams identified this
process with a series of events in the years 1578 and 1579, by which the
radicals accommodated themselves to, and reconciled themselves with, the
broader Reformation.[24] James Stayer treats this as a more complicated
process. He suggests that by the late 1530s the movements which comprised the Radical Reformation had lost their »utopian impulse« to change
society as a whole, and hence their radicalism, but that their acceptance
into society was delayed until the 1560s for the Hutterites in Moravia and
the 1570s for the Mennonites in the Low Countries.[25] In the case of the
latter process, he draws on the work of Hans-Jürgen Goertz and subsequently Michael Driedger which describes how the initial anticlericalism
of the radicals was gradually internalized and led them to police their own
communities in a process similar to that of confessionalization in the
mainstream churches, resulting in the establishment of what Goertz and
Driedger refer to as »conforming nonconformity«. More recent work by
Astrid von Schlachta and Andrea Chudaska reveals the extent to which
similar activities appeared among the Hutterites.[26]

While valuable for understanding the subsequent history of the Mennonites and Hutterites, this focus on what I would label the »successful«
dissenter traditions has, I fear, given us a lop-sided view of the religious
dissent in the Holy Roman Empire and elsewhere on the continent in the
sixteenth and seventeenth centuries. In the place of caged thinking which
approaches the history of early modern dissenters from the perspective of

---

[24] Williams, »Radical Reformation« (see note 4).

[25] James Stayer, »The Passing of the Radical Moment in the Radical Reformation«,
Mennonite Quarterly Review 71 (1997), 148–52.

[26] Goertz, »Kleruskritik, Kirchenzucht und Sozialdiziplinierung in den täuferischen
Bewegungen der frühen Neuzeit«, in *Kirchenzucht und Sozialdiziplinierung in frühneuzeitlichen Europa*, Heinz Schilling, ed. (Berlin: Duncker & Humblot, 1994), 183–98;
idem, »Zucht und Ordnung in nonkonformistischer Manier«, in *Antiklerikalismus und
Reformation: Sozialgeschichtliche Untersuchungen* (Göttingen: Vandenhoeck & Ruprecht, 1995), 103–14; Michael Driedger, *Obedient Heretics: Mennonite Identities in
Lutheran Hamburg and Altona During the Confessional Age* (Aldershot: Ashgate,
2002), 75–106; Andrea Chudaska, *Peter Riedemann: Konfessionbildendes Täufertum im
16. Jahrhundert* (Heidelberg: Gütersloher Verlagshaus, 2003); Astrid von Schlachta,
*Hutterische Konfession und Tradition (1578–1619): Etabliertes Leben zwischen Ordnung
und Ambivalenz* (Mainz: von Zabern, 2003). On Mennonite confessionalism, cf. Karl
Koop, *Anabaptist-Mennonite Confessions of Faith: The Development of a Tradition*
(Kitchener, Ont: Pandora Press, 2004).

magisterial polemics against them, it provides a history from the perspective of some dissenter apologetics, which sounds suspiciously like a Biblical narrative of suffering through years of persecution in the wilderness until the faithful are delivered into the promised land.

3. Reconsidering Dissent in the Confessional Age

Recent research into religious dissent in the Duchy of Württemberg during the Reformation and confessional age provides an interesting alternative to the usual narrative derived from events in the Netherlands and Moravia.[27] There are several reasons to focus on this region. First, there were in the duchy several dissenting traditions, most notably not only different strands of Anabaptism, but also a vibrant Schwenckfelder movement. Second, early on the duchy's rulers developed a clearly defined and articulated church order that became a model for church reform in several other territories.[28] This established fairly consistent definitions of religious dissent and policies for dealing with it. However, despite this level of organization, Württemberg's treatment of religious dissenters was relatively mild, as is especially evident in its reluctance to execute Anabaptists. As a result, it represents an important middle ground in the treatment of dissenters, especially Anabaptists, between the relative toleration they ultimately experienced in the Netherlands and Moravia and the continued harsh persecution in Swiss territories like Zurich, Berne, and Basel. Consequently, it provides us with a different perspective on the dynamics of interactions between authorities and dissenters than those observed in the better known cases of Mennonites, Hutterites, and the Swiss Brethren.

Anabaptism arrived in Württemberg from the neighbouring imperial cities, especially Horb, Rottenburg, and Esslingen, where the prominent Swiss Anabaptists Wilhelm Reublin and Michael Sattler were active in 1526 and 1527. In time, the activities of Hutterite missionaries supplemented the influences from Swiss Anabaptism, although, as we will see, Anabaptism in Württemberg took on contours of its own. In 1529, Casper Schwenckfeld left his home in Silesia for voluntary exile in southern Germany. After 1539 he spent a significant amount of time in Württemberg, especially on an estate of the powerful noble Ludwig von Freyberg. As a

---

[27] For example, see Gritschke, »*Via Media*« (see note 22); Räisänen, *Ketzer im Dorf* (see note 22).

[28] See James Estes, trans. and ed. *Godly Magistrates and Church Order: Johannes Brenz and the Establishment of the Lutheran Territorial Church in Germany 1524–1559* (Toronto: Centre for Reformation and Renaissance Studies, 2001), 22.

result, he was able to develop a significant following in the region, particularly among the politically influential in the cities and the nobility in the countryside. Schwenckfeldianism has traditionally been regarded as a thinking man's dissent in contrast to more popular Anabaptism. Especially after news became current of the Anabaptist takeover of the city of Münster in 1534 and 1535 and of communitarian experiments by Anabaptists in Moravia, it allowed dissent against the increasingly restrictive state churches without the social and political radicalism associated with Anabaptism.[29]

The 1527 execution of the Anabaptist leader Michael Sattler in Rottenberg is indicative of the initial repression of religious dissent in southern Germany. Matters were no different within the Duchy of Württemberg, which was under Habsburg administration when the Reformation arrived. Its approach to Anabaptism, derived from the imperial mandates of 1528 and 1529, prescribed the death penalty for Anabaptist leaders and preachers along with the obstinate and those who relapsed. However, those accused of Anabaptism who were willing to recant as well as fellow travelers of the movement were to be shown mercy.[30]

In 1534 Duke Ulrich of Württemberg regained control of the duchy. His reign laid the foundations for a dissenter policy that was both comprehensive and relatively consistent for the rest of the century and into the next. In June 1534, even before he had possession of his lands, he issued an order for the detention of Anabaptists.[31] The following year he devoted considerable attention to the matter, culminating in an Anabaptist Ordinance in June. This was then supplemented by a second Anabaptist Ordinance, inspired at least in part by the events in Münster and news from Moravia.[32] Ulrich's successor, Duke Christoph, is said to have been consumed by his desire to fight sectarianism.[33] Christoph dedicated a major Visitation Order (1553), two mandates (1554 and 1558) and two sets of instructions (1557 and 1559) to the problem of Anabaptists and other

---

[29] John Oyer, »Nicodemites among Württemberg Anabaptists«, *Mennonite Quarterly Review* 71 (1997), 513; idem., »Anabaptists in Esslingen: A Viable Congregation under Periodic Siege«, in »*The Harry the Good People out of the Land*«: *Essays on the Persecution, Survival, and Flourishing of Anabaptists and Mennonites* (Goshen: Mennonite Historical Society, 2000), 195.

[30] Gustav Bossert, ed. *Quellen zur Geschichte der Täufer*, vol. 1: *Herzogtum Württemberg* (Leipzig: M. Heinsius Nachfolger Eger & Sievers, 1930), 1: 1*–5*, 1–4.

[31] Ibid., 36–37.

[32] Ibid., 57–60.

[33] James Estes, *Christian Magistrate and Territorial Church: Johannes Brenz and the German Reformation* (Toronto: Centre for Reformation and Renaissance Studies, 2007), 208.

dissenters. The mandate of 1558 was incorporated into the Great Church Order of 1559, which established the Lutheran state church in the duchy. Christoph's concerns continued during the reign of his successor, Duke Ludwig. In 1571 he issued new instructions for dealing with dissenters which were revised in 1584. Subsequent dukes, Friedrich and Johann Friedrich, largely continued the policies of their predecessors. It is usually thought that by the end of Johann Friedrich's reign in 1628 ducal policy finally succeeded when Anabaptism and Schwenckfeldianism had largely died out in the duchy.[34]

There are several noteworthy features about the policies of the Württemberg dukes toward religious dissenters. The first is their relative tolerance. After the departure of the Habsburg authorities, Württemberg is said to have been one of the most tolerant places for dissenters in the empire. By the terms of the Peace of Kaaden, according to which Ulrich regained his duchy, the duke was required to pursue »sectarians« within his lands.[35] Nonetheless, while he retained the death penalty as a possible threat, especially against leaders, preachers, and relapsed dissenters, the focus of his efforts was more on banishment of those hardened in their beliefs and instruction for those willing to recant. And in practice, punishments for all dissenters were milder than those stipulated in the duke's instructions. Not surprisingly, Duke Christoph's zeal to end the »sectarian« presence in the duchy led to consideration of stricter punishments.[36] In general, his policies sharpened the distinction between the leaders of the sects, who deserved more serious punishment, and the simple and misled who deserved mercy and for whom instruction in true doctrine was the remedy. Likely this reflected the influence of Johannes Brenz whom Christoph called to Stuttgart and who is usually seen as responsible for much of the Great Church Order. There is little change observable among subsequent dukes under whom, as under Christoph, punishments actually meted out were milder than those on the books.

A second noteworthy feature of this policy is that while it does deal extensively with Anabaptism, that focus is only part of a broader concern with dangerous sects in general. By the Peace of Kaaden, Duke Ulrich committed himself to pursuing Sacramentarians (Zwinglians), Anabaptists and other new sects.[37] The following year, officials in the duchy delibe-

---

[34] Claus-Peter Clasen, *Die Wiedertäufer im Herzogtum Württemberg und benachbarten Herrschaften: Ausbreitung, Geisteswelt und Soziologie* (Stuttgart: W. Kohlhammer, 1965) takes his analysis only to the opening years of the Thirty Years War.

[35] Bossert, *Quellen: Württemberg* (see note 30), 37.

[36] Ibid., 187–95, 1022–47.

[37] Ibid., 37.

rated on how to deal with the appearance of Schwenckfelders, »a new sect of Anabaptists«.[38] And in an order of 1535 to his officials, the duke encouraged pursuit of Anabaptists and other similar sects and rebellious rabble (Rotten).[39] By way of contrast, though, the mandates of 1535 and 1536 were aimed specifically at the Anabaptists. Christoph's approach appears to have been more discerning and, arguably, more comprehensive. His statements of policy and instructions to his officials consistently identify the offending parties as Schwenckfelders, Anabaptists, and other erring sects. In some cases, as in the mandate of 1558, Sacramentarians, too, come in for special mention.[40] Interestingly, Ludwig's instructions from 1571 add papists to this list.[41]

The final feature of these policies to which I want to call attention is the graduated structure of both interrogations and punishments. From the outset, the ducal legislation maintained a sharp distinction between leaders and followers, between the obstinate and the »reasonable« among the sectarians. These distinctions appear under the Habsburg administration and no less than under the administrations of the dukes. The threat of death or physical harm was consistently reserved for leaders, preachers, the obstinate, and the relapsed. They were more likely to be incarcerated during questioning and faced the possibility of being tortured. Even if these physical threats were not carried out, they were more likely to be banished and have their goods confiscated. On the other hand, especially from the reign of Christoph on, there was greater emphasis on the instruction of followers, who were characterized as simple and misled.

In addition, there appears a growing distinction over time between punishments meted out to Anabaptists and those imposed on other dissenters. This is least obvious in the legislation and activities of Duke Ulrich who largely treated other sects as subsets of the Anabaptists. But a growing awareness appears under Duke Christoph whose policies discuss punishments of other dissenters as worthy of a distinct discussion from that focused on the punishments of Anabaptists.[42] Discussions around the development of the 1558 mandate make explicit the assumption that milder procedures and punishments should be applied more to the Schwenckfelders and especially the Sacramentarians than to the Anabaptists.[43] And Ludwig's instructions of 1571 call for new consideration of the approach

---

[38] Ibid., 994.
[39] Ibid., 38.
[40] Ibid., 168–71.
[41] Ibid., 295.
[42] Eg. ibid., 128–30.
[43] Ibid., 1022–38.

to the problem posed by Anabaptists, but indicate that existing policy toward Schwenckfelders and Sacramentarians will suffice.[44]

The significance of these policies for the development of dissent in the duchy is probably clearest in the case of Anabaptism. Here the classic research of John Oyer has been enlightening. Oyer identified Nicodemism as one of, if not the, distinguishing feature of Anabaptism in Württemberg. Nicodemism he defined as the willingness to participate in the activities of the state church, while maintaining one's own Anabaptist beliefs and traditions or being willing to recant one's beliefs but return to them after the recantation. He also identified as an additional characteristic of Anabaptism in Württemberg its lack of ordained or clearly defined leaders. He described both of these characteristics as the result of survival strategies likely developed in response to the policies of the dukes: Nicodemism was a response to the relative toleration accorded to rank and file Anabaptists, and the lack of clearly defined leadership to the harsher penalties imposed on leaders.[45] However, Oyer did allow as well that the Anabaptists may have borrowed these tactics from the Schwenckfelders in the region, with whom they had significant contact and for whom these were central strategies as well.[46]

As Oyer observed, there were, indeed, significant contacts between Anabaptists and Schwenckfelders in Württemberg. Probably most famously, Schwenckfelder nobles or nobles with Schwenckfelder sympathies provided refuge and protection not only to other Schwenckfelders but to Anabaptists as well. The best known of these nobles was likely Hans Konrad Thumb of Neufeld, although a quick scan of the *Täuferakten* reveals the names of at least seventeen other noble families known to have sheltered Anabaptists.[47] More striking in some ways are the examples of families in which both Schwenckfelders and Anabaptists were represented. Here the most famous example is the Greiners, who figure prominently in studies of both Schwenckfelders and Anabaptists in Württemberg.[48] Scholars have recognized that the border between Anabaptism and

---

[44] Ibid., 295.

[45] Oyer, »Württemberg« (see note 29), 491, 494–96; idem, »Essllingen« (see note 29), 196–97, 246–47.

[46] Oyer, »Württemberg« (see note 29), 491, 500; idem, »Esslingen« (see note 29), 242; Gritschke, *»Via Media«* (see note 22), 239–41, 274, 338–54.

[47] Bossert, *Quellen: Württemberg* (see note 30), 1187; on the relationship between nobles and their dissenter subjects, especially Anabaptists, see Clasen, *Wiedertäufer im Württemberg* (see note 34), 30–31, 162–66; Gritschke, *»Via Media«* (see note 22), 314–19, 324–33.

[48] Clasen, *Wiedertäufer im Württemberg* (see note 34), 186; Oyer, »Württemberg« (see note 29), 502–05; Gritschke, *»Via Media«* (see note 22), 342; Räisänen, *Ketzer im Dorf* (see note 22), 272.

Schwenckfeldianism in Württemberg was a porous one, although they have usually seen the movements as a one-way street from Anabaptism to Schwenckfeldianism, especially in the wake of the Münster disaster.[49]

I suspect that the interconnections between Anabaptism and Schwenckfeldianism were, in fact, much more extensive than we have realized, but that these interconnections have been obscured by the categories both their contemporaries and we have imposed on early modern dissenters. In the early 1540s, Caspar Schwenckfeld entered into a heated exchange with the Anabaptist leader Pilgram Marpeck that is often seen as a defining moment in the separation between Anabaptism and Spiritualism. However, the likely impetus for this exchange – competition for the allegiance of two noblewomen – highlights as well the extent to which these two traditions appealed to many of the same people.[50] Ulrich Bubenheimer discovered evidence in Württemberg in the early seventeenth century of private or underground dissent which allowed conformity to the demands of the state church, but which was not identified with any dissenting tradition. This practice he labelled *Kryptoheterodoxie* and characterized it as quasi-Pietist. As a result, he suggested that assumptions that the ideas of Anabaptism and Schwenckfeldianism largely disappeared in Württemberg during the course of the seventeenth century are premature.[51] I would hazard that the phenomenon Bubenheimer observed is the result of a process of synthesis between Anabaptism and Schwenckfeldianism that developed throughout the sixteenth century, disagreements between Schwenckfeld and Marpeck notwithstanding.

We see in the policies of the Württemberg dukes that over the course of the sixteenth century there developed greater sophistication not only in discerning the roles of individuals within suspected dissenting traditions, but also in distinguishing between those traditions.[52] Instructions for interrogations after mid-century include detailed questions on aspects of both Anabaptist and Schwenckfelder belief.[53] Yet the information these

---

[49] Ulrich Bubenheimer, »Von Heterodoxie zur Kryptoheterodoxie: Die nachreformatorische Ketzerbekämpfung im Herzogtum Württemberg und ihre Wirkung im Spiegel des Prozesses gegen Eberhard Wild im Jahre 1622/23«, *Zeitschrift der Savigny-Stiftung für Rechtsgeschichte. Kanonistische Abteilung* 110 (1993), 312; Räisänen, *Ketzer im Dorf* (see note 22), 97–98.

[50] Williams, *Radical Reformation* (see note 3), 703–21; Stephen Boyd, *Pilgram Marpeck: His Life and Social Theology* (Durham, NC: Duke University Press, 1992), 104–07, 115–26; Walter Klaassen and William Klassen, *Marpeck: A Life of Dissent and Conformity* (Waterloo, Ont: Herald Press, 2008), 210–14.

[51] Bubenheimer, »Von Heterodoxie zur Kryptoheterodoxie« (see note 49), 308, 314, 339–41.

[52] Räisänen, *Ketzer im Dorf* (see note 22), 111–46.

[53] Eg. Bossert, *Quellen: Württemberg* (see note 30), 169–70, 193–95, 296–303.

interrogations yielded appears to have produced less than the desired clarity. Certainly, at times officials appear to have had difficulty deciding where on the scale of dissenters individuals fit, as with Claus Frey and Michel Kleinmayer, who were deemed »likely more Schwenckfelder than Anabaptist«.[54] In other cases, judgments changed, as with Hans Walter's widow, who was originally judged a Schwenckfelder, but subsequently found to be an Anabaptist.[55] At least some of this confusion appears to have stemmed from the fact that some of the dissenters did not adhere to a specific tradition. The records include a number of references to Anabaptists reading Schwenckfelder books, for example the miller Matthäus Weiß, who was suspected of harbouring Anabaptists and who was discovered to have had both Anabaptist and Schwenckfelder books in his house.[56] Michel Kleinmayer mentioned above was initially identified as a Schwenckfelder on the basis of his opinions about the relationship between the written word and the Spirit which were found in Schwenckfelder books he possessed and notes taken from those books. However, he was subsequently judged to be an Anabaptist because he refused to attend the Lutheran church since it did not properly institute the ban against sinners, a teaching regarded as central to Anabaptism.[57]

My suspicions about this blending of religious traditions in the sixteenth century is reinforced by a closer look at the Greiner family. John Oyer highlighted the distinctive features of Württemberg Anabaptism when he indicated that the Greiners were both Nicodemites and important pillars of Anabaptist communities in several regions of the duchy.[58] My comments will focus on the branch of the family in Walkersbach, a forest hamlet near Urbach. Of particular interest are three brothers, Georg, Melchior, and Jacob, the sons of Blasius, a Nicodemite Anabaptist with a long history of friction with the church. The three brothers appear in ducal records in the 1570s in a variety of ways. Georg is first described as an Anabaptist who harbours other Anabaptists and whose son criticizes pedobaptism. At the same time, Melchior and Jacob were judged to be more Schwenckfeldian than Anabaptist.[59] Later the same year, all three were described as Schwenckfelders and Anabaptists. Jacob and his wife were labelled Schwenckfelders who openly read Schwenckfelder books during sermons in the local church. Georg, his wife Clara, and their son sheltered

[54] Ibid., 257–58, 467.
[55] Ibid., 558.
[56] Ibid., 635–36, see also 651.
[57] Ibid., 491.
[58] Oyer, »Württemberg« (see note 29), 502–05.
[59] Bossert, *Quellen: Württemberg* (see note 30), 492–93.

known Anabaptists, and Jacob was known to associate with Anabaptists and to have claimed that he absented himself from the sermons in church because the pastor criticized Anabaptists.[60] The following year, Jacob and Melchior were described as evil Anabaptists and Schwenckfelders.[61] Six years later, Jacob and his wife were accused of despising the office of the ministry like all Schwenckfelders, and shortly thereafter Jacob's wife was denied burial rites because she was a Schwenckfelder, although shortly thereafter she was labelled a Schwenckfelder and an Anabaptist.[62]

I would suggest that this blending of traditions was likely the result, at least in part, of two unintended consequences of ducal policy. First, officials initially lumped all dissidents together under one umbrella, thereby encouraging a common identity. Second, they increasingly distinguished between types of dissent and assigned harsher penalties to the Anabaptists than to the other categories of dissent. John Oyer claimed that in cases like those of the Greiners referred to above, where individuals appeared to be both Schwenckfelders and Anabaptists, authorities identified them as Anabaptists.[63] At the same time, as Päivi Räisänen has noted, it was in the interest of the accused to be placed on the less dangerous end of the dissenter spectrum.[64] Dissenters usually came to the attention of the authorities because of a refusal to attend sermons and participate in the Lord's Supper at the state church. There were a range of reasons for such refusals, especially to participate in the Eucharist. Importantly, though, these were common tactics of both Schwenckfelders and Anabaptists.[65] After one was identified in this way, it was the purpose of subsequent interrogations to determine the reasons that one absented oneself from these activities through more detailed questioning, which in turn determined not only the possible range of punishments one faced, but also the nature of the interrogations to follow. Studies of Anabaptists and Schwenckfelders in Württemberg indicate that individuals assigned to both groups adopted strikingly similar strategies to avoid being pinned down in this way.[66]

I do not mean to suggest that there were no steadfast Anabaptists or Schwenckfelders in Württemberg of the type the historiography on the

---

[60] Ibid., 504–05.

[61] Ibid., 513.

[62] Ibid., 567, 585.

[63] Oyer, »Württemberg« (see note 29), 504.

[64] Räisänen, *Ketzer im Dorf* (see note 22), 289–90.

[65] Gritschke, »*Via Media*« (see note 22), 276, 281–82; Räisänen, *Ketzer im Dorf* (see note 22), 261–69; Bruce Tolley, *Pastors and Parishioners in Württemberg During the Late Reformation 1581–1621* (Stanford, CA: Stanford University Press, 1995), 78–82.

[66] Gritschke, »*Via Media*« (see note 22), 338–54; Räisänen, *Ketzer im Dorf* (see note 22), 289–305.

Radical Reformation has taught us to expect. The cases of clearly defined Anabaptists in the *Täuferakten* vastly outnumber the ambiguous cases like those described above. A steady flow of Hutterite missionaries into the duchy in the latter part of the sixteenth century certainly held up to dissenters a clearly defined and exclusive Anabaptist model. And similar voices are evident among the Schwenckfelders. For example, in 1579 Johann Martt, a former priest and Schwenckfelder leader, described a confessional unholy trinity: the devil was the Father, Catholics the Son, and Lutherans, Zwinglians, and Anabaptists the Holy Spirit.[67] However, as with the Schwenckfeld-Marpeck controversy, this can also be read as evidence of the similar attraction the two groups held for the same dissenters and the need to head off the appeal of the other dissenting tradition.

The dissident landscape in Württemberg, as elsewhere on the continent, thus was much more complex than we have realized. As noted above, research into the transition from dissenting movements to churches among Hutterites and Mennonites has yielded a model of Anabaptist confessionalism which parallels in important ways the confessionalizing activities of the early modern state. Evidence from Württemberg indicates the existence of another model – one that research into Anabaptist experiences in the Swiss territories and central Germany suggests is also significant. Dissenters in these regions, especially those identified as Anabaptists, were much more fully integrated into local communities than we have realized. Often they synthesized elements from different dissenting traditions, which remained distinct and clearly defined more in the eyes of the authorities than those of the dissenters.[68] Michael Driedger has distinguished between poles of fixed and flexible standards in identity formation among religious minorities in early modern Europe.[69] While the Mennonites and Hutterites provide evidence of the former, the Nicodemite Anabaptists and Schwenckfelders on their way to *Kryptoheterodoxie* in Württemberg provide evidence of the latter. But as both Driedger and Mark Furner have observed, a transformation in the direction of more flexible standards of confessional identity does not mean religion and belief were not important to the people involved.[70]

---

[67] Gritschke, »*Via Media*« (see note 22), 330–31.

[68] See, for example, Mark Furner, »Lay Casuistry and the Survival of Later Anabaptists in Bern«, *Mennonite Quarterly Review* 75 (2001): 429–69; Urs Leu, »Täuferische Netzwerke in der Eidgenossenschaft«, in Schubert, von Schlachta, and Driedger, eds., *Grenzen des Täufertums – Boundaries of Anabaptism* (see note 22), 168–85; Mathilde Monge, »Überleben durch Vernetzung. Die täuferischen Gruppen in Köln und am Niederrhein im 16. Jahrhundert, in ibid., 214–31; Hill, *Baptism, Brotherhood, and Belief* (see note 22).

[69] Driedger, *Obedient Heretics* (see note 26), 173.

The creation of fixed standards of confessional identity even among religious radicals often involved not only establishing clearly defined beliefs and practices, but also identifying traditions with lengthy historical pedigrees.[71] Such an appeal to tradition seems absent among the dissenters in Württemberg who hovered along the border between Anabaptism and Schwenckfeldianism. They chose elements from both traditions to develop a new tradition. Interestingly, this was, at least in part, a response to the retention of those very traditions by authorities intent on distinguishing Anabaptists from Schwenckfelders, and each from Sacramentarians.

4. Radicalism and Dissent in the English Reformation

I promised to conclude by suggesting possible implications of this research for our understanding of the Reformation in England. In response to a longstanding thesis suggesting continuity between religious radicals in sixteenth-century in England and their seventeenth-century counterparts, Patrick Collinson suggested three ways we could think about this relationship:

1. that Lollardy largely disappeared in the sixteenth century, that there was little subsequent separatist dissent, and that the seventeenth-century radicals were novel phenomena arising out of the circumstances of their own time;
2. that there was an on-going, underground, at least semi-separatist tradition of dissent which resurfaced in the seventeenth century; or
3. that environment rather than tradition is more significant in terms of the continuity of dissent and that specific geographic regions fostered these attitudes.

Collinson allowed that these explanations were not mutually exclusive and that a combination of all three might reflect the forces at work in English society. In the end, he concluded that if the proponents of continuity of dissent are suggesting that there was an ongoing tradition of religious voluntarism, which was neither wholly in nor entirely out of the church, he had no objections.[72] Yet, this sort of continuity is appearing in the most recent research into religious radicalism and dissent on the continent.

---

[70] Furner, »Lay Casuistry« (see note 68), 431; Driedger, *Obedient Heretics* (see note 26), 177.

[71] Driedger, *Obedient Heretics* (see note 26), 51–60, 75–82; Brad Gregory, *Salvation at Stake: Christian Martyrdom in Early Modern Europe* (Cambridge, MA: Harvard University Press, 1999), 197–249; Geoffrey Dipple, *»Just as in the time of the Apostles«: Uses of History in the Radical Reformation* (Kitchener, Ont: Pandora Press, 2005), 251–76.

In fact, in important ways, Reformation era dissenters in England look like their counterparts in Württemberg and other regions on the continent. However, these similarities derive not from the importation of radical ideas and practices from the continent, but from general patterns of dissent in late medieval western Europe and common practices used to discover and punish dissenters. Recent research into late fifteenth- and early sixteenth-century Lollardy paints a picture of a movement that looks surprisingly familiar to some scholars of continental dissent: the Lollards came from across the social and economic scale; they were often integrated into their communities, in some of which they held positions of prominence; and they were often connected to family groupings across generations.[73] Furthermore, by the sixteenth century they had adopted a number of practices very similar to those used on the continent to avoid running afoul of, or to minimize exposure to, religious and secular authorities. From the middle of the fourteenth century Nicodemism was common among the Lollards; Anne Hudson calculated that for every Lollard burned by authorities fifty escaped burning by retracting their beliefs or by employing strategies of evasion and vagueness in answering difficult questions about their beliefs.[74] Some scholars have heralded this model of dissent as the source of later English religious radicalism rather than the alleged separatist traditions from the continent.[75] The experiences of dissenters in Württemberg suggest that perceived differences between English conformists and continental separatists are not as clear as historians have presumed.

The failure to recognize this fact highlights the importance of the recent recognition that »radicals« were defined as such by their opponents. Within the context of the English Reformation, this discussion, like so many about radicalism, has usually focused specifically on the Anabaptists. When authorities first identified the Anabaptist threat, the movement was

---

[72] Collinson is here responding directly to the work of Margaret Spufford and her students, although he notes that Christopher Hill made similar arguments, with some variations, throughout his career. Patrick Collinson, »Critical Conclusion«, in Margaret Spufford, ed., *The World of Rural Dissenters, 1520–1725* (Cambridge: Cambridge University Press, 1995), 394, 396; cf. idem, »Night Schools, Conventicles and Churches: Continuities and Discontinuities in Early Protestant Ecclesiology, in Marshall and Ryrie, eds., *Beginnings of English Protestantism* (see note 19), 213–14.

[73] Derek Plumb, »The Social and Economic Status of the Later Lollards«, in Spufford, ed., *World of the Rural Dissenters* (see note 72), 103–31; idem, »A Gathered Church? Lollards and Their Society«, in ibid., 132–63; Nesta Evans, »The Descent of Dissenters in the Chiltern Hundreds«, in ibid., 288–308.

[74] Anne Hudson, *The Premature Reformation: Wycliffite Texts and Lollard History* (Oxford: Clarendon Press, 1988), 158–61.

[75] Eg. Loades, »Anabaptism and English Sectarianism« (see note 8), 64.

identified largely with foreigners and its essential characteristics associated with teachings and practices from the Melchiorite Anabaptist tradition in the Netherlands. However, according to Horst, the term took on greater currency in official circles and the movement itself became more fully integrated into the English dissenting tradition during the reign of Edward VI.[76] Interestingly, at least some of the increased concern with Anabaptists, and certainly the greater precision in defining the nature and threat of the movement at this time, came from continental not domestic sources. Crucial polemics written against the Anabaptists in England amounted to translations or paraphrases of works written by Heinrich Bullinger and Jean Calvin, which in the latter case involved an explicit response to the archetypical prescriptive Anabaptist text, *The Schleitheim Articles*.[77] Interestingly, though, while the polemics against the Anabaptists became more specific, there is little evidence that official understandings followed suit. From about the middle of the fifteenth century, »Lollard« had been used as a term synonymous with »heretic«, and this usage continued into the 1530s.[78] However, in the 1540s it was gradually replaced by »Anabaptist« as the catch-all term to define dissenters.[79] I suspect that similar forces were at work here as in Württemberg. There is reason to be as skeptical about doctrinal statements derived from English records as from those on the continent and evidence that »sectarians« were more severely punished than other dissenters.[80] Here, too, as the authorities looked for distinct, and possibly new, dissenters, they may have helped to integrate and supplement existing traditions of dissent.

This dynamic has largely escaped the attention of historians, who generally have taken the hard and fast definitions of dissenting groups from polemics against, and official pronouncements about, them as evidence of hard and fast lines between the dissenting groups. This tendency is obvious in the emphasis on separatism or sectarianism as leitmotiv of Anabaptism, and hence radicalism, in the historiography of the English Reformation. But the problem goes much further, and even in cases where

---

[76] Horst, *Radical Brethren* (see note 7), 100, 137. Cf. J. W. Martin, *Religious Radicals in Tudor England* (London: Hambledon Press, 1989), 18–20.

[77] Carrie Euler, »Anabaptism and Anti-Anabaptism in the Early English Reformation: Defining Protestant Heresy and Orthodoxy During the Reign of Edward VI«, in *Heresy, Literature and Politics in Early Modern English Culture*, David Loewenstein and John Marshall, eds. (Cambridge: Cambridge University Press, 2006), 45–52.

[78] Hudson, *Premature Reformation* (see note 74), 446.

[79] Martin, *Religious Radicals* (see note 76), 18–19.

[80] Hudson, *Premature Reformation* (see note 74), 32–33; idem, *Lollards and Their Books* (London: Hambledon Press, 1985), 125–40; Martin, *Religious Radicals* (see note 76), 42.

this characteristic appears, as in Thomas Freeman's assessment of the Free-willers, who he claims were *de facto* separatists, distinctions are drawn on the basis of theological tenets like the Incarnation or the Trinity.[81] The failure to recognize an ongoing, largely conformist tradition of dissent in the English Reformation as radical is, I suspect, a symptom of a deeper dynamic going back to the time of the Reformation and especially to the time when religious movements institutionalized and became, or did not become, churches. Scholarship on the history of religious dissent in early modern England has emphasized the importance of Mary I's reign for the development of sectarian or separatist traditions. At this time Protestant Reformers were forced into opposition, and those who did not flee to the continent either conformed or went underground. While some scholars trace the roots of the English separatist tradition to Edward's reign, most accept that under Mary the tradition came into its own.[82]

This matter intersects with another essential question in the historiography of the English Reformation: the extent to which the confessionalization thesis applies in the English context. Peter Marshall has added interesting insights to this ongoing discussion, arguing that the religious pluralism that arose in the English context came not from the failure by the English state to apply confessionalist methods but from the failure of the methods that were applied. A crucial stage in this process came with Mary's attempt to return England to Catholicism which was more a re-direction of the confessionalist agenda than an abandonment of it.[83] Assuming for the sake of argument that Marshall's analysis is correct, I would counter that in at least one important way, the Elizabethan church did manage to carry through a confessionalist agenda: by controlling the past, especially the dissenting past. In doing so, it pre-empted an important component of identity formation in dissenting religious groups, which, as we have seen, could take on some of the contours of confessionalization in areas where dissenting traditions gained some element of independence. A crucial component in the success of the Elizabethan church in this area is John Foxe's *Acts and Monuments*, which Thomas Freeman has compared to a blanket of snow, »imposing frozen, pristine

---

[81] Thomas Freeman, »Dissenters from a Dissenting Church: the Challenge of the Freewillers 1550–1558«, in Marshall and Ryrie, eds., *Beginnings of English Protestantism* (see note 19), 129–34.

[82] Loades, »Anabaptism and English Sectarianism« (see note 8), 65, 69–70; Martin, *Religious Radicals* (see note 76), 25–27, 30, 128–29, 145; Collinson, »Night Schools, Conventicles and Churches«, (see note 72), 230–35; Freeman, »Dissenters from a Dissenting Church« (see note 81), 132–34, 156.

[83] Peter Marshall, »Confessionalization, Confessionalism and Confusion in the English Reformation«, in Mayer, ed. *Reforming Reformation* (see note 10), 55.

uniformity upon a variegated landscape«.[84] However, research of the last few years has begun to melt that snow and to highlight the extent to which Foxe appropriated the English dissenting tradition for the Elizabethan church. In the process, he turned Lollards into proto-Elizabethan Protestants and wrote out of the story not only other dissenting trajectories, but also almost all accounts of Nicodemite behaviour. However, Andrew Pettegree has highlighted the importance of Nicodemism for Marian Protestantism, going so far as to call the Elizabethan settlement a Nicodemite Reformation.[85] I. B. Horst had claimed that many of the Marian martyrs may have been, in fact, Anabaptists.[86] Given the nature of the English dissenting tradition, it seems more valuable to look for the Anabaptists, or other radicals, among the Marian Nicodemites. Likely there, no less than among the Protestant Nicodemites, we will find the core of subsequent dissenting traditions. And among the Nicodemites and grudging conformists we will find the shared experiences of radical spirits on the continent and in England.

---

[84] Freeman, »Dissenters from a Dissenting Church« (see note 81), 155.

[85] On the exclusion of »unorthodox« Marian martyrs from Foxe's text or their conversion into mainstream Protestants, see Martin, *Religious Radicals* (see note 76), 176–78; Freeman, »Dissenters from a Dissenting Church« (see note 81), 152–55. Andrew Pettegree, »Nicodemism and the English Reformation«, in *Marian Protestantism: Six Studies* (Aldershot: Scolar Press, 1996), 86–117.

[86] Horst, *Radical Brethren* (see note 7), 154–58.

IV.

Das Bild der Reformation von sich selbst
The Reformation's Self Image

The Reformation's Self-Image:
The perspective of the Wittenberg and Swiss Reformations

Euan Cameron

The purpose of this section of the volume is to consider an essential part of the process by which the Reformation movements became »churches«: namely, their awakening self-understanding that they occupied a distinct and unique moment in the unfolding history of the Christian Church. This inquiry takes us into the historical writing and historical arguments which the reformers made about the place of their movement, and their understanding of the Gospel, in Christian history.

Yet there is a paradox here. In the first place, the reformers' self-understanding was undoubtedly theological and dogmatic rather than historical. The first reformers did not embrace any idea that Christian *doctrine*, as such, evolved or developed over time. The Gospel had been fully, and in a sense finally, delivered in the message of Jesus Christ as foretold by the prophets and recorded by the evangelists and apostles. That was the meaning and implication of the doctrine usually described as *sola scriptura*. The life of the Church lived out in the days of the apostles and the earliest church was, as we shall see, *in principle* (if not always in practice) definitive of what the Church should be. That implied that the reformers rejected any idea of a dynamic tradition, in which the Holy Spirit progressively led the Church into new practices, or new expressions of old truths. Neither did they accept the presumption that the institutional Church could, in a continuous and authoritative way, determine how the Scriptural revelation was to be interpreted.[1] They would certainly not have embraced the idea proposed three centuries later by John Henry Newman, where doctrine itself emerges within the Church through a dynamic process of development.[2]

---

[1] See the decree of the Council of Trent on Scripture and Tradition, as ed. in Norman P. Tanner (ed.), *Decrees of the Ecumenical Councils*, 2 vols (paginated continuously) (London: Sheed & Ward; Washington, D. C.: Georgetown University Press, 1990), 662–65.

[2] John Henry Newman, *An Essay on the Development of Christian Doctrine* (London: J. Toovey, 1845).

On the other hand, the reformers believed that their moment in the history of Christianity entailed a uniquely important *rediscovery* of the pristine witness of the Church. Most if not all of the mainstream reformers believed themselves to be living in an age when the Gospel had been brought back into the light after centuries of widespread and serious error. They hoped that the recovery of the true meaning of the Gospel would redress the consequences of centuries of disorder and decay, and restore the Church to something like the more nearly ideal state, at least as to teachings and practices, that it had enjoyed in the earliest years after Pentecost. Consequently, several major historical questions remained to be answered. How had such a gross difference opened up between the Church as described in the apostolic writings and those of the early Fathers, versus the Church of c. 1500? At what point ought one to regard the visible Church as not only flawed (which, in a sense it always was) but as so far removed from its fundamental principles that it could no longer be regarded as a valid expression of the visible Church, and must be seen as a »false church«? How would the present-day churches – the churches of the Reformation and their adversaries – look when compared against the witness of the early Church and the early Fathers? Some even deeper theological questions arose, and were asked and explored: what made a »heresy« or a »schism« against the true Church? In what senses should even a grievously faulty church be regarded as an expression of the true or ideal Church, the Church as an object of belief?

Many of these questions trespass on to theological ecclesiology rather than history, and not all will be explored in equal detail in this essay. As a preliminary point, one should note a partial analogy between the admiration of antiquity (partial and qualified as that sometimes was) in the writings of the reformers, with the admiration for the old Church expressed by some of their forbears a century or more before them. One of the most persistent medieval legends of lost purity was the so-called »Sylvester-legend«. The story told how the Emperor Constantine, suffering from leprosy, offered vast rewards to any who could heal him. Sylvester I, bishop of Rome, offered prayers for his healing and was rewarded with authority over the Western Empire, while Constantine went East to found Constantinople. The acceptance of this power and wealth was, depending on the account, described as »poison poured into the Church« leading to wealth, power, and the accompanying corruption. The legend apparently originated with the apocryphal *Acts of Sylvester*, written around 500. It was copied in detail in the notorious but widely accepted eighth-century forgery, the »Donation of Constantine«; that text in turn was incorporated into both Gratian's *Decretum* in the mid–12th century and summarized in the *Golden Legend* of Jacobus de Voragine in the 13th century.[3] The legend circulated in the Middle Ages in both orthodox and heretical forms.[4] More generally, the reforming writers of the era of the Great Schism looked with sometimes naïve wistfulness back to the early Church. Conciliarist reformers such as Dietrich of Niem, Heinrich of Langenstein or above all Nicolas de Clamanges, in his *De Ruina et Reparatione Ecclesiae*, imagined the early Church as an age of gold, when not only the Church but the whole world enjoyed the fruits of virtue in a time of prosperity and well-being.[5]

However, the differences between the medieval and the Reformation era images of a fallen church cast some important light on the special character of the reformers' critique. For the Middle Ages, the perfection of the Church in a remote past was conceived of in essentially moral terms: sacrificial dedication to mission, voluntary poverty, readiness for martyrdom. The early monastics were celebrated for their spectacular abstinences and mortifications and for their miraculous gifts. Many early Christians were credited with exceptional abilities in detecting and resisting evil spirits. Correspondingly, the flaws of the modern Church were conceived of in similarly moral terms: the pursuit of wealth, self-indulgence, the desire to achieve political power and dominion. The Protestant reformers of the sixteenth century would view the ideal state, and the corresponding decline, of the Church in quite different terms. The reformers understood the Church to be defined by the Gospel, and in particular, by the insights into the justification and sanctification of sinners which they discerned in Paul's epistles and in John's Gospel. The Church suffered decline insofar as it lapsed from those principles, and embraced practices and rituals which contradicted them. When the visible Church embraced and encouraged customs which derogated from sole dependence on Christ's merits for salvation, such as monastic vows or sacrificial masses, it departed from

---

[3] See *The Cambridge Companion to the Age of Constantine*, edited by N. E. Lenski, (Cambridge: Cambridge University Press, 2006), 298 seqq., for the *Acts of Sylvester*. For the text of the Donation see Lorenzo Valla, *The Treatise of Lorenzo Valla on the Donation of Constantine*, ed. and trans. Christopher B. Coleman (New Haven: Yale University Press, 1922), 10–19. See also Jacobus de Voragine, *The Golden Legend; or, Lives of the saints, as Englished by William Caxton*, 2 vols. (London: J. M. Dent and Co., 1900) II, 84–86.

[4] For the adaptation of the legend in Waldensian contexts see for instance Euan Cameron, »Waldensian and Protestant Visions of the Christian Past« in Marina Benedetti (ed.), *Valdesi medievali: Bilanci e prospettive di ricerca* (Turin: Claudiana, 2009), 197–209.

[5] É. Delaruelle, E.-R. Labande [et] Paul Ourliac, *L'Église au temps du grand schisme et de la crise conciliaire (1378–1449)* 2 vols. paginated continuously (Paris: Bloud & Gay, 1962), II, 894–5 and references.

the Gospel in a potentially fatal way. For the leaders of the sixteenth-century Reformation the well-being or failure of the Church was conceived in terms of theology as reflected in practice. That did not mean that there was no overlap between the priorities of medieval and early modern reformers: as will be seen, the critique of political dominion in the papacy to a certain degree bound the two together. However, the priorities of the Reformation leaders were essentially theological rather than concerned with ethical performance. Insofar as there was a purity in the early Church, it consisted not in any moral perfection (which was impossible) but in its scriptural simplicity of doctrine and of worship, which the reformers sought to restore. Purity of belief and simplicity of worship was, in fact, more important to the Protestants than sanctity or purity of life, which they knew must be for ever elusive.

1. Luther and the true and false Church

Consistent with Protestant theological anthropology, there had to be room for the fact that, at all ages and among all people, the church was made up of justified sinners who were still sinners. Especially for Luther, who reflected more carefully on this question than most, the Church, even at its best, was always an object of belief rather than perception. As Luther wrote in a series of lectures on the Psalms begun in 1532:

»Therefore we should know and believe that the church is holy, but we are not to see it as such, since the article of faith says: ›I believe a holy church‹, not, ›I see a holy church‹. But if you want to judge by sight, you will see that it is sinful. You will see many, in fact, countless occasions for offense, brethren dominated by their passions [...] one person incited by impatience, another by anger, another in some other way. It is not written: ›I see a holy church‹, but, ›I believe‹; for it does not have its own righteousness but Christ's, who is its head. In that faith I perceive its holiness, which is a holiness that is believed and not one that is palpable or visible.«[6]

Luther, perhaps even more than the reformers who followed him and respected him, approached the question of the Church theologically first, and historically only as a distant second. For Luther, the true Church – the Church as defined in the creeds and an object of faith, as in the above extract – was always a gathering of the hidden, unidentifiably few elect.

---

[6] *Luther's Works*, American edition, ed. Jaroslav Pelikan, H. C. Oswald, and H. T. Lehmann, 55 vols. (St. Louis, MO: Concordia; Philadelphia, PA: Fortress, 1955–86 and now continuing) [hereafter *LW*] vol. 12 (Ps 45:7). Compare *Luthers Werke: Kritische Gesamtausgabe*, 73 vols. (Weimar: H. Böhlau, 1883–2009) [hereafter *WA*] XL, 472–610.

The true Church exists hidden, in part, by its own sinfulness. For practical purposes, one may recognize the many participating bodies in the universal Church by their demonstrating the essential »marks«, of which the most important, and the most widely shared, were the preaching of the Gospel and the administration of baptism and the Eucharist.[7] The Church exists in a dynamic relationship of mutual dependence on the Word of God; it transcends the faults of its participants, including its ministers. However, Luther also believed, crucially for this chapter, that a particular manifestation of the Church could become so fundamentally estranged from the Gospel that it ceased to be a true Church altogether and became a »false church«. Nevertheless, for Luther this relationship between true and false churches never resolved itself into a simple or naïve opposition between false Catholicism and true Protestantism. There could have been elements of truth in the Catholic past, and there was always a risk that structural falsehood would take root in the reformed traditions, or breakaway movements from them, as well.[8]

2. The Reformers and the Early Church

The greatest and most predictable challenge to the reformers' vision of themselves as the rediscoverers of the true Church and its message came from the Catholic tradition's claim to continuity. More specifically, the Catholic tradition claimed an unbroken sequence of fathers and doctors of the Church, whose testimony allegedly validated the existing institution. In broad and general terms, most of the leading reformers believed that one could find valid statements of Gospel truth in the writings of the early fathers and the early councils. However, defining the relationship of the primitive Church to the Fathers, and of the Fathers to the churches of the Reformation, posed an intellectual challenge. Theologically speaking the question was not a difficult one: only the canonical Scriptures could claim absolute authority as the expression of the Holy Spirit. The Fathers and Councils would only have a derivative or second-hand authority, insofar

---

[7] These two marks were also identified in Melanchthon's *De Ecclesia et de Autoritate Verbi Dei*, in [Philip Melanchthon], *Philippi Melanchthonis Opera Quae Supersunt Omnia*, ed. C. G. Bretschneider et al., 28 vols. (Halle: C. A. Schwetschke and Son, 1834–60), vol. 23, cols. 585–642, at col 640. Cited hereafter as *CR* 23.

[8] For this summary, based on extensive research in Luther's works, I gratefully acknowledge Prof. Dr. Dorothea Wendebourg's paper on »Luther's Ecclesiology« delivered to the conference of the Roman-Catholic bishops of the US at the Catholic University in Washington DC in 2017, forthcoming in the volume of proceedings of that conference and kindly shared with me by Professor Wendebourg.

as by their teachings and decisions they expounded, upheld and confirmed
the Word of Scripture and refuted error. Yet even within the terms of this
reduced role, the Fathers presented the reformers with a delicate question
of periodization. At what point did the teachers of the historic church
tend to become less, rather than more reliable? How could the progressive
departing of the visible Catholic Church from the truth of the Gospel be
charted through the evolution of their writings? The question, be it noted,
was always one of doctrine: the fathers stood or fell by their teachings, not
by their personalities or moral qualities.

In the spirit of comparing Wittenberg and British testimonies, it is
interesting here to compare two works which addressed the question of
the Fathers and Councils in parallel but by no means identical ways: Philip
Melanchthon's short work published as *On the Authority of the Church
and on the writings of the Ancients*, first published as a separate treatise in
1539;[9] and the *Apology of the Church of England* published in 1562 by the
formerly exiled bishop John Jewel, and translated into English in the same
year by Lady Anne Bacon.[10] Both these works were written under the
shadow of Catholic attempts to impose authority on the churches, and to
reclaim control of the tradition through councils. In the case of Melanchthon (whose work appeared in the same year as Luther's *On Councils
and the Churches*) it was the calling of a council to Mantua which did not
in fact materialize. In that of Jewel it was the concluding stages of the
Council of Trent. Both works focused substantially on the issue of the
credibility to be assigned to the early fathers, and the degree to which
sixteenth-century Catholics could legitimately claim the early Fathers as
patrons and defenders of the present-day Catholic Church, its teachings
and its rituals.

Several core principles informed both these works. First, both Melanchthon and Jewel emphasized that only Scripture held definitive authority
as the basis of Christian teaching. Melanchthon rejected the Catholic claim
that the Church was prior to Scripture and had authority over it.[11] On the
contrary, the Church was only credible because of the Word.[12] Jewel ar-

---

[9] Philip Melanchthon, *De Ecclesiae Autoritate et de veterum scriptis libellus* (Wittenberg: Joseph Klug, 1539); also published in *CR* 23: 585–642, as note 7.

[10] John Jewel (1522–1571), *Apologia ecclesiæ anglicanæ* (London: Reginald Wolf,
1562); translated as *An Apologie or answere in defence of the Churche of Englande, with
a briefe and plaine declaration of the true Religion professed and vsed in the same*
(London: Reginald Wolf, 1562). The edition cited here will be that found in [John Jewel],
The Works of John Jewel, ed. for the Parker Society (vols. 23–26) by John Ayre, 4 vols.
(Cambridge: Cambridge University Press, 1845–1850), III, 1–48 (Latin) and 49–112
(English).

[11] *CR* 23: 595.

[12] Ibid., 603.

gued, perhaps paradoxically, that some of the strongest support for *sola scriptura* came from the Fathers themselves.[13] Secondly, both these reformers quoted with approval arguments that the earliest form of the Church should usually be expected to be the best and purest.[14] Thirdly, both were well aware that while the early Church might be the ideal on principle, it was not always perfect in practice: there were always weaker members even in the heroic ages.[15] Nevertheless, Melanchthon and Jewel both considered that the standard of the early Church was the one against which the present-day Catholic Church must be judged, and severely criticized.[16]

However, subtle and important differences separate the arguments of Melanchthon and Jewel. Melanchthon argued, essentially, that even if the Fathers or the early Councils could sometimes be quoted in defence of a Catholic practice (monasticism, or prayers for the dead, for example) that did not justify the practice: it only showed that the Fathers were in error on that point. A large part of his treatise consisted of reviewing the writings of the early Church to demonstrate that, while remaining essentially true to the Gospel, it went badly astray on one point or another. Ambrose, Basil and Cyprian were all members of the true Church but all gave bad advice on certain questions.[17] Early Councils could mix »ridiculous« decrees with good ones, such as forbidding priests to attend second weddings.[18] Councils progressively, and wrongly, took away from clergy the right to marry.[19] Among the Fathers, Melanchthon argued, one could find the gradual growth of errors over such things as sacrificial masses or other ceremonies: even if some of the works attributed to them and most used by Catholic polemics were suppositious.[20] Yet within Melanchthon's at times highly critical catalogue of sayings of the Fathers, a clear narrative strand emerged. Error was cumulative; while from time to time a church Father would correct earlier errors – as Augustine had recalled the Church to correct teaching on faith and justification – the general chronological drift was towards greater and greater error. Gregory I's pontificate, coinciding with the barbarian domination in Europe, marked a particular point of decline.[21] While the Catholics of Melanchthon's day might claim some

---

[13] Jewel, *Works* (as note 10), III, 57, 62, 106.

[14] *CR* 23: 596, 605; Jewel, *Works* (as note 10), III, 77–79, 100, 106.

[15] *CR* 23: 602, 609: »Hoc exemplum monet, ne ita miremur antiquitatem, ut eam omnibus vitiis liberemus«; also *CR* 23: 617; compare Jewel, *Works* (as note 10), III, 71, 79.

[16] *CR* 23: 634; compare Jewel, *Works* (as note 10), III, 77, 78–79, 106.

[17] *CR* 23: 600.

[18] Ibid., 606.

[19] Ibid., 608.

[20] Ibid., 619.

[21] Ibid., 626–632.

support from some of the more erroneous of the Fathers' remarks, never-theless, the teaching of the reformed churches represented

»the consensus of the Catholic Church of Christ, as is shown by the Creeds, the more sound of the Councils, and the more learned of the Fathers«.[22]

John Jewel took a rather more optimistic, or perhaps naïve view of the Fathers. Jewel was convinced, or claimed to be, that the reformers over-whelmingly had the Fathers on their side on all the issues that mattered. In contrast, sometimes Catholic polemics even tried to suppress patristic evi-dence which did not agree with them, as when an English Catholic called John Clement tried to destroy some pages in Theodoret on the Eucharist which could not be reconciled with transubstantiation.[23] Selectively, Jewel quoted the patristic passages which most effectively supported the Swiss reformed position which he espoused, for example on the sacraments and Eucharistic presence.[24] Jewel mocked Catholic polemicists who claimed to have the Fathers on their side by noting the disagreements between them: the Fathers urged the general reading of the scriptures, which modern Catholics reject. The Fathers considered that a vow of chastity might law-fully be set aside; the Council of Gangra considered a married priest to be as worthy as a celibate one.[25] Councils were a doubtful benefit in many respects, and sometimes even those Councils that the Catholics summoned they did not obey, as with Trent's decrees on pluralism.[26] In all this Jewel concluded that

»But yet for all this, from the primatiue Church, from the Apostles, and from Christ wee haue not departed, true it is.«[27]

Two slightly inconsistent arguments were jostling for attention here. On one hand, the testimony of the Fathers was only ever persuasive rather than decisive. If they agreed with Scripture, well and good: if they did not (in the reformers' opinions) they could be set aside. And yet, at the same time the theologians of the Reformation believed that the Fathers' argu-ments leaned far more often on their side than on the side of their op-ponents. Moreover, they suspected that the Church had departed further and further from the truth as time had passed. One was more likely to find the Gospel in Augustine than in Gregory the Great, and perhaps in Gre-gory than in Bernard, let alone Innocent III: though occasional sparks of

---

[22] Ibid., 634.
[23] Jewel, *Works* (as note 10), III, 85–87.
[24] Ibid., 62–64, 66–67.
[25] Ibid., 86–87; compare *CR* 23: 608, which also approves of the Council of Gangra.
[26] Jewel, *Works* (as note 10), III, 87–88, 96–99.
[27] Ibid., 91.

divine insight might be seen at almost any point in the history of the Church.

The churches that emerged from the Reformation therefore defined themselves *in contrast to and against* a Catholicism that had, they were convinced, progressively degraded from its original state. That act of definition required fairly detailed investigations into how the Church had been in antiquity. The remainder of is paper will explore only a few themes, themes which recur again and again in the writings of both the Wittenberg reformers, especially the Philippist writers who gathered around and learned from Philip Melanchthon, and the Swiss reformers based in Zürich and Saint-Gallen. Those themes, however, addressed some of the most sensitive issues between the reformers and their critics.

First, consideration will be given to how the history of monasticism was understood in Reformation historical writing: since there was no doubt that (i) contemporary monasticism was unacceptable to the reformers and (ii) that monastic communities existed in the early Church, the issue needed to be addressed. Secondly, this paper will explore how the reformers' writings dealt with the papacy in the Western Church. Again, there had clearly been bishops of Rome for a long time; but the question that could then be raised was, what was their episcopate like in the past, and how did it validate or invalidate the present form that it had assumed? Thirdly, this piece will consider some of the historical observations made concerning the Eucharist or Mass. Given the traumatic effect that debates over the Eucharist caused between different groups of reformers in the early Reformation, one might expect the reformers to be very wary of this topic. However, as well as serious and fatal disagreements, there were also broad areas of consensus between Lutherans and reformed: chiefly that the Mass, as practiced c. 1500 with the heavy overtones of propitiatory sacrifice, had no foundation in Scripture or Christian antiquity.

3. Monasticism in Protestant historiography

Monasticism represented an early challenge to the reformers' historical vision. Martin Luther was a monastic himself, and signed himself as »Augustinian«, or some variant of this expression, fairly regularly until early 1521 and occasionally thereafter.[28] Yet as early as the address *To the Chris-*

---

[28] For Luther's later uses of this signature see e.g. *LW* 48, 141 (Luther to Thomas Fuchs, December 23, 1519); *LW* 48, 159 (Luther to Georg Spalatin, April 13, 1520); *LW* 48, 173 (Luther to Spalatin, August 23, 1520); one of the last occurrences of this si-

tian Nobility of the German Nation Luther was convinced of one fundamental point, that monasteries were established as places of education, and
were not at all like modern monasteries. He wrote:

>»[I]n those days [*the early church*] convents and monasteries were all open to
everyone to stay in them as long as he pleased. What else were the convents and
monasteries but Christian schools where Scripture and the Christian life were
taught, and where people were trained to rule and to preach? [...] And in truth all
monasteries and convents ought to be so free that God is served freely and not
under compulsion. Later on, however, they became tied up with vows and became
an eternal prison.«[29]

The *historical* claim, that monasteries in antiquity were quite different
from those of Luther's own time, had an unlikely source, but one that we
can almost certainly identify. Desiderius Erasmus wrote a brief *Life of
Jerome*, to accompany the edition of Jerome's writings which Erasmus
completed in 1516.[30] In a crucial passage, Erasmus wrote that Jerome chose, after careful consideration, to become a monk. However, Erasmus insisted that the monasticism of Jerome's time was nothing like the monasticism of his own age. Monks in those early years were not bound to strict
rules. They would choose when to worship and how. They would wear
sober but not special clothing. Above all, they were allowed to leave
whenever they wished, and there was no punishment for leaving the house
except for potential harm to one's reputation.[31]

Luther was sure that something was theologically wrong with the very
idea of the monastic life, as he argued in the *Theses on Vows* prepared
around 1521, and in the *Judgment of Martin Luther on Monastic Vows*
which he published in the same year. The fatal theological error made by
nearly all those who took vows, he claimed, was that they believed that by
doing so they would gain spiritual »merit« before God, especially by the
commitment to lifelong and unalterable service. In his *Judgment On Monastic Vows*, Luther said that the vow was »not altogether ridiculous« if
taken for a limited time and for a specific purpose, as for instance to study
with those who were more learned in the faith. Christian schools for boys

---

gnature form appears to be in *LW* 48, 313 (Luther to Spalatin, September 17, 1521) by
which time Luther was already living at the Wartburg and dressing as a layman.

[29] *WA* 6: 439–40; *LW* 44: 174.

[30] Desiderius Erasmus (ed.) *Omnium operum Divi Eusebii Hieronymi Stridonensis*, 9
vols. (Basel: Froben, 1516).

[31] Desiderius Erasmus, *Eximii doctoris Hieronymi Stridonensis vita, ex ipsius potis-
simum literis contexta* (Cologne: In aedibus Eucharii Cervicorni, 1517), b 2^{r/v}. Erasmus
in turn cited as evidence several writings of Jerome which he claimed supported this
portrait of fourth-century monasticism: the life of Hilarion, the letters to Rusticus and
Paulinus, or the letter entitled *Hear, daughter* where Jerome described the threefold
pattern of monks in Egypt.

and girls grew from this practice, and some developed into monasteries. It was only with the degradation of the custom in later years that lifelong vows were used to ensnare recruits who were no longer taught.[32] If this point were observed, monasteries would then have the character God intended them to have, and nothing else. They would simply be Christian schools for youth, designed to establish ardent young people in the faith by means of a godly upbringing, until they reached the years of maturity.[33]

It is difficult to be absolutely sure whether the historical conviction about early monasticism was generated by the theological argument about vows, or *vice versa*. What is clear, however, is that the image of monasticism expressed both by Erasmus and Luther was a highly selective one. They said as little as possible about the extravagant and dangerous practices of abstinence and mortification of the flesh found in some early monasteries. They avoided discussion of the claims to the miraculous, or the spectacular abilities of ascetics to discern and resist the power of demons, which figure largely in the works of such early historians of monastic communities as Palladius or Cassian.[34] However, Luther and the reformers seemed certain that monasteries were first and foremost places of education. That was what they had been in the past, and that was what they should be once more, if they were to survive at all.

The same point was made in the massive expansion of Johannes Carion's world chronicle planned by Philip Melanchthon and completed after his death by his son-in-law, the theologian, physician and mathematician Caspar Peucer. When writing about the 12th century emperor Lothair of Supplinburg (r. 1133–7) Peucer wrote:

»It also appears that monasteries had not yet been entirely transformed from their first and most ancient form and purpose, but had preserved something of their ancient custom in exercises of piety, learning and studies. Collegiate churches were formed in the beginning that they might be schools, and the custom was in these colleges to form the youth in Christian letters and manners. This plan, since it seemed useful for public conduct, our ancestors endowed with devout zeal, so that there would never be lacking the necessary resources for students. Afterwards, when superstition succeeded devotion, and the laws of the pontiffs were received in place of the doctrine of the Gospel, these colleges, which up to that point had been assemblies of students, were gradually handed over to sacrificing [priests], and the wealth of the colleges was poured out on the indulgence of Roman pride and the pleasures of lazy people, with the schools abolished.«[35]

---

[32] *WA* 8: 614–15; *LW* 44: 312–13.

[33] *WA* 8: 641; *LW* 44: 355.

[34] Palladius, Bishop of Aspuna, *The Lausiac History*, translated by John Wortley (Athens, Ohio: Cistercian Publications; Collegeville, Minnesota: Liturgical Press, 2015); John Cassian, *The Conferences* ed. and trans. Boniface Ramsey (New York: Paulist Press, 1997).

Almost exactly the same argument can be found in the writings of several of the Swiss reformers. In his *Epitome* of 1534, an exercise in historical geography to assist readers of scripture, Joachim Vadian of St-Gallen made the following observation:

»Then, as this pattern of life grew, and pupils were attracted to it, monasteries were founded everywhere, that is, schools for the conducting of the ancient pattern of education: just as the mind was to be exercised by the reading and the learning of the Scriptures, so the body was to be exercised in turn by regular physical work«.[36]

Much later in his work Vadian observed how Basil of Caesarea

»is also said to have founded monasteries, that is schools, where the cares of the world were cast aside and there was space to attend to learning, manners, modesty and continence, for a purer worship of God and service of one's neighbour. For that was what monasteries were at that time.«[37]

He mocked the idea that modern monastics should boast of following Basil's rule, when »they offer nothing of the ancient monasticism save the name«.

Joachim Vadian had, of course, every reason to resent contemporary monasticism. As Bürgermeister of St-Gallen he struggled without success to reform the great abbey that dominated his community. Yet he wrote a surprisingly even-handed *Chronicle of the Abbots* of the monastery that made, nevertheless, powerful critiques of contemporary monasticism. Ancient monasteries were like schools, for training in evangelism: just as soldiers undergo training for combat. Hence the fasts and other disciplines were not ends in themselves but preparation for evangelism.[38] In four chapters Vadian echoed Luther to the effect that monastic vows as taken in his own time (what he called the »new monkery«) failed to achieve their objectives. Their insincere and self-defeating claims to chastity, poverty and obedience proved that modern monasticism had betrayed its own roots, such that it took vows but failed to perform them in the spirit in which they were originally devised.[39]

---

[35] [Johannes Carion], ed. Philip Melanchthon and Caspar Peucer, *Chronicon Carionis expositum et auctum multis et veteribus et recentibus historiis [...] ab exordio mundi usque ad Carolum Quintum imperatorem, a Philippo Melanthone et Casparo Peucero: Adjecta est narratio historica de electione et coronatione Caroli V imperatoris* (Wittenberg: J. Crato, 1572), 436.

[36] Joachim Vadian, *Epitome Trium Terrae Partium, Asiae, Africae et Europae compendiarum locorum descriptionem continens, praecipue autem quorum in Actis Lucas, passim autem Evangelistae et Apostoli meminere* (Zürich: Froschauer, 1534), 187–88.

[37] Vadian, *Epitome* (as note 36), 433.

[38] Joachim Vadian, *Chronik der Aebte des Klosters St Gallen*, in *Deutsche historische Schriften: Joachim v. Watt (Vadian)*, ed. Ernst Götzinger, 3 vols. (St. Gallen: Zollikofer'schen Buchdruckerei, 1875–1879), vol. 1, 14–15.

[39] Vadian, *Chronik der Aebte* (as note 38), vol. 1, 16–33.

So how had things gone so badly wrong? The reformers, both German and Swiss, tended to combine two arguments which did not entirely sit well together. First, the *idea* that vows were meritorious was, and always had been, deeply wrong. Secondly, however, the degradation of religious practices, those that might have been a good idea in the ancient world, happened progressively, as human beings forgot vital principles in the quest for something new.

In Luther's *On Councils and the Churches*, published in 1539 in the wake of the summons to the abortive Council of Mantua, he charted the failure of councils to stop the growth of wealthy, depraved monasticism.

»Just as happens in a garden, where the weeds grow much higher than the true fruit-bearing shoots, so it also happens in the garden of the church: these new saints, who sprout and grow out from the side and yet want to be Christians, nourished by the sap of the tree, grow far better than the true old saints of the Christian faith and life.«

In the middle ages the numbers of house and the range of orders proliferated so that

»one could well say it rained and snowed monks«.[40]

Similarly Heinrich Bullinger in his *Origin of Error*, completed in its definitive form also in 1539, saw the monasteries as victims of their own material success:

»Religion begat wealth, and the daughter devoured the mother, that is, wealth drove out piety and introduced luxury. With piety neglected, a way was open for error; error in turn filled everywhere with superstition; superstition then suppressed good letters, and in their place implanted barbarism.«[41]

4. The papacy

As other scholars have demonstrated, the estrangement of the reformers, Luther above all, from the *ideal* of the papacy took some time to mature.[42] Within the same short period Luther could refer to the papal bull of excommunication as *The Execrable Bull of Antichrist*, and dedicate his *On Christian Freedom* to Leo X in hope against hope of a more considerate

---

[40] WA 50: 610–11; LW 41: 125–27.

[41] Heinrich Bullinger, *De Origine Erroris Libri Duo Heinrychi Bullingeri: In priore agitur de Dei veri iusta invocatione & cultu vero, [...] In posteriore disseritur de Institutione & vi sacrae Coenae domini, & de origine ac progressu Missae Papisticae* (Zurich: Froschauer, 1539), fos. 36ʳ–37ʳ. Compare Carion, *Chronica* (as note 35), 417–22.

[42] See for instance Scott H. Hendrix, *Luther and the Papacy: Stages in a Reformation Conflict* (Philadelphia: Fortress Press, 1981).

hearing.[43] However, once the breach with the papacy was complete, a historical problem remained. There had, as it seemed beyond doubt, been a succession of bishops in Rome. To Catholic apologists, the existence of this succession, and the Petrine commission handed down in Scripture, proved that the Catholic Church was the true one. If the reformers were to argue that their Church represented the true Church founded by Christ and sustained by the Holy Spirit, some way had to be found to argue away the history of the papacy.

That was not a pressing concern for the early reformers, but it became so as the years passed, and as the movement became a group of churches. It is a most interesting coincidence – given the premise of this volume – that the earliest major contribution to a Lutheran perspective on the history of the papacy was in fact written by an Englishman. In 1536 the English émigré and future martyr Robert Barnes (1495–1540) published his *Lives of the Roman Pontiffs, whom we call the popes* in Latin at Wittenberg.[44] Luther himself supplied a characteristic preface. As Paul had foretold, God had

»sent a spirit of error, that people should believe iniquity who were unwilling to believe the truth. So, little by little, [when Christ was abolished, with his faithful witnesses the Apostles, Martyrs and Confessors,] there finally succeeded that new Christ, that is, Antichrist in the temple of God, with his new saints. He taught us to worship those whom neither our fathers nor he nor we knew«.

This, Luther continued, could not have happened, or at least not so easily,

»if there had been some accounts of his acts handed down truthfully by faithful historians, by which devout people could have been warned: given that there seemed to be no shortage of those who could smell the foul stench of that Satanic drain«.

Luther, not a historian himself, welcomed Barnes's efforts to prove historically what Luther had argued from Scripture.[45]

In fact Barnes's work did not quite achieve its aims of a truly independent and critical history of the papacy.[46] For the most part he excerpted and summarized from a range of earlier authors, notably Bartolomeo Platina, whom he duly cited in his short paragraphs. Some of the legends, for

---

[43] Given the theological sophistication of Luther's thoughts on the Church, a case can be made that even such apparently contradictory positions concealed an inner consistency. See Dr. Wendebourg's paper as cited above, note 8.

[44] [Robert Barnes], *Vitæ Romanorum Pontificum: quos Papas vocamus, diligenter & fideliter collectæ per D. Doctorem R. Barns* (Wittenberg: Iosephus Clug, 1536).

[45] Ibid., A ii^r-A iiii^v.

[46] A more generous assessment of Barnes's work is found in Korey D. Maas, *The Reformation and Robert Barnes: History, Theology and Polemic in Early Modern England* (Woodbridge, UK; Rochester, NY: Boydell & Brewer, 2010).

example of the compilation of the Canon of the Mass by a succession of early popes, he quoted uncritically even though others, such as Bullinger, had already treated these with more scepticism.[47] However, Barnes developed across the pages of his compilation a habit of adding waspish marginal remarks about the ever-growing arrogance and assertiveness of the papacy. A Lutheran historical narrative emerged: the popes became progressively more and more ambitious for political power, especially at the expense of secular rulers. The popes bullied the church of Ravenna, which had not been subject to them, into obedience to Rome.[48] The Roman Empire was translated to the Franks by the authority of »the pope and not of Christ«.[49] Barnes reported the legend that Sylvester II was a dedicated magician.[50] By the 11th century he claimed that »for the most part the popes are either unlearned, bellicose, necromancers, seditious, or just downright evil«.[51] By the time that he reached the age of Hildebrand, elected pope as Gregory VII in 1073, Barnes felt free to editorialize copiously against those Catholic authors who had praised the pope for his elevation of the clerical estate. The contest between empire and papacy became, in Lutheran hands, a narrative of the improper assertion of ecclesiastical authority in the affairs of secular rulers, precisely the *confusio regnorum* that Luther had denounced in *On Secular Authority* in 1523.[52] It goes without saying that this historical argument helped to reinforce the later Lutheran appeal to the prince as protector and patron of the Church (although that role remained somewhat problematical within Luther's own theology).

By the mid–16th century this historical argument, that the fundamental error of the papacy consisted in its assertion of political power and authority, appears to have become established in Lutheran historical thinking. In the Carion-Melanchthon-Peucer *Chronicle*, Peucer interrupted his narrative of political events to lament the degradation of the Church. When

---

[47] Barnes, *Vitae Pontificum* (as note 44), B i[r/v]. For another account that would later be regarded as spurious, see Barnes's reference to Pope Eleutherius's letter to King Lucius of Britain on B viii[v]. This text also formed part of Henry VIII's propaganda campaign against papal monarchy.

[48] Ibid., G[v]-vi[r], G vii[r/v], K viii[r/v].

[49] Ibid., H vii[v].

[50] Ibid., O ii[r/v].

[51] Ibid., O v[v].

[52] Luther's *Secular Authority: To What Extent it should be Obeyed* (1523), is ed. in WA 11: 245–80; *LW* 45: 77–129. On *confusio regnorum* see W. D. J. Cargill Thompson, *The Political Thought of Martin Luther* (Brighton: Harvester, 1984), 55–56; and Eike Wolgast, »Luther's Treatment of Political and Societal Life« in *The Oxford Handbook of Martin Luther's Theology*, edited by Robert Kolb, Irene Dingel and L'ubomír Batka (Oxford: Oxford University Press, 2014), 397–413, at p. 399–400, 404.

discussing the Church around the year 1000, Peucer looked back to the days of the Synod of Nicea, when, he claimed, the church held no political authority, and indeed the patriarchs could not themselves convene synods: that power rested with emperors until the High Middle Ages.[53] By degrees, the popes clawed more and more authority from secular rulers through the early medieval centuries.[54] All this served as prelude to a narrative of the Investiture controversy, with Gregory VII as the villain of the piece.[55] Following that campaign the emperors and secular rulers were reduced to servitude under the papal tyranny.[56] By the time that he reached the 15th century, Peucer determined that the separation between the Roman hierarchy and the true Church was complete:

»For we do not, as some think, only disapprove of the corrupt manners and crimes of the priests and pontiffs: we deny to them the title of Church of Christ, in that they departed from the foundation of Christ and the Apostles, and in truth we judge the religion of Rome to be the abomination of desolation, of which the Son of God foretold, that is, the idol which wrought universal devastation in the Church.«[57]

A Swiss version of the same argument was compiled by Johannes Kessler (1502–74), pupil and follower of Vadian and educator at St-Gallen, in the work that he entitled *Sabbata*. Kessler had visited and studied at Wittenberg before returning home to write and teach: he affords an interesting example of crossover between the Lutheran and Swiss traditions. In a key chapter of *Sabbata* he addressed the history of the papacy and its degradation. He argued that for the first centuries of the Church there were no monarchical leaders, only godly pastoral bishops. The alliance with imperial power and the struggle against heresy led to greater assertiveness in church leaders, until Boniface III claimed the title of *Pater patrum*. Over the course of time the popes set themselves up over kings and claimed authority to confer imperial dignity on Charlemagne.[58]

---

[53] Carion, *Chronica* (as note 35), 417–18.
[54] Ibid., 419–20.
[55] Ibid., 422–33.
[56] Ibid., 462.
[57] Ibid., 508.
[58] Johannes Kessler, *Johannes Kesslers Sabbata mit kleineren Schriften und Briefen*, ed. Der Historische Vereins des Kantons St Gallen, (St. Gallen: Fehr'sche Buchhandlung, 1902), 28–62.

5. The Eucharist

On the one hand, all are aware just how dangerous a topic the Eucharist became to touch in the early Reformation and beyond. On the other, it was just as essential, in this case as in the previous two instances, to explain how a rite that was fundamental to the primitive Christian experience had been distorted and transformed into a travesty of its original intent. Once again, polemical historians of the Church told a story of progressive, gradual, incremental decay. Time and space allows for only brief discussion of two examples.

Philip Melanchthon, in an almost casual reference in his *De Ecclesia*, observed that on the authority of [ps-]Dionysius, early Eucharists consisted solely of prayers, a communion and dismissal: there were no private masses, and the then current Catholic practice was by those standards an abuse.[59] In the Melanchthon-Peucer revision of Carion's chronicle, the [corrupt] Catholic Mass was on two occasions referred to as the »Maozim«, the [plural] name of a false idol referred to in Daniel 11:38, which was long regarded as a prophecy of the Antichrist.[60] There followed a review of the steps by which the Mass became more sumptuous, and the laity were progressively excluded from frequent communion and from receiving the consecrated wine. In a later passage Peucer associated these changes with the rise of the papal monarchy, when the ›theatrical‹ aspect of the Mass replaced the voice of teaching.[61]

A very similar argument had been developed in far more comprehensive detail by Heinrich Bullinger in his *De Origine erroris, in negocio eucharistiae, ac missae*, which was first published separately in 1528[62] and then re-worked into the larger and more complete version of *On the Origin of Error* in 1539.[63] After praising the value of the sacrament, Bullinger claimed that it was celebrated in the very simplest possible fashion by the first Christians.[64] As time went by the rite was made more splendid,

---

[59] CR 23: 612.

[60] Carion, *Chronica* (as note 35), 367: »Sparsa etiam tunc semina, et fundamenta iacta mutationis et profanationis Coenae Dominicae et ἀρτολατρείας Pontificiae, quae pro Christo coluit Deum Maozim prorsus ritu et furore Ethnico, qui cultus est Idolum vastans, de quo vaticinatus est Daniel Propheta.«

[61] Ibid., 420: »Introductus est in Ecclesiam ad priores idolatrias et abusus cultus Idoli Maozim, quod occupavit in Ecclesia locum et honorem adorationis soli Deo debitum, et ad se oculos hominum mentesque convertit.«

[62] Heinrich Bullinger, *De Origine erroris, in negocio eucharistiae, ac missae* (Basel: Thomas Wolff, 1528). Amy Nelson Burnett has commented that this work was one of Bullinger's earliest theological treatises, compiled some years before its first publication.

[63] Ibid.

[64] Ibid., 133ʳ–134ᵛ.

and the details about its celebration were specified in a detail unknown to the early church.[65] Bullinger reported the story told by Platina of the introduction of different parts of the rite by successive famous popes, and was (unlike Barnes) extremely sceptical about most of the details. Bullinger went on to document the rise of multiple sacrificial masses, and the doctrine of transubstantiation, in granular detail. He ended the work with a call to return to the primitive simplicity of the early Church – as, of course, he believed that the Zürich church had already done.

In the fullness of time, the apologists of the Reformation would write histories of their own movement, and describe in detail the processes by which it came to be established. Beginning that process, however, took a few decades – and, one might add, required the lapse of a sufficient period of time that the reformers could no longer expect the Second Coming to render a history of their movement redundant.[66] Probably the first narrative of the early Reformation to be written was composed by Friedrich Myconius of Gotha around 1540; but it would not be published until the early 18th century in an edition by Ernst Salomo Semler.[67] The history of the Reformation proper would develop in the latter decades of the sixteenth century, through the Martyrologies of the reformed churches, and in due course through the confessional accounts of (for example) the Lutheran Lucas Osiander the Elder and the reformed apologist Abraham Scultetus.[68] However, for a long time the historical energies of the partisans of the Reformation, and of many of their opponents, were consumed with looking backwards. Reflecting on the early church supplied crucial arguments for the new churches which were coming into being.

---

[65] Ibid., 137[v]–142[r]. This passage may be compared with Barnes's far less critical summary noted above, note 47.

[66] For an argument that the Second Coming loomed large in Luther's vision of the place of the Reformation in history, see Heiko A. Oberman, »Martin Luther – Forerunner of the Reformation« in [Oberman], *The Reformation: Roots and Ramifications* (Edinburgh: T. & T. Clark, 1994), 21–52. As late as his *Supputatio Annorum Mundi* of 1541 Luther was convinced that history would not run for much longer.

[67] [Friedrich Myconius], *Friderici Myconii historia reformationis: vom jahr Christi 1517 bis 1542* (Gotha: Andreas Schallen, 1715).

[68] Lucas Osiander [the Elder], *Epitomes Historiae Ecclesiasticae, Centuriae I.-XVI.*, 10 vols. (Tübingen: Georgius Gruppenbachius, 1592–1604); Abraham Scultetus, *Annalium Evangelii passim per Europam* [...] *Renovati Decades Duae*, 2 vols. (Heidelberg: J. Lancelloti, 1618–20); for discussions see Euan Cameron, »One Reformation or Many: Protestant Identities in the Later Reformation in Germany«, in *Tolerance and Intolerance in the European Reformation*, ed. O. P. Grell and R. W. Scribner (Cambridge: Cambridge University Press, 1996), 108–27; »Primitivism, Patristics and Polemic in Protestant Visions of Early Christianity« in *Sacred History: Uses of the Christian Past in the Renaissance World*, ed. Katherine van Liere, Simon Ditchfield, and Howard Louthan (Oxford: Oxford University Press, 2012), 27–51.

The Scottish Reformation: Vision, Implementation, Memory

Kristen Post Walton

The Scots came late to the Reformation. The ideas of Luther did not break far into the Scottish consciousness until almost a decade after Wittenberg. The Scots did not reform their nation formally until 1560, twenty-four years after Calvin published his *Institutes*. Often, showing up »late to a party« can result in missing some major opportunities, but Scottish Reformers were able to take the delay to engage with reformers across the continent and in England, to engage with the intellectual developments of the Reformation, and to create a vision for their kingdom that would result in what Alec Ryrie termed »the first modern Revolution« in 1560s Scotland.[1] Using the knowledge gained by observing the path of the Reformation across Europe and taking Scottish traditions under consideration, the Sixteenth Century Scottish reformers were able to implement a far-reaching reformation in the country that not only transformed its religion, but also changed society and politics. The Scottish Reformation was deep and extremely successful, with a very high rate of conversion to the new faith and the creation of a Protestant state. Though this did not happen overnight, the groundwork for the political, social, and religious reformation of Scotland was laid in the 1560s. By the end of the decade, even the memory of the Scots was being transformed, as authors such as George Buchanan rewrote Scottish history to demonstrate that Scotland was not the last to reform, but instead, she possessed a native reformed Scottish church that had simply been perverted by Rome. The belated Scottish Reformation succeeded thoroughly because of the vision of the reformers, the manner in which they implemented the new faith, and the creation of a historical tradition that made Scottish Protestantism a part of Scottish Nationalism. Scotland was a Sister of Lutheran, Swiss, and English Reformations, but she was a younger sister, who observed the success and failures of her elder siblings before entering into her adulthood.

---

[1] Alec Ryrie, *The Origins of the Scottish Reformation* (Manchester: Manchester University Press, 2006), 1.

This chapter concentrates on the period before the Melvillian transformation of the church, emphasizing the roots of the Scottish Reformation and then focusing on its story during the first decade of its implementation. As such, this work explores three areas of the Reformation: the first is the vision gained for the Kirk based on international observation, highlighting the earliest connections with the continent and England, debate, and intellectual exchange. The second relates how that vision was implemented in Scotland to create, or at least attempt to create, an early universal Kirk. The final part considers how George Buchanan, among others, created a new historical memory for Scotland to help make the reformation permanent by tying the ideas of the new Kirk to ancient Scottish traditions. As a result, though not going into the details of the Scottish Reformation, this chapter lays a framework for the story of Knox and the political and religious reformation of 1557–67.

When discussing the Scottish Reformation, most historians note quickly that in 1528, Patrick Hamilton was burned as a heretic, and then they jump directly to the 1540s and the spread of Reformation ideas by Protestant leaders such as George Wishart and John Knox. The early Scottish Reformation, though, should not be ignored as it shows the very close continental connections of the Scots (all important in view of the recent Brexit vote), and the early introduction of Lutheran ideas through, largely, the foreign-educated university man. The 1560 Reformation was primarily a Calvinist one, but the roots of that Reformation were not simply Calvinist. Early (if weak) challenges to the church had occurred in Scotland during the fifteenth century, but the true reformed ideas first entered Scotland in the early 1520s. Master Patrick Hamilton, descendant of kings and an absentee cleric himself, was one of the central voices that brought the early Lutheran ideas across the North Sea. His internationalism introduced him to the ideas of Luther, and his passion for the ideas led to his execution as Scotland's first martyr of the Protestant Reformation. From the 1530s to 1560, the Scots reformers also were influenced by Zurich, Basel, and the Erasmian reformations. The introduction of Reformation ideas did not cause an immediate Scottish Reformation (the king was against that, with the benefits he received from the Pope), but Hamilton, like other early reformers, laid the groundwork for the 1560 Scottish Reformation by introducing ideas he adopted in Paris, Louvain, and Marburg, to St. Andrews, and from there, the kingdom of the Scots.

Patrick Hamilton had noble connections. His uncles were the Regent Albany from the minority of James V and the Regent Arran from the minority of Mary, Queen of Scots. Hamilton's noble connections allowed his ideas to carry to more people and offered him some early protection as he preached the ideas of Luther, but also ensured his quick martyrdom upon his final conviction of heresy. Master (as Knox refers to him) Patrick Hamilton was given a living in 1517 at the age of 14: Commendatory Abbot of Fearn Abbey in a remote area of East Ross-shire, a Premonstratensian order of friars founded in the 13th century.[2] Hamilton quickly used the money he received as a teenage leader of the Abbey to go to Paris for his education, shortly after his half-uncle Albany had returned to Scotland from France to act as Regent. Little is known about his time at Paris – his registration record remains, in which he lists himself as »Patricius Hamelto, Glassguensis, nobilis« – but there remains no definite answer as to which College he attended, though it is likely that he was at Montague where John Major was teaching.[3] During his time at Paris, he would likely have learned much of Erasmus's ideas as well as some of the early discussions of Luther's work. We know from Bulaeus that by late 1519, many copies of the Leipzig debate between Luther and Eck had come to Paris.[4] Hamilton is listed as receiving a Master's degree from Paris after 9 August 1520, and according to his friend Alesius, he next went to Louvain, where he possibly met Erasmus himself, particularly as Patrick's noble connections would have made it fairly easy to open the door, but no records remain and only Alesius's comment tells us that he visited Louvain.[5]

On the 9th of June 1523, Patrick Hamilton returned to St. Andrews, Scotland and quickly began implementing the ideas he had learned on the continent. He arrived the same day as John Major, who had been brought there by Archbishop James Beaton. Most believe that Hamilton at this point was more an ›Erasmian Humanist‹ than a Lutheran, having been convinced of Erasmus' philosophies while on the continent between 1517–

---

[2] For more on Commendators, see Mark Dilworth, »The Commendator System in Scotland«, *The Innes Review*, Volume 37, Issue 2, 51–72.

[3] Iain Torrance, »Hamilton, Patrick (1504?–1528)«, *Oxford Dictionary of National Biography*, Oxford University Press, 2004 (http://www.oxforddnb.com/view/article/12116, accessed 5 Aug 2016).

[4] Peter Lorimer, *The first preacher and martyr of the Scottish Reformation: an historical biography, collected from original sources, including a view of Hamilton's influence upon the Reformation down to the time of George Wishart, with an appendix of original letters and other papers* (Edinburgh, Thomas Constable, 1857), 38. Also see Caesar Egassius Bulaeus [César Egasse du Boulay], *Historia Universitatis Parisiensis*, 6 vols. (Paris: F. Noel, Petrus de Bresche et Iacobus de Laize-de-Bresche, 1665–1673), vol. vi, 108–09.

[5] Lorimer (see note 4), 28, 40–44 on Louvain, Alexander Alesius, *Primus liber Psalmorum iuxta Hebraeorum et divi Hieronymi Supputationem, expositus ab Alexandro Alesio* (1554), 164[v]. Alec Ryrie states that Hamilton likely became exposed first to the ideas of Luther at St. Andrews, but the higher likelihood is for Paris (Alec Ryrie, *The Age of Reformation: Religion, Politics and Society in Britain, The Tudor and Stewart realm, 1485–1603*, chapter 4).

23.[6] He was originally just incorporated into the University and only on 3 October 1524 was he admitted to the Faculty of Arts. He attached himself to St. Leonard's, where men such as Alexander Alane (Alesius) and John Winram were young canons of the Priory.[7] During his time in St. Andrews, »he called for implementation of humanist methodology in university teaching as a means to combat clerical ignorance«.[8] Hamilton was not yet a declared Lutheran during this time, but he was moving further away from the Roman Church and refused to wear his monk's habit, despite remaining Abbot of Fearn.[9] Only in 1526 did Hamilton turn more fully to Lutheranism and start to declare his reformed convictions more openly. As a result, he soon was forced to flee Scotland. By the winter of 1527, Beaton had begun to inquire into Hamilton's views and found the scholar »inflamed with heresy, disputing, holding and maintaining divers heresies of Martin Luther and his followers, repugnant to the faith«.[10] Hamilton then decided to go into exile as opposed to recant or suffer formal accusation from the Archbishop. He fled to Wittenberg with a servant and two friends – John Hamilton of Linlithgow and Gilbert Winram of Edinburgh. He did not stay long in Luther's town – plague had descended upon the city – and though he might have met Melancthon and Luther, there is no mention of Hamilton in their letters. He soon proceeded to the new university Philip of Hesse was founding in Marburg as the first new evangelical university, whose department of theology was under the oversight of Francis Lambert.[11] The University opened in spring of 1527 (some places give a formal opening date of 1 July) and Hamilton and his friends matriculated in May, when Hamilton named himself from Linlithgow. Lambert and Hamilton developed a close relationship, and Hamilton became the first member of the university to publish a set of theses for open debate.[12] These became known as *Patrick's Places* and laid out the details of many of his beliefs. Although the work would not have a huge impact on Scottish theological developments, it was published on the continent and translated into English by John Frith before Frith's burning at Smithfield in June 1533.

---

[6] Torrance (see note 3).

[7] Lorimer (see note 4), 56–57.

[8] James Edward McGoldrick, »Patrick Hamilton, Luther's Scottish Disciple«, *Sixteenth Century Journal*, Vol. 18, No. 1 (Spring, 1987), 83.

[9] Alesius, quoted in Lorimer (see note 4), 62.

[10] Lorimer (see note 4), 82–83.

[11] Ibid., 87–88.

[12] Torrance (see note 3), also Lorimer (see note 4), 96.

Patrick's Places was Hamilton's first written attestation of his faith. The work looked at the distinction between law and gospel, stressed sola fide when discussing faith and works, and addressed justification and holiness. His ideas were not new – they did not add anything significant to the developing theology of the reformation – but clearly laid out his beliefs and are important as the earliest »doctrinal production of the Scottish reformation«.[13] Hamilton produced these so quickly on his arrival that it is now believed that he had composed most of the ideas in his personal commonplace book he had in St Andrews. »His theses were directly and explicitly Biblical. Emphasis was laid on human powerlessness under sin and utter dependence upon God's grace«.[14] His ideas relate directly to Luther's 1520 Of the Liberty of a Christian Man and Melanchthon's 1521 Loci Communes. Throughout the work, he stresses the important of sola fide. He starts the work with the 10 Commandments and states that Loving God and Loving thy neighbor are the two most important, for if those two are followed, all the rest of the commandments will be followed as well. He uses syllogism to defend his arguments, with every example coming directly from scripture. Hamilton's primary argument was that one can only get to heaven by Grace alone, but at the same time, he went with the Lutheran concept that »good works are necessary fruits of faith. [...] He denied vigorously that the Protestant doctrine of justification encourages moral laxity and indifference toward good works«.[15] Hamilton had confirmed his beliefs and soon realized that he was prepared for whatever would meet him at home. His friends stayed in Germany while Patrick Hamilton crossed back across the North Sea to preach and spread his evangelical zeal in Scotland. His determination to spread the faith led to his eventual arrest and execution. He knew his return would not end well and did not take advantage of opportunities to avoid martyrdom. Hamilton knew his position in society would mean that his martyrdom would have a lasting impact – and it did. His debating skills won him converts, including Alesius, who was first sent to argue with him and ended up converted, and the story of his asking for »dry wood« while being burned helped to turn him into one of Scotland's best known martyrs, whose initials still lie in on North Street in St. Andrews (where first year students work hard not to step on them!). Hamilton and his foreign education affected the growth of Protestant ideas in Scotland, and although his Lutheran beliefs were soon eclipsed by the Calvinist Refor-

---

[13] Lorimer (see note 4), 96–97.
[14] Torrance (see note 3).
[15] McGoldrick (see note 8), 86.

mation of 1560, Hamilton's preaching and his martyrdom did fan the flames of the Scottish Reformation.

Patrick Hamilton was not the first person to bring up the idea of reforming the Roman Church in Scotland, nor was he likely the first to bring Lutheran ideas into the kingdom. »His trial, for all its fame and importance, was neither the genesis nor the matrix of religious dissent in Scotland«.[16] His Martyrdom, combined with his place in society would mean that he had a greater impact than the earlier attempts to reform the church. Although Scotland did not have its own major home-grown heresy during the middle ages, the ideas of Wycliff and the English Lollards crossed over the northern border. Englishmen and Bohemians both brought the teachings of Wycliffe and Hus to Scotland, so that in 1425, the parliament passed an act prohibiting the heretical beliefs. Scotland did have some of her own native Lollards, though. Martin Dotterweich argued strongly for the role of Quintin Folkhyrde – a Scot with connections in Prague and England – who preached in the vernacular at the beginning of the 15th century, highlighting that his work was actually even translated into Czech! His ideas were largely anti-clerical in nature, but he embraced the evangelism of the later Protestants as he rode through Scotland, likely around Ayrshire.[17] In addition, Knox showed how thirty Lollards of Kyle were brought to trial by Blackadder in 1494 on thirty-four charges of heresy. Many of these Lollards had personal connections to King James IV, and they did not receive formal sentencing, but had been accused of crimes from rejecting the worship of images to allowing priests to marry and stating that prayer could be made directly to God outside a church to weakening the overall position of the Pope, stating Peter was the only one who received rights from Christ, not his heirs or successors to other Lollard-like beliefs.[18] Another man from Ayrshire, John Campbell of Cessnock who Alesius describes as having been allowed to study the Testament at home by James IV. When he was accused of heresy, he appealed to the king, who interviewed both him and his wife,

»So clearly and convincingly, by quotations from Scripture, did she disprove the charges made, that the king not only acquitted Campbell, his wife, and his priest,who were all accused, but even rose and embraced the lady, greatly praised her study of Christian doctrine«.[19]

---

[16] Martin Dotterweich, *The Emergence of Evangelical Theology in Scotland to 1550* (unpublished PhD thesis, University of Edinburgh, 2002), 116.

[17] Ibid., 19–25. Ian Cowan has stated that the Protestantism in Ayrshire should not be overstated, but the fact is that it is emphasized because it was not the norm, not because it was. Ian B. Cowan, *Regional Aspects of the Scottish Reformation* (London, The Historical Association, 1978), 6.

[18] Dotterweich (see note 16), 25–42.

Alesius uses this as an example of how James IV had been open to some of the ideas embraced by the reformers. In any case, before Hamilton returned from the continent, some early aspects of Reformation theology had found a foothold, no matter how small, in at least Ayrshire.

Even Luther's Reformation and its followers had an impact on Scotland before Hamilton's full conversion to the reformed faith. The Frenchman, Monsieur De La Tour, who came to Scotland with the Duke of Albany was later burned for heresy in France after spreading Lutheran ideas in Scotland before 1525 (he left with Albany in 1524).[20] In 1525, the Parliament of Scotland legislated against Luther for the first time, not forbidding Lutheran ideas (as the legislation states that Scots »persist in the holy faith«), but forbidding their importation

»That no manner of stranger who happens to arrive with their ships within any part of this realm bring with them any books or works of the said Luther, his disciples or servants, dispute or rehearse his heresies or opinions, unless it be to disprove them, and that by clerks in the schools only«.[21]

The legislation, though, had also required that the act be published in all ports and burghs of Scotland. This would mean that any person who had not previously been aware of the ideas of Luther would learn about them (nothing like being on the Index of forbidden books to get an immediate best seller). By 7 August, the king had sent out a mandate to the Sheriffs of Aberdeen, on the request of Gavyn Dunbar, an order to take inquisition of all people in Aberdeen who »have such books or favour such errors of the said Luther«, bringing the act beyond just the foreigners who might be importing the books. The act was formally reinforced later in 1527 to address all men, not just foreigners, but despite both acts, Lutheran books and pamphlets did spread in the country. The 1527 Act also challenged the earlier ability to dispute the new opinions by »limiting the freedom of disputation to clerks in school alone«.[22] In January 1527 as well, Hackett, Wolsey's man in Antwerp, sent a letter describing the spread of ideas to Scotland, »divers merchants of Scotland bought many of such like books, and took them to Scotland a part to Edinburgh and most part to the town of St. Andrew«. The English had attempted to seize and burn them, but the ships had already set sail.[23] The government of James V did not see

---

[19] *Principum addam iudicia, et ut omitta[m] reliquos, domesticum tibi exemplum recitabo* [D vii]ʳ, 28–29, quoted in Dotterweich, 51.

[20] Alec Ryrie, *The Origins of the Scottish Reformation* (see note 1), 31.

[21] *The Records of the Parliaments of Scotland to 1707*, K. M. Brown et al eds (St Andrews, 2007–2016), 1525/7/32. Date accessed: 5 August 2016.

[22] Lorimer (see note 4), 67–69.

[23] Robert Demaus, *William Tyndale: A Biography. A Contribution to the Early History of the English Bible*, (Longon: The Religious Tract Society, 1886), 170.

much of a native threat to the Church in the 1520s, and even most of the
Scots who embraced the new theology had overseas experience. Ryrie
notes Melville and Gilbert's trips to Germany; the Zwingli-influenced
Wishart and others also shared the foreign experience with Patrick Hamilton – George Buchanan notes about himself that »he fell into the flame
of Lutheranism then spreading far and wide« when he left St Andrews in
1527.[24]

Most historians jump directly from the martyrdom of Hamilton to that
of Wishart when discussing the origins of the Scottish Reformation. The
early reformed church, though, was fanned by the close international connections held by the literate classes of Scotland, and reformed ideas did
not disappear in the almost twenty years between the two martyrdoms.
After Hamilton's death, others, including Alesius, were firmly convinced
of the new faith. In Scotland during the 1530s and early 40s, Reformed
thought was not rampant, but it was there. Between 1528–32, Ayrshire
churches were desecrated. In 1533, the state legislated against a vernacular
Bible, and Hamilton's colleague Henry Forrest was executed for his beliefs. Many fled Scotland in the 1530s, but more martyrdoms did occur,
especially in St Andrews in 1538–9. Though James V encouraged some
challenges to the church in his own court (he actually commissioned George Buchanan to satirize the Franciscan Friars), in 1541 the king put forth
strong acts against the Reformation. Notwithstanding, he pushed for reform within the clergy.[25] Although in 1543 the Vernacular Bible was allowed, other craftsmen were burned for their beliefs in Perth. Many of the
reformers, including Alesius (who spent much of his life in exile, ending in
Leipzig in 1565) and Hamilton's sister, left the country, building even
further early connections with the international reforming community.
During this time, and for the years leading up to 1560, those connections
grew exponentially. The story of Patrick Hamilton and the early reformers shows much of the truth of Jenny Wormald's contention on the
spread of the early Reformation in Scotland: »Those men who went to
England and Europe, rejecting Rome and adopting Lutheran beliefs, seem
to have been strongly influenced by the Scottish Lutheran, Patrick Hamilton. They had something else in common; they all began as clerics,
even priests, in the old church. [...] It was the pre-Reformation church that
provided the education at home that opened the way to further study
abroad. Those who remained within the church and were receptive to
what was happening in Europe had, through that contact, given it its

---

[24] Ryrie, *Origins* (see note 1), 31, Lorimer (see note 4), 81.
[25] Ryrie, *Origins* (see note 1), 44–47.

strongest hope of life. But those whom it sent abroad who found themselves convinced by the new beliefs created a rival and very powerful group, with the same appeal to a strongly self-conscious European society as their orthodox counterparts, and the additional appeal of the modern as opposed to the traditional«.[26]

From the days of Hamilton through the martyrdom of Wishart, Reformation ideas were the exception in Scotland, but many of those who did believe traveled out of the country. Many of the ideas that entered and spread were from more of the Zwinglian and Calvinist than the Lutheran traditions from the 1530s through the Reformation itself.[27] These connections grew as the exile of Protestants became even more noticeable during the late 1540s and 1550s.

John Knox is the most famous of the Scottish reformers, and the best example of how exile influenced the development of his faith and ideas about religion, but he was not the only Scottish reformer to go into self-exile during the regency of Mary of Guise. In addition, those friendly to reform kept up extensive correspondence with others on the continent, which helped Scottish ideas about the faith to develop and grow. Knox is the best example of the movement of person and ideas in this period. After leaving the French galleys, Knox was exiled to England in 1549, where he throve and embraced the more Calvinist ideas of the Edwardian church. Mary Tudor's accession to the throne saw him fleeing: as opposed to traveling with English Protestants through the Low Countries, he landed in Dieppe and first went to the Scottish community. While there, he strongly rejected Nicodemite principles as he learned that many of his English colleagues were attending mass to hide their Protestant leanings. The 1554 rebellion in England encouraged him to move on towards Zurich to consult with the great reformers in Switzerland. En route to Zurich, he stopped in Geneva to speak with Calvin. He went to Lausanne to meet Beza and Viret and finally landed in Zurich to speak with Bullinger. His European exile then took him to back to Dieppe, where he was more easily able to be in contact with other Scots exiles such as John Willock, before returning to Geneva to study further the Reformation ideas, particularly in relation to the cause of England.[28] Knox went to Frankfurt (where he was expelled due to a disagreement over liturgy), and returned

---

[26] Jenny Wormald, *Court, Kirk and Community* (Edinburgh, Edinburgh University Press, 1981), 103.

[27] Duncan Shaw, *Renaissance and Zwinglian Influences in Sixteenth-Century Scotland* (Edinburgh: Edinburgh University Press, 2012), passim.

[28] Jane Dawson, *John Knox* (New Haven and London: Yale University Press, 2015), 82–89.

to Geneva, leading to his strengthened connection with the Swiss reformers. In many ways, Frankfurt was the pivotal moment for the Scottish Reformation, if we give Knox as much credit as he gives himself for the establishment of the Kirk. It was the break with the English congregation in Frankfurt that led Knox to return to Geneva and to return as well to Scotland, both figuratively and with his visit of 1555–6. Knox, though, was not the only Scot to be influenced during this period by time on the continent. John Wedderburn who died in 1556, wrote his Gude and Godlie Ballatis, many of which had obvious links to the Protestant ideals, such as

»God send euerie Priest ane wife / And everie Nunne ane man / That thay mycht live that haly lyfe / As first the Kirk began«.[29]

William Ramsay, the second Master of St. Salvator's in 1560, went to Wittenberg in 1544, and others also connected with the continent.[30]

When Knox did return to Scotland first in 1555–56, he brought with him the ideas he had been learning on the continent. Having recently been expelled from the Frankfurt English congregation, Knox began to look more to the Scottish Church, where the preacher excitedly rediscovered that his »ministerial talents were in considerable demand«.[31] While there, Knox also connected with William Harlaw, John Willock (who had previously been in Emden), John Lockhart, John Erskine of Dun and others who together helped to build the Protestant networks within Scotland.[32] During his time back from the continent, Knox not only married, he also helped to encourage Protestantism across Scotland and also built connections with many of the lairds and lords through his departure in July 1556. Knox's visit was crucial for the development of a collective identity for the Protestants, and even after his return to Geneva, he continued to build the idea of a rebellion to Catholic rule through letters to the magnates and the commons. The wars of 1558–1560 were based on religion *and* politics – if not for the growing French presence and Mary of Guise's apparent turn away from the passive toleration of Protestants with the burning of Walter Mylne – the 1560 Reformation would likely not have occurred.[33] Knox

---

[29] John Wedderburn, *Ane Compendious Book of Godlie Psalmes and spirituall sangis collected forth of Sindrie par Scripture* (Edinburgh: Henry Charter, 1576), 165.

[30] James K. Cameron, »Aspects of the Lutheran Contribution to the Scottish Reformation 1528–1552«, *Records of the Scottish Church History Society*, v. 22, issue 1, (1984) 2.

[31] Dawson, *Knox* (see note 28), 111.

[32] Ibid., 112.

[33] Amy Blakeaway has recently published an article arguing convincingly that the wars of the Scottish Reformation really began with 1558 and an open war between England and Scotland, before the Scots join forces with the English in 1560 (Amy

arrived back in Scotland in May 1559, and he had a vision for Scotland – he wanted to create a reformed nation that would be his own, expanded version of Calvin's Geneva. »The Godly reformers quickly enacted their plan. Over a few days that May, Scottish Protestantism went from ›being an underground movement in an outwardly Catholic country to an armed revolt against established authority.‹«[34] The reformers started with iconoclasm, spreading in May from Perth to Fife. Knox next began to hold assemblies of the new kirk, preaching to those who would listen. By October 1559, the reformers had begun to shift any remaining French loyalties in the country and began a major propaganda war (of real or imagined events) that helped to consolidate the Scots (even those not in favor of the new religion) against the Regent Mary of Guise.[35] The rebels even named a new government which deprived the regent of her rule in Scotland in name if not fact on the 23rd of October.[36] On 27 February 1560, the Scots created a secret diplomatic alliance with England and by the end of June, Mary of Guise was dead, and it was obvious the new Scottish government and the reformers had succeeded. On 16 June, commissioners from France arrived in Scotland to entreat of peace, and by July, the Scottish situation was settled. The English Cecil laid out a plan for the governance of Scotland, which left the chief offices of state and justice in Scottish hands and placed the governance of Scotland with safeguards over their selection linked to the Three Estates of Parliament.[37] The King of France (Francis II) »engaged [...] that the government of Scotland should be administered by twelve commissioners, all Scotsmen; and that in case there should arise any dispute about matters of religion or civil polity, the decision thereof should rest with the parliament of the whole kingdom.« The Scots were free to call their Parliament, and in August, they moved to reform the kingdom, without their Queen's formal consent.

When the Confession of Faith was presented to the Parliament, only the Catholic Bishops and the Lords of Atholl, Somerville and Borthwick voted against its institution. The new religion was confirmed in Scotland

---

Blakeaway, »The Anglo-Scottish War of 1558 and the Scottish Reformation«, *History, The Journal of the Historical Association*, 2017, 201–224).

[34] Kristen Post Walton, »Scotland's ›Cittie on a Hill‹« in Halvorson and Spierling, eds., *Defining Community in Early Modern Europe* (Surrey: Ashgate, 2008), 249–50.

[35] Ryrie, *Origins* (see note 1), 172–73.

[36] *Selections from Unpublished Manuscripts in the College of Arms and the British Museum illustrating the reign of Mary, Queen of Scotland, MDXLIII-MDLXVIII* (Glasgow, 1837), 73–76.

[37] Jane Dawson, *The Politics of Religion in the Age of Mary, Queen of Scots: The Earl of Argyll and the Struggle for Britain and Ireland,* (Cambridge: Cambridge UP, 2002), 102.

by the Parliament (though Mary, Queen of Scots would not ratify it formally). Knox argued strongly for the legality of the Reformation, even without the formal ratification by the monarch, and defended strongly the legality of the Parliament itself, stating:

»The Queen's person was absent, and that to no small grief of our hearts. But were not the Estates of her realm assembled in her name? Yea, had they not her full power and commission, yea, the commission and commandment of her head, the King of France, to convocate that Parliament, and to do all things that may be done in lawful Parliament, even as if our Sovereigns had been there in proper person? That Parliemant, we are bold to affirm, was more lawful, and more free than any Parliament that they are able to produce for a hundred years before it, or any that hath since ensued; for in it the votes of men were free and given of conscience; in others, they were bought or given at the devotion of the prince.«[38]

Knox's desire to justify the reformation of religion and establishment of his form of Protestantism also showed a transformation in the role of Parliament itself and in the governance of the state. Although he still gave an oral nod to the role of the monarch within the state, he argued clearly that the lack of a monarch actually made the Parliament into a more free and more legal Parliament than it would have been had the Queen been in residence. The Scottish situation remained confused during the fall. The French King refused to nominate his governors of Scotland, the reformers worked to create a Book of Discipline (which finally was accepted the following winter). Under the ideas espoused with the Book of Discipline, the state would continue to govern the country until the church reforms could be implemented, thereby reducing the state's power, so that eventually, the state would largely be concerned just with foreign policy and some aspects of civil and criminal law, while most of the rest of the governance in Scotland would be done by the parishes and the church.[39] The death of Francis, though, on 5 December 1560 had changed somewhat the trajectory of the governance of the newly formed Scotland, if not its religion. Mary, Queen of Scots would return to the country the following August and take over the reins of government, meaning that the monarchy would be restored in fact as well as in name. Despite once again having a Catholic monarch, Knox's vision for the implementation of a Godly State in Scotland did not end, and during the 1560s, the vision laid the groundwork for the Scottish Kirk, including creating the Scots Confession of Faith, laying out the basic theology, which would be largely upheld until

---

[38] John Knox, *The History of the Reformation of Religion in Scotland, Book III*, ed. William McGavin (Glasgow: Blackie, Fullarton & Co., 1831), 216–17.

[39] Roderick Graham, *John Knox, Man of Action* (Edinburgh: St Andrew Press, 2013), 194–95.

replaced by the Westminster Confession. The six Johns' vision for Scotland was not fully implemented, but their idealistic vision, based on years of observation of international reformations, is important for setting up the longer trajectory of the Scottish Church.

In December 1560, the Scots had called the first meeting of the General Assembly (the Convention) of the new Kirk, starting the religious transformation from the center. The Scots Confession had determined that the state would support religion and religion would support the state from that day forward in Scotland. Kirk session meetings had already started in a few communities around Scotland, including St. Andrews, where Knox had imposed Discipline. Eighty percent of the cases brought in front of the St. Andrews session in 1560 were concerned with adultery and fornication. These sessions were all local in nature, and the Convention was supposed to help implement a broader policy to create a godly society not just on a local, but on a national level. Interested in all aspects of society, the Convention looked into everything from marriage, to weights and measurements, from alms for the poor to the election of ministers and place of civil magistrates. The Convention, combined with the Book of Discipline was to implement an entire reformed society and government in Scotland, and included over fifty pages of details covering all aspects of both.[40] As the Book stated:

»As no citie, toun, house, or familie, can maintaine their estate, and prosper, without policie and governance, even so the church of God, which requireth more purelie to be governed than anie citie or familie, cannot without spirituall policie and ecclesiasticall Discipline, continue, increase, and floorishe.«[41]

As John McCallum so rightly pointed out, the implementation of the ideas of the Book of Discipline, the Convention, and the local Kirk Sessions was not immediate across the entire kingdom, but by early 1561, the ideas for how to create a Godly state were not only formalized, but they were slowly beginning to be implemented across Scotland. Ideas for poor relief and the establishment of education (especially with universities) were particularly slow to be implemented, but remained a concern for the Kirk.[42] Despite that, other aspects of the new kirk did begin to be implemented, from the calendar of observance (Knox was well-known to require atten-

---

[40] Walton (see note 34), 256–57.

[41] *The First and Second Book of Discipline. Together with some Acts of the Generall Assemblies, clearing and confirming the same: and An Act of Parliament* ([Amsterdam], 1621), A 2$^{r/v}$, 23 STC 22015 (Hereafter *BoD*). This quote was also cited in Walton, 257.

[42] James Kirk, »Melvillian Reform in the Scottish Universities«, in Michael Lynch and Ian B. Cowan, eds., *The Renaissance in Scotland* (Leiden: Brill, 1994), 276–300. Also see Steven J. Reid, *Humanism and Calvinism, Andrew Melville and the Universities of Scotland, 1560–1625* (London: Routledge, 2011), 268.

dance at a General Assembly on Christmas day), the acceptance of a vernacular Bible, and even Knox's Book of Common Order (which was the
first book printed in Gaelic in 1563).[43] Of the approximately 1080 parishes
in Scotland, 240 places were filled by 1561 and around 850 by 1567; mostly in the lowlands and often not full ministers but instead readers, but this
does demonstrate an attempt to move towards local implementation of the
new religion.[44] Finally, although presbyteries would not emerge for some
time, by 1563, some locations in Scotland had both kirk sessions and
moderators, who would preside over the meeting of the Kirk. As a result,
although some historians have tried to negate the importance of the 1560
reformation and the first decade of the Kirk, the vision of 1560 did have a
large impact on the creation of the Scottish Kirk.[45]

The final section of this paper looks at how the Scots not only implemented their vision through the arms of both the Kirk and the Government, but also how they worked to change Scottish culture and tradition
by claiming that the new kirk was not fully new – but instead was part of a
deep Scottish history. George Buchanan and others, starting in the 1560s,
rewrote the Scottish history books to create a national myth that demonstrated that the new Kirk was in many ways a recreation of the traditional
Scottish Church that had been corrupted by Rome in the middle ages.
Buchanan published his History of Scotland (*Rerum Scoticarum Historia*)
in 1579. Following the path of the early fifteenth century Walter Bower
who wrote the Scotichronicon (building on the work of John of Fordun)
to build a strong Scottish historical tradition, Buchanan states he wrote his
work to ›purge‹ Scottish history »of sum Inglis lyis and Scottis vanite«[46] in
part of what was helped to tie together the Scottish Reformation with a
strong Scottish identity, rejecting the English and Roman past attempts to
control the northern British kingdom. Craig, Spottiswoode, Calderwell
and others would later build on Buchanan's traditions to create a national
history tied largely around the church, but Buchanan led the way with his
establishment of a new historical memory for the Scottish Kirk. The story
of the Sixteenth Century Scottish Reformers' interpretations of the pre-
Roman church in Scotland allows us to gain further insight into the idea of

---

[43] Dawson, *Scotland Re-Formed, 1488–1587* (Edinburgh: Edinburgh UP, 2007), 227–
29.

[44] Michael Lynch, *Scotland, A New History* (London: Pimlico, 2001), 198–99.

[45] Gordon Donaldson, *The Scottish Reformation* (Cambridge: Cambridge UP, 1960),
74.

[46] »George Buchanan to Mr. Thomas Randolph; jeering him upon his second Marriage. Busied on the Story of Scotland. Knox's History/ Commends Beza's poetry.
1572«, in Henry Ellis, ed., *Original letters: illustrative of English History; Including
numerous Royal Letters* (London: Richard Bentley, 1846), I, i.

the development of a pure Church in Scotland and an increasing Scottish communal identity.

Briefly, Buchanan idealizes Celtic figures like the Culdees whom he states were far more impressive »in learning and piety« than the Roman monks who expelled them, yet »exceeded them in Wealth, Ceremonies, and in Pomp of outward Worship; by all which they pleased the Eye, but infatuated the Mind.«[47] In describing the trajectory of Scottish History, particularly the morality, asceticism, and discipline the Scottish Kirk come to light. In addition, Buchanan, also the author of *De Iure Regni Apud Scotos*, highlights the fact that kings were always supposed to listen to their councils and many of the kings were chosen by the Scots nobles. These ideas correspond well with his own Protestant resistance theory developed in response to the rule and forced abdication of Mary Stuart. The idea of a council also corresponds well with the concept of the Scottish General Assembly and the participation of the greater population in the Presbyterian government, not only the highest church members or the King. For Buchanan, the roots of these ideas date to the original King Fergus, whom he sees as being elected king by the commonality. To Buchanan, the crown was under the law from the beginning[48] – something that ties directly into his Protestant Resistance theory.

Buchanan clearly denotes the negativities of being moral versus immoral in terms that come straight from the reformers, by giving very specific punishments to those historical figures who act immorally. He importantly, though, addresses the question of discipline as a feature of the early church, defining it differently from earlier historians. John Major noted how during the time of Oswald, »children of the English were instructed by Scottish teachers in the study and observance of the discipline known among the regulars.«[49] Major's discussion of discipline, though (he mentions it multiple times in his work) largely refers to the actions of church members, discipline as the study of a subject (albeit the subject is religion) or discipline as punishment. Buchanan's discipline reflects the more Calvinist ideas that correspond with the state and a government imposed discipline from the king. Buchanan refers multiple

---

[47] George Buchanan, *History of Scotland, Book IV* (London: J. Bettenham et al., 1733), 157.

[48] Roger A. Mason, *Scots and Britons: Scottish Political Thought and the Union of 1603* (Cambridge, Cambridge UP, 1994), 118. Also see his work on Boece: Roger A. Mason, »'s cotching the Brut: politics, history and national myth in sixteenth-century Britain«, in Roger A Mason, ed. *Scotland and England 1286–1815* (Edinburgh: John Donald, 1987), 60–84.

[49] John Major, *A History of Greater Britain as Well England as Scotland 1521, vol. 10*, ed. Archibald Constable (Edinburgh: Edinburgh UP, 1892), 93.

times to the »ancient discipline« of Scotland: first, when describing Scotland and noting that the common people had given up their ancient discipline to embrace indulgences, but later he uses the term in a more political sense.[50] Constantine II in the 860s »corrected the public discipline« by »severe laws«; he was particularly harsh in his laws, bringing the priests back to frugality, making effeminate young soldiers lie on the ground and eat only one meal a day to harden them, prohibiting games except those that strengthened mind or body, and punishing drunkenness with death. Buchanan praised Constantine's mind and virtue in his description, presenting him as a model king.[51] One hundred years later, Buchanan has Kenneth III purifying court and country to bring the people back to their »ancient discipline«.[52] Buchanan's descriptions of the kings do not diverge greatly from those of earlier historians – Boece, for example, describes the laws of Constantine and how he made drunkards leave the country on pain of death[53] – but Buchanan specifically uses the term discipline, which ties in well with the gospel and the ideas of the Reformers. He also addresses even the early monks, defining them as pure in relation to the corrupt monks of the Roman church. Buchanan worked to create both a religious and political tradition in Scotland that promoted his own beliefs.

Buchanan had a specific agenda to promote his political ideas of »»popular‹ sovereignty and the legitimacy of resistance to tyranny« that he embraces in his *De Iure Regni*[54] and his ideas about the Catholic Church and new Scottish Kirk. It is hard to believe that Buchanan did not realize that he was creating history, more than describing facts, despite using rhetoric of how he was fixing all of the errors of past historians from Bower to Major to, especially, Boece. Throughout his History are references to a Scottish Kirk, unpolluted by Roman influence, that was much more pure than what developed in the later Middle Ages. Buchanan, though, like those before him, was creating historical memory that future Scots would be able to call on in order to argue for a Scottish religious tradition with roots that reached back much further than the year 1560. Nineteenth Century scholars embraced his version of Scottish Kirk history that was also expounded upon by Calderwood who refers to him di-

---

[50] Buchanan (see note 48), 58.

[51] Ibid., 284.

[52] Ibid., 305.

[53] Hector Boece, *The History and Chronicles of Scotland, Book 10*, ed. John Bellenden (Edinburgh: W and C Tait, 1821).

[54] Roger A Mason, »Buchanan in Reformation Britain: From Buchanan to Blaeu: the politics of Scottish chorography 1582–1654«, in *George Buchanan: Political Thought in Early Modern Britain and Europe*, eds. Caroline Erskine and Roger A Mason, (Aldershot: Ashgate, 2012), Chapter 1.

rectly in his 17th century History.[55] Two years after Buchanan's death in 1582, the Scottish Parliament challenged the truth of both of Buchanan's great works – not banning them outright, but demanding that they be turned into to the Lord Secretary to be purged of

»offensive and extraordinary matters specified therein, not suitable to remain as accords of truth to posterity«.[56]

Part of the notorious Black Acts of 1584, this act likely passed more because of Buchanan's political than religious descriptions (James VI much preferred the idea that Fergus I conquered Scotland than that he was declared King by the people in Assembly), but it demonstrates the effect that his history was having on the Scots. The government rarely suppresses something that is not being read and believed by people within the State. Buchanan's creation of a historical memory strongly promoted the ideals of Buchanan and established a Scottish lineage for the faith of the Reformers.

The Scottish reformation is complex, but also builds on the traditions of other European reformers who paved the way for the Scottish Kirk. Continental and English connections helped to build the faith, but also helped the Scots determine the direction of their own religious path. When Knox, the other Johns, and the Lords of Congregation worked to develop the direction of the Scottish faith, they were influenced greatly, but not solely, by Geneva. As they moved forward, though, they worked to create a thorough Protestant state that connected history, tradition, society, culture, the political sphere, and religion.

---

[55] David Calderwood, *The History of the Kirk of Scotland*, ed. Thomas Thomson (Edinburgh: Wodrow Society, 1842).

[56] *An act for punishment of the authors of the slanderous and untrue calumnies spoken against the king's majesty, his council and proceedings, or to the dishonour and prejudice of his highness, his parents, progenitors, crown and estate«* NAS, PA2/12, 118^{r/v} [1584/5/14], accessed at http://www.rps.ac.uk/trans/1584/5/95 , 10/20/15.

Das Selbstbild der englischen Reformation
Eine Fallstudie

Martin Ohst

Die Aufgabe, über *das* Bild zu berichten, das die englische Reformation von sich selbst gezeichnet hat, ist strukturell unlösbar. Wie in allen Spielarten der reformatorischen Bewegung und Kirchenbildung konkurrierten ja auch in England unterschiedliche Konzeptionen und Selbstdeutungen der Reformation miteinander, und so entstanden ganz unterschiedliche, in Konkurrenz und Widerstreit sich aufeinander beziehende Selbstbilder.

Aus diesen Selbstbildern wird im Folgenden eines herausgegriffen, und zwar dasjenige, das die maßgeblichen Gestalter derjenigen Reformmaßnahmen, welche im *Elizabethan Settlement* zu einem vorläufigen Abschluss gelangten, gezeichnet haben – mit der Absicht, es in einer langfristigen, geduldigen Erziehungs- und Bildungsanstrengung den Gliedern der Ecclesia Anglicana als das normativ-verbindliche argumentativ darzulegen und einzuprägen.

Es findet sich in den beiden *Books of Homilies*, also zwei Sammlungen von Lesepredigten, deren jeweilige Erstfassungen in Schwellenjahren der Reformation erschienen: 1547 gleich nach der Thronbesteigung Eduards VI. und 1563 nach der Thronbesteigung seiner Halbschwester Elisabeth; aus gegebenem Anlass[1] wurde der zweiten Sammlung 1571 noch ein weiterer Text gegen Ungehorsam und Rebellion angefügt, und damit stand der Textbestand für die Folgezeit fest. Eine nach den Maßstäben ihrer Zeit sehr sorgfältige kritische Edition dieses Textcorpus hat John Griffiths 1859 vorgelegt.[2] 2015 hat Gerald Bray eine Neuausgabe veranstaltet.[3] Sie beruht

---

[1] Papst Pius V. hatte 1570 in der Bulle *Regnans in excelsis* Elisabeth I. zur Häretikerin erklärt, sie deshalb des Thrones für unwürdig erklärt und die Untertanen von ihren Treueiden entbunden (Quellen zur Geschichte des Papsttums und des Römischen Katholizismus, hg. v. Carl Mirbt, Tübingen [4]1924, 348f. [Nr. 491]).

[2] The Two Books of Homilies Appointed to be Read in Churches, Oxford 1859. Diese Ausgabe ist vollständig und kostenlos im Internet unter Google Books abrufbar.

[3] The Books of Homilies. A Critical Edition, hg. v. Gerald Bray, Cambridge 2015. Da sich diese Ausgabe sicherlich künftig schlichtweg wegen ihrer leichteren Verfügbarkeit und Lesbarkeit durchsetzen wird, zitiere ich sie im Folgenden. Ich gebe dabei zunächst die Nummer der Sammlung, dann die des Einzelstücks und dann die Seitenzahl an. »I/4, ed. Bray, 32« heißt also: First Book of Homilies, 4. Predigt, S. 32 in Brays Edition.

text- und quellenkritisch wesentlich auf den Ergebnissen von Griffiths' Untersuchungen und modernisiert die Texte orthographisch. Einen Fortschritt gegenüber der alten Edition markiert sie insofern, als dass sie auch die Homiliensammlung des Londoner Bischofs Bonner enthält: Die sollte in der Regierungszeit Marias das *First Book of Homilies* verdrängen und attestierte diesem damit wider Willen einen hohen Grad an Wirksamkeit.

Eine ganz vorzügliche Einführung in diese Texte erschien 2011 aus der Feder von Ashley Null.[4]

I.

Die beiden corpora bilden miteinander ein durchkomponiertes Ganzes. Die erste Sammlung hat ganz eindeutig ihren Schwerpunkt in der Entfaltung kirchlicher Lehre, und in diesem Zusammenhang kommt den ersten fünf Homilien noch einmal hervorgehobene Bedeutung zu: Bis auf die zweite, die wohl von John Harpsfield verfasst wurde, stammen sie von Thomas Cranmer und legen in Grundzügen die für alles weitere grundlegenden kategorialen Leitlinien des reformatorischen Christentumsverständnisses dar – eben in der Fassung, die es in Cranmers Bildungs- und Gedankenwelt gewonnen hat.

Die Sequenz der ersten Sammlung nimmt ihren Ausgang bei einer Anleitung zur fruchtbaren Bibellektüre (I/1) und beginnt dann materialiter mit dem eben schon erwähnten Traktat zur Erbsündenlehre (I/2). Die Lehre von der Erlösung durch Christus (I/3) wird operationalisiert durch Sermone über den lebendigen Glauben (I/4) und die guten Werke in ihrer notwendigen Verbindung mit dem Glauben (I/5). I/6 spezifiziert hier noch einmal, indem das Wechselverhältnis von Gottes- und Nächstenliebe erörtert wird. Die folgenden Homilien widmen sich Problemen praktischer christlicher Lebensgestaltung: Fluchen und Meineide (I/7) stehen exemplarisch für die Gefahren, die im Abfall von Gott durch Tatsünden (I/8) liegen. Positive Impulse geben die Ermunterungen (»Exhortations«) gegen die Todesfurcht und zum Gehorsam gegen Herrscher (I/9) und Obrigkeiten (I/10), und die beiden letzten Stücke der Sammlung widmen sich dann wieder dem Kampf gegen Laster: Hurerei und Unsauberkeit (I/11) sowie Streitsucht und Gezänk (I/12).

---

[4] Ashley Null, Official Tudor Homilies (in: The Oxford Handbook of the Early Modern Sermon, hg. v. Peter McCullough, Hugh Adlington u. Emma Rhatigan, Oxford 2011, 348–365).

Profil und Schwerpunkte der zweiten Sammlung unterscheiden sich hiervon deutlich. Im Mittelpunkt steht hier christliches Leben, sofern es sich in festen Institutionen sowie in Regeln, Sitten und Bräuchen gestaltet, welche die unterschiedlichen Lebenszyklen umspielen. Hier geht es weniger um die kategorialen Grundlagen christlichen Glaubens und Lebens als um dessen gesellschaftlich geprägte und prägende Gestalt, welche durch die Reformation eine tiefgreifende, kaum ein Gebiet des Kultus wie des Alltags unberührt lassende Transformation erfahren hat. Die erste Predigt gibt Leitlinien für die angemessene Wertschätzung von Kirchengebäuden (II/1). Es folgt das längste Stück der gesamten Sammlung, die wohl von John Jewel verfasste *Homily Against Peril of Idolatry and Superfluous Decking of Churches* (II/2) – eine immerhin über siebzig Druckseiten lange Stellungnahme zur Bilderfrage; ihr kritischer Radikalismus wurde durch Elisabeth I. persönlich an zwei Stellen durch Eingriffe in den Text abgemildert.[5] Das positive Gegenstück hierzu bietet auf gerade einmal fünf Seiten die Predigt über die angemessene Instandhaltung und Ausschmückung von Kirchengebäuden (II/3). Die nächsten Sermone bilden eine kleine Trilogie: II/4 widmet sich dem Fasten als gutem Werk, und II/5 wendet sich gegen Völlerei und Trunkenheit; hiermit hängt dann auch eng der Kampf gegen überflüssigen Aufwand für Kleidung und Schmuck zusammen (II/6). Schon rein thematisch ist hier das Ineinander von Kontinuität und Diskontinuität in den spätmittelalterlichen und frühneuzeitlich-reformatorischen kirchlichen Anstrengungen zur Sozialdisziplinierung mit Händen zu greifen.

Unter dem Leitwort »Prayer« (II/7) thematisieren die beiden folgenden Homilien den öffentlichen Gottesdienst: Dessen Ort und Zeit (II/8) sowie dessen Volkssprachlichkeit (II/9). Ein hiermit verwandtes Problem thematisiert II/10, nämlich den Umgang mit solchen Stellen der Heiligen Schrift, die zum hier leitenden reformatorischen Bibelverständnis im (scheinbaren) Widerspruch stehen.

II/11 behandelt die Liebestätigkeit an Armen und Bedürftigen. II/12–17 sind für Hauptfeste des Kirchenjahres und deren würdige Feier konzipiert: Weihnachten (II/12), Karfreitag (II/13) und Ostern (II/14) leiten die Sequenz ein, die durch II/15 (Kommunion) nur scheinbar unterbrochen wird, denn hier ist offensichtlich die herkömmliche Regel leitend, dass eben in der Osterzeit kommuniziert wird. An die Homilie zum Pfingstfest (II/16) schließt sich als Annex die volkskundlich und frömmigkeitsgeschichtlich besonders beziehungsreiche Homilie zu den traditionellen Feldumgängen am Sonntag Rogate an. – Auch die beiden folgenden Ho-

---

[5] Vgl. II/2 (ed. Bray, 227, 249).

milien gehören wider den ersten Augenschein thematisch eng zusammen: II/18 ist der Ehe gewidmet, und mit der »Idleness«, gegen welche sich II/19 wendet, ist das Mönchtum gemeint. II/20, also das ursprüngliche Schlussstück der Sammlung, ist der Christenbuße gewidmet; die Predigt »Against Disobedience and Wilful Rebellion« ist, wie gesagt, erst 1571 angefügt worden.

Der normative Rang ist diesen Texten nicht nachträglich zugewachsen, sondern die einzelnen Homilien, die ja ihrerseits bisweilen Reihen von selbständigen Predigten sind, sind, ebenso wie die durchkomponierten Sammlungen, von Anfang an mit normativem Geltungsanspruch konzipiert worden.

Die Verwirklichung dieses Anspruchs haben die Initiatoren strategisch ins Werk gesetzt, indem sie die gottesdienstliche Verlesung dieser Texte verpflichtend anordneten. Am striktesten ist hier das königliche Vorwort zur ersten Ausgabe des 1st Book: Dort wird allen kirchlichen Amtsträgern mit Seelsorgeaufgaben die allsonntägliche Verlesung einer solchen Homilie bzw. des Teils einer solchen vorgeschrieben, und wenn jemand – ausnahmsweise – eine eigene Predigt hält, dann muss die ausgefallene Homily-Lesung am darauffolgenden Sonn- oder Feiertag nachgeholt werden.[6] In der Endfassung der *39 Articles* ist das dann erheblich gemildert:

»The second Book of Homilies, the several titles whereof we have joined under this Article, doth contain a godly and wholesome Doctrine, and necessary for these times, as doth the former Book of Homilies, which were set forth in the time of Edward the Sixth; and therefore we judge them to be read in Churches by the Ministers, diligently and distinctly, that they may be understanded of the people.«[7]

Diese Homilien stammen von unterschiedlichen Autoren, die inhaltlich je eigene Akzente setzen und stilistisch individuelle Konturen aufweisen. In einigen Homilien sind umfängliche Textbestände patristischer oder kontinentaleuropäischer Provenienz verarbeitet. All das ist in den Einleitungen der Editionen von Bray und besser noch von Griffiths detailliert nachzulesen und wird hier im Folgenden vernachlässigt – zugunsten einer Perspektive, aus der die beiden Homilien-Bücher miteinander als Ausdruck eines gestaltenden Willens zu stehen kommen, also so wahrgenommen werden, wie sie wohl von den Gottesdienstgemeinden, welche ihre Verfasser und Redaktoren vor Augen hatten, rezipiert werden sollten.

---

[6] Vgl. ed. Bray, 5f.
[7] Die Kirche von England. Ihr Gebetbuch, Bekenntnis und Kanonisches Recht, hg. v. Cajus Fabricius, Corpus Confessionum 17/I, Berlin u. Leipzig 1937, 397.

II.

Natürlich werden diese Gemeinden nirgends im Stil heutiger Homiletik thematisiert. Aber wenn man die Texte im Zusammenhang liest und sie in der Auswahl ihrer Themen auf sich wirken lässt, dann stellt sich ohne unzulässigen Phantasieaufwand doch ein ziemlich deutliches Bild davon ein. Es fällt ja schon bei oberflächlichem Lesen auf, dass immer wieder von Götzendienst etc. die Rede ist – das ist schon in den doktrinären Texten der ersten Sammlung der Fall, aber dann massiert in denen der zweiten Sammlung, die den Zyklus der kirchlichen Feste und Feiertage traktieren. Insbesondere spricht die Tatsache für sich, dass der Sermon zur Bilderfrage mit seiner fast schon grotesken Überlänge gut ein Viertel jener zweiten Sammlung in Anspruch nimmt. Offenbar haben die Autoren und Redaktoren Menschen vor Augen, für welche das vorreformatorische kirchlich geprägte Leben mit allen seinen Riten und Gebräuchen zwar verschwunden sein mag, aber es ist doch präsent – als eben nicht verwundener, verarbeiteter, bewältigter Verlust. Und genau deshalb muss darauf immer wieder zurückgekommen werden; es gilt zu erklären, warum der Bruch stattfinden musste und warum die Mittel und Prozesse, die ihn herbeigeführt haben, dem höherrangigen göttlichen Willen gemäß waren und sind. Der Grundton der *Homilies* ist also apologetisch, und die Gemeinden, auf deren angenommene Verstehensvoraussetzungen hin sie konzipiert sind, werden als den Neuerungen gegenüber skeptisch-reserviert imaginiert.

Die Reformation ist also in diesen Lesepredigten omnipräsent – ausdrücklich und noch mehr unausdrücklich. Sie markiert einen tiefen Einschnitt in das zuvor gültige, althergebrachte Gefüge von Lebensgewohnheiten und Lebensgewissheiten. Dieser Einschnitt ist geschehen, und er hat eine neue Gestalt kirchlichen Lebens hervorgebracht. Er ist allerdings immer noch im kollektiven und individuellen Gedächtnis als Einschnitt präsent: Den Predigthörern, welche den Autoren vor dem inneren Auge stehen, kommt er in allen Bereichen des kirchlichen Lebens im Wochen-, Jahres- und Lebenszyklus immer neu zu Bewusstsein, und deshalb bedarf er immer wieder neu der Erklärung und der Rechtfertigung. Diese Rechtfertigungsanstrengungen haben ihr positives Widerlager im Angebot eines erneuerten geschichtlichen Selbstverständnisses: Sicher, die Kontinuität zum papstkirchlichen Christentum der Vorfahren mit seinem Reichtum an Riten und Gebräuchen ist abgebrochen. Aber an die Stelle der alten religiösen Ritual- und Vorstellungswelt ist ein neues Angebot der Identifikation und Selbsteinordnung getreten: Das einst im biblischen Israel und Juda sowie in der Frühen Kirche archetypisch realisierte Gottesvolk mit seinen allein wahrhaft ewiges Heil und zeitliches Wohl verheißenden Lebensnormen und Lebensformen. Die Reformation kommt in diesem Bild zu stehen als Abkehr von zeitweiligen verderblichen Devianzen, bewerkstelligt durch die dazu dem Gottesvolk eingestifteten Institutionen. Ihre Legitimität erweist sich darin, dass sie selbst samt der Problemkonstellation, welche sie hervorgebracht hat, in der normativen Geschichte des Gottesvolkes unmissverständlich präfiguriert ist.

III.

Die zu diesem Zweck aufgebotenen Gedankengänge werden fundiert durch ein normatives Grundgefüge, welches die Kategorien bereitstellt, anhand derer sich argumentativ darlegen lässt, dass es sich bei dem, was der reformatorische Umbruch beseitigt hat, um Missbildungen handelte, während die Neuerungen, welche die Reformation hervorgebracht hat, in Übereinstimmung stehen mit den allgemeinverbindlichen Norminstanzen allen christlichen Glaubens und Lebens. All das wird entfaltet in den ersten fünf Homilien der ersten Sammlung; bis auf die (relativ unbedeutende) über den Sündenfall und die Sünde stammen sie, wie gesagt, aus Cranmers Feder.

Die alles bestimmende Leitvorstellung gleicht einer Ellipse mit zwei Brennpunkten, welche die Bibel und das Gottesvolk bilden: »Denn Gottes wort kann nicht on Gottes volck sein, widerumb Gottes volck kann nicht on Gottes wort sein«[8] – an diese Maxime Luthers erinnert jenes elliptische Interdependenzverhältnis rein formal. Sieht man jedoch näher hin, dann treten die inhaltlich-materialen Differenzen deutlich hervor.

Nach Cranmers Homilie ist das Gotteswort die Bibel als geschlossener Kanon. Sie ist das gültige, in sich wirkmächtige Zeugnis von Gottes Wesen und Gottes Willen. Das gilt einmal hinsichtlich des Menschen als des Sünders, der sich im Glauben die Heilstat Christi aneignet und so im werktätigen Gehorsam gegen die göttlichen Gebote zum Heil gelangt. Und das gilt ebenso für die sozialen Lebensstrukturen, in denen der Glaube des gerechtfertigten Sünders sich zu bewähren und zu betätigen hat.

Die Bibel ist in corpore, als Kanon, Gegenstand des Glaubens: Rechtfertigender Glaube hat zu seiner unwandelbaren und unentbehrlichen Grundlage den Glauben an das Bibelbuch. Der nimmt die Geschichtserzählungen der Schrift zur Kenntnis und eignet sich die mit ihnen verbundenen religiösen Deutungs- und Wertungsmuster an, und die werden dann zu Matrizen seiner eigenen Wirklichkeitsorientierung und -gestaltung.

---

[8] Martin Luther, Von den Konziliis und Kirchen (WA 50,629).

Dieser Glaube lässt sich eben auch die Lehre von der Erbsünde und die Verheißung der rein geschenkhaften Sündenvergebung und Rechtfertigung um Christi willen gesagt sein. Er impliziert die Einsicht, dass die Teilhabe an den ihm verheißenen Heilsgütern daran gebunden ist, dass der Glaube seinerseits zum Motiv einer ihm authentisch entsprechenden Lebenspraxis wird:

»And yet that faith doth not exclude repentance, hope, love, dread and the fear of God, to be joined with faith in every man that is justified. But it excludeth them from the office of justifying. So that although they be all present together in him that is justified, yet they justify not altogether. Nor that faith doth not exclude the justice of our good works, necessarily to be done afterward of duty towards God, (for we are most bounden to serve God in doing good deeds commanded by him in his Holy Scripture all the days of our life).«[9]

In Cranmers Fassung ist die Lehre von der Rechtfertigung aus dem Glauben, anders als bei Luther, aber auch bei Melanchthon, nicht die Gesamttheorie christlichen Glaubens und Lebens. Vielmehr ist sie, wie in der Scholastik, eng bezogen auf die Taufe und auf die als punktueller Akt des Christenlebens verstandene Buße.[10]

Dieses Profil zeigt sich nochmals deutlicher, wenn man sich die biblischen Leitbezüge ansieht: Sie stammen vorwiegend aus den Deuteropaulinen, aus den Pastoralbriefen und aus den Katholischen Briefen des Neuen Testaments, und der eigentliche Leittext für Cranmers Verständnis des rechtfertigenden *Glaubens* ist das Glaubenskapitel des Hebräerbriefs, den Cranmer, wie er mehrfach betont, für paulinisch hält.[11]

Und was dabei herauskommt, ist eine Rechtfertigungslehre, die völlig problemlos an die einschlägigen patristischen Ausführungen angeknüpft werden kann; eng verwandt ist sie mit Augustins – natürlich ihrerseits durch eine reformatorisch gefärbte Brille gelesener – Schrift *De fide et bonis operibus*.[12]

---

[9] I/3 (ed. Bray, 24). Im letzten Teil des Zitats klingt Eph. 2,10 an; der gedankliche Gehalt dieses Verses ist in den einschlägigen Ausführungen der *Homilies* sehr viel intensiver präsent, als die Zahl der im Register vermerkten förmlichen Zitate es vermuten lässt.

[10] »[A]nd therefore we must trust only in God's mercy and that sacrifice which our high priest and Saviour Christ Jesus, the Son of God, once offered for us upon the cross, to obtain thereby God's grace and remission, as well of our original sin in baptism as of all actual sin committed by us after our baptism, if we truly repent and convert unfeignedly to him again« (I/3, ed. Bray, 27).

[11] Vgl. exemplarisch I/4 (ed. Bray, 34–36).

[12] Von Cranmer zitiert I/4 (ed. Bray, 34).

Exkurs

An dieser Stelle drängt sich unwiderstehlich eine profilierende dogmengeschichtliche Zwischenbetrachtung auf: Martin Luthers reformatorisches Verständnis der christlichen Religion erschließt sich der dogmengeschichtlich fragenden Rückschau als kongeniale Neuaneignung bestimmter Leitelemente des ursprünglichen Paulinismus, die im Römerbrief und im Galaterbrief vertreten werden, also in denjenigen Texten, in denen das paulinische Evangelium sich gerade darin zur Geltung bringt, dass es eingespielte Muster religiöser menschlicher Selbstdeutung ins Unrecht setzt und in staunenswerter Weise neu konfiguriert: Nach Luther ist Christsein Erlöstwerden im Hineingezogenwerden in das Ursprungsgeschehen der christlichen Religion, dessen Mit- und Nacherleben. Gottes Fordern und Sichschenken in Jesu Christi Wort, Weg und Werk aktualisieren sich im und am einzelnen Christenmenschen mit derselben erschütternden und beseligenden Dramatik wie bei den Zeitgenossen, insbesondere bei Paulus selbst. Das Hineingezogenwerden in die Ursprungsdramatik der christlichen Religion, deren worthaft vermitteltes Miterleben im angefochtenen Glauben ist das dynamische Zentrum sich in unendliche individuelle Lebensgeschichten ausdifferenzierender christlicher Existenz.

Auch die Books of Homilies *sind durch und durch von paulinischer Terminologie geprägt. Ihre Quellenbasis ist jedoch eine charakteristisch andere. Sie umfasst vor allem solche Texte und Textkomplexe, in denen die paulinische Terminologie in urchristliche Konsense eingeschmolzen worden ist. So sind gedankliche Muster entstanden, die sich von der sperrigen Eigenart des originären Paulinismus durch »Popularisirung und Vereinfachung« unterscheiden. Sie bezeugen also ein »theoretisch vereinfachtes, praktisch fruchtbar gemachtes Christenthum«, wie es die historistische Exegese vor etwa 100 Jahren in den Deuteropaulinen, in den Katholischen Briefen und in den Pastoralbriefen vorfand und als dasjenige Reservoir von Vorstellungen und Gedanken identifizierte, aus dem sich die »alte Kirche [...] einen mittleren Durchschnitt apostolischer Lehre construirt« hat.[13] Die Ursprungsdramatik der christlichen Religion ist hier mental in die Ferne gerückt und kommt nicht im modus der Selbstvergegenwärtigung in Betracht, sondern eher als ätiologische Erzählung, auf welche gegenwärtige Glaubenssätze und Lebensregeln sich legitimierend zurückbeziehen.*

An der so verstandenen Bibel vermag also der Christ Gottes Willen für ihn und mit ihm abzulesen – im Sinne einer Rechtfertigungslehre, die ihn in die Erfüllung der göttlichen Gebote einweist.

Ebenfalls eröffnet ihm die Bibel ein Verständnis der gegebenen geschichtlich-sozialen Welt, welches ihm diese eben als Ort seines werktätigen Gehorsams vor Augen stellt.[14] Es ist der Bibelglaube, der Lebensorientierung und Lebensleitung gewährt. Charakteristisch ist das folgende Zitat mit seiner Anlehnung an 2.Kor 5,6f.:

---

[13] Alle Zitate aus HEINRICH JULIUS HOLTZMANN, Zur praktischen Erklärung des Hebräerbriefs (in: Zeitschrift für praktische Theologie 13, 1891, 219–238, hier: 221).

[14] Grundlegend hierzu ist I/1 (ed. Bray, 7–13).

»›Therefore let us be always of good comfort, for we know that so long as we be in the body we be as it were far from God‹ in a strange country, subject to many perils, ›walking without‹ perfect ›sight‹ and knowledge of Almighty God, only seeing him by faith *in the Holy Scriptures*.«[15]

Die Leitvorstellung, die als hermeneutischer Zentralbegriff die Orientierungspotentiale der Bibel erschließt, ist der Begriff des Gottesvolkes, dessen Glieder alle Christen durch ihre Taufe sind.

Deren Geschichtserzählungen, insbesondere die des Alten Testaments, dokumentieren archetypisch und somit für alle Zeiten gültig Gottes durch Lohn und Strafe erziehendes Heilshandeln an seinem Volk; besonders schön wird das am folgenden Zitat deutlich, das sich auf das alttestamentliche Bilderverbot bezieht:

»You will say peradventure, these things pertain to the Jews; what have we to do with them? Indeed, they pertain no less to us Christians than to them. For if we be the people of God, how can the Word and law of God not appertain to us? Saint Paul, alleging one text out of the Old Testament, concludeth generally for other Scriptures of the Old Testament as well as that, saying: ›Whatsoever is written before (meaning the Old Testament) is written for our instruction‹ [Röm. 15,4]; which sentence is most specially true of such writings of the Old Testament as contain the immutable law and ordinances of God, in no age or time to be altered, nor of any persons or nations or age to be disobeyed.«[16]

Gemäß den vereinfachten Grundstrukturen Augustinischer Geschichtstheologie war dieses Gottesvolk im Alten Bund im Biblischen Israel verkörpert; im Neuen Bund ist es universalisiert; es lebt unter ganz unterschiedlichen weltlichen Herrschern in verschiedenen Gemeinwesen. Eine exklusive Identifikation des englischen Volkes mit dem Gottesvolk sucht man in den Homilies vergeblich. Sicher, England kann darauf angesprochen werden, dass es sich in besonderer Weise der göttlichen Zuwendung erfreut[17] oder es kann wegen seiner starren Undankbarkeit getadelt werden,[18] aber das ist nie exklusiv gemeint. Das Gottesvolk ist vielmehr die umfassende Gemeinschaft derjenigen Menschen, die trotz des Sündenfalles von Gott zum Heil berufen und erwählt sind, und es lebt in unterschiedlichen, gottgewollten weltlich-politischen Ordnungsgefügen. Der Bibelglaube ist also keineswegs das Fundament hierokratischer oder theokratischer Konstruktionen, sondern er lehrt gerade die gegebene weltliche

---

[15] I/9 (ed. Bray, 78). Die kursivierte Passage hat keinen Anhalt am Paulus-Text.

[16] II/2 (ed. Bray, 225).

[17] »But blessed be God that we in this realm of England feel not the horrible calamities, miseries and wretchedness which all they undoubtedly feel and suffer that lack this godly order« (I/10, ed. Bray, 86).

[18] »O England, ponder the time of God's merciful visitation, showed thee from day to day, and yet will not regard it, neither wilt thou with his punishment be driven to duty, nor with his benefits provoked to thanks« (II/17, ed. Bray, 465; vgl. Lk. 19,41ff.).

Obrigkeit richtig einzuschätzen; der jeweilige König ist »God's lieutenant, vicegerent and highest minister in that country where he is king«.[19]

Weil das so ist, darum kann in unverkennbarer Anknüpfung an die Terminologie henricianischer und edwardianischer Kirchenpolitik die Bibel geradezu als Inbegriff der

»holy rules, injunctions and statutes of our Christian religion, [...] that we have made profession to God at our baptism«[20]

bezeichnet werden. Und die gibt den Christenmenschen hinsichtlich ihres Verhältnisses zu den weltlichen Herrschern die folgende Leitmaxime ihres Handelns:

»Let us all obey, even from the bottom of our hearts, all their godly proceedings, laws statutes, proclamations and injunctions, with all other their godly orders«.[21]

IV.

Dieses Gesamtkonzept christlichen Lebens, das sein Fundament in der als Lebensordnung verstandenen Bibel besitzt, ist für das Orientierungsprogramm, das die *Homilies* entfalten, konstitutiv. Das bezeugt eindrücklich die Komposition der ersten Homiliensammlung, die mit *A Fruitful Exhortation to the Reading and Knowledge of Holy Scripture*[22] beginnt und mit einem Sermon gegen Zank und Streit in Glaubensdingen endet. Dort wird die Situation vorausgesetzt, dass selbst beim Bier die Vorwürfe hin- und herfliegen:

»›He is a Pharisee, he is a gospeller, he is of the new sort, he is of the old faith, he is a new-broached brother, he is a good catholic father, he is a papist, he is an heretic‹«.[23]

Das Programm zur Überwindung dieser religiösen Fragmentierung lautet:

»Let us so read the Scripture that by reading thereof we may be made the better livers, rather than the more contentious disputers«.[24]

Wer also die Bibel liest, der lebt sich förmlich ein in die Lebensweisungen und Lebensordnungen des Gottesvolkes. Er lernt Gottes Willen mit seinem Volk und für sein Volk kennen, er erkennt, wo und wie der Teufel immer wieder in Gottes Reich eindringt – verführend, irreleitend, spal-

---

[19] I/10 (ed. Bray, 92).
[20] I/1 (ed. Bray, 13).
[21] I/10 (ed. Bray, 87).
[22] I/1 (ed. Bray, 7–13).
[23] I/12 (ed. Bray, 109).
[24] I/12 (ed. Bray, 111).

tend. Und ihm erschließt sich eben auch, dass die Reformation in England als Transformation des Kirchenwesens auf königliche Weisung hin und als Aufrichtung der königlichen Suprematie in der Ecclesia Anglicana und über sie ein Akt des Gehorsams gegen die dem Gottesvolk eingestiftete Ordnung war und als solcher zu akzeptieren ist.

Die archetypisch-normative Geschichte des Gottesvolkes hat im Paradies begonnen, aber sie hat ihr Ende weder in Christi Himmelfahrt noch beim Abschluss des neutestamentlichen Kanons gefunden. Sie umfasst neben der biblischen Geschichte des Alten Bundes und der Zeit Christi und der Apostel auch die Zeit der Kirchenväter. Wie über die Bibel, so beansprucht diese Selbstdeutung der Reformation auch über die allgemein als normativ angesehene patristische Periode[25] die alleinige Deutungshoheit.

V.

Wenn man sich diesen Anspruch und seine Gründe vor Augen führt, dann fällt es auch leichter, ein Charakteristikum der *Homilies* zu verstehen, das bisher nicht erwähnt wurde, nämlich deren überreiche Bezugnahmen auf Autoren aus der patristischen, aber auch aus der frühmittelalterlichen Periode.[26] Als unbefangener Leser drängt sich einem ja zunächst die Frage auf, wem mit diesen Präsentationen von Exzerpten und Lesefrüchten gedient sein sollte – ein durchschnittlicher Predigthörer des späten 16. Jahrhunderts konnte doch sicher etwa mit dem Namen Johannes Chrysostomos nicht mehr anfangen als ein heutiger! Hier soll sicherlich keine laientheologische Kompetenz gefördert werden, sondern die Namen und Zitate sollen den Predigthörern ebenso wie die Rekurse auf biblische Erzählungen Identifikations- und Deutungsmöglichkeiten eröffnen. Durch Horizontverschmelzungen wird die Situation im nachreformatorischen England daraufhin transparent, dass ihre charakteristischen Eigenheiten in der normativ-archetypischen Geschichte des Gottesvolkes präfiguriert sind: Israelitischer Götzendienst und mönchische Zeremonialfrömmigkeit

---

[25] Vgl. die folgende Passage zum Bilderverbot: »that this truth and doctrine concerning the forbidding of images and worshipping of them, taken out of the Holy Scriptures as well of the Old Testament as the New, was believed and taught of the old holy fathers and most ancient learned doctors, and received in the old primitive church which was most uncorrupt and pure« (II/2, ed. Bray, 228).

[26] Exemplarisch sei verwiesen auf die Wolke von Zeugen, die Cranmer in I/3 (ed. Bray, 25 f.) für den von ihm entfalteten Begriff des lebendig-tätigen rechtfertigenden Glaubens ins Feld führt. Charakteristisch ist weiterhin, wie Johannes Chrysostomos die Doktrin bekräftigt, dass auch die Angehörigen des Geistlichen Standes dem weltlichen Herrscher zum Gehorsam verpflichtet sind (vgl. I/10, ed. Bray, 88).

bzw. der Kampf gegen diese beiden Entartungen werden so als lediglich zeitgeschichtlich differente Ausprägung eines identischen Konfliktmusters durchsichtig,[27] und das wiederum zeigt: Die Entfernung der Heiligenbilder aus den Kirchen, die Auflösung der Klöster und das Ende monastischen Lebens in England haben Land und Volk nicht etwa aus der Kontinuität genuin christlicher Lebensgestaltung herausgerissen, sondern sie, ganz im Gegenteil, nach einer Periode der Perversion wieder in diese legitimierende Kontinuität eingegliedert.

Das zeigt nicht nur der Blick ins Alte Testament, sondern auch die Geschichte der Alten Kirche. Die Kirche der Spätantike ist eben nicht organisch-stufenlos in die Papstkirche des Mittelalters übergegangen, sondern hier hat sich ein Abbruch ereignet: Die Bildlosigkeit des frühchristlichen Gottesdienstes wurde allmählich aufgeweicht. Und maßgeblich beteiligt an diesem Verfallsprozess waren die römischen Bischöfe, die gerade im Zuge dieser politischen und kirchenpolitischen Aktionen illegitime Machtansprüche erhoben und durchsetzten, welche das Römische Reich mit katastrophalen Langzeitfolgen schädigten und schwächten. In seiner Homilie über den Kirchenschmuck schildert John Jewel das alles in einer ausführlichen, weitgehend von Heinrich Bullinger entlehnten Erzählung des Bilderstreits im 8. und 9. Jahrhundert. Diese ganze Erzählung ist durch und durch didaktisch-tendenziös gestaltet; zweifelsohne hatte sie für Predigthörer aber auch einen beträchtlichen Unterhaltungswert.[28]

In dem Geschichtsbild, das die *Homilies* ihren Hörern vor Augen malen, liegt hier der Wendepunkt, von welchem ab diejenigen Verfallsprozesse begannen, die dann mit und seit der Reformation umgekehrt wurden.

Wir halten fest: Die archetypisch-normative Geschichte des Gottesvolkes, die sich dem Glauben erschließt und die den Predigthörer sich selbst[29] sowie den Weg zum zeitlichen Wohl und zum ewigen Heil eröffnet,[30] also der Hintergrund, auf den die *Homilies* ihr Bild der Reformation auftragen, ist dreigliedrig und reicht von der Schöpfung und dem Sündenfall bis zum Übergang der Spätantike in das Frühe Mittelalter.

---

[27] Vgl. I/5 (ed. Bray, 44 f.).

[28] Vgl. II/2 (ed. Bray, 234–249).

[29] »And as drink is pleasant to them that be dry and meat to them that be hungry, so is the reading, hearing and searching and studying of Holy Scripture to them that be desirous to know God, or themselves, and to do his will« (I/1, ed. Bray, 7).

[30] »It giveth good counsel in all doubtful things. It showeth of whom we shall look for aid and help in all perils, and that God is the only giver of victory in all battles and temptations of our enemies, bodily and ghostly« (I/1, ed. Bray, 9).

Was so vor den Hörern bzw. Lesern entfaltet wird, ist, formal gesprochen, ein umfängliches Identifikationsangebot. Worin liegt dessen Attraktivität und Plausibilität? Nun, hier muss man dem Vorstellungsvermögen etwas Raum geben.

VI.

Augenscheinlich ist es auf die Erwartungshaltung von Menschen hin konzipiert, denen die Papstkirche des Spätmittelalters einmal orientierende Heimat gewesen ist – als göttliche Stiftung, in der und durch die Gottes gnädiger Heilswille erfahrbar in ihre Gegenwart und Lebenswelt hereingriff. In ihrer sakramentalen Vollmacht und in deren Trägern war sie die Heilsgegenwart Gottes auf Erden – zuvörderst dadurch, dass sich in der Messe / Eucharistie allenthalben und zu aller Zeit die Heilsereignisse der Weihnacht und des Karfreitags wirksam vergegenwärtigten. Volkstümliche Vermittlergestalten, welche den gegenwärtigen Gläubigen ihre Teilhabe an den Heilsfrüchten der Heiligen Geschichte vor Augen führten, waren die Heiligen: Durch ihre in Kunstwerken und in den Legenden vergegenwärtigten Lebens- und Sterbensgeschicke, durch die Wunder, mittels derer sie ihren Status dokumentierten und die Gläubigen dazu einluden, sich auf den Weg des Glaubensgehorsams zu machen – in der Hoffnung auf zeitliches Wohl und ewiges Heil.

Gerade die Heiligenverehrung in allen ihren kulturellen Ausdrucksformen ist in den *Homilies* in geradezu obsessiver Weise präsent – zentral natürlich in John Jewels Homilie über die Gefahr des Götzendienstes und den überflüssigen Kirchenschmuck, dem mit großem Abstand umfänglichsten Stück der beiden Sammlungen, aber auch sonst ist das Thema geradezu omnipräsent – aus der Perspektive, dass es sich hierbei um Götzendienst, um falschen Kultus handelt, also um jene Versuchung, die auf das Gottesvolk schon in der Zeit des Alten Bundes fortwährend eingedrungen ist und der es dann in der Zeit der Apostel und der Kirchenväter in neuen Gestalten erneut zu widerstehen hatte.

Und hieraus ergibt sich ein erster wichtiger Zug im Bild der Reformation, das wir uns aus den Homilies konstruieren können: Die Hörer werden nicht so sehr darauf angesprochen, dass der reformatorische Umbruch sie aus Verängstigung und Heteronomie in einem heillosen System der Leistungs- und Verdienstreligion herausgeführt hat, sondern ihnen wird eingeschärft, dass die erneuerte Kirche es ihnen möglich macht, Gott so zu dienen, wie der selbst es von den Gliedern seines Volkes für ihr zeitliches Wohl und für ihr ewiges Heil fordert. Und diese göttliche For-

derung mitsamt den an sie geknüpften Strafandrohungen und Lohnver-
heißungen wiederum ist ablesbar an der Geschichte des Gottesvolkes, die,
modern gesprochen, aus deuteronomisch-deuteronomistischer Perspektive
wahrgenommen wird: Der selbsterwählte, von Gott so nicht gebotene
Gottesdienst, der Fremdkultus, der Götzendienst – dieses ganze Syndrom
irregeleiteter Religion war es, das das biblische Gottesvolk immer wieder
vom rechten, heilsamen Weg abbrachte, gegen das Jesus kämpfte und das
dann den Aposteln und Kirchenvätern im Römischen Reich der Kaiserzeit
in den Weg trat. Es ist deutlich: Menschen, denen der herkömmliche
papstkirchliche Deutungskontext ihres Lebens abhanden gekommen ist,
wird nahegelegt, sich in diesem narrativ-normativen Orientierungsrahmen
beheimaten zu lassen.

Und hier tut sich nun ein weiterer Bedeutungshorizont der Einfügung
in die Geschichte des biblischen Gottesvolkes auf und mit ihm ein weiterer charakteristischer Zug im Bild der Reformation: Nach dem Bibelverständnis, das die Homilien praktizieren, waren es ja in erster Linie
nicht etwa die Propheten, die im biblischen Israel bzw. Juda den Götzendienst bekämpft bzw. die deuteronomistische Forderung der Kultus-
Zentralisation durchgesetzt haben, sondern vielmehr die Könige. Und genau darin liegt das geschichtstheologische Motiv, welches den folgenden
Panegyrikus auf Heinrich VIII., den Cranmer im Sermon über den Glauben und die Guten Werke anstimmt, zu mehr macht als zu einer bloßen
unehrlichen Lobeshymne auf den jüngst verstorbenen Herrscher:

»Honour be to God who did put light in the heart of his faithful and true minister
of most famous memory, King Henry VIII, and gave him the knowledge of his
Word and an earnest affection to seek his glory, and to put away all such superstitions and pharisaical acts by antichrist invented, and set up against the true Word of
God and glory of his most blessed name, as he gave the like spirit unto the most
noble and famous princes Jehosaphat, Josiah and Hezekiah.«[31]

Und die der zweiten Sammlung nachträglich angefügte Homilie gegen
Ungehorsam und Rebellion bezeichnet es als Strafe Gottes, dass Edward
VI. so früh verstorben ist – »our good Josiah«.[32] Gerade die Einführung
der Reformation in England durch die Krone und ihre Eigenart als Inbe-
sitznahme der Herrschaft in der Kirche und über sie durch die Krone wird
aus diesem Blickwinkel zum beglaubigenden Siegel ihrer Legitimität: Die
Könige und ihre Berater haben sich in die archetypischen Verhaltensmuster eingefügt, welche die guten judäischen Könige und später die christlichen Kaiser nach Konstantin einst ausgeprägt haben. Die Übernahme des

---

[31] I/5 (ed. Bray, 50). Vgl. dieselbe Zusammenstellung auch II/2 (ed. Bray, 224). Zu
Josaphat siehe den erhellenden Artikel von Udo Rüterswörden in RGG⁴ 4, 575.
[32] II/21 (ed. Bray, 515).

Supremats in der Ecclesia Anglicana durch die Krone wird also nicht etwa gerechtfertigt als Notmaßnahme, die zur Abstellung bestimmter kirchlicher Missstände bzw. zur Durchsetzung von Reformmaßnahmen gegen einen sich verweigernden Klerus unumgänglich war, sondern als die in sich selbst heilsame und notwendige Wiederaufrichtung der gottgewollten Ordnung. Das zehnte Stück der ersten Sammlung, *An Exhortation Concerning Good Order and Obedience to Rulers and Magistrates*[33] führt das aus. In einer Weise, die auf die Hierarchienlehre des Areopagiten zurück- und damit auf Richard Hooker vorausverweist, entfaltet sie einleitend eine Ontologie der alle Wirklichkeit durchwaltenden hierarchischen Ordnungsstrukturen und stellt fest, woher der Träger der Krone seine Macht hat: »not from Rome, but immediately of God most highest«.[34] Die Argumente hierfür sind charakteristisch. Einmal wird das Rache-Verbot in Dtn. 32,25 angeführt – im Gottesvolk ist alle Privatrache verboten und, modernisiert und verkürzt gesagt, das Gewaltmonopol des Herrschers aufgerichtet. Sodann: Jedes Wesen, das eine Seele hat, ist, so stellt die Homilie im Anschluss an eine sehr wörtliche Übersetzung von Röm. 13,1 fest, dem weltlichen Herrscher zum Gehorsam verpflichtet – und davon sind weder Priester noch Apostel und Propheten ausgenommen, wie unter Verweis auf den Kirchenvater Johannes Chrysostomos ausgeführt wird. Charakteristisch ist hier die Dreizahl der Instanzen beieinander, die im Konsens miteinander die unverbrüchlichen Lebensordnungen des Gottesvolkes bezeugen. Im Kontrast hierzu erschließt sich das wahre Wesen des Papsttums:

»And here let us take heed that we understand not these or such other like places which so straitly command obedience to superiors and so straitly punisheth rebellion and disobedience to the same, to be meant in any condition of the pretensed power of the Bishop of Rome. For truly the Scripture of God alloweth no such usurped power, full of enormities, abusions and blasphemies, but the true meaning of these and such places be to extol and set forth God's true ordinance and the authority of God's anointed kings, and of their officers appointed under them. And concerning the usurped power of the bishop of Rome which he most wrongfully challengeth as the successor of Christ and Peter, we may easily percieve how false, feigned and forged it is, not only in that it hath no sufficient ground in Holy Scripture, but also by the fruits and doctrine thereof. For our Saviour Christ and Saint Peter teach most earnestly and agreeably obedience to kings, as to the chief and supreme rulers in this world next under God, but the bishop of Rome teacheth immunities, privileges, exemptions and disobedience most clearly against Christ's doctrine and Saint Peter's. He ought therefore rather to be called antichrist and the successor of the scribes and Pharisees than Christ's vicar or Saint Peter's successor,

---

[33] I/10 (ed. Bray, 96–108).
[34] I/10 (ed. Bray, 87).

seeing that not only in this point but also in other weighty matters of Christian religion, in matters of remission of sins and of salvation, he teacheth us so directly against both Saint Peter and against our Saviour Christ.«[35]

Es liegt vor Augen: All das soll den durch die Reformation vollzogenen Bruch erklären und legitimieren. Hierbei ist die Anordnung und Abstufung der Argumente signifikant: Vorrang hat eindeutig die Wiedergewinnung des königlichen Supremats in der Kirche, der zeitweilig durch dessen Usurpation an den römischen Bischof verloren gegangen war. Dass das Papsttum die Zentral- und Symbolgestalt einer inneren Fehlentwicklung christlichen Glaubens- und Heilsverständnisses ist, wird eher pflichtschuldig nach- bzw. eingeschoben. Zugespitzt könnte man sagen: Die Reformation hat in allererster Linie die in der gregorianischen Kirchenreform revolutionär umgestaltete kirchliche Ordnung wieder vom Kopf auf die Füße gestellt.

VII.

Und an dieser Stelle stoßen wir nun gleich wieder auf einen ganz eigentümlichen Befund. Man erwartet ja vor dem eben umrissenen Hintergrund, dass in den Invektiven gegen Papsttum und Päpste, welche die Homilies wie ein cantus firmus durchziehen, die großen Kämpfe als Illustrationsmaterial herangezogen werden, welche zwischen Päpsten und weltlichen Herrschern des 11. und 12. Jahrhunderts ausgefochten wurden und das lateineuropäische Ordnungsdenken zu neuen Ufern trieben. Aber genau das ist nicht der Fall: Papst Gregor VII. wird gerade einmal genannt – weil er (angeblich) Heinrich IV. und dessen Familie in Canossa grausam behandelt hat.[36]

Und noch erstaunlicher: Die englischen Ereignisse dieses Streits um das Verhältnis der geistlichen zur weltlichen Herrschaft werden ausnahmslos mit Schweigen übergangen: Anselm von Canterbury wird genau einmal erwähnt, und zwar als Gewährsmann für die Lehre von der Rechtfertigung allein durch den Glauben,[37] seine Rolle als Kirchenpolitiker wird beschwiegen. Aber der erstaunlichste Befund ist doch der folgende: Weder König Heinrich II. oder sein gleichnamiger Sohn und Mitregent noch vor allem Thomas Becket, *der* heilige Märtyrer der Gregorianischen Kirchenreform schlechthin, wird in diesen Homilien auch nur an einer einzigen

---

[35] I/10 (ed. Bray, 93, mit Bezug auf 1.Petr. 2,13–17).
[36] II/16 (ed. Bray, 446). Die zweite im Register genannte Stelle (ed. Bray, 561) bezieht sich lediglich auf eine Bemerkung Brays im Apparat.
[37] I/3 (ed. Bray, 26).

Stelle erwähnt, und das heißt: Eine der für die spätmittelalterliche Frömmigkeit und Mentalität nicht nur Englands prägende Gestalt und Episode
wird einfach mit dem Mantel des Schweigens zugedeckt – von den Angehörigen einer Generation, in der der Heilige als Namenspatron allgegenwärtig war – man denke nur an *Thomas* Wolsey, *Thomas* Cromwell, *Thomas* Morus, *Thomas* Cranmer …

Über die hier waltende Leitabsicht kann man lediglich Vermutungen
anstellen, man muss es aber auch: Die eigene, spezifisch englische papstkirchliche Vergangenheit wird mit Schweigen bedeckt, um das papstkirchliche Christentum überhaupt zu externalisieren. Das Papsttum und mit
ihm das papstkirchliche Christentum überhaupt wird nicht kritisch als
Bestandteil der eigenen Glaubens- und Herkunftsgeschichte bearbeitet
und verarbeitet, sondern es wird aus der kulturellen Identität und Geschichte der eigenen Gesellschaft bzw. des eigenen Volkes gleichsam herausgeschrieben und in die Distanz des Ausländischen gerückt.

Anders als in der lutherischen Frömmigkeit und Theologie, welche das
bleibende, sich im und am Gewissen immer neu ereignende Widerspiel
von Gesetz und Evangelium in ihre konstitutiven Grundlagen aufgenommen hat, und der damit, wenngleich in verallgemeinerter und verschlüsselter Weise, die Erinnerung an ihre Herkunft aus dem reformatorischen
Bruch mit dem papstkirchlichen Christentum dauerhaft eingeschrieben
blieb,[38] wird hier die Bedeutung der Reformation klar und eindeutig festgelegt und vor allem begrenzt: Sie war ein geschichtlich-einmaliger Wechsel zurück von der verfälschten zur berichtigten Ordnung in Kirche und
Gesellschaft. Nicht das Geschehen des Umschwunges selbst ist primär
erinnerungswürdig, sondern im Zentrum steht die neue bzw. erneut ins
Recht gesetzte alte Ordnung, die er hervorgebracht hat.

Dieser Eindruck verstärkt sich noch einmal, wenn man sich vor Augen
führt, welche geschichtlichen Vorgänge im Gesamtzusammenhang der
Homilies am ausführlichsten bemüht werden, um zu zeigen, dass es sich
bei der seit der Spätantike entstandenen Herrschaft des Papsttums in der
westlichen Kirche um ein Devianzphänomen gehandelt hat, das durch die
Rückeroberung des Supremats in der Ecclesia Anglicana durch die Krone
sein verdientes Ende gefunden hat: Als Gegenstand der Leiterzählung fungieren die byzantinischen Bilderstreitigkeiten des 8. Jahrhunderts und in
ihnen die Rolle, welche Päpste als Gegenspieler bilderfeindlicher byzantinischer Kaiser in ihnen gespielt haben. Es findet sich in der schon erwähnten Homilien-Reihe über den Kirchenschmuck. Bei oberflächlichem

---

[38] Vgl. dazu MARTIN OHST, Vom Leistungsprinzip zum Bildungsgedanken. Motive
und Tendenzen in Martin Luthers Verständnis der Buße (in: BThZ 34, 2017, 47–72).

Lesen schüttelt man lediglich den Kopf und fragt sich, was dieses Vorführen patristischer und frühmittelalterlicher Gelehrsamkeit samt Zitaten-Wust in einer Predigt für Laien soll. Sieht man genauer hin, dann erkennt man besonders deutlich das in den *Homilies* nicht allein hier, sondern durchgehend leitende geschichtstheologische und geschichtspolitische Motivgeflecht: Der Kampf gegen den Bilderkultus hat schon die Geschichte des alten Gottesvolkes bestimmt. Und schon bald ist durch Neophyten aus dem Heidentum die Versuchung zum Bilderkultus in die frühchristlichen Gemeinden eingedrungen, dort aber zunächst konsequent abgewiesen worden, wie Euseb und Hieronymus bezeugen. Die werden damit in der geschichtstheologischen Dramaturgie gleichsam zu Funktionsäquivalenten alttestamentlicher Propheten bzw. Geschichtsschreiber erhoben und vom Autor, wohl John Jewel, expressis verbis als »authorities«[39] angeführt. Im Westen markiert dann Gregor d. Gr. eine Wasserscheide, der zwar zu Unrecht als Befürworter der Bilderverehrung in Anspruch genommen wird, aber dennoch mit seinem berühmten Appell zur Duldung der Bilder in Kirchen als Bibeln für die Leseunkundigen dem verderblichen Unfug letztlich Tür und Tor geöffnet hat. Und es beginnt dann eine Skandalgeschichte, in der Ostreich und Westreich, östliche und westliche Kirche auseinanderdrifteten, weil die Päpste im Bilderstreit ihre Machtgier befriedigten, indem sie die Bilderverehrung begünstigten, während die byzantinischen Kaiser sie tapfer bekämpften:

»Now on the contrary part, note ye that the bishops of Rome, being no ordinary magistrates appointed of God out of their diocese, but usurpers of princes' authorities contrary to God's Word, were the maintainers of images against God's Word and stirrers up of sedition and rebellion and workers of continual treason against their sovereign lords, contrary to God's law and the ordinances of all human laws, being not only enemies to God, but also rebels and traitors against their princes«.[40]

Und so haben sie Unheil über das Reich und die Kirche gebracht:

»And so there became two emperors, and the empire, which was before one, was divided into two parts upon occasion of idols and images and the worshipping of them, even as the kingdom of the Israelites was in old time for the like cause of idolatry divided in King Rehoboam his time. And so the bishop of Rome, having the favour of Charles the Great by this means assured to him, was wondrously enhanced in power and authority and did in all the west church, specially in Italy, what he lust, where images were set up, garnished and worshipped of all sorts of men«.[41]

---

[39] II/2 (ed. Bray, 237–239).
[40] II/2 (ed. Bray, 242).
[41] II/2 (ed. Bray, 247).

All das ist natürlich nicht der Versuch, ein ganzes Volk historisch zu bilden, sondern hier wird exzessiv die Geschichte als Lehrmeisterin für das Leben instrumentalisiert.[42] Die Geschichtserzählung steht im Dienste der religiös-politischen Bußpredigt, wie die zweite Sammlung sie in einem anderen Zusammenhang laut werden lässt:

»O England, ponder the time of God's merciful visitation, showed thee from day to day, and yet wilt not regard it, neither wilt thou with his punishment be driven to duty, nor with his benefits provoked to thanks, if thou knewest what may fall upon thee for thine unthankfulness, thou wouldest provide for thy peace«.[43]

VIII.

Die Reformation war also derjenige Akt, in dem England die Usurpation des Papsttums abgeschüttelt hat. In und mit der Reformation hat die Krone wieder die Rechte und Pflichten übernommen, die ihr im Gottesvolk zustehen, und sie hat aufgeräumt mit allem Götzendienst. Diejenigen Menschen, die damit ihre geistliche Heimat in der religiösen Vorstellungswelt der Papstkirche verloren haben, sollen aufhören, der Pracht der vorreformatorischen Kirchen und Gottesdienste und den Heiligenbildern und ihrem Kultus nachzutrauern und sich stattdessen als Glieder des Gottesvolkes glücklich schätzen: In dem Gemeinwesen, dem anzugehören ihnen ganz unverdient gewährt ist, walten durch die Reformation und seit ihr wieder die von Gott seinem Volk geschenkten und auferlegten heilsamen Ordnungen, welche miteinander das biblische Israel, die Apostelzeit sowie die Zeit der Kirchenväter und der ersten christlichen Kaiser widerspiegeln.

Wie unterschiedlich diese Ordnungen jedoch hinsichtlich ihres normativen Gehalts, aber auch hinsichtlich der zu ihrer Deutung und Durchsetzung berufenen Institutionen ausgelegt werden konnten, das deutete die Kontroverse um die liturgischen Gewänder schon während der Zeit, in der das *Second Book of Homilies* entstand, an, und es sollte immer deutlicher werden.

---

[42] Vgl. expressis verbis II/2 (ed. Bray, 273).
[43] II/17 (ed. Bray, 465). Vgl. Lk. 19,41–44.

The self-perception of the English Reformation:
A case study

Martin Ohst

The task of describing *the* [single] image that the English Reformation projected of itself cannot be accomplished – for structural reasons. As with all permutations of the Reformation movement and of church formation, England too witnessed competition between various concepts and self-interpretations of the Reformation that led to the emergence of wholly different self-images, each competing and conflicting with the others.

This study singles out one of these, i.e. the one drawn by the leading figures behind the Reformation measures that temporarily culminated in the Elizabethan Settlement; their intention was to argumentatively expound and imprint this image upon the members of the Ecclesia Anglicana as a binding norm during the course of a patient long-term campaign of instruction and indoctrination.

This image is found in the *Books of Homilies*, two collections of sermons that were first published during the years that ushered in the Reformation: in 1547, immediately after Edward VI's accession to the throne, and in 1563, after the accession of his half-sister Elizabeth. In 1571, an additional exhortation against disobedience and rebellion was added to the second volume in response to certain events at that time;[1] this was the final addition made to the body of text for the period that followed. In 1859, John Griffiths published a critical edition of this text corpus that by the standards of the time was compiled very carefully.[2] Gerald Bray published a new edition in 2015.[3] In terms of textual criticism and source analysis,

---

[1] In 1570, Pope Pius V issued the papal bull »Regnans in excelsis«, in which he declared Elizabeth I a heretic, i.e. unfit to rule, and dispensed her subjects from their oaths of fealty (cf.: Quellen zur Geschichte des Papsttums und des Römischen Katholizismus, ed. Carl Mirbt, Tübingen [4]1924, 348–9 [no. 491]).

[2] The Two Books of Homilies Appointed to be Read in Churches, Oxford 1859. The full text of this edition can be retrieved online through Google Books at no cost.

[3] The Books of Homilies. A Critical Edition, ed. Gerald Bray, Cambridge 2015. As this edition is sure to become definitive in the future due simply to its ready availability and readability, this is the edition I quote from below. When referencing these quotations, I cite the number of the collection followed by the individual homily and then the page number. »I/4 ed. Bray, 32« therefore refers to the *First Book of Homilies*, 4th Homily, 32 in Bray's edition.

Bray's edition is largely based on the results of Griffiths' research but modernises the orthography of the texts. It is an improvement on the old editions inasmuch as it also contains the collection of homilies by Bishop Bonner of London; this was intended to supplant the First Book of Homilies during the reign of Queen Mary and thus unintentionally attested to the First Book's great effectiveness.

Ashley Null wrote an excellent introduction to these texts in 2011.[4]

I.

The two bodies of text form an integral whole. The first collection clearly focuses on the exposition of ecclesiastical teachings; the first five homilies are particularly significant in this respect. Except for the second one, which was probably composed by John Harpsfield, they were all written by Thomas Cranmer and set forth the categorical outlines of the Reformation understanding of Christianity that laid the foundations for everything that followed – in a form shaped by Cranmer's education and thinking.

The sequence of homilies in the first collection opens with *A Fruitful Exhortation to the Reading of Holy Scripture* (I/1), the material part beginning with the above-mentioned tract on original sin (I/2). The doctrine of Christian salvation (I/3) is given practical expression by sermons on »lively faith« (I/4) and the conjunction of faith and good works (I/5). I/6 goes into greater detail on this subject and expounds on the interrelationship between charity, the love of God and the love of the neighbour. The homilies that follow are devoted to problems of practical Christian living. Swearing and perjury (I/7) are used to illustrate the dangers of falling from God through sins of commission (I/8). Positive inspiration is provided by the »exhortations« against the fear of death (I/9) and on obedience to rulers and authorities (I/10), while the last two homilies in the collection are again devoted to the struggle against sin, in this case »whoredom and uncleanness« (I/11), and contention and brawling (I/12).

The profile and focal areas of the second collection are clearly quite different. These homilies focus on Christian life as regulated by established institutions and the rules, customs and traditions that surround the various cycles of life. This collection is less concerned with the categorical

---

[4] ASHLEY NULL, Official Tudor Homilies (in: The Oxford Handbook of the Early Modern Sermon, eds. Peter McCullough, Hugh Adlington and Emma Rhatigan, Oxford 2011, 348–365).

foundations of Christian life and faith than with the form in which they shape and are shaped by society. During the Reformation this relationship underwent a profound transformation that left hardly any element of worship or any aspect of everyday life untouched. The first homily contains guidelines on the right use of church buildings (II/1). This is followed by the longest work in the entire collection, the *Homily Against Peril of Idolatry and Superfluous Decking of Churches* (II/2), probably written by John Jewel. This three-part treatise on the problem of using images encompasses more than seventy printed pages; the critical radicalism of this homily was toned down by Elizabeth I herself, who made changes to two passages in the text.[5] The positive counterpart to this tract, encompassing just five pages, is the sermon on the *Repairing and Keeping Clean and Comely Adorning of Churches* (II/3). The next homilies make up a small trilogy: II/4 is devoted to fasting as a good work, while II/5 inveighs against gluttony and drunkenness; these are closely linked with an exhortation against excessive expenditure on clothing and jewellery (II/6). The alternation of continuity and discontinuity in the Church's efforts to impose social discipline during late medieval and early modern (Reformation) times is already clear from the subjects addressed.

Under the heading »Prayer« (II/7), the next two homilies expound on the subject of public church services, i.e. the time and place at which they should be held (II/8) and their use of the vernacular (II/9). II/10 addresses a related problem, i.e. how to treat those passages of Holy Scripture that (seem to) contradict the understanding of the Bible prevalent within the Reformation movement.

II/11 deals with acts of charity towards the poor and needy. II/12–17 were composed for the main festivals of the Church year and describe how they should be fittingly celebrated: the sequence starts with Christmas (II/12), Good Friday (II/13) and Easter (II/14), and only appears to be interrupted by II/15 (Communion), because the tradition had been to take Communion only at Easter. The homily on Whitsun (II/16) is followed by the homily on the tradition of beating the bounds on Rogation Sunday, one which is particularly rich in information on folklore and the history of piety. – The two homilies that follow are also closely linked in terms of subject matter, although this does not initially appear to be the case: II/18 is devoted to matrimony, while the »Idleness« inveighed against in II/19 actually refers to monasticism. II/20, originally the final work in the collection, addresses the subject of Christian repentance. As mentioned above, the sermon *Against Disobedience and Wilful Rebellion* was not added until 1571.

---

[5] Cf. II/2 (ed. Bray, 227, 249).

The status of normative texts was not added to these homilies after the fact; rather, the individual homilies, which for their part sometimes constitute series of independent sermons, were – like the integrated collections – intended to have a normative effect right from the time of their conception.

The proponents of the Homilies achieved their normative effect strategically, by making it compulsory for these texts to be read to the congregations in all church services. This rule is enforced most strictly in the royal preface to the first edition of the 1st Book: here all church ministers with pastoral duties are enjoined to read such a homily or part of one every Sunday; if anyone – in exceptional circumstances – preaches his own sermon, the omitted homily must be read on the following Sunday or church holiday.[6] The final version of the *39 Articles* is much more lenient:

»The second Book of Homilies, the several titles whereof we have joined under this Article, doth contain a godly and wholesome Doctrine, and necessary for these times, as doth the former Book of Homilies, which were set forth in the time of Edward the Sixth; and therefore we judge them to be read in Churches by the Ministers, diligently and distinctly, that they may be understanded of the people«.[7]

These homilies were composed by various authors, each of whom inserted their own emphases and used individual stylistic contours. Some of the homilies contain extensive passages that are patristic or Continental European in origin. These aspects are explained in detail in the editions by Bray and even better by Griffiths, and are ignored here in favour of a perspective from which the two Books of Homilies are viewed collectively as an expression of a formative will, i.e. they are perceived as they would probably have been received by the congregations which their authors and editors had in mind.

II.

It goes without saying that these collections were in no way organized by presuppositions regarding congregations and their sets of mind according to the style of modern homiletics. However, if we read the texts in context and allow the choice of topics to sink in, no undue exercise of the imagination is required to obtain a relatively clear picture. It is evident even from a superficial reading that the subject of idolatry etc. is addressed

---

[6] Cf. ed. Bray, 5–6.

[7] Die Kirche von England. Ihr Gebetbuch, Bekenntnis und Kanonisches Recht, ed. Cajus Fabricius, Corpus Confessionum 17/I, Berlin and Leipzig 1937, 397.

repeatedly; this is already the case in the doctrinal texts of the first collection, but occurs even more frequently in the second, which is devoted to church festivals and holidays. The fact that the excessively – almost grotesquely – long sermon on imagery takes up a good quarter of the second collection speaks for itself. The authors and editors apparently had people in mind for whom the pre-Reformation, church-centred lifestyle with all its rites and customs had disappeared and who still felt this to be a loss that had to be confronted, processed and overcome. This is exactly why it still had to be repeatedly addressed; it was important to explain why the break had to be made and why the means and processes that effected the break were and still are in keeping with the supreme will of God. The basic tone of the homilies is therefore apologetic, and the congregations to whose presumed powers of comprehension they were tailored were imagined to have a cautious, sceptical attitude towards these innovations.

The Reformation is consequently omnipresent in these homilies, both explicitly and – even more so – implicitly. It marks a significant break with the traditional structure of habits and certainties that prevailed in earlier times. Once effected, this break caused a new form of church life to emerge. However, it was still present as a breach in the collective and individual memories of the faithful: the congregations which the authors had in mind were continually reminded of it in the weekly, annual and life cycles governing all areas of Christianity, which was why it had to be repeatedly explained and justified. These attempts at justification had a positive counterpart in the possibility of a renewed historical understanding of self. To be sure, there had been a break in continuity from the papal Christianity of ancestral congregations with its wealth of rites and customs; however, the old world of religious ritual and ideas was replaced by new scope for identification and self-classification as the people of God once archetypally realised in biblical Israel and Judah and in the early Church, with forms and standards of living that alone promised true eternal salvation and temporal well-being. Here the Reformation is understood as a renunciation of transient detrimental aberrations brought about by the institutions established for God's people with this purpose in mind. Its legitimacy is evident inasmuch as the Reformation itself, together with the constellation of problems that created it, is unmistakably prefigured in the normative history of God's people.

III.

The trains of thought pursued with this end in mind are substantiated by a normative basic structure supplying the categories on the basis of which the following can be argued: first, that the upheaval of the Reformation eliminated aberrations; secondly, the innovations which it produced were aligned with the universally binding normative instances of all Christian faith and life. All this is expressed in the first five homilies in the first collection; except for the (relatively insignificant) homily on sin and the fall of humankind, these – as mentioned above – were all composed by Cranmer.

The universal guiding principle is similar to an ellipse with two focal points, i.e. the Bible and God's people: »for God's Word cannot be present without God's people, and God's people cannot be without God's Word«[8] – in formal terms, this elliptical interdependence is reflected in this maxim by Luther. However, if we look more closely, the material differences in content become apparent.

According to Cranmer's homily, the Bible, as the Word of God, is a closed canon. It is the valid, inherently powerful testimony to God's nature and will. It applies to Christians as sinners who acknowledge Christ's act of salvation and are redeemed by active obedience to the divine commandments. It also applies to the social structures within which the faith of the redeemed sinner must be upheld and expressed in good works.

The Bible is, in its entirety, as canon, an object of faith: the immutable, indispensable basis of justificatory faith is belief in the Bible. This faith appropriates Scriptural narratives, assimilates the patterns of religious interpretation and evaluation associated with them, and turns them into matrices of its own understanding and shaping of reality. The content of this faith can be summarised as the doctrine of original sin together with the promise of justification and the merciful forgiveness of sins for Christ's sake. It implies that participation in the salvation it promises is conditional on faith becoming the guiding principle of a style of living that authentically reflects it:

>And yet that faith doth not exclude repentance, hope, love, dread and the fear of God, to be joined with faith in every man that is justified. But it excludeth them from the office of justifying. So that although they be all present together in him that is justified, yet they justify not altogether. Nor that faith doth not exclude the justice of our good works, necessarily to be done afterward of duty towards God, (for we are most bounden to serve God in doing good deeds commanded by him in his Holy Scripture all the days of our life)«.[9]

---

[8] MARTIN LUTHER, Von den Konziliis und Kirchen [On the Councils and the Church] (WA 50,629).

In Cranmer's version, like Melanchthon's but different from that of Luther, the doctrine of justification by faith does not encompass the entire
theory of Christian living and belief. As with scholasticism, it is instead
closely linked with baptism and repentance, which is understood to be an
individual act of Christian life.[10]

A glance at the biblical references makes this profile even clearer: they
are mostly taken from Deutero-Pauline writings, the pastoral letters and
Catholic epistles of the New Testament, while the text that serves as the
primary source for Cranmer's understanding of justification by faith is the
chapter on faith in the Letter to the Hebrews, which Cranmer – as he
emphasised on several occasions – believed to be a Pauline text.[11]

What emerges is a doctrine of justification that can easily be linked with
the relevant patristic remarks; this is closely related to Augustine's treatise
De fide et bonis operibus – naturally read through Reformation-tinted
spectacles.[12]

Digression

*A short digression into the history of Christian doctrine is unavoidable at this point:
viewed retrospectively in the light of doctrinal history, Martin Luther's reformatory
understanding of the Christian religion reveals itself as a congenial appropriation of
certain essential elements of original Pauline theology as presented in the Letters to
the Romans and the Galatians, i.e. in the texts in which the Pauline gospel is ex-
plicated in invectives against established patterns of religious self-interpretations of
humanity and reconfigures them in a remarkable way. According to Luther, Christians are redeemed by being drawn into the formative process of the Christian
religion, bearing witness to them and reliving them. God's commandments and
giving of Himself in the words, life and works of Jesus Christ are actualised in and
by the Christian people with the same earth-shattering, beatific drama as that experienced by Jesus' contemporaries, particularly St. Paul himself. They are drawn
into the original drama of the Christian religion, in which verbal testimonies made
in response to tests of faith form the dynamic core of endless individual stories
bearing witness to different types of Christian existence.*

*The Books of Homilies are likewise dominated by Pauline terminology. How-
ever, the sources on which they draw are characteristically different. They specifically encompass texts and groups of texts in which Pauline terminology has become*

---

[9] I/3 (ed. Bray, 24). – The last part of the quotation touches on Ephesians 2:10. The
intellectual content of this verse is much more immanent in the relevant remarks in the
homilies than the number of formal quotations noted in the index would lead one to
think.

[10] »[A]nd therefore we must trust only in God's mercy and that sacrifice which our
high priest and Saviour Christ Jesus, the Son of God, once offered for us upon the cross,
to obtain thereby God's grace and remission, as well of our original sin in baptism as of
all actual sin committed by us after our baptism, if we truly repent and convert unfeignedly to him again« (I/3, ed. Bray, 27).

[11] Cf. for example I/4 (ed. Bray, 34–36).

[12] Cited by Cranmer I/4 (ed. Bray, 34).

part of early Christian consensus. This has given rise to patterns of thought which through »popularisation and simplification« have shaken off the cumbersome nature of original Paulinism. They therefore testify to a »theoretically simplified Christianity made fruitful in practice« which was perceived around 100 years ago through the historicist exegesis of Deutero-Pauline scripture, the Catholic epistles and the pastoral letters, and which was identified as the pool of thoughts and ideas from which the »old Church [...] constructed a middle-of-the-road apostolic dogma«.[13] Here the original drama of the Christian religion has been mentally pushed into the background and, rather than being seen as reenacting itself, is considered to be an aetiological narrative to which current doctrines and rules for living can apply for legitimation.

If the Bible is understood in this way, Christians can use it to determine God's will for them – in the sense of a doctrine of justification that instructs them in the fulfilment of God's commandments.

The Bible also gives them an understanding of the socio-historical world put before them as the place where their acts of obedience are to be performed.[14] It is belief in the Bible that gives guidance and orientation throughout the Christian's life. The following quotation, based on 2 Corinthians 5:6–7, is characteristic:

»›Therefore let us be always of good comfort, for we know that so long as we be in the body we be as it were far from God‹ in a strange country, subject to many perils, ›walking without‹ perfect ›sight‹ and knowledge of Almighty God, only seeing him by faith *in the Holy Scriptures*.«[15]

The guiding principle which, as a central hermeneutical concept, opens up the Bible's potential for orientation is the principle of God's people, whose members are all Christians by baptism.

The biblical narratives, especially those in the Old Testament, document God's salvation of His people by reward and punishment in an archetypal manner that is thus valid for all time; this is particularly evident from the following quotation, which refers to the ban on imagery in the Old Testament:

»You will say peradventure, these things pertain to the Jews; what have we to do with them? Indeed, they pertain no less to us Christians than to them. For if we be the people of God, how can the Word and law of God not appertain to us? Saint Paul, alleging one text out of the Old Testament, concludeth generally for other Scriptures of the Old Testament as well as that, saying: ›Whatsoever is written before (meaning the Old Testament) is written for our instruction‹ [Romans 15:4]; which sentence is most specially true of such writings of the Old Testament as

---

[13] All quotations from HEINRICH JULIUS HOLTZMANN, Zur praktischen Erklärung des Hebräerbriefs [A Practical Explanation of the Letter to the Hebrews] (in: Zeitschrift für praktische Theologie 13, 1891, 219–238, here: 221).

[14] The foundation of this is I/1 (ed. Bray, 7–13).

[15] I/9 (ed. Bray, 78). The passage in italics has no points of reference to St. Paul's text.

contain the immutable law and ordinances of God, in no age or time to be altered, nor of any persons or nations or age to be disobeyed«.[16]

According to the simplified basic structures of the Augustinian theology of history, God's people were embodied in the Old Covenant in biblical Israel, while in the New Covenant they are universalised; they live in various communities under very different worldly rulers. We search the homilies in vain for any exclusive identification of the English people as the people of God. To be sure, England can be said to enjoy special divine blessings[17] or criticised for its stubborn ingratitude,[18] but such descriptions are never applied to England alone. Instead, God's people are referred to as an extensive community of Christians who despite the Fall of Man are chosen by God for salvation; they live in different worldly, political structures willed by God. Rather than laying the foundations for hierocratic or theocratic constructions, biblical belief therefore teaches due respect for existing worldly authorities; the respective king is

»God's lieutenant, vicegerent and highest minister in that country where he is king«.[19]

Because this is the case, the Bible can be described as the embodiment of the

»holy rules, injunctions and statutes of our Christian religion, [...] that we have made profession to God at our baptism«[20],

a description that is unmistakeably linked with the terminology used in Church policy in the age of Henry VIII and Edward VI. The Christian people are given the following guiding principles with regard to their relationship with worldly rulers:

»Let us all obey, even from the bottom of our hearts, all their godly proceedings, laws statutes, proclamations and injunctions, with all other their godly orders«.[21]

---

[16] II/2 (ed. Bray, 225).

[17] »But blessed be God that we in this realm of England feel not the horrible calamities, miseries and wretchedness which all they undoubtedly feel and suffer that lack this godly order« (I/10; ed. Bray, 86).

[18] »O England, ponder the time of God's merciful visitation, showed thee from day to day, and yet will not regard it, neither wilt thou with his punishment be driven to duty, nor with his benefits provoked to thanks« (II/17, ed. Bray, 465; cf. Luke 19:41 seqq.).

[19] I/10 (ed. Bray, 92).

[20] I/1 (ed. Bray, 13).

[21] I/10 (ed. Bray, 87).

IV.

This comprehensive concept of Christian life, rooted in the Bible as a set of rules for living, is constitutive for the programme of orientation set forth in the homilies. Impressive evidence of this is provided in the composition of the first collection of homilies, which begins with *A Fruitful Exhortation to the Reading and Knowledge of Holy Scripture*[22] and ends with a sermon against quarrelling and strife in matters of faith. Here it is assumed that accusations fly backwards and forwards even in the taverns:

»›He is a Pharisee, he is a gospeller, he is of the new sort, he is of the old faith, he is a new-broached brother, he is a good catholic father, he is a papist, he is an heretic‹«.[23]

The programme for overcoming this religious fragmentation is:

»Let us so read the Scripture that by reading thereof we may be made the better livers, rather than the more contentious disputers«.[24]

In other words, people who read the Bible become accustomed to the rules and instructions for living that are followed by God's people. They become familiar with God's will for His people, and they recognise how and where Satan repeatedly penetrates God's kingdom – by beguilement, misdirection and division. It also becomes apparent that the Reformation in England was a transformation of ecclesiastical life brought about by royal decree with the aim of establishing royal supremacy in the *Ecclesia Anglicana*; it was therefore an act of obedience to the institutions given to God's people and had to be accepted as such.

The normative, archetypal history of God's people began in Eden but did not end with the Ascension of Christ or the conclusion of New Testament canon. Along with the biblical history of the Old Covenant and the time of Christ and the Apostles, it also encompassed the age of the Church Fathers. As with the Bible, this self-interpretation of the Reformation claims the sole authority over the patristic period, which was generally regarded as normative.[25]

---

[22] I/1 (ed. Bray, 7–13).

[23] I/12 (ed. Bray, 109).

[24] I/12 (ed. Bray, 111).

[25] Cf. the following passage on the prohibition of images: »that this truth and doctrine concerning the forbidding of images and worshipping of them, taken out of the Holy Scriptures as well of the Old Testament as the New, was believed and taught of the old holy fathers and most ancient learned doctors, and received in the old primitive church which was most uncorrupt and pure« (II/2, ed. Bray, 228).

V.

If we keep this claim and the reasons behind it in mind, it becomes easier to understand one of the characteristics of the homilies that has not yet been mentioned, i.e. the abundance of references to authors dating not only from the patristic period but also from early medieval times.[26] To an unbiased reader, the first question that arises is whom these presentations of excerpts and gleanings from books were actually intended for – the name of John Chrysostom was certainly no more familiar to the average person listening to a sermon in the late 16th century than it would be to a modern-day churchgoer! The intention was certainly not to instil theological competence in the laity; instead, the names and quotations, like the allusions to biblical narratives, were meant to facilitate identification and interpretation for those listening. By merging horizons, the situation in post-Reformation England becomes more transparent when it is made clear that its characteristic attributes were preconfigured in the normative, archetypal history of God's people. The idolatry of the Israelites, monastic ceremonial piety and the struggle against these two forms of degeneracy are accordingly explained simply as different manifestations of the same pattern of conflict arising at two different points in history.[27] This in turn shows that the removal of religious imagery from the churches, the dissolution of the monasteries and the end of monastic life in England did not tear the country and people away from the continuity of genuine Christian life; on the contrary, these actions returned them to this legitimising continuity after a period of perversion.

This is shown not only by a glance at the Old Testament but also by the history of the early Church. The Church of late antiquity did not transition organically and seamlessly into the papal Church of the Middle Ages; there was in fact a break. The aniconism of early Christian divine services was gradually relaxed, this process of decay being significantly accelerated by the Roman bishops, who during the course of these political and ecclesio-political activities made and enforced claims to power that damaged and weakened the Roman Empire with disastrous long-term consequences. In his homily on the »superfluous decking of churches«, John Jewel described all this in a detailed account of the 8th and 9th century

---

[26] One example is the cloud of witnesses, which Cranmer cites in I/3 (ed. Bray, 25 seqq.) as an instance of active justification by faith, a concept that he himself developed; characteristic reference is also made to John Chrysostom in support of the doctrine that members of the clergy are also bound to obey worldly rulers (cf. I/10, ed. Bray, 88).

[27] Cf. I/5 (ed. Bray, 44–5).

iconoclastic controversy that was probably largely borrowed from Heinrich Bullinger. This whole narrative is biased and didactic through and through; however, it probably had considerable entertainment value for the congregation.[28]

The image of history that the homilies paint for their listeners encompasses the turning point marking the commencement of the processes of decay that were reversed with and from the time of the Reformation. One thing is certain: the normative, archetypal history of God's people, which is revealed by faith, conveys self-understanding to the listener[29] and paves his way to temporal rewards and eternal salvation.[30] The background on which the homilies paint their image of the Reformation is tripartite and ranges from the Creation and the Fall of Man to the period bridging late antiquity and the early Middle Ages. In formal terms, the listener/reader is presented with an array of options to identify with. What makes them seem attractive and plausible? Here we have to give free rein to our imagination.

VI.

It seems that they were conceived to meet the expectations of people for whom the papal Church of the late Middle Ages was once the guide and home, as a divine institution in and through which God's merciful design for salvation was tangible in the present day and in their daily lives. With its sacramental authority and bearers, it was the redeeming presence of God on earth – first and foremost because the salvific events of Christmas and Good Friday were effectively recalled in every place and at every time in the Mass/Eucharist. Traditionally, the saints were mediating examples illustrating the promises of Christian religion in the eyes of present-day believers: through their lives and deaths as visualised in legends and works of art, and by the miracles with which they documented their status and invited believers to join them on their path of faithful obedience in the hope of temporal rewards and eternal salvation.

---

[28] Cf. II/2 (ed. Bray, 234–49).

[29] »And as drink is pleasant to them that be dry and meat to them that be hungry, so is the reading, hearing and searching and studying of Holy Scripture to them that be desirous to know God, or themselves, and to do his will« (I/1, ed. Bray, 7).

[30] »It giveth good counsel in all doubtful things. It showeth of whom we shall look for aid and help in all perils, and that God is the only giver of victory in all battles and temptations of our enemies, bodily and ghostly« (I/1, ed. Bray, 9).

The veneration of saints in all its cultural forms of expression is addressed almost obsessively in the homilies – primarily, of course, in John Jewel's homily on the dangers of idolatry and the »Superfluous Decking of Churches«, which is by far the lengthiest sermon in the two collections; however, the subject is almost omnipresent in many other respects – from the viewpoint that this is idolatry, false worship, i.e. the temptation that continually pursued God's people even in the times of the Old Covenant and that assumed new forms during the ages of the Apostles and the Church Fathers.

This constitutes the first major brushstroke in the image of the Reformation that we can reconstruct from the homilies: congregations are not so much made aware that the Reformation led them out of an unholy system of religious performance and merit dominated by fear and heteronomy; instead, it is inculcated in them that the renewed Church makes it possible for them to serve God in the way that He demands from His people if they are to receive temporal rewards and eternal salvation. In turn, these divine demands together with the associated threats of punishment and promises of rewards can be elicited from the history of God's people, which – in modern terms – is perceived from a Deuteronomic viewpoint. The choice of a divine service by the people rather than the use of that commanded by God, idolatry, the worship of other gods – it was this whole system of misguided religion that repeatedly diverted the biblical people of God from the true road to salvation. It was a system against which Jesus fought and which later obstructed the path of the Apostles and Church Fathers during the age of the Roman Empire. It is clear that people who have lost the traditional interpretation of their lives provided by the papal Church are exhorted to find themselves a home in this narrative, normative framework for orientation.

Here another horizon of interpretation is integrated into the history of the biblical people and God, adding another characteristic brushstroke to the image of the Reformation: according to the understanding of the Bible postulated by the homilies, it was not the prophets who led the fight against idolatry in biblical Israel and Judah and who imposed the Deuteronomistic centralisation of worship, but rather the kings. This is precisely the historico-theological motif that makes the following panegyric to Henry VIII uttered by Cranmer in his sermon on faith and good works more than just an insincere hymn of praise to the recently deceased ruler:

»Honour be to God who did put light in the heart of his faithful and true minister of most famous memory, King Henry VIII, and gave him the knowledge of his Word and an earnest affection to seek his glory, and to put away all such superstitions and pharisaical acts by antichrist invented, and set up against the true Word of

God and glory of his most blessed name, as he gave the like spirit unto the most noble and famous princes Jehoshaphat, Josiah and Hezekiah«.[31]

It is also the motive that causes the *Homily against Disobedience and Wilful Rebellion*, added retrospectively to the second collection, to describe the early death of Edward VI – »our good Josiah«[32] – as a punishment by God. From this perspective, it is precisely the introduction of the Reformation to England by the Crown and the fact that it was implemented as a seizure of Church power by the Crown that seals its legitimacy: the monarchs and their advisers integrated themselves into the archetypal patterns of behaviour that once characterised the good Jewish kings and later the Christian emperors after Constantine. The Crown's assumption of supremacy over the *Ecclesia Anglicana* is accordingly not justified as an emergency measure necessary to suppress certain forms of ecclesiastical abuse or implement measures to reform a non-conforming clergy, but rather as a necessary, inherently salvific re-establishment of divine order. The tenth homily in the first collection, *An Exhortation Concerning Good Order and Obedience to Rulers and Magistrates*[33] explains this in depth. It begins by presenting an ontology of the hierarchical orders governing all reality in a way that looks back to ps-Dionysius the Areopagite and forward to Richard Hooker, and specifies the source from which the wearer of the Crown has his power: »not from Rome, but immediately of God most highest«.[34] The arguments that back this up are characteristic. There is one reference to the threat of vengeance in Deuteronomy 32:25; God's people are forbidden to avenge themselves privately and – put briefly in modern terms – the ruler's monopoly on the use of force is made absolute. This applies to every being that has a soul, as stipulated in the homily following a very literal translation of Romans 13:1 that binds the worldly ruler to obedience; no exceptions are made for priests, prophets and Apostles, as explained with reference to Church Father John Chrysostom. Characteristic here is the trinity of instances that consensually bear testimony to the steadfast way of life of God's people. The true nature of the papacy is described by way of contrast:

»And here let us take heed that we understand not these or such other like places which so straitly command obedience to superiors and so straitly punisheth rebellion and disobedience to the same, to be meant in any condition of the pretensed power of the Bishop of Rome. For truly the Scripture of God alloweth no such

---

[31] I/5 (ed. Bray, 50; cf. the same collocation in II/2, ed. Bray, 224). Cf. Udo Rüterswörden's enlightening article on Jehoshaphat in RGG⁴ 4,575.

[32] II/21 (ed. Bray, 515).

[33] I/10 (ed. Bray, 96–108).

[34] I/10 (ed. Bray, 87).

usurped power, full of enormities, abusions and blasphemies, but the true meaning of these and such places be to extol and set forth God's true ordinance and the authority of God's anointed kings, and of their officers appointed under them. And concerning the usurped power of the bishop of Rome which he most wrongfully challengeth as the successor of Christ and Peter, we may easily perceive how false, feigned and forged it is, not only in that it hath no sufficient ground in Holy Scripture, but also by the fruits and doctrine thereof. For our Saviour Christ and Saint Peter teach most earnestly and agreeably obedience to kings, as to the chief and supreme rulers in this world next under God, but the bishop of Rome teacheth immunities, privileges, exemptions and disobedience most clearly against Christ's doctrine and Saint Peter's. He ought therefore rather to be called antichrist and the successor of the scribes and Pharisees than Christ's vicar or Saint Peter's successor, seeing that not only in this point but also in other weighty matters of Christian religion, in matters of remission of sins and of salvation, he teacheth us so directly against both Saint Peter and against our Saviour Christ«.[35]

It is perfectly clear that all this was intended to explain and legitimise the break brought about by the Reformation. Here the arrangement and nuances of the arguments are significant: priority is clearly given to the reclamation of royal supremacy over the Church, which had sporadically been lost due to its usurpation by the Bishop of Rome. The postulation that the papacy is the central, symbolic manifestation of an inner aberration of Christian faith and understanding of salvation is incorporated or added as it needed to be. In short, it could be said that the Reformation first and foremost reversed the overturning of ecclesiastical order implemented by Gregorian church reform and brought it back to the right way up.

VII.

Here we make yet another curious finding: against the background outlined above, we would expect the invectives against popes and the papacy that pervade the homilies like a *cantus firmus* to be illustrated by the great battles between the popes and secular rulers of the 11th and 12th centuries that broke new ground in the Latin European understanding of order. However, this is by no means the case: Pope Gregory VII is mentioned just once – because of the cruel treatment he (allegedly) meted out to Henry IV and his family in Canossa.[36]

---

[35] I/10 (ed. Bray, 93, with reference to 1 Peter 2:13–17).

[36] Cf. II/16 (ed. Bray, 446). The second passage mentioned in the index (ibid., 561) refers solely to a remark made by Bray in the critical apparatus.

Even more surprising: the events that took place in England during the course of this dispute on the relationship between ecclesiastical and secular rulership are ignored without exception. Anselm of Canterbury is mentioned just once, i.e. as a source for the doctrine of justification by faith alone;[37] nothing is said about his role as a church politician. However, the most astonishing discovery is as follows: neither King Henry II, his son and co-regent of the same name nor, above all, Thomas Becket, the doyen of holy martyrs in Gregorian church reform, are mentioned even once in these homilies. In other words, a figure and episode that shaped medieval piety and thinking in more countries than England is simply cloaked in silence – by members of a generation among whom many were named after this saint – we just have to think of *Thomas* Wolsey, *Thomas* Cromwell, *Thomas* More, *Thomas* Cranmer ...

We can only make assumptions about the intentions that guided this decision; however, this is essential: the country's own, specifically English papal past is never referred to in order to facilitate the externalisation of papal Christianity. The papacy, and with it papal Christianity, are not critically processed and integrated as part of the country's history of faith and origins, but effectively written out of the cultural identity and history of England's society and people and pushed away as something foreign.

Unlike Lutheran piety and theology, the constitutive principles of which incorporate the ongoing contradictions between the law and the Gospel that are a regular matter of conscience and which accordingly keep in mind their origins from the Reformation's break with papal Christianity, albeit in a general, codified way,[38] the significance of the Reformation is clearly defined and above all limited: it was an event unique in history, a turning back from a distorted order of Church and society to a true one. The actual events of this turnaround are not what should primarily be remembered; instead, the focus is on the new or newly rectified old order that they produced.

This impression is enhanced still further when we consider which historical events were expounded upon in the greatest detail within the overall context of the homilies in order to demonstrate that the rise of Papal governance in the western Church since late antiquity was an aberrant phenomenon that came to its proper conclusion when the Crown regained supremacy over the *Ecclesia Anglicana*. The subject of the main narrative

---

[37] I/3 (ed. Bray, 26).

[38] Cf. MARTIN OHST, Vom Leistungsprinzip zum Bildungsgedanken. Motive und Tendenzen in Martin Luthers Verständnis der Buße [From Performance Principle to Formative Concept. Themes and Tendencies in Martin Luther's Understanding of Penance] (in: BThZ 34, 2017, 47–72).

is the iconoclastic controversy in 8th century Byzantium and the role played by the popes as the antagonists of the Byzantine emperors who were opposed to imagery. This subject is referred to in the above-mentioned homilies on church adornment. When reading them superficially, we can only shake our heads and ask ourselves what this display of patristic, early medieval scholarship with its jumble of citations is doing in a sermon for the laity. If we look more closely, we see the complex of historico-theological and historico-political motives not only here but throughout the homilies as a whole: the struggle against idolatry shaped even the early history of God's people. Heathen neophytes soon caused the temptation to commit idolatry to penetrate the early Christian communities, where they were however initially consistently rebuffed, as Eusebius and Jerome testify. In the theological dramaturgy of history, these figures are consequently elevated to the status of functional equivalents of Old Testament prophets or historiographers and expressly cited as »authorities«[39] by the author, probably John Jewel. Gregory the Great later marked a turning point in the history of the Western church: he was incorrectly said to have condoned the worship of images but actually threw open the doors for the whole pernicious nonsense with his famous appeal in favour of images being tolerated in churches as bibles for the illiterate. This was the beginning of a scandal that caused the Eastern and Western kingdoms and churches to drift apart, as the Popes satisfied their greed for power by encouraging idolatry while the Byzantine emperors bravely fought against it:

»Now on the contrary part, note ye that the bishops of Rome, being no ordinary magistrates appointed of God out of their diocese, but usurpers of princes' authorities contrary to God's Word, were the maintainers of images against God's Word and stirrers up of sedition and rebellion and workers of continual treason against their sovereign lords, contrary to God's law and the ordinances of all human laws, being not only enemies to God, but also rebels and traitors against their princes«.[40]

They consequently brought disaster to the kingdom and the Church:

»And so there became two emperors, and the empire, which was before one, was divided into two parts upon occasion of idols and images and the worshipping of them, even as the kingdom of the Israelites was in old time for the like cause of idolatry divided in King Rehoboam his time. And so the bishop of Rome, having the favour of Charles the Great by this means assured to him, was wondrously enhanced in power and authority and did in all the west church, specially in Italy, what he lust, where images were set up, garnished and worshipped of all sorts of men«.[41]

---

[39] Cf. II/2 (ed. Bray, 237–239).
[40] II/2 (ed. Bray, 242).
[41] II/2 (ed. Bray, 247).

This is naturally not an attempt at a historical instruction and education of an entire people; rather history is here, to an excessive degree, made instrumental as a teacher for life.[42] The historical narrative is put to the service of the politico-theological sermon on repentance, as the 2nd collection exhorts in a different context:

»O England, ponder the time of God's merciful visitation, showed thee from day to day, and yet wilt not regard it, neither wilt thou with his punishment be driven to duty, nor with his benefits provoked to thanks, if thou knewest what may fall upon thee for thine unthankfulness, thou wouldest provide for thy peace«.[43]

VIII.

The Reformation was accordingly the act with which England shook off the usurpation of the Papacy. Through and during the Reformation, the Crown again assumed its due rights and obligations towards the people of God and did away with all idolatry. People who had lost the spiritual home they had found in the Papal church's world of religious ideas were exhorted to stop mourning the magnificence of the pre-Reformation churches and church services with their institutions and religious images and instead to value their status as members of the people of God. The community in which they were gratuitously permitted to live without precedent merit was pervaded by the redeeming orders once again given by God to His people and imposed on them in the wake of the Reformation, orders that in general reflected biblical Israel, the time of the Apostles and the age of the Church Fathers and early Christian emperors.

However, the widely different interpretation of these orders, both in terms of their normative content and the institutions called upon to interpret and enforce them, is indicated by the liturgical controversy that arose during the period in which the Second Book of Homilies was compiled and was to become even more marked as time went on.

---

[42] Cf. expressis verbis II/2 (ed. Bray, 273).
[43] II/17 (ed. Bray, 465). Cf. Luke 19:41–44.

Autoren – Authors

Albrecht Beutel, Professor für Kirchengeschichte, Evangelisch-Theologische Fakultät, Westfälische Wilhelms-Universität Münster (D)

Amy Nelson Burnett, Paula and D. B. Varner University Professor of History, University of Nebraska, Lincoln (USA)

Euan Cameron, Henry Luce III Professor of Reformation Church History, Union Theological Seminary, New York (USA)

Geoffrey Dipple, Professor of History and Chair of Social Sciences, Augustana Faculty, University of Alberta, Camrose (Canada)

Susan Karant-Nunn, Director em. of the Division for Late Medieval and Reformation Studies and Regents' Professor em. of History, University of Arizona, Tucson (USA)

Thomas Kaufmann, Professor für Kirchengeschichte, Theologische Fakultät, Georg-August-Universität Göttingen (D)

Konrad Klek, Professor für Kirchenmusik und Universitätsmusikdirektor, Fachbereich Theologie, Friedrich-Alexander-Universität Erlangen-Nürnberg (D)

John McCallum, Senior Lecturer in History, Nottingham Trent University, Nottingham (UK)

John Ashley Null, DFG-Projektmitarbeiter, Theologische Fakultät der Humboldt-Universität zu Berlin (D)

Martin Ohst, Professor für Historische und Systematische Theologie, Seminar für Evangelische Theologie, Bergische Universität Wuppertal (D)

Wolf-Friedrich Schäufele, Professor für Kirchengeschichte, Fachbereich Evangelische Theologie, Philipps-Universität Marburg (D)

Andrew Spicer, Professor of Early Modern European History, Brookes University, Oxford (UK)

Andreas Stegmann, Privatdozent für Kirchengeschichte, Theologische Fakultät der Humboldt-Universität zu Berlin (D)

Christopher Voigt-Goy, Privatdozent für Kirchengeschichte, Kirchliche Hochschule Wuppertal-Bethel (D)

Alexandra Walsham, Professor of Modern History, University of Cambridge (UK)

Kristen Post Walton, Professor of History, Salisbury University, Maryland (USA)

Dorothea Wendebourg, Professorin em. für Kirchengeschichte, Theologische Fakultät der Humboldt-Universität zu Berlin (D)

Abkürzungen – Abbreviations

AEH	Anglican and Episcopal History
ARG	Archiv für Reformationsgeschichte / Archive for Reformation History
ARF	Augsburger Religionsfriede
BKVAR	Die brandenburgischen Kirchenvisitations-Abschiede und -Register des XVI. und XVII. Jahrhunderts, hg. v. Victor Herold, Bd. 1ff., Berlin 1931ff.
BPfKG	Blätter für Pfälzische Kirchengeschichte
BSRK	Bekenntnisschriften der Reformierten Kirche, hg. v. E. F. K. Müller, Leipzig 1903
BThZ	Berliner Theologische Zeitschrift
BWKG	Blätter für Württembergische Kirchengeschichte
ChH	Church History
CR	Philippi Melanchtonis opera quae supersunt omnia, hg. v. Carl Gottlieb Bretschneider, Corpus Reformatorum Bd. 1–28, 1838–1860
DNB	Dictionary of National Biography
DRTA.JR	Deutsche Reichstagsakten, Jüngere Reihe
EdN	Enzyklopädie der Neuzeit
EEBO	Early English Books Online
EHR	English Historical Review
EKO	Die evangelischen Kirchenordnungen des XVI. Jahrhunderts, begründet von Emil Sehling
ESTC	English Short Title Catalogue
FS	Festschrift
GStAPK	Geheimes Staatsarchiv Preußischer Kulturbesitz, Berlin
HJ	Historisches Jahrbuch der Görresgesellschaft
JBBKG	Jahrbuch für Berlin-Brandenburgische Kirchengeschichte
JBrKG	Jahrbuch für Brandenburgische Kirchengeschichte
JEH	Journal of Ecclesiastical History
LStA	Martin Luther: Studienausgabe, hg. v. Hans-Ulrich Delius
LThK³	Lexikon für Theologie und Kirche
LuJ	Lutherjahrbuch
LW	Luther's Works
MBW	Melanchthons Briefwechsel. Kritische und kommentierte Gesamtausgabe

RE[3]	Realencyklopädie für protestantische Theologie und Kirche
RGG[4]	Religion in Geschichte und Gegenwart
SBBPK	Staatsbibliothek Berlin, Preußischer Kulturbesittz
SCJ	Sixteenth Century Journal
STC	A Short-Title Catalogue of Books Printed in England, Scotland, & Ireland and of English Books Printed Abroad, 1574–1640, 4 vol., 1976–1998
TRE	Theologische Realenzyklopädie
USTC	Universal Short Title Catalogue
VD16	Verzeichnis der im deutschen Sprachbereich erschienenen Drucke des 16. Jahrhunderts
VD17	Verzeichnis der im deutschen Sprachbereich erschienenen Drucke des 17. Jahrhunderts
WA	D. Martin Luthers Werke. Kritische Gesamtausgabe, 73 Bände, Weimar 1883–2009
WA.Br	D. Martin Luthers Werke. Kritische Gesamtausgabe. Briefwechsel, 18 Bände, Weimar 1930–1985
WA.DB	D. Martin Luthers Werke. Kritische Gesamtausgabe. Deutsche Bibel, 12 Bände, Weimar 1906–1961
WA.TR	D. Martin Luthers Werke. Kritische Gesamtausgabe. Tischreden, 6 Bände, Weimar 1912–1921
ZevKR	Zeitschrift für evangelisches Kirchenrecht
ZHF	Zeitschrift für Historische Forschung
ZKG	Zeitschrift für Kirchengeschichte
ZSRG.K	Zeitschrift der Savigny-Stiftung für Rechtsgeschichte, Kanonistische Abteilung
ZThK	Zeitschrift für Theologie und Kirche

Personenregister – Index of names